THE LINCOLN COUNTY WAR

THE LINCOLN COUNTY WAR

A DOCUMENTARY HISTORY

By Frederick Nolan

UNIVERSITY OF OKLAHOMA PRESS : NORMAN AND LONDON

Dedicated
with unqualified admiration
and abiding affection
to the memory of
Robert N. Mullin, 1893–1981
who showed me the way.

BY FREDERICK NOLAN

The Life and Death of John Henry Tunstall (Albuquerque, 1965)
The Algonquin Project (New York, 1975, 1976; reissued as *Brass Target*,
   New York, 1978)
The Mittenwald Syndicate (New York, 1977)
The Sound of Their Music: The Story of Rodgers and Hammerstein (New York, 1978)
White Nights, Red Dawn (New York, 1981, 1983)
Wolf Trap (New York, 1984, 1986)
Red Center (New York, 1987, 1988)
The Lincoln County War: A Documentary History (Norman, 1992)

This book is published with the generous assistance of the McCasland Foundation,
   Duncan, Oklahoma.

Nolan, Frederick W., 1931–
    The Lincoln County War : a documentary history / by Frederick
Nolan.
      p.   cm.
    Includes bibliographical references and index.
    ISBN 0-8061-2377-X
    1. Lincoln County (N.M.)—History.   2. Violence—New Mexico—
Lincoln County—History—19th century.   3. Frontier and pioneer
life—New Mexico—Lincoln County.   I. Title.
F802.L7N65   1991
978.9′64—dc20   91-22210
                                                                          CIP

Text and jacket design by Bill Cason

The paper in this book meets the guidelines for permanence and durability of the
Committee on Production Guidelines for Book Longevity of the Council on Library
Resources, Inc. ♾

2   3   4   5   6   7   8   9   10   11

CONTENTS

ILLUSTRATIONS

MAPS

PREFACE

THE Lincoln County War took place at a time when territorial New Mexico in general, and Lincoln County in particular, was a burgeoning microcosm of money-mad, power-hungry nineteenth-century America, America before the dream had soured, America on the brink of becoming a world power, America the promised land where a pushcart immigrant could overnight become a millionaire, America in the Gilded Age when the robber barons of Wall Street were the uncrowned kings.

Men like Jay Gould, Jim Fisk, William Tweed, Collis Huntington, and Leland Stanford early learned a simple fact of American life—the man who has the gold makes the rules. They used wealth and influence as a weapon to break any man or group that stood in the way of their ambitions; in their world there were only lions and lambs, hunters and prey. Ordinary people, their rights, and their future, were irrelevant. The only things that counted were money and power.

In their headlong pursuit of that money and power all of them fell victim to the classic misbeliefs that have forever bedeviled the American dream: that success is preferable to excellence, that wealth is the equivalent of honor, that rules are the same as ethics, that profits are more important than standards, that power places its possessor above justice, that strength is superior to reason, and that losing is the worst disgrace.

A decade later in New Mexico Territory, opportunities of the kind that the robber barons had grabbed in the early Seventies were just beginning to present themselves. Men like Tom Catron and Steve Elkins, William Rynerson and Lawrence Murphy—aye, and John Tunstall and Alexander McSween—were only emulating, in a cruder way and on a smaller scale, the methods perfected by the Goulds and Tweeds. There is no difference at all, except one of location, between the arrogance of "Boss" Tweed's "as long as I count the votes, what are you going to do about it?" and Lawrence G. Murphy's "It don't make any difference who the government sends out here. We control these Indians."

The name of the game was monopoly: get it and keep it, no matter how. Murphy and Dolan perceived the challenge of Tunstall and McSween not as rivalry but as effrontery. Their response was conditioned by that arrogance, and they acted—overreacted—accordingly, bringing the full power of the machinery of which they were a part to bear upon the interlopers. First, threats and when those failed, local law, county law, territorial law, even federal law were shamelessly and ruthlessly manipulated to bring down their enemies and to protect from those same laws those who effected that downfall.

Tunstall and McSween—the latter and his wife especially—also appear to have abandoned their principles and adopted the belief that any tactic which resulted in victory was defensible. First Tunstall's wealth was used as a club; when that failed, they raised the stakes—to what extent John Chisum was involved is almost impossible to determine—by using the same kind of smear tactics and dubious legal ploys as their opponents, and backing them up with hired guns. The result of this escalation was inevitable.

The Lincoln County War was unique among the many so-called frontier "wars" in that it was waged simultaneously on three different levels of American society. It was debated and discussed in the highest offices of the land, between presidents and secretaries of state, prime ministers and ambassadors. It was argued, manipulated, and justified at a slightly less exalted level by local politicians, attorneys, businessmen, and army officers in the press of half a dozen states and territories. And while they debated and manipulated and argued and justified, it was fought in bloody earnest at the grass-roots level by cowboys and farmers, hired guns and rustlers.

Each one of these had his own reasons, and expectations, for getting involved. This man had his pride, that one his reputation; this one office, that one ambition; this one had money, that one had none; this one hoped to land a job, that one to swing a deal. In defense of what they owned or in the hope of perhaps acquiring what someone else owned, decent, honest men found themselves committing or condoning robbery, looting, arson, and murder. The pattern of events in Lincoln County is one repeated over and over in American history: one mob tries to "muscle in," the other resists, and violence flares. Someone gets killed, and retaliation follows. Neither side will give ground or back down; guns rule. Newspapers fulminate, the law is powerless, politicians wash their hands. Citizens become vigilantes, vigilantes become murderers; and all in pursuit of those same mad misbeliefs: ambition, pride, wealth, and power.

For all that the pattern is familiar, there is something more to the story of the Lincoln County War than a mere chronicle of civil disturbance: the abundance of its literature alone suggests that it offers us something of special significance. Yet it was an inconclusive and futile struggle, a war, as one respected historian has suggested, without heroes. But if there were no heroes, what is the reason for its enduring appeal? Could it be that ultimately what we find most admirable about it is the continuing strength and faith in the future of the ordinary people, the dirt-poor Hispanics who had defied the Apaches and settled the valleys, and the determined, scratch-ankle Anglo farmers who followed them and held on, come hell or high water?

What vision of a future they cannot possibly have envisaged possessed them? Their lives were a litany of deprivation: no doctors, no dentists, no schools, no churches, no decent houses, no sanitation, no roads, no law and order. And yet they stayed. Mistreated, manipulated, exploited, cheated, lied to, and robbed for decades, still they hung on, still somehow managing to believe that up ahead, somewhere, there was a rainbow and a pot of gold beneath it. How did they do it? Why, in the face of such unremitting discouragement, did they go on believing it was worth persisting? What would America be today if they had not?

This faith and courage remains to me the most remarkable aspect of the story of Lincoln County, and indeed, the American West. Perhaps after all it was the ordinary people who were the heroes of the Lincoln County War. Perhaps this is why we return to it again and again, for it contains that ultimate reassurance we all so badly need: that in the end, the people survived, the people triumphed not by the gun but by the rule of democracy and law. Let us hope, in this time of falling tyrannies, that it will always be so.

FREDERICK NOLAN

Chalfont St. Giles, England

 # ACKNOWLEDGMENTS

ALTHOUGH this book has been some thirty years in the making, and nearly four years in the writing, I would not be so foolish as to suggest it is the last word on the subject: indeed, the very opposite. Doubtless there are not only errors, but conclusions here with which others may take issue: so be it. I do not seek to excuse myself by pointing out that the bulk of the research has been conducted from a distance never less than four and often nearer ten thousand miles from the scene; I offer the observation only to convince anyone who believes there is no more to be found that they are wrong. As further support for this observation I refer the reader to the remarkable detective work of Lewis A. Ketring, Jr., of Los Angeles, of Jerry Weddle of Catalina, Arizona, and of Robert G. McCubbin of El Paso, some of whose unique photographic archive appears here for the first time. His treasures are a perfect illustration of my contention: seek—diligently enough—and ye shall find.

There is still a great deal to be done. Someone must one day write this story from the Hispanic point of view. Someone must write a proper study of the rise of the House of Murphy. There are still many lives unexplored, many riddles left to answer. I have written this book in the hope that it may fire someone with the determination to set out on that exploration.

I have never been fortunate enough to conduct extended research in the United States; it is therefore with great humility that I acknowledge my profound debt to the many talented and dedicated people, professional and amateur, who have done so much over the past three decades to help me arrive at my understanding of the events this book seeks to reexamine.

I would like particularly to salute the memories of Eve Ball, Col. Maurice G. Fulton, Pearl Hendricks, William A. Keleher, Robert N. Mullin, Edward Penfield, and Belle Wilson, all of whom I am privileged to have known. I am equally privileged to have been able to share my doubts, my queries, and my theories with a band of aficionados I dubbed "the Lincoln County Irregulars" and who include Bob Barron, Donald Cline, Nora Henn, Harwood Hinton, Jr., Jeffrey Jackson, Lewis Ketring, Jr., Donald Lavash, Robert McCubbin, Herb Marsh, Leon Metz, Paul Northrup, Doyce Nunis, Jr., Philip Rasch, C. L. "Doc" Sonnichsen, Robert Utley, Jerry Weddle, Herman Weisner, and John Wilson. It has also been my good fortune to locate descendants of some of the principal participants: to Bob Widenmann, Baird Hershey, and most especially to Hilary Tunstall Behrens, who made all the Tunstall family material available to me—and therefore, to all of us—go my sincerest thanks.

I wish to pay special tribute to the hard-pressed staffs of the many museums and historical societies who have assisted me in the preparation of this work, notably those of the National Archives in Washington, the British Public Records Office, the Haley History Center, and the New Mexico State Records Center and Archive. There are many, many others: I have done my best to acknowledge them appropriately in the notes to the main text.

To the many friends in Lincoln County who have guided and supported me since my first visit there in 1971: Walter and Nora, Ralph and Rosalie, Jerry and Cleis, Lynda and Jim, Bob and Linda, Gary and Dee, Billie and Myrna Lee, Art and Cora, Ralph and Gloria, Tom and Anne, Morgan and Joyce, Paul, Michael, Betty, Ann, Rafaelita, Rosina, Mickey, Karl, Tom, Joe-Ben, Dave, Carol, Ernestine, Jack, everyone at the Flying H, and others too numerous to mention: thank you, thank you for your many kindnesses.

In conclusion I would like to honor Robert O. Anderson and his son, Phelps Anderson, of the Lincoln County Heritage Trust, who believed enough in my project to offer to underwrite, without strings, some of my research costs. Such generous patronage is rare, and I salute it, as I salute their enlightened contribution to the physical preservation of Lincoln County history. May it prove in their work, as in the work of historical detection which we all share, that the best is yet to come.

THE LINCOLN COUNTY WAR

FIG. 1. Lincoln, N.M. USAF aerial photograph, ca. 1980.

CHAPTER 1

BEGINNINGS: BILLY THE KID

A legend is a legend: Marilyn or Mike Fink, Kennedy or Custer, Evita or Elvis. No matter how determinedly the historian sets out to place them in proper context, legends remain curiously elusive. It is rare to be able to pinpoint the moment when history ends and legend takes over: the alchemy is usually too subtle. In the case of Billy the Kid, however, it can be said without hesitation that his legend began around one o'clock in the afternoon of Thursday, April 28, 1881, in the little town of Lincoln, New Mexico.

Until that bloody Thursday, when he killed the two deputies guarding him at the old Murphy-Dolan store and rode out of town, laughing, the Kid was hardly more than a well-known horse thief, rustler, and badman, a member of one of the many gangs that terrorized the southeastern quadrant of the Territory after what was called the Lincoln County War. Seventy-eight days later, he was dead. Yet somehow, somewhere between these two events, Billy the Kid's life began its apotheosis: history into legend.

Over the succeeding century, an avalanche of dime novels, books, poems, movies, plays, musicals, and even comic books, some learned, others laughable, first enhanced the legend and then enshrined it. The Kid became the Robin Hood of New Mexico, a gallant young man fighting for justice on the wrong side of the law, *caballero muy simpático*, immortal. Doubtless he would laugh if he knew, for one of the few things that can be said about him with certainty is that he was not expecting immortality.

Paradoxically, his immortality kept alive the story, however garbled, of the Lincoln County War. For that, if nothing else, history owes Billy the Kid a debt. It is doubtful if any of the writers and historians who have examined its causes and events would have done so had their interest not been fired by an earlier fascination with that short and violent life.

No apology is necessary for beginning with his story. The legend will not suffer by being once again dissected and examined for the truths it conceals; and if, in the process, Billy the Kid is removed briefly from the shining armor of myth and placed properly in his historical context, it will not be for long: he will return to legend unaltered. Indeed, those who savor the ironies of history may find a certain sweet justice in the fact that today, of all the powerful, rich, and famous men of his era, it is the Kid who is remembered best—and at that, for things he never did.

But who was he? The same questions have remained unanswered almost since the time of his death in 1881. Where was he born? Who was his father? Where did he spend his childhood? Thousands of writers have offered solutions, many of them persuasive, not a few seductive, none of them anywhere remotely near definitive. Like Alexander McSween, principal on one side, like Lawrence G. Murphy, principal on the other, the Kid lived his early years—two thirds of his life—in circumstances that remain shrouded in mystery.

No wonder he has fascinated us all for so long. No wonder such a legend has sprung up around him that it almost defies analysis, changing form and color to adapt to the era in which it finds itself. To arrive at any approximation of the truth, it becomes necessary to begin again at the beginning, to put away guesswork, hopeful conjecture, and wishful thinking, and concentrate instead, here as elsewhere, upon *documentary* evidence. Perhaps thus we may, if nothing else, do away with some of the misconceptions.

The first full-length account of his life was, of course, Pat Garrett's *An Authentic Life of Billy the Kid.* Most of it was written, as is well known, by Garrett's friend and amanuensis, Marshal Ashmun "Ash" Upson. Upson had been, if not an eyewitness, a longtime resident of Lincoln County who knew where more than a few of its family skeletons were closeted. He was personally acquainted with most, if not all, of the characters about whom he wrote. Most authorities dismiss the book more or less out of hand as a farrago of mendacities, inventions, and hyperbole, but carefully read, it can still yield a great deal of information to a sharp-eyed researcher.

Upson stated categorically that William H. Bonney, Billy the Kid, was born in New York City on November 23, 1859.[1] Suspicion has been cast upon this statement because November 23 was also Upson's birthday, although it might as fairly be claimed that he remembered it so well because of that simple fact. Indeed, although immediately thereafter Upson went on to make other biographical claims that later research has totally confounded, this date has not yet been so satisfactorily discredited as to be dismissed out of hand.

Others who knew the Kid as a youth supported the proposition that he was born in New York, but the strength of their testimony (and Upson's) is diluted by the fact that they could have read it elsewhere first and then "remembered" it. Several cheap novels that appeared between his death and the appearance of Garrett's book located the Kid's birth in New York; newspaper reports published within weeks of his death not only stated that he was a New York native but also that his real name was McCarty or McCarthy.

The bare and brutal truth is this: All that can be stated as a fact is that most accounts—including many that precede Upson's—aver that the Kid was born in New York. Such accounts are to some extent borne out by the testimony of William Antrim, the Kid's stepfather, who testified in pension applications to the U.S. government that his wife's "first husband was named McCarty," that McCarty had "died in New York City," and that he had "no military service to [Antrim's] knoladge."[2]

More than thirty years ago, Philip Rasch and Robert Mullin diligently endeavored to solve the mystery of the Kid's origins.[3] In the intervening years, assisted by enormous improvements in information retrieval, other, equally diligent researchers have devoted perhaps as much time and effort again in an attempt to solve the riddle. One of these holds that his date of birth was November 20, 1859. The other is convinced it was November 17.

The November 20 theory has much to commend it, notably some convincing documentation.[4] One Patrick McCarthy married Catherine Devane in New York on June 19, 1851. Their son, Patrick Henry, was born in Ward One of Manhattan on September 17, 1859, and baptized at St Peter's Church, Barclay St., September 28, by the Rev. J. Conron, the sponsors being Thomas Cooney and Mary Clark. In further support, the census records for 1860 are offered, showing that Patrick, age thirty, and Catherine, twenty-nine, also had a daughter, Bridget, six years older than their son. New York directories list a Patrick McCarthy (or McCarty) operating a boarding house at 87 Washington St. in 1860–61; in 1863, his widow is shown living at 210 Greene St.; she in turn disappears thereafter.

Since a Catherine McCarty with two children appears in the life of William Antrim, the Kid's stepfather, in 1864, this looks very promising; but it begs a number of genealogical questions. The first is, what happened to Bridget McCarthy? The second and more important one is, why is Henry McCarty's brother Joseph not shown in the census return? While willing to accept the proposition that Bridget might well have died and therefore never made the trip west to New Mexico, we cannot accept the census records as the correct McCarty family unless they also show Joseph McCarty, who would have been six years old at the time.

The alternative proposition is appealing because it takes into account the indisputable existence of Joseph McCarty.[5] The Kid's older brother died November 25, 1930, at the age of seventy-six, making the date of his birth 1854. During the years 1852–56, only one male child named Joseph McCarty was born in the entire city of New York. The date was August 24, 1854, the place the New York Hospital, the mother Catherine McCarty.

The fact that no father's name is listed suggests that the birth was illegitimate; other than that the records tell us nothing. The New York Hospital offered free services to the poor and indigent of the city. The upper East Side was still open country; farms and shanties dotted the landscape above Fiftieth St., so the question of where Catherine McCarty lived at the time of Joseph's birth is impossible to answer, just as it is impossible to tell which of the dozens of Catherine McCartys who appear in the 1850 census might be the right one.

She may well have been that cliché of the time: the servant girl with her fatherless baby, labeled "a fallen woman" and cast out onto the streets. If—the word is used apologetically—they are the same woman, this might explain how the Catherine McCarty who had her first baby in the relative comfort of a hospital gave birth to her second in the squalor of the lower East Side. It was a very long way indeed—and not just in miles—from East Sixty-eighth St. to Allen St.

Close to the notorious Five Points, Allen St. was at the center of the most wretched and criminal area in the city.[6] Between Fourteenth St. and the Battery, half of Manhattan's million citizens were crowded into an area that occupied only one fifth of the island. Within this section were some thirteen thousand tenements, seven thousand of which were "in bad condition." Since nearly all tenements were filthy and unhealthy, the phrase may be taken as a euphemism for utterly squalid. Rev. W. C. van de Meter, who ran the Howard Mission and Home for Little Wanderers on the Bowery only a few hundred yards from Allen Street described the area as

> the very concentration of evil and the headquarters of the most desperate and degraded representatives of many nations. It swarms with poor little helpless victims, who are born in sin and shame, nursed in misery, want and woe, and carefully trained to all manner of degradation, vice and shame. The packing of these poor creatures is incredible. In this ward there are less than two dwelling houses for each low rum hole gambling house, and den of infamy. Near us, on a small lot but 150

by 240 feet, are twenty tenant houses, 111 families, 5 stables, a soap and candle factory, and a tan yard. On four blocks, close to the Mission, are 517 children, 318 Roman Catholic and 10 Protestant families, 35 rum holes, and 18 brothels. In number 14 Baxter Street, but three or four blocks from us, are 92 families, consisting of 92 men, 81 women, 54 boys and 53 girls. Of these 151 are Italians, 92 Irish, 28 Chinese, 3 English, 2 Africans, 2 Jews, 1 German, and but 7 Americans.

According to the census of 1870, the population of Ward Four, which covered an area of eighty-three acres, consisted of 10,546 natives and 13,292 foreigners, a total population of 23,748. It held 500 tenement houses of which 300 were—that euphemism again—"in bad sanitary condition." One small block in the Five Points district was said to contain 382 families.

On November 20, 1859, an unnamed male child was born at 70 Allen St.[7] The parents of this child were listed as Edward and Catherine McCarty; they were not married to each other. This woman was thirty; the fact that the Catherine McCarty who died in Silver City was born in 1829 adds resonance to the proposition that this was the baby who became Billy the Kid. It cannot, however, be said to have been proven; the 1860 and 1870 census reports for the second, third, and fourth wards of Manhattan have failed to reveal any listing of a family unit consisting of Catherine, Joseph, and Henry McCarty. Additionally, acceptance of 1859 as the year of birth is complicated not only by the fact that all his friends said that the Kid was only twelve when he came to Silver City, which would mean he was born in 1860 or 1861, but also by the possibility that the Allen St. child may have been the Michael Henry McCarty who in 1876 gained brief notoriety as a street hoodlum and murderer.[8]

The inescapable conclusion of all the foregoing is that the only birth that can be stated to be even probably that of a participant in the story of Billy the Kid is that of Joseph McCarty, and even this is open to considerable doubt.

As for the Kid himself, in spite of the absence of definitive documentation, the tradition of a New York birth must be respected. It is anyway as likely to have been there as Ohio, Illinois, Kansas, Missouri, Indiana, or even New Mexico, all of which have been offered as alternatives. If it was, the question of whether it took place in Greene St. or Allen St. is largely immaterial, since one was as much of a cesspool as the other.

There is, however, one further witness to be heard from, and he is a potent one: the Kid himself.[9] Between June 17 and 19, 1880, while taking census records at Fort Sumner, N.M., Lorenzo Labadie—former Indian agent and brother-in-law of Juan Patrón—noted down the vital statistics of one William Bonny. Since he was living adjacent to Charlie Bowdre and his wife Manuela, there does not seem to be any reason to doubt that this was the Billy Bonney of Lincoln County fame. What is interesting about the entry is that he gave his age as twenty-five, and the place of his birth not as New York but as Missouri. His occupation, he said (no doubt with a grin), was "working in cattle," and both his parents had also been born in Missouri. Was the Kid having mischievous fun with the census taker, or is he telling us, across the century, that the search has not yet properly begun?

William Henry Harrison Antrim, born at Huntsville, Ind., on December 1, 1842, was one of the eight children of Levi and Ida (Lawson) Antrim.[10] In later times he said he "lived at Wichita, Kansas, first year after leaving service," but his memory may have betrayed him: the family bible suggests it was in 1870 that the move to Kansas was made. Levi Antrim settled in the area that would become Newton with the arrival of the Atchison, Topeka & Santa Fe Railroad in the spring of 1871. William and his brother James Madison filed on land a little farther south.

Beginning in June 1870, William and James homesteaded 160 acres of Osage Trust land at Augusta, Butler County, Kans.; a month later a Catherine McCarty took up a homestead nearby. This Catherine McCarty was from Indianapolis. In supporting her application for this land, Antrim testified, "I have known Catherine McCarty for 6 years past; she is a single woman over the age of twenty one years, the head of a family consisting of two children and a citizen of the United States."

This at first seems to indicate that Antrim and the Kid's mother met in Indiana in 1864; add to it the statement made by Sheriff Harvey Whitehill of Silver City, who knew the Kid well, that the Kid's name was Henry McCarty "and he was born in Anderson, Indiana," and the testimonies more or less coincide. The existing documentation, however, seems to indicate that the Catherine McCarty who farmed adjacent to Antrim is not the Catherine McCarty he married. A Henry J. Cook testified in 1892 that after selling him her property in August 1871, Catherine McCarty and her children moved to New Orleans, and she died there in 1873.

To accept this is to stand probability on its head. What would seem likelier is that Cook got it half right: it was to New Mexico, not New Orleans, that Catherine McCarty went, and he was a year out with the date of death. It demands too much from history that the woman Antrim described in a statement supporting her land purchase could be unrelated to the woman he married three years later. All that remains in the realm of speculation is the question of how—and why, if they were New Yorkers—Catherine McCarty and her two sons came out to Indiana at all.

The pattern of their movements thereafter, however, is entirely plausible. If we assume an attachment between Catherine McCarty and the much younger Antrim—at the time of their meeting she was thirty-five, and he but four and twenty—her joining him in Kansas when the Antrim clan moved southwest seems a reasonable hypothesis. It is infinitely easier to imagine young Henry McCarty as a farm boy in Indiana, and near Wichita, Kans., than as a slum dweller—and a murderer—in the dark streets of Manhattan.

They remained in the Wichita area for two years; Antrim is on record as saying that he left there in October 1872. Whether Catherine McCarty left with him, whether she followed, or whether he was to effect the most astonishing historical coincidence of all time by meeting another Catherine McCarty in Santa Fe and marrying her, without prior acquaintance, readers must decide for themselves. From this point on, at least, history provides solid ground. On March 1, 1873, the first documentary evidence appears of the existence of the boy who became Billy the Kid: witness to his mother's marriage in the First Presbyterian Church of Santa Fe, N.M.[11]

On that Saturday in March 1873, "Mr William H. Antrim and Mrs Catherine McCarty, both of Santa Fe, New Mexico," were joined in matrimony by the Rev. David F. McFarland of the First Presbyterian Church of Santa Fe. The witnesses were Harvey Edmonds, Mrs. A. R. McFarland, her daughter Katie, and Mrs. McCarty's two sons, Joseph, who was called Josie, and Henry.

Shortly thereafter, the family left for Silver City, then favored for its location nearly six thousand feet above sea level as a healthful climate for sufferers from asthma and tuberculosis—"consumption," as they called it—a disease that Catherine Antrim, as she now was, had contracted some years earlier. Antrim, who was to become an inveterate prospector, was doubtless also attracted by the reports of rich silver strikes in that district. The family settled in a two- or three-roomed frame house facing Main at Broadway, near the Enterprise Building, and not far from the Opera House.[12]

Little is known of Henry McCarty Antrim's life in the mining town, and much of what is known appears to have been "misremembered." But the burden of the oral tradition is that he was, for the time and place, a more than usually well-behaved boy. Anthony B. Conner, whose sister Sarah Ann married the Richard Knight at whose home Henry lived for a time after his mother's death, recalled that "Billy was one of the best boys in town. . . . I knew he was a better boy than I was. I never remember Billy doing anything out of the way any more than the rest of us. We had our chores to do, like washing dishes and other duties around the house."[13] One schoolmate, Louis Abraham, recalled that Henry was "full of fun and mischief."[14] Another, Harry Whitehill, son of the later sheriff of Silver City, testified that "he wasn't a bad fellow." His teacher, Miss Mary Richards, recalled that he "was no more of a problem than any other boy" and that "he was always quite willing to help with the chores around the schoolhouse."[15]

His contemporaries largely concur that the boy they knew there as Henry Antrim was 5 ft. 5 in. tall, with blue eyes, brown or dark blond hair, and prominent buck teeth. Like his mother, Henry was ambidextrous. He liked to sing and dance and may have performed in amateur theatricals at Morrill's Opera House.[16] It is important to keep this personality profile in mind when examining the theories advanced about the character of this same youngster only two or three years later.

On September 19, 1874, the weekly *Silver City Mining Life* noted:

Died in Silver City on Wednesday, the 16th, Catherine, wife of William Antrim, aged 45 years.
    Mrs. Antrim with her husband and family came to Silver City about one year and a half ago, since which time her health has not been good, having suffered from an affection of the lungs, and for the last four months she has been confined to her bed. The funeral occurred from the family residence on Main Street at 2 o'clock on Thursday.

Catherine Antrim was buried in the cemetery at Silver City beneath a head-board that misspelled her name and recorded the date of her death as September 13. Antrim, who could never remember the place or date of his marriage either, misquoted this date as the real one for the rest of his life.

There is some evidence that Antrim and his stepson did not get along well; this was seized on by many writers as an explanation of why the Kid went bad.[17] George Coe related a not-untypical story that Henry entered their room one day and found Antrim abusing his mother. He picked up a chair and laid Antrim out; thinking he had killed his stepfather, he left Silver City and never went back.

Henry did not flee Silver City before his mother's death. All accounts concur that Antrim treated his family in general, and Henry in particular, much more kindly than many a man in his place would have done, and if there ever was any trouble between them, Henry was probably the cause of it. In later years "Uncle

Billy" described Henry as a cruel little sneak thief who stole everything he could get his hands on, and who, when given a Barlow knife as a present, immediately used it to decapitate a neighbor's kitten.[18] This is a picture of Henry widely at variance with the recollections of his friends, not to mention Henry himself.

After Catherine's death, Henry went to stay for a while with the Truesdell family.[19] Later, Antrim found work at Richard Knight's butcher shop, where the boy helped out. Still later, Antrim—who was a real rolling stone—got a job at Ed Moulton's sawmill in nearby Georgetown; his stepson remained in Silver City, lodging with Canadian-born Mrs. Sarah Brown, who ran the town's only boardinghouse, working for his keep by washing dishes and waiting table after school.

It was not to be for long, however: Destiny had other things in mind for Henry Antrim.

CHAPTER 2

ALEXANDER MCSWEEN
HEADS WEST

AT around the same time that young Henry McCarty would have been doing chores on the Antrim farm outside of Wichita, a young lawyer named Alexander Anderson McSween was hanging out his shingle fifty-five miles away in Eureka, Kans. A former Presbyterian minister, McSween had come to Eureka only a little while earlier, sometime between the extremely hot summer and the early cold fall of 1872.[1]

Eureka was first settled in 1857 by colonists from Mississippi who came with the avowed intention of making Kansas an ally of the slaveholding states. Until 1872, it had stood on the edge of the frontier. Not much farther west lay wild, uninhabited prairie known only to Indians, buffalo hunters, trail drivers, and the soldiers at faraway Fort Dodge.

When the trail herds started coming north to Newton after the Atchison, Topeka & Santa Fe Railroad reached there in the spring of 1872, the little town managed to avoid the worst excesses of the cattle-drovers and those who preyed upon them by first making liquor sales illegal, and second giving its "addition," nearby Greenwood City, self-rule, promising never to interfere with its activities in any way.

By the end of the year, Eureka was fast becoming a backwater. The railroad was already at the Kansas-Colorado border; Dodge City, that booming, bibulous Babylon of the frontier, had taken over as the cowboy capital. Over at Greenwood City, it was discovered that the man who had laid out the town had swindled everyone, and nobody owned the lots on which their properties stood, whereupon the saloonkeepers and madams loaded their cabins and shacks onto wagons and moved on; and that was the end of Eureka's "addition."

Why McSween (fig. 2) chose to settle in Eureka is not known. Indeed, like that of Billy the Kid, practically nothing is known about the first two thirds of his life. Once again it is necessary to peel away the layers of disinformation that have grown over the truth to reveal something of the real man beneath them.

In April 1878, McSween gave his age as thirty-five; other evidence supports the proposition that the year of his birth was 1843, and the place probably Prince Edward Island in Canada.[2] In other accounts of McSween's life—and most of what is known about him comes from her—Mrs. McSween gave the birthplace as Charlestown (Charlottetown), P.E.I.[3] It is impossible to corroborate this, since birth records in that province go back only as far as 1906. Diligent searching in census and baptismal records there has proven largely inconclusive, although in

FIG. 2. Alexander Anderson McSween. Date and photographer unknown. Said to have been taken at Topeka, Kan. There is evidence that McSween was clean-shaven at the time of the war; from this photograph it might be deduced he was also balding.

the 1861 census the family of Alex McSwein (*sic*) shows two males under the age of sixteen.[4]

On a number of occasions, McSween referred to himself as a Scot or Scotch-man—not "of Scots descent" or "of Scottish parentage"—which might be taken as contradiction of his widow's statements were it not for the fact that McSween, unusually in a lawyer, was given to imprecision. There are two Alexander McSweens of the right age in the 1851 census of the parish of Duirnish, Isle of Skye—the McSweens of Prince Edward Island were largely emigrants from there.[5] Whether any of these is the Alexander McSween of Kansas and later Lincoln County has yet to be established. Of his early years all that is known is that he "had been educated for a Presbyterian minister. He was a wonderful orator and a fine writer. When a young man he wrote for sixteen prominent journals. After his death a cousin of his, a member of Parliament from Canada, wrote me and told me McSwain was chosen from a family of five boys as the most intelligent one. He was writing for magazines when he was sixteen years of age."[6]

No confirmation of McSween's education for the Presbyterian ministry has yet been located; or indeed, of his wife's statement that she first met him in Pekin, Ill., in 1870.[7] In fact, it has proven impossible to find any conclusive documentation of his movements before 1871, when the name of Alex A. McSween, from White-hall, Ill., lodging at 1511 Carr St., St. Louis, appears as one of the thirty-five members of the junior class of the Law Department of Washington University for 1871–72.[8]

The law school at Washington University began operations in the 1867–68 academic year, making it the oldest law school west of the Mississippi. Candidates for the Bachelor of Laws degree were required to pass both written and oral examinations. The period of study extended over two "years" of six months' duration. McSween either chose not to, or was unable to, complete the course, for his name appears neither in the 1872–73 yearbook nor in any subsequent list of Washington University graduates.

St. Louis city directories show that in 1872 McSween, listed as a student, occupied lodgings at 1801 Olive St., close to the campus. Other evidence, in the form of an item in the *Eureka Herald* of January 2, 1873, indicates that he had already moved to that town.

ROLL OF HONOR

For a reason satisfactory to all concerned, the ordinary mode of promotion ("go up") was abolished in District School No. 29 on the farm of D. E. Miles, Esq., Spring Creek. But the abandonment of that time-honored and effectual incentive to study led to the devising of a *quasi* substitute. It was decided to publish the names of all scholars who should prove themselves worthy at the end of the term in the Eureka *Herald.* In conformity with the above, mention is made of J. Edgar Miles and George B. McFarrar, James E. Stepter and Jessie Lowery (colored); Ida Rodebaugh, and Artie Stepter, (colored), in recognition of their constant and punctual attendance, perseverance and good behavior during the past term.

A. A. McSween.

No school records from that time have been preserved, but since the fall school term ran from July to December, it would appear McSween came west from St. Louis in the late spring of 1872, attended the Institute of the Teachers of Greenwood County, took the teacher's examination, and taught school that fall to pick up a little money. By another astonishing coincidence, the Ida Rodebaugh he taught at the Miles farm was the sister of a local boy who would also make a name for himself as a desperado and sidekick of Billy the Kid: "Dirty Dave" Rudabaugh.[9]

On April 3, 1873, the *Herald* reported that "Mr. McSween, whose card appears in this issue," had rented the office south of the *Herald* building. His card:

Alex A. McSween
   Attorney-at-law, will faithfully attend to all business with which he may be entrusted. Collections made and promptly remitted.
   Eureka, Kansas.

On the same day, McSween was one of seventy-five signatories calling for a meeting "at Earhart's Hall on Saturday evening, April 5th, at 7½ p.m. sharp, for the purpose of putting into nomination anti-licence, anti-salary, anti-saloon candidates for the city office of Mayor and Councilmen." As has been remarked, the good people of Eureka were largely successful in keeping liquor out of the town. McSween, a lifelong teetotaler, was taking a popular stance opposing liquor licenses.

The following week his card appeared again, but this time in the regular front-page column reserved for a listing of local attorneys, of whom by now there were seven. McSween's next appearance in the *Herald,* on April 24, was to issue this stern injunction:

Notice is hereby given to all persons indebted to the late Dr. J. B. Bennett that his books have been placed in my hands for collection. An immediate settlement will save unnecessary trouble and expense.

Alex A. McSween.

James B. Bennett was a young, unmarried physician who died intestate and whose father, Elijah Bennett, claimed the estate as sole heir. The probate documents record the appearance of "A. A. McSween, Justice of the Peace in and for Eureka Township, County and State aforesaid." McSween's election as a justice of the peace—which probably took place the preceding fall—raises the question of his citizenship.[10] In order to vote or stand for election, McSween had to prove citizenship; yet no record of his naturalization has been found.

That same month, McSween purchased three town lots on Sycamore and Ninth streets for the sum of fifty-two dollars. His name continued to appear regularly in the columns of the newspaper: he was clearly on good personal terms with its editor, Samuel G. Mead. The following week, Mead ran an item half-news, half-advertisement that is revealing:

We advise all parties whose indebtedness is left with Mr. McSween for collection to call at his office as soon as they receive notice of that fact. He will do just as he says, regardless of the consequences.

The *Wichita Eagle* of June 12, 1873, indicates that McSween was taking his duties as a justice of the peace seriously.

HORSE THIEVES

Francis M. Carson and John Jefferson were arrested in this city [Eureka] Tuesday morning charged with stealing four mules from Mr. Frank Wilkin of Wichita. They were traced here from that place and the mules found in their possession. At the preliminary examination before Judge McSween, Carson plead[ed] guilty. The judge considered the evidence against Jefferson sufficient to hold him for trial. Both were committed to jail to await trial at next district court. The arrest was made by Sheriff Baker as the parties were crawling down from the hay mow where they had slept. They were terribly afraid of being taken to Wichita, as they knew the result of such a trip. They were confined in the jail of the new court house, where they remain at present. It is reported that one is a desperado who is wanted by the authorities elsewhere.—*Eureka Herald*[11]

During July, McSween's name was among those of the Teachers and Friends of Education attending the Fourth Annual Institute of the Teachers of Greenwood County. Then on August 28, the *Herald* carried the following announcement:

Married.

At the Presbyterian Manse, Atchison, by the Rev. E. Cooper, D.D., on Saturday, August 23, Judge McSween of Eureka and Miss Sue E. Homer.

We congratulate our legal friend upon the successful termination of this case. His petition was evidently in proper form and his pleading so strong and earnest [that it] did not fall on unwilling ears. This is one of those rare cases where the judgment for plaintiff is also judgment for the other party. For while our gallant friend Mac thought, as well he might, that he was securing a glorious prize, he was obliged to surrender himself in return, and the fair bride has at least as much to boast of as Mac himself. Both have our good wishes.

May they live as long as the patriarchs, may their olive branches be as numerous as the leaves of the forest, and may all the joys of life attend them.

The *Herald* reproduced extracts from other Atchison papers designed to show that the blushing bride was "not without honor in her own city and among her own people." But was she?

Marriage License number 765, issued August 13, 1873, by Probate Judge S. A. Frazier, authorizes the marriage of Alex A. McSween of Eureka, Kans., aged twenty-nine, and Sue E. Homer of Atchison County, aged twenty-seven.[12] The ceremony was performed by New York-born, fifty-four-year-old Edward Cooper, pastor of the First Presbyterian Church of Atchison at 302 N. Fifth St., with his wife Mary as witness. The glowing newspaper encomiums to the bride seem to indicate that she was well known in the town, yet the only documentary record of Sue E. Homer that can be found in Atchison is her registration with the First Presbyterian Church in Atchison on April 13, 1873.

According to her own statement, she was attending a convent there, but like much of what she said about her early life, this statement raises more questions than it answers.[13] There was only one convent in Atchison, and Sue E. Homer was twenty-seven, too old to have become a student, and unlikely, since she was not Catholic, to have been a teacher. The Atchison census for 1870 lists all students and teachers at the convent. Her name is not among them, nor for that matter does it appear anywhere else in that census.

These anomalies give rise to serious questions. If Sue Homer was in a convent, she would have had little opportunity to cultivate the wide popularity claimed for her by the newspaper articles. If she was not, her arrival on the scene only four months before her wedding would have given her even less chance to cast her "genial glow" over her "many friends."

Further doubt is cast on her account by the fact that she claimed to have met McSween not in Kansas, but in Pekin, Ill., in 1870. "He was stopping at an hotel there and I was stopping with some friends of mine. He was in the parlor writing. I was there telling an old grandmother about the Indians, as I had been down near Indian Territory. He overheard me and that evening he met me and got to joking and kind of flirting."[14] McSween told her he was going to Emporia, Kans., on business, presumably the Lord's, since "he was not a lawyer then, but a minister." After two weeks he came back. "We engaged in repartee and I gave him about as good as he gave."

There is no documentary record of either of them in Pekin, Ill., a river town that saw plenty of transients.[15] At the time in question it was a terminus of the ill-fated Chicago & St.Louis Railway, "two streaks of rust" that ferried passengers the 154 miles from the Windy City. Neither has it been possible to find any trace of McSween in Whitehall, Ill., so we must again fall back upon the recollections of his wife.

He had no money. He was not a lawyer then, but a minister. After we were engaged [soon after the Pekin meeting in 1870] he said he wanted to study for some other profession before we got married. He said he wanted to go to Washington University at St. Louis. He was detained and got there some two weeks after it opened. The Dean did not take him that late, and he told the Dean he could catch up. He left disconsolate, but then had a letter from the Dean. It said that he had decided he would take him in, as he felt he could catch up with the work. He went back and caught up, but he nearly killed himself. He ruined his health.[16]

To summarize: by her own account, Sue E. Homer has traveled from "near Indian Territory" to Pekin, Ill., in 1870. She becomes engaged to McSween, who at the end of 1871 and the beginning of 1872 is attending law school in St. Louis; while he is there, and even when he moves to Eureka, she is in Atchison, Kans., where she attends a "convent," but leaves no record of her passing. Nor does she indicate how she got there, what she was using for money, or where she was living. There are enough oddities in all this to prompt a more thorough examination of the story she told her many biographers.

To begin with, she was born not Homer, but Hummer, on December 30, 1845, and appears in the 1850 and 1860 censuses for Adams County, Pa., not as Sue E. or Susan, but Susanna (fig. 3).[17]

FIG. 3. Susanna Hummer as a young woman. Date and photographer unknown.

Nor was she born, as she always claimed, in Gettysburg, but on a ninety-four-acre farm some twelve miles north of that town, in Tyrone Township, Adams County. Her father was Peter Hummer, born 1808 in Adams County; her mother Elizabeth Stauffer, born 1812 in Front Royal, Va. They were married by Rev. Daniel Gottwald on November 22, 1832, and there were eight children of their union: Savilla, Delilah, Rebecca, Elizabeth, Susanna, Amanda, Lydia, and Leander.

Elizabeth Stauffer Hummer died on October 20, 1851; five months later, on March 17, 1852, Peter Hummer married his wife's younger sister Lydia Stauffer. There were to be a further eight children of this union: Addison, Laura, Ida, Florella, Harvey, Emma, Ellsworth, and Hattie. By the time the fifth child, Harvey, had been born, however, Susanna Hummer had left Tyrone Township. Her last appearance is in the 1860 census.

The Hummers were Dunkards. Now known as the Church of the Brethren, the Dunkards were a sect of German Baptist Brethren who fled from Germany and settled in Germantown, Pa., in 1719. Dunkards dressed simply and were opposed to oaths, alcohol, tobacco, and war, all of which they doubtless experienced in superabundance when the fury of the Civil War burst over them during the battle of Gettysburg.

The family tradition is that either immediately after the battle, or immediately after the end of the war, Susanna ran away from home and went west with, or fled west to, the home of a married sister.[18] "Adventure began for Aunt Sue when she, rebelling at the strict discipline of that Plain [Dunkard] Sect, ran away from home shortly after the Civil War. During the night the young girl left by a second-story window of her family home at [what is now] Chestnut Hill, near Biglersville, and headed west with a married sister and the latter's family."[19]

Only two of Susanna's siblings went west.[20] The first was her immediate elder sister, Elizabeth, who married David Pugh Shield of Columbus, Ohio. The second was a younger sister, Amanda or Annie; all that is known about her is that she married a man named Frank Guilloma, and that in 1895 they were living at New Baltimore, Ohio.

The Shields were married on November 11, 1859.[21] The ceremony was conducted in Adams County by the same pastor who had married Peter and Lydia Hummer; it is safe to assume it was celebrated at the family home. Sometime following the wedding the bride and groom returned to Ohio, where the twenty-seven-year-old Shield was a lawyer in his father's practice. Their first child, George, was born in Ohio, but in late 1862 or early 1863 the Shield family left Ohio for Stockton, Mo., where David Shield's brother George Whitelaw Shield practiced law. So if Susanna Hummer left home anytime after Gettysburg to visit Elizabeth Shield, it was to Missouri she went, not Ohio. The fact that on the same day the battle of Gettysburg began, David Shield enlisted in the Missouri Militia might be considered as support for the possibility that his departure for the wars prompted Susanna to join her sister, who was expecting a second child.

The tradition among her Pennsylvania relatives, however, is that she "headed west with a married sister and the latter's family," to Ohio, not Missouri. This suggests that perhaps it was to or with her other sister Annie that Susanna decamped. The fact that Ohio is a contiguous state adds support to this proposition, but in the ultimate analysis, neither theory jibes with what the lady herself said. If she was living with her sister Elizabeth (was that the "down near Indian Territory" she referred to?) or, for that matter, with her sister Annie in New Baltimore, why did she not simply say so? And if she was not, where was she between the time she left home and her first documented appearance in Atchison, in April 1873?

Not one of all the people who talked to her at such great length ever asked her this question. As a result, Susanna Hummer's life between 1860 and 1873 remains a complete mystery. Until that missing decade is accounted for, it is difficult not to suspect she deliberately concealed the truth about her past, leading ineluctably to the conclusion that there was something in it of which she was considerably less than proud.

The 1873 "panic" sent shock waves right across the country, so it is no surprise that McSween's appearances in the *Eureka Herald* that summer hint that money was tight. In the first three weeks of October, the following notice appeared:

> Parties knowing themselves indebted to the Lantier estate are requested to call at once at my office and settle. Produce of every kind taken as payment. Delinquents will be forced.
>
> Alex A. McSween.

The warning obviously had its effect: a week later, McSween was offering for sale "four oxen, one cow, one pig, hay and corn on one, two, or three years' time, well secured. Also two farms to let with desirable conveniences." Taken in conjunction with the item describing his renovation of the Gregory house, this might be seen as reasonable indication that the McSweens intended to remain in Eureka a lot longer than in fact they did.

Meanwhile, the Presbyterians finished their remodeling at the town hall, at a cost of $3,400 exclusive of donated labor. The Methodists were not so lucky:

Reverend Doctor Buckner, who had gone back east to raise some money, deposited it in a bank in Chicago, one of the many that failed that year; he even had to borrow to get back to Eureka.

That same October, an exchange of correspondence between McSween and J. H. Yeoman, postmaster at Charleston, a small town in the southern part of the county, revealed that McSween was skilled in "phonography," an early form of shorthand. On December 11 he placed another ad in the *Herald*.

Indiana.
I have a piece of land near Terre Houte [*sic*] which I would sell or exchange for city property at a reasonable rate. Also a house and lot in town for $750, the house alone cost $900.
Alex A. McSween.[22]

The phrasing of the item implies that the house in Terre Haute was McSween's own, and not one for which he was acting as an agent, but if McSween ever did live on the banks of the Wabash, he left not a single trace there of having done so.

For the good people of Eureka, 1874 started well. J. Evenhack was advertising the largest stock of groceries in southern Kansas, with salt at two cents a pound; sugar, seven cents; sorghum, fifty-five cents a gallon. F. A. Tuttle, 81 Main St., advertised three pounds of coffee for a dollar; seven pounds of sugar, one dollar; seven boxes of matches, twenty-five cents; and a pound of oysters for fifteen cents. There were two new blacksmith shops in town, and "the ring of the anvils sounded throughout the streets like an Aeolian harp in a high wind." Wood was four dollars a cord and abundant. Orders for fruit trees, shrubs, and bulbs grown by Albertson and Richey on Walnut Creek could be left, and picked up at the post office or the treasurer's office. J. M. Smith was starting a class in vocal music, at a dollar-fifty for twelve lessons. Mrs. L. M. Flint opened a dry goods and millinery store at the corner of Fourth and Main.

It would appear Alexander McSween's law practice was also thriving, because in February 1874, he paid two hundred dollars for two town lots, the second parcel of land he had bought since his arrival about two years earlier. The same month, he also bought a property formerly occupied by a family named Gregory. "He is fitting it up to live in," reported the *Herald*. "He hopes it will be large enough for him and his for several years. We see that he proposes to have it thoroughly renovated."

As summer came on, and residents were warned to keep their hogs shut up, the *Herald* noted on June 18 that the "rennovations" were still going on at the McSween place. "His house received the third and last coat of paint yesterday," the paper reported. Clearly, the McSweens were planning to settle down in Eureka: four months of renovation indicates extensive, and perhaps expensive, changes. And while there is no perfect proof of this, it would appear that McSween may have been making them with someone else's money.

One of his clients was Samuel Webster, a Canadian from Lindsay, Ont., then living in Eureka.[23] As well as cash for investment, Webster gave McSween a number of promissory notes, due for collection between October 1873 and April 1875, all of which were paid before due. The total sum involved was $746, against which, in May 1874, McSween made one payment of $100, leaving $646 outstanding. It was still outstanding three years after the McSweens had left

Kansas forever, and Samuel Webster later testified that he believed "the said monies and the proceeds of said promissory notes and mortgage were appropriated by the said Alexander A. McSween to his own use and for his sole benefit."[24]

Coming events cast their shadow before. What pressures McSween was under can only be guessed, but if his probity buckled under them at this juncture, and for such a relatively small amount, how much more easily it may have collapsed beneath the weight of his temptations and trials in Lincoln County.

The summer of 1874 brought considerable hardship to the Sunflower State.[25] Although Greenwood County seems to have escaped the worst (after all, it was the richest county in the state in proportion to its population, with a million dollars' worth of cattle on its ranges), times became increasingly hard as the economic depression that had hit the eastern seaboard the preceding year sent shock waves throughout the country.

"Why not pay cash to the merchants in Eureka?" exhorted editor Mead of the *Herald*. "They give you credit when you are out of money, but when you have money you trade elsewhere. This is so in every town in the United States. Is it right?"

At the end of July 1874, Eureka was rocked by a financial scandal. The books of County Treasurer A. F. Nicholas—old settler, good Methodist, Eureka Bank stockholder and signer of the town's charter of incorporation—were examined and found incorrect. Shortages of over twenty-five thousand dollars were reported. Although responsibility for these was never conclusively proved, many said that the bank's officers must have known of the deficit. It was evident that for six years there had been bungled bookkeeping. The failure of the bank followed; this might easily have contributed to McSween's financial difficulties.

To add to the troubles of the people of Kansas, an extreme summer drought in July was followed in August by a plague of chinch bugs and grasshoppers, which wiped out everything the farmers had labored so long to grow. In the longer established eastern counties, farmers were entrenched well enough to weather the devastation. In central and western Kansas, where the new settlers were still putting down roots, famine threatened, forcing Governor Osborn to appeal to the federal government and the governors of neighboring states for aid. An eyewitness in Abilene described the plague:

> [C]oming home late one afternoon for supper I stepped back surprised to see what came to be known as Rocky Mountain locusts covering the side of the house. Already inside, they feasted on the curtains. Clouds of them promptly settled down on the whole country—everywhere, unavoidable. People set about killing them to save gardens, but this soon proved ridiculous. Specially contrived machines, pushed by horses, scooped up the 'hoppers in grain fields by the barrelful to burn them. This, too, was nonsensical. In a week grain fields, gardens, trees, shrubs, vines had been eaten down to the ground or bark. Nothing could be done. You sat by and saw everything go.[26]

Sixteen days later, the hoppers were back: "a cloud of them reached fourteen miles east and seven miles west of Eureka," taking four hours to pass over going south. Next day another cloud went south. "Some of them stopped in the county," the *Herald* reported, "the most went on." Those that did not created the usual havoc.

McSween attended the Fifth Annual Institute in July, and his card appeared as usual on the front page of the *Herald.* But by September 23, his fortunes reversed, he was selling up. The two town lots bought the preceding February were conveyed to one B. S. Bennett of Greenwood County for $700, the buyer assuming a mortgage of $333, the vendors retaining profits of the premises for one year. Whether, as seems likely, B. S. Bennett was related to the doctor whose estate McSween had handled has proven impossible to determine, although it is tempting to surmise that McSween was indebted to that estate as well. The following day his card appeared in the *Herald* for what was to be the last time.

In later years, Susan McSween stated that they left Eureka in September, but if this is so, it must have been at the very end of the month, and hard on the sale of their property. She always gave as their reason for the trip to New Mexico the fact that McSween suffered badly from asthma. If illness was the only reason for their leaving, it is hard to understand why McSween's friend Mead, editor of the *Herald,* did not run a story, full of the fulsome valedictions so beloved of frontier editors, to mark their departure.

McSween's name appeared on February 11, 1875, and the following March 4 and May 20 in a list published in the *Herald* of letters uncalled for at the Eureka post office. This confirms the impression that they decamped, leaving no forwarding address, and is reinforced by the fact that not only did they take Samuel Webster's money with them, but left behind unsold the three town lots they had bought in April 1873. These were finally sold for nonpayment of taxes at a sheriff's sale in 1884.

In her account of their journey, Susan McSween said they started out from Eureka with a horse-team and wagon, traveling west via Dodge City. "We stopped at Granada [Colo.] two months. The railroad had built beyond there. This was in 1874. We took care of a house there for two men who wanted to go out on the plains hunting buffalo. We were going to Silver City."[27]

Upon resuming their journey they fell in with a Mexican freighter who spoke good English and went with him to Punta de Agua, N.M., known today as Punta, a few miles south of Manzano on the old military road to the south. There they met Miguel Otero, a U.S. congressman, who advised them to try Lincoln. "He said it was a new place and the only town in the county, and that he thought McSwain would do well to come. He gave us a letter of introduction to the Murphy firm. We came on down the road to Lincoln."

CHAPTER 3

THE PROVING
OF JOHN TUNSTALL

ON March 6, 1874, while Alexander McSween and his wife were busily fixing up the former Gregory house in Eureka, a young Englishman named John Henry Tunstall was celebrating his twenty-first birthday in Victoria, British Columbia. Perhaps "celebrating" is not quite the right word: in fact, he wrote his parents, he had "a dull kind of day."

Tunstall, the only son of a prosperous London businessman, had come to Canada in September 1872 to take his place in the overseas branch of the family business, Turner, Beeton & Tunstall. Established in 1868, the company was managed by the Canadian partner, John H. Turner. It was now considered the "first house" in the town, with a wholesale establishment on Fort St., another building on Government St., and the imposing three-story emporium called London House on the town's principal thoroughfare, Wharf St. It was at the latter location young Tunstall worked as a clerk.

Although, through the family's preservation of Tunstall's letters and diaries, his life is probably better documented than that of any other participant in the Lincoln County War, only a little is known about his early years.[1] He was born in the east London suburb of Dalston on March 6, 1853, the son of John Partridge and Emily (Ramié) Tunstall. At the time of his son's birth, J. P. Tunstall was a commercial traveler—traveling salesman—in East Anglia.[2]

Little is known about Tunstall's childhood, or where and how he was educated. The letters briefly mention his having attended a polytechnic, possibly the London Polytechnic, and on another occasion hint at a boarding school. Apart from a sometimes cavalier attitude toward punctuation and spelling, his command of his own language indicates he received a decent education. He spoke some French (probably learned from his mother, the daughter of a prominent family of Jersey, Channel Islands) and German (the Tunstalls employed German nannies).

At the age of fifteen he worked for a year alongside the owner's son, later a partner, in the firm of E. C. Foreman at 32 Gresham St. in the City of London. He left that position in the summer of 1869 to make a "grand tour" of Europe, which included visits to Paris, Hamburg, Cologne, Frankfurt, Baden, Dresden, Berlin, Vienna, and Switzerland. On his return he continued his business apprenticeship with another London firm, Ayers & Saunders, presumably remaining with them until he left for Canada. No trace of either of these companies exists today.

When he left London in 1872, John Henry Tunstall was not yet twenty.[3] Five feet eleven inches tall, weighing 138 pounds, sandy-haired, clean-shaven, and only partially sighted, he was the one son in a family of five, which consisted of two older sisters, Emily Frances, nicknamed "Minnie," and Clara, and two much younger girls, both of delicate constitution: Lillian, born in 1868, and Mabel, born two years later. The two "sprats," as John called them, were given the pet names of "Jack" and "Punch."

The house in which John was born, 14 Liscombes Cottages, Dalston (now 224 Queensland Rd.), in the London borough of Hackney, still stands. The family left there in 1863, after the death of twelve-year-old Clara; in 1869 they left Dalston altogether, and moved to a pleasant cottage at 7 Belsize Terrace in Hampstead, then a green, wooded, hilly neighborhood that John and his sister Minnie referred to as "our Switzerland." It was from here, on August 18, 1872, that young Tunstall made his optimistic departure for the New World.

Traveling to New York on the Cunard steamer *Calabria,* and then across to San Francisco by rail, Tunstall kept his solemn promise to his "Trinity"—his mother, father, and dearly loved sister Minnie—that he would not only write frequent, long, and detailed letters, but also maintain a journal in which he would record everything—events, places, even his innermost feelings—for his sister. There is mention also of a "business" diary, but no trace of this has ever been found.

Tunstall's situation in the Victoria firm was not altogether comfortable. He was something of a supernumerary, an extra hand reluctantly accommodated at the wish of the senior partner. John clearly tried very hard not to be the typical father's son in the family firm: his early letters contained much information on business matters and comments about the running of the store.

Arriving in Victoria on September 26, 1872, having spent some time in both New York and San Francisco, he moved in as a paying guest at the home of his father's partner, John Herbert Turner, whom he described as "a most agreeable & gentlemanly man. . . . I am living with him at his residence which is a pretty, English-looking villa, about a mile out of town [at Point Ellice, on the corner of what are now Bay and Pleasant streets] & I have every prospect of happiness."[4]

He had little to say about the physical appearance of his new home town, although it was a pretty, English sort of place (fig. 4). Settled as Fort Victoria by James Douglas in 1842, its magnificent harbor at Esquimalt had become the Pacific base for the British Navy. The main commercial streets, most of which were sixty feet wide, ran north-south: skirting the harbor was Wharf, then Government, Douglas, and Blanshard; crossing these at right angles were Courtney, Fort, Yates, and Johnson. Starting from the corner of Fort and Government streets, with a radius of three quarters of a mile, Victoria covered two thirds of a circle stretching around the harbor; to the south of the town center on a high knoll stood Beacon Hill, a large park set aside for public use that contained a racecourse and a cricket ground and was a favorite destination of local citizens out for a walk or a ride.

Tunstall's early letters indicate that he saw his job in Victoria as an apprenticeship preparing him in ten or fifteen years to take over the Canadian end of the business, or perhaps assume his father's place in it. He and Turner seem to have got along famously at first, although Turner was twenty years older. When Tunstall first arrived in Victoria, Turner's wife Elizabeth and their son Arthur, known as Artie, were in London on an extended visit. Several friendly souls advised him

FIG. 4. The Turner family at home, Victoria, B.C., ca. 1873. Photographer unknown.

to get out of the Turner household before she returned, causing him to remark that "I quite dread Mrs. T's return, for the people here dislike her, as much as the Beetons do, & to tell you the truth, I am afraid I could not get on with her."[5]

As for the other people at the store, Tunstall needed only a couple of months' acquaintance to make up his mind: he reported on January 2, 1873 that

> Mr. Harvey & I are first rate friends, though he is a man I should be very shy of giving power to, & one who wants, well looking after, though he is a first rate man if you keep him in the right place (& know which is the right place for him). Next comes old Stannard, we are on the best possible footing, he is as much like a mill horse as a man can be, he knows the stock, the customers, & his position, as well as any man knows his pocket, But he is a mill horse & you cant alter him. [Walter] Shears & I are very good friends but being the same age as myself, & his having lived with me in London, it is more difficult to keep the line; he is not such a success as I anticipated, & does not seem to take as much interest in the business as he should do. Bob Byrn & I get on A.1. he is a first class man for us to have, & keeps his books like a picture.[6]

The intensity of John Tunstall's relationship with his sister Emily, his "dear darling Old Pet," "the only girl I'll ever love," is apparent in all his letters. Theirs was a very special bond that went back to childhood—perhaps at the time of Clara's death—when each had made a solemn, lifetime promise always to be true to the other. Minnie's love and thoughtfulness never failed to move the sentimental Tunstall; how much so is apparent in a letter of Sunday, January 12, 1873, in which he speaks of finding the ring she sent him in a Christmas pudding:

> Mr. Turner & I admire it very much. I have of course looked up the word Mizpah, which I failed to see the point of till now, I find that it means a beacon, or watch tower, I hope never to pass it over the first joint of the third finger of my right hand, & I will look upon it as an engagement ring, never to be broken but by your wish. The thought of it makes me feel quite sentimental, & had not Mr. Turner been present, I fear I should have bedewed it.[7]

Victoria must have seemed a provincial place to a young man of Tunstall's predilections and background. Raised to horses, he decided to risk his father's wrath—little risk at all, for the old man fairly doted on his son—and bought one for $150. In this April letter he sets out his reasons:

> there is no amusement here save riding, fishing, shooting, rowing, reading, drinking, smoking, playing billiards, cricket, or baseball here. Now there is only one place to row namely up the arm, which once taken, the novelty ceases & there are no clubs or rowing conveniences, the boats are all "hulks" & expensive so the attractions are not great. Shooting takes so much time that much as I should like it, I have only been out about half a dozen times with my gun *atall.* Reading after being in business all day, when it is so fine out of doors, one canot be for-ever poreing over a book or a newspaper. Drinking, smoking & playing billiards, I hear my dear Mother groan & her muttered "God forbid that any son of mine &c &c" at the very thought of the first of these three, now let me candidly & truthfully tell you, that I believe with the exception of myself & all but perhaps two other exceptions, there is not a young man of my age & caste, in this town, who does not "drink" & to excess, this may surprise you, but it is none the less true, smoking does not amount to anything either one way, or the other, I rarely smoke, & then not more than one pipe in the evening. playing billiards necessitates the previous two. . . . if I am seen down town in the evening, I am thought mean for not drinking with my friends, whom I pass in the Colonial & other places when ever I go down after business & if there is one thing which "damns", eh! "damns" a man's prospects here more than anything else, it is for him to be thought mean. billiards would be so costly that I will only say that I could hardly touch a cue under 10/- shillings, cricket or baseball are played while I am in business so I need say no more of them, now all I have said Mr. Turner endorses to the letter, he considers that I am *economical,* & do the right thing, which requires tact, for people expect a great deal from a young man who has no family & is connected with the "first house" in the town.[8]

Social life in Victoria, such as it was, had few attractions: Tunstall found most of the people he had to mix with extremely provincial, what he punnishly called "deuxieme seconde categorie de jambons [gens bons]." His position, as a partner's son, a guest of the Turner family, and a member of the firm with "great expectations," required that he socialize.

He made regular calls on the "first families" of the town: the Wilson Browns, the Roderick Finlaysons, the Alfred Langleys, the Rhodeses, the Heywoods, the Wilsons, and the Palmers, whose daughter Fanny he had met earlier in the year at dancing classes.[9] Fanny had returned to England for eight months, and the Palmers called him in to see her photograph, which was "wonderfully pretty, though not flattered." He listened to Mrs. Palmer's dissertation upon the subject of Mrs. Heywood and her vulgarity, which was almost more than he could stand without laughing, as he had just left the Heywoods, where the lady of the house had bent his ear in similar vein about Mrs. Palmer.

On August 7 the officers of the flagship *Repulse* issued invitations to a ball for Admiral Hillyer, who was about to leave the colony, a gala occasion. Events such as this were rare in Victoria, however: entries in Tunstall's journal most often begin with the words, "Nothing worthy of note happened today."

In September 1873 the young merchant took a hunting vacation in the Cowichan Bay area on the eastern coast of Vancouver Island. His account of the trip is full of adventures; clearly he did not mind roughing it, and was confident about his ability to survive in the wilderness. He got back to Victoria on September 13 and noted in his diary that "Mr. & Mrs. Turner & Arty seemed very pleased to see me back again, though they thought I looked very thin, I told them it was the leanness one sees in a well trained race horse, & that I never felt better in my life."[10]

Hardly surprising that after such adventures, his first day back at the store elicited the comment "precious dull" in his journal. Indeed, life in this genteel little backwater could scarcely have been otherwise. The only excitements were typical small-town ones: a fire, a runaway horse, affairs at the store, local gossip, none of which held any charm for Tunstall.

He was a perfect example of that curious mixture that makes up the English personality, courting popularity while affecting not to want it, liberal yet prejudiced, a certain charm taking the edge off arrogance, self-deprecation concealing self-righteousness. He could also be mercilessly judgmental, as in this record of a day in the domestic life of the Turners. It began when Mrs. Turner

> snubbed her lord, at the dinner table, most atrociously, & in a way that shewed her nature up most thoroughly. It happened thus. Mrs. Turner seldom drinks beer, though as butler I always offer her some; Mr. Turner was filling his glass, & holding the bottle, said, "Won't you take some today, Liz" he said this very kindly, Mrs. Turner put her head on one side & slightly caricaturing his tone, said, "Won't you take a glass today, Liz, you know I wont, you know I never drink beer." As much as to say what a hypocrite you are, Turner swallowed it, & said nothing; If I ever have a wife, & she treats me that way, she'll get beer, & bottle, both, straight in the eye; unless my temper gets pretty well tamed down before that period.[11]

Writing as much as Tunstall did—he was answering long and frequent letters from his father, his sister, and also the occasional one from his mother—took up most of his spare time and nearly all of his weekend. He records on October 22 that he "sat up till three o'clock in the morning writing home." That "budget" consisted of a letter to Minnie, "My Dearly Beloved Sister," in reply to hers of August 7 (their letters took about a month each way in transit, so his reply to her questions of that date would reach her about two months later); one to his "Dearly Beloved Mother"; another to his father, whom he frequently addressed affectionately as "Dear Governor"; another to "My Dearly Beloved Sister" answering hers of August 11; another to "My Dear Governor"; "My Darling Sister" again; "My Dear Governor" again; "My Dearly Beloved Sister" (replying to hers of July 30); and yet another to "My Dearest Min," covering seventeen pages in all.

Replying to their questions, he ranged across such topics as the profit margins at the Victoria store ("Flowers, Feathers, Millinery & Jewellery & fancy articles, such as card cases &c &c we get 200 [percent] on, Haberdashery about 130, a few black goods bear 125 or 130 per cent. Carpets we get about 75 per cent upon, on an average"); his feelings about his cousin Harry Beeton, who had come out for two months in Victoria and was now back in London ("gassy & superficial in the extreme"); his own popularity ("I can candidly say that I think [the people here] like me, & are likely to like me better as time goes on"); and even his acne ("I can assure you that my face is neither spotty, nor unattractive, nor unsightly, that is, if I can believe my lady friends on the subject, hem! hem!").

When it came to lady friends, Tunstall, like many a young man before him, told his parents no more than they needed to know. On Monday, November 10, he noted in his journal that "the steamer came in this morning, among the passengers is Miss Fanny Palmer, who has been away for nearly eight months, her mother has been continually telling me that she always remembers me in her letters &c, to which I always say . . . I felt very much flattered &c with variations."[12] Two days later, he joined the skating club at a new hall that had been built on Fort Street.

I asked Fanny Palmer to come, which she was very pleased to do, as she is very fond of skating, she looked exceedingly pretty & skates most gracefully. Imagine my vexation after putting on her skates & my own, to find I could not skate on them *one bit.* . . . I must confess that I never was so anxious to learn anything in my life, as I was to learn to skate, the idea of my taking a girl to a skating rink, for others to skate with, was maddening, there were about half a dozen beginners in the room tumbling about like lobsters, & I could not but feel that I looked like a lobster too, however, I was so determined to learn that I learnt in an hour. . . .

Fanny asked me how I managed to learn so quickly, so I thought of the Governor & his gallant speeches, & said, "who could not learn quickly, for the pleasure of skating with you?"

I stayed for about half an hour at the Palmer's after escorting Miss Fanny home, Mrs. Palmer is really most intensely bad style, I think I shall have to "let up" on them . . . though this girl is about the prettiest girl in Victoria, & no trouble to get along with, "nous verrons"; Now my dear Parents dont run off with the idea that I am smitten for if you do, you will run off with a useless load, My only feeling in the matter is that the girl has a pretty face & as much brains behind it, as the ugly ones, & it is quite as much pleasure to talk to a pretty face as an ugly one. In London I would not cross the road to be kissed by her, but here she could make all the youth of Victoria, except myself, walk barefooted for a mile for that reward, I would not go the distance unless I was allowed to *ride.*[13]

In spite of such disavowals, Tunstall was taking a lively interest in the young ladies of Victoria, while always assuring his London readers that they need have no fear of his becoming entangled. There was Jinny Cooper,"that girl is a devil to flirt, I never saw her equal, but its very good fun"; a Miss Archer, to whom he paid a great deal of attention because "it sets all the girls talking at a great rate"; and Miss Baxter, "*an awfully smart girl* who has flirted with everyone here but myself." Fanny Palmer, of course, whom he took on a sleigh ride through town on January 22, and added that "I shall ask Fanny for one of her photos, I should like you to see it, she is such a nice looking girl, she would not be to be sneezed at even in London, though I would not give a snap of the fingers for a score like her." At Mrs. Sutro's dance there were "two extremely charming young ladies names [sic] Munro there, whom I am very much taken with. . . . I shall cultivate them, by and bye." It is hardly surprising, then, that on February 14, he "received a lot of valentines which I put in the stove without opening them. I sent some to Fanny Palmer, which I altered and wrote on, to suit her case, I met her at the Skating Rink & she shewed them to me, which amused me very much, as she never suspected who had sent them."[14]

Friday, March 6, was John Tunstall's twenty-first birthday. It is noted in the journal only as "a dull kind of day," principally because he did not mention his majority to the Turners, they having only a week earlier thrown a substantial party, and "I should have been sorry for them to feel, either the burden of anything of the kind on my account, or for them to regret their not doing so."[15] As for his feelings,

> I need not tell you that I thought of you a great deal . . . & felt that no matter what the future held in store for me, in my *manhood*, that my *childhood* had been one long scene of Happiness & pleasure; & I felt that of all the boys *throughout* the *world*, who might be entering upon their majority on that day, that there were very few, who could look back upon more happiness than myself, & none who could feel that they were more truly loved than I am.

In April 1874, John Turner left Victoria for a business trip to London. In his absence, the combustible combination of Tunstall and Elizabeth Turner was not long in igniting, and within a few weeks they had what Tunstall described as "a considerable row." It was passed over lightly, but it was a precursor of worse to come: these two liked each other not at all. Meanwhile, Tunstall assured his sister that he did not share her opinion that he was "made much of" in Victoria. Indeed,

> I go out visiting very little, though in future I intend to do more of that sort of thing; but I am not atall a "*cock of the village.*" I leave all "beauing" to those who have the time & inclination to do it, up to now, I have shewn more politeness to my horse, & my dog, than I have to the girls, for they are really not worth "killing" since they are none of them fit for the "bag" of an old country sportsman.
>
> Those two Miss Munroes, are about the only two girls on the island who have been carefully brought up (at least, so I think) they are very nice in their behaviour, I dont think they are immensely well educated, I have not called at their house more than once & I therefore dont know very much of them, but I intend to get to know them, the eldest is engaged to a man named Rithet, the younger & prettier of the two, though I don't know if the elder is not the most attractive, is yet free to enter into an engagement if she sees fit, I need not say that in my wildest moments I am never tempted to dream of breaking off my engagement with you.[16]

So time went by. He dined with the Byrns; Jinny Cooper was there, "about as much inclined to flirt as ever, it is a sort of habit with her, I think, I fancy she cant help it." He was summoned for riding his horse faster than at a walk across one of the bridges. Most days, however, Tunstall found himself writing "Uneventful" so often that he complained, "Oh, Hang it! I could write uneventful from one years end to the other, I wish the place would burn down, if it was only to give us something to talk about."

Tunstall had something to talk about soon enough: the steamer arrived on Tuesday, June 9, bearing a thirty-seven-page letter from his father. After a few pages about business—the preceding year's turnover had been £35,246, net profit

£2,788—and other parental cautioning, Papa Tunstall outlined the contents of a letter he had received from John Turner about John's behavior.

Turner complained that John had too many dogs; that he stayed late at people's homes, keeping them up when they would have preferred to be abed; stayed out later than he should; that when he did come home he never read; that he was hard to get out of bed in the mornings, and had to be told if he was not down in time for breakfast, it would be cleared away; that he often took his horse to town unfed and ungroomed; that he was untidy and careless in his work; that he was overly familiar with some of the lady shoppers; that he did not set a good example to Shears and Stannard; and more, and more.

Tunstall set out to justify himself, something necessity would make him very adept at doing as time went by. His reply was seventeen pages long; it is revelatory of a young man's inability—or unwillingness—to see himself as perhaps others saw him. It is clear that his patrician attitude irritated Turner and that the older man disapproved strongly of Tunstall's friendship with "unsuitable" local girls. Turner's criticisms were not entirely unfounded; unfortunately for him, he was dealing with a young man who not only refused to admit he could be in the wrong, but who now—very plausibly—set out to undermine Turner's position by making his criticisms look like victimization.

> I consider as I said at starting that you did right in asking Mr. Turner all the faults he had ever found with me; but for you to feel the smallest shadow of vexation over events that occurred between a year & two years ago, I consider was good vexation *wasted, thrown-away completely.*
>
> In addition to which, when you consider that I have been in business under the eye of a man of forty who is looked upon as a *firstrate* man of business, in a new sphere as this was to me, where I have to enact the part of a servant, & a master at the same time, in which I am brought into contact with *female* customers, all of whom I know socially, & that notice everything I *do*, or *say*, *& don't fail to repeat it*; I think that when that overseer tells you, that the only faults he has had to find during the 22 months I have been here, from a business point of view, were carelessness & on one or two occasions not being quite distant enough to an out-of-business friend; & that he thought & said, that when trade was lively I was quite up to the mark, you *ought*, & I *ought*, to feel *more* than satisfied, & when you consider that I am *even* out of business, always under his eye, live in *his* household, & mix with *his* friends, that *he* has a wife whom *nobody* has good words for, *that he* can't get along with [himself] or anyone else either, & that he is supposed to possess, & I think that if there is any truth in the proverb, "that the proof of the pudding is in the eating", that he *does* possess, a vast amount of tact, since every soul in the place speaks well of him & that the only thing he can say in the shape of fault finding is, that I don't get up very readily, & that he thinks I stay at people's houses longer than he would, which is a thing he is no judge of, & *can't be*, as I explained before. I think also that you should be *more* than satisfied for you all know that. . . . None of you, Father, Mother, Sister, Aunt & cousins, *none* of you, with all your french tact, Staid ideas, experience & everything, *begin* to get on with Mrs. Turner, you *all* quarrelled with her, but when I took the reins, & was clear of all advice, & other obstacles, I put a smooth snaffle in her mouth & *by Jove*, I've kept her up to the bit, for more than twelve months.[17]

Two days later he had cause to rue his words, for he witnessed Mrs. Turner "in the 'role' of virago." Tunstall was sharp with little Arty Turner, who ran to his Mama in tears.

Mrs Turner began a tirade, such as few others can equal . . . and when she began going on, I was fairly "riled" as we say; (as though it mattered whether he howled 99 times, or a 100 in the 24 hours) she began telling me, I was always unkind, & cruel to the boy, & one thing & the other, which I denied, & she repeated, till I got mad, she said "you're a most disagreeable young man" so I told her "she was a most detestable woman" at last she went on & on, till I told her, I hated wordy warfare & she had better cease, as I should not listen to her any longer. . . . In the course of her rage she told me "Arty had a much better right to be here than me, & I had better pack up my traps & go". I *shall* go, as soon as I find a place to suit me, she really is not worth the trouble of working. To be perpetually angling, to keep right with a beast of that description is a perfect farce. "le jeu ne vau pas la chandeles" I *cannot* stand it any longer . . . so far as I can judge, she has but one sense of affection or but one byas, in her nature and that is, a *stupid, pigheaded, ill judged, ignorant* fondness for that boy, who is like herself, devoid [of] all love, human kindness,or generosity, either of thought, feeling or action.[18]

The game was indeed not worth the candle, as Tunstall put it in his fractured French. There was nothing for it but to get out of the Turner household as soon as he possibly could. But the collision with Mrs Turner was not the only vexation he had to face.

On Saturday, July 4, he called on Fanny Palmer to take her for a buggy ride. As he handed her aboard outside her home, the skittish little mare he had traded for his big horse, Jim, ran away, spilling Fanny in the road.

> another man & myself carried the girl home senseless (it was not eighty yards from her house) after a while she came to & went off again, almost at once, we felt all her bones, to see if any were broken, & were relieved to find that they were sound,or at any rate appeared to be. I will cut all this short & tell you the sequel which was. That after fainting three or four times before night, she finally got to sleep. She has a bruise on her cheek bone, & her hip is bruised & shaken by the fall, but the doctor says, that there is nothing the matter, but what she will be well of, in a few days. I am happy to say that no blame attaches to me in the slightest degree[19]

Although he knew perfectly well that everyone in town was talking about his "romance" and expected it to conclude in matrimony, Tunstall dropped Fanny Palmer like a hot brick, and concentrated instead upon finding new quarters as far away as possible from Elizabeth Turner. By Friday, July 31, he recorded having "called on Papa's friend Mrs. Francis and have concluded to live there."

> Monday, August 10th.
> I moved to my new quarters & the improvement is *great*. I have two rooms, one was their drawing room, a nice room, though I must buy a table for it. I will draw a plan of it some time soon, to give you an idea of what it is like. the bedroom above, rather larger than the drawing room, is a *very very* nice room, the people Papa knows & can tell you more about than I can up to now. There is one thing I can say which is that I feel more comfortable, than I have done since I left home.
> I have two rooms, gas in each, breakfast on Sunday, a fire in winter whenever I wish it, towels & bed linen found me, a stable (which I must spend £10 on, to make a beautiful stable of it) two enclosed yards & another large piece of ground for the horse to run in; for $25 a month (& I can tell you it is the cheapest thing, in lodgings on this coast.)

Saturday, 15th [August]

I like my quarters more & more every day, I feel as happy as a"big sun flower", so far as my lodgings, or rather *home* is concerned, the people (Mrs. Francis and her daughter Mrs. [Eliza] Gillihan) are as kind as they can be. Mr. Turner's house could not compare with this, as far as my comfort was concerned. They feed my dogs & do everything they can think of, to make me comfortable. I have bought a table for 18/- which with a cloth to cover it completes my sitting room which is the picture of comfort. My bedroom is very nicely furnished, having, a double bed, a marble topped chest of drawers with a large looking glass attached, a large cupboard for my clothes, a sofa & easy chair, a marble topped washstand & other bedroom furniture to match.[20]

Tunstall's stay at the Francis home on Pandora Avenue was to be one of the happiest periods of his life. With old Mrs Francis (fig. 5) and her daughter Eliza to minister to all his needs, he fell to planning his forthcoming "shooting tour" up-country. "There is not a boy in the world that has a right to be more happy than I am now," he wrote.

Over the last four or five days before he left, he wrote another long "budget" to his family. Minnie had told him that the drawing room at 7 Belsize Terrace had been refurnished, eliciting from her brother this charming picture of life *chez* Tunstall:

I picture the drawing room as rather more darkly furnished than before, without any trace of a heavy or hearse-like appearance. . . . I can see the governor in the armchair cross legged, & talking over the subjects of interest at the present, such as the future of the business, my future, Mr. Turner's late arrival in Victoria, I fancy I hear him saying, "Well, you know, John will just tell Mr. Turner how the thing was, & there will be an end of it, & that is *exactly* how it will be." I can picture my Dearly beloved Mother, shaking her coil & comb-crowned head & looking as straight at the blackest possible side of the picture as it is possible for mortal to do. I see you, my Darling Sister Min sitting at the table pouring out the tea, talking to the little ones in German, listening to the conversation & representing the hopeful side of the question, & contrasting it with Mamma's doleful picture & saying "you are not afraid but that John will work it right in the end." & as to my two dear Old boys, Jack & Punch, whom I love & yearn for, till I feel my heart will swell to double the size. . . . why! I see them sitting side by side, on your right, seeing which can behave in the most dignified & ladylike manner & most resemble sister Min.[21]

At 7.30 in the morning of September 1, he set off for New Westminster on the steamer *Enterprise* with his "gun case & a change of clothes, done up in a pair of indigo four point blankets, with [the cocker spaniel] Punch at heel."

I felt in starting on this outing a little of the Governor's old feeling, of "coute qui coute" I *should* go, I felt in the first place quite used up; in the second, quite disgusted; and in the third, that my health required it; so although I took so long a holiday at the expense of others, as through Mr. Turner's late arrival, the boys had to take their holidays late, if they took them at all & my taking such a one, curtailed *theirs* considerably; but they all knew that I needed change more than they,, & were very glad that I got it. Therefore, when I set foot on the steamer . . . I made up my mind to leave all my vexations to take care of themselves, till I came back & that I would not once think of them till I returned.[22]

He was off to the Similkameen Valley above Hope with his friends Price and Nicholson, a trip that would last thirty-three days, the diary account of which

FIG. 5. Mrs. Allen Bunn Francis. Date and photographer unknown.

covers nearly seventy closely written pages. In it he referred to his poor sight—he was all but blind in one eye—with easy jocularity: obviously the condition was of long standing. He had shot some prairie chickens, which he remarked "ain't so bad for a poor blind man." He described all his adventures in great detail, with drawings and topographical detail that would enable his "Trinity" to follow his route on the map he sent them.

On Monday, September 28, the party headed back to civilization. While they were waiting for the steamer at Hope, Tunstall remarked to the storekeeper that he

> had never eaten so little as two meals a day before I came on this trip (two is the most we ever made) or done so much really hard work consecutively; he asked what I weighed when I left? I told him "148 lbs, but I did not suppose I weighed more than 140 now", he "Guessed I'd gained eight instead of losing it as I imagined". I got onto the scales & what was my astonishment to find that I weighed 156 pounds, I never turned the scale properly at 150 before, in my life, & I weighed very light just before leaving, I never felt so well to my knowledge as I did when I came off this trip, so you can judge what fresh air & exercise will do for me.[23]

He returned to the store on Monday, October 5, to find that they had "not been *overdone* with business" in his absence.[24] "Mr. Turner seemed very pleased to see me," he wrote, "& never so much as hinted that I had been away *too* long, or a long while."

On Wednesday, October 14, after recording a ride to Beacon Hill, where the bishop of Victoria and his wife had expressed their amazement at the improvement in the mare they had traded with him, Tunstall's journal of his life in Victoria ceased; the next page is written from San Francisco, more than a year later. There is no explanation for this in the letters, which continued and indeed, over the following year, increased in frequency and volume. In his final entry for 1874, he had this to say to his sister, and perhaps also to history.

> I have the greatest objection (*personally*) to making a wild beast show of myself. I have no objection to giving you a history of myself, as you say, that nothing is too trivial to have interest for you, but to make a living "biographer of *myself*" for the amusement of others, is not atall to my taste. . . . *what on earth* can anyone else care to know about me, but yourself & if they want to hear about any of my doings let them invest a penny in the "London Journal" & they will find adventures without end, far more exciting than ever befall me, & much better expressed than I am able to express anything.[25]

History may beg leave to differ.

CHAPTER 4

THE RISE OF THE HOUSE OF MURPHY

FOR Lawrence Gustave Murphy, June 3, 1874, must have been a memorable day. On this otherwise unremarkable Wednesday, the Irish immigrant laborer who had arrived in America a quarter of a century earlier threw open the doors of his new store in the county seat town of Lincoln, N.M., a grand building that would comfortably house all the activities of the company in which he was the dominant partner.

Standing at the western end of the town's single street, the "House," as it came to be called, was the physical expression of Murphy's power and influence: a store, a saloon, a meeting place for the firm's military cronies from nearby Fort Stanton, a bunkhouse for the cowboys it employed, a Masonic Hall. Dwarfing every other building in town, two stories high, more than 180 feet long, each floor 2,800 square feet in extent, with 11-foot-high ceilings and spacious living quarters on the upper floor, the new home of L. G. Murphy & Co. was the largest civilian structure in Lincoln County; there were few larger in all New Mexico.

It is not too difficult to imagine him up there on his second-floor balcony, a glass of Double Anchor whiskey in his hand, "a slender, sandy 'complected' man, a little above average height . . . dressed carefully and expensively in the best of broadcloth suits," smiling benignly down upon his little empire, the leonine head back, the shrewd narrow eyes beneath the high, sloping forehead missing nothing.[1]

This was no beardless boy, no small-town lawyer, no clerk bemoaning his petty tribulations. Lawrence Gustave Murphy was a ruthless and powerful man—"the Lord of the Mountains," as one writer would call him—and he ruled his domain with an iron hand.[2] Brooking opposition from no one, the firm of L. G. Murphy & Co. had dictated the political and economic fortunes of Lincoln County ever since it began doing business. Murphy had learned well from the "gombeen men" of his boyhood in Ireland.

Over thirty years ago, writing about Lawrence G. Murphy, Philip J. Rasch said that "almost nothing is known of his early years."[3] It is a sad reflection on the generations of historians who have followed that this is still very largely so. Murphy remains one of the most enigmatic figures of his era.

His obituary stated that he was born in County Wexford, Ireland, about 1831; that he had graduated from Maynooth College; and that he served as a sergeant-major in the Regular Army.[4] Although honored patriots in Wexford bore the name Murphy, it is almost impossible to check the first statement, since records of births were not centralized in Ireland before 1864, and there are thirty-five parishes in County Wexford alone. As for the second, no student named Lawrence Gustave Murphy ever attended St. Patrick's College at Maynooth.

Murphy's Army record suggests that if he ever went to college, he stayed there but a short time, since at the age of seventeen he was in Buffalo, N.Y., where he enlisted in the Fifth Infantry, U.S. Army, declaring his age as twenty-one.[5] He told the recruiting officer that he was a laborer, born in Wexford, Ireland.

That was in July 1851, so it would appear that he began his service in Texas, for in 1851 the Fifth Infantry was building Fort Belknap on the Brazos River.[6] On May 21, 1856, Murphy's first tour came to an end, and he was discharged with the rank of sergeant at Fort McIntosh, Tex.; his rank may be read as indication that he was strong, tough, and a scrapper, for no man became a sergeant in the U.S. Army who was not the physical equal or superior of every man in his detachment. His civilian status did not last very long; five days later he re-enlisted at the same post.

In July 1857 Brigham Young, founder of the "State of Deseret"—the Mormon Zion in Utah—led his people into what was virtually insurrection against the federal government. President Buchanan acted decisively, appointing a capable Georgian named Alfred Cumming governor of Utah Territory. Twenty-five hundred troops under the command of Col. and Bvt. Brig. Gen. Albert Sidney Johnston—among them a young officer named Nathan Dudley—were detailed to accompany Cumming to Salt Lake City, there to enforce Mormon obedience to national laws.

This news filled the Mormons with fury, and armed resistance followed. While the "Utah Expedition" was still being organized at Leavenworth, the Mormons began to wage war on any unauthorized party entering their domain. On September 11, a group of emigrants bound for California was butchered in what was to become known as the Mountain Meadows Massacre. Four days later Brigham Young issued a proclamation forbidding any armed force to enter Utah and ordered mobilization under martial law.

The Fifth Infantry—Murphy's regiment—together with the Tenth Infantry, the Second Cavalry, and two artillery battalions, left Fort Leavenworth on September 16. The beginning of October found Col. E. B. Alexander's forward command of about five hundred cavalry approaching Fort Bridger, although the rear of the expedition had only reached Fort Laramie. At this juncture, Mormon Maj. Lot Smith led an attack on the expedition that resulted in the destruction of seventy-four army wagons containing several months' troop provisions.

The loss of their supplies visited fearful hardships on the soldiers. Horses, mules, oxen, and men died of cold and disease as they struggled to reach winter quarters at Fort Bridger, Utah (now Wyoming), only to find that the angry Mormons had already destroyed it. Capt. Randolph B. Marcy and forty enlisted men trekked a thousand miles overland to Fort Massachusetts, N.M., to obtain supplies. The journey took them fifty-one days: when they arrived, they were so emaciated and ailing that the troops at that station had difficulty recognizing them as fellow soldiers.

The plight of the men at Fort Bridger was scarcely less parlous, but fortunately for all of them, a mediator, Thomas L. Kane, son of a Philadelphia judge, made his way to Salt Lake City, conferred with Brigham Young, and found a solution satisfactory to both sides. Although the military men were spoiling for a confrontation, no fighting ever took place.

As two federal peace commissioners reached complete agreement with Young in June 1858, Marcy got back to Fort Bridger with reinforcements and fifteen hundred animals. On June 10, Johnson's little army entered Salt Lake City—which it found deserted—and set up an encampment at Cedar Valley, about thirty-six miles south of the city. Although, as one cynic commented, the outcome of the so-called war was "Wounded, none; killed, none; fooled, everybody," Sgt. Lawrence G. Murphy had certainly seen his share of tough soldiering.

Now holding the rank of quartermaster sergeant, Lawrence Murphy was next discharged on Friday, April 26, 1861, just a fortnight after Brig. Gen. P.G.T. Beauregard fired the opening shots of the Civil War at Fort Sumter. He left the service at Fort Fauntleroy, later Fort Wingate, 170 miles west of Santa Fe, with the highest commendations, plus a recommendation for a commission in the regular army. Instead, having made his way to Santa Fe, he accepted a commission on July 17 as a first lieutenant in the First Regiment of the New Mexico Volunteers being organized in Santa Fe by Col. Ceran St. Vrain and Lt. Col. Christopher "Kit" Carson.

He began his service at Fort Union on July 27 and was appointed Regimental Quartermaster. Whether he was with Carson at the battle of Valverde on February 22 is not clear. He was "unofficially reported" to have been on detached service with Col. John P. Slough's First Colorado Volunteers at the time; that being so, he may have participated in the skirmishes at Pigeon's Ranch and Apache Canyon (Glorieta Pass) near Las Vegas, N.M., in which the "Pike's Peakers," commanded by Slough and John M. "Preacher" Chivington, together with several companies of Murphy's old regiment, the Fifth Infantry, collided with the Confederate Army, and between March 26 and 28, stopped its thrust towards Fort Union.

In April 1862, writing from Hot Springs, Las Vegas, his tour of duty completed, Murphy requested that instead of returning to Fort Union, he be posted to Santa Fe "or wherever else my services may be most needed." On May 31, before his request could be acted upon, the First Regiment was reorganized. In the process, Murphy was discharged.

He sat out the rest of the war in the west, as Sibley's Army of New Mexico retreated down the Rio Grande valley and out of the Territory. Not until the fall, with the Confederate threat entirely removed by the arrival of the California Column, was Murphy able to take his case to his friend Kit Carson and seek reinstatement.

Gen. James H. Carleton, leader of the force that had so anticlimactically come to the rescue of New Mexico, had been appointed commander of the department, succeeding General E.R.S. Canby. On September 23, just a few days after Carleton's arrival in Santa Fe, Carson wrote him as follows:

> During the time that Lieut. Murphy served in my Regiment, he performed his duties with zeal and ability . . . although in the organization of a new Regiment like this, he had many difficulties to contend with.
>
> Lieut. Murphy has been during his service with the Regiment of nearly a year prompt and efficient in the performance of his duties, and although in the performance thereof, he made some enemies at first, yet all eventually saw that he had

acted for the best interests of the service, and in a manner to learn their duties to those unacquainted with them.

Lieut. Murphy was well liked in the Regiment, and I would respectfully ask that he be recommended to the Governor for a Commission in the Regiment as a First Lieutenant as I feel confident that he will perform the duty with advantage to the public service.[7]

Carson's request was acted on with commendable promptitude; four days later Murphy got his first lieutenancy, and by October 12 he was with the regiment when it reoccupied Fort Stanton, which had been abandoned in August 1861.

With no war for them to fight, General Carleton employed his army in repairing roads and rehabilitating army posts. Aware of the discontent among his officers and men, he fastened upon the idea of using the army to suppress the local Indians, the Mescalero Apaches, who had a virtually free hand while the army was otherwise engaged. He decided that Carson would be the ideal man to lead the campaign; although the assignment was not to Carson's liking, he accepted.

He began his war upon the Mescaleros forthwith, sending patrols down the Rio Hondo to its junction with the Pecos River, with orders from General Carleton to kill "all Indian men of the Mescalero tribe . . . whenever and wherever you find them."[8] Within a week, Carson's men had shot and killed thirty-two Mescaleros, among them the headmen José Largo and Manuelito. A few weeks more, and five hundred Mescalero men, women, and children had been sent to Bosque Redondo as "prisoners of war."

Kit Carson was the very antithesis of a "book" soldier. His command was more like a committee than a military organization, and as Carleton's instructions, orders, counterorders, and exhortations to kill Indians poured in, Carson, who had no great regard for army rules and regulations, obeyed those he approved and ignored those he did not. He let his officers see to the running of the post; the officers, as was the wont of officers, delegated the task to their noncoms, and discipline was less than stringent. The laissez-faire atmosphere fostered by Carson's methods and encouraged by the post's isolation, the manner in which the captive Mescaleros were treated and fed, were matters of which Lawrence G. Murphy doubtless took careful note.

Appointed regimental adjutant on Christmas Eve, 1862, he spent the next three months at Fort Stanton as recruiting officer.[9] By this time Carleton was reporting to the War Department that the Mescaleros, "this long dreaded tribe of murderers and robbers," was in a "promising condition," and that "the country around Fort Stanton is filling up with settlers."[10]

Recruiting clearly held no attraction for Murphy: there was still a war going on, and in common with many of his fellow soldiers, he wanted to be in on it. On April 10, 1863, he tendered his resignation, giving as his reason the fact that he was "desirous of joining the Army in the East." Carson dissuaded him: the regiment was preparing to move. Chastising the Apaches was not enough; Carleton now wanted the Navajos punished for their transgressions and had set July 20 as the deadline for their surrender.

On May 23 Murphy received orders to accompany Colonel Carson to Fort Garland for special duties as ordnance officer and assistant adjutant general of the "Navajo Expedition." On Tuesday, July 10, as the news came in of the federal victory at Gettysburg and the lifting of the siege of Vicksburg the command, which had been assembled at Los Pinos and consisted of 27 officers, 476 mounted and 260 dismounted men, marched off to Fort Wingate.[11] Pausing at Fort Defiance on July 20 to pick up a band of Ute scouts, Carson and his men set out to make war on the Navajo Indians.

It was not so much war as simple slaughter. The military statistics for 1863 were: 301 Indians killed, 87 wounded, 703 captured; 14 soldiers killed, 21 wounded; and 3 officers killed, 4 wounded.[12] Murphy was active throughout this campaign, and his contribution was acknowledged by Carson in his report: "I am especially indebted to the zeal and intelligence of my acting assistant adjutant general, Lieut. Lawrence G. Murphy, First Cavalry, New Mexico Volunteers, and I particularly recommend him to the notice of the general commanding as a most efficient and energetic officer."[13]

On January 6, 1864, Carson left Fort Canby and marched his 375 men through deep snow to Canyon de Chelly, arriving there six days later and immediately engaging the Indians, killing 23 and wounding many more. The following morning more than two hundred men, women, and children surrendered; it was the beginning of the end. By January 25, Carson reported he had five hundred prisoners at Fort Canby and a thousand more on their way in to surrender. By March the figure was twenty-five hundred; well over a hundred had meanwhile died of malnutrition, disease, or wounds.

"The Long Walk" that would take the Navajos to the reservation at Bosque Redondo began at daybreak on March 5. While Murphy does not appear to have had a direct hand in that sad and shabby episode, he was to be responsible for policing the Navajos for a long time to come. Acting on Carson's report, Carleton promoted Murphy; he was mustered in as captain at Fort Canby on March 19 and sent on detached service to Santa Fe.

On August 22, Lawrence G. Murphy took command of Company G, First New Mexico Cavalry, stationed at Fort Sumner and formerly commanded by Capt. William Brady. By this time there were over seven thousand Navajo "prisoners of war" on the prairie a mile and a half south of the post, guarded day and night by sentries instructed to kill any who tried to escape. The reservation was some forty square miles in area; a seven-mile-long communal irrigation ditch, or *acequia*, supplied the lateral canals that watered the land. The Navajos had some two thousand acres under cultivation; vines, fruit trees, and "a fine growth of young cottonwoods" were coming forward well. Four hundred soldiers policed the Indians, no easy task, for the Navajos and Apaches were enemies.

Murphy was still at Fort Sumner when the Civil War came to an end. He had learned a great deal about the mechanics of clothing, feeding, and supplying the needs of the army and the Indians, and perhaps also not a little about the money that could be made doing so. The reservation's beef requirements alone had spawned a whole new cattle trade in New Mexico. John Chisum of Paris, Tex., had staked out a range at Bosque Grande, a few miles south of Bosque Redondo on the Pecos River; by year's end the army had purchased thousands of cattle from him (fig. 6).

In June 1865, Murphy was given special duties as acting agent to the Mescalero Apaches at Bosque Redondo. It was a difficult task. When first imprisoned there, the Apaches had been amenable to their new life; after the arrival of the Navajos they grew increasingly dissatisfied and unhappy. Murphy seems to have established a good relationship with them for all that; it would stand him in good stead when he quit the service and went into business.

On October 27, General Carleton nominated Murphy brevet major "for gallant and meritorious services in the Navajo war."[14] On the same day, two brother officers were also brevetted: Emil Fritz, for gallantry at the battle of Adobe Fort in 1864, and William Brady, for gallantry against the Navajos in July 1865.

On November 10 the entire Mescalero population at Fort Stanton decamped for their own country. Carleton sent a characteristically garbled message to Maj. Emil Fritz, commanding Fort Stanton since October 13.

> Those Indians have got to be recaptured or killed, the men, and I want your zealous help at once, and with no relaxation, to do it until it is done. Raise the whole of that part of the country to a determined spirit to get those Indians now, or they will never enjoy quiet or security. Keep a record of all you do. If the people will rise as one man the Indians will soon succumb; but if there is dilly dallying and talk and no energy on the part of the troops and the people that part of the country might as well be given up to the Indians first as last.[15]

An expedition was put into the field to pursue the Mescaleros, commanded by Brevet Major Murphy. What results it achieved are not indicated in Murphy's records, but since he was back

FIG. 6. John Simpson Chisum, aged forty-two, ca. 1866. Photographer unknown.

commanding his company the following month, it would appear they were minimal. After a leave of absence in March 1866, Murphy was transferred to Fort Stanton; he arrived there April 7 and took command four days later. All the good friends he had made in the service were there: Emil Fritz, Paul Dowlin, William Brady. It must have seemed like coming home.

Originally established in 1855, Fort Stanton occupied a military reservation that covered 144 square miles (In 1872, this was reduced to an area that stretched 8 miles along the Bonito River and extended approximately 1 mile on either side of it, with the post in the center.) It was 191 miles from Santa Fe, 207 from Fort

FIG. 7. Emil Christian Adolf Fritz, aged about forty, ca. 1871. Photographer possibly Nicolas Brown.

Union. The nearest settlement was La Placita, a village of about sixty houses 9 miles east of the fort.

During the war the fort had been abandoned, and the Confederates had burned it, leaving only the corrals and the building walls standing. The following year, as has already been related, Carson used it as his headquarters during the expeditions against the Mescalero Apaches. Some rebuilding took place, but not much, as may be gauged from the comments of a post surgeon who reported on arrival in 1870: "These dilapidated walls were rudely and temporarily repaired on the reoccupation of the post, and with earth floors [and] earth roofs in the barracks, constituted the quarters of the troops until the present time."[16]

In the late summer or fall of 1866, their military service over, Lawrence Murphy, with Emil Fritz (fig. 7) as his partner, opened a brewery and store under the name L. G. Murphy & Co. just beyond the eastern boundary of the Fort Stanton reservation.[17] They were a good team. Fritz was German: energetic, thorough, possessed of that quality Germans call *zuverlässig* and which means so much more than merely dependable; Murphy convivial, shrewd, pragmatic, popular. Both had commanded Fort Stanton; both had excellent military records. Indeed Fritz is said to have refused a regular army appointment as second lieutenant, Eighteenth Infantry, to go into business with Murphy. They were well connected, hospitable, expansive; their business prospered.

By the time the rebuilding of the fort had been completed in 1868, they had erected a substantial eighteen-room trading post upstream of the fort, as well as a branch store, a saloon, and a "sort of hotel" at the settlement nine miles downriver. They had also obtained a license from the War Department to operate as Indian traders. Though money was short, L. G. Murphy & Co. flourished. The firm bought local produce by extending credit for merchandise at its stores; with little or no real competition to hamper it, the firm set its own prices for what it sold and its own interest rates on what it loaned.

In the process of becoming the dominant merchant of the area, L. G. Murphy & Co. also became the de facto Indian agent, furnishing the predatory Apaches with supplies in exchange for horses and cattle into whose provenance the firm did not inquire too diligently.

On January 16, 1869, just two months after the landslide victory of Ulysses S. Grant in the presidential election, a bill was introduced in the territorial legislature by Capt. Saturnino Baca proposing that a new county be created out of eastern

Socorro County. Baca declined the honor of having it named after himself and suggested instead that it bear the name of the assassinated president; in due course the placita on the Rio Bonito would also adopt the Lincoln name. The census of 1870 listed a population of 2,904 souls, 588 of whom lived in Precinct One, the area around Lincoln. About two thirds of the population was made up of Hispanic New Mexican settlers, and showed a considerable increase on the fifty-four families, including sixteen Anglos, listed a decade earlier.

The new county was in the Territory's third judicial district centered on La Mesilla (the second district was at Albuquerque, the first at Santa Fe). Justice was administered by a federally appointed judge and a district attorney, who traveled to the county seat twice yearly, in April and October, to hold district, or circuit, court. The population of Lincoln multiplied two- or threefold when court was in session.

For the rest of the year, the most important local official was the probate judge, ex-officio tax assessor. Each precinct also had a justice of the peace, who fulfilled a role not dissimilar to that of the earlier alcalde. The decisions of the courts were enforced by the federally appointed U.S. marshal, the sheriffs of each county— who also served as tax collectors—and their deputies. Each town also elected a constable who in turn could appoint deputies.

Lincoln had no public school; it did not even have a church. Not until 1874 would the stagecoach from Las Vegas visit the new county seat. There were no hotels or restaurants; visitors either camped in their wagons or stayed with friends. Amelia Bolton Church, who arrived with her family from Ireland in 1871, recalled that

> there were two general stores—small affairs—in Lincoln when we arrived; one owned by Jose Montaño, the other by Elisha Dow. . . . All freight was hauled in by ox-team or mule-team from Santa Fe. . . . Thus everything not raised locally was very expensive. . . . Help was plentiful; men worked for $1.00 a day and women for 50¢. However few people could afford paid help. Everyone kept one or more milk cows, some hens, pigs, a few sheep, and raised their own beef when possible.[18]

On April 3, 1869, James Joseph Dolan, just a month short of his majority, was mustered out of the army at Fort Stanton and obtained a job as a clerk with L. G. Murphy & Co (fig. 8).[19] He was a bright, direct, active, and ambitious young man, slim, dapper, and dark, with startlingly blue eyes. Murphy took an immediate shine to him; maybe he saw in Dolan a young man not unlike himself at the same age. Indeed, he took such a fatherly interest in the young man that in later years, many believed Dolan to be his adopted son.

Dolan immersed himself in the activities of his new employer and the firm's bewilderingly complicated maneuvers with the government and those appointed to look after its Indian wards. In April 1868 Congress had appropriated two million dollars to be spent on the "Indian problem." This enormous sum was to be used to pacify the hostile tribes and put them on the road to self-sufficiency.

A Board of Indian Commissioners was set up; although toothless, it did the best it could with a huge and intractable problem. One of the board's decisions was to invite the participation of religious organizations in the selection of Indian agents, the theory being that men of God might prove more uplifting and considerably less venial than the current crop of candidates. By the summer of

FIG. 8. Lawrence Gustave Murphy (seated) and James Joseph Dolan, Fort Stanton, Christmas, 1871. Photographer Nicolas Brown & Son. One of a series taken at this time. Dolan is about twenty-three; Murphy perhaps thirty-eight.

1869, Quakers were running sixteen Indian agencies; in 1870 other religious groups would be invited to participate.

In New Mexico, however, responsibility for the Indian posts still remained with the army. In July 1869 Lt. Argalus G. Hennisee was detailed to replace civilian agent Lorenzo Labadie in taking care of the warlike and unpredictable Mescaleros, who were still jumping the reservation and forming raiding parties.[20] Early in May they ambushed a wagon train in the San Agustin Pass, killed two soldiers, and wounded four more, for the loss of five of their own men; on August 15, Captain Stanwood, leading Troops F and H, Third Cavalry, had another run-in at the same location. Three times in the fall of 1869 the troops were out after hostile bands. In the last of these engagements, Lt. Franklin Yeaton received wounds from which he later died.

In spite of the fact that he considered the Mescaleros "the worst Indians in the country," adding that "talk and promises do not amount to anything among these treacherous and suspicious beings," Hennisee set to work vigorously.[21] He began by recommending the reestablishment of the reservation at Fort Stanton and

FIG. 9. Fort Stanton Trader's Post, ca. 1871. Photographer possibly Nicolas Brown.

negotiating with some of the Indian leaders about coming in and settling down. In February 1870, a minor chief named José de la Paz brought in a small band. Hennissee sent him off to Comanche country to see if he could persuade any of his fellow tribesmen to come in. José was back on April 12 with about thirty more Indians, and a promise from Cadete, the Mescalero leader, that he would come in soon. "If the Indians could be established on a reservation," Hennissee told Washington

> the influence of bad men (of which there is no scarcity in this country) would be in a great degree broken; and the Indians would have more liberty to hunt. At present they are compelled to depend almost entirely upon the food issued by the Department, as they are afraid of scouting parties when they are away from the immediate vicinity of their established camps. . . . The Indians who now receive food from the Department seem to be as well satisfied as it is reasonable to expect them to be, under the circumstances, the allowance of food per day to each Indian being only one half of one pound of corn and one half of one pound of fresh beef.[22]

Before Hennissee could get much further, the army was relieved of responsibility for the Indians. One Robert S. Clark was appointed agent for the Mescaleros, but he seems never to have tried to reach Fort Stanton (figs. 9, 10). His place was taken by the first agent appointed by the Department of the Interior, Andrew J. Curtis, a protégé of the American Unitarian Association. On arrival in company with Nathaniel Pope, superintendent of Indian affairs for New Mexico, Curtis found only José de la Paz and twenty-seven of his band on the reservation. There were still plenty of hostiles in the mountains. In June 1870, Indians thought to be Navajos killed two Mexicans, stampeded sheep, killed cattle, stole horses. Three braves rode up within a quarter of a mile of the Murphy & Fritz brewery, but left without trouble.

At Fort Stanton, Murphy and Fritz were waiting, oozing with a helpfulness and charm that quite swept Pope and Curtis off their feet (fig. 11). Curtis reported

> I take pleasure in mentioning in this connection that the fact of these Indians being now in and at peace is mainly, if not entirely, the result of efforts put forth by

FIG. 10. Brewery and saloon at Fort Stanton. Date unknown. Photo by A. F. Randall, Willcox, Ariz. Said to have been the brewery owned by Murphy and Fritz.

[Probate] Judge Murphy and Colonel Fritz. . . . They have several times, at their own expense, sent out clothing and other presents with messengers to communicate with the tribe, and on one occasion sent a team and wagon laden with presents into the Comanche country, to induce them if possible, to come in and make peace. These efforts were at last crowned with success, and the Government not only, but the people of this county as well, are largely indebted to these gentlemen for the important results obtained by their efforts.[23]

Murphy & Co. knew, of course, that the continuation of the firm's prosperity depended upon the presence of a sympathetic, or better still, malleable agent. On a number of occasions the firm petitioned to have Saturnino Baca, William Brady, or Paul Dowlin—army cronies, malleable men all—appointed to the post.

If fair means did not work Murphy & Co. did not hesitate to use the other kind.[24] On October 14, 1870, A. M. Stephens was appointed post trader by the secretary of war, whereupon Murphy and Fritz made a trip to Washington to petition Secretary Belknap for permission to retain their holdings and continue their business, supported by a sheaf of glowing testimonials from every officer at Fort Stanton. When they were informed that they would be permitted to keep their property and no more, they riposted by securing the Interior Department's license as Indian trader. This appointment, dated March 20, 1871, led inevitably to the departure of Stephens the following month.

Next, Frank T. Bliss of Bliss & Lombard of Chicago, new post trader, requested that Murphy & Co. be ordered off the reservation in accordance with the provisions of the June 7, 1871, circular which provided that the legal post trader have exclusive privileges to trade upon the grounds of the post. The officer commanding, Lt. Col. August V. Kautz, did not feel authorized to accede to Bliss's request; apart from the fact that Murphy and Fritz were intimate friends of his, he considered that removing Murphy would create difficulties with the Indians. It would appear Murphy & Co. then bought out Bliss & Lombard, but when Washington learned this, the appointment was revoked.

On March 12, 1872, C. F. Tracy was appointed post trader. He lasted only until August 12 and was replaced by William Dayton, who rented his appointment

FIG. 11. Standing, rear: Dr. Charles Styer (left) and James Dolan; seated. Indian Agent Andrew Jackson Curtis (left) and Emil Fritz. This was also one of the Christmas, 1871, sequence by Nicolas Brown & Son (see Fig. 8).

to Murphy & Co. for $125 a month and promptly returned east. Seeing the government rendered powerless, its official appointees frustrated and blocked at every turn, it is hardly surprising that both the military and the Indians took the path of least resistance and continued to do business with Murphy & Co.

Indian Agent Curtis and Superintendent Pope seem to have been as unable to influence events as their predecessors. In 1871, Curtis claimed he had 325 Indians. By the fall of 1872 he clearly had surrendered to the pressures of the House: the figure increased to nearly 1,900, and eventually to 2,679—"a rapidity of increase," a later agent noted sardonically, "which leaves rabbits, rats and mice in the shade."[25]

On December 14, 1872, yet another superintendent of Indian affairs, Col. L. Edwin Dudley, was appointed; within three months Curtis was replaced. The new agent, Samuel B. Bushnell, reported to Superintendent Dudley that only two hundred Apaches had visited the agency during April; that he was presented with vouchers by Murphy & Co., which he was expected to sign without question; that Murphy and "his confidential clerk, J. J. Dolan" (Fritz, who had heart trouble and a kidney disease, was spending more and more time at his Spring ranch, east of Lincoln) controlled the issues made from their storerooms; and that when he complained, Murphy told him: "It don't make any difference who the Government sends here as agent. *We* control these Indians."[26]

With Superintendent Dudley's blessing, Bushnell decided to try buying out Murphy & Co. Murphy coolly set a price of ten thousand dollars on his building. Declining this bargain, Bushnell concluded that if he couldn't keep the Indians away from the agency, and more importantly, Murphy's brewery, the next best thing was to move the Indians. He decided to look at nearby ranches with a view to doing just that. Meanwhile Superintendent Dudley drew the attention of the commissioner of Indian affairs to the fact that

> the post trader at Fort Stanton, Mr. Dayton by name, appointed several months since, has never opened his store, and from what I can learn has probably sold out to the firm of L. G. Murphy & Co., who seem to have been able to annul in fact the appointment of post trader at this point.
>
> The Indian Department is interested in this from the fact that no other store exists there, and these men are also in fact the Indian traders. What I desire is that some man friendly to the Administration, and of good character and reputation, should be appointed as post trader, who shall have sufficient capital and will open a business of his own, and that I can also appoint an Indian trader.[27]

On Sunday, May 18, 1873, Sam Bushnell invited an officer of the Eighth Cavalry, Capt. James F. Randlett (fig. 12), to join him and John H. Riley in scouting a new location for the agency. Riley, who was acting as agent for Van C. Smith, beef contractor to the Mescalero Agency, owned a ranch just a few miles from the fort: a possible site for the relocation Bushnell had in mind.

On their return to the post, Randlett—a combative character and an outspoken critic of the Murphy company's methods and its personnel—invited Riley to stay in his quarters.[28] He then went off to dinner with his commanding officer. On his return, he found Jimmy Dolan abusing Riley and threatening to kill him unless he retracted certain statements he had made.

Dolan was quieted down; Randlett suggested Riley accompany him to church. Murphy and Dolan were also there. Riley told Randlett he "believed Dolan meant to assassinate him, as he had seen him arranging his pistol as if for use." After the service, Dolan again accosted Riley, but told him not to be afraid, he wasn't armed. Randlett "spoke kindly" to Dolan, warning him he would get into trouble if he started a fracas at the fort.

"He replied in a boisterous manner that he could not help it," Randlett reported, "that Riley was a d-n lying coward."

Randlett grabbed Dolan's arm and summoned the sergeant of the guard.

"Let me go!" Dolan said. Randlett refused, whereupon Dolan pulled out a Smith & Wesson pistol. "Damn you, I will kill you then right here!" he snapped, and fired. Randlett managed to thrust Dolan's arm up, and thus "prevented the shot from taking effect in my head." The sergeant of the guard grabbed Dolan and marched him off to the guardhouse. When Murphy attempted to intervene he, too, was arrested.

On the face of it, the attack seems to have been motivated by the fact that Riley had been "interfering" in Murphy & Co. affairs by working with Van C. Smith and John Chisum to undercut Emil Fritz in tendering for the Mescalero beef contracts, and further by aiding and abetting Bushnell in his attempt to take the Indians away from the post. It might have been just a drunken brawl—both Dolan and Murphy were "somewhat under the influence of liquor." But was it?

It is hard to believe Dolan had any real quarrel with Riley: indeed, they were good friends and later, partners. Randlett, however, was another matter: he was threatening the cozy relationship that existed between the military and the House of Murphy & Co. It is entirely possible that the real reason for the fracas was to provide Dolan with a way of getting rid of him: start a fake fight with Riley, in which process, regrettably, Randlett would be killed.

Dolan—Murphy was not held—spent the night in the guardhouse along with eleven soldiers jailed for theft, drunkenness, or desertion.[29] The following morning a writ of habeas corpus effected his release to the civil authorities in the shape of Sheriff Jacob L. "Jack" (or "Jackicito") Gylam. Randlett, Bushnell, 2nd Lt. John W. Wilkinson, and a civilian employee of the agency gave testimony about the Fort

FIG. 12. James Franklin Randlett. Date and photographer unknown.

Stanton fracas at a preliminary hearing in Lincoln before Probate Judge Baca, with Dolan no doubt testifying there, as he had to Captain McKibbin immediately following the fracas at the fort, that it was only a minor disagreement in which his pistol had been discharged accidentally. Judge Baca found no grounds for formal charges. Dolan was released; pausing only to file charges maliciously against Randlett of assault with intent to kill, he went back to doing what he had been doing. But not for long.

Capt. Chambers McKibbin, Fifteenth Infantry, commanding Fort Stanton, issued an order that Dolan was to "leave this military reservation immediately and remain away from it," but on May 29, on his return to the fort from Santa Fe, where he had been for medical treatment, Emil Fritz interceded.[30] He told McKibbin "from the opinion expressed by the Doctors it would be well for him to arrange his affairs and beg'd me not to be offended if he asked that Dolan be allowed to return to their store for this purpose." Fritz gave his personal guarantee that there would be no trouble if Dolan was allowed to stay. McKibbin agreed, and Randlett concurred, for Fritz was highly respected. Dolan stayed to help him draw up his last will and testament.

Emil Fritz had decided to go home to die. He left Fort Stanton for the last time on June 10, 1873. Murphy accompanied him as far as Santa Fe, where on June 13, they sold their Fort Stanton sutler store to L. Edwin Dudley for eight thousand dollars. Fritz then continued on to his father's home in Stuttgart, arriving there August 9, "very sick." In a letter published in the *Santa Fe New Mexican* on

October 6, 1873, he expressed the hope that he would be back in December; he must have known better.

When word came up from Lincoln that a writ was on its way, Captain Randlett wrote a series of letters to the Adjutant General's Office (AGO) asking for advice and legal assistance.[31] The first, dated July 18, pointed out that there had been no authorized post trader at the fort since April 1872; that L. G. Murphy & Co. was selling goods to enlisted men at outrageously extortionate prices, and the "manner in which they have supplied the Indians I believe to be scandalously dishonest."

He followed up with another letter on July 22, advising the AGO that the writ had been served. He was in no doubt as to the source of his troubles:

> I came to this Post with my Troop in April, 1872. I found the tradership of the Post in the hands of L. G. Murphy & Co (Indian traders) and their prices for goods sold to enlisted men extortionate almost to robbery. These parties have also been engaged in supplying the Indians supposed to be on this Reservation; I soon became convinced that they were swindling the Government in the matter outrageously. . . . I have spoken freely my condemnation of which I have every reason to believe of the dishonesty of their transactions connected with the supplies furnished to the Indians, and I believe it is generally understood that I have no better opinion of their place than that it is a den of infamy and its toleration a disgrace to the Public Service. . . .[T]he War Department will understand the situation when it is considered that one officer of the Army has told me that Murphy has said he would kill me, another that so mighty was the power of the firm that they could get false testimony enough to deprive me of my Commission as an officer. Murphy I am told on what I believe is good authority has said that if he could not have his way in feeding the Indians he would put them on the Warpath and corral me and my command here in the Post and one of their employees "Dolan" I believe said that he would put on a breech clout and lead the Apaches against me.[32]

Randlett's allegations did not end there. Speaking of his own indictment for assault on Dolan by the grand jury the preceding day he added: "The officers of the Civil Law here are nearly all parasites of Murphy's, the Magistrate and Probate Judge before whom Dolan's case was examined is said and so believed by everybody I know, holds a relation to Murphy the most unnatural and disgustingly brutal. The people of the County are nearly all considered peons of Murphy's."[33]

This was strong meat. Randlett's accusations were enough, when taken in conjunction with the mass of similar complaints that had been received about the activities of L. G. Murphy & Co., for Secretary of War William W. Belknap to order Captain McKibbin on September 30 to "remove from the Post Murphy, Fritz and every man who is in any way in their employ, and *keep them off the reservation*; and further, if the new trader who is to come to Fort Stanton has, or attains, any interest whatever with Murphy and Fritz, that you remove *him* also."[34]

Bowing to the inevitable, Murphy & Co. moved their headquarters to Lincoln, a placita or "little plaza" of about sixty buildings. They set up business in temporary quarters—the exact location of these is uncertain, but may have been a small, two-story adobe on the north side of the street managed by Alec Duval and known as the "Placita Store"—while construction on the big new building at the western edge of town was completed.

Lawrence G. Murphy was not a man to admit defeat lightly. He refused to vacate the Fort Stanton building he and Fritz had sold to the superintendent of

Indian affairs, and when Maj. William Redwood Price of the Eighth Cavalry (sent to investigate Randlett's allegations) refused to consult with him, stating that his business was with the legitimate Indian agent, Murphy (who had been drinking heavily even by his standards) threatened to send the Mescaleros back to the mountains if he could not retain control over them. Superintendent Dudley finally cut the Gordian knot during his visit in early September. Backed by eight soldiers, he "at once demanded possession [of the buildings] and promised to take the trouble of vacating the premises myself unless the agent received possession within twenty four hours. The buildings were vacated."[35]

Unabashed by this reverse, Murphy & Co. simply found another way to skin the same cat: after the firm's removal, Jimmy Dolan obtained the Indian tradership, thereby effectively making it a branch of the House. Forgetting its differences with Riley—if any there had ever been—the firm made a quid-pro-quo arrangement with him. Now Riley's partner was Col. William L. Rynerson, a former officer and territorial attorney general. This, in spite of their politics—Murphy was a staunch Democrat—brought the firm into the orbit of what was known as "The Santa Fe Ring."

With Republican presidents occupying the White House since 1860, a well-entrenched Republican machine, feeding on the beneficence of Washington, controlled New Mexico. At its head was Thomas B. Catron, U.S. district attorney and president of the First National Bank of Santa Fe. This loosely knit freemasonry of lawyers, soldiers, and Republican leaders with influential ties in Washington maintained a ruthless domination over federal patronage and the favors emanating from the territorial capitol in Santa Fe.

Most of the members of the Ring were Masons. Murphy and Dolan became the Lincoln County extension of this powerful group; indeed, Catron, Murphy, Dolan, and William Brady were among those who organized the first Grand Lodge in New Mexico. Joined fraternally as well as by a common desire for wealth and power, the Ring had little trouble disposing of Agent Bushnell, who was gone by December. But not even the Santa Fe Ring could secure Murphy's reinstatement on the military reservation.

In the final analysis, it made little difference: the War Department appointed Paul Dowlin post trader. Murphy must have laughed out loud. Dowlin was a fellow soldier, a close friend of the House: Murphy & Co. supplied the goods and, more especially, the whiskey Dowlin sold to the Indians. In addition, Rynerson and Riley, as subcontractors to William Rosenthal & Co., cattle broker and paid-up member of the Santa Fe Ring, were nicely placed to supply Murphy & Co. with low-priced beef to fill government contracts. That was how the Santa Fe Ring worked: wheels within wheels, within wheels.

From Lincoln, Murphy & Co. continued to tighten its political and economic hold upon the county. The military and Indian contracts were the only source of real money in the region; clouds of graft surrounded them at every reservation in the West. As a retailer, L. G. Murphy & Co. seems to have been considerably less than successful, permanently bedeviled by cash-flow problems, and "carrying" many of the local settlers, sometimes for quite startling amounts. It would be a brave businessman who advanced credit equal to today's equivalent of over fifty thousand dollars to his customers as Murphy did in 1873–74: Saturnino Baca alone was on the books for over five thousand.[36]

Of course the real money was in supplying the army and the Indians and in "liberating" supplies sold to the Indian agency, which were then sold to a network of customers as far away as Las Cruces and Albuquerque. The mercantile debts carried, and the names of the people who owed them, suggest that the real reason for continuing them was to render the debtors, their produce—and perhaps their votes—at the disposal of the House.

One of the methods used by the House to effect this control was to "sell" to incoming settlers ranches or land for which they had no real title, advancing goods and credit at the firm's store against future crops or stock increase to get the newcomers started. After awhile the settlers would realize the trap they were in and do one of two things: balk, or move on. If the first, the House would use the law to attach goods and property for debts owed the company; if the latter, it would simply repossess and begin the cycle all over again with some unsuspecting new arrival. The trick, as John Tunstall would later so carefully explain to his parents, was never to give more credit than the land, the stock, and the crops were worth.

There is some ground for believing this was the case with some newcomers who arrived in Lincoln County shortly after Murphy & Co. settled in the plaza.[37] These were the Horrell brothers—Ben, Martin, Merritt, Sam, and Thomas— and their kin from Lampasas County, Tex., where they were well known for, among other things, "the branding, killing, and skinning of other people's cattle."

This was not their first exodus to New Mexico: the family had started out for California with a herd of about fifteen hundred cattle in 1868, but sold them at Las Cruces where, in an argument over wages, John Horrell was shot and killed by an employee named Early Hubbard.[38] Early in 1869, paterfamilias Samuel Horrell was killed by Apaches in the San Agustin Pass; Tom Horrell and John's widow Sally managed to fight the Indians off and escape. The family returned to Texas in March 1869 and resettled at Lampasas, where Tom Horrell soon married an orphan girl who had come back with the family from New Mexico.

"They were not really quarrelsome," a man who knew them said, "but clannish. They drank considerable but none of them were topers, but they always loaded for bear, drunk or sober."[39]

The Horrells were on the run: on March 14, 1873, protecting Merritt's brother-in-law Bill Bowen, they had killed five officers of the state police in a shootout at Jerry Scott's saloon in Lampasas. A second detachment of state police was sent in a few days later, and Mart Horrell, Jerry Scott, Allen Whitecraft, and James Grizzell were arrested and lodged in jail at Georgetown. On May 2 a mob of about thirty-five men treed the town, broke open the jail, and freed the prisoners. The Horrells took to the breaks and stayed there until around September, when the whole clan gathered for a move to New Mexico. All except Ben brought their wives and children along; they were left at Seven Rivers until the boys could get settled in.[40]

On arrival they purchased from Heiskell Jones and Frank Regan a homestead in the Ruidoso valley, where most of the Americans in the region had settled; the Hispanics favored the area around La Placita and the Bonito valley. "They tended to their business and bothered no one that I know of," Bill Jones recalled, with chilling understatement. "But you could not bother them."[41] Unfortunately, the Horrells had arrived just in time to run straight into a race war.

From the point of view of the Hispanic New Mexican population, Texans— *Tejanos*—were bad news. The first of them had come to New Mexico with the conquering Confederate Army in 1861; shortly after investing Fort Stanton they rode down the river to La Placita, breaking into homes to plunder and rape. The cowboys who came north with the herds were of the same breed, raised with the belief that Hispanics—"Mexicans" or "greasers," as they called them—were subhuman, and they treated them accordingly. Killing a "greaser" was such low sport a man didn't even put a notch on his gun for it. This arrogant attitude created widespread resentment among those of Hispanic ancestry; racial tension simmered just below the surface of everyday life, erupting occasionally, as it had done earlier in the year at John Copeland's ranch on Eagle Creek eight miles west of Fort Stanton.

Two young Hispanic employees went missing, taking—Copeland claimed—a rifle, pistol, blankets, and household goods, as well as a valuable pair of matched horses.[42] Copeland's neighbor John H. Riley claimed to have lost a new saddle. They caught up with one of the men and "persuaded" him—by threatening to hang him on the spot—to reveal the destination of his fellow thief. Copeland pursued the second man and killed him. He returned to his ranch, where Riley was holding the first man, and they set out for Fort Stanton. Somewhere along the way this man, too, was killed "while trying to escape."

The local Hispanics were incensed, and young Juan B. Patrón, the well-educated probate clerk in Lincoln, demanded Copeland and Riley's arrest pending a grand jury investigation. Judge Lawrence G. Murphy demurred, whereupon Patrón signed his own warrant, gathered a dozen neighbors into a posse, and set out for Copeland's ranch. Copeland was absent when they got there, but Riley met the posse and agreed to go with them to his own ranch nearby. Dr. H. G. Tiedemann, post surgeon at Fort Stanton, was visiting the Copeland place; at Riley's bidding he headed back to the fort to obtain assistance as soon as the posse left.

Meanwhile Copeland turned up; the posse made the two men take them to the place where the second of the two Hispanics had been killed. A well-known Lincoln hotblood named Lucas Gallegos cocked his pistol and put it to Riley's head.[43] "You shoot that man?" he asked. Fortunately for Riley and Copeland, the contingent of cavalry from Fort Stanton dispatched by Tiedemann hove into view at this juncture, and whatever plans Patrón and his friends had in mind were temporarily shelved.

Some versions of these events have it that as the posse departed, Riley shot Patrón in the back.[44] In fact that fracas was two years in the future, although there can be little doubt the bad feelings that caused it and several other later fights had their origins in what happened around this time.

In May there was another collision—the first of many—between Hispanics and Anglos on Tularosa Creek.[45] This time it was over water rights. Some thirty-five local men, infuriated by the way the incoming Anglo settlers regularly and arbitrarily cut their irrigation ditches and appropriated land they had been working for a decade, attacked the settlement there, destroying dams and ditches put in by the Anglos. Troops were sent for, and the infuriated locals fired on them. The soldiers returned the fire and killed one of the mob. This flare-up fizzled out, but the feelings of resentment remained.

What exactly sparked "the Horrell War" is unclear: The Texans said Hispanics had tried to rob them of the proceeds of the sale of their Texas cattle, a sizable sum in gold. The Hispanics claimed "one of the Horrells shot and killed one of the neighboring Mexicans while the latter was cutting a ditch"; that is, trouble was over water rights, which seems likelier. Whatever the cause, the tension was bowstring tight; all it needed was an incident to touch off the explosion. It was not long in coming.

On December 1, 1873, Ben Horrell and some cronies—Zachariah Crumpton, ex-Lampasas saloonkeeper Jerry Scott, local resident Texans David C. Warner and Sheriff Jacob L. Gylam (known to the locals as "Jackicito")—tanked up on Pike's Magnolia or some similar ninety-proof brain shriveler and proceeded to "run" (i.e., shoot up) the town. Town Constable Juan Martín—"a high strung fellow who thought a good deal of himself"—tried to get them to surrender their weapons, an insult scarcely to be borne by sons of the Lone Star.[46] Gylam told them he was

> a damned greaser. "Don't pay no attention to him," he says. "I'm sheriff and I'm responsible for this thing." Then he gathered up a crowd of his own to arrest them and take them in. In the meantime Dave Warner was an old citizen and he seen trouble brewing and told them what they were going to get into. He says, "Let's us go and get us a supply of whisky and go down here to my sister-in-law's and we can stay down there and have a good time."[47]

Other, less emotive accounts suggest the boys actually surrendered their weapons when they were first braced.[48] Before long they were re-armed and threatening the life of Probate Judge Jacinto Gonzalez, with whom they suspected their weapons had been deposited. They went to John Bolton's house looking for trouble, but Bolton chided them for making so much noise when his wife was ill and they quieted down and left.[49] It was at this juncture they headed for the brothel, firing in every direction as they went. Martín, realizing he needed reinforcements if he was to stop them a second time, summoned four or five of his fellow police guards, taking along William Warnick, a local butcher, to act as an interpreter, and followed the boys down to Francisco Romero y Valencia's place

> and this fellow told him where they were and begged them to let them alone. No, he was going down there to arrest them. He was deputy sheriff. . . . Well, they went down there, and the Horrells come from a desperate country, and they were as quick with a six shooter as could be. So he went in there and tried to arrest them, and they wouldn't surrender. He made a dive for his pistol and got half-way to it, and Tom Horrell shot him through, and he sent out and told the crowd not to stop shooting until they killed the last one of them. Well, they done it.[50]

Other testimony in the shape of Frank Coe's recollections paints a darker picture: he claims Murphy hired Juan Patrón to kill Ben Horrell and Dave Warner.[51] It may well be young Juan was one of those who went "to the house where these two were with some women. They knocked at the doors, both Mexicans knocking at the same time. The two rooms in which Horrell and Warner were adjoined, and when they came to the doors they were shot down. . . . Warner jerked his gun and shot it, killing the Mexican before he fell. The Mexicans probably got $100 for the deed."[52]

Other versions have it that Warnick had scarcely begun to explain the purposes of the party when Tom Horrell—or Dave Warner—shot Martín dead. The locals who had accompanied the deputy now opened up, killing Warner; Ben Horrell and Jack Gylam burst out of the house and ran for it. They were pursued down to the river by a mob that probably included Juan Gonzalez, Juan Patrón, Seferino Trujillo, and perhaps José Montaño and Joe Haskins. It was said both men surrendered and were shot in cold blood: Gylam's body was riddled by thirteen shots, Ben Horrell's by nine.[53]

Fearing reprisals, Lincoln justice of the peace Manuel Gutierrez invoked the protection of the military at Fort Stanton, but the commanding officer, Maj. John Sanford Mason, told them troops could only be used for protection against the Indians.[54] He did, however, send a detachment under the command of Capt. Chambers McKibbin, recently removed from the post Mason now occupied, downriver to keep an eye on things (fig. 13).

The Horrells came up to Lincoln and demanded the arrest of the murderers. The request was denied; the men had been killed while resisting arrest. It was a dressed-up variation of the unwritten *ley fuga* and the Horrells knew it; they took steps accordingly. Two days later Seferino Trujillo and another Hispanic were found dead in a pasture on their ranch.[55] The Horrells denied involvement; there were stories that the two men had been killed by a herder who saw them driving off Horrell cattle.

FIG. 13. Chambers McKibbin. Date and photographer unknown.

Feelings in Lincoln were running high; there was talk among some of the Hispanic population of making a clean sweep of it, killing all the Anglos or running them out of the country. Mason reported that the Catholic priest was urging the citizens to set fire to the Horrell ranch and kill them as they fled, that Juan Gonzales had gone to Tularosa for reinforcements, and that "there was every evidence of a large gathering of armed Mexicans."[56]

He was right: on December 5, Sheriff Alexander H. "Ham" Mills, appointed without election by Probate Judge L. G. Murphy, and without benefit of warrants, led a posse of about forty local men down to Eagle Creek, and demanded that the forted-up Horrells surrender. The Texans knew better than to put themselves at the mercy of a mainly Hispanic posse, especially since it was evident that the noted local hard case Juan Gonzales and not Mills was the real leader of the band.

The two parties exchanged sporadic shots throughout the day, watched by the detachment led by McKibbin, which was constrained from interfering by army regulations that forbade the intervention of the military in civil process. Eventually the posse abandoned the bloodless fight and returned to Lincoln. Frank Coe suggested the whole episode was a bluff organized by Murphy to drive the Horrells out and make them surrender their cattle.

On Saturday night, December 20, a large armed band composed of the Horrells and their supporters rode into Lincoln, where they found a wedding *baile* in progress.[57] "Come on," they said, "we'll make them dance to our music."[58]

> At about midnight they went to the house, shot out the lights first, and then began shooting at random. They shot a woman, Ponia [*sic*] Garcia, through the knee crippling her for life. They killed three Mexicans and captured [wounded?] several more. The Horrells knew that Murphy & Dolan were behind the killing of their brother.[59]

When the smoke cleared, Jose Candelaria, Isidro Padilla, Mario Balazan, and Isidro Patrón, Juan Patrón's father, lay dead. Another man—Balazan's nephew—and two women, Apolonia García and Pilar Candelaria, were wounded. On the basis of the warrants later issued, it would appear the principal attackers included Sam, Merritt, and Tom Horrell, Zack Crumpton, Jerry Scott, Robert Honeycutt, James Wilson, C. W. King, James McLaine, and John Wilson, a soldier from Fort Stanton who was observed firing two pistols indiscriminately into the crowd.

The following morning Juan Patrón slipped out of town (fled?) and headed for Santa Fe to request protection from Marsh Giddings, governor of the Territory. On Christmas Eve, Capt. E. G. Fechét led a detachment of soldiers from Fort Stanton to bivouac half a mile from the town, hoping thereby to prevent further bloodshed, although quite how the troops were supposed to do so when they could not act without a presidential authorization is difficult to understand.

Just how the citizens of Lincoln—or indeed, the Horrells—celebrated the holy feast of Christ's birth at this time is not recorded; but on Boxing Day, December 26, Lawrence G. Murphy, Jacinto Gonzalez, and Manuel Gutierrez all addressed letters to Governor Giddings appealing for help. Fortunately for all concerned, heavy falls of snow brought movement of any kind to a standstill. For a couple of weeks hostilities ceased.

Early in January the citizens of Lincoln held a mass meeting; presided over by Lawrence G. Murphy, with Jimmy Dolan as secretary, it appointed Murphy, José Montaño and William Brady to organize a vigilance committee to act in the emergency. Letters flew between Fort Stanton, Lincoln, and the territorial capitol, reporting that the civil authorities were powerless to maintain order or to bring offenders to justice.

Help was soon forthcoming: on January 7 the governor issued a proclamation offering a reward of one hundred dollars each for Crumpton, Scott, and the three Horrell brothers, thereby effectively declaring open season on the Texans.[60] Sheriff Mills and a posse of sixty men set off to the Ruidoso to arrest the Horrells. Surrounding the ranch, they shot or drove off all the remaining horses. During the night, the Horrells decamped down the Hondo to Casey's ranch. There they made a deal with Frank McCullum, Heiskell Jones, Jerry Hocradle, and young Billy Casey to bring their remaining livestock, food, and household goods down-river to Missouri Bottom, their destination. On their way back, the quartet was waylaid by a mob of Hispanics who made off with everything the Horrells owned.

At this juncture the clan decided discretion was the better part of valor. On January 19, they sold 1,098 head of cattle, 4 yoke of oxen, and 13 horses to Charles Miller for $9,802.50. (A week later, Miller sold them to Dolan.) A day or two later, Ben Turner was ambushed when he and a boy named Edward "Little"

Hart went to the house of a Hispanic to get some corn. There is a tradition the killer was Martin Chaves, but Maj. John Mason at Fort Stanton reported that

> the man who killed him came to the Placita, boasted of the act and it was proposed to raise a purse of $100 for him. He is well known having murdered a Mexican a short time since. No attempt was made to arrest him.
>
> Their provisions were all carried away, and the house the Texans occupied was burned shortly after they left. Parties who have seen them since the death of Turner say that their entire number twenty-two took a solemn oath, that they would work together, and while five of them lived, they would be revenged. . . .
>
> Lt. Wilkinson . . . says that the town is deserted, that Murphy was very drunk, but told him that Jimmy Dolen was heading the Posse and they had gone down after the Texans.[61]

On Sunday, January 25, the "posse" led by Jimmy Dolan rode down to the Ruidoso, burned down the Horrell ranch house, and hauled all the crops and corn back to Lincoln.[62] Steve Stanley, drunk as a skunk, got into a fight with Hondo valley farmer Billy Gill, who had been heard to say he would sooner pay the fine than ride in Mills's posse, and was wounded; the next day Gill was discovered, also wounded, in a house three miles west of Lincoln, having run that far in an attempt to reach the safety of the fort. The same Monday night, a mob tried to lynch a man named (William) Little, but he got away and reached Casey's ranch.

When news of all this reached them, the Horrells decided it was time for some reprisals of their own. On Friday, January 30, they headed back upriver, making no secret of their coming. They sent word ahead that they wanted a reckoning with Murphy, Dolan, Stanley, Mills, Patrón, Juan Gonzales, Bill Warnick, and Joe Haskins, among others. En route, "Little" Hart, aided by Tom Keenan and C. W. King, went over to the Haskins place adjacent to the Casey ranch, called the young settler, who was Ham Mills's brother-in-law, to the door, and shot him dead in front of his Hispanic wife. The motive for this killing is unclear: Haskins may have been involved in the shooting of Ben Horrell and Jackicito Gylam, or he may have been killed because he was related to Martin Chaves, suspected of killing Ben Turner, or for no other reason than he had a Hispanic wife. In the eyes of Texans, of course, any man who married a "greaser" automatically forfeited all rights as a member of the human race. The incensed Texans had nothing less in mind now than the wholesale slaughter of every Hispanic in the vicinity of Lincoln.[63] By the time they got as far as Casey's Mill, however, the plan had fizzled out; perhaps Robert Casey, who came from the same part of Texas as they, persuaded them to abandon it. The Texans contented themselves by splitting into two groups. One of these slaughtered a party of five Hispanic freighters hauling corn to the Chisum ranch whom they met on the road; the others stole stock from the ranches of Steve Stanley, his half-brother Ham Mills (both were married to Hispanic women), and Aaron Wilburn, and on the highway relieved twenty-four-year-old Robert Beckwith (whose mother was Hispanic) of his horse, saddle, and pistol. Then—knowing he could scarcely impede them—they joined forces to steal horses and mules from Beckwith's ranch at Seven Rivers before heading for Hueco Tanks, east of El Paso.

The testimony concerning these and ensuing events is garbled and unreliable;

the entire county was in a ferment. The *Santa Fe New Mexican* of January 27, 1874, reported that

> a private letter of the 21st inst. which has been shown us from Placitas, county seat of Lincoln County, gives the following concerning the unfortunate war between the Texans and the Mexicans. "All here is war and rumors of war. The Sheriff left here yesterday with sixty men to arrest the Harrolds and from a courier just returned we learned a fight was going on last night. A general distrust prevails throughout the whole section. Every man met is armed to the teeth. Up and down the Rio Hondo a number of ranches have been deserted, and now many fine places could be purchased for a song, their owners and occupants being determined and anxious to depart from a place where the reign of peace and order will not apparently, be re-established for a long time to come.[64]

Prophetic words indeed.

With the Horrells apparently gone for good, Murphy & Co. went back to doing what the firm did best. On April 1, 1874, Williamson D. Crothers succeeded Samuel Bushnell as Indian agent for the Mescaleros. His first appalled reaction to conditions at Fort Stanton was to request Maj. David R. Clendenin, commanding, to put an end to the illegal sale of whiskey to the Indians, carried on by Paul Dowlin.[65] Clendenin (fig. 14), another Murphy crony, did absolutely no more than he had to do.

The same month, charges were also preferred against two more of the House's *bêtes noir*, Robert Casey and Capt. James F. Randlett, citing both for murder and as accessories to the murder of the four Hispanics killed by the Horrell gang the preceding December.[66] Randlett renewed his protests to the AGO, requesting permission to appoint counsel to conduct his defense, and claiming he was being railroaded.

On May 25, 1874, Murphy riposted with a printed twenty-two-page letter of rebuttal addressed to Secretary of War William Belknap, contesting—indeed, ridiculing—all the charges made against him by Randlett both now and in the preceding year, submitting testimonials from officers previously stationed at Fort Stanton and from citizens of Lincoln County, all lauding the good character and reputation for fair dealing of Murphy & Co.[67]

"Testimony of this nature could be introduced without limit did I consider it necessary," Murphy concluded, inviting Secretary Belknap to conclude, like "all right-minded, honorable men, that Capt. Randlett is occupying a false position in society, and is a disgrace to the service."

In spite of the undoubted force of Murphy's arguments, and the glowing testimonials appended—one, notably, from former Indian agent Samuel Bushnell—Belknap was not swayed. He ordered the attorney general of the Territory, Thomas B. Catron, to defend Randlett personally.

Possibly more aware of Catron's sympathies than Belknap, Randlett had already retained attorney D. B. Rea who, "by affidavits showing an undue prejudice against the defendant," obtained a change of venue to Socorro County.[68] There the Randlett case was thrown out without the jury even leaving their seats; the charges against Casey were also dropped when the Territory concluded after examining the evidence that it wasn't worth going to trial.

As the year progressed Crothers, like his predecessors, found the hold of the

House on Indian agency affairs almost impossible to break.[69] After three months, during which he was totally unable to stop the illegal traffic, Crothers was informed by the post commander that he was occupying the building in which his agency was located only "at the sufferance of the military." Knowing it had been purchased by the Interior Department, Crothers wired the Bureau of Indian Affairs in Washington for instructions. They replied that no record of the transfer or title could be found.

Unable to influence Crothers as he wished, Murphy—and Dolan—resorted to other means. A program of harassment was begun, commencing with allegations that Crothers had sold 125 pounds of sugar and 106 pounds of coffee belonging to the agency to Rushwood Black, husband of Dr. Blazer's housekeeper, followed by a charge of operating a hotel without a license.[70]

By the time all this happened, however, sad news had reached Lincoln County: Emil Fritz had died of heart and kidney disease in a Stuttgart hospital on June 26, just three weeks after the grand

FIG. 14. David Ramsey Clendenin. Date and photographer unknown.

opening of the new store. A legal notice dated August 29 was published later that year in the *Santa Fe New Mexican,* which read

> Death having dissolved the partnership heretofore existing between L. G. Murphy and Emil Fritz, under the style and title of L. G. Murphy & Co., it is requested that persons having claims against said firm will present them within thirty days from date, and all persons indebted to same firm will please settle within that time or have their accounts placed in the hands of an attorney for collection.
> (Signed) Lawrence G. Murphy.

In that same issue, December 28, 1874, was a further notice, confirming in print what everyone in Lincoln had long been aware of: that the firm was now being run by the partnership of L. G. Murphy and J. J. Dolan.

In five years, Jimmy Dolan had come a long way.

CHAPTER 5

THE KID GROWS UP

TRADITION—not always a bad star to follow—suggests that Henry Antrim started to go to the bad after the death of his mother, learning to play poker and monte and falling under the spell of older street toughs like George Shaffer (or Schaefer), alias "Sombrero Jack." Evidence of petty theft and general juvenile delinquency would be hard to come by in any frontier town: all of them had their daily quotient of brawls and shootings, and Silver City was no exception. Henry Antrim did not make his appearance in the public prints immediately, leaving his biographers nothing on which to work but supposition.

Garrett's ghost writer Ash Upson had the same problem, and remedied his lack of knowledge by propagating the fanciful tale of twelve-year-old Billy stabbing to death a man who insulted his mother, resulting in the boy's being driven "out into the night, an outcast and a wanderer, a murderer, self-baptized in human blood."[1] While it is scarcely necessary to comment upon the accuracy of Upson's account, it is rather more difficult to put genuine meat on the bones of Henry's adolescence. In seeking to do so, even Maurice Fulton, who viewed Kid legends with proper academic disdain, fell into the trap of propagating an apocryphal story to the effect that the boy stole a keg of butter and sold it to a Chinese man who reported him to the owner of the hotel where he worked.[2] In revenge the Kid stole the informer's coat and was arrested. When he escaped, he went to the Chinese fellow's cabin and slit his throat.

This fanciful tale is a perfect example of how one small acorn of truth can be exaggerated into an oak tree. The facts of the matter appear to be somewhat more prosaic.[3] Sometime during early 1875, a rancher identified only as Webb left his buckboard unattended on the street in Silver City. In the wagon was a keg of butter, which Henry Antrim appropriated and sold to some of the local merchants. It took Sheriff Harvey Whitehill no time at all to track down the culprit. Whitehill, elected earlier in the year, was a former miner who stood 6 feet 2 inches tall and weighed 240 pounds. He had boys of his own, and no doubt thought the best way of handling the matter was to sequester Henry's ill-gotten gains and thoroughly paddle the boy's backside.

If Whitehill hoped this would act as a deterrent, however, he was doomed to disappointment.[4] The following September, Henry got into rather more serious trouble. Charlie Sun, twenty-five, one of two westernized Chinese (hence the description "sans cue [queue], sans joss sticks") who ran a laundry in town, reported that their shack had been burglarized. According to the *Grant County*

Herald, the thieves got away with clothes and two pistols valued at $150–$200. This was rather more than a youthful prank: in fact, it was fairly serious larceny.

Henry's part in the theft seems to have been as the lookout for a gang of youths led by "Sombrero Jack," who got Henry to hide some of the stolen clothes in a trunk in his room at the Star Hotel. A few days later, Mrs. Brown found the clothes and reported the fact to Sheriff Whitehill, who arrested the boy on Thursday, September 23, 1875, and lodged him in the town jail. Henry spent only two nights in the hoosegow: the following Sunday, the *Herald* noted that "Henry McCarty, who was arrested on Thursday and committed to jail to await the action of the grand jury, upon the charge of stealing clothes from Charlie Sun and Sam Chung, Celestials sans cue, sans joss sticks, escaped from prison yesterday through the chimney. It is believed that Henry was simply the tool of 'Sombrero Jack' who done the actual stealing while Henry done the hiding. Jack has skinned out."[5]

Henry did likewise. Conflicting claims exist as to where he went: the Truesdells said he came to them and they put him on a stagecoach to Globe; Sarah Brown said it was she and a woman named Holson who put the boy on the stagecoach, not the Truesdells.[6] The Knights claimed he walked fifteen miles to their ranch and stayed there; Daniel and Mary Richards Casey told a similar story; and Robert Black insisted it was to his house that Henry came after the escape. All seem unlikely; what seems infinitely more probable is that the boy went directly to the mines at Chloride Flats, where his peripatetic stepfather was working. Antrim's coworker Dan McMillan recalled how "Mr Antrim was called out of the mines one day to talk to his son who said the matter was urgent. When he returned he told [me] that his boy had gotten himself in a great deal of trouble and he had given him all of the money he had on him at that time and told him to leave town."[7]

Until recently, no one has been able to trace Henry Antrim's movements between that September Saturday and the day, almost exactly two years later, when he added murder to his criminal record. As in other instances, theories rushed into the vacuum, the most seductive of them being the "New York theory."[8] This proposes that Antrim—there is no explanation how—sent both Henry and his brother Joe back whence they had come: New York. Henry resumed his real name—Michael Henry McCarty—and on September 6, 1876, stabbed another street rowdy, a Thomas Moore, to death at the corner of Hague and Pearl streets. Subsequent to this apparently motiveless killing, McCarty eluded capture and disappeared. Five years later, Patrolman Thomas Dwyer of the Oak St. police station and "twenty Fourth Warders, all of whom had known McCarthy," averred that the youth who had killed Tom Moore was none other than Billy the Kid, whose death had just been reported.

McCarthy, they claimed, was born in Vandewater St. about 1859, attended school there, and later became an apprentice tinsmith. His father, Edward, kept a fruit stand on the corner of Nassau and John streets. When Michael was about thirteen he was "bound out" to a western farmer by the Children's Aid Society. He ran away and came back to New York, where he killed Moore and then disappeared.

Anyone familiar with the folklore version of the Kid's life might be understand- ably tempted to read into the Moore killing the origin of the legend that the Kid stabbed a man to death in Silver City for insulting his mother. More than that, however: if what Dwyer and the twenty Fourth Warders said was true, it would explain why for fifty years researchers have been unable to track down Henry Antrim in Arizona and New Mexico. Tempting it may be; true it is not.

While it is impossible to be precise about where the Kid went in the months immediately after he left Silver City (although there may be merit in the old tradition that he herded sheep for Amado Chavez), the Kid's trail through Arizona has been traced.[9] Throughout the spring and summer of 1876, he earned a hand-to-mouth living as a cowboy, part-time gambler, and occasional thief. He is even said to have made a couple of rustling sorties down into Mexico—perhaps Upson's flights of fancy were not so fanciful after all—and to have worked as a cowboy in the fall roundup on the Hooker ranch in Arizona. In between times he ran stolen horses from settlements along the Gila River west into the newly established mining district of Globe.

By the summer of 1877 the abolition of the Chiricahua reservation and the apparent abatement of Apache trouble had brought ranchers and miners flooding into the former reservation land. The big cattlemen preempted the new ranges along the San Pedro valley. Between Tucson and Camp Grant lay Sulphur Springs, where John Chisum's cattle herds ranged; their proximity might account for the persistent legend that the Kid worked for and was fired by Chisum. On the heels of the cattlemen came the rustlers and horse thieves, making their hideouts in the rugged hills bordering the San Pedro valley. And right behind them came the gamblers and whores. Settlements sprang up near the military camps, some taking their names: at the Camp Grant settlement, sometimes called Bonita, Miles L. Wood, sixteenth Anglo settler in Arizona, doubled as sheriff and justice of the peace.

There had been two military establishments of that name. The first, now abandoned, was notorious for the massacre there, six years earlier, of more than 140 Apaches, most of them women and children. The second Camp Grant, established the following year, was located at the foot of the Pinaleno Mountains southwest of Safford. It was this area that young Henry Antrim made his stamping ground. One source has him working for a forage contractor in the Gila valley below Solomonville and as a civilian teamster at Camp Grant.[10] Some little while later he was called a pimp, which suggests he might also have been practicing a still older trade.

Henry Antrim was nearly eighteen now; he had also acquired the nickname "Kid"—not that there was anything unusual about that, since most youngsters of his age were given the same patronizing nickname. It implied an inferiority to grown men, a lack of status and strength. "Hell," a man might say, in either contempt or lofty forbearance, "he's only a kid." A vivid word picture of him exists at just this time: "dressed like a 'country jake', with 'store pants' on and shoes instead of boots. He wore a sixgun stuffed in his trousers."[11]

He needed the gun; kid or not, Henry was getting himself a bad name. He was a member of a gang running horses and cattle between the mining camps and Camp Grant, which was being used as a relay station for stolen stock. His methods were crude but effective. "The soldiers would ride down to Bonita and tie their horses in front of the saloon known as the 'hog ranch'," Miles Wood recalled, "and go in for a drink, and while [they were] doing so [Henry] and his chum

Macky would steal the saddles from the horses and some times would take the horses and hide them until they got a chance to dispose of them."[12]

In late November 1876, Henry stole a saddled horse belonging to a cavalry sergeant named Louis Hartman from outside McDowell's store and lit out toward the Globe mining camp.[13] Hartman got up a detachment of four soldiers and went after Henry, recovering the horse. But since he had no warrant, he had to turn Henry loose. On February 16, 1877, Hartman remedied that lack and swore a warrant for the arrest of "Henry Antrim, alias Kid."

The old man Miles Wood enrolled as a constable claimed he couldn't find Henry; the truth was, he didn't want to. It wasn't until March 25 that the opportunity presented itself for Miles Wood to make the arrest; he saw Henry and his sidekick Johnny Mackie going into the dining room of the Bonita hotel for breakfast.

"I told the waiter I would wait on them," Wood recalled.[14] He got a large salver and put it on the table in front of them; underneath it he had a gun. He got the drop on them and marched them over to the post, where he requested that Maj. Charles Compton, commanding, hold them for trial in the guardhouse, to which the officer agreed. Henry had no intention of remaining in jail, however; that evening, in spite of having been shackled after he threw salt in a soldier's eyes in an attempt to make a break, he escaped custody "shackles and all," and went right back to doing what he was good at. Another arrest warrant, again for larceny, was issued early in August. Again the Kid was taken into custody, and yet again he broke free.

With two arrests for thieving in one six-month period notched up against him, a more careful man might have distanced himself from an area where he was clearly well known, but it appears the Kid's method of handling problems was to pretend they didn't exist: he would make the same mistake just a few years later at Fort Sumner. Later that month he was back at Camp Grant, and back in trouble again.

Bad trouble, this time: murder.

CHAPTER 6

LINCOLN COUNTY: THE VIOLENT PARADISE

ALEXANDER McSween and his wife Susan reached Lincoln late in the afternoon of March 3, 1875. They arrived, one eyewitness said, in a covered wagon drawn by a yoke of black oxen; and penniless, according to another.[1] What truth there is in this statement, made years later by Marion Turner, is difficult to ascertain: McSween certainly had money—even if it wasn't his own—when he quit Eureka.

They made their way to the home of postmaster (annual salary, nine dollars) John Bolton and his wife, who made them tea and helped them to find temporary accommodation at the home of Lucas Gallegos, near the *torreón* and just across the street from the Sanchez Building, which was used as a combination civic center, dance hall, and courthouse.[2] After the relative comfort of life in Eureka, Kans., the newcomers must have found Lincoln primitive (maps 1, 2). For all that, as Amelia Bolton Church recorded, they said they had come to find their El Dorado.

If McSween was looking for an El Dorado, he must soon have concluded he had come to the right place. There was no attorney in Lincoln or, for that matter, within 150 miles in any direction. As a result, there was no shortage of clients. In addition, he had arrived just in time to capitalize on the spring 1875 term of court.

McSween rented a room at the courthouse for his office and, as was the custom at that time, applied for and was granted permission to practice. His first client was W. W. Paul, who had a ranch on the Peñasco River. Paul was charged with larceny (a term usually employed to cover cattle or horse theft). McSween's defense was successful, and the rancher was acquitted.

It was not very long before the McSweens witnessed the violent side of life in Lincoln County. Susan McSween recalled that "they had a sheriff and no jail, so one night he wished to go to a dance so he told his prisoner he could run away and when he got a good distance from him, to run faster. When he did he shot him and went to the dance."[3] The sheriff in question was Ham Mills; other than the fact that the victim was black, his identity is not known.

When the McSweens first came to Lincoln, the county officers were not even keeping books; McSween took on that task soon after his arrival. At the time "Major Murphy was Probate Judge and he handled all the County money just as he saw fit. Mr McSween got everything running straight & Murphy did not like that to begin with."[4]

A number of other matters at the April term of court had a direct bearing on the newcomers' future. During the first week of court, the grand jury heard testimony in the matter of Lincoln County taxes, which the territorial auditor reported to be two years in arrears.[5] Probate Judge Lawrence G. Murphy, ex-officio receiver of taxes, charged the defalcation of 1873 taxes to the former sheriff, Jacob L. Gylam, killed in the "Horrell War" (as related in chapter 4). Concerning the 1874 taxes, he claimed that Apache raids had made it impossible to collect them.

The grand jury's reaction to this was to indict for dereliction of duty tax collector Sheriff Mills, County Treasurer Jośe Montaño, probate court clerk Juan Patrón, and the local justice of the peace, Pablo Piño y Piño. Because they had failed to collect taxes, the grand jury said, it had not been possible to make a start on building a school, a courthouse, or a jail. The jury expressed the pious hope that its actions would have a salutary effect.

His feathers ruffled, Probate Judge Murphy tendered his resignation. Owing to the illness and subsequent death of Gov. Marsh Giddings, however, no action was taken on the resignation. Thus Murphy was still holding office when, on April 21, he appointed William Brady as administrator of the estate of Murphy's former partner, Emil Fritz.

Discharged from the army in May 1866, Brady had settled with his wife of four years, Maria, on a ranch of about a thousand acres four miles east of Lincoln in a fertile valley he named Walnut Grove. He campaigned successfully to become Lincoln County's sheriff in 1869; in the same election Murphy became probate judge. Between the two of them they just about ran the county.

At the fall term of court in 1871, Brady was foreman of the grand jury; his actions left him open to the accusation that he had sought to persuade other jurors to hand down indictments on parties unsympathetic to the Murphy regime. Nonetheless, he almost simultaneously became the first elected representative from Lincoln County to serve in the territorial house of representatives.

Murphy probably thought he was conferring a favor on Brady by appointing him administrator of the Fritz estate, since the fees would be substantial. There was an additional reason: Murphy wanted someone "reliable" looking after the estate. Brady was a former fellow officer and a friend; he was also deeply in debt to the House, and effectively relied on Murphy for his paycheck, which assured his reliability. As it happened, however, Murphy had done his old comrade a disservice, because the matter of Fritz's estate turned out to be a veritable minefield.

Thanks to Miguel Otero's letter of introduction, McSween was retained by L. G. Murphy & Co.; Brady now hired him to make collections of House accounts receivable on behalf of the estate. In such cases there was no fee: McSween would be paid 10 percent of whatever he collected.

McSween's acceptance of the task is one of many instances of a curious, almost wilful insensitivity that seems to have been part of his personality. By taking it on he allied himself with, and by inference supported, men whose philosophy, religion, and predilections were the antitheses of his own. Whatever their motives, Murphy and Dolan were openhanded and easygoing with their friends. They made no bones about their Catholicism, their Democrat politics, or their liking for whiskey, and they ruled almost by *droit de seigneur*—the complete antithesis of Presbyterian, Republican, teetotal, civic-minded, parsimonious "Mac." In addition, the job of being Murphy's bill collector was not calculated to endear McSween to those he must perforce pursue and perhaps prosecute for their debts to the House.

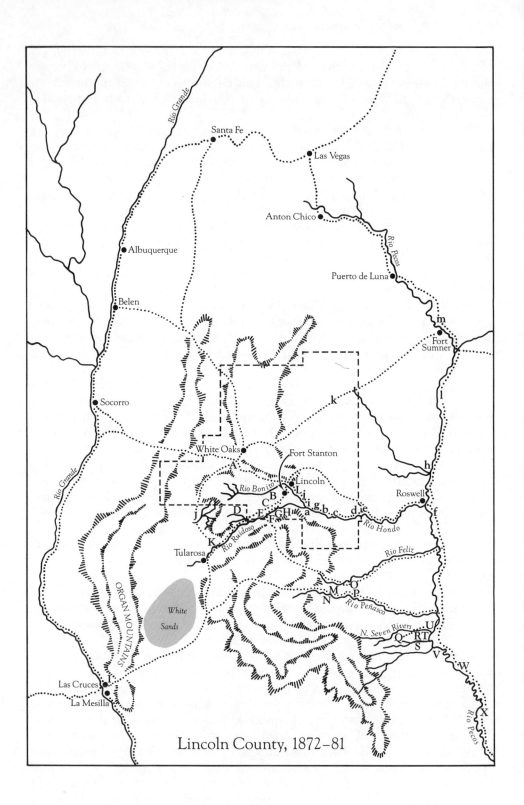

Lincoln County, 1872–81

Lincoln County, 1872–81

Principal Locations and Ranches

Dotted Line ------ indicates boundaries of present-day county
Dotted Line ..... indicates principal roads

Key

- A. L.G. Murphy Carriso ranch
- B. John Copeland ranch
- C. John H. Riley ranch
- D. J.G. "Doc" Scurlock farm
- E. Charlie Bowdre farm
- F. Horrell family/Dick Brewer farm
- G. John Newcomb farm
- H. Ham Mills/Andrew Boyle farm
- I. Shedd's San Agustin ranch
- J. Pat Coghlan Three Rivers ranch
- K. Blazer's mill
- L. Bartlett's mill
- M. John Tunstall Feliz ranch
- N. George van Sickle ranch
- O. Billy Mathews-Frank Freeman ranch
- P. W.W. Paul ranch
- Q. Andrew and Joe Boyle ranch
- R. Buck Powell ranch
- S. Johnson and Olinger ranch
- T. Lewis Paxton and Milo Pierce ranch
- U. Hugh Beckwith ranch
- V. Underwood and Nash ranch
- W. Dolan-Riley cow camp
- X. Loving's Bend/R.K. Wiley cow camp

- a. Ab Saunders and Frank Coe ranch
- b. Avery Clenny ranch
- c. Will Lloyd ranch
- d. Martin Sanchez farm
- e. Jake Harris ranch
- f. Chisum South Spring River ranch
- g. Ham Mills ranch
- h. Lloyd's Crossing/Dedrick Brothers ranch
- i. Robert Casey ranch
- j. Fritz Spring ranch
- k. Kuch and Greathouse ranch
- l. Chisum Bosque Grande ranch
- m. Thomas Yerby ranch
- n. Dowlin's mill

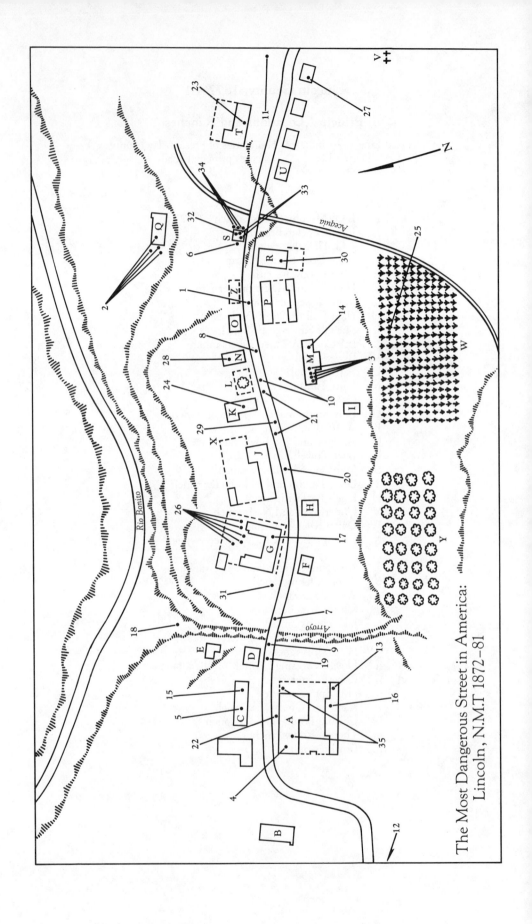

The Most Dangerous Street in America:
Lincoln, N.M.T 1872–81

The Most Dangerous Street in America
Lincoln, N.M.T., 1878–81

Key to Lettering

A. L.G. Murphy & Co., later Jas. J. Dolan & Co.
B. George Peppin house
C. Wortley hotel
D. A.H. "Ham" Mills house
E. Schon house (may have been further north)
F. Stephen Stanley house
G. McSween house
H. Lola Sisneros house
I. John B. Wilson house

J. Tunstall store and rooms
K. Daniel Huff house
L. Torreon
M. Courthouse
N. Saturnino Baca (later Mrs. McSween) house
O. Lucas Gallegos house (may have been further north)
P. Jose Montaño store and house
Q. Francisco Romero y Valencia house
R. Juan Patrón store and house

S. Jail
T. Isaac Ellis store and house
U. John Bolton house
V. Campo Santo (town cemetery)
W. Cornfield
X. Burial place of Tunstall, McSween, MacNab, Morris
Y. Orchard
Z. Site of Dudley's Camp, July 19–20, 1878

Key to Numbering

1872

1. ——— After Van C. Smith and Cal Dotson beat up Avery M. Clenny, saloonkeeper Pete Bishop kills Dotson. *

1873

2. Dec. 1. Sheriff J.L. "Jack" Gylam, Ben Horrell, Dave Warner, and Juan Martín killed in gunfight near here.
3. Dec. 20. Horrell gang shoots up a wedding dance here, killing Isidro Patrón and three others, wounding one man and two women.

1874

4. Oct. 21. Lyon Phillipowski killed by William Burns.
5. Nov. — Daniel Fisher killed by José Valencia.

1875

6. Spring. "Escaping" prisoner killed by Sheriff Ham Mills. *
7. Aug. 1. William Wilson shoots Robert Casey; Casey dies next day. *
8. Sept. 15. John H. Riley shoots and cripples Juan B. Patrón. *
9. Oct. 10. Ham Mills kills Gregorio Balansuela. *
10. Dec. 18. William Wilson publicly hanged for murder of Casey. Tomas Archuleta, McSween servant, killed by "men from Doña Ana County."*

1876

11. Feb. 18. Stephen W. "Will" Lloyd fights a duel with Stephen Stanley, who is seriously wounded, but recovers. *
12. July 18. Horse thief Jesús Largo taken from custody of Sheriff Saturnino Baca and lynched between Lincoln and Fort Stanton.

1877

13. Sept. 2. Josiah G. "Doc" Scurlock accidentally shoots Mike Harkins.
14. Dec. 6. W.W. "Billy" Campbell kills Thomas King at a *baile.*
15. Dec. — Frank Freeman shoots and cripples a black soldier.

1878

16. May 3. James J. Dolan kills Hiraldo Jaramillo.
17. Aug. 5. Frank Freeman and Charlie Bowdre shoot up the McSween house and wound a soldier.
18. Aug. 12. [?] Armstrong killed by sheriff's posse. *
19. Mar. 10. Jimmy Dolan breaks his leg jumping off his horse trying to kill an unarmed man. *

20. Mar. 28. Billy the Kid tries to kill J.B. "Billy" Mathews. *
21. Apr. 1. Billy the Kid, Jim French, et al., kill sheriff William Brady and deputy George Hindman.
22. A soldier is killed trying to pass a sentry and another man dies on hearing of ambush of Brady when an old wound bursts open.
23. Apr. 30. Open fight between "Regulators" and "Seven Rivers Warriors" results in death of two and wounding of four of latter; from roof of the Ellis house George Coe shatters the ankle of "Dutch Charlie" Kruling, 440 yds. away.
24. July 15. Daniel Huff dies, probably of poisoning.
25. July 16. Charlie Crawford, a.k.a. "Mr. Lallercooler," mortally wounded by shots from Montaño store; dies at Fort Stanton, July 23.
26. July 19. The Big Killing: Sheriff George Peppin and posse besiege and set fire to the McSween house, killing Alexander McSween, Harvey Morris, Francisco Zamora, Vincente Romero, and Robert Beckwith; Yginio Salazar and Ignacio Gonzales wounded. Another man, Bowers, may have died in the burning house.
27. Dec. 13. John Copeland shoots but does not kill Juan Mes, a.k.a. Johnny Mace. *
28. Lt. J.H. French tries to make lawyer Huston Chapman fight him.

1879

29. Feb. 18. Billy Campbell, Jimmy Dolan, et al., kill Huston Chapman.
30. Apr. 25. Unknown parties attempt to kill lawyer Ira E. Leonard.
31. June 14. George Washington, trying to shoot a dog, accidentally kills his own wife and child. *

1880

32. Nov. 23. Dick Hardman killed by unknown parties while in custody.
33. May — A youth named Stone killed by "One Armed Joe" Murphy. Next day, while in custody, Murphy is shot to death by unknown parties. *
34. July 3–5. On succeeding days a man named Harriman, another who is a deputy sheriff, and a third, a prisoner, are lynched at the jail.

1881

35. Apr. 28. Billy the Kid escapes from confinement in the old Murphy store, killing deputies Jas. W. Bell and Robert Olinger.

*Asterisks indicate unconfirmed locations.

That first April he cannot have been unaware of the machinations being carried out by his new employers against the Indian agent, Williamson D. Crothers, who had been arrested on a charge of larceny.[6] In La Mesilla, District Attorney Albert J. Fountain categorically refused to recognize the writ, declaring the whole matter "out and out persecution in order to injure [Crothers's] standing with the Interior Department." In spite of this, a Mesilla grand jury indicted Crothers in June, and John H. Riley among others testified that Crothers had used government supplies to provide hotel accommodation for travelers, falsified ration reports, and forged cattle receipts. Once again, Fountain refused to prosecute.

Later that month, the Department of the Interior sent Illinois Congressman John McNulta to Fort Stanton to investigate the cause of the raids made by— and upon—the Mescalero Apaches during the preceding year. His second brief from Secretary of War William Belknap was to look into the charges made against Agent Crothers.

McNulta spent most of July investigating and taking affidavits. Crothers testified that "L. G. Murphy & Co is the chief troublemaker. . . . Once Murphy presented a bill for salt for $400, which amounted to only $40. John Riley said to me, "We have always made some money out of this agency until you came here, but we can't make money out of you. The department at Washington expects us to make money and it is expected the agent will aid us. We all make money, including the agent.""[7]

McNulta's report exonerated the Indians from any guilt in the recent troubles. Crothers, too, was adjudged blameless, although he was criticized for his lack of business acumen. It surprised no one in Lincoln County other than Congressman McNulta to learn that Murphy had begun planning to get rid of Crothers within three months of his arrival.

McSween's law practice continued to thrive; he was an aggressive and ambitious man, and soon won a reputation for being a "smart," if expensive, lawyer—that is, one who usually could find in the laws some technicality he could use to the advantage of his client. His manner was curt and abrasive: when John Riley haggled with him over an account for one hundred dollars, McSween contemptuously cut the bill by half. "I consider it worth fifty dollars," he told Riley, "to find out the sort of man you are."

He soon plunged into community affairs and local politics. He began to make plans for a school and a Presbyterian church in Lincoln and became active in the local Republican party, actions that again illustrate his curious lack of sensitivity. Lincoln was an almost exclusively Catholic community, its politics dominated by the Democratic party in the persons of L. G. Murphy and James J. Dolan. Giving offense to the Hispanic population on matters of religion while taking a political stance against the House was a dangerous game, as was linking one's destiny with John Chisum, which McSween proceeded next to do.

At the time, Chisum, "Cattle King of the Pecos," was beginning to divest himself of the huge cattle herds that had won him that name. In the spring of 1875, he had relocated his headquarters to a sprawling adobe ranch house at South Spring River, a few miles south of Roswell. In spite of the fact that more than eighty thousand of his cattle were grazing in the Pecos valley on a 150-mile stretch of public-domain land held "by right of discovery" reinforced by a small army of well-armed cowboys, Chisum was really as much a cattle dealer as rancher. His herds contained animals bearing many different brands belonging to his former neighbors in Texas, who had given him bills of sale or powers of attorney (on credit) to sell their cattle. These documents, often claimed to be spurious, were to form the basis of the avalanche of lawsuits that would overtake Chisum in a few years' time.

Chisum had bid successfully for the 1874–75 contract to supply beef to the Mescalero reservation—one million pounds of beef on the hoof at $1.98 a hundredweight. His fulfillment of this lucrative contract was beset with difficulties. That summer the Mescaleros stampeded his entire horse herd, leaving a hundred of his cowboys without mounts. When he finally managed to round up a herd to drive it to Fort Stanton in September, Agent Crothers at first refused to accept delivery, because he had a surplus of beef on hand. Chisum insisted—he needed the money—but when Crothers reported his problem to Washington he was instructed to tell Chisum not to deliver any more cattle until they were called for. The result was that when the contract expired, Chisum had delivered only one third of the specified quantity of beef.

Having planned for income of more than $17,500 and received something less than $6,000, Chisum was caught in a financial bind. He arranged to sell his ranch at Bosque Grande and most of his cattle to the St. Louis cattle brokerage of Hunter and Evans.[8] Alexander McSween acted as his attorney in these negotiations, which were newsworthy enough to reach the attention of John Tunstall in California, who later wrote to his father about the sale. Tunstall reported the price as $350,000. The *Las Vegas Gazette* said it was $319,000. The *Pueblo Colorado Chieftain* put the figure at $219,000. Whatever the amount, a celebratory buffalo hunt was staged; Chisum's bookkeeper, Abneth McCabe, wrote to a friend that McSween had killed a buffalo "and now thinks he is a second Kit Carson."[9]

McCabe, who had once worked for Robert Casey, had no very high opinion of lawyer McSween, or his reputation for being smart, shrewd, and tight-fisted.

> Mr John Chisum has gone to Arizona by way of [Las] Vegas and Santa Fe. He will take the stage at Santa Fe and send his buggy and horses back by the Honorable Judge McSween, Mrs. Casey's particular *friend* (?).
>
> The lawyer was with us over a week. Mr. Chisum had him employed in fixing up some papers and accounts which he wished placed in the hands of someone to collect; and as no other lawyer would come to Bosque for such little accounts, he had to get McSween, and if McSween does not collect anything, he gets no pay— that is the sum and substance of his big fees.[10]

It is not apparent whether McSween, immersed throughout the summer in Chisum's business, was a witness to the gratuitous murder of mill owner Robert Casey. It happened in Lincoln on August 1, just one day after a new governor, Samuel Beach Axtell, was sworn in at Santa Fe to replace Marsh Giddings, who had died on June 3. Rescued from a particularly unsavory political controversy by his friends in Washington, Axtell would play an important role in what was to become known as the Lincoln County War. At this juncture it is doubtful if he even knew of the existence of that violent quarter of the Territory.

Casey was another ex-soldier who had settled down in the Lincoln area following his discharge from the post–Civil War Army.[11] His family—the father was a blacksmith—had emigrated from Ireland to Canada, then moved to Lowell, Mass., where Robert was born in 1828. At the age of sixteen, he joined the Second U.S. Dragoons and served a five-year hitch as a farrier on the Indian frontier in Texas. On June 21, 1856, he married Ellen Evelyn Shellenbarger at Waco, Tex., and they settled on Elm Creek, near Menard, where they raised cattle under the "KC" brand.

In the summer of 1867, Casey drove a herd north to Fort Sumner, following the trail blazed by his fellow Texans Charles Goodnight, Oliver Loving, and John Chisum. In July 1870 Casey sold his ranch in Texas, joined forces with a trail herd being taken to Fort Sumner by two brothers named Bridges, and driving seventeen hundred head of cattle, headed north into New Mexico with his family. Soon after they crossed into New Mexico they were attacked by Apaches, who ran off most of Casey's cattle and all his horses, mules, and draft oxen. Breaking steers to harness, the resourceful Casey eventually got his family to the Hondo valley. There, for 60 head of cattle and a note promising later delivery of 220 more, he bought the ranch of a Frenchman named Leopold Chene.

The ranch was at what was then called La Junta, six miles east of the point at which the rivers Bonito and Ruidoso become the Rio Hondo, which is in turn ten miles east of Lincoln. When Casey settled on the Hondo, there were only four houses between his ranch and Lincoln, then still called Placita. As the ranch and mill flourished, however, other Americans—many of them Texans—moved into the region. Among them were Alexander H. "Ham" Mills, who was married to a Hispanic woman, and his half-brother, Steve Stanley. Dave Warner, who also had a Mexican family, and who was killed during the Horrell troubles (see chapter 4), lived where the hamlet of Tinnie now stands. The Caseys' nearest neighbors were ex-army sergeant Will Lloyd and his wife, Eliza, who worked for Murphy as a housekeeper and was said to be able to outcuss a muleskinner.

In the opposite direction, farther down the Hondo, the nearest settlement was Missouri Plaza, also known as Missouri Bottom and La Plaza de San Jose Valle de Missouri. Established by Kansas City–St. Louis freighters from Valencia County soon after the Civil War, it was a huddle of flat-topped adobes, with a general store run by Frank Regan selling groceries, hardware, and liquor. Most of the families who lived there were Hispanic: Sanchez, Valdono, de Vaca, Torres, Cordoba, Sedillo, Lucero, Garcia, Baragon, Melindes, Trujillo, Sisneros, Anaya; the Americans included Heiskell Jones and John Newcomb, who was married to one of the Anaya girls. By 1872, due to the drop in the level of the river caused by the irrigation ditches of the upstream settlers, the hamlet had been abandoned.

A letter written in 1872 by M. A."Ash" Upson shows that in spite of Indian depredations, Robert Casey's ranch on the Hondo—known far and wide as "Casey's Mill"—had become a substantial and flourishing establishment.

> I went down with [Calvin] Simpson [from Las Vegas] to Placita (newly named Lincoln) stayed a few days, met an old Texan, Robert Casey, who lives about twenty five miles below the Fort [Stanton]. The valley is very pretty, well settled by American rancheros, and most of them married to Mexican women.
>
> Casey is the wealthiest of them all. He has the only grist mill in the valley, over 600 acres of land under cultivation, hundreds of head of stock—horses, cattle, mules, burros, sheep and house fowls; and last but not least a splendid American wife and seven fine, healthy, handsome, well-behaved children. He is one of Nature's noblemen. No education but a gentleman by intuition—it is no credit to him—he can't help it, his wife is a lady for the same reason.[12]

Casey took a liking to Ash Upson, and persuaded him to stay on as a clerk in the store that was operated in a one-room building near the ranch house and the mill. Upson began teaching Casey's eight-year-old daughter Lily some English, and ended up teaching not only all the Casey children, but also those of their neighbors. It was not long before he was also giving simple arithmetic lessons to some of the adults as well.

> You can't guess how we live here. A large family, lots of peons (Mexican laborers). They kill a steer or a hog or a sheep, half a dozen chickens, every two or three days, 'bite the dust'. Sweet milk, buttermilk, whey, fresh eggs, butter, broiled chicken, fish and wild duck! Oh, there's no use talking—I can't do justice to the subject. Great nice clean bed-colchen (mattresses) a foot thick. Fishing tackle, shot gun and rifle, choice of twenty horses to ride. Deer in the mountains, antelope on the plains, ducks on the river, and fish in it. Why should I not be happy?[13]

Casey continued to gain in stature in the tiny community. His mill, ranch, and store kept him more and more from his irrigated fields, which he leased to local families on a sharecrop basis, thus increasing the trade of his commissary. The presence of the latter attracted more Anglo families, many of them fellow Texans, who settled east of the mill and nearby. Before 1873, Casey's only direct competition was from the merchants of the little town up the river, Jose Montaño and Isidro Patrón. After L. G. Murphy & Co. moved to Lincoln, however, Casey's presence was looked upon less benevolently.

In addition, the well-liked Casey was becoming politically active, and something of a leader of that American faction in the Lincoln area which openly resented the abuses, both political and financial, practiced by the House.

On Sunday, August 1, a political convention was held in Lincoln to select candidates for the various county offices. During it, Casey made a strong speech, highly critical of Murphy and the stranglehold the Murphy machine had on the lives of the local people. The effect of such effrontery upon Murphy and Dolan, who were present, may be gauged by Juan Patrón's testimony that on a similar occasion—or perhaps this one—the enraged Murphy had roared into the room, overturned the tables, destroyed the papers, and told the people there, "You might as well try to stop the waves of the ocean with a fork as oppose me!"[14]

With the Murphy party roundly defeated, the convention broke up around noon, and Casey went to eat lunch at the Wortley Hotel with his clerk Edmond Welch, and a former employee, William Wilson. The Wortley, which was a sort of mess hall for the Murphy firm's employees and visitors, was at this time owned by Richard Ewan (the name is often given as Ewing) and managed by Charlie Myrick.

After lunch, Casey and Wilson went their separate ways. As Casey came back up the street, Wilson ambushed him from behind an adobe wall. His first shot hit Casey in the side, and the rancher staggered to the shelter of a nearby house. Wilson ran around the other side and fired again, his bullet hitting Casey near the corner of his mouth. Casey collapsed, mortally wounded. He was carried into Steve Stanley's house where the Fort Stanton post surgeon, Doctor Carvallo, tried to save the wounded man's life. His efforts were in vain; Casey died the next day.

The brutal killing enraged the town to such a degree that Wilson would have been lynched had he not been immediately whisked into protective custody. He claimed that he had killed Casey, who had employed him for several months, in an argument over eight dollars in back pay. He was taken to Fort Stanton and placed in the guardhouse to await the action of the grand jury.

An unsigned letter from Lincoln dated August 3, 1875, purporting to give the facts of the case appeared in the *Santa Fe New Mexican* on August 10.

The community has received a terrible shock. Robert Casey was fatally shot by William Wilson on Sunday last. Mr. Casey died about four p.m. yesterday and was buried today. It appears they had some difference (words only) about eight dollars in the forenoon of that day. About noon Mr Wilson left town, but returned in due course of two hours with a Henry rifle. He stationed himself in the Hotel and watched for Mr Casey's approach, and soon the opportunity offered. When Mr Casey was within sixty yards of him he fired; the ball taking effect in the left hip. After the first shot Mr Casey ran away but only to be shot again immediately below the right eye. Wilson was understood to be under the influence of liquor. An effort was made to raise a crowd to lynch Mr Wilson but he turned his back to a house and kept the crowd at bay. Upon consultation amongst his friends with assurances of fair play Wilson surrendered his rifle and himself to the sheriff; the latter swore in ten persons to assist in preserving the peace.

He had an examination and was sent to Fort Stanton guard house to await the action of the grand jury.

Susan McSween, who insisted throughout her life that the Caseys in general and Robert Casey in particular were beneath contempt, provided one version of the killing.[15] "Casey hired men to work for him until he owed them a big bill, then he would run him off with a gun an American came along and worked for him when he left Casey still owed him eight dollars and when he asked Casey for the money in Lincoln Casey cursed him. then he borrowed a gun and went to him for the amount again when he repeated what he said before he killed Casey, that was in Sept. 1875."

The *New Mexican's* correspondent was quickly challenged.[16] Clearly determined not to let anyone whitewash Wilson, someone signing himself "Citizen" wrote:

Fort Stanton, N.M. August 28, 1875.
Gentlemen:—In the issue of your paper of the 9th inst. appears a communication purporting to be dated at Lincoln, referring to the killing of Robert Casey, the writer's evident intention being to make his murderer out a hero. Here is what he says: "At the distance of sixty yards he fired; the ball taking effect in the left hip. Mr Casey ran away." And again: "Wilson turned his back to a house and kept the crowd (he should have said mob) at bay". Now the whole truth is this: Casey was first shot at the distance of 15 or 20 paces or possibly less, the ball striking in the region of the hip and lodging in the spine. How a man could run away after such a shot I leave your readers to judge. Moreover, as Casey was not one of that stamp that run away, I am of the opinion that your correspondent must have some other motive in view besides the truth in making such an assertion. There are few persons that would have the temerity to charge Casey with "running away" had he been alive. That Casey and Wilson were near each other at the first shot is evident for as Casey turned round the corner of a house after having been shot to have time to revolve his pistol, he was met by Wilson who had turned the other corner face to face and he placed the muzzle of his rifle near Casey's head shooting him the second time. And as regards the lynching of Wilson, your correspondent knows better. He had too many friends on hand for any person or persons to try anything of the kind. And that this was so, was proved subsequently on his examination before the justice of the peace where all nearly all [sic] the testimony adduced was in his favor. And had it not been for a few men Wilson would have been loose at present, and no doubt presented with a rifle for his meritorious conduct by his admirers.

When Casey was first shot, one person made a remark about lynching, but he had found that he was in the wrong community and left in quick time. Therefore Wilson putting his back toward a house and keeping the crowd at bay who were going to lynch him is simply poppycock and shows the animus or ignorance of your correspondent. That Wilson was in any danger unless by being hugged to death by his friends those that know won't believe. In matters of this nature, newspaper correspondents should not pervert facts either through maliciousness or ignorance, but should state the truth not only on account of the newspaper publishing the same but for the public.

Very respectfully
CITIZEN.

"Citizen's" shafts were well-aimed. At the time the first letter appeared in the paper, Jimmy Dolan was in Santa Fe, which perhaps accounts for "Citizen's" jibe at the Lincoln dateline. It is tempting to try to guess his identity: whoever it was certainly had no admiration for the House and its minions, but that hardly narrows the field.

Casey's funeral service was conducted by L. G. Murphy, who was generally believed to have been educated for the priesthood. The audacity of it is worthy of Shakespeare's Richard III: here is a man who, having conspired to bring about the murder of another, shamelessly accepts the widow's invitation to speak an oration over the corpse! We are assured the widow had no idea at the time it might be so; but suspicions grew as tongues wagged. Casey's son, Robert, who was fourteen when his father was killed, gave this version of what was later more generally believed:

[My father] was killed by a fellow named Wilson. He was just a renegade. He told me once of being a prisoner on an island and swimming four or five miles to get himself out.

There was a traitor in that [plot to kill my father]. They had a horse saddled for [Wilson] to get away on, and when [my father] was killed one of the mob [Charlie Myrick] got afraid that he'd get implicated in it, and he jumps on the horse and leaves the country himself. Wilson was afoot and that was where he was caught.[17]

Casey's friends speculated that Murphy had paid Wilson to kill Casey, promising him protection from the law if he was arrested or brought to trial. Cynics confidently expected that the murderer would be pardoned. There was a muttering of vigilante talk. In a letter dated November 3 addressed to the widow Casey, Abneth W. McCabe wrote, "I am in hopes that Wilson will be hung according to law, for I know he will never leave the post alive, even should the Governor reprieve him or commute his sentence. Fifty men would leave the Pecos any day to hang or kill him if it was necessary."[18]

Hardly had the anger generated by the murder of Robert Casey abated than another blatant murder attempt took place. This time, the victim was Juan Patrón, another of those who had been actively outspoken against Murphy at the August convention.

The reason given for this attack was as tenuous as the one Wilson had given. On September 11 or 15 (sources vary) John H. Riley, well known to be a supporter and affiliate of the Murphy organization, shot Patrón on the street of Lincoln (figs. 15, 16). The *New Mexican* gave the details as it had received them "by letter from Fort Stanton":

FIG. 15. John Henry Riley, aged about thirty-five, ca. 1885. Photo by Fredricks, New York.

[W]e learn that on last Wednesday [September 15] the notorious Juan Patrón was shot by John H. Riley at that place. Patrón's wound is believed to be fatal. Our informant states that Patrón had been following Riley round the post as if seeking a quarrel, and at last drew a pistol on him, when Riley shot him down. Our informant further states that Riley is sustained by the best portion of the people of Lincoln county.[19]

Why the *New Mexican* chose to refer to Patrón as "notorious" is hard to understand; perhaps they had him confused with Juan Gonzales. Their correspondent seems to be the only one who places the shooting at Fort Stanton. Riley appeared before Justice of the Peace Wilson. He testified that Patrón had followed him around all day, verbally abusing him and eventually going so far as to draw a pistol. At this point Riley, who was—fortuitously, no doubt—carrying a carbine, shot Patrón down. His plea of self-defense was accepted and he was released, apparently without having had to explain how it had come about that he shot Patrón in the back, the ball entering near the spine and passing through to the abdomen.

As the *New Mexican* noted, it was believed that Patrón was mortally wounded, but thanks to the ministrations of Post Surgeon Carlos Carvallo, a graduate of the Royal University of Berlin, Patrón recovered, although he was a cripple for the rest of his life.

Although no contemporary account suggests it, there is a distinct possibility that the shooting was a flare-up of the smoldering embers of the racial violence of 1873: only a month later, there was yet another brutal affray. A Mexican named Gregorio Balansuela (Valenzuela) made the fatal error of calling the quick-tempered Ham Mills a "damned gringo."[20] Mills shot him dead on the spot.

Some sources state that Mills was wounded, which indicates a gunfight rather than outright murder; the fact that the grand jury indicted him for manslaughter tends to confirm this. McSween's defense was unsuccessful; Mills was sentenced to a year in prison. Released on bail furnished by Murphy, Mills seems to have decided to go to Texas until local feeling subsided.

At the same October session, the grand jury handed down a murder indictment against William Wilson and another as accessory against Charlie Myrick, who had fled to Arizona. At the subsequent petit jury trial on October 18, William Wilson was sentenced to hang, the date set for November 11. Soon after his trial Wilson tried to break out of the guardhouse but was shot and "dangerously wounded" by the guard in the attempt.[21]

Strenuous efforts were made to obtain a commutation of his sentence. His lawyers—William L. Rynerson and Simon B. Newcomb—appealed for a stay of execution, which was granted by Governor Axtell, who claimed he needed extra time to consider the evidence and seemed inclined to extend the reprieve. District attorney Col. Albert J. Fountain went to Santa Fe, "disabused [Axtell's] mind and gave him a correct history of the affair, and he concluded to let justice take her course."[22]

Wilson's hanging was scheduled for Friday, December 10. Because of rumors that some kind of attempt would be made to prevent the execution, Company G, Eighth U.S. Cavalry, under the command of Lieutenant Gilmore, escorted the ambulance carrying the condemned man, post commander Captain Stewart, Post Surgeon Carlos Carvallo, and Reverend Lamy of Manzano, from Fort Stanton to Lincoln.

On arrival, the prisoner was taken to the house of Sheriff Saturnino Baca, elected the preceding September. Wilson put on his funeral suit (supplied by Murphy & Co.) and, after shaking

FIG. 16. Juan Batista Patrón. Date and photographer unknown.

hands with several acquaintances, mounted the scaffold set up near the courthouse. The death warrant was read to the large crowd of watchers in both English and Spanish, followed by Wilson's dying declaration. As the visiting priest gave Wilson extreme unction, Sheriff Baca unaccountably announced that the execution was to be postponed for thirty minutes. This produced such a storm of protest that the sheriff was forced to rescind his decision.

Casey family tradition has it that with Wilson on the scaffold were the priest, the sheriff, and L. G. Murphy. Wilson turned to Murphy and said bitterly, "Major, you know you are the cause of this. You promised to save me, but . . ." At this point, the Casey version goes, Murphy kicked the lever that sprang the trap, and Wilson's body plunged down.[23]

After nine and a half minutes—the time was reported in the *New Mexican*; one cannot help but wonder who was ghoulish enough to record it so precisely—Wilson's body was cut down and put in the waiting coffin.[24] The crowd had begun to disperse when a Mexican woman lifted the coffin lid and screamed, "The dead has come to life!". On examination it appeared that Wilson was indeed still alive, and those present demanded the murderer be strung up again.

At this juncture, Lawrence Murphy intervened. Wilson, he said, had been legally hanged, and could not be hanged again. This was a point of law that not even Murphy could make stick, and his protests—which Casey's friends saw as an extension of Murphy's plan to cheat justice and spirit Wilson to safety—were ineffectual. The unfortunate Wilson was dragged out of the coffin and hanged—lynched would be more accurate—for another twenty minutes. There was no doubt, when they let the body down this time, that Wilson was well and truly dead.

CHAPTER 7

JOHN TUNSTALL
DREAMS OF SHEEP

IT might be said with some justification that but for John Coffee Hays, there would have been no Lincoln County War. For it was "Captain Jack" who, shortly after John Tunstall's arrival in San Francisco, convinced the young Englishman that he was too late to start up sheep ranching in California, and that he should go instead to New Mexico.

The idea of getting out of the drapery business and into a man's world had come to Tunstall late in the summer of 1875. In writing to his father, he speculated on what he might do with his life if he left Turner, Beeton & Tunstall.

> I would not care to go into any Drapery House to work for a salary, so that my position in London, would be a very indefinite one, [such] as doing odds jobs in your office; I could start in many things on this coast with a far better prospect both immediately and in the future than that is.
>
> Sheep farming for instance as carried [out], on the islands here, is far more profitable & does not involve more capital than any other business. Stock farming likewise & should you decide that you would like me to return I should like to spend a couple of months in Oregon & Washington Territory, & have a look around to see how these businesses are carried on, there is great scope in these countries now, & I am not at all sure that I could not make far more in something or other here, than we shall ever do by pedalling dry goods in Victoria.[1]

Within a fortnight Tunstall was to meet Capt. Martin Morse Kimberly, a former California sheep farmer (fig. 17). From the moment he began talking to Kimberly, John Tunstall's mind was made up. If he could persuade his father to finance him, he would fling off the shackles that bound him to Victoria, B.C., and seek his fortune elsewhere.

His first plan was to go into partnership with Kimberly and establish a sheep farm on the Aleutian island of Oukamok, one of the Semidi Islands, about seventy miles southwest of Kodiak. Fired by this prospect, his correspondence touched less and less upon business at London House; he thought of "nothing else but sheep farming all the time, whether I am riding, walking, sitting, standing, eating or sleeping."[2] Even the tragic death of his friend Fanny Palmer, lost at sea when the steamer *Pacific* was wrecked in November 1875, got very short shrift.

His preoccupations obviously affected his work at the store. This led to a collision with Turner, resulting in Tunstall's leaving in high dudgeon.[3] At about the same time, it became apparent that the Oukamok scheme with Kimberly was not going to materialize, so Tunstall made other plans. He would go down to Santa Barbara and use his contact with Kimberly to get introductions to the big

FIG. 17. Martin Morse Kimberly. Date and photographer unknown.

sheep ranchers in that area. He would "bone up" on sheep ranching and then, when he was ready, file on some land and start making his fortune.

On Monday, February 14, 1876, after drawing fifteen hundred dollars through Turner at the store, Tunstall made his preparations to leave Victoria. "You can . . . very well imagine that leaving such a place does not call forth many sighs of regret," he wrote.[4] There followed a series of last-minute vexations, farewell calls, and uncertainty as to whether he would actually leave or not. But when the steamer rolled out past Ogden Point on Friday, February 18, Tunstall was aboard. He had a rough ride ahead of him.

Tunstall reached San Francisco on Monday, February 21, after a three-day ordeal on the "Ox Team" (as the packet plying the Pacific coast was known). She was, he said, "the most infernal roller that was ever turned out of a ship-yard," and he "suffered a great deal."[5]

He reached the Palace Hotel on Market Street at about half past eleven that night and doubtless collapsed gratefully into its luxurious embrace. The next day he awoke to find San Francisco in festive mood. "The great $30,000^{00} four mile & repeat, Horse Race comes off today, it is a general holiday here, so I can't attend to business," Tunstall reported, and set off for the racetrack, signing his first brief note from California "Your affectionate son, (& for the present) 'Adventurer'" (fig. 18).

> The sight of a city after such a long absence from its busy scenes, made a peculiar impression upon me. I *never* till yesterday (I am writing on Wednesday [February 23]) understood how the *excitement* of a city would "*carry away*" the weak (don't misunderstand me & think I was *carried away*, I am far too serious & sober an individual, for any such feelings to possess me) but I felt that to people brought up in the country, it would not be at all impossible to be drawn into the vortex of the whirl of pleasure & folly, & till checked by ruin, not to have power to resist its influence; San Francisco was very crowded yesterday; the climate was that of May, and very pleasant after the rains of Victoria.[6]

Next day he went to see R. Guy McLellan, who had offices at 330 Pine St. McLellan, whom he found "very pleasant," promised to help him gain all the information he would need for acquiring land. It was a complex business. There was, for instance,

> Public land unsurveyed, & untenable save by preemption . . . there is Public land surveyed & untenable save by purchase at $1.25 per acre. There is land held under Spanish Grants; grazing & agricultural land at prices varying according to locality

& quality. There is land held by speculators at various prices, also according to quality & location. There is railway land at various prices from the same causes [sources?] (Railway Land is land given to Railway companies, by the state as an inducement to them to build their railroad & is usually alternate sections of 20 miles square along both sides of the road) Then again there are sheep ranches already made & located for sale by heirs, executors, assigns & others.[7]

What there did not seem to be was any land he could get for free. He had met a man from Oregon who told him that the kind of land necessary for raising sheep there was already taken up, and convinced him that looking for a place in that part of the country would be a "very long job."

The form it now takes is that *securing* a run won't be so very easy, & will necessitate a larger disbursement than I calculated; I am by no means sure of this last assumption, but that is the appearance of things at present. I shall probably call upon Major New's friend [Colonel Hays] tomorrow, he lives over at Oakland. I don't wish to remain here longer than I am obliged as it is rather a costly place to stop in.[8]

FIG. 18. John Henry Tunstall, aged twenty-two, 1876. Photographer, Watkins Yosemite Art Gallery, San Francisco. The better-known photograph of Tunstall was probably taken in San Francisco in 1872.

That evening, he dined with young Allen Francis, son of his Victoria landlady, who was going back to his old post with the Alaska Fur Co. at New Church. On Saturday, he had his photograph taken ("Much as I dislike adding to the number of photographs extant of myself"), presciently feeling "as I should probably spend an adventurous 12 months before Feby. 1877, that I might not survive to see that date &c &c &c & that you would perhaps like to know what sort of corpse I made, though the vultures were my undertakers, I decided . . . to have my photograph taken for your benefit, & shall probably be able to enclose it with this letter."[9]

In view of subsequent events, Tunstall's gallows humor here has a distinctly unsettling flavor: it was in fact to be his last photograph. Next he visited McLellan again, and then "crossed over to Oakland to call on Capt. Jack Hayes."

At the time John Tunstall met him, Hays was approaching his sixtieth year and had retired from public life, although he was still active in real estate ventures, banking, and industrial interests (fig. 19). According to Tunstall, Hays owned ten thousand acres of land near Visalia and was "thoroughly posted upon the value of lands, in *money* as well as their *productive value*."

FIG. 19. John Coffee Hays, ca. 1876. Steel engraving from a photograph, photographer unknown.

I told him I was going to settle in this state if I could find a location, that I intended to start sheep farming. His reply was "*Too late, sir! Too late, sir!* Six years too late, sir, There is not a patch of Tulare, Kern or Fresno [counties] left. If you had capital to invest in it six years ago, you could have secured your run, made a *pile* out of sheep, & sold every acre you bought for $1.00 for $8.00 and lived independently for the rest of your life. My land down at Visalia is worth $20.00 per acre today. That country is quite full!" My jaw lengthened at this information, till I declare it fairly ached. "Goodbye to the sunny south," thought I. "Australia will have to be my home then after all." I can assure you I felt quite sick at the stomach. I told Captain Hays, in as jocular a manner as I could summon up, though I believe I must have looked as though I had just swall[ow]ed some aloes that quite dissolved my el dorado, that the orange groves I had pictured surrounding my log mansion and my 150,000 sheep were sent higher than a kite. "Not at all," he said. "Not a bit! not a bit! New Mexico is the place for *you*! just you *jump right in*, buy up all the land you can, start your sheep & turn every cent you make into Spanish Grants. New Mexico today is just where California was 10 years ago."[10]

In the face of such contagious enthusiasm, it would not have been surprising had Tunstall rushed back to his hotel, packed a bag, and taken the next train to New Mexico. In spite of Hays's advice, however—or perhaps because of it—he decided to

> go down & see Dr Shaw & study sheep & land a little down there [in Santa Barbara] & I expect I shall attach myself to a party going through New Mexico somewhere about June or July, that will be in plenty of time, & a cheap way of doing it.
>
> Captain Hayes considers that of all the ways of making money, that taking up land & raising sheep, is the quickest & safest, he knows all about the whole thing, you see he has grown up with the country & you may say that there is not a thing to do with the land that he is not familiar with. He said that a Spanish grant in New Mexico, covering about 2,500,000 acres was sold in San Francisco the other day for 25 cents per acre, 5 or so parties each of whom he knew each taking a part of it, at which price he says one could buy lots of smaller grants, his advice was "*buy land!!!!!!* he said it was the safest investment in the united states. . . ."[11]

He spent his final evening in San Francisco with attorney Guy McLellan and his wife, to whom he had come with a letter of introduction from Mrs. Ann Clarke, a saleslady at the Victoria store. The lawyer had already concurred with Hays that New Mexico was the coming place. He promised to give Tunstall a letter of introduction to "one of his most intimate friends" Samuel B. Axtell, recently installed as governor of New Mexico. Even so, he suggested, Tunstall could do no better than to go down to Santa Barbara as he had originally intended, and then make his way to Santa Fe.

On Saturday, March 4, Tunstall left on the packet *Mohongo* for Santa Barbara, a "cozy nest of New England and Western New York people" as one writer described it in 1873. His first call was on Mrs. Jane Kimberly, who had some letters from London for him. On Monday, March 6, his birthday, Tunstall called on Doctor and Mrs. Shaw (fig. 20). They seemed, he told his "Trinity" of parents and sister who had entertained the Shaws in London, "quite what you represented them."

Doctor Shaw took him uptown, introduced him around, and put his name down for the local club. He spent much of the next couple of days with Shaw, talking sheep. A trip upcountry with a

FIG. 20. James Barron Shaw. Date and photographer unknown.

real estate agent named Barnard was called off because heavy rains had made the roads impassable.

During this time, Tunstall also acquainted himself—and through his diary, his family—with the ins and outs of acquiring land in either Arizona or New Mexico. He dined with Mrs. Kimberly, who told Tunstall her brother was "in charge of an indian reserve in Arizona & has lived in New Mexico & Arizona for the last 16 years, at her suggestion I have written him a letter of enquiry upon those countries. He says Indians are not troublesome atall, nor likely to be again."[12]

Doctor Shaw also introduced Tunstall to one of the most prominent of southern California's movers and shakers, Col. William Wells Hollister (fig. 21). "Mr. Tunstall is from London, England," Shaw said, as he introduced the two men, "and comes here with a view to starting sheep farming." "Then," Hollister boomed

"he has come here *too late* Doctor. *Too late,* the day is passed for starting sheep here, New Mexico, Arizona, Southern Colorado & Northern Texas are the places for him to look at."

Dr. Shaw said "Oh Colonel don't discourage him so much as that," Col. Hollister replied "Better to tell the truth if it does hurt a little you know, Doctor. No, those countries are today just where California was 20 years ago." we said good day & walked on.

Now allow me to introduce you to Col. Hollister. Twenty six years ago, Col. Hollister owed his creditors in Illinois, more than he could pay, & they took what he could give them & released him. He borrowed some money of his sister & bought some sheep; his sister & he mounted a wagon & drove them through to California

FIG. 21. William Wells Hollister. Date and photographer unknown.

where he sold them, & returned for more; he drove two or three such bands through, & made enough by the operation to repay his sister, & start a ranch in Southern California, he bought land as fast as he had money to do it with, which as sheep were rather scarce he was enabled to do after a few years, he extended his ranches as his sheep increased, & in comparatively few years he became a wool grower, of some standing; with every dollar he could spare he bought land; he now owns I believe altogether about 250,000 acres, he has been selling some lately, in large tracts, for about 20 times as much as he gave for it, & is today supposed to be worth about two million & a half of dollars.

Now I say "that unless the Devil is in it, I'll be as rich as Hollister before long". He did nothing that is not within my reach.[13]

Of course, Hays told him, there was another way to acquire land. What he ought to do was look out for

a girl that had a Spanish Grant, & he would secure two good things at once; for said he, "some of those Spanish girls, *you know*, by Jove! are *mighty* nice looking girls, *I tell yer.*

I was telling Mrs. Kimberly this, when I got to Santa Barbara, & she took all the illusion from the long eyelashes. She said that a squaw would be infinitely preferable for a wife, she says [the Spanish girls] would degrade & lower the proudest man, that ever was, to the level of a brute; But I dont know what I should say if I had the chance of getting 250,000 acres, I fancy I might say, "*Squaw or no squaw*, give me the acres."[14]

Tunstall remained in Santa Barbara until March 26, "posting up" on land speculations and sheep farming from anyone he could get hold of. "I am quite convinced that next year is *the* year for New Mexico," he enthused. Why, Colonel Hollister had told him

"that his brother was through there last year, & that it was a splendid country, & that anyone going in next year could make a magnificent fortune, if they would only stick to it"

You will see that we are going to hold a hand *full* of trumps directly, & the deal is just coming round. I am as sure of it, as I am that I am sitting here, that if I only live 15 years longer, & you back me up as I shall see necessary, when the time comes, that I shall be very rich indeed besides making plenty of money for you as I go along. I am a little more careful of my neck than I used to be, as I feel it belongs to our pets.[15]

On March 28, Tunstall left Santa Barbara to stay on Doctor Shaw's ranch, about fifty miles from town. A fortnight later he headed upcountry to the San Julian rancho, owned by Diblee and Hollister, and from there to Santa Rosa, where he stayed with Joseph Wright Cooper (fig. 22), who had married one of Hollister's nieces. By April 22 he was back at La Laguna and Bell's Los Alamos ranch. On May 2 he summed up his situation: "I can but say that I am not leaving a *grain of sand* (to say nothing of a stone) unturned to get posted in the knowledge I am seeking, & that up to now I think I have had marvelous luck, in my opportunities; I shall (when I *do go*) go to New Mexico by a stage coach, that passes through Arizona."[16]

He left Shaw's ranch to go back to Diblee and Hollister's via Cooper's ranch at Santa Rosa "about an hour & a half's ride over the top of a young mountain from the Laguna." While there, he was suffering badly from rheumatism, which had settled in his left hip and right elbow; "I very much re-

FIG. 22. Joseph Wright Cooper. Date and photographer unknown.

semble the Governor [his father], when he has lumbago," he said.

By May 9, with his Spanish "not progressing so fast as to be dangerous," Tunstall was ready to leave the friendly atmosphere of Cooper's ranch for San Julian, with a stop on the way at the Lompoc ranch owned by a man named McLeod. He left with this advice of Cooper's ringing in his ears:

"You be sure & buy the right sort of *dirt*, & your fortune is made; I learned *that* when I was a boy. My Father taught me; I have seen everything else that ever changes hands for money, *get* low & *keep* low, but I never saw land go back one cent in value, in my life, & I have acted on that principle; I was left at 22 years of age, without a cent; in fact, worse than that, for I had two sisters dependent upon me; I worked for years, till I got a small sum of money, then I slapped it into land quicker than lightening; where is the war that can carry off the land? where is the thief who can steal your land? or the Political ring who can swamp it? *NO! SIR, land is land*, & when your money is *there*; you have it *safe*; I bought land & *kept* on buying & that is how I made my money; I consider that I have made $200 000⁰⁰ during the last ten years, & lived all the time as well, almost out of nothing; & yet I have done nothing smart & nothing that you cant do."[17]

Good advice—but in the final analysis Tunstall chose to disregard it completely, and settled in precisely the sort of place he had been warned against, where a war would indeed carry off his land, where thieves would indeed steal him blind, and a political ring swamp him. For the moment, however, he was "feeling very impatient to get on the move for New Mexico," but guessed he would wait until August.

Tunstall's next stop was at the home of Wigmore and Sage, "wool growers" who had purchased land not far from the Shaw ranch. On June 11, shortly after treating his father to an explanation of the term *greaser* that would probably get him lynched today, Tunstall went on to say that he was on his way to San Luis Obispo to see Robert G. Flint, a sheep raiser who had already sent him some information on New Mexico and promised him more if he wanted it. Flint's San Juan ranch was some fifty miles beyond San Luis; the temperature was 110 in the shade.

"By Jove! It came near killing me, I believe," said Tunstall. "My mouth got dry & rough & my tongue felt like a nutmeg grater."[18] He reached the ranch without incident, however; but on his arrival found that the rancher was away till the following Sunday, June 19. However, when Mrs. Flint and her sister-in-law Mrs. Elson indicated they looked upon his staying till Flint's return as a matter of course, Tunstall killed a couple of days speculating over the various land grants in New Mexico about which the rancher had written him, and toughing out the unbearable heat

> with the water in the pitcher at blood heat, ones bed as though it had been warmed with warming pans till it was hot right down to the castors; where the tumbler on the wash stand was quite *hot* & the very floors, carpets, walls, pillows & sheets were all alike *blood* heat; on taking off ones clothes before an open window, to be fanned as if with the breath of a furnace, that came on one in fitful gusts, but very hot. I tell you this climate makes one very glad that New Mexico is not so hot by a great deal. Mrs Flint has just told me that the thermometre is at 90 in an inner room. I heard the foreman say "that a man might go right to Hell, without knowing when he first entered, in such times as these" & I believe him.[19]

On Sunday, Flint returned from his cattle delivery, and Tunstall reported on the rancher to his father on Tuesday, June 20. Flint, he said, was "a tall, coarse looking man of about 55 or 60," whose ramblings provided the information that the climate of New Mexico was cold in winter, that the American population was very small, that the day of Indian raids was pretty well over, and that "the politics were in the hands of a ring who control things as they like." Flint also offered Tunstall the further misinformation that

> there are very few sheep & cattle there. As soon as I go there, he says everyone will know my business & that it is a "rare field full of razors". He speaks very highly of [Elias] Brevoort, also of [Wilson Waddingham] the owner of the Armendaris Grant, whom he says is an Englishman. . . . He says it is a much better cattle than sheep country, & strongly advised me to get posted on cattle. He has had both cattle & sheep, & he says that cattle pay best to raise anywhere. . . . I think I shall study that question, it is not so intricate as sheep & there is a great deal to recommend it.[20]

If Tunstall had the wherewithal to buy the Armendaris Grant, Flint said, he would be "a *Prince* (as far as power was concerned) in a very few years," commanding through the lay of the land, "what would be 'tant amount' to a kingdom." Tunstall asked Flint how much he thought one would have to pay for the grant.

Flint thought that fifteen thousand pounds sterling (seventy-five thousand dollars) would do it. Why not then just buy half of it? asked Tunstall.

His answer was, "Well, you see Mr Tunstall New Mexico is today, where California was 20 years ago, they are going to go through the same process of laws & changes, that we have done, & the man that is going to win this game must legislate today whilst he has but the few to deal with, so as to reach beyond all that the many can do in future. . . . [I]f you want to win the game you must look 20 years a head, or you will have worked for nothing, if you buy half that grant, as soon as you begin to succeed someone will buy up the other half, & then you will have interminable trouble & bother with your neighbor's cattle.

This Mr. Waddingham (the owner of the Armendaris Grant) has been in that country for a number of years, he owns three other Grants as well, he is mixed up with the politics of the place & the Armendaris has *been* & *is* quite an unproductive property to him & Waddingham wants to realize & leave the country.

That railroad [down the Rio Grande valley] will be completed I should think without *any* doubt in less than ten years.[21]

Tunstall had now been in California more than four months; he was just beginning to see the direction he might go. From Shaw's ranch, on June 24, 1876, he once again addressed his "Much Beloved Governor." Of all his voluminous correspondence with his father on the subject this letter most clearly indicates the way his mind was working.

There is Land in New Mexico today that can be bought for about one twentieth of what it will be worth in ten or 15 years time; & the *question* for *us* to consider is, whether we can make a living out of the land when we have got it, for those ten or 15 years.

I will just endeavour to examine the chances, from my present knowledge, *but mark me*, that this is only for your *education*. I have not been there & I cant speak in any but a speculative way.

The nearer you are to an empty stomach, the nearer you are to a market, unless the stomach be your own, & even then, the chances are greatly in favour of your getting to market, as soon as possible. The stomach of New Mexico, is at present not very large, & the owners thereof are for the most part poor, & as a man of the World, the farther I am off an empty stomach & an empty purse, the better I like it; & I come at once to the conclusion that I don't want to go into a business, which will compel me to have as my customers the empty purses & stomachs of New Mexico. I must cater for the wants of those who can pay for what they want; The roads are inferior & communications bad, so I must if possible produce something that does not need a vehicle to get it to market, or at least in proportion as the means of conveyance are bad, the produce that will walk to market is the most desirable.

Therefore a *stock* business is *the thing*, either sheep or cattle, & the question between the two is rather a hard one to solve, but before attempting to solve that question there are some facts that we can look at, concerning the country generally, some of which favour our stock & sheep business & some which do not. The taxes in N.M. are at present very low; here in California a man is taxed on every head of stock he owns, & every improvement he has on his ranch, if he puts up a fence he gets taxed upon it, if he builds a pig pen, he gets taxed upon it. Of course, in return the State builds roads, bridges, &c. but on a man of property this comes "kind of heavy" & in course of time all these laws will be made in N.M. that are so inconvenient in California today, & if we can contrive to make the running, & get

the race into our hands before the judges crowd on the weights, we shall be all right
& have made use of our opportunities. . . .

Now I want you to look at the south Eastern corner of the map of New Mexico,
& you will see a spot on the Pecos River marked Chisum's Rancho; This man
Chisum started raising cattle, without a rood of land, 15 years ago, he had a partner
at some part of the time, & dissolved with him some time ago; a short time since,
he "sold out" for $350,000 or £70,000, his former partner brought an action claiming
some part of that sum, but he lost the suit. The day for making a business on public
land in the United States is gone, I think, for no one could calculate upon not being
interrupted for ten years in the future.

I expect that New Mexico is better adapted for a stock, than a sheep country, by
the lay of the water, & the means of communication, & I would as far as I am
concerned, as soon have a stock as a sheep business, I don't think there is much
choice between them as far as the life & the profits are concerned, they are both
very good businesses. . . .

New Mexico will be to me a new country, with a new language, a new people,
a new climate, a new diet, new laws, new animals, & a new religion. I must learn
them all, the same as I have the Californian, & see whether I can live from hand
to mouth off the property which must in 15 years be worth a large fortune & which
is now within our reach, until the golden future arrives; & see whether by studying
its peculiarities now, I can't use them so as to be in the right position when that
time comes. . . .

I shall on reaching Santa Fe present my letters of introduction & arrange to board
& lodge in a Spanish family, if possible; for until I know the language & the people,
I can do nothing atall there. During that time (I mean the time it takes me to learn
the language) I shall get posted upon nearly everything else which is of the least
importance.[22]

It was obviously at this juncture that Tunstall's thoughts began to turn toward
the idea of a cattle rather than a sheep ranch. He reported having "gleaned some
very good ideas" on the subject from Bell before leaving La Laguna to return to
Santa Barbara. When he got there he learned that tragedy had struck the Shaw
family: their youngest child, Donnie, had died. Tunstall arrived just in time to
attend the funeral, on Wednesday, June 28. He implored his "Dear Little Mother"
to write to the Shaws, for "no one ever needed the precious healing oil, more
than those two poor stricken hearts."

On July 10, concerned by his continued expenses, Tunstall moved into a
cheaper hotel in Santa Barbara; he was now planning to leave about July 26, as
he could live more cheaply in San Francisco.

I intend to go across by train to Denver in the rough, by which I mean that I shall
dress as though I was going to the mines, & travel 2nd or 3rd class. The whole trip
wont take much more than a week, & I may be able to effect quite a saving that
way. . . .

I expect to find the climate in the neighborhood of the Armendaris Grant very
preferable in winter to that of the grants situated in the northern portion of the
Territory, but the garden of New Mexico is in the country near Mesilla; & I regret
to say that I can only hear of small grants there. But all this speculation before hand
is very vain, & can not be of any earthly use, still it is the subject that runs in my
head.

He went to a dance; he went sea bathing with half a dozen young ladies; but
he wasted no ink describing these social events to his Trinity. His mind was
always on his future plans.

I inclined towards [cattle] for New Mexico more & more. They need no outlay of money for buildings, you see & can live w[h]ere water is more sparsely distributed, are not molested by wolves or cayotes, get to market without a wagon or conveyance of any kind, & when bred on a place, need little or no herding; besides leaving the owner of them free, through 2/3rd of the year.

If that Armendaris Grant is what I take it to be, you will see that I shall own it someday.[23]

The news from London was that Henry Beeton was offering to buy Papa Tunstall's share of the business for a cash payment; Tunstall advised his father to accept. "If you can get out of the affair about the same amount of cash (or good bills, it does not matter which) as the last balance sheet declared to be yours, you will be doing *immensely* well, if you can get more than that, well *so much* the better." As for his own plans, he wrote, "My hopes are as high as ever, I feel quite confident that if I live, I shall make a success of this enterprize. . . . [T]he more I think of the Armendaris Grant the more I want it, it looks to me richer than any gold mine."[24]

This July 21 letter was his last from Santa Barbara. The next was from the Cosmopolitan Hotel in San Francisco dated August 4; he had put off his departure for New Mexico for a few days after meeting a certain Mr. Jenkins, who managed the San Francisco end of Elias Brevoort's real estate business. Jenkins had put him on to a "California gentleman [who] was going to take a month's tour through the land grants of N.M. about the 12th of the month & he suggested that if I was on the spot, I could join the party."

Tunstall asked his father to send him a letter of credit at Santa Fe, "as I shan't have a great deal of money left by about that time, & it would be a bad place to be 'broke' in." He reported meeting a Cornishman who had been in the surveyor general's office for nearly six years, his time "about equally divided between Colorado, New Mexico & Arizona," who confirmed Tunstall's feelings about investing in land and stock in New Mexico. All this made him "quite impatient" to reach Santa Fe.

He met his friend Ann Clarke, who was in San Francisco on a visit. She told him that trade had been awful at Victoria; he made no attempt hide his satisfaction: "You know Turner *has* said, in the times passed, 'that I was a drawback to the business', I am afraid he has not got on much better without me than he did with me; she says he has walked about the place, looking very quiet & serious of late; Poor Devil! I guess he will look more serious & quiet after a while than he does now."[25]

A long discussion with Jenkins about the various grants available for sale in New Mexico was followed by another with a Californian sheep raiser named Pinkerton, who owned one seventh of the Amarilla Grant and a large interest in the Nolan Grant. Pinkerton asked what kind of acreage Tunstall was thinking of taking up. "Oh, about 100,000 acres," Tunstall told him.

He asked me how much I had any idea I could pay down & what time I should like to get on the balance? I asked him what sort of arrangements of that kind were usually made. He replied that in such new countries "cash" was the usual time & he repeated his former question.

I told him that if 100,000 acres would cost £4,000 [$20,000] if I could pay from £1500 to £2000 down, & get from 5 to 10 years to pay the balance, I should consider it very convenient providing the interest were not too high.

He told me he would sell me his land in the Horse lake country at those terms, if I could satisfy him that I was a responsible party. I asked him the interest he would require? he said 8 per cent if the money were advanced for 5 years & 10 per cent if advanced for 10 years.[26]

Promising to think the offer over, Tunstall took his leave of Pinkerton. He did not, apparently, contact him again. Just before leaving, Tunstall told his parents he had appointed his lawyer friend McLellan his "American correspondent" and inside the cover of his pocketbook inscribed the following message:

In case of any accident happening to me, I have here written my name, viz., *J. H. Tunstall.*

My nearest friend is R. Guy McLellan, 585 Clay Street, San Francisco who will, if communicated with, render me any assistance that I may need.[27]

He had learned all he could, and now he was impatient to be on his way. And when the Central and Union Pacific's "Emigrant Train" left San Francisco at four o'clock in the afternoon of Friday, August 11, twenty-three-year-old Tunstall was on board. His hopes were high, the future was bright. "Really," he wrote, "luck seems to follow me now, nearly wherever I go." He ended with a flourish, signing the letter—not inappropriately—"Yours, Adventurer."[28]

CHAPTER 8

 # FATEFUL ENCOUNTERS

JOHN Tunstall professed himself "much grieved" to find that the train he had taken passed through the Sierra Nevada range at night. "I had seen them before when I came out from England (That was four years ago this month) but would have liked to see them again very much."[1] Of the Union Pacific's much-vaunted Day Coaches, of Buck's Reclining Car Chairs, Pullman's Palace Sleeping Coaches, of the Miller Safety Platform and the Celebrated Westinghouse Air Brakes boasted of in the Union Pacific prospectus he sent to his parents, adventurer Tunstall had nothing to say in his first letter from Santa Fe; only that

> Yankees are the "cussedest" set of leeches that I ever struck. I went via the Union Pacific line as far as Cheyenne, which took 3½ days & 3 nights during which time I did not undress & barely slept, I however survived. We reached Cheyenne at 2 p.m. [on August 12] the train left for Denver at 5 a.m. the next morning so I did not get much sleep that night. I reached Denver at 9 a.m. [August 13] I had a couple of letters to gentlemen there, whom I interviewed (as the train did not leave for Trinidad till 2 P.m.).
> . . . We reached El Moro the terminus of the Denver & Rio Grande R.R. at 1 o clock at night, we had to wait till about 2.30 for the coach to take us on to Trinidad, which is three miles south. I lay down on three wooden chairs & slept for about an hour at Trinidad before the machine (drawn by four mules & very appropriately called a jerkey which was to convey me some 220 miles) started; this machine, somewhat resembles a stagecoach, insomuch as it is painted red, & has a sort of box middle, & a boot behind, but the wretched affair has no springs, the body is fixed to the running gear with straps about 8 inches long, fixed to rigid bars, & I can assure you one soon discovers why it is called a "jerkey".

Today's traveler driving through the 7,834-foot Raton Pass sees one of the West's most breathtaking panoramas: the curving road, the ruined church across the gully with gravestones scattered down the steep hillside, the enormous vista stretching out ahead, and the smoke-blue mountains away to the west. What it must have been like to come through it in Barlow and Sanderson's Southern Overland Stage Company jerky in 1876 can only be imagined.[2] Tunstall remarked only that "from the south side of the Raton Mountains to Las Vegas the road is one of the finest I ever saw, & entirely a natural road."[3] While he found the scenery "very pretty," living conditions were less prepossessing. "Everything here is in a very crude state," he observed, "adobe houses with mud roofs, cattle do all the hauling & freighting, horses are scarce, & mules & donkeys very much used. The meals on the road were execrable & a dollar each."

Santa Fe was readying itself for the Republican and Democratic territorial conventions; an announcement of the dates of both appeared in the *New Mexican* the day of Tunstall's arrival.[4] If Tunstall picked up a copy, he could also have read that Tim Shay, "a Colorado rough," had been killed in La Junta by saloon owner Rufe Edwards after a difference over a card game; that Mr. William H. Manderfield's apricot garden was flourishing; that mountain raspberries were plentiful and new potatoes could be had for twelve cents a pound. From Lincoln County there was a story signed "Rover," datelined Blazer's Mill, August 6, which recounted how a party of Mexicans from there led by a Mr. Morris J. Bernstein had recovered eight stolen horses, seven in Puerta de Luna and one in Fort Sumner.[5]

None of this would have meant any more to Tunstall than the announcement that the firm of Paul Dowlin & Co. had been dissolved by mutual consent, and would in future be known as Paul Dowlin & Bro., or the "card" that had appeared regularly in the *New Mexican* since 1874, advertising the firm of L. G. Murphy & Co., Wholesale and Retail Dealers in General Merchandise, offering Groceries, Liquor and Mining Implements. Highest prices for country produce, cattle &c. The address was given as "Licoln, Rio Bonito, N.M." and in all the years the card appeared, the error was never corrected.

Obviously feeling that William Pool's Exchange Hotel was too expensive for his purse, Tunstall took a room at Paul Herlow's hotel on San Francisco St.— "Burro Alley." Despite its scruffy appearance in the few contemporary photographs that exist, San Francisco St. was a bustling little thoroughfare in which could be found W. W. Tate's New Era Restaurant and Chop House, Joe Stinson's saloon, Esselbach's Bath Rooms and the store of F. Abeytia & Brothers, manufacturers of Mexican jewelry. Herlow's was a "very 2nd class hotel" but

> mine host is a good honest german, has been in the cattle business for years & I think I can get plenty of information out of him, so I get a slight setoff against the mud walls, floor & roof & inferior cookery. . . . I have had dinner & a chat with mine host, on the subject of cattle; he has dealt in cattle for years (some 20 years) all through Texas, Colorado, & New Mexico, & understands the whole thing, cattle are a sort of second nature to him, he got broken through a mule speculation, in which the indians stole all the herd, & he had to do the first thing that came along to make some sort of raise & he went into the hotel business (as it is called) but he is just as essentially a cattle man, as some men you know, are *horse* men, who have been horse dealers & jobbers all their lives. I tell you all this that you may understand this man; we went into some figures, or rather I made him figure out a business which would come within the compass I spoke of, in fact I made him figure out my plan, without having anything to say about the land, & his result came out more satisfactorily than I had made it.
>
> In addition to this he gave me the history of the cattle trade of the last 15 years, & I can see just as clearly as any turn of trade (in which the whole market can be reviewed, both supply & demand) can be seen; that this is a *most* favorable time to go into cattle. The life for the 1st three years in that business, conducted as I should consider it advisable to run it; would be rather rough, but the smooth water would come almost before one was aware of it. Sheep are going to be good in this country, & a brick business will be a most paying business, for the next 10 or 15 years, but they need so many more fixtures, more men, time & attention than cattle, that I think cattle would be the most desirable.[6]

He set forth in considerable detail how he envisaged starting up—he had been in Santa Fe fewer than seventy-two hours when he wrote this—and what he thought it might all cost.

> The only permanent, safe & scientific way to run a stock business, is to own land enough to be independent of the world. The history of California is going to be reenacted here & the successful men will be those who have foreseen the day when free range would be a thing of the past, & who provided for it. . . .
>
> In choosing land, I don't intend to look out for what might be called wheat land, but for well watered stock country. Stock land with a clear title will in less than 12 years be worth $5^{00} per acre, though I don't think it will be worth more than that, for a great many years, however that is quite rise enough, & there will in two or three years be a market right at one's elbow, for all the meat one can produce. . . .
>
> My reason for leaning towards cattle is as much as anything, that a man is so much freer & more independent with them than sheep if the business is properly conducted. I could leave my stock ranch, to take a run over to England 2 years sooner than I could a sheep ranch. Lumber [for fencing and outbuildings] is much cheaper here than in California & the prospects of a stock business are better here in every way than there, as far as I can judge. I feel in excellent spirits about myself though I feel *serious,* as the time for decisive action seems very close now, for I may say I know now where to find what I want.

Tunstall was unable to make use of the letters of introduction written by Guy McLellan and a sheep raiser named Gray that he had brought from California. Gov. Samuel Axtell had gone to the Centennial Exhibition in Philadelphia and would not be back for two or three months; and a lawyer to whom he had also been given an introduction was away on a legal circuit, so for the moment he had "no acquaintances here yet, worth the speaking of." Looking around him, he assessed his new surroundings.

> It is quite necessary that I should have either a horse or a wagon & horses to get around upon; the latter would be the best in some respects, though I guess I can do with the former; where one has long stretches of dry country to cross, a wagon is very much ahead of a horse to get around with, as one can carry water in it. I shall however hire a wagon if I want one & then I shall not have so much on my hands which is a disadvantage in its way.
>
> This is the first place I have been in, where every one goes armed, all the men have a great "six shooter" slung on their hip, & a knife on the other as a counter poise; I keep my revolver *mighty* handy all the time, though I don't show it; it carries a fearful ball, & shoots quick, but I don't calculate to have to use it. That sort of experience & adventure depends somewhat upon a man's disposition & habits & the places he frequents; a man who gambles & drinks is very apt to be "*thar,* or thar abouts" when any shooting takes place, as he belongs to the shooting crowd; & will be with his crowd; but a man who attends to his own business only & above everything else does not figure in politics may live in this country a great while without smelling powder. . . .
>
> I ought to keep on travelling for about 4 or 5 months on horseback, till I know the whole country, & I expect I shall do so, too. I shall acquire a bull terrier to watch my interests, & I shall christen him Blucher, so that in case a greaser sneaks up to my horse's picket rope, I shall get wind of him before he reaches it.

It was Tunstall's belief that he could invest about seven thousand pounds sterling (thirty-five thousand dollars) in such a way as to own a hundred thousand acres, cover his own expenses, and pay his father 5 percent interest on the money for the first three years. The indigenous stock was not much improved, he reported, the Texas steer being about the average. "When I start, if I can afford it, I shall breed towards a Durham model, as persistently as I can." He went on,

> When you write again, tell me if you think you could let me have £7,000 next spring, I should I believe be able to pay you between £250 and £350 of interest at the end of 12 months. I should then be indebted to no one but you, the items would be Land £4,000, Cattle, Horses, Fixtures, wages, food &c about £3,000, & I could realize about £750 the first year, & keep it up right along, till about the 3rd or 4th year when it would nearly double, it might double sooner, but with the worst kind of luck it would double then. More money might be used to advantage in buying fine breeding stock in a business of the same size; but it is not necessary to endeavor to do too much when one's means are not large.
>
> . . . [I]f things turned out exactly as I expected at the end of the first year, & you could spare more capital, £2,500 more capital would nearly double the amount of the profit, but I consider the amount that I have talked about, viz. £3,000, is as much as one ought to put into stock to *start* with, an addition the next year would be all right though. . . .
>
> P.S. I believe than in ten years I could buy out the Turners & Beetons just as they stand, & give them a champagne supper to top the bargain.

John's mother Emily Tunstall had warned him not to take any unnecessary risks out in that wild country. He assured her he did not propose to do so, although

> all countries more or less thickly populated with a *needy, ignorant* population are unsafe in a measure. A man's safety does not depend on the *people* here, if it did he would have *none*, it lies with *himself*. If he offers no reward for molestation, provokes no hatred or malice, & avoids the neighborhood of drunkenness, where wanton attacks & insults are sometimes offered, & made, he is but open to what may be called a casualty, & he has to take that chance. I tell you all this, as I tell you *everything*, but fear for my life never occurs to me. I have contracted the habit of keeping my hand on my "shooting iron" & should any trouble arise (which is *very far* from likely, as I get on as smoothly with the motly crew I meet, in my fashion, as you do with the friends in your drawing room) I expect I shall gain the honour of the first shot.[7]

Since his arrival in Santa Fe, Tunstall had also been working, in sporadic bursts, upon a long letter to his "Dearly Beloved Sister," Emily or "Minnie," to whom he had not written for several months. Apologizing for this and for not having described the scenery in the places he visited, Tunstall explained that these days he usually saw land "from a ranchero's point of view; that is, with a view to how many sheep or cattle it would carry to the acre."[8] Nevertheless, he endeavored to convey something of the flavor of the country to his sister.

> If you get the [military] map of New Mexico [sent some time ago] you will find on the northern boundary of the Maxwell Grant, a town marked Trinidad. This town . . . is they say the last one going south, that has any traces of an American population; that is, going south to Old Mexico (or more properly speaking Mexico) & is the terminus of the Denver & Rio Grande R.R. The altitudes throughout this country are very high; the mean is about 6000 feet, through a very large country; & about here (that is in Colorado) if you look at a large map you will see that the watershed of America divides East, West & South. The air is intensively pure, one can see about 10 times the distance that one can in any other place I have been in.

With my one eye, I distinguished a man riding a white horse quite easily at nine miles; at three miles, I distinguished the breed of some sheep that were grazing; & so on, the clearness of the atmosphere is most disceptive, and at first seems quite absurd.

Asthmatical people live here without any inconvenience. Mexican towns are built pretty much upon one model & the houses are built like the towns . . . in the form of a square, as they all are, with a garden in the centre; . . . these houses are but one story high for the most part & built of sun dried mud slabs about 4 Ins. thick, 14 In. long, & 10 In. wide, called adobes; these are laid in mud in place of mortar & in a good house built of three tiers of adobes, make a very thick wall, for they put plenty of mud between them, thereby making a wall about 36 in. wide, the roofs are nearly flat & simply a cake of flat mud which of course cracks a good deal in the sun, & often lets in rain, if it rains very hard, though as very little rain falls that does not amount to much; a town has a garden in the centre called a plaza, & houses of this style built all around it. . . . [T]he windows of the houses give most upon the garden or inside court, many of them have no windows facing outside & only one door; an adobe house, as you can imagine, when well ventillated (which they rarely are) is cool in summer & owing to its thick walls almost like a cave; & warm in winter. if ill ventilated they are close & stuffy. . . .

Santa Fe is a mud town claiming about 5000 inhabitants but I dont think it contains 3000. I find that New Mexico is almost entirely owned or controlled by jews, who have come in at an early day & farmed the advantages of the country up to this point. There are not very many nice people here, the old Spanish familys are settled further south at Albuquerque & in that section of country. Take it altogether, however, I think I shall do very well here when I start; The climate is superb & the chances of success seem to me to be at present at a focus. . . .

In these frontier towns one meets some very singular people from time to time. For instance I was sitting at dinner at Santa Barbara next to a man who looked like a complete fool, & very shabbily dressed; I got into conversation with him & found him to be one of the most extraordinary men I ever met. He had travelled *all over* the world, & *thoroughly*; he had travelled on this coast from Alaska to Cape Horn & knows the place by heart, he had travelled through every state in the Union, there were men around from ½ a dozen different, out of the way state[s], who said he knew them by heart, Colorado, New Mexico, & Arizona he appeared to have at his fingers ends, not only the people & districts, but the vegetable, animal & mineral kingdom of each section as well. Canada, Europe, Asia & Africa he seemed just as well acquainted with. My friend & I looked upon him as a sort of mystery, he was a Scotch man who looked a litle over 30. He seemed to know every thing, & at the same time he appeared soft & yet I don't think anyone could score a single point off him.

Who this remarkable individual was, Tunstall irritatingly neglects to mention; he does exactly the same thing in his next paragraph, but this time we know that the young adventurer is recounting the circumstances of his first meeting with the man he would come to consider his closest friend: Robert A. Widenmann.

Yesterday in leaving my bedroom, I saw a very common looking man lying on a rough bed, & saying to mine host, "I wish I could sweat". I told him that "if he ran 50 yards in the road he could do so" he told me "he had a slight sunstroke two days ago", he got up after a while, dressed in a very shoddy suit of clothes, a flannel shirt, & no collar, a wretched pair of boots & no sox; I got into conversation with him & found him a *very* highly educated man & possessed of a flow of language & accuracy of information that but very few possess. He had been educated in Germany, France & England & is a Southern American. He speaks English *very* correctly.

As, of course, someone educated in Germany would have done: Widenmann had grown up in that country and clearly spoke as he wrote. There was more about him in a September 5 letter:

> I have met a particularly nice fellow here (I forget his name) he was born in Georgia, & was educated in Europe. He is 24 years old, he appears to be quite well off & is going into sheep farming just as I am, he has been sheep farming in Colorado & is moving down to the Pecos. He is not going to buy any land, but I am sure he is wrong in that. It is strange how much our tastes agree, if I could be tempted to go into partnership with anyone it would be with him; he has a partner, but he attended to buying bucks, selling wool &c.[9]

Widenmann was being somewhat less than truthful with Tunstall, understandably so. If later accusations aimed at him are to be believed, Widenmann was living from hand to mouth on whatever credit he could get against mythical "remittances from home." So perhaps he saw the chance of a meal ticket shaping up, and determined to latch on to it. There was no further reference to Widenmann in Tunstall's correspondence until the following year, making it difficult to avoid the conclusion that when he ran out of credit in Santa Fe, Widenmann invited himself down to Lincoln, where he turned up around the middle of February 1877 and began making himself indispensable to Tunstall and objectionable to everyone else.

On August 27, Tunstall gave his father some of the facts and figures of "prospecting":

> This country is even less advanced than British Columbia, as far as accomodation for travellers is concerned. A teamster camps under his wagon & fries his beans & bacon outside; a chance traveller like myself has to stop at some house & pay $1^{00} per meal . . . & nights lodging to pretty much the same tune. I ordered a bottle of tonic Dr Bates recommended me in Santa Barbara, & which I found did me a great deal of good & it cost the modest sum of 12 shillings [$3] "No more tonic for me" I said to the drugist; but that will give you an idea of how things are, the first hotel here [The Exchange] charges £13. 0.0 [$65] per month for board & lodging. The one I am at [Herlow's] £9.0.0 [$45] & that is the cheapest in town. Then going into a new country like this . . . there is a certain amount of treating that *has* to be done & cant be got out of. I tell you all this to explain to you how it is that my funds are drawing to a close.[10]

He spoke of making a trip with a party going down to Reed's ranch on the Pecos near Seven Rivers, and then striking across country from there to Las Cruces, returning to Santa Fe up the Rio Grande valley; it did not come to fruition. One of the unusual aspects of Tunstall's letters home is the fact that he rarely if ever remarked on current events. Not a word, for instance, about the killing of "Wild Bill" Hickok at Deadwood City in the Black Hills on August 2, noted in the August 22 issue of the *New Mexican;* or the vast swarm of grasshoppers that flew over Santa Fe on Monday, September 4. Tunstall spent his time "posting" himself on the means of acquiring land, and filled his letters with his findings. There were two more ways of obtaining land he had not heard of before: "public sale" land, and "school fund" land in Texas. He explained the pros and cons of all this, vis á vis grant land, and promised to write to the land office in Texas for details. He roguishly remarked that there was "a family in town just now, I don't know how many there are in it, I think 4. They own 300,000 sheep, if I married one of the daughters I should have quite a nice flock to start with, should I not? I think I had better get introduced."[11]

He had "lots of masculine friends now," he said; he had been told on half a dozen different occasions that "they like me better than any Englishman they ever met." He was "sorely tempted" by the offer of a two-hundred-thousand-acre cattle ranch on the Cieneguilla Grant, up near Taos: price twenty-five thousand dollars, title as good as "99 out of 100 [percent]." Paul Herlow put him off it, saying he did not think, from what he knew of it, that it would suit Tunstall.

> I think that the land on the Pecos & Canadian rivers is really the best; but of that even I am not sure; I hope you will have sent me some money when I wrote for it, or I fear I shant be able to go on my prospecting trip. We succeeded in getting a clear title to the mule, so that you need not fear that I shall get killed by a horse for some time. I am not a bit less hopeful than ever, I dont think there is any doubt but that I shall make a fortune as fast as I anticipated. . . .
>
> There is a man here [named Gwynne] who owns 75000 acres of the Montoya grant, which I think could be bought for $20,000 this grant has about the *most* perfect title in the territory, & is said to be very desirable property.
>
> The lands further out on the Canadian river are very subject to raids by the Comanchee indians, who are the finest & most determined warriors left of the indian race. two years ago they ran off all Chisum's horses (some 250 head) in spite of his never having less than 50 men on the ranch. West of Fort Bascom is pretty safe. In taking a ranch subject to Indian raids one might lose every head of cattle that one had, in a single night. I am working back to sheep a good deal in my ideas, but it is altogether a *two-sided* question.[12]

On September 11 he received a draft from his father for $485. "I can't *begin* to express my appreciation of your generosity," he wrote. Had it not arrived, "my present exchequer would very likly have prevented my taking a very desirable trip."

> I was invited to go on a hunting & prospecting trip by a Gentleman named [Van C.] Smith who has a ranch about at the junction of the Hondo & Pecos. He (Mr. S.) was not going himself, the party consisted or was to consist of a Mr [P. D.] Elkins, Sen[r] one or two other gentlemen & myself. Mr. E. is the father of the Delegate in congress for the Territory, he is a man of about 55, has lived here about 26 years & knows the country very well & is a very experienced hand in bush life. We proposed to leave here about the 20th of this month; In the meantime a Mr.[George] Hogg (who has a ranch very near the one I have just alluded to) was in Santa Fe & stopping at this Hotel & invited me to go with him back to his ranch, & stop as long as I felt inclined; I was afraid to go lest I should get "broke" down there, besides your letters were coming in thick & fast & I did not want to miss any of them; I therefore decided at the last not to go with him, though his invite still holds good when I get to that part of the country. Which (you understand) I will do with Elkins & Co.
>
> The other trip was to Taos, to inspect that Grant of Brevoort's which I wrote about, there was a friend of his here, who was to go with me to show me the bounds &c. This friend left town before he could conclude all the arrangement, so it is still pending, as it were.[13]

Tunstall put both these plans to one side in order to take a forty-five-mile ride to Lagunas to see the sheep camp of a newly arrived drover, who had "accomplished the hitherto unparalleled feat of driving 10,000 sheep from California through Arizona into New Mexico, with the trifling loss of 600 head." The name of this "Lion" was George Stoneroad, one of three brothers who owned one hundred fifty thousand acres of the Beck Grant and operated as the firm of Stoneroad Brothers in Las Vegas.

Stoneroad was a six-foot-two Texan, "brought up to cattle," who had emigrated to the San Joaquin valley before settling in New Mexico. He told Tunstall that the cattle business was "a killing life to lead, the work was so hard & incessant." Sheep were easier and paid better, he said, giving the young Englishman once more furiously to think.

On September 21, Tunstall wrote his father that he had just returned from a week's trip to Taos to look over the Cieneguilla Grant and was starting off immediately on another tour, this time to look at the Beck, Gallinas, and Montoya grants.

The Cieneguilla trip had come about when Tunstall and Anthony Joseph were introduced by Paul Herlow on Thursday, September 14. Joseph said he was going back to Taos next day via the Ojo Caliente, and he invited John to go with him. They met at Plaza de Alcalde; on the way to Ojo Caliente, Tunstall learned that Joseph was

> the son of Portuguese parents, he came to this country with his parents when he was 2 years old, he was educated in the eastern states & is more refined in his manner & feelings than I think anyone I have met here, we became good friends at once. Of course a great part of our conversation turned upon Spanish Land Grant questions; I found him very well posted & he gave me several points of which I was ignorant till then. He employed his time up to a few years ago, to a great extent, in what we call "working up" Spanish Grants, that is, seeking out the heirs to Grants & buying up their interests. He has a better knowledge of the Spanish language than most men here, which gives him a great advantage, besides which his father & himself have always commanded great respect from the Mexicans. He was the first to take hold of the Ciniguilla Grant & get it in shape, which he held in company with two others for some time; he then sold out his share, & bought a grant out to himself, which lies right alongside & to which he took a great fancy on account of some highly virtuous mineral hot springs, situated upon it. I could not nor have I yet been able to discover that he has any interest in the sale of the Ciniguilla property; & it is my belief at present that he was disinterested in what he told me & in his conversation.[14]

Tunstall spent the weekend at Ojo Caliente, during the course of which he doubtless learned that, although Anthony Joseph was only thirty, he was already a highly successful entrepreneur: he owned one hundred fifty thousand acres of the Ojo Caliente Grant, a further thirty thousand acres in Colfax County, the Hot Springs Hotel and Spa, a store, and other property in Taos. Tunstall related how Joseph "said that if I bought the Ciniquilla property & put some sheep upon it (we did not specify any numbers though from the style of the conversation, I think from 2 to 4 thousand would be implied) he would go into partnership with me if I liked, he said that his business was spread out rather much for one man to attend to at present, though he did not want to drop any of it."[15]

Although he was disinclined to take a partner, Tunstall promised to think it over. His letter touched on two more items of local interest.

> At Plaza Alcalde at which place I stopped a little while in going to Taos the other day, about 6 months ago [on April 15, 1876] the best & richest man in the village

[Louis Clark] was shot in cold blood; everyone knows who did it, & they are not taking any steps towards justice. They kill a man about every month through that country. About four months ago two men at Santa Fe fought a duel in the Plaza at midday, which was just about as much of an outrage, as for two men to do the same thing in the square of St. Hellier, [Jersey] they were indicted but got off all right.[16]

The "duel" Tunstall refers to (more accurately, it was a drunken brawl) took place late in the afternoon of June 27; the principals were saloonkeepers Joseph Stinson and Van C. Smith, the same Van Smith who had invited Tunstall to join him on a hunting trip a week or two earlier.[17] Smith was wounded in the hand and hip, although apparently not seriously; a number of windows around the square were shattered by their wild shots. The case had just come to trial in the Rio Arriba district court; both defendants were discharged for lack of evidence sufficient to convict on Wednesday, September 20 (Tunstall was writing on September 22).

When he got back to Santa Fe, he talked over Joseph's offer with Paul Herlow, who told him Joseph was "about the best man in the Territory, & that if I did not want him, I had better never take a partner."[18] He confessed that the more he thought about the Cieneguilla land, the more he thought "we shant find so good an investment elsewhere." Brevoort's price was twenty-five thousand dollars, but John might be able to get him down to twenty thousand if he could offer him ready money. Although this was more than his father had expressed himself able to do, Tunstall was "in hopes that such a chance of investment might tempt you a great deal."

If I entered into a partnership with Mr. Joseph we could I think take this grant up with ease, but I jib at a partnership very much. Still I consider that his was a most flattering offer, I am sure if I told anyone here that I had had such an offer, they would call me a fool for not accepting it, *every* one seems to look upon him as a rich and reliable man in *every* way. There would be a great advantage in it at first through his knowledge of the country & its capabilities & he could I think get all the sheep on shares, that he wanted, he is so well known . . . [but] I am not any more in favor of a partnership than you are.

Another excursion loomed, this time a trip to Fort Bascom to look over the Montoya Grant in the company of another young Englishman, George D. Greenwood, whose home was in Bradford, Yorkshire, but who had been living in New Zealand. Passing through California, he had met Tunstall's friend Pinkerton, who suggested he look up his fellow countryman when he got to Santa Fe. He was a "short, rather fat sort of fellow of about twenty, most *unmistakably* English," Tunstall reported.

They got away late on Sunday, September 24, in "a hooded wagon with very little spring to it & in exterior appearance very much resembling the wagon in which Mr. Barkis drove Peggoty & David Copperfield in," and drawn by "the sorriest looking plugs I ever set eyes on." He continued, "Our 'jehu' [driver] was a Mexican gambler, a long slim fellow with an Italian magenta scarf around his waist by way of a belt which gave him an appearance which suggested in a very distant way a kinship to a Greek brigand, though he was a very good sort of a fellow & not in the least like one."[19]

Their route took them southeast through the Pecos and Tricos grants, on to San Jose ("pronounced san hosay," said the ever-didactic Tunstall) to La Cuesta and Gallinas Springs, Stoneroad's headquarters. On the sixth day of their journey, they were caught in a violent storm. They took shelter in the home of "a very wealthy mexican" near the *placita* of Lorez.[20] An abortive try to push on next day met with failure, so Tunstall and his friend Greenwood, who had diarrhea and was as "grumpy as English men generally get, when they are somewhat out of sorts," spent the day with their unnamed host and his pretty daughter, upon whom Tunstall unsuccessfully tried his shaky Spanish.

> I tried bantering the young lady by suggesting that she looked sad, then that perhaps she was cold &c, she laughed & said "no" &c &c but I could not get any ideas out of them, & having made them teach me some dozen new words, & having gone through my whole vocabulary three times, from beginning to end, I left them. I found the next day that the father had had a long chat with our Jehu concerning me & had passed some most flattering remarks upon me, so I at least impressed them more favorably than they did me. Jehu told me that Mexicans, that is the girls, never had anything to say; that if one spoke to them, it was all right; if not, well, that was just as good; he (Jehu) married a white woman at Salt Lake, & knows more than most mexicans, both of English & the manners & customs of the whites.
>
> We had by this time exhausted all the time we had to spare before returning, so turned the horses heads west again for Las Vegas. I was sorry not to see this grant better, or rather not to see more of it, altho I had already made up my mind that it was too far off to suit me, for there wont be a rail road through it for years & years to come & hauling the wool would cost a fortune every year. Cattle would do first rate out there though. Three days brought us to Las Vegas, where I took leave of Greenwood.

Tunstall got back to Santa Fe two days later, having walked the last twelve miles in "high spirits superinduced by this exhillerating climate & this very healthy style of living; I felt & still feel almost as fine as if I were slightly under the effects of laughing gas; I dont think that anything does one so much good as a camping out expedition, one has such an appetite all the time, I have increased 5 pounds over my usual weight in the fortnight."[21]

There were three letters waiting for him at Herlow's, which "in no way damped my spirits. I don't know when I have gone to bed feeling more confidant & hopeful than I did that night." On Friday, October 7, he buckled down to answering all the questions his own letters had inspired from his loving, curious, apprehensive family.

He explained how land grants were "worked up" by agents like Brevoort and Gwynne. He wrote a whimsical little page about the "fearful fire" to which the fair sex was exposed when he gazed upon them with his blind eye. He commented upon affairs at Victoria, where his father was entering another three-year agreement with his former partners. And he set straight any misapprehensions under which his loved ones might be laboring.

> You refer to this country as being destitute of religion, that is hardly the case, though your impresion of the people & their actions I guess is not far wrong, but I was rather surprised to hear the other day that the priests take a toll of one seventh of every man's income, who is within the pale of the Roman Catholic Church, I could hardly credit it, but the people stand it "poor degraded superstitious devils" it is no great wonder they are poor.
>
> You speak of mine host the German [Herlow] as if he were a private individual

I had struck by chance, he keeps this hotel, but is nevertheless a very nice fellow to deal with, & very clever in a business point of view.

I seem to have excited your sympathy over my description of my journey here, I could stand a great deal more discomfort than I did on that journey, it was not so pleasant as a trip to Edinburgh 1ˢᵗ class by the Night Express, but I can assure you, I dont look upon any such trifles as a jolty, dusty, ride as anything more than incidental inconveniences not worthy of two thoughts. I would just as soon sleep out of doors by my camp fire & cook for myself, as I would stop at the Palace Hotel & I know I should live the longer for it.[22]

Brevoort came to see if he was still interested in buying the Cieneguilla for twenty-five thousand; Tunstall told him he wasn't ready to move just yet. He had also decided to forget about Texas: apart from the fact that the information he had received from the land office there did not tally in any way with the information he had been given, that part of the world was "*very* unsafe. I don't think I shall entertain any views of prospecting there."

"They have fandangos here, once or twice a week," Tunstall noted disdainfully on Sunday, October 22. "Last night," he said, "they got shooting down there, killed one man on the spot & there are lots of wounded, they say. A fandango is a public dance, in fact the Argyle Rooms of Santa Fe. Shooting is by no means uncommon there, no one seems at all excited about it."[23]

This fracas had taken place at Harry Mottley's Centennial Hall and Terpsichorean Academy on the Levee. As a result of it Mottley and his partner Allen were arrested. Their preliminary hearing took place before Esquire Ortiz the following Tuesday, when Mottley, charged with the murder of Pedro Barbero and the wounding of two Vijil brothers, was remanded to jail in default of twenty-five thousand dollars' bail. His partner Allen was discharged. The *New Mexican* reported that one of the wounded men, Antonio Vijil, was still in critical condition, but he later recovered.

For all of his investigations into the pros and cons of cattle vs. sheep, land grants or ranches he might buy, and many other possibilities, Tunstall had still not come to any decision when, on October 28, he wrote to his "Much Beloved Father" that

as regards cattle, I have ceased to think of them since my conversation with Stoneroad on that head, but if I were well fixed with sheep, I think it not unlikely that I should invest in a few hundred *well* bred cows, they would of course pay very well, & *well* bred stock is so much more gentle than the stock cattle of this country, that they are not at all the same thing; one could not afford to stock a ranch with well bred cattle at first (they would cost too much for a beginner) but I daresay that after a while, I might be tempted by them, when I could afford it.[24]

He broke off at this juncture to talk to Elias Brevoort, who told him that a group of Chicago investors was interested in the Cieneguilla grant; did he want primary consideration in the matter? Tunstall replied that he was "not over favorably impressed with the grant, & did not think I should make any move until the spring under *any* circumstances; I did not even ask any questions about it, as I *of course am not* in a position to move *at once*; & as I am *obliged* to wait till the spring I thought it as well, to keep his mind in as good a shape as the circumstances allowed."

The following afternoon, Sunday, September 29, he picked up the letter where he had left off; no sooner had he done so than there was another interruption in the shape of a fellow guest at Herlow's, "an elderly man (I guess near 60 years old)" named Col. John M. Isaacs. Isaacs had heard Tunstall was looking for grazing lands, and volunteered to give him "some most useful advice concerning the lands, titles & grant agents & land lawyers in this territory."

> I gained the Old Boy's friendship quite accidentally; Herlow had rheumatism, & I gave him a couple of powders, which fixed him up, the next morning he was speaking of it, & recommended my selling them at $2^{50} for ½ Doz. powders & said "I could sell all I wanted to" I said laughing "that I considered the pleasure of curing anyone was worth two & a half". This pleased the old Gentleman very much & he has always been friendly ever since. So you see one never knows when one is making a useful friend; he knows more about grants than I do, has seen more, & been on the point of buying several.

An attack of rheumatism some time earlier had prevented Tunstall's joining the hotelkeeper on a trip to the Albuquerque area.

> Herlow as you can tell from my letters did not go to Bernallio, he has so much business here that I dont see how he will ever spare the time; I may start upon a trip down into Lincoln County the day after tomorrow, that is the place I should start in if we could not afford to buy land, but it is like building a house upon the sand, to start a stock business upon the public domain; I am certain ten years is the limit of time to do so in this country, viz. build a range upon public land, & 10 years is just long enough to build up a business, large enough to make a fortune out of. . . .
>
> There is a very nice young fellow here from Lincoln County just now, a lawyer by profession, who has the outward appearance of an honest man (Herlow speaks very highly of him) he has been trying to persuade me to go into stock & not buy land, there is quite a point in what he says, but I have seen too much of California, to do so unless I am obliged. He has not seen that side of the question as I have. But I must say that his plan has a good deal to recommend it.[25]

The nice young fellow with (at least) the outward appearance of an honest man was Alexander McSween, on his way to New York in connection with the Emil Fritz will. Parsimonious Mac, like Tunstall, preferred Herlow's prices to those of the Exchange; they seem to have hit it off at once, perhaps because both of them considered themselves a cut, both socially and intellectually, above the common herd. Tunstall's plans meshed neatly with McSween's ambitions; doubtless each saw in the other a means of achieving his goals. McSween, who had audited the firm's books, knew exactly how rocky was the financial situation of L.G. Murphy & Co. It may well be he told Tunstall the time was ripe for someone to take over their monopoly. Whatever the nature of the plan he outlined, it must have been appeared very attractive indeed to the young Englishman, for by the following Thursday, November 3, Tunstall was on his way to Lincoln.

CHAPTER 9

THE FACTIONS ALIGN

WHEN John Henry Tunstall first arrived there in November 1876, Lincoln County was isolated from civilization as if on another planet. Vast and at best sparsely populated—as it remains to this day—it was a place of astonishing physical contrasts, of rich, fertile grasslands and barren desert, of forbidding mountain ranges rearing twelve thousand feet above volcanic *malpais*. Its rolling hills closely clad with pine and aspen, it was a wild, empty, beautiful country teeming with wildlife: bear, antelope, deer, wild turkey, quail, grouse, duck in profusion; one man records taking 126 trout out of the Bonito in a single afternoon.[1]

It was also a place of random violence and danger. To the safety of its empty mountain fastnesses fled the wanted and the hunted, murderers and horse thieves, defaulters and desperadoes from all the surrounding territories: Arizona, Texas, Colorado, Kansas. Life here was always lived at risk: the absence of law, the presence of godless men, and the volatile mixture of whiskey and deadly weapons created a climate in which any argument or difference of opinion could end in gunfire. It was a place where to kill a man was much less a sin than to steal his horse; and to steal his cattle was no sin at all.

Lincoln, the county seat, was the axis upon which the life of the entire area revolved. From here, Murphy and Dolan controlled the financial and political affairs of the county. The native farmers who relied upon them for the staples of life were as dependent upon them as serfs in the Middle Ages upon their liege lord.

Since Alexander McSween was his adviser, there can be no doubt that Tunstall was aware of all this long before his arrival; or that in fact his trip to Lincoln was made in order to examine the ways in which the House's hegemony worked. His decision to stay, with a view to challenging it, was probably the most significant event in the history of Lincoln County; had Tunstall decided to locate elsewhere subsequent events would have taken a very different course.

He left Santa Fe on Thursday, November 2, spending the night at the house of a man named Davis at Galisteo.[2] The following morning, Juan Patrón picked him up there at around nine. They left an hour or so later. Colonel Isaacs, who was en route to the placer mines in the Jicarilla Mountains, had intended to join the party, which consisted of Patrón, Saturnino Baca, and Baca's brother-in-law. Isaacs's business prevented his going, however, so Tunstall set off with the others.

Baca and Brent rode in one wagon; Tunstall in a second with Patrón, "a very good sort of fellow & the best educated mexican I have met, he appears to have good principles & [is] certainly kindhearted." But not, apparently, to his horses: the journey down to Lincoln took four days of what Tunstall records as "mental torment," and watching Patrón's style of buggy driving was "nothing short of agony." Baca soon left them far behind; Tunstall endured various other forms of torture—including a scanty campfire, no blankets, little sleep, poor food, and a seven-mile trek at dawn to recover a strayed horse—before they reached their destination. On the way, Patrón related the circumstances of his difference with John Riley a year earlier. Tunstall noted only that Patrón had been

> shot through the back about 12 months ago about ½ an inch to the left of the spine, in about the hollow of the back, the bullet was taken out from just under the skin of his stomach, & strange to say he survived it, though it seems to have touched the nerves that command his left leg, he has very little control over it, this is the only ill effect he feels from it & at the time he was shot, he thought he was shot in the leg & not in the back.[3]

They got in at about two on Monday afternoon, November 6. Writing home later, Tunstall referred to the place as "Lincoln (alias) Placita" and said it consisted of

> a small collection of adobe houses scattered up a pretty creek called the Rio Bonito (which means Pretty River) & is in miner's parlance about the "toughest" little spot in America, which means the most lawless; a man can commit murder here with impunity; in talking of a man who had shot another here the other day, for calling him a "gringo" (which is the same as calling a frenchman a "frog") & who afterwards rode quietly up the town & told the sheriff "he would like to see the man who could capture him" I said "he is rather bad medicine, I guess" The man I was talking to replied "Who? Ham Mills? (which is his name) No! Not a bit of it! you never saw a better fellow than Ham anywhere; he gets mad quick, & shoots quick, but he's a good shot & never cripples; none of his men have ever known what hurt them & I really think he is sorry for it afterwards when he cools off."[4]

Because Ham Mills's unexpected return to Lincoln was on everyone's tongues, Tunstall was misled into the belief that the Balansuela killing had just occurred. In fact, the hulking ex-sheriff had elected to face the music for last year's sins.[5] In the event, he never spent a day in jail: over a hundred citizens petitioned the governor for clemency, and the following December Axtell granted the popular Mills a pardon. Nevertheless, as Tunstall remarked, "Placita is a rather dangerous place at present, at least I think so, a man was shot for the sake of $40.00 (which, by the way, he had not got) but was supposed to have & the murderers got off all right. They have a vigilance committee, which is an abuse instead of an amender of abuses & when such is the case it is worse than bad."[6]

The identity of the man who was shot for forty dollars is not known. The only shooting in Lincoln around this time was the one in which Thomas King was killed at a local *baile* by Billy Campbell.[7] This appears to have been shortly before Tunstall arrived; King—"an interesting old freak" who had been a Forty-niner— was killed when Campbell took exception to his goosing a girl. An unsigned item in the *New Mexican* datelined December 14 from Lincoln gave details of the fracas and commented sardonically on the way justice was dispensed in the little town on the pretty river.

> A recent decision of Judge Wilson, our Justice of the Peace, deserves to be placed on record. Some eight days ago, W. W. Campbell shot and killed Thomas King, as

it is alleged, in self defense. He came over and surrendered himself and stood his examination before Judge Wilson, and was acquitted after fifteen hours deliberation. On the next day, Campbell and I. S. Tesson were re-arrested, the former as principal, the latter as accomplice for the *same* matter. At the second examination it was proved to the sapient judge that he could not try a man twice for the same offence, so he discharged Mr. Campbell, but activated by a desire to impress us heathens with due respect for his talents, he held Tesson in $500 bonds to await the action of the grand jury as an accomplice. Comment is unnecessary.[8]

The time frame given here is suspect: justice of the peace Wilson was voted out of office in the November 7 elections, which took place the day after Tunstall arrived, so the shooting happened some time earlier than the date given. Billy Campbell was shortly thereafter arrested at Fort Stanton by U.S. Mail special agent Charles Adams on a charge of having robbed the Las Vegas stage, and taken in irons to Santa Fe; Campbell, as we shall see, was later to make a further notable contribution to the annals of Lincoln County.

John Tunstall spent his first night in Lincoln at Juan Patrón's, where he slept "soundly and well. I really regret feeling so impatient at him on the road for his bad driving, for he is a very good fellow & considering [how limited] the chances he has had I think him a wonder."

The next day the local elections were held, and passed off "without anyone getting shot," unlike those of the preceding February. Patrón had campaigned successfully for one of the three posts of county commissioner: the other two were filled by Will Dowlin and Francisco Romero y Luceras. Mill owner Paul Dowlin was elected representative to the territorial house, James Farmer replaced Green Wilson as justice of the peace, and William Brady became sheriff.

Tunstall's first impressions of Lincoln are, alas, lost; doubtless he found it raw and primitive, even by Santa Fe standards (fig. 23). At the western end of the street stood the Murphy-Dolan store; around it a scattering of flat-roofed adobe buildings that included Sam Wortley's "hotel," a few private houses, and (it is said) a brothel. Between the House and "the plaza," the old center of town, were four or five boxlike adobes, one of which was the original Murphy branch store, now the home of Alexander and Susan McSween. At the plaza were Montaño's store, the *torreón*, and the courthouse, with Patrón's store a little farther east. Many of the Hispanic New Mexicans lived in *jacals*, the typical small houses of the time, crude constructions of cedar posts and plaster, with dirt roofs.

It is still possible to find such *placitas* in New Mexico, even today. No soldiers walk the street, of course, no blacksmith's anvil clangs, and there are fewer animals, but all the rest is much the same. Most visitors rarely go to such places, however, and so can only try to imagine how it once was: bats flickering through the twilight, the air full of the smell of burning charcoal. Children and dogs everywhere, gamecocks flapping and settling in the branches of the trees. Bare adobe walls; music and raucous male laughter coming from a saloon. A water cart trundling down the street, a little building where an old man beats out metal horseshoes over a glowing forge fire. Every house has animals in its yard: pigs, sheep, goats, milk cows. Chickens wandering everywhere; horses and mules hitched outside the buildings. The dusty street thronged with people, Anglos, Mexicans, black soldiers from the nearby fort, sometimes Indians, for the Apaches live nearby, and the Pueblos come into Lincoln each fall, their burros carrying panniers loaded with apples, peaches, and grapes, which they sell from their camp

FIG. 23. A view of Lincoln from the southeast, ca. 1885. Photographer unknown.

in the middle of the plaza, not fifty yards from where present-day visitors buy apples by the roadside.

John Tunstall lost no time in calling on Susan McSween, whom he described as "the wife of the lawyer I met in Santa Fe the other day":

> [I] found her a very pleasant woman in every way, she told me as much about the place as any man could have done, she is the only white woman here & has a good many enemies in consequence of her husband's profession. I slept at Patron's as before & on Wednesday I waited for a mail cart to arrive upon which there might be some letters for Messrs. Taylor &c. There were none & I left at 12 to travel 45 miles. My horse was not very fresh, but he went fairly well nevertheless, so I reached the Jicarilla station at 8 p.m.[9]

The Jicarilla Station was an army forage post near present-day White Oaks. Since McSween was away in the East and not due back until mid-December, Tunstall decided to await his return among friends there. Col. John Isaacs arrived soon afterwards, staying, as did Tunstall, with Dr. George Ginn and Col. L. G. Taylor, district recorder and notary public. According to Tunstall the latter had served in the Tenth Kentucky Cavalry and been a member of General Morgan's staff in the Confederate Army.

Altogether Tunstall spent about a month there, interrupting his vacation only to ride across to Lincoln, "50 miles across the mountains," to send Christmas greetings to his family and to pick up mail forwarded to him there from Santa Fe.[10] He stayed in Lincoln until Christmas Eve; it was during this visit he first met Dick Brewer, either at the McSween home or at the time of the formation, on December 14, of the Lincoln County Farmers' Club (fig. 24).[11]

Its officers were Lawrence G. Murphy, president; William Brady and Joseph Storms (known locally as "El Gallo," "the rooster"), vice presidents; Morris J. Bernstein, secretary; and Charles Fritz, treasurer. A committee consisting of Will Lloyd, Saturnino Baca, and Francisco Romero y Lueras was elected, and motions were heard from John Newcomb, who proposed that news of the formation of the club be sent to the Department of Agriculture in Washington and the territorial press; and Richard M. Brewer, who moved an adjournment until the first Monday in January.

Overshadowed completely by the other events of this violent month, the formation of the Farmer's Club is important evidence that in spite of the town's reputation, the hardworking local farmers were trying to make it a decent place to live. Some of them, like Brewer, would be caught up in the storm to come. Many of them would not: Storms, Lloyd, Newcomb, and many others would stay out of it, hanging on to what they had until the tempest subsided. If the war that was to come produced any heroes, it was men like these.

FIG. 24. Richard M. Brewer. Said to have been taken at Carthage, Mo., in 1870, at which time Dick would have been twenty. Photographer unknown.

Soon after the Farmer's Club was formed, Lincoln witnessed yet another scene of mindless violence. Alabama-born Frank Freeman, a noted rowdy from Colfax County who shared squatter's rights on a small ranch in the Peñasco valley with J. B. "Billy" Mathews, shot and crippled a black soldier who had the temerity to sit next to him at table in the Wortley Hotel. Sheriff Saturnino Baca was summoned, but by the time he arrived, Freeman had run for the hills. He kept going till he reached Texas.

At about the same time—the festive spirit seems to have been sadly lacking in Lincoln County—there was another shooting. Although it took place a long way from Lincoln, it was significant because it was the precursor of what was called the "Pecos War," a new outbreak of violence that would unite the smaller ranchers around Seven Rivers against John Chisum. Later, these same ranchers would oppose Alexander McSween, with whom Chisum was considered to be allied. According to an item excerpted from the *New York Sun* by the *New Mexican*, a man named Yopp, who was in charge of Fort Worth cattle rancher Robert K. Wylie's cow camp at Eighteen Mile Bend on the Pecos

became enraged at an employee, "Buck" Powell [fig. 25]. He drew his revolver and fired three shots at him. Buck woke up, seized a Winchester, and shot Yopp in the

FIG. 25. Thomas Benton "Buck" Powell with wife and baby. Date and photographer unknown. The attire is typical of citizens of Lincoln County at the time of the war.

mouth, the ball coming out at the back of the neck. Yopp fell and remained for a few moments insensible. Suddenly recovering he reopened fire on Powell. Powell's gun hung fire. He then seized Yopp's own gun and shot him through the heart. Powell did not receive a scratch. He wanted to go some 150 miles [to Lincoln] and give himself up for trial but was persuaded not to. So the matter ended.[12]

Tunstall seems to have had adventures of his own getting back to the Jicarilla Station: in a letter commenting on his description of the trip, his mother remarked "As to your Xmas eve experiences to reach [there], well if you can go through such, all I can say is you bear a charmed life."[13] Could he have had an encounter with roving Apaches?

Tunstall returned to Lincoln after Christmas. A new mail service from Santa Fe to Fort Stanton via Galisteo and Manzano, operated by his friend Herlow and a man named Williston, had begun on the first of the year, and Alexander McSween had a bundle of five letters from London for the Englishman.[14] Writing to his eight-year-old sister Lillian ("Jack") on January 14, Tunstall bared the deeply sentimental streak he usually kept so well hidden:

> and when I read the Dear kind words you wrote to me, I thought I had never wished to go home as much before. I saw a grand, great, bald headed eagle, sailing & sailing & *sailing* round in the sky, above my head; I looked up wih my eyes full of tears, & thought, "if only I had that eagle's great, strong wings, how swiftly I would fly across the land & the sea, & how straight I would go, to my Dear Old Sister Jack" then I thought how I should kiss & hug you, till I thought there would be nothing left of you, for I could never make you know, how much I love my two Dear Little Sisters. I love you *all the time* till my left leg nearly breaks. I never think of being happy unless I think of my three Pets; & whenever I *am* happy, I am sorry that you cant share whatever it is that is making me so, whether it is the "drumstick" of some old turkey "gobbler" or a ride on a fine day under a blue sky, & a shining sun. I sometimes dream that I see you all, & I wake up so happy that I nearly cry.[15]

Tunstall had taken upon himself the responsibility of becoming the financial mainstay of his family. He envisioned relieving his father and mother from the necessity of providing for their children; when John had made his fortune, he and his sister Minnie would set up house together and look after the "little Pets" for the rest of their lives. So, when he had to be "out in the cold & sleep out of doors at night, I always think of you all & I think 'well it does not matter, its for the sake of my Dear Old Boys [his little sisters] & they are worth all I can ever do for them'."

He had left his new dog, Biddy, with Taylor in the mountains: "It was so cold the day I left there, I would not bring her away," he told Lillian. This letter is the only one surviving of the several Tunstall wrote during the next couple of months, including a long one containing his impressions of Lincoln and the comparison he drew between his travel-stained self and the elegant Mrs. McSween. While it is possible—thanks to that didacticism we have noted before—to reconstruct most of what he said about his plans, it is sad not to have one of his vivid word-pictures of Susan McSween, and any comments he might have made on events in Lincoln, such as the Freeman fracas at the Wortley and the mid-January murder of a youngster named Sostero García at San Patricio by another hot-tempered local, Lucas Gallegos.[16]

Alexander McSween got back from the East in mid-December, having successfully untangled the complications—he did not hesitate to refer to them as a swindle—of the Emil Fritz insurance policy. The actuary of the defunct Merchants Life Assurance Co., a man named Hobby, had put his head together with the receiver and a third party—"someone who is well known" was all McSween would say, but we may read the name Levi Spiegelberg into his lawyerly caution—to defraud the heirs out of half the value of the policy. This McSween successfully forestalled.

On his return to Lincoln he learned that Emilie Scholand (fig. 26) had moved to Las Cruces, leaving the matter of the estate in the hands of her brother, who had begun proceedings to have McSween removed as attorney. Fritz sent for the lawyer on his return from the East. On December 12, McSween excused himself as follows:

Mr. Fritz:

Dr. Sir;—Yours was handed to me late this p.m. My horses are at the Rio Ruidoso, and I was unable to secure others to go down to your place today.

FIG. 26. Luise Marie Emilie Fritz Scholand, aged about thirty, ca. 1879. Photo by Dames & Butler, San Francisco.

I would suggest to you, that Lieut. Wilkinson and yourself come up to-morrow evening, as I have no time to go down during week days, owing to the fact that I have been absent so long.

It was my intention to have seen the Lieut. yesterday and explained this matter to him. Naturally, you will have greater confidence in what he endorses, and I think I can make this matter so plain to him, as a business-man, that he can set your fears and doubts at rest.

This matter is of the first impor-tance to you, and I hope that you will defer your handling [?] until its attended to.

I live by the Public, and must ex-pect to be criticised by the Public, and am, therefore, to a great extent, indifferent to praise or censure, when I have an inward consciousness of do-ing right. $10,000 is a very large amount of money, but I can assure you that it's not large enough to buy me. Whilst there was a reasonable hope of using me as a tool, I was the "whiteheaded boy" but no sooner was that hope dispelled than I was repre-sented as everything but a *man*. I cer-tainly never acted otherwise than right and honestly with you, and we should always praise the bridge that carries us safely over.

If you are determined to protect the interests you represent, you can easily do so; if on the other hand, you allow parties who, legally and morally, have no interests in the matter, to dictate to you, you'll find yourself swamped, and that ere long.

I like to be on good terms with mankind, but I'll incur their displeasure rather than sell the interests of those who confide in me.

[P.S.] I'll expect you and W; if you don't like to come let W. come. I have no other feelings than those of goodwill towards you. Don't fail to com as I want to write the Bankers this week.[17]

The bold flourishes that underline his signature indicate that McSween felt he had stated his side of things well. He knew, of course, that Jimmy Dolan was stirring up trouble for him with Fritz; he felt that explaining himself to Fritz's brother-in-law, Lieutenant Wilkinson, would be easier than trying to make mat-ters clear to Fritz, whose grasp of English was too limited for him to understand the complexities of the insurance settlement (fig. 27).

His English was not, however, so limited as to prevent Fritz from accepting

McSween's proposal. Two days later, the lawyer sent him another, and this time more exasperated, note setting out his own case, the difficulties placed in his way by Spiegelberg, and the fact that, thanks to his own efforts, the settlement on the policy would be made in full.

FIG. 27. Carl Phillip Friedrich "Charlie" Fritz, aged about forty, ca. 1871. Photo by A. W. Warner, Montrose, Pa.

> Whoever tells you I am trying to get the money for Mrs. Scholand states something of which he knows nothing—something manufactured by himself. Both of you made a contract with me in behalf of the estate, and not in behalf of either or both of you. I intend to collect every dollar I possibly can for the estate and the division is an entirely different matter. The Probate Court has the sole ordering of the division, and not I. You may rely on this, that I'll not pay anyone a dollar. If I should collect the money, I'll place it to your credit at the 1st National Bank and that releases me. I regret that you should mistrust me when I was working for you in good faith, spending even my own funds in further cause of the interests you represent. If you entertain any fears, you can have an order for the proceeds when collected. I excuse you on account of the pressure that may have been brought to bear upon you.[18]

McSween was not too obliquely pointing out that he was aware of Jimmy Dolan's hand in Fritz's actions.

> I understand you are very mad at me; I would like to know why. Come at your earliest convenience and let me know the cause of your discontent. I can't chase the wind nor idle tales, but if you really distrust me I want to know; then you can give, doubtless, your reasons and I'll be satisfied. When I see you and state all the facts, I think you'll change your mind. I know I worked in good faith, and supposed you had the requisite amount in me.

Charles Fritz's reaction to this catalogue of wounded feelings is not known; and anyway, McSween's statement of his fees and expenses, presented at the January 1877 session of probate court, would certainly have dissipated any sympathy the lawyer's letter might have evoked. This was in the not-inconsiderable sum of $3,815.15, comprising the agreed $500 retainer, travel and legal expenses of $542.20, $2,573.30 representing 10 percent of the accounts receivable he had collected for the estate, and $200 for his own lost income during the period he had been in the East. When the court approved these charges, Fritz had no option but to pay up and look happy.

Dolan's interest in the Fritz estate was simply motivated: the House was strapped for cash. When Tunstall returned to Lincoln, Dolan offered McSween $5,000 if he successfully induced Tunstall to buy Murphy's thirty-thousand-acre "Fairview" ranch at Carrizo Spring.[19] McSween not only refused but, to add insult to injury, warned Tunstall off, stating that Murphy did not have clear title to the place.

On top of all this, McSween now proposed that Emil Fritz's still-unvalidated will be set aside, and the estate divided equally among all the heirs, of whom there were a large number in Germany. This did not sit well with Charlie Fritz, and even less well with Dolan and the ailing Lawrence Murphy, who were hoping to annex a large chunk of the proceeds on a "debt" they claimed Emil Fritz had with the House. Every time it looked like they might get their hands on some hard cash, McSween seemed to get in the way.

Tunstall and McSween set up an agreement: the lawyer would become a participant in Tunstall's schemes, on a percentage basis, in return for legal advice and—if and when necessary—advances of money against expected remittances from England. Having begun by steering Tunstall away from Murphy's Fairview ranch, McSween now pointed him instead in the direction of land in the Feliz valley. There is an abiding tradition that Robert Casey, murdered in Lincoln two years earlier, had preempted this land, claiming "squatter's rights"; his widow and her family considered it theirs. Perhaps they were responsible for the tradition.

Susan McSween, who had no time at all for the Caseys, said otherwise. "I dont know from whom Tunstall acquired the Felix ranch . . . but I know that the Casey did not claim it & that some one owned the ranch and sold to Tunstall."[20] She later recalled the name of this party as Dexter, but was never asked to elaborate. No Dexter appears in any of the available census or tax records of Lincoln County at that time.

The question of who owned the squatter's rights was in any case irrelevant: by taking advantage of the forthcoming Desert Land Act, Tunstall could—arbitrarily, but quite legally—make the land his own.[21] Under this act, to be promulgated in March 1877, any person would be able to file on 640 acres of desert—i.e., unirrigated—land by making a down payment of twenty-five cents an acre. He would then have three years to make the necessary improvements—irrigation and occupation—before a further payment of a dollar an acre gave him perpetual title to the land.

Since it was not certain that, as a British subject, Tunstall would be able to take up land under his own name, it would be necessary to file on the sections he wanted in the names of nominees. However, there was a snag: he could not file these claims until the Desert Land Act came into force in March; if anyone else preempted the land in the intervening period, Tunstall would be forced either to buy him out or abandon his plan. This explains the secrecy, nervousness, and uncertainty that can be detected throughout his correspondence at this time.

The Feliz valley, some eighty miles southeast of Lincoln, was ideal cattle country. Two large springs formed the river's headwaters. The land was verdant and lush. McSween's suggestions became Tunstall's plan: he would file on some four thousand acres of desert land; ownership of the water rights would give him control of the whole range. It would appear he planned to lay claim to a strip of land taking up both sides of the Feliz River from its headwaters to a point some seven or eight miles east, and another "ranch" on the Peñasco, which Frank Freeman and Billy Mathews held by "squatters' rights." Others would follow as and when he could afford them.

By January 23, Tunstall had put together the parameters of his cattle and land scheme, and wrote to his father from Lincoln asking him to try to get together the sum of thirty-two hundred pounds (about sixteen thousand dollars) that he would need to make a start on his venture. If this sum had been applied only to desert land, it would have bought him twelve thousand acres, so he obviously had plans farther afield than the valley of the Feliz; his later distress when Mormon settlers moved in there suggests these may have been in the Pecos valley.

His principal allies were to be lawyer McSween and Dick Brewer, who had ranched for a while on the Feliz when he first arrived in Lincoln County, not far from where Tunstall planned to locate. Other proxies would include Sam Corbet, Avery Clenny, Florencio Gonzales, Trinidad Delgado, and Dr. Spencer Gurney.

Shortly thereafter Tunstall accompanied McSween to Las Cruces. As well as making his long-delayed inspection trip to the "garden of New Mexico" and Bernalillo County, Tunstall wanted to visit the land office at Mesilla. There he could make preliminary inquiries about filings under the Desert Land Act, which was to be passed into law in March.

Apart from the inherent dangers of travel at this time—there were Apache raiders loose in the Fort Bayard area,[22] and marauding gangs of Mexican and American horse thieves and cattle rustlers in the area—a new peril lurked in the valley of the Rio Grande: a particularly virulent strain of smallpox, which had already advanced as far north as Belen.

By February 27, Tunstall and McSween were in Albuquerque. It would be safe to guess McSween was doing a circuit of his clients: lawyering in territorial New Mexico was a farther flung business than it is today. At Belen, on March 9, Tunstall noted that they had

> now travelled over 700 miles, our ponies are looking somewhat gaunt, as they, like ourselves, never get more than 2 feeds per diem, & they are often scanty enough; they, however, usually manage to take us 40 miles a day at a stretch, our vehicle is light, though the roads, owing to snow, rain & sand, have been, so far, very heavy. I dont like this Rio Grande country atall, it is a complete waste, & in my opinion one long den of thieves & murderers, at the present time they are getting somewhat scourged with smallpox, & by that means a number of the young male fry are being prevented from developing into horse thieves, & the female fry from developing into fit mates for same.[23]

From some clues in a letter written by Emily Tunstall to her son on February 27, it would seem that Tunstall and Dick Brewer (Mrs. Tunstall calls him "Dick Patterson," but Tunstall knew no one of that name) had been on an expedition together, perhaps as far as the Texas line, with a view to buying cattle.[24] A strong friendship had sprung up between the two men, in spite of the difference in their backgrounds. Brewer had fallen prey to smallpox, and was being nursed by his parents, who had come out from Wisconsin around Christmas 1876 to help Dick get his new farm started.

> I am very anxious to hear after the health of my friend Dick Brewer, as I esteem him highly, I should be much shocked by his succumbing to the malady he has taken, as he is a very fine specimen of humanity, both physically & morally; He repeatedly told me, as we drove on our journey, when I would allude to the risk we had run, (which vexed me *very much* but did not *frighten* me atall, as I knew the thing was done, could not be undone, & we could only wait & see how it might act upon us) "You will just scare yourself into having the smallpox, as sure as you live."[25]

As it turned out, it was Dick Brewer who got the smallpox, not Tunstall, although he continued to fret over the unavoidable delays that jeopardized his plans.

You see, I am unable to lay a scheme before you, until it is perfected throughout, & in the interim I have nothing to do, but bite my nails & fret, at the slow flight of time; & my anxiety is such, that the slightest breath of rumour that anything is happening which endangers my carrying out my scheme, makes me as nervous as a culprit, & the fact of not being able to confide my plans to anyone does not in any way make the matter more bearable.

His hopes of being back in Lincoln by March 13 or 14 were dashed when McSween agreed to defend another case; it was unlikely they would be back in Lincoln before March 16, he reported from Belen on March 12.[26] This long letter contains a great deal of comment on the business at Victoria, for Papa Tunstall made sure to keep his son completely informed of everything that was going on there. The "Governor" also expressed the fear that his son might get shot. Possibly, said Tunstall, but

I *don't expect it.* There are two very prolific causes for shooting in this country, viz., Drink & jealousy. I don't frequent the locality of the former, nor the company of those who do; & I dont make myself an object for the excitement of the latter, neither do I calculate to; & if formerly I had not the knack of making friends, I seem to possess it now to a sufficiently useful extent; & then again, I have a presentiment that I shall *not* get killed, but that I *shall live* to accomplish my schemes, & give those three Pets "*such a time* as will make their heads swim" (as we say on the frontier).

He was much moved by his sister's description of the family's Christmas, and Minnie's account of taking Mabel and Lillian to their first pantomime, a particularly British theatrical entertainment. Of course, he missed them all enormously; all the same, he entreated his "Dear Darling Mother,"

don't imagine that I am overcome, from morning till night, with a sense of lonely ness, & depression, or that what seem hardships to you are any inconveniences to me, for that is not the case; My heart always feels as light as a *feather;* ambition will help a man to disregard the *present entirely,* & if you could see me building a fire to dry the ground upon which I was going to spread my blanket for the night, under the star spangled (not banner, of Uncle Sam) but vault of heaven, you would probably hear me whistling at the same time (the nearest I could get with my unmusical mouth) "I wish I were a fish with a great long tail" & if the matches would not strike & I had to gather twigs to raise me off the ground, the expression my "fiz" [slang for physiognomy, i.e., face] would wear, would be far more indicative of wrath at the trouble, than sadness.

My mind is never off my schemes, I am always, studying to strengthen what is completed & enlarge the borders of my net & diminish the size of the mesh, so as to catch the small fry as well. I never get the "blues" they result from a mind drained of its last resource, & that is not my case. If I make my schemes a *reality* (which I feel as sure of, as I do of anything connected with the future) I shall need no sympathy from anyone. The *present* & all connected with it, will seem to me like the labour of turning a machine (that poured out gold at the rate of a bushel per hour) would seem to you; I shall only begrudge the time as it passes.

If I could explain my plans for making money to you, it would sound like a sort of fairy tale; I have kept up a "*terrible thinking*" (like that speechless parrot [in the joke]) all the time, to puzzle, & twist, & turn & patch, & alter my scheme until I have made it fit my requirements, but I believe that if I had the money I want (I can *make do* with £3,200 this year, but could do much more with £5200) you would be astonished at the result I would bring about.

He had asked his father to send him five hundred pounds immediately to secure some cattle—lawyer McSween had tipped him off that some of Ellen Casey's stock, attached for debt, would be coming up for auction at a sheriff's sale. The thirty-two hundred pounds was to be sent five hundred at a time "*as soon as you possibly* can."

"As regards indians," he reassured them, "it is much better to be *quite* close to an indian reservation, than 150 miles off one, as indians never raid near home, as their cattle & horses would then be recognised. the comanches are at a safe distance, you see the Pecos river flows between & the "cow boys" *there* have but little love for the "varmints" as they style them."[27]

Tunstall and McSween finally left Belen on Sunday, March 18. They made about fifty miles that day, and slept in an adobe at the village of Abo.[28] The people there were "miserably poor & had smallpox in every house." Next day, carrying no food except a loaf, they left for the Gallinas spring, about sixty miles away, under the impression that a man named (Elisha M.?) Dow had a ranch there. They had traveled about thirty miles when McSween's offside mare, Molly, collapsed with what appeared to be flatulent colic. Faced with the prospect of one of them retracing their route on foot while the other remained for eighteen hours alone on the prairie, the two men seem to have been paralyzed by indecision:

[W]e sat down & watched her, & the carrion crows came around & watched her, & soon many came, to wait for their promised orgie. The sun was high & hot & burning & we soon got very thirsty. The mare would get up & lie down again, & roll & groan, & lay with her legs stretched out & held off the ground. This went on from about 11, until about 4, it grew cooler & evening seemed approaching, the mare seemed more peaceful but refused to move; at 5 it was the same & I began to study how Mc & I could travel 85 miles with nothing but 1lb of bread between us & how the poor exhausted, hungry & sick cattle could do it, the grass was so poor that they could not get a feed off it.

Fortunately for both of them, an ox wagon came rumbling over the hill. Tunstall's next words indicate the tenor of their conversation before its arrival: "There you are, Mac!" Tunstall said. "I told you that I wasn't going to be left in the lurch. I *told* you my people believe that Providence has a special commission out to protect me, and I didn't think they could be fooled this time any more than they ever had been. You see, there it is, come just in the nick of time!"

The Mexican teamsters loaned them a pony to hitch up with their sounder animal, and they limped on until sunset, pitching camp for a couple of hours to make some coffee and eat their bread. They hitched up again and by 2 a.m. had made another fifteen miles. At this point they bedded down for the night.

Next day Molly was sufficiently recovered for them to limp on to Gallinas spring. There was no ranch there: they had no option but to carry on the remaining forty miles to the Livingston and Winters place at Jicarilla Station. Here they learned of the mysterious death of Tunstall's friend Col. John M. Isaacs, who had "fallen into the fire" at post trader Paul Dowlin's house at Fort Stanton.

Isaacs had come down to the Jicarilla Mountains around the beginning of December, and located a good claim with another Santa Fe acquaintance, Charles Thayer.[29] Early in March he went to Fort Stanton on business, and took a room at Dowlin's. Late one night he was found unconscious in front of the huge fire, his legs burned to a crisp from the knees down. Stewart Martin and others at the post did what they could for the old man, but after days of agony, he died on March 13. There were dark rumors of foul play; the old man had written a letter to his friend William Miller at White Oaks, in which he said a "detective" named Adams had thrown him into the fire.

At Livingstone's Tunstall also learned that a party of Mormons were "on their way to the Hondo river where it joins the Pecos, which is terribly near my country, I sweated all night long over these apparently insurmountable details."[30]

The settlers were a group of immigrants led by Jacob and George Harris and Ezra Lee who had staked out an area close to the junction of the Peñasco and the Pecos. Clearly Tunstall had ideas about that area himself, although what they were it is impossible to conjecture: perhaps the Feliz valley was his second, rather than his first choice.

When they got back to Lincoln next day, Tunstall was overjoyed to find letters from London agreeing to fund his scheme: he felt almost intoxicated, he said. He had complained of having no one to confide in, no one he could trust—an indication of the distance he kept between himself and McSween—and now that problem too was banished, for Robert Widenmann, who would become Tunstall's intimate friend and confidant, had arrived in Lincoln during his absence. "I was very pleased to see him," Tunstall wrote. "He is a man I can depend upon, & whom I like *very* much."

> I introduced him to Mr & Mrs McSween, & he left for his room at about 9 P.M. When he was gone, Mrs McSween told us that a number of rich Mexicans had been down to look at my country, & were just going to come in like locusts, also that some white men proposed to do the same thing. I was almost overcome; I was tired almost to death, not having slept worth a fig for two nights, I was starved down as well, & this nearly floored me. I could not think my way round the difficulty *atall*, I was too tired to *think* worth a cent, & I knew that these confounded squatters could "bust" my whole scheme like a rotten egg. I went to bed disgusted & disheartened, & rose at sun rise, after a restless miserable night.
>
> "However the game is not lost till its won" they say, & after revolving the thing round & round till my brain grew feverish from *friction* alone (I believe) I concluded that I would "buck it" out. I know how I can win the game *yet* in spite of all the scrubs & the terrific odds they get in the handicap. It needs a bold swift policy & if there is any chance for me to adopt it, I will do it. There is no real risk in the fight, though the munitions of war are costly, but the force & energy needed, to say nothing of the work, is very considerable.[31]

These thoughts were doubtless prompted by two things: McSween's purchase, just before they left Lincoln, of some six acres of land adjacent to the plaza in Lincoln, formerly the property of L. G. Murphy & Co.; and the withdrawal from his business of the Lord of the Mountains himself, Lawrence G. Murphy, formally concluded on March 14. McSween got the land for the statutory "$1.00 and other good and sufficient considerations," probably settlement of his legal fees, a further indication of the low ebb of the House's finances.[32] The firm was continued under the name of Jas. J. Dolan & Co.; Dolan's partners were John H. Riley, who had just successfully bid on the fresh beef and beef cattle contracts for forts Bayard and Stanton, and Billy Mathews.[33] Mathews had bought a secret, silent share of the business with seven hundred dollars Tunstall paid him for his Peñasco ranch, an ambulance (a small, covered wagon like those used by the army), and a pair of mules; he now lived in dread of the return of his partner, Frank Freeman, who was unaware of the deal.

Tunstall's plan—fueled with information provided by Alexander McSween—was to go into competition with Jas. J. Dolan & Co. on all fronts: a mercantile establishment built on the newly acquired land in Lincoln that would completely take away the House's trade on the one hand, and a cattle ranch that would enable Tunstall to outbid them for military and Indian contracts on the other. To woo the House's customers away, he would advance goods against forthcoming crops of corn, hay, and grain by means of what he called "grain notes." In addition, to keep the Santa Fe Ring from knowing their secrets (and also because it would be more profitable), they would establish their own bank to provide loans and mortgages; these would give the new firm first refusal on any defaulter's crops or land. All these were well-thumbed leaves from the book of L. G. Murphy & Co. It may be imagined that Jimmy Dolan did not look upon their being appropriated by Tunstall with any great degree of favor.

On Monday, March 26, Tunstall reported that the preceding Saturday he and Widenmann had walked over to Brewer's ranch—an athletic ten-mile hike—"with a plan of battle set." He wrote that "on Sunday the elements in opposition, made moves which necessitated a complete change of tactics. We have, I think, proved equal to the occasion, however. I can't tell when your first remittance will come to hand, but I want it *very badly.*"[34]

The opposition's moves concerned Dick Brewer, who on March 13 had signed a three-month promissory note to L. G. Murphy & Co. for $2038.75 "at ten percent per annum until paid."[35] This would appear to have been his purchase of the former Horrell ranch on the Ruidoso, and perfectly illustrates House procedures: First, although you have no clear title, claim possession of a ranch. Then "sell" it, slapping a healthy rate of interest on the loan. Allow its owner to run up bills at the store until he cannot pay either his loan, his interest, or his account, then foreclose, taking back the improved ranch, crops, livestock, and anything else the man owns. As soon as he has moved on, repeat the process, upping the price accordingly. It was a good racket, but it was about to be bust. On their return, no doubt having checked the records in the Land Office at Las Cruces, McSween and Tunstall informed Brewer that the House had no title to the land, and that by filing on it under the Desert Land Act he could make it his own.

This strike at the very heart of the Murphy-Dolan operation could not be countenanced. Dolan, accompanied by Mathews and Billy Morton, went over to the Brewer place armed to the teeth, and demanded that he either pay up or move out. Brewer, whose father had once been swindled out of his farm by an unscrupulous land speculator, was not bamboozled. He told them they had no title to the place, but they could have it if they would pay him for the improvements he had put in. Dolan angrily declined this offer, and warned Brewer that if he did not do as he was bid, it would become "a personal matter" between them. Brewer stood his ground: he wasn't looking for a fight, but he wouldn't run from one, either.

Promising Brewer the matter was not over yet, Dolan and his henchmen left for Lincoln. Dolan felt—with some justification—that he had been swindled out of the value of the ranch, and it appears that he had; Brewer's debt was still outstanding at the time of his death. In point of fact it was Tunstall, not McSween, who took over Brewer's debt with the House; McSween had no interest in acquiring ranches. Whether this was what Tunstall was referring to there is no way of knowing. The facts of the affair are buried in the Byzantine coils of their business arrangements, and Tunstall's elliptical comments do little to clarify them.

If you could but be in my boots for a little while, you would appreciate the position, it is not unlike a squirrel in one of those wire barrels, in which the poor little rascal is running up hill all the time, & can't make anything stick. I keep on engineering & planning; & planning & engineering, but as I have not that most solid of hammers (viz., Cash) in my hand, I have missed some welding heats. But the game is not lost *yet;* and *By Jove!!* if it does get lost it shant be my fault.

As Regards, how when & where to buy cattle; I shant make any mistake over that, to amount to anything, *under any circumstances;* if you were here, your mind would be easy on that score, there is *no* fear about it. . . .

Dick Brewer has got over his small pox & is well & hearty. I am as well as ever. Brewer's father & mother have gone back to Wisconsin so this is a Bachelor's hall, there is nothing very polished about it, but the welcome is as hearty as it can be.[36]

His celebration of Brewer's recovery was premature: the following Friday, Tunstall reported from the Ruidoso that on Wednesday, March 28, he and Brewer had started in Dick's wagon

to get some wheat ground at Dowlin's Mill & fetch some hay from a ranch (known as the Coe & Saunders ranch situated about 12 miles from Brewer's) we reached there early; after lunch Dick became very ill; he took his wheat on to the mill & left it, however; when he came back he could not unharness his team & all the afternoon, evening & night he was in great pain, in all his joints, his back & his head. I was afraid he had spinal meningitis or a congestive chill, he was delirious some part of the time. He is a *very* powerful man & very strong minded, to see him suffering to such an extent that his mind could not bear it, was very trying & to be so many miles from the simplest kind of medicine, & not having a saddle or a saddle horse, to use (for such was the case) made the situation a very anxious one, I gave him an emetic, & put his feet into hot water, which I think helped him, though not to amount to a very great deal.

He slept towards morning, but got up in considerable pain, looking very ill & being *very* weak. I fetched the flour from the mill & loaded the wagon with hay (my first experience at that work). At the mill, there are several cases of small pox (I ought to say here, that the *whole* county is full of that epidemic, the garrison at Fort Stanton is quarantined, & the whole county is down with small pox) McSween & I, have been in the midst of it, for ever so long, on our trip down the Rio Grande, but neither of us have shown any signs of it up to now.

Well, to return to my own adventures, when I was returning from the mill, I met a man whom I knew very well & who has just had the disease *most frightfully* he was one mass of sores; he stopped me to ask me to take him down to Brewer's, as he was not getting well treated where he was; I had no authority to take him, & of course got out of the job, but the sight of him gave me such a turn that I nearly fainted.

. . . I have no fear of the small pox, in fact if I could take it, & not be in anybody's way, I would as soon have it as not, for it is one of the finest scavengers of the system "that ever was". [It was then believed that smallpox "purified" the entire system like a purge!] Well, Dick & I managed to get home, in spite of all our difficulties, which were many, & not over trifling; as the wagon & harness we were using was borrowed & was a very poor rig; & the horses, though good, were in poor condition, & the road along the river was a very bad one. Today [Friday, March 30] Dick has gone to Lincoln to get some medicine; Widenmann left on one of my horses to go & take up a ranch & Oliver,(who is working here) is away attending to the cattle, so I am alone for a while.[37]

Tunstall asked his father to get him half a dozen copies of the *Bell's Life* newspaper for Oliver, "a Canadian of good family, he has travelled all over the United States & England, & is a very intelligent, well-informed man." He continued, "Now, as regards the main chance, I have finally decided upon my course, & we have to win the race upon that line; the game has already commenced. When we have won it, (which we *must* & *shall* do) it will be worth three times as much, as it can *possibly* cost us."

For the first time he outlined his specific intentions over seven more pages, following it with a nine-pager the next day.

I shall acquire property, which in the event of my death, you could recover every cent out of, that it would have cost; & more too; & in my safe, I shall always keep full particulars, both of the property acquired & speculations *gone into*, & the full directions of how to work out of them, properly, & I will always endeavor to have my affairs in such a shape that you could get over here, in time to handle them, before they could get in any way "mixed up", the solution of all this & the way to work it is very simple, though it would entail a fuller understanding of things out here, than you can possibly have at that distance, or I could give you by letter.

. . . I am now going to introduce you to my *latest* scheme for making money. . . . First of all let me tell you that groceries, in this country realize a profit of 50 per cent upon the *return*, & they are a cash article. In the second place there are two cash customers for four staple articles in this country, viz., The Indian department & the Army & the articles they buy are corn, hay, flour & beef.

In the third place let me tell you that the Mexican is essentially a "*borrowing animal*" if anyone will lend, he cant help borrowing, any more than the needle can help turning to the pole; but unlike most borrowers, he pays willingly as soon as it is in his power. These two last are *axioms,* so accept them as such. Fourthly this country is so far away from any other (I mean this *district*) that produce raised here is as it were protected from foreign produce, by a tariff of 1½ cents per lb. (for it costs 1½ cents per lb. for wagon freight from any other produce market). Fifth, this district is not large, & one can arrive within a few lbs. of the amount of grain that will be realized at harvest, by the *whole* community, *or any member of it.* Just bear all this in mind, for they are facts, which exist.

Now the question arises; Out of the existing circumstances & with these ascertained points, What scheme if practicable would catch the ready money of the Indian department & the Army & avoid the danger of too many debtors among a needy & improvident class?

The answer to the first part of the question is simple: By having Hay, beef, flour, or corn, raised within the district, Uncle Sam is compelled to patronize you, & pour his almighty dollars into your cap. The answer to the second is simple likewise.

Dont credit the *poor shiftless* wretches with what they cant pay. *Now,* you see, we know what we want to do; we are like the wise men whom Columbus told to balance the egg. The question then arises, why on earth should we not happen to find a solution, of a given question?

The solution, I think you will agree, is found in the following problem. T. opens a grocery store, M. applies for groceries; T. supplies him with groceries in return for promissory notes to deliver x lbs. of corn at his store, of fair merchantable quality upon the 20th day of August; T. having ascertained beyond doubt that the crop planted by M. will (when gathered) equal x.

The same problem can be solved in the same way upon the flour question. By this means I can acquire a *controlling* interest in both those articles.

The question then arises, Is T. sure to get the contracts? perhaps he may not, but whoever *does* get the contract, *must* come to T. to buy, or get "bust". The next question arises as to hay. How can T. "or any other man" think for a moment, that in a country where every mesa is a hayfield, or would be if it was cut, that he can secure the hay contracts *at his own price? Solution,* T. looks around & sees 4 mowing machines in the country, 3 of which would be opposition mowers. He sees that the 3 opposition mowers are out of repair, that they are in fact ineffective, that they are 8 weeks off any supply house, from which the ineffective parts could be replaced & he knows that the hay season is not much more than 6 weeks long. He leagues himself with the one effective mower; early in the season he secures his men & horses, sends east & buys three mowers & three horse rakes & with these properly handled the market can be cornered & a profit made, according to Poor Uncle Sam's necessities. There is a large margin to *win* on this hay contract & a very small one to lose. I cant touch the beef contract *yet,* "But the time will come."

"But!" (I hear you say) "this is not going into a ranch business *atall.* We don't see what all this means." "Just you hold on for a spell. . . ." You see the mexicans would bring their cows, steers, calves, yearlings, 2 year olds, ranches &c &c to trade for groceries, just as sure as anyone would sell to them that way. Now you see I would sell for any good property they brought.

If their title was good, I would take their ranch as payment & let it; It would be *splendid property* to hold & There is nothing more profitable than buying *young stock* (if one can but get the chance, *even for cash*) & this way it would be more so & I shall be able to acquire stock by degrees, which I would much rather do, than in one big lump, as I can gain experience more easily that way . . . & I can acquire the cattle for at least 1/3rd less than any other way. This country is different to any other, & if a man is somewhat supple, & accomodates himself to *circumstances* & twists his business into shape, to fit the circumstances, he can make far more than if he tried to run his affairs, just as he would & could in an old country.

. . . To make all this work easily, so as not to kill me with anxiety, I ought to have the *land* & the *stock* money as soon as possible, for you see as I acquire cattle, I shall reduce the capital I have to run my store with; or else I shall have to turn my acquired property into money again, before they have had time to increase in value.

All the fixtures necessary to run my store business will be, a desk, a safe, & a pair of scales & I should need all three if I had nothing but a cattle ranch. The mowers would sell at once if I were disappointed in my hay project. I hear there is to be a sale of condemned effects at Fort Stanton in about 6 weeks; at these sales there are always a lot of things sold that have no earthly defect that anyone can discover; for instance, this time I hear there are 50 horses condemned, because they don't match in colour; they will all go for next to nothing & be very desirable horses, as they will all be very well broken acclimated (which is a *great* advantage) & most of them about the right age. In addition to the horses there will be blankets & a lot of miscellaneous stuff, which one cant get as a general thing in this country, save at very high prices, & which one needs in starting a ranch business.[38]

He wondered whether McSween had any mail for him; he was still waiting for a reply to the letter of January 27, posted on the 31st, in which he had asked for five hundred pounds; since Widenmann was using his horse, he had no way of getting to Lincoln to find out. He was in good health and spirits,

though I feel serious as a judge, owing to my mind being so fully occupied & my having so much to make me anxious & thoughtful; My most earnest desire is for success & more on account of my three Pets than for myself; for if I can but win,

I would be content, to cast the fruits of my success at their feet, knowing I had won the means, of smoothing away a vast proportion of the rocks in their path, & given them the means of beautifying their lives & I could retire from the scene without a sigh.

That night Dick Brewer returned from Lincoln bringing letters for John: two from his father, one from his mother, and a fourth from "My Old Boy Jack" (his sister Lillian). In replying next day, Tunstall recalled an old family tradition.

You used always to reserve to yourselves & constituted it a *Tunstall's Privilige*, to express any opinion you or we might have, whether *reasonable* or *otherwise*, providing always that it was done modestly & politely & put more in the form of an interrogation than an assertion.

That act passed the Tribunal of the Trinity, so long ago, that the document recording the date of its passage has crumbled away; but the right has become so firmly implanted in the breast of the race, that it is never disputed.

The beauty of the form of government adopted by this *peculiar* & *individual* race, is to be seen & admired in its fruit; The original lawmakers (who are, we are happy to say, still in the land of the quick, & are known to the initiated respectively as the "Head" and the "Neck") are never known (we are proud to say) to infringe upon their self constituted limits, viz., Of interrogation & politeness, save we think upon one occasion, when the "Neck" (in *entire* subversion of the orders & laws before laid down & through long use, found to be perfect in their acting & working, Peremtorily, uninterrogatively & unpolitely) was known to say "For God's sake, give me some brandy". I repeat that we are *proud* to have to testify that this was the *exception* that proves the rule. . . .

Now, let me tell you at the start, that I have read your letters over again this morning, & I am very pleased to be able to inform you that I propose to prove (as I feel every confidence that I can do, *every* time) that my schemes are *perfect*. And that the fears you have had; & that you expressed in *accordance* with *your rights* are nought but *Ghosts*.

And if I succeed (as I ought to do) in making all that as clear to you, as it is to me, you will have the extreme pleasure of finding you are WRONG.[39]

Taking each point or doubt they had raised in their letters, Tunstall examined it, explained it, or elaborated on earlier comments he had made, patient as a teacher with a wilful child. What he wanted them to realize was that they were

already started on *one* race, I call it the "Fortune Stakes" & "*win or die*" is my motto. We are playing for a higher prize than we shall ever play for again.

You say "you dont fear that I dont weigh all matters before to act", you may *well* have that opinion; *Night* & *day* I think of nothing else, & I turn & turn everything round & round, until I get completely dizzy. I know the game I am playing pretty well by this time, my mind has never quitted the subject since I first wrote the word "sheep" to you, nearly two years ago.

I know this country better than most of the old settlers & I have the run of all the clues that touch my interest. A land agent could just about as soon palm a sell off on Old Nick, as he could on me; A land agent goes away *sick at the stomach*, after I have riddled his tract & title for him, for about 15 minutes, "You bet your boots" they only "trot out" their best when they talk trade *to me*; I know every flaw in the climate, water or grass from El Paso to the Raton mountains, I *know* where the Comanches & Apaches raid, & where the horse thieves plunder & hide; I can tell them the contingent disadvantage, for every advantage they can boast; & the first thing they know will be, that that brown coated, steak eating Englishman has got the nut out of the pudding.

There were more parental fears to be allayed: "I sometimes think you must think me *very* innocent," he complained. But no, rapid water carrying away cattle was not a problem. "I would not mind driving a herd of our cattle across the Thames, anywhere above Richmond, & outside of the Rio Grande, I have never yet seen a stream in this Territory that the Rajah could not clear with me on his back." Yes, it was perfectly safe for his letters to be sent via McSween. No, if he bought cattle in Texas they wouldn't be run off by Indians en route. No, traveling around as much as he did, he could not keep a diary; but he would write at every opportunity. No, he did not think Col. Jack Hays was related to U.S. president Rutherford Hayes. Yes, if he called a spot a good watering place the water supply was permanent. No, they need not be alarmed that he would let anyone bring an unexpected bill against him, either McSween or anyone else. Finally, "as regards my getting shot; Well, this is a free country, & people some times use each other as targets pretty freely, but I am not going to get shot, so dont be uneasy about that."

Strangely enough, on March 28, just a day or two before Tunstall wrote these words, one of John Chisum's warriors, Jim Highsaw, shot and killed R. K. Wiley's onetime foreman, Richard Smith, at Loving's Bend on the Pecos. This affray brought the Pecos War, or what some people preferred to name more accurately as "Chisum's War," to a head. No mention of it appears anywhere in Tunstall's letters: perhaps he believed Chisum's troubles did not concern him. In this, time would prove him badly wrong. For the moment, however, he was too wrapped up in his plans.

> I am going to order a stock of groceries tomorrow from St. Louis Missouri, & a safe, the combination of which I have already sent you; I shall get a book in which I shall keep a business diary, & description of the way to work out, all the unfinished schemes I start, so that in the event of any accident happening, you could come & haul in the nets I had cast. The only conclusion I put to this letter, to satisfy me, is

---

**I know I am right, & I intend to go
ahead with all my strength.**

Tunstall clearly enjoyed playing cat and mouse with the opposition; but it was a dangerous game. For all his vaunted knowledge of conditions in his new domain, he was being very naive about the hostility his plans were arousing. He told his parents, "I go by the name of 'The Englishman' as a general thing & they say to Dick from time to time, 'Confound that Englishman, what is he going to do in this country anyhow?' "

What Tunstall had in mind was fairly simple: to usurp all the "rackets" by which the real money was made in Lincoln County. A cattle ranch on which to run stock either bought, foreclosed upon or—even—stolen. The store to ensure—particularly with the House put out of business—the indebtedness to him of the majority of the citizens. McSween handling all the legal business, Widenmann over at the fort as post trader or perhaps Indian agent. With all those channels controlled, and a few of his other "flyers" (such as buying and selling county scrip) making extra money, Tunstall would have been in a fair way to realize his ambition to pocket half of every dollar that was spent in the county.

Had the market economy of Lincoln County remained as it was, fixed around the dollars generated by the fort and the Indian agency—and that it would do so was the basis of Tunstall's planning—he might indeed have become the wealthy *milord* he so often imagined himself as, spending six months of the year in London and "popping over" to check on his empire every summer. Herein lay Tunstall's—and McSween's—fundamental misconception. They confidently expected the little world of Lincoln County to remain locked in its 1870s time-warp. It could not, and it did not.

Of course, Tunstall could not see into the future. Perhaps he didn't really want to. His very words "Confound that Englishman, what is he going to do in this country anyhow?" suggest he was thoroughly enjoying every "point" he was making at the expense of his rivals. By Jove! one can almost hear him saying, that's got the blighters on the run, what?

At this juncture, Tunstall believed his rivals were completely unaware of his machinations. He could not have been more wrong. Since the beginning of April, the Lincoln post office had been moved into the Murphy-Dolan building, and Murphy's fiery-tempered troubleshooter Jimmy Dolan was not the man to have scruples about reading Tunstall's—or anyone else's—letters. Nor was he about to sit idly by while Tunstall and his legal adviser McSween muscled in on the hegemony the House had enjoyed for more than a decade. "The Englishman" had completely underestimated the caliber and determination of the opposition. It was to prove a fatal error.

CHAPTER 10

LITTLE WARS IN LINCOLN COUNTY

JOHN Tunstall had come to Lincoln County at a particularly volatile time. Not only was the race hatred engendered by the Horrell War of 1873 and subsequent events still simmering, but now the long-standing animosity between John Chisum and the smaller ranchers in the area known as Seven Rivers turned to out-and-out violence.

Chisum's headquarters was now the fortlike South Spring ranch near the tiny settlement of Roswell. His range, held by right of preemption and the hardcase cowboys he employed to patrol it, stretched from old Fort Sumner in the north a hundred and fifty miles south to the Texas line. On this vast stretch of land grazed some seventy-five thousand cattle.

At Seven Rivers, which lay between the present-day towns of Artesia and Carlsbad, there was a scattering of smaller ranches and a trading post run by the Jones family. Among those who had settled in the area were Hugh Beckwith, his sons Robert and John, his son-in-law William H. Johnson, Lewis Paxton and Nathan Underwood, Charles Woltz, Andrew Boyle, Milo L. Pierce, Thomas B. "Buck" Powell, and the Olinger brothers. Beckwith, as volatile a character as old "Uncle John" Chisum, was the patriarch of this scattered community.

Susan McSween thought highly of Hugh Beckwith; John Chisum did not. She characterized him as

> a good man honest and upright had a mexican wife but he himself taught his children in every way, and worshiped his son Robert, but a man by the name of Johnson envagled himslf into the good thoughts of the family by making them believe how rich he was and married one of the girls and when those troubles broke out he joined in with them [Murphy and Dolan] with the inducements Dolan had out that they could all get rich by taking cattle from John Chissum.[1]

Mrs. McSween's version is a little simplistic, because it was a byword of the time that no one could live at Seven Rivers who did not steal from Chisum, just as it was a byword that L. G. Murphy & Co.'s "miracle herd"—so called because no matter how many cattle were sold from it, it never got any smaller—was replenished from Chisum's stock. She went on to say that "Dolan [moved] his herd of Cattle from off the Carrizozo Range to the lower edge of Mr Chisum's to increase his herd. Billy Morton was his Foreman in about a month after they were down there John Chisum took a lot of cowboys went down and cut out about 40 head of cows with their brands on them he asked Billie "what do you mean by this" Billy responded "I thought I could get away with them."[2]

Chisum believed, not to put too fine a point on it, that most of the Seven Rivers ranchers were a bunch of damned cow thieves, and that Dolan and Riley bought from them knowing the stock was stolen. Yet an uneasy truce existed: the two factions were in many ways interdependent. Chisum's warriors kept the Indians at bay, thus securing the livelihood of the Seven Rivers ranchers. Chisum frequently needed experienced extra trail bosses and foremen; these he found at Seven Rivers.

As his best biographer has remarked, 1877 was the most demanding year of Chisum's ranching career.[3] Coincident with his massive spring movements of cattle in response to the orders coming out of Kansas City from his partners and assignees Hunter & Evans, Chisum noted a significant increase in the theft of his cattle. His disaffection for the Seven Rivers ranchers waxed in direct proportion to his losses. When these losses were exacerbated by the shooting of his foreman Yopp, his hostility became open. Out of Chisum's antagonism, fostered by his Jinglebob cowboys, grew further violence.

The Jinglebob was Chisum's trademark: a method of cutting the steer's ears in such a way as to form the eponymous dangling strip of cartilage, a much surer way of marking his stock than the "Long Rail" brand he used, a straight line that could be (and was) converted by stock thieves into an arrow, a bow, a "lazy P," and even in one case, a square dubbed a "pigpen." The only way to rustle a Jinglebob steer was to cut off its ears altogether.

On March 28, 1877, a Chisum foreman, James M. Highsaw, accompanied by some Jinglebob cowboys, rode into the public corral used jointly by the local stockmen at Loving's Bend on the Pecos River. The Chisum faction's version had it that when he discovered a few gallons of freshly cut ears obviously taken off Chisum cattle, Highsaw confronted one of the Seven Rivers cowboys, Dick Smith, and accused him of stealing Chisum's stock. Gunfire erupted; when it ended, Smith was dead. On hearing the news, Chisum expressed satisfaction: the war had commenced, he said, and there were six more thieves at Seven Rivers who needed killing: Underwood, Paxton, Woltz, Beckwith, Johnson, and Powell.

The source for Chisum's remark is a contentious "history" of the "War on the Pecos" written in the form of a report to District Attorney Thomas B. Catron by one of the Seven Rivers ranchers, Andrew Boyle, a former British soldier who held a commission as a deputy sheriff of Doña Ana County.[4] He was partisan, of course: which of them was not? His account of Dick Smith's death, for instance, states that Smith was "shot in the back five times with a Colt's improved 45 cal. six shooter," which puts a totally different perspective on the whole affair.

Although Boyle does not mention it, immediately after the Smith shooting a party of about twenty men pursued Highsaw to the Chisum ranch, where he had taken refuge; on arrival, they found the fortlike building defended by well-armed Jinglebob riders ensconced behind the parapet of the roof, and they retreated without firing a shot in anger.

A fortnight later, on April 10, the situation worsened: Jimmy Dolan came down to Seven Rivers to buy cattle from Paxton and Underwood. En route to his cattle camp to fill the order, Nathan Underwood and his party came up on six Chisum warriors not far from Wiley's camp. Fearing ambush (they claimed), the Underwood party fired on Chisum's men, fortunately without inflicting any damage.

Seeing this as a declaration of hostilities, Chisum drove up to Fort Stanton to request support from the military. Col. George Purington, commanding, turned him down flat; the cavalry did not act as anybody's private police force. Chisum next tried Sheriff Brady in Lincoln, but Brady pointed out that the shooting had occurred in Doña Ana County, outside his jurisdiction. The angry Chisum took himself away: it looked like he was going to have to kill his own snakes, and now was as good a time as any.

As it happened, Lewis Paxton was in Lincoln; Sheriff Brady warned him that Chisum was planning to go to war, and Paxton hurried back to Seven Rivers to warn his friends, who quit their isolated camps and gathered inside the protective walls of Hugh Beckwith's fortlike ranch house.

On April 20, Chisum, Wiley, and some thirty Jinglebob warriors rode up the river, loaded for bear. When they got to the Hugh Beckwith ranch (a few miles north of where present-day Lakewood stands) they surrounded it, drove off all the horses and mules, and cut off the water supply. By late afternoon the place was under siege.

The standoff lasted all night. Under cover of darkness, Charlie Woltz and Buck Powell slipped through the lines and headed for La Mesilla to get help in the form of arrest warrants and manpower. Next morning Chisum sent a note to the house urging that the women and children leave. These—a Mrs. Stafford (mother of the Olinger boys), Beckwith's daughter Helen, and two younger Beckwith children—replied that they would take their chances in the house rather than trust themselves to the tender mercies of Chisum's warriors.

On April 22, according to the Boyle account, "Chisum advanced his threats into execution telling his men they would try and take the walls of the other party, and kill them all who were in there. They commenced shooting at about 700 or 800 yards distance, the besieged returning the fire. Chisum's men lost courage and would not advance any closer, saying they were not going to get killed for $30 a month, that they had hired to herd cattle and not to fight."

A parley was proposed. William Johnson rejected the suggestion, stating that he was not authorized to act as a spokesman for the others, to many of whom Chisum owed back wages; until Chisum paid his debts, talk was out of the question. Faced with this impasse, the wily Chisum withdrew, restoring the water supply and returning the livestock. He led his men back south to begin the spring roundup. A few days later he was stricken with smallpox.

Powell got back from La Mesilla on May 7 with warrants for the arrest of Chisum, Wiley, and Jim Highsaw, the latter for murder. Boyle, as deputy sheriff, raised a posse consisting of about fourteen Seven Rivers men and rode down to Wiley's cow camp. There they found Chisum, too sick to be moved. From there they rode up to Chisum's ranch at South Spring. Boyle reported, "On May 10, got to Chisum's ranche. Wylie [sic] seeing we were there, sent out a man by the name of Charles Moore, whom we had seen at the cow camp, with a note stating that there were men in there who did not want to fight. . . . I sent him an answer that we did not want to kill any person, that I had warrants to serve and I was going to serve them, that there was no use resisting."

Wiley came out to parley with Powell and Robert Beckwith, telling them Chisum would honor his debts if they would make out proper claims. While they were talking, Jim Highsaw made good his escape from the rear of the huge ranch house. When the parleying was done, Boyle and his posse "all went down and saw Chisum, and Wylie got the checks and paid the men and I served the warrant on John S. Chisum and placed him under bond as he was still sick."

"Chisum's War" was over, although the animosity remained. We have remarked that Boyle's account was partisan. That Boyle was perhaps other than he represented himself is indicated by the following communication sent to him by one of Chisum's "warriors," Charles H. Brady.

> Dear Sir, you red-headed —— of—b——— if you do not bring them horses back you stole you shall hear the gentle report of my needle gun; that is the kind of hair pin I am, this thing of being on a sheriff's posse for a band of horse thieves may do in some places but it has got too thin with me, yours on the first dark stormy night.[5]

At the June term of court, the Doña Ana County grand jury handed down indictments against Chisum, Wiley, Highsaw, Nathan Hendricks, Brady, Thomas Easton, Cicero Knight, Edward Jackson, and "divers other persons whose names are not known" for their part in the attack on the Beckwith ranch. Highsaw was indicted for murder, and Robert Beckwith, Louis Paxton, Buck Powell, and George Hindman for various offenses. No action appears to have been taken on any of these warrants. For the moment, at least, peace—or what passed for peace—returned to Lincoln County.

John Tunstall's schemes were coming together fast. In spite of earlier uncertainties, he told his "Much Beloved Father," he had not

> changed my intention of going into a stock business by one single shade of opinion; I still think it the most lasting & profitable business I ever heard of; the only change I have made in that regard since my first letter on sheep, is that I have by reason of added experience, & change of circumstances been compelled to alter my opinion as to the best time & place & means of starting, or in other words "as to the *how, when & where* to start". I now consider that my present scheme is so near perfection in all its bearings, that if I succeed in working it out (which I *will do* if it costs my last drop of blood) that I shall have the *finest property* I have ever seen since I have been in the United States. . . .
>
> You are right in supposing that Mr. McSween is to be instrumental in working my points & you can take my word for it, that my arrangements with him are such as will be the most likely or the surest to bring everything out as I wish it. I have been in a field full of razors far too long, ever to close an eye for a single moment to the possibility of being cut or skinned. I have all the confidence in him that is necessary, in so important an affair, but nevertheless I never give a chance away, or have a corner out of which he could make a cent out of me, against my will. I hav worked his affairs & mine into such a shape, that they spur him the way I want him to go.[6]

A newly discovered sheet written by Tunstall sometime in April 1877 (the only date on it is Papa Tunstall's notation "Rec'd 8 May 77") indicates that he also at least considered the idea of buying from black soldiers serving at Fort Stanton the homestead rights automatically conferred upon them by a grateful government.[7]

> This is in further explanation & elucidation of the laws governing "soldiers Homesteads" from Sec. 2304 to sec. 2309.
>
> Sec 2305, you see underscored the first two lines; these shew that the time the

man served during the war, counts to his advantage, in reducing the usual time necessary to complete his title to a homestead, *viz.,5 years. but* if he had served 7 years in the war, he would still have to live one year on his tract of land, *to complete his title.*

The United States understand living on a tract to mean "Not being absent from it more than six months at one time" But Sec. 2308. says that if he still be in the service of the U.S.A. or [illegible], he need not reside upon the land atall & yet complete his title.

Thus you see by getting these fellows to file a declaration on the land, the title will be perfect in 12 months, & by lending them the money at a high rate they will be in my debt to such an extent, that they will secure me in any event. But these nigger soldiers care less for their homestead rights, than they do for a chew of tobacco.

For The rest, the laws speak for themselves.

Now you see that I cant have any deeds in less than 12 months & as I cant get any filing done until the land is surveyed and that takes 6 months, I shall probably not be able to get any deeds in less than 18, but when I do the title will be a virgin title to the land, as before that was issued none existed, no unsatisfied claims can arise, or old documents turn up to set me aside & no tax can be levied upon the land I use save that to which I have a title.

In addition I will say that I feel *every* confidence in the future.

I never need a card but on looking through my hand, I find it. & I never meet an obstacle but I find a way round it.

I am in the best of spirits, though anxious & very much occupied. If you could but see just how my affairs are situated you would feel as I do, I feel sure.

Tunstall never put this scheme into operation: he was too canny to have advanced loans to soldiers who could at any time be transferred out of the area. That McSween would have encouraged him to do so seems equally unlikely. What he did do was go ahead with his ranch scheme, enlisting the assistance of McSween, Brewer, Sam Corbet, Widenmann, and others to make filings in the Peñasco, Feliz, and Ruidoso valleys. It appears that his "stock scheme" encompassed not one ranch but a number of ranches, each to be managed by one or more of the men he eventually had working for him. Two young cowboys, a half-breed called Fred Waite and a callow youngster known variously as Henry Antrim, William Bonney, or just plain "Kid," were to run stock on the former Mathews place; Brewer would manage the Ruidoso ranch, Gauss and Middleton the Feliz, and so on.

In discussing money matters with his father, Tunstall said that he planned to invest in land "between now and December by degrees," and if Papa Tunstall could provide a further infusion of money "it would help me immensely. . . . Another £3000 would complete everything as far as I can *possibly* see. But *any how* we have time to think of all that before we shall need it"(fig. 28).[8] His closing comment, "I don't see that you need burn this," may be a clue as to what happened to the missing letters referred to earlier.

By the middle of April, his schemes were matured. He would buy cattle, put them on the Feliz land, and hire men to squat on the land until it could be surveyed. He explained what this entailed in a letter written from Brewer's ranch to his father on April 21.

To *hold unsurveyed land* is a sort of game of "bluff" [poker]; for instance suppose I want to do so; I would if I could, run a herd of cattle upon it & I could to a great extent keep people off it, for I should call all the best locations "camps" & have men in my employ to represent that they owned them & I should have force enough to carry out any intentions I might have with regard to them. This explains the use of a herd of cattle in that capacity.

To run a small herd of cattle will cost as much as it will to run one twice or three times as large, for one needs a cook, if one has but two herders, a stable, a mowing machine, a wagon, a work team, a couple of houses, a cattle corral, camp cooking outfits for the ranch & the road, a barn &c &c which cost just as much for the running of 20 as for 1000 head of stock. So you see that the more cattle a man has up to almost any amount, the more economically they can be worked.[9]

Tunstall already had his eye on a man to be his cook; this was Godfrey Gauss, an ex-regular soldier of German origin who had no reason to admire the House (fig. 29). Dick Brewer was clearly to be a participant, for the Englishman had

FIG. 28. John Partridge Tunstall, aged sixty-two, 1877. Cabinet photo by W. Nicholson, Ventnor, Isle of Wight.

been staying at the Brewer ranch pretty much since his arrival in the county. The third member of Tunstall's team was the recently arrived Robert A. Widenmann; he had already insinuated himself into Tunstall's confidence, as the following shows:

I keep on the tramp nearly every day, as I have arrangements to make, letters to write & to receive, plans to work up & chances to hear of & consider, all the while, which take me from here to the Plaza & back. My grey horse is fit to ride again now, which saves me a great deal & my friend Widenmann who is with me here is a wonderful assistance, he has I guess saved me near £100 already; I am going to do my utmost to keep him around me, he is such a splendid fellow, he is one of the very few men of my own age, that I ever cared a "red cent" about. His parents are German & live in Georgia. He was educated in Germany & has travelled nearly all over it & Switzerland on foot, he speaks french nearly as well as I do, German perfectly, & has a very varied experience, he has been engaged in a banking business, a chemical factory, he held a very nice position in the Bremen Steamship Co. of New York, & has run a ranch in Colorado for a year & a half, he is a very smart fellow & is as nice a dispositioned man as any I ever met; he stands six feet & is very broad, he weighs 175 lbs & is 25 years old. should anything happen to me you will find that he can put you up to all the points necessary to finish up all my business, so as not to lose anything; you would like him immensely. I think myself very lucky to have met him, he is only in the position of a friend at present, but I shall make *some* business arrangement with him, as soon as I start into anything.[10]

Tunstall seems to have accepted Widenmann's uneasy mixture of falsehood and fact at its face value, even to enclosing "Rob's" picture with his letter.

FIG. 29. Gottfried G. (Godfrey) Gauss.
Date and photographer unknown.

McSween was less enamored of the newcomer; he told Tunstall that "a young man in health, who had no money nor clothing, and was willing to work for another for board and clothing, was not the man for him."[11]

On April 22, Tunstall acknowledged receipt of his father's registered letters of March 21 and 28, each containing drafts for $4,812.00 in gold, $9,624.00 in all, a small fortune.[12] Adding another note two days later, he said he was still having "very anxious times."

Nothing can be done in one direction in consequence of some surveys not being complete; & in another, I have no harness yet & I need some on Friday [April 27] at the latest. . . . I need it to take the necessaries of life over to a ranch, upon which a location has been made, & upon which someone must live.

I am about to buy some wool at 12½ cents, I hope to sell it at 18 & get the money back in two months & be out about 3 cents expenses, thereby making 14 per cent in the time; 18 cents is the *very* lowest it can bring & 3 cents the *most* it can cost, I hope to sell it for more than 18 but I quote you the lowest; I also save $150⁰⁰ on some freight by making this turn, as I give a man a load both ways, (to & from the railroad) instead of only one way. I have a good deal to occupy my mind just now, as starting *anything* is always a job, though everything is going better than I anticipated.[13]

Frontier life had its share of aggravations; just as he reached Lincoln from Brewer's, he was thrown by a "*confounded, treacherous* beast of a mule," landing on a rock that put an inch-long gash in his head; en route to Fort Stanton from there he was caught in a snowstorm; then "to crown the boiling," he learned that the much-needed harness had not arrived. He returned to Brewer's ranch in a sour mood; there he continued the letter, which set out his intentions.

The land scheme will take as I have told you £3200.0.0 [$16,000] from first to last. The payments have already commenced & will continue to have to be made, until about next Decr. or Jany, after which there will only be a small payment left to be made about 12 months after that.

In the mean time I am going to try & turn this money, that might otherwise lie idle in the bank, to some advantage. This "advantage" will consist I hope of good interest in the substantial line, & a lot of what one might call negative benefit in the shape of influence; I really *need* a stock of cattle for the fortification of any land scheme, & I am afraid that I shall have to have them, though they will lock up some capital which I would like much better to have loose. As regards credit on a land purchase from government, the government give *none atall* to *any* body.[14]

Tunstall was aware, of course, of the impending sale of the widow Ellen Casey's cattle; he was hoping to pick them up for around seven dollars a head, cash on the barrelhead. His agent would be McSween, of whom he had this to say:

> I believe I have him in such a shape, that he cant slide back a single point; any how he cant make anything by so doing, whereas he can by doing the right thing; & it is not in his power to hurt me other than by causing a delay, never mind what he does. But I have good reason to have confidence in him. Others put more confidence in him a great deal than I have occasion to do, & they seem to have done so for years & not suffered.

The reason for his confidence was that he had already proposed an arrangement with the attorney that would enable McSween to become a partner in Tunstall's "ring." In return for legal advice and acting as Tunstall's agent over the coming year, McSween would receive 1 percent of the profits, after a deduction of 8 percent on Tunstall's capital. When a formal partnership was effected in May 1878, McSween would receive 8 percent of what was then on the books, thus acquiring an interest without having to put up capital.

Susan McSween was strongly opposed to their plans. "I told Tunstall and Mr McSwain they would be murdered if they went into the store business," she said. "I did my best to keep McSwain from entering the business, but he went in against my will. Tunstall was the cause of his getting into it."[15]

The older Tunstall had obviously asked his son to explain how his schemes for making money would work. As an example, John told him of his plan to buy county scrip at a discount for cash, enabling him to make a 50 percent profit "without *any* risk in the world." His account book shows that he purchased $250 worth of scrip for $137; obviously he planned to buy more. He said he did not yet know how much scrip the county issued every year, but "I intend to control *all* of it if I can."

> *Everything* in New Mexico that *pays* at all (you may say) is worked by a "*ring*," there is the "indian ring" "the army ring" "the political ring" "the legal ring" "the Roman Catholic ring" "the cattle ring" "the horsethieves ring" "the land ring" & half a dozen other rings; now to make thing stick to do any good, it is necessary to either get into a ring, or make one for yourself, I am at present at work making a ring, & I have succeeded admirably so far; you see an adventurer like myself does not present a very formidable aspect if *in the ring* but anyone as well posted as myself can nearly break up an insipient ring single handed; by skirmishing on the outskirts a little. . . .
>
> My ring is forming itself as fast & faster than I had ever hoped, & in such a way that I will get the finest plum of the lot, always providing that I can make my points, which up to now I have done quite successfully. I propose to confine my operations to Lincoln County, but I intend to handle it in such a way, as to get the half of every dollar that is made in the county *by anyone*. And with our means we could get things into that shape in three years, if we only used two thirds of our capital in the undertaking.[16]

His "ring" was to be composed of himself, McSween, and as a silent partner, John Chisum. The "finest plum of the lot" was the post tradership, which Tunstall seems to have had his eye on right from the start. Papa Tunstall sounded a warning note.

As regards the banking and storekeeping & the intricate way of making money, of course it is quite impossible for me to see that as you see it, my not being on the spot; but I have no doubt but you may be right & were we to meet, you would make me see it the same as yourself. But in a poverty-stricken, cutthroat country like New Mexico, you would be always liable to be broken into & liable to be shot by some of your drunken customers, and that occupation would not be so good for your health.[17]

These were prescient words; and indeed, Tunstall was well aware of that very danger: there were two fatal shootings within days of his reading his father's letter. At Lincoln, Jimmy Dolan killed a young Mexican named Hiraldo Jaramillo. A few days later, Paul Dowlin was killed by an employee at his mill. Details appeared in the *New Mexican* of May 8.

The news reached the city this morning of the cold blooded murder of Mr Paul Dowlin at his mill in Fort Stanton, by one Jere [Jerry] Dillon. Upon receipt of the melancholy news at Fort Stanton several of the officers, with Mr William Dowlin, proceeded to the scene of the murder. They found Mr Dowlin alive—but sinking fast—the wound being on the head. At 12 o'clock midnight he died. Lieut. Pague, 15th Infantry, send word to the commanding officer that the murder was cold blooded; and further advices state that after firing two shots with a carbine, Dillon drew a revolver and kept firing until Dowlin fell. During the firing Dowlin kept advancing on Dillon—although unarmed—begging Dillon to stop firing for God's sake and listen to reason. To the large circle of his friends in this place the sad death of Paul Dowlin is cause for heartfelt sorrow.[18]

The *New Mexican* had more news of the Dowlin killing—and first news of the death of Jaramillo—in its issue of May 22, which quoted a "private letter to a gentleman in this city dated Fort Stanton, May 9, 1877." The writer was clearly a friend of Dolan's: note how as the account proceeds James J. Dolan becomes Jimmy. The letter touched first on the Dowlin murder:

The man who killed Paul Dowlin has lit out for Texas. The [motive for the] murder is still a mystery. Paul had an idea that he would be killed by Dillon. A day or two before his death he made out his will and was to have signed it in a day or two.

James J. Dolan killed a Mexican about 20 years of age a day or two before Dowlin was killed named Hiraldo Jaramillo. He was working at the house for James Dolan. He was working for Dolan at the time and had put up a job to kill him. It seems that day the Mexican had put a hammer under his pillow. Jimmy saw it and took it away. When Jimmy told him to clean off the horses, they went to the corral together, when the Mexican caught hold of Dolan's arm and commenced to cut him. He had a tight hold on Jimmy and would not let go, when Jimmy pulled his pocket pistol and shot him in the hand; still the Mexican would not let go, when Jimmy fired the second time and shot him in the arm. The Mexican continued to cut away at his arm, when Jimmy fired again and shot him through the heart, killing him instantly. Jimmy gave himself up but was discharged, as he killed him in self-defense.

Jaramillo's apparent inability to kill Dolan with a knife is only marginally less difficult to believe than Dolan's astonishing forbearance. And anyway, this sanitized version of events fooled no one in Lincoln. People whispered that the real reason for the killing was that widower George W. Peppin, thirty-four, an ex-soldier and good friend of the House (fig. 30), had been having an affair with Jaramillo's sixteen-year-old wife. Jaramillo, who was working for the House, found out about it and threatened to kill Peppin on sight. Dolan-style, Jimmy intervened, provoked a quarrel, and killed Jaramillo "in self defense."

Whatever his reasons—probably no more than that he did not wish to worry his family—Tunstall failed to mention either of these killings in his letters. Perhaps it was just that he had other, to him more important, things in mind. Acknowledging receipt of a third draft of £1,000, making the total he had received something in the region of $14,500, Tunstall recorded on May 7 that he hoped that night to "conclude a most economical, & advantageous stroke in the cattle line. I can't explain all its ramifications, but if succesful, which we hope [to] make it, I shall acquire about $5000 worth of cattle for less than $1300 & I can't possibly lose in any event."[19]

The cattle concerned belonged to Ellen Casey. According to Susan McSween, the widow Casey had gone to Santa Fe

FIG. 30. George Warden Peppin at about twenty-nine years of age, ca. 1870. Photographer unknown; the original is a tintype.

and bought $1300⁰⁰ worth of goods from the Speigleburg Bros on credit when the time came to collect it she would not pay it and I think refused to. She told a lady friend who was with her on the way back from Santa Fe that she would not pay for them. she was just so ignorant that she believed she could do so. After the Speigleburgs could not get it, they sent the bill to Mr. McSween to collect it he had to sew her and got judgement and then attached the cattle.[20]

The court ordered Sheriff Brady to seize and impound four hundred head of KC cattle and, if Mrs. Casey did not pay up, to dispose of them at a public auction, which was held on May 11. Quite what went wrong with Tunstall's plan is not clear, but on May 20 he told his father that he had only made

half the turn I expected to make in the cattle line, one of my points failed to stick, but in any case I have made a splendid arrangement, it is too long to go into now, but I can give you the sum of it; if all works out as I expect it to do, I shall get $2000 worth of cattle, this is their very lowest value, for $1000. should it work out the way not expected to do, I shall have had six months experience in the cattle business & receive 2 per cent per month on a loan of $900 & on all expenses incurred during the six months. I at present hold an absolute bill of sale for the cattle, but have given in exchange a promise to sell at stated figures on a certain day, in case the party is so minded.[21]

The price Tunstall quotes makes nonsense of the tradition that he bought four hundred head for about fifteen hundred dollars; his use of the word *loan* indicates that he made an arrangement with Mrs. Casey, not the sheriff. His account book with McSween shows the purchase of 209 head of cattle for $987.40. A later reference to "the mulishness of an old woman" suggests that the widow Casey somehow scuttled his plan to get all four hundred head.

It would appear Mrs. Casey refused to part with her cattle at such a price, whereupon McSween, acting as her attorney (and also as Tunstall's agent), proposed that Tunstall advance Mrs. Casey the money to pay off part of her judgment and avert the total loss of the cattle; if she could repay the loan, plus interest, she would get her animals back. If not, Tunstall would keep them and profit by the low price. This is confirmed by Susan McSween, who maintained that "both M[c] & Tunstall told her that they would put the cattle out on the Felix they would let her have them for the amount they brought at the sale and the interest on the money for the time they would be out."[22]

While all this was going on, Tunstall was "working like a horse & worried out of my seven senses" as he wrote from Fort Stanton on May 17. His hasty scrawl to his father explains why.

> Please tell me in your next if the letters you have received from me have ever appeared to have been tampered with & if you have received letters with instructions to burn them, from me during last month & if so, how many.
>
> There is a ring here opening letters I think, & I am sorry I ever wrote you those that I allude to. I have not a moment more.

Burn This[23]

The reason for Tunstall's unease is obvious: the "ring" was of course J. J. Dolan, who as postmaster would have had ample opportunity to read the letters containing the plans and schemes Tunstall had laid before his father. The young adventurer determined to find some other way to send his mail to London, but it was to be some months before he could make a satisfactory alternative arrangement.

On May 20 he was still "fearfully worried."[24] He had been working from sunup to sundown the last two days branding the cattle he had bought. "It is the hardest work I ever did, or looked on at; to lasso & throw a heavy wild steer & then hold him down while he is branded takes muscle skill & nerve & if it is not a little the finest sport I ever had a hand in I am very much mistaken."

Two days later he took up his pen once more. "I expected to be on the road today moving my stock onto their range," he said, "but Dick is using my 2nd saddle so I am anchored until his return."

> I am in splendid health in spite of my working so hard, as I have done lately; & having so much to worry me; I came near "getting blue" the other day, I require so many things that I have not got, & owing to the stupidity of others, dont seem to be able to get; for instance I ordered a set of harness 2 months ago from Santa Fe, it is 4 days drive from here & it has not reached me yet.
>
> I have had to herd these cattle (which are (so cattle men tell me) as awkward a bunch of cattle as you could find in the Territory) around this ranch, where the wheat is all up, & no fences around it; upon the old crocks of horses that Dick has loose, over & above his work horses, which makes altogether about as wearysome a job of it one could well get hold of. I have run my poor sick grey down after them until he is quite unservicable & will probably be for 2 months to come. And the most agravating circumstance of the whole thing *is*, that all of it might have been avoided, had it not been for the mulishness of an old woman.

Then my horses get upon other people's wheat, & I write to people for one class of information which I need badly & they send me another that I dont want; I write to set things going in different quarters, & get no reply; letters get lost in the post, people prospect & settle on my land, & a thousand & one things happen to keep me on the boil, toil, & spoil all the while.[25]

On Sunday night, May 27, Tunstall sat down to write to his father. This ten-page letter presents the clearest existing statement of his plans.[26]

He was planning, he said, to take the cattle over to their range—probably the Peñasco ranch he had bought from Mathews—the next day. Due to the shortage of horses and the natural propensity of cattle to prefer wheat and corn to grass, he had had "a very trying time," but these were "minor anxieties & dont hurt but for the moment." The more serious ones were "Land scheming & finance."

I at first wrote you that I had at last decided upon working a land scheme in this section & that it would cost *net* £3200, these figures are about right, though I once thought I could do it for less. At the same time I told you that to start a cattle ranch on a paying basis would cost £3000 more.

I set to work towards those ends, & I have found that the sums needed to work my first scheme would not exhaust my capital, for nearly 12 months & I saw (like anyon else) that there would be great waste of interest, in allowing money to lie idle in that way; so I began to look around for paying investments, for short periods; I did not expect to find *any* at all but to my surprise I found a *great many*, that would pay marvellously better than I had any idea of, & at the same time be safe. Then, the question arose, (as I had a choice of investments) Which will aid my ulterior projects the most? & be the most easily handled while I am working on my land & cattle schemes?

Loans on cattle, at once suggested itself as they could if not repaid be carried over to the cattle scheme.

Then I saw that by getting a shipment of goods, I could make large profits on cash transactions, & acquire cattle.

Then I saw that contracts if worked for, were almost better than cash, as there was the profit on the merchandise sold, & the flour or corn sold to the government, or in other words there was a profit on what was given in exchange by me & taken in exchange by me.

Then I saw that certain ranches, if controlled, could control the prices of grain, & that in this country, it was more easy to cover the market, than in any other part of America.

Then I saw that I could acquire a title to a great many ranches, already improved & very valuable, & by a little engineering be able to control things almost entirely.

And I at last came to the conclusion, that there was a wonderfully paying & safe business, only waiting for someone to seize, which involved but a small capital as compared with the profits that must accrue from it, & which I could set on fast, & very likely keep hold of, & run my original schemes as well.

On further examination I find all this to be real & safe & easily handled. I have not done much with it yet though I am prepared to do *all* that I can see I can "turn" round quickly enough to suit me. I have, I expect, acquired a small herd of cattle at 50 percent below their value; & as cattle are a staple article, that is like clear profit; & if I continue as I hope I shall do (that is to folow out my schemes) that will of course be *clear profit*. I have purchased some few dollars worth of that scrip, & will make over 50 per cent upon its cost, within a few months of its purchase.

I have made arrangements to corner all the corn in the county & will make a large profit upon it.

I am "going-to-work" to corner the wheat & I guess I shall make my point.

I have found a lot of ranches that I can buy for a *trifle*, that are worth in many instances 4 & 5 times what they would cost me & in fact that I can make more out of, in one year, than they will cost me to buy.

I have worked into a strong, young & independent ring, who are working things upon a basis that I am certain is bound to stand, & to succeed, & my stand therein is an independent one.

I shall also make quite a neat thing out of hay this year, unless things go very differently to what I expect them to do, & if they do, I shant lose atall.

This soliloquy helps a little in understanding the cryptic entries in the McSween-Tunstall account book, reproduced in appendix 3. The remark about "loans on cattle" supports the theory advanced in the matter of the Casey animals, and perhaps explains the transactions with Hunter & Evans. Most of the other entries, however, remain an infuriating puzzle.

Tunstall credited McSween with the first two drafts he received from his father, a total of £1,500 that converted to $7,695.45. The second infusion of money was used to open an account at the Merchants National Bank in St. Louis, Mo. His finances and those of McSween thereafter became bewilderingly intertwined. Both later operated accounts at the First National Bank in Santa Fe, and there is some evidence that McSween also had bank accounts in New York and St. Louis, or possibly East St. Louis, Ill.

To make the financial puzzle even more confusing, Tunstall neglected to date the account book entries after July 21, 1877. Widenmann was to say later that "the business is so intricate, the books were kept in such a shape by [Tunstall] that only one who is thoroughly acquainted with the business can handle it. Then the landmatters are so arranged and there are so many secrets connected with it purposely, so that a stranger should not be able to interfere or hinder the workings, that no outsider could arrange them."[27]

One might offer a guess, from Tunstall's entries, that he loaned John Farmer, Felix McKittrick, and Ham Mills money against their crops or land or both; and that in addition to the Mathews place, he had an interest in Brewer's ranch. It can be seen that he paid taxes for, or in behalf of, R. D. Hunter, John Copeland, John Newcomb, Francisco Romero y Trujillo, McKittrick, Chisum, Brewer, Corbet, and J. H. Blazer but not why, or for that matter, when. The same applies to most of the other entries: the best one can apply to them is an informed guess, and in the case of one or two—like the payment of seventy-five dollars to W. L. Rynerson—not even that. Tunstall was playing his cards very close to his chest, but he had his reasons.

All that is necessary to win the game I am playing is to get possession of the corners. And *now* is *the* time to do it. There is *no* speculation about it, & *nothing* that you cant wash your hands *quite* clean of, in a moment, should you desire it.

My funds will carry everything along for me that I need, comfortably, easily & profitably until Dec', & I may be able to make things work slick enough, to tide me over that date, but I hardly expect it. It depends upon how the "turns" can be made, for instance, if I could deliver all my corn & wheat before that date, I should have made the "turn" in that time, as the government vouchers are better than cash, as they are eastern exchange as well.

I wish you *never* to forget, that I dont speculate *atall*, a profit & a good one is *certain*, on every investment I make, & the chances are three to one every time, that it will be a very large one.

In addition to all this, a chance is looming away in the distance (though only at the distance of 12 months) of acquiring a *very* profitable business, viz., The Post Trader ship of Fort Stanton. The Post Trader will resign his position then, & if I get a chance of playing the right cards, I may very likly get the position. From what I can see, I think £2000 would run the business, the profits would be not less than £1000 a year & be *absolutely safe.*

And if I could but get that position, I could make a *great deal* of money every year, as I should so entirely control the county, that I could make the prices of everything just to suit myself. At the distance you are from here, it is hard to realize how all this works, but if you will imagine that this county is like an island, in which there is an import duty of from 1d. [2¢] to 2½d. [5¢] per lb. you will see how it works, to a great extent; if you were on such an island, & you bought up all the breadstuff at 4d per lb. & it could not be raised elsewhere for less than 4d per lb., you could sell as fast as you pleased for 5d, as you would have no opposition, & suppose it was corn or wheat at 1d per lb. you could sell it for 2d without opposition & make *quite* a *decent* profit "*n'est [ce] pas?*"[28]

If he only had his father's capital, Tunstall went on, he was sure he would be able to retire in ten years' time with a splendid fortune. "Capitalists make money by controling markets; I have found a market that *we* can control, if we will."

In the short time he had been in Lincoln Robert Widenmann had become the companion Tunstall had so often wished for, someone with whom he could share his hopes, his plans, his worries, his disappointments. In this letter, John referred to Widenmann as his "confidential friend & adviser" and told his father that he had

executed a small deed, constituting him my legal representative in case of my death, until you write, come over, or instruct some other person, to attend to my affairs in your interest. He is a man I have great confidence in, both as regards his ability & integrity, & I feel sure that in case you ever need his assistance, that he can save every cent that I "have out" for you. The history of his interest & mine would be somewhat lengthy, but I consider them parallel & not at all liable to clash. So that should anything happen to me, there wont be any chance of your coming out here, to find my affairs entangled, & your property all subject to a set of influences that you cant make head or tail of. Two of Widenmann's leading traits are obstinacy & combativeness, he will hold a point longer & fight harder to keep it, than any man of his age I ever met. And he has consequently a great deal of what I call "force" in his character; if he decides that a horse wants throwing down, he throws him; & if a mule gets its own way with someone one & he concludes that she has to learn that she cant do it with others, he teaches her. I consider myself very lucky in meeting him, he so exactly suits me, we are sufficiently good friends to be able to get as mad as we like with each other, without its affecting our friendship in the slightest.[29]

It seems hardly necessary to belabor the point that, for once, Tunstall had badly misjudged his man. The truth of Widenmann's situation was that he was a penniless, homeless exile. Tunstall's friendship gave him a roof over his head, food in his belly, money in his pocket—the account book shows he had already received a payment of more than two hundred dollars—and bright prospects. The parallel interests Tunstall mentions might refer to the possibility of Widenmann's becoming Indian agent at the Mescalero Agency, with Tunstall as post trader.

In closing this May 27 letter to his father, Tunstall expressed himself "fairly satisfied" with his progress.

[T]hough I have not yet done anything final, I have got everything into good shape; & see my way clearly to accomplish shortly. There are so many "wheels within wheels" that one *cannot* get at, to hurry; & that retard the whole machine, that I *often* feel very impatient; but the only thing to do is oil where necessary, scan the movements that are beyond one's reach, calculate the time when the impediment will be turned around to where it can be reached, & stand ready & make preparations so as to remove it then; & not allow it, in its necessary rotation, to get beyond ones reach again, & thereby retard ones progress for another revolution. "Cut the sucker when it is young, & before the life of the tree is endangered or weakened" is my motto. . . .

I feel as a man might feel, who would be asked to describe water, to someone who had not seen it; I could tell you the use of it, the way to use it, & that it was simple. *But I am blessed!* if anyone could convey an adequate idea of it, to anyone who had not seen it.

Well! my plans are like water; as simple, as profitable, & as easily handled; & to me *now* almost as necessary as water to a thirsty traveller; We have all heard of people being wrecked & drowned in water, but where we use it only as a drink, as a motive power, & to water plants, we are safe. & where we can measure the force of every stream & current, the height of every fall & how many bucketsfull there are in the well, as (we may say) we can do here, there is not much chance of a shipwreck, for we are not liable to get out of our depth.

He likened his situation to that of a soldier who has been inside the enemy's fortress, carefully gauged his strength and what he will need to conquer him; and, he says, "*we can, & we will* accomplish it."

I feel when I think of my plans & my chances that I will never survive failure in them; I will succeed, or I will die. . . .

I dont choose to leave all that I hold dear upon earth, to spend my life amongst foreigners & strangers, & battle & "rough it out" in a wild country without knowing that I am getting or going to get a commensurate advantage, & unless we get as much of the juice out of our orange as we can, we are wasting time.

You know that the country is a rough one to live in, but you have *no* idea *how* rough, nor will you *ever* have; But if I can make enough to be able to live with my Pets [his sisters], at the end of ten years, I wont care how rough it is, or *anything else;* & if it is the roughest, at the same time it pays best, but let us start our ten years as soon as possible & crowd sail the whole journey. For I live in the anticipation of being amongst you all again, my *Much* Beloved Pets.

One of his "Pets," however, had a surprise for him. Just seven days later he reached Lincoln to find letters from his family announcing that his sister Minnie— the central figure in all his ambitions, the sister with whom he had sworn an everlasting "engagement"—was to become engaged to a young lawyer from Germany named Louis Behrens.

 # THE DANGEROUS SUMMER

IT will have become apparent that, as far as his parents were concerned, Tunstall's *modus operandi* was to set his plans before them as a proposition, meanwhile proceeding with them in fact. A further instance of this is his failure to mention at this time that work had already begun on his store in Lincoln.

He and McSween had grandiose plans for the headquarters of their "ring." On the land the attorney had purchased from L. G. Murphy & Co., which stretched along the north side of the Bonito River from near the Wortley Hotel in the west to a point opposite the Montaño store in the east, McSween planned to build an imposing home, the showpiece of Lincoln County. Adjacent to it, Tunstall would erect a store, which would also house McSween's law practice and a new enterprise, the Lincoln County Bank. Farther along, in due course, there would be a school and a Presbyterian church.

As has been remarked, entries in his account book, dated March 20, 1877, support the theory that Tunstall's mercantile business was under way by early spring.[1] One shows a payment of five hundred dollars to Otero, Sellar & Co., wholesale merchants of Las Vegas; the second is for "Freight on Store Stationery." If Tunstall was shipping in goods from Las Vegas and had stationery printed as early as March, he must have been selling goods from somewhere other than the store that today bears his name.

Exactly where this was is unknown; at one time there were upwards of twenty "stores" in Lincoln. For what it is worth, a scribbled note of Susan McSween's states, "They started their store in a small house before [the] other was built they threatened Mac's life all this time & poisoned the old man who worked on it."[2]

It is at least possible to date accurately when work was begun on Tunstall's store. His account book shows that the first expenditure on the building was incurred on June 2, 1877. This sum of $166.50 was followed by others: $191.25 on June 9, $83.00 on June 16, $110.50 on June 23, and $32.37 on the last day of the month. Another $133.14 was paid on July 7, $35.63 a week later, and $25.95 the following week. The fact that the payments were all made on Saturdays suggests they were laborers' wages, dating the construction of the store between the beginning of June and mid-July.

The building was constructed as if in anticipation of a siege. Although the three-foot-thick walls were proof against anything short of a howitzer, Tunstall specified window shutters made with a double thickness of heavy wood sandwiching a steel plate. With these closed, the building would have been well-nigh impregnable: but against what, or whose, expected attack were these precautions taken?

At the western end of the building was the room housing the Lincoln County Bank; adjacent to it, McSween's law office. Tunstall's office and bedroom were in the rear of the building at the opposite end. They were spartanly furnished: a woven wire bed, a safe, a chair and table on which were set photographs of Tunstall's family were all they contained. At the rear of the building was a corral with a ten-foot-high adobe wall, entered from the street by means of a board gate. In its northwestern corner was a smaller building that was to be used to store grain.

Of the building of the McSween house, other than that it was wholly or partially overseen by George Peppin during the summer of 1877, little is known. Even more surprisingly, no contemporary picture exists, although one would have thought such a "showpiece" must have attracted widespread attention.

The house was U-shaped, the open end looking over the Bonito; it probably had a large front parlor, a sitting room, two dining rooms, two kitchens and three bedrooms, with a corral, stable, privy, and chicken house (in 1878, the McSweens had seventy chickens) in the rear; there was a picket fence on three sides and a wall at the back. A contemporary description of a typical residential adobe of the time provides a flavor of how it might have looked:

> A tier of rooms on each side of a square, comprising as many as required, encompassing an open patio with a door or gate wide enough to admit the family coach. The back tier was generally occupied with a kitchen, provision store, or granary, and other offices. Most of the apartments except the winter rooms open into the patio, but the latter are entered through the hall. The roofs are flat—a layer of two or thre feet of earth supported by stout joists or horizontal rafters. The terrace also forms a pleasant promenade, the surrounding walls usually rising so high as to serve for a balustrade and also for a breastwork in times of trouble.
>
> The floors are constructed of beaten earth "slicked over" with soft mortar and covered with coarse carpet of domestic manufacture. Plank floors are the exception rather than the rule. The interior of each apartment is roughly plastered over with a clay mortar unmixed with lime by females who supply the place of trowels with their hands. It is then whitewashed with calcined gypsum. To obviate this [rubbing off on clothing] the parlors and family rooms are usually lined with wallpaper or calico to the height of five or six feet. The front of the house is completely plastered in a similar manner, although not always whitewashed.[3]

By the standards of the time, and especially the place, the McSween home was lavishly furnished.[4] In the carpeted parlor there were curtains on the windows and pictures on the walls, and against one wall stood an organ; there was also a center table and six stuffed chairs, a sofa, a corner rack, and a mirror. In the sitting room was a bookcase containing over a hundred law books, part of McSween's extensive library (there were another 550 books in his office). Susan McSween's sewing machine stood in one corner; there was a stove, two lamps, two clocks, a sofa, a table, and eight chairs. Later, there would also be a grand piano. The south bedroom was carpeted and curtained, with a bureau in one corner, a washstand in another, and a small table beside the bed.

McSween's office, too, was handsomely appointed: three bookcases filled with law books lined the walls; McSween's desk stood at one end of the room, and a stove in the corner; there was a carpet on the floor, a dozen chairs for clients or visitors. Bearing in mind that the McSweens had arrived in Lincoln penniless, and that every single item they owned had been bought after their arrival, Tunstall's remark that Mrs. McSween had many enemies on account of her husband's profession becomes more understandable. Not a few people in Lincoln County muttered darkly that McSween could never have honestly come by enough money to buy all these possessions.

What with supervising the building of his store, moving his cattle onto their range, and making preparations for a trip to St. Louis and Kansas City, Tunstall more than had his hands full.[5] Aided by Widenmann and a Hispanic laborer, he moved the stock from Brewer's place on Monday, May 28, covering the fifty miles to the new ranch in two days. They reached their destination after dark, and could not find the house; after a "meal" of stale bread and fresh water, they spread their blankets. Next morning, Widenmann located the house about four miles upstream, and came back to the campsite with "a man named Johnson," probably Hugh Beckwith's son-in-law, William H. Johnson, who ran a ranch on the Pecos near Seven Rivers with Wallace Olinger.

As well as his cattle, Tunstall had brought all his horses down from Brewer's ranch; these included his original grey horse and a pair of mules that had cost him $150 plus

> a large chestnut horse that cost £13 [$65], a bay pony that cost £11 [$55] & is named Billy; a Bay horse with white hind legs that cost £16.8 [$82] named Bill; a white horse that cost £10 [$50] named Sam; & a bay horse named Frank that cost £5 [$25]. These, at the prices I paid, are all *good property,* My object in getting them now, is this, the grass is good & they will all recruit, & get fat, Sam & Billy & the mules are the only sound ones at the present time. The grey will be all right again soon, the chestnut is poor, when he is fat I will trade him off either for horses or cows; Bill is a fine horse but at present rather tender footed, he needs shoing & a little rest, when he will be worth £25. Frank needs rest when he will be worth about £10. The mules are worth about £50.

Tunstall's investment in so much horseflesh had been occasioned by his learning that "to do a cow range justice, each hand should have three horses," and he wanted the animals to be fit in six months' time when he expected he would be needing them. He did not mention, although of course he knew, that by putting them on the range, he was making them a target: horse thieving was a worse plague in Lincoln County than the smallpox.

In the year before Tunstall's arrival in Lincoln County, most of the horse stealing had been done by a local gang led by a triumvirate of Mexicans named Nicas Meras, Jesús Largo, and Juan Gonzales, the latter a notable thug who had distinguished himself, if that is the word, during the Horrell War of 1873 (see chapter 4). In the summer of 1876, after stealing horses belonging to Frank Coe and Ab Saunders from their ranch on the Ruidoso, the gang was pursued by a posse of local citizens that included Coe, Saunders, "Doc" Scurlock, and Charlie Bowdre. Two of the gang, one of them Meras himself, were killed in the canyon that now bears his name.

A week or two later, Jesús Largo was captured and lodged in the inadequate pit jail in Lincoln. Hearing that Bowdre, Saunders, Coe, and Scurlock were on their way into town, Sheriff Baca decided to move his prisoner to the safer surroundings of Fort Stanton. En route, Largo was taken from him by the Ruidoso men and lynched.[6] Juan Gonzales was tracked down and killed by a sheriff's posse in Bernalillo County in November 1876. Commenting on his demise, the *New Mexican* callously remarked that

[h]is death is a benefit to honest men and those who helped him to an early grave have the good wishes of all law-abiding people. . . . The Territory is well rid of a very bad man and Bernalillo and Lincoln counties are greatly benefitted by his summary taking off.[7]

Then there was the Mes gang, operating out of a fortified *placita* on the Hondo called La Boquilla.[8] Juan Mes, José (or Jesús) Paz, and Juanito Mes and their followers preyed rapaciously on Chisum's herds, or anything else they could steal. There are conflicting stories concerning how they got their comeuppance. One version has it that the Mes boys finally went too far, killing a man named Oliver Thomas in Lincoln in December 1875. Soon thereafter a detachment of cavalry from Fort Stanton was sent to clean out La Boquilla. A running fight resulted in seven of the gang being killed, including two of the Mes brothers. The rest decamped to Puerto de Luna on the Pecos, taking along with them a number of horses stolen from the Mescalero reservation.

Version two has the imprimatur of the *Mesilla News* of August 11, 1875.

Jesus Mes, Pas Mes, Thomas Madrid and Jermin Aguirre had headquarters at the Boquilla in Lincoln county. They stole thirty head of horses and made for Mexico, arriving at San Ignacio. Juan Mes had preceded them. James McDaniel and a posse of four men followed the trail. The Mexican authorities arrested the men and horses and turned them over to McDaniel upon his word of honor that he would return them to Lincoln. Juan Mes surrendered voluntarily, but as he had no horses with him, he was not turned over, but remained in jail.

McDaniel arrived at the San Agustin ranch and asked for help in returning the men to Lincoln as he had rumors that friends in Las Cruces would attempt a rescue. At 11 p.m. a group of armed men arrived, forced McDaniel and the one guard to one side and shot the prisoners.

McDaniel reported the matter to Las Cruces. He said that he knew none of the masked party. All four were thieves and murderers who had operated from California to the end of the railway.

The *News* account begs several questions, such as what happened to the four possemen who accompanied McDaniels, said to have included Jessie Evans, Tom Bostic, and Sam Bass, the last a Hondo valley resident soon to find his own little place in the pantheon of western badmen.[9] Taking whichever version one prefers, the result comes out much the same: Lincoln County was shot of the Mes gang.

All this meant, however, was that the county's bad luck had changed to worse: its home-grown thugs were about to be replaced by a much more ruthless and professional gang from Doña Ana County. They were known as "the Boys" and— casting deep doubt upon his account of the demise of the Mes brothers—one of their founding members was that very same Jim McDaniels. The leader of this gang, which numbered between twenty-five and thirty men at full strength, was Jessie J. Evans. Other leading lights included Nicholas Provencio, Frank Baker, and Tom Hill. A number of the Boys had worked for John Chisum, and knew the back trails of Lincoln County as well as the backs of their own hands.

Although the Boys were not yet the direct threat they would later become—for the moment their operations were confined to the Mesilla area—there were more than enough deadbeats hanging around Lincoln with an eye to the main chance for Tunstall to be wary. He said goodbye to Johnson, who was taking his "boss" Beckwith half of the steer they had butchered, and left Widenmann in charge of the "ranch," probably nothing more grand than a *choza,* or dugout house.[10] "He has a pretty 'rough deal'," Tunstall reported, "the cabin is tiny & lets the air in all around & the equipment is fearfully scanty."

I saddled up the mule "Nancy" (a large reachy handsome grey mule) & started for Lincoln, over a mountain trail that runs for 35 miles without striking water; The sun was very hot, but Old "Nance" stretched away in a gallop a good part of the time, & for the rest she took a jog between a walk & a trot that covered the ground very fast; I left my carbine with Rob (as I considered he needed it the most) so all I had was my [Webley] "British Bull Dog five shooter" I am however so used to travelling about now, that I never bother my head about danger, or no danger. By about 2 P.M. I reached the first water, the heat was terrific, I went to a ranch nearby & gave the mule some corn & lay off for two hours or so, I felt quite used up. I reached Lincoln (15 miles further on) at Sundown, & set to work to get some grub for myself & "Old Nance."[11]

He went over to Sam Wortley's for supper and read his business letters; he said he knew their contents before he opened them. Then he walked over to McSween's house, carrying the letters from London that contained news of the engagement of his favorite sister Emily (Minnie) (fig. 31).

Mr & Mrs McSween had retired, so I took off my shoes & sat down to what I expected to find a nice long stretch of family news.
    You know the contents of those letters *as well as I do,* so I need not remind you of them; you know I must have been surprised, so I need not tell you *that;* I am not a *woman* so I could not weep with excitement, bereavement, surprise, & uncertainty. I am not a *Christian* so I could not kneel down & pour forth a prayer for your guidance & welfare, to the God of the Christian; I am only a man, with cold ideas as regards the unseen, but you *know, My Sister* that I love you *more dearly* than I do my own life, *or anything this world contains* & that none will delight in your joys, or grieve for your sorrows more deeply than I will, as long as we are spared to each other. That you may be happy; is my *only* wish, & whatever will tend most to your permanent welfare & *true* happiness, *that do,* & you will do as I would have you do.
    My ideas as regards marriage have become far more set during the last 18 months than they were before & (like many others) I consider that marriage & its results form the only real & lasting happiness in this World, domestic joys are the only ones that do not pall, & that outlive us.
    You know my admiration for you is unbounded, & that it would be impossible to find a man, in my estimation, too good for you; You *know* that I consider that *no* woman *breaths,* who is likely to be able to make a home as happy as you will do; & the man who undertakes to make your joy, or your sorrow through life, undertakes *that* which (if there is a hereafter) I shudder to think of.
    My feelings in the matter are so deep that I am quite unable to express them. . . . [T]ears wrung from me by my anxiety for your happiness have been streaming down my face for the last hour, I feel quite unmanned at the thought of the slightest hazard of your happiness. . . .
    If Mr Behrens proves to be, what we all expect *your* husband to be, I can ride

FIG. 31. Emily Frances Tunstall, aged twenty-seven, 1877. Photo by Elliott & Fry, Baker St., London. In this portrait study, probably taken on the eve of her wedding, "Minnie" is holding a photograph of herself as a child.

over my lonely mountains, & round the edges of precipices & amongst robbers & murderers with a lighter heart, as I can feel that you have a protector, should aught befall me.[12]

Writing to his father, who had sounded a note of caution about his lending money to the poor Mexican families, Tunstall agreed that they were "as improvident as butterflies" but that the only trick one needed to know in dealing with them was to know how much they could pay.[13] Once again Tunstall exhorted him to "strain every nerve" to raise two or three thousand pounds more and let him have the first instalment by December.

I shall do all I can to turn quickly enough not to get squeezed, but by Jove! the chances one gets here, are like passing banknotes in the street, & not picking them up.

If you could let me have that money soon, I could get so much control of this country that I could make money *very* fast. Everything appears to be working very nicely, a card I needed came to me in the last deal.

I shant be right until I have secured my land, I mean my cattle range & I might get squeezed in Decr there is no knowing.

If I had the capital out here that you have in that rotten, waterlogged business in Victoria, in ten year from now, I would go home, & live on grilled £5 notes.

If all goes right, *that is,* if you can let me have that money in the fall or spring, I shall have the chance of starting in the most profitable business I have ever yet struck, viz., The breeding of angora goats, the story of how the affair stands would be too long to tell, but the offer is as good as a fortune in ten years if I can embrace it.

That Post Tradership I am sorry to say will be open in January next, I say sorry, because I want it, have a good show to get it & you dont appear to think you can raise the coin by then, it is worth a cool £1000 per annum, & could be run on £2000 like a charm & would afford such a grip on the country that, I would make money so fast, that you would think I stole it, I believe. But unless you were here you could never understand all these things, about the army & indian contracts, the post traderships, the cattle range & the way one range secures the other, & the ranches, & the water rights, & the mills, & the squatters & a thousand other corners that have to be tucked up & w[o]rked "& then dont the grist just come in Stranger? No I guess not!" as a Yankee would say, & wink with his right eye & squirt some tobacco juice out of the left side of his mouth.

On June 8 a hasty note announced that he was off on an eight-day trip.[14] Whether there is any significance in the fact that he made the trip while Murphy, Dolan, and Riley were away in Santa Fe is not certain; since his next letter is dated June 23, it would appear it took longer than he had expected, for he had

> just returned from a tramp of 300 miles through rather a dangerous country, as the indians are out on the warpath, & the outlaws are making strong headquarters in that section, I am well acquainted with the greater part of the latter & we always meet as friends, but upholders of law & order are not much loved by them at bottom. I had a pleasant trip enough, I took an old man [Gottfried Gauss] along with me who is cooking for Dick Brewer, so I had some one to growl with, when I came to a fork in the trail, & did not know which branch to take. The trip was one I was *compelled* to take & very useful to me.[15]

It would appear he had been making further inquiries at the land office in La Mesilla, because towards the end of the letter he inserted a very unusual request.

> I want you to do something for me that requires a good deal of judgement. I want you to procure me the power of attorney of two different men to control & sell land for them in New Mexico. They ought not to be related to us, or known to each other & they must be men of honour who would not withdraw their power of attorney, as I shall get land conveyed into one of their names, hold it there for some time, then sell to the other, & finally sell it to myself, & whilst it is in their names they could, if they would, defraud us. Unless (it strikes me) they gave me an absolute power of Attorney for a *stated* time, subject to no alteration until the expiration of the time specified. Hughes [a family friend] & Smallfield [Tunstall's one-time employer] might answer our purpose. I only want one at a time.

No further mention of this scheme appears in Tunstall's correspondence or in that of Papa Tunstall which has survived: what its purpose may have been can only be conjectured.

On July 1 Tunstall reported that Widenmann had ridden over from the Peñasco for treatment: he had contracted smallpox and "just managed to reach here."[16] It must have been a rough ride, since the early symptoms of the disease are headaches, vomiting, backache, and a temperature of 103 degrees. It was a good fifty miles from the Peñasco, and the temperature was 95 in the shade.

In those days, treatment for smallpox was considerably less than sophisticated.[17] The three rocks upon which frontier medicine stood were "purge, blister and bleed." A "certain, never failing remedy" published in the *New Mexican* recommended mixing an ounce of cream of tartar into a pint of water and drinking it at intervals: the result was no doubt violent vomiting and sweating, thought then to be beneficial. Tunstall had his own methods. "My first move was to put him into my bed, & administer a good dose of castor oil, the next to put his feet into hot water, & mix him a sour drink. I kept up the oil & vinegar treatment, for four days, abused him like a pickpocket all the time & now he is well, all but having lost his appetite & found a horse's."[18]

Such rapid recovery is unusual in smallpox, which usually takes two or three weeks to run its course. It is tempting to wonder whether it was something else Widenmann was sick of: the desolate loneliness of life on Tunstall's ranch, for example.

Apart from Widenmann's illness, Tunstall reported, business was "all right so far." He had made some "good quick turns, & profitable & economical ones too." No mention was made of news he must have read in the *New Mexican* (doubtless breathing a huge sigh of relief at his luck as he read it), that half to two thirds of the sheep in California had died of starvation during the current season.

> I expect to drive a nail in the course of two days, that is worth the driving "*You! bet! your boots!!*" & if I can but drive one more where I want it, we shall have the whip hand with a vengeance.
>
> I am about to make a business trip to St. Louis Missouri I shall start in a few days. I have decided *to do* in more lines than I at first intended, I find that it will be necessary, to bring in the right class of customers. The trip there, will be a terrible one, "*mais il faut soufrir pour etre beau.*"
>
> My health is A.1. & my business seems to promise the fairest possible. I am under those circumstances of course in good spirits. I dont mean to infer that I have no earthly vexations, for *I have*, & their name is Legion, but I see no impassable barriers ahead & that is the principal thing.

Once again, there is no knowing what his "nail driving" refers to: unless it is some unspecified arrangements he had with various taxpayers to advance them money. The 1877 tax assessments had been completed in May and certified by Juan Patrón, chairman of the county commissioners. The principal taxpayers were:

Robert D. Hunter	$3,059.75
J. J. Dolan & Co.	336.65
Dowlin Bros.	282.44
L. G. Murphy	175.24
J. H. Blazer	119.05
Casey Estate	116.21
P. Coghlan	107.35
A. A. McSween	105.95

These eight taxpayers contributed $4,302.64 of the total county tax assessment of $5,248.06. Most of the other property owners in the county paid less than $30 each.[19]

The McSween-Tunstall account book indicates a debit of Tunstall's account, listed "R. D. Hunter Taxes" in the amount of $3,059.75; of $121.05 listed "Taxes J. H. Blazer"; of $51.11 for John Copeland's taxes; of $24.87 covering John Newcomb's; and nominal amounts in the names of Romero y Trujillo, Brewer, Corbet, McKittrick & Chisum, Gonzales, Ellis, and Daniel Dow. The total involved is $3,321.01.

On July 2, before he left for the East, Tunstall wrote McSween a check, drawn on his St. Louis bank, for two thousand dollars. He also arranged for a gold draft on Boatman's Exchange & Savings Bank in Kansas City in the sum of one thousand dollars to be paid to the lawyer. These appear as the eighth and ninth items on the debit side of the McSween-Tunstall notebook. McSween deposited the two-thousand-dollar check in his Santa Fe bank account on July 19; the draft appears as one of two in McSween's account early in August. The second of these is probably the Chisum & Hunter draft that appears as item eleven in the notebook.[20]

What the purpose of this financial manipulation was can no longer be ascertained; in the cases of Hunter and Blazer, Tunstall was probably "hiring out" his money at good interest rather than leave it lying idle in the bank. His loans to Lincoln residents were perhaps made with an ulterior motive: if they defaulted, he could foreclose on their properties. All this, of course, lies in the realm of speculation.

There is, however, no speculation about the fact that on July 31, his account now sufficiently in credit, McSween drew a check on the First National Bank of Santa Fe for $1,545.13 in favor of William Brady, sheriff and ex-officio collector of taxes for Lincoln County. It has been suggested that Brady endorsed the check and handed it to the county court, which used the money to pay in full the civil suit brought by J. J. Dolan & Co. against Mrs. Casey, although there is no such endorsement on the check, and it is difficult to understand why the county court would use money collected for taxes to settle a civil suit.[21]

Nevertheless someone, either the court or Sheriff Brady, handed the check to J. J. Dolan & Co., because when it finally turned up canceled, it bore a further endorsement by John H. Riley, showing that the money had been used to pay for cattle purchased by the House from Underwood & Nash at Seven Rivers. Upon this fact John Tunstall would later pounce, with far-reaching results, in defense of his friend McSween.

All this, however, was in the future. At the moment, Tunstall set off for the East

> under the most favorable auspices. I shall have a very strong letter to "Dunn's commercial Agency" who are *the* reference of the whole United States, also to Messrs Hunter & Evans who control the price of cattle *entirely* west of the Missouri River. The cashier at my bank at St Louis is [Robert P. Eagle] a Suffolk man & my balance there is pretty large at present, so I guess I am apt to find people to post me as to the markets, facility of trading, shipping &c &c when I get there. I shant stop half a day longer than I am obliged, though I shall drive nails enough before I leave, to hold everything together for 12 months at least.[22]

He ruminated philosophically on the change in his thinking brought about by the news of Minnie's engagement: he was still trying to get used to the idea of returning to England to find her married, and quite possibly, to find that his "pets" had also found homes of their own, leaving him "the lonely one of the outfit."

> I have however fought alone (though not unaided) for so long, & shall by that time, have done without sympathy for so long, that I shant command much pity. And in the vista of the future I see myself reading Hood's poem [*The Bachelor's Dream*] of "What do you think of that my cat? What do you think of that my dog?" with a curl on my lip as I look around my "growlery", & think over the vicissitudes & changes of life, & look back at the day dreams of youth, when Dear Min was to run my house, & the grounds were to be enclosed in so many miles of oak palings; & then I guess my needs will be smaller & the objects I shall take pleasure in, very different from what I used to think they would be. I feel like an *Old, Old* Bachelor *already* & my mind runs only on dollars & cents, & the chances of making them, & dodging the bullets the while. I have entirely lost my liking for dogs, I think I dont care much about horses, I always use the worst one I can find, that is able to do my work, so as to spare the better ones. . . . I enjoy every meal I eat, if it be but bread & coffee (& sugar & milk, are rare additions to the extract of the bean of Arabia, in New Mexico). I never hanker after the flesh pots, or wish for finer diet, & all other

appetites are equally under control, so you may imagine that my tastes & inclinations are no hindrance to my success in business.

My present idea is to fight this thing out on my present line for ten years, live for nothing but money during that time, & if I have enough to retire on, *do it*, & I daresay a short apprenticeship will suffice to teach me the way to employ leisure agreably.

It does not seem to have occurred to him that it could come out any other way. But the "gombeen men"—the Irish epithet for loansharks—of Lincoln County were planning to drive a few nails of their own. Lacking the financial muscle to compete with Tunstall, Dolan and Riley hit upon another strategy: they would "steal the Englishman poor." To help them realize this aim, they looked towards Doña Ana County.

 # BATTLE LINES

SUMMER, 1877.

In Taos and the Rio Arriba country, grasshoppers were four inches deep on the ground.[1] In a letter to the *New Mexican*, Antonio Joseph reported that every trace of vegetation was destroyed and that the people were starving. Other letters from Abiquiu and Santa Cruz confirmed the devastation: corn, melons, fruit trees, everything gone. The Pecos valley seems to have been more fortunate; returning to Santa Fe from a fishing trip, John Elkins informed the newspaper that the crops down there were in a flourishing condition.

A new weekly newspaper, the *Mesilla Valley Independent*, began publication; an annual subscription was three dollars. In one of its earliest issues, that of July 28, a contribution from the irrepressible Ash Upson continued the notion that apart from the smallpox, which was sweeping the county from east to west,

> everything has been very quiet in this vicinity—disgustingly, aggravatingly so. . . . It is probable that [Chisum] will drive over 10,000 head of cattle this year, and mark and brand near 20,000 head of calves. His principal, Col. R. D. Hunter, has already sent for and received about 3,000 head of select beef cattle, which are on their way to Kansas. The remainder will go to Arizona.

Upson was doing Chisum no favors: advertising that herds of cattle would be coming through the Mesilla valley was like sending Jessie Evans and the Boys an engraved invitation to steal them.

Wily old John Chisum knew the Boys as well as most: many of them had worked for him at one time or another.[2] A herd that started for Arizona in mid-July was routed across the Rio Grande at Fort Craig, something like a hundred miles above the usual crossing point.[3] Foiled in their plans to steal this consignment, the Boys let it be known that when the next Chisum herd came their way they planned to steal it "if it takes 100 men to accomplish the job."[4] In fact, the *Independent* reported, they had already gone so far as to sell the cattle at ten dollars per head in advance.

If this news daunted Chisum or his longtime herd boss Emery Peter, they evinced no sign of it. The next Arizona-bound herd, consisting of about twenty-five hundred head, was started for Sulphur Springs early in August. Once it was on its way, Chisum and his neighbor George Hogg rode up to Lincoln to visit the McSweens; Chisum was said to be especially fond of the lawyer's wife.

As Upson had remarked, things were fairly quiet in Lincoln—by Lincoln standards. But the battle lines had been drawn, for all that. On the one side were L. G. Murphy and Jimmy Dolan, a powerful partnership of arrogance and shrewdness, strength and cunning. Murphy had learned, in the army and out of it, that you had to back what you said with muscle; Dolan knew how, with a wink and a nod and a nudge of the elbow, to work people around to his way of thinking and how, when they wouldn't budge, to manipulate them.

On the other side were Tunstall and McSween, almost equally powerful. Tunstall was clever, ambitious, and rich. Taking every leaf he turned out of the House's book, he intended to be as much the boss of Lincoln County as Murphy once had been, but hid that intention behind a facade of English dissimulation. McSween, his none-too-honest lawyer and partner, was equally ambitious for position and money, and not too particular about how he got either, willing to show Tunstall how to bend the law to their own purpose.

To the poverty-stricken farmers of Lincoln County Tunstall's advent must have seemed like a miracle: here was a man who would pay them a fair price for their crops, advance them money when times were hard, make available to them a range of goods from the East such as Lincoln had never before seen. Whether, once he had the whip hand, Tunstall's attitude would have remained quite as benevolent is another matter.

The summer advanced. George Peppin and his laborers finished the McSween house, a palace by Lincoln standards. The Tunstall store was fast taking shape fifty yards farther along the street. Pat Coghlan, Jimmy Dolan (just back from his trip to Santa Fe, accompanied by William and Mrs. Rosenthal), and Juan Patrón were among those bidding for the contracts to supply forage to the military at Fort Stanton.[5] John Tunstall had departed for St. Louis soon after the Fourth of July holiday, leaving McSween and Widenmann in charge of his interests.

If the accusations made against her have any foundation in fact, and there is absolutely no reason to suppose that they did not, what was most occupying the attention of the citizens of Lincoln town at this juncture was the scandalous behavior of Susan McSween (fig. 32).[6] Almost from the time of her arrival, her actions and her ostentation had shocked and alienated the largely Mexican female population.

Lincoln tradition has it that Alexander McSween was impotent, and that as a consequence his wife took her pleasures elsewhere. Saturnino Baca was to testify that she "had deservedly borne the reputation of being a profane, lewd, and unreliable woman" since 1876, and that he had heard her charged to her face in the public street and in front of her husband, with having come from a brothel to Lincoln. He also reported hearing her say that a woman who had a pretty face and a good appearance was a fool if she did not make money when she could get a chance.

While he was building McSween's house, George Peppin, who did not hesitate to label Mrs. McSween "a common prostitute" on one occasion and "bad, unprincipled, lewd and untruthful" on another, told her that her boldness was going to get some man killed on her account.

"You know me to be a bad woman and think hard of me," she is alleged to have said, "but you do not know what is the matter between me and Mac."

Whatever it was, there seems little doubt that tall, slender, handsome, red-haired thirty-two-year-old Susan McSween was also vain, headstrong, proud, and promiscuous. That summer, she is said to have outraged local opinion by brazenly conducting an affair with twenty-one-year-old Francisco Gomez, who was working for Peppin, taking her pleasures in the brush near the river and by all accounts making little effort to conceal them.

If the allegations made about his wife have any foundation in fact—and in considering them, not only who made them but the reason for their having been made must be closely examined—it is difficult to understand how Alexander McSween was able to function so successfully as an attorney. It seems most unlikely that respectable citizens would have put their legal affairs into the hands of a man whose wife was a common trollop; that being so, the accusations leveled against Susan McSween may well be no more than the vicious lies she maintained to her dying day they were. It is certainly almost impossible to believe that Taylor Ealy, the straitlaced Presbyterian missionary who brought his family to Lincoln the following year, would have remained under the same roof as a woman with a reputation as scarlet as that imputed to Susan McSween.

FIG. 32. Susan E. McSween. She had this picture and the portrait of McSween copied at the studios of her nephew Kirkness in Baltimore, which suggests that both may have been taken at the time of their marriage, when she was twenty-seven.

McSween himself was becoming increasingly preoccupied with the complex affairs of the Fritz estate.[7] At the urging and with the cooperation of co-administrator Charles Fritz, Probate Judge Florencio Gonzales had written to the New York lawyers, Donnell, Lawson & Co., instructing them, after deduction of their fees for collection, to

> deposit the amount remaining at the First National Bank at Santa Fe to the credit of Charles Fritz, administrator of the estate of Emil Fritz, deceased, and subject to the order of the Probate Court of the County of Lincoln and the Territory of New Mexico, as previously ordered by the said Probate Court and agreed upon and understood by all the parties, any documents and directions sent you by A. A. McSween notwithstanding, and such directions and documents are hereby revoked and amended.

This was no longer possible: in a letter dated July 19, Donnell, Lawson had advised McSween that $7,148.49, the proceeds of the Emil Fritz life insurance policy, had been credited to him.[8] Even allowing for the firm's not insubstantial charges, Donnell, Lawson had done considerably better for the estate than the settlement of $5,800 originally proposed.

McSween advised the court that he had already been paid the money, and asked for its assistance, before he made settlement, in obtaining an audit of the books of L. G. Murphy & Co. with a view to ascertaining the value of the estate's interest in that firm.[9] This audit Jimmy Dolan, already in sufficient financial trouble to be borrowing a thousand from Tunstall, not unnaturally resisted.

The court ruled in McSween's favor, and appointed three examiners: Morris J. Bernstein, Juan Patrón, and McSween. Dolan enlisted the aid of Charles Fritz and Emilie (Fritz) Scholand in continuing to resist the audit, whereupon McSween, certain that if Dolan got his hands on the money the other heirs would never see a penny of it, formally petitioned Probate Judge Florencio Gonzales for release from his responsibility as a bondsman.

He gave as his reasons first, the fact that Emilie Scholand had left Lincoln County the preceding November and despite his written requests would not return to perform her duties as co-administrator of the estate. Second, that neither she nor Charles Fritz had taken any effective steps to wind up the estate. Third, that both were incompetent to handle its assets; and finally, that if they were permitted to do so, they would misapply them, leaving their sureties—himself in the sum of eight thousand dollars—to make good their defalcation.

Judge Gonzales was faced with an impasse.[10] McSween had the money but would not pay it over. Dolan, Fritz, and Emilie Scholand could petition the court as many times as they wished: McSween could continue to refuse payment on the grounds already stated. There, for the moment, at least, the matter rested.

Meanwhile, what of Henry McCarty, or Henry Antrim? As we have already seen, his horse-thieving escapades in Arizona had resulted in quite a lot of local notoriety. Nevertheless, he remained in the area of Camp Grant, in the heart of Apachería, throughout the summer of 1877.

On Friday, August 17, he was in Bonita, the civilian settlement hard by the military establishment, and got into an altercation outside a *cantina* with a thirty-two-year-old Irishman named Frank Cahill.[11] It has been variously stated that he was a soldier, a blacksmith, and that he was black, but apparently none of these is true. Be that as it may, Cahill and the Kid collided outside Adkins's *cantina*, and the argument turned into a brawl. Cahill had picked on the youngster before; Henry wasn't having any more. When Cahill grabbed him, the Kid shot him in the belly. The fracas was reported in the *Arizona Weekly Star* six days later.

> Frank P. Cahill was shot by Henry Antrim alias Kid at Camp Grant on the 17th, and died on the 18th. The following are the dying words of the deceased:
> I, Frank P. Cahill, being convinced that I am about to die, do make the following as my final statement: My name is Frank P. Cahill. I was born in the county and town of Galway, Ireland. Yesterday, Aug. 17th, 1877, I had some trouble with Henry Antrem, otherwise known as Kid, during which he shot me. I had called him a pimp, and he called me a s—— of a b——, we then took hold of each other: I did not hit him, I think: saw him go for his pistol, and tried to get hold of it, but could not and he shot me in the belly. I have a sister named Margaret Flannigan living at East Cambridge, Mass., and another named Kate Conden, living in San Francisco.

As always, there are conflicting versions of what happened next.[12] One has it that the Kid made no attempt to get away; Miles L. Wood, thirty-nine, a Canadian who had come to Arizona in 1869, enlisted the aid of a local rancher, arrested him at a nearby boardinghouse, and lodged him in the army guardhouse. Wood was magistrate and justice of the peace at Bonita; it was he who conducted the inquest on Cahill.[13]

A couple of days later, Tucson's second newspaper, the weekly *Arizona Citizen*, published an account of the Cahill killing.[14] This added the news that Cahill was about thirty-two, that a coroner's jury had found the killing "criminal and unjustifiable, and that 'Henry Antrim alias Kid' [was] guilty thereof." It did not, however, give any indication of what had happened to him. If he was lodged in jail, it certainly was not the military one: no civilian was put in the Camp Grant guardhouse between March and November of that year.[15]

A telegram from Maj. Charles E. Compton, commanding, replying to an inquiry made by deputy U.S. marshal W. J. Osborn in Tucson, seems to support the likelier proposition that after the Kid killed Cahill, he simply stole a horse and skinned out.[16] "Cahill was not killed on the military reservation. His Murderer Antrim, alias 'Kid', was allowed to escape and I believe is still at large."

So the Kid was on the run once more, this time with a murder charge hanging over him. He took to the owlhoot trail and slipped over the border into New Mexico Territory. There were so many criminals there one more would not make the slightest difference. By October the Kid was stealing horses wherever and whenever he could find any. Finding a market for them, however, was another matter. The best place to do this was in the Mesilla valley.

The area around La Mesilla might well be called the garden of New Mexico, but it was also renowned as the headquarters of the man who was known as the "King of the Rustlers," John W. Kinney. Kinney was the head of what was arguably the largest horse- and cattle-rustling operation in the Territory. His "boys" stole all over west Texas, eastern Arizona, and southern New Mexico. His ranch outside of town had "the reputation for being the headquarters and rendezvous for all the evil doers in the county," according to the *Independent*.[17]

If, as tradition insists, the Kid joined Jessie Evans and the Boys down at La Mesilla, he did so at a particularly volatile moment, as this item in the *New Mexican*, datelined Socorro, August 9, indicates:

Some parties just up from the Mimbres district assert that the gang of thieves organized in and about Mesilla numbers 25; that they have threatened to take the life of Mr. A. J. Fountain of Mesilla; that they propose to injure the telegraph line while committing plunder, and just now it is rumored that they are watching the coach with bullion which left Silver City on Tuesday last. They are pictured up as the terror of that vicinity.

The Boys were a phenomenon unknown up to that time in New Mexico, the nearest thing the Territory had to organized crime. Before proceeding to the story of the calamitous effect of their descent upon Lincoln County, it is instructive to examine their careers in a little more detail.

The "prime men" of the gang, according to the *Independent*, were Tom Hill, Frank Baker, Bob Martin, George Davis, George "Buffalo Bill" Spawn, and Nicolas Provencio.[18] All of them had half a dozen aliases. The leader of the gang was Jessie Evans, twenty-six, alias Graham, alias Davis, a Texas hardcase who is said to have originated in Missouri (fig. 33). By his own account Jessie arrived in New Mexico in 1872, working for Borrowson and Grier, and in the summer of 1873 for Chisum. A couple of years of punching cows obviously convinced him there was an easier way to make a living; by 1875 he was already well known as

FIG. 33. Jessie J. Evans. Date and photographer unknown; the original is a tintype. Unverified; identified as Evans by W. G. Carrell of Saginaw, Mich., to Walter Noble Burns, April 15, 1930. The identity of the woman is unknown.

a cattle and horse thief. And killer: he was a probable participant in the August 1875 murder of the Mes brothers at Shedd's ranch, along with his longtime sidekick, Jim McDaniels.

On New Year's Eve, 1875, Kinney, Evans, McDaniels, and Charles Ray "Pony" Diehl got into a brawl with some troopers from Fort Selden at a local *baile*; the soldiers thrashed them and threw them out of the place.[19] The quartet slunk off, tanked up on tonsil paint, and returned to the dance hall around midnight when, in best Texas tradition, they opened fire through the windows: a soldier, shot through the forehead, and a civilian, shot through the breast, died immediately. Another civilian and three soldiers were severely wounded; one of these later died.

Little more than two weeks later, on January 19, at Las Cruces, a man named Quirino Fletcher made the mistake of boasting publicly that a few months earlier, he and three other Mexicans had killed and robbed two Texans in Mexico.[20] That night at around 10:30, somebody put six bullets into Fletcher. The *New Mexican* offered a hypothesis:

> He had returned escaping from prison in Chihuahua, where he had been imprisoned for the killing of Mansfield. As several Texas friends of Mansfield are in town, it is supposed that Quirino may have come to his death by some of them.

No one was in any doubt as to the identity of Mansfield's "Texas friends"; but when witnesses of the shooting tried to obtain action from a justice of the peace, the first one claimed to be too sick and the second "could not be roused up at all."[21] (The Doña Ana County grand jury eventually indicted Evans, Samuel Blanton, and a man known only by his first name, Morris.) Nobody wanted to be thought the dead man's sympathizer lest Jessie Evans and his cronies take it personally, so Fletcher's body lay where it had fallen in the street until next morning, when Mr. C. Duper of the Montezuma Hotel had someone carry it inside.

Throughout 1876 and the early part of 1877, the Boys stole as they pleased throughout southeastern New Mexico, west Texas, and the Rio Grande valley. No one lifted a finger against them until the summer, when Col. Albert J. Fountain, editor of the *Independent*, decided it was time to stand up and be counted (fig. 34).

FIG. 34. Albert Jennings Fountain, aged about thirty, ca. 1868. Photo by F. Parker, El Paso.

The first issue of his paper appeared on June 23. By mid-July, Fountain was blasting the Boys mercilessly. Under the masthead "A Fair Warning," he wrote a scathing article that offered the Boys twelve ropes and twelve cottonwood trees if room could not be found for them in the county jail.[22] Not content with this, he went on to ridicule a *Mesilla News* report that Evans, Nicholas Provencio, Frank Baker, and two other "outraged citizens" had been arrested and "ruthlessly imprisoned" by the Mexican authorities while in Paso del Norte (later Juarez) on "important business."[23]

Fountain knew—and knew his readers knew—what kind of "important business" Jessie Evans and the Boys had on the far side of the Mexican border: that was where they disposed of all their stolen horses. What kind of important business, Fountain wondered, required its principals to conduct it under the assumed names of Jessie Williams (Evans), Frank Johnson (Baker), and Mariano Baltier (Provencio)?

Such effrontery was not to be tolerated by such bravos as the Boys: Evans and Baker sent word to Fountain that they planned to kill him on sight. Fountain turned for protection to Sheriff Mariano Barela and District Attorney Rynerson; the latter telegraphed Governor Axtell for authority to call out the militia. In short order Axtell's authority arrived.

Word was received that John Kinney had gathered together "a band of desperadoes said to number from 10 to 30 at his Ranch, he crossed river and disarmed teamsters of [wagon] train about an hour ago."[24]

A posse of fifty picked men set out to arrest Kinney, but Kinney had planted a fifth columnist among them and was long gone when the posse arrived. Next day Fountain telegraphed his friend John Crouch that there was

> a formidable band of thieves in this county. Their headquarters are at Kinney's. They include Jessie Evans, Frank Baker, Nicholas Provencia and several Texans recently from Pecos. . . . [T]hey sent word to me that I would be shot down on sight, they are all together and are determined to make things hot as they call it. They say they will reenact the Pecos War in this valley, other good citizens have been threatened with assassination. I took out a warrant yesterday against Kinney, Baker and Evans, a posse was summoned to assist in making arrest, the posse was held in this town three hours and runners were sent out who notified accused persons of our intentions; of course we made no arrests. Kinney has been riding day and night through the county, gathering all members of band, he publicly threatens to raid Mesilla and kill certain men. There is great excitement here.

The "excitement" resulted in the Boys deciding on a change of climate for a while, and Doña Ana County's gain became Lincoln's loss. What this short essay graphically illustrates is the yawning chasm that lay between the characters of the Boys and the Englishman. Tunstall was later to delude himself into believing that he had an understanding with these rapacious thieves, and even that he was on good terms with them. He might as well have expected to have an understanding with a school of barracuda.

So in late July, with the Mesilla valley closed to them, the Boys transferred their activities to Lincoln County, perhaps with the implicit encouragement of the House. Knowing his methods, it is not too difficult to imagine a scenario in which Jimmy Dolan pointed out the rich pickings awaiting the rustlers in Lincoln County: the vast cattle herds of Chisum, Hunter & Evans; the herds of horses owned by the Mescalero Apaches; Tunstall's growing operation. It would be easy street for the Boys, especially since they could be reasonably assured that Sheriff Brady would interfere as little as possible, and the House would buy every head of cattle they could steal.

Whatever the reasons, the Boys headed up the trail almost immediately. Whether the tough little teenage killer they called "the Kid" was with them cannot be ascertained; he does not appear in the historical record again until October 1877.

When John Chisum and George Hogg arrived for their stay at McSween's newly completed house early in August, not only were the lawyer and his wife living there, but also Mrs. McSween's sister Elizabeth and her husband David P. Shield (figs. 35, 36).

The Shield family had left Osceola, Mo., where Shield was a prominent attorney, persuaded by Susan McSween that the mountain air of New Mexico would mend her sister's health as it had McSween's, and by the promise of a partnership for David Shield.[25] Susan McSween bought Tunstall's ambulance and mules and sent it up to Trinidad to bring them down to Lincoln. The Shields and their five children—the oldest, George, was sixteen, the youngest a babe in arms—occupied the eastern wing of the house; McSween and his wife the west.

On August 5, with John Chisum and George Hogg as their guests, this extended family sat down to Sunday dinner, unaware of the fact that a hundred yards down the street, shooting trouble was brewing.[26] Frank Freeman, who had left Lincoln two jumps ahead of the law the preceding December, had returned to the area. He joined forces with Charlie Bowdre on the Ruidoso, and the two of them rode into Lincoln, where they forced José Montaño to open up his store and provide them with liquor.

FIG. 35. David Pugh Shield. Date and photographer unknown.

> [T]hey then commenced smashing things generally, breaking lamps, bottles, glasses, etc. Meeting with an innocent sergeant from Fort Stanton and there being no other victim at hand Freeman, who had one of his murder fits on, took the sergeant by the hand in a friendly manner, and with his other hand reached around and placed the muzzle of his pistol at the back of the sergeant's head and fired. Fortunately, the wound was not mortal; Freeman, supposing that he had killed the sergeant, accompanied by Bowdre rushed through the streets of the town shooting at every object that met their view, Freeman shouting that "his name was Frank Freeman and no twenty men could arrest him", that "he had his man for all meals in the day and that he intended to kill every man in town that he didn't like". Thus they paraded the streets, shooting and yelling like demons. After awhile another idea seemed to strike them. Coolly reloading their weapons they proceeded to the residence of A. A. McSween, attorney at law, a prominent and good citizen, where John S. Chisum was stopping as a guest. Two ladies and five children were also in the house. They fired a number of shots promiscuously in the house, broke a window open, and forced an entrance. The inmates fled for shelter. The ruffians then riddled a sewing machine with bullets, and shouted that "if John S. Chisum or his corpse was not turned over to them, they would burn the d—d house down". About this time a Mexican servant in the employ of Mr. McSween obtained a firearm and discharged it at the ruffians, slightly grazing Freeman in the arm, whereupon they ingloriously fled, and made their way to the store of J. J. Dolan & Co., where they had intruded and left their horses on their arrival in town.

Sheriff William Brady, summoned from his farm east of town, hastily obtained arrest warrants, raised a posse, and went after the two miscreants.

> About this time Freeman leaped into his saddle and declared his intention of shooting every man he met. Brady arrested Bowdre, and Freeman interfered and pulled his six shooter. Brady done the same, and would have shot Freeman but for the interference of Bowdre. Messrs. J. J. Dolan and J. B. Mathews then came to the assistance of Brady and probably saved his life. A scuffle ensued, resulting in the sheriff mastering the situation. Freeman and Bowdre were turned over to the posse. The citizens being greatly enraged and excited, Sheriff Brady deemed it prudent to apply to Col. George E. Purington, commanding officer at Fort Stanton, for an escort to take the prisoners to the fort for safe keeping.[27]

FIG. 36. Elizabeth Hummer Shield. Date and photographer unknown, but probably late 1880s in Las Vegas, N.M. Elizabeth Shield was Susan McSween's elder sister.

This is not quite the full story. What actually happened was that Bowdre knocked Brady down and Freeman was about to kill him when Dolan and Mathews (who had his own reasons for wanting Freeman locked up) intervened. The "enraged and excited" citizens were all set to lynch the two men; Brady forestalled this by calling in the military. Taken before Justice Wilson, the two thugs were required to post bail: five hundred in Bowdre's case, which he was able to furnish, and a thousand in Freeman's, which he could not. Freeman was carted off to the fort by the cavalry; George Coe suggests the black troopers were all set to lynch Freeman themselves—as well they might have been, bearing in mind his boast that he was a "nigger killer"—but somehow he managed to escape from them en route and head for the hills.[28]

About a week later one of Freeman's sidekicks, a man known only as Armstrong, rode into Lincoln, tanked up on Double Anchor, and commenced firing off his gun, yelling that he was on his way to meet Freeman, and they were coming back to burn the place down, aided by "a desperate character from Grant county" known as "Nelson from the Gila."[29] One of Sheriff Brady's deputies, Francisco Romero y Valencia, obtained a warrant, raised a posse, and went after Armstrong. The desperado fled towards the river, shooting as he ran; whereupon he was shot down. The *Independent* continues the story:

> Fearing that the [Freeman] band on the Ruidoso would now carry their threats into execution, the sheriff took ten of the best citizens of the county as a posse and determined to endeavor to arrest the outlaws at their rendezvous. Having obtained reliable information that they had a comparatively large and well-armed force, Sheriff Brady deemed it prudent to apply to Col. Purington for a military force, and that officer kindly responded by sending Lieutenant G. W. Smith and fifteen cavalrymen to assist the sheriff. The party proceeded to the ranch of Charles Bowdre on the Ruidoso, which was known to be the rendezvous of the outlaws.
>
> Upon arriving at this place the sheriff deployed his men on each side of the creek. His presence was soon discovered by Freeman, who rushed out and fired at Brady—and missed. He then sprang on to his horse which stood ready saddled. In an instant the horse fell, riddled with bullets. Freeman, still unhurt, endeavored to make his escape through a cornfield, firing as he retreated. He was pursued and killed. Bowdre escaped by wading down the bed of the stream; others of the party were captured and taken to Lincoln where they were examined and committed for trial.

Who the "others of the party" were—only the name of Nicholas Provencio, well known to be one of the Boys, appears in the *Independent's* account—is not known, but that they were all hogs from the same wallow is apparent because, within days, the Boys launched a raid on the Mescalero Indian Agency. Frederick C. Godfroy, the agent, reported that

> [o]n the evening of August 11, it being yet daylight, some of these men made a descent on the agency herd under our very noses. Having no arms to furnish my employees, it was impossible to pursue the thieves until assistance had been obtained; so I dispatched my clerk [Morris Bernstein] to Fort Stanton with a requisition on Captain Purington, the post commander, for troops to pursue the robbers. The next morning a detachment of fifteen men under command of Lieutenant Davenport started from the post. The pursuit by the military was unsuccessful, in spite of their promptitude, on account of severe rainstorms having obliterated the trail.[30]

Once again, Lincoln County was in turmoil, armed men riding, danger at every fork of the trail. Someone signing himself "Eyewitness" wrote to the *Independent* from Lincoln on August 16 to report that there had been "a fight between the outlaws and the troops. We do not know of the result except that the thieves got whipped. Nelson was at the head of the band who no doubt will be run down into your country. We are organizing a militia company here for the protection of our lives and property."[31]

Whether this skirmish actually took place is open to doubt. Nelson—no doubt the one from the Gila—does not appear again in the annals of Lincoln County, unless he be the John Nelson who appeared two years later among the predators known as the Rustlers, whose activities would make the exploits of the Boys look like schoolboy pranks.

No sooner had things calmed down a little than trouble flared up again at Dowlin's Mill, where Chisum's Arizona-bound herd was making its slow way southwest.[32] Some of the Jinglebob riders got hold of a supply of whiskey. On August 23, one of them, Johnny Ewer, shot himself in the leg and had to be rushed off to the hospital at Fort Stanton. Next a half-Comanche man named Ramon Garcia, alias Capitan, got blind drunk and shot J. M. Franklin in the back, killing him instantly. Garcia was captured by some men from Mesilla and taken away by them to be lodged in the guardhouse at Stanton. He never reached the fort.

While all this mayhem was going on, John Tunstall was in St. Louis, whither he had gone after a brief stay in Kansas City.[33] Using as his base of operations Griswold, Clement & Scudder's Lindell Hotel, he made extensive purchases of stock for his store in Lincoln (fig. 37). He laid out $1,062.55 for goods at Edward Martin & Co., "manufacturers & wholesale dealers in clothing & gents' furnishing goods" on Washington Ave.; $417.50 at H. A. Wells & Co., "importers & jobbers in china, glass and queensware" at 423 N. Fifth St.; $1,464.10 on haberdashery at Dodd, Brown & Co. He also bought more than $500 worth of firearms from H. Folsom & Co., and made arrangements for the shipment of all his purchases to Lincoln via Otero, Sellar of Las Vegas. "I came out here to buy goods," he told his father on August 1, "& see so many things that I could sell to advantage, that I have to be horribly careful not to buy too much; it makes me feel almost nervous, though my health & youth dont allow my nerves to trouble me much. I am in magnificent health; I never felt better."[34]

There is much in these letters on the subject of his father's business in Victoria,

FIG. 37. The Tunstall store ca. 1886. Photographer unknown. This picture was taken during the time the store was being operated by Jimmy Dolan. Probably the closest likeness to the way it looked at the time of the war.

and the impending marriage of his sister Minnie. There was even a rare touch of homesickness in one passage.

> I think a great deal about my two Dear *Little* Sisters, & wonder often how much longer the waves of fate will keep my feet from the Shores of Dear Old England & what sort of an idea they have & are forming of their "rough back woodsman of a brother" & whether they will rush up to this mass of gipsey colored humanity clothed in buck skin, & hold up their dear little fair faces to be kissed, or whether they will shrink a little from me, & feel that they could love me ever so much better at a distance. I look at all the little girls I see, & wonder if my two pets resemble them, & if so? how much?

His affairs were progressing all right, he said; he was dining that night with his banker, Robert Eagle, an Englishman from Bury St. Edmunds. He liked St. Louis "better than any American City I have visited so far; it seems to be less different to London somehow or other, though it is laid off with all the streets at right angles like any other American town."[35] Unfortunately

> [t]he air here is too relaxing, after *our* dry, crisp air, that braces every fiber & tissue; that I feel very much weakened & oppressed by it, & in addition the fruit or the water or something or other has disagreed with me, with the usual result, nearly all the time I have been here, which has not added to the pleasure of being within the pale of civilization again.
> . . . On the whole I shant sigh when I leave this wilderness of walls & streets (pretty as they may be) & return to coarse food, fine air, outdoor exercise & within

the sound of the roar of one of the leaders of the herd of cattle I expect to call mine before long.

I expect to leave here in about 4 days, I have been delayed by the contrariety of some men who need killing very badly & live at Lincoln.

Quite what contrariety Dolan and Riley were up to—they were undoubtedly the "men who needed killing very badly"—is not clear, but Tunstall's words indicate just how much his own attitudes had been altered by the environment in which he found himself. The House in fact negotiated a loan of a thousand dollars from Tunstall during his absence: the arrangements were made in his behalf by McSween on or about August 29.[36] This was probably the "point very near my heart" Tunstall referred to in a letter from Kansas City: to have Dolan and Riley over a financial barrel was solid proof that his master plan was working.

He left for New Mexico on August 27: a scrawled postscript to the letter of August 1 dates his departure: "I am just leaving & dread the journey awfully but 'Needs Must.' "

He did not add the rest of that well-known proverb, but he might well have done. Ahead of him, driven by a devil of a kind he had not before encountered but "needs must," lay troubles that would stretch Tunstall to the limit.

And they went by the name of "the Boys."

CHAPTER 13

THE TRIBULATIONS OF JOHN TUNSTALL

THE Boys lost no time in continuing their reign of thievery and intimidation: the activities of Frank Freeman, Armstrong, and "Nelson from the Gila" and the raid on the Mescalero Agency were but precursors of what was to come. In the middle of September they swept through Lincoln County on another raid; on September 18 they hit Brewer's ranch on the Ruidoso, stealing horses and mules belonging to Brewer, McSween, and Tunstall. McSween passed the news to the *Independent.*

> This forenoon my horses and those of Mr. Tunstall were stolen from a ranch on the Rio Ruidoso. I valued my horses at seven hundred dollars. Tunstall's cost over a thousand dollars. Two of mine were fine American horses. Among Tunstall's were the handsomest team of mules in this section of the country.
>
> Good citizens are in pursuit of the thieves and I hope they will overtake them and plunder.
>
> For the recovery of these animals we will pay a liberal reward. The thieves were seen driving off the animals. "The boys" are known.[1]

In view of Tunstall's May 30 statement that all his animals had cost him $425, McSween's valuation of the horses and mules is open to question: it appears that only two of Tunstall's horses—a matched pair he called "the dapple grays"—were taken. The "good citizens" who were in pursuit were Dick Brewer and his Ruidoso neighbors Charlie Bowdre and Doc Scurlock, both of whom had careers speckled enough to make their sympathies vis à vis the Boys somewhat uncertain. They needed no trackers to tell them where their quarry was headed: down the long trail through the Tularosa valley, skirting the White Sands, and on to Shedd's ranch, that well-known clearinghouse for stolen stock on the eastern slope of the San Agustin pass.

When the three pursuers reached Shedd's, according to Tunstall's later account (and therefore, presumably, Brewer's), both the Boys and "the animals were 'right there' in sight."

> Dick had a long parley with them & they finally said, "Well we will give you back your horses, & keep the balance to pay our expenses in the matter" (there were 7 of the rascals at the place at the time) he returned them the only answer that could come from him, for he is as brave as a lion, "If you can't give me 'the Englishman's' you can keep them & go to Hell." after doing all that could be done, he went on to Las Cruces & tried to get men to assist him to go back & take these fellows, but Las Cruces is just full of this band & their friends, the sheriff is in with them

alltogether; he staid there three days saw he could do nothing & returned, Widenmann met him [at San Nicolas spring] not quite halfway to Las Cruces. Widenmann was as mad as a battleaxe [and] swore he would have those mules or the scalps of the rascals who stole them.[2]

Whether Sheriff Barela was altogether in with the Boys or not—and all the evidence indicates he was—he could excuse himself from issuing warrants to Brewer by pointing out that the crimes had been committed in Lincoln County.[3] Unwilling to use any means but lawful ones to recover the stolen stock, Brewer and his two companions returned to Lincoln to report to McSween.

Whether the Kid participated in this particular horse-thieving sweep is uncertain. On balance of probability he did: the evidence that he was at least an occasional, if not a regular, member of the gang is far too convincing to ignore. Susan McSween was emphatically against the proposition. The Kid, she said, was just a cowboy who "worked where he could [and] worked for Chisum about six months, when Chisum 'fired' him he came up to Lincoln and Tunstall sent him out to the Felix and he never was associated with Tom Hill, Frank Baker & the other [I] dont remember his name, and I doubt if he knew Jessie Evens before the time they met in Lincoln the night Chapman was killed. Those four were the Murphey & Dolan thieves."[4]

Lily Klasner, however, had nothing but contempt for the idea of the Kid as an honest cowpuncher. In an undated document, probably early draft notes for what became her autobiography, she stated categorically that "Billy the Kid was never at no time nor place a Chisum Cowboy nor ever drove or worked in any way. . . . [N]ot one day in any way or maner did he work for them and the only times he was ever there was while on the dodge with the McSween outlaws. All the cow boy and cow men resent him being given the honorable name of cowboy when he was never associated with cattle except to steal them."[5]

Even if he did not take an active part in the theft of Tunstall's horses, an item in the *Independent* of October 13 shows quite clearly that Henry was out there stealing with the best—or worst—of them.[6] The singling out of his name suggests that the Kid was already well known; the inference here that he was one of the gang is equally inescapable. On Monday, October 8, it said,

three horses belonging respectively to Col. Ledbetter, John Swishelm, and [a man named] Mendoza, were stolen from Pass coal camp in the Burro Mountains. On learning the facts Col. Ledbetter and Swishelm went out to the camp and trailed them in on the road at Apache Tahoe. Sometime on Tuesday [October 9] the party of thieves, among whom was Henry Antrim, were met at Cook's cañon by Mr. Carpenter. Telegrams have been sent to Sheriff Barela at Mesilla, and we hope to hear of the Arrest of the thieves and the recovery of the horses.

The thieves who stole the horses from the Burro Mountains last Monday, stopped the western bound coach 7 miles east of Fort Cummings, asked the driver if he "had anything on" and on his replying no, said, "Well, we'll let you pass this time" insisting on Morehead taking a drink with them and finally rode off remarking that they were leaving the country. There were nine of them each armed with two revolvers and a Winchester rifle, and carrying two belts of cartridges.

They fired at Geo. Williams at Warm Spring Ranche, but as George very promptly returned their fire, they left without unnecessary delay.

The gang is constantly on the road, and it is time that the citizens turned out and strung them up.

Lily Klasner said the Kid told her he had stolen a racing mare that belonged to the daughter of Sheriff Mariano Barela in Las Cruces.[7] He then rode over to the Hondo valley and stayed with Frank McCullum, with whom he traded the stolen mare for a fresh horse so he could ride down the Pecos valley to join Jessie Evans and maybe get work.

In spite of the fact that the theft of Barela's horse caused bad blood between them—Barela and Evans were, literally, as thick as thieves—Jessie apparently let the Kid stick around. He was still there when the Brewer-Brady posse came down after Evans and the Boys, on October 17. The fact that they had one of Colonel Ledbetter's horses with them at the time of the arrest may be taken as further proof of earlier collaboration. So the Kid was brought back to Lincoln and was thrown into the underground jail with the Boys, there to languish until released by "the Pecos warriors" in November.

There are some problems of chronology with the Klasner account: the Tunstall horses were stolen September 18 and taken to Shedd's ranch, but Lily does not have the Kid arriving in Lincoln until just before Ellen Casey's departure (with Tunstall's cattle) on October 20, at which time he is describing his deliverance from the "dungen" jail which did not take place until November 16. All the same, it remains a persuasive version of events.

Other accounts have the Kid arriving in Lincoln County around October.[8] Ash Upson's fantasies of Indian fights and reckless rides can be unhesitatingly ignored, but it is not so easy to set aside the claims of the Jones family, of George Coe, or of the descendants of Sheriff Brady, all of whom aver that the Kid came to Lincoln County that fall. It may be that all are in small part correct: all that matters anyway is that the Kid got out of the Mesilla valley around the middle or end of October and then drifted up into Lincoln County. There is even doubt as to what name he gave: the Brady family insist he was using the name Henry Antrim when he worked briefly for the sheriff; yet the following February he was going by the name William H. Bonney.

The Lily Klasner memoir adds one further valuable dimension to the activities of The Boys at this time.

> What we arrived at from all [the Kid's] talk and tales was that he was just a trifling no acount street urchen and little bum arround the town had never been made iether to go to school nor work, had picked up a lot of bad raising and habits with the vicious element he run with, got in bad [trouble and] was about to be caught and prosecuted, so stole this mare [belonging to Mariano Barela at Las Cruces] and came to the Lower Pecos. He was now large enough to ride and belong in a way to the Jessie Evans Chain Gang. . . . By Chain gang is meant that at first it was Evans, Baker, Jimmy McDonald [McDaniels] and others would russel the stuff down in this part of the Pecos valley and take it up by the Penascos, La Luz, Tuleroso, and to The white Sands, and there [at Shedd's ranch] they would be met by a gang from that country who would take the bunch and push them out in to Arizona and then an other one fa[r]ther out to Colorado. These gangs were well oiled up and in good working order. The Murphy Dolan Co on the Pecos. The Jessie Evans [gang] between who turned them over to the McKinley [Kinney] gang of Las Cruces, who shoved on out to The Arizona Gang and so on, even as far as the Black Hills.[9]

Maybe the Kid stayed awhile with the Jones family down at Seven Rivers; maybe he worked briefly for Sheriff Brady and John Chisum, and bunked with George Coe during the winter. Maybe, as Lily Klasner suggests, Tunstall

> pretended he took a great liking to the Kid he being so young and a poor orphan boy in bad company he Hunstal [sic] would give him work and a chance to reform and go straight and make a man out of himself. This was [what he said] but the truth was he thought he would get [on] the good side of the Kid and get him to turn state's evidence. . . . This was why this good, honest Englishman took such a fancy to the Kid, to use him as a tool, and the Kid was smart enough and crooked enough to change crowdes.[10]

Whatever his reasons, the Kid went to work for "the Englishman." Exactly when it is impossible to say: his name does not once appear in Tunstall's letters.[11]

Having left St. Louis for the trip west on August 27, John Tunstall got to end of track on September 3, where he found letters from home awaiting him, forwarded from Lincoln. These brought the news of the marriage of his sister Emily (Minnie) to Louis Behrens on July 30 at Ventnor, Isle of Wight. In his reply to her, dated September 6, John assured his sister that he did not in any way feel that her marriage would "rob" him of her.[12] For all his assurances, the following sentences seem more accurately to mirror his mood: "Of course, when anyone has lived as long as I have with a certain point in mind, as the end of his hope, the height of his ambition, & the desire nearest his heart, & he is all of a sudden informed, that however right & proper his ambition, he must of necessity find another goal for it; he can but for a time feel somewhat stunned & bewildered."

Stunned, bewildered? But Tunstall knew that his sister had become engaged; the natural outcome of an engagement was marriage. Had he perhaps allowed himself to think it might yet come to nothing, as an earlier romance had done? Was it the realization that the solemn pact he had shared with his sister since their teens—that one day she would keep house for him and be a mother to their two "pets" (younger sisters)—would now never come true that made him feel "stunned and bewildered"?

One thing is certain: Tunstall's tactics changed dramatically upon his return to Lincoln. No longer did he carefully consider his "points" and take care to avoid risks; in fact he seems to have determined to confront danger head-on. Yet since he cannot have been under any possible misapprehension about the kind of men he was dealing with, the change can only be explained as either a massive misjudgment of his own capabilities or a complete disregard for the possible outcome. If it was the latter, then perhaps it was no coincidence that he signed the same day's letter to his parents "Yours till Death."

He prepared to leave Trinidad for Lincoln, only to discover the truth of the old adage "Man is born to trouble as the sparks fly upwards."[13] He was still there on September 12 when he gave his "Much Beloved Parents" an account of his tribulations:

> I had proceeded south towards my headquarters some 15 miles when the near front axle of the travelling conveyance [I] have had built at a cost of $100[00] heated and stuck immovably. I returned to Trinidad to repair damages, lost rather more than a day in the operation, & proceeded on my journey I reached a point called "Sweet

Water" some 80 miles from anywhere when the nut & end of the spindle upon which the wheel turns (or in other words the point of the axle) of my off hind wheel broke off. I rigged up a temporary contrivance to keep the wheel on & I have had to return here for permanent repairs. "Telle est la vie" The vexatiousness of this accident to me can not well be exaggerated, as I am most impatient to get back to Lincoln.

It was to be another month before he got there. Four days after his third departure from Trinidad, he came down with smallpox at Las Vegas, where

ten corpses a day were being carried to their last resting place, victims to this scourge, & bad treatment, out of a population of 3000; it is not worthwhile for me to describe my feelings as I lay listening to the "knell for the parting souls" which was rung almost incessantly during the time I was there, as there always seemed to be someone to ring for; I got mighty sick, but they could not make me believe, that that bell would ring for me, "Not if I know myself" I would tell my Dr [J. H. Shout] when he shook his head; I had a hard time though I did not have a great many spots & I did not seem to get over it, but kept sick; one night a man came into Las Vegas from Lincoln, with the news that all my best horses were stolen & Dick Brewer's as well; I had been down about three weeks at that time, but you bet! I had a resurrection as soon as I heard that![14]

Still far from well, Tunstall clambered into his traveling conveyance, hitched up "Long Tom," and headed for Lincoln, covering forty miles each day until he got to his destination. He pulled in on Sunday night, October 14, and hurried to McSween's to find out what had been happening during his absence.

He learned there was illness in the Shield family; it was sufficiently serious for Shield and McSween to have declined to defend Lucas Gallegos and Catarino Romero on a charge of murder at the district court session held in San Patricio the preceding week.[15] It may well be that the youngest Shield children had succumbed to smallpox; there is a persistent tradition in Lincoln that one, or possibly two, of their babies were buried there, but no graves have ever been found.

The news that Isaac Ellis, a recent arrival from Colfax County who had bought Daniel Dow's property, had made more improvements and was doing a thriving mercantile business at his new store at the eastern end of town cannot have cheered Tunstall much.[16] But what he was really anxious to know was who had stolen his horses. McSween told him: Jessie Evans and the Boys. They had had Lincoln County by the tail for weeks. The *Independent* of October 13 painted a vivid picture of their movements—and their methods—subsequent to Brewer's pursuit to the San Agustin pass.

After having supplied themselves with a fresh outfit of horses in Grant County and elsewhere, "Captain" Evans and his party crossed the Rio Grande moving eastward. They stopped awhile at San Augustin, where they supplied the inner man with the choicest viands to be found on Mr. Shedd's table, and then took the main road to Tulerosa. Near Whitewater they left a fine bay horse dead on the road, probably one of the animals recently appropriated in Grant County. On arriving at Tulerosa, the "Captain" and his party extended to themselves the hospitality of that quiet village and manifested a creditable degree of modesty in their demands. After indulging in a big drunk, and having fired a hundred or more shots promiscuously about the town as a parting salute, they moved on up the Tulerosa.

At the house of one Sylvestre ———— (who on a former occasion had appeared as a witness against one of "the boys") they made another familiar call and treated the humble and defenceless occupants to a specimen of their marksmanship by shooting a dog and riddling the entire house with bullets. The frantic appeals of the helpless man to spare the lives of his sick children only excited these "gentlemen" to shouts of derisive laughter. Late in the afternoon they halted at a store of the Trader near the Indian Agency; here they interviewed our old friend John Ryan who was in charge of the store, and demanded provisions and other supplies, which were, of course, furnished. A portion of the proceeds of the former raid made by these gentlemen upon the Indian Agency was the mare belonging to Miss Lou Godfroy, daughter of Major Godfroy, the Indian Agent. Miss Godfroy prized the animal highly and was deeply grieved at her loss. The bold raiders had this animal with them, and "Captain" Evans upon his arrival at the store, informed Mr Ryan that he had heard the mare belonged to a young lady and that his gallantry forbade his retaining her property without her consent—in fact he would scorn to retain the animal under such circumstances (especially as the mare had been badly used and was no longer serviceable) and requested Mr. Ryan to deliver the animal to its owner with his ("Captain" Evans) affectionate kiss. Here they made inquiries as to when the members of the court from Lincoln would be along, asked as to the whereabouts of other obnoxious parties, and moved on.

Near the summit of the Sacramento Mountains they went into camp for the night, placing sentinels out to guard against surprise. About 8 o'clock p.m. Messrs. Riley and Longwell came along in a buggy; the sentinel, on hearing their approach, gave an "owl hoot" as a warning to his comrades, which was responded to at once by those in camp. Riley and Longwell passed within a few feet of the guard, an American, who responded to their greeting in Spanish, and on passing, the entire party, numbering seventeen well armed and mounted men, paraded on the roadside. Near the Agency they separated, one party going up the Tulerosa; the other went toward the Ruidoso.

Quite how Riley and Longwell managed to get "near the summit of the Sacramento Mountains" in a buggy (a not inconsiderable climb on a surefooted horse) the *Independent* failed to explain; but the piece does indicate the friendly relationship that existed between the Boys and the House. Fountain was wrong about the rustlers' destination, however: they were on their way to Seven Rivers.

When he learned that the Boys were down there, McSween went to Sheriff Brady and demanded that he appoint Brewer a deputy sheriff, raise a posse, and go after them. He, McSween, would furnish arms and provisions from Tunstall's stocks, which had just arrived and were piled up in the store. Brady very reluctantly complied, and on Friday, October 12, the fifteen-man posse thundered down the valley toward the Pecos and Seven Rivers.

Of all these developments Tunstall told his parents not a word until the following January; now, a brief note on McSween's letterhead dated October 16 reported only that he had reached Lincoln the preceding night (he later corrected this statement to Sunday), that he was alive and well, that he had read all their letters, and that he would be "on the road again tomorrow morning at sunrise, only a short trip (200 miles there & back). . . . In a week I will write to you at length, I positively cant say any more at present for lack of time."[17]

John Chisum had sent an order for goods; Tunstall wanted to see him anyway on "some special matters," so he hunted up what the cattleman wanted and set out for the Pecos.[18]

"Long Tom" was used up by hard work little feed & alkali water; so I had to press a little rat of a white pony into the service that Dick had thought was not even fit for service under the saddle. & from driving a large bay horse that stood 16½ hands high & that I had broken to work just as I like a horse to work; to have to drive a mouse that had never been in single harness, that was ignorant of the uses of a bridle, & was not strong enough for the work I put him at, was nearly martyrdom to me; but when he got tired 10 miles out from my destination that night & it came on to sleet & freeze so that I had to sit on the reins & pull on them with my fists, my hands being too stiff to hold them, I can assure you that it was not short of martyrdom; there were some bad crossings of the river, but the mail carrier met me at the worst one & piloted me across. I reached the house I was making for two hours after sundown, I could not unharness my horse, & I really dont think I could have stood another half hour of such suffering.

Next morning he set off on the second half of his journey; as he crested a rise he saw a party of riders up ahead coming his way. A mile farther down the road he met the sheriff's posse, on its way back to Lincoln with Jessie Evans, Frank Baker, Tom Hill, and George Davis—and the Kid?—under arrest. "I must say it did me good to shake Dick's great paw," Tunstall said.[19] "I was afraid lest they might have drilled a hole through him." He looked around the posse; he had seen two of the Boys when he first came to Lincoln County, but failed to recognize any of them.

"Why, I thought you boys went out to round up some wild stock," he said to the possemen. Brewer laughed; so did the Boys. Tunstall must have looked a bit uncertain: were the Boys under arrest, or what?

"By Jove!" sneered one of them, mocking the Englishman. "He don't know if Dick has got us or we've got him."

"Well," said Tom Hill, whom Tunstall described as the hardest nut in all the gang, "have you got any whiskey, Englishman?"

"Merely a dram," Tunstall retorted, confidence returning. "If you knew me you would know that I don't need any to keep my blood warm, but if you met me at Lincoln, I'd soak you if you wished."

"Well, we'll be in the jug by then, you get back and you can soak us there if you like."

Tunstall promised to do just that, and the posse moved on towards Lincoln; they had been riding all night and had not yet broken their fast. Brewer remained behind to share the contents of Tunstall's mess box and provide him with an account of what had happened at Seven Rivers.

In between mouthfulls he told me that when at the Penasco the sheriff had wanted to turn back but that he [Brewer] asked what men would follow him? "as he intended to go on even if he had to go on alone" they all wanted to follow him, so they went on; the second night, they rode all night & in the grey dawn surrounded the house the thieves were in, it was a strong place called in this country a "choaser" (that is a house built over a hole in the ground in such a way that when you are inside, there is as much of the house under, as over the ground) a good many shots were fired, Jesse Evans says he cant tell how he failed to hit Dick as he had three fair, square shots at him, & he was saving his shots for him alone. The bullets struck within 4 or 5 inches of him each time. Jesse seemed as cool as if he was not interested; the end of it was, that some men in Dick's party who knew these fellows well, told them that they meant taking them dead or alive, & that if they surrendered they would not be lynched, & they surrendered.[20]

Brewer was under no illusions about what would happen when the Boys got to Lincoln. "They will get out of gaol sure as fate," he told Tunstall. "They have more friends in the country than enemies, and you mark me, those chaps will get let out, Brady will let them go for sure."

He mounted up and rode off to catch up with the posse, which reached Lincoln at about two in the afternoon. Tunstall continued on down the Hondo valley. Having some sardonic fun at the expense of the sheriff, whose reluctance to pursue the Boys was well known, R. H. Ewan wrote to the *Independent* to report the arrest and to make sure that the sheriff got all the "credit" that was due him.

To Sheriff Brady is owing *entirely* the projection and skillful consummation of the order of arrest from the last district court. Too frequent sins against our worthy and vigilant sheriff have been bandied about in reference to his ability to carry out justice in opposition to certain friends of his. To all such "croakers" I can now safely say: forever afterwards hold your peace.

In the face of a sudden and terrible storm of snow and rain, insufficiently appointed in food and clothing, facing expected death in case of collision, our sheriff boldly pushed on and crowned his arduous pursuit with complete success.

As chief, all hail to our noble and deserving Sheriff Brady. We are proud of that noble and self-sacrificing posse (all residents of our renowned county) who so cheerfully followed and ventured with the determined leader.

The chiefs of that band are now lodged securely in the new jail at this place. And, we trust, being now cared for by the law's course will be permitted to go to its finality.[21]

That night, Tunstall's "white mouse" gave out about ten miles from his destination, "at a place where I could get neither wood nor water; the night was bitter cold, I walked about a good deal & did not sleep much."[22] In the morning he hitched up and drove on, aching in every joint. He stayed the night at Jacob Harris's place and learned that Chisum had gone upriver to Bosque Grande, turning his trip into one nearer three hundred miles than two. He found that his aches "increased instead of decreased & that rheumatism had got me at a disadvantage when my 'white mouse' gave out the night before."

He exchanged the white pony for a mare called Mormon Pussy he had bought from Harris for $110 before going east. She

had never been in single harness, her disposition was said to be good, she was described as free to a fault, fast, & true as steel, a good walker & trotter. She is a pretty piebald, stands about 14¾ hands high, & is well made. She was said not to take the whip, that she would runaway but not kick. We hitched her up & she went off all right but as if she did not care to go.

I drove up to Bosque Grande but it took me all day, the mare seemed jaded from the start. I concluded my business with Chisum & left the next morning. I had to whip her all the way back & she stood it like an "old plug". It was night when I reached Harris'. . . . [W]hen I told him how she behaved he shewed great astonishment, & his wife & children raved at my description of their favorite. "Well Jake" said his wife (his name is Jacob) you told the Englishman she could trot, & you must make her do it if it kills her tomorrow. We started out the next morning & he whipped a good gait out of her, but she behaved as if she was completely worn out though she was in fair flesh.

Surprisingly, neither Harris nor Tunstall, who might have been expected to know, realized that the mare was in foal. She aborted while Tunstall was riding her to Lincoln a month or two later.

He set off for Lincoln, arriving there at about sundown on October 23. The first person he met was Justice of the Peace Wilson, whom Tunstall characterized as an old fool who was "about as much use as a fifth wheel would be to a coach."

"Well, Englishman," Wilson said, with what seems to have been some relish, "they seem bound to drive you out of the country."

"How is that?" asked Tunstall.

"Well, all your cattle are driven off, and I guess they're in Texas before now," Wilson told him, and doubtless went on to explain that the widow Ellen Casey and her brood had rounded up all their own cattle, added the ones Tunstall had "bought" to the herd, and headed south for Texas.

Tunstall told his parents that he merely bade Wilson good night and went over to McSween's to find out what had happened. Picture him: dusty, dirty, tired, rheumatic, and hungry, still suffering from the after-effects of smallpox, washed out after driving three hundred bone-jolting miles, and spending those bitterly cold nights on the prairie. He may have said something to old Wilson, but it would be safe to wager that it most certainly was not "good night."

CHAPTER 14

JESSIE EVANS AND THE BOYS

TUNSTALL'S spirits must have sunk into his boots as McSween told him what had happened.

> [T]he man I got those cattle of had taken advantage of Widenmann's Dick's & my absence to see if he could not turn a dishonest penny and By Jove! he came within an ace of turning it for he gathered a little crowd, his 2 sons & 4 other men, & started for Texas where he has relations.
>
> Dick, however got wind of it as he came up the river, & asked 6 men in the Sheriff's posse to join him & bring back the cattle. As soon as he got to town he went to see McSween & said "All Tunstall's cattle are in Texas or mighty near there by this time". "Well, what's to be done, Dick?" said Mc[Sween]. "Why I must 'rack out' on the road again & bring them back, to be sure I ain't going to see him run over" [said Brewer].[1]

Tunstall's identifying as a man the party from whom he got his cattle is puzzling. The drive was in fact made by the widow Casey and her two sons, Adam and Will. According to her daughter Lily's somewhat erratic account, Mrs. Casey decided to quit Lincoln County temporarily. No reason is given for this decision. The family loaded everything they needed into two wagons, and with four or five men to help him, Mrs. Casey's friend Abneth McCabe pointed the eight hundred or so head down the Pecos, leaving "Old Man Turner" to look after the Hondo ranch. About fifteen or twenty miles across the Texas line they were overtaken by Brewer and "at least fifteen men, most of whom were Mexicans."

> Brewer demanded a portion of the cattle, which he said were the property of Tunstall and McSween. After some heated discussion, about all my brothers could do was to let Brewer take about 400 head. . . .
>
> When we told Mother what had occurred she hurried us to Lincoln to see her lawyer, McSween. It so happened that Brewer, having taken our stolen cattle back to the Feliz ranch, had reached Lincoln ahead of us and reported the incident to Tunstall and McSween. I do not know what his story was but next day, just after Mother reached home, Brewer and pretty much the same crowd came to our ranch and threw their guns down on my two brothers, saying they would have to accompany them back to Lincoln. The boys wanted to know what it was all about, but Brewer would say only, "You'll have to go to Lincoln with us and find out." They never showed any warrant, but simply took the boys by force of arms.
>
> Of course, Mother would not submit to such treatment of her sons. . . . She was fortunate in catching up with Uncle John [Chisum] who returned with her to Lincoln and used his influence to get Add and Will released.[2]

Lily Casey Klasner's account features Abneth McCabe and "four or five men," at least two of whom were her brothers. Will was then eighteen, his younger brother not yet seventeen. Compare Tunstall's version:

Mc[Sween] made out the documents, Dick hunted up saddles & bridles & called out which of my poor horses could stand the most after what they had [already] gone through & the next night they slept 50 miles from town. "Long Tom" was pressed into service, jaded as he was. They rode night & day, only stopping to eat & sleep a few hours here & there, when the horses played out; two of their horses gave out under them & Dick had to buy others; as they neared the Texas line people told them they might as well turn back as there were 26 Texans with the cattle & they could not take them away. Dick said "he did not care if there were 126, he meant to get back that herd." The end of it was that one fine afternoon, 5 of Dick's outfit overtook the herd in charge of 7 men. Dick & another of the party had been detained buying the two horses I spoke of. A man named [John] Middleton was in charge of Dick's outfit. Middleton is about the most desperate looking man I ever set eyes on (& that is not saying a little) I could fancy him doing anything ruffianly that I ever heard of, that is from his appearance, but he is as mild & composed as any man can be, but his arms are never out of his reach; Dick had the papers so they held a council of war & decided to stop the herd until he came up, as they were within 10 miles of the Texas line & had they crossed it it would have cost as much as the cattle were worth to bring them back legally; upon this they rode out over the hill & towards the lead cattle & the seven men made for the vantage ground of a hill nearby, upon this Middleton "racked out" & cut them off & rode up towards them; they dismounted & unsheathed their rifles but Middleton still advanced only scattering his men out so as to give less for them to aim at. (I had a case of carbines in just before they left & they each carried one of them, they are the finest weapon manufactured & you bet there was no discount on the way those boys could handle them.)

As they drew on to about 150 yards, Middleton called to dismount & at the glitter of those 5 lean barrels the rascals backed down & threw down their guns rather than stand a volley. Then came the parley; the owner of the cattle had given them in charge of a man named McCabe. McCabe swore & charged & stormed about "an armed mob stopping peaceable people &c &c" for a long time until at last Middleton said "Well, now, I have heard enough of that so dont let me hear another word out of you; we will have it as we say & take chances how it turns out," & that settled his hash.[3]

Brewer caught up the next day; Tunstall's 209 cattle were cut out of the herd and turned back toward the Feliz. Remaining with the cattle, Brewer sent some of the posse—which included Fred Waite, Sam Corbet, Florencio Chavez, "and a few others"—on ahead to Lincoln to let Tunstall know his animals were safe. The Englishman decided to go to meet them; he loaded a wagon with food, hitched up his "white mouse," tied the mare Mormon Pussy (whose condition, not surprisingly, was getting "worse and worse") to the tailgate, and set off.

I got as far as Dick's ranch on the Ruidoso when a man met me from town with a note from McSween saying that the Plaza was likly to be attacked by the band of desperadoes to which those 4 belonged who were in jail & that I had better return at once by the road as the mountain trail was likly to be being watched. I ate at Dick's & in the afternoon saddled Pussy & started. She seemed very sick, the road was 20 miles & the trail 7, so I said to the mare, "Old Girl, we'll go the trail whether it's watched or not" & I took the trail, keeping a bright look out ahead & around[4]

The mare traveled more and more slowly; when the sun dropped behind the mountains, Tunstall was still three miles from Lincoln. He was within "half a mile of the point from which the rest of the journey would be safe" when the mare heard something. "The next moment I heard it too, swung her around & threw up my carbine. I had not much time to waste as the horse I heard was coming on a keen run; my heart was in my mouth, for the rascals had sworn to kill 'that Englishman' on sight."

Once again his words reveal the dichotomy of Tunstall's relationship with the Boys: here he relates that they have sworn to kill him on sight; a little later he is swapping jokes with them and sending them a bottle of whiskey in the Lincoln jail.

As it turned out, the rider coming towards him that October night was "all right," so Tunstall proceeded into town. There he learned that McSween had received an anonymous note, from a source that had previously proven reliable, to the effect that the Boys were "dropping in a few at a time at a point [in the Roswell area] about 80 miles from here & that the 4 'Boys' we had in gaol would be liberated by a strong party. I should, had I continued my journey, have passed through a country where they would be, so it was as well to come back that night & for many a night everyone was on the lookout & in a state of excitement but *nothing happened*."

Tunstall discontinued writing at this point, and did not return to the letter until January 9. It is quite clear he decided to refrain from telling his family what had been happening. In the period between his return to Lincoln on October 14 and February 2, when this letter arrived in London, they knew nothing of his difficulties; all they had were a few brief notes from either John or his friend Widenman... This of November 16 is typical:

My Dear Parents,
    I am still alive & well.
        your son,
          John.
P.S. you have no idea of the press of business & annoyance I am staggering under.

He was not exaggerating. Some time preceding, he had hired twenty-eight-year-old Sam Corbet as a sales clerk, and the store was open for business.[5] Most of its transactions were being done on credit: the local farmers and townspeople pledging their crops of corn and hay to Tunstall in exchange for "grain notes," a form of scrip invented by Tunstall. Earlier, you made it sound as if this were his own idea that enabled them to buy goods at the store. He was doing land office business: every farmer in the area was clamoring for the chance to obtain credit.

In addition to the affairs of the store, and the Lincoln County Bank—president, John Chisum, vice president, A. A. McSween, and cashier, Tunstall—the "stock scheme" was also in operation. Dick Brewer, John Middleton, "Dutch" Martin Martz, Frederick Waite, the Kid, and Godfrey Gauss had already been hired either to work on the Feliz ranch or "squat" on others until Tunstall could enter formal filings after Christmas.

There are some clues as to which ranches these might have been.[6] On October 13 Tunstall advanced Avery M. Clenny and his wife, Antonia Torres de Clenny, the sum of two hundred dollars for ninety days: the interest rate was a stunning

24 percent annually, the security Clenny's 160-acre homestead "near Hondo." Presumably Tunstall advanced George van Sickle a hundred on the same basis. He had purchased a quitclaim from Billy Mathews for his Peñasco valley ranch, another for the Feliz ranch. Other entries in his account book in the names of Brewer, James Farmer, Felix McKittrick, Ham Mills, John Copeland, and Will Lloyd probably refer to similar investments. It should perhaps be pointed out that such whopping interest rates were fairly normal at the time on short-term loans.

In addition to all this, Tunstall and McSween were intensifying their assault upon the interests of J. J. Dolan & Co. Conditional upon Tunstall's thousand-dollar loan to the firm in August had been its sale to McSween of a second tract of land in Lincoln, the balance of forty acres originally owned by L. G. Murphy. The new "ring" now owned one of the largest pieces of real estate in town. To add to Dolan and Riley's problems, McSween had also begun preparing a suit against the House for $23,376.10. This was the sum that he and the other two examiners appointed by the probate court had established as Emil Fritz's equity in the firm of L. G. Murphy & Co.

The Boys had been put in irons and lodged together with Lucas Gallegos and Catarino Romero in the recently completed county jail.[7] This was an adobe structure built by George Peppin; it comprised a house for the jailer, beneath which were two log-lined underground rooms reached by means of a ladder lowered through a trapdoor. Because of the fetid conditions below ground, the shackled prisoners were taken outside once a day for exercise. It was during one such break that Tunstall

> went to see them one Sunday [October 31?] & chatted with them for a while. I got them pretty mad over a few things I told them that were too true to be palatable, but I was never notorious for "rubbing the right way" & the people here know that I usually say about what I think & take chances on how it suits the audience. They asked me if I remembered promising them some whiskey? I said "yes" & they chaffed me about the mules, told me they were sold to a priest down in Old Mexico &c &c. They found that I could joke as well as they could & we laughed a good deal. Some time after that I sent them a bottle of whiskey. I went to see them in gaol after that & joked them a good deal.[8]

It is difficult to imagine the Boys laughing with Tunstall; easier by far to picture them laughing at him. They had nothing in common with such a man. They were worlds apart, in education, in attitude, in experience; can Tunstall have been so naive as to believe he could befriend these case-hardened frontier thugs? Apparently so.

> One Sunday Dick came in from the Feliz (my ranch). I had been to see "the boys" & asked him to come and see them. He came & we laughed & joked a good deal more. They were outside the gaol for exercise, bye & bye Jesse Evans said "it amuses me to see 'the Englishman' come around & he don't get any satisfaction". "Satisfaction! the Devil!" said I, "what do you mean?" "Why! what you want to know is where your mules are, & you don't get to find out" said he. "Find out my Great Uncle!!!" said I. "Do you think I have no sense. I never went begging for a woman & I'll swear the mules aint foaled that I would pay for. You have stolen my mules and horses, they are worth an easy $700⁰⁰ & you know I want them, without being told, & I know that if you want to return them you can do it, but you should go to Hell & the mules too before I would ask you for them!" he turned on his heel & said "Bully for you". They were then ordered below & Jesse asked us to try & go

down with them to "talk over matters & things" We could not go down without an order from the Sheriff. I went to try & get one but he refused me; he is an Irishman, a slave of whiskey, & a man I think very little of, he is a tool.

As they left, Brewer again told Tunstall he was sure the Boys would get out; if they did, he was equally sure they would return the stock they had stolen. After all, he had protected them after their arrest at Seven Rivers, "and they bore him a big debt of gratitude as they expected he would have been the first to lynch them," said Tunstall.

Tunstall's second Sunday visit must have taken place on November 4; on or about November 7, Juan Patrón received information from Catarino Romero, who had managed to escape from custody, that the Boys had gotten hold of tools, filed through their shackles, and cut holes in the log walls of the jail. He informed Brady accordingly; accompanied by Patrón and McSween's partner David Shield, the sheriff examined the prisoners in jail and found that this was so. The jailer, Maximiano de Guevara, suggested obtaining new shackles; Brady vacillated. McSween takes up the story

A few days afterwards Sheriff Brady came into Tunstall's store in a half intoxicated condition and indirectly accused Mr Tunstall of giving the credit of the arrest of said outlaws to R. M. Brewer . . . and had considerable talk with Mr Tunstall and among other things accused Mr Tunstall of having tried to aid Baker Evans Hill and Davis to escape. Mr Tunstall told him "You know their shackles are filed and there are holes cut in the logs and you take no pains to secure them and do you dare to accuse me, who have aided in the arrest of these persons, who have threatened my life, with assisting them to escape?"

Brady thereupon put his hand upon his revolver as though he was going to draw it and I stepped between them and placing my hand on his shoulder and said "It ill becomes you as a Peace Officer to violate the law by shooting. Brady replied "I won't shoot you now, you haven't long to run, I ain't always agoing to be sheriff" and then left the store.[9]

Tunstall told it differently; in his version he is in control.[10] McSween is a witness, not a participant.

Brady commenced making some insinuations, which I took up & told him what I thought of. I was leaning my back against a counter at the time; he called me "a fool"; I affixed a couple of adjectives & raised my voice one note louder than his & returned the compliment. He reached around to his left hip for his Colt's revolver, but he did not get his hand on it; & I would think for his sake that it was as well he did not, for I had him covered with my pocket pistol that carried a half inch ball & I should have turned loose had his hand once touched the butt of his pistol; as it was I did not move a muscle & I guess he did not think it good for his health to stay around there any longer & after raving a little he left. He had the audacity to insinuate that Brewer & I were wishing to go & see the prisoners to assist them in making their escape. He said "he had put them in gaol & they should stay there in spite of Brewer or anyone else.". . .

He remained in town that day, the gaoler resigned his position, a responsible Mexican then took charge of the gaol temporarily. The next day a new gaoler [Diego Archuleta] was found, Brady was in town, The Mexican gave the keys to Brady, but he omitted to turn the gaol over to the new gaoler. The next morning, on getting up, I met a man at the door who said "Well! the Boys are out & the gaol empty!" "Didn't I told you so," said I.

Tunstall, Patrón, and McSween went over to the jail.[11] There, according to McSween, they found

> several sacks in which rocks weighing 20 or 25 lbs were hid, augers and files. Upon further investigation I found that no one had been left in charge of the Jail that night and that the doors had not been even locked though Brady was at Murphy's house where he made his headquarters. I am informed . . . that the augers and files referred to above were packed in goods bought in the store of J. J. Dolan & Co. where Murphy resided and by one of their employees (Pantaleon Gallegos) delivered to the said prisoners.

An unexpected beneficiary of the delivery of the Boys was Lucas Gallegos, still languishing in jail for the murder of Sostero García. He took advantage of this opportunity to "go to Texas."

The three men marched back uptown to ask Brady to raise a posse to go after the Boys; McSween stated later that they offered him twenty men; Tunstall makes a liar of him.[12] Not that it mattered one way or the other: Brady turned them down flat. "I arrested them once, and I'm damned if I'm going to do it again," he snapped. "Hereafter I'm going to look after Brady's interests!"

At around eleven o'clock that same Saturday morning, old John B. Wilson rode into town from the Ruidoso in a great state of excitement. He said the Boys had descended on Brewer's ranch and that they had been firing there since daylight. In all likelihood Brewer was dead. Tunstall unhesitatingly prepared to ride down to the Ruidoso.

> I saddled Mormon Pussy & filled up my rifle revolver & belt, & started out to hunt some help to go to the rescue, McSween tried, & others, but we could not raise a man; They told me I should get picked off before I got within a mile of the house, that thirty of "the boys" had composed the rescuing party. "We don't back down," said I & started alone. I thought I could not do much as they must have been besieged since sun up, it was then 11 a.m. I expected to find the whole crowd killed at Dick's, or else besieged & near given out. but I had to go if only for the sake of appearances.[13]

That last sentence indicates his true motivation: Tunstall had no hankering for a shoot-out with Jessie Evans and the Boys. When he got to the Ruidoso and came within sight of the house, he saw smoke crawling over the flat roof and a haystack apparently burning in the corner of the corral. Since it was "impossible to get within a mile of the house without being seen," he galloped straight into the corral as fast as the horse would go. To his astonishment three of Dick's men appeared at the door.

"Where's Dick?" shouted the anguished Tunstall.

"Up the river," was the reply.

"Confound you!" fumed Tunstall. "Ain't any of you killed, and I've got up all this agony for nothing! Where are Jesse Evans and the Boys?"

Brewer's men explained what had happened. The smoke on the roof was due to a broken chimney. The haystack was not afire; someone had built a campfire in the corral and it was smoldering. As for Jessie Evans, Frank Baker, Tom Hill, and George Davis, they had ridden up to Brewer's ranch that morning with thirty men,

> ordered breakfast & sat around the fire, as cosy as could be, told the fellows there just how they were rescued. Ten men went right into the gaol at about 3 a.m., put

a pistol to the man's head who was sleeping there, broke open the [trap]door with rocks & let the boys out. Not a soul stirred in town. After they had breakfasted they knocked their irons off & drove up Dick's & my horses (I had 8 there just then, & the poor beasts were off their feet already from the work they had done, some had sore backs & not one was in order) They lassoed them & enquired whose horse each on[e] was as they caught him, when they found they were all mine but the cart horses (they left the cart horses, as a man told them Dick could not haul his corn without them) they said "You tell Mr Tunstall we are very sorry to have to use his horses, but we are on foot & need them more than he does, but that we will return them to him & every hoof we ever took from him; We were put up to that job on Dick & him, but we see the stuff they are made of, & we will never take a thing of theirs again."

Did Tunstall put this pretty speech into the Boys' mouths, or did they actually utter these flowery sentiments? And if the latter, did Brewer or Tunstall really believe one word of them?

I listened to all this, & let it go, but my heart ached for my poor horses, when I thought what they had been called upon to do, & were now under the saddles of men who could not stop to feed them even if they wished to. I waited for Dick & returned that night. He said I should get them back.

"The boys" went from Dick's that morning over to my cattle ranch (where my cattle are all safe & sound) & found the redoubtable John Middleton in sole control & possession, they (15 of them) stayed with him all night, told him "that they would die for Dick Brewer if it would ever do him any good, & that they would never touch another hoof of the Englishman's stock as long as he was in the country."

One of them, a low lived, sneaking, cayote of a fellow, was playing with his six shooter & it occasionally pointed at Middleton, (he (M) would not care a snuff, for any man that ever walked, or any number of men, he would never back down) & he told him "to point that thing somewhere else, as he did not wish to be shot by a fool" bye & bye Mr Lallercooler (as we have christened the fellow [Charlie Crawford]) saw John's carbine standing in the corner & asked whose it was? "Mr Tunstall's" said John. "Well, I guess I'll take it along, I need one & I want something to remember him by anyhow" said he. "Well, I just guess you'l leave that right where it is & try & remember Mr. Tunstall some other way, anyhow!" said John, & you bet he left it, right there.

Since then they have sent my horses back one at a time & I think that I have them all back except one. He was an old favorite, the first horse I bought in New Mexico. He has been taken into Texas, & I cant say whether I shall get him back or not. They were of course worn out when returned, but it was much better to get their bones than nothing at all.

A letter to the *Independent,* dated December 3, signed "Lincoln" (probably McSween), amplifies one or two points in Tunstall's account.

Since that Saturday morning that shrouded us in disgrace we have maintained the silence of the dead in these matters. Among the rescuers of "the boys" was their ally and champion, the famous Pasha Boyle, the distinguished historian of the "Pecos War", having by that history gained a clear right to be called "the champion falsifier of 1877."

On their way to the Feliz, they met Juan Trujillo and borrowed his saddle, gun and pistol, for Don Lucas Gallegos. They refreshed the inner man and cleaned the outer at the Feliz. From there they went to R. M. Beckwith's. Here they related their hairbreadth escape, left their jaded horses, and started to hunt for others.

We have recently heard from them. They were between Fort Stanton and Major Murphy's cow camp, and were there seen and interviewed. Lucas Gallegos was the spokesman. He told our informant that McSween's, Patrón's and Montaño's death warrants had been signed.[14]

Surprisingly enough the Boys kept their florid promise; they never did lay another finger on any of Tunstall's horses, or Brewer's either. This uncharacteristic streak of gratitude does add weight to Sheriff Brady's accusation that Tunstall and Brewer had made a deal: escape from jail in return for getting their animals back. Tunstall was more devious than that, however: one suspects that if he engineered an escape it was to rid himself once and for all of the threat of Captain Evans and his followers, at the same time persuading Jessie he was doing him a favor, to be repaid by returning the horses that would be provided.

Is that how it happened? Jessie Evans later testified that McSween was implicated; so did Andrew Boyle. Of course neither was renowned for strict adherence to the truth. And we must make what we can of Lily Casey Klasner's statement that Billy the Kid, a member of the gang that helped the Boys escape, was then taken on and "cultivated" by Tunstall in the hope that the Kid would in due course turn state's evidence against the others in the rescue party.[15] Clever he might have been; but it is a little difficult to imagine Tunstall as quite such an accomplished disciple of Macchiavelli.

On December 6, Tunstall wrote a hasty note to let his parents know he was "still alive & well."

> [T]he last battle is about over, I can count the dead & the living very nearly exactly, some of the wounded are hard to classify but the waters are calm enough now for me to settle down & write to you.
>
> I have a letter in course of completion for you & you will get it I daresay a fortnight after this scrap.
>
> I hope you will have spent a very merry Christmas when you receive this [the letter arrived in London on December 26] & that a happy new year will follow it. You know you have all my love.[16]

Clearly, Tunstall thought his tribulations were at an end; in fact, both he and McSween were making plans to leave Lincoln County for some time, Tunstall to visit England, McSween to spend up to six months in the States. Tunstall's error is understandable. After all, the new store was flourishing. Widenmann had returned from Las Cruces with the mules stolen by the Boys the preceding September. And, most important of all, Jessie Evans and the Boys had quit Lincoln County.

Not, as Tunstall perhaps believed, because of his devious planning, however.[17] Some twenty-five miles south of El Paso, at San Elizario, a full-scale race war had blown up when new American proprietors tried to deprive the local population of their traditional right to haul salt from the saline lakes near the town. The enraged Mexicans killed a number of Anglos and the state troopers seemed powerless to stop further bloodshed. Charles Kerber, sheriff of El Paso County, telegraphed to Las Cruces for men to aid the forces of law and order.

Among those who raised men to go down to San Elizario was John Kinney; no doubt attracted by the likelihood of pay and plunder, the Boys hastened to rally to Kinney's banner. Coincident with their departure the second plague blighting

Lincoln County waned; frosty nights and bitterly cold days virtually removed the threat of smallpox.

Widenmann got back to Lincoln around the end of November.[18] From the moment he got to Las Cruces in September, "Rob" realized

> he was in a den of thieves, cut throats & desperadoes & corrupt officials, he has a hot temper & does not care who knows it, & I promised him long ago that if he ever got shot, I would see that his man reached the throne very soon after him & I began to think that his chances were getting slim.
>
> I had dropped onto one of these bravo boys, down the Pecos, got him scared & manipulated him in such a way as to find out where the mules were & written Rob concerning them. I got one letter from him saying "he intended to bring home either the mules or some scalps" but it is no use for me to describe the uncertainty I was in about him to you when you want to know what happened.
>
> He hired a couple of Mexicans to use as spies &c, got hold of leading business men in that country, went to the Old Mexican line & made friends with the customhouse officials, went into Texas & worked some of the officers in the army that are stationed there & got people on the look out all round for the stock, then he took his rifle & sixshooter & hunted them inside his guarded circle, he made things so hot down there for himself, that it is more than a miracle that he was not killed, he & another man took one of Dick's horses & another stolen horse, from the teeth of 5 men; he finally met the man who was taking care of the mules, & told him, that unless he sent the mules to the place where he was stopping by seven o'clock the next morning, he would shoot the top of his head off; the fellow knew right well that he would do it, or try so hard that there would be no fun in it, so he sent back the mules.
>
> When he took those horses they rode 50 miles in six hours, to run them to a place of safety. One of the Mexicans got shot & killed over the business & the other got shot through the face from one cheek to the other. Finally he slipped out of town with his prizes one dark night & reached Lincoln safely in the course of four days.

The matter of Widenmann's adventures raises some very interesting questions, particularly since it would appear that the shooting referred to was done by none other than John Kinney (fig. 38).[19] According to information given by that worthy to the *Mesilla News,* he learned of a plot by two men to kill him for a large sum of money. He decided to leave town, only to encounter on his way one Ysabel Barela. A "difficulty" ensued; Kinney shot Barela through the jaw, the ball going in one cheek and out the other.

As Kinney continued in the general direction of Texas, Barela's friend Leandro Urieta grabbed a Henry rifle and rode up the main street, throwing shots at innocent passers-by, including Messrs. Sledd, Rosencrans, Montgomery, and Caldwell, and another man. Deputy sheriff Manuel Barela, brother of the sheriff, went unarmed after Urieta and pulled him off his horse.

Shouting "You're the one that I wanted, anyway!" Urieta fired at Barela, the gun flash burning his clothes. Before he could fire again, Sheriff Mariano Barela ran to his brother's aid, mortally wounding Urieta, who died at four o'clock the same day. The newspaper reported that Ysabel Barela recovered; other sources differ.

The similarities between Widenmann's story and this "difficulty," which happened on or about November 9, are striking. Is it possible that Widenmann hired Urieta and Ysabel Barela to kill Kinney or Manuel Barela ("the man who was taking care of [Widenmann's way of saying "holding"] the mules") or both, and that the shootings were the result? Is that why Urieta shouted what he did? If

FIG. 38. John Kinney and his daughter Mary Lynn. Date and photographer unknown. Thought to have been taken toward the end of his life, possibly at Prescott, Ariz.

Widenmann was behind all this, where did he get the money to hire the killers? Was he hired as an intermediary or acting on his own initiative? Or is it more likely, knowing the man's proclivity for self-aggrandizement, that he heard of the fracas and assigned to himself the principal role in it?

Regardless of how he did it, Widenmann had recovered Tunstall's mules; and doubtless Tunstall was happy to have his friend and confidant at his side once more. "All this stealing has put me back terribly," he told his parents.[20] "It has cost a lot of money, for men expect to be well paid for going on the war path."

His account book seems to confirm this: he paid Brewer $62.00 to cover the cost of his excursion to Shedd's ranch in pursuit of the Boys; other entries note several payments to Widenmann totaling $142.40; and one to "C. Bowder" (Charlie Bowdre) for $36.30. It was not just the drain on his finances that hampered Tunstall.

> I have had to expose myself a great deal in raking over the country, on expeditions arising out of all this, when I was by no means in a fit state to go; I feel pretty badly used up just now. I dont know whether (like the horses) I shall be able to get on my pins as soon as the new grass comes. When a fellow has to go through what I have done in the last 4 months, & just has sand enough left to play the last card, & wins the odd trick; I can asure you that untill the excitement of the next rubber moves him, he feels more like a dead man than a live one; I hardly like to write it, but I feel awfully used up.

Used up or not, he made another trip out of Lincoln early in December, the details of which he did not see fit to record.[21] Wherever he went, it was far enough away that he could not get to a post office, for on December 7 Widenmann penned a short note to the Tunstall family to advise them that Tunstall was "away and not able to write to you this mail, but is, as he says, 'alive and well.' He will doubtless send you his letter shortly." A postscript adds "We have been in great trouble but it is now all over."

Not for the first time (or the last), Widenmann was wrong: their troubles were only just beginning.

CHAPTER 15

THE TRIALS OF
ALEXANDER MCSWEEN

ALEXANDER McSween and his wife had decided late in the year to take a trip back east. With David Shield on hand to take care of business, the McSweens planned to be away for perhaps as long as six months. They planned to rendezvous at Anton Chico with John Chisum, and travel together to St. Louis, where Mrs. McSween would remain, visiting friends and relatives and continuing her music training. Some of the arrangements the lawyer made before departure persuaded not a few people that he had no intention of returning.

On December 4, for instance, McSween executed a warranty deed in favor of his sister-in-law Elizabeth Shield, giving her title to the five-room east wing of the McSween house and that portion of his land on which it stood, "in consideration of love and affection" cherished for his sister-in-law "and the sum of $1.00."[1]

Three days later, Charles Fritz petitioned the probate court to order McSween to pay over the proceeds of the Fritz insurance. Using as his reason (or excuse) the fact that Emilie Scholand had again failed to appear, McSween demurred; he would pay over the money only if Mrs. Scholand or her representative, carrying her signed authority, was present. Charles Fritz assured the court that his sister would appear in person the following month.

McSween was still conducting business right up to the morning of his departure, as shown by a bill of exchange in favor of Richard Ewing [Ewan] in the sum of $186.03 drawn on L. G. Murphy & Co., "the balance due me from you," dated December 18.[2] No doubt there were many other arrangements to be made: the handing over of his caseload to his partner David Shield; a final conference with Tunstall about their mutual interests, and so on. The McSweens left town during the course of that Tuesday en route to Anton Chico.

Immediately following the probate court hearing on December 7, Jimmy Dolan had made straight tracks for Las Cruces.[3] His version of events, given later to Frank Warner Angel, was that he went there to obtain legal advice and secure counsel to represent him at the next hearing, scheduled for January 21, where he planned to show the court that the Fritz estate was substantially indebted to the House. While he was there, James Longwell brought him the news that the McSweens had left. "I do not remember whether I called on [Mrs. Scholand] before I received the information or whether I called on her afterwards," he testified later with characteristic evasiveness.

Whatever the facts, he easily persuaded Emilie Scholand, whose command of English was even worse than her brother's, that the McSweens were leaving the country for good and taking her money with them.[4] A letter he wrote to the *New*

Mexican much later indicates what he might have told her: that the hundred-dollar payment McSween had made to her and her brother was "hush money" to keep them quiet while he made good his escape; that he was going to St. Louis to complete his education as a lawyer and would not come back for at least two years, if ever.

On December 21, Emilie Scholand signed an affidavit that said what Dolan wanted it to say.[5] He took it to his friend, District Attorney W. L. Rynerson, who immediately requested their mutual ally in Santa Fe, U.S. District Attorney Thomas B. Catron, to ensure that McSween did not leave the Territory before a warrant for his arrest could be sent to Las Vegas. At the same time, an order prohibiting John Chisum from leaving the jurisdiction of the court of New Mexico was cited as cause for his arrest and detention.

Catron telegraphed the sheriff of San Miguel County to hold McSween and Chisum pending the arrival of warrants. McSween was to be arrested for embezzlement; in the case of Chisum, Catron used an almost unheard-of legal ploy, a writ of *ne exeat regno* (let him not leave the kingdom), an obscure piece of legislation that had its origins in English common law.

Although the sheriff of San Miguel County had no legal right to detain either of them, McSween and Chisum agreed to wait, meanwhile consulting lawyers in Las Vegas; when after forty-eight hours the warrants did not materialize, their attorneys insisted on their release, and the trio left Las Vegas for Trinidad. They had not been gone more than half an hour when the awaited warrants arrived. According to an account of events written by John Chisum, they were overtaken by the sheriff and a posse armed with guns, rocks, and clubs, which surrounded the ambulance in which Chisum and the McSweens were riding.

> Chisum was jerked out head foremost & fell upon his face on the hard road and [was] siezed by the throat. . . . [H]e still helt his grip until Chisum said to the Sheriff Will you please be so kind as to loosen the grip of this . . . cur? The Sheriff spoke and the cur loosed his holt so Chisum breathed once more the fresh air of New Mexico they brag so much of.
>
> McSween was also jerked out of the ambulanch and drug off by a lot of the gang & Mrs McSween left siting all alone crying in the ambulanch without a driver or even a protector. The Sheriff and his possey very much excited McSween was somewhat confused Chisum laughing and cool. He looked the gang over & noticest one . . . that had on a clean shirt & had just arrived at the scene of excitement. Chisum asked him if he would be kind enough to drive Mrs McSween to the [Wagoner] Hotel which he consented and drove her there. Chisum and McSween were then marched to the Court house McSween put in jailors room & Chisum in the Court house and arrested under a charge sworn out by the Sheriff of resisting the Sheriff of San Magil County in the discharge of his duties as Sheriff aforesaid.[6]

Chisum's lurid account dates these events January 28, 1878; if they ever happened—in McSween's version, he was required to remain in his hotel room until he was taken to jail—they actually took place between Christmas Eve and December 28. The old cattle baron knew as well as McSween who was behind their arrest; his jaunty account of subsequent events shows that Chisum had determined to tough it out his own way. As for McSween, Chisum added, "feeling it his duty to protect those he represented [he] suffered himself imprisoned and after he had suffered in the Cold Dungeon 4 day & nights was then let out and told if he would pay over the money he could go on to St. Louis. McSween refused to Compromise saying he was [either] guilty or not guilty. And after being kept at Las Vegas some 8 or 10 day he was carried before Judge Bristol for an examination."

Not quite: the San Miguel court ordered that McSween be taken under arrest to La Mesilla, there to be examined by the court of the judicial district in which the alleged offenses had been committed. Faced with an involuntary return to Lincoln County, McSween urged his wife to go on to St. Louis; she let herself be so persuaded. That she went would seem to indicate either supreme confidence in her husband's ability to vindicate himself, or supreme indifference to his fate. Since McSween's actions at this point indicate clearly that he felt he had nothing to fear, there seems no reason to suppose it was the latter.

McSween placed himself at the disposal of the law. Chisum elected otherwise; required to list his assets in the lawsuits being brought against him, the old cattle rancher refused and was duly imprisoned. He remained in Las Vegas for eight weeks all told, occupying his time by composing an idiosyncratic account of his troubles with the Santa Fe Ring, and writing letters to his friends in the same cocky, ironic style.

December in Lincoln County was bitterly cold; the temperature did not rise above zero once in the week preceding the holiday, and snow fell on Christmas Day. There seems to have been little festivity at Tunstall's ranch on the Feliz: he had a bad attack of the blues.

> I had quite made up my mind to go over to England this winter & I had been looking forward to it for months, picturing all sorts of joy in seeing you all again & in explaining to you all I had done & all I hoped to do, & amongst my troubles I would think of that hope marred & it was by no means the least of them. When I shall be able to get over now I can not atall say, though I shall seize the first opportunity.
>
> My Xmas day was not a success, though I had a very fair dinner, I need not tell you that I thought of you all, perhaps more on that day than any other, & regretted that I was not amongst you. Your photos have been a great pleasure to me, you cant imagine how I long to see Lillian and Mabel, even more than the rest of you; if I had not those two little pets to live for I should often consider the battle long & the stakes not worth the game, but I feel that I have a trust to guard for them, & things will go hard indeed but what I will hold my own & theirs too.[7]

In a later letter he revealed that not only was he "a good many degrees below par" at Christmas, but also that he

> had a lot of bothering business to attend to, that compelled me to be out in the cold, a great deal, & a careless Mexican let all my horses out, & sent me galloping all over creation to fetch them in, when I was not fit to be away from the fire.
>
> But I looked at all your likenesses in the evening, & loved you all a great deal, first one at a time then collectively, I nearly felt home sick (a weakness I never allowed to come over me since I left you) but I had too much fighting on hand, to think about leaving the front.

Further indication of his state of mind comes from a recently found snippet of a letter he wrote around this time to his old friends the Francises in Victoria. "I am in a fair way to make a fortune," he told them. "[I]f I live I shall acquire it, but what a price I am giving for it. I am sacrificing the presents of a Father's smiles, a Mother's love & sisters caresses, the enjoyment of home and all that makes life [worth] living."[8]

Concluding the twenty-four-page letter he had commenced at the end of November, he told his family that he had had

> a great deal of book work to do lately, though that is of course comparitively, rest.
>
> I have the arrangements made to milk 100 cows this year, I dont expect to make very much out of it directly; but indirectly I shall; the cattle will get more gentle, I shall get buildings & improvements put up, & I shall sell a good many goods to the hands at work & the butter will pay the piper.[9]

Tunstall's two greatest weak spots, according to McSween, were his fondness for horses and his friendship with Robert Widenmann. In closing, Tunstall touched on both subjects.

> I bought a blind horse the other day at a sale of condemned army stuff, I gave 27½ dollars for him, & I think I never saw a prettier horse, & I never threw my leg over a finer saddle horse, he walks fast enough to keep my Long Tom horse in a slow jog trot, he paces, trots, & goes a single foot gait, that I never saw in England, he can canter on a cabbage leaf & gallop very finely, he is coal black, his mane & tail are as fine as I ever saw, I should think he is nearly thoroughbred, he is not over 7 years old. I would not take $150[00] for him today. He has never had his eyes doctored, & I think I may cure him, if I could do that, he could not be bought. . . . I bought another horse there, a white one, he weighs about 1300 lbs, he is quite sound only 9 years old, he was condemned because the government saddles hurt his back, I paid $25[00] for him, I put him in harness & he works splendidly, I would not take $125[00] for him today.
>
> This winter is a very cold one; or else, being fagged out & rheumatic I feel it more than I did last year, though I seem to be able to drive a hard pulling horse against the wind without gloves, when others cannot, & I guess when I "pick up" again I shall get as tough as ever. . . . Widenmann or rather Rob (as I always call him) sticks to me like a brick & takes as much care of me, & spares me as much bother & exposure as is possible. . . . I think I need rest & care more than anything else, as I have done too much, & it will be time that will pull me through.

Of McSween's difficulties there was not a hint, although word of the lawyer's predicament reached Lincoln twenty-four hours before he himself did. Tunstall's letter to his parents was written the same day that McSween arrived in the custody of two San Miguel County deputy sheriffs, Antonio Campos and Adolph P. Barrier. Upon arrival, they learned that Judge Warren Bristol was seriously ill and that McSween's hearing at La Mesilla had been postponed (fig. 39).[10] Deputy Campos returned to Las Vegas, leaving McSween under house arrest in Barrier's custody.

The following morning, McSween appeared in probate court to hear Judge Florencio Gonzales disallow, for lack of evidence, a claim from L. G. Murphy against the Fritz estate.[11] McSween said the amount claimed was seventy-six thousand dollars. Dolan put it at fifty-seven thousand. The actual records do not show any figure. The ruling was a bitter blow to the House, for Dolan and Riley were on the verge of bankruptcy. Lawrence G. Murphy, wasted and frail, was terminally ill.

McSween left court and immediately sat down to compose a letter to the Las Cruces newspaper *Eco del Rio Grande,* which had published on January 3 an editorial deploring his actions in the matter of the Fritz estate.[12] Claiming that it did him "great injustice," McSween set out his version of events. He had become attorney for the estate in October 1876; refused to settle for fifty cents on the dollar with "certain parties" in New York; paid over seven to eight hundred dollars to get the policy out of the hands of Spiegelberg Bros.; and filed a complete accounting of his costs with the probate clerk on his return. In January 1877 he had presented his account for $3,815.15, which was approved by the probate court and Charles Fritz. On August 1, Donnell, Lawson advised him they had credited his account in the sum of $7,148.94, whereupon he had advised Fritz and Mrs. Scholand that he was ready to settle, after paying approved claims totaling $280.00 to Juan Patrón and J. B. Wilson.

I was never asked to settle, nor did I promise or agree "to surrender the amount at the next session of probate court."

I was requested to go to St Louis on business for Col. Hunter. Every man, woman and child in the town knew I was going three weeks before I left. Before leaving I wrote Captain Crouch, Judge Bristol, Judge Newcomb, and Mrs. Fountain of my contemplated trip, how long I expected to be absent, &c. Two or three days

FIG. 39. Warren Henry Bristol. Date unknown; photographer William H. Brown.

before leaving Mr Fritz called at my office and asked if I would pay him a specific sum of money; I replied in the affirmative. I told him I was going; how long I expected to be absent; that Mr Shield of this place would have charge of my business during my absence; that when Mrs Scholand came over or sent her order, the balance in my hands would be paid. I remitted Mrs Scholand some money at the suggestion of a member of the Doña Ana bar. L. G. Murphy, surviving partner &c, recently filed claims against the estate to the amount of $76,000 (seventy six thousand dollars!). The whole of this claim was this day disallowed by Judge Gonzales, for want of evidence. On the other hand, taking Maj. Murphy's own statement, the surviving partner owes the estate over thirty thousand dollars, so that his claim to the insurance money has "faded."[13]

Desperate for money, Jimmy Dolan and John Riley executed a mortgage deed two days later to—who else?—Thomas B. Catron of Santa Fe.[14] For the sum of ten dollars, plus Catron's "accommodation endorsement" of their various notes and "a certain note this day in the amount of $25,000," they surrendered their interest in everything they owned: the forty acres of land in Lincoln on which the House and Dolan's home stood, their entire stock and all their book accounts, their inventory of grain and hay, as well as fifteen hundred cattle, thirty-five horses, and twelve mules at Black River. The deed was witnessed by William S. "Buck" Morton, foreman of the Murphy cow camp, and Edgar Walz, Catron's brother-in-law, who had arrived at Santa Fe from Minnesota at the beginning of the year.

On Monday, January 14, McSween and Tunstall went in for the kill. McSween acted first: he presented to Charles Fritz, as co-administrator of the Fritz estate, his suit against L. G. Murphy & Co. in the amount of $23,376.10. The alarmed Fritz, according to McSween's later testimony, told him "not to commence a suit against L. G. Murphy for the money due said estate . . . as he intended to compromise same and look out for his own interests, and that he did not care for the absent heirs and did not propose to work for their benefit."[15]

Next, John Tunstall joined the fray.[16] At the twenty-third legislative assembly, convened in Santa Fe on January 7, Governor Axtell had presented his annual message to the assembly. Tunstall seized on one passage and used it to strike at those who were responsible for the harassment McSween was being forced to endure.

OFFICE OF JOHN H. TUNSTALL
Lincoln, Lincoln County.
January 18, 1878.

"The present sheriff of Lincoln County has paid nothing during his present term of office."—Governor's Message for 1878.

Editor of the Independent.

The above extract is a sad an unanswerable comment on the efficiency of Sheriff Brady and cannot be charged upon "croakers". Major Brady, as the records of this county show, collected over Twenty Five Hundred Dollars, Territorial funds. Of this sum, Alexander A. McSween, Esq., of this place paid him over Fifteen Hundred Dollars by cheque on the First National Bank of Santa Fe. Said cheque was presented for payment by John H. Riley, Esq. of the firm of J. J. Dolan & Co. This last amount was paid by the last named gentleman to Underwood & Nash for cattle. Thus passed away over Fifteen Hundred Dollars belonging to the Territory of New Mexico. With the exception of Thirty-nine Dollars, all the taxes of Lincoln County for 1877 were promptly paid when due.

Let not Lincoln County suffer the delinquency of one, two, or three men.

By the exercise of proper vigilance, the taxpayer can readily ascertain what has become of what he had paid for the implied protection of the commonwealth. It is not only his privilege but his duty. A delinquent taxpayer is bad; a delinquent tax collector is worse.

Jimmy Dolan was in La Mesilla when this letter was published in the *Independent*; its effect on him was electric. Seething with anger, the little Irishman vowed to confront Tunstall at the earliest opportunity and see if the Englishman would say to his face what he had been saying for so long behind his back.[17]

If Tunstall was aware of how rash an act he had committed, he gives no sign of it.[18] He was probably too preoccupied: as he told his parents on January 20, he was up to his neck in worries and aggravations

but with the luck that seems to stick to me, I seem to light on my feet when no one else would. I have been very much under the weather during the last fortnight, but I am feeling somewhat better now. I have to start out on the road tomorrow, on a trip 6 days long, it is a hard trip & I dread it, but I believe that if ever I reach the point of death, I shall be called upon to make some disagreeable trip, before I am allowed to go to the next world. I am going to drive my blind horse Colonel, to save other horses, that are not in such good flesh & that I want to build up. I rode him today, & he is a beauty, the best road horse I ever crossed, he never makes a mistake unless I get careless (which I dont get) & he moves along as easy as a chair & makes about 6 miles an hour without moving one in the saddle. I am afraid I shant be able to cure his eyes, as he was run blind.

He was going to La Mesilla, he told his parents, once again concealing from them the underlying reasons for the trip. Instead he talked about the "points" he was making. He had things in such a shape now, he said, that the only risk he ran was of Indians stealing his horses. If they did so, he would "gather up a few of the boys & have a little war of my own & I expect the result would be that I should bring back about 4 horses for [every] one stolen." This was all preliminary to asking his father whether he was going to be able to put up some more money.

I cant look into your pocket & tell how well you are able to answer this call, just at present; though of course you have expected me to write in about this shape before long. I would write you at greater length but I am as I told you, about to start tomorrow for a two or three weeks trip, & I have no time to go into every detail of my business, & I would like to hear what you will be able to do, as soon as possible after my return. If you could not respond to the call atall, I reckon I could survive it, for I have been playing my hand very slick. But as I have told you from the start, it takes a certain number of cattle to make enough increase to pay herding expenses &c &c. . . .

There are 8 men talking around me & I have to have a little business conference with one of them, so I must close this. I will take writing materials along with me & write to you from Mesilla.

The following morning, a Saturday, Tunstall, McSween, David Shield, J. B. Wilson, and Deputy Sheriff Barrier left Lincoln; according to Tunstall's account they reached La Mesilla five days later, on Wednesday, January 30. McSween's hearing was set for the following Saturday.

Meanwhile Jimmy Dolan had prepared a reply to Tunstall's "taxpayer's complaint": addressed to the *Independent* and datelined Las Cruces, January 29, it flatly refuted Tunstall's allegations.[19]

In answer to a communication in reference to taxpayers of Lincoln County published in your issue of the 26th and signed J. H. T., I wish to state that everything contained therein is false.

In reference to Sheriff Brady, I will state that he deposited with our House Territorial funds amounting to nearly $2000, subject to his order and payable on demand. Owing to sickness in the family of Sheriff Brady he was unable to be in Santa Fe in time to settle his account with the Territory. This I hope will explain satisfactorily how the Governor in his message had our county delinquent.

If Mr. J. H. T. was recognized as a gentleman and could be admitted into respectable circles in our community, he might be better posted on public affairs. For my part I can't see the object of Mr. J. H. T.'s letter, unless it is to have the public believe that Alexander A. McSween is one of the largest taxpayers in our county, when in fact he is one of the smallest.

Sheriff Brady is ready at any time to show uneasy taxpayers what disposition he has made of the money paid by them; he can also show clean receipts from the Territorial Treasurer for his account.

And so, indeed, Brady could: the office of the territorial treasurer published a statement in the *New Mexican* of February 9 to the effect that Brady's accounts had been properly kept and payment had been made in full. This was true as far as it went; payment had been made, but not by Brady. Thomas B. Catron had paid in the monies on the sheriff's behalf, using for funds the proceeds of Indian Department vouchers made out by John Riley and forwarded to the First National Bank in Santa Fe.

While they awaited Judge Bristol's pleasure, Tunstall took the opportunity to write—for what would be the last time—to his "Much Beloved Governor."[20] He was still "very much below par," he reported, and had suffered badly with rheumatism on the trip.

> [T]here is a local peculiarity in the atmosphere for 70 miles of that journey, that catches a rheumatic subject every time, & my knees ached a good deal.
>
> I came here on some land business & was just in time to save a very important filing I had made in the land office, which some of those confounded squatters had tried & nearly succeeded in upsetting; I saw their filing & discovered an irregularity in it & had it set aside, those fellows would steal the eyes out of a man's head, if he did not keep them peeled all the time, they have not, however, scored a single point in my game. . . .
>
> I came here to make a very fine point in my game, & I think I have made it; those cursed squatters (I cant call them by any other name) have the laws all made to suit them; they are handicapped in such a way, that it is only by strategy that I can win; but win I will, in spite of everything.

Like the earlier letter from Lincoln, the main purpose of this one was to show his father why he needed a further three thousand pounds (fifteen thousand dollars) to complete his schemes.

> I would of course like the money I write for, as soon as possible as I have been put off writing for it for a long time, as until I had made good every piece in the game, that I had lost, & until I had proved to myself, that I could win the game on the line of play I had adopted, I would not risk another cent of your money in my hands, but now that I have turned every piece of apparently bad luck around, until every misfortune looks like a blessing, I have confidence in what I am doing & that I run no risk. If you can raise all the money at once, to send me, it would suit me that much the better; if not, you could send me £1000 at a time, as soon as you could manage it, that would be the next best thing.

The very last lines Tunstall wrote home as he concluded his letter on January 31 were in praise of his friend Widenmann (fig. 40). During his pursuit of Tunstall's stolen mules to La Mesilla, Widenmann had

> made quite a name for himself here, for coolness, courage, & general manly virtues, he is a splendid fellow & takes as much care of me when I am sick as if I were a woman; I get impatient at him sometimes, one night I threatened to set my bull dog on him if he would not stop coddling me up; he had fed and taken care of the dog a good deal & said "he would not hurt *him*," & kept up his kind treatment, I fetched Punch in, & made a strike at Widenmann, & if I had not held him Punch would have had him in a trice, we tied master Punch up again, & Rob did not brag over his superior health & strength again for a while.

He closed by saying he was expecting to leave La Mesilla in two days; obviously, he did not expect McSween's hearing to be more than a formality. It turned out to be anything but. Due to Judge Bristol's illness, the examination took place at his home on February 2 and 4. During it, McSween was subjected to harsh and partisan questioning by both District Attorney Rynerson and Bristol himself.

The hearing, which overran Saturday and had to be continued on Monday, was a curious affair: testimony was given not under oath but "on honor." No record of the proceedings seems to have been kept; once again there is conflicting evidence concerning what was said. Addressing the grand jury in Lincoln the following April, Bristol stated that McSween had taken it upon himself to show

that he was a large property owner in Lincoln county. That the value of his property was estimated not by hundreds but by thousands of dollars . . . he had an interest in a large amount of stock scattered here and there over the country, and that he was in the mercantile business with Mr. Tunstall, and had an extensive stock of goods in this town. Among the witnesses to prove this was Mr Tunstall himself. I will call your attention to a single item of his testimony. It was this—that he and McSween were

FIG. 40. Robert Adolf Widenmann, aged twenty-seven, early 1879. Photo by Thomas Fall, Baker St., London.

partners in trade; that they owned as partners the stock of goods in the store on Mr McSween's premises here; that the stock of goods was worth a considerable amount, I forget how much; and that Mr McSween had a half interest or thereabouts.[21]

James Longwell, who was present at the hearing, confirmed that he heard Tunstall testify that McSween was his partner.[22] David Shield and Deputy Sheriff Adolf Barrier said otherwise; they jointly testified that "they were present during the entire examination and heard all the evidence; that A. A. McSween was not sworn as a witness, nor did he make in person a statement in his defence; [and] that Mr Tunstall made oath that no articles of co-partnership were ever executed by and between him and said McSween."

That Tunstall and McSween were not partners is a matter of record; there is more than enough evidence of Tunstall's dispassionate attitude toward McSween—and partnerships in general—to justify the statement that he would never have jeopardized all his plans by entering into any such arrangement with the lawyer, or anyone else.

The hearing proved inconclusive: because of the absence of his most important witnesses—Juan Patrón was attending the legislature then in session, and Florencio Gonzales had been unable to come to La Mesilla—McSween's case was continued to the April term of court in Lincoln. In closing the hearing, Judge Bristol, prejudiced throughout against McSween, delivered a lecture to the lawyer, which Deputy Barrier described as "very unbecoming," and which he felt showed Bristol to be "a bitter partizan."[23]

Bail was set at eight thousand dollars on condition that it be approved by Rynerson. That worthy, however, categorically refused to accept any and all bondsmen offered by McSween, in any sum or for any reason. Deputy Barrier was thereupon ordered by Judge Bristol to take McSween back to Lincoln and there deliver him to Sheriff Brady, who would hold him in custody until acceptable bond was effected. In other words, if nothing else, the bastard could rot in the pit jail until April.

The party set out on the return journey on Tuesday, February 5.[24] They reached Shedd's ranch, on the eastern slope of the Organ Mountains, at sundown that night and proceeded to make camp in the corral. To what can have been only their dismay and consternation, they saw Jessie Evans, Frank Baker, and John Long (alias Frank Rivers) coming toward them. Shedd's ranch was dangerous territory: the Boys could do anything they liked in this part of the world and get away with it.

David Shield went over to talk to the Boys, who asked if the McSween party had by any chance passed Jimmy Dolan on the road. Shield told them that they had not seen him. Frank Baker made a remark to the effect that they had an appointment to meet Dolan, and when Jimmy said he would be somewhere at a stated time, he was there. Indeed, Dolan did arrive in the small hours of the morning, together with Charles Fritz and James Longwell. They joined the Boys in their bivouac.

Dolan's arrival must have unsettled them even more. Bitterly angry over his letter to the *Independent,* the Irishman had confronted Tunstall in La Mesilla, calling him names and challenging him to fight; to Dolan's disgust, Tunstall demurred. The McSween party spent an uneasy night contemplating a journey during which at any time Dolan, backed up by the Boys, might come after them. They awoke early and breakfasted at about eight. As usual, there are contradictory versions of what happened next. McSween's was as follows:

> About 8 or 9 o'clock . . . [I] saw J. J. Dolan, with gun in hand, and another man descending from a house occupied by Mr Shedd, said house being situated about 70 or 80 yards due south of where [I], Tunstall, Wilson, Shield and Barrier were camped: said J. J. Dolan and the person accompanying him appeared to be going in a westerly direction, thus hiding themselves from us by the southeast corner of said corral. In a few minutes said J. J. Dolan and Jesse Evans came around the southeast corner of said corral. In a few minutes said J. J. Dolan drew his Winchester carbine on Mr Tunstall, and asked him if he was ready to fight and settle their differences. Mr Tunstall asked him if he asked him to fight a duel. Mr Dolan replied "You d——d coward, I want you to fight and settle our difficulties." Dolan drew his gun cocked on Mr Tunstall three times. Mr Barrier placed himself between or in line with Dolan and Evans, and saved, as I believe, the lives of Tunstall and myself; when Mr Dolan was leaving he used these words, "You won't fight this morning, you d——d coward, but I'll get you soon." After he had gone off about 20 yards he turned around and said to Tunstall "When you write to the 'Independent' again say I am with the 'boys.'"
> " . . . [A]fter the occurrence of the attempted killing of Tunstall and myself above related, we started for Lincoln; after travelling about 20 miles we were passed on the road by said J. J. Dolan, Evans, Baker, Hill and Long alias "Rivers." Evans and Baker rode with Mr Dolan in his ambulance. It was known to Mr Dolan at this time that all these men were highwaymen and escaped prisoners.

McSween's statement places him in harm's way; Deputy Barrier remembered it differently.

> Dolan and Evans came to our camp both well armed; Dolan wished to fight Tunstall; drew his gun on Tunstall three times. Tunstall said he was not a fighting man; did not get his living that way.
> Dolan as he left the camp said, "Damn you, I'll get you yet, you damned coward!" or words to that effect as near as I can recollect.

Predictably, Dolan's account contradicted everything said by Barrier and McSween:

> I left Mesilla on February 5th. At San Augustin I heard that Tunstall, McSween, Barrier, Shields and Squire Wilson were there. The next morning I went to their camp to see Tunstall about the letter he had written to the Independent, which was untruthful, and about his attempt to injure us. These facts made me very angry; I was armed; I talked to Tunstall in a very severe manner. He acted in a very childish manner. I tried in every way to see if he was a man. He made no resistance although he was armed. I did not drop my carbine on him; I only threw it over my shoulder with the butt towards him.
> I told him I was ready to give him any satisfaction he wanted. I made no threats against him. I never said "When you write the Independent say I am with the 'boys,' " or any words to that effect. Any assertion to the contrary by any one is absolutely false. I went there to take no advantage of him. My gun was neither loaded nor cocked, nor did I sneak up to where he was. I wanted him to stop his lying statements about me or stand accountable for his assertions to me personally. That was the only object I had in going to see him.
> Jesse Evans was standing in the corner of the stable near McSween's party's camp. He evidently saw that I was excited and followed after me. He did not follow me by request, either directly or indirectly. I had no appointment with either Baker, Evans, or Rivers to meet me at San Augustin or anywhere on the road, and any assertions to the contrary are absolutely false.

Dolan's testimony always has the same curiously evasive quality about it, that of someone never quite willing to state that black is black and white is white. This specimen is no different. He explained that Evans was riding in the ambulance because he had been wounded. This tallies with a story that appeared in the *Independent* on January 26, which stated that after stealing some horses on January 19, Jessie Evans and two others were chased by three Hispanics near Lloyd's ranch, about thirty miles north of Las Cruces. In the ensuing exchange of gunfire, several horses were killed and Evans was slightly wounded in the groin; it would appear he was convalescing at Shedd's.

Dolan also claimed he was glad to have the Boys along because he was afraid he would be killed on the road. Although McSween made no such claim, it is not difficult to imagine the alarm his party must have felt when Dolan and the Boys overtook and passed them about twenty miles out from the San Agustin pass. Ahead of them lay the trackless White Sands, perfect terrain for ambush.

They reached the Mescalero Agency without incident, to find not only that Baker, Hill, and Long were awaiting them, but that Agent Fred Godfroy was apparently on very friendly terms with the three badmen, their raids on the Mescalero horse herds some months earlier seemingly forgotten.

Godfroy told Tunstall that he had bought a horse from Hill that once belonged to McSween and had been among those stolen by the Boys and later brought back and put on Tunstall's ranch. Since neither Tunstall nor McSween had any claim to the animal, Godfroy asked Tunstall to give him a paper releasing it; Tunstall obliged. McSween's account of this exchange gives no hint of the electric tension that must have been in the air. With the lowering Hill, the plug-ugly Baker, and Jack Long stalking about, Tunstall had little option but to hand over the animal whether the claim was valid or otherwise. The Boys, especially Tom Hill, were just looking for an excuse to kill him, and he knew it.

After they left South Fork, according to Barrier, an ambush was laid for them between Dowlin's Mill and Fort Stanton; this would indicate they used back trails to reach their destination safely on Sunday, February 10. On arrival McSween learned that

> a courier had preceded me from Mesilla with a writ of attachment. That Riley, Dolan, and Murphy, and Sheriff Brady were in ecstasy over [my] prospective confinement in the county jail, and I was informed that Sheriff Brady was making the occasion a subject of merriment by making contracts to grind corn in Mexican mills to make gruel for my maintenance. That said Riley swept out the jail, in order that he might in future have it to say that he swept out the room in which I was incarcerated; that said Brady expressed himself, in the presence of E[lisha] A. Dow and others, to the effect that Tunstall and I had reported that he (Brady) was a defaulter to the Territory, but that he meant to show us that he would not make a default in confining [me] in jail and taking the spirit out of [me]; that he may have allowed Baker, Evans and Hill to escape, but he would not allow [me] to do so.

It was Dolan's machinations that had provided the occasion for Brady's elephantine humor. On February 6, prompted by Dolan, Charles Fritz had appeared before John S. Crouch in the Doña Ana County district court at La Mesilla and sworn an affidavit to the effect that McSween owed him and his sister eight thousand dollars, that the debt had been fraudulently contracted, and that McSween was "about to remove his property and effects out of this Territory."[25] With Rynerson and Dolan providing the required sixteen-thousand-dollar bond, the court next day issued a writ of attachment in the amount of eight thousand dollars against the person and property of Alexander McSween.

A small miracle was worked getting this writ from La Mesilla to Lincoln, more than one hundred and fifty miles away; it arrived there early enough on February 8 for Brady to commence attaching McSween's property before the lawyer's arrival. Because it had been adjudged that McSween and Tunstall were partners in everything, he also went to the Tunstall store to attach it and its contents. There he was confronted by Robert Widenmann.

> I told him that the property belonged to J. H. Tunstall, that I protested against any attachment, and would hold him and his bondsmen responsible for any loss or damages. Sheriff Brady said that he knew better; that the property belonged to A. A. McSween and he would attach it as such. He proceeded to take an inventory, without placing a value on any article or thing attached. He demanded the keys of different doors leading from the store, and upon my refusal to deliver the same had me arrested and searched without warrant or legal process, and forcibly took the keys from me. He was at the time accompanied by G. W. Peppin, Jack Long, James Longwell, and F. G. Christie.[26]

Widenmann's complaint was justified: Brady simply attached everything in sight, attributing no value to anything. As a result, when McSween reached

Lincoln he discovered Brady had attached "not only my personal property, but also my real, together with the property of J. H. Tunstall and others, even pictures of the family of the latter, as also a notarial seal belonging to D. P. Shield. He (the Sheriff) was commanded to attach and safely keep so much property as would secure the sum of 8,000 dollars, but he attached property, both real and personal, worth over 40,000 dollars."[27]

Persuaded that to do so would jeopardize McSween's life, Deputy Sheriff Adolph Barrier refused to hand his prisoner over to Brady. Instead McSween was held under a form of house arrest, with Barrier as his custodian. The lawyer immediately set to work trying to make bond that would satisfy Rynerson. At once he found the subtle hand of Dolan working against him: José Montaño had been warned that his business would be ruined if he supported McSween; Doctor Blazer was told that he would find himself facing charges of cutting timber on federal land if he subscribed.

Unable to spare time to write his father, Tunstall bade Widenmann scribble a note on February 9.[28] "Your son is 'all right,'" he wrote, "but we are very buisy. Should anything occur [i.e., happen] to him you will be sure to hear from me at once." Tunstall was not too preoccupied, however (according to the *New Mexican*), to write to John Chisum, still imprisoned in Las Vegas.[29] "The Sheriff has attached my store and threatens to attach my stock," he is alleged to have said, "but God damn him, he'll find I can't stand everything." It does not sound at all out of character: Tunstall was in a mounting rage. Even though he was in imminent danger of death, he realized he had no alternative: it was fight back, or be destroyed.

CHAPTER 16

PRELUDE TO MURDER

ON Monday, February 11, Tunstall and Widenmann, with Fred Waite (fig. 41) and "Kid" Antrim—now going by the name of William Bonney—as bodyguards, went to the store, which was being guarded by Brady's deputies Follett Christie, James Longwell, George Peppin, Jack Long, Charles Martin, and John Clark, the last a black man.[1] Tunstall was good and angry—Longwell testified that the Englishman put his hand on his gun and called him a damned thief—at having his property attached for a debt of McSween's. Brady's men were not impressed.

When Tunstall promised to make everyone involved in this "damned high hand business" suffer, Longwell suggested Tunstall seek legal redress. Fresh from watching McSween suffer at Rynerson's hands, Tunstall was scornful. "The courts be damned!" he snapped.

"Well," Longwell said, "if the courts here don't do you justice, you can appeal it to the Supreme Court or go to the United States court at Santa Fe."

"God damn that ring," Tunstall said, exasperatedly. "It's the worst God damn outfit of them all."

Following this exchange, Tunstall managed to convince Sheriff Brady that six horses and two mules in the corral behind the store were indisputably his personal property. Brady promptly released them from attachment, and Tunstall had the animals taken to the safety of his ranch. Widenmann takes up the story:

> [W]e succeeded in getting all the horses released (two mules and six horses) and at once started a man named G. Gauss, with three horses, for the ranch, I think, and on the afternoon of the same day started Wm. McCloskey and John Middleton for the ranch on two other horses, and subsequently I followed, in company with F. T. Waite and Wm. Bonnie, and arrived at the ranch on the morning of the 12th. R. M. Brewer was there in charge of the ranch, as well as the above-named persons, who had been sent on, and who were employed at the ranch then and prior to this.[2]

Meanwhile, back in Lincoln, the validity of Dolan's old boast that he had the Santa Fe Ring behind him, and that they controlled everything in New Mexico, including the law, was now apparent. Tunstall and McSween decided upon a new strategy, one perhaps suggested by Widenmann. That evening, McSween wrote a long and detailed letter to Carl Schurz, secretary of the interior, accusing Mescalero agent Fred Godfroy and J. J. Dolan & Co. of collusion and fraud.

> *Sir:* Your commendable efforts to improve the working of your Department induces me to write you in relation to the management of the Mescalero Apache Indian

FIG. 41. Frederick T. Waite (left). Date and photographer unknown. The second man is almost certainly Henry Newton Brown.

Agency in this County, and in doing so, I am not without the hope that you may give the matter immediate attention.

Before stating particulars I may mention that Maj. Godfroy, the present Agent, boasts of the fact that the Commissioner of Indian affairs sends him a copy of all letters of complaints and accusations; if he should be favored with a copy of this no possible good could result from this letter, for wherever you forewarn you forearm.

It looks as though the Agent were the property of J. J. Dolan and J. H. Riley, known here as J. J. Dolan & Co. For the past two years these men have had the flour & beef contracts (as sub-contractors I think) and have delivered articles unfit for use. Sprouted half rotten wheat has been mashed and turned in as first rate flour. The flour for this agency is principally ground on a Mexican Mill without a bolt or smutter—in other words the wheat is mashed. Frequently Corn has been bought and turned in as flour. Occasionally these fellows patronize a good grist mill situated within 18 miles of the Agency. For example, when Gen. Vandeveer was here inspecting, the Clerk at the Agency under direction of the Agent, placed a few sacks of good flour at different points, into these the Gen. placed his Knife and was, of course, highly satisfied with the flour!

These fellows are also Indian Traders. At their store they receive "surplus" by an underground Railroad process. Frequently they load wagons with Indian coffee and sugar and send over here to sell—these same men have a store here.

The beef they furnish is of the poorest quality. The cattle they kill are frequently too poor to walk to the butcher pen and have to be killed on the range and carted to the issue house. They *never* kill the number reported, nor do they feed the number of Indians they report.

Indian Blankets have been given or sold citizens. It's well known that these men deal in stolen cattle and thus encourage stealing—the Agent is certainly aware of this.

M. J. Bernstein, Clerk, kept books for said J. J. Dolan & Co during six months of the past year, during which period he received salary, as we believe, from the Government.

The Indians are continually depredating on citizens owing to the fact that the Agent fails to give them what the Govt. has allotted them.

I suggest that you send a Detective here who will ferret this matter; he'll find things as I have stated them. Or you might suspend the Agent until an investigation was had. If this course were adopted, the Agent should know nothing of it until the temporary Agent should present the papers to take charge, so that there could be no putting in order of "fixing up"; for, certainly, if the Agent gets word, the object of your investigation will have been to a great extent defeated. A thorough search will disclose fearful villainy on the part of all concerned.

I can furnish unimpeachable affidavits in support of the hints given herein should you require them.

Should you appoint a *temporary* Agent, I would recommend Robt. A. Weidenmann of this place as a competent and responsible man who will discharge his duty without fear or favor. For my responsibility I refer to Soule Thomas & Wentworth, 208 S. 4th St., St. Louis, Mo. and Col. R. D.Hunter, Nat. Stock Yards, East St. Louis Ills.

In confidence.

P.S. Said Dolan is Post Master here and the mails passing thro' are always *well* examined; to such an extent is this true that many here have had to change their P.O.

Govt. officers are interest[ed] in these frauds so that those on whom the duty of prosecution is by law cast are not to be trusted.

A. A. McS.[3]

Next day, the lawyer completed his arrangements to raise bond and submitted his sureties in the sum of $34,500 to Rynerson.[4] These were: Tunstall, $20,000; James West, $4,000; John Copeland, $3,000; Isaac Ellis, $4,000; Refugio Valencia, $2,000; and José Montaño, showing his defiance of Dolan's threats, $1,500. McSween was not sanguine about their acceptance: his black manservant George Washington had heard Dolan and Riley say there was no use in McSween trying to give bonds, as Rynerson would not approve any he might offer, and he would have to go to jail. Sure enough, Rynerson rejected them, on the grounds that the sureties were not worth the amounts proposed.

Although he had already sequestered goods and property far in excess of the sum specified in the writ, Brady now deputized Billy Mathews (fig. 42), Dolan and Riley's silent partner, to take a posse down to Tunstall's ranch and attach "McSween's" cattle. Widenmann was there when it arrived on the morning of February 13.

J. B. Matthews (claiming to be Deputy Sheriff) rode up to the ranch of Tunstall's on the Rio Feliz in company with George Hindman, John Hurley, an Indian [Manuel Segovia], Roberts, Evans, Baker and Hill. Seeing the last three in the party, and knowing they had threatened to kill me on sight, I stepped out and asked the party to stop where they were (which was about 50 yards from the house) and asked Matthews to come forward and state his business; Matthews said that he was Deputy Sheriff, and had come to attach the cattle of A. A. McSween, to which I answered that McSween had no cattle there, but if there were any he might take them. I offered no resistance, nor did the people with me, nor did we make any threats.

R. M. Brewer told Matthews in my presence and the rest of the party that he could round up the cattle and if he (Matthews) claimed that Brewer's cattle (there being some of Brewer's cattle on the range) belonged to McSween, he could leave a man there to take care of them until the Courts could settle the question. I then

FIG. 42. Jacob Basil "Billy" Mathews and his wife, Dora Bates Mathews, ca. 1882. Photographer unknown. Mathews was thirty-five years old at this time.

told Brewer that I was agoing to arrest Evans, Baker and Hill under my United States warrants, whereupon Brewer and the rest of the parties that were at the ranch with me said that it could not be done, that they were all ranch men and living at their places, and if they assisted in arresting Evans, Baker, and Hill, Dolan and Murphy would have them killed as soon as they got back to their ranches.[5]

Tunstall's cook, Godfrey Gauss, said that Brewer told Widenmann not to try to arrest the Boys, "for if he did we would all surely be killed."[6] As it was, things nearly developed into gunplay anyway. Brewer invited the possemen up to get something to eat. Then, as Widenmann recounted it, Jessie Evans advanced on him swinging his carbine and catching it at full cock pointed at Widenmann.[7]

"Are you looking for me?" he asked. "Have you got any warrant for me?"

"That is my business," Widenmann replied, defensively.

"If you ever come after me, you're the first man I'm agoing to shoot at," Evans warned him.

"That's all right," Widenmann said. "I can play at that game, too."

Widenmann demanded to know what the Boys were doing with the posse. Mathews told him that Evans had come over to find out if Widenmann had a warrant for him. While they were speaking Widenmann heard Baker say to

"Buckshot" Roberts, "What the hell's the use of talking? Pitch in and fight and kill the sons of bitches!"

Widenmann again turned to Evans and asked him what he had come to the ranch for.

"Mathews wanted me to come along," Evans said. "Besides, I wanted to see you."

As they spoke Frank Baker walked towards Widenmann with his pistol held butt forward as if in surrender, then swung it over in the maneuver known as the "road agent's spin" so that it ended up fully cocked and pointing at Widenmann.

The showdown did not come; although he indeed had warrants for the Boys, Widenmann was not so foolhardy as to try to arrest them singlehanded. After the posse had eaten, Mathews decided to go back to Lincoln and get further instructions from Sheriff Brady regarding the cattle, and told Widenmann and Brewer he would come back with just one man.[8]

Mathews, Hurley, and Segovia left for Lincoln; the rest of the party headed for W. W. Paul's ranch on the Peñasco. Widenmann rode with Mathews for a while; on the way, Mathews asked him

> if they attached Tunstall's cattle too, whether we would resist. I told him not if he left them there, but that if they attempted to drive the cattle to the Indian Agency, as they had said they would do, in order to kill them for beef, that we would do all that was in our power to defeat them, since if the cattle were driven there and killed, we could not collect a cent from Sheriff Brady's bondsmen [Dolan and Riley] who were known to be insolvent. On my journey to the town I had Waite and Bonney with me part of the time. We rode ahead part of the time; Matthews and his party last mentioned rode ahead.[9]

Widenmann arrived at the plaza on Wednesday evening, February 13, and reported to Tunstall and McSween. The latter takes up the story at the point where Widenmann told Tunstall

> he was satisfied that Matthews intended to raise a large posse, and take the cattle by force; for that purpose . . . Baker [and "Buckshot" Roberts, according to Middleton] had gone down to Dolan & Co's cow camp on the Pecos with instructions to William Morton, their foreman, to raise all the men he could, and meet Matthews with his posse at Turkey Springs, a few miles from Tunstall's cattle ranch, on the evening of the 18th February, 1878. [The next day] Mr Tunstall was informed in my hearing by George Washington that Murphy, Riley and Dolan had helped Matthews raise a force to the number of forty three men; that said Riley informed him (Washington) that there was no use in McSween's and Tunstall's trying to get away from them this time, as they had them completely in their power; that they could not possibly be beat, as they had the District Attorney (meaning Rynerson) the Court, and all the power in Santa Fe to back them; that their plan was to take the cattle from Tunstall's ranch by sending two Mexicans they had in the posse to make a sham "round up" of the cattle and horses, so as to draw the men in Tunstall's house out of it; then the balance of the posse were to take possession of the house and get Tunstall's men.[10]

Riley's was no idle boast: he had just received a letter written by Rynerson a few days earlier (fig. 43).

LAW OFFICE OF
WILLIAM L. RYNERSON
District Attorney, 3rd Judicial
District, New Mexico
Las Cruces, New Mexico,
February 14, 1878.
Friends Riley and Dolan,

I have just received letters from you mailed 10th inst. Glad to know that you (Dolan) got home O.K. and that business was going on O.K. If Mr Weidman interfered with or resisted the Sheriff in Discharge of his duty Brady did right in arresting him and anyone else who does so must receive the same attention. Brady goes into the store in McS's place and takes his interest. Tunstall will have same right then he had heretofore but he neither must obstruct the Sheriff or resist him in the discharge of his duties. If he tries to make trouble the Sheriff must meet the occasion firmly and legally.

FIG. 43. William Logan Rynerson, aged forty-six, ca. 1874. Photographer unknown; the original is a tintype.

I believe Tunstall is in with the swindles with the rogue McSween. They have the money belonging Fritz' estate and they know it. It must be made hot for them all, the hotter the better; especially is this necessary now that it has been discovered that there is no hell.

It may be that the villain Green "Juan Bautista" Wilson will play into their hands as Alcalde. If so, he should be moved around a little. Shake that McSween outfit up till it shells out and squares up, and then shake it out of Lincoln. I will aid to punish the scoundrels all I can. Get the people with you Control Juan Patron if possible You know how to do it. Have good men about to aid Brady and be assured I shall help you all I can for I believe there was never found a more scoundrelly set than that outfit.

Tunstall was much agitated by Widenmann's report, but remained firm in his decision not to take any step that would give their enemies an excuse to resort to violence. Rumors drifting in throughout Thursday confirmed Widenmann's story: Mathews was indeed recruiting a posse, largely composed of men from the Seven Rivers area and more than forty strong; they were to assemble not later than Saturday afternoon at Paul's ranch on the Peñasco.

Next morning, Bonney and Waite stopped Sam Wortley at gunpoint as he carried food to the men guarding the Tunstall store, and made him take it back to the hotel.[11] Later that day, Bonney saw James Longwell in the doorway of Tunstall's store and took aim at him. Fortunately for Longwell, Steve Stanley wandered into the Kid's line of fire and Longwell was able to duck inside. The Kid stood in the street with his carbine pointed at the store and shouted, "Turn loose now, you sons of bitches, I'll give you a game!"

Nobody inside accepted the challenge. After a while the Kid slouched away.

Early the following morning, Saturday, February 16, Widenmann left Lincoln in order to be back at the Feliz when Mathews arrived.[12] Waite, Bonney, Middleton, and Henry Brown went with him. Later that day, Dolan disappeared from town. Uncertain what his next step should be, Tunstall decided to go down to Chisum's ranch to see if he could get any help there. He left Lincoln on Saturday evening. As he said goodbye to McSween, the Englishman wrung the lawyer's hand.

"Mac, I want you to promise me that if I'm killed, you'll wind up my estate and give every cent in it to my two little sisters," he said. "If you die, I'll do the same for you, and give every cent to Mrs. McSween."

Then Tunstall rode off down the street on the horse he was training as a present for Mrs. McSween on her return to Lincoln. It was the last time the lawyer saw him alive.

McSween went back into his office and turned to his own problems. The *Grant County Herald* of February 9 had published an article about the Fritz estate squabble, and McSween felt he must contest the allegations it contained. He also now composed a supplementary plea for presentation at the March term of probate court.[13] In it, he averred that the co-administrators were wasting and mismanaging the estate by commencing and prosecuting a suit against him; that in spite of his offers to settle they had refused to do so, at the instance of J. J. Dolan "who is striving to obtain said monies and who is not entitled thereto"; that Dolan, the administrators' bondsman, was insolvent and guilty of fraud; that Charles Fritz and Emilie Scholand had perjured themselves at McSween's hearing in La Mesilla, and a number of other charges designed to persuade the court to revoke the letters of administration granted to Fritz and his sister.

Tunstall headed first for Chisum's ranch hoping to get assistance there, but with their brother still in jail in Las Vegas, James and Pitzer Chisum were reluctant to commit the Jinglebob to Tunstall's fight.[14] Vastly disappointed, Tunstall ate and snatched a few hours' sleep before heading down the Pecos and up the Feliz to his ranch. He reached the Feliz at about ten p.m. on Sunday, having ridden well over a hundred miles in twenty-four hours.

Widenmann, Brewer, Middleton, Bonney, Waite, McCloskey, Gauss, and Brown had done what they could to fortify the place by piling up sandbags and drilling holes in the walls of the house, and every man jack of them was ready for a fight. Tunstall immediately vetoed any such action. There was to be no resistance, he told them; no bloodshed.[15] He would not risk the life of one man for all the cattle in New Mexico; everyone must leave first thing in the morning.

"We'll leave Gauss here," he told Widenmann. "He's an old man. They won't touch him."

At about 3 a.m., McCloskey was dispatched to the Peñasco to get "Dutch" Martin Martz, an acknowledged neutral, to come over to the Feliz and help turn over the cattle to the posse. Since he had friends among the possemen, McCloskey was to stop at Turkey Springs and inform whoever was in charge that although the attachment was being made against Tunstall's consent, there would be no resistance.

Preparations made, the exhausted Tunstall turned in for a few hours' sleep. On what was to be his last night on earth he shared a bed with old Gauss; the others spread their blankets wherever they could. Next morning, Monday, February 18,

Tunstall, Brewer, Middleton, Bonney, Waite and myself [Widenmann] started for the Plaza about 8 o'clock . . . Waite driving the wagon; the rest of us driving about eight horses besides those we were riding. The horses were the property of J. H. Tunstall, R. M. Brewer, and myself. None of the horses then or ever belonged to A. A. McSween, and all but three had been released by the Sheriff, and of those three horses, one belonged to Brewer, one to Bonney, and the third was traded by Brewer to Tunstall for one of the horses the Sheriff had attached [in Lincoln].[16]

Henry Brown rode with them for a mile or so; then he peeled off to make his own way to Lincoln. Soon after their departure the posse arrived at Tunstall's ranch.[17] According to Billy Mathews they "had been informed by 'Dutch Martin' that if it was not for Widenmann there would be no trouble, as Brewer would make no resistance. We went to the ranch carefully, one party in front of the other from the rear, myself and Roberts being the party in front. We found that there was no one there except Gauss and, I think, 'Dutch Martin'."[18]

When Mathews came up to the ranch, he asked Gauss where Brewer and the rest were.

[I] told him they had all left this morning. There was a large party with him (Matthews); I should judge at least thirty. I gave them something to eat, or, rather, they helped themselves to what they wanted.

Matthews then said to me "Why did not someone remain to turn over the property?" I said Mertz would be here to do that. They commenced shoeing their horses out of Tunstall's property: three or four horses were shod. Matthews said, "If only Jim (meaning Dolan) was here. I have a notion to send after them and bring them back." I do not know whether they sent for Dolan, or whether he came of his own accord. He came about this time, and he picked out the men to follow after Tunstall's party to bring them back if they caught them before they reached the Plaza. From their actions I thought that some of the party of Tunstall's would be killed. I heard, I think it was Morton, cry out "Hurry up, boys, my knife is sharp, and I feel like scalping some one." They were all excited and seemed as though they were agoing to kill someone.[19]

Pantaleon Gallegos started to make a list of the posse; when he saw that Gallegos was writing down the names of Evans, Baker, Hill, and Davis, Mathews spoke to him sharply and said, "Don't put them boys down at all."

"I heard no one object to Baker, Evans, Hill and Davis going with the party," Gauss continued. "I am positive that Matthews and Dolan picked out the men. They would say 'You go; you go,' and so on, point out each person, and these persons commenced to examine their arms and horses."

Having selected the possemen and deputized Morton, Mathews instructed his men to "go with him after the horses, and they left, I having instructed them to overtake the horses and bring them back, and, in case there was any resistance, to arrest the men and bring them back too. If they did not overtake them before reaching the Plaza, if they found they were going to Lincoln, there to follow them in, and have Sheriff Brady attach the horses."[20]

At a later date, Mathews was asked to name on oath every man in the posse that went after the horses.[21] He listed John Hurley, Manuel Segovia, George Hindman, Pantaleon Gallegos, J. W. Olinger, R. W. Beckwith, Ramon Montoya, Thomas Green, Thomas Cochrane, Charles Kruling, George Kitt, Charles Marshall, Sam Perry, and Buck Morton, whose knife was sharp and who felt like scalping someone. Notably absent from his testimony were the names of Jessie Evans, Tom Hill, and Frank Baker. Sam Perry claimed the Boys "volunteered" to go along with the posse because

they had a horse among the horses Tunstall had taken away, and . . . wished to go after it. I do not remember whether there was any objection made by anyone to their accompanying us, except that Dolan said to either Matthews or Morton that they (Baker, Evans and Hill) had better not go. Either Baker, Evans or Hill replied that a person had a right to go for their property or something to that effect. I am positive that Dolan did not go with us.[22]

February 18 was a fine winter day, with a gentle west wind blowing and the temperature in the high forties. About ten miles from the ranch, Fred Waite left the main party and took the wagon road. Tunstall and his men headed up the mountain trail, and passed Pajarito Spring around five in the afternoon. As evening drew in, they entered a long canyon that would lead them down to the Ruidoso valley.[23] "Brewer, Tunstall and I were riding along driving the horses," said Widenmann,

> Middleton and Bonney being about 500 yards in the rear, and we three had just come over the brow of the hill when a flock of turkeys rose to the left of the trail. I offered Tunstall my gun, he having none with him, to shoot some of them, but he declined the use of it, saying that I was a better shot than he was. Brewer and I started off for the turkeys, leaving Tunstall with the horses, and had got about 300 yards from the trail, when I heard a noise behind me. Turning in my saddle I saw a party of men come over the brow of the hill on a gallop. I said, "Look there, Dick," and hardly spoken the words when a ball whizzed between me and Brewer, and the attacking party all commenced shooting at us without speaking a word to us. I said to Brewer, "We can't hold this place, it being a perfectly barren and rocky hillside; let us ride to the hill over there and make a stand;" the hill being covered with trees and large boulders. We rode towards the hill, the whole party coming after us, until they had reached the hillside; they had been continually firing at us; when they reached the hillside they evidently saw Tunstall, for they all turned down to where he was: in going to the hill we were met by Bonney and Middleton, who had partly rode around us to get away from the attacking party.

John Middleton's account of the same events was less florid and more immediate.[24] He said they had all scattered for the purpose of hunting the turkeys.

> Whilst so hunting we heard yelling, and saw a large crowd of men coming over the hill firing as they were coming. Tunstall and I were on the side of a hill about 700 yards from some horses we were bringing from the Feliz ranch to Lincoln. . . . The horses numbered nine. If they wanted the horses they could easily have got them without coming within 700 yards of us. Not one of those . . . with Tunstall fired a shot. We endeavored to escape for our lives. I was within thirty steps of Tunstall when we heard the shooting first. I sung out to Tunstall to follow me. He was on a good horse; he appeared to be very much excited and confused. I kept singing out to him "For God's sake, follow me." His last words were, "What, John? what, John?"

 # MURDER IN THE CANYON

THERE is no eyewitness account of the death of John Tunstall. Although a number of the men in the posse that pursued him from his ranch made affidavits setting down their recollections of the event, only three men knew exactly what happened up there in the canyon: Jessie Evans, Buck Morton, and Tom Hill. The story they told, that Tunstall had fired upon them first, and then been killed by their return fire, received little serious credence.

Widenmann and Middleton of course set down what they believed to have happened, but neither was an eyewitness. The most convincing testimony concerning the manner of Tunstall's death—although it, too, is only hearsay—came from two men who played no serious part in the fighting thereafter: John Patton and Albert H. Howe. Both appear to have obtained their information from one of the possemen, George Kitt. Patton said Tunstall was murdered in cold blood by Morton and Hill. Kitt told him

> that Tunstall was some distance off and was coming towards them; that Morton wished to shoot him, and Hill said, "Hold on, till he comes nearer." That after Tunstall came a little nearer, Morton shot him in the heart, and then Hill shot him in the head; that both Hill and Morton told Tunstall that if he would give up he would not be hurt; that notwithstanding this promise they shot Tunstall.[1]

Albert Howe's affidavit told essentially the same story in more—and equally convincing—detail. Although he had not seen the actual shooting, he said, Kitt

> was informed how Tunstall was killed by "the Boys"; that Tunstall was some distance off from the road, and when he found he had been deserted by his party, he turned and rode towards Hill and Morton; that when he came in sight of them he seemed very much surprised and hesitated; that Hill called to him to come up and that he would not be hurt; at the same time both Hill and Morton threw up their guns, resting the stocks on their knees; that after Tunstall came nearer, Morton fired and shot Tunstall through the breast, and then Hill fired and shot Tunstall through the head; someone else fired and wounded or killed Tunstall's horse at the time Tunstall was shot through the head by Hill; that two barrels of Tunstall's revolver were emptied after he was killed; that Tunstall fired no shots, and that Tunstall was killed in cold blood; that deponent knows said Hill, and considered him a desperate man, who would kill a man on sight that he had any dispute with or spite against.[2]

Widenmann and the others, having stopped at John Newcomb's farm on the Ruidoso to arrange for him to take a party out to find Tunstall's body and bring it in to Lincoln, brought the news into town between ten and eleven o'clock that night. Immediately thereafter, Widenmann, as a deputy U.S. marshal, went to the fort to ask for help from the military in arresting Tunstall's murderers; since he had no warrants, his request was denied.

The news of Tunstall's murder spread like wildfire. Some forty or fifty angry local men who had assembled at the McSween house during the day to protect the lawyer, and to render Tunstall assistance if he needed it, immediately pledged their support for any effort that might be made to bring Tunstall's murderers to justice.

At some point during these proceedings, it was alleged, John Riley, much the worse for liquor, reeled into the house and tried to dissociate himself from the murder.[3] Having laid down his gun, Riley proceeded to empty his pockets to prove he had no hostile intentions. From one of them fell a memorandum book that contained detailed notations of the shady transactions the House had conducted with the Indian agency, lists of the stolen cattle Dolan had bought from the Boys, notes on McSween and the Fritz estate, and a list of "code names" for use in correspondence. Inside this notebook was the letter from District Attorney Rynerson dated February 14, which exhorted "Friends Riley and Dolan" to "shake up" the McSween outfit (see chapter 16).

The providentiality of Riley's carelessness in this instance seems highly suspect: what a moment to put into the McSween faction's hands such damning evidence of the House's criminal activities! Was the Rynerson letter genuine? It has been pointed out that Wilson's appointment as alcalde (i.e., justice of the peace), was only made the day that Rynerson's letter was allegedly written. How did he find out about it so fast? The notebook, if it ever existed, came into McSween's hands by other means. It is hard to imagine Jimmy Dolan sanctioning the keeping of such a record; and in the unlikely event that he did, it is even harder to believe that the canny Riley would have been carrying it around. Possibly Widenmann kept Riley's notebook and took it back to Ann Arbor; if so, it was destroyed with all his personal papers when he died.

Either way, the town had turned into an armed camp; most of the posse that had gone to the Feliz had now returned, although Dolan was still conspicuously absent. Miraculously, there was no collision between the two parties, and the night passed without further incident.

At first light next day, John Newcomb assembled a search party at his farm on the Ruidoso consisting of himself, Florencio Gonzales, Patricio Trujillo, Lázaro Gallegos, and Ramón Baragón.[4] The last-named was an experienced tracker; it was he who found the body, concealed in the trees some distance away from where Tunstall had been killed. The body was "lying closely by the side of his horse," said Gonzales.

> The corpse had evidently been carried by some persons and laid in the position in which we found it; a blanket was found under the corpse and one over it. Tunstall's overcoat was placed under his head, and his hat placed under the head of his dead horse. By the apparent naturalness of the scene we were forced to conclude that the murderers of Mr Tunstall placed his dead horse in the position indicated, considering the whole affair a burlesque. It has been claimed that Mr Tunstall fired upon the posse, and had some horses they wished to attach, and that he fired two shots at them out of a Colt's improved revolver. We found his revolver quite close to the scabbard on the corpse.

It must have been placed there by some one after Tunstall's death. We found two chambers empty, but there were no hulls or cartridge shells in the empty chambers; the other four chambers had cartridges in them. On examination we found the skull broken; we found that a rifle or carbine bullet had entered his breast, and a pistol bullet entered the back of his head, coming out in the forehead. The corpse of Mr Tunstall was found over 100 yards off the trail on which the horses travelled, in advance of those said to have been driven by Mr Tunstall, showing clearly, by fresh horse tracks which were seen by us distinctly and plainly, that the horses the posse claimed to have been trying to recover from Mr Tunstall must have been quite a distance behind Mr Tunstall, and must have been passed by the posse before they could get Mr Tunstall.[5]

Tunstall's body was strapped onto a pack animal and brought down the steeply sloping canyon to Newcomb's farm. There it was transferred to a wagon, and brought up to the plaza. As soon as it arrived, Justice of the Peace Wilson empaneled a coroner's jury consisting of George B. Barber, John Newcomb, Robert M. Gilbert, Samuel Smith, Frank Coe, and Benjamin Ellis.[6] On the evidence placed before them by Widenmann, Brewer, Bonney, and Middleton, they arrived at the verdict that Tunstall had been killed "by one or more of the persons whose names are herewith written, to wit, Jessie Evans, William Morton, Frank Baker, Thomas Hill, George Hindman, J. J. Dolan, and others not identified by the witnesses who testified."

At about midday on that same Tuesday, while Tunstall's body was still being brought in from the canyon, a party consisting of Dr. Taylor F. Ealy, his wife Mary, their two children, and a schoolteacher, Susan Gates, had arrived in town. They had come to Lincoln at the behest of the Presbyterian Board of Missions, to whom McSween had during the preceding year addressed a request for a missionary.

They had learned about the murder of Tunstall the preceding night at Fort Stanton.[7] Apprised of conditions in Lincoln, and advised to turn right around and go back whence he had come, Ealy determined to carry out the task assigned to him, and the party left the fort for the plaza the next morning. A baptism of fire awaited.

About three miles out of town the party was stopped by a group of Dolan supporters, who searched their wagon for arms. Stopping to ask directions to McSween's house as he passed the Dolan store, Ealy was jeered at and told that while Lincoln had no need of his Bible-punching, he'd find plenty of work if he was a sawbones. When they got to McSween's house, "two or three armed men called out halt & we found ourselves in the center of a battlefield—about 40 men armed in full fighting trim—double belts of cartridges, one for the revolvers and the other for the Winchester rifles."

The reactions of the genteel Ealy family to what they found waiting for them at the end of their long journey can be easily imagined; the good reverend can hardly have been reassured by McSween's sardonic comment that he was likely to find Lincoln stony ground. Nevertheless, he told McSween he was ready to do what he had come to do, and temporary accommodation was found for them all in the east wing of the McSween house.

Tunstall's body lay all night in McSween's house. Next morning, at the request of McSween and Widenmann, the assistant post surgeon, Daniel M. Appel, came in from the fort and with the assistance of Doctor Ealy carried out a post-mortem examination, after which the body was embalmed, in the expectation that the Tunstall family would wish to take their son's body back to England.

Among the contentious statements made in his account of the examination, given the following July, Appel opined that both of Tunstall's wounds had been caused by rifle bullets, contradicted Doctor Ealy's testimony that in addition to the bullet wounds, Tunstall's head had been badly mutilated, and added that he had found "evidence of venereal disease."[8] This can scarcely have accorded with McSween's wishes; he wrote later of sending the report to the Tunstalls when Appel put it "in intelligent form." Appel obviously did not choose to compromise his findings; this may account for the fact that he was never paid for his services.

Well aware that Sheriff Brady would never arrest the men who had killed Tunstall, McSween, adept at using the law's technicalities, bade Dick Brewer and Bonney to appear before Justice of the Peace Wilson to swear affidavits against those of the posse they had recognized. On the strength of these, Wilson issued warrants, which were placed in the hands of the town constable, Atanacio Martínez. Martínez was considerably less than enthusiastic about bearding the Dolan lions in their own den, but he was bluntly told he would be killed if he did not.

On Wednesday morning, with Kid Bonney and Fred Waite as deputies, Martínez went to the Dolan store to arrest the men named in the warrants. When the trio got there they found the place guarded by troops from Fort Stanton commanded by Lt. C. M. DeLany, who had come to the plaza at Brady's request when the sheriff learned of the gathering of angry citizens at McSween's on the night of Tunstall's murder.[9]

Backed by the soldiers and his own heavily armed party, Brady not only refused to let Martínez make any arrests, taking the position that the men named in the warrants had been members of a legally constituted posse, but there and then placed the constable and his two deputies under arrest, disarmed them, and marched them down the street to the jail in full sight of the entire town. The humiliation of this experience may well have been the cause of the Kid's implacable hatred of Brady.

Martínez was released that same evening; Waite and the Kid remained in jail, as preparations for Tunstall's funeral were made. A grave was dug out by Sebrian Bates beyond the northeast corner of the corral wall behind the Tunstall store. McSween dressed the body himself and placed it in a coffin in his parlor. Doctor Ealy remarked in his diary that the atmosphere was "warlike. Soldiers and citizens armed. Great danger of being shot."[10] His sentiments are echoed in an official communication written that Thursday to the acting assistant adjutant general at Santa Fe by Col. George Purington, commanding Fort Stanton.

> Sir:
>
> I have the honor to report that the usual Lincoln County war has broken out and a terrible state of affairs exist. As I understand it the Sheriff of the County levied on the property of Mr McSween in obedience to writ of attachment issued by the Hon. Judge Bristol. After the attachment Mr McSween organized a party of twenty five or thirty armed men and have set at defiance the Sheriff and his posse. The Sheriff is utterly powerless, and to prevent the destruction of property and the loss

of life I sent a detachment of troops to Lincoln. Last night the mob fired on the soldiers and wounded a horse.

Threats were made that the life of J. J. Dolan and Co shall be sacrificed. Mr Tunstall was killed by one of the Sheriff's party which has greatly exasperated the mob. Mr Riley is at this Post demanding protection from the military. I have communicated the facts to Judge Bristol. I respectfully request instructions what to do in the premises. I am fully satisfied that the lives of Sheriff Brady, Dolan, Riley and others would not be worth a farthing if turned over to the McSween party. I shall this evening re-enforce my detachment to a Company, instructing the Officer in Charge to use every means in his power to keep the peace until civil Law can be restored. [11]

Next day, Friday, February 22, Tunstall was buried. The wound in his forehead had been concealed with sticking plaster; according to McSween the corpse looked very natural. From his house the coffin was carried along the street to the burial lot beyond the store by pallbearers John Newcomb, Dick Brewer, and Frank and George Coe. His grave was out beyond the corral wall behind his store. [12]

Mary Ealy played Susan McSween's organ, carried out to the graveside. The congregation sang "Jesu Lover of My Soul," and Doctor Ealy read from 1 Corinthians 15:13–25; this was followed by a funeral sermon in English, translated into Spanish by John B. Wilson, which took as its text Job 14:14, "If a man die shall he live again?" The service ended with the hymn "My Faith Looks Up to Thee." Then Tunstall's remains were lowered into the unmarked grave in which they still lie. As he watched the coffin being covered, Dick Brewer made a vow that every one of the men who had had a hand in Tunstall's death would pay for it with his life.

After the funeral there was a mass meeting in the McSween home. Angry citizens, gathered to ensure that the threats voiced against McSween were not carried out, determined to demand an explanation of Sheriff Brady's actions in arresting Martínez and refusing to apprehend the murderers of Tunstall. A deputation consisting of Florencio Gonzales, Isaac Ellis, John Newcomb, and José Montaño, all respected citizens, confronted the sheriff at the Dolan store. When asked why he had arrested the constable and his deputies, Brady's reply was blunt: "because I had the power." [13] As to his intentions with regard to arresting the Boys, Brady was evasive; but his Irish temper flared when he was asked whether he was now willing to accept McSween's bond in the matter of the Fritz estate. "I will not take a bond of McSween of any kind or amount," he snapped.

This was not at all what McSween and Widenmann wanted. Dolan and his group were more than content to weather the present storm, and leave everything to the grand jury due to convene at the beginning of April. McSween knew that if Tunstall's murderers were not arrested immediately, they would be out of the country and beyond the reach of the grand jury long before it sat. He also knew that Jimmy Dolan had slipped out of town and headed for La Mesilla, hoping there to obtain an alias warrant through District Attorney Rynerson. This would make possible the re-arrest of McSween by Sheriff Brady, thus removing the attorney from the protection of Deputy Barrier, who still had him in his "custody." Rumor had it that Dolan also planned to enlist a more direct kind of assistance in the form of desperado John Kinney, and as many ruffians as the King of the Rustlers could recruit.

McSween and Widenmann needed some big guns of their own. Certain that the murder of a British subject would bring about a federal investigation of the affairs of Lincoln County, the two men set themselves the task of involving the British government. First, however, they had to break the news of John Tunstall's death to his family in London.

Although they are long and in many ways repetitive of what has gone before, because of their intrinsic value and for the insight they offer into each man's priorities, both McSween's and Widenmann's letters are reproduced here in their entirety for the first time (fig. 44).[14]

LAW OFFICE OF
ALEX A. MCSWEEN
LINCOLN COUNTY
Lincoln, New Mexico, Feby. 23 1878.

J. P. Tunstall, Esq.,
    London, England.

My Dear Friend:—Would to God that I could in some way that would not pierce and wound your heart tell you that your son John is dead! The duty of communicating you the sad fact is to me sad and painful in the extreme, but how much more so must the news be received by you and his mother; his sister Minnie and two little sisters. It seems to me that were I able to state that he died a natural death and left some kind message for you all that you and we would feel less keenly his untimely death, but I cannot so record, for he fell by the hand of the cruel assassin, about twenty miles from our place.

On Saturday he left here for his cattle range on the Rio Feliz, distant about fifty miles. On Monday following he left his range for this place in company with Richard M. Brewer, W. Bony, John Middleton and R. A. Weidinmann. When about thirty miles from the Feliz they were overtaken by about twenty men, composed of murderers and horsethieves. Not expecting any danger on a route they had travelled so often, they rested their horses and went hunting Turkeys, and in this way got separated. Soon they saw the outlaws trying to cut them off from each other. They used every effort amidst a shower of bullets to get together, but your son was killed before that could be done. They fired one shot at his right breast and another in the back of the head, the ball coming out at the left forehead. They then mashed in his skull. Mr. Middleton informs me that when escaping for his life, he used every effort to save your son, but without avail, he says he kept singing out: "Come this way, Mr. Tunstall; follow me, for God's sake". That John would say "What, John? What do you say, John?" I believe that even at that deadly moment your son thought for the others more than he did for himself; they were his bosom friends and he was entirely devoid of selfishness when it came to friends. They were few who knew him but those who did loved him, and are determined to avenge his death upon those who planned and executed it.

His murderers took his ring; his watch and two pistols were left untouched. His horse was killed.

We received the news of his death about eleven o'clock of the night (18th) of his death, and next morning I sent a man after his corpse. It was brought in here on the night of the 19th inst. News of his death had spread near and far and brought together large crowds to view his mutilated body. On the 20th I had his body embalmed by Dr. D. M. Appell, U.S.A., Fort Stanton, N. Mex., who also, at my request, made a *post mortem* examination, the result of which I'll forward you soon—

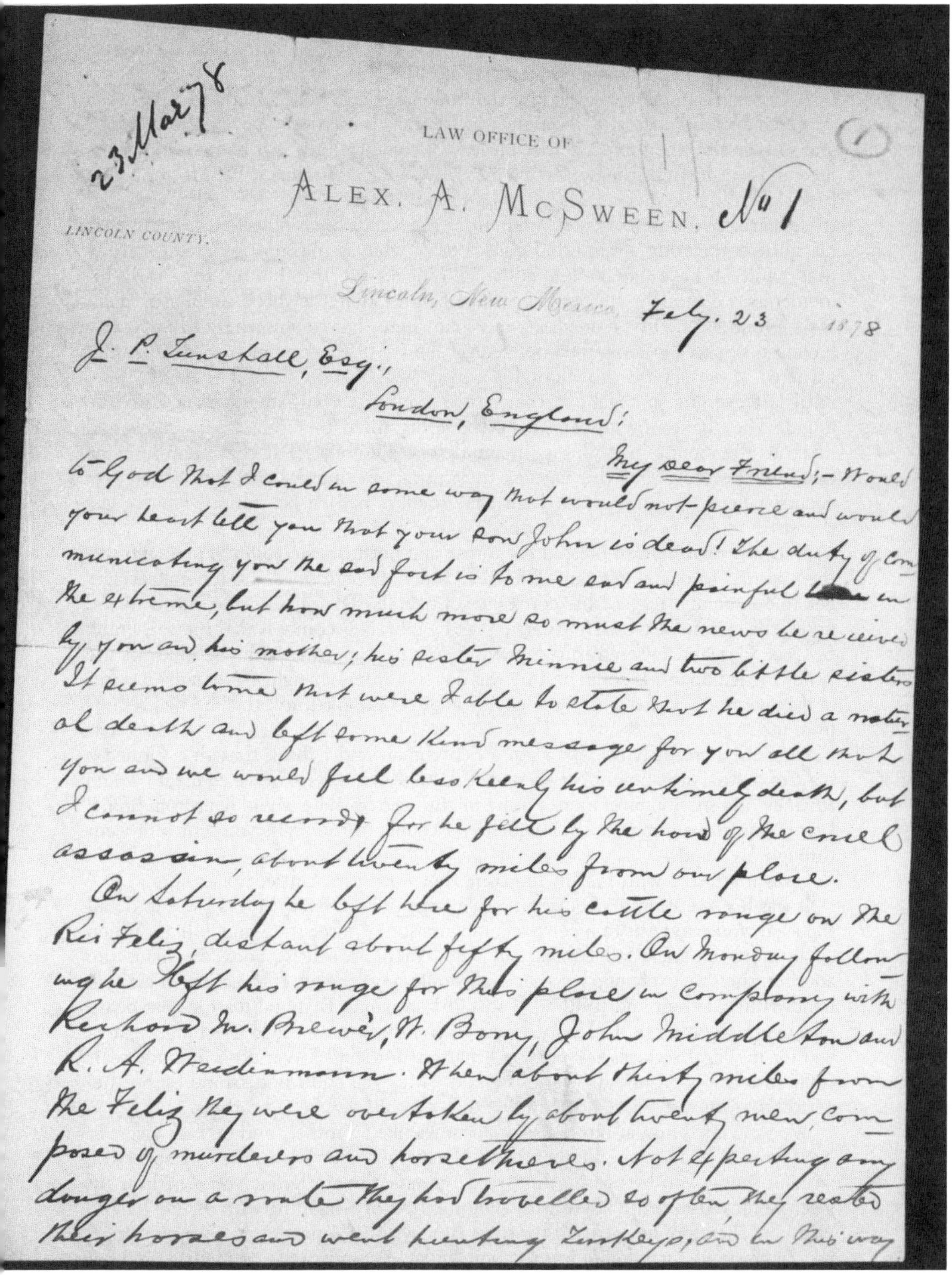

LAW OFFICE OF

ALEX. A. McSWEEN. Nᵒ 1

LINCOLN COUNTY.

Lincoln, New Mexico. Feby. 23 1878

J. P. Tunstall, Esq.,

London, England:

My dear Friend;— Would to God that I could in some way that would not pierce and would your heart tell you that your son John is dead! The duty of communicating you the sad fact is to me sad and painful in the extreme, but how much more so must the news be received by you and his mother; his sister Minnie and two little sisters It seems time that were I able to state that he died a natural death and left some kind message for you all that you and we would feel less keenly his untimely death, but I cannot so record, for he fell by the hand of the cruel assassin, about twenty miles from our place.

On Saturday he left here for his cattle range on the Rio Feliz, distant about fifty miles. On Monday following he left his range for this place in company with Richard M. Brewer, H. Bonny, John Middleton and R. A. Weidinmann. When about thirty miles from the Feliz they were overtaken by about twenty men, composed of murderers and horsethieves. Not expecting any danger on a route they had travelled so often they rested their horses and went hunting turkeys, and in this way

FIG. 44. McSween's letter to Tunstall's father informing him of the murder of John Tunstall. The old man dated it (top left) on receipt and numbered it (top right) as part of material submitted to the British Foreign Office supporting his claim for indemnification.

just as soon as he puts it in intelligent form. I had him embalmed for the reason that I believe you will some day remove his ashes.

A Coroner's Inquest was held on the body on the 19th according to our laws. I appeared for the Territory and examined witnesses. It was developed by the evidence and so found by the jury that "the [deceased] came to his death by reason of shots fired and sent forth by the hands of James J. Dolan, G. Hindman, W. Morton, Jesse Evans, Frank Baker, Tom Hill,——Long and others to the jury unknown." For these men I had warrants issued and put in the hands of an officer. Confident that his spirit is hovering around and conscious of what is transpiring here, I can say that whilst I have life and a dollar, I'll never let this matter rest until his murderers are brought to justice. Still, I believe that they'll be summarily dealt with if found. The first named is a merchant here, but he's nowhere to be found, having taken to the mountains for refuge. Thirty of the best men in this County gathered at our house the night his corpse was brought in and remained here until last evening in the hope that parties connected with the murder could be found. They have now dispersed, but have organized themselves into bands and taken to the mountains to hunt the murderers. The officers at Fort Stanton came down to see me about the matter; they think the murder the worst that ever occurred here. Feeling was so high that soldiers had to be stationed here, lest the store of Dolan should be burned.

With my own hands I dressed his corpse and put it in the coffin. The coffin was then carried to our best room. The Rev. Mr. Ealy performed the funeral services before a large and respectable concourse of people. The organ pealed forth its sad notes; the coffin was closed and carried out by John Newcomb, R. M. Brewer, Frank & Geo. Coe and lowered into a grave in my private graveyard; the clods of the valley rattled upon his coffin and he was covered from our sight—*Not a dry eye was in the audience. I knew John—I knew his affairs*—I don't think that he had secrets from me.

He came here in Nov. '76. I am a Scotchman and I think that that formed a bond of mutual attachment between us. When he came here, he asked me if I would advance him such sums of money as he might need until he would hear from home; I replied in the affirmative. Subsequently a couple of the drafts you sent him went through my hands.

I was interested with him in the store, but not in his cattle, horses, &c.

It was his intention to acquire title to a large tract of land. In this I was to do all the legal work, and was to receive a compensation of three thousand dollars. When about going East last fall I made out a statement in a little book, he made out another; then we exchanged so that each would have the a/c of the other in his own handwriting. I then said to him: "Tunstall I am going East and fearing that death may overtake either of us, I want to say to you that I have made no charge against you for my legal services in your land matters nor shall I ever do so." Large tears came into the poor fellow's eyes as he said, "Mc, you and I understand each other perfectly—you won't lose anything by that—I consider we're brothers."

We welcomed him at our house at all times like a brother, and he had access to every part of it, from the kitchen to the Drawing room. We learnt to respect you without seeing you by hearing him read the affectionate letters you sent him. In Dec. he moved into the house with the intention of remaining with us. He had no vices and therefore he spent all his spare time with us. I never saw a young man in his circumstances whose life was so commendable. Never a day or night passed but he mentioned you all. He kept your photographs carefully, but he would look them over, and make affectionate comments, three or four nights each week. He loved you all as only a son and brother could or should love.

J. J. Dolan & Co entertained fearful malice toward him and me on account of business. They could not stand to see competition. Without a doubt they planned and executed his death, and it's equally certain that business jealousy was the cause of it. Nobody could have anything against him. Both of us feared violent deaths, but not so soon. He feared more for my life than he did for his own. He understood well from the U.S. Attorney to the lowest magistrate that there was a combination and determination to keep down independence. This combination is known as the "Santa Fe Ring." To the branch of the Ring down here he had become particularly obnoxious owing to the fact that he was acquiring so much land, and because I aided him.

In the event of anything happening [to] us, it was understood that the one who survived would close up the estate of the other without charge. The evening he left he took me into his room and said: "Mc, I want you to promise me that if I am killed that you'll wind up my estate and give every cent in it to my two little sisters—for God's sake remember my two little sisters. If you die I'll wind up your estate and give every cent in it to Mrs. McSween, this we'll do without charge. of course I promised.

After his death Mr. R. A. Weidenmann showed me what he called a will dated May 23, '77, signed by John—it's his handwriting without doubt. At the time it was given your son had no property to amount to anything and I think the power of atty. was only intended to cover what he had then. He never mentioned the fact to me, and it's the only thing I have *known* him to withhold from me. I think the matter escaped his mind. He met Mr. W. in Santa Fe and took strong liking to him. Mr. W. being "hard up" as they say here, John invited him to share his hospitalities until something turned up. Mr. W. accepted the invitation and came here in March last. John frequently told me that the fellow had many points that he admired, but he was paying him no wages—only giving him his board and clothing. Now, so far as my knowledge goes, Mr. W. was a strong friend of your son's and your son was a very strong friend of W's.

Mr. W. informs me that he too promised your son to wind up his estate as I did and that was his only reason for wanting to be Administrator. I told him that for my part I would accept no trust of that character so long as there were other good, honest and competent men to fill the position who could give good bonds, that I would much sooner write you as John's friend than as his Administrator, that I could not consent to have the Court issue him Letters [of Administration] without Bonds, for however faithfully he might discharge his duties, I considered it would be unjust to his representatives and against my promise. That it was immaterial who was *appointed*, it was my intention to watch their administration and report their irregularities, if any occurred, to the Court. I recommended the Court to appoint Isaac Ellis, a good, honest and substantial property holder as administrator. He done so. Bonds, until the Inventory is taken, we put at $20,000—After Inventory is made will be put at *double* the amount. I have promised the Admr. to do all the legal portion of the administration free of charge.

He had between 3000 & 4000 acres [of] Land the title to which has not yet been perfected—he had three years in which to do that, tho' it was his intention to perfect the title the coming summer. Tho' the title is in this condition, the interest he had is safe and will so remain for 3 years. But should his heirs desire to withdraw the money invested I think they can easily do so with interest—

His other property consists of Merchandise, horses and cattle—he had about four hundred head of cattle.

I forgot to state that the evening he left he gave me a penny which he had carried a long time. After his corpse came in I put the penny and a silver dollar of mine on his eyes—I enclose both of them for you.

Since he and I first met never an unkind or unpleasant word passed between us. We felt like brothers; we acted like brothers; I buried him like a brother; I mourn for him as a brother.

FIG. 45. Death card for John Tunstall, March 1878.

His corpse when embalmed looked *very* natural. The wound on the forehead was skillfully fixed with sticking plaster. Few could have told but what he died a natural death. If I can serve you at this distance I'll cheerfully do so.

My wife is in the City of St. Louis on a visit. I have not had the heart to tell her this sad news as yet. I'll write her this a.m.

Your friend, A. A. McSween

McSween's letter manages to convey his lack of regard for Robert Widenmann without ever actually putting it into words. There is throughout the letters of both men a sense of rivalry, as if each was trying to prove to the family that he was the truer friend to Tunstall. McSween felt Widenmann's relationship with Tunstall was, for one of such brief duration, unhealthily close. Widenmann had "roughed it" with Tunstall, and seems to have felt an entitlement to represent the Englishman's interests. In the matter of Tunstall's death he had the advantage (fig. 45). Unlike McSween, he had been with Tunstall moments before the Englishman was killed. His letter to Tunstall's father in London, written later on the same day as McSween's, is the closest that exists to an eyewitness account of what happened as darkness fell that February afternoon.[15]

Lincoln, Lincoln Co. N.M. Feby 23rd 1878

Honored Sir!

Would to God that this letter were spared me, you alone and dear Harrie's mother can judge what pain it gives me to write it. But I must do it in order to keep my promise to my dear friend my brother. In his last letter to you, extracts of which he read to me before he sent it, he informed you of the troubles we had had here. But they did not end there. After Mr. McSween's return from Las Vegas, dear Harry accompanied him and a few others to La Mesilla on the Rio Grande where Mr McSween had a preliminary trial. it was soon evident though that the whole case was in the hands of the New Mexican ring and Mr. McS. concluded to have the trial deferred until the regular session of the court here next April. While there in La Mesilla dear Harries life was threatened by one J. J. Dolan whom he had never injured. On the road returning at San Augustine the same J. J. Dolan again approached dear Harry in company with one Jessy Evans a noted desperado and murderer, pointed his rifle at Harry and told him to come on and fight. Harry answered that he did not make his living by fighting and murdering and as to fighting a duel he, if he ever did it, would only meet gentlemen and his equals in that way. After a great deal of abuse Dolan said, "You won't fight now but I'll get you yet" and left. Near here the same parties, who are acting for and with the New Mexican ring, had the road waylaid, but fortunately our party took an other road and thereby evaded the danger.

During the time Harry and the others were away, I took charge of the business as in fact I always did when here. On the 10th [9th] inst.(Saturday) in the morning Sheriff Brady walked into the store read a writ of attachment, attaching McSween's property to me and said he would at once take possession of all the goods and property. I protested, saying that this was the property of J. H. Tunstall and not of McSween and refused to deliver the keys, whereupon I was arrested and shamefully treated.

In the evening I was released. Sunday night Harry and McSween arrived and Monday, after Harry and I had tried our best to have the property released, but had been unsuccessfull we thought it best that I should go to the ranch and take care of things there. I rode all night and arrived there early Tuesday morning. I had not been there long before a deputy Sheriff and 7 others, among them 4 desperados for whom the sheriff has warrants in his hands, among them the same Evans, rode up to the ranch and demanded the delivery of McSween's cattle. I informed them, that Mr. McS. had no cattle there and after much talk they concluded to return to Lincoln and get new instructions. It leaked out afterwards that they came there to kill and get me out of the way and the only thing that saved me was that I kept my hand on my pistol and watched them closely.—I returned to town and there found that a new party was being organised to drive off the cattle. I started back to the ranch the same night and Harry started for the Pecos to get help. In this he was not successful and therefore came to the ranch last Sunday night. After much consideration we came to the conclusion that, as the other party were very strong having gathered together 31 of the worst men in the county, being encamped 8 miles from the ranch and having sent us word that they only wished to gather the cattle and count them, we would mount our horses and drive the spare horses with us to town. We sent the other party word that we would leave one good man at the ranch and they might have an other, of their own selection, to take care of the cattle, until things would be settled by the courts. We started about 8 Ocl. in the morning and rode on leisurely. Our party comprised Harry, Dick Brewer, John Middleton, F. Waite, William Bonnie and myself. Harry and I rode together most of the time and in talking over the situation he made the remark: Robert, old fellow if you die or get killed first I will take care of all there is left of you and all your effects and will see that your parents get everything that is yours; you will do the same with me, won't you? I answered in the affirmative and we shook hands. We rode along slowly, not expecting any trouble.—I will stop here just to tell you, that we are just informed, 9 O'cl.P.M. that there are 20 or 30 of the mob here in town and that they say openly that they will kill McSween and I tonight or die in the attempt. I will write as long as permitted and will contrive to get this letter to you in one way or another. If I die or am killed tonight, I die for right, justice and honor and am contented to die for them. God knows best for all of us. His ways are inexplicable but always for the best. Harry is looking down upon me from above, and, I feel certain, approves of what I do.

Although the situation in Lincoln was tense, Widenmann was in no great danger of being killed that night: Colonel Purington had detailed three troopers to guard the house. Widenmann seems to have needed to dramatize every situation in which he found himself. Whether this was to ingratiate himself with the Tunstall family or to make his own part in events appear more important than it actually was is not clear: probably both.

—Now to continue with my letter.

We were about 11 miles from town, Harry, Brewer and I were riding along driving the loose horses Bonnie and Middleton were about 500 yards in the rear, when a large flock of turkies rose close to the road and Brewer and I started to kill some of them to take home with us. We had got about fifty yards from the road when I heard a noise behind us and looking around I saw a bunch of horsemen come over the brow of the hill in our rear, as fast as their horses could carry them, and in front of them about 200 yards, were Middleton and Bonnie. The latter, as soon as he caught sight of us, rode towards us, while Middleton rode towards Harry, calling him to ride over to us. Harry urged on his horse, a splendid animal, but seems to have lost all his presence of mind, for instead of keeping direct for us, he rode a circle. As soon as he started towards us we struck out for

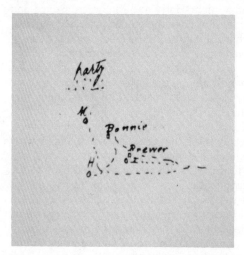

some tall timber and rocks where we could defend ourselves. By this time bullets were flying thick around us. Harry never reached us and after we had taken our position the murderers, 18 in number, rode around us but did not come within range of our rifles. They placed a guard over dear Harries body, killed his horse, laid him (Harry) on his blankets, crossed his hands, and the balance of the party rode on and tried to waylay us. We rode around them, seeing we could not get to Harry, I ordered Brewer and Middleton to see and get some men to look for Harry. Bonnie and I rode to town and informed them of what had happened. We reached town about 10 O'cl. P.M. I had a horse saddled and while he was being saddled had something to eat, not having had anything to eat or drink since morning. I then rode to the fort (Fort Stanton) to inform the authorities and then rode the next 3 days and nights continually, mounting fresh horses as soon as I had rode down the one I was on. I tried my utmost to apprehend the murderers but did not succeed and then when I had cornered them the sheriff, who is in league with them, would not allow them to be arrested. Dear Harries remains arrived here Wednesday evening and I had them embalmed and they were buried with proper ceremony, a presbeterian minister officiating. God knows how I feel in writing all this, it is hard, fearful hard for a father to read them and I can only pray that God may give you, his mother and his sisters strength to bear the blow. He loved you all so dearly and would often when he and I were alone, we always slept in the same room, take the photographs out of the box he kept them in, look at them and give each an endearing name. To me he was more than a brother and I feel as if I had lost part of myself. I am pretty well worn out and only the thought that I must succeed in apprehending and bringing those men to justice keeps me up. And with God's help I will and shall succeed.— I would not write in regard to business were it not *imperatively necessary*. You will see by the enclosed paper, a copy, that dear Harry left a will. Mr. McSween thought it prudent that another person, a Mr. Ellis a good and honest man should be appointed administrator for the present under $10,000—bonds, but after the appraisement the bond will according to law have to be twice the amount of the appraisement or about $50,000—.

Now there is not a man in the county who could give this bond and according to law, if the bond cannot be furnished the sheriff takes the property into custody. But the sheriff is indirectly the cause of dear Harrys death and a *scoundrel* and a

FIG. 46. Lt. Millard Fillmore Goodwin (left) with Lt. Charles H. Gatewood, ca. 1880. Taken at the time of their return from the campaign against Victorio. Photographer unknown.

villain, and the property would go to *ruin* and be *stolen.* To avoid this I would advise you to send me or some other honest and reliable person a full and complete power of attorney so that everything can be properly managed and every cent saved. I promised Harry that I would see to this. It would certainly also be best that you should come as soon as possible. Undoubtedly you will wish to take the earthly remains of poor dear Harry to the home of his childhood. If so please inform me by return mail so that I can order an [*sic*] metallic casket. Any other orders you may have for me will be promptly executed and I only beg to impress upon you that the *utmost dispatch is necessary* in regard to the property. I again assure you and dear Harry's mother and sisters of my heartfelt sympathy. Words are inadequate to express what I feel, God alone can see my heart and he knows that and how deeply I feel for and with you. May my dear parents be spared this.—I hope to hear from you by the earliest opportunity. You have undoubtedly by this time received Mr. McSween's dispatch.

    In deepest grief.   Yours sincerely,

                                                 Robt. A. Widenmann.

P.S. Dear Harry died the 18th inst. about 5½ O'cl.P.M.

It would seem that this letter was either written the night before and dated next day, or written early in the morning of February 23, for it makes no mention of his activities that day, and in his dealings with the Tunstall family, Widenmann was not the man to forgo any credit he might bestow upon himself.

    Widenmann still had the federal warrants he held for Evans, Hill, Baker, and Davis—the selfsame ones he had not dared to serve when the Boys came down to Tunstall's ranch. By invoking his power as a deputy U.S. marshal, he had the right to demand the assistance of troops in serving them. He placed his request before Colonel Purington, who had no option but to put Lt. Millard F. Goodwin and a detachment of soldiers at Widenmann's disposal (fig. 46). Widenmann led them back to Lincoln with blood in his eye.

CHAPTER 18

THE FACTIONS POLARIZE

BACKED by Lieutenant Goodwin's detachment, and supported by a sizable group of McSween supporters, Widenmann threw a cordon around the Dolan store and proceeded to search it (or, as Dolan's people presented the matter, ransack it).[1] No trace of the four wanted men was found, but it was persuasively claimed by the Dolan faction, supported by Colonel Purington, that it was by this means that the Rynerson letter of February 14 came into McSween's possession.

From the House, Widenmann led his men to the Tunstall store, still guarded by Brady's deputies, and proceeded to "search" for the wanted men. Of course he knew perfectly well they were not there. His intention was to wrest back possession of Tunstall's store, at any cost. They'd made him run in the canyon, forced him to abandon Tunstall and let him be killed: now the boot was on the other foot. Widenmann was physically large and aggressive, with a mean streak a yard wide.[2] Whether he was as tough as he acted is another matter, but rash and imprudent he most certainly was.

Clear evidence of this foolhardiness appears in the testimony of Lieutenant Goodwin, who stated that Widenmann proposed at this juncture that he withdraw his troops and let the two sides shoot it out.[3] Goodwin said forcefully that if a fight broke out, he would immediately place his troops between the two factions, forcing them either to stop shooting or to run the risk of wounding or killing soldiers. Widenmann was not prepared to take that chance and backed off.

In the version of ensuing events given by Sheriff Brady's deputy George W. Peppin, "a number of armed men" [who included]

Atanacio Martines, Richard Brewer, Doc Scurlock, John Middleton, William H. Antrim alias "Kid", Samuel Smith, Samuel Corbett, —— Wayt, —— McNab, —— Edwards, Frank Coe and George Coe, George Washington (colored) George Robinson (colored) Ignacio Gonzales, Jesus Rodrigues, Esiquio Sanches, Roman Burgan [Baragón] and other persons whose names are to [me] unknown entered the [Tunstall] store and said Martines by virtue of what purported to be a warrant arrested [myself] and all persons placed in charge by said William Brady of said goods chattels and premises and took the keys of said store and premises from Sheriff William Brady's men so placed in charge of said property and took said last named persons out of said store. Subsequently [I] and others who were in charge of said goods and store as aforesaid to wit Jack Long, James Longwell, Charles Martin and John Clark (colored) were released and [I] applied for some property belonging to [me] left in said store and premises. Was told that the keys were down at McSween's house (the defendant in attachment suit) and Mr Corbett went after them and after bringing keys and taking out some of [my] property (blankets) from said store proceeded to the house of said Alexr. McSween and then and there [I] saw said Corbett deliver said keys to said Alexr A. McSween. The Sheriff's posse in charge of said goods and said store as aforesaid were by the said Martines and party disarmed. Sheriff Brady was also subsequently arrested and since said Brady was so dispossessed he has not been in possession of said property.[4]

Peppin's affidavit was made in the middle of April, so it is apparent that once ensconced therein, the McSween supporters did not give Brady any opportunity to repossess the store. Brady in fact did not try; according to Peppin, the sheriff felt he would be "unable to do so without bloodshed which he . . . was anxious to avoid." Especially, one feels, if it might be his own. Instead, Brady preferred charges against the repossessors for rioting, swore out warrants, and arrested them all. After a hearing before Justice Wilson, all were bound over to the April grand jury.

On the 24th, even as Doctor Ealy organized the first Sabbath school ever held in Lincoln, McSween was writing again to the elder Tunstall, a brief note but of considerable import.

> My Dear Sir:—I would suggest that you communicate with Mr. Isaac Ellis, Administrator of the Estate of J. H. Tunstall, Lincoln, N.M. in regard to what you wish done. I feel confident that he will follow your instructions.
>
> In this connection I wish you would authorize me to offer a reward for the apprehension of the murderers of your son. This would be well, tho' I feel satisfied that some of them shall have been sent to their "long homes" before this reaches you.[5]

In Doctor Ealy's idiosyncratic letters another of the day's dramas was reported: "Mr. Weedman, U.S. Deputy Marshall, was poisoned here but recovered. He is a german well educated. Makes his headquarters in this house."[6]

Ealy's terse report gives no further details, but Widenmann later recorded that his life had been saved by a large quantity of butter he ate on some batter cakes. Which of the adherents of the Ring might have poisoned him, and how, if not perhaps why, must be left to conjecture; he did not nominate a suspect.

Following the evening Sabbath school, which had an attendance of twenty, a further meeting of the citizens of Lincoln ended with the resolution that for his own safety, McSween had best leave town, and soon. Rumors coming up from the Mesilla valley were of a kind to make his friends fear for his life. McSween promised to leave as soon as he got his affairs in order. On the following day, having made his will, which was witnessed by his brother-in-law and partner David P. Shield, Samuel Corbet, and Doctor Ealy, McSween wrote to Sir Edward Thornton, British ambassador in Washington.

> Sir,
>
> I would call your attention to the murder of John H. Tunstall, a British subject, at this county, on the 18th inst., by James J. Dolan et al.
>
> Mr. Tunstall had no relatives in the United States. His father, J. P. Tunstall, of the mercantile house of J. P. Tunstall & Co., resides at 7, Belsize Terrace, London.
>
> An impartial investigation of the circumstances which led to his foul murder will show a disgraceful state of affairs, not only as regards the Territorial, but the United States officials also.

After the murderers arrived in this town, I had warrants issued for their arrest, and put into the hands of a constable for their apprehension. I did not put them in the hands of the Sheriff of the County, for the reason that I believe he was indirectly connected with the murder. When the constable and posse went to serve the warrants he was met by the Sheriff, who took him and posse prisoners, and refused to allow them to make any arrests, although the alleged murderers of Mr. Tunstall were then and there with the Sheriff. The public regard this as the most inexcusable murder that has ever taken place here, but unless you cause the matter to be looked into, I have but small hopes of the matter being properly prosecuted. "Rings" are so common throughout our Territory that the probability is that a genuine prosecution of the murderers would interfere with "ring interests."

In confidence, your &c.
A. A. McSween.

P.S. Mr. Tunstall died seized of property to the amount of about 25,000 dollars in this county.[7]

Perhaps it was the recent arrival of Doctor Ealy that prompted McSween's next move: on the following day, February 25, he made a further attack on Indian agent Frederick Godfroy (fig. 47), this time through John C. Lowrie, head of the Presbyterian Board of Missions in New York.

Rev. Dear Sir:—A Presbyterian by birth, education and choice, I regret that our church cannot endorse a more competent and better qualified Indian Agent for the Mescalero Apaches in this County than the present incumbent, Maj. Godfroy.

Maj. Godfroy is familiarly known here, a Roman Catholic community, as the "Presbyterian fraud". It's a fact well known here that he's in league with the parties furnishing Beef, flour &c to cheat & defraud the Indians. He sells them blankets, sugar, coffee &c; accepts *mashed* rotten wheat for flour; the beef so poor as to have to be killed on the range and carted to the issue house. The result of all this is, that the Indians here nearly all left the Reservation and are robbing and murdering citizens.

He keeps nobody, outside his family, about him but Roman Catholics, tho' others could be had. Rev. T. F. Ealy has just arrived here and can inquire into this matter. The fraud, corruption and dishonesty of the agent can be established by cumulative evidence in the shape of affidavits.[8]

This broadside fired, McSween slipped out of town escorted still by Deputy Sheriff Adolph Barrier. The next day Widenmann, apparently fully recovered from the poisoning attempt, wrote to the British ambassador in Washington echoing McSween's earlier appeal for an investigation. He also addressed himself, for the first time, to Tunstall's mother.

Dear Mrs. Tunstall:

You can not imagine what a task it is for me to write these letters, but I must do it. dear Harry (he always liked me to call him so) would have done the same for me. Even on the day of his death, while we were riding along together, he said to me: ["]Old fellow, one of us will probably have to go soon and if you go first I will write to your parents and if I am the one you do the same for me and attend to my matters." You have lost a son and an only son, one of whom any mother could be proud of, a son who was the embodiment of honor and all that was manly and good. I have lost a brother whom I can never replace. It is so hard for me now, the days seem so long and I can't remain at one place or occupy myself with anything any length of time. I feel as if I had lost the best part of myself and am vainly seeking

FIG. 47. Frederick Charles Godfroy. Date
and photographer unknown.

to find it again. I miss him at every step and don't see how I am going to get along without him.

Whenever I returned from some trip, and I was away very often, he would meet me while I was getting of[f] my horse and say: "Thank God, old boy, that you are back again; I have been so lonely while you were gone." And it was the same with me when he was away—We slept in the same room and being much occupied during the day and evening we most always had our little private and confidential chats before going to sleep. People about here often said that we were more like man and wife than anything else. Most every evening when we had our private chats he would speak of the dear ones at home and used such loving and endearing terms, that one could easily see how much he loved you all. He often said to me: You know, Robert, that what I make here is for the dear ones at home. You and I will make our stake here and then go back to the old country, establish ourselves in good snug bachelors quarters, have plenty of horses and dogs and live in peace and quiet. Speaking of you one evening he said: Rob, old fellow, you adore your Mother (and I do) but I tell you there is not an other Mother like mine in the world and my father has no equal. In speaking of Mrs Behrens [Minnie] he more than once said: I don't think I could find another young lady like her and as she is my beau ideal of what a woman should be, I think I shall always be an old bachelor. Of his little chicks, as he called his little sisters, he spoke with unbounded love and praise and he always looked forward with joy to the time when he could visit home again. Poor dear boy, he is now with the blessed ones above and I feel as if he were looking down upon us and watching us.—

At the funeral, the services were conducted by a Presbeterian clergyman, we sang the old hymn "Jesus lover of my soul," then the clergyman read from the I Carinthians XV Chapter 13 to 25 verses exclusive. after this a few appropriate remarks were made on the text "If a man die shall he live again" Jobe XIV 14. and then sang "My faith looks up to Thee." At the grave a short prayer was said and with Earth to earth, dust to dust and ashes to ashes the one whom I loved better than a brother, and I parted for this life. It brings the tears to my eyes to think of it; he often said that he and I must never part while we were alive, and yet the parting came so soon.—I have copied the hymns that were sung and enclose them. All his letters from home I have taken and put under lock and key so that no stranger can desecrate the love expressed in them by reading them. He most always read me the greater parts of the letters he received from home, read them to me to show how dear you all were to him and how much you thought of him. Even on the morning of the day of his death he showed me a letter received from home the day before and made me translate the german happy new year's wish sent me so kindly by Mrs. Behrens. Please tell Mrs. Behrens [there follows some writing in almost illegible old German script: it has so far defeated everyone asked to try to translate it, but it appears to express, among other sentiments, the hope that God will grant Minnie a happy New Year].

I have written all these details, thinking that you would wish to know them as much as my dear mother were she burdened with the same great loss. I know that a mothers love is unfathomable and every word spoken by a dear departed one is treasured as a jewel. I pray God that he may strengthen you to bear this great loss.

P.S. I forgot to state that dear Harries favorite songs were: The tear by Gumbert and The Mill and when ever I touched the organ or guitar he asked me to sing them for him.[9]

This letter displays clearly the intimacy Widenmann claimed with Tunstall, and which McSween so distrusted. He felt that Tunstall had placed far more confidence in Widenmann than was justified by the man's background and character. The Tunstall family entertained no such reservations. Their letters to Widenmann show that they accepted him entirely at his own valuation.

Next Widenmann addressed "Henry Tunstall, Esq." in Victoria, B.C., clearly under the impression that the Uncle Henry of whom Tunstall had spoken bore the same surname. This letter was followed by one to R. Guy McLellan in San Francisco. The lawyer, who it will be remembered had given Tunstall a letter of introduction to Governor Axtell, wrote to his friend in Santa Fe enclosing a copy of Widenmann's letter. Since Widenmann had stated categorically that the murder had been committed "in the interest of the New Mexican ring", Axtell sent it to the *New Mexican,* where it was later published alongside his scorching reply.

On February 28, replying to a letter from Tunstall's father acknowledging one of the telegraph-length notes he had written at John's request, Widenmann wrote:

Your kind letter of the 2nd came to hand yesterday and I only wish that I could in this as in my former letter say that everything was all right. You are undoubtedly in receipt of my sad letter written a few days ago, when this reaches you. Since then dear Harrys effects have gone into the hands of an administrator Mr. Isaac Ellis, an honest and good man but of no great business ability, and they [sic] effects are now being appraised by a commission appointed for the purpose. I am attentively watching all the proceedings and fulfilling my promise to dear Harry as near as possible. His letters from home I have under lock and key, so that strangers can not get at them. The murderers took his shirtstuds, ring (the one given him by his sister, which he prised very highly) and spurs from his body. I hope to be able to get them back for you at some future time. His clothes and other trinkets I have placed in a large case, where they will be faithfully kept until your orders in regard to them are received. I must again impress upon you that something must be done as soon as possible to prevent the goods cattle and horses from being sold at auction. If this were done you would be forced to sustain a heavy loss, for auctions here never allow the realisation of anything on articles sold in this way. Then the landed interest should also be looked after. If the land entries which have been made are allowed to run out uncompleted they will be a complete loss. I will do my utmost to defeat any attempt to sell at auction until I can hear from you and will also try to keep the expenses down to the lowest possible limit.

As I said in my last letter it would be best to send a power of attorney and then come on yourself. If you should come I would meet you at the end of the rail or send some good reliable man, probably Brewer, to bring you down. In this way the journey could be made without much fatigue to yourself. You could reach here from El Moro in five or six days and I could provide every possible comfort for you on the road.—

The situation here is not the best. The murderers are the tools of the New Mexican ring and knowing dear Harrie's death will be avenged by me they have tried their utmost to get me out of the way. Knowing that I am not afraid of their bullets in a fair fight, they attempted, the other day to have me poisoned and I had a hairbreadth escape. I was only saved by the large quantity of butter I ate on some battercakes. I hope to get through all right though. Brewer is out now to make some arrests. I expect him back in 6 or 7 days. All the respectable citizens in the country are on our side. I hope to hear from you soon, and remain,

Sincerely and respectfully yours.

March 1st. 9 A.M. Mr McSween was forced to flee for safety last night, as we had discovered a plot to murder us. I am going to stand by my post to the last and, if fate decrees, will die for honor, honesty and right. I yet feel that right and justice will gain the day although the mills of the Gods grind slow, but they *grind fine*.[10]

That same March day, Taylor Ealy wrote to his mother in Pennsylvania.

Your letter . . . finds us keeping house. Mr. McSween a lawyer—whose wife is at present in St. Louis—has kindly allowed us to occupy her house for the present & in the meantime we can get one in readiness. Think we will like it here better than we thought. At present we have all kinds of kitchen furniture—but of course it is not our own.

Mr. McSween has about 70 chickens. We boarded a week with Mr. Shield, his partner-in-law. Mr. McSween had an interest in a store here, but Mr. Tunstall, his partner in the store, was shot by men who do not want anybody to do business but themselves. The store may be auctioned or retailed out, or it may run on, we do not know yet.

There is not any [news]paper printed here yet, but in another year I have no doubt there will be.

The county I believe nos. about two thirds Americans. Indians & Mexicans are not troublesome—it is the whites. One party trying to elbow the other out of the country.[11]

"One party trying to elbow the other out of the country": hardly elegant, but succinctly accurate. The murder of Tunstall had polarized the loyalties of the population. The farmers of the Ruidoso and Hondo valleys and the Hispanic New Mexicans who had availed themselves of Tunstall's credit, unaware of what his intentions towards them had been, allied themselves with McSween. Behind McSween, it was believed, stood Chisum.

The small ranchers from the Seven Rivers area, their memories of the preceding year's "War" still vivid, were hostile towards Chisum and anybody who allied themselves with him, and therefore threw in their lot with Dolan and Riley, behind whom stood Rynerson, Catron, and the Santa Fe Ring.

By the beginning of March, the lines were clearly drawn. Shortly thereafter, battle commenced.

CHAPTER 19

WAR: THE REVENGE
OF THE REGULATORS

IN the weeks following Tunstall's death, his friends' and former employees' desire for revenge grew in the face of Sheriff Brady's disinclination—which they saw as refusal—to arrest the men who had killed Tunstall, and the reluctance of the military—which they saw as partisanship—to further assist Deputy U.S. Marshal Robert Widenmann in doing the same (after his misuse of their forces in Lincoln). The result was the formation of a vigilante group.

Calling themselves "the Regulators," Dick Brewer, John Middleton, Fred Waite, and William Bonney were joined by Josiah Scurlock, Charlie Bowdre, Henry Brown, Sam Smith, and Jim French (figs. 48, 49). To their ranks came also Frank MacNab, who had known Bowdre and Middleton in Kansas and was employed as a detective by the cattle firm of Hunter & Evans.

What prompted these men to take up arms?[1] There can be little doubt that they were motivated by the complex mixture of emotion and rationalization that military historian John Keegan calls "the will to combat," a mixture made up in varying degrees of personal loyalties and resentments, the pressure of unavoidable compulsion, the prospect of personal enrichment, the endorsement of religion (making killing lawful in time of "war") and not at all the least, drink, which we have already seen as a major factor in the violence of the times. Fueled in greater or lesser part by the "will to combat," inured by upbringing and experience to the commonplace character of violence in frontier life, decent men could—and would—justify to themselves actions they would—and did—condemn outright in other circumstances.

As we have seen, Justice of the Peace Wilson, acting on testimony sworn before him by Brewer and Bonney, issued warrants for the arrest of those named in that testimony. He then appointed Brewer a constable, and Brewer duly deputized the others. Hearing that some of the wanted men were at the Dolan cattle camp on the Pecos, the Regulators mounted up and headed down to the valley, sixty miles away.

After scouting unsuccessfully for a couple of days, they sighted five men just below the crossing on the Peñasco—the exact location is something of a movable feast—late in the afternoon of March 6.[2] The men fled, splitting into two groups. The posse went after a party of three consisting of Dick Lloyd, Frank Baker, and Buck Morton. After a headlong pursuit that became a running fight in which over a hundred shots were fired, Lloyd's horse gave out. Brewer's posse ignored him and thundered past after the other two. Their horses, too, fell exhausted and the two men hid among tule reeds until the posse threatened to burn them out,

FIG. 48. Josiah Gordon "Doc" Scurlock, aged about nineteen. Date and photographer unknown.

leaving Morton and Baker no option but to surrender. Understandably, they expected to be summarily dealt with: both had been in the group that had killed Tunstall. Brewer told them bluntly he would have preferred not to have taken them alive; now that he had, however, he gave them his word they would not be harmed.

Others in the party, notably the Kid, objected strongly. If they took Morton and Baker back to Lincoln, Brady would set them free. Why not avenge Tunstall right now? Brewer was adamant, and it speaks eloquently of the power of his personality that his companions capitulated and agreed to take the prisoners back to Lincoln.

In Lincoln, on that same March Tuesday, Widenmann was writing yet again to J. P. Tunstall, returning unopened two letters addressed to John Tunstall, or "dear Harry," as he referred to the dead Englishman.[3] "Everything is quiet here now," Widenmann reported, "like the calm before a storm which is certainly brewing. We are prepared for it, and will meet it firmly."

What those preparations included is noted by Taylor Ealy in his diary for March 8, a bitterly cold, windy day.[4] McSween, he wrote, was having "a wall 12 feet high built of stone and adobe around his house." It would appear the lawyer, too, felt a storm was brewing. And it was, it was.

Down on the Pecos, the Regulators and their prisoners had reached the Chisum ranch, where they heard a rumor that Jimmy Dolan was gathering twenty or more men at Lincoln to intercept the posse and free Morton and Baker. As an added irritant, William McCloskey had attached himself to the posse at one of the cow camps the men had stayed at on their way upriver.[5] McCloskey made a living working for anyone who needed an extra hand at roundup or branding time; he had done some casual work for Tunstall. On the morning of February 18 he had been sent to tell Mathews that no resistance would be offered to the attachment; instead of coming back to rejoin Tunstall, he remained with Mathews's men and was with them when they came to the Tunstall ranch that morning. Some of the Regulators thought McCloskey had turned his coat.

Morton, the eldest son of a prominent Virginia family, asked permission to write to one of his kinsmen, H. H. Marshall of Richmond, setting forth his version of the events leading to his arrest. His brief account of Tunstall's murder—the only written record by any of the actual participants—is notably at variance with the stories told by the other possemen. The tenor of the letter and the fact that Morton chose to write a cousin rather than his own family suggest that Marshall may have been a lawyer.

FIG. 49. Charles Bowdre and his wife, Manuela Herrera, ca. 1880. Photo by Furlong, Las Vegas, N.M. *Carte de visite* taken off Bowdre's body by Pat Garrett December 22, 1880 (note bloodstains). One of a pair, taken at the same sitting; this has never been published before and is unretouched. Bowdre would have been about forty-two at this time.

The 6th March I was arrested by a Constable party accused of the murder of Tunstall. Nearly all the sheriff's party fired at him and it is impossible for any one to say who killed him. When the party which came to arrest me and one man who was with me, first saw us about one hundred yards distant we started in another direction when they (eleven in number) fired nearly one hundred shots at us. We ran about five miles when both of our horses fell and we made a stand when they came up they told us if we would give up they would not harm us; after talking awhile we gave up our arms and were made prisoners. There was one man in the party who wanted to kill me after I had surrendered, and was restrained with the greatest difficulty by others of the party. The constable himself said he was sorry we gave up as he had not wished to take us alive. We arrived here last night enroute to Lincoln. I have heard that we were not to be taken alive to that place. I am not at all afraid of their killing me, but if they should do so I wish that the matter should be investigated and the parties dealt with according to law. If you do not hear from me in four days after receipt of this I would like you to make inquiries about the affair.[6]

At about ten o'clock the following morning, Brewer's posse left the Chisum ranch, stopping at the post office in Roswell to register and mail Morton's letter. Instead of following the direct route to Lincoln, Brewer led his men off on a trail that swung around the base of Capitan Mountain to the north before turning toward Lincoln. Although frequently used by the military, this road was much less traveled than the one that followed the Hondo down its valley.

Brewer's reasoning is easy to follow: If Dolan really was getting up a rescue party, the posse would avoid it by taking the less used route and, no small additional benefit, this would have the effect of bringing the posse to Lincoln under cover of darkness.

What happened next no one will ever know. The best known account was written by Roswell postmaster and born romancer Ash Upson, who sent this dispatch to the editor of the *Independent*.

Richard Brewer and a Constable's posse with legal process arrested Wm. S. Morton and Frank Baker on the banks of the Pecos after an 8 mile chase. The prisoners are charged with the killing of J. H. Tunstall.

The posse arrived at Chisum's ranch on Friday, 6th inst. It left for Roswell where Morton registered a letter about 10 o'clock on Saturday morning. Morton at the post office expressed fears that he would be lynched and declared his willingness to stand trial.

About half after ten the party left with their prisoners ostensibly for Lincoln. About 5 o'clock P.M. Martin Chavez reported here that the party had left the road to their left and gone toward Black Water holes. This Sunday morning Frank McNab, one of the arresting party, returned. His statement of events after leaving here are in substance as follows:

"When we had ridden some 20 miles and had reached a point about 5 or 6 miles from Black Water, Morton was riding side by side with one of the posse, when he suddenly snatched McClosky's pistol from his scabbard and shot him dead.

"Although mounted on a slow horse, he put him to his best speed, closely followed by Frank Baker. They were speedily overtaken and killed."

McNab said as he had no further business in that direction he returned. Whatever face or color future developments may put on the face of the affair, there is no doubt but that McClosky, Morton and Baker are dead.[7]

It is as well to be wary of any account of events written by Upson. Fortunately, his is not the only one available: Support for MacNab's version appears in a letter from Alexander McSween to Tunstall's father dated April 4, in which the lawyer undertook to bring the old man up to date on events in Lincoln.

> After the burial of your son, our resident m[a]gistrate issued warrants for the arrest of his murderers and placed the same in the hands of his constable. Eight of the men who participated in that fearful deed were known to be at the house of L. G. Murphy & Co, this place with the Sheriff. Hither the constable with a posse of two citizens went to arrest the murderers. Instead of aiding the constable, as he should have done, the Sheriff took him and posse prisoners! Without any authority of law he kept them prisoners twenty four hours. He finally released them but refused to allow them to make any arrests. On the heels of this, said magistrate issued another warrant for others of the murderers living about 150 miles distant; this he empowered, as our law under certain circumstances allows, Richard M. Brewer, a young man of irreproachable character and an ardent friend of your son's, to serve. Mr. Brewer, with nine others, went to execute the warrants. After a hot chase two of them were arrested. When within 25 miles of this place on the 8th ult., one of them made an effort to escape. He took a pistol from an inattentive man riding by him and, after having shot the latter in the head, made for the mountains with his partner in crime, and as they refused to surrender they were shot dead—the three, am told, died within 20 minutes.[8]

Widenmann hewed to the party line.[9] In a letter to the *Cimarron News and Press,* dated March 30, he gave the following version of what had happened in Black Water Canyon: "Morton killed McClusky while riding [at the] side of the latter with McC's own pistol and he and Baker then started to run, firing back at the posse at the same time."

That the two prisoners would have attempted anything so foolhardy defies belief: little wonder the Dolan faction put the story about that Morton and Baker had been shot while on their knees begging for their lives.[10] Such evidence as has emerged over the years indicates that what happened may well have been an execution. Morton's body is said to have had nine bullets in it, all in the back; if indeed he fled, this would indicate remarkable marksmanship on the part of the Regulators. Whatever the truth, the three men were just as dead. The Regulators rode to the nearby camp of sheepherder Francisco Gutierrez and made arrangements for the bodies to be buried, then headed for San Patricio, leaving Brewer to go on alone to Lincoln. More bad news awaited him there.

That day, escorted by Col. George A. Purington, Gov. Samuel B. Axtell had arrived in Lincoln to investigate the trouble (figs. 50, 51). He stayed only three hours, all of which time was spent in the company of L. G. Murphy and Jimmy Dolan.

Although he spoke briefly with Isaac Ellis, Widenmann, and McSween's partner David P. Shield, Axtell declined to listen to their views on the recent troubles. Instead, he performed a series of official acts as extraordinary as any ever executed by a public servant in the history of New Mexico. By proclamation, Axtell arbitrarily removed Justice of the Peace Wilson from office and voided all processes issued by him; revoked Widenmann's appointment as a deputy U.S. marshal; and declared that henceforth the only valid legal processes would be those issuing from Judge Bristol in La Mesilla, and Sheriff Brady and his deputies the only officers empowered to enforce them.

His intention in making the proclamation, Axtell announced, was "to assist good citizens to uphold the laws and keep the peace." Understandably, others

FIG. 50. George Augustus Purington. The identification provided by the archive is vague; by process of elimination, it can be established that there were only two officers with the rank of major in the photograph: Major Surgeon Benjamin Franklin Pope, seated far left, front row, and Purington, seated what looks like third but is actually second from right, front row, with Dundreary whiskers (note the major's rosette on his cap). Taken at Fort Clark, Tex., 1887; photographer unknown.

saw his actions differently, Widenmann for one.[11] In his March 30 letter to the *Cimarron News and Press*, he asked:

What did the Governor do here? Did he call a meeting of citizens to ascertain from them the cause of the trouble? Did he take the opinions of good and respectable citizens, weigh them as to their merits, and then form his course of action? No! When one of our most esteemed citizens attempted to give him a history of the trouble and its causes, he quietly remarked "I know all about this matter and its cause, and I have already taken such action as I deem necessary." The question is, where did he learn the facts, and what were they? Powers behind the throne are generally well posted as to the facts on their side of the case. The Governor also said "God deliver us from such citizens as there are in Lincoln County," to which I answered that the citizens were all right, but "*God deliver me from such executive officers.*"

FIG. 51. Samuel Beach Axtell, ca. 1875. Photo by Broadbent & Taylor.

Axtell's partisanship was evident to even the most uninformed citizen. In declaring Wilson's appointment illegal, he was nullifying a law he himself had signed only two years earlier, and in saying Widenmann's commission as a deputy U.S. marshal had been revoked, he was misrepresenting the fact that this had been done in error and that the commission had since been reinstated by U.S. Marshal John Sherman.

The real object of the proclamation lay, of course, in its third section, which was to deliver all legal power into the hands of the minions of the Santa Fe Ring. Axtell cannot have been unaware of the fact that there were at least four other justices of the peace in Lincoln County besides Wilson, all of them unquestionably still empowered.

Knowing Axtell had made an error of judgment for which he could later be made to pay dearly was of little consolation to McSween and Widenmann. The governor's arbitrary action placed them squarely in the legal power of their enemies. By invalidating the warrants issued by Wilson, he simultaneously rendered the "lawful" killing of Morton and Baker murder, and turned the Regulators into wanted men.

Axtell left town as abruptly as he had appeared, and headed back to the capital. The depth of his concern is illustrated by a small item in the March 16 *New Mexican*, in which the governor appears to attach roughly equal importance to Jimmy Dolan's drunken accident and the murder of John Tunstall.

Governor Axtell returned from as far south as Fort Stanton with [U.S. Army] Paymaster Towar on Wednesday [March 13]. The Governor reports the troubles in Lincoln county between the Dolan and McSween parties as quieting down, the result being the death of a man named Tunstall. Mr. Dolan had a leg broken by a fall from a horse a few days before the Governor's arrival there.[12]

As soon as Brewer returned to Lincoln on the night of the governor's proclamation, McSween told him that Axtell's proclamation effectively made him an outlaw. Brewer left town immediately; two days later McSween, still in the custody of Deputy Sheriff Adolph Barrier, headed down the valley to the safer shelter of the Chisum ranch. "Uncle John" had only recently returned there after his incarceration in Las Vegas. Perhaps now he might be persuaded to take a more active part in what was happening.

Among the blizzard of letter writers firing off their broadsides in the months preceding the shooting war, there are notable absentees. Not once during this time did either Lawrence G. Murphy, John Riley, or Jimmy Dolan set pen to paper in their own defense. Perhaps the old despot was too proud to debate his case in the public prints with the likes of Widenmann and McSween; perhaps also it was his restraining hand that kept Dolan and Riley from the lists.

When, finally, the House did see fit to defend itself in print, all Murphy, Riley, or Dolan seemed able to muster was a catalogue of flat and undocumented denials that lacked conviction when set next to the voluble accusations of their enemies. The lack of any documentary representation of their case has left history to judge Murphy, Dolan, and Riley on the highly unsatisfactory evidence of their actions alone. It seems unlikely now that this situation will ever be redressed: so McSween and Widenmann dominate the war of words.

The paper war was conducted on a strange, triangular basis. William Manderfield and Thomas J. Tucker's *New Mexican* was the acknowledged mouthpiece of the Santa Fe Ring; also sympathetic was Ira M. Bond, editor of the *Mesilla News*. Accusations leveled against McSween or Widenmann in either of those papers would be answered by them in Harry Whigham and Thomas Henderson's *Cimarron News and Press* or Fountain's *Independent*.

The *New Mexican* went after Widenmann's scalp early in March when R. Guy McLellan, to whom Widenmann had written immediately following the murder of Tunstall, wrote to his old friend Governor Axtell enclosing Widenmann's letter and requesting information. Axtell passed the correspondence to the newspaper, which reproduced it with an editorial excoriating Widenmann, saying in part:

> It will be noticed that Widenmann wrote [to McLellan] within a few days after the death of Tunstall and before it was possible for the district court to take any action. Its regular meeting is on the second day of April, where there will be a grand jury called and the whole affair fully investigated. Since Widenmann's letter was written, arrests made under color of law by some of the party who were with Tunstall, of the two men accused of assisting to kill him; these two men were killed by the party who had them in charge. One of the arresting party was also killed. The facts of the case have not yet been fully ascertained.[13]

The editorial continued by praising Axtell for the way he had handled matters in Lincoln during his recent visit, and added a sardonic description of the place itself, "partly inhabited by Indians . . . Texas cattle men, a few traders and business men, and a few skeleton companies of United States troops." As for "this man Widenmann," he had been

> appointed a deputy United States marshal by Marshal Sherman to take a company of United States troops from Fort Stanton and arrest the worst of the band, dead or alive; unfortunately he failed to do so, and the life of Tunstall, a worthy and valuable citizen, has been lost. All the facts in this case are yet to be investigated by a grand jury, and we do not think it proper to speak about them further at present. The slanders on the courts by Widenmann are without any foundation in fact. He has forfeited the confidence of Marshal Sherman and all good men here, and has been removed from office. Col. Geo. A Purington, 9th Cavalry, Sheriff Brady of Lincoln County, Col. W. L. Rynerson, district attorney for the third district, and Hon. Warren Bristol, United States judge presiding over the district—each and every one of them enjoy and deserve the confidence and esteem of the best men in New Mexico.

Widenmann was not about to let the *New Mexican* saddle him with the implication that Tunstall had been killed because of his failure to arrest the Boys. He sent a long letter to the editors of the *Cimarron News and Press*, parts of which have already been quoted above, describing Axtell's activities in Lincoln. As for arresting the Boys:

> I tried my utmost to arrest Evans, Baker and others, but with such powerful friends ready to aid them, to harbor and conceal them, to furnish them horses and supplies as J. J. Dolan, J. H. Riley and others, no one who knows this country will doubt that their arrest was a matter of the utmost difficulty. One of the parties who escaped from jail, and for whose arrest Brady had a warrant, only the other day was one of his posse, and was at the house of J. J. Dolan with him.

The editors of the *News and Press* (one of whom, Henry Whigham, was English) followed up with their own editorial in support of Widenmann, but the *New Mexican* was not done with him yet. Another attack appeared, and this time some of the accusations it contains ring too true to be as summarily dismissed.

> Widenmann is to a great degree responsible for the disturbed condition of affairs in Lincoln County. Col. G. A. Purington reports officially that he (Widenmann) abused his trust and use[d] the U.S. troops to break into houses and plunder them of valuable papers and other property, and also to oust the Sheriff from custody of property attached by writ legally issued from the court of which Widenmann is an officer. . . . [H]e has excited the ignorant and vicious class to violence; and at a military post, on a military reservation, in presence of Col. Purington and other officers, and in the hearing of ladies, declared with great violence that he had a warrant for J. J. Dolan and *that he intended to kill him on sight!* This warrant charged Dolan with killing Tunstall, and Widenmann has obtained it by committing the crime of perjury, for Dolan was not within 30 miles of the spot when Tunstall fell. This man obtained a warrant by perjury and used it as a shield to kill his victim on sight; and this man holds a commission as a deputy U.S. Marshall.
>   We have said U.S. Marshal Sherman by reappointing him endorsed his acts. This would be true if Sherman knew of these acts. We are informed by trustworthy persons that Marshal Sherman did not know of Widenmann's base conduct when he reappointed him; that he will at once investigate the case, and if these statements prove true, dismiss the scrub from his service. And if he didn't write the letter to Guy McLellan of San Francisco, and that other letter to the British minister at Washington; and didn't abuse his authority and use U.S. troops to rob the house and oust Sheriff Brady from the custody of the goods; and didn't commit perjury to

obtain a warrant against J. J. Dolan for murder, and didn't violate all the rules of decency, and good breeding, by boasting at the post, in the presence of officers and their ladies, that he would kill the said Dolan on sight—then we will take back all we have said, and humbly eat our peck of dirt.[14]

To this further attack Widenmann made no response. By the time it was published he had other things on his mind.

Shortly after what would have been Tunstall's twenty-fifth birthday, and about a week after Morton and Baker were killed, it was Tom Hill's turn unreadily to meet his Maker. It happened at a lonely spot in the San Andres Mountains called Alamo Springs. On that particular day Jessie Evans, accompanied by the dark, swarthy, low-browed Hill, known as Tom Chelson in his native Texas, chanced upon the camp of an old German named John Wagner, who was taking a herd of four thousand sheep from California to Texas.

There are several versions of what happened next: this is one of them.[15] Hill and Evans sneaked in, held up the herdsman who was guarding the camp, and began ransacking the place. The herdsman, whose nationality is given in some accounts as German and in others as Cherokee Indian, made the mistake of picking up a Winchester, whereupon he was unhesitatingly shot down. Thinking him dead, Hill and Evans proceeded with their robbery, which was an even bigger mistake. The herdsman was only wounded, and opened up on them with the carbine. His first shot killed Hill on the spot, and his second shattered Evans's right arm so badly that it was feared he would never have the proper use of it again.

Bleeding profusely, Evans fled on Wagner's horse and painfully made his way to W. F. Shedd's ranch some ten miles to the southeast, where he knew he could obtain aid and comfort. It would appear Evans's luck continued bad: while at Shedd's he was arrested by a railroad constable named David Wood, and taken under arrest to Fort Stanton.

Exactly when these events took place is a matter of conjecture: March 14 seems the likeliest date. The shoot-out at the Wagner camp was reported in the *Independent* on March 16, and Evans's arrest is confirmed in a note from U.S. Marshal John Sherman to U.S. Attorney General Charles Devens on April 3. At this juncture, of course, Evans's name meant nothing to Devens, although that deficiency was shortly to be remedied.

Widenmann's letter to "Henry Tunstall"—the "Uncle Henry" of whom he had heard his friend speak—reached Victoria, B.C., on March 19. It was opened by John Turner, who immediately cabled Henry C. Beeton, John Tunstall's uncle, in Milwaukee.

LETTER JUST RECEIVED FROM LINCOLN NEW MEXICO JOHN TUNSTALL MURDERED ON EIGHTEENTH FEBRUARY BY GANG OF DESPERADOES THE SHERIFF OF THAT PLACE MEMBER OF THE GANG THAT PLANNED THE MURDER, HE REFUSES TO ARREST MURDERER. LETTER SIGNED ROBERT J WIDENMAN ADDRESS ROSWELL LINCOLN COUNTY NEW MEXICO. TELEGRAPH ME IF I CAN DO ANYTHING RESPECTING THE BUSINESS AT LINCOLN. I HAVE PLACED MATTER IN ATTORNEY GENERAL'S HANDS HERE YOU HAD BETTER DO SAME. WIDELMAN HAS WRITTEN SIR EDWARD THORNTON.[16]

Beeton wrote at once to Sir Edward Thornton, the British ambassador in Washington. On the same day, he replied to Widenmann that "I should esteem it a great favour if you will write me at once all the particulars of this melancholy and sad affair and also what steps are being taken to bring the criminal to justice and to protect my nephew's property."[17]

Next day, Beeton wrote to his brother-in-law J. P. Tunstall that "something serious" had happened to John, and that he must be prepared for the worst. Two days later, Beeton's daughter Florence, called "Flo," wrote at greater length from the Palmer House in Chicago breaking the news her father had only hinted at. "I only wish I need not tell you," she wrote,"but if you do not already know by other means, you must know sooner or later and it would be wrong to keep it from you."[18]

Flo Beeton's letter also indicates some of the difficulties that would later beset John Tunstall's father. None of them had more than the most general idea of where Lincoln was, and knew nothing at all about conditions there. With hindsight it is easy to smile at Henry Beeton's fussbudget efforts to secure advice from (of all people) Stephen B. Elkins, but neither he nor, it would appear, anyone in Washington seems to have had much more than the vaguest idea of how things were run out in New Mexico Territory.

> We have referred the matter to the Rev. Brooke Herford who has two sons in New Mexico and would be likely to give us information [Flo continued].
> On reference to a military map, which we send you, we find that Lincoln is in a south-easterly direction, and at least 200 miles from the stage road. The Herfords are near the northern boundary at a place [called Clifton which] we have marked with a cross. Santa Fe is the nearest staging point, the distance intervening between that and Lincoln is to be done only on horseback. Now Papa was in hopes that he could have got at any rate at some point in the neighbourhood of Lincoln and there met this Widelman and consulted with him, but we are told it would be madness for a man like Papa to attempt it. It is necessary in a matter of this kind to know something of the Mexican tongue, to know the people you have to deal with, and the country besides, and to go alone and inexperienced into such a den of desperadoes would be folly in the extreme.
> It seems that murders are of almost everyday occurrence and that those who dwell in such a country are not safe at any moment. Only the other day we hear that two young Englishmen have been murdered by some sheep stealers in those parts so that the thief is identical with the murderer.
> We are waiting further particulars from Victoria and Washington as Mr. Turner will have sent the letter on and we ought to receive it in a week from this, and the Minister's reply may reach us here tomorrow.
> Finding that a young fellow, Warren by name, a friend of the Herfords is leaving today for New Mexico to join them there, Papa put the matter before him and gave him what money he would need. Mr. Herford most kindly offers his son's services and Papa is now writing to William Herford the eldest, giving him the particulars as far as we know and authorising him to take all the necessary steps to recover the property and see that all is right.

Beeton meanwhile wrote William Brooke Herford the facts as he knew them, adding that he had sent Warren off with a hundred dollars to cover any expenses Herford might incur.[19] He enclosed with the letter his power of attorney and affidavit as next of kin, together with an introduction to Col. Stephen Elkins, "a friend of Judge Strong's and the most influential man in connection with the Courts of New Mexico."

> You must endeavour to see him, and if Santa Fe is out of your route, telegraph him to meet you at the nearest point; it may be necessary for you however to see the Governor of the State, should Col. Elkins be absent, and in that case you would have to go to Santa Fe, but of all this you will be the best judge.

Next day, the 23rd, Beeton wrote at length to J. P. Tunstall, giving him full details of everything he had done: his initial contact with the English Unitarian minister, Rev. Brooke Herford; his visit with that worthy to the office of Gen. Philip Sheridan's office to obtain maps; his commissioning of young William Herford to go down to Lincoln and sending a hundred dollars by Warren to cover expenses; obtaining a letter of introduction to the commander at Fort Stanton from Sheridan's aide, Gen. George A. Forsyth, and another from Judge Strong to Stephen Elkins. Herford, he said, was a "first rate fellow, educated at Owen's College, Manchester, for the Ministry, and is in every way the very one to undertake this work."[20]

> You will notice in my letter to Will. Herford that I speak of a letter John had written to Mr. Francis the U.S. Consul at Victoria. Just previous to my leaving Mr. Francis told me they had received a long and satisfactory letter from John, after a very long interval, wherein he said he had started a Store and Ranch at Lincoln, New Mexico, and had just returned from St. Louis where he had been buying goods. He seemed to write in very good spirits; this was the last account of him received in Victoria.

By March 30, Robert Widenmann had received Beeton's letter of the 19th, and replied to him in care of the Windsor Hotel, New York.

> Full particulars of the murder have been by me forwarded to dear Harries (he always liked me to call him so) parents as also to Sir Edward Thornton. The murder was one of the many committed in the interest of the New Mexican ring. Their organs among the press of the Territory and even the Governor are doing all in their power to protect the murderers. My life is daily threatened and the papers attack me for trying to expose them. I enclose you a copy of one of my [March 30] answers to an attack by one of the papers, also a brief and condensed statement regarding the cause of and maner in which Harry was murdered. 3 others and I only escaped (we were with Harry at the time) by making a stand on protected ground against 18 of the murdering party.
>
> I also enclose copy of a will made by Harry. My life being in such great danger we thought it best to have a Mr. Isaac Ellis, a thoroughly honest and upright man appointed administrator until after the meeting of court, when things will probably quieten down.
>
> The murderers will never be punished if an investigation is left to the U.S. officials in this Territory, since all or most of them are members of the ring. I would therefore politely request you to use all your *utmost endeavours* to have a commission of investigation *appointed in Washington* which commission should *embrace at least one Englishman.* A Mr. Montague R. Leverson, an Englishman of education and refinement who is thoroughly acquainted with western manners and customs and who is at present visiting this section would be eminently fitted for the appointment and he would insure thorough honesty in the investigation. Would it not be well for you to make the short run to Washington and personally use your influence with Sir Edward Thornton. You can there at the same time get a thorough insight into the whole matter.

The persons Dolan & Riley mentioned in my statement as well as the Governor are the tools of the ring whose head Thos. B. Catron U.S. District Atty. at Santa Fe is.

As regards the property it is in safe hands and I am giving it my attention and will see that nothing is lost or squandered. I promised Harry I would do this should he die and he promised to do the same for me should my time come first.

I should be glad to hear from you before you leave for England.[21]

With his letter Widenmann enclosed a copy of the "will" (McSween referred to it as what it was, a power of attorney) that John Tunstall had written in May 1877 and a four-page summary of Tunstall's difficulties and the events that led up to his death. Although garbled, the statement merits reproduction inasmuch as it was the first full account of those events that the Tunstall family had seen.

When Mr. Tunstall first came to Lincoln, he was treated well by L. G. Murphy & Co. They tried to sell him some of the ranches to which they had no title, but seeing that he would not bite at this bait, they began to be mean and run him down. They controlled Lincoln County politically and commercially. T[unstall], seeing a good opening here, decided to open a store here and establish himself permanently here. No sooner had this decision been made than L. G. Murphy & Co., who in the meantime had been transformed into J. J. Dolan & Co., showed their hatred and opposition. They saw that as soon as any man with capital came into the country they would lose their control, that as soon as the people, whom they had so persistently robbed and kept on the verge of poverty, saw that they could deal with an honest man who would always give them their just dues, they would lose the greater part of the trade. Riley, one of the firm of J. J. Dolan & Co., told McSween he would have him and T[unstall] stolen poor, that he would not do it himself, but would get others to do it. T[unstall] went to St. Louis and while there, most all of his horses were stolen by Jesse Evans, Frank Baker, Tom Hill and George Davis.

Dolan borrowed $1,000 from McSween, who loaned it to J. J. Dolan & Co. on T[unstall]'s a/c. The note was not paid and Dolan refused to recognize T[unstall] in the transaction. T[unstall] upbraided Sheriff Brady for the escape of Evans and party from the county jail. Brady at the time reached for his revolver, but McSween prevented his using it. The governor's message showed that Sheriff Brady had not paid any of the Territorial taxes into the territorial treasury. T[unstall] wrote to the Mesilla Independent stating the fact and showing how the money had been used, which information Dolan himself supplied. T[unstall] went to Mesilla and while there, his life was threatened by Dolan. In the return from Mesilla, Dolan and Jesse Evans again threatened T[unstall] Dolan drew down his carbine on T[unstall] three times, cursed T[unstall] and before leaving him said: "You won't fight now, you coward, but I'll get you yet." T[unstall] and party were [to have been] waylaid between Dowlin's mill and Fort Stanton but fortunately they came the lower road and thereby escaped being murdered. On January 19th, 1878, J. J. Dolan & Co. transferred all their property to T. B. Catron of Santa Fe. Before T[unstall]'s arrival here, Brady attached all of T[unstall]'s property under writ of attachment on A. A. McSween. They (Brady) also sent a posse to attach T[unstall]'s cattle. On February 17th, T[unstall] arrived at the ranch about 10 o'clock P.M. and it was decided to return to Lincoln the next day with the loose horses. McClusky was sent to the sheriff's posse, which consisted of some 30 or 40 men, among them the greatest outlaws in the country, on the Peñasco, to tell them they could take the cattle and leave a good man with them, and that we would also have a good man to take care of the cattle. Our party consisted of T[unstall], R. M. Brewer, Wm. Bonnie, John Middleton, and R. A. Widenmann. Wait was sent around with the wagon by the road.

We started about 8 o'clock A.M. and traveled slowly. About 5 o'clock P.M. (February 18th) while Tunstall, Brewer and I (Widenmann) were driving the horses, Middleton, & Bonnie were about 500 yards in the rear, a flock of wild turkies rose near the trail. Brewer and I had got some 50 or 100 yards from the trail when we heard a noise in our rear. Turning in our saddles we saw a body of horsemen coming over the hill at a gallop. No sooner did these men see us than they turned in our direction and commenced firing at us. There were 18 men in the party. We saw at once that we had no chance against such odds on the ground we were on and therefore made for the opposite hill which was covered with rocks and timber. On our way there we were met by Middleton and Bonnie and we took our stand on the top of the hill. Middleton at once said that T[unstall] had been murdered, that he had tried to induce him to come our way, but T[unstall] evidently excited did not understand him and rode up to the attacking party. It was afterwards ascertained that T[unstall] rode up to the party, that Morton commenced cursing him and ordered him off his horse, and when on the ground, Jesse Evans shot him through the chest, which shot felled him to the ground. Morton then jumped from his horse, drew T[unstall]'s pistol from its scabbard, shot T[unstall] through the head, shot T[unstall]'s horse in the head with the same pistol, returned the pistol to its scabbard and then mashed T[unstall]'s skull with the butt of his (Morton's) gun. We kept our position, the murdering party, after killing T[unstall], rode partly around us and then disappeared behind another hill, not coming within range of our rifles. It was also ascertained that the sheriff's posse had, while on the Penasco plotted to kill T[unstall], Brewer and myself. We made the best of our way to town, where we arrived about 10 o'clock P.M.[22]

What Henry Beeton—who knew nothing about the background to his nephew's killing—made of Widenmann's summary it is hard to imagine, but no doubt he went armed with it to Washington at the end of March, where he was to confer with Sir Edward Thornton, and in due course, with President Rutherford B. Hayes himself. By the time he did so, however, Henry Beeton's concern was irrelevant: all hell had broken loose in Lincoln County.

WAR: THE ASSASSINATION OF WILLIAM BRADY

ON Monday, April 1, at about 9:30 a.m., Sheriff William Brady and his deputy George Hindman were assassinated on the street in Lincoln by a group of the Regulators. Brady died instantly, his body riddled by nine shots; mortally wounded, Hindman staggered a few yards before collapsing.[1]

George Peppin's oldest son, Juan Peppin, was ten or twelve in 1878.[2] In 1930, at the behest of Maurice Garland Fulton, he set down what he had seen and heard that April day.

> [That morning] I was doing some work on a fence my father, George Peppin, was building on our place, just outside the town of Lincoln at the west. My father had gone to the Murphy store. About 9 o'clock I heard shooting in the town, but did not give it much thought until someone came by the house with the news that Sheriff Brady had been killed. As my father was one of his deputies, I thought it more than likely that he had been with the Sheriff. So I left my work and went into town. Seeing a large number of people in the vicinity of the Tunstall store, I went there. I saw Major Brady lying on his back in the street dead, all covered with blood, and one of his deputies, George Hindman, lying mortally wounded a few yards further along the street. My father was alive but had had a narrow escape.
>
> From hearing him tell about it, I am able to give what happened just before I came on the scene. A fellow by the name of Henry, Brown I believe was his last name, had created a disturbance at the east end of the town and Sheriff Brady had set out to arrest him, accompanied by George Hindman, Billy Mathews and my father. They were walking down the street abreast, my father being nearest the side of the street on which the Tunstall store was. Sheriff Brady came next, then George Hindman, and finally Billy Mathews. These four had just passed the gateway to the corral, when five or six of the McSween men fired at them from behind the adobe wall of the corral. These men slipped into town during the night and placed themselves in the corral. They had drilled port holes in the east wall of the corral, so they could level their rifles through them. Brady and Hindman fell, as I have said, but Billy Mathews and my father ran for their lives and got protection behind a house on the opposite side of the street. It is generally believed that Billy the Kid took a shot at Billy Mathews but did not come closer to him than to splinter the door facing where he stood. My father saw Billy the Kid go out and try to take Brady's rifle, but a shot from Billy Mathews put a stop to his attempt. Green Wilson was working in his garden, and a stray bullet struck him in the rear.

If Juan Peppin's account might be said to express the attitude taken by the Murphy supporters, that of the excitable and partisan Dr. Taylor F. Ealy, who classed those who were persecuting McSween as "a dirty set of Irish cut throats," presents the viewpoint of the other side. As Ealy's biographer has pointed out, to the missionary's prejudiced Presbyterian eye, Irish meant Catholic meant wicked: thus there is no hint of sympathy in his account of Brady's death.

> I saw some men with guns pass our house and opposite our house Sheriff Brady stopped to talk to a woman I took to be Mrs. Ham Mills. He was laughing—then he hurried up to overtake his posse at the east end of the big house—which was unoccupied—the house with the bank, law office, store and drug room—where we afterwards lived was a wide door made for wagons to drive into the corral. This door swung open and the sheriff fell mortally wounded. I did not hear him groaning— but the women in our house said they did—when George Hindman fell; he called for water and some one helped him up, and as he was being helped towards Stoc[k]ton's saloon, he received another wound and fell dead.[3]

These would seem to be the closest thing to eyewitness accounts that exist. Neither McSween nor Widenmann spared much more than a sentence in informing Tunstall's family that the sheriff had been killed, and neither went into any sort of detail about the event. Lest this be considered significant, it should be added that neither described in any greater detail the deaths of Morton, Baker, or later, Roberts.

On the face of it, then, Brady's death was an execution, pure and simple. But why was he killed? Was it because Alexander McSween, as one piece of evidence indicates, had only a short while before promised that the man who killed the sheriff would get a five-hundred-dollar reward? Was it because, as other testimony suggests, the Regulators had learned Brady was on his way to arrest—i.e., kill— McSween as the lawyer came into town? Or was it, after all, a spur-of-the-moment assassination carried out by half a dozen of the hotter heads among the Regulators? To arrive at any sort of conclusion we must examine the events that preceded the murders (fig. 52).

As has already been remarked, the principals of the House seem to have been reluctant to commit their side of the case to paper. Some of their supporters, however, were less inhibited: Sheriff William Brady, for one, was busily justifying his actions to his nominal superior, District Attorney William L. Rynerson in La Mesilla.

SHERIFF'S OFFICE, LINCOLN CO. N.M.
March 4, 1878.

SIR:
> Deeming it my duty, I beg to submit for your information the following report of events which have transpired within the county since the receipt of the attachment papers on property of A. A. McSween of this place, on the night of February 8 last. On the following day I proceeded to the store of A. A. McSween, or of J. H. Tunstall & Co. and levied the attachment in conformity with law, and with the assistance of two others commenced taking an inventory of the stock etc. During the whole of this time I was met at every step by insult, vituperation and obstacles of every degree, and I am justified in believing that while inventorying the property in the private residence of McSween, an accident alone saved me from assassination.[4]

What this "accident" was, or who the assassin, neither Brady nor anyone else seems to have seen fit to record; even his biographer avoids making a guess. Brady continued:

On the 10th [of February, 1878] I deputised one of my assistants [Mathews] to proceed to the Rio Feliz distant some 50 miles from this point where the company herd of horses and cattle were held, to attach the same. He took with him four men and on his arrival he found there one Wiedimann in charge of some 15 armed men, and some men against whom the same Wiedimann claims as Deputy U.S.Marshal to have warrants of arrest. These men he invited to partake of his hospitality while the posse were not allowed to approach the house.

After the reading of the attachment said Wiedimann informed my deputy sheriff that he could not make the attachment, and the threatening attitude of the armed men around him convinced my deputy that the destruction of himself and party would speedily follow any attempt to enforce the attachment, and he wisely returned to report. I then increased his posse to about twenty four of the best citizens procurable, and again sent him to enforce the attachment which he did, except as to the horse herd, which they attempted to run off, and while a portion of the posse were in pursuit of the party, J. H. Tunstall fired on the posse and in the return fire he was shot and killed. It has

FIG. 52. William Brady, ca. 1877. Photo by W. T. Hiester, Santa Fe, N.M. As he looked at age forty-eight, shortly before his death.

falsely been averred that attached to my deputy's posse were men against whom U.S. warrants had been issued. To disprove this, I present you a letter which reached him before he attached, and in addition to my minute verbal instructions:

LINCOLN, N.M. Feb.15th, 1878.

J.B.Mathews,
Deputy-Sheriff.
DEAR SIR: You must not by any means call on or allow to travel with your posse any person or persons who are known to be outlaws. Let your Mexicans round up the cattle and protect them with the balance. Be firm and do your duty according to law and I will be responsible for your acts.

I am, sir, respectfully yours,
WILLIAM BRADY, Sheriff, Lincoln Co.

When I had completed the inventory, I placed three men in charge of the property attached. On return of Wiedimann and his party he was joined by another party of reckless men, and by stating to the military authorities that one of the men [Jessie Evans] against whom he had a warrant was closeted with the men I had in charge, he obtained possession, arrested the men on trumped up charges, and by force retook all the property I had attached, and for all I know still has possession, unless, as I incidentally learn, the Probate Judge has placed in charge of the store a Mr. [Isaac] Ellis as administrator of the estate of the late J. H. Tunstall. Anarchy is the only word which would truly describe the situation here for the past month, and the quiet and order now prevailing I fear very much that this condition of things will not last. I regret to say that our Justice of the Peace J. B. Wilson became a willing instrument in the hands of the leaders of the mob, and at their instance and without a shadow of justice issued warrants of search and arrest indiscriminately against my posse, and all who in any manner countenanced us against the mob. I was myself arrested by his warrant and on examination before him was held in two hundred dollars bond. Private houses were entered under cover of these search warrants and the inhabitants robbed and insulted by his so-called constables. I trust the law will not be found powerless to punish such violation of it in his person.

I await further instructions as to obtaining repossession of the property I attached.

Simultaneously, using the office of District Attorney Thomas B. Catron in Santa Fe as his conduit, Brady sought by telegraph the support of the governor.

Dear Sir:

A. A. McSween, wridaman [Widenmann] and others have collected a well armed mob of about fifty men and are getting more to join them. They defy the law. They threaten the lives and property of our best citizens. The good and law abiding citizens although far in majority are not able to compete with them for want of arms. I cannot serve any legal documents or carry out the law if I am not assisted by the military. Please see his Excellency the Governor and ask him to obtain an order from Gen. Hatch to the Post Commander of Fort Stanton to protect me in the discharge of my official duties.

I am, very respectfully,
Your obedient servant,
Wm. Brady, Sheriff.[5]

The message was passed to Governor Axtell, who endorsed it to the effect that he knew Brady and believed what he said. "One man an Englishman named Tunsdell has been killed. I start in the morning for the scene of action. It will take me four days to go there. I hope orders may be given to Gen. Hatch to send us such assistance as will enable me to keep the peace and protect life and property."[6]

Covered by this note, Brady's letter was forwarded to Washington, where President Rutherford B. Hayes acted at once. Secretary of War George McCrary authorized military support for Brady; by the time Axtell reached Fort Stanton

I was informed by Col. Purington, commanding the post, that my request for help had been granted, and that he had orders to assist the civil authorities. He also informed me that there appeared to be a dispute as to who were civil officers. The Sheriff of the County had certain writs issued out of the District Court. A Deputy Sheriff of San Miguel County had McSween in charge and declined to deliver him to Brady. Wilson, Justice of the Peace, had issued warrants against the Sheriff and his deputies, and a Deputy U.S. Marshal for Lincoln County claimed the right to direct the movement of the troops. Under these circumstances, Col. Purington asked my advice as to whom he should render assistance. I told him that Wiedderman's appointment as Deputy Marshal had been revoked; that Wilson had been appointed Justice of the Peace by the County Commissioners, and that appointment was good for nothing—that a Justice of the Peace must be elected, could not be appointed, that it was so established in our Territorial Constitution, the Organic Act. Col. Purington went with me to Wiederman's office and saw him, and he admitted that his appointment had been revoked. We also went to the office of Wilson, Justice of the Peace, and informed him what was the law in his case. He said he would not act as Judge any more, and bundled up his papers and retreated in good order into his bar room. I did not remove him from office—he was not in office. Col. Purington asked me to put these facts in writing for the information of the people. I did so. This is my proclamation of March 9, 1878. If it makes anybody an outlaw the fault is in the facts not in me.

Up to March 9, 1878, no man had been killed except Tunstall. I conversed with all the citizens of Lincoln County I could meet. I advised them to seek peace and pursue it, to be in earnest to uphold the law. I told them I would use my best exertions to have every man who was present when Tunstall was killed, and who took any part whatever against him, indicted and tried, and as they claimed to justify as officers resisted in the discharge of duty, they must make this claim good on their trial and in open court. I told them Judge Bristol would be with them in about three weeks, and would organise a grand jury, and investigate all the facts. There were four men said to have been in the Sheriff's party spoken of by what is called the McSween party, as outlaws, said to be very bad men. It was feared by the McSween men that Sheriff Brady would not be active in their arrest. I talked to Col. Purington about this, and I told him I would give him a request in writing to arrest these four men and to keep them in his guard house till the court should sit. We did not think [it] best to inform anyone of this for fear it might thwart our purpose.[7]

As we have seen, the "McSween men"—most notably Robert Widenmann and David P. Shield—claimed that Axtell had acted illegally in removing Wilson, and that in fact he had spent his entire time in Lincoln in the company of Lawrence Murphy and Jimmy Dolan; but the damage was done. By removing the justice of the peace and revoking his warrants, Axtell accomplished the end desired by the Dolan faction. District Attorney Rynerson and Sheriff William Brady were now the only authorized law in Lincoln County.

Charged now with murder, little better off than outlaws, the Regulators re-treated to the mountains. Perhaps prompted by the sight of a drunken Jimmy Dolan falling off his horse and breaking a leg while trying to kill an unarmed man—this happened within twenty-four hours of Axtell's proclamation—Alexander McSween had also left town, heading hastily down the valley to a hideout near Roswell.[8] It was at this crucial time that there arrived in Lincoln, as the guest of Juan Patrón, a man destined to become a formidable ally of the McSween faction: Montague R. Leverson of Douglas County, Colo.

British-Born Leverson—who had supported Chisum in his trials at Las Vegas—was a lawyer, a crusader, and an experienced political agitator. He now espoused the cause of McSween and Widenmann and wasted no time in making himself heard at the highest levels. On March 16 he addressed a long letter to Sir Edward Thornton, the British ambassador.[9] District Attorney Rynerson, he claimed, had "incited" the murder of John Tunstall; Governor Axtell and Judge Bristol were "screening"—i.e., protecting—the murderers. In addition, he said, "excepting perhaps the U.S. marshall and his deputies there is not a single U.S. officer in this Territory who is not either a thief and assassin, or the protector of thieves and assassins."

He went on to damn Axtell's actions of a week earlier by enclosing copies of the Act of the Legislative Assembly dated January 13, 1876, which gave the county commissioners power to appoint any county officer in the event of death,

resignation, or removal; the document confirming the appointment by the commissioners of John B. Wilson to replace John H. Farmer, justice of the peace,
resigned, dated February 14, 1877; and Axtell's March 9 proclamation.

That done, he addressed himself to President Hayes.[10] Leverson claimed he
had a considerable amount of "pull" with the Hayes administration, although it
was perhaps less considerable than he represented it to be. Clearly Widenmann,
McSween, and Chisum, his likeliest source for the information contained in his
letters, were not averse to taking whatever advantage of it they could.

That this was not Leverson's first contact with Hayes is evident; he began by
referring to his "last letter to your Excellency on the state of affairs in this
Territory" and later to the "base and brutal murder of Mr. Tunstall referred to in
my first letter on this subject." Again he states that "investigation will prove
conclusively that the murder was plotted and continued by the District Attorney
of the third Judicial District by whom the District Judge is used as a tool" and
that "the Governor has *illegally* and *despotically* exerted his powers to screen the
murderers." He explained that "Mr. Axtell is a freemason (so am I) and so is the
Irishman who is here the leader of the thieves and assassins of this region, and
I think it probable that in violation of the *spirit of the order*, the Governor has
chosen to believe what his brother free-mason has told him instead of inquiring
into the truth."

With the confident expectation "as an Englishman" that the British government
would soon intervene in the matter of Tunstall's murder, Leverson entreated
Hayes to order, "immediately and by telegraph," the suspension of the governor
and the district attorney, and the appointment of an acting governor who would
in turn nominate someone to take possession of Rynerson's books and papers
"before they can be destroyed."

> Similar measures would be desirable if you wish to get at the truth with regard to
> the embezzlements committed by the Surveyor General. Charges against the judge
> of the 3rd Judicial District were (I am informed) presented about two years ago and
> are now on file in the Attorney General's Office. [These charges] have never been
> investigated, owing, it is alleged, to the influence brought to bear . . . by the U.S.
> District Attorney for New Mexico through Mr. Elkins.

Leverson was aiming high with these charges. The U.S. district attorney for
the Territory was Thomas B. Catron (fig. 53). He and Stephen B. Elkins, his
former law partner, were the most powerful members of the hydra-headed Santa
Fe Ring, ruthless and blatant controllers of everything worth controlling in the
Territory of New Mexico.

Next, on March 20, Leverson wrote to U.S. Marshal John Sherman, Jr., from
Lincoln (on Tunstall's letterhead, further indication of the advisory presence of
Robert Widenmann), canvassing his support. "I am the person" he told Sherman,
"by whom the naturalization frauds of New York in 1868 were detected and
exposed over my signature in the New York Tribune. I having refused $3000
offered and shewn to me by an emissary from Tammany to suppress my report
before it was published & then told to state what I would take & to remember
that 'Tammany never goes back on its friends.' "[11]

After thus establishing his incorruptibility, Leverson set out the matter of
Axtell's removal of Wilson and subsequent proclamation. He went on to claim
that Sheriff William Brady was

the very man who to the knowledge of the governor himself as shewn by the previous message to the Legislature was until 9 July last a defaulter to the Territory & had never paid in a dollar since he came into office!

The amount thus defaulted was paid by Mr. Catron on the 9 Jany out of the proceeds of Indian vouchers & moneys forwarded by Mr. Riley of the firm of J. J. Dolan of this place.

Under the warrants issued by Mr. J. Wilson, 2 of Mr. Tunstall's murderers were arrested. While riding to jail they succeeded in shooting one of the guard and were then shot down.

Under the governor's proclamation the troops are now at the beck and call of the sheriff pursuing the men who made the arrest to the indignation and dismay of every honest citizen in the county.

Two more of the sheriff's posse by whom Mr. Tunstall was murdered stopped and were robbing a Mr. Wagner who was bringing a herd of sheep from California, when one of his hands—a german whom they had wantonly shot—shot & Killed one of them & shot & wounded the other. Both of these men were "wanted" by the U.S. for robbery & had been gen-

FIG. 53. Thomas Benton Catron. Date unknown. Photographer Brands Studios, Chicago, Ill.

erously furnished mules saddles and arms by Mr. Riley of the firm of J. J. Dolan & Co being 2 of the men so kindly let out of jail last fall by the governor's protege sheriff Brady. I assure you I have done my very best to get at the truth and have listened to & questioned *both* sides. I am acquainted with the statements, denials and explanations furnished by the sheriff's lot, but they are too flimsy & too thoroughly contradicted by *facts* which are patent & can't be gainsaid to need further notice here.

So soon as I return to Santa Fe I will call & give you further information but in the meantime in the interests of justice & honesty & *to avoid further bloodshed so far as possible,* I earnestly recommend you to telegraph to Washington that orders be given for the troops to be retired to the fort and that they be ordered out only on the call of the U.S. Marshall or of his deputies and only in aid of U.S. process in their hands also & above all things do not fail to sustain your present deputy Mr. Wideman; the citizens can be relied on to do their duty so soon as the demoralizing spectacle of the U.S. troops aiding and abetting thieves and assassins under the orders of the government is put an end to.

Leverson's—and Widenmann's—motivation here, of course, is clear. Brady and his deputies, backed by a detachment of troops from Fort Stanton commanded by Lt. George W. Smith, were scouring the area between Lincoln and the Pecos looking for McSween and the Regulators. Let Deputy U.S. Marshal Widenmann gain control of those troops, and the tables would be turned with a vengeance. Evidently someone at the Lincoln post office in the Murphy store thought so, too, for the following notes are appended to Leverson's letter in a different hand.

> Wilson was appointed a Justice of the Peace by the Co. Commissioners. As the organic Act provides that Justices of the Peace shall be elected he was not a lawful Justice of the Peace. "Justice" Wilson issued warrants of arrest for members of the Sheriff's posse who had been charged before him as the murderers of Tunstall.
>
> The story of the shooting of the guard and the two men charged with the murder of Tunstall will be found to have quite a different coloring. McC[loskey] the guard is claimed by Morton, one of the prisoners, to have been his friend. He so wrote to his friends in West Va. & in anticipation that he would be killed by the arresting party. McC. was simply shot & killed Morton & Baker were badly mutilated with many shots. Such appears to be a well received & believed statement.
>
> Morton counted McC. as his friend. The idea was that the arresting party (McC. being one of them) intended to kill Morton & Baker before reaching Lincoln, but McC. was opposed to it & acted friendly to M & B.

The industrious Leverson now dashed off notes to Sen. H. B. Anthony of Rhode Island and the colorful Gen. Benjamin F. Butler of Massachusetts.[12] Enclosing a copy of his letter to Sherman, he entreated them to call upon Secretary Schurz and ask him to show them the letters Leverson had written to Schurz and the president concerning the murder of John Tunstall.

Next day, while the citizens of Lincoln were "plowing and making gardens," Widenmann and Leverson continued their campaign. Writing to Alfred Bury, a Kansas City merchant whose acquaintance Tunstall had made while buying goods there in the summer of 1877, Widenmann described the events of the preceding six months. He named Jessie Evans and Buck Morton as Tunstall's murderers, told how Axtell had "placed every obstacle in his power in our way to hinder us from bringing the murderers to justice," and requested Bury's cooperation in obtaining the appointment of an investigatory commission in Washington. Leverson, Widenmann said, would be an ideal member of such a commission.

Leverson, meanwhile, was exhorting Sir Edward Thornton to action. It had occurred to him, he wrote, that Sir Edward "might still be inclined to think that a charge so sweeping and severe as that which I made against the United States officials in this Territory was either rashly made or made in a spirit of partisanship."[13]

Not so, he assured Thornton. He had no interest whatever in the matter beyond a desire for truth and justice. So far from partisan bias was he, a stranger to New Mexico, that in fact he would make his home there were life and property secure.

> Did these depend on the citizens they would be so, but unhappily the corruption and wickedness of most of the United States officials render them unsafe. Rynerson, of whom I am about to speak, the *District Attorney of the 3rd Judicial District* having himself murdered in cold blood the Chief Justice of this Territory about seven years ago.
>
> I could bring proofs against every one of these men that I have accused, but they will come best when the Commission of Enquiry meets; yet to convince you that my sweeping charge against the U.S. officials is not too severe, I send as a supplement to what I sent you against the Governor *one* of the proofs against Rynerson, the *District Attorney*. Enclosed please find copy of a letter in *Rynerson's own handwriting*

to his confederates Dolan and Riley, and when you read it please bear in mind that the letter is written by a lawyer holding the position of prosecuting attorney in whose absolute power (practically) lies the prosecution or *letting loose* of all criminals in this 3rd Judicial District of New Mexico. Can anything more directly amounting to an invitation to the murder which followed be conceived? He had already "non-prossed" [*nolle prosequi*: the prosecutor discontinues his action] an indictment for assault with intent to kill pending against Riley who had shot and crippled for life Juan B. Patron, the present Chairman of the County Commissioners.

As a lawyer, Leverson really should have known that away from the context in which it had been written, Rynerson's letter to "Friends Riley and Dolan" dated February 14 would not appear to any casual reader to be an "invitation to murder"; partisan, certainly, but nothing more.

Undaunted, Leverson next went into the matter of Rynerson's categorical refusal of McSween's bail. Ordered to put up $8,000, McSween had offered sureties of $34,500, but Rynerson rejected them all on the grounds that the sureties had not justified before him. The reason for this, Leverson said, was to require McSween's bondsmen to travel from Lincoln to La Mesilla, so that they could be murdered en route. This was an artful inversion of the truth: that fear of assassination had kept McSween's bondsmen from traveling to La Mesilla to support him. The end result, however, was the same.

When Deputy Sheriff Adolph Barrier of San Miguel County, who had been McSween's custodian since his arrest at Las Vegas just before Christmas, was instructed to turn his prisoner over to Sheriff Brady, Leverson continued, "he pointedly and publicly told the sheriff that he saw it was intended to murder Mr. McSween and that he would not turn him over, but would himself keep him in custody in this County. This [deputy] Sheriff now holds Mr. McSween, hiding him from the Sheriff, and the United States troops, who at the insistence of the Governor, are being sent after them."

Leverson remained in Lincoln only a few more days after writing this long and involved letter. Informing Thornton that he expected to be back in Santa Fe by April 3 or 4, and that he would be "happy to furnish all the assistance and information in [his] power" to the ambassador, Leverson left for the Chisum ranch. On March 25, he mailed a postcard to Carl Schurz from Roswell.

I have written to Senator Anthony of Rhode Island and General B. F. Butler of Massachusetts, asking them to call on you and to ask you to show them the letters you have received touching the murder of Mr. Tunstall, with a view to their getting a Congressional investigation in the event of the President failing to have a proper one.

I write to beg you to give them every aid in your power. New Mexico is a volcano which may burst forth at any moment and hang every member of the Ring.[14]

A flurry of shooting early in the morning of Saturday, March 30, convinced Doctor Ealy that more trouble was brewing, but whatever its cause (and Ealy does not say) things calmed down.[15] Robert Widenmann spent the day pursuing his campaign of correspondence. His first task was to compose a rebuttal of the charges made against him in the March 23 issue of the *New Mexican*, which he did in a five-page letter to the editors of the *Cimarron News and Press*. The charges leveled against him, said Widenmann, using a phrase he can only have learned from Tunstall, were nothing but "Billingsgate and Blatherskite."

Since his rebuttal has appeared earlier, it is enough to note here that the editors of the *News and Press* were more than happy to publish it in its entirety, and in a later editorial, to drive a coach and horses through the holes in the arguments adduced by the Santa Fe paper.[16]

On March 19, Henry Beeton, John Tunstall's uncle, had written to Widenmann from New York's Windsor Hotel where he had just received a telegram from John H. Turner in Victoria advising him of the murder of Tunstall. Widenmann's reply, on the letterhead of the Lincoln County Bank, was written the same day as his rebuttal.

Next day, Sunday, a further letter arrived from Beeton.[17] Explaining that his knowledge of his nephew's death was limited to what he had learned in Turner's telegram, Beeton asked Widenmann to provide him with some specific information.

I know his father sent him within the last six or nine months 15,000 dollars to commence Store-keeping and I also know just before leaving Victoria, a month or more ago, [Allen Francis], a friend of my nephew's received a long letter from him, stating he had a Store and Ranch at Lincoln, New Mexico, and that he had been to St. Louis to purchase goods.

You have already acted the part of a true friend of the family in doing what you have, I therefore do not hesitate to ask you to furnish me with all the information in your power concerning his affairs, that I may know what [to] do before leaving and be able to satisfy his father when I return to London.

The following questions I should like answered if possible, viz.

Who did he buy the Store and Ranche from? What was the price? Had he paid the money? Was he alone in the business, or had he an assistant, if so is he in charge?

Where are the books, and what balance do they show?

Are there any creditors in St. Louis and elsewhere?

Can I by coming to Lincoln do any good over and above the Govt. Official in the way of settling his affairs and securing for the family the balance of his property?

When I get to Chicago this evening I intend to get a newspaper from St Louis which may contain an account of the murder. Can you send me one?

Henry Beeton's naive belief that news of Tunstall's murder might have been reported in the St. Louis newspapers again emphasizes how little conception he had of just how far from civilization Lincoln really was, a distance not measured merely in miles. Widenmann settled down to reply.

I have just rec'd your kind favor of the 21st inst. in answer to which I beg, in part, to refer to my respects of yesterday, and wil now answer your questions as briefly as possible. By going into the matter thoroughly I would not be able to finish this letter in time to catch the outgoing mail which leaves in about an hour.

The ground the store is built on was bought of A. A. McSween. Harry built the store.

The ranches were all taken up and entered under the Desert Land Act, and, this law requiring that 25¢ per acre entered should be paid at the time of entry and allowing the payment of the balance at $1 per acre within 3 years from the date of entry, part payment has been made. The entries embrace between 3 and 4000 acres and are all well located. One tract embraces a waterfrontage of between 8 and 9 miles and will in time be worth at least $10000 as a cattle ranch.

A. A. McSween was to receive a share of the profits of the business in consideration for his knowledge of the country and people but this agreement was annulled some months ago.—I was generally in charge of the business, although at first I gave my attention to the land and cattle matters.—The store is inventoried and closed, the cattle of which there are about 300 head are at the ranch and being taken care of.—The books are in possession of the administrator Isaac Ellis of this place. They have not as yet been balanced. The disturbed condition of affairs in this county making it very difficult to transact much business. The whole county is clamoring for the arrest of the murderers but the sheriff has refused to allow them to be arrested. The creditors in St. Louis are: H.A. Wells Co $417.50. Henry Folsom, about $500. Dodd Brown Co. $1477.11 as per statement of Octob.8, and Edward Martin Co. about $500 and A.A. McSween, Lincoln about $5000. I give you the above state-ment from memory not having the books before me.

On the other hand the inventorying of the personal property without the cattle and real estate and notes and book accounts, shows an appraised value of a little over $14000. The book accounts will beyond a doubt with the notes realize at the lowest estimation $8000. the cattle are worth here, sold in open market, between $2500 and $3000 but sold in the proper man[n]er will undoubtedly bring more. The real estate it would be difficult to give the exact value of, but if handled properly it will realize as handsome profit on the investment.

I have given dear Harrie's parents all the facts as above stated, excepting the figures. I did this very reluctantly knowing how the simple mention of business would grate on their feelings after this terrible affliction. I do not think your presence here would do much unless you came with a power of attorney from the heir. The matters are in the hands of the probate court of the county and only a power of attorney would enable you to remove them therefrom. I advised dear Harrie's father to send an instrument to me or some honest and reliable man here and expect to hear from him by an early mail. This step woul[d] save much expense and make an early settlement of the business possible. If you will allow me, I would again suggest that you go to Washington and call on Sir Edward Thornton and President Hayes and request to see and examine all papers sent these gentlemen from this place. Such papers will give you a full and complete history of the whole matter. The New Mexican ring is straining itself to its utmost and I doubt not that they will attempt to take my life at the first opportunity. In fact some of its tools have and still openly threaten to do so, but I am prepared for them.

I deserve no thanks for what I am doing for dear Harry and his poor parents and sisters. I am simply living up to the promise I gave him and he would have done the same for me had I been in his place. He was a brother in every sense of the word. I have had his remains embalmed so that they can be removed to the home of his birth which he loved so dearly, when desired. Any farther information you desire I will gladly furnish and shall be happy to hear from you at any time.[18]

About noon that day Sheriff Brady and eight cavalrymen rode through town on their way back to the fort. With the soldiers as his posse, Brady had gone down to the Pecos valley to summon veniremen for grand and petit jury duty, and—if he could find him—to arrest Alexander McSween. When the party stopped at the Chisum ranch, they were met by Montague Leverson and Susan McSween, newly returned from her extended visit to St. Louis and Kansas City.[19]

According to Leverson, Brady apologized for coming with troops, confessing that none of the civilian population would serve as possemen. Leverson said he believed Brady's life was in danger and advised him to resign. Meanwhile Captain Smith "pressed and exhorted" Mrs. McSween to persuade her husband to come in to Fort Stanton and there in safety await the imminent April term of court. He gave his word as an officer and a gentleman that Brady would make no attempt to serve the warrant he had for McSween's arrest. "You may make a football of my head," Smith assured her, "if a hair of his head is injured or if the least insult be given him by word or sign from the highest to the lowest."

Mrs. McSween promised to talk to her husband. On learning that McSween had been guaranteed the protection of the military, Deputy Sheriff Barrier, who had effectively been the lawyer's bodyguard for the last three months, left at once, anxious to return to his family.[20] The following day, Saturday, McSween came in, either bringing the Regulators with him or summoning them soon afterwards. For what transpired next, we have only the testimony of an eighty-five-year-old man, Francisco Trujillo, who recalled in a 1937 interview, almost sixty years after the events he witnessed as a young man, that

> we found Macky Swin [McSween] at John Chisum's ranch. Breakfast being over Macky Swin told us to go into the store and take anything that we wished. At this point it was decided to leave Captain Stock [Smith?] to guard over Macky Swin. Of the original eight Mexicans in the party, four were left to join the Americans. Macky Swin then asked us to meet him the following Monday at Lincoln because he said: "As soon as I arrive, Brady is going to try to arrest me. You shouldn't let him get away with it. If I am arrested they'll lynch me, while if you kill Brady, you shall earn a reward."[21]

It is difficult to know how much weight to give to Trujillo's statement, which is at best imprecise. He goes on to say that the Regulators went to Berrendo, a small hamlet east of Roswell, where there was a fandango in progress. They were enjoying themselves when word came in that a gang of "about fifty Murfes" [Murphies, i.e. men of the Murphy-Dolan faction] was coming. They saddled up and rode off; after riding about half a mile they heard shouts and gunshots. They decided to make a stand, but the Murphy men failed to show up, so the Regulators headed for Agua Negra, arriving there at daybreak on Sunday.

At this point the party broke up, the Anglos going to Lincoln, the Mexicans to San Patricio where they arrived Sunday afternoon.

> There Billy the Kid said to Jose Chaves, "Let us draw lots to see who has to wait for McSween at Lincoln tomorrow." The lots fell to Charlie Barber [Bowdre] John Milton [Middleton] and Jim French White. The leader decided that only nine Anglos should go. Billy said, "None of you Mexican boys will go!"
> Jose Chaves y Chaves then said,"Why don't you want the Mexicans? You know the other Americans aren't any braver than I am."
> Billy then said, "Don't be annoyed, Jose, it's for this reason, Brady is married to a Mexican woman, and you are always sympathetic to your own kind."

Garbled though the Trujillo account is, this could still be read to indicate that the decision to kill Brady had already been taken; whether it was taken at the bidding of McSween, however, is another matter entirely. To begin with, it is inconceivable that Dick Brewer would have agreed to become Alexander McSween's paid assassin. It would seem far likelier that Brewer's decision to return to his ranch on the Ruidoso, rather than go to Lincoln with the Regulators, was a crucial factor in what ensued. Without the commanding presence of Brewer to restrain them, Frank MacNab, Fred Waite, Henry Brown, Jim French, John Middleton, and Billy the Kid may well have decided to take matters into their own hands.

The *New Mexican,* when it finally pronounced on the murder, offered yet another proposition.[22]

We quote from an article in the "Independent" of March 16th under the heading of Criminal Justice.

"It is a misfortune for a county to lose confidence in the courts.

Men are disposed to take the law into their own hands when they are forced to feel that the courts cannot be depended on to mete out even-handed justice to its violators. This is an evil but one degree less than the failure of the courts to administer the criminal law and is to be deprecated under any circumstances but the most urgent and extreme.

It is a terrible alternative, and all that can be said in its behalf is that mob law is better than no law.

But when the public has reason to lose confidence in its courts and jurors and to realize that life and property are not guarded as thoroughly as they should be, the disposition to execute justice without the leave or authority of law is natural and inevitable, however to be deplored."

We are informed by parties who are every way responsible for their statements that when the "Independent" citing the above arrived in Lincoln county it was seized upon and used by two prominent influential men there who have taken an active and important part in the late troubles, to incite the ———— and "Regulators" to murder Sheriff Brady and George Hindman in cold blood.

First the persuasive talents of one influential individual was used upon McNab and the "Regulators" for an hour or so; then the cunning appliances and efforts of a wealthy individual were "put where they would do the most good" with McNab and the "Regulators" and each of them used this article in the "Independent" to clinch the villainous scheme. The result is known to everybody.

The Regulators rode on up to Lincoln and spent Sunday night with Robert Widenmann and Sam Corbet behind the stout walls of the Tunstall store. The sequence of events here is important, especially when examining the statement of Francisco Trujillo. The McSween party, en route from Chisum's ranch, was due to arrive on the same Sunday evening. Heavy rains in the valley delayed them, and they were obliged to spend the night at San Patricio, ten miles below Lincoln.

In spite of Captain Smith's promises, the military escort that was to have ridden into Lincoln with the party to ensure its safety pushed on to the fort without them. Since he had come up with them, Sheriff Brady knew that when McSween reached Lincoln next day, there would be no soldiers around to protect him; it is equally certain the Regulators were also aware of this. The scene was set for tragedy.

In the matter of Brady's murder there are three completely different propositions to examine. The first is that—at McSween's explicit command—the Regulators staged a disturbance to draw Brady and his deputies into a planned, cold-blooded ambush. The second is that the Regulators, knowing McSween was coming in from the fort without the escort promised by Captain Smith, saw Brady and his deputies heading towards where McSween must come, assumed the sheriff was on his way to arrest and/or kill the lawyer, and did the only thing they could to stop him. The third is that the "hothead" faction of the Regulators had taken over, and the murder of Brady was an act of pure opportunism.

Juan Peppin's testimony supports the first proposition: a "disturbance" staged to lure Brady onto the street where he could be gunned down. But how could the Regulators have been sure that Brady would not just send one or more of his deputies? The proposition is further weakened by Doctor Ealy's eyewitness testimony that Brady stopped to laugh and joke with Ham Mills's wife Maria—unlikely, surely, if he was on his way to quell a disturbance? Most important, Henry Brown was not at the east end of town making a disturbance. He was in the Tunstall corral with the execution squad.

Testimony supporting the second proposition, that Brady was killed on his way to arrest/kill McSween, appears in letters Montague R. Leverson wrote the following day to Carl Schurz and President Hayes.

> I have *not yet been able to get a trustworthy account* of the affray; what I have been informed but still not from any of the men active in the tragedy is this: that in violation of the pledges made by himself and Captain Smith, who failed in leaving any escort (a corporal's guard would have sufficed) for McSween at Lincoln, Brady had started out with Heineman [sic] his deputy Peppin, and 2 other men, to go down the creek and arrest McSween (really there can be no doubt, to murder him) and who he knew in reliance on Captain Smith's plighted word, was on his road to the fort but had to pass through Lincoln to reach it. Brady and his party were met by citizens, some of them, I am assured on excellent authority, being among the best citizens in the county; how the firing commenced I have been unable as yet to learn.[23]

Leverson's *faux naif* description of Billy the Kid, Jim French, Charlie Bowdre, Frank MacNab, Henry Brown, and John Middleton as "being among the best citizens in the county" does not inspire confidence in his account, and his conclusion that Brady and his deputies were en route to kill McSween begs the question of how they hoped to do this with impunity before witnesses like Mrs. McSween, Chisum, Calvin Simpson, Albert Howe, and Leverson himself.

The "hothead" theory is tempting: "It was not McSween's wishes it was those fool boys, but they were driven into it by the persecutions thrust upon them by the other party," said Susan McSween, many years later.[24] How much weight her colored recollections lend to the proposition that the decision to kill Brady was taken on impulse, and that her husband knew nothing about it, is debatable; it remains a possibility.

In examining exactly what happened on the day of the assassination it becomes apparent that even the physical evidence is confused (see map 2). Juan Peppin indicates that Brady and his deputies were going east on the street of Lincoln, that is, towards Roswell. Leverson says that McSween was coming into town on his way to the fort; that being so, Brady would have had to go to the east end of town to meet him. But if, as has been most recently suggested, Brady met his deputies at the courthouse and then walked east down the street, the party would not have had to pass the Tunstall building, and no ambush would have been possible.

Brady's biographer states categorically that they were going in the opposite direction: "[they] left the courthouse and headed west for the Tunstall store."[25] This would only make sense if McSween's party had—as some versions state—made a detour via Fort Stanton. To add further to the confusion over what happened next, at least one writer contends the sheriff and his men were on horseback, not on foot.

It is possible that the confusion has arisen out of the use of the word *courthouse*.

In 1878, the courthouse was the building opposite the *torreón* now known as the "convento." In 1881, however, the county purchased the Murphy-Dolan store and it became the courthouse (fig. 54). Over the intervening years, this building became known as "the old Court House"; in fact, it still is. Could it be that the witnesses who have said Brady met his deputies at the courthouse were actually referring to the Murphy-Dolan store (i.e., "the Court House")? If so, then everything would make sense.

The Lincoln tradition has it that Brady had slept that Sunday night at the Murphy store or the courthouse ("the Court House"?). Only lately has it been suggested that in fact Brady rode into Lincoln from his farm that morning, the warrant for McSween's arrest and the writ authorizing attachment of the lawyer's property in his pocket.[26]

If Brady rode into town—his farm was a few miles east of Lincoln—the Regulators certainly saw him go by. The sheriff is known to have eaten breakfast at the Wortley. What more natural place to meet his men than across the street in the Murphy-Dolan store, which he always used as his headquarters? Juan Peppin confirms that his father had gone there.

It is quite certain that the sheriff had made no secret of his intention to arrest McSween, and that the Regulators knew this. Since McSween had not arrived the night before as planned, they knew he must appear that morning. To establish with any certainty the direction Brady and his men took, it becomes necessary to know for sure whether McSween entered town from the east or the west. Although some authorities state he had gone to Fort Stanton first, the eyewitness testimony of Montague Leverson, who came up from Chisum's ranch with McSween, indicates otherwise.

Therefore Brady had to walk—or ride—from one end of town to the other to arrest the lawyer at the Ellis house. This places Brady at the Murphy store; had he been at the 1878 courthouse, he could not have walked past the Tunstall store because the courthouse was east of it. Further support for this proposition comes from the fact that he was shot in the left side.

Just as it seems clear the Regulators knew Brady's intentions, it would appear some word of theirs had also leaked out. There is a tradition in the Brady family that on the morning of the shooting, Francisco Anaya sent his twelve-year-old son Timoteo to warn the sheriff that an ambush was being planned near the Tunstall store.[27] Brady seems not to have taken the warning seriously.

Now, did he ride—or walk—down to the Ellis store to quell a "disturbance" set up by Henry Brown? Apparently not. To begin with, Brown was not there, but with the other Regulators at the Tunstall store. And would Brady have needed four deputies to arrest one man?

Was he then on his way back from the courthouse, after posting notice that due to an error, the commencement of the April term of court had been announced for this, instead of the following, Monday? This would at least account for the statement that he was walking west when he was killed. But again, the answer is no, for this tradition has also been discredited. There was no misunderstanding about the date court would open.

"When you have eliminated the impossible," as Holmes said to Doctor Watson, "whatever remains, *however improbable,* must be the truth." Which leaves us with the inescapable conclusion that Brady was on his way to arrest McSween as the lawyer rode unprotected into Brady's eminent domain. There was absolutely no

FIG. 54. The Murphy-Dolan store at the time it was serving as courthouse. This may be the earliest photograph of the building so far located; note the hitching rail and the original covered porch. Using the growth of the tree for guidance, it may be judged to have been taken on some special occasion (there is a family group on the balcony), possibly ca. 1881–82, at the time Dowlin & DeLany sold the building to the county.

need for Brady to try to kill him on the street. Once in Brady's power, McSween's life would not be worth a plugged nickel.

In the ultimate analysis, the question of where the sheriff met his men and which direction they walked, or rode, is irrelevant. They were out in the open, an easy target. The ambushers made ready in the corral behind the Tunstall store. The sheriff and his four deputies—Billy Mathews, George Hindman, George Peppin, and Jack Long—were not bunched together in a tight group, but scattered across the street. As they drew level with the Tunstall store, rifle fire shattered the morning stillness. Hit in the head, back, and left side, Brady was killed instantaneously. Hindman, felled by a single shot, lurched a few steps and then collapsed. Jack Long was also hit, but skittered to safety near the *torreón*, while Peppin and Mathews ran for the shelter of Lola Sisneros's house. Old John Wilson, hoeing his onion patch some distance up the hill, was struck by a stray bullet that passed through the upper portion of both his thighs.

The assassination squad consisted of Frank MacNab, Jim French, Fred Waite, John Middleton, Henry Brown, and Billy the Kid.[28] Chavez y Chavez claimed in later years to have been there, too; indeed, he said it was he who killed Brady. Robert Widenmann was also in the corral, but whether he participated in the shooting was never ascertained: he claimed he was feeding Tunstall's dog. Hardly had the gunsmoke wafted away, Doctor Ealy wrote, than

> [o]ne of the men in the corral ran out to pick up Hindman or Brady's gun and as he stooped was shot, likely by Mathews. The report was that he shot him through the bowels but it was a mistake. I dressed his wound. He came walking into our back door, The ball passed through his left thigh. I drew a silk handkerchief through the wound, bound it up, and he was taken charge of by Sam Corbet.[29]

Two men ran out: Billy the Kid and Jim French. It has been suggested that the Kid's motive was to steal Brady's Winchester. Bearing in mind the Kid's highly developed sense of self-preservation, this seems unlikely: and anyway, the rifle Brady was carrying was the Kid's own weapon, confiscated by the sheriff at the time of Billy's February arrest. Another proposition is that Widenmann, "the dog feeder," urged someone to get the warrant for McSween's arrest out of the sheriff's pocket. If this was so, the Kid's effort was unsuccessful: Peppin served the warrant on McSween the same afternoon.

From the shelter of the Sisneros house across the street, Billy Mathews took a shot at the Kid that clipped him just above the hip and went through French's thigh. Thus wounded, "Big Jim" was unable to ride. Sam Corbet came up with a plan to hide him; the other five got on their horses and erupted out of the corral behind the store, heading for San Patricio. As they thundered out of town, men ran into the street firing after them.[30] At the edge of town, John Middleton dismounted, knelt and took aim, and fired back at the crowd, which scattered. Then the Regulators disappeared from sight.

CHAPTER 21

WAR: THE FIGHT AT BLAZER'S MILL

THE two blood-spattered bodies lay in the muddy street for several hours. The entire town was in an uproar. A galloper was dispatched to Fort Stanton to summon the military. According to Taylor Ealy, "the Murphy, Dolan and Riley men were soon hunting for the wounded man. They searched the house, for they said they tracked him by the blood. I learned that Sam Corbet had sawed a hole through the floor under a bed [in the Tunstall store] and as there was not any cellar under the house laid him on a blanket on his back with 2 revolvers in his hands."[1]

It is not hard to picture Jim French flat on his back in the darkness, two pistols clutched in sweating hands, listening for the angry voices of the Dolan men, tense and ready to cut loose if his hiding place was discovered. His luck—or theirs—prevailed: although they searched the McSween house three times, they did not find French.

A little while later, about eleven o'clock, the two wagons carrying McSween and his friends arrived in town. Only now did the party—which apart from the McSweens and John Chisum included Montague Leverson, Las Vegas salesman Calvin Simpson, and Albert Howe, a merchant from South Fork—learn what had happened that morning. It has been said they rode by the sprawled bodies without so much as looking at them.[2] This cannot have been so: they stopped at the Ellis house—the McSween home was occupied by Doctor Ealy and his family—well below the spot where the bodies lay.

Almost immediately after their arrival, Montague R. Leverson excitedly composed another letter to President Hayes, advising him that

> two more of Mr. Tunstall's murderers had been killed, viz., the sheriff who employed the ruffians in his posse & a noted cattle thief who was also one of the sheriff's deputies on the occasion of Mr. Tunstall's murder.
>
> More bloodshed will follow unless the Governor be at once removed. He is the main-stay of the thieves and murderers. . . . I again urge on your Excellency the fact that the native element had nothing to do with these troubles and it is of no use looking on it as a Mexican anarchy. This county alone ought to have a population today of 30 to 40,000 persons & would have it but for the thieves being supported by the Government.[3]

He now proceeded to relate information Chisum must have given him. Only last year, Leverson said, referring to the Pecos War, Chisum had been *refused all aid* by the Sheriff, by the military and by the governor to protect him from the bandits who in bands of twenty and thirty were stealing the cattle of his employers (Mr. R. W. [*sic*] Hunter of St. Louis). I am informed that Mr. Elkins the ex-Delegate offered to pay him $5000.00 if he (Mr. Hunter) would give up a contract to him for supplying beef which had been awarded to him (Hunter) and *would guarantee* him that none of his (Hunter's) cattle *should be stolen* to supply that contract.

Mr. Hunter had only tendered in self-defence, because the year previously, *his* cattle had been stolen and the Indian agent (Godfroy) had knowingly received such stolen cattle from the contractors.

Leverson can hardly have laid down his pen when a troop of twenty-five cavalrymen led by Captain Purington thundered and jingled into town in response to Deputy Sheriff Peppin's frantic summons. Still shaken by his own close call with death, Peppin now assumed the role of sheriff and stormed about making arrests. Going first to the McSween house, he arrested David P. Shield and McSween's two black servants, George Washington and George Robinson. That done, he and his soldier escort went to the Tunstall store and arrested Robert Widenmann before proceeding down the street to the Ellis house to get McSween.

Isaac Ellis met him at the door, and Peppin informed him that he had come to arrest the lawyer. McSween refused to recognize Peppin's authority, in which he was entirely correct: Peppin's office had dissolved upon the death of the sheriff. Lieutenant Smith, who with two troopers had accompanied Peppin to the Ellis house, asked whether McSween would surrender to him. McSween agreed, but at this juncture Captain Purington arrived and refused to take the lawyer into protective custody unless Peppin approved. Peppin agreed to this, and then announced his intention of searching the McSween house for Brady's killers, requesting the assistance of Purington's troopers. Montague Leverson takes up the story.

> On reaching Lincoln I went to the house of Mr. John B. Patron, chairman of the Co. Commissioners as whose guest I came down (as by the way did poor Mr. Tunstall when he first came 2 years ago) and presently I went up the street for my mail.
>
> On my way I saw a company of Cavalry under the command of Brevet Col. Purington (and Capt. Smith) and was informed by Mr. Shield that he and Mr. Weideman deputy U.S. Marshall and two colored boys had been arrested by *Colonel Purington* without warrant, color or authority of any kind, none of them having anything to do with the affray, that his (Mr. Shield's) house had been invaded and *searched by soldiers* and by Peppin, still claiming to be deputy sheriff and then (as you will see presently, later in *my hearing*,) supported in such claim by Col. Purington and Captain Smith. . . .
>
> I then went to the house of the administrator of Mr. Tunstall's estate and on my road saw *soldiers* forcing open and coming out of the corral gates and soldiers getting over the corral walls of Mr. Tunstall's house.[4]

Leverson urged Isaac Ellis to deny either Peppin or the soldiers admission to the Tunstall store until they had a warrant, and to shoot them down if they attempted to force entrance(!). He also warned the troopers that the conduct of their officers was illegal and criminal, and that they, too, would be liable to criminal proceedings if they followed illegal orders.

> Mr. John Chisum returned in about half an hour and informed us that after a heap of difficulty Col. Purrington had at last consented to take MacSween and the other

prisoners to the fort. I went up to say goodbye to Mr. MacSween, and it will perhaps help you to an understanding of matters here, for me to state, that when I went for my mail *in the forenoon,* one of the ruffians, armed to the teeth (I being wholly unarmed) brushed up against me saying "Damned son of a bitch," although up to that time *unless the sanctity of the mails had been violated* nothing had transpired on my part to show the judgement I had formed.[5]

It has already been shown that Leverson's mail was being read and commented upon: even a short note he penned to Carl Schurz in the wake of Peppin's arrests and searches carried a comment added in a different hand.[6]

As McSween prepared to leave with the soldiers, he asked Leverson to see Juan Patrón about getting some men to protect his house.[7] At this point, after a whispered aside to Purington, Peppin announced he was going to take three men into the McSween house. McSween forbade his doing so. Peppin hesitated, then laughed.

"Colonel Purington has ordered me to search for arms," he said. Leverson turned to the officer.

"Have you or these men a search warrant?" he asked.

"No," Purington said. "Peppin asked me if he could search, and I told him he could do as he pleased."

"But he purports to do it under your authority!" McSween protested. Purington ignored his remark, whereupon Leverson reminded him that the Constitution of the United States provided that no citizen's house could be searched without a warrant. Purington had had his bellyful of the loquacious Mr. Leverson.

"Damn the Constitution," he barked, "and you for an ass!"

Shocked at hearing an officer of the U.S. Army damn the Constitution, Leverson began to harangue Purington's men. Purington told the Englishman to shut up because he was making a damned fool of himself.

"God knows," Leverson said angrily, "I would not live in a country where outrages such as those I have witnessed this afternoon are countenanced."

"Sir," Purington growled, "you have my permission to suit yourself!" He turned to Peppin. "Here, Peppin, take your prisoners."

"That's what I want to do," Peppin said. "I'm ready to take them."

Both McSween and his wife protested vociferously that to be given up to Peppin was to be given up to be murdered. Leverson turned to Lieutenant Smith and reminded him of the promises of protection he had given Mrs. McSween.

"Shut up!" Smith snapped. "I had enough of your damned talk down on the Pecos."

At this juncture, Leverson withdrew, fearing that his further intervention might endanger McSween's life. McSween and his wife climbed into the wagon with the other prisoners, and the cavalcade moved off up the street towards Fort Stanton. When they got there, Purington did nothing to assist them. McSween managed to arrange two rooms at the post trader's, one for his wife and himself, the other for Shield and Widenmann. Robinson and Washington had no option but the guardhouse.

There is an abiding legend to the effect that on that same afternoon, his flesh wound healed enough to ride, the Kid emerged from hiding and made his dramatic exit from Lincoln. Bullets whistling around him, he galloped out of town towards San Patricio. When he got out of bullet range, he turned, dismounted, doffed his hat, and made a mocking bow in the direction of the town. It's a good story. It may even be true.

That night, under the pen name of "Stanton," McSween wrote a long, detailed account of the day's events and those following on Governor Axtell's visit and proclamation, which he sent to the *Cimarron News & Press.* Back in Lincoln, Montague Leverson wrote his longest letter yet to President Hayes.[8] His was the outrage of a cultured man—had he not entertained, in his London home, such luminaries as Mazzini, Garibaldi, Kinkel, Victor Hugo?—whose nose has been rubbed in the dirt. Reminding the president (as he had earlier reminded Marshal John Sherman) of the service he had done the nation in 1868 when he exposed the naturalization frauds in New York, Leverson set out the events that had occurred since he had gone down to the Pecos.

He exhorted Hayes to protect the "unhappy citizens of this county" from "the thieves and assassins whom the officials of the United States encourage in their crimes," and also demanded "a court martial upon Col. Purrington and Captain Smith."

If any letter could be said to have started the wheels of Washington bureaucracy turning, this—notwithstanding the sardonic postscripts added by the same anonymous writer at the Murphy-Dolan store—may well have been the one. It arrived in the capital at the precise moment when the administration was being made painfully aware that it could no longer avoid conducting an investigation of affairs in Lincoln County.

That same first day of April, Carl Schurz forwarded a copy of Leverson's March 16 letter to U.S. Attorney General Charles Devens, pointedly remarking that some of the charges in it were "against certain officers of your Department."[9] On April 2, in Ottawa, Henry Beeton brought the murder of Tunstall to the attention of the secretary of state for Canada; that worthy promised that Earl Dufferin would intercede with the U.S government.

On the 4th, Brook Herford wrote from Chicago to General Philip Sheridan, commanding the Military Division of Missouri, requesting the suspension of action by the military in Lincoln County. On the 5th, Doctor Ealy wrote to his uncle, Congressman Rush Clark (an Iowa lawyer who was active in the Republican party and had entered Congress March 4, 1877), recording the deaths of Brady and Hindman, and describing the subsequent activities of Peppin and Purington.

By April 6, Henry Beeton was in Washington, conferring with Sir Edward Thornton, who in turn was "doing all he could to get the U.S. government to move."[10] Next day, Beeton talked at length with Stephen Elkins. This was a bizarre experience for Elkins; his reactions give some indication of just what a smooth operator he must have been. Writing to J. P. Tunstall, Beeton reported that Elkins

> had heard a great deal about our unhappy business and listened to all I had to say and promised to do all in his power to have justice done. He, like everyone else, feels that a brave and honorable young man, the best and most innocent down there, has been sacrificed and that for the sake of his friends, and on every other account, the whole affair must be thoroughly investigated and full justice meted out.
>
> You will see by William Herford's letter that the man who killed John has himself been killed and two others of the gang. Mr. Elkins believes Widerman acted the

coward and ran off leaving John alone. He thinks his statements are to be received with caution. Mr. Elkins is expecting to hear from the Governor of the Territory about Dolan, as to his participation in the affair. . . .

Tomorrow morning I shall see the President, Mr. Hayes, and his War Minister [George W. McCrary] and lay our case before them. I shall give the British Minister another call. . . . I was glad to hear Col. Elkins speak so highly of the Judge, Warren Bristol, who will try the case, and he also thinks well of the Governor Axtel. By the advice of Sir Edward Thornton I have telegraphed Herford to stimulate Secretary [of State William M.] Evarts who is now in Chicago.

On April 8, Beeton presented his case to President Rutherford B. Hayes.[11] On the 9th, from Cimarron, Frank Springer, one of the foremost attorneys in northern New Mexico, and a sturdy opponent of the Santa Fe Ring, especially in the troubles of Colfax County and the Maxwell Land Grant, also addressed himself to Congressman Clark. Clark forwarded Springer's letter to the attorney general. Slowly, slowly, the mills of God began to grind.

On April 2, Col. Nathan Augustus Monroe Dudley, Ninth Cavalry, arrived at Fort Stanton. Although he did not officially assume command until Friday, April 5, one of his first acts was to concur in granting permission to the prisoners already at the fort to remain in protective custody until the April term of court began the following Monday.[12] That same day the Regulators (the Kid had rejoined them at San Patricio) received word that some of Tunstall's cattle had been driven off toward Shedd's ranch in the San Agustin Pass, that notorious rendezvous for stolen cattle and the people who bought them.

That, at any rate, was one story the Regulators put out. There are others: George Coe, who was a member of the band, claimed they had heard George Davis, one of the Boys, was heading for a rendezvous at Rinconada, and they decided to "blot him off the map." His cousin Frank gave several different versions; in later years he claimed that "Brewer had heard that several men we were looking for were in Rinconada in the Mescalero Reservation," although he failed to mention his own statements to the Doña Ana County District Court in 1881 that he actually went to the agency alone and met the Regulators there. Still another story is that the Regulators were hunting for Andrew L. "Buckshot" Roberts and George Kitt, who had been members of the posse that killed Tunstall.[13]

Whatever their motives, they set off up the Ruidoso. Surprisingly—he had quit the group for awhile to do some much needed work on his farm—Dick Brewer agreed to be their leader, thus tacitly giving his approval to the murder of Brady. The party consisted of Brewer, John Middleton, Charlie Bowdre, Frank MacNab, Henry Brown, Fred Waite, Jim French, Doc Scurlock, Frank and George Coe, Steve Stephens, John Scroggins, Ignacio Gonzales, and Billy Bonney, "the Kid." They camped overnight on the Rinconada, where the Apaches saw them butchering a steer. Next morning they rode down to Blazer's Mill.

Dr. Joseph Hoy Blazer was a former dentist who had drifted into Lincoln County from Texas in 1867, and traded a freighting outfit for the sawmill two miles west of Mescalero, which became known thereafter by his name. The mill had been on this spot for many years before Blazer's arrival; timber from it had been used to construct or repair buildings as far apart as Fort Davis, Tex., and Fort Selden, N.M.

Soon after he bought the mill, Blazer built a two-story house on the site big enough to shelter everyone in the community in the event of Indian trouble. The place was a veritable fortress.[14] The adobe walls of the lower story were twenty-seven inches thick; those above about half that, with portholes under the eaves. The wooden cupola on the top, which commanded the entire area, had an interlining of adobe bricks also pierced for portholes.

When the Mescalero Indian Reservation was established by executive order on May 29, 1873, the government leased Doctor Blazer's house for use as an office and living quarters for the Indian agent and his family. Blazer retained the northwest corner room as his own office. Built onto the north side of the house was a large, one-story room that served as Blazer's store. The door to this, like Blazer's office, opened on the west side of the building, where an uncovered porch ran the length of the building.

The front of the building faced the road and opened to the south. Along the south side of the road, the creek ran for about half a mile before reaching the floodgate above the mill. Immediately south of the creek and in line with the house was a horse corral, reached from the house by a footbridge. The sawmill itself was about two hundred yards to the south and west and fifty feet lower than the rise on which the house stood. Directly to the west of the big house was a huddle of other buildings which included the Blazer home, a blacksmith shop, and a barn.

Indian Agent Frederick C. Godfroy, his wife, their two daughters Kate and Louisa, and a hired man who did the cooking lived at the house. Soon after her husband was appointed in 1876, Mrs. Godfroy began to take in lodgers and serve meals to travelers. At the time of these events, her daughter Kate was engaged to be married to Maj. Daniel M. Appel.

Shortly before noon, the Regulators arrived.[15] They stopped at the big house to order food, then took their horses to the plank corral on the other side of the creek. Leaving the animals to be taken care of by Doctor Blazer's son Almer and two other teenage boys, they trooped back to the house to eat. If they were really looking for Andrew L. Roberts, they were being exceedingly lackadaisical about it. Roberts, on his way to the mill, had seen them coming down from Rinconada and detoured via an old Indian trail in the high timber to the south.

Roberts was in something of a dilemma. Obviously he did not want to run into a gang of fifteen Regulators. At the same time he was anxious to go down to the post office at the mill to see whether the mail carrier had brought a letter containing the check covering the sale of his farm on the Ruidoso. He rode to the edge of the mesa. Below him lay the scattering of buildings: blacksmith shop off to the left, the long low sawmill down below, Doctor Blazer's house on the far side of the Stanton road, the big house off to the right on its commanding bluff. He could not now see the Regulators, who were in the house eating, nor their horses, which were in the plank corral. Leaving his packhorse up on the hillside, Roberts rode on in.

For what happened next, we must rely upon the testimony of Frank and George Coe, the only participants who set down their recollections of what happened (figs. 55, 56). Blazer's foreman, David M. Easton, later described in some detail what happened that morning; his testimony by and large coincides with that of the cousins Coe, although his opinion of some of the Regulators does not.

The fullest version of Frank Coe's account is the one he gave to Walter Noble Burns. He claimed Middleton was left outside to guard the horses, a statement

FIG. 55. Benjamin Franklin Coe and his wife, Helena Anne Tully Coe. A wedding portrait by John Hodges, Durango, Colo., February 7, 1881.

that may be attributed to forgetfulness, since the horses were in the corral and Middleton ate with the rest. George Coe, another fellow with a selective memory, had it that he and Middleton were keeping guard while the others were eating; it was at this juncture that Roberts rode in. Then George Coe and Middleton went in to eat while the Regulators stood to one side, awaiting the outcome of Roberts's talk with Frank Coe. There is support for some of this in Easton's testimony; he said he was talking to the Kid outside the house while Roberts and Coe had their talk.

In his version of events, Frank Coe was first to finish eating; he went outside and saw Roberts coming up from the corral, where he had tethered his mule. In accordance with Doctor Blazer's well-known requirement that guests leave their weapons outside when they came into the house, Roberts had hitched his gunbelt over his saddlehorn but was carrying his rifle. Frank Coe called hello: he and Roberts—apparently an alias, because Coe knew him as Bill Williams—were on neighborly terms. They shook hands, then went around the house and sat on the porch. Frank Coe told the little man that the Regulators had a warrant for his arrest.

"The hell you have," said Roberts.

"Yes, and I'm glad you rode up because now we won't have the trouble of hunting for you. You better come in the house and see Brewer and surrender."

"Me surrender?" said Roberts.

"Why, of course. There ain't any way out of it now."

"Well, we'll see about that."

"There are thirteen in the gang, Bill," Frank Coe said, "and if you don't surrender peaceable, it means simply they'll kill you. You wouldn't have a chance on earth."

"As long as I've got a load in old Betsy here," replied Roberts, patting the butt of his Winchester, "there ain't nobody going to arrest me, least of all this gang."

"Now, don't be foolish, Bill," Coe argued. "There ain't no sense in resisting and getting yourself killed."

"I'd be killed if I surrendered."

"What makes you think that?"

"Didn't I try to kill Billy the Kid and Charlie Bowdre last week? If those two fellows got their hands on me now, they'd kill me sure."

"No, they wouldn't. You surrender and nobody will hurt you."

"Yes," said Roberts, "that's what they told Morton and Baker. I know this gang."

FIG. 56. George Washington Coe and his wife, Phoebe. Date and photographer unknown.

Roberts was employed herding cattle for Dolan; there is no direct record of any fracas involving him with Bowdre and the Kid. However, if he had indeed tried to kill them, the time frame suggests he must have been one of the posse that collided with the McSween party at San Patricio. His remarks add extra piquancy to the fact that it was Bowdre whom he first shot at, and that it was Bowdre who fatally wounded him.

Frank Coe sat with Roberts for nearly half an hour trying to persuade him to surrender, but Roberts wasn't having any truck with the Regulators. Oddly enough, he made no move to leave. George Coe takes up the story at this point:

Dick Brewer's mind was fully made up to take Roberts regardless of consequences. He counseled with us by saying: "Boys, he's a bad *hombre*, well-armed, and I ain't going to ask anyone to go and get him, but who will volunteer? Anybody?"

"You bet, I'll go for one," Charlie Bowdre said. "I'll be another to go, Dick," said I.

And then Billy the Kid stepped forward and said: "I'd hate to miss this little frolic, so I guess I'll go, too."

"Good!" said Brewer. "If he kills that little bunch, the rest of us will take a hand."

We three buckled up, cocked our guns, and started around the house, Bowdre taking the lead. . . . Roberts had his cocked rifle lying in his lap as he and Frank talked, and as Charlie Bowdre turned the corner of the house, he dropped his gun on Roberts and commanded him to throw up his hands.

"Not much, Mary Ann," answered Roberts.

Bowdre had the drop on Roberts, as the latter had to raise his gun from his lap. With his refusal to throw up his hands, they fired simultaneously. Bowdre's bullet entered Roberts right through the middle, while Roberts's ball glanced off Bowdre's cartridge belt, and with my usual luck, I arrived just in time to stop the bullet with my right hand. It knocked the gun out of my hand, took off my trigger finger and shattered my hand. . . . I was stunned, not knowing just what to do. Instead of offering my back as a target for his bullets, I ran forward right in front of Roberts. He shot once at John Middleton, and the bullet entered his breast. He fired three more times at me, but missed.

Dick Brewer was enraged and swore vengeance at Roberts declaring: "I'll get him now at any cost."

It was not to be quite that easy. Mortally wounded, Roberts had dragged himself along the porch on the west side of the building and fallen into Doctor Blazer's office on the northwest corner. His carbine was empty, and his pistol and cartridge belt were still hanging on his saddlehorn. He looked around: on a peg on the wall hung Doctor Blazer's silver-mounted .45-60 Springfield hunting rifle. There was a box of shells nearby. Grunting in agony from his wounds, Roberts dragged the mattress off the cot in the corner and threw it down before the partly open door.

Outside, the Regulators were milling about in confusion: Middleton was down, coughing blood, George Coe nursing his shattered hand, Charlie Bowdre *hors de combat* from the punishing belly blow he had received when Roberts's bullet hit his belt buckle and severed his cartridge belt. Brewer hunted up David Easton and told him to go into the office and bring Roberts out. Easton refused, begging Brewer to take his men and leave. The enraged Brewer replied that he would have Roberts out if he had to pull the house down. Frank Coe's version is tellingly different:

Brewer was determined to have Roberts dead or alive. He called Doctor Blazer to bring Roberts out of the house. Doctor Blazer wouldn't do it. Brewer threatened, if he didn't, he would burn the house down. Still Doctor Blazer refused. This made Brewer mad clear through; he didn't want to give Roberts time to die but was bound to kill him at once, if possible, and have it over with. He crept down around the barn and outhouses and, keeping under cover, got into position behind a pile of saw logs near the mill and a hundred yards directly in front of the house.

Roberts was dying, but he was a long way from dead. According to his own version of events, he was feeling "very ill" when he heard a bullet thud into the wall behind him. He saw a puff of smoke among the logs down by the mill, which stood on a level about fifty feet lower than the house. He trained his sights on the spot and waited for the gunsmoke to clear. As it did he saw a gun appear over a big log. A man's head came in sight and he fired. He knew neither whom he had fired at, nor whether he had hit the man.

Frank Coe testified that Roberts's bullet struck Dick Brewer square in the middle of the forehead and tore off the top of his head; most other accounts state the bullet hit him in the eye. Either way, "Brewer simply slumped over dead where he lay at full length behind the logs and never made another move."

The demoralized Regulators got out of there, leaving their captain dead in the dust. Borrowing a government wagon from Godfroy to carry their wounded, they headed up the trail towards Fort Stanton. En route they met Assistant Surgeon Appel, on his way to answer Godfroy's urgent telegraphic summons for medical assistance. He did what he could for Middleton and Coe, then hurried on.

At the agency, Johnny Ryan, who worked at the Dolan branch store, warily approached the house, carrying a white cloth.[16] Roberts recognized Ryan, a gnomelike old fellow with a bald head and a long white beard, and allowed him in. Godfroy's family did what they could to make Roberts comfortable while they awaited the arrival of Doctor Appel.

The day had been very hot. Brewer's body had been lying out in the sun since shortly after noon, and it was decided to bury him immediately. The carpenter made a good coffin from finished lumber—the traditional shape, not just a rough box—and it was lined with white muslin and covered with black. Because no minister was available, Doctor Blazer's married daughter Ellie Hedges read the burial service and passages from the bible. Everyone in the little community attended.

By the time Assistant Surgeon Appel got to the mill it was night.[17] He examined Roberts's wound. The bullet had entered just above the left hipbone and ranged downward. Appel told him there was no hope. Roberts accepted the news philosophically. For several hours, according to Paul Blazer, he was able to talk.

Roberts's account of the fight was brief. One shot was fired at him as he reached the corner of the house. It missed. As he moved backward toward the recessed door of Doctor Blazer's office, Middleton came in sight and he fired. Middleton fell. Because of the smoke he could not identify the others who appeared. He kept firing and did not know whom he had hit. As he started to open the door behind him, the Kid poked the barrel of his gun at him and fired. Roberts pulled the trigger but his gun was empty. The Kid, he said, had seen his pistol and cartridge belt on the saddle, and let his *compadres* draw his fire until he counted the shots; then, knowing himself to be safe, he got into the fight.

Roberts lapsed into a coma during the night and died shortly after noon the next day. Both coffin and grave had been prepared; he was buried next to Brewer with a service identical to the one held the previous day. It is one of history's little ironies that no one any longer knows which grave is which.

CHAPTER 22

WAR: MCSWEEN ASCENDANT

ON the same day that Buckshot Roberts was fighting for his life at Blazer's Mill, Alexander McSween was busily at work, writing a long letter to John Tunstall's father in London. In it, he harked back to the day following Tunstall's funeral, when John Wilson had issued warrants for the arrest of John's murderers.

Eight of the men who participated in that fearful deed were known to be at the house of L. G. Murphy & Co., this place, with the Sheriff. Hither the constable with a *posse* of two citizens went to arrest the murderers. Instead of aiding the constable, as he should have done, the Sheriff took him and *posse* prisoners! Without any authority of law he kept them prisoners twenty four hours. He finally released them but refused to allow them to make any arrests.[1]

Recounting briefly (without naming any of them) the manner in which Morton, Baker, and McCloskey had died, McSween went on to more recent events.

Since that time three more of the murderers have gone "the way of all the earth"— the Sheriff referred to was killed yesterday. About 40 of the best citizens in this County have taken to the mountains and will not leave until John Tunstall's cruel and foul murder is avenged. Oh, I *trust* his soul *sees* the number of friends he had here. . . .

I have really thought that I would have followed John before this. His friends came to me about 12 o'clock one night and obliged me to absent myself from town for some time; I reluctantly done so. My wife as soon as she was informed of his death returned [from St. Louis]; she feels dreadfully about his untimely end—we considered him as one of our family.

He went on to say that the British minister in Washington had asked the U.S. secretary of state for an investigation, and that Montague R. Leverson, who had been in Lincoln for the past two weeks, had taken an interest and "published the brutal affair near and far." As for himself, "owing to the persistency of my wife I came to Fort Stanton, 9 miles west of Lincoln; she is afraid that I'll be killed [by] some *hired* assassin. It's currently reported that some murderer from a neighboring County is concealed at L. G. Murphy & Co's who is to receive $500[xx] for killing me."

Tunstall, he claimed, had owed him five thousand dollars at the time of the murder, "as shown by an account [book] in his own handwriting" (see appendix 3).

As I am subject to a heavy expense and expect that to continue for some time to come, I thought, perhaps, that you would be willing to pay me that sum without waiting for its payment from the Administrator, *provided* I could satisfy you that the amount is due . . . I hope to be able to pay the men who have left their ploughs and fields a fitting recompense in the shape of a liberal reward.

If you can without any inconvenience to yourself, remit me said sum as directed, I'll be greatly relieved; but if you cannot, I'll continue defraying the expense of the party who are pursuing his slayers as long as I can command a dollar—that is what he would have done for me if our positions were reversed . . . I always gave him any sum of money he might want if he were in need and I had it. He would have paid me soon had he lived.

Next day, word was received at the fort of the gunfight at Blazer's Mill, and McSween, using the pseudonym "Stanton," wrote an account "as I received it from an eyewitness," which he sent to the *Cimarron News & Press*.[2]

Labeling Roberts "one of the famous Jesse Evans gang," McSween added that since his service with the posse that murdered Tunstall, the dead man had been in the employ of Murphy, Dolan, and Riley. Middleton and Coe's wounds, he reported, were not considered serious; Bowdre was not even mentioned. All McSween's sympathies were for Dick Brewer, "one of Nature's noblemen."

Physically faultless; generous to a fault; a giant in friendship; possessing an irreproachable character and unsullied honor; kind, amiable and gentle in disposition, he has fallen early into the "three by six" promised him some eighteen months ago.

Outside the "House" no one knew Mr. Brewer but to respect him. He was a young man without vices of any kind. Had he been content to enslave himself he would, no doubt, be living now, but to a man of his kingly nature, existence would be intolerable under the conditions sought to be imposed. Murderers and horse thieves hated him; their friends hated him. But the people, Mexican and American, held him in the highest possible esteem. He had a fine ranch on the Rio Ruidoso, which he had been cultivating for the past four years. Peace be to your ashes, Dick! as you were familiarly called. Sweet and pleasant be your slumbers. Ever green and fresh be your memory. Some will malign you but that will not disturb you, for when mist has cleared away and the horizon of truth be clearly seen, even they will be shamed to silence. Death has deprived your father and mother of an obedient and loving son; your sister and brother of the prince of brothers; the county of Lincoln one of her best, most industrious, sober, upright and honest citizens. He died young—27 years of age. His father and family live in Wisconsin.

On the Saturday, McSween scribbled a couple of hasty notes. The first was to the new commanding officer at Fort Stanton.[3] "Owing to the troubled condition of affairs in the County of Lincoln, I hereby apply to you . . . for military protection until the meeting of the District Court in said County of Lincoln believing as I do that unless such military protection is granted me, I will lose my life."

The second note was addressed to Tunstall's father.[4]

Since writing my last in which I mentioned the killing of Brady and Hindman, two of your son's murderers, John's *best* friend has been killed by them, and [one] of the men he had caring for his cattle was wounded; another man was shot in the hand. The difficulty was started by one of John's murderers; he was mortally wounded. They only fan the blaze by killing Richard M. Brewer, a young man of 27 years of age and of unreproachable character. He was one of Nature's noblemen. John thought so much of him that I think he must have written of him. The dear souls! I knew them as nobody here knew them. . . . Brewer was universally esteemed as one of our best citizens. I have cared for [the] wounded men bountifully.

My wife feels fearfully bad for the untimely death of our two friends. She esteemed John highly on account of his natural goodness. Until she is able to write she asks me to convey to you her sympathy in this dreadful bereavement.

McSween had no time for more correspondence; he had but two days to prepare for the all-important April court term beginning on Monday, April 8. Even as he was writing these notes, Lawrence Murphy was warning Colonel Dudley that the real reason the Regulators were in the agency area was because they were planning to ambush Judge Bristol and District Attorney Rynerson on their way to Lincoln. "It is currently reported here," he wrote, "that a party of mounted outlaws are somewhere in the vicinity of Copeland's Ranch where they command the roads and it is believed to be with a view to capture or kill the Judge and members of the court while en route to Fort Stanton or this place. I am advised that the Judge and his party will leave Las Cruces today."[5]

Dudley took Murphy's warning seriously; he dispatched Lt. Millard F. Goodwin and ten cavalrymen to meet Bristol, Rynerson, and those traveling with them. Goodwin and his men rode all night and the following day met the Bristol party at Blazer's Mill, escorting them from there to the fort, where they arrived safely on the Sunday afternoon.

Taking no chances on the mood of the Regulators, Judge Bristol elected to stay at the fort and be escorted each day to Lincoln by a detachment of troops. On the appointed Monday, he opened court at Lincoln.

Finding that the county commissioners—mindful of Governor Axtell's proclamation—had not appointed a sheriff to replace the murdered Brady, Bristol empowered John Copeland to serve warrants. Two days later, on April 10, county commissioners Will Dowlin, Francisco Romero y Lueras, and Juan B. Patrón—apparently no longer hostile towards Copeland in the matter of the two Hispanics killed on his ranch some years earlier—nominated Copeland as sheriff. Judge Bristol promptly arranged for Copeland to have the assistance of a detachment of soldiers from the fort to help him serve warrants.

On Wednesday, April 12, Robert Widenmann was startled to receive a letter from John Tunstall's father dated March 21 that indicated clearly that his and McSween's letters containing the details of Tunstall's death had not then reached England. He dashed off a hasty note.

Your kind letter of the 21st ulto. just reaches me. I am astonished that you had not at that time received my letter giving you full particulars, but undoubtedly you have it by this time. Since then we have had a rough time here but I think with the aid of God right and truth will soon triumph. We are doing our utmost to bring the murderers of dear Harry to justice and we will do it if it takes our lives and all we have. The whole Country is aroused and with us and should the courts not do their duty the people will take the matter in their own hands.—The property is in good shape. I have done all in my power and will continue to do so, so that you will not lose a cent if I can help it. All your instructions will be carried out to the letter. I will write you a long letter by next mail, can't do it today as the mail leaves in a few moments.[6]

By Saturday, a grand jury had been selected, with Dr. J. H. Blazer as foreman.[7] Bristol charged the jury with a lengthy review of recent events: the murders of John H. Tunstall, of Sheriff Brady and George Hindman, and of Andrew L. Roberts. When he came to the charges of embezzlement against McSween, Bristol went out of his way to castigate the lawyer for his part in the insurance controversy. The jury retired to consider the evidence.

McSween's and Widenmann's letters containing the details of Tunstall's death had arrived in London on March 23. J. P. Tunstall replied to both of them three days later. His letters arrived in Lincoln the day before the grand jury was due to deliver its verdicts.

In their replies, the characters of the two men leap from the page: McSween's odd mixture of shrewdness and sentimentality, Widenmann's bombastic self-aggrandizement and clumsy unctuousness. Widenmann clearly wished the Tunstalls to believe him the leader of the forces avenging their son and McSween little more than a discarded former partner; McSween, who had disliked him from the beginning, resented Widenmann's stealing his thunder and suspected his motives where Tunstall's family—and more important, his estate—were concerned. Their antipathy is evident throughout the correspondence. Widenmann was first to reply, on April 16.

> Your kind letter of the 26th ulto. just reaches me. I am very thankful for it, for I had feared that my letter had been intercepted or lost. I have been so anxious to hear from you, and yet, always feared to open it when it should come. I so feared that our letters, though we tried to break the dreadful news to you as gently as possible, would be too great a shock for you, knowing from the letters dear Harry so often read to me, how dearly you all loved him. Dear Harrie's health had been rather poor after his return from St Louis, but while he and I were here alone, Mr. & Mrs. McSween were away, it improved greatly and I feel certain he would have entirely recovered within a year.
>
> As regards the business I will as soon as I get things in shape and can balance the books, give you a clear statement of its standing. The estate excepting the cattle, some of the horses and the land has been appraised, at I think something over $15,000—. I can not give the exact figures as the papers are not before me. On the other hand there are some ammounts due in St. Louis and to Mr. McSween, I forgot to state that the book accounts are not included in the appraisement. Everything is being well taken care of and I hope and will endeavour to show through my future actions, that the great trust you and dear Harry place in me is not misplaced.
>
> The land you speak of and which dear Harry intended to buy for $150 has been purchased, but the disturbances coming on at the same time made it impossible for us to perfect all the papers at the time. I hope though to acomplish this in a few days. I do not think it safe to give you the details until all the titles are perfected as I have good reasons to fear that the mails are tampered with.—
>
> Since my last letter many startling things have occurred here. Two of the murderers while trying to escape from Dick Brewer and the posse which had arrested them and after they had killed one of the posse were killed. Then one of the murderers was killed while robbing some emigrants while an other was wounded at the same time and afterwards captured and is now under arrest at Fort Stanton. Then on the 1st inst. the County Sheriff who was indirectly one of the murderers and an other of the murderers were killed, within 300 yards of where I am now sitting, by a party of infuriated citizens. An other died at the house of J. J. Dolan & Co. where during the excitement, an old wound he had received broke.[8]

Not for the first time, Widenmann presents history with an insoluble problem. Who was the Dolan supporter who died so dramatically on the day Brady was assassinated?[9] It would appear that this must remain among the many unsolved mysteries engendered by the Lincoln County War. So, it would seem, must another incident of that bloody April Fool's Day, in which, the *Independent* reported on April 13, a soldier had been "shot and killed by mistake while attempting to pass a sentry at Murphy's house."

Widenmann continued his letter with an account of the Blazer's Mill fight and the death of Roberts, who

was killed while resisting arrest, but his life was sold at a fearful price to all of us. After being wounded he shot and killed poor Dick Brewer, wounded trusty John Middleton severely, and several others slightly. Poor, honest, faithful Dick! He said he would get every one of the murderers or perish in the attempt and he has faithfully kept his word. Middleton is said to be getting well again and improving very rapidly. The whole County is in arms, now, and should the courts not do *their duty* there is no telling what they, the people will do. Every person feels that as long as the country is under the controll of such cutthroats life is not safe and if the courts do not right the matter the people will. I give you only the outlines since I can't trust more to paper. There is a powerful ring in New Mexico which has always had its own way in everything and all its members are at work against me because I dared to come out against them, as you will have seen by the papers I sent you. But I will fight them to the bitter end, they have had one whom I loved dearer than a brother murdered and I will break them up if such a thing is possible.

They have succeeded in placing me under arrest and are now trying their utmost to get me out of the way, but never fear; we are strugling for justice and right, the honest people throughout the country are with me and right will triumph in the end. Never fear for me. My dear father, from whom I received a letter today, says: "Pursue the course you have taken, no matter what the consequences, you are fighting for truth, justice, honesty and right, and with God's aid you will succeed. Do not give up an inch of the ground you have gained." With such encouragement by his and your letter I am bound to win the fight.—Since my last letter to you I have again been shot at, but dear Harrie's protecting spirit seems to guard me.—

It will be impossible to close up the business next fall specially the book accounts, since it is only then, that debts can be collected and I have thought that it might be best that I should get everything in running order and then start to see you [in London]. There is much information in regard to the land matters that you will need to give you a clear insight and enable you to decide as to the course to be pursued, which I dare not trust to the mails. During the summer months business here is always dull and I could then so arrange as to get in time and I believe that it would facilitate a thorough adjustment of everything. Of course I await your decision and will act upon your suggestion. I could return in time for the harvest and then be on hand to close everything out and to collect all the outstanding accounts. An other thing that induces me to think that this is the best course is that life is very insecure and I should like very much to see you and explain everything before it is too late. There is no telling what the "ring" may do. . . .

I have just seen Mr. Ellis and find that the power of attorney arrived safe. I have requested him to put it in his safe and keep it until the May meeting of the probate court when it will be acted on.

Mr. Beeton received my letter addressed to Victoria in Milwaukee and sent a power of attorney to Mr. Will Brook Herford son of Revd Brook Herford of Chicago, empowering him, Mr. W. Brook Herford to take charge of everything in his, Mr. Beeton's name. Mr. Herford is at a loss how to proceed since your power of attorney arrived but I think everything will be arranged without any trouble. I will write to Mrs. Behrens by next mail. Today's mail is now waiting for me.

McSween's reservations about the wisdom of giving their power of attorney to Robert Widenmann—and indeed, his feelings about Widenmann—are evident in the first of three letters he wrote to the Tunstalls the following day.

On account of the imperishable esteem in which we held your son and with which we'll cherish his memory, we permit Mr. Weidenman still to share the hospitalities of our home, knowing as we do the friendship your son cherished for him. W. informs me that you do not purpose removing the remains; of this am glad as this will enable us to sleep by him and Brewer when we shall have been "gathered to our fathers" With tears in my eyes I say to you, that I think I shall sleep that long sleep easier by their side! Since these troubles commenced, I often feel that I would [like] to share [that] sleep. Dear boys, are you not witnessing my struggles and triumphs? Do you not, while anchored in the tranquil harbor, feel interested in that little *barque* you left in the tumultuous seas! Or are you so wrapt up in felicities of your celestial home as to be unmindful of the ones on *this* side! Peace be to your ashes! Green be your memory. As long as we live, flowers will bloom on your graves, and at your heads we'll place marble stones with suitable inscriptions. When the grave shall unclasp its frigid arms, our corruptible bodies shall put on *in*corruption; then we'll see each other. I miss you, the best friends I have ever had outside my own family.

The world is a *furnace.* Happy we if we can come out like the refiner's gold or purer.

Our Dist. Court is in session and my time for writing is limited

Mr. Herford, son of the Rev. Mr. Herford, Rector of the Church of the Messiah, Chicago, Ills., is here to attend to the affairs of your son. He is a resident of Colfax Co., in this Territory, and is favorably known by some of our best citizens. He has a power of atty. from Mr. Beeton, your brother-in-law. Of course this power of atty. is of no value whatsoever as against yours. I will accept no responsibility, but I'll help anyone you empower to close up the estate to your advantage; this trust I have and will surely carry out. I have given you, in a former letter, my views of the propriety of letting Weideman wind up the estate; there are many reasons why I cannot approve it. But if you think it proper to so empower him, I'll only promise to *watch* your interests. Mr. Herford's family is well known in England, and he'll be over there in July—or in fall—and could give you particulars. No one here would act jointly with W. I would rather not say this much, but I must give you an honest opinion. Aside from his incompetency, I think it inadvisable to entrust a young man who has not one dollar with the management of your means. We know not from whence he comes nor whither he will go. I advise you to revoke the power of atty. sent by you & make to Mr. Herford as done by Mr. Beeton.

Will furnish estimate of land cost shortly. I'll have to examine some papers before giving figures. The title can be made absolutely safe. Notwithstanding the troubles, parties in St Louis have written regarding these lands, desiring to purchase them. The fact of the Territory becoming a state will in no way affect the title.

In one way I am glad that your son wrote nothing to you of me. Often he has told parties here that he would not attempt to describe me to you until he went home. Our home and my office were open to him at all times.

The murderers are energetically pursued. They [will] all be brought to account for the fearful crime. The men who were wounded are doing well. Thank God. Ever your friend.[10]

Next, McSween addressed himself to Tunstall's sister Minnie, who had also written to him and Widenmann.

Are the happy spirits cognizant of what transpires here? If so, your brother John will be gladdened by my telling you what I have so frequently heard him say. He would take a seat by the table and look over the family pictures so dear to him. He would say "There's dear old Minnie—she's the best girl that ever lived—God bless her"

He invariably read us the affectionate portions of the letters sent and rec'd by him. He read us the letters written by him to you and Mr. Behrens before you were married—with tears in his eyes. He frequently spoke of Mr. Behrens:—and loved him because the Governor, his mother, Jack & Punch liked him after he took Min.

Seven of his murderers are now dead; two are wounded. There will be no peace here untill his murderers shall have paid the debt—the whole country is in arms. But this news is marred by the fact your brother's best friend, R. M. Brewer, was killed; John Middleton, James French, W. Bony, Charles Bowdre and George Coe wounded. They are recovering rapidly. I have had all that human skill could do for them done. Some of them are farmers and you may imagine what actual state of things existed when they took up their guns. They knew, and so did the whole community, that your brother's murderers would never get their due in our courts. He always said that the man who killed Mc would die before the Throne in short time after committing the deed if he could see him; that he would devote his life and means to the avenging of my death: I would gladly do the same for him. To know that all who planned and executed the inhuman deed had each rec'd their due I would part with every dollar I have. Never, whilst I live shall I turn aside from the accomplishment of [this] mission. But it will only endear his memory more, to state to you that I am not alone in these feelings and designs. Even women, such as Mrs. Isaac Ellis and Mrs. McSween, and Mexican women want to hear of the murderers having paid the debt. John S. Chisum, a man worth a half million Dollars, is doing all he can in the same direction—he's been here over three weeks working for that purpose. He is a bosom friend of ours and John took him as such. He always calls himself, my wife and myself "the family". Your brother asked Chisum to include him in the term which was done. Chisum is an old single man, John was single, we had no children; I tell you that we were happy. Your brother thought a great deal of Chisum and Chisum did of him. I can say, that I have never known Mr. Chisum to think so much of a young stranger as he did of John H. Tunstall at the time of his death. The tears shed when the funeral services were performed at our house are a sure indication of the general esteem in which he was held and the abhorrence cherished for the horrible deed. I can only give you a few names of those who are willingly trying to avenge his death, such as John N. Copeland, Isaac Ellis & Sons, Geo. Barber, Sam. Corbett, Frank & Geo. Coe, A. Sanders, those wounded, McNab (a brother Scot) D. P. Shield, John Newcomb and a hundred others. On account of John you have friends with warm hearts, here whom you will never see in the flesh. In thought we can bridge the distance and hold sweet and sympathetic communion; so we commune with the dear departed.

I am glad that your brother never wrote anything of me. He frequently told my wife and others of his friends that he would not write of me, as he could not do me justice in a letter; he wanted to wait until he saw you all. I knew him thoroughly and he did me, and to know him was to become wedded to him in eternal friendship. It's not broken.

He was continually talking about all of you. He considered his life your property and himself only a steward.

We are glad that his ashes is to remain where we laid it. We'll guard and honor it. And tho' far from the scene of his youth, his grave and that of his trusty friend Brewer who died avenging his death shall annually bear fragrant flowers.

The man who, I wrote your father as having killed Brewer is dead. My wife sends her loving regards.[11]

Widenmann's letter to Minnie has a different tone: here he seems to be trying to elect himself to membership of the Tunstall family.

Your kind and welcom letter reached me yesterday and it is with very great comfort that I see that our letters conveying to you the dreadful news only reached you after you had at least been prepared to receive them. It is a great and real satisfaction for me to read the letters. I feel so fearfully lonely and deserted since dear Harrie's death. He and I were always together when business did not seperate us. Many and many a pleasant and quiet evening did we spend while we were alone here. After supper we would generally post up the books together, write the necessary business letters and then light our segars and enjoy a good comfortable talk and smoke. Often I would take up the guitar and play and sing some of the old German Wolkslieder and before finishing he would always request me to sing "The Mill" and would sing it through with me, every verse of it. How often did he say that you used to sing it to him and how much he enjoyed it. And how dearly and devotedly did he love you all. After he had received the photographs he would take them out of the box he kept them in and look at them, hand them over to me and say "Now old fellow I know you have good and dear parents and sisters, but look at that. You can't beat that!" and then he would praise one after the other. He almost worshiped you all. When the letter informing him of your engagement to Mr. Behrens arrived he looked like a disappointed lover, and for a time, did not seem to be able to grasp the idea. I often joked him about it. We had agreed that should I marry first he would come and live with me, and should he be the first to marry I would live with him; but he would often say "Rob, you can't get around it I'm sure to come and live with you" I would ask why? "Because", he would say, "I won't marry unless I find some one exactly like dear Minn (excuse my using this expression, but I am using his words) and that's next to an impossibility." When he wrote his first letter to Mr. Behrens he read it to me and I laughed immoderately at him. But he was serious and said "Now look here I mean it and you know it and there's no foolishness about it." Often afterwards I joked him about it. Poor dear fellow I always feel as if he were looking down approvingly on all of us.

Since my letter of Feby 23rd, 2 of the murderers have been killed one died through an old wound reopening during the excitement and an other was wounded and is now in prison at Fort Stanton. On the other hand poor Dick Brewer has been killed while endeavouring to arrest one of the murderers. We will have the honest fellows remains buried by the side of those of dear Harry. I have been shot at a number of times, only the other day a bullet passed within an inch of my head and struck the wall near which I was standing. But I have no fear, dear Harrie's protecting spirits is guarding me. I only desire that I may be spared to see you all and give you all the details which it is impossible to give on paper.

The New Mexican ring is attacking me on all sides, but I am giving them back their pay with interest and shall continue to do so. . . .

I am keeping dear Harrie's dog Punch and will bring him with me when I come. I have recovered his spurs but could not as yet succeed in getting the ring. If I ever can get it though or get track of it I will have it no *matter what the consequences*. There are many other articles and trinkets he was fond of which I will bring with me.—[12]

Widenmann speaks of going to England as if it were all arranged. In fact, he was still trying to sell the idea. Widenmann went on to propose again, as he had to Tunstall's father, that he close up the business and head for England "about the 1st of June." Since McSween's comments indicate that Widenmann was penniless, it is clear he expected the Tunstalls—or John's estate—to pay for the trip.

Dear Harry so often spoke to me of the dear ones at home, scarcely a day passed but what he mentioned the one or the other of you if not all, and he read to me so many of your letters to him and his to you that I have always felt that you were not strangers to me. In fact dear Harry and I were so closely bound together through the ties of friendship and more than brotherly love that I often felt that though the ocean seperated us and I had never had the pleasure of seeing you, there still was a strong tie which connected us and now, since I am left here *all alone* I feel this more with every day. I suppose I am somewhat peculiarly constituted. During my life I have formed very few intimate friendships, though in the course of my travels I have met very many persons, but from the time dear Harry and I first met we were irresistably drawn together and the tie grew stronger with each passing day so that it may safely be said that neither of us had a thought but that the other was informed of it at the first opportunity. But it has pleased God to seperate us and leave me alone here. Hard though it be, Gods will be done. True there are many pleasant persons here, but none like dear Harry. There are but few such noble wholesouled men in the world as dear Harry was. We have lost a brother like whom there are but few. Oh when I think of the dastardly outrageous deed it makes my blood boil in every artery and swear vengeance.

It is impossible to believe the foregoing to have been artless; and while there is no evidence to suggest that he ever saw a line of Widenmann's correspondence, McSween's third letter, written on the same day, offers a usefully corrective view of Tunstall's friend.

Your son and I never differed but [on] two subject matters—his retention of Weiden-mann & his passion for horses. Tho' these formed no part of my relations with him he would insist upon my giving my judgment. I told him that a young man in health who had no money nor clothing & was willing to work for another for board & clothing was not the man for him. Never had a cross word with John and am glad of it.

Weidenmann is still stopping at my house. This we suffer on account of the friendship [John] entertained for him. He is now charged with the murder of Brady & Hindman, so was my brother in law and two colored servants of mine. The last named three have been released by order of the Grand Jury who failed to find any evidence against them. Am equally certain that W. is entirely innocent, tho' unfortunately he was near where the shooting took place. I purpose defending him and sustaining him until the last; not for any admiration I entertain for him but because John H. Tunstall considered him his friend. Understand me, I have nothing against him more than his laziness, youthful pomposity, lack of discretion, so indispensable now, and, in the language of this country, poking his nose where it does not belong. Any favors that he'll get here from me or any other man here will be *only* on account of your son.

I do not wish to refer to it any more. Whatever you instruct him to do will be all right so far as I am concerned. I deemed it my duty to say what I have. One thing, if nothing else, bothers me: he tells me that he promised Tunstall that he would wind up his Estate; so did I, but for all of it I would not take the responsibility. I can fulfil my promise by watching those upon [whom] you or the law throw the duty. Mine will be gratuitous: his ought to be so, too. I'll be free from responsibility to be compensated in dollars & cents. The Administrator only gets 1 per cent. W. has no means and must draw his support from the assets. He will have a retinue of servants. I don't think that that will do. Still if you think it best to let him manage it without any responsibility, all well, I'll do all I can with him, without any financial trust, to close up to your advantage.

Should he go over there, you would have to remit a sufficient sum to take him from here, as he has not one dollar or anything from which to realize it. Then I think you'll want to get rid of him before he'll want to leave you. I would rather not say this much, but I think I should not hold it back.[13]

In response to J. P. Tunstall's queries, McSween went into some detail about the land Tunstall had filed on.

1st. It will take $3840.xx to *perfect* the title. This sum is to be paid the U.S. Government, and does not include any costs. There will be fees to officers of the land office and the expenses of the party making the proofs at the office as witnesses. I promised John that I should make no charges nor shall I, these fees will not exceed $200xx

2nd. When proofs shall have been made the title will hold good, tumults cannot affect it. These roughs will *all* be *obliged* to leave the country. This will be [true?] for the best part of the Territory.

3rd. The fact of the Territory becoming a State will in no way affect a title now obtained from the U.S. Govt.

You have two years in which to perfect the title—a little better. There is another piece [of land] that he wished to secure, and if you desire to carry out his wish you should lose no time in doing so. Notwithstanding our troubles, the country is being eager[ly] sought after. A few days ago I rec'd a letter from a party in St Louis with whom your son was acquainted asking in regards to his lands. I understand them to say they will purchase. An answer at length to their queries would consume time, so I deferred until writing you.

I feared to trust my own judgment with the value of the land, for I feel that to recommend the perfecting of the title would be too much of a responsibility as I am not an expert in land valuation. Mr. Chisum, of whom your son, I think, must have written, gives it as his judgment that the land will some day prove valuable. Mr. C. is a business man, worth about half a million Dollars.

I am fascinated with the climate and the Geography of the country. To me it will be a source of pleasure to answer all inquiries you may address me in regard to the land or any other matter affecting your interests.

Your daughter Mrs. Behrens speaks of an armor[—]He shall be around us as a wall of fire that no danger can come near us. I have never carried a firearm in my life—don't now—don't expect [to]. I have lived 35 years without them & without drinking Whiskey, and I can I hope get along the bal. of my days without.[14]

On Wednesday, April 18, the grand jury completed its deliberations on the territorial cases, and its findings were delivered to Judge Bristol by foreman Joseph H. Blazer.[15] They can hardly have made the judge's day.

In the matter of the murder of John Tunstall, which "for brutality and malice is without parallel and without a shadow of justification," the grand jury found indictments against Jessie Evans, George Davis, Miguel Seguro (Manuel Segovia), and Frank Rivers (an alias of John Long) as principals. Also named as accessories were James J. Dolan and J. B. Mathews. Bond in the sum of five thousand dollars was fixed for Evans, and at two thousand each for Dolan and Mathews.

"We equally condemn the most brutal murder of our late Sheriff William Brady, and his deputy, George Hindman," the jury continued, bringing in indictments against John Middleton, Fred Waite, Henry Brown, and Wm. H. Bonney. Bonney also appeared in the indictments brought in against the killers of Roberts at Blazer's Mill, although this time under the more familiar moniker of Henry Antrim alias "Kid." Middleton, Stephen Stevens, John Scroggins, George Coe, Frederick Wait (sic), Charles Bowdre, Dock (sic) Scurlock and Hendry (sic) Brown were also named. Then came the verdict for which Alexander McSween had been waiting so long.

> Your Honor charged us to investigate the case of Alex. A. McSween, Esq., charged with the embezzlement of ten thousand dollars belonging to the estate of Emil Fritz, deceased; this we did, but are unable to find any evidence that would justify that accusation. We fully exonerate him of the charge and regret that a spirit of persecution has been shown in this matter.

Finally—icing on the cake to the McSween faction—Dolan and Riley were indicted for cattle theft. All this was a complete repudiation of Judge Bristol's recommendations, and a thorough vindication of the McSween cause.

Dolan and Riley threw in the towel; the following item appeared in both the *Independent* and the *New Mexican.*

A CARD TO THE PUBLIC
The condition of affairs now existing in the county is such as to make it unsafe for the undersigned to further continue business as they have heretofore done. They take this occasion to assure their friends and the public that the suspension will be only temporary, and that they will resume when peace and quiet shall take the place of lawlessness, and order be restored in the county. Asking for continued confidence, and hoping for a renewal of business relations, we remain,

> Very respectfully,
> Jas. J. Dolan & Co.

Lincoln, N.M., April 17, 1878.[16]

In point of fact, Thomas B. Catron had taken control of their assets, mortgaged three months earlier. He sent his brother-in-law, Edgar Walz, to manage the Lincoln store pro tem. McSween put the pressure on. That same day, acting on the authority of J. P. Tunstall, he composed for the newspapers a "card" which clearly indicated that no quarter was to be shown.[17]

$5000 REWARD
I am authorized by J. P. Tunstall of London, England, to offer the above reward for the apprehension and conviction of the murderers of his son, John H. Tunstall, at Lincoln county, New Mexico, on the 18th day of February, 1878. The actual murderers are about twenty in number, and I will pay a proportionate sum for the apprehension and conviction of any of them.

> A. A. McSween

Lincoln, N.M., April 17, 1878.

Belatedly, Murphy, Dolan, and Riley's friends rallied to their defense. The *New Mexican,* having obtained a copy of Montague Leverson's March 16 letter, published a biting response to the Englishman's accusations. In answer to its own question, "Who is Levison [sic]?" the newspaper went on to label him a liar, a lawbreaker, an impudent ass, and a fool.

HE IS CRAZY!
No such letter was ever written by a sane man. No language is adequate to describe its folly. Its foolishness is even greater than its mendacity!

. . . We publish it without farther comment. We would no more attempt to analyze it and point out its falsehoods than we would attempt to analyze the mind of an idiot and attempt to show in what respect he was a fool. He is simply all fool as the letter is all lie! Look at Tunstall's death! with his own pistol! before he was asked for it! His Excellency the President of the United States and his august Cabinet! pondering with serious faces, over such an awful state of facts! To think that a former member of Congress and present Governor of a Territory, a U.S. District Judge, a U.S. Attorney, a Territorial District Attorney, and a Surveyor General should have gone and done it! And all *colleaguing* together to keep on doing it! Plotting assassinations! Shielding murderers, forging indictments, buying testimony, embezzling public funds! Here's richness! Angel, blow your horn![18]

This was all good knockabout stuff, but of course, the editors of the *New Mexican* knew perfectly well who Leverson was: only a few months earlier, on February 23, they had lauded his "splendid blooded bulls," and for three months before the appearance of its editorial, the newspaper had regularly carried the Englishman's paid advertisement:

IMPROVE YOUR STOCK

My Blooded Stock Will Stand For service for a few weeks at Herlow's corral on the following terms:-

The Thoroughbred Jersey "Comet" at $20 per leap. In New York $23 was paid. Any of my Durhams $10 per leap. The thoroughbred racehorse "Sunset" at $50 per leap.

Montague R. Leverson
of Douglas county, Colorado.[19]

More interestingly, the *New Mexican's* reference to Frank Warner Angel indicates that by the time the editorial appeared, news had already reached the Territory of the Justice Department's decision to investigate the charges the paper was at such pains to dismiss. This could be why, at long last, Dolan and Riley decided to put pen to paper in their own defense. On April 20, a long letter from Riley appeared in the *New Mexican*. Its stated intention was to reply to the "tissue of falsehoods" reported in the *Cimarron News & Press* of April 11—the article McSween had written under the pseudonym "Stanton."

Apart from the embezzlement charges and the fact that he owed J. J. Dolan & Co. seventeen hundred dollars, McSween was "an unprincipled, scheming villain who, when he thought justice would overtake him . . . threw Lincoln County into a state of anarchy," said Riley.[20] In this, his willing tool had been Widenmann, "a worthless scoundrel and [dis?]respectable loafer devoid of honor who left Santa Fe without paying his board bill." It was Widenmann who, claimed Riley, had assassinated Sheriff Brady on McSween's instructions.

Poor Brady! After an honorable record of twenty years as a soldier and an officer, a greater portion of which was served in the war of the rebellion, to be so assassinated by a cowardly sneaking tool of an unprincipled and ambitious man—and yet the article referred to in the *News and Press* seems to justify this foul murder. Who in New Mexico can say aught against Sheriff Brady? As an officer he was respected and feared by citizens in our county, and as such was in the way of the man McSween. He leaves a wife and nine children to mourn his untimely death—and while Widenmann is trying, through his usual hypocritical lying and the medium of far-off newspapers, to hurt his fair name, the best men in New Mexico are determined to see this man and his co-murderers legally brought to justice.

A further letter, signed "Cow Boy," which appeared in the same issue of the *New Mexican,* is one of the most fascinating documents of the Lincoln County War, the more so because the identity of the writer is unknown.[21] If nothing else, he did a fine line in character assassination. Harking back to the preceding summer and the escape of Jessie Evans and the Boys from the jail in Lincoln, "Cow-Boy" claimed he could

> prove that Brewer was in Lincoln plaza the evening of the night of the rescue. I can prove that Brewer met Evans, Baker & Co.'s friends in a cañon near Charley Bowder's ranch and there informed them that a new jailer would be put in at the jail that night, because McSween had told him that Brady was afraid of the old jailer, for he had let one prisoner get away. I can prove that the rescuing party went from the cañon near Bowder's ranch to a spring nearby, who and how many there were, what they came for, who held the horses on top of the hill above Lincoln plaza, who asked the jailer for the keys, and after Baker, Evans & Co. were taken from jail, they went per agreement to Brewer's ranch and there armed and mounted themselves, Brewer as a blind keeping away from his ranch. Brewer wrote a note to McSween stating that Evans, Baker & Co. had been to his ranch that morning and helped themselves. Brewer aided and abetted the rescue of Evans, Baker & Co. with the knowledge and consent of Tunstall and McSween. I can prove that Tunstall arranged on his way to the Felice ranch to meet Evans, Baker & Co.; said that he knew "the boys" would bring his horses and mules to him and that he was not afraid to meet them. I can prove that Tunstall tried to hire Baker as foreman of his horses and cattle. Evans, Baker & Co. did return the horses and mules to Tunstall, Brewer and McSween, Brewer going as far as Seven Rivers for some of the horses.
>
> Robert A. Widerman, a man who bummed his way in Colorado, who was kicked out of the hotel and decent society in Santa Fe, and came to Lincoln county a deadbeat, was cognizant of these facts, he being in the employ of Tunstall and McSween. Dick Brewer to avoid the payment of a debt due to L. G. Murphy & Co. had placed all of his property in the hands of A. A. McSween. A. A. McSween as attorney for Charles Fritz, deceased, had gone to New York and collected ten thousand dollars, the amount of the policy on the life of Emil Fritz. McSween at first denied collecting the ten thousand dollars and used it twelve months before Charles Fritz obtained evidence sufficient to satisfy the Probate Judge of Lincoln county to order McSween to turn over the money to the administrators of Emil Fritz. McSween in open court told the Probate Judge that he had the money in his pocket and to get it if he could, and instead of obeying the order of the Probate Judge he made over all of his property, including that of Dick Brewer, to Tunstall, excepting a house and lot which he deeded to Shields' wife, a sister of McSween's wife. Shields ran off from his creditors, came to Lincoln last summer a pauper, Dick Brewer going to the end of the railroad for him.
>
> McSween started to the States but was arrested at Las Vegas and brought back and placed under bonds. Charles Fritz sued out an attachment against the property of A. A. McSween. Tunstall had the property in his possession on the Rio Felice. Tunstall and McSween had armed and equipped a band of as mean men as he could find, and informed every person that the Sheriff could not attach the property. With Tunstall were John Middleton, an escaped jailbird from Texas, from whom there is a large reward, Wait, part Indian, also a refugee from Justice, Dick Brewer the releaser of Evans, Baker & Co., "the Kid" a boy who was arrested for stealing horses from Col. Hunter and the rest just as bad characters. Tunstall's party had cut portholes in the house and fortified around with bags filled with sand.
>
> When Deputy Sheriff Matthews and posse arrived at the Felice ranch Tunstall and party had been gone about two hours and a half. Some of the McSween party

had sent a runner to Tunstall with word that the Sheriff was coming and had the Pecos cow-boys with him. Brewer remarked "If the Pecos cow-boys are with the Sheriff I am not going to fight."

J. J. Dolan and others of the Sheriff's party stopped at the Felice with the cattle; the rest went in pursuit of Tunstall and party to attach the horses. A running fight took place. How and by whom Tunstall was killed the courts can only decide. If he was killed by thieves, murderers and escaped prisoners, as Brewer and party say, then those thieves, murderers and escaped prisoners were turned loose upon the county by Brewer with the knowledge and consent of Tunstall and McSween.

Tunstall and Brewer had with them thieves, murderers and escaped prisoners. All of these facts were well known to Robert A. Widerman. If you sow the wind you will reap the whirlwind. After court, you will hear again from

COW-BOY.

Simultaneously, and surprisingly—examples of his written intervention in Lincoln County affairs are very few and far between—the frail and ailing Lawrence G. Murphy took issue with the editor of the *Trinidad Enterprise and Chronicle.* On the same day the *News & Press* had published "Stanton's" letter, that "far-off" newspaper printed a markedly similar version of events signed "Thine in the Right," a salutation used frequently by Isaac Ellis. For all its lofty tone, however, Murphy's reply answers not one of the accusations leveled against the House.[22]

Insofar as my friends and I are concerned, I only hold you accountable for the selection you made of your correspondent. You could not have made a worse one, and it is to be hoped, for your sake, that when you knew him he bore a better character than he shows in his "history". It is greatly to be regretted that a public journal will lend itself to the publication of such a series of falsehoods as is contained in that "history". And I repeat that no matter what his previous character may have been, he has now shown himself alike destitute of common honesty, decency, and truth. Without intending advice, it is permitted me to suggest that it would have shown more wisdom on your part and his to have awaited the action of the court now investigating the very matter therein treated of. It is not a little strange that your "history" had to leave the territory, where the facts are known and understood, to enlighten the outside world with falsehoods.

I have studiously refrained from noticing the slanders previously published since the lawlessness of which "Thine in the Right" is the apologist and defender commenced; nor do I propose to do more now than enter the general denial herein made, leaving it to a more appropriate occasion to show the correctness of my position.

The old lion could still roar his contempt, but exactly why Murphy for so long "studiously refrained" from replying to his detractors remains a mystery; perhaps because he was, to use his own phrase, extremely indisposed. Whatever the case, his denials had no real effect upon public sentiment, which had once more swung firmly in favor of the McSween faction. Some indication of how far is indicated by the letter Murphy addressed to Colonel Dudley on April 23. "At the earnest request of the District Attorney Rynerson and others, I left Lincoln yesterday to seek protection for my life at this post but extreme indisposition prevented my reporting to you on my arrival and presenting my request. I do so now in the hope that my sixteen years of faithful service in the Army, and the evident danger, will justify you in granting my request, until an opportunity offers of my getting to Santa Fe."[23]

His fears were well founded. No sooner had the district court adjourned on the following Tuesday, April 24, than the room it had occupied was the scene "pursuant to an hour's notice" of a mass meeting of Lincoln citizens. Called to order by Juan B. Patrón, those assembled nominated Probate Judge Florencio Gonzales chairman of the citizen's committee (John Chisum, Juan Patrón, and Avery Clenny), with Saturnino Baca and José Montaño as vice chairmen. McSween and Ben Ellis, Isaac Ellis's son, were named secretaries.

There were speeches and more speeches, including one by Brook Herford, who closed with this ringing appeal: "I trust that the pledges of good feeling made this evening in so solemn and appropriate a manner, may never be marred or broken."[24] After the speeches, resolutions were proposed by Juan Patrón, John Chisum, and others. Among them were a condemnation of the actions of Governor Axtell during his March visit to Lincoln, and a fulsome vote of thanks to Lieutenant Colonel Dudley, the new commanding officer at Fort Stanton, and to the soldiers from the fort who had been in town during the session of court.

Thanks were also rendered to John Copeland for his "important and efficient" discharge of the office of sheriff. The secretaries were bidden to send copies of these resolutions to the president of the United States, the secretary of war, Governor Axtell, the *Independent,* and the *News & Press,* and "as a token of respect"—in English and Spanish, borne by a committee consisting of Gonzalez, Patrón, and Ellis—to Lieutenant Colonel Dudley.

These are clear indications of the feelings of the ordinary citizens of Lincoln County, hard-working, God-fearing farmers who wanted only to return to their fields and be done with the killings and counter-killings that had begun with the death of Tunstall. The strength of their hostility to Murphy and Dolan was demonstrated at once: Although it is not mentioned in any of the proceedings, it appears that McSween was instrumental in having everyone present sign a petition to be presented to what he called "the Irish firm."[25] The men were asked "for the sake of peace and safety" to leave the county and return no more. The beleaguered partners had little choice but to acquiesce.

The tables had been completely turned. The pro-Dolan sheriff Brady had been replaced by Copeland who, since he owed his appointment to McSween, was no more eager to arrest McSween's supporters than Brady had been to arrest his enemies. The Department of Justice's special investigator, Frank Warner Angel, was on his way to New Mexico, to probe the actions of the federal officials there. An inspector from the Department of the Interior was coming to look into the running of the Indian agency. Another investigation into Dolan's handling of the post office at Lincoln was also expected momentarily.

The enemy was in disarray: McSween had the field.

CHAPTER 23

WAR: THE TABLES TURNED AGAIN

ON April 25, a Thursday, Robert Widenmann gave Tunstall's father an update on events. His account is as interesting for what it omits as for what it contains.

> The Court of the District has been in session here. Its officers, with two exceptions, showed their partiality in all their actions And had it not been for our Grand Jury, composed of the best men of the County, the country would now be in open revolt. But the truth is beginning to dawn even here. The people are united and determined to exterminate all thieves and murderers. Dear Harrie's murderers were indicted but they escaped arrest through the disgraceful action of our District attorny Col. Rynerson; but Dolan and Riley were arrested, but this same District attorney allowed them to give bonds for their appearance at the next session of the court. He also had me arraigned before the Grand Jury for the killing of Brady, but the Jury acquitted me. No sooner had the Jury done this than he had me rearrested for resisting the sheriff when he made the illegal attachment of dear Harrie's property.
>
> He then took a change of venue in the case, which will force me to appear before the Court at La Mesilla, 150 miles from here, the second Monday of June [in fact, it was the third Monday, June 17], but he will be unable to make a case against me. They see how we are fighting them to keep them from getting the property into their hands and are doing their utmost.[1]

The courts, in the persons of District Attorney Rynerson and Judge Warren Bristol, had always maintained that Tunstall testified he and McSween were partners, thus justifying the issuing of writs of attachment against Tunstall's property. In view of McSween's later testimony on the subject to Judge Angel, what Widenmann had to say next is of especial interest:

> When dear Harry commenced business here he allowed A. A. McSween a share of his profits for his knowledge of the people and the country and for legal advice, but this arrangement was dissolved 4 or 5 months ago, because McS. was getting into trouble about some funds he had collected for an estate. It was before this arrangement was entered into with McS. that the will of which I sent you a copy was made. Dear Harry thought that, should anything happen to him, everything should be done to keep the property from going into his partners (if he could so be called) hands. As I have said, this arrangement was annulled before these troubles began and the writs of attachment were issued.
>
> The Judge of this district was informed of this, nevertheless a few days ago he issued new writs of attachment for the property and placed them in the hands of the sheriff. Thereupon I informed the sheriff, who is an honorable man, that if he should proceed to attach dear Harrie's property under a writ against McS. I would hold him pecuniarily responsible for all damages and losses. Your power of attorney will be

presented and no doubt recognised by the [probate] court at its next session on the 5th prox. The sheriff will today see the Judge and tell him that knowing that the property belongs to you and not to McS.,he will not proceed to attach it unless he is given an indemnity bond to secure him against any suit for damages which may afterwards be instituted. I think it doubtful that the bonds can be secured since everyone knows how things stand and should the bonds not be given the sheriff will not proceed on the writ. I am now trying to get some amicable settlement between McS. and the heir for whom he has collected the money and have the suit and the attachment dissmissed, but doubt whether I will be successful. Come what may though I am going to stay right here until things get straightened out, no difference what ruses and threats they make to get me out of the country.—

After I get the books and property I will make a thorough balance sheet and send it to you, so that you can see the exact status of things. In regard to the land matters I will make explanations when I see you personally. The lands are now perfectly safe and there is ample time to complete the titles, there remaining two to two years and a half to do it in. Of course this should be done as economical as possible and I hope to be able to propose to you a plan which will greatly aid in doing it. The cattle are all safe and in excellent condition. I will write you at least once a week and keep you fully posted.

It was beginning to look as if Widenmann and McSween were in contention for control of Tunstall's not inconsiderable assets. That Brook Herford suspected something of the sort is indicated by the fact that he telegraphed J. P. Tunstall in London advising that the power of attorney given to Robert Widenmann be revoked and made over to him. Tunstall telegraphed Widenmann of his intentions: the dispatch arrived on April 28; Widenmann immediately telegraphed a reply: "Await my letter today before acting." In the letter written later that day he said that McSween and he were

perfectly astonished at your dispatch, it is inexplicable to us especially compared with the actions of Mr. Herford. When Mr. H arrived here I had just received your letter informing me that the power of attorney had been sent.—

I told Mr. H of this to which he simply remarked, that in this case the Probate Judge would decide as to the validity of the two documents. Nothing more was said and he never informed me that he had telegraphed you. What his reasons for doing so were I can not imagine, and Mr. McS is also at a loss to comprehend his action. Mr. H is now at Fort Stanton but as soon as he returns I shall ask for an explanation.[2]

Widenmann's next remarks give some indication of the underlying reasons for the eventual loss of Tunstall's holdings, and why his bewildered parents could never make head or tail of John's business arrangements. He had advanced money on crops not yet harvested, corn not yet ripe, and hay not yet cut, and had invested heavily in cattle and horses, with a view to eventually bidding on army contracts. He had bought out a number of small ranchers, then filed on their land in the names of other men, as well as making extensive filings along the Feliz River through nominees. Since these filings had been made under the Desert Land Act, they may have been of questionable legality, which might explain why Widenmann wrote that

Mr. McSween and I are both of the opinion, that if a stranger, who is unacquainted with the business, people and country, tries to settle up the estate, there will be a considerable loss. The business is so intricate, the books were kept in such a shape purposely by dear Harrie that only one who is thoroughly acquainted with the business can handle it. Then the landmatters are so arranged and there are so many secrets connected with it purposely, so that a stranger should not be able to interfere or hinder the workings, that no outsider could arrange them. Besides there are arrangements regarding the land matters and different ranches that were only known to dear Harry and myself, although Mr. McSween made out the papers and filings at the land office. I also fear that should Mr. Herford handle the business, it would be a great drawback to the men who are now in the mountains after dear Harrie's murderers. I have been aiding them in every possible way and they being naturally disinclined to deal and communicate with a stranger and many things would be left undone which otherwise would be done.

When Mr. H's explanation for his action reaches you, I should be happy to hear what it is. Would it not be best to act on the information Mr. H will undoubtedly give you, only after you have my answer to it? . . . I cannot but think that Mr. H has shown considerable duplicity in his action but in saying this I may be doing him an injustice and will therefore not say anything more about it until I can get at the facts.—

In a postscript to this letter, Widenmann hypothesized that perhaps Herford had suggested the change due to the fact that he, Widenmann, was in trouble over the killing of Brady, because Herford seemed "too honest and honorable a man to have any other reason for what he has done."

If Alexander McSween was as concerned as Widenmann claimed, no sign of it showed in the scribbled note he sent to Tunstall's father that same day. With it he enclosed an account book in John Tunstall's handwriting setting out the transactions between them.

As has already been shown (see appendix 3), this neat little notebook raises a number of fascinating—if probably unanswerable—questions. Taken at face value, it appeared to indicate that at the time of his death, Tunstall owed McSween $6,598.04.[3]

> After writing you that I would send it to his banker for identification [wrote McSween] I began to think that it might seem to you that I mistrusted you in some way; and that for that reason I failed to send it to you for identification.
>
> Those of his murder[er]s living are indicted. Justice will overtake all of them.
>
> The Irish firm that really caused his death has been obliged to flee for safety. A Petition signed by 9/10 of our people was presented to them asking them for the sake of peace and safety to leave the County and return no more; they have done so.[4]

"The Irish firm" was unable to leave immediately; conditions were just too dangerous. It was not until a week or so later that Riley left for Las Cruces and Jimmy Dolan for Santa Fe, taking his protector and mentor Lawrence G. Murphy there to obtain the medical treatment he now so urgently needed.[5] The *New Mexican* noted on May 11 that Murphy, Dolan, and James Longwell had arrived in the city the preceding day. A few days later Fountain's *Independent* claimed that they had been kicked out of Fort Stanton by Colonel Dudley.

Their side's "victory" in the courts had put the Regulators into an aggressive mood: just how aggressive may be gauged from an anonymous item which appeared in the *Grant County Herald* on June 8, 1878.[6] Writing from Silver City on May 31, the writer—identified only as "S"—painted a picture of life in Lincoln County radically different to the one described in McSween and Widenmann's letters to the Tunstalls.

MR. EDITOR OF THE HERALD

I have been going through your town from Lincoln county and in talking to your people I find that you would not be afraid to tell the truth about the Lincoln county row, if you had a fair show. I think the thing ought to be showed up and I believe you will publish my letter. I use poor grammar but you can fix it up to look right in the paper.

I was in Lincoln county through the whole fight and this is just how it was. I had a ranche down on the Penasco. I came in there last summer and went through the whole trouble and am pretty well posted. The difficulty was because McSween won't pay over the life insurance of $10,000 to Fritz's sister who ought to have it. Tunstall came in the county and tried to run out Murphy and Dolan. McSween thought Murphy was throwing off on him, and then for spite went in with Tunstall. In the fight afterwards, Widerman the marshal, crowded down everybody who was not in favor of Tunstall and McSwain. If it hadn't been for Brady he would have had everything in his own hands.

Where I lived on my ranche I tried to be a fair man to both sides. Men on both sides were going by nearly every day, and I tried to treat both the same. I wouldn't hold up one side or the other. I went in, on business to Lincoln and Widerman says to me that he killed a lot of my friends the other day. I told him they were no friends of mine nor no particular enemies. Then Widerman says why don't you come in with us if you are no friend of theirs you ought to be with us. And I said it was no fight of mine, and I didn't intend to put myself up to be shot as long as I could make a living by work.

I went back to my ranche and a day after a friend of mine came out to the ranche from Lincoln and said, you better leave because Widerman and his party think you are no friend and say they intend to put you out of the way if you stay here. The next day I thought the matter over and then traded my ranche for a horse to travel on. I left nearly fifteen acres of grain and it was the 7th of May and before long I could have had a good crop, but I considered my life worth more. I had no quarrel with either party but was afraid Widerman might send someone to kill me in the dark.

Then I left my ranche and started for Tularosa and at daylight I came to the ranche south of Fort Stanton. One of Widerman's men met me. He says Widerman wants to see you at the plaza in Lincoln. I went back to the plaza because I was afraid I would be killed on the road if I refused. Widerman told me he wanted to know what Murphy and Dolan's party intended to do. I said I knew nothing about it and they let me go. Then I started for Mesilla and on the road met two other men who were afraid of their lives from Widerman and his party. After I met these men a party met us and spread out on both sides of the road. We jumped off the horses and showed fight. Then they said they were looking for cattle, but I knew three of them to belong to Widerman's party.

Roberts was killed only because Dolan had him to work for him taking charge of his herd. The whole fight was because McSween and Tunstall wanted to run Murphy and Dolan out, and then when I didn't want to do anything on either side, they drove me out, too, because they thought I was a friend of Dolan's, when I was just as much a friend of Widerman before he commenced to try to make me fight for him.

I wouldn't have left even by the threats of my life, only I found out that John Chisum, who before hated Widerman, was making a job with him and McSween to go together and clean out the whole county. I knew that Chisum would be glad to see me killed and so I just left my crops and sailed out. Lots of men are leaving the county in the same way, because they say that McSween and Widerman and Chisum are paying four dollars a day for a man and his rifle and intend to drive everybody else out. It was no fight of mine, but they drove me away from a good ranche where I thought I could make a first class farm, and I think the thing ought to be showed up. If you will publish this you will do justice to many men who have been crowded almost to the death, only because they wouldn't take up Widerman's and McSween's fight, and although they were not the friends of the other side, because that party had the power they drove them out of the country or left them with no show for their lifes. It ought to be published and I think you will do it. I have left there and now I ain't afraid to tell just how the thing was. Every word I write is true and the people ought to know it.

This remarkable little document—could it have been written by Ham Mills's brother-in-law Steve Stanley?—captures more fully than most the atmosphere of the time: its portrayal of Robert Widenmann as a swaggering bully is a convincing one. Whether it is accurate it is impossible to say, although it is not difficult to believe it was seen as accurate down Seven Rivers way.

So when the new "captain" of the Regulators, Frank MacNab, was heard to state publicly that their next priority would be to ride down to the Seven Rivers area and "close out" that nest of cattle rustlers, a posse—its avowed purpose to "help" the new sheriff, John Copeland, make the arrests of the men responsible for killing Brady—was formed there under the command of W. H. Johnson, a former Brady deputy.

By the time it was ready to leave for Lincoln, 125 miles away to the northwest, the "posse" consisted of about thirty-five men, among whom were George Peppin, Marion Turner, Buck Powell, Milo Pierce, Bob and John Beckwith, Lewis Paxton, Sam Perry, Joe Nash, Tom Cochrane, Wallace and Bob Olinger, Follett Christie, Ruben Kelly, Jim Patterson, Charles Martin, Frank Catlin, J. W. Gauce, Thomas Gaffney, Dick Lloyd, John Long, Tom Green, Billy Mathews, John Hurley (fig. 57), Dutch Charlie Kruling, John Galvin, and Jim Ramer. A number of these men had been in the posse that had pursued and murdered John Tunstall.

Word of the formation of this group seems to have reached Lincoln ahead of its arrival: George Coe said they heard the Seven Rivers crowd were coming "to clean up Billy the Kid's gang."[7] Rumors were also circulating to the effect that at the invitation of District Attorney Rynerson, John Kinney had organized a gang to make war on the McSween party; but no one knew for sure from which direction, if any, his attack might come. If Widenmann's letter of April 28 is anything to go by, they certainly knew something was afoot. "We are expecting an attack on the town tonight and are having guards out. But I am happy to say that I think peace and quiet are slowly returning. We have succeeded in driving Dolan and his party out of town, they have been indicted by the Grand Jury and will, sooner or later be brought to justice. We yet expect to have many a skirmish, but right is sure to win in the end."[8]

The first skirmish was not long in coming. On the following evening, after eating supper in Lincoln, Frank Coe and his partner Ab Saunders set off down the trail for their farm on the Hondo (fig. 58). With them rode Frank MacNab. Their lack of caution, in view of the aforementioned rumors, is difficult to understand, but it is clear they were not expecting trouble. About eight miles below Lincoln, they stopped to water their horses at the Fritz ranch, completely unaware that the Seven Rivers "posse" had come up the Hondo and stopped to rest there.

The Seven Rivers men saw the trio approaching; they held their fire until the

FIG. 57. John Hurley, aged about thirty, ca. 1884. Photo by Baker & Johnston, Roswell, N.M.

three dismounted at the spring for which the ranch was named. MacNab and Saunders were gravely wounded in the first murderous fusillade. Frank Coe, still in the saddle, attempted to spur his horse away, but it was shot in the head and killed instantaneously. Coe leaped from the saddle and rolled into a declivity, keeping the Seven Rivers men at bay until he ran out of ammunition. Frank MacNab, mortally wounded, tried to drag himself to safety, but was pursued and finished off with a shotgun. Coe, after some parleying—he was friendly with a number of the men in the party—was allowed to surrender and was "arrested." Saunders was brought into the Fritz ranch house and found to be still alive, although in bad shape from bullet wounds that had shattered his left hip and ankle.

After dark the Seven Rivers men headed for Lincoln. Ten or twelve of them stationed themselves at the Dolan store, the remainder in the breaks east of town. Four or five others, led by Johnson and Marion Turner, slid into the plaza, their plan to use the Baca house to set an ambush for McSween and his adherents, just as McSween's men had done with Brady and Hindman. The outraged Captain Baca flatly refused, so they regrouped at the eastern edge of town and made ready to attack the Ellis store, which had become the rendezvous and commissary of the Regulators.

On May 9 and 11, first McSween and then Widenmann wrote accounts of what had happened at the Fritz ranch and in Lincoln the following day, May 1. McSween began with an account of the killing of MacNab.

> Frank McNab, James A. Sanders and Frank Coe left here on the evening of the 30th ult for a ranch 12 miles east of here. When 8 miles from here they were fired upon by a party of 25 men who waylaid them—7 of them were the murderers of John—killing McNab and seriously wounding Sanders in the left hip and left ankle.
>
> Next day the 25 attacked the town of Lincoln & lost 6 of their men—none in the town was injured.[9]

Widenmann went into more detail; his letter again contains the implication that an attack had been expected.

> On the morning of the 30th ulto., 25 men rode up to the town, divided into two parties, one stationing itself above town in the house of J. J. Dolan & Co. while the other half stationed themselves in the brush about 250 yards below the house of Mr. Ellis. Before coming to town the same party (they are in the employ of J. J. Dolan & Co. and L. G. Murphy) killed one Frank McNab and severely wounded

A. Sanders while these latter were riding home to their ranches. They stated at several places that they were going to kill Mr. Ellis, McSween and myself.

Our party took the best stand we could and awaited their attack. The first shot was fired about 9 O'cl and the bullett struck within 2 inches of my head. We then opened out on them and poured the lead into them so rapidly that in less than an hour we had them routed and had them cut off from their horses. The fighting continued throughout the day, the murderers trying to regain their horses, while we beat them back at every attempt. About 5 O'cl P.M. a company of cavalry was sent into town by the commander of Fort Stanton who had been informed that we were fighting.

The thieves were captured and taken to Fort Stanton, but things soon took a turn there. The commander, after having been thoroughly soft-soaped by Murphy, constituted himself Judge, declared the murderers innocent, though one of their victims lay wounded in the Fort hospital. He refused to disarm them and would have liberated them had not our sher-

FIG. 58. James Albert "Ab" Saunders, late 1878. Photographer A. W. Fell, Lompoc, Calif.

iff declared that if he did this he would hold him personally responsible, whereupon they were held at the Fort but allowed to keep their arms. You can imagine our astonishment when the second day after this occurred a company of soldiers rode into town and arrested all of us under the plea of assault and battery with intent to kill. Why did they not say murder at once, for in defending our lives we killed 2 and wounded 4 of them. We were all taken to Fort Stanton and closely confined while the murderers were allowed the limits of the post and their arms. A few days afterwards the murderers were liberated while we were sent back to town as prisoners and stood our trial. Such is military justice!

We are daily expecting a renewed attack, and should they come, will give them the best we have.

As usual, Widenmann is disingenuous; Capt. G. W. Smith who, at the frantic behest of John Copeland, led a troop of soldiers down to Lincoln to investigate the sheriff's report that there were three dead men lying in the road below town and that the U.S. mails had been stopped, paints in his report a picture at once more accurate and more confused.[10] He rode into town between 3:30 and 4:00 p.m. on May 1st, to the accompaniment of "sharp skirmish fire which was well sustained until after I had entered the main street from the upper end of town."

There were men on top of, and hidden behind, the houses along the street. Arrayed against them were twenty or twenty-five men dismounted "along a line of trees bordering the Rio Bonito [and] another party on the bluff on the opposite bank."

I was soon met by the Sheriff of Lincoln County, Mr. John N Copeland with his gun in his hand. He was considerably excited and . . . said there was a party of men below the town who he wanted to arrest but could not. Passing through the town and within rifle range of the party on the bluffs . . . I left my detachment in line with orders to cover me with their carbines and rode forward to the river bank signaling with my cap to the men on the bluff and calling to those nearer to come over to me.

The whole party complied and calling Mr. Copeland up, after some parley asked him to point out the parties he wanted to arrest. He replied "I want the whole damn business."

Three of the party then said for themselves and the rest that they would surrender to me and would go to Fort Stanton, but would not give up their arms to Sheriff Copeland as they believed he would turn them over to the party in Lincoln to be murdered.

"From all the information obtainable and contradictory in the extreme owing to the excited state of the people (the Sheriff being the most so of any man I saw)," Smith concluded that the Seven Rivers men had not responded until several volleys had been fired at them by the McSween faction, and that the men Copeland wanted to arrest had in fact been deputized by William H. Johnson to assist Copeland. He decided to take them all back to the fort and let Dudley sort it out.

Who the dead and wounded men were, history does not record; most accounts have followed that of George Coe, who described taking a shot at Dutch Charlie Kruling.[11] Coe claimed to have "struck through both legs without breaking a bone. However, it did tear off quite a slice of ham." Others accounts have it that Kruling's ankle was shattered badly enough to keep him in hospital for four months. An ambulance brought Saunders up from the Fritz ranch at about noon on the day of the fight. Kruling was taken to the post hospital in the same conveyance. MacNab's body was also in the ambulance; McSween had his fellow Scot buried next to Tunstall.

One other account, written to the *Cimarron News & Press* by Indian Agency clerk Morris J. Bernstein, using the pseudonym "Soapweed," confirms Widenmann's figure: "Six of the 'Boys' were seriously, perhaps fatally, injured," he states. "This is the grandest victory yet won by the people."[12]

The people were not out of trouble yet, however: the long tentacles of the Santa Fe Ring were reaching out yet again to entangle McSween.[13] While still in custody at Fort Stanton, he received a letter, dated May 2, from District Attorney William L. Rynerson, replying to a request he had made some time earlier. Its tone indicates precisely the esteem in which Rynerson held the Lincoln attorney.

I am just in receipt of your[s] of the date of the 27th ulto., directed to me, in which you say, "If the parties have been indicted by the last grand jury for the murder of John H. Tunstall, I wish to ask you to place warrants in the hands of our sheriff for their arrest. Please reply."

In reply I have to say that I shall discharge my duty without let or hindrance from any one, and when warrants are necessary, in every case they will be issued and placed in the hands of the proper officer. Just whom you mean by "our sheriff" is not clear to me, as in the past few months it is said you have had some interest in more than one sheriff. You may mean Martinez, you may mean Barrier, or you may mean some one else whom I do not know, whom you have reduced to possession and are pleased to designate as "our (your) sheriff"; and since you have undertaken the task of directing me in my duties, I may be permitted to suggest that you seem to have forgotten to dictate or direct as to what should be done as to the warrants "if parties have been indicted by the last grand jury" for the murder of Sheriff Brady, George Hindman, A. L. Roberts, and others in Lincoln County. Passing strange!

Rynerson was not the only one who viewed "McSween's sheriff" with a jaundiced eye. An anonymous correspondent, signing himself only "J," sent the following dispatch from Lincoln to the *New Mexican* on May 3.

Matters have now taken a turn which will lead to a final settlement of the troubles of the county. The new sheriff is a McSween man and is to be found at all times in the society of the very men for whom he has warrants in his possession.

These warrants he refuses or neglects to serve until compelled thereto by Gen. Dudley, the commanding officer at Fort Stanton. It is a notorious fact that Copeland (the new sheriff) has been carousing with the murderers of Brady, Hindman and Roberts ever since the court adjourned. There are at present seventeen of Dolan's party under arrest at the Fort, and eight of McSween's. Troops are out under command of Lieutenants Smith and Goodwin with warrants for the arrest of McSween and his party.[14]

McSween can hardly have been surprised at Rynerson's lack of cooperation; his letter had in all probability been written to document it, and to cloak his next step in legality. On May 3, he appeared before Justice of the Peace Gregorio Trujillo at San Patricio and made affidavits charging Robert Beckwith, W. H. Johnson, and others—Seven Rivers men all—with "assault with intent to kill" Frank MacNab and Ab Saunders. Judge Trujillo signed the warrant (it is in McSween's handwriting), which Sheriff Copeland duly served on the men in custody at Fort Stanton, informing them that the preliminary hearing was set for May 6 at San Patricio. It was at this point that Col. N.A.M. Dudley made a significant intervention.

Until now, Dudley had studiously avoided partisanship: indeed, the citizens of Lincoln had sent him a vote of thanks subsequent to the April term of court there.[15] From this time on, however, his hostility toward McSween's cause became increasingly evident. Understandably, perhaps: Lawrence Murphy and Jimmy Dolan had taken advantage of their extended stay at the post to "softsoap him," as Widenmann put it—in other words, to put to him, vigorously and convincingly, the case against McSween. He was doubtless further influenced not only by the protestations of the Seven Rivers men, every one of whom signed a petition begging him to send them before J. P. David Easton at Blazer's Mill, "where they will get justice," but also the reports that he had received about Copeland's erratic, drunken conduct during the skirmish in Lincoln.

Some indication of this appears in a letter that appeared in the *New Mexican* as a corrective to Fountain's piece in the *Independent* claiming Dudley had kicked Murphy, Dolan, and Riley out of Fort Stanton.

Headquarters, Fort Stanton,
May 6, 1878.
J. J. Dolan, Esq.,
  Sir:—I have the honor to acknowledge the receipt of your note referring to a newspaper paragraph published in one of the territorial newspapers charging that I had ordered you and others out of the garrison. I consider it hardly worth your notice to make any contradiction of the statement. My treatment of yourself, Messrs.

Murphy, Riley, and Mr. Waltz, and the aid my officers and myself had given you in protecting your lives and property, is sufficient refutation to any such report.

Yours in haste and truly,

N. A. M. Dudley, Lt. Col. 9th Cavalry Commanding.[16]

Dudley had already given Murphy and his men a convincing demonstration of his partiality while they were still at the Fort.[17] On May 1, Copeland asked for troops to take the prisoners at the fort over to San Patricio and to remain until they had appeared before Justice Trujillo. Instead, on May 2, Dudley ordered Lieutenants Goodwin and Smith and a troop of cavalry to "escort" Sheriff Copeland over to Lincoln and San Patricio and "assist" him in serving a batch of tit-for-tat warrants. These had been issued the preceding day by Justice of the Peace David M. Easton at Blazer's Mill on affidavits made before him by George Peppin and Billy Mathews charging McSween, Isaac Ellis, Widenmann, and a dozen others with assault with intent to kill.

With such an "escort," the hapless Copeland had little choice but to comply. Lieutenant Goodwin's report to the post adjutant, dated May 6, tersely summarizes subsequent events.

In compliance with S[tanding] O[rder] 17 from this post dated May 2nd 1878 I accompanied the Sheriff of Lincoln County to Lincoln to assist him in arresting certain citizens charged with riot. the following named persons were arrested by the Sheriff. Scurlock, Ellis Sen., Wm. Ellis, Scroggins, Gonzales, Corbet, Widerman these I sent at the Sheriff's request under guard to Fort Stanton.

we then proceeded to San Patricia 16 miles from the town of Lincoln and there the Sheriff arrested McSween and with him returned to this post.[18]

Before the prisoners could be brought before him, however, Justice of the Peace Easton affirmed his neutrality by abruptly resigning, unwilling to let Murphy & Co. sandbag him into choosing between its supporters and those of McSween. This left Dudley in a quandary: now the only magistrate available was Gregorio Trujillo at San Patricio. If he sent McSween down there, he also had to send the other arrestees. Trujillo would undoubtedly free the Lincoln men and throw the book at the party from Seven Rivers.

When Copeland requested that he turn all the prisoners over to him, pointing out he could only hold them for thirty-six hours before bringing them before a magistrate, Dudley complied at once, no doubt happy to wash his hands of the whole business.[19]

Without military assistance—which Dudley did not volunteer and Copeland apparently did not request—there was no way the sheriff could get twenty Seven Rivers "prisoners" before a court; he "signed" for them all on May 4, and turned them loose with a mumbled injunction to go home and quit feuding. His main concern, anyway, had been to effect the release of the McSween men also confined at the fort. He returned to the fort three days later to get Doc Scurlock and his rifle belt and pistol and—significantly—to ask for and receive a military escort back to Lincoln with his prisoner. Once there, he turned Doc loose; whereupon, with a commission as Copeland's deputy in his pocket, the twenty-nine-year-old Alabaman immediately assumed the leadership of the McSween fighting men.

In his May 11 letter to the Tunstalls Robert Widenmann related some of his difficulties in getting appointed administrator of the Tunstall estate.[20] The probate judge had decided he could not turn the property over to Widenmann until all the debts had been paid,

> and could therefore only appoint me administrator under $10,000 bonds. I had no other alternative than to act on this decision. The disturbed condition of affairs making it almost impossible to transact any business, I, under the advice of Mr. McSween, who acted as my atty. gave a chattel mortgage on the goods and cattle with the condition that these and I be released from bonds as soon as the indebtedness is paid, which I can do in 30 to 60 days without any trouble. The Judge said he would not make any other arrangement if you had been here yourself and I therefore hope this will be satisfactory to you. I have made a balance sheet as well as I possibly could from the condition of things, showing the standing of the estate at the time of dear Harrie's death and when Mr. Ellis took the estate in hand and will make another one as soon as I can, showing how it stands at present. These statements will be subject to some alteration, as the claims have not all been presented, but these alterations will be small and I think the statements will, in the main points, be correct.

> *Assets*
> Merchandise, etc. on hand
> and Grain Notes as per
> Inventory of Appraisers
>   (Feby 25/78)   13803.08
> Cash in Bank at St. Louis   41.89
> Book Accounts   7812.98
> County Scrip $303 @ 40¢   125.20
> Bills receivable   2125.97
>   23909.12
>
> *Liabilities*
> Accounts due
> in St. Louis and New Mexico   4667.15
>   Balance   18241.97

The statement does not embrace the cattle nor the account of A. A. McSween, the two very nearly offsett each other. On the whole I think that you will not sustain any loss on your original investment especially as I will do my utmost to sell the goods at the prices ruling here. To do this I will probably have to order some staple articles, such as sugar, coffee, candles, etc. of which there are none on hand and they greatly facilitate the sale of the other goods.

I am also wholly out of arms and amunition with which to protect the property and I will have to order enough for this purpose at once. The arms and amunition which were on hand were loaned out for protection of life and property and to catch the murderers.

I think I can pay off the indebtedness in from 30 to 60 days as there are about $3500—due in St Louis which will be placed to the credit of the business with the Bank in St Louis as soon as I can forward the proper papers and bills, which I will do in a few days. I will always keep you fully posted.

Next, Widenmann touched on the forward plans of the Regulators. After the fight at the Fritz ranch, the Seven Rivers men had appropriated Frank MacNab's and Ab Saunders's horses, and on their way home, had also stolen six of Tunstall's horses from the ranch. When news of the theft came in from the Feliz, the punitive expedition to "close out" the Dolan cattle camp that MacNab had planned was mounted.

Yesterday the news came in that 6 horses, which were at the ranch had been stolen by the party which attacked the town. I am afraid this is true. A party of about thirty is now organising to follow them and I have not the slightest doubt but they will overtake them and capture both horses and thieves and hope in my next to be able to give you some definite information. I am afraid that the cattle will also be stolen and am therefore going to have them brought nearer town and kept under close herd. The expenses in holding them either at the ranch or here are great and I will try to dispose of them as soon as possible. But I am afraid that to do this without a sacrifice, it will take some time, as at present there is absolutely no money in the country and property of all kinds is exposed to great risks.

He told the Tunstalls that he had asked Brook Herford for an explanation of his actions, which Herford clearly did not feel obliged to provide, so Widenmann offered his own.

Mr. Herford was, during his stay in this section, much in the company of the officers at Fort Stanton. But these officers, or the greatest number of them, are controlled by the Quartermasters ring, which is a part of the New Mexican ring, against which we are fighting, and it is therefore not to be wondered at that he has been thoroughly plied with lies and slanders against us, and his actions towards Mr. Ellis, McSween and myself seem to indicate that this has been thoroughly done. A stranger who comes to this place at present without thoroughly being acquainted with things will find it difficult to understand them and it is therefore not to be wondered at if he becomes prejudiced after being plied by the officers of the U.S. army who are generally supposed to be gentlemen, though I beg to be allowed to have my own opinion on the subject.

As a further indication of Herford's unreliability, Widenmann related another sad little tale.

When the murderers killed McNab and wounded Sanders, the latter was riding dear Harrie's saddle. They captured the saddle and I afterwards found it in the Quartermasters corral at Fort Stanton, but the quartermaster would not deliver it to me. I told him (the q.m.) that if he allowed the murderers to take the saddle I would hold him responsible for it. He thereupon held the saddle, but Mr. Herford also herd of its being there, demanded it, and rode it off on his leaving here for home. It is not the value of the saddle that I grieve for but dear Harry always rode the saddle and no other, had rode it for some 3 or more years and it was one of the things which I desired to bring to England when I go, feeling that a momento of this kind would be valuable to you. I shall try to have it returned.

Herford's character thus successfully assassinated, Widenmann went on to remit a copy of Assistant Surgeon Daniel Appel's post-mortem report, so that they would "see that dear Harry did at least not suffer." It is instructive to compare this document with the one Appel later gave to investigator Angel.

Copy of Surgeon's report
John H. Tunstall, Feb. 20th & 21st, 1878. Wounded in the head, entered 3 in. behind and in a line with the superior border of the right ear, made its exit 1½ in. above the left orbit and ¼in. left of the middle line of the forehead.
The wound in the chest entered 2 in. to the right of the medium line, breaking the Clavicle, and made its exit 3½ in from the external border of the Acromian process and scraping the upper border of the Scapula.
The fracture of the bones of the skull extended completely around its circumference, passing through the two wounds and extending downward through the hori-

zontal plate of the frontal bone, the greater [illegible] of the ephinoid bone and cribuform plate of the ethmoid bone.

Apologizing for the fact that his letter was "necessarily all business," and promising within the next few days to reply to the letter he had received from Emily Tunstall, Widenmann now painted an evocative picture of himself for their benefit: "It is really a difficult task to write a readable, connected letter, when one is expecting to be attacked or shot every minute, and when one sits in his chair with a rifle close at hand and two belts of cartridges and a revolver strapped on."

Here is a different Robert Widenmann, fighting man, banded about by cartridge belts, six-shooter at his side, rifle by his hand, the personification of the "walking Gatling gun" described by Dudley and the threatening bully of the anonymous "S." As to the accuracy of the portrait, it can only be said that in all the annals of the Lincoln County War, there is no documentary evidence that Widenmann ever fired a shot in anger.

Meanwhile, the many representations being made in Washington had set the ponderous machinery of government in motion.[21] Following Sir Edward Thornton's letters of March 9 and 27 to William Evarts, U.S. secretary of state, concerning the murder of Tunstall, Evarts referred the matter to the attorney general, requesting an investigation. On April 9 S. F. Phillips, acting attorney general, reported to Evarts that he had requested the district attorney for New Mexico to "institute a thorough inquiry into the circumstances of the murder, and to report promptly to me whether from the facts any steps can or should be taken by the Government in the matter. I have not yet received a reply, but I have taken other measures to have the subject thoroughly investigated than through the officers of this Department now in New Mexico."

Among the "other measures" taken by the Department of Justice were the appointment of a thirty-three-year-old New York lawyer, Frank Warner Angel, to go to New Mexico with a wide-ranging brief as the department's special investigator (fig. 59). Among the problems he was assigned to investigate were the allegations of land grant frauds in Colfax County and the outbreak of violence there which had resulted in the murder of Rev. Franklin J. Tolby in September 1877; the murder of John Tunstall and the mounting anarchy in Lincoln County; and allegations of corruption among federal officials—notably Governor Axtell and District Attorney Thomas B. Catron.[22]

Angel, who was hoping to obtain a federal appointment, accepted the assignment and on April 15 began making arrangements to travel to Santa Fe. On April 16, the attorney general wrote to John Sherman, U.S. marshal for New Mexico, identifying Angel as having been authorized "to make certain investigations in matters in New Mexico in which the United States is concerned." The news of Angel's impending arrival spread rapidly.

He reached Santa Fe on May 4, coming down from El Moro by buckboard, and installed himself in the Exchange Hotel. That same day, the attorney general wrote asking him to obtain certain information concerning the Una de Gato Grant and also the murder at Las Vegas of Pierre Buisson.[23]

After a week in Santa Fe, during which time he called upon Axtell, Catron, Sherman, and others to explain his mission, Angel left for Lincoln County. He arrived on the heels of yet another outbreak of violence.

FIG. 59. Frank Warner Angel, 1868. Photographer unknown. This law-school graduation photograph was taken when Angel was twenty-three. He was ten years older at the time of his investigation.

On May 14, the Regulators, made "lawful" again by their new "captain" and Copeland deputy, Doc Scurlock, swept down on the Dolan-Riley cattle camp at Black River. This was the "party of about 30" which Widenmann had said was organizing in Lincoln on May 11, ostensibly to retrieve MacNab's and Saunders's horses and others stolen from the Tunstall ranch.

Driving off the men who were guarding the livestock, killing Manuel Segovia, alias "The Indian"—unfounded reports said a teenage boy and a man named Wair (Billy Wier) were also killed—as well as wounding two others, the Regulators then gathered up all the horses and mules, regardless of ownership, and drove them back to Lincoln.[24] Not only had they retrieved the stolen animals, but they had struck another blow to avenge Tunstall: Segovia had been in the February 18 posse.

The *New Mexican* report—of course—puts a slightly different face on the raid. Copeland, it said, had sent "a body of about thirty armed men under a notorious outlaw and assassin as his deputy to obtain a pony said to belong to the estate of the young man Morton, whom these same men had murdered while a prisoner in their hands, *and upon whose estate they were now administering*. They went armed with an order of the probate judge to take this pony. That is what they ostensibly went to do in the name of law and order."[25]

Having scattered the cattle and stolen the horses, the newspaper reported, the Scurlock party "proceeded, as usual, to get drunk and 'whoop up' the country at their leisure." Of all this, and the killing or killings, Widenmann, writing to the Tunstalls that evening, says nothing; but he had no scruples about taking the credit. "It gives me great pleasure to inform you," he said,

that of the 6 horses reported stolen in my last letter I have succeeded in recovering 4 and have some hopes of getting these back also. It was at first my intention of moving the cattle nearer town but on consideration I have abandoned the plan. If I moved the cattle many of the young calves would be lost and it would be almost impossible to hold the herd on a new range without going to an unwarranted expense. It would cost at least $250—or $300—and even if I should succeed in retaining them all they would greatly deteriorate in value. I have therefore resolved to hold them at the ranch on the Feliz under close herd and corral them every night. This will make it impossible for them to be stolen unless a large party comes to take them and if this is done, though I think there is very little danger of it, I can be after them within 12 hours of the time they are taken. In managing in this way the expenses will not be one half of what they would be if I brought them near here, and the cattle and horses will be in better condition.

As poor Dick Brewer's cattle are also at the ranch and the administrator of his estate desires to take them to his ranch preparatory to their being sold, a party of us go to the ranch tonight to seperate them. It is rather a dangerous trip but then it must be done and with Gods help we will get through all right.[26]

Widenmann had just finished his letter when the mails arrived bringing J. P. Tunstall's letter of April 23. He scribbled a postscript to the effect that the trip to the Feliz would take about four or five days, and, obviously in reply to a question, added that "the title deeds to the land are in the safe at my side and as I sleep in the same room there is no danger of their being stolen. But they are all recorded and even if stolen would be of no value to the thief and could easily be duplicated by the land office."

Strangely, neither Widenmann nor McSween saw fit at this time to tell the Tunstalls that Department of Justice investigator Frank W. Angel was in Lincoln, or that both of them were making sure that a large body of citizens was on hand to provide affidavits. Indeed, Widenmann besought the aid, via the columns of the *Cimarron News & Press,* of "every man and woman in New Mexico knowing the damaging facts against U.S. officials."[27]

What effect his exhortations had, if any, is uncertain; however, he and McSween, after the latter's return on May 25, threw themselves wholeheartedly behind Angel. Before the end of the month, John Middleton, George van Sickle, Godfrey Gauss, Henry Brown, and William Bonney had appeared to make statements before John Wilson. A great many of these affidavits are in the handwriting of McSween, Corbet, or Widenmann; the fighting men like Middleton and the Kid merely signed them. Juan Patrón and Jose Montaño gave depositions on May 22 before Morris J. Bernstein, who among his many other hats also wore that of notary public. Alexander McSween, Assistant Surgeon Appel, Sam Perry, Wallace Olinger, Bob Beckwith, and Jimmy Dolan were among those whom Angel interviewed personally.

On May 19, Taylor Ealy recorded hearing that Widenmann had been killed.[28] The rumor proved false, as the next day Widenmann returned to Lincoln, bringing Dick Brewer's cattle with him. It is possible he had some kind of run-in with the Seven Rivers warriors, who were at Johnson's ranch at the time of the Regulator raid. Mention of an incident involving "19 of Dolan's cutthroats" appears in Widenmann's May 27 letter to J. P. Tunstall; perhaps this was the basis for the rumor that he had been killed, which was sent to the *New Mexican* and repeated in the *Las Vegas Gazette* at this time.

> Everything is quiet in Lincoln County. A truce seems to have been tacitly agreed upon. The telegram to the *New Mexican* reporting the death of Sam Smith, Newcomb, Widenmann and others, was a canard. Easton has charge of Murphy, Dolan and Riley's house. McSween is at Chisum's ranch. W. H. Johnson and his party from Seven Rivers are at the Indian Agency. Murphy has sold his ranch at the Carrizo Springs to the Hall Brothers, young Englishmen with capital, for the sum of $18,000.[29]

The "quiet" of Lincoln County was soon to be shattered. During the weeks he was in Santa Fe getting Murphy settled in, Jimmy Dolan had also done some serious thinking. He knew perfectly well that to dominate Lincoln County his

PROCLAMATION
BY THE GOVERNOR.

For the information of all the citizens of Lincoln County I do hereby make this Public Proclamation:

First---John N. Copeland, Esq., appointed Sheriff by the County Commissioners, having failed for more than thirty days to file his bond as Collector of Taxes, is hereby removed from the office of Sheriff, and I have appointed **GEORGE W. PEPPIN**, Esq., Sheriff of Lincoln County. This has been done in compliance with the laws, passed at the twenty-second session of the Legislative Assembly, relating to Sheriffs.

Second---I command all men and bodies of men, now under arms and traveling about the county, to disarm and return to their homes and their usual pursuits, and so long as the present Sheriff has authority to call upon U. S. troops for assistance, not to act as a sheriff's posse.

And, in conclusion, I urge upon all good citizens to submit to the law, remembering that violence begets violence, and that they who take the sword shall perish by the sword.

S. B. AXTELL,
Governor of New Mexico.

FIG. 60. Axtell's proclamation removing Copeland.

people had to have the support of the military. But the military could support only the elected or appointed sheriff, and the sheriff was unquestionably hostile to the House and sympathetic to the McSween party. The solution was simple: get rid of the sheriff. But how?

Dolan was clever, devious, and persuasive. It is not too difficult to imagine him in creative discussions with the House's most influential friends: Catron,

Thornton, Axtell, Murphy, and Dolan constituted a powerful brain trust, which would not have taken too long to realize that there was a way to be shut of Copeland.

The law required a new sheriff to post bond as tax collector. Copeland had failed to do so inside the required thirty days. There was a perfectly good reason for this, of course: conditions in Lincoln had made it impossible for anyone even to compile the tax lists needed to assess the amount of the bond. No matter: Copeland had failed to file before the deadline, and on that omission the governor could act. On May 28, Axtell promulgated yet another proclamation, the main purpose of which was to remove Copeland and appoint as sheriff in his place George W. Peppin (fig. 60).[30] Albeit on a technicality, the tables had been turned yet again.

CHAPTER 24

WAR: MCSWEEN EMBATTLED

THE appointment of Peppin as sheriff was bad news for the McSween faction. Their discomfiture was noted by one of the more sardonic of Lincoln's letter writers, the anonymous party who signed himself "El Gato."[1] On May 10 he gave the *New Mexican* a somewhat slanted but nonetheless telling update on events.

The position taken by the McSween party was that the men who joined the Seven Rivers posse led by Deputy Johnson did so in order to kill Isaac Ellis, John Copeland, and McSween. Speaking for the other side, "El Gato" claimed they had come to Lincoln to "report to our new and inefficient Sheriff, John Copeland, to aid and assist him in serving the warrants he held in his possession against the murderers of Brady, Hindman, Roberts and others." On their way they killed MacNab and captured Frank Coe and Ab Saunders who "begged like dogs for their lives."

> This, however, was unnecessary; their captors were no hired assassins fighting for pay. No, on the contrary, they are the men whose names head the tax list of this unfortunate county; men who leaving their families, their homes, and their properties, have come over a hundred and fifty miles, willing to sacrifice their lives in order to restore peace to this distracted section of the territory.
>
> On arriving at Lincoln they found the new sheriff in town carousing with the very men whom he was bound to arrest under writs issued by the court on indictments which even McSween's grand jury was compelled to find.[2] At this sight their indignation knew no bounds, but with a praise-worthy desire to respect the law, they sent to Copeland and placed their lives and services at his disposal, should he attempt to do his duty and serve the warrants which he at that time carried in his pocket. To use a vulgar phrase, "he was having a good time," and it would be ingratitude of the blackest kind should he arrest and confine the gentlemen who were providing him with amusement.
>
> He immediately gathered McSween's band of assassins and led them to the attack, having in the meantime sent for U.S. troops. Johnson and his men were unwilling to fight the authorities and more unwilling to surrender to McSween's butchers; and retreated to the mountains until the arrival of the troops, when they immediately surrendered to Lieut. G. W. Smith, 9th Cavalry. On their arrival at Fort Stanton they immediately made affidavits and had warrants issued against the men who fired on them when they entered the town. These warrants were issued by the Justice of the Peace at Blazer's Mill, Mr. Easton. Some of them were served nominally by Copeland with the assistance of the military, but in reality by officers in command

of the detachment. Copeland was compelled to accompany this expedition by the firm and determined action of Col. Dudley, commanding Fort Stanton, and this alone can account for the fact of his once having attempted to do his duty. When the day arrived for the trial of these cases Mr. Easton, from motives unknown to your correspondent, handed in his resignation and refused to try the cases. Both parties who had until now been under arrest were therefore released.

This is the state of affairs at present; the two parties are at liberty, and a desperate fight is daily expected. As a natural consequence of the present state of affairs, there are a thousand and one rumors afloat; among the principal are the following:

1st. That McSween has paid John Copeland $3000 for acting as sheriff.[3]

2d. That McSween has paid various sums to procure false evidence against Dolan and Riley.

3d. That McSween has hired the services of a Presbyterian minister to give his actions a religious flavor.

These rumors I give with all due reserve. The only one corroborated is the first, and that is, as far as I can learn, grounded on a statement made by Copeland while under the influence of liquor. "In vino veritas."

This was a carefully weighted attack. By inferring that the Seven Rivers posse was composed exclusively of decent, taxpaying citizens—some were, but as many were not—the opposing party could be vilified as "hired assassins fighting for pay." "El Gato" implies that the Blazer's Mill affidavits were sworn by the entire posse— a group of public-spirited men acting in concert and without malice. In fact the warrants were issued on testimony sworn by George Peppin and Billy Mathews, widely known as "Dolan's affidavit men."

As for the "rumors," "El Gato" was seeding fertile ground. Copeland was living at the McSween house, and his sympathies were a matter of common knowledge; it was not difficult to believe that McSween was paying him handsomely, or that the lawyer was buying perjured testimony against Dolan and Riley. Why he should have wanted to give his actions a religious flavor, however, is not explained.

In Santa Fe, Murphy and Dolan added their weight to the lists with letters to the *New Mexican*, attacking John S. Crouch and Albert Fountain of the *Independent* for the inaccuracy of editorials the paper had published concerning Lincoln County affairs.[4] Indeed, although most of his letter was couched in surprisingly mild terms, Murphy went so far as to threaten a libel suit. It would have made for some interesting litigation.

Meanwhile, Robert Widenmann was having trouble with the mails. He was not the only one. As Taylor Ealy testified, "it was a trying matter for others as well as myself to go for our mail to the Dolan, Riley headquarters, as the Post Office was standing and sitting full of men with revolvers, and to people who did not have any use for those things, it seemd quite out of place in a U.S.P.O.[5] This was a daily occurrence, and as there seemed no stop to it after a time I quit going for my mail."

Apparently some of Widenmann's letters to Tunstall's father had not gotten through; the old man was to aver later that several of his more important letters addressed to Lincoln were never delivered. Acknowledging on May 27 receipt of a letter from London dated May 2, Widenmann said, "I am unable to find where our letters are detained, the mails have been robbed several times lately, and this may be one cause. We hope to fathom the difficulty before long though."[6]

J. P. Tunstall had sent Widenmann copies of correspondence he had exchanged with San Francisco lawyer Guy McLellan. The attorney, a personal friend of Governor Axtell, had expressed reservations about the accusations leveled against him.[7] Widenmann assured Tunstall Sr. "that the judgment passed on the U.S. and Territorial officials of this Territory" would hold good. To substantiate his opinion, he forwarded a copy of District Attorney Rynerson's letter to his "Friends Riley and Dolan," written a few days before the murder of Tunstall, which letter, said Widenmann—and the verb is important—had been "captured by us shortly after dear Harrie's death."

J. P. Tunstall had asked about letters sent by him to his son which would have arrived after John's death. These, Widenmann reported, had been

> received by Mr. Ellis and by him opened, he probably thinking that they contained some matter of importance. I enclose them as directed. There are a large number of dear Harrie's letters from home here. Soon after his death I collected them and placed them under lock and key. The Probate Judge once wished to have them but I refused to give them up, telling him that I would not have them profaned by strangers being allowed to read them. It would make too large a package to send them by mail and I will therefore, unless otherwise directed by you, bring them with me.[8]

Both the *Las Vegas Gazette* and Taylor Ealy, it will be recalled, had recorded the rumor that Widenmann had been killed along with Sam Smith and John Newcomb. Widenmann's letter indicates the source of that rumor.

> At the ranch I found things quiet and in good shape, but had a narrow escape from 19 of Dolan's cutthroats who were in the neighbourhood. I stayed at the ranch until they left for the Pecos River so as to make sure that they did not steal any of the horses or cattle. We [presumably Widenmann had taken Newcomb and Smith along as herders] brought poor Dick's cattle away from the ranch and [they] are now in the hands of the administrators of his estate.

His being appointed administrator of Tunstall's estate would necessitate a delay in his departure for England, Widenmann continued.

> I start for Mesilla in about a week and as I am assured by all parties that this is a plan to get me murdered, I am going to take all possible precautions; the balance I must leave in God's hands.
>
> The U.S. central Government has sent out a Mr. Angel from New York who is now here, to investigate dear Harrie's death and also all territorial and government officials. He gives me to understand that, no sooner had he reached Santa Fe, than the ring there offered to bribe him. I think that up to date that has not been accomplished, and Mr. Angel says that if we will give him the testimony, he will have every U.S. officer from the Governor down removed providing the testimony will warrant. You can imagine that we will leave no stone unturned.
>
> Catrone, the U.S. attys partner [W. T. Thornton] who is now here, advises me to leave the country. On being asked his reason for this he said that a large party throughout the Territory (the ring of course) were bound to kill me and would kill me because I brought too many accusations against them, and brought them out flatfooted without any reserve. My work in Washington is beginning to tell on them and I should not at any time be astonished to be shot. But I am using all possible caution and should they attempt to kill me hope to get a shot at the would be murderers.

It would seem that Frank Angel was something of a diplomat as well as a lawyer, more than able to keep to himself the opinions he formed while taking testimony.[9] Widenmann obviously had no idea of Angel's assessment of him; the investigator was later to write, "Given to boasting—veracity doubtful," thus capturing the essence of the fellow in five words.

On June 3, Widenmann wrote J. P. Tunstall another long letter, this one mainly concerned with the management of the estate.[10] The balance now credited to it, he reported, was up by $477.59, this being the healthy 40 percent net profit on $1,206.42 worth of merchandise sold since the end of February. José Montaño had presented a bill against the estate for $192.20, and Isaac Ellis his for some $250. Widenmann said he had asked them to swear their bill because

> besides the merchandise bought, they charge $160 for corn and $160 for board furnished the men who are after dear Harrie's murderers who were here to protect the town when it was attacked and at other times; my understanding had heretofore been that all parties were to beare these expenses together, each his part, and I therefore consider the above charges exhorbitant. Mr. Ellis also charges $50 for taking care of the horses here, while he was in charge [of the estate] and $138 for his fees as administrator.

Obviously Isaac Ellis subscribed to the precept once expressed by John Tunstall of not losing a dollar for the sake of sentiment. His house and store were the Regulators' commissary in Lincoln, and he was sympathetic to their cause; but business was business.

Widenmann went on to report that about $450 worth of lumber with which to put a roof on the Tunstall store had been bought and paid for before John's death. Confident the family would sanction his carrying out Tunstall's original plan, Widenmann had contracted with a local carpenter, Daniel Huff, to do the work for $275.[11] Both the carpenter and the further $200 worth of lumber necessary to complete the job would be paid in goods. Another expense looming was the projected purchase of Brewer's cattle, which would probably soon be sold "as you are about the only creditor." He went on, "Everything is quiet here and Mr. Angel, the gentleman sent out here to investigate things, is busily engaged taking testimony. Mr. McSween's and my testimony covers about 250 pages and the citizens are now pouring in to give their evidence. If our present endeavours are not crowned with success it will not be our fault; we are doing our utmost."

He was still not sure exactly when he would leave for Mesilla, and wished that "disagreeable" trip was over with. At this point, Widenmann gives a picture of himself somewhat at variance with that of the bandoliered gunfighter he had earlier described. "Mr. Angel and the business keep me thoroughly occupied during the day, and I am at work nearly every evening until 11 or 12 0'cl Cooking and writing business letters. I am thankful that I have plenty of work, for were I forced to remain idle, thinking of the murderous villains who are pestering us, would drive me mad with anger."

On June 5, McSween dashed off a hasty letter to J. P. Tunstall. The pressure he was under is as evident in his handwriting as it is absent in Widenmann's. The contents of this letter confirm that there was no comparison of notes between the two men. Nonetheless, he was in good spirits, because they had "succeeded in getting the U.S. Government to appoint and send out" a gentleman from N.Y. to inquire into the murder of John. For the past week or ten days I have been very busy in taking testimony. Parties for years in the employ of Murphy have testified that sentence of death had been passed on your son and myself long before he was killed. One man testified that Dolan, of the Murphy & Co. party before John was killed offered him $1000—if he would kill me as I would be leaving my house in the morning for my office. It's notorious that I have never owned or carried a more formidable weapon than a penknife and it would be an easy matter to kill me.

I have no doubt but that the U.S. Govt as the result of the investigation will be obliged to award you a large sum for your son's death. The testimony will be as full as it can be made.

On their side there has been killed on account of John's death Morton, Baker, Roberts, Hill—Evans crippled and now in U.S. Hospital—Brady, Hindman, and two others whose name is unknown—but *helped* murder John.

Full particulars of the trouble, cause and result will shortly be published by Officers of this County and will be sent you. There is not much use in sending Newspapers having excited paragraphs for the purpose of making them enterprising and spicy when they are ignorant of the status of things here.

On our side were killed Brewer & McNab, wounded badly— [indecipherable: Lothe?], Middleton, Coe, Antrim, French and Bowdre and Sanders.

I think the Estate is above, not under, what I represented. I have not received a dollar from anyone yet. Mr. Ellis is in business and is not in a condition to advance anything. It takes time to realize on assets here with profit, consisting, as they do, of stock and produce.

P.S. Mr. W. has the *sole* management of the Estate. By way of advising, I'll do all I can. Will try and send particulars of Brewer's death by next mail and will also write my ideas about a monument for John. [12]

Strangely, McSween made no mention of the governor's proclamation dismissing Copeland and appointing George Peppin sheriff, although newspapers containing the text of that document had arrived in Lincoln the preceding day, June 4. [13] Needless to say, they threw the town into a ferment.

There was no question where Peppin's allegiance lay: all Lincoln knew he was in Dolan's pocket. As Brady's deputy, Peppin had narrowly escaped death in the April ambush; he had also been among the crowd that killed MacNab at the Fritz ranch. His appointment was seen as conclusive proof that Thomas B. Catron— via Axtell—was furnishing the Murphy-Dolan cause all the assistance he could.

Widenmann had his say on the subject when he got around to telling J. P. Tunstall the news on June 11. "Affairs have somewhat changed here," he began.

Last Tuesday morning we were astonished to see in the papers what purported to be a governors proclamation though having neither date, place of issue, Territorial seal, nor being countersigned by the Secretary of State. I send you one of the papers containing this interesting document. You will see by the same that our present sheriff, an honest and honorable man, has been dismissed and one Geo. W. Peppin put in his place. Our objections to this are, first that under the laws of this Territory, the Governor has neither the power nor the right to do this. Second: that this Peppin is one of the murderers of McNab. Third: that he is one of a band of thieves and murderers. Fourth: that he is a highwayman and at the present time one of a party of men who are waylaying the roads for the purpose of killing me and others. I should think these sufficient reasons to object to his appointment. Many more can be given though if desired. This act of the Governor's shows him and the other officials of this Territory in their true light, and it is difficult to see what the result may be. I think, though, that if we give them enough rope they will hang themselves. Mr. Angel, who is investigating the conduct of officials in this Territory seemed rather disgusted with their proceedings when I last saw him. May he prove an angel to us not only in name, but in deed.[14]

On June 7, a large detachment of troops commanded by Captain Purington started down to Roswell to safeguard Catron's cattle. Cynics did not fail to note that soldiers could be quickly put in the field as "Catron's cowboys" when the request came from the right quarter.

There was a lull, but it was shortlived; the new sheriff wasted no time in mounting his campaign against the McSween party. His first task was to appoint a staff of deputies to assist him: John Long, Marion Turner, Buck Powell, and Jose Chavez y Baca were duly sworn. With these as his right-hand men, Peppin began gathering together a posse to serve not only civil warrants but also the federal warrants he now held as deputy U.S. marshal. These, naming more or less all of the original Regulator group, had been issued in connection with the killing of Roberts on the Mescalero Apache Reservation.

How much terror these arrangements threw into the hearts of the Regulators may be gauged from a letter John Middleton wrote to Buck Powell on June 3.

Dear Friend Buck, Dear Sir,

I want to ask you a few questions, will you please answer them.

Where do you live at?

Are you a citizen of Lincoln co.

Did you ever live in Lincoln co.

Do you and your posse think we are a set of damned fools, that we would recognize you as a deputy sheriff, if you do you are badly fooled.

Look at the Governor's proclamation and see what he says. dont he [say] all citizens to go home and lay down his arms, and not allow themselves to be summoned as a sheriff's posse. Look at Peppin the first thing he did was to go into the Plaza with a band of masked men and a posse do you call this wrong or right, if right where is the wrong?

Buck if you had staid on your own range and took no hand in this thing you would never Been Molested the same with many others, do you think that a half a dozen of us would run from the posse you have—we would like to see them too well. Come and you can find us. I want to lift the Belt John B[eckwith] has on. We have run them too often to try to get out of the way. Please answer this and tell me all the news, and what you think of these lines.[15]

McSween's letters to Carl Schurz and the Presbyterian Board of Missions had also borne fruit; on June 13, the Department of the Interior's Indian inspector, E. C. Watkins, arrived at the Mescalero reservation to investigate the allegations made against Godfroy. For a fortnight, Watkins diligently took affidavits and examined the records of the agency.[16] His discursive report, supplemented by material gathered by Frank Angel, who completed the investigation when Watkins was reassigned, was submitted on June 27 to Ezra A. Hayt, commissioner of Indian affairs. It was sufficiently damning to result in the eventual removal of Godfroy; but in the process it did nothing to bolster the causes of either Alexander McSween or John Chisum.

The latter had entered a $47,000 claim for reimbursement for Mescalero depredations, notably the loss of his entire horse herd in 1875. Jessie Evans, still recuperating under the wing of the officers of the fort, made a particularly damaging affidavit in which he claimed that Chisum had employed him and others to steal horses from the Indians, providing horses and arms for them to do it.[17] About 140 or 150 horses had been run off since 1873; one raid alone netted 60.

Watkins then asked if Evans connected McSween with these thefts.

> Yes sir I do, he was acting as Agent for Mr. Chisum since 1873. I have heard him talk with the men who were engaged in stealing horses and in such a way as to connect him with Mr. Chisum. I have known of Mr. McSween's buying stolen horses and paying for them do not know whether for himself or as Agent for Mr. Chisum. Mr. McSween has made me offers to engage in stealing horses the same as Mr. Chisum did.

Watkins asked Evans whether McSween had helped him to escape from the Lincoln jail in October 1877. "Yes. Mr. McSween and party helped us out. I and the boys with me rode his horses from his ranche with his consent, he told us to take his horses and anything else he had. We took his horses, saddles, and bridles, also arms we returned the horses but did not return the arms."

Confirming that McSween had bought the horses knowing them to have been stolen from the Indians, Jessie scrawled an approximation of a signature with his left hand. Watkins added a postscript: "The above statement was made by Jessie Evans—a notorious horse thief—while under the charge of the U.S. Marshal and suffering from a wound received while attempting to rob a [wagon] train. Although a horse thief he has the reputation for telling the truth."

Inspector Watkins evinces a touching faith in his fellow man, but the evidence he gathered cannot be dismissed out of hand. The names of Frank Baker, Tom Hill, Frank Rivers [John Long], Jim McDaniels, and Marion Turner were prominent among those said to have been hired by Chisum specifically to rustle horses.

Andrew Boyle and others testified that McSween had offered to buy cattle without questioning their provenance providing they were not Chisum's.[18] Inspector Watkins commented drily that he had found it difficult to contact McSween, "the head and moving spirit of a Banditti [a gang of bandits]," because the attorney had fled to the mountains. He had not persisted because Colonel Dudley had assured him that the lawyer was "a dangerous, unreliable man whose reputation was very bad and who could not be believed under oath where his own interests were concerned."

Insofar as it had been charged that the Indians were being systematically robbed by Godfroy, Dolan, and Riley, Watkins took the testimony of Taylor Ealy, who claimed to have "seen groceries at Dolan and Riley's store said to have been brought from the Agency. His evidence is mostly hearsay," wrote Watkins. "Apparently he is much under the influence of McSween in whose family he has been living. He is the man whom McSween desired to have appointed Agent in case Godfroy was removed."[19]

Actually, in his testimony Ealy had denied any interest in the post of Indian agent; it will be recalled that McSween had suggested Widenmann for the job. Nevertheless, Watkins was able to establish that Godfroy had "loaned" government supplies to Dolan and Riley, to Pat Coghlan, and to Doctor Blazer. Godfroy contended that this was common practice on all reservations, and that the supplies were invariably returned. However, when Watkins discovered that no record of any of these transactions had ever been kept, and that the official count of

Apaches receiving rations at the agency was less than 400, rather than the 1,150 Godfroy had been reporting, he drew his own conclusions.[20] These, augmented by the findings of Frank Angel, were more than sufficient to lead to Godfroy's downfall.

No mention of any of this appears in Robert Widenmann's letter to the Tunstalls of June 11.[21] If it is read with the knowledge that Peppin's mercenaries were forgathering, however, Widenmann's relief at obtaining an escort to Mesilla is easy to understand.

> I fear I shall not be able to start for England as soon as I first thought I would. Next Thursday the 13th inst., I start for Mesilla, and am happy to inform you that I think the trip will be less dangerous since I have succeeded in obtaining a military escort there and back. All the roads leading to Mesilla are blocked by Dolan and Riley's cuthroats, but with a military escort I do not think there is as much danger. Dolan and Riley are now at Mesilla and it is at that place that I think we will have trouble, if we do not have an open fight there I will be much astonished.

He was anxious, he said, to settle the debts of the estate and withdraw it from the probate court before he left. Apparently J. P. Tunstall had asked him whether he would need money for the trip; Widenmann airily assured him that

> the business can furnish that when required. On the other hand I would not advise giving away money on the estate under any circumstances. Money in this country brings from 18 to 25 % per annum which rate of interest is ruinous. I think things can be arranged easier.—
>
> From a statement of Mr. R. D. Hunter's a/c made out a few days ago, and embracing also the accounts of his employees, I find that there are $3028.46 due from him. Then I think that some of the notes can be collected soon and these with the above mentioned account will enable me to clear off the indebtedness of $653.98, as per my last statement. Then I have a plan by which the cattle can be sold at reasonable figures, which will enable me to pay Mr. McSween's claim. I can not give you the cattle plan, having good reasons to fear, that most of my letters are tampered with, no difference whether registered or not.

Sheriff Peppin's posse was ready to ride.[22] It consisted of about twenty men, many of whom had come to Lincoln under the banner of that malodorous thug John Kinney, said to have been sent to Dolan's aid by his friend Rynerson. On June 18, in his role of deputy U.S. marshal, Peppin made a formal request for military assistance in arresting McSween and his supporters.[23] Unable to refuse aid to a federal officer, Dudley sent a detachment of twenty-seven men commanded by Lieutenant Goodwin.

Peppin met the soldiers about halfway between the fort and Lincoln. When Goodwin saw the caliber of Peppin's possemen, he flatly refused to accompany the posse unless Peppin got rid of Kinney and his bandits.[24] Peppin promised to do so, and the party moved on towards Lincoln.

Word of its impending arrival had already reached the town, creating great uneasiness. Old John Wilson offered the courthouse and the land it stood on to Taylor Ealy for two thousand dollars and, when Ealy demurred, dropped the price to seven hundred and a span of mules.[25] A general exodus of citizens took place over the following few days: in fear of gratuitous assassination, a number of them, including John Copeland, Florencio Gonzales, and Juan Patrón, sought the safety of the fort.

There is understandable confusion about the movements both of Peppin's posses and the McSween crowd around this time; but there seems no doubt that Peppin took control of the town about June 20 and held it until July 14.[26] How much control Peppin actually had is another matter: the *Independent* of June 22 noted that

> Colonel John Kinney holds Lincoln, and Lincoln, I regret to say, presents an appearance as melancholy as an old toper when about to join the Sons of Temperance.
>
> While a dozen or so graveyards scattered around town adds a little cheerfulness to the place, nevertheless, notwithstanding the late arrival of a $900 piano for Mrs. McSween and a $500 set of Scotch bagpipes for Honest Mac, Lincoln is terribly dull.[27]

McSween was apparently not among those who fled from Lincoln at the approach of the Peppin-Kinney posse.[28] On June 19, he mortgaged his wife's recently arrived Beatty grand piano—the same one sardonically referred to above—to Isaac Ellis for five hundred dollars, presumably to pay his fighting men the three dollars a day it was said they received.

Five days later, he wrote his last letter to the Tunstalls. Dated Lincoln, June 24, it implies he was still at that place in spite of the presence of his enemies. In it he again asked for the money Tunstall "owed" him, now so desperately needed to fund his cause. Without a word about his own difficulties, he began by offering advice on the family's plan to erect a tombstone over John Tunstall's grave.

> Any design of monument you may suggest can be executed in this country. I suggest that you entrust securing such as you want to Mr. Eagle, Cashr. Merchants' National Bank. St. Louis, Mo. He was a friend of John's and could and would attend to the matter in person. St. Louis is the nearest point that I know of where acceptable work could be secured, and the result [?] would be more satisfactory if conducted in person than by mail.
>
> The evidence in regard to the murder of John has been taken and I have no doubt but that it's of such a character as will entitle you to an indemnity. Mr. Angel, the commissioner, called upon me today and said that Mr. Tunstall was killed by a mob. Many of the old mob have come in again and are determined to kill me. In view of this Mr. Angel and other friends here advise me to leave for a while. I'll go off about 65 miles where, I think, I'll be safer.
>
> I have not received anything from the Estate as yet. Mr. Widenmann has only produce on hand, and he thinks he can do better for the Estate than sell it now. The same is true of the cattle. I rec'd nothing as yet from any one. I have spent nearly all my available means in prosecuting the murderers and I wish you could advance me the amount itemized on my Pass Book with John, if you can possibly do it. I regret having to make this appeal to you, but my expense has been fearful. If you can, without injury to yourself, remit me this amount I'll cheerfully keep expending until I bring all these fellows to justice.
>
> *Do this if you can*[29]

The letter was written on what had in happier times been Lincoln's noisiest and most festive holiday, St. John's Day; if the annual fiesta was observed at all, it was surely a more muted affair than usual.[30] Sometime during the day McSween left town, apparently intending to go to Chisum's; he ended up at San Patricio.

It appears he and his bodyguards ran into some of Peppin's men en route to the Pecos, since the following day Doctor Ealy recorded in his diary that there had been fighting on the Ruidoso and that the sheriff's posse came in at dark.[31]

Next day, June 26, Peppin authorized John Long to raise another posse to arrest McSween and his adherents on the warrants Peppin held; they left that evening for San Patricio. A "private letter" from Lincoln to the *New Mexican* describes ensuing events:

"The town was surrounded about daylight. . . . [A] thorough search was made and no one found; when the posse was leaving they saw a man crossing a wheat field where he had evidently slept during the night; it was George Washington, one of the accessories to the murder of Sheriff Brady; he turned to run, but a few shots stopped his flight, and he surrendered and gave his gun to one of the posse and begged for his life. He is now a prisoner here. After leaving San Patricio the posse ran into eleven more of the assassins, consisting according to Washington's statement of A. A. McSween, John Copeland, Waite, Kid, Bowdre, Jim French, Scroggins, 'Dirty Steve' [Stephens], Jesus Rodriguez, Atanacio Martinez and Eusebio Sanchez. Several shots were exchanged but no one was hurt on either side. As the posse was only six in number, a courier was dispatched for the troops, but they arrived too late to effect a capture. Washington will be examined by Judge Angell in the morning, and his testimony taken down. From what Washington had already stated it is positive that Widerman was with the party that murdered Brady and fired one of the fatal bullets."

From the above [the newspaper editorialized] it appears that McSween has at last thrown off the mask and is now *openly* operating with the band of assassins who have so long made Lincoln county the theatre of their crimes and outrages. It is to be hoped that Sheriff Peppin will not stop until he has the whole gang, including the villainous and unscrupulous leaders, with the strong grasp of the law that they may suffer the just punishment of their crimes.[32]

Sheriff Peppin was certainly doing his best to oblige.[33] On the 27th, he appeared at Fort Stanton to make an affidavit before Capt. Thomas Blair to the effect that Long's posse "had been resisted in trying to execute said warrants and had been fired upon by certain persons against whom said warrants had been issued and that said deputy and his posse had two horses shot by said persons so resisting the said deputy, and unless he had assistance they would not be able to enforce the said warrants and prevent blood shed."

By the time the troops were in the field, word came in that McSween and his men had retreated in the direction of the Pecos. Long's posse returned to Lincoln, where the deputy proceeded to swear affidavits against McSween and the Kid, whom he claimed to have recognized, charging assault with intent to kill. The implication is that for the first time in his life, McSween was carrying a firearm.[34]

At this juncture, a further set of representations was made to President Hayes and Secretary of the Interior Carl Schurz, probably orchestrated by Montague R. Leverson, now beginning to see himself as a natural appointee for the governorship of New Mexico.[35] The first salvo was a long letter to Hayes from Coe's ranch, Chicores Park, Colfax County, dated June 22. The writers were "two residents of Lincoln County," Jasper N. Coe and one J. Isaacs. "Jap" Coe was Frank Coe's brother; Ab Saunders had been his brother-in-law. His claim to be a resident of Lincoln County was marginally stronger than that of Isaacs, an artist from New

Jersey who by his own account had been there only four months. Nevertheless, Coe said,

> after incurring the greatest peril to life and property at the hands of the thieves and murderers whom the Governor and the U.S. troops aid and abet in their crimes [we] have succeeded in bringing whole skins to this section where the brother of one of us possesses this ranch. We respectfully desire to call your attention to the necessity of immediately removing the present Governor of New Mexico, unless in your Excellency's opinion the people of the territory are to be regarded as his peonage.

The letter went on to cover much of the ground already plowed by Leverson: the governor's proclamation removing Copeland and substituting Peppin, the failure to apprehend Tunstall's murderers, the danger of Angel's being either bought off or bumped off—a familiar threnody. This letter was forwarded via the office of Carl Schurz the following day. To that already overburdened worthy, artist Isaacs addressed himself as follows:

> I have joined with Mr. Coe in a letter to the president, forwarded to your care by this mail, but I think it right to explain that although I have been resident in Lincoln Co. for the last four months, I did not go there with the intention of making it my home. I hail from New Jersey, and am by profession an artist. I have been travelling through California, Arizona and Dona Ana & Lincoln Co's. New Mexico, for the purpose of making sketches, and seeing the deplorable state of affairs existing in this territory, I made inquiries for myself and deemed it to be my duty as an American citizen, and I hope an honest man, to join in any effort which might be made to rescue the people of the territory from the thieving and murdering bands to which unfortunately they were handed over by the late administration, while their continuance in office is a *lasting stigma upon the present.* Wherever I have been I have heard the name of Dr. Leverson of Douglas Co. Colorado spoken as that of one who had done the most signal services to the people, and as a gentleman they would rejoice to see appointed Governor, and further that if the appointment of the Governor were determined by the desire to do what would benefit the people, he would certainly be appointed, and they feel confident that he would restore peace and order throughout the country within thirty days. . . .
>
> Ascertain from Mr. Angel whether I have correctly represented the opinion of the people and ask his own estimate of Dr. Leverson, and if you find that I have correctly represented the facts, his appointment to be Governor would be a noble illustration of the president's administration, and rescue the country from the deplorable condition to which the U.S. officials have reduced it.

On June 28, as Jack Long's posse returned to Lincoln licking its wounds, Montague Leverson added a salvo, addressing Schurz from his ranch near Larkspur, Colo.

> It is with the greatest reluctance that I yield to the solicitations which have reached me in great numbers by every mail since my return, to address you once more upon the affairs of New Mexico. I have been the more reluctant to again intrude myself upon your notice because Mr. Angel, the gentleman charged to investigate & report to the administration, has impressed me most favorably, and inspired me with great confidence both in his ability and integrity.

By all indications, Leverson had made no such favorable impression upon Angel when the commissioner had visited him en route to New Mexico. At that time, Angel succinctly noted that the Englishman knew "6 times more than he can prove & 6 times more than any one else." Once again, Angel's diplomacy is in evidence; Leverson had no inkling of the investigator's private opinion of him.

Once more trumpeting his services both to the Union during the Civil War, which he claimed the Hon. Charles Francis Adams had declared "worth an army corps," and to the Republican party since he had lived in the United States, Leverson appealed to Hayes, calling himself "a simple citizen whose only desire is to *see the right prevail.*"

He went on to cite the reasons why—in his humble opinion—Samuel B. Axtell should be removed from office: the governor's failure to maintain peace and order, his appointment of "Rynerson the murderer" as district attorney, his March proclamation in Lincoln, his dismissal of Copeland and substitution of Peppin, the use of troops to disarm honest men and leave thieves and murderers armed.

> It is impossible for me to express to you in a letter the mistrust & fear evinced by the people of the Territory, even in the bona fides of the present investigation, & I must in all honesty acknowledge that the past and present course even of the present administration affords but too much ground for such mistrust; nothing indeed but the very strong faith I have in *you* personally, in president Hayes and the very favorable impression produced upon me by Mr. Angel would have overcome like mistrust even on my part.

He then set forth in considerable detail what he described as "the causes of the present prevailing mistrust" of even Angel's bona fides: the fact that Axtell was continued in office, that troops were still being used to police civil matters, that charges leveled against the governor in 1877 had been disregarded and the affidavits given in confidence at that time betrayed to Stephen B. Elkins, "the brains of the Santa Fe ring." There was much, much more. What Leverson had in mind was a visit to Washington, paid for by the government, so that he could lay before the president a fuller statement than could be made in writing of "the oppression under which the honest and downtrodden citizens of New Mexico were laboring."

No such invitation appears to have been forthcoming. For the moment, at least, the loquacious Doctor Leverson fell silent.

CHAPTER 25

WAR: COLLISION COURSE

BOLD Rob Widenmann, the "walking Gatling gun," had been summoned to appear before the district court at La Mesilla on June 17 as a witness for the Territory against Jessie Evans, accused of murdering Tunstall.[1] Evans, in custody at Fort Stanton since being wounded and later arrested, had filed through his attorneys for a writ of habeas corpus on the grounds that he was being held illegally. Also summoned to La Mesilla were Juan Patrón (petit jury), George Washington and Atanacio Martinez (under bond to appear on charges of resisting an officer), George Robinson, Godfrey Gauss, and Jose Chaves y Chaves.

These, together with John Copeland, having official business before the court, petitioned Colonel Dudley for a military escort on the grounds that their lives would be in danger on the road.[2] Dudley agreed to furnish an escort if they would swear an affidavit to that effect, and on June 10 Patrón, Widenmann, Copeland, Washington, and Martinez so swore.

They were instructed to assemble at the fort on the morning of June 13, where a four-man escort, issued with twenty days' rations and one hundred rounds of ammunition each and commanded by a noncom from Company F, Ninth Cavalry, was waiting to escort them. The party, augmented by U.S. Marshal John Sherman and his deputy, David H. Montgomery, who had come down from Santa Fe to take some U.S. prisoners—notably Evans—to La Mesilla, left that day.[3] Jimmy Dolan was already there: he had left Santa Fe for the south on June 8.

Six weeks later, Robert Widenmann wrote J. P. Tunstall an account of subsequent events.[4] It is instructive that at no time does he mention any of the others summoned to appear with him.

> As I told you I came over here with a military escort which was to return with me, but no sooner had I arrived than T. B. Catron the head of the New Mexican ring, had the escort ordered back and then began cathauling me here. He soon found he had got hold of the wrong man and that he had better leave me in peace. Nevertheless I had trouble enough. He and his tools blocked all proceedings in court so that justice is out of the question, and then he had all the roads blocked so that I have not been able to get back to Lincoln. Coming over here I ran into a band of his cutthroats, and only quickness in covering the three leaders with my rifle until the soldiers came up saved my life.

Widenmann's slang, though arcane to our ears, is very apposite; to "cathaul" means to subject a person to prolonged, severe questioning, from the earlier literal sense of dragging a clawing cat down the bare back of someone tied prone. It was not Thomas Catron who gave him his "cathauling," however, but the giant Rynerson and diminutive Judge Warren Bristol. Examining him in the matter of Tunstall's murder, both gave Widenmann a very hard time.[5]

Widenmann related how he, Brewer, Bonney, Middleton, and Tunstall had been driving the horses towards Lincoln that February afternoon.

> We saw a large party coming after us, fifteen to twenty strong. We started to run to get out of their way. When within 300 yards of us they fired at us. I looked back and recognized Jessie Evans, Frank Baker, J. J. Dolan, Tom Hill, George Hindman, A. L. Roberts and Billy Morton. I ran into a ravine to the left of the mountain. Tunstall ran into a ravine to the right of the mountain. The party followed Tunstall. I had run some distance when I heard shots, on the other side of the mountain.
>
> Rynerson: Then you did not see defendant shoot at all?
> Widenmann: No, I could not see him at all.
> Rynerson: Did you ever hear defendant use threats towards you?
> Widenmann: A man said that he heard—
> [At this point, Simon B. Newcomb objected that hearsay was inadmissible. Objection sustained.]
> Newcomb: Mr. Widenmann, you did not see Tunstall killed?
> Widenmann: No.
> Newcomb: You did not see defendant shoot?
> Widenmann: No.
> Newcomb: Then you don't know of your own knowledge that Tunstall was killed at all.
> Widenmann: Well I think he was killed.

At this point in Widenmann's uninspiring performance the court, in the person of Judge Warren Bristol, swooped like a hawk on what had always been the fundamental weakness in his account of the murder of Tunstall.

> Mr. Widenmann, you say you were running horseback, dust flying, balls whistling around, yet you could casually look back, see a large party of fifteen or twenty coming at full speed 300 yards behind; that you recognized Mr. Dolan in the party, when everybody knows that a number of reliable witnesses swear positively that Mr. Dolan was 25 miles from there at the time.
>
> Widenmann: Yes, I know a number of men swear Dolan was at another place but I recognized Dolan there.
> The Court: Well, Mr. Widenmann, I know by experience something about riding at full speed under such circumstances and looking back at a party three hundred yards off and recognizing persons. Mr. Widenmann, your testimony in this matter will be taken with a good deal of allowance.

In the end, Widenmann was forced to admit that he had not seen Tunstall shot, and that he could not name the man or men who had shot him. On cross-examination he had to admit that he had not even seen Tunstall's body after the shooting. In effect, he admitted what he had always hitherto strenuously denied: that he and his companions fled headlong for their lives on the approach of the posse, abandoning Tunstall to his fate.

Further humiliation awaited.[6] Throughout the hearing, Widenmann kept his hands constantly in the pockets of the linen duster coat he was wearing. No sooner had he stepped down from the witness stand than Sheriff Mariano Barela braced him in the doorway of the courtroom.

"What right you got to carry concealed weapons in your pockets?" he growled.

Unceremoniously thrusting his hands into Widenmann's pockets, Barela relieved him of two pistols. The shamefaced Widenmann "changed color, but said nothing."

Evans took the stand in his own defense, and on oath testified that on the morning of February 18, he had seen Jimmy Dolan at the Tunstall ranch, twenty miles from where Tunstall was killed. No, he had not seen Tunstall on the day Tunstall was killed; no, he had had nothing to do with the shooting; no, neither he nor Frank Baker was even with the sheriff's posse that day. Having thus provided Dolan with a cast-iron alibi and himself with a halo, Evans posted the requisite five-thousand-dollar bail without apparent difficulty, plus another thousand required on a cattle theft charge. His cases were bound over, and Jessie walked free.

The *New Mexican* rejoiced in Widenmann's discomfiture and proceeded to blackguard him unmercifully.

> Our attention has been called to the testimony of R. A. Weideman given before Judge Warren Bristol in the habeas corpus case of Jesse Evans. . . . We are neither surprised nor disappointed, as we have long since pronounced him an unmitigated liar and scoundrel. He is also a cowardly murderer. His conduct in Lincoln County shows him to be in every way a villain; and how, with all the crimes surrounding him, he has been permitted to escape to Silver City, is more than we can understand. It looks to us as though it was putting a premium on crime. Since this man Weideman made his advent amongst us he has made it his business to earn for himself the character of a first class liar and fraud, and concluded his successful efforts with perjury in the testimony referred to. We warn the good people of Grant County that he is a dangerous man, and they cannot be too well guarded against his cheek and plausibility. He "done" many persons in Santa Fe by mythical remittances from Europe, which of course, never arrived. To be forewarned is to be forearmed.[7]

It is doubtful Widenmann "escaped" to Silver City. The court session over, he found himself blockaded in La Mesilla. It is equally doubtful he ever made any serious attempt to get back to Lincoln: somewhere along that route might lurk John Kinney, who had a long-standing score to settle with him. To cap it all, the news coming down from that section was all bad, and Widenmann was not so enamored of McSween as to lay down his own life in the lawyer's cause or, for that matter, anyone else's. So as the storm in Lincoln County swelled to a climax, Widenmann elected to remain in the relative safety of the Mesilla valley.

Alexander McSween had no such safe option: he was on the run. Driven from his home, harried by Peppin's posses, McSween and the men with him were constantly on the move throughout late June and early July. The mobile force of between a dozen and twenty men riding with—guarding—McSween consisted of old Regulators like Scurlock, Brown, Middleton, Bowdre, the Coes, Jim French, and Billy the Kid, and newer faces, a number of them Hispanics who had rallied to McSween's banner.

Why now, rather than earlier, did the Hispanic population rally to McSween's banner? Could his oratorical skills alone have swayed them? Hardly. Can it have been for the promise of money, or land, or both? Doubtful. Was there perhaps not a strong motivation of vengeance involved, the opportunity to repay a decade of slights from the men from the south, the Tejanos? More than possibly: note how few of the Hispanic population threw in their lot with Jimmy Dolan's faction.[8]

Their leader was Martin Chaves, a farmer from Picacho; as a young fellow of nineteen or so, he had nearly re-ignited the race war of 1874 when he ambushed Ben Turner as the Horrell clan made their way down the Hondo valley en route to Texas. Now at twenty-three he had replaced Juan Patrón as the leader and spokesman of the local Hispanic farmers.

How young they all were! All of McSween's fighting men were in their twenties, and many—like Yginio Salazar—still in their teens. Scurlock and Bowdre were the oldest members of the group at twenty-nine. Frank Coe was twenty-seven, Middleton twenty-four, George Coe twenty-two, and Henry Brown and the Kid both nineteen.

This was less true of the forces ranged against them: men like Peppin, Mathews, Sam Perry, Buck Powell, Andrew Boyle, and Milo Pierce were in their middle or late thirties, Dolan and Kinney both thirty. Even so, many of Dolan's supporters were also young men: Wallace Olinger was twenty-nine; Bob Beckwith, twenty-seven; Jessie Evans, twenty-five; John Beckwith, Lucio Montoya, Joe Nash, and Johnnie Hurley, twenty-three; and Jack Thornton twenty-two.

Armed and dangerous, these hotblooded, reckless young men, every one of them fired with the "will to combat," were the volatile elements of an inevitable conflagration, a bloodbath looking for a place to happen. That it would happen was no longer in doubt: a collision was inevitable.

The McSween party camped each night somewhere in the lonely hills between Lincoln and Roswell, using the Chisum ranch as their commissary. Chisum himself was diplomatically absent from South Spring, having elected to remain at Bosque Redondo supervising the clearance from the Pecos valley of the cattle he had sold to Hunter & Evans.

On July 3 a small posse led by Peppin's deputy Jose Chaves y Baca stumbled on the McSween party at San Patricio. They were well entrenched and their heavy fire drove the posse back. Sheriff Peppin immediately sent an urgent request for assistance to Colonel Dudley at Fort Stanton.[9] Dudley's records show that the messenger who brought Peppin's request reported a noncombatant (Julian López?) wounded and two or more horses killed.[10] Even so, Dudley was unable to assist Peppin. Just twenty-four hours earlier he had received a directive from headquarters in Santa Fe which precluded his further intervention in the affairs of Lincoln County.

Perturbed by the increasing use of federal troops in the enforcement of civil law, Congress had passed into law on June 18 the *Posse Comitatus* Act, which henceforth prohibited the use of soldiers in any civil action unless personally sanctioned by the president of the United States. Dudley received notification of the terms of the new act on June 28; he immediately recalled the detachment under Capt. Henry Carroll that was in the field with the sheriff (fig. 61).[11]

The resulting lack of military support does not seem to have much inhibited Peppin's posse: according to an account of the events of early July sent to the *Cimarron News & Press* by someone signing himself "Lincoln" (probably McSween), they tore San Patricio apart.

Headed by Axtell's sheriff and J. J. Dolan the Rio Grande posse killed and stole horses . . . broke windows and doors, smashed boxes and robbed them of their contents; from an old woman who was living alone they stole $438. They tore the roof off of Dow Bros. store; threw the goods out on the street and took what they wanted. Towards women they used the vilest language. Citizens working in the fields were fired upon but made good their escape up the river. Dolan and Pantaleon

FIG. 61. Maj. Henry Carroll, 1898.
Photographer unknown.

Gallegos, late clerk to the "House", killed a horse lariated near the town because the owner was supposed to sympathize with the Regulators. Dolan informed the people that there was no law in the county that he could recognize and that when certain Regulators and sympathizers were killed, he would leave the d——d country. Kinney, who was present, remarked those were his sentiments. Kinney said in town he was employed by the Governor and that he and his men would have to be paid $3.50 a day by the county, and that the sooner the people helped him to arrest the Regulators, the sooner their county would be relieved of this expense; Dolan endorsed this speech. Peppin stated that he would turn those who sympathized with the Regulators out of their houses, that he would take all their property, that he had power to do as he pleased. Dolan and Kinney enthusiastically endorsed this sentiment.[12]

There is substantiation in the military files for most of "Lincoln's" allegations; the population was terrorized.[13] A delegation of women from San Patricio presented to Colonel Dudley a petition signed by twenty-seven citizens of that village begging for his protection, but he was unable to provide it. All he could do was offer the safety of the post to any who wished to avail themselves of it.

A letter to the *Mesilla News* of July 13, signed "Paul Knox," alleged a confrontation between the returning possemen and Susan McSween. Learning that one of the two horses they had captured after their San Patricio skirmish was her mare, Pet, and convinced that therefore her husband must be dead, she grabbed a shotgun and ran screaming up the street to the Dolan store, insisting she "must have her Pet, talk to 'Jemmy', or someone must die." If this ever happened—it is not out of character—the outcome of the confrontation was inconclusive. Perhaps this was the occasion on which John Kinney told her, "We know that McSween is hiding out and has no gun but I will find him and run him into some place and I will shoot him, I've killed fourteen men and I'll kill him, too."[14]

At any rate Susan, having heard the name Baca mentioned as leader of the posse, stomped down the street to the home of Saturnino Baca (fig. 62).[15] Calling him outside, and in full view of his family and friends, she accused him of sending the posse to San Patricio to kill her husband. Baca replied that he did not have authority to send men anywhere. Susan was too fired up to listen: those men were thieves, she stormed; they had stolen her husband's horse. Baca refused to put up with any more of this and told her to go away. "Then she told me," Baca said, "that she had money and men to kill me and all my family." In making this threat

FIG. 62. Saturnino Baca. Date and photographer unknown. Taken in old age, probably around the turn of the century, at Lincoln, N.M.

Susan McSween incurred the undying enmity of the Baca family, and most especially Jose Chaves y Baca's kinswoman Juana Maria Baca. One day it would cost her dear.

Fleeing from San Patricio, the McSween force moved downriver toward the safety of the Chisum ranch, only to find themselves now besieged by another posse, this time consisting of some dozen men from the Seven Rivers area under the command of Deputy Buck Powell. Safe inside the massive walls of South Spring ranch, the McSween men had no fear of their pursuers. The walls of Chisum's ranch were four feet thick, and—barring the use of artillery—a dozen men could hold it against an army. "There was not a shot fired all day," said Will Chisum, who was up on the flat roof of the ranch house with the Kid and others. "The Seven Rivers party, as it was called, stayed all day about one mile from the ranch till dark, then they rode out in the flat and stayed all night."[16]

Next morning, unable to break the deadlock, Powell withdrew to Seven Rivers for reinforcements. Two days later he was back, this time with some extra men commanded by another of Peppin's special deputies, Marion Turner. They were looking for a fight to the finish, but when they reached the Chisum place, their birds had flown. The Seven Rivers men set off after them.

The *Las Vegas Gazette* made a valiant try at clarifying affairs:

McSween's party also started up the Pecos [towards Bosque Grande]. Powell had been reinforced by Marion Turner and some 12 or 14 men, making about 35 in all;

Turner was also deputized to make arrests. The two parties combined pursued the fugitives. They found the break up the river was a blind, as the McSween crowd had left the river and struck off by the Capitan in the direction of Lincoln. Turner, Powell and their friends pursued, and word was given out that they were between Lincoln and Capitan on the morning of July 10th. At that time McSween's forces were at San Patricio with 40 men. The danger of a severe battle is imminent.[17]

The Seven Rivers men were in a jubilant mood: they had their enemies on the run.[18] On July 11, Bob Beckwith, who was with them, wrote to his sister Josie that the posse had

arrived here yesterday in persuit of McSween's mob but did not overtake them. We were under the impression they were coming to recapture the town but they had not been near it. Today we will start to look after them.

we do not know where about in the country they are at Ruidozo or the Feliz. they have recruted to twenty five McSween[ites] with them in person our party or Sheriff posee numbers about 35 men. the mob are too cowardly to come to us and fight. we have to look for them like indians, the mob was Routed from this part of the country on the 3d and had the sheriff persuid them down to the Pecos we would have captured them, but they returned to the plaza and twelve of us only had to contend against them at South Spring River ranch we held them there the [Fourth of July] all day and they did not dare come out and fight us they shot a few shots at us from the houses but did not tuch any of us.

had the men from here come to our assistance we would have provable [sic] got some of them but they did not come untill we sent for them and when they come Mcsween's mob had escapted.

Now Dear Sister do not fret yourself about us it does no good. And tell Mother and Camilia and Ellen not to either, God will be with us and those murderers will not tuch a hair on our heads. Dear Sister we are having a Ruff time of it but hope era long we will be about to go home again.

That the McSween men were in an equally belligerent mood there can be no doubt. One of them (the handwriting was recognized as that of Charlie Bowdre) sent this letter to Catron's brother-in-law, Edgar Walz.

In Camp, July 13, 1878.
Mr. Walz. Sir:—We are all aware that your brother in law, T. B. Catron, sustains the Murphy-Kinney party, and take this method of informing you that if any property belonging to the residents of this county is stolen or destroyed, Mr. Catron's property will be dealt with as nearly as can be in the way in which the party he sustains deals with the property stolen or destroyed by them.

We returned Mr. Thornton [Catron's partner and representative in Lincoln County] the horses we took for the purpose of keeping the Murphy crowd from pursuing us with the promise that these horses should not again be used for that purpose. Now we know that the identical horses returned are used by the party with whom you are clearly identified.

We know that the Tunstall estate cattle are pledged to Kinney and party. If they are taken, a similar number will be taken from your brother [in law]. It is our object and efforts to protect property, but the man who plans destruction shall have destruction measured him. Steal from the poorest or richest American or Mexican, and the full measure of the injury you do, shall be visited upon the property of Mr. Catron. This murderous band is harbored by you as your guest, and with the consent of Catron occupies your property.

Regulator.[19]

Apart from the arrogant politeness with which they were delivered, Bowdre's threats scarcely differ from those of Charlie Crawford (that same "Mr. Lallacooler" who had once tried to steal Tunstall's carbine), who had told Isaac Ellis the preceding day in Lincoln that he intended "to tear down the lower end of town and kill all the damn sons of bitches that live in that part of town."[20]

Such behavior emphasizes the true plight of the hapless citizens of Lincoln County, who were at the mercy of both parties. A man working alone on his farm might see a heavily armed band approaching: friends or foe? He would not know until they arrived, and then it would be too late. The best he could hope for was that they would take no more than all his food, ammunition, and horses. If he had sympathized with the wrong people, they might just as readily kill him on the spot. Nor were his wife and children any likelier to be safe from their mindless violence.

Further evidence of these conditions appears in Colonel Dudley's official report, dated July 13. It has been the fashion to present the commandant of Fort Stanton as a despotic martinet in thrall to the Murphy-Dolan clique. If it was so, the old martinet was a master of dissimulation, because his reports consistently refute the calumny, none more than this affecting document.[21]

Yesterday Mrs. Brady the widow of the late Sheriff Brady and the mother of eight little children presented herself at my quarters weeping, and in apparent great distress, stating to me and others present that Scurlock of the McSween party an two other men fired three shots at her eldest boy, in a Cañon only half a mile from his home. This is not the first instance as she stated of their attempt to kill her children as the bullet holes in her residence go to prove. It was a sad scene to witness the grief and fears of the poor woman as she told her pitiful story saying "They have murdered my poor husband and not satisfied with this they now want to kill my boy." I offered to receive the boy in the garrison but she said she could not get along on the farm without him, so I sent a guard of one man to remain at the house for a few days hoping that as the factions are now at full strength, and within a few miles of each other, the one or the other side will be driven out of the country. The present status of affairs in the County is simply shameful and disgraceful.

The action of leading men on both sides, some of whom are holding prominent relations to the Government is infamous, and instead of matters improving, they are growing more and more lawless daily. I trust the District Commander will pardon me for expressing my opinion so plainly.

Up to this date, as all my weekly official reports will show, I have refrained from doing so for various reasons, but I feel it a duty to that portion of community that are law abiding to state what I here do. That a large portion of the farmers are in a state of fear not only for themselves but even for their wives and children. They do not know what may turn up the next hour. I am credibly informed that McSween has over fifty armed men under his personal control in one body. The Sheriff and Dolan party has nearly the same number, twenty two of the latter force camped on the 10th inst. two miles below the Garrison, drawing their supply of beef as they frequently have before from the Government Contractors butcher at the post. A similar force of some fifteen men belonging to Sheriff Peppin was at the same time in Lincoln, holding to the town against the McSween party. So alarmed I am informed are the laboring classes in some sections of the County that they do not dare to leave their homes to work in the fields.

The Crops are now maturing and unless properly cared for the labor of the spring and summer will be lost to the people and much suffering will be brought on the poorer residents of the county during the winter.

The Officers of the Post one and all feel the mortifying fact that they can do nothing under existing laws and instructions to protect parties against the troubles that surround the original settlers of the country, who are guiltless of the origins of these difficulties, neither can they take any action to assist in driving out of the country the well known desperadoes who are now here aiding both sides to keep up the strife, many of whom are non-residents of not only the County but even the Territory. Several parties owning more or less Stock and other property have expressed fears that no matter which side is successful, that when these men's services are no longer required in the capacity of partisan warriors, that they will compensate themselves by taking out sufficient property to indemnify them for time and expenses. It is alleged that McSween pays the men three Dollars per day, how true this is I cannot say; state it only as common rumor, and have been told so by men claiming to have been offered this sum. I do not wish to be understood as giving an opinion as to the right or wrong of either of these factions; under the circumstances as they have been presented to me I consider it a difficult problem to solve.

Dudley was to see his direst predictions all too soon fulfilled; the "war" was about to move into its final, fatal phase.

On Sunday, July 14, taking George Peppin and his small force completely by surprise, the McSween party, armed to the teeth, thundered into Lincoln in full strength. McSween, the Kid, Jim French, Tom O'Folliard, Joe Smith, Thomas Cullins, George Bowers, Jose Chaves y Chaves, Yginio Salazar, Ignacio Gonzales, Florencio Chaves, Francisco Zamora, and Vincente Romero invested the McSween house, at this time occupied by Mrs. McSween, her sister Elizabeth Shield and children, and Harvey Morris, a thirty-year-old native of New York state who was reading law with the firm. David Shield had gone to Santa Fe to attend court.

Henry Brown, George Coe, and Sam Smith took over the Tunstall store. Doctor Ealy and his family, together with the schoolteacher Susan Gates, were also in the building, occupying the rooms that had once been Tunstall's quarters.

Martin Chaves, Fernando Herrera, and a group of Hispanics—perhaps as many as twenty—manned the Montaño store; its owner was on a buying trip to Santa Fe. Bowdre, Scurlock, Middleton, Stevens, and another eight or ten men took over the Ellis store and house, in which Isaac Ellis and his wife and sons were living.

This massive force completely outnumbered—and drove a wedge between— Peppin's men. Jack Long was forted up in the *torreón* with Billy Mathews, Jim Reese, Sam Perry, Jim McDaniels, George "Roxy" Rose, and a mystery man known as "The Dummy," who pretended to be deaf and dumb but in fact was neither. Up the street at the Wortley were Jimmy Dolan—still nursing a broken leg but able now to walk without crutches—George Peppin, Pantaleon Gallegos, Lucio Montoya, Andy Boyle, and a couple of others.

Peppin sent a messenger down the valley to urgently summon Buck Powell and the rest of the posse, still in the San Patricio area.[22] They arrived at around six in the evening, and were greeted by volleys of firing from the McSween faction. A horse was killed, but there were no other casualties.

McSween moved quickly to empty the *torreón* of Peppin's men occupying it; these seven were drawing their food and water from Saturnino Baca, who lived in a house about fifty yards from the old tower. Unfortunately for Baca, the house belonged to McSween, who sent a brusque note to the old soldier.

Sir:—

I want you to vacate the property now occupied by you at once. Unless you leave the house within three days, proceedings will be instituted against you without further notice.

You have consented to improper use of the property by murderers for the purpose of taking my life, and I can no longer consent to your occupancy thereof.[23]

Faced with eviction in such dangerous circumstances, the hapless Baca appealed to the only person who could help him, Colonel Dudley at Fort Stanton.

McSween with about thirty five men—he (McS) says he has sixty—threatens my family and the sheriff's posse is out of town, and no one knows when they will return. My wife has just given birth to a child, and is almost scared to death.

Couldn't you do me the favor to let me have a few soldiers to remain with my family for a few days, by granting this you will confer an everlasting favor.

His hands tied by the new regulations, Dudley could only send Assistant Surgeon Daniel Appel to Lincoln to see if he could help. Appel called on McSween, who waspishly told him to tell Baca that "he was on his ground and was harboring his enemies there and they would have to leave, if they would not leave in any other way he would burn them out. He also stated . . . that he had been out in the hills long enough, that as he had now returned to his house they would not drive him away again alive."[24]

Appel managed to persuade McSween to allow soldiers to occupy the *torreón*, but Saturnino Baca decided to take no chances and requested that Colonel Dudley send a wagon to take his wife to the fort.

By Monday afternoon, then, Peppin's force was up to around forty; it included Jimmy Dolan (fig. 63), of course, and such Seven Rivers stalwarts as Bob Beckwith, John, Tom, and Jim Jones, Bob and Wallace Olinger, Milo Pierce, and W. H. Johnson, as well as John Kinney, Charlie Hart, John Chambers, Charlie Crawford, John and Jim Hurley, Jessie Evans, Tom Cochrane, Jose Chaves y Baca, and others.

They watched as the men occupying the McSween house drilled portholes in the walls and barricaded the windows with adobe bricks, readying for siege. It looked as if McSween had decided to make it a fight to the finish.

Prompted by Dolan, the sheriff sent Jack Long to the McSween house with instructions to serve the warrants he held. Long marched up to the McSween house and called for the surrender of the wanted men. A fusillade of bullets caused him to beat a hasty retreat back to the Wortley.

Mary Ealy's later recollections flesh out the other events of this dramatic day.

There was a lot of shooting that day, but I don't think anyone was killed; that evening or sometime in the night a Mr. Green [Wilson] who lived close to us came to the window and called the Doctor saying, "There is a man over here dying," and asked him to go see him; they started off and immediately those in the tower started shooting. Wilson, or Green, called to them. "Don't shoot, I am taking the Doctor to see a dying man." It was some time before the Doctor came home. The house where the man lived was just beside the tower, and the man told the Doctor the cursing and swearing was awful. The man was very low and died before morning.

Arrangements were made to bury him that same evening. Two colored boys, Bates and Washington, dug a grave along side where Tunstall was buried and about the time they lowered the body into the grave, the desperadoes from the tower

FIG. 63. James J. Dolan (seated) and Robert Olinger, ca. 1879. Photo by Bennett & Brown, Santa Fe, N.M. Another photograph, taken at the same time, shows Olinger alone, standing. Dolan is about thirty-two here, and Olinger going on thirty.

opened fire and frightened the boys so much that they just dropped the body into the grave and ran for their lives. In a short time the widow and two children came and stayed until sometime the next day. She couldn't talk English, so it was hard for us to talk to her. We all sat up as it would have been impossible to sleep. The shooting, yelling and screaming were distressing.[25]

The man who died was Daniel Huff, the carpenter and odd-job man Widenmann had hired to repair the Tunstall store. His hasty burial and subsequent events precluded any kind of a postmortem, so the cause of his death is unknown. Lincoln tradition has always leaned to his having been poisoned by a relative who objected to his friendship with the McSweens. Who the—Hispanic—relative may have been is a matter for conjecture.

"Firing all day and after dark," Doctor Ealy recorded glumly on Tuesday, July 16.[26] "Two of McSween's windows were shot to pieces." His wife again adds human dimensions to the Doctor's shorthand.

We got all our drinking water from the neighbors, but all the other water for cooking, etc., from the river at the foot of a little hill back of our corral. The children and all of us were suffering for water; Susan said, "If we don't get water we will die anyway." So we started and were not molested. We carried several buckets of water which lasted while we were in Lincoln. At the same time, the lady, Mrs. Huff, whose husband had just died, went home with her children. We told her to come back again, but the shooting began so fiercely, I suppose she went somewhere else or someone got her.

Dolan and Peppin had deployed their forces as best they could behind the two houses nearest McSween's: those of Ham Mills (who had abandoned his wife and child and fled the Territory) and Juan Chaves. The two factions kept up steady fire most of the day, but it was clear that the Dolan crowd were making no impression on the well-protected McSween forces behind their stout adobe walls. At this juncture Peppin had a brain wave.[27] He scribbled a note to Colonel Dudley. "If it is within your power to loan me one of your howitzers, I am of the opinion that parties for whom I have warrants would surrender without a shot being fired. Should it be in your power to do this in favor of the law, you would confer a great favor on the majority of the people of this county, who are being persecuted by a lawless mob."

His letter arrived just as Dudley sat down to write his weekly report to General Hatch at headquarters in Santa Fe. The colonel's comments read almost like a soliloquy.

Affairs in Lincoln have become serious, seeming approaching a crisis. The town is at the present writing in a perfect state of War. About one hundred men, nearly equally divided, are holding the several prominent buildings. Both parties commenced firing last evening and have kept it up at intervals since. I have heard of no casualties as yet. Dr. Appel and Capt Blair have just returned from the seat of war, and report both parties under cover. Streets wholly deserted, women and children much alarmed.

The ——— alias late Dolan and Riley faction (I will be better able to fill up the blank in a few days) [He was referring to the frequent changes of name the Dolan party indulged in.] I fear will get the worst of it. McSween occupies his own house with a force of about twenty men. He seems to openly defy the Sheriff, if the latter's written reports can be believed.

I have just received a letter from Geo. W. Peppin, deputy U.S. Marshal and Sheriff of Lincoln County asking for the loan of a howitzer, stating that the men he has warrants for are in town and he cannot arrest them without it.

I after careful consideration and a long conversation with my officers, came to the conclusion to refuse the request, deeply regretting that I was compelled to do so.[28]

A black trooper, Pvt. Berry Robinson, was sent to Lincoln carrying a letter from Dudley regretfully denying Peppin's request. He left the fort at about 6:30 and "made pretty fast" to get to Lincoln before dark.[29] Some distance outside Lincoln he was stopped by four men "painted like Indians" who demanded to know where he was going.

"To attend to my business," Robinson replied. The men again asked him where he was going.

"I'm on government business," Robinson told them. "I'm not a citizen."

"You talk pretty damn saucy," one of the men said.

"I talk no more damn saucy than you do," Robinson retorted. At this juncture the four men surrounded him and drew their six shooters. Unfazed, Robinson put a cartridge in his gun, brought it to an advance, and rode on.

I saw no one else . . . until I got to the wheat field just at the outskirts of Lincoln. There the men at the McSween house shot at me through portholes on the top,

FIG. 64. Daniel Mitchell Appel. Date and photographer unknown.

one ball whistled past my horse's head. He got scared and fell. I got off but held on to his bridle and remounted.

Mr. Dolan motioned me to come on fast and I ran the horse until the hotel was between me and the party firing at me when I walked for the hotel. The sun had not yet set and I am sure they could see I was a soldier.

Peppin had sent five men up on the hill south of town, where they ensconced themselves behind rocks and poured shots down on the Montaño house below. Pinned down, the men inside put sacks of flour into the windows, but were unable to go outside for water until after dark, when a black man filled a washtub, which was set in the middle of the floor for communal use.

On the morning of Wednesday, July 17, Colonel Dudley appointed a board of officers, consisting of captains George Purington and Thomas Blair, together with Doctor Appel (fig. 64), to go to Lincoln and investigate the Robinson incident. Even as the officers saddled up, the shooting began again.

The day had begun quietly; so quietly, in fact, that the men Peppin had posted up on the hill south of town behind the Montaño store were misled into believing the McSween party had decamped. They started down to rejoin the posse. There are two versions of what happened next. The first is that of Saturnino Baca, who was "looking out from the front of my door and saw two men coming down the hill towards Mr. Montaño's house, and when [they were] about three or four hundred yards from the house I saw firing from McSween's, Montaño's, and Ellis's house, and I saw a man fall and the other man I saw running down the hill but did not know what became of him."[30]

The other version holds that Charlie Bowdre's father-in-law, Fernando Herrera, who was in the Montaño store, saw the movement up on the hill, aimed his buffalo gun and fired.[31] The same tradition has it that the distance was nine hundred yards, a little more than half a mile. The bullet whanged off the hammer of Charlie Crawford's rifle and tore through his body from hip to hip.

Whichever version is true, Crawford was mortally wounded. He collapsed and lay groaning in agony on the hillside as the summer sun scaled the sky, and the temperature climbed into the high eighties. No one dared go up there and help him.

At around noon, Purington, Blair, and Appel, escorted by five troopers, arrived in town.[32] "I went from one end of town or village to the other," Purington later testified, "and saw everything closed, every home closed, no one in the street. In one end of town there was a body of 50 men, or such a number, men in the hills to the right [south] of town and these men were keeping up a continuous fire into the town and from the town."

They talked first to the Peppin possemen at the Wortley, who included B. N. Waters, Roscoe Bryant (alias "Rustling Bob"), John Beckwith, Tom Cochrane, K. L. Bryan, and Jessie Evans.[33] Dolan and Peppin confirmed courier Robinson's story, adding that they had shouted to the men in the McSween house that they were firing on a soldier, but that no one had taken any notice. The officers proceeded to the McSween house and questioned the lawyer about the Robinson incident; they concluded, in spite of McSween's denials, that the shots had come from his home. No attempt seems to have been made to establish the identity of the four men who had stopped Robinson outside the town.

At this juncture, the officers learned that Crawford was still lying wounded in the cornfield on the hill above the Montaño store. Although there was still shooting going on, Doctor Appel and Lieutenant Blair went to see what they could do for the wounded man (Appel refers to him as "a murdered man"); as they scrambled up the hill, they were fired on by the men in the Montaño house. "We distinctly heard the bullets pass within a few feet of us," Appel recalled later.

The three officers returned to the fort, taking Crawford with them; he died in the post hospital a week later. The fight continued. Wednesday night, Mrs. Ealy recorded,

> was worse and worse. We barricaded our windows with our trunks and laid our beds on the floor. That night Ben Ellis was shot while looking after his horses. A couple of men from their place waded up the river until they reached where we were living; then they crawled up to the corral and managed to reach the door, although many shots were fired at them from the tower. The Doctor went with them and tried to reach Ellis' but he was not able to wade the river and could not get there. It was a long time before he came back. He tapped on the door; I asked who was there, then I let him in.[34]

The night passed; July 18 dawned bright and clear. At Fort Stanton, Sergeant Keefe of the Fifteenth Infantry acted as translator for three Hispanic women who had come to the post to ask Dudley to repossess their homes: "One of the women told me Peppin and part of his posse drove her out of her house and the other two women told me Scurlock and a party of men drove them out of their houses [the preceding night]."[35]

It could be that one of these women was Ham Mills's wife Maria; the Mills house was strategically placed next to the McSween place. This might account for the old Lincoln tradition that she or her daughter Juanita walked all the way to the post to beg Dudley for help. In the event, Dudley was unable to do more than offer the women the shelter of the post.

In Lincoln, Taylor Ealy determined to do what he could for Ben Ellis, who had been severely wounded in the neck and had lost a lot of blood.[36] The missionary and his wife, their baby daughter Ruth in her arms and their older daughter Pearl holding her father's hand, defiantly marched down the middle of the street to the Ellis place.

In a way, Ealy's action symbolized the growing confidence of the McSween party. The situation of the Peppin force was becoming less and less tenable. They could make no impression upon the men in the heavily-fortified McSween house, nor dislodge those in the other buildings. Crawford was dying; Johnson and two others were wounded. Many of the possemen were discouraged and wanted to quit. Not so the Regulators: Joseph Smith wrote to his former employer, Howard Capper of Roswell, in jaunty mood.

> I thought I would write you a few lines to let you know what the people are doing up here. We have taken the town. One was killed day before yesterday and one wounded. Ben Ellis was shot through the neck by one of the guards. Everything is fair in war. Seen Jim Reese the other morning walking down the street. I heard Collins sing hunger the other morning. I heard Jim Reese cried because he is on the other side. He says he is in it and can't get out of it. All of them have taken an oath to stand by each other until death, so I guess we will get to kill a lot of them fore they get away. Capper, you must not think hard of a fellow for quitting you; but I wanted to go, so I went. The U.S. troops have stepped aside, and given us full swing. There is 45 of us citizens have turned out. I tell you it makes a fellow's hair stand up when bullets coming whistling through the air; then I get cooled down, I don't mind it much. Best respects to Sam. Harvey Morris sends his respects to all. Had a little excitement yesterday. The Murphys told some woman in town that they got a condemned cannon and was going to bombard the town. Tried to scare us out but we didn't scare worth a damn.
>   Well, I must quit writing. Good luck to you.
>   Tell Bill Nagle he can have them gloves.[37]

It was alleged—although he not unnaturally denied it—that at this juncture Jimmy Dolan decided to go up to the fort and talk to Dudley in person.[38] With him he took John Kinney, Sam Perry, George "Roxy" Rose and possibly one or two others. The question of whether or not this conversation took place—and it is disputed—brings into contention the highly charged matter of Colonel Dudley's disinterest.

His reports time and again intimate that he had little sympathy for either of the feuding factions: yet witnesses stated categorically that he promised Dolan help. When Dolan was later called upon to confirm or deny this conversation, his testimony took the usual form. In the first place, he had never been at the fort; in the second place, if he had, the conversation in question had never taken place; and in the third place, he wasn't there in the first place. Nevertheless Samuel Beard, who lived at Cienega la Mancha, stated that he had overheard part of their discussion. "I heard him (Col. Dudley) tell Mr. Dolan as he was getting on his horse to leave; to go down and stand them off, and he would be there by twelve o'clock. I [also] heard him tell Mr. Dolan to take all his men away from the Fort. If he found any of them here by sundown he would put them in the guardhouse."

Another earwitness was photographer James A. Tomlinson. He overheard John Kinney and another, unnamed man talking things over. As far as the unnamed man was concerned, Tomlinson testified, he and others

> were getting tired of the Lincoln County fight and that he and others had come for the purpose of making a raise, and that he thought there was no use of waiting any longer as they could do nothing without the assistance of the Military. Kinney's reply was that to wait a day or two longer; that he was assured that assistance would be had. He then commenced complaining about having nothing to eat down there; and also that there were friends of the McSween party in the Garrison, or the Fort,

that were constantly giving them (the McSween party) information as to their plans and so forth. He thought it would be a good idea to commence killing here first. Kinney replied no, that would not do; that they must make a killing down there, other parties would be or could be attended to afterwards.

From the context, the unnamed man has to have been Roxy Rose, one of the local toughs who had thrown in his lot with Kinney "for the purpose of making a raise," that is, for the pickings. In the interests of accuracy, it should be placed on record that Tomlinson was considered by the Dolan crowd to be a McSween spy; so too was Juan Patrón, still sheltering at the post.

Dudley accosted the latter brusquely and ordered him off the post, saying he did not want anyone spying on his movements and actions.[39] Patrón protested he was not a spy. Dudley threatened to send him to McSween's house in a wagon. Patrón instead left for Las Vegas; he was on the Rio Hondo when the final fight took place in Lincoln. No one ever asked Dudley why he felt it necessary to keep his movements and actions secret.

That evening Dudley called an informal meeting of his officers in his quarters; it lasted about half an hour.[40] Those present were Captains Purington and Blair, Lieutenants Goodwin and Pague; Asst. Surgeon Appel was at the hospital when the meeting commenced and joined them midway through. They were all aware of conditions in Lincoln; it is doubtful if there was any other topic of conversation at the post. Dudley wanted their opinion on the advisability of taking troops down there. They concluded jointly to sign a resolution supporting his decision to "place soldiers in the town of Lincoln for the preservation of the lives of the women and Children."

The brass mountain howitzer that stood on the parade ground was broken; the blacksmith, Mr. Nelson, was ordered to repair it, and worked all night to do so.[41] Lieutenant Pague was detailed to remain at the post in command; all other available officers and men would accompany Dudley to Lincoln.

The following morning at about 7:30, "Boots and Saddles" was sounded. By 8:00 a.m., the command—four officers, one company of cavalry, and another of infantry, for a total of thirty-five men—was en route to Lincoln. With them went the brass twelve-pounder, a Gatling gun with two thousand rounds of ammunition, and three days' rations.

A little after 9:30 a.m. the command halted at the Miranda ranch, on top of a hill to the west of town; John B. Wilson, who had taken his family there for safety, was informed that the board of officers which had investigated the Robinson incident required him to prepare a warrant for the arrest of those who had fired on the courier.[42] Wilson promised to come down to his office directly. During the conversation shots were heard from the direction of town.

Four hundred yards west of town the command halted yet again while the infantrymen got out of the wagons and formed up. Then, with Captain Purington leading the column, Colonel Dudley and his detachment marched into Lincoln.

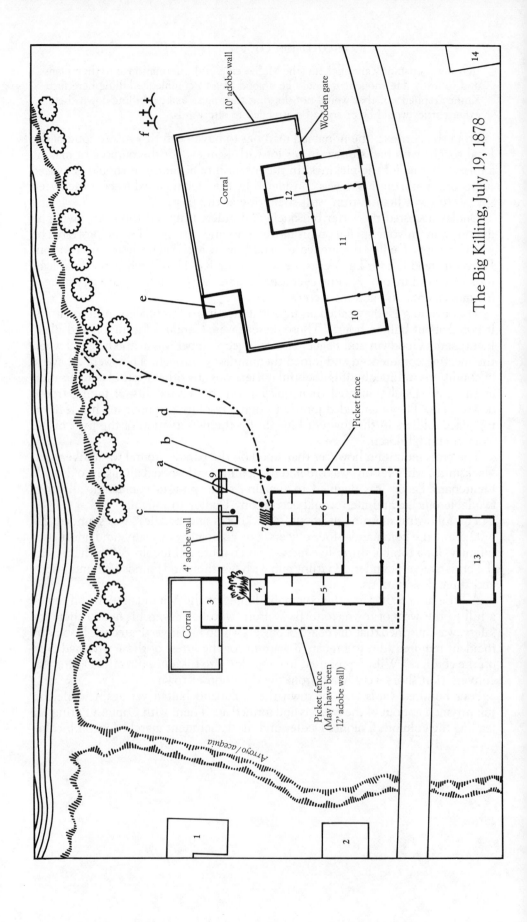

The Big Killing, July 19, 1878

The Big Killing

July 19, 1878

Key

1. Schon house
2. Ham Mills house
3. Stable with lumber pile on roof where Boyle, et al., hid.
4. Lean-to summer kitchen; fire set here
5. McSween quarters
6. Shield quarters
7. Woodpile
8. Chicken house
9. Privy where Jack Long hid
10. McSween law office

11. Tunstall store
12. Ealy family and Susan Gates (formerly Tunstall) quarters
13. Stephen Stanley house
14. John B. Wilson house
a. McSween and Beckwith killed here
b. Harvey Morris killed here
c. Francisco Zamora and Vicente Romero killed here
d. Escape route of Kid, OFolliard, and the others
e. Tunstall grain store. 3 McSween sharpshooters on roof
f. Graves of Tunstall, MacNab, et al.

CHAPTER 26

WAR: THE BIG KILLING

MORNING sun glancing flashes of light off their accouterments, the cavalry came around the bend in the road and into Lincoln town (see map 3, fig. 65). When they reached the Wortley Hotel, Dudley again halted the command. He summoned Sheriff Peppin and, by his own account, delivered these words (fig. 66).

> I want you to understand that I have not come to Lincoln to assist you in any way. I have come solely to protect the women and children; the men can take care of themselves. I propose to go into camp within half a mile of the town. If my camp is attacked, or an officer or man killed or wounded by a shot fired by either party from any house, I shall demand the parties be turned over to me, and in case of failure I shall request the women and children to leave the house, and I shall open fire on it with my howitzer, and arrest the parties in the house. I do not know what houses your party or McSween's occupy; I shall treat both parties exactly alike.[1]

Bearing in mind the testimony indicating that Dudley had promised Dolan help, it is at least possible that this speech was made "for the record," as it were. Dolan and his supporters certainly knew the soldiers would be arriving that Friday morning; but then, Doctor Ealy's account of events indicates that McSween did, too.

> The night before McSween was murdered, a messenger came to warn him that they were coming to kill him. If he had taken the warning his life would have been spared. Ft. Stanton was 9 miles west of Lincoln. The officers were playing billiards and through a transom over the door a woman heard Colonel or General Dudley late at night give the command, *all the command* will move early in the morning to Lincoln with the Gatling and Howitzer cannon, etc. This angel of mercy walked all the way from Ft. Stanton to Lincoln 9 miles to tell him what the bandits and the military intended to do.[2]

The "angel of mercy" was probably one of the local Hispanic women whose arrival at the fort had been recorded by Doctor Appel. If the news she brought perturbed McSween, there is no indication of it in the jaunty little note he wrote that morning to postmaster Ash Upson in Roswell.

> Dear Ash:—Please send me $3^{00} in stamps.
>   I am here O.K. I suppose you hear queer versions. Right will triumph.
>   Just as soon as the Commissioners can come together, your School business will be attended to.[3]

FIG. 65. Lincoln scene, looking east, ca. 1905. Photographer unknown. This is how the street must have looked as Dudley led his troops through town.

Significantly, Dudley made no stop in front of the McSween house to deliver there the warning he had given Peppin. The troops marched past the house and on beyond the Tunstall store, the *torreón*, and the Baca house.[4] They did not see a living soul after leaving the Wortley. When they reached the Montaño store, Dudley again gave the command to halt.

He stated later that his original intention had been to camp on the edge of town, remain overnight in Lincoln, and make a reconnaissance of one day's march downriver next day. Instead, however, he elected to camp on a vacant space directly opposite the Montaño store and stretching almost as far as the jail. The land was leased by George Washington, who gave Dudley permission to use it.

Camp was pitched "immediately below and on the side of an unfinished adobe building opposite the Montaño house."[5] It is more than likely this was the shell of either the school at which Susy Gates was to teach, or the church that McSween had promised Doctor Ealy.

In those days, the ground on which the camp was pitched sloped downhill below the McSween house. This rise concealed the western end of town completely; in fact, only the front part of the roof of the McSween house was visible from that location.

Whether with Dudley's sanction or otherwise, Peppin and his men took advantage of the cease-fire occasioned by the column's march through the town to occupy strategic locations all around the McSween house.[6] Bob Olinger led one group to Steve Stanley's house; Johnny Hurley occupied Green Wilson's *jacal*. Andy Boyle led a party to McSween's stable, and Billy Mathews, Pantaleon Gallegos, and Sam Perry forted up in the Schon place. Jimmy Dolan—moving

FIG. 66. Nathan Augustus Monroe Dudley, aged fifty-six, 1881. The mourning band probably marks the assassination of President Garfield, who died Sept. 19, 1881. Dudley is wearing dress uniform of lieutenant colonel, Ninth Cavalry. Note the monocle!

as fast as his gimpy leg would permit—took over the Mills house, and Peppin moved into the *torreón*.

Susan McSween later testified that when the column passed the McSween house "men broke into the [Stanley] house opposite ours immediately afterwards [and] hung out a black flag" from the top of the front doorway.[7] No one could mistake its import: at the battle of the Alamo, Santa Anna's soldiers had raised a black flag, signaling to the Texan defenders that they would be given no quarter. Peppin's *Tejanos* were telling the McSween faction the same thing.

Before the soldiers had even finished pitching their tents, the men occupying Patrón's house abandoned it and joined the others in the Ellis place.[8] Dudley ordered the howitzer trained on the door of the Montaño house. As the gun crew shouted the cadences of their loading drill, Dudley dispatched Captain Blair to repeat his injunction to Martin Chaves and the men inside, and to advise the women there—Mrs. Montaño, Mrs. Teresa Phillipowski, and Mrs. Bolton—to leave forthwith.

After a while Chaves and his men came out of the house, their heads covered with blankets to conceal their identities, and Chaves led them down to the Ellis house. The women remained: Mrs. Montaño came across the street and offered Dudley and his officers the use of her home for the night; he demurred, saying they would remain in camp.

Doctor Appel went down to warn Ellis and the men there that the troops were in town and why.[9] Finding Ben Ellis's wound in need of dressing, he returned to the camp for his bag, bringing Isaac Ellis along to talk to Dudley in person. Sergeant Keefe had meanwhile been ordered to tour the village to reassure the people and inform them that the army had come to protect them. He found only about a dozen families still present.

In the space of a mere half hour, the McSween party's strategic domination of the town was broken. They were vastly uneasy: what was the military going to do? About five minutes later, Susan McSween "saw three soldiers going up the street to the hotel. I went out to ask the soldiers why they were in town or why they had come here and what their intentions were. After a few minutes I saw the same three soldiers going back to camp with Mr. Peppin. Well, after this we all became alarmed, all who were in the house seeing Peppin guarded by the soldiers."[10]

Moments after this, the men in the house opposite hung out the black flag of no quarter. McSween scribbled a note to Dudley and gave it to his ten-year-old niece, Minnie Shield, to take to the military camp. All his euphoria was gone; the note clearly indicates his apprehensiveness: "Would you have the kindness to let me know why soldiers surround my house. Before blowing up my property I would like to know the reason. The constable is here and has warrants for the arrest of Sheriff Peppin and his posse for murder and larceny."[11]

Cynically choosing to misinterpret McSween's distraught request, Dudley ordered his adjutant, Lieutenant Goodwin, to reply as follows: "I am directed by the Commanding Officer to inform you that no soldiers have surrounded your house, and that he desires to hold no correspondence with you; if you desire to blow up your house, the commanding officer does not object providing it does not injure any U.S. soldiers."[12]

While this exchange was going on, Dudley sent for Peppin to tell him that the men from the Montaño store had gone down to the Ellis place, and suggested Peppin head them off.[13] Accompanied by Robert Beckwith, John Jones, John Hurley, and one or two others, Peppin ran down towards the Ellis place, yelling for the men there to come out and surrender.

The defenders of the Ellis house, including Bowdre, Middleton, and Scurlock, and the men under Martin Chaves who had just joined them, were already saddling up in Ellis's corral. They rode out, firing back at the advancing Peppin party, wounding John Jones slightly. One or more of the retreating McSween men was also hit: the following day, blood was tracked over a mile and a half of the trail they had taken.

The Peppin party found and appropriated thirteen saddles at the Ellis place. One of them was Dick Brewer's and another, according to Doctor Appel, belonged to a man named Meeten (probably Morton) who had been killed. Peppin led his men back up the street to the plaza, Bob Beckwith carrying a bucket of coal oil he had picked up in the Ellis place. There they were met by the disgruntled Dudley, who told Peppin that if he'd come as soon as he was sent for, he would have captured the whole party.

Dudley had not been inactive during the sheriff's short absence.[14] He had summoned Justice of the Peace Wilson to his quarters and demanded Wilson now issue the warrant for McSween's arrest that he had been asked for earlier. Wilson told him he could not issue a warrant without the necessary affidavit, whereupon Dudley sent Purington, Appel, and Blair back to Wilson's office to make one. Wilson still hesitated.

> I told him that I doubted my authority to issue such warrant believing that it was the duty of the U.S. Commissioner. . . . [H]e called me a coward and told me I was issuing just such warrants every few days and if I did not issue the warrant right off . . . he would put me in double irons and report me to the Governor for neglect of duty and . . . if it was one of the McSween party wished such warrants that I would issue it right off or at once.

Wilson went back to his office, drew up the warrant, and handed it to the waiting Peppin. Peppin thereupon deputized a less than enthusiastic Bob Beckwith to serve it forthwith. He then instructed three black men who worked for the McSweens—George Washington, Sebrian Bates, and Joe Dixon—to join the posse and carry lumber to burn the McSween house. As a paroled prisoner, Washington pleaded and was granted exemption.

Susan McSween saw Bates and Dixon, together with Beckwith, Hurley, and a man she did not recognize (the Kid said it was John Kinney) piling lumber against the east side of the house.[15] Much alarmed, she decided to seek aid from Dudley. Crawling on her hands and knees because of the danger from bullets, she got clear of the house and hurried up the street towards Dudley's camp. Near the *torreón* she encountered George Peppin, and demanded to know why he was forcing her servants to help him burn down her house.[16]

"If you don't want your house burned down, make the men in there get out of it," Peppin retorted. "I am bound to have the men inside there today, dead or alive."

"Then I shall go to Colonel Dudley's camp to get protection!"

"You needn't think you'll get protection from Colonel Dudley or anyone else when you harbor such men in your house!" Peppin told her angrily. She brushed past him and hurried on towards the military encampment, where she demanded to see Dudley. He received her outside his tent, not twenty yards from the Montaño house.

What follows is an attempt to reconstruct their conversation.[17] Most of it comes from Dudley's version; Mrs. McSween later claimed that during their talk he was profane and cast aspersions on her morals. Being a lady, she could not repeat his actual words, but others testified later that officers, soldiers, and civilians standing within earshot clearly enjoyed the spectacle of Dudley taking hoity-toity Mrs. McSween down a peg.

"My husband and I hold you in the highest respect, Colonel Dudley," she began.

"Thank you for the compliment," Dudley said, doffing his hat.

"I have come to find out what you are doing in the plaza on such a day as this," Mrs. McSween said.

"I am not aware that I have to report to you about my movements, Madam," Dudley replied stiffly. "However, people from the plaza have been coming to the

Fort for a month past demanding protection. I have given some of them quarters. I am here today to protect the women and children and anyone who requests protection."

"Why then do you not protect myself, my sister and her children?"

"She has no business being there. I cannot give you protection while you allow such men as Billy Kid, Jim French, and others of like character to be in your house."

Mrs. McSween said that it looked strange his soldiers guarding Peppin back and forth through the town, and his putting soldiers around their house and sending them such word as he had sent them.

"It is none of your business," Dudley snapped. "I will send my soldiers where I please."

"Why is your cannon pointed at my house?"

"If you will look more closely at the gun you will see that it is pointed in the opposite direction."

"I have been told you are going to blow up my house," Mrs. McSween persisted.

"You have been misinformed," Dudley said. "In fact I have a letter sent to me by your husband stating that he intends to blow his house up himself."

"I don't believe my husband ever wrote such a letter!" she said. "Or that you ever received it."

Dudley was on sure ground here. He went into his tent, got McSween's note, and read it out loud.

"I don't believe my husband wrote that!" Mrs. McSween said. Dudley held it up so that she could see the handwriting, but when she reached out to take it from his hand, he whisked it away.

"I don't trust you to handle the letter yourself. I believe you would tear it up if you got the chance," Dudley said. He turned towards Sgt. Thomas Baker, standing nearby.

"If this woman attempts to take this letter out of my hand, you are to shoot her," he told Baker. He was smiling as he said it, clearly enjoying himself.

"Then you will not help us?" said Mrs. McSween.

"If your husband will surrender himself to the military, I will give you my word and honor as an officer of the army that he will not be molested or in any way hurt," Dudley replied. "I will take him to the post with me and give him all the protection I can."

Susan McSween shook her head and turned to leave.

"I must say one thing before I leave your camp, Colonel Dudley. Your being in town with your troops today looks a little too thin to me."

"I don't understand what you said," Dudley told her. "Please repeat it."

"I said your being in town with your troops today looks a little too thin."

"I don't understand such slang phrases. The ladies I associate with don't use such language, and I don't know what you mean by the phrase 'too thin'."

Frustrated, angry, frightened, and confused, Susan McSween returned to her home to tell her husband what Dudley had said. Meanwhile, the combined Scurlock-Chaves group which had fled under fire from the Ellis house now reappeared on the crest of the hills north of town and began shooting at the possemen scattered around the McSween house.[18] Firing became general until the soldiers in the camp wheeled the howitzer around so that its muzzle was pointing at the

Regulators. As the gun crew made great show of swabbing out the barrel and trimming the elevation, the attacking party turned tail and disappeared. McSween was now vastly outnumbered.

Under heavy fire, Marion Turner led a party of a dozen or so men dashing across the street under heavy fire.[19] They flattened themselves against the walls alongside the front windows and poked their guns inside, demanding the occupants surrender.

"We have warrants here for all of you!" Turner shouted.

"And we've got warrants for you, too!" Jim French yelled back.

"Where are they?" Turner yelled.

"In our guns, you cock-sucking bastard!" retorted the defiant French.

Turner and his men were repulsed; Jack Long and the pseudo-deaf-mute they called "The Dummy" were next to try. Moving carefully from McSween's stable along the rear wall to the gate, Long and the Dummy sneaked up to the kitchen door and sloshed coal oil on the wooden floor. "Minnie Shield . . . was on her way to the river with buckets to bring water to the men when the full blast of shooting commenced and scared her back, and when she reached their dining room two men were dashing torpedos on the floor to set their house on fire at the same time the others were putting the coal oil on our back windows."[20]

Minnie's mother, Elizabeth Shield, who was pregnant, threw water on the flames, extinguishing them.[21] Long and the Dummy, retreating from the house, were fired on by George Coe, Henry Brown, and Sam Smith, concealed in the grain warehouse behind the Tunstall store. The two men had no option but to dive into the open privy, which was located outside the fence and dug into the bank. Whenever things got slack, the trio in the Tunstall store would pepper the outhouse with bullets, forcing its occupants below ground level. "It was not a good place to sit down," as Long later sardonically observed.[22]

The two men were joined shortly thereafter by Buck Powell, who had been spotted coming up from the river with water and had to run for cover in a hail of bullets. They were pinned down in the privy until dark; doubtless a malodorous experience but, as Long admitted later to George Coe, it beat dying all hollow at that.[23]

At about two o'clock in the afternoon, Andy Boyle, in spite of having been nicked alongside the neck by a bullet from the Tunstall grain store, managed to get a pile of kindling and wood shavings alight at the northwest corner of the house. That he may have been a more reluctant hero than his actions indicated is testified to by Susan McSween, who said the men who set the fire were a group of four or five men "whom they had invagled into their crowd and that morning when they saw what was comming they concluded the[y] did not want any part in the strife, but old man Peirce threw his gun down on them saying "now ("God Dam") you, you have been with us several days eating &c and you have got to go & set fire to the house."[24]

Boyle set his fire against a wood-frame lean-to known as the summer kitchen. This began to burn furiously, the fire gathering strength as the possemen threw coal oil onto it. Those inside the house tried desperately to staunch the flames, but were driven back by heavy fire from the men hidden in McSween's stable.

The house burned slowly but inexorably; the occupants moved back from the advancing flames room by room. They carried Susan McSween's piano with them for awhile; eventually it was abandoned to the flames. She was always outraged by the suggestion that she had played it during the fighting.[25] "God forbid," she said, "that I could ever be so void of sentimen[t as] to sit down and play on it under such grave moments."

As the flames advanced, Peppin's men closed in; late in the afternoon, the gunfire being directed into and issuing from the burning house reached a crescendo so intense that Dudley stationed his sentries behind the unfinished adobe walls of the building by the camp, and ordered his men to stay under cover. Still later, a small keg of gunpowder stored in the house exploded; after that the fire began to gain rapidly. Susan McSween painted a vivid word picture of the scene inside.

> The boys talked to each other and McSwain and I were sitting in one corner. The boys decided I should leave. They were fighting the fire then in my sister's house. McSwain said he guessed that was better. The neighbors told me [later] that Dudley got uneasy then. They said he stood on a hill near the store and said: "My God, why does that woman not come out?"
>
> The Kid was lively and McSwain was sad. McSwain sat with his head down, and the Kid shook him and told him to get up, that they were going to make a break.[26]

Susan Gates appeared at the camp with a note from Doctor Ealy asking for an escort of soldiers to help him remove his family and effects from the Tunstall store, which he had been told was next to be burned down.[27] In spite of his antipathy towards Ealy, whom he perceived as a man of the cloth sympathizing with murderers, Dudley sent three men and a wagon to do what they could. The soldiers went down to the Tunstall store and piled the wagon high with the family's belongings. When they got it back to the camp one of the soldiers, making no allowances for the missionary's distraught state of mind, reported that Ealy had used "threatening and impudent language," whereupon Dudley ordered them back to their tents.

About half an hour later, Mary Ealy sent him a note apologizing for her husband's behavior and asking for an escort to bring herself, her family, and Susy Gates to safety.[28] Because the gunfire was now so heavy—experienced officers in the command estimated that *more than two thousand rounds* were fired during the evening—Dudley was unwilling to expose any man to it on his orders.[29] He asked for volunteers: Appel, Blair, Corporal Pergold, and five enlisted men stepped forward. They hitched up the wagon and returned to the Tunstall store.

When she saw the officers helping the Ealy family into the wagon, Susan McSween ran out of her burning home and begged Captain Blair for his protection for herself and her sister; he immediately agreed, and hostilities were momentarily suspended as she, Elizabeth Shield, and the five terrified children came out of the house and, protected by the watchful officers, ran along the street to the waiting wagon. They were given quarters at the Patrón house, a safe distance from the firing zone.

As darkness fell, Doctor Appel recalled, "the house was in a great blaze lighting up the hills on both sides of the town."[30] The situation of the defenders was now desperate. McSween was in a state of near collapse, sitting in one corner of the northeast kitchen, his head in his hands. The heat was intense; all of them were filthy, sweaty, thirsty. It was a straight choice: run or die.

A desperate strategy was evolved. The "lively" Kid, assuming the mantle of command in the face of McSween's collapse, proposed that he and four others would make a break for the gate in the fence along the eastern edge of the

FIG. 67. Robert Beckwith. Date and photographer unknown.

McSween property and try to reach the safety of the Tunstall store. While the attention of the Peppin men was focused on them, McSween and the others would run for the gate in the rear adobe wall, shielded by the chickenhouse from the fire of the men in the stable, dash down the steep, tamarisk-clad banks of the Bonito and across the river to safety.

The Kid said they made their move "about dusk that evening, a little after dark."[31] Not that darkness made much difference: the leaping flames illuminated the whole scene with a hellish light. The decoy party consisted of the Kid, French, Chaves y Chaves, Harvey Morris, and Tom O'Folliard. They edged to the door, poised and tense. Then they ran, firing at anything that moved.

Harvey Morris was killed before he had gone three yards, a single bullet dropping him in his tracks. The Kid and the others ran dodging and weaving through a storm of bullets towards the Tunstall store, only to be met by more shots fired by men hiding behind its northeast wall. The Kid said these men were soldiers, an accusation not unnaturally denied by the military. "I ran towards Tunstall's store, was fired at and then turned towards the river," he said. Followed by his companions, he stumbled and slid down the steep riverbank to safety. McSween and the others were not so fortunate. Andy Boyle told what came next:

> When the first party escaped McSween and two Mexicans got as far as the back house, and Harvey Morris fell as he was going out the gate. McSween and the two men was back in the corner and stayed about five minutes. They then tried to run out the gate a second time, we shot at them and they again ran back, stayed there about 10 minutes more. McSween called out I shall surrender. Robert Beckwith replied I have got a warrant for you. He went then at the back door to Serve the Warrant. McSween replied I shall never surrender, then the fire became Promiscuous and that was the time the Big Killing was made.
>
> When McSween said he would not surrender everyone of them commenced to shoot. Robert Beckwith fell first with McSween on top of him and two Mexicans right beside them. Two more Mexicans went into the Chicken House, and two fell between the door and the back of the house.[32]

Susan McSween's account of her husband's death is not that of an eyewitness, but it is infinitely more poignant.

In the evening my husband and his friends blinded by smoke weried by battling the flames and the no less remorseless enemies outside driven from room to room as the fire increased till the last room was consumed at last sallied from the home and Oh, my God my heart almost fails to write it, was shot down like a dog on his own threshold when he had fallen upon his knees calling out I surrender Oh my God save me, Oh Lord my lord save me, & after he fell they tore up burning boards and piled them to his body & left it to burn.[33]

The Big Killing was over. Later testimony would establish that Florencio Chaves and Jose Maria Sanchez had escaped unhurt in the confusion, and that Ignacio Gonzales was severely wounded in the arm as he ran for safety.[34] Lying near the smoldering ruins of the house were the bodies of five men: Alexander McSween, Francisco Zamora, Vicente Romero, Harvey Morris, and Robert Beckwith. One, possibly two more were dead inside the house. Fifteen-year-old Yginio Salazar, badly wounded, sprawled unconscious near the adobe wall, was presumed dead. Andy Boyle kicked the body a couple of times to make sure; he was about to put another bullet into Salazar for luck when Milo Pierce said, "Don't waste your shot on that greaser, he's long gone and dead as a herring."[35] Bob Beckwith's body was retrieved by his friends and taken to the Murphy store (fig. 67).

Somebody got liquor; the Peppin posse whooped and screeched and cavorted about, firing their guns into the air. Others rounded up Sebrian Bates and George Washington, and forced them to sit up on an adobe wall and play their fiddles "all through the long hours of that sad night," as George Coe put it.[36] Still others broke open the Tunstall store, long since abandoned by its defenders, and helped themselves to anything they wanted. The officers and men from Fort Stanton watched all this as impassively as they had observed the burning of the McSween house and the killings that followed; not one of them made so much as a murmur of protest.

Around midnight the victors reeled off to their beds. During the night, when they were gone, Yginio Salazar somehow managed to crawl to the Otero house, more than half an agonizing mile away.[37] The bodies of McSween and his followers lay where they had fallen; no one dared go near them until morning.

WAR: THE AFTERMATH

ON Saturday, July 20, 1878, the army day started early. At 5 a.m. the bugles blew assembly and the noncoms shouted the enlisted men into formation for roll call.[1] The smell of coffee from the mess tents mingled with the acrid tang of burned timber from the ruins of the McSween house. The few citizens left in town emerged timidly from their houses to fetch water or tend their animals; one or two went across to where the bodies of McSween, Morris, Zamora, Romero, and Beckwith still lay in the yard, rapidly stiffening as rigor mortis set in. McSween's chickens were picking at the corpses. Flies clustered on the bloody wounds. The copper stink of death was everywhere. Dudley ordered some of his men to cover McSween's body with a bed quilt that was lying in the yard.

George Peppin busied himself rounding up enough men to form a coroner's jury.[2] Foreman John B. Wilson, Felipe Miranda, Jose Garcia, Maximiano Chaves, Octaviano Salas, Felipe Mes, and Jose Serna were taken to see the bodies. They testified that McSween had five shots in his body, Morris one, Romero three in body and legs, Zamora eight, and Beckwith two in wrist and head. They then and there rendered their verdict, to wit:

> We, the Coroner's Jury under our oaths do say that A. A. McSween, Harvey Morris, Francisco Samora and Becente Romero came to their deaths by rifle shots from the hands of the Sheriff's posse, while they the above named persons were resisting the Sheriff's posse with force and arms, and that Robert Beckwith came to his death by two rifle shots from the hands of the above named persons . . . while they were resisting the Sheriff's posse as afore said with force and arms, he (Robert Beckwith) then and there being a deputy Sheriff and in the discharge of his duty as such, and trying to arrest parties for whom he had warrants to arrest.

The sun was climbing higher; the bodies had to be removed.[3] Bob Beckwith's had already been taken to the Dolan store; later in the day, when Dudley's command returned to Fort Stanton, they took Beckwith's body with them, and interred it with full military honors in the cemetery there. Friends and family removed the bodies of Zamora and Romero. Peppin sent one of the Shield children to ask Mrs. McSween if she wished him to bury her husband: she forbade him to so much as touch him. For the moment, David Easton detailed a couple of Mexicans to carry the bodies of McSween and Morris into the Tunstall store.

Following them there, he discovered that the place was full of Peppin's men. Jessie Evans and John Kinney were trying on new suits. Jake Owens, Andy Boyle, and others were helping themselves to anything that took their fancy.

Easton sent for Peppin and Sam Corbet (fig. 68). Peppin confessed he was powerless to stop the looting but offered to send two men to help Corbet, who declined. Dudley and Appel came in; the latter promised to have the looters arrested if Corbet would swear out warrants. Corbet again declined: he was afraid he would be killed if he did. Aided by the presence of the officers, they got the looters out; Easton helped him to board up the store, and they left. Corbet went to the Ellis house and scribbled a hasty note to Robert Widenmann.

FIG. 68. Samuel R. Corbet at about thirty-six years of age, ca. 1886. Photographer Furlong & Crispell, Las Vegas, N.M.

Dear Rob
Yesterday morning Genl Dudley, Capt Purington, Capt Blair and Lieut Goodwin with a detachment of cavalary and a detachment of infantry marched down to the Plaza. Just as soon as they came in sight, Peppin and his posse got themselves ready for a fight. Peppin's posse went to McSween's and told them to surrender which they refused to do. They then set fire to the house & burned everything Mrs. McSween & Mrs. Shield had, killed McSween, Harvey Morris, Bicente Romero and Francisco Parinio [Zamora] these have been found. I do not know if any more were found or killed. Last night or soon this morning the Store was busted open and every thing taken that was wanted. I went to Peppin and talked to him, he said he was not responsible for anything in the store. I nailed it up the best I could, but think it will be opened again or burned. I do not know what to do, am liable to be killed any moment. I have not heard from you since Court adjourned, why dont you write to me.—I have written 3 letters and received no answer.—Mrs. McSween and Mrs. Shield have not a change of clothing left. Dr. Ealy is going to leave, he is going straight to Washington he has gone to the Fort now. I will not describe the conduct of some Gentlemen but you will find it out soon.—For God sake don't make anything I say public.—God knows what will turn up next.—I am still stopping at Ellis's.—The cattle on the Felix are liable to go any day.—Please let me hear from you.—[4]

As soon as he finished this note, Corbet left town for the safer environs of Magado, a *placita* near what is now Capitan. He did not even stay to see McSween and Morris buried in a grave dug by Sebrian Bates in the plot behind the store. "My wife, out of her scanty supply, furnished the winding sheet," Doctor Ealy recalled later.[5] There was "no coffin, no hymn, no prayer." Dudley was harsh and unsympathetic.[6] "McSween's body, unwashed, was wrapped up in a blanket, placed in a box, and buried without ceremony," he reported that night.

By following the bloodstains the wounded youth, Yginio Salazar, had left in his agonizing midnight crawl, John Kinney and three of his men had meanwhile tracked him to the home of Jose Otero, and threatened to kill him. Fortunately for Salazar, his sister-in-law Nicolasita Pacheco had sent for Doctor Appel, who told Kinney that if they harmed Salazar he would see them hanged.[7] They slouched off. Appel summoned Justice of the Peace Wilson and had Salazar execute an affidavit giving an account of the fight.

At about four in the afternoon, Dudley ordered camp struck and prepared to leave Lincoln.[8] Before he departed, he posted a small guard at the Baca house; Saturnino Baca believed the Regulators held him responsible for bringing the troops to town, and claimed they had threatened to burn him out in retaliation for the burning of the McSween house. Dudley then made a general offer to take with him in an ambulance anyone who wished to go to the fort for protection. Elizabeth Shield and her children, Doctor Ealy and family, and Susan Gates elected to go. Susan McSween, nursing her grief and her bitterness toward Dudley, refused to place herself under any obligation to him and remained in town, in spite of the threatening presence of Kinney and his bravos.

By any sensible reckoning, the war should have ended that bloody Friday, but it did not. As Dudley presciently noted in his report, written at midnight after his return to his quarters: "One thing is sure, both parties are still determined, the fearful sacrafice of McSween's clique on the 19th inst does not seem to satisfy either side. A deep revenge will be sought by the sheriffs posse for the loss of their pet leader *Beckwith*, and a still stronger spirit exists on the part of the McSween men to retaliate for the death of their headman, McSween."[9]

Men who had the "reckless courage" to attack as well defended a position as the McSween house, and for that matter men who defended as stubbornly as those inside the house had, were "not of a character to abandon a course they believe is only half completed," Dudley said, and he was right.[10] The fire had not gone out; it would flare into life all too soon.

Next morning, David Easton and Edgar Walz found a mob of local Hispanics pillaging the Tunstall store.[11] When challenged, they said Mrs. McSween had given them permission to take whatever they wanted. Easton went across to the Patrón store to ask the widow if this was so.

"I'd rather have the Mexicans living on the creek have the goods than any of Peppin's gang of murderers," she said.

"You can do as you please," Easton replied. "If you have any interest in having the goods saved, I will aid you, but if the goods are allowed to be stolen by anyone I will go home."

"If you think the store will not be burned down and that the goods can be saved, I would be glad to have you help to put them back," Mrs. McSween told him. Easton went back to the store and nailed up the doors and windows again. That afternoon there was yet another break-in. Sam Corbet was sent for but refused to leave Magado. David Easton told Sebrian Bates and Joe Dixon to nail the store up again; thereafter—there was probably nothing left worth stealing by this time—it was left undisturbed.

On Tuesday, July 23, twenty-seven-year-old Charlie "Lallacooler" Crawford died at the Fort Stanton hospital, far from his Iowa home.[12] He was buried the following day after a service led by Doctor Ealy, who preached a sermon, the text of which he recorded as verse sixteen of the last chapter of Ecclesiastes. It is a measure of Doctor Ealy's distraught and confused state of mind: there are only fourteen verses in that chapter.

Ealy's distress stemmed from the fact that Dudley and his officers were making no secret of their displeasure in having a party of missionaries camping on their doorstep. The day after their arrival, Dudley had slapped a censorship order on Ealy, forbidding him to correspond with anyone unless the letters first passed through his adjutant's office.[13] Ealy then further put his foot in it by asking Dudley to send a soldier to cut the wood in their quarters because it was too long to go into the stove. The irascible Dudley exploded.

> Sir: I am in receipt of your note of this evening and in reply have to say, I have ordered an ax to be sent to you for the purpose of shortening the wood to suit your fireplace or stove . . . which you will be required to use or go without wood. Soldiers at present under my command have other more important duties to attend to than waiting on parties holding your position.
> If these views do not meet your expectations . . . the sooner you leave the post the better I shall be pleased. I am surprised that a Minister of the Gospel, a missionary at that, should be so indolent as to be unable to cut a few sticks of wood to aid his wife in cooking for himself and small family at a time when you have nothing in the world to do besides.[14]

Dudley's impatience is understandable; he had a lot more on his mind than Taylor Ealy's firewood. The civil unrest in Lincoln was only part of his problems, for he also had to contend with hostile Mescaleros who had left the reservation and were hiding out in the mountains, raiding and stealing stock.[15]

In Lincoln, meanwhile, Susan McSween had ventured out for the first time.[16] Accompanied by Sebrian Bates and George Washington, she went across the street to the ruins of her once lovely home and began poking about in the ruins to see if there was anything worth salvaging. As she lifted up a strip of burned carpet she looked up to see Andrew Boyle and John Kinney watching her.

"What's the good of trying to save that?" Boyle asked her, roughly. "By God, we've killed McSween and we'll get you yet!"

"I'll not leave that for you vandals to carry off," she snapped, pointing at the carpet. "I'd rather see the Mexicans get it than you."

Her words angered John Kinney so much he threatened to shoot her on the spot if she didn't shut her mouth.

"Well, kill me!" she shouted defiantly. "You've already taken away all that was precious to me, my husband and my home. I'd just as soon you take my life!"

Standing defiant in the broken ruins of her home, teetering on the edge of a complete breakdown, wearing the same stained, soot-soiled dress she had worn since the day her husband was killed—now the only clothing she owned in the world—her pride and courage seem to have shamed the two men. They turned away without another word and headed toward the western end of town.

On July 25, six days after the Big Killing, Susan McSween wrote to John P. Tunstall in London. It is a curiously uneven letter: at one moment truly moving, yet the next so apparently calculated as to render suspect all the sentiments it contains.

> My dear Sir,
> Oh, it is painful indeed that I am at last left to convey to you the sad news of my dear dear Husband's death, he was killed in the evening of the 19th at home and the house and everything in it burned to ashes, was not able to save even a change of clothing for myself. Oh that day was the most horrible Sight that could be imagined,

he was murdered even worse than poor John. Those thieves and murderers gathered around the house, set it on fire, & commenced shooting in every door & window, when he, Mr. McSween, found there was no chance of escape, he begged them not to shoot him, but that availed nothing. I buried him by the side of your dear Son, that always was his wish; you cannot imagine the love he bore for your son. I would have written before this, but the subject was too painful, and now it is only more painful. Oh! how can I survive all this, do pray for me. Mr. McSween was not himself from the day of your son's death, he has not left a thing undone to prove that he was a murdered man, & I fear too, that Mr. Widenmann is killed; he started for Mesilla about four or five weeks ago to attend Court and we have not heard from him for about three weeks & whilst those men were here they swore they would kill him, others said we would never see him again; now we don't know what to think of it. After those men killed my dear Husband, they broke into your son's store and dressed themselves from head to foot & invited all others to help them selves which many of them did, they broke into your son's the [sic] office, rummaged through the papers, took what they wanted of them, opened the trunk and took all his clothing. Oh, but it pained me to see all this done. John has given me many little keepsakes that I prized very highly but they too had to burn up with the balance of my things. They have also threatened my life because I have defended both Mr. McSween and your son, and many believe that I am really in danger. I will write you more particularly when I recover from the shock.

I hope you will pardon me for speaking of a matter which is entirely business, but as I am left entirely destitute, with not even a change of clothing, I deem it necessary to speak of the matter, but I was aware of your son owing Mr. McSween about four or five thousand dollars & also knew he had asked you to pay it, now I fear you have sent it, and that somebody will find it, they are beginning to claim his debts already, can you not pay it me or could you not send a small portion of it to me that I may have something to depend on for a while at least, nothing can be done yet about Mr. McSween's business, nearly every man has left the Town & gone to the mountains to save their lives. I will write you soon again, am very sick at present. I am of a very nervous disposition & cannot stand under too much. Excuse this for I scarcely know what I am doing.[17]

Staying at the Patrón place, from which its owner had long since fled, she was guarded by a rota of ex-Regulators, including Charlie Bowdre, Doc Scurlock, Jim French, and the Kid. It was at this time the rumor was circulated that French had become the widow's lover: there were always ears in Lincoln eager to hear such slanders. French's own words repudiate the calumny: "John [Middleton] and I took turns sleeping in front of the door of the house where widow McSween was staying. The old hag got an idea they were going to kill her. I guess we owed it to the wife of old penny pincher Mac, but she never even thanked us, she never even offered either of us a breakfast."[18]

Hardly the recollections of a lover, one feels. Even in such perilous times, however, lighter moments intervened. One night a polecat walked over the sleeping body of Sam Corbet, who let out a yell that wakened not only his companions but also the sleeping woman, who thought Dolan's men had finally come to carry out their threat to kill her.

David Shield was in Las Vegas, where he had remained after attending court in Santa Fe. When he received the news of McSween's death and the loss of all his family's possessions, he addressed himself to Montague R. Leverson, with whom he had been in regular correspondence, requesting a business loan of one hundred dollars for ninety days. "I do not wish to place myself under any obligations to the ring or their clique & they control everything here," he said.

Shield's letter re-ignited the crusading zeal of the formidable Leverson, who immediately wrote to Carl Schurz, enclosing Shield's note.[19] "If the president still hesitates to remove the wretches who are desolating New Mex., you must resign," he told Schurz, "if you would not share the responsibility for the horrid crimes there daily committed." Thereafter he once more turned his attention to President Hayes himself.

Excellency

I enclose you a letter I have just received advising me of the murder of another admirable gentleman A. A. McSween. For this murder—as also for that of McNab committed some weeks ago *your Excellency's administration* is accountable before God & man.

You have now known long enough the character of the wretches appointed to office by your predecessor. Your Excellency was warned that this would be the result of continuing them in office and all you have done has been to send down an able and upright gentleman *to investigate!* Meanwhile men equal to yourself in every quality of heart and mind are being daily murdered by procurement of the villains your predecessor appointed to office and you maintain there!

Excellency I have in no way sought the office— dangerous indeed for a man who does his duty as governor of New Mexico, but I know that my name has been mentioned in that connection to the administration.

Tho' it would entail also heavy pecuniary sacrifices on my part I would accept the office & pledge myself to restore peace and order to New Mexico within 60 days of my installation or perish in the attempt.[20]

Clearly believing that his appointment to the governorship was but a matter of days away, Leverson next wrote to the *Denver News,* which had published an account of the events of July 19.

NEW MEXICO
Heavy Charges Against the Santa Fe
Ring

LEVERSON'S RANCH, July 31—

I have just read with surprise your insertion of a communication from Santa Fe, written for the purpose of giving a legal color to the atrocious murder of that admirable gentleman, A. A. McSween, by the assassins employed by the United States officials—the infamous Governor Axtell at their head—for that purpose. Having closely examined the state of affairs in that unhappy territory, I state positively that for every murder committed in that country, from the Colfax county troubles to this day, the governor and the United States attorney (and in Lincoln county Judge Bristol also) are directly answerable, as well as for the insecurity of property there prevailing.

These infamous men were all appointed by President Grant, heedless of the qualifications of the men he appointed, and the very worst features of carpet-bag government in the south have been outdone in unhappy New Mexico.

The man Peppin, called the sheriff, and who was so appointed by the scoundrel Axtell, but who has never been able to qualify, was, at the time Axtell appointed him, charged, and warrants were out for his arrest, for the murder of two men in Doña Anna county, before he came to Lincoln.

The present administration sent an able and upright gentleman "to investigate," but it is the general belief that the Santa Fe ring will not allow him to leave New

Mexico alive! Meanwhile, the administration was warned on all hands that unless it immediately removed Axtell and Catron, the United States district attorney, more good and true men would be murdered. Yet the administration does nothing, and, before God and man, it is morally responsible for the murder of McSween and his followers.

Take no stock of anything sent you from Santa Fe. So terrible a reign of terror prevails in New Mexico that no journal, except the *Cimarron News and Press*, has dared to tell the truth.[21]

Immediately this appeared (it was reprinted in the *Las Animas Leader* on August 9) Leverson sent a copy to Schurz with yet another letter, this time more or less giving the secretary of the interior his final opportunity to appoint Leverson governor of New Mexico.[22] His letter, Leverson revealed, had led to his being requested "to stump this State for the Democratic party this Fall." The leaders of the Republican party both in Colorado and New Mexico were so bad, he stated, that he would in all probability comply with the request,

chiefly I must say for the purpose of denouncing the atrocities committed in New Mex. and so doing something towards securing relief to its people, *if the administration should not anticipate my efforts by affording* the needed relief. . . .

I am told that my name has been urged on the administration as a fitting person to be appointed Governor of New Mex *for the benefit of the people.*

I do not seek, I have not sought, I do not desire the appointment: not because I dread the danger (as you will presently observe) although strongly persuaded I should not live 3 months in New Mexico, for even now, further plots have been laid for my life by the ruffians now holding power, one of which lately failed signally. They laid their plans—of course neither Axtell nor Catron has appeared openly in the matter—to get hold of some 5 or 6,000.00 [dollars] worth of my property expecting I should go down in person to save it. The coach was stopped the day they expected me by 2 masked and armed ruffians who demanded the way bill & who cursed and swore when they found *I* was *not* in the coach but allowed it to proceed without robbing it!

Nevertheless, *I would cheerfully sacrifice my own private business & peril my life,* to furnish security for the lives and property of the citizens; the only purpose for which government should be tolerated at all!

Were I appointed governor my first act would be to request that the U.S. troops be ordered to confine their activities to protecting the citizens from the Indians & to aiding the *U.S. Marshall,* instead of as heretofore, aiding the thieves and murderers to rob and murder, making searches and arrests without warrant, depriving the good citizens of their arms (all in violation of the constitution) & helping the U.S. Attorney of New Mex to steal Mr. Hunter's cattle!

Without the use of a man of the U.S. Army an efficient and *upright* governor would restore peace to New Mexico within 60 days relying on the people only to aid him!

Carl Schurz obviously agreed that an efficient and upright governor was clearly what New Mexico needed, and an efficient and upright governor it would have. That man, however, would not be Montague Leverson, for Schurz had another candidate in mind. But before he could be appointed, guns were blazing yet again in Lincoln County.

Nathan Dudley's observation that the two sides were as hostile as ever was absolutely correct. Fortunately for all concerned, they now seemed unable to find each other. "From the most reliable information I have," Dudley reported to headquarters in Santa Fe, "I believe the Sheriffs posse has traced the McSween party to the Pecos; the last report places them only six miles ahead of the sheriff's party. Another fight may be expected anyway. If they will only keep out of towns it matters little how much shooting they do."[23]

George Peppin and his deputies, scouring the countryside for the remnants of the McSween force—"Modocs," as Gus Gildea had so contemptuously dubbed them—were misled in the assumption they would be on the Pecos in the neighborhood of the Chisum ranch. In fact, they were somewhere in the mountains between San Patricio and South Fork, whence they emerged on the afternoon of August 5 to precipitate a fracas in which Morris Bernstein was to meet his death.

What prompted their appearance at the Mescalero Agency? One reason given is that they planned to steal some horses from the Indians; another that they were in pursuit of a gang of rustlers, led by Frank Wheeler, who had run off Tunstall's horses; a third, that they planned to kill Godfroy; and least likely of all, a reason lamely suggested by Frank Coe, was that they had gone to visit Dick Brewer's grave.[24] The meticulous records of the U.S. Army, however, suggest quite a different motive for the murder.

Capt. Thomas Blair was detailed to make a complete investigation and to interview any and all witnesses. He took statements from Doctor Blazer, interpreter Jose Carrillo, Fred Godfroy, his wife, and their daughter Kate. In his report to Dudley, dated August 9, Blair concluded that the gang numbered nineteen; the Kid, Scurlock, Middleton, Bowdre, French, O'Folliard, Brown, Scroggins, Stevens, Bowers, and the Coes, together with half a dozen Hispanics, among whom were Fernando Herrera and Ignacio Gonzales.[25] These latter were in the van, and were fired on by Indians who feared they had come to steal the ponies grazing along the creek. Godfroy and Bernstein were at the issue house giving out supplies when the firing began. "The Indians who came in that day had pretty much all gone," said Godfroy.[26]

All at once, I saw the squaws in the vicinity of the issue window throw up their hands and halloa and shout, that there was some shooting going on. Those near the window threw back their rations for safe keeping, and ran in all directions.

Mr. Bernstein immediately ran out, going towards the shooting. I called him back and told him he had better take a horse. I councilled him to be very cautious as we did not know who the firing was [being] done by That I was afraid that the wild Indians had just come in had met some of the Indians here and were fighting with them There were then some Indians in sight shooting over the crest of the hill. Finding they were not supported, they all retreated, except two, who kept up an incessant fire at the (to us) unseen enemy. The last words I said to Mr. Bernstein were: If you get there before I do and find it is the Indians fighting, try and pursuade them to stop, and if it becomes necessary shoot back, dont shoot until the last moment. I immediately got another horse, and as I left the issue room, I saw him ride over the crest of the hill, from behind which the shooting was done, and before I got halfway, I saw the horse had been riderless.

I knew then that he was killed, but not by the Indians. I pushed on till I got to the crest, and I satisfied myself that we were attacked by others than Indians. Suddenly a man appeared, a white man, with his gun in his hand and looking alternately at me and the Indian who was pressing him close. He shot at the Indian, and immediately another man appeared and shot in my direction. At the same time three shots came from the right side and rear of him in the same direction, the balls passing over my head; I knew it would be folly to remain there longer, as I would certainly be killed if I did. Knowing that Lieut Smith and four soldiers were at my house which is a mile distant I started to get their assistance. Lieut. Smith and three of the soldiers returned with me, leaving one to protect the house.

When we returned shooting was still going on between the two Indians and the unknown assailants. As soon as they saw me returning with soldiers the firing ceased and they left, taking with them all the agency animals and leaving four of their own horses, saddled and bridled, which had got away from them during the fight. After some searching I found the body of Mr. Bernstein lying on its face, with four bullet holes in it. His Winchester rifle, pistol and cartridges were gone, his pockets were turned out and contents gone.

Immediately following the raid on the agency, Dudley, outraged and mortified—after all, Bernstein had been killed under the noses of Lieutenant Smith's squad, detailed to guard the agency—ordered a detachment led by Captain Carroll out after the fugitives.[27] Godfroy meantime sent a runner across to Fort Stanton with two telegraph messages, one to the Bureau of Indian Affairs in Washington, this to Governor Axtell in Santa Fe.

SOUTH FORK VIA MESILLA

August 5, 1878.

Morris J. Bernstein my clerk today was brutally murdered by McSween outlaws near the issue room. Myself and Indians were also fired upon but escaped unhurt. Attacking party supposed to number forty. Business at this office will be somewhat delayed in consequence.[28]

Axtell in turn advised Carl Schurz in Washington that Bernstein had been murdered, that government and Indian horses had been stolen, that the Indians were fighting the outlaws, and that Godfroy's life was in danger. Schurz's reaction can scarcely have been what either Axtell or Godfroy expected: he suspended both of them.

It all seems quite straightforward: the McSween gang rode in to steal horses, ran into unexpected opposition, and killed Bernstein. Yet Captain Blair's report recorded tensions at the agency which suggest that there might have been a great deal more to the murder of Bernstein than is at first apparent. Blair seems to have thought so, too, and as a result he put some particularly pointed questions to Doctor Blazer.[29] Was it true, he asked, that a few nights before Bernstein was killed, Bernstein had called Blazer a liar; whereupon Blazer smote the table with his fist and shouted that no man could him a liar and live, and that he could have sixty Mexicans there in ten hours? Blazer's reply was hardly a model of clarity.

He said I had injured him personally by reporting the absence of beef to Genl. Dudley. I told him I had not. I had reported the absence of beef first to Capt. Smith in a conversation in regard to the condition of the county, not as reporting a wrong[doing] but fearing from threats that San Juan, Gregorcia, and other Indians had made to me that it would bring on an Indian war . . . that Capt Smith had insisted on my going with him, that it was my duty to report the same thing to Genl. Dudley. I had done so at his [Smith's] request and not to injure him [Bernstein] or Riley or any other person. . . . I insisted on him retracting the assertion that I had sworn to a falsehood, that I would prove by Capt. Smith and Genl. Dudley what I had sworn, and could prove the assertion was true by Mr. Easton. That Mr. Riley had admitted in writing the truth of the assertion I had made, at least that Riley had told me and that Genl. Dudley had told me so.

Blazer went on to say that one Benito Montoya had brought him a note from George "Roxy" Rose, asking him to come to Tularosa, where during the evening of August 2, Jim Reese had been shot in the head during an altercation with the Sanches brothers. Blazer told him his horses were out, but he would come as soon as he could.

> In the morning after sun up I was standing on my porch. Mr. Bernstein came around the corner of the house to my porch asked me if there was a horseman come to my room during the night. I told him yes. . . . He said he knew Jim Reese and would like to see the letter. He went into my room, read it, and asked me to write to him on my arrival at Tulerosa, if there was any hope of benefitting Reese, that he might write to Dr. Appel. When I got to Tulerosa Reese was dead and I did not write to him.
>
> I returned the same evening. Mr. Bernstein and I talked together. He appeared satisfied with my explanation, and I thought there was no more trouble between us on that subject.
>
> I would say further that Mr. Farr went with me to Tulerosa. I believe he was present at the conversation with Mr. Bernstein, both in the morning and evening. A few evenings before this, a citizen, whose name I will not give came to me, and told me, he was satisfied from what he had heard, that my life was in danger, that Mr. Bernstein was very much incensed against me.

Captain Blair's conclusions are the most interesting part of his lengthy report. He expressed himself convinced that Bernstein had been murdered by the McSween party. It was quite evident, he said, that

> the manner of attack was premeditated, and that the first shots were fired at the Indians, in order to draw Maj. Godfroy, Bernstein, and some other employe [interpreter Jose Carrillo] outside the buildings and then murder them.
>
> I did not obtain sufficient evidence to warrant me in connecting others with the murder, than the party already mentioned, that is the McSween party.[30]

Nevertheless, Captain Blair still had his suspicions. "I invite special attention to the Statement[s] of Dr. Blazer," he wrote in his report. "To a person disinterested in the affair, they are remarkable."

> It appears that Dr. Blazer has been in various way[s] insinuating and making innuendoes against Maj. Godfroy since the latter refused to discharge Mr. Bernstein. . . .
>
> He neither expressed surprise nor regret at the murder of Mr. Bernstein, nor sympathy for his friends. He also insinuated to me that Mr. Bernstein had frequently tampered with his letters. I consider the life of Mr. Godfroy in very great danger, unless he has a guard of soldiers.

A month later, the *Cimarron News and Press* printed an article that attempted to write *finis* to the story of the brief and bloody flurry at the agency. Morris Bernstein had been killed, it claimed,

> by a Mexican who was with a party going from San Patricio to Tularosa to assist in recovering a lot of stolen stock in the possession of Frank Wheeler and others then at San Nicolas. When the Mexicans reached the water along side of the road above the Agency, they stopped to water their horses. Bernstein saw them and probably supposing them to be a party of the "Regulators" attacked them with a party of

Indians; he rode up to one Mexican and fired two shots at him; the man took shelter behind a tree. Bernstein still advancing rode close to the tree and fired again at the man, who returned the fire and killed Bernstein. The Mexican says he acted strictly in self-defense and will at any time deliver himself up for trial. His name is Atanacio Martínez.[31]

Although the reasons given for the party's being at the agency are debatable (whom were they going to "assist"?), the account of how Bernstein actually died rings true. Atanacio Martínez's support of the McSween cause dated back to the days immediately following the murder of Tunstall. In spite of this "confession," he was never indicted for the murder. Instead, that dubious honor belongs to George Coe, Henry Brown, Fred Waite, and the Kid.

Nearly a month after the killing, Cpl. Thomas Baker of the Fifteenth Infantry reported to the post adjutant that on the night of August 30,

> an employe of Dr. Blazer (Mr. Stracie) while sleeping at Browns Ranche over heard a conversation between the Coe's Bros and other parties to the effect that they did not want to kill him (Bernstein) but that while they were firing at the Indians he rode up and asked what do you S- of B- want here, at the same time firing his pistol at the man most nearest to him (a Mexican) which fire was immediately returned by the whole party.[32]

Whichever of them fired the fatal shots, there remains the suspicion that Bernstein's death was more than the random killing it appeared to be. What importance should be given to the quarrel between Bernstein and Doctor Blazer?[33] What was the significance of interpreter Carrillo's remarks about the man and woman killed by Navajo scouts? How did Jimmy Dolan and Pantaleon Gallegos come to be with the pursuit detachment commanded by Captain Carroll? Perhaps one day history will permit the untangling of the web of concealed motives that seem to have been involved. Until then, the verdict remains open.

CHAPTER 28

ANARCHY IN LINCOLN COUNTY

IN the weeks following the death of Morris Bernstein, Sheriff Peppin abandoned all pretense of upholding law and order and took refuge at Fort Stanton, where he held down the not inapposite job of post butcher. What was left of the old Regulator group—Billy the Kid, Doc Scurlock, Charlie Bowdre, Sam Smith, Jim French, and Tom O'Folliard (fig. 69) prominent among them—headed for the mountains two jumps ahead of the decidedly pro-Dolan Lieutenant Goodwin and his pursuit detachment.

On August 13, loyal Sam Corbet undertook to bring Tunstall's father up to date on conditions in Lincoln County.[1] He began by saying he had just read a letter written by Dudley

in which he charges Mr. Widenmann and Mr. McSween of the Murder of Your Son. Well does Genl. Dudley know that his murder was premeditated and the same parties have since succeeded in murdering Mr. McSween. And I am afraid they will do the same with Mr. Widenmann if he does not leave the country. Mr. Dolan with a company of Soldiers (from Fort Stanton) and about 20 Apache Indians are out hunting the citizens of this county who are friends of Mr. McSween and your Son. Genl Dudley cannot get enough Soldiers to catch them so he armed the Indians and turned them out. I suppose Mr. Widenmann explained to you how Genl Dudley managed to have him and Mr. McSween and others arrested about the time he wrote you that letter. It was by warrants sworn out by Murphy Dolan and Riley's affidavid men, Mathews and Peppin, the latter is now the Governors *Pet* Sheriff who had in his posse the day they killed McSween about 8 of the Murderers of Mr. Tunstall for whom he had warrants in his possession for their arrest for his murder and many other crimes. Peppin is one of the Party who waylaid and killed Frank McNab and is now acting the sheriff and assisted by Genl Dudley. I wrote you some time since of the conduct of Genl Dudley in the murdering of McSween and others on the 19th of July. on the following morning when I went into the Store, Genl Dudley himself was in the store where Peppin & his Banditti was carrying of goods and since I learn that the United States Troops help carry of[f] goods from the Store. I left town to save my scalp until Peppin and his Banditti left. They are some where on the Pacos now.

I came back yesterday and am stoping with Mr. Ellis will remain here until I hear from Mr. Widenmann I have not heard from him since the 19th of May. I have written sevral letters to him but received no answers. I am satisfied that he has wrote but the letters are destroyed at the office as it belongs to Catron & Dolan. P[ost].M[aster]. since McSween was killed everything has been quiet in Town but Peppin is liabl to come in any day. Burnstien was killed at the Indian Agency on the 5 inst (Murphyite) The Cattle are still on the Felix and I am at a loss to know what to do with them for I am satisfied when Peppin's Posse leaves the county they

FIG. 69. Tom O'Folliard. Date and photographer unknown. In view of the subject's evident youth, and apparent slimness—he is said to have weighed 175 lbs. at the time of his death—this probably was taken before he left Texas, aged nineteen.

will take them. But I have no orders from Mr. Widenmann to dispose of them and would not like to do it otherwise.

It is to be hoped that Mr. Angel will do something for us soon, if not all the citizens in the county who have even sympathized with Mr. Tunstalls friends will have to leave or be killed.

Only four days later, old embers blazed yet again. This time it was at "Henpeck Ranch," as the Beckwith place on Seven Rivers had come to be known. Hugh Beckwith had never liked his son-in-law William Johnson, and they quarreled constantly. After the Big Killing, Beckwith came to hold Johnson responsible for the death of the son he had idolized. As Susan Barber said, "Beckwith did everything to keep his boys out of [the Lincoln troubles] but Johnson overpowered him and got them on the last trip when 'Bob' was killed."[2] Beckwith's grief festered for a month, and then exploded in violence.

What happened next is set forth in a letter written by Refugia Beckwith and her son John on the day of the murder.

We have to inform you that Hugh M Beckwith shot and killed Mr W H Johnston [sic], the husband of his daughter, on the 17th day of August.

The killing was premeditated and without provication as can be proven.

The circumstances are these. Mr Johnston, Wallace Olinger, W A Alexander and A R Bennett were stringing some snap beans in the yard of our house, when Mr Johnston started to go to his room & on his way had to pass by a small adobe house. Just as Mr Johnston passed the house H M Beckwith come out of his room with a double barrel shotgun loaded with buck shot and fired one barrel into Mr Johnston killing him almost instantly. H M Beckwith then aimed the other barrel of his gun at Wallace Olinger, but Mr Olinger shot him first in the face. We then disarmed H M Beckwith and placed him under guard. We sent him up to be tried by the law & to suffer whatever penalty the law may impose, though he is the husband of one of us and the father of the other.

Abneth McCabe, now at Seven Rivers, was chosen to escort the badly wounded Beckwith up to Fort Stanton; they arrived there five days later. Post surgeon Daniel Appel examined Beckwith and pronounced his life in danger, whereupon Beckwith was placed in the hospital.[3]

Susan McSween, who had gone to Las Vegas for medical attention, had there met Frank Angel, the special investigator of the Justice Department. Angel had returned to New Mexico to examine further the accusations leveled against

Governor Axtell, notably by Cimarron attorney Frank Springer. Angel asked for, and Mrs. McSween provided, further affidavits from herself and others relating to the death of her husband and the burning of the McSween house.

Angel headed back East at the end of August, and Mrs. McSween returned to Lincoln, where she soon realized that her situation was, to say the least of it, precarious.[4] Without the protection of "those foolhardy boys" she was at the mercy of any swaggering tough who wished to insult her on the street; and many did. Had it not been for the intermittent presence of the Kid, French, Scurlock, and Sam Corbet, worse might have ensued.

Worse was to ensue anyway: The hard-core toughs of the old Peppin posse—Kinney and Jake Owens, Jessie Evans and Jim McDaniels, Gus Gildea, Roscoe "Rustling Bob" Bryant, John Collins, John Irvin, and Bob Speakes among them—now joined forces with thirty-nine-year-old John Selman and his brother, Tom, who liked to call himself "Tom Cat." Tom Selman was a deserter, pimp, rustler, and fugitive from vigilante justice. Brazenly dubbing themselves "the Rustlers" and enlisting as many thugs of like spirit as could be found, the gang made ready to ride.

On Sunday, August 18, some of this crowd rode up to the Feliz and helped themselves to Tunstall's cattle, which were guarded only by old Martin Martz. Godfrey Gauss advised Tunstall's father the following Thursday, August 22, that the war was once again

raging as fiercely as ever, the county is overrun by horse and cattle thieves, and there is no law in force.

The thieves took last Sunday the herd of cows about 200 in number worth perhaps $2500.00, the last of the property belonging to your son's estate which could have been at present turned into ready money. The thieves took one man—who with me was taken [sic] care of the cowherd—along with them, & I arrived here yesterday giving information of the heavy loss we sustained. I am thrown out of employment & as there is no means on hand to get paid I am truly in a pitiable condition. Wages are due to me to this date of $175.00 & if I canot get payment, without all means as I am, I canot even leave this godforsaken country & have to look starvation into the face.

Mr. Widenmann is absent from here since June, his whereabouts unknown & he surely canot show himself here now without sharing the fate of your son. Mr. Ellis a merchant here who has been administrator before Mr. Widenmann advised me to write to You, Sir, for help in this dilemma. Would you not have the kindness to put to the disposition of Mr. Ellis so much fund that he could pay me off? I beg most respectfully to consider the case well & to set yourself in my miserable position.[5]

Gauss was not exaggerating. The *Independent* of August 24 noted a *Las Vegas Gazette* report that six wagons bearing Jacob Harris and all the settlers from the North and South Spring area had passed through town, "driven out by the lawless element of the section."

They tried hard to take no part in the conflict and preferred to leave rather than take up either side. About twenty horses had been stolen from them. A deputy sheriff [Marion Turner] rode up with a posse and demanded that they take up arms and go with them and fight. This they refused to do and loaded up and left the country. They left their lands, houses, standing crops, gardens, and everything pertaining to comfortable homes.[6]

The old Regulator gang—making now only token pretense of being anything but what they were, rustlers—was at Bosque Grande; from there, on August 30, John Middleton wrote to Robert Widenmann, still blockaded in La Mesilla.

Dear Rob,

Yours came to hand this morning. I was glad to hear from you. There is nothing can be done by your coming out here The 7 Rivers outfit has stolen your cattle they are at Black River now. We all will start from here the day after tomorrow will do the best we can. old man Beckwith killed (Johnson) his son in law so much for him.

If we dont get Tunstalls cattle we will get more in there place.

10 Buffalo men have joined us we are about 36 in number. there was something flying R[ound] about your killing B[rady] but George [Washington] says it is not so. He helped (George) us in the Plaza the last fight, I dont think he said it, tho while he was a prisoner Peps taken Him to Stanton where Angell interviewed Him. Everything is running pretty, you stay where you are and take care of yourself I dont want you to go like poor Tunstall & Mc has gone we can manage what is here as well without as with you. Old John [Chisum] has gone back on us & Ellis & Son the same, we dont ask no favors of them God dem them. Old uncle Jesse Evans [of Hunter & Evans] is doing all he can for us this say nothing about whatever you do. The reason I dont want you come here is this Everything is stoled out of the country by Peps posse, and we intend to play the same game, at this we will back ourselves. Old Peps has resigned and gone they are Basted in completely. Jim Dolan is on the road to 7 Rivers with the Carrasosa cattle camped at Elk Springs 3 nights ago aims to join the rest of the outfit at B[lack] River we will get him if he dont watch. Take care of yourself I want to see you again Before we die.

Your friend John Middleton.[7]

Middleton had promised that "if we dont get Tunstalls cattle we will get more in there place," and he and the others were as good as their word. On September 6, the gang raided the Fritz ranch below Lincoln, driving off 15 horses and 150 head of cattle.[8] The Fritz ranch was an acknowledged House stronghold; the fact that less than six months earlier it had been the scene of the gunfight in which Ab Saunders was crippled and Frank MacNab killed no doubt afforded the gang additional pleasure.

In La Mesilla on Monday, September 2, Robert Widenmann once more addressed himself to Tunstall *père.* "All my mail matter, going and coming has been held by the tools of the New Mexican ring," he complained, "and it is with only with the greatest difficulty that I can get any letters through. I fear that all or most of my letters to you have been held and will never reach their destination."[9]

His letters to Lincoln were certainly not getting through; Sam Corbet complained of not having had not heard from him since his departure. "It is impossible at present to get back to Lincoln from here," he continued,

as all the roads are guarded and they are only waiting to get a chance to kill me. I have concluded to adopt the following plan: I have ordered all the notes and land certificates to be sent here to me, where I can probably negotiate some of them. Corbett is to keep the books with Mr. Ellis and I have requested them to keep the safe for this purpose. If the cattle are recovered, and I think they will be, I have made arrangements to sell them to Mr. Chisum. After the notes and papers arrive here I will go to Santa Fe and arrange with Mr. [Thomas] Conway, a thoroughly trustworthy attorney, to collect the Dolan note of $1000 and some other accounts. I will then go to Las Vegas and if the cattle are not recovered by that time organize a party and pursue them until I overtake them. This done I will try to arrange with some reliable person if I can not find one here I will bring my brother out, to collect all the outstanding accounts. As soon as this is arranged I will go [to] St. Louis, collect the a/c against R. D. Hunter amounting to a little over $3000.—and pay pro rata on all the claims against the estate. This done I will start for England and can give you then all the facts.

Tunstall's father, who had received Susan McSween's distraught letter of July 25, apparently asked Widenmann to clarify the situation vis à vis the debt she had claimed.

Now as regards McSween's claim allow me to advise you not to send over one pence until you have heard all the facts of the case. I feel that after I have explained everything to you you will look at matters in a somewhat different light. The turn things have taken now will beyond a doubt for a time at least subject you to considerable losses and though I am now doing all in my power to collect the evidence to hold the Territory and the U.S. responsible for all the losses, yet, should I be successful, it will be some time before I can collect the amount which would be payable upon the establishment of the claim. I do not see how in right and equity you, an englishman, are to bear all the losses, and I think you will agree with me when you hear my explanation. I would therefore again advise you to make no remittance at present and I will not telegraph you to do so except under the utmost necessity.

I think I see my way clear and will do my utmost to save you from any losses. Of course I am only human and can not hope to accomplish miracles but I will use my utmost efforts to save all I can. All the things and dear Harrie's effects and trinkets which I had gathered together to bring to you have been stolen as also everything I had even to my clothes, photograph album, etc. As to my things that does not in the least trouble me, but I greatly feel the loss you sustain by having all these momentoes stolen.

Mr. F. W. Angel the U.S. commissioner sent out to examine matters in the Territory was forced to return to Washington because his life was in iminent danger and had been frequently and openly threatened by the New Mex. ring. But I am certain that his labour will carry severe retribution with it. This feeling is already evident through the Territory and the members of the ring are trembling in their boots. Where I once had one outspoken friend in my fight against the ring, I now have 10, simply because the reign of terrorism is broken, and the people dare to begin to speak their thoughts openly. My life is daily threatened, but I have become so thoroughly accustomed to it, that I dont mind it much. I am always on the look out and dont think I will be caught napping. The man that succeeds in killing me will get £500 [$2,500] so I am reliably informed. . . .

You can not imagine how I long for a few weeks rest. I am continually on the qui vive and mind and body are at all times so thoroughly alert and the anxiety about your interests is so strong that it is beginning to wear upon me. The seeming and real bodily inactivity which I am condemned to until I can get the necessary papers here and make arrangements so that I can move on is very disagreeable and trying but this will soon be over.

And soon it was. Five days after he wrote, the newspapers were full of the news that Governor Axtell had been suspended, and reports of strong rumors that U.S. District Attorney Catron would be next to go. Within a week, Widenmann was making plans to leave for Santa Fe.

On September 23, Sam Corbet wrote a jubilant letter to J. P. Tunstall in London.

I have just received yours of the 24 Augt, and the latest and best news I have to tell
you is the removal of Gov *Axtell*, United States Attorney T. B. *Catron* Judge *Bristol*
United States *Marshall Sherman* and Indian Agent *Godfroy*. All belonging to the
Santa [Fe] Ring. I wrote you some time last month and told you about the Sheriff's
Posse stealing all the cattle and the Horses from the Felix. for some time I could
not get any letters from Mr. Widenmann but for the last 2 weeks I have had sevral
letters from him. he is still at La Mesilla and cannot get back until something is
done to get rid of those outlaws who are runing loose in this county headed by Gov
Axtells Pet Sheriff Peppin, these outlaws who stoled the cattle [have] taken them
to the Pecos about 150 miles below here and have rebranded them and they say
they will have 1000 head before they leave the county.

Mr. Ellis is still here and since the [Tunstall] Store was robbed I have been keeping
Books for them (Ellis & Sons). Salazar, the man who was wounded when Mr.
McSween was killed has got well and left Town for awhile until things change a
little. I have not been able to see him since he was wounded but he has not left the
county, he will have to stay out until the outlaws are run out of the country. He
will be on hand at Court if we have any this fall. There is sevral more men living
who was with Mr. McSween when he was killed, Mr. Angel has done good work
for this Territory and I hope his work is not done yet, we will not be satisfied until
General Dudley is court marshalled and the murderers of Mr. Tunstall Caught.
Dudley ought to be Indicted for the Murder of Mr. McSween and I think will be
when we have court at Lincoln.[10]

Corbet's letter was hardly in the mailbox when the Rustlers descended upon
Lincoln and the nearby settlements in a scything sweep of mindless violence.[11]
During their three-week reign of terror they wrecked Will Hudgens's saloon (the
old brewery) near Fort Stanton, abused Hudgens's wife and sister, and seriously
injured a man who tried to intervene. They then rode into Lincoln intending to
loot the Ellis store. Stood off by armed men posted inside, they amused themselves
by instead breaking into houses up and down the town. Susan McSween later
claimed, and clearly believed, that the Rustlers came to Lincoln to kill her, but
having been warned of their intentions, she had already fled to Las Vegas.

At La Junta the Rustlers ransacked and wrecked the Avery Clenny store. On
the Hondo they looted and then burned the Coe and Saunders ranch, and
wantonly shot down Clato and Desiderio Chaves, and a retarded youngster named
Lorenzo Lucero, three harmless boys cutting hay. Stealing horses wherever they
found them, they went down the river to the Martin Sanches farm at Picacho,
where they brutally murdered his fourteen-year-old son, Gregorio. A few nights
later they raped two young Hispanic women, the wives of workers at Bartlett's
Mill.

This was no longer civil disorder, nor even war; this was outright anarchy, in
which the lawless outnumbered and outgunned the law-abiding citizens.[12] In spite
of the odds, the citizens made a spirited attempt to fight back, as Sam Corbet's
October 1 letter to J. P. Tunstall reveals.

The Dolan party came up again last week. Dolan Capt. Evans (of the Banditti)
came up with [Lieutenant Goodwin?] to Ft. Stanton and stoped their where they
could get protection from the Military, while the "Rustlers" as they call themselves
robbed the citizens. they broke open many houses taking evry thing out braking
dishes &c took Blanketts, Jewelry, Stock and any thing they wanted even strip[p]ed
women of their clothes. They came to Mess. I Ellis & Sons Store to rob it but we
were fixed for them and stood them off they went below here to a store at the

Junction 9 miles from Lincoln and took $800⁰⁰ worth of goods. they killed two Men and two boys only about 14 Years old, unarmed and in the Hay field at work rode right up to them and shot them down. some of the citizens I and Mr. Ellis together with them got after them and run them two days and one night nearly to Seven Rivers, but could not get close enough to kill any of them. We captured all the loose horses they were driving back animals and all their Blankets and Provisions. Mr. Dolan and Capt. Evans stoped in the Fort until yestard they started to Santa Fe, I suppose to try to get in with the New Govenor. We are going to start to Seven Rivers friday with all the Citizens that can raise a gun and try and stop their murdering and stealing. I am satisfied they will make a desprate fight and I expect will out number us, but we have concluded it was better to die fighting for our right all in a pile than to be murdered one at a time at our homes, I am satisfied that some of us will never get back to Lincoln, but I am willing to take my chance with the good citizens of the county, although I have nothing to loose but my life, which is as dear to me as any one's but the time has come when we have to fight or leave the country and some of our best citizens have died for their rights and the few who have been spared this long might as well go the same way, or stop the Murderers at once. Mr. Ellis went to Ft. Stanton to get some cartridges today and Genl Dudley order[ed] the Post Trader not to sell a cartridge without an order from him, which he refused to give to our party, we managed to get 8000 rounds by slipping them out to night. Of all the men in the world old Dudley is the worst, an old drunken sot and is Col in the U.S. Army, but I hope he will not be Col long. If I have luck to get back I will try and keep you posted. We have warrants for all the outfit below and are ready to start Friday. I sent your son's Watch, Pin and other little things to Mr. Widenmann I have his Books A/c &c Most of his private letters were destroyed I have a few of his letters from home.

Hoping I will be spared to give you a good account of our trip, I remain as ever Your Obt Servt S. R. Corbet.[13]

The thought of yet another band of armed men on the warpath, this one carrying *eight thousand rounds* of ammunition, clearly put the fear of God into the few settlers still left in Lincoln County. Down at Seven Rivers the Beckwiths, the Pierces, Buck Powell, and Lewis Paxton fled the country. The post offices at Roswell, Seven Rivers, and Lloyd's station were abandoned. A steady stream of families was flowing out of the Territory. Draconian measures were needed. The new governor of New Mexico, General Lew Wallace, determined to enact them.

It is fair to say that had Lew Wallace had even the faintest idea of just what tribulations awaited him, he would have refused the appointment of governor of New Mexico; he had anyway been less than eager to accept it. Nevertheless he was determined to make something of this opportunity in the hope that it would lead to the ambassadorship he really coveted. Fifty-one years of age, tall, slender, frank, courteous, and decisive, he was a marked change from the previous incumbent, and much was expected of him (fig. 70). Upon his arrival from the East, the citizens of Cimarron greeted him with a fifty-gun salute; out of deference to Axtell, there were no such demonstrations in Santa Fe when Wallace got there on Sunday evening, September 29. A few days later, he wrote an account of his meeting with Axtell to his wife Susan.

The Governor was sitting at the table when I entered. He arose to receive me, giving me to see a good looking, gray haired, dark eyed, pleasant featured man, about fifty five years old, and a gentleman. As you may imagine, the interview was

FIG. 70. Lew Wallace. Date and photographer unknown.

not a pleasant one; yet he went through it very well. After the introductions, we shook hands, and I said, "I have come to pay my respects to you, Governor, and to ask when it will be agreeable to you to present my papers." He replied: "I have been expecting you, General, and of course know all about your business. It is not my pleasure that is to be consulted, but yours." "Will tomorrow suit you, then?" I asked. "Certainly," he replied. "I do not want any ceremony about it." "Well, then, Governor, I will write you a note with an enclosure—the President's order—tomorrow. And it shall follow immediately that I have qualified by taking the oath."

"Yes," he replied, "when you have qualified, you are governor."[14]

On October 3—the same day Dudley reported that the Rustlers had committed the brutal rape of the two girls near Lincoln—Wallace requested a report on conditions there from U.S. Marshal John Sherman who, Sam Corbet's report to the contrary, had not been dismissed. Two days later the bumbling, drink-sodden Sherman produced a report which, when reduced to its essentials, said what everyone already knew, that there had been a complete breakdown of law and order in Lincoln County. Attached to Sherman's report was a letter from Warren Bristol, giving the reasons behind his decision to abandon the October term of court there. First, Bristol pointed out,

the Sheriff has either abandoned or been driven from his office or duty, and taken refuge at Fort Stanton for protection. He refuses to go out. Second, the prosecuting attorney is absent from the Territory. Third, a large part of the better class of the population from which jurors should be drawn have fled the county. Fourth, the county is completely demoralized, the troubles having arisen from two contending parties both in my opinion equally bad each having in its employ professional assassins whose crimes it seeks to shield and if necessary defend. Fifth, to accomplish these ends witnesses are intimidated, killed, or driven from the country. Sixth, it is impossible at present to obtain fair juries whose findings and verdicts will not be tainted with gross partisanship. Seventh, the court can meet only through such subordinate officials as are furnished by election or appointment and juries taken directly from the people. When these from any cause utterly fail in their duties the holding of court for the time being could be but a mockery. Eighth, it is believed by those well informed as to the affairs in that county that during the present state of public feeling and animosity the assemblage of a body of men by attempting to hold court unrestrained by the military or any adequate force as they would be, would be more likely to result in serious disturbance than otherwise and do more harm than good. Ninth, there seems to be lacking that degree of force which is necessary to render the execution of the mandates of the court at all.[15]

Wallace sent the Sherman report and Bristol's letter to Secretary of the Interior Schurz by telegraph the same day, together with a recommendation for a presidential declaration of insurrection and the imposition of martial law.[16] This was something of a hot potato in view of the *Posse Comitatus* Act. It was one thing for troops to assist in catching criminals; to set them up as police, court, judge, and jury was another matter entirely. President Hayes backed away from the idea of martial law and instead, two days later, issued a proclamation admonishing "all good citizens of the United States, and especially of the Territory of New Mexico" who had been committing lawless acts "to disperse and return peaceably to their respective abodes on or before noon of the thirteenth of October."[17]

After that date, he decreed, the army would when necessary again be permitted to furnish troops to support civil authorities. Astonishingly enough, this seemed to work. Though some thousands of head of stock were stolen and three more women raped during the fortnight that followed, there were no killings.[18] For the first time since the death of John Tunstall, civil order was reestablished in Lincoln County. As the beginning of the reign of terror had been marked with one death, so the restoration of the fragile peace was marked with another when, in the small hours of the morning of October 20, Lawrence Gustave Murphy, the Lord of the Mountains, died an alcoholic wreck in a Santa Fe hospital.[19] He was only forty-four years old.

CHAPTER 29

BILLY THE KID TAKES OVER

FROM the beginning of September, when Charlie Bowdre and Doc Scurlock abandoned their farms on the Ruidoso and moved lock, stock, and barrel to Fort Sumner, only one or two of the old Regulator gang remained in Lincoln.[1] Everybody else was getting out; even old Uncle John Chisum had moved his blooded stock away from the Pecos valley to new range in the Texas Panhandle.

Frank and George Coe decided to go back to Colfax County and help Frank's brother Lou move his cattle to the San Juan country. "We had had enough of outlaw life," George Coe said, "and we begged [the rest of] them to give up this way of living which promised nothing but eventual disaster." Billy the Kid was having none of such talk. "Well, boys, you may do exactly as you please. As for me, I propose to stay right here in this country, steal myself a living," he said. "I'm off now, with any of my *compadres* who will follow me, after a bunch of horses at the Charlie Fritz ranch. He has more horses than he can manage, and I need *dinero*. I'm broke fellows, and I've got to make a killing."[2]

The Kid was making no bones about it, he and his sidekicks had enthusiastically joined in the outright thievery commonplace throughout the county. After Susan McSween fled Lincoln on September 17, they came there no more. They took their stolen stock up to the Fort Sumner–Anton Chico region, where they had reliable friends and could get from Jim Greathouse and Alexander Grzelachowski on credit the food, drink, and other supplies now denied them by Isaac Ellis and the Chisums.

The old gang was breaking up.[3] Doc Scurlock forswore rustling for honest work at Fort Sumner. John Middleton got a job herding Hunter & Evans beef north to Kansas. Henry Brown quit, too, and cowboyed for a while on George Littlefield's LIT ranch near Tascosa. Fred Waite cut out for his home in the Indian Territory and never lifted a hand in anger for the rest of his life. Even Charlie Bowdre was losing his enthusiasm for the owlhoot trail, but he stuck with the Kid out of loyalty. Billy the Kid, his acolyte Tom O'Folliard, and the rest settled down to rustling other people's horses and cattle. Their preferred modus operandi was to steal stock in New Mexico to sell in the Texas Panhandle, and vice versa.

On October 24, 1878, the Kid sold his sorrel horse, Dandy Dick, to Dr. Henry F. Hoyt, a young doctor who was "adventuring" in the Southwest.[4] The horse, branded BB on the left hip, is said to have been the one Sheriff William Brady rode into Lincoln the day he was ambushed. Hoyt made the Kid a present of a little gold ladies' watch he had won in a poker game. Attached to it was "a handsome long chain of braided hair." It is this chain, according to Hoyt, that can be seen crossing his shirt front in the only authenticated photograph of the Kid, the tintype taken at Fort Sumner late in 1879 or early the following year (see fig. 74 in chapter 34 below).

By the time the Kid and O'Folliard made the long trek back north to Sumner, things had changed drastically in Lincoln County. The deadline set by President Hayes expired on October 13. From now on, lawbreakers would have the army to contend with. Even the Rustlers had gone to ground. In an October 22 letter to Carl Schurz, Wallace was jubilant, if not strictly truthful.

> I have the honor to inform you that since the posting of the President's proclamation of the 7th inst. in Lincoln and Dona Ana counties there has been no report of violence or wrong in those localities. For the time at least the order has had a sufficient effect, and as yet but one paper in the Territory has uttered a word of protest against it, and that one pretends to be Democratic. The better people everywhere have heartily approved the measure. The result will doubtless be gratifying to the President and all his advisers. It certainly is to me.[5]

His jubilation was shortlived. Two days later, he received the first of what was to be many letters from a Las Vegas lawyer, Huston I. Chapman, acting in behalf of Susan McSween. She had declared war to the knife upon those she judged responsible for the death of her husband—especially, particularly, and vengefully, upon Col. Nathan A. M. Dudley.

Susan McSween had begun an account of the death of McSween for the Tunstall family while she was still in Lincoln.[6] Her long letter, dated August 28, was not completed until October 7. In it she enlarged with quite religious fervor upon "the painful subject" of the death of her "loved husband."

> This world is such a cold and selfish place, that I many time[s] wish I could leave it & go to that beautiful home we're promised beyond & where I have no doubt my life companion has gone. Oh it is so hard to live without him but I try to console myself with the thought that he is free from the persecution he so long & so nobly opposed for the sole honor of right. *I know he was a good Christian* I believe he has gone to that beautiful land of which he so many times spoke & I hope I shall meet him ere long, he was robbed of his deserving crown here on Earth, but he will were it in heaven, he was cut down in the prime of his manhood when his ability and energy had placed him in a position to enjoy life & without a chance to vindicate his character, but I shall work every day I live after him to vindicate it for him, he was murdered in the most brutal cold blood & with the assistance of our army officer and all just because he so bravely and nobly tryed to prosicute the death of your poor son who had gone before him, these officers were bitter enemies of John & for no reason unless it was jealousy & Mr. McSween knowing this he would never go to them for favour or bow to them as the other party would therefore they grew more bitter towards Mr. McSween. I have just sent a large amount of evidence to Washington to Mr. Angel who has just left the country from having investigated the murder of your poor son & I pray that it will be favourable. I have also written a letter to General Sherman the head of the United States Army for an investigation of the murder of my dear husband, he is now expected in this country. I am determined to prosicute his death.

By the beginning of October, this determination had become a crusade. "When that party heard that I was making an effort to prosicute the death of my poor husband, they solemnly swore that they would kill me & started for our town," she said, "but I happened to hear of it & left immediately at the request of my friends. We have now got a new Governor & we have great faith he will make a great change soon, & they will soon remove all United States officers & put new men in their places. I think the cause of your sons and Mr. McSweens death is very plain to them now in Washington City, think their will be a full report of everything soon."

Next day, October 8, she wrote again, this time reminiscing at considerable length about John Tunstall. "There were no two better friends than John & myself," she told his parents.

I had just received a letter from him a few days before I heard of his death & in that letter he told me he was tired of this world & its perplexity & beged me to come home, that my home was desolate without me, that he thought to have me there thing[s] would be different & my husband told me after I returned that he used to beg him to send for me he used to say "Mac you have the best wife that ever lived" & "I know things would be different if she were here." I do think he was one of the most inocent men I have ever met. When your daughter was married he would shed tears about it, & would beg me to be his sister now that he had lost his sister "Minn" as he would call her. We promised one another to be sister & brother the ballance of our lives, that we would never allow anything to come up between us to cause a hard feeling . . . & that my home should be his home ever afterward, that we would never have anything but that we would think well a portion of it belonged to the other. I furnished one of my rooms for him, he helped tack down the carpet then said now that never should be taken up because I taked it down I dont think that he ever kept one business thought or plan from me he had great confidence in my business qualifications. He gave me some beautiful pictures for my house, one of them was a cross with ivy winding up on the cross, & at the bottom was the motto "I cling too the[e]." When I left he told me he would have a nice riding horse for me when I got back & the day he started for his Ranche, as he was putting his foot into the stirrup, he remarked to Samuel Corbet, "Sam I bought this horse for Mrs. McSween & I want to train him nicely before she gets back." this horse was killed by his side, he would say to Mr. McSween "Mac, I love your wife," & after I left my home when some of his friends would praise anything they had to eat he would say "Oh! but their is no one can have thing[s] as nice as Mrs. McSween["]. Now we know there are but few husbands would like to hear many such expressions from any man, but it would only please Mr. McSween as it came from him, he loved him so much thought he was so noble & good that he would not be guilty of committing a wrong. Mr. Chisum Mr. McSween Mr. Weidenman Richard Brewer John & myself were all the warmest friends, we called ourselves the family, & they would all say I was the "het" of the family, when we left home [in December 1877] John went with us one days drive, I could see all that day that he was terribly grieved at our going & the look he gave me when he bade us good bye & turned from us will haunt me the ballance of my life.[7]

Of McSween she had this to say:

I had a noble husband, I loved him dearly & was so proud of him, he had no bad habits & I could see no fault in him. I buried him by Johns side because he requested me to burry him there for two or three weeks before he was killed he would say he knew he would be killed . . . I would not advise you to have a tomb stone or monument for John untill the troubles are settled & then I want to get one for my dear husband if am able & I think we ought to have the epataph suitable for the cause in which the[y] fell, they are not buried in the regular burrian [sic] ground but in a private burrial ground that we had laid out on our own ground & there are now 7 burried there 4 who fell in the cause the ballance are friends, the ground has not been consecrated but I will have all that attended to just as soon as I can.[8]

By October 18, her decision to "prosicute" her enemies was firmed up by the arrival in Las Vegas of Robert Widenmann, bearing with him a gift of one hundred pounds sterling (five hundred dollars) sent by J. P. Tunstall.[9] "I am truely grateful," Mrs. McSween wrote him, "as I was so very much in kneed."

I do not want to ask you for more, but I am afraid I shall kneed it soon I shall have to use a good portion of this to bring suits against the murderers of my husband & I intend to sue the county for damages & all parties who were conected with those trouble[s] that are property holders, say Dudley & a few others who we know to be worth something & as our county is now under Martial Law I am going to have every man (who was implicated in burning our house & killing my dear husband) arrested & tried for murder. I do think we will come out all right yet, though right is slow comming. Our new Governer appears to want to do what is right, he promises to give me all the assistance he can in bringing those men to justice, & I shall never give up so long as I have one ray of hope. I wish you could send me about five hundred dollars more it would make me independent for some time & I will not trouble you again for a long time, I do not want to lose any point by not having the means to carry it out. Mr. Weidenmann left this place for Washington City and your place nine days ago [October 9].

Thus, financed by the Tunstall family, Susan McSween declared war on her enemies. Her lawyer was a relative newcomer to New Mexico, a former civil engineer of the Atchison, Topeka & Santa Fe Railroad who had recently begun a law partnership in Las Vegas. In spite of poor health and the loss of an arm in his youth, Chapman was energetic, outspoken, and fearless almost to the point of foolhardiness. In writing to Wallace he wasted no time blasting Dudley:

I desire to call your attention to one person whose actions have been offensive in the extreme to a large number of the best citizens of Lincoln county, and that man is Col. Dudley. I am in possession of facts which make Col. Dudley criminally responsible for the killing of McSween and he has threatened that in case martial law was declared that he would arrest Mrs. McSween and her friends immediately. Through fear of his threats Mrs. McSween left Lincoln and is now residing here until such time as she may safely return to her home.[10]

Although, as his covering letter indicates, Wallace found Chapman's accusations "incredible," he could not ignore them. He forwarded Chapman's letter at once to Col. Edward Hatch.[11]

I enclose you copy of a letter received from Las Vegas, which will explain itself.

Candidly speaking, the accusations therein against Col. Dudley strike me as incredible; at the same time, it is apparent that Mrs. McSween, whether with or without cause, is alarmed; wherefore, as it appears she has business in Lincoln county requiring her personal attention, with a view wholly to put her at rest, I respectfully request a special safeguard for her, which, if forwarded to me, I will cause to be duly transmitted.

You will further oblige me by calling Col. Dudley's attention to this letter. As he will be directly in charge of the troops to be moved into Lincoln and Dona Ana counties, the charges preferred by Mr. Chapman seriously affect his fitness for the very delicate duty.

When Hatch in turn sent the letter to Fort Stanton, Dudley's reaction was, predictably, explosive. He had of course heard all the gossip about Susan McSween's reputation, and more besides. Within a week he had eight affidavits, five from citizens of Lincoln and three from his own officers—Appel, Smith, and Pague—attesting that not only had Dudley been the blameless savior of the defenseless women and children of Lincoln, but also that Mrs. McSween was a scandalous, immoral, lewd, licentious, dishonest, and ruthless woman.

First on parade was George Peppin, who said he had known the McSweens since the day they came to Lincoln County, and that Mrs. McSween was "a bad unprincipled, lewd and untruthful woman, one that would not hesitate to use any means in her power to accomplish her ends, even to the sacrifice of life."[12] In June 1878 she had told him "she would be damned if she would not clean the County of Lincoln out, of the parties who opposed her husband's action if she had to spent twenty five thousand dollars to do it." He further "unhesitatingly" declared that he "would not believe [her] under oath. Further that he knows [her] to have been false to her marriage vows . . . having witnessed [her] in actual criminal contact with a well known Citizen of said Lincoln County, this in the spring of 1877."

He promised to reveal the citizen's name before a proper tribunal when called on to do so. Of course, he did not need to, since anyone in Lincoln county who read his testimony would know he was talking about John Chisum. Peppin attested that he knew Francisco Gómes, a truthful, honest and reliable man," and that he had been forced (by whom, one wonders?) "to witness the said Mrs. McSween's lascivious conduct towards Francisco Gómes and that the same was too disgusting to relate. That he can find an abundance of witnesses who will corraberate all that is here deposed to in regard to the said Mrs. McSween's character."

There was a great deal more: Peppin told of Mrs. McSween's consorting with "well known and recognized outlaws" as well as of the events of July 19, contesting the accusations made in Chapman's letter, which Peppin said he had read.

Next in line was John Priest, citizen, making his sole appearance in the annals of Lincoln County.[13] He had been living there "most of the time" for the past two years, and claimed he was "perfectly free from any partisan feeling whatever," even though he had accepted an appointment as Peppin's deputy sheriff just two days earlier. He had frequently heard Mrs. McSween being talked about, and had become convinced that she had "a bad reputation for veracity, and is not looked upon in the community of Lincoln and neighborhood as a virtuous woman."

Next day, farmer Francisco Gómes, now twenty, ten years a resident of Lincoln, made a particularly damning statement.[14] He swore that he had become acquainted with Mrs. McSween soon after her arrival in the county and that

soon after he got acquainted with her she began to make improper advances to him . . . [and] persisted in these advances in such a palpably lewd and libidinous manner that he . . . held sexual intercourse with the said Mrs. McSween. This in the life time of the said A. A. McSween her husband. That this sexual intercourse . . . subsequently became of frequent occurrence. That these sexual acts were committed at various places, chiefly in the brush near the river and mostly while he, the Deponent, was employed on the buildings then (in 1877) being erected in the town of Lincoln.

Whether such words as *sexual intercourse, lewd,* and *libidinous* would have tripped naturally off the tongue of the untutored Gómes we may take leave to doubt, at the same time keeping in mind the fact that he was Saturnino Baca's son-in-law. There seems good reason to believe that Baca's wife, Juana, who loathed Susan McSween, took particular pleasure in wreaking revenge on her for the threats she and her husband had made against the Baca family. The same day, Saturnino Baca appeared before Lieutenant Pague to attest that he had known the McSweens for several years, and that he knew her character "to be bad for both veracity and chastity," and that "for the last two years Mrs. McSween has deservedly borne the reputation of being a profane, lewd, and unreliable woman."[15] Why, he had even heard Mrs. McSween charged to her face with having come from a house of ill fame to Lincoln, and furthermore, "the character of Mrs. McSween has been frequently discussed in his presence and hearing during the last two years, as a bad woman that the facts of her loose character was notorious." Baca confirmed that he had read the affidavit of Francisco Gómes, who was "a reliable truthful honest boy." "During the years 1876 and 1877," he stated, "Mrs. McSween had repeatedly stated to him and to others in his presence that she and McSween, meaning her late husband, came to this County to make money, and that she did not care how she did it. That a woman who had a pretty face and good appearance was a fool, if she did not make money when she could get a chance."

Lt. G. W. Smith deposed before Lieutenant Pague that "from common report," Mrs. McSween's reputation was bad and that "in a matter of interest to her, he would not believe her under oath."[16] He then changed chairs with Pague, who in turn stated that he had "repeatedly" heard Mrs. McSween characterized "as a lewd bad woman, and from her general notorious reputation . . . would not believe her under oath."

Last came John Long, or Frank Rivers as he had once called himself, who made a long affidavit on November 9 that gives a valuable and well-considered overview of the events leading up to and including the final fight in Lincoln as perceived by Dolan's adherents.[17] As for Mrs. McSween, he had known her since she first came to the country, and had

> more than twenty times heard her character discussed by all classes. That her reputation is universally bad. That she is not now, and has not been since he first knew her, recognized by respectable people, who know her. That she is a lewd woman, without principle, and would stoop to any artifice to accomplish her purpose, regardless of means . . . that he would not believe [her] under oath. That she is both profane and vulgar, and that her general reputation is that she has no respect for her marriage obligations, and has violated them time and time again.

Disregarding for a moment the question of whether gathering such scurrilous filth and presenting it as evidence was conduct becoming the officers and gentlemen of Fort Stanton, the fact remained that Susan McSween's morals, or lack of them, had absolutely nothing to do with her accusations against Dudley. Wallace, a lawyer himself, ought certainly to have forcefully said so, and rejected such "evidence" out of hand, but he did not. Perhaps this was because he thought he had already resolved the problems of Lincoln County. On November 8, barely two months after taking office, he wrote to Carl Schurz, "The task assigned to me, as my special mission here, has been accomplished. Do you not think," he asked, "that I am now entitled to promotion? As the field in which your hand has to appear is a very wide one, with much to be done in it, I would be particularly happy if you would entrust me with some fitting part of the work."[18]

Wallace was soon disabused of this notion, probably by Huston Chapman, who visited him in Santa Fe a few days later to serve notice that he intended to begin criminal proceedings against Dudley for arson and murder at the next term of district court. Further concerned that the officer he had nominated to exercise complete control of Lincoln and Doña Ana counties might find himself hauled into the very court he would be responsible for protecting, Wallace added to a proclamation of general amnesty, which he had drafted but not yet promulgated, a clause extending that amnesty to officers of the U.S. Army.

Thereupon, thirty days having elapsed since the presidential proclamation with "no report of disturbance or outrage," Wallace released his document.[19]

> For the information of the people of the United States, and of the citizens of the Territory of New Mexico in especial, the undersigned announces that the disorders lately prevalent in Lincoln County in said Territory, have been happily brought to an end. Persons having business and property interests therein and who are themselves peaceably disposed, may go to and from the County without hinderance or molestation. Individuals resident there but who have been driven away, or who from choice sought safety elsewhere, are invited to return, under assurance that ample measures have been taken and are now and will be continued in force, to make them secure in person and property. And that the people of Lincoln County may be helped more speedily to the management of their civil affairs, as contemplated by law, and to induce them to lay aside forever the divisions and feuds which, by national notoriety, have been so prejudicial to their locality and the whole Territory, the undersigned, by virtue of authority in him vested, further proclaims a general pardon for misdemeanors and offenses committed in the said County of Lincoln against the laws of the said Territory in connection with the aforesaid disorders, between the first day of February, 1878, and the date of this proclamation.
>
> And it is expressly understood that the foregoing pardon is upon the conditions and limitations following:
>
> It shall not apply except to officers of the United States Army stationed in the said County during the said disorders, and to persons who, at the time of the commission of the offense or misdemeanor of which they may be accused were with good intent, resident citizens of the said Territory, and who shall have hereafter kept the peace, and conducted themselves in all respects as becomes good citizens.
>
> Neither shall it be pleaded by any person in bar of conviction under indictment now found and returned for any such crimes or misdemeanors, nor operate the release of any party undergoing pains and penalties consequent upon sentence heretofore had for any crime or misdemeanor.

Unfortunately for Wallace, his amnesty had the opposite effect to what he had intended. Anyone who had fled the county—for whatever reason—was now at liberty to come back, all his sins forgiven. If all were pardoned, whom would the civil authorities arrest? And worse, the choleric Dudley read into the paragraph concerning officers that Wallace had added to the proclamation the basest slander, that he and his officers were by implication guilty of crimes for which they had to be offered amnesty. Without further ado, Dudley wrote a long, angry, and insulting "open letter" to the *New Mexican*, which published it with poorly disguised pleasure on December 14.[20] Dudley's closing paragraph went straight for the jugular.

> I am aware that it is not within the province of an officer of the Army, to make suggestions to a civil functionary, occupying the high position held by yourself, much less criticize his official course; but when false and unjust accusations are

made, either against myself, or the gallant officers of my command, it becomes my duty to demand for them and myself a hearing, and not allow a general pardon to be promulgated for them or myself, for offenses that we know not of, and of which we feel ourselves guiltless.

Supporting this bitter attack was a round robin to Dudley signed by Asst. Post Surgeon Daniel M. Appel, and Lieutenants Smith, Goodwin, Pague, and French: "We, the undersigned officers of the U.S. Army stationed at this post during the recent troubles in Lincoln county, have heard read an open letter addressed by you to his Excellency, the Governor of New Mexico, and desire to say that the said letter expresses most fully and spiritedly our feelings on the subject, thus publicly declining to accept the pardon tendered to us by His Excellency."

This outright slap in the face strengthened the conclusion at which Wallace had already arrived: Dudley would have to go. This decision was reinforced by information coming to him—deluging him—from Huston Chapman in Lincoln.[21] On November 25, Chapman singled out the men at Fort Stanton for further excoriation.

> You attach much importance to the awe-inspiring influence of the military, but it would pain you to see in what contempt they are held by the people whose confidence they have so shamefully abused. These depraved specimens of humanity who disgrace the name of soldier by their debauchery and immoral conduct are little to be relied upon in any matter where they are interested.
>
> It is a matter of surprise to me that a man like Col. Dudley, who is a whiskey barrel in the morning and a barrel of whiskey at night, is entrusted with so important a position, or even retained in the army where his debaucheries must work such a damaging influence upon younger and better officers, and thus destroy their usefulness.
>
> Col. Dudley is continually under the influence of liquor and has used his position as commandant of Ft. Stanton to insult and abuse unoffending citizens until his conduct has become a reproach to the military service of the country and an insult to every officer who tries to maintain the dignity of his position. I desire particularly to call your attention to the conduct of this man Dudley to the end that in the future we may know upon whom to place the responsibility for his wrongdoings.

Two days later, Chapman penned another long and eloquent letter, confirming that Lincoln was still as much of a hell town as it had ever been and that, as usual, it was the unarmed, law-abiding citizens who were getting the worst of it. On that very day, he reported, the town had once again been

> thrown into a panic by two drunken deputy sheriffs charging into town on their horses with their guns cocked and directed at the house of Mrs. McSween. A few minutes afterwards a posse of soldiers under command of one Lieut. Goodwin came riding into town with three horse-thieves who had formerly been of Sheriff Peppin's posse and were brought in for examination before the justice of the peace. What I have to complain of is the riotous manner in which the military, sheriff and deputies charge about over the country giving unnecessary alarm to peaceably disposed citizens. The sheriffs deputies who were with the military were drunk and had with them a flask of whiskey from which they were continually drinking and their conduct was any thing but that of a peace officer. One of the deputies . . . fired his gun into the street to the great danger of peaceable citizens, and in fact there was no disturbance except that made by the military and drunken deputies. I will tell you candidly that the people have more fear of outrages from the military and the quasi

sheriff who is harbored and protected at Fort Stanton than from any other source. The people have too painful a remembrance of the murder of McSween by order of that "brave and accomplished" soldier Col. Dudley, to rest quietly while he is permitted to continue his acts of rapine and murder.

I wrote you [on November 25] of the acts of the military in arresting a merchant, Mr. [A. J.] Ballard, and taking him out in his night clothes and keeping him exposed to the cold for several hours, from the effect of which he is suffering a very severe sickness. Such outrages by the military are becoming too common and unless a stop is put to it at once serious trouble may be expected. Your own proclamation that peace had been restored in Lincoln County supercedes the necessity of further aid from the Government and prevents the use of the military to aid the civil authorities in Lincoln County, and I have advised the citizens here to shoot any officer who shall in any manner attempt their arrest, or interfere with their rights.[22]

It is difficult to know if the hotheaded Chapman really believed that the way to further the cause of peace was to counsel the citizens to start a war with the military, but as Isaac Ellis wrote later, Chapman was "a 'rule or ruin' fellow whom nobody liked."[23] The McSween men were willing to stand trial if the other side would do so as well, Chapman continued, but they would never allow themselves to be arrested by "murderers" like Dudley and Peppin.[24]

There is not an honest man in Lincoln who would believe Col. Dudley on oath, yet you rely on him for all your information, and you have pardoned him for the murder of an innocent man. I can assure you that the people take no stock in your amnesty proclamation and they think you have been derelict in your sworn duty as governor in not visiting Lincoln County and acquainting yourself with the true status of affairs. The people of Lincoln County are disgusted and tired of neglect and the indifference shown them by you, and next week [he was writing on Friday] they intend holding a mass meeting to give expression to their sentiments; and unless you come here before that time, you may expect to be severely denounced in language more forcible than polite.

To show you in what contempt and distrust the military are held by the people I will cite one instance: When your proclamation was received at Fort Stanton by Col. Dudley, he at once sent for the leading citizens of Lincoln County to come to the Fort and [counsel?] with him, but not *one* man responded to his invitation. They had been treacherously betrayed once before, and they refused to be duped again.
. . .

I am now preparing a statement of facts for publication, which, I am sorry to say will reflect upon you for not coming here in person, for no one can get a correct idea of the outrages that have [been] committed here by quietly sitting in Santa Fe and depending on drunken officers for information. . . .

Fort Stanton is today, and has been during all the troubles, the rendezvous of the worst outlaws that have infested Lincoln County, and today the disreputable class who are harbored there is a disgrace to the Government. The horse and cattle thieves who are, and have been, depredating throughout the county were deputies under that notorious murderer the *quasi* sheriff, Peppin, and they have always been found associates of the officers at the Fort.

While Chapman flailed away at Dudley and Peppin, Susan McSween was getting her own priorities in order.[25] In what appears to have been her last letter to the Tunstalls, she reported that she had arrived in Lincoln

a week ago today & find everything badly mixed up & very little more security than when I left here although the Governer has issued a proclamation that there is peace here I send you a coppy of it.

The store building has been greatly damaged by the recent heave [sic] rains & it will take at least $1,000 to repair it [and] put the roof on the building Mr. Weiden before he left here offered your sons half of the building & lot for $1,000 to Mr. Ellis but since the building has been so much damaged by the rain he does not want it at that price. I think that he wants the building but he does not want to pay any [un]reasonable price for it. I would like to own the whole building myself because it was built by my husband & your son. If you do not ask too much for your half of the store I [am] willing [to] buy it although I feel very poor & feel although I could not spare the means but as it was build by my Dear husband & your dear son & laid out & plan[n]ed by myself I would like to clame it as my homestead. My home was burned & unless I can hold that building I will have but little left me, please let me know at once if you will lett me have it dont wait for Mr. Weidenman to return as that will be too late. I [want to] go to work to fix it up to live in & that must be done soon or else the building will go to destruction. I do not think that half the building is worth more than $8,000 [sic, but almost certainly Mrs. McSween intended to write $800] if you will take that tell me.

Some of your cattle have returned to the old range & Mr. Ellis gathered them up & is killing them & branding them I fear few will be left when Mr. Weidenman returns.

I have a power of attorney from Richard Brewer's Father to settle his Estate I will see that they do not rob it as they are trying to do.

I will write you again in a few days in reguard to a monument for my dear husband & your son which I intend having placed over their graves.

By the time this letter was posted, Chapman had canvassed opinion in town as to the usefulness of a mass meeting of citizens; the Ellises and Jose Montaño urged him to forget it. Doubtless encouraged by Susan McSween, with whom he was sharing the old Baca house near the *torreón*—from which the captain and his family had been evicted on Susan's return to Lincoln—Chapman persisted. The following Sunday, he posted notices around town.

THERE WILL BE A MASS MEETING OF THE CITIZENS OF LINCOLN COUNTY ON SATURDAY, DECEMBER 7TH, 1878, AT THE COURT HOUSE IN LINCOLN, FOR THE PURPOSE OF EXPRESSING THEIR SENTIMENTS IN REGARD TO THE OUTRAGES COMMITTED IN THIS COUNTY AND TO DENOUNCE THE MANNER IN WHICH THE PEOPLE HAVE BEEN MISREPRE- SENTED AND MALIGNED; AND ALSO TO ADOPT SUCH MEASURES AS WILL INFORM THE PRESIDENT OF THE UNITED STATES AS TO THE TRUE STATE OF AFFAIRS IN LINCOLN COUNTY.

ALL CITIZENS ARE INVITED TO ATTEND.[26]

There seems to be no record of the meeting, if it ever actually took place. One way or the other, however, such activities clearly showed that Huston Chapman was a dangerous troublemaker who, if something wasn't done to put a spoke in his wheel, would get the whole damned war started up again.

CHAPTER 30

CLAIM AND COUNTERCLAIM

FOR anyone of a superstitious nature, Friday, December 13, 1878, fulfilled all the requirements of a bad-luck day. It started out innocuously enough, with Sheriff George Peppin requesting a military escort "to protect him from violence and being killed by well known murderers" while he was attending probate court.[1] He knew as well as anyone that the likes of the Kid, Scurlock, French, and others were coming and going in the town as they pleased, and he had no desire to run into them without reinforcements on hand.

Dudley acquiesced, and 2nd Lt. J. H. French, two noncoms, and fifteen soldiers, each carrying forty rounds of ammunition, reported to Peppin at the courthouse in Lincoln at 8:30 a.m.[2] "When we arrived there," Peppin testified,

> [Lieutenant French] left his command at Montanas and he with his Sergeant went with me to the Court house to attend court. He stayed with me entirely through the day in court and out of court while I was doing business around the town. At five o'clock the court adjourned, not having finished its business and the weather being so bad. I requested the Lieut. to remain with me until the next day as I said I would not stay there in my official position unless he stayed to protect me. He got quarters for his men and stayed after supper we went into Montanas private rooms and talked to him (Montana) and the Probate Judge until about nine o'clock.
>
> Montana and Gonzales (the judge) then left us and I told the Lieut that . . . I had been informed Jim French and others were in town and that some of them were always in town. He made the remark to me that I ought to go after them. I told him I would rather not and he said he would go if I would deputize him. I told him I would and he said "Well I'll go" and he called up the Sergeant to send him three men. I told him to begin at the lower end of the town and search all the houses the men would be likely to be in.

James Hansell French, a second lieutenant in the Ninth Cavalry, was twenty-six years of age. He had thrown his cap into the air on the parade ground at West Point just four years earlier, and had seen two years' service in Texas and Colorado before ill health brought about his resignation from the army in August 1876. After two years as a civilian, he was reappointed and ordered to Fort Union, and transferred to Fort Stanton in November 1878. For all his youth, French was something of a firebrand, and also a heavy drinker.

Following Peppin's suggestion, French and his men went first to the home of Maximiano de Guevara, broke the board he had propped against the door, and burst into the house. The former jailer testified that French, drunk but not staggering, sat on a bench near the fire, pulled out a lot of papers, and asked him if he knew where Doc Scurlock was.[3] Guevara said no.

"You're a sonofabitch and a liar!" French said. "If you don't tell me where Scurlock is I'll kill you!" He pulled a cartridge from the gun lying across his lap. "Smell it," he ordered. "See how nice the powder smells."

Guevara repeated that he did not know where the men French was looking for were. French cocked his gun and pointed it at him, at which Mrs. Guevara screeched, "For God sake don't do anything to him!"

"Shut up, you bitch!" French shouted. After a few minutes more, he left.

Peppin added a corrective rider to Guevara's testimony. The house was a known haunt of the men he had warrants for—Scurlock, French, Stevens, Scroggins, Bowdre, Brown, and the Kid among them. The Guevara woman was a common prostitute, and these men went to see her. In fact he learned later they went to the house after French left.

In his own account of what happened, French said that next he divided his men, sending Pvt. Shannon Keton and Pvt. Louis Horton to the upper end of town, while he and trumpeter George Washington (no relation to the Lincoln one) checked out Copeland's place.[4] He told his men to rendezvous at "H. J. Chapman's house [the Baca house] because his Mistress Mrs. McSween is at the head of an infamous party of Murderers, some in fact the most of whose names were on my warrants."

At John Copeland's house, French arrested a Hispanic boy who was carrying a pistol, disarmed him, and took him along to the Baca house. When he got there he found that Keton and Horton had arrested Huston Chapman, assuming him to be one of the wanted men. There are—of course—two versions of what happened next. The first is Chapman's.[5]

French told Chapman to swear the boy; Chapman replied that he had no authority so to do. French cursed him and insisted; Chapman acquiesced. French questioned the boy, who said he had gotten the gun from Sheriff Brady's son. French then dismissed the boy and told him to come and get his gun in the morning. At this juncture, Chapman demanded to know by what authority French had arrested him.

"By God, sir, if I have any authority I will show it to you!" French said, and sat down at the table, taking papers from his pocket. Then he stood up again. "God damn you, sir, I'm a better lawyer than you are!"

"You may well be," Chapman replied, "but you have a poor way of showing it."

French sat down again, saying he had warrants for the arrests of certain men, and he would see if he had one for Chapman, abusing him the while.

"Lieutenant French, if you have a warrant for Mr. Chapman, show it to him and he will go with you," Mrs. McSween said.

"You keep your mouth shut!" French said, then turned to Chapman. "By God, you are the man I am after."

"Lieutenant, I know my rights as a citizen and I mean to protect them," Chapman said. "If you have a warrant for my arrest, I want you to produce it. If not, I wish you to leave."

"God damn you, sir, you were never arrested."

"Yes I was," Chapman said, pointing at the soldier who still had him covered with his gun. "And there is the man who arrested me."

"You are a God damned liar, sir!" French shouted.

"But it is true, Lieutenant," Mrs. McSween said. "Mr. Chapman was arrested."

"That is a lie, madam!" French repeated.

"Your men are more gentleman[ly] than you, sir!" Chapman told him, nettled by French's rudeness. At this French jumped up, cocked his revolver, and told his men to stand back. "Stand back now," he repeated. "God damn him I'll fix him."

"For God's sake, Lieutenant," Mrs. McSween said, "don't have any trouble in my house." She started to cry. "I've been ill. I cannot stand such excitement."

"That will do, I don't want any of that strategy. I have seen that played back in the states," French sneered. He peeled off his uniform: overcoat, jacket, and vest. "God damn you, Sir, you have got to fight me," he told Chapman. "Are you armed?"

"No," Chapman replied. "And I want to know by what right you curse me."

French ignored him, calling one of the troopers over to bind one of his arms behind his back so he could fight Chapman. The lawyer touched him on the chest.

"You are a United States officer, Lieutenant," he said, "but you must get out of this house, we have had enough of it." He went to the door to open it, and French said, "Men, take him in charge."

Chapman again told French he must leave. French put on his greatcoat, leaving one of the enlisted men to bring along the rest. At the doorway he stopped dramatically.

"My name is Lieutenant French, Company M, Ninth Cavalry, United States Army," he said. "I will see you again, Mr. Chapman."

By this time, Mrs. McSween had fainted.

"Look at that woman!" Chapman shouted. "Look what you have done. Now you must get out of here!"

"If I have caused all this I'll go," French said, and left. As soon as they had gone, Chapman ran down the street looking for a doctor, only to collide yet again with French and his men.

"Who goes there?" French called, as he and his men cocked their guns.

"Chapman," the lawyer replied.

"Where the hell are you going now?"

"To fetch a doctor."

"Pass on!" French said, impatiently. "My name is Lieutenant French, 9th Cavalry, United States Army, and I'll meet you again."

Challenged on his way back, and again allowed to pass, for the moment Chapman's involvement in the events of the evening was at an end. That is version one.

Version two is taken from the testimony of Keton, Horton, Washington, and French.[6] Needless to say, it differs radically from Chapman's story. The Hispanic boy was arrested, Horton said, because French had asked him if he could identify Scurlock, and the boy said he could. When they went into the house, French said a polite good evening to Mrs. McSween, who replied in like manner.

"Do you have a warrant for me?" Chapman asked.

"I don't know if I have," French replied.

"By what right have you arrested me?"

"Chapman," French said, "I didn't arrest you."

"Well, your men did."

"If my men arrested you, that is a mistake of mine," French said, "and I am responsible for it."

At this juncture, according to Washington, words passed between them, and French said something about being versed in law, and such like. Chapman shook his finger in French's face. French stood up.

"If you will allow me I will give you an understanding in this thing," he offered.

"It is no use to allow you, you have acted ungentlemanly with me," Chapman replied.

"Hush," Mrs. McSween told him, "and let the Lieutenant realize this thing."

At this point, French took off his clothing preparatory to fighting, and asked Chapman if he was armed. Chapman said he was not, and called French a scoundrel.

"You have abused me as I was never before abused in my life," French told him. Then, Washington said, "Mrs. McSween commenced hallowing. Saying she was dying. She was very much excited, appeared to be very badly scared."

All the soldiers denied French was drunk; Washington and Horton contradicted Chapman's assertion that cocked guns were being brandished.

Whichever version of these events is closer to the truth, Lieutenant French's ill-judged attack on the one-armed Chapman has attracted so much attention that it has tended to obscure something perhaps more significant: the actions and identity of the "boy" French disarmed and arrested. Who was he? Why was he at Copeland's house, armed, with a pistol given to him by Sheriff Brady's son? Is it not likely that he was the very same Juan Mes whom, several hours after the Chapman incident, Copeland shot? Very few of the shootings that happened in Lincoln were without motive, and there seems to be no question that Mes was a supporter of the Dolan faction. Was he skulking around the Copeland place trying to get a crack at one of the Regulator gang? Was this why Copeland got into an argument with him?

In most accounts of this day, Chapman's altercation with French has assumed greater importance than the one that followed it.[7] As a result, little is known about it other than the basic facts: around midnight John Copeland got into a brawl with a nineteen-year-old Mexican boy named Juan Mes, known locally as Johnny, which ended with Copeland putting one bullet through the boy's belly and another through his chest.

Copeland immediately surrendered to James Tomlinson, who went across to the Montaño house and woke French and Peppin, who were sleeping in the same room.[8] Copeland, "a big burly *man*" who had shot a "*boy*," begged French's protection "in such vehement terms that the Sheriff had to delay in turning him over to me for safe keeping."

Why was Copeland so afraid? He had shot a nineteen-year-old Hispanic, which on the normal Lincoln scale was scarcely much more of an offense than spitting in the street. Yet here was this "big, stout, powerful man" quaking in his boots and begging French to protect him: from whom?

French detailed his sergeant to take Copeland in charge and went up to where the wounded Mes, "a good looking fellow about nineteen years of age," still lay, and remained with him until daylight, when a doctor arrived from the fort.

Next day, at about 9:30 a.m., Chapman and Sidney Wilson, a Las Vegas lawyer who had located in Lincoln the preceding month, went down to Montaño's to talk to Copeland. From this point onward, the testimonies diverge sharply. Sidney Wilson, who had no visible axe to grind, indicates that French was either still drunk or drunk again.

I went into Mr. Montana's house . . . and asked permission to see Mr. Copeland. Lieut. French said I could if I would see him in his presence [and] ordered Mr. Copeland to be brought in. On his coming into a room I wanted to ask him a few questions as to his case, when Lieut. French asked him whether he killed that man. I ordered Mr. Copeland, as his attorney, not to answer the question as it was improper and should not be answered. Lieut French then demanded an answer a second time [and again I] ordered Mr. Copeland not to answer it. He Lieut. French then ordered me out of the room and I left with an injunction to Mr. Copeland not to say a word, no matter how much force was used to compel him. After I had left the room and just as I stepped outside the door I overheard Lieut. French give the order to take Mr. Copeland back to where he had been taken from. I had passed into the yard when Lieut. French called me back and also ordered Mr. Copeland brought back. I came back into the house, at the request of some of the soldiers. Mr. French apologized, and said he thought he was too fast, and I replied that I thought he was. He said that perhaps in his anxiety to do his duty he had probably overreached himself; that he did not desire to do anything to injure me or hurt my feelings or any one else. He then stated to me "If you want to hold your conversation with Mr. Copeland you are now at liberty to do so." I then talked with Mr. Copeland as much as I desired to. Lieut. French stopped me while I was conversing with Mr. Copeland. After I got through with Mr. Copeland Lieut French came in and ordered Mr. Copeland taken out. He then stated to me that he had some warrants placed in [his] hands or that the sheriff had some warrants, I do not recollect which, and he said that he had gone to several houses that evening; and had searched for the parties, that the Sheriff had warrants for; that they had good reason to believe that the parties were at the houses which were searched, and also said: ["]I think they are getting out some criminal warrants for me, or some kind of criminal process, and in the event of their doing so, I desire you to defend me. I think I was fully justified under the law in doing what I did, in searching the houses" and asked me what I thought about it. I told him that my legal opinion was, that he was justified in doing what he did if he was properly armed with warrants for the apprehension of thieves and murderers. My opinion is that he Lieut French was under the influence of liquor when the conversation took place between us but I do not think he was incapacitated from properly performing his duty. he seemed anxious to do what he had been ordered to do by his superior officers, as he repeatedly told me he was. in the Court Room he . . . made a request of the Justice, that he the Justice was to ask leave of him Lieut. French to talk to the prisoner in his charge meaning Mr. Copeland. He afterwards went out doors and asked me if I thought that was proper. I told him it was not. He then requested me to apologize to the Court for him, as he thought he was doing what was his duty in the premises. I saw no other misconduct, have seen much worse in the court rooms, and no notice taken of it.[9]

Juan Patrón, George Barber, Jose Montaño, and Bonnie Baca all made affidavits that French was not drunk at any time during his stay in Lincoln, nor had he committed any wrongful acts. All this, of course, clashes violently with the fiery Chapman's testimony.[10]

Chapman said he went down to the Montaño place with Wilson: when Copeland was brought in, Chapman asked to speak with him alone.

"Whatever you say must be said in my presence," French told him. "I have to hear what you say."

"I am Mr. Copeland's attorney," Chapman claimed. "I have a right to speak with him privately."

"God damn you, sir, get out of my house!" French snapped.

"All right, sir," Chapman said and went to the door. As he did French stripped off his shirt, saying, "God damn you, sir, I'll whip you anyhow!"

"Don't you lay a finger on me, sir!" Chapman warned him.

"Then get off these premises, God damn you!" French snarled. Chapman left and went up the street to the courthouse, where he appeared before Justice of the Peace John B. Wilson to lodge his complaints against French. After hearing these, Wilson adjourned for lunch. At this juncture French and Chapman collided yet again.

"You are the God-damnedest meanest man and scoundrel in the country, sir!" French told Chapman. "I'll fight you with one arm tied behind my back ."

"If you don't get away from here, Lieutenant," Chapman warned, "you'll need more arms than you have to protect yourself. I don't want any trouble with you. Just keep away."

Peppin came across and hustled French away. Court was resumed, and Copeland's hearing commenced. French returned to the courtroom in time to see one of his soldiers talking to Chapman. He picked up a rifle and, placing it between the two men, told Chapman he did not want him talking to any of his men.

"I have already spoken to him," Chapman said, "and he has spoken to me."

"God damn you, I don't want my men to speak to you!" French shouted, as Judge Wilson called for order.

"Anyone that wants to speak to me can do so," Chapman retorted. "I can't stop people talking to me."

Judge Wilson called on Peppin to restore order in court.[11] Peppin made French resume his seat, and the officer remained quiescent as Copeland's case was heard.

Once again, George Peppin's corrective testimony restores some sense of perspective to this opéra bouffe:

> Shortly after Chapman and Wilson came down to speak to Copeland . . . I didn't want them to speak in private to him so the Lieut had Copeland brought into our room and Chapman wanted to take Copeland out and talk to him privately. Lieut French told him that wouldn't be allowed, what he had to say he had to say out loud, and Chapman replied, "Damn you, I'll talk to him if I like to." then Lieut French told him "You can't speak to him at all, you leave this room, here is the door, get outside it as quickly as you can. I am on duty and don't want any trouble with you." Chapman said when outside the door "Come out here, step outside, I am not afraid of you." He [French] stepped out of the door and said do you mean this personally and he said he would tie one arm behind him (French) and whip him. I told Chapman to leave and not come around there any more, if he pleased, he was trying to get trouble started and if he kept on he was liable to do it.

Chapman followed Sheriff Peppin out into the street.

"I will have warrants for Lieutenant French," he said, "and I expect you to serve them right away."

"I'll know it's time for me to serve warrants when I've got them," Peppin told him.

"Lieutenant French should not ride out of this town without being arrested!" Chapman insisted.

"I think he will," Peppin said. "It's not my place to arrest him. Even if I had warrants I would have to serve them on his commanding officer."

"I'll be damned if I don't have men enough in this town to arrest all the shoulder straps in the county and you too!" Chapman said, hotly.

"You can't trot them out too soon for me," Peppin said. "But you better not. You keep away from me. I don't want any trouble with you."

When court resumed after lunch, Chapman made it his business to meet them three or four times; every time, "he had something insulting to say." He called French "a damned scunk" and "a damned fool." At no time was French under the influence of liquor, Peppin said, "but [he] was excited and [I] think he had good cause to be so. I don't think any other officer in this post would have stood what he did without striking the man."

In his final sentences, Peppin came as close as anyone to the real reason for all this brouhaha: "I believe the persecutions against him are intended to provoke General Dudley, and not Lieut. French particularly."

No matter: Chapman had his cause. He, Susan McSween, and Maximiano de Guevara swore out warrants charging French with felonious entry and assault with intent to kill, and on his return to the fort, Dudley put him under military arrest. At the same time Dudley ordered a board of inquiry to convene the following day.

At 8:30 a.m. on December 15, the officers of the board proceeded to Lincoln, with instructions from Dudley not only to investigate French's actions, but also to apologize to Chapman.[12] The detachment arrived at 9:45 a.m., and the statements upon which all the foregoing is based were taken: Chapman, Mrs. McSween, Sebrian Bates, Maximiano de Guevara, J. B. Wilson, Sidney Wilson, Peppin, Patrón, Barber, Montaño, and Baca. At 5 p.m. the officers returned to the fort, where Washington, Horton, and Keton were interviewed, and where Lieutenant French prepared his own flowery version of events.

On the 16th, the civil warrant for French's arrest was served on Dudley. He had refused to countenance handing French over to the civil authorities. Dudley considered Justice Wilson, who the preceding day had acquitted Copeland on a plea of self-defense, an object of contempt and his administration of civil law "a farce and disgrace." Dudley went so far as to recommend in his report that Wilson be replaced by "an honest, independent person whose soul and body does not belong to one party."[13]

In the interim, however, he had instructed Doctor Appel to find out what had happened; Appel's report convinced him to reverse his position.[14] He ordered Lieutenant Dawson to go to town immediately to act as escort for French. Dawson's departure coincided with the arrival of Will Hudgens, who had hurried over to the fort to report that a mob had gathered in Lincoln, and made known that it planned to take Johnny Mes and Johnny Hurley, who was looking after the wounded man, and kill the pair of them. Dudley followed up on Appel's recommendation, and sent the doctor to town to bring the two men up to the fort in an ambulance.

Once again, the question arises: why had the shooting of Johnny Mes aroused such strong feelings? Now, instead of Copeland, it was Mes and Johnny Hurley— Dolan supporters both—who were being terrorized by the "mob" (the old Regulator gang). There was clearly much more to all this than a drunken brawl.

The only hint of what might have been the cause is in Dudley's December 17 report: "I feel quite confident that if Mace [sic] had been left in the Plaza last night an attempt would have been made to kill him. Copeland well knows if

Peace and order is ever restored in Lincoln County, he will be indicted by the Grand Jury if the witnesses are not put out of the way."[15]

A Hispanic might have had a grudge against Copeland because of his involvement in the killing of his compatriots in 1873, although there is no evidence of any connection between that event and this. Or was this Juan Mes related in some way to the leader of the horse thieves who had plagued Lincoln some years earlier? Like many of Lincoln town's mysteries, this one seems destined to remain unsolved.

Almost as his officers left the fort on that bright, sharp, bitterly cold Monday morning, Dudley received a note from Charles Fritz requesting protection: he had seen some of the old Regulator gang skulking around his cattle. If no protection was forthcoming, Fritz said, he would have to leave the country. Dudley's reaction was choleric: he declared himself "sick and tired of forwarding such statements, and propose to pay no attention to such complaints in future. If his Excellency Governor Wallace thinks peace and order prevails in Lincoln county he is the worst fooled official I ever saw."[16]

On December 21, the board of officers recommended that no further action be taken in the case of Lieutenant French. Three civil charges had already been preferred, they said,

> on the first of which he was tried, the proceedings lasting three days, and every effort made to convict him, but he was acquitted and plaintiff made to pay the costs. The second charge was dismissed . . . and on the third charge, knowing the Justice of the Peace was prejudiced against him, and fearing his desire to conciliate the prosecuting parties would further influence him, he waived an examination, and was bound over to appear before the district court, at which [on] the facts of the case we expect a dismissal.

No doubt consigning the citizens of Lincoln, and Huston I. Chapman in particular, to a merry Christmas in hell, Dudley retaliated on December 20 by promulgating an order which effectively put Lincoln off limits to his soldiers and—more important—put the fort off limits to the citizens, most especially Copeland, Wortley, Chapman, French, Scurlock, the Kid, Bowdre, Brown, the Coes, and "all other parties recognized as the murderers of Roberts, Brady, Tunstall, Beckwith and Bernstein."[17]

If the one-time Regulators gave a damn for Dudley's proscription, they did not show it. The town was theirs, so much so that on December 27, Jimmy Dolan, Billy Mathews, and John Long sought sanctuary at the fort, claiming that the presence of outlaws in Lincoln made it unsafe to do business there.[18] They were just in time for a celebration—and no doubt the whiskey flowed like water—for General Sherman had decisively refused to accede to Wallace's request that Dudley be relieved.

Four days later, Dolan addressed an ominous note to the governor in Santa Fe.

> Your friend Chapman appears to be the only man in this county who is trying to Continue the old feud. I and Many Citizens feel Confident that if this man was silenced, the trouble would End . . . I have learned Enough since I returned here that should I remain in this County, my fate will be that of Major Brady and others. I only intend remaining until such time as I can Straighten up my business as to the interests of my Creditors, and as per Agreement with them. It makes me and my friends feel Mighty Sore, that we are compelled to leave our homes and business,

which we are Compelled to do, or put ourselves on Equal footing with the outlaw and assassin.[19]

A letter like this was a beautifully camouflaged way of giving its writer the opportunity later to say, "I told you so." Whether Lew Wallace realized it is another matter. He could scarcely be expected to know that when a devious and dangerous man like Jimmy Dolan said, "If this man was silenced, the trouble would end," it meant only one thing: Huston I. Chapman had been sentenced to death.

CHAPTER 31

THE LITTLE WAR
OF HUSTON CHAPMAN

THE events of mid-December had another significant by-product—the resignation of Sheriff George Peppin.[1] Complaining to Governor Wallace that he had not received so much as five dollars in salary in the five hazardous months he had held office, he turned in his star, thus annulling the appointments of every one of those who had been his deputies: John Long, Abneth McCabe, Chavez y Baca, Marion Turner, and the rest.

One of them, John Kinney, had been brought before the district court in La Mesilla during November, charged with the murder of Ysabel Barela a year earlier.[2] To absolutely nobody's surprise, all the witnesses in the case discovered they had pressing business elsewhere. Kinney took a change of venue to Grant County where, on December 14, he was acquitted by twelve good men and true.

Peppin's replacement was George Kimbrell, appointed by the county commissioners to fill out the unexpired term of the former sheriff. A few months short of his thirty-seventh birthday, Arkansas-born Kimbrell had farmed at Chaves Flats near Lincoln for thirteen years, and now owned a homestead at Picacho with his Hispanic wife Paulita and their children. He had taken no part in the Lincoln troubles and was respected as a decent and honest man.

Huston Chapman and Susan McSween busied themselves with the problems of probating the McSween and Dick Brewer estates. Widenmann, it will be remembered, had mortgaged the Tunstall estate to secure his bondsmen. Now, Chapman learned that under the terms of the mortgage those bondsmen—Juan Patrón, John Copeland, Jose Montaño, and Francisco Romero y Valencia—had served notice on Sam Corbet, as Widenmann's agent, that they planned to remove Widenmann as administrator. Chapman stepped in and had Mrs. McSween appointed administratrix of the estate in Widenmann's place.

On December 16, with Copeland, Patrón, Montaño, and A. J. Ballard serving as her bondsmen, Susan McSween took her oath as administratrix, and Isaac Ellis and Jose Montaño were appointed appraisers, as they were also for McSween's estate. In their January 16 report, Tunstall's property was valued at $534.00, collectible notes $3,909.76, uncollectible notes $1,442.63, and his real estate— a half-interest in the store, the land on the Feliz, and the George van Sickle ranch—$1,300.00, a significant drop in value from the appraisal made in the early summer.[3]

On January 17, Montaño and Ellis submitted a report valuing McSween's estate at $1,853.50 in personal property, $1,910.00 in real estate, and $10,023.21 in collectible notes.[4] The bulk of this last sum was made up of claims of $6,500.00 against the estate of Tunstall and $2,437.42 against that of Brewer.

Once all his legal affairs were taken care of, Chapman returned to his feud, appearing before J. B. Wilson to swear out a warrant charging Colonel Dudley with arson and complicity in the murder of McSween. This can hardly have been good news for Wilson who had on January 11 proclaimed, in a letter to the *Independent* (its text polished up by the editors, as Wilson was barely literate) that peace had returned to Lincoln County.

> Gentlemen: I see by an article in your paper in which you predict that the peace in this country is by no means assured, Sirs, if you will be so kind as to publish this answer to your article I will state that to the best of my knowledge that there are no serious troubles existing in the county at the moment.
>
> I speak from personal knowledge when I say that many persons of the two parties heretofore at war with each other are getting together and settleing all old difficulties, several such reconciliations having taken place in my office within the last few days, and through my advice have become friends again and as far as I can judge it is the intention of all parties to use their best efforts to settle and forget old quarrels and disputes, and again become friends and aid the enforcement of the law. Our board of County Commissioners has been in session four days regulating the County . . . with Hon Isaac Ellis as chairman of the board it may be expected that everything will be done in a legal and business[like] manner. The corn contractors are filling their contracts with fine American corn such as this country can boast of raising in great abundance. I can safely say that we are now enjoying peace and plenty and those who doubt it can come and see for themselves.[5]

There is evidence to suggest that Wilson was promoting peace at the behest and with the approval of Governor Wallace.[6] Whether this is also true of Doctor Blazer is not known, but on February 8 he too asserted that things were much better. On Monday, February 4, Kate Godfroy, daughter of the former Indian agent, was married at the agency to Asst. Surgeon Daniel Appel in a ceremony conducted by Rev. Thomas Harwood of La Junta, superintendent of the Methodist Mission in New Mexico. This happy occasion was just one instance that

> the "war element" in Lincoln is fast fading from view and peace and quiet prevails. The paraphernalia of war is being exchanged for implements of husbandry and the mailed warriors are adopting peaceful pursuits and turning their attention to stock raising and agriculture. Those who fled to a land of safety are returning to their former homes bringing with them others who will aid in building up the wealth and property of the county.[7]

Dudley was unconvinced, and said so.[8] If Wallace was of the opinion, as interviews he had given to the press seemed to indicate, that "a full restoration to good order and security exists in Lincoln County," then perhaps this would be a good time for the troops stationed at Roswell to be withdrawn and the command readied for any Indian outbreak that might occur in the spring. "I would here state," he went on, "that the new Sheriff Mr. Kimball made unofficial call on the Post Commander during the last week. He stated that he felt confident he could not make a single arrest of any of the parties for whom he had warrants turned over to him by Sheriff Peppin, without the aid of the military."

On January 20, Chapman had bidden adieu to Susan McSween and gone to Las Vegas in her buggy. From that place on February 10 he wrote a long letter to the Tunstall family about the affairs of the estate, which must have severely embarrassed Robert Widenmann, who—having apparently "escaped" from La Mesilla without too much trouble and visited Susan McSween in Las Vegas and his family in Ann Arbor en route—had been staying with the family in London since Christmastime.

> I find that your son was the owner of over 2,500 acres of land entered under the Desert Land Law, all of which is in the names of other men, and unless immediate steps are taken, all or most of this land will be lost. I think that Mr. Widenmann was derelict in his duty in not appointing some one to look after your son's estate in his absence. Several thousand dollars might have been saved to the estate had there been someone to look after the property. . . .
>
> I am certain that you could not entrust the management to a more competent and careful person and one [who] was a true and devoted friend to your son. Mrs. McSween is so very popular in Lincoln county and can do more towards settling your son's estate than any other person.[9]

It is difficult to know whether Chapman was deceived or just besotted; perhaps it is generous to assume the latter. Whatever the reason, he seems to have believed without question whatever Susan McSween told him. The letter went on to make a plea in behalf of the old Regulator gang.

> I also desire to call your attention to the circumstances in which are left the men who fought for your son and done all in their power to avenge his murder. They have been indicted for the killing of some of the murderers of your son, and are without any means of defending themselves when the trial comes on. They were promised by both McSween and Widenmann that they should receive pay for hunting down the murderers of your son, but they do not ask for pay, but think that something should be done to assist them out of their present trouble, as it would be a vindication of your son. If you can do something for them, I think that they deserve it. They have asked me to write you and explain their situation, and you can take such action as you may think proper.
>
> I shall leave here tomorrow for Lincoln.

Since it did not directly concern them, he did not add that he planned to stop off en route in Santa Fe. This he did in the company of David Shield, who accompanied Chapman to the territorial capitol because he had heard about the "eight long affidavits" made against his sister-in-law, and had written to Wallace requesting permission to inspect and copy them. Wallace refused, whereupon Shield addressed Colonel Hatch directly, stating that it was his intention to present the affidavits to the Masonic order for investigation.[10] He explained that McSween had been a master mason and said he was informed that Dudley was also a member of the order. Hatch demurred, noting that permission to see the documents could only be granted by the secretary of war.

Determined to take his case to Washington in person if need be, the angry Chapman set off back for Lincoln. His friends, attorney Ira E. Leonard and J. H. Koogler, editor of the Las Vegas Gazette, tried to persuade him not to go, warning him that he was taking his life in his hands.[11] Chapman admitted that he feared violence, but said that no matter what obstacles the military establishment put in his way, or what dangers he encountered, he was determined to bring Colonel Dudley and Lieutenant French to justice.

In Chapman's absence, one or two developments had occurred which radically altered the domination of Lincoln by the old Regulator group. It was well known that the Rustlers were now concentrating their efforts on the lower Pecos and Seven Rivers area. Shortly after Chapman's departure, Susan McSween hired Charlie Scase, who worked at the agency, as a "detective." Scase succeeded in tracing John Tunstall's cattle, which were in the possession of Robert Speakes, one of the more dangerous members of the gang that had raped the girls at Bartlett's Mill and killed the boys at the Chaves farm. When she received Scase's report on February 11, Mrs. McSween swallowed her pride sufficiently to pen a request to Colonel Dudley.

> I am in receipt of positive information through my agent, who was just returned from Seven Rivers, that two hundred and seventy five head of Cattle, belonging to the Tunstall estate of which I am the legal Administratrix, are in the hands of Robert Speake, and other parties, who are now at or near the point referred to, with this herd, and that they intend to drive it into Old Mexico, and there dispose of it for their own interest.
>
> All of the cattle can be positively identified, I send you the brands of this stock and respectfully request, that you will give me all the aid in your power in protecting the interests of this estate.
>
> These parties are now endeavoring to dispose of the herd at Seven Rivers. No reliable parties will purchase it in this section of the Country, as it is well known that they are stolen property, therefore I feel confident that they will attempt to drive it off.[12]

Although in his official report he termed her request "farcical," Dudley smoothly assured her that upon proper requisition by the sheriff, he would provide assistance; in the meantime he had written to the commanding officer at Fort Bliss, and the Texas Rangers, to take steps to ensure that the cattle were not driven into Old Mexico.[13] "I am expecting a report from Capt. Carroll, daily," he added, "who is now supposed to be en route to Stanton from Seven Rivers, where he has been with the new sheriff several days. He no doubt will be fully informed in regard to the stock in question, and if possible secure it."

Carroll's detachment had in fact recovered 275 head of cattle stolen by the Rustlers, half of which were Tunstall's. Carroll and his soldiers drove them north up the Pecos Valley; en route,

> all stock men on the river were requested to go through the herd . . . and cut out any cattle known to belong on their ranges . . . Evidence goes to show that the Hunter & Evans cattle were driven off by John Jones, Jim Jones, Tom Jones alias George Davis, Tom Cockner [Cochrane] and have new brands supposed to be theirs, also brand supposed to belong to Marion Turner, all of Seven Rivers.[14]

Delayed by these proceedings, Carroll would not reach Roswell until February 25. Meanwhile, six of his men were sent on special orders to escort to the agency from the old Dolan cow camp a herd of twenty-one hundred head belonging to Thomas B. Catron. Dudley authorized this on the assurances of Edgar Walz that the cattle were destined for the Mescalero Agency. He was considerably less than amused when he discovered that they were being driven to Catron's (formerly Murphy's) ranch.

This herd arrived at Stanton on February 15, accompanied by Jimmy Dolan, Jessie Evans, and chief herder Billy Campbell. They pushed on to the ranch, avoiding Lincoln for the time being. In that place the Kid, now generally seen as leader of the old Regulator group, was echoing the sentiments Alexander McSween had spoken just seven months earlier. At that time the Kid had been eager and energetic, while McSween was tired and depressed. Now, the Kid in his turn was tired of fighting, tired of running from Dolan warriors and lawmen with warrants for his arrest.[15] Knowing that Jessie Evans was at the fort, he sent him a note proposing a parley.[16]

Evans agreed. He, Dolan, Edgar Walz, Billy Mathews, and Billy Campbell would come to the plaza on Tuesday night to talk things over. Waiting for them would be the Kid, Tom O'Folliard, Doc Scurlock, George Bowers, and Jose Salazar. The ingredients could not have been more explosive, nor the date more significant: February 18, a year to the day since Tunstall had been killed.

Who exactly was there, and where exactly the initial meeting took place, is uncertain. Some say they met on either side of facing adobe walls, others say in a neutral bar.[17] The mood was hostile. Evans, the *Independent* reported, said the Kid was "impossible to treat with," and suggested killing him then and there.

"I don't care to open negotiations with a fight," the Kid shouted, "but if you'll come at me three at a time, I'll whip the whole damned bunch of you!"

Edgar Walz managed to cool things down and got the leaders to shake hands. They repaired to a bar to formulate a peace treaty remarkable—in such circumstances—for its comprehensiveness. It was agreed that neither party would kill any member of the other party without having first given notice of withdrawal from the agreement.[18] All persons who had acted as "friends" were included in the agreement and were not to be molested. No officer or soldier was to be killed for an act previous to the date of the agreement. Neither party would appear or give evidence against the other in any civil prosecution. Each party would give individual members of the other party every aid in their power to resist arrests on civil warrants and, if arrested, would try to secure their release. If any member of either faction failed to carry out the terms of this compact he was to be killed on sight.

Peace declared, the participants began to celebrate in earnest. By ten o'clock they were roaring drunk. Wise citizens hastily barred their doors and shuttered their windows as the revels grew increasingly raucous. Sheriff George Kimbrell, able to enlist the aid of only one man, slipped out of town and hurried to the fort to request assistance in arresting Bonney and Salazar, for whom he had warrants.[19]

Meanwhile, the celebrants arrived at the home of Juan Patrón (fig. 71), who had arrived in town a little earlier from Las Vegas, accompanied by Huston Chapman. No sooner did he lay eyes on Patrón than Campbell pulled out his gun and threw down on him. Patrón scuttled behind one of the others, and thus saved his own life. He watched ashen-faced as the noisy crowd spilled out onto the frozen mud of the street and lurched towards Frank McCullum's saloon and eating house, recently erected adjacent to the ruins of the McSween house.

Chapman had put up Mrs. McSween's horses and buggy in the corral. His face was swathed in bandages, for he was in great pain with neuralgia, exacerbated by the bitter winter winds he had endured on the long drive south. He decided to go down the street to get some bread to make a poultice for his face. On his way back he encountered the mob: Dolan, Evans, Campbell, Walz, the Kid, Salazar, George van Sickle, Billy Mathews, Joe Bowers, and the rest. Campbell stopped in front of Chapman, blocking his path.[20]

FIG. 71. The Juan Patrón house and store, ca. 1890. Photographer unknown. Standing far right is Miguel Otero; the woman in the doorway is thought to be Natividad, daughter of José Montaño.

"Who are you and where are you going?" he rasped.

Chapman was in severe pain, tired, and in no mood to be pushed around. "My name is Chapman," he said crisply, "and I am attending to my business."

"Then you dance," Campbell growled, pulling his six-shooter and jamming it against Chapman's chest.

Chapman shook his head. "I don't propose to dance for a drunken mob," he snapped.

"You better watch how you talk, mister," Campbell said, "or we'll make you."

Chapman lifted the bandage away from his face so he could see more clearly.

"You can't scare me, boys," he said. "I know it's you, and it's no use. You've tried that before. Am I talking to Mr. Dolan?"

"No," Jessie Evans said, "but you're talking to a damned good friend of his."

At this moment Dolan fired his pistol, and almost simultaneously Campbell's trigger finger tightened in reflex. Chapman gasped, "My God, I am killed!" and collapsed, his clothes set alight by the powder flash from the guns. Reeling away from the stink of burning flesh and cloth, Campbell led the way up the street to McCullum's, proclaiming as he went that he had "promised my God and General Dudley that he would kill Chapman, and now he had done it." He added that he was now going to Fort Stanton to kill Charlie Scase, Mrs. McSween's cattle detective. "I promised General Dudley that I would not kill Scase on the post, but now I am going to kill him wherever I find him," he declared.

They went into McCullum's and ordered drinks and canned oysters. Dolan handed a pistol to Edgar Walz and told him to go and put it in Chapman's hands. Walz sagely declined, whereupon the Kid offered to do it. Once out of the saloon, he did nothing of the sort. Taking no chances on the volatile mood of Dolan and his cronies, he hurried down to the Ellis place, where he was joined by O'Folliard, who had slipped out of the saloon unseen. They saddled up and headed for San Patricio. At 11:30 p.m. Sheriff Kimbrell, escorted by Lieutenant Dawson, Doctor Lyon, and twenty cavalrymen entered town from the east.[21] Dawson reported that he

> accompanied the Sheriff with my command to several houses for the purposes of arresting the parties [Bonney and Salazar] named in the order, but did not succeed in finding any of them. In our search through the town, we came across the dead body of H. J. [sic] Chapman, late a resident of Lincoln who had evidently been killed a few hours previous to our arrival in the town, the body was very badly burned and most of the clothing off the upper portion of the body was burned. We then proceeded to the Justice of the Peace (Wilson) and informed him of the fact that the body was lying in the road, he said he was aware of it, but was unable to get any person to assist him in removing it. I then gave him the necessary assistance and the body was removed to the Courthouse. I then returned to this Post, arriving about 5:30 o'clock A.M.

Next day, every citizen in Lincoln signed a petition to Dudley, supplemented by a formal request from Sheriff Kimbrell, that troops be stationed immediately in the town.[22] Less than an hour after its receipt, Lieutenant Goodwin and a detachment of soldiers, towing a Gatling gun, were on their way down. The people of Lincoln welcomed the troops with open arms; Susan McSween even turned the Tunstall store over to them as barracks. Everyone in the place was convinced that the old troubles had burst into flame once again. In fact, apart from a few dying kicks, the shooting war was over.

CHAPTER 32

LEW WALLACE STEPS IN

IN the four and a half months since his inauguration, Lew Wallace had devoted to the Lincoln County troubles little more than the impatient attention of a preoccupied parent with a fretful child. His concern for the terrorized citizens of that area had to vie with his preparations for the arrival of his wife Sue and their son, Henry, and his nightly immersion in the complexities of plotting and writing his novel, *Ben-Hur*. The murder of Huston Chapman altered all that.

Wallace could see all his hopes of promotion being wrecked by Dudley who, scoffing at Wallace's claims that all was well in Lincoln, sent weekly reports to Santa Fe which clearly demonstrated that the opposite was the case. The man simply had to go. Almost exasperatedly, and without any clear idea of what he hoped to achieve, Wallace decided to go to Lincoln in person. Some indication of his uncertainties can be had from the fact that on February 27, he formally suggested to Colonel Hatch (fig. 72) that there might well be a case for the declaration of martial law in Lincoln County (the military disagreed). He then in a letter to Carl Schurz pointed out that

> a request was sent to Col. Dudley, at Fort Stanton, for troops to protect the lives and property. The affair seems to have stopped with the murder of Chapman; yet Col. Dudley went over in person, carrying with him the equivalent of two companies. He also took a Gatling gun. Upon his own showing, a sergeant with a patrol would have been sufficient. The effect of this ridiculous action will be, I fear, to throw the people into a state of unnecessary alarm.
>
> I have further information that certain notorious characters, who have long been under indictment, but by skilful dodging, have managed to escape arrests, have formed an alliance which looks like preparation for raids when the spring opens. If so, their seizure now will put a quietus upon this operation. With that idea, I proposed a plan of campaign—the word may be excused—against them. To prevent interferences by justices of the peace who are for the most part terrorized past recollection of duty to the public, the intention is to make use of the warrants issued from U.S. courts for offenses against the United States, thus removing the old obstacle found in *preliminary* examinations by justices.
>
> The outlaws have always run to the mountains, in my judgement the only way to get at them was by untiring use of the troops and Indian scouts. The plan was submitted to General Hatch, commanding the District of New Mexico, and he has approved and entered heartily into it. He will go with me and in person direct the movements of the troops. I will rely greatly upon his judgment and energy.
>
> Accordingly I will leave for Lincoln tomorrow. . . . The disposition of the resident

citizens there continues excellent. If they can be protected there for a season against raiders from abroad, the morale of the community will restore itself, so it is important that we take the initiative, and make the country too hot for the harborage of their enemies.[1]

How he arrived at the conclusion that Dudley's stationing troops in the town was "ridiculous," while simultaneously suggesting that Colonel Hatch declare martial law, Wallace did not make clear. And anyway, the citizens of Lincoln were less confident in the excellence of their disposition than Wallace seemed to think: around the time he was setting off for Lincoln, Justice of the Peace J. B. Wilson was writing to Dudley suggesting the formation of some kind of local militia.[2]

FIG. 72. Edward Hatch. Date and photographer unknown.

General Dudly. Hon Sir. it past my mind to ask you if we can form an organisation Here if you can Send us arms to put in the Hands of the people for mutual protection if you can do so please Let me know as soon as you can as I am going to try to effect such steps Here at once in this matter an early answer will be a great favor to our cause of action.

I am yours in truth,
John B. Wilson JP

Dudley replied that he had no arms to loan the citizens, and even if he had, he would need authorization from the secretary of war. As always, he was playing it exactly by the book; he was an old hand at documenting, and thus justifying, every action he took. He knew perfectly well that the impending visit of Wallace and Hatch was not a friendly one—the governor had already requested his dismissal—and Dudley had no intention of giving them any ammunition to use against him.

Wallace and Hatch did not in fact leave Santa Fe until March 2, part of a caravanserai made up of ten supply wagons, three ambulances, sixty horses and mules, and a detachment of cavalry. They reached Lincoln in the afternoon of Wednesday, March 5. Hatch installed himself at Fort Stanton, but the governor decided to stay in the rooming house in back of the Montaño store in Lincoln.

Wallace seems to have kept no detailed record of his activities during the six weeks he was in Lincoln County, but he did make a series of reports to Carl Schurz that give an insight into his decisions.[3] He certainly wasted no time going into action.

A short interview with the leading citizens satisfied me that it would not be possible in the beginning to obtain affidavits against parties well known to be guilty of crimes;

this on account of the terrorism so general after the brutal assassination of H. J. Chapman. . . . Accepting the necessity of the situation I decided to proceed immediately without warrants. After the criminals were in custody, the popular fear would be removed, and with the toning up of confidence, testimony come in abundance— such was my hope. Accordingly, the following request was sent up to the Fort. . . .

March 5, 1879.

I have information that William Campbell, J. B. Mathews, and Jesse Evans . . . are now with J. J. Dolan at Carisosa ranche. You will please send a sufficient force to arrest them . . . have them brought to Fort Stanton, and held securely until their cases can be investigated by the grand jury.

General Hatch promptly complied, and the next day the three—Campbell, Evans and Mathews—were secured, and in due time lodged in the Fort. These men, you should understand, were all principals in the Chapman murder. Two of them are the most desperate of the outlaws. Evans is one of the murderers of Tunstall. He and Campbell have to answer for several other lives feloniously taken. Of the same gang is J. J. Dolan; but as I had hopes that his large money interests in this county, amounting to $70,000 or $80,000, would make him pliant for me as a witness, he was not included in the order of arrest. Two days afterwards he came and voluntarily surrendered himself to me; whereupon with the same object in view, I took his parole confining him to the limits of the Fort. Subsequently he violated his parole, and by my order was put in close confinement.

The governor had more work for Hatch: another note (on the letterhead of John H. Tunstall) was hurried to the fort saying that Wallace had discovered that "the Kid is at a place called Las Tablas, a plazita up near Coghlin's ranch."[4]

He has with him Thomas Folliard, and was going out of the Territory, but stopped there to rest his horses, saying he would stay a few days. He was at the house of one Higinio Salazar.

You will oblige me by sending a detachment after the two men; and if they are caught, secure them in the Fort Stanton for trial as accessories to the murder of Chapman.

If the men are found to have left Las Tablas, I beg they be pursued until caught. The details are commended to your good judgment.

Whether the Kid really was leaving the Territory we shall never know, although it is quite within the bounds of likelihood, given his frame of mind at this time. Of the fact that he wanted to quit fighting there is no doubt; his later actions confirm it. So, on March 6, another cavalry detail commanded by 1st Sgt. Israel Murphy, consisting of two noncoms and seven enlisted men, was ordered to proceed "without delay to Las Tablas or plazeta near Coghlans ranche and arrest Kid alias Bonney and Thomas Folliard." They came back empty-handed; the Kid was not there.

Wallace's most significant action came the next day. In the course of his interviews with the people, he said, it had become apparent to him that his attempts to restore confidence would be "long delayed, if not fruitless," while Dudley was in command at Fort Stanton.[5] He addressed a long letter to Colonel Hatch requesting that Dudley be relieved.

I will state in general terms that it is charged here that Lt. Col. Dudley is responsible for the killing of McSween and the men who were shot with that person; that he was an influential participant in that affair, and yet is an active partisan. I have information connecting him also with the more recent murder of H. J. Chapman; to the effect that he knew the man would be killed, and announced it the day of the night of the killing, and that one of the murderers stated publicly that he had promised Col. Dudley to do the deed. I am further informed that another man was driven in fear of life from Lincoln to Fort Stanton; that a band of armed men followed him there, and hunted about the Trader's store, avowing a purpose to kill him; that the party pursued appealed to Col. Dudley to give him protection, but was turned away, and escaped with difficulty; that there was no investigation of the affair by Col. Dudley, and that the would-be murderers were not interrupted in their hunt, which was repeated through two days, but were permitted to leave at their leisure, and within a night or two after, engaged in the killing of Chapman.

Hatch obliged—not without considerable satisfaction, one suspects—by relieving Dudley immediately, placing Capt. Henry Carroll in temporary command until the return from leave of the next ranking officer, Capt. George Purington. Angered at what he perceived as unjustified and high-handed treatment, Dudley exploded, protesting to his superiors in the most indignant terms and demanding a court of inquiry to clear his name.

Dudley's protests reached Washington coincidentally with a series of charges and specifications preferred against him with Secretary of War McCrary by Susan McSween's new lawyer, Chapman's Las Vegas friend Ira E. Leonard.[6] These included having abetted the murder of McSween, the burning of his home, and the plundering of the Tunstall store; having threatened Justice of the Peace Wilson; and making slanderous accusations against Mrs. McSween.

Dudley's request for a court of inquiry was granted, and the arrangements put in hand; meanwhile, Wallace continued his vigorous campaign to end the violence in Lincoln County.[7] On March 11, he provided the pliant Carroll with a list of the outlaws he wanted brought in; in every case but one (Andrew Boyle was wanted only for horse theft) the charge was murder.[8] The men named were

John Slaughter, Andrew Boyle, John Selman, Tom Selman alias Tom Catt, Gus Gildea, James Irwin, Reese Gobles, "Rustling Bob" [Roscoe L. Bryant], Robert Speakes, "the Pilgrim," John Beckwith, Hugh Beckwith, Jim French, Joe Scurlock, William Bonney alias the Kid, Tom O'Folliard, Charlie Bowdre, Henry Brown, John Middleton, Fred Waite, J. B. Mathews, Jessie Evans, Jimmy Dolan, George Davis alias Tom Jones, Frank Rivers alias John Long and A. L. Mont, Yginio Salazar, John Jones, William Jones, James Jones, Marion Turner, Caleb Hall alias Sam Collins, Heiskell Jones, Joseph Hall alias Olney, Buck Powell, James Highsaw, Jake Owens, and Frank Wheeler.

"The list, I stop to remark," Wallace told Schurz, "is by no means perfect; yet it was enough to begin with."

Some of those named are guilty of double murders; some of triple. . . . Another party butchered an entire family of Mexicans—men, women and children—nine in all. The other day Capt Carroll passed by the place of the butchery, and found the skeleton of a boy in a sitting posture, leaning against a tree. The head had rolled off the shoulders, and lay upon the ground *with a cigar in its mouth.* These illustrations will furnish an idea of the natures of the men against whom I find it necessary to proceed in a kind of war. I cannot hope to get them all on account of the country, which for brigandage is better even than northern Italy; yet there will be enough for wholesome examples.[9]

The next part of Wallace's clean-up plan was to launch an all-out war on the rustlers—at Shedd's ranch at San Agustin, at Slaughter's cow camp, at Beckwith's, and all over the Seven Rivers area. To assist him in this task, Wallace furnished Carroll with a complete list of all the cattle brands recorded at the county clerk's office. Carroll was to send troops to "every cattle camp, corral and herding place they may hear of in the county of Lincoln." If he found cattle, horses, or mules without brands there, or branded stock held by anyone not having bona fide bills of sale, he was to confiscate the animals and turn them over to Florencio Gonzales, probate judge. Gonzales would in turn place them in the keeping of John Newcomb, whom Wallace had designated "cattlekeeper of the county."

While all this was going on, Fate placed in Lew Wallace's hands a willing informant who was prepared to provide him with all the "wholesome examples" he required.

> Dear Sir I have heard that You will give one thousand $ dollars for my body which as I can understand it means alive as a Witness. I know it is as a witness against those that Murdered Mr. Chapman. if it was so as that I could appear at Court I could give the desired information, but I have indictments against me for things that happened in the late Lincoln County War and am afraid to give up because my Enemies would Kill me. the day Mr. Chapman was murderded I was in Lincoln, at the request of good Citizens to meet Mr. J. J. Dolan to meet as Friends, so as to be able to lay aside our arms and go to Work. I was present When Mr. Chapman was Murderded and know who did it and if it were not for those indictments I would have made it clear before now. if it is in your power to Annully those indictments I hope you will do so so a[s] to give me a chance to explain. please send me an annser telling me what you can do You can send annser by bearer I have no Wish to fight any more indeed I have not raised an arm since Your proclamation. as to my Character I refer to any of the Citizens, for the majority of them are my Friends and have been helping me all they could. I am called Kid Antrim but Antrim is my stepfathers name. Waiting for an annser I remain Your Obedeint Servant,
>
> W. H. Bonney.

An eyewitness to the Chapman murder! This was exactly what Wallace wanted. He scribbled a hasty reply.

> Lincoln, March 15, 1879.
> W. H. Bonney.
> Come to the house of old Squire Wilson (not the lawyer) at nine (9) o'clock next Monday night alone. I don't mean his office, but his residence. Follow along the foot of the mountain south of the town, come in on that side, and knock on the east door. I have authority to exempt you from prosecution, if you will testify to what you say you know.
> The object of the meeting at Squire Wilson's is to arrange the matter in a way to make your life safe. To do that the utmost secrecy is to be used. So *come alone.* Don't tell anybody—not a living soul—where you are coming or the object. If you could trust Jesse Evans, you can trust me.
>
> Lew Wallace.

These two letters were the beginning of a correspondence unique in the annals of outlawry.[10] In the weeks that followed, the Kid put his life on the line for Lew Wallace. He knew, even if the governor did not, that Billy Campbell and Jessie Evans took agreements like the one made on the night of February 18 quite literally. Anyone who broke the compact was to be killed on sight, and turning informer certainly qualified.

Unfortunately for the Kid, however, he was just a means to an end. Wallace never had any real intention of fulfilling any of the promises he made. That he was a sophisticated, intelligent man dealing with an unlettered thief who, no matter what his origins and crimes, deserved better than the cynical exploitation of his naïve desire to clear himself, redounds less than favorably upon Wallace. No doubt he justified his later actions by telling himself that deals struck with the likes of William H. Bonney were as worthless as the "precious specimens" who struck them.

The story of their meeting at Wilson's *jacal*, set back on the hill amidst trees behind where San Juan church now stands, is an oft-told tale. Wallace the novelist is much in evidence in the account he gave of it in later years.[11] The details lent themselves to dramatization: the shabby old man's room, dimly lit by a coal oil lamp; the governor in his dark broadcloth suit, tense with waiting; the quiet knock at the door at nine; the youthful Kid easing in carrying a Winchester in one hand and a six-gun in the other.

The plan Wallace proposed was simple: the Kid would submit to a fake arrest by Sheriff Kimbrell, remain in jail until the grand jury met, and identify the murderers of Chapman. In return, Wallace said, "I will let you go scot free, with a pardon in your pocket for all your misdeeds."

The Kid agreed, and left as noiselessly as he had arrived: whether his meeting with the governor was as secret as they both believed is another matter. In a matter of hours, Billy Campbell and Jessie Evans, assisted by a Fort Stanton recruit known as "Texas Jack," a member of Captain Carroll's company, escaped from the guardhouse and rode off into the mountains.[12] This put a considerably different complexion on the Kid's plan: to turn state's evidence with Campbell and Evans in prison was one thing. To do it while they were both free and armed was quite another. He wrote an edgy note to Wilson:

> Please tell You know who that I do not know what to do now as those Prisoners have escaped. to send word by a bearer a note through You it may be he has made different arrangements if not and he still wants it the same to Send "William Hudgins" as Deputy, to the Junction tomorrow at three o'clock, with some men you know to be all right. Send a note telling me what to do.
>
> W. H. Bonney.
>
> P.S. Do not send soldiers.

Wallace had other, more immediate preoccupations. To begin with, Capt. George Purington, who had returned from leave in Ohio, was proving considerably less cooperative and eager to please than young Henry Carroll. Purington was and always had been a Murphy supporter, and was doing everything he could to undermine Wallace's efforts by the simple means of doing as little as possible.

To counter Purington's foot-dragging, Wallace formed a militia company, the Lincoln County Rifles.[13] Less friendly observers dubbed it "the Governor's Heelflies," using a pejorative Texas term for the rabblelike Home Guards that had been raised during the Civil War.[14] Its rolls indicate that the organization was strongly pro-McSween in its sympathies: commanded by Captain Juan B. Patrón, with 1st Lt. Ben Ellis, and 2nd Lt. Martin Sanches, it included among its members such familiar names as George Washington, Martin, Florencio, and Maximiano Chaves, Jose Maria and Esequio Sanchez, Francisco Sanchez y Gonzales, Jose Chaves y Chaves, Ramon Montoya, Fernando Herrera, and Yginio and Jose Salazar.

Among the first tasks allotted to the Riflemen (together with the offer of a thousand-dollar reward if they succeeded) was the pursuit of Evans, Campbell, and Texas Jack. A patrol led by Private Fletcher, Ninth Cavalry, captured the latter; but both military and militia were unsuccessful in bringing in the wily Evans and his dangerous sidekick, who had slid off down the Pecos to John Slaughter's cattle camp.[15] Patrón also led his men up to the Fort Sumner region after Charlie Bowdre and Doc Scurlock. Bowdre was hiding out, but Scurlock was arrested and brought down to Fort Stanton, where the guardhouse was now beginning to resemble the Bastille.

Wallace was also perturbed by the number of prisoners at that place being signed up as clients by attorney Sidney Wilson. Sooner or later Wilson would appear with writs of habeas corpus, the prisoners would be released, and chaos would again ensue. Meanwhile Wallace sent a note to the Kid telling him that the escape of Evans and Campbell made no difference to their arrangements. The Kid wrote back on March 20.

> I will keep the appointment I made, but be Sure and have men come that you can depend on I am not afraid to die like a man fighting but I would not like to be killed like a dog unarmed. tell Kimbal to let his men be placed around the house and for him to come in alone, and he can arrest us. all I am afraid of is that in the Fort We might be poisoned or killed through a Window at night, but You can arrange that all right. tell the Commanding Officer to watch Lt. Goodwin he would not hesitate to do anything There will be danger on the road of somebody waylaying us to kill us on the road to the Fort. You will never catch those fellows on the Road. Watch Fritzes, Captain Bacas ranch and the Brewery. They will either go to Seven Rivers or to Jicarilla mountains. They will stay close untill the scouting parties come in give a spy a pair of glasses and let him get on the mountain back of Fritzes and watch and if they are there will be provision carried to them. It is not my place to advise you but I am anxious to have them caught and perhaps know how men hid from soldiers better than you. Please excuse me for having so much to say and still remain,
>   Yours truly,
>
>   W. H. Bonney.
> P.S. I have changed my mind. Send Kimbal to Gutierrz just below San Patricio one mile, because Sanger and Ballard are or were great friends of Camuls [Campbell's]. Ballard told me yesterday to leave for you were doing everything to catch me. It was a blind to get me to leave. Tell Kimbal not to come before 3 o clock for I may not be there before.

Next day, true to his word, the Kid surrendered to Sheriff Kimbrell and a posse of citizens. So, at the same time, did his now inseparable friend, fat Tom O'Folliard. They were brought in to Lincoln and stuck into the old cellar jail; next day they were moved to Patrón's store, opposite. Wallace sent a note to Purington to say he would keep the prisoners under guard in Lincoln for a couple of days and then send them to the fort. His true attitude towards the Kid is revealed in another of his letters to Schurz, in which he remarked, "A precious specimen named 'The Kid' whom the Sheriff is holding here in the Plaza, as it is called, is an object of tender regard. I heard singing and music the other night; going to the door I found the minstrels of the village actually serenading the fellow in his prison."[16]

The "precious specimen" was not so contemptible that the governor could not visit him in his room the following Sunday and make copious notes of the Kid's answers to his questions about the gangs of rustlers that had been terrorizing the county, their hideouts, their safe houses, the back trails they used, and their present whereabouts.[17]

Gus Gildea (wanted at San Antonio for killing Mexicans) Gildea is carrying the mail now from Stockton to Seven Rivers—James Irvin and Reese Gobles (rumored that their bodies were found in a drift down the Pecos)—Rustling Bob (found dead on the Pecos killed by his own party)—John Selman (whereabouts unknown) came to Roswell while Captain Carroll was there. The R[ustler]s stayed at Seven Rivers; which they left on their second trip via the Berenda for Fort Stanton. On their return back they killed the Chaves boys and the crazy Lorenzo, and the Sanchez boy, 14 yrs old. They also committed many robberies. They broke up after reaching the Pecos, promising to return when some more horses got fat.

The Kid held nothing back. He told Wallace all about the way stock was translated at Shedd's ranch, Mimbres Spring, San Nicolas Springs, and other rustler hideouts, and provided an insightful rundown of the careers of the Jones family. But this was all small beer; Wallace wanted a big coup.

His thoughts now were all of the forthcoming term of district court, scheduled to begin its deliberations on Monday, April 14. He felt it was doomed before it got started, for finding jurymen would be next to impossible, and the witnesses presently held at Fort Stanton might either escape or be set free by process of habeas corpus, rendering the securing of convictions unlikely. He had been in Lincoln County a month, and he was really no further forward than he had been when he arrived.

There was only one answer.[18] He again telegraphed the president requesting the proclamation of martial law; and was without ceremony again refused. That left him no option but to try for a civil solution to the problems confronting him. His April 4 report to Schurz indicates that he was not optimistic of achieving one.

My work goes forward somewhat slowly, but well enough to keep me in hope. The third detachment of which I spoke in my last is returned, and there are now fifteen prisoners in custody, some of them very desperate characters. Henceforward everything depends on the conduct of jurors and witnesses. I confess to much doubt on the subject. Still it is my opinion that the experiment should be tried; if there is failure, if, on account of intimidation, partiality, prejudice or corruption, there be acquittals grossly wrong, then the last civil resort will have been spent, leaving only martial law.

Privately, he decided to leave Lincoln as soon as the jurors were empaneled, leaving his interests in the capable hands of Ira Leonard and his assistant George Taylor. Wallace justified his departure by claiming that he had to prepare for the forthcoming Dudley Court of Inquiry, scheduled to convene on May 2. It seems much likelier he smelled impending failure and did not want to be associated with it.

Leonard was himself uneasy; in a note to Wallace written the day before the court party arrived at Fort Stanton from La Mesilla, he noted that there were

some suspicious circumstances that require vigilance to ascertain whether there is any meaning attached to them or not. For the last two or three days there have straggled in here from four to six hard looking characters a day. Cow boys from Texas and Buffalo hunters one gives this reason another that for coming here but I have an idea that the object is to rescue their friends if brought here for trial. they are all camping about or near the town so I am informed. . . .

I am satisfied that old Dr. Gurney is in the camp with Campbell & Evans. He left here three days ago on a pretended prospecting tour. This morning he sent in for medicines. If I had known it in time I should have put someone on his trail. Ballard is also gone, it is said to his store but I dont believe it.[19]

On Sunday, April 13, Judge Warren Bristol, District Attorney Rynerson, District Clerk A. L. Baldy, and attorneys Albert J. Fountain and Simon B. Newcomb arrived at Fort Stanton, where Bristol proceeded to confirm Wallace's premonitions by releasing, on habeas corpus petitions filed by attorney Sidney Wilson, fifteen of the prisoners held there. The following day, court was convened, and Judge Bristol addressed a lengthy and salutary opening statement to the grand jury.[20] "We are all aware that partisan feeling has run very high," he told them, "that it has been very intense and very bitter; and for this reason I warn and admonish you that you cannot permit this partisan feeling to influence your action as grand jurors without violating the solemn oath you have taken as grand jurors that 'you will present no person by indictment through malice, hatred or ill will, nor leave any unrepresented through favor or affection.'"

He might as well have saved his breath. The grand jury, with Isaac Ellis as foreman and many of its members (Avery Clenny, John Newcomb, James Farmer, Martin Sanchez, Francisco Romero y Valencia, Juan Trujillo, Trinidad Vigil, and Frank McCullum) sympathetic to the old McSween cause, generated indictments as if they were receiving commission for quantity. In a county with scarcely more than the same number of voters, some two hundred indictments were returned, most of them against men who had been identified with the Dolan faction.

In the matter of the death of Alexander McSween, the grand jury fixed the actual murder on Marion Turner and John Jones. Dudley and George Peppin were indicted for arson incident to the burning of the McSween house, Campbell and Dolan for the murder of Chapman, Jessie Evans as an accessory. Indictments were also returned against John Selman and eight Rustlers for the murderous atrocities of the preceding September and some two dozen more against Peppin and his possemen for the murder of Frank MacNab. Lucas Gallegos, who had been awaiting trial for two years, was finally tried and sentenced to one year's imprisonment for the murder of his nephew, Sostero García. The only McSween supporters indicted by this grand jury were Tom O'Folliard and Sam Smith, who took the rap for the theft of Charles Fritz's horses.

"No civil case was tried," said a sardonic reporter in the Grant County Herald of May 10. "In nearly all of them one or the other party was dead." This meant that the two suits instituted against McSween, the one by L. G. Murphy & Co. for some four thousand dollars, and the other by Charles Fritz and Emilie Fritz Scholand for the Fritz insurance money, were continued to become cases against Mrs. McSween as administratrix of her husband's estate.

Some of the indicted men, notably Jack Long, Billy Mathews, Buck Powell, Johnny Hurley, and Tom O'Folliard, pleaded and were granted immunity under the Wallace amnesty. Attorney Sidney Wilson, appearing for Dolan, submitted that his client could not hope to obtain a fair trial in Lincoln; the judge agreed and granted change of venue to Doña Ana County. Among the others who made the same submission were John Beckwith, Lewis Paxton, Robert Olinger, Buck Powell, Sam Perry, George Peppin, John Galvin, Tom Cochrane, Charley Kruling, Wallace Olinger, and Johnny Mes, all of whom had been indicted for murder or assault with intent to kill. Change of venue was granted in every instance. Colonel Dudley, still defiantly rejecting Wallace's amnesty, also elected for a change of venue to Doña Ana County.

By the time all this came to pass, Lew Wallace had long since left Lincoln for Santa Fe, leaving the Kid wondering whether the governor's promise had been anything more than hot air. He had kept his word and testified against Dolan, Campbell, and Evans—Dolan alone, really, since the other two were long gone—in the Chapman case. He expected his own hearing, in the matter of the Brady murder, to be a mere formality in which, his having turned state's evidence being taken into account, the district attorney would decline to prosecute. But Rynerson refused to play ball. Instead he pressed the charges, challenging Wallace's right to offer the Kid or anyone else immunity from prosecution.[21] On Sunday, April 20, Ira Leonard sent a worried note to Wallace in Santa Fe. "I tell you, Governor," he wrote, "the District Attorney here is no friend to law enforcement. He is bent on going after the Kid. He proposes to distroy his evidence and influence and is bent on pushing him to the wall. He is a Dolan man and is defending him in every manner possible."

Rynerson went on to secure a conviction for murder and a change of venue to Doña Ana County, which must have given the Kid plenty of food for thought. He had no illusions about his fate if he was tried there. The Santa Fe Ring looked after its own, and Rynerson would see him hanged long before Jimmy Dolan's case ever came to court. But the trial was not until July, so the governor could still come through. He might as well hold on to that—what else did he have?

No sooner had the district court at Lincoln terminated than another trial began: the military court of inquiry into the conduct of Colonel Dudley.[22] After a preliminary assembly on May 2, the full court convened at Fort Stanton on Friday, May 9, Col. Galusha Pennypacker, Sixteenth Infantry, Fort Union, presiding. The recorder (who fulfilled in a court of inquiry the role that would be played by a prosecuting attorney) was Capt. Henry H. Humphreys, Fifteenth Infantry, Fort Bliss, who was assisted energetically (in spite of Dudley's objections that he was both a witness and Mrs. McSween's attorney) by Ira Leonard. A quarrel with Thomas B. Catron had robbed Dudley of that powerful ally; instead he was defended by Santa Fe attorney Henry L. Waldo.

The charges and specifications set forth by attorney Leonard accused Dudley of being a party to the murder of McSween, the burning of his house, and the looting of the Tunstall store, of threatening J. B. Wilson, slandering Susan McSween, publishing an "open letter" calculated to foment disturbances, and taking no action in the matter of Lieutenant French's assault on Chapman and Mrs. McSween.

This was a hearing, not a trial; the purpose of a court of inquiry was to establish whether, on the evidence adduced, there were grounds for court-martial proceedings. In all, well over a hundred witnesses were summoned to appear, and Leonard was confident that they would secure a favorable verdict.

Dudley's attorney, Henry Waldo, was equally confident they would not. A former member of the law firm of Catron & Elkins, one-time chief justice and attorney general, he was one of the Territory's top lawyers. His strategy was fairly simple: to restrict the examination of Dudley's actions to the single day of July 19 rather than everything he had done since his arrival in April, and to turn the proceedings into a trial of Wallace's handling of the troubles rather than Dudley's part in them. Waldo had seen to it that a good proportion of those scheduled to appear as witnesses were military or former Peppin possemen, none of whom was likely to blacken Dudley's name.

Governor Wallace was the first to testify in proceedings that eventually stretched over six weeks. He stated that when he had first arrived in Lincoln, the people were in dread of Dudley, and so intimidated by him that it was impossible to secure affidavits against murderers who were known to be his friends. Judge Waldo, a most able attorney, gave him a very hard time, cross-examining him ruthlessly. He made Wallace admit that before April 5, he had no personal knowledge of affairs in Lincoln County, having relied on information received from others, thereby denying Wallace any opportunity to introduce evidence he had gathered in Lincoln on the grounds that it was all hearsay. Wallace was excused further attendance and returned to Santa Fe while the court of inquiry proceeded.

In spite of the governor's poor performance, Ira Leonard still felt confident.[23] On May 19, he scribbled a pencil note to Wallace to tell him "we are pouring 'hot shot' into Dudley so fiercely that his face for the last three days has strikingly resembled the wattles of an enraged turkey gobbler."

His euphoria did not last long. After the testimony of Capt. Casper Conrad, Alex Rudder, Samuel Beard, James Tomlinson, Juan Patrón, Isaac Ellis, David Easton, and J. B. Wilson, Leonard called Susan McSween, the prosecution's star witness. To what can only have been Leonard's utter dismay, her testimony was confused, hesitant, querulous, and unimpressive. She said little or nothing to harm Dudley's case and, by what the court can only have deemed her apathy, did even less to advance her own. For instance, when she was asked about the affidavit she had executed charging Dudley with the murder of her husband, she replied, "I made an affidavit but I cannot remember anything contained in it. It was made by my attorney and carelessly read to me [and] I did not pay much attention to it."

It may well be that her experiences the preceding year had finally caught up with Susan McSween, and that she was in a state of mental near-collapse which might partially account for her poor performance. In any case, Leonard's failure to ask her the right questions and Waldo's refusal to give her any room to enlist sympathy did nothing to improve matters.

Recorder Humphreys and Leonard then produced witnesses to support the accusation that Dudley had sent soldiers to help burn the McSween house, and had stationed his men in such a way as to prevent McSween's friends from coming to his rescue. The main witnesses to this were George Washington, Sebrian Bates, Joe Dixon, Mrs. Teresa Phillipowski, William Bonney, and Jose Chaves y Chaves. Both the latter swore that they had been fired on by three soldiers as they fled the burning house.

Sam Corbet testified to the looting of the store, and Doctor Ealy recalled his arguments with Dudley; minor contributions that Leonard was unable to capitalize upon. When Leonard himself took the stand, Waldo was able to show that since Leonard had not arrived in Lincoln until early in April 1879 anything he might have to say on the subject was also hearsay, and therefore inadmissible evidence. Challenged to give his reasons for bringing charges against Dudley, Leonard claimed to be acting for the public good, said he had "no malice or ill will" against Dudley, and said that he was contributing his services in this matter without fee or reward. The court took his public zeal under advisement, and Leonard began to realize he was losing ground. When Pennypacker refused to allow the introduction of material relating to the causes of the troubles, confining him to Dudley's conduct on July 19, it became apparent that Waldo's strategy was working, and there was nothing Leonard could do about it.[24] He wrote again to Wallace on June 6.

> They mean to whitewash and excuse [Dudley's] glaring [mis]conduct. They have transcended all rules of evidence to allow hearsay coming through other channels than direct parties, and are allowing liberally to Dudley what they peremptorily refused us. I am thoroughly and completely disgusted with their proceedings. . . . I had a good notion to show my disgust by abandoning the case and let them have it their own way. There is nothing to be looked or hoped for from the tribunal. It is a farce on judicial investigation and ought to be called and designated "The Mutual Admiration Inquiry."

The parade of witnesses supporting Dudley was formidable. They included Jimmy Dolan—doing his "know nothing" act again—Saturnino Baca, Jose Maria de Aguayo, David Easton again, Mrs. Baca and her daughter Juana, Sgt. John Kellike, Sgt. G. Davis, Sgt. Ezra Shanks, George Peppin, John Long, Buck Powell, Billy Mathews, Joe Nash, Andy Boyle, Milo Pierce, Marion Turner, Bob Olinger, Johnny Hurley, Private Shiply, Sergeant Murison, Corporal Bugold, O. D. Kelsy, Sgt. Andrew Keefe, Lieutenant Goodwin, Captain Purington, Asst. Surgeon Appel, Lieutenant Garst, Doctor Lyon, and finally, Lieutenant Colonel Dudley himself.

On July 5, Henry Waldo presented his closing argument, a powerful and persuasive peroration that must have taken several hours to deliver. He vilified Leonard, suggesting that the court of inquiry was just a further instance of that attorney's persecution of his client. He called into question the credibility and character of the witnesses in general and Mrs. McSween in particular and concluded by proclaiming that the foul conspiracy concocted by Wallace, Leonard, and Mrs. McSween had "ended in utter and ignominious failure."

Recorder Humphreys then somewhat less inspiringly put the case for the prosecution, claiming that the hearing had proved Dudley's partisanship, both pro-Dolan and anti-McSween. The killing of McSween and the burning of his home had been murder and arson, and all involved, actively or passively, were equally guilty. In conclusion, he stated that it was his belief that all the charges made against Dudley, with the exception of his implication in the murder of Chapman, had been proven.

On July 18, "after careful investigation and mature deliberation," the officers of the court found in favor of Dudley. He had not been guilty of violating either the civil law or military orders. Furthermore, his actions on July 19 had been prompted "by the most human and worthy motives and by good military judgment under exceptional circumstances."[25] Proceedings before a court-martial were therefore unnecessary.

Long before the board reached its verdict, at least one streetwise witness had read the writing on the wall: the cause was lost, the fight was finished. Maybe Lew Wallace would come through, maybe he wouldn't. The Kid wasn't about to wait and find out. So on June 17, twenty days after he appeared at the court of inquiry, he walked unhindered out of his "prison" in the Patrón store, and with Tom O'Folliard at his side, headed out through the Capitan gap and northeast towards Fort Sumner.

He was through with promises. Tunstall had promised him a ranch. McSween had promised him pay. Wallace had promised him a pardon. None of them had delivered. He had put the only things he had to offer—his loyalty and his life—on the line for two years, and what did he have to show for it? Nothing. The only thing life had taught him was how to stay alive. The only things he had ever owned he had stolen. From here on in, he would profit by the lesson: look out for Number One, and never buy anything you can steal.

CHAPTER 33

DOLAN CLEARS HIS NAME

JIMMY Dolan and his supporters were in the ascendant once again. Lew Wallace complained helplessly to Carl Schurz that

> the people go to Fort Stanton . . . and witness strange sights; they see Dolan, admittedly the leader of the fiercest refractories, at large and busy in Col. Dudley's behalf, although he is under two indictments for murder, one a murder in the first degree. They know he is not at large by the consent or connivance of the sheriff. They know that the commandant of the fort has my official request in writing to keep him in close confinement. Knowing this, and seeing what they see—Dolan free to come and go, a boarder at the trader's store, attended by a gang well understood as ready to do his bidding to any extreme—they are further met by threats of bloody things intended when Col. Dudley is acquitted by his court and restored to command of the post, and are afraid, and so constantly as to find it impossible to settle down.[1]

Dolan was taken to La Mesilla for a habeas corpus examination just as soon as his testimony at the court of inquiry was completed. Before his departure he made all the arrangements necessary for his marriage on July 13 to Caroline, daughter of Charles Fritz—some indication of the depth of his concern about the outcome. The hearing was reported in the *Las Cruces Thirty Four*:

> Dolan has been released on $3000 bail to appear at the next term of court at Socorro. E. A. Walz, Billy Mathews and others testified. Dolan claimed to have been very drunk and could not have hit Chapman without firing through Walz. Dolan fired, according to his admission, but said he knew nothing of what was happening, and simply fired into the ground "to call the boys off." Campbell said he had promised his God and General Dudley to kill Chapman when the party was in a saloon after the shooting.[2]

A few days later, the *Independent* sardonically drew attention to some of the flaws in Dolan's testimony.

> He saw nothing, neither did he know anything about the shooting of Chapman; he did not see Chapman shot and did not know that he was killed until after his arrival at the hotel. He acknowledged that he fired a shot, but stated that he fired it "to attract the attention of the party"—to call the boys off. Heard Evans talking, but did not know who he was talking to. In short, Mr Dolan knew nothing about the killing of Chapman, although he was not ten feet away.
>
> It will be remembered by those who read the newspapers that Mr Dolan once denied over his own signature that he was present when Chapman was killed. He

afterwards admitted that he was present but unarmed. He now admits that he was present and he was armed, and that he fired the first shot but that he fired it to attract the attention of the party. He stood in the midst of a party of eight or ten men and had to fire his pistol in order to attract their attention! Fatal shot! Whether it was fired by collusion with Evans and Campbell, or whether he meant it as a signal or merely to attract attention, it caused the death of Chapman.[3]

Once again, Dolan's defense was in the classic style he had so often employed, represented in this instance by the proposition that (a) he had not been there when it happened; (b) if he was there, he didn't have a gun; (c) if he did have a gun, he didn't fire it at anybody; and anyway (d) he couldn't have fired the gun because he wasn't there in the first place.[4]

No doubt laughing up his sleeve the whole way, Jimmy bade adieu to La Mesilla and hurried back to Lincoln where, on Sunday, July 13, he was married to Caroline Fritz.[5] The ceremony, which was conducted by Rev. J. S. Tafoya, assisted by Mickey Cronin, took place in the home of Allen Ballard at La Junta. "There being present few personal friends of the bride and bridegroom," gushed the *Mesilla News*, "who through all the vicissitudes of fortune, prosperity, slander and calumny, still were ever their true and devoted friends." The fact that the wedding did not take place at the bride's home, and that Ballard gave the bride away, suggests coolness, perhaps even opposition, on the part of Charles Fritz, who does not appear to have attended the wedding.

Dolan's best man was Jack Long. It is tempting to wonder if the two of them found any irony in the fact that the ceremony was taking place on the anniversary of the opening of last year's fighting. After the celebrations, Dolan and his eighteen-year-old bride left on a two-month honeymoon.

The question has to be asked, did Dolan shoot Chapman? Every account of the killing agrees that only two shots were fired. Dolan claimed he fired into the ground; those present would seem to have concurred by not disputing his statement. But it is important to bear in mind that all of them were so abjectly afraid of Billy Campbell that they would probably have sworn a horse was a giraffe if required. The answer may lie in two unargued facts: the first, that Campbell fired only once, and the second, that there were *two* bullets in Chapman's body.

The following November, Jimmy appeared at Socorro to stand trial on two charges of murder.[6] Cynics were not slow to point out that all the witnesses who might have testified against him were either dead or outlawed, and Dolan's attorneys—Catron & Thornton, of course—had no difficulty in securing a dismissal. At the same session of court, the charges of arson and participation in the murder of Frank MacNab brought against George Peppin were also dropped.

All his sins forgiven, Jimmy Dolan was restored to the community. His acquittal marks the point at which Dolan started to rehabilitate himself, and although as the years went by his drinking reached the same heroic proportions as that of his one-time friend and mentor, Lawrence G. Murphy, he remained thereafter on the (anyway, comparatively) straight and narrow path.

During the summer and autumn of 1879 the citizens of Lincoln County—and indeed, the whole of southern New Mexico and western Arizona—were preoccupied by the raids of warring Apaches led by Victorio.[7] In October 1878 the decision had been taken by the Bureau of Indian Affairs to transfer the Apache leader and his people from Warm Springs to the barren and overcrowded San Carlos reservation. Rather than go there, Victorio led his warriors off into the mountains. Their families were transferred to the Arizona reservation, further angering the Apache leader.

He remained "out" until February, then "surrendered" long enough to get fed, clothed, and rested up. In April, Victorio left for the mountains again. It was not until June that he led his men back in, surrendering this time at the Mescalero Agency in Lincoln County. Indian Agent S. A. Russell told him he would try to have the women and children brought back from Arizona if Victorio would stay in. The Apache agreed.

Meanwhile in Silver City angry citizens, denouncing the army and the Indian Bureau for harboring a "band of cutthroats," assembled a grand jury and indicted Victorio and his followers for murder and theft. The plan was to give Victorio a fair trial and then hang him. A group of them formed a "hunting party" and came up to the reservation.

At the beginning of September, Victorio confronted Russell and furiously accused him of doublespeak: he pulled the Indian agent's beard and threatened to raid the agency and steal everything in it. Russell tried to persuade the Indian leader that the men from Silver City were not looking for him, and issued ration tickets to Victorio and his men. The angry Apache tore them up, threw them in Russell's face, and stamped out, swearing he would take his men on the warpath in three days. Terrified, Russell sent for the troops at Fort Stanton; by the time they got to the agency, Victorio was gone. As he left he stopped to shake hands with Doctor Blazer, whom he considered a friend. He said he would never come back to the reservation again.

"From now on it will be war," he said. "War to the death. There is no other way."

He was as good as his word. His raiders swept west, butchering sheep—and two herders—in Temporal Canyon. On September 4, near Ojo Caliente, they surprised a company of the Ninth Cavalry commanded by Capt. Ambrose E. Hooker, killed five troopers and three civilian herders, and stole forty-six horses. Their trail across the San Andres Mountains was marked by burning ranches and dead settlers.

On September 17, the Apaches had a running fight with a party of citizens, killing ten of them and stealing all their stock. Next day, they caught a detachment of forty-six troops commanded by Capt. Byron Dawson—the same officer who had found Huston Chapman lying dead in the street in Lincoln—in a clever ambush near the headwaters of Las Animas Creek, killing five soldiers, one civilian, and two Indian scouts. After a rearguard action lasting thirty-six hours, and reinforced by a further two troops of cavalry commanded by Capt. Charles D. Beyer, the beleaguered Dawson retreated, leaving behind thirty-two dead horses and most of his baggage and supplies. Several more running fights took place, on September 26, September 30, October 1, and October 27; and thirty-five more Anglos were slain before Victorio disappeared across the border into Mexico.

The citizens of New Mexico and Arizona breathed a sigh of relief, and so, too, no doubt, did Lew Wallace, for the Indian war had effectively removed the other "war" from the headlines. Devoting more and more of his time to working on his

FIG. 73. John Beckwith. Date and
photographer unknown.

novel, which was close to completion, he made little or no mention of the subject in his reports to Schurz until September, when he received news that old scores were still being settled in Lincoln County.[8]

Although they had been indicted for the murder of Alexander McSween, no serious attempt ever seems to have been made to arrest and bring to trial Marion Turner or John Jones, who continued to run their cattle camp at Seven Rivers. There, during the summer of 1879, they got into contention with John Beckwith about the ownership of some cattle (fig. 73). Matters came to a head at Joe Nash's *choza* in Pierce Canyon on August 26. An anonymous correspondent sent a report of ensuing events to the *Mesilla News*, which was "condensed" in the September 20 issue of the *New Mexican*.

Jones and Beckwith got into a conversation about some cattle which Beckwith had stolen from Jones; when Jones demanded payment for the stock, Beckwith refused to pay and drew his pistol to kill Jones, but was too slow, Jones killing Beckwith. Jones expressed himself as being very sorry of having to kill Beckwith.

On yesterday, August 29, John A. Jones started up to the nearest justice of the peace to give himself up; when he got as far as Pierce & Paxton's camp on his way he was brutally and wilfully murdered by Robert Ollinger and others who were friends of Beckwith.[9]

This all seems straightforward enough, but murder in Lincoln County was seldom that simple. Apparently Jones had already threatened to kill Beckwith in front of Milo Pierce, who warned him grimly that if he did, he would have to kill him too. Lew Paxton, Pierce's partner, also sent an account of the killing of Jones to the *News*.

This morning John Jones came riding into our camp. Bob Ollinger a man that belongs to John Beckwith's camp was here at the time. As Jones got off his horse and came to the house, the two men, that is Jones and Ollinger, grappled in with each other and they both began shooting with their revolvers. Ollinger got his work in and killed Jones. After the shooting was over Buck Powell and myself examined things and found six shooters and guns scattered all over the yard. Ollinger's pistol was empty and two loads only were discharged and all six from Jones's pistol.

My partner M. L. Pierce was sitting or lying on the bed outside of the house and there was a stray ball struck him in the hip. Pierce is not badly hurt; we rigged up a wagon at once and sent him to Fort Stockton, Texas, where he can get the ball taken out as it lodged in his hip. Three days before this John Jones killed John Beckwith.[10]

Paxton's account indicates a noisy and violent scrimmage; other sources suggest that what happened was that Milo Pierce faked being ill (hence his lying on the couch or bed) and called Jones over to shake hands. When he had hold of Jones's hand, Milo hung onto it so John couldn't unlimber his gun, and Bob Olinger, who was said to be Bob Beckwith's cousin, shot him twice in the back, one of the bullets going through Jones's body and hitting Pierce in the hip. That there is a lot more to the story than this is evidenced by the fact that the grand jury later indicted both Jones and Marion Turner for the murder of John Beckwith.

It is extremely doubtful that anything further will emerge to illuminate the dark doings that occurred at Seven Rivers during the summer of 1879, but there was obviously a great deal more to them than reached the newspapers. Whether any of the motivation stemmed from the manner of Bob Beckwith's death during the Big Killing is now impossible to ascertain. Either way, tradition has it that the Kid's hatred of Bob Olinger stemmed from the death of the Kid's friend. Either way, the man who had killed Alexander McSween was dead. When the news reached him, Governor Wallace was moved to report somewhat inaccurately to Carl Schurz that "one 'Jim Beckwith' was shot and killed by one 'Tom Jones' and that 'Jones' was then killed by one 'Olinger' to which, as the three are amongst the most bloody of the 'Bandits of the Pecos', all the good people cried 'Amen.'"[11]

The Dudley Court of Inquiry was finished, but Dudley's trials were not over. The judge advocate general of the Department of the Missouri expressed his disagreement with the verdict in the strongest terms, arguing that the evidence indicated that Dudley's actions had been partisan in the extreme. General John Pope concurred; the report was forwarded to the War Department with a curt notation: "The Department Commander disapproves the opinion expressed by the court of inquiry." Simultaneously, Pope submitted another set of charges and specifications against Dudley, with a view to holding a court-martial. The judge advocate general declined to proceed further against Dudley, with "deference to the view of General Pope," on the grounds that it would not be in the public interest to investigate the matter further.

The verdict must have been of considerable satisfaction to Dudley, who left Fort Stanton immediately after the court of inquiry adjourned, and took the stagecoach north.[12] The *Trinidad News* of August 5 reported that he had been in town on his way "to meet Mrs Dudley and escort her to Fort Stanton, N.M., his post of duty. The General has just passed through a long investigation of his conduct of affairs in Lincoln county and we hope when the finding is made public, he will be found exonerated for the blame sought to be laid on his shoulders."

On his return, Dudley began preparing his defense against the indictments for arson and libel filed by Ira Leonard on behalf of Susan McSween. The case was slated to be heard in the La Mesilla district court term commencing November 10, Judge Warren Bristol presiding.[13] Dudley, who had spent a part of the preceding week in Santa Fe, left for La Mesilla on the Sunday stagecoach. "From parties well informed in the premises, we learn that there is no case against him," the *New Mexican* reported on November 15.

To Dudley's intense annoyance—his court of inquiry had cost him several thousand dollars in legal fees and expenses, and it was costing him fifty dollars a day to stay in La Mesilla—Susan McSween failed to appear.[14] In a letter to the court, she explained that her attorney Ira Leonard had not turned up to escort her to La Mesilla, having been detained on business elsewhere; and that with Victorio's Apaches off the reservation she had been afraid to travel alone. She asked for a continuance, which Bristol curtly refused, ordering her bail forfeited and issuing a warrant for her arrest.

His action had the desired effect; she arrived a week later, escorted by Sebrian Bates, her only witness. Beginning Monday, November 27, the case was heard over three days and parts of two nights. Dudley was certain he would be acquitted.[15] "Before the trial," Susan McSween said, "he had strutted along the street and said: 'It will all be over in an hour. There ain't nothing in it.'" In fact it did not take anything like an hour; the jury was out only two minutes before returning with a verdict of not guilty, at which point the spectators in the courtroom burst into applause.[16] "Thus," said the *New Mexican* with evident satisfaction, "ends a most infamous persecution."[17]

So it did; it appears that the libel suit filed by Leonard on July 14 charging Dudley with bringing Mrs. McSween "into public scandal and disgrace" never even came to trial. Although he was not allowed to return to command at Stanton, Dudley was restored to duty at Fort Union and went on to live a long and full life.[18]

From the summer of 1879 onward the Kid made his headquarters in the area around Fort Sumner, Puerto de Luna, and Anton Chico.[19] Doc Scurlock and his wife were living at the old fort; Charlie Bowdre was near at hand, working on Thomas J. Yerby's ranch about twenty miles northeast. The Kid made a living the only way he could—by stealing, by dealing cards, by gambling. The once sleepy little village of Las Vegas to the north had turned into a booming end-of-track hell town with the arrival of the AT&SF railroad on July 4. There were plenty of people there who would buy horses or cattle without asking too many questions. A new boom town, White Oaks, had also sprung up with the discovery of gold in the Jicarilla Mountains not far from where John Tunstall had spent his first Christmas in New Mexico. A trio of brothers named Dedrick had a livery stable in the town; they also had a place nearby where stolen stock could be driven, butchered, and sold to the miners.[20] The Dedricks, who owned another ranch near Bosque Grande, were associates of Whiskey Jim Greathouse in some of his shadier enterprises. Greathouse and his partner Fred Kuch had a trading post and rooming house about forty miles north of White Oaks; the Kid and his *compadres* could get food, supplies, and credit there.

Documentation of the Kid's career at this time is, not surprisingly, sparse.[21] In August 1879 he was charged in the San Miguel County court at Las Vegas with keeping a gaming table. A charge of cattle theft was dismissed for lack of evidence, and in yet another appearance for cattle theft, this time with William Wilson, Tom Pickett, and Samuel Cook, the Kid was released on three hundred dollars' bail.

Garrett—or rather Upson—claims the Kid, O'Folliard, Bowdre, Scurlock, and two Mexicans stole 118 head of Chisum cattle from Bosque Grande, drove them up to Yerby's ranch where they rebranded them, and later sold them to some

Colorado men at Grzelachowski's ranch at Alamogordo.[22] Around October or November, Scurlock and his wife decided to leave New Mexico for Texas, possibly after a dispute over the division of the spoils from this transaction.[23] They located in the Panhandle, where Doc settled down and became a highly respected citizen until his death at Eastland nearly fifty years later.

In January 1880 the Kid killed Joe Grant in Bob Hargrove's saloon at Fort Sumner. Grant was said by some to be a bounty hunter; maybe, maybe not. There is a version of events by the ever-unreliable Upson, which is probably as good as any other. The Kid was beginning now to realize what so many men who rode the owlhoot trail found out the hard way: that every theft that took place was blamed on him, and that every drunken tough looking for a "reputation" was liable to come looking for a fight with him. As for Grant, the Kid's only recorded comment on the fracas was made to Milnor Rudolph, postmaster at Sunnyside near Fort Sumner. Talking to Charlie Bowdre, Rudolph learned that "another man had turned his toes up at Sumner." As the Las Vegas Daily Optic reported it, "upon being asked who it was, he [Bowdre] said the man's name was Joe Grant. Rudolph asked Billy what occasioned the trouble, and he remarked: 'Oh, nothing; it was a game of two and I got there first.'"[24]

Upson's catalog of the Kid's thievery is as likely to be accurate as any other. It paints a believable picture of his activities, and confirms why he and his compadres were soon to be considered as big a menace as the original gang whose name they now bore—the Rustlers.[25]

In February 1880 the Kid, Mose Dedrick, Yginio Salazar, and Paz Chavez stole forty-eight head of horses from the Mescalero reservation and traded them off all up and down the Pecos. In May, he and Charlie Bowdre, one Pruett, and another accomplice stole fifty-four head of cattle in the Panhandle and drove them to White Oaks, where they sold them for ten dollars a head to Thomas Cooper. In June the same gang returned to Fort Sumner driving horses stolen around the White Oaks area.

In July they stole a "bunch" of cattle belonging to John Newcomb at Agua Azul, about fifteen miles from Lincoln. During the summer they made "various successful raids," including one in which they drove off ten head of work steers, the property of a Fort Sumner resident, and sold them together with twenty more to John Singer in Las Vegas.

But the times at last were changing, and a cold new wind of law and order was beginning to blow. At Fort Sumner there lived a lean, lanky giant of a fellow, a former buffalo hunter and saloonkeeper named Pat Garrett.[26] John Chisum and Joseph C. Lea, the two most prominent citizens of the Roswell area, approached Garrett with a proposition: move to Lincoln, qualify for the election, and run against George Kimbrell as sheriff. Kimbrell was a good enough fellow, but he was as paralyzed by fear of the outlaws as his predecessor George Peppin had been a year earlier.

Garrett had powerful support.[27] Backed by Chisum, Lea, and Joseph LaRue, a Lincoln storekeeper who had made a lot of money grubstaking miners, and with David Easton, Will Dowlin, and Jimmy Dolan making impassioned speeches (and raising funds) in his behalf, Garrett succeeded in winning the nomination. On November 2, by a majority of 141 votes out of a total of 499, he was elected sheriff of Lincoln County on a ticket to rid the Territory, once and for all, of the Kid.

Although his term of office did not begin officially until the first of the year, Sheriff Kimbrell was pressured to appoint Garrett a deputy for November and December 1880. His appointment coincided with the arrival in New Mexico of Azariah F. Wild, an agent of the Treasury Department who had been sent out to investigate a rash of counterfeit money that had appeared in Lincoln County.[28] At Lincoln, Wild examined a "queer" hundred-dollar bill that had been passed by Billy Wilson on—of all people—Jimmy Dolan. Wild's inquiries led him to the conclusion that the dud money was being circulated by Wilson, Tom Cooper, and W. W. West and Sam Dedrick, partners in that livery stable and other enterprises in White Oaks.

Wild sought a simple solution: he asked U.S. Marshal John Sherman to issue warrants and arrest the suspects.[29] He was astonished when Sherman refused. "I prefer not do do so," was all he would say. Wild concluded that Sherman's reason was the same one that kept George Kimbrell home—he was terrified. It was dangerous to travel the lonely trails between Las Vegas and Roswell unless as one of a well-armed party. The bandits, forty or fifty strong, rode where they pleased and stole what they wanted. No one dared to grapple with a gang that included men like the Kid, the Texas outlaw Joe Cook, the Las Vegas killer John Webb, or the hulking, murderous Dave Rudabaugh. The terrorized citizens of the county had learned, like the village people in the Kipling poem, that the smart thing to do was to ask no questions and "Watch the wall, my darling, while the gentlemen go by."

Wild decided to put together his own gang, consisting of Ben Ellis, George Kimbrell, Johnny Hurley, Captain Lea, Frank Stewart, and Pat Garrett.[30] If Sherman would commission them all deputy U.S. marshals, he would start to clean up Lincoln County. Sherman hastened to comply, and Wild drew up a plan to make a three-pronged attack on the outlaws. Kimbrell and Hurley would go to White Oaks and flush them out. Stewart would block their entry into Texas. Garrett and Captain Lea would push the fugitives north, while two other posses waited until called on. Before the plan could be put into operation, however, the outlaws robbed the U.S. mail and read some of Wild's confidential reports to Washington. The undercover agent found himself out in the cold, and temporarily abandoned the operation.

The Rustlers had not abandoned theirs, in spite of a "polar wave" of weather sweeping across the country. On the night of November 22 (there is conflicting evidence about the date, which is given as anywhere between November 20 and 28, depending upon the source consulted), an attempt was made to steal horses from a ranch on the edge of White Oaks. The next morning it was rumored in town that the Kid and some of the gang were at Blake's sawmill, some distance out of town on the trail to Coyote Spring. Storekeeper Will Hudgens, one of the many Lincoln residents who had moved to White Oaks following the gold strike, was deputy sheriff. He raised a posse that included his brother John, George Neil, Tom Longworth, Jim Carlyle, Jim Redman, James W. Bell, J. P. Eaker, and William Stone.

On their way out of town, the posse encountered Mose Dedrick and W. J. Lamper coming in. Suspecting that the two men had come from a rendezvous with the Kid's band, Hudgens arrested them. Pushing on, the posse stumbled on the Kid's camp. The startled outlaws ran for their horses, shooting as they went, killing John Hudgens's horse. Return fire killed Billy Wilson's and the Kid's horses; the outlaws fled, abandoning their camp.

The posse scouted around, taking a good saddle off the Kid's horse. Blacksmith Jim Carlyle picked up a nearly new pair of gloves and appropriated them. Near the abandoned fire the possemen found Mose Dedrick's overcoat, dropped by the Kid, together with canned goods, provisions, and other dry goods known to have been bought that morning at White Oaks. They had Mose dead to rights, and decided to take him back to town; he appeared with Lamper before Probate Judge James A. Tomlinson, another transplanted Lincolnite, who put him under bond to appear before the next district court. Mose promptly skinned out.

Meanwhile, another posse was raised in White Oaks to push on after the Kid and his gang. This one consisted of about fourteen men, including the brothers Hudgens, Tom Longworth, James Brent, Jim Carlyle, and James Bell. Leaving White Oaks on the evening of November 23, they rode through heavy snow towards the Greathouse and Kuch ranch. On the morning of November 27 (the same strictures apply to this date as to the earlier one), the posse surrounded the place and awaited daylight. The first movement from the house was that of the German cook, Joseph Steck, who came out to harness a team of horses.[31] Eaker and Brent jumped him, guns drawn. They made him lie flat on the ground while they questioned him about the men inside. From the descriptions they gave him he was able to confirm that the Kid, Dave Rudabaugh, and Billy Wilson were stopping at the house.

Jim Carlyle scribbled a note to the Kid, informing him that the posse had the place surrounded, and demanding his surrender; Steck was ordered to take it in to him. The Kid "read the paper to his *compadres*, who all laughed at the idea of surrender."

The Kid's party sent me out with a note demanding to know who the leader of the party was, and invited him into the house to talk the matter over. Carlyle, the leader of the White Oaks crowd, at first objected, but Greathouse putting himself as hostage for his safety while he was in there, he took off his arms and walked into the trap. In the meantime I was backward and forward between the two parties, carrying dispatches.

Getting hungry, about 11 o'clock, I went into the house to rustle up a dinner. I found Carlyle getting under the influence of liquor and insisting on going out, while the others insisted on his staying. While I was getting dinner, Mr Cook [Kuch], Greathouse's partner, carried dispatches between the camps. For some reason the White Oaks boys became suspicious; things were not as they should be with their leader, and they decided to storm the fort. Therefore they sent me word by Mr Cook to come out as war would commence in earnest. I stepped outdoors to go to some safe place and witness the bloody conflict. After being out a moment, Cook stopped and turned, when with a crash a man came through a window. Bang, bang, the man's dying yell, and poor Carlyle tumbles to the ground, with three bullets in him, dead.

I started to run away from the house, with Cook behind me, and towards a barricade of the White Oaks boys when they commenced to shoot at us, and so did all the boys behind the different barricades. About 60 or 75 shots were fired at us, bullets flying in all directions. . . .

We crawled out amongst the boys when they told us it was all a mistake; that they thought we were making a feint to cover the retreat of the desperadoes.

Kuch and Steck, accompanied by Greathouse who had slipped away from the posse during the shooting, got horses and headed for a nearby ranch, where they remained until next morning. When they returned the posse was gone. "We found poor Carlyle frozen stiff where he fell," Steck said. "We tied a blanket around him and buried him the best we could. He was afterwards taken up and put in a box by the Sheriff's posse."

Two nights later, the Greathouse and Kuch ranch was burned to the ground. Nobody claimed the credit—if there was credit attached—but it is safe to assume that the cowed White Oaks possemen, who had slunk off after the death of their leader, returned as a drunken mob. After torching Greathouse and Kuch's place, they went on to the Spencer ranch, where Greathouse, Kuch, and Steck had hidden the night after Jim Carlyle was killed. They burned that down as well.

On December 3 the editors of the *Las Vegas Gazette* published a stirring editorial denouncing the "powerful gang of outlaws harrassing the stockmen of the Pecos and Panhandle country, and terrorizing the people of Fort Sumner and vicinity," including the Kid, Rudabaugh, Charlie Bowdre, and "others of equally unsavory reputation."[32] All the members of the gang were "hard characters, the off scouring of society, fugitives from justice, and desperadoes by profession." The *Gazette* called upon the citizens of San Miguel County to "unite in forever wiping out this band."

The Kid decided to reply to these accusations directly to Governor Wallace.[33] On December 12, from Fort Sumner, writing in red ink on ruled paper, he told his side of the story.

I noticed in the Las Vegas Gazette a piece which stated that Billy "the" Kid, the name by which I am known in the Country was the captian of a Band of Outlaws who hold Forth at the Portales. There is no such Organization in Existence. So the Gentleman must have drawn very heavily on his Imagination. My business at the White Oaks the time I was waylaid and my horse killed was to See Judge Leonard who has my case in hand. he had written me to Come up, that he thought he could get everything straightened up I did not find him at the Oaks & Should have gone to Lincoln if I had met with no accident. After mine and Billie Wilsons horses were killed we both made our way to a Station, forty miles from the Oaks kept by Mr Greathouse. When I got up next morning the house was Surrounded by an outfit led by one Carlyle, who came into the house and Demanded a Surrender. I asked for their Papers and they had none. So I concluded it amounted to nothing more than a mob and told Carlyle that he would have to Stay in the house and lead the way out that night. Soon after a note was brought in Stating that if Carlyle did not come out inside of five minutes they would Kill the Station Keeper (Greathouse) who had left the house and was with them. in a Short time a Shot was fired on the outside and Carlyle thinking Greathouse was Killed jumped through the window breaking the Sash as he went and was killed by his own Party they think it was me trying to make my Escape. the Party then withdrew.

they returned the next day and burned an old man named Spencer's house and Greathouse's, also I made my way to this Place afoot and During my absence Deputy Sheriff Garrett Acting under Chisum's orders went to Portales and found Nothing. on his way back he went by Mr Yerbery's ranch and took a pair of mules of mine which I had left with Mr Bowdre who is in Charge of mr Yerby's cattle he claimed that they were stolen and even if they were not he had a right to Confiscate any Outlaws property.

I have been at Sumner Since I left Lincoln making my living Gambling The mules were bought by me the truth of which I can prove by the best citizens around Sumner. J. S. Chisum is the man who got me into Trouble and was benefited Thousands by it and is now doing all he can against me. There is no Doubt but what there is a great deal of stealing going on in the Territory and a great deal of the Property is taken across the [Staked] Plains as it is a good outlet but so far as my being at the head of a Band there is nothing of it in Several Instances I have recovered stolen property when there was no chance to get an officer to do it.

One instance for Hugo Zuber Postoffice Puerto de Luna another for Pablo Analla Same Place

if some impartial Party were to investigate this matter they would find it far Different from the impression put out by Chisum and his Tools.

Yours respect
William Bonney

Governor Wallace's reaction to this catalog of half-truths and self-justification was one of indifference; he had already decided that there was only one way to get rid of the Kid. It was simple, brutal, and unequivocal.

BILLY THE KID

$500 REWARD

I will pay $500 reward to any person or persons
who will capture William Bonny, alias The Kid, and
deliver him to any sheriff of New Mexico.
Satisfactory proofs of identity will be required.
LEW. WALLACE,
Governor of New Mexico.[34]

CHAPTER 34

THE PURSUIT OF BILLY THE KID

EVEN as Wallace published his reward notice, Chisum's men were breathing down the Kid's neck. On Friday, December 10, Frank Stewart, one of Azariah Wild's deputy U.S. marshals who was also employed as a detective by a Panhandle cattlemen's association, left Las Vegas with twenty men, provisioned and equipped to stay on the trail of the rustlers for at least two weeks. The following day Pat Garrett and his Lincoln County posse moved into the Fort Sumner area to join up with Stewart and his men.

Another group, led by Charles Siringo, had come up from the Panhandle where Outlaw Bill Moore, owner of the LX ranch, had told him to take the toughest men on the place and go and close down the Kid's operation. Siringo selected Jim East, Lon Chambers, Lee Hall, and eighteen-year-old Cal Polk to hunt down the Kid (figs. 74, 75).

Fifteen years later, Polk wrote down his recollections of the pursuit that ensued. It is a remarkable document, and is reproduced here exactly as Polk wrote it.[1]

They was a heep of cattle stealing goin on at that time and they was several ranches up and down the Canadian River hired a man by the name of Frank Stuart to stay in New Mexico and watch to find out if inney of the Panhandle cattle was stolen & carried that way. In the winter Moor received a letter from Stuart telling him that Billy the Kid and his men was going to worge the White Oaks with five hundred head of stolen cattle from the Panhandle so Moor started five of us down there to see about it. He put Jim McClarrity boss of the crowd. After traveling a few days we caught up with Billy. He had a hurd and 23 white men and a niggro with him. They was in camp for dinner when we rode up. Billy asked us down to take dinner with him. We got down and eate dinner, then Jim told him we wanted to look through his hurd. He said all rite, and told some of his hands to go and round them up. We all mounted our horses and started toworge the hurd. I nodist that Billy kept his winchester in his hand and when we got to the hurd, Billy said there they are, go in and look at them. As soon as we got in the hurd we saw they all belonged to the—X and LIT Ranches. Jim Rode back to Billy and said old boy these are our cattle.

He wheeled his horse a round and said, there they are. you can take themm, but you will take a heap of hot led before you do. Of corse we did not want any cattle then. We turned and rode easy and I did not try to keep from riding in the lead for about 5 miles. We returned to the Ranch and told all about it. The cattlemen up and down the river all raised cane and said they was going to send 150 men after them desperadoes and the cattle. The Ranch men sent down to Austin, Texas and got papers to go into New Mexico after Billy the Kid and his outfit. Me and Jim

East started south with Charley Cirringo's out fit. after we had traveled three days Moor sent a man over to take us and bring the out fit back. He wanted to send us after Billy the Kid. . . .

When we got ready to go Moor did not have but five men that would go out of 25. These was C. W. Polk, James East, Lon Chambers, Lee Smith and Charley Cirringo, he was the bosss. and a cook, chuck wagon with 4 good mules. Each one of us carried one good horse a peace. . . . We started on the 22nd day of Nov 1880 and went up to the LIT Ranch above Tascosa that night. The LIT out fit sent a wagon, cook and five men named as follows Louis Bosman [Louis Bousman], Monroe Harris, Tom Emray [Emory], Billy McKoley, and Bob Roberson for a boss. While the LS Ranch sent three boys by the name of Bob Williams, Uncle Jimmie and Big Foot Wallace [Frank Clifford]. The Panhandle cattle men could not get [any] men to go. The boys would quit there jobs in the dead of winter before they would go out. Out of 300 men they was only 13 that would go. [They got to Anton Chico on a Sunday at noon]. Just as we all rode up into town the cathlick church broke [up] and the Maxacans [began] coming out of it. They all stoped and gazed at us, and wondered what was the matter. We all had 2 belts full of cartidges a peace around us and was armed to the teeth with six shooters Bowie knives and Winchesters on our sadles.

Siringo went on to Las Vegas "for corn"; in fact, he could not wait to get at the gambling tables, and when he got back, ten days later, he was flat broke. To top it all, his men—who had been drinking and shivareeing the town, and had gotten into a shooting scrape—were practically at war with the citizens of Anton Chico. Siringo hastily removed them over to White Oaks, where they went into winter camp.

In the intervening period, Garrett had been doing what the boys from Texas were only talking about: leading a twenty-man posse that included Azariah Wild, Bob Olinger, and Barney Mason. He had left Roswell at the end of November for the Fort Sumner region.[2] His dragnet quickly worked. The possemen picked up Joe Cook, one of the Kid's sidekicks, with two stolen horses in his possession. Garrett sent him back to Roswell escorted by Wild and two deputies, then headed up the Pecos to the Dan Dedrick ranch at Bosque Grande.

Once again Garrett's knowledge of the Kid's hideouts paid off. Although this time the main gang had gone, the posse captured John J. Webb and Tom Jones, alias George Davis. The manacled prisoners were taken along as the posse pushed cautiously into the Kid's home base, Fort Sumner, where they learned that their quarry had left one jump ahead of them, going north.

Dropping off the prisoners and four more possemen, Garrett headed for Thomas Yerby's ranch at Las Cañaditas. On the way they flushed Tom O'Folliard, but he outran them. By the time the posse got to the ranch, their birds had flown, and only Charlie Bowdre's wife Manuela and another woman remained. Garrett led his men and their worn-out animals back to Fort Sumner.

After the animals were rested a little, Garrett led the posse out again, this time to Los Portales, supposed to be the stronghold of the rustlers, about fifty miles southeast of Fort Sumner. Once again the foray was a water haul; the Kid seemed to have vanished off the face of the earth. They retraced their tracks, stopping at the Wilcox-Brazil ranch to eat. Wilcox told Garrett that Charlie Bowdre wanted to parley, and would he meet him, alone, on the Sumner road? Garrett

showed him a letter from Capt. J. C. Lea, of Roswell, wherein it was promised that if he, Bowdre, would change his evil life and forsake his disreputable associates,

FIG. 74. Henry McCarty, alias Henry Antrim, William H. Bonney. Date and photographer unknown; the original is a tintype. Said to have been taken outside Beaver Smith's saloon late 1879 or early 1880, by an itinerant photographer. This is the only authenticated tintype known to be still in existence. Given by the Kid to Dan Dedrick, it remained in the Dedrick family until 1985, when it was donated to the Lincoln County Heritage Trust. Note the hand holding the reflector to the left of the Kid's head.

FIG. 75. Billy the Kid. An "enhanced" portrait obtained by photographing the tintype, reversing the image, and restoring the facial tones.

every effort would be made by good citizens to procure his release on bail and give him an opportunity to redeem himself.

Bowdre did not seem to place much faith in these promises and evidently thought I was playing a game to get him in my power. He, however, promised to cease all commerce with the Kid and his gang. He said that he could not help but feed them when they came to his ranch, but that he would not harbor them more than he could help. I told him if he did not quit them or surrender he would be pretty sure to get captured or killed, as we were after the gang and would sleep on their trail until we took them in, dead or alive. And thus we parted.[3]

The letter from Captain Lea that Garrett gave Bowdre was probably one sent in reply to an earlier request for assistance. On December 15, obviously having taken Garrett's advice to heart, Bowdre wrote to Lea to say he had

broke up housekeeping and am camping around, first one place & then another on the range, so that no one can say that Yerbey's ranch is the stoping place for any one. So no party will have any excuse for going there unless they are after me. I thought this a duty due Mr. Yerby, for if there is nothing to eat at the ranch no one will go there & there will be no chance for a fight coming off & Mr. Yerbys property injured. If I dont get clear I intend to leave some time this winter, for I dont intend to take any hand fighting the territory, for it is a different thing from what the

Lincoln Co War was. The only difference in my case & some of the officers in Lincoln Co is that I had the misfortune to be indicted before the fight was over & did not come under the Gov's pardon. It seems to me that this would come to their minds once & awhile, when they are running around after me, but I supose it is human nature to give a man a kick when you have the upper hand. I saw the two Billies the other day & they say they are going to leave this country. That was my advice to them for I believe it is the best thing they can do. Don't you think if you can get the Gov interested in my case, that it could be thrown out by the Dist Att without my appearing at court. I dont doubt your good intentions, but during the present state of the country I think there is some danger of mobing.

For my name has been used in connection with a good many things that I have had nothing to do with, which outside parties can't know. I have taken your advice in regards to writing to Mr. Yerby & have no doubt but what he will do all he can for me.

I know of nothing to urge in my favor, more than that others were pardoned for like offences. Experience is a good but stern teacher & I think if I keep my mind, I will let every man do his own fighting, so far as I am concerned, & I will do my own.

Respt.

Chas Bowdre[4]

Before the ink on Charlie Bowdre's letter had dried, the last, long, relentless pursuit of Billy the Kid had begun. Garrett gathered all the posses together at White Oaks—Frank Stewart and his men, Siringo and his. From the men available Garrett selected the ones he wanted as possemen: Stewart, Hall, East, Chambers, Emory, Bousman, and Williams. Although Garrett does not mention Cal Polk, the latter's persuasive account indicates that he was there. "Then the sheriff of Lancon County taken charge of us. All except a nuff of the men to take the wagons on to the White Oaks. So Pat started with us south east to old Ft. Sumner."[5]

They set out on the 15th, making forty-five miles that day, cold camped, and got to Puerto de Luna the following morning at about nine, where they spent the day at Grzelachowski's store, "eating apples and drawing corks."[6] From there they pushed on to Fort Sumner, arriving at Gayheart's ranch, twenty-five miles above the fort, about nine o'clock at night on December 17 "in a terrible snowstorm from the northwest." Garrett sent Juan Roibal into Sumner to see if the Kid and his men were there; Roibal reported they were. Next day Garrett and Mason sneaked in to check the place out, learning that the fugitives had left town and were at the Wilcox-Brazil ranch.

Garrett tried a subterfuge. He coerced one José Valdéz to write the Kid a note saying the posse had left for Roswell. He figured, correctly, that thinking him gone, the Kid and his men would ride back into Sumner to celebrate. Garrett laid his plans accordingly. Cal Polk takes up the story again:

We got there just before night [on December 19]. We stoped and put our horses in an old soldier hospittle that had been deserted and we camped in a little house clos to it that night. We was all in the room playing poker, but Lon Chambers he was on gard outside. The snow was about 12 inches deep and the moon was shining bright on it that made it light so you could see a man 300 yards off. All at once Lon come to the door and said see some well armed men comming. We grabed up our guns and stept out in the shade of a high doby wall. They come on up until about 10 yards of us. When Pat Garrett spoke and said throw up your hands, at that moment they jerked their gons out and they big shooting came off. They was about 40 shots fired. When the smoke got out of my face so I could see I saw one man's horse running in a circle and come back to us. When he got close he said don't shood me for I am killed. We went to him. His name was Tom Ofalyar. We taken him off his horse. He was shoot thrue the breast and only lived about ten minutes and died. Garrett then ordered us to get on our horses and follow the trail in the snow which we could see for 50 yards a head. You see Billy had lots of Mexacans friends that was carrying him nuse all the time so he knew where we was and where our horses was and he thought he would come and steal our horses and then whip us. But he sliped up on that.[7]

As the gang thundered away, Rudabaugh's horse was hit; after running on a few miles, it collapsed.[8] Rudabaugh doubled up behind Billy Wilson and the party headed back towards the Wilcox-Brazil ranch, about twenty miles east of the old fort. Bad enough that Garrett and his posse were still around, but the question plaguing them now was, what would Garrett do next? The Kid sent Emanuel Brazil into Sumner to ask around. Brazil came straight to Garrett and told him where the outlaws were. Garrett gave him some well-thought-out disinformation to feed to the outlaws and told Brazil to go back to his ranch and let him know when they made their move.

Brazil came back around midnight on December 20. The Kid and his men had gone. The posse saddled up and headed out, the whining wind whipping up long tendrils of icy snow that melted as it touched their faces then froze again instantly. Icicles hung from the muzzles of horses. Saddles and harness were as hard as iron.

Straight as an arrow across the open land the trail of their quarry ran before them. Garrett must have smiled grimly as he realized there was only one place they could be going—the old forage station built by Alejandro Perea at Stinking Springs. The Kid had forgotten that Garrett knew his hideouts as well as he knew them himself. "We rode on ther trail untill about 2 oclock in the morning," said Polk.

When we come in sight of there horses tide in front of a little house that had been a ranch, but was vacant. We got down tide our horses and left too men with them. The ballance of us sliped up to a little spring branch which run along in front about 20 steps from the door. There they all stoped except me and Jim East. We crauld up and went all around the little house to see if they was any port holes in it. The house was sollid made of rock and no holes in it. Only one door, and no shuter to it. They horses was tide to a pole that stuck out over the door. We could heer them snooring inside the wall which was about 4 feet from me and jim. We then went back to the crowd at the branch and told them how everything was shaped up. We put some blankets down on the snow under the bow of the hill and lay down on them. We could raise our heads one foot and see rite in the door. We lay there until day lite half froze. Just at sun up we heard them talkin and getting up and in a few minutes a man come out with a morat [nosebag] in his ha[n]d to feed his horse. His name was Charley Bodder. Just as he was putting the morat on his horse we all raised up on our kneese and drewe a beede on him with our winchesters. He looked over his sholder and saw us. Pat told him to throw up his hands.

He said all right in the minnet as he taken his hands down from the horses head, he jerked out 2 pistols and fired at us and at the same time we fired. They was three shots hit him one in the leg and too in the body. He droped his pistols and come realing to worge us. He said something like I wish, I wish, and then said blood is cloging in my mouth and fell acrost one of our boys, Lee Smith. He roled him over to one side and there he froze in a short time and lay there all day. In a few minutes after the shooting, Billy cried out is that you Pat out there. Pat says yes, then Billy says Pat why dont you come up like a man and give us a fair fite. Pat said I dont aim to. Billy says that is what I thought of you, you old long logged S..B and then every thing hushed for a while.

All at once some of the boys nodist that they was reaching out at the door and cutting the horses loose and leading them in the hourse. They had got 2 in, and just as they got another one in the door, we fired on him and droped the horse dead in the door. We then shot the ropes in to the others was tide with and turned them loose. Billy and his men was afraid to get in front of the door to pull the dead horse out of the way, and this blocked every thing. They aimed to get the horses in and mount them and come out a fiting for their lives. But they couldnt get over the dead horse in the door.

They was 2 boys went up on a little hill and comence shooting at the house. The horses in side got scard and was a bout to run over Billy and his men, so they turned them loose and out they come over the dead horse. As quick as they got out from the house we rounded them up and caught them. Pat sent a man to Willcoxes ranch after some grub which was about 6 or 8 miles while we build up a big fire to warm by. While we was warming Billy said Pat have you got any thing out there to eat. Pat said yes. Billy said we have got some in here if you will let us come and get wood to cook it with. Pat says all rite you can all can come out after wood if you want too. Billy says you go to H. . . you cowardly S. . .B and then he hushed. He would crack jokes where we could here them all as if nothing was the mater. we garded there all day and built up a big fire up the branch about 200 yards and all got warm and cooked super and while we was eating just at sundown, we saw a little white rag stuck out the winder on a stick. . . . And in a few minutes Mr. Ruderbay come out with his hands up. He then come on up to us where we was eating supper and told Pat that Billy wanted to surrender under sun up and wanted to know where Pat would carry them. Pat says to Las Vegas. Ruderbay says if we hafto go to Las Vegas, we will die rite here for the Mexacans will mob us there. Pat says we will carry you to Santfee.

Ruderbay says if you will see us safe to Santefee jale we will surrender. This was agree on. So the boys come out and left the arms in the house. When they got to us they all shuck hands with every man and then set down and eat supper. After supper we all mounted our horses. I took Billy the Kid up behind me while the other boys doubled up on ther horses and we started to Willcoxes ranch about 6 miles. Billy made me a present of his Winchester and Frank Stuart took his fine Bay mair.[9]

Garrett sent a wagon back to the stone house to bring in Bowdre's body lest scavenging coyotes should get to it.[10] The posse set out for Fort Sumner, where Garrett had the sad task of informing Manuela Bowdre that her husband was dead. He paid for a burying suit out of his own pocket.

The prisoners were shackled in the blacksmith shop, and by sundown Garrett was on the move again heading for Gayheart's, where they stayed overnight before pushing on to Puerto de Luna. Garrett was trying to get to Las Vegas as fast as he could: "to beet the male hack," as Cal Polk put it, "so the nuse would not get there first."

They arrived at Grzelachowski's at about two o'clock in the afternoon of Christmas Day, 1880.[11] A "capacious" dinner was being served, and the hospitable "Padre Polaco" assured Garrett there was plenty for all. If he held any grudge against the Kid for stealing his horses and cattle, it did not prevent him from seeing that "his plate was kept filled."

The posse reached Las Vegas the next afternoon to find that "the nuse" had reached the town ahead of them. There was a sizable crowd lining the streets to cheer Garrett and his men and get a look at the Kid, and more particularly to shout threats at Dave Rudabaugh, with whom the citizens of the town had a long-outstanding score to settle. The two-mule wagon rumbled through town, turned over the Gallinas bridge and fetched up outside the San Miguel County jail on the north side of the plaza.

Next day the Las Vegas newspapers, the *Optic* and the *Gazette*, vied with each other to tell the whole story of the capture of the desperadoes.[12] "Kid is about 24 years of age," said the *Optic*, "and has a bold and yet pleasant cast of countenance." When interviewed between the bars, the reporter went on, the Kid was in a talkative mood, "but said that anything he might say would not be believed by the people."

> He laughed heartily when informed that the papers of the Territory had built him up a reputation second only to that of Victorio. Kid claims never to have had a large number of men with him, and that the few who were with him when captured were employed on a ranch. This is his statement and is given for what it is worth.

"Dirty Dave," who was renowned for his aversion to washing, didn't appear to have raided any clothing stores lately, the report went on. He expressed anxiety about the strong feelings of the locals against him. Pickett, a former policeman in West Las Vegas, shook hands heartily and seemed anxious to talk. Wilson lay on his cot and did not participate.

The *Gazette's* man, as if sensing he had a chance at immortality, immediately got some quotes out of the Kid. "You appear to take it easy," he said.

"Yea! What's the use of looking on the gloomy side of everything," the Kid replied. "The laugh's on me this time." He looked out of the window, then asked, "Is the jail at Santa Fe any better than this? This is a terrible place to put a fellow in."

When told conditions in the capital were no better, he shrugged and said something about putting up with what he had to.

"There was a big crowd gazing at me, wasn't there?" he exclaimed, smiling. "Well, perhaps some of them will think me half man now; everyone seems to think I was some sort of animal."

Actually, the reporter told his readers, the Kid was "quite a handsome looking fellow." He was about five feet eight or nine, with clear blue eyes, light hair and complexion, slightly built, weighing about 140 lbs. "A frank, open countenance, looking like a schoolboy, with the traditional silky fuzz on his upper lip," the reporter summed up, "the only imperfection being two prominent front teeth slightly protruding like squirrel's teeth."

The Kid told his side of the story one more time for the reporter. Perhaps he was still naïve enough to believe there was someone in New Mexico Territory who would believe it.

> "I wasn't the leader of any gang—I was for Billy all the time. About that Portales business, I owned the Ranche with Charlie Bowdre. I took it up and was holding it because I knew that sometime a stage line would run by there and I wanted to keep it for a station. But, I found there were certain men who wouldn't let me live in the country and so I was going to leave. We had all our grub in the house when they took us in, and we were going to a place six miles away in the morning to cook it

and then 'light' out. I haven't stolen any stock. I made my living by gambling but that was the only way I could live. They wouldn't let me settle down; if they had I wouldn't be here today." and he held up his right arm on which was the bracelet. "Chisum got me into all this trouble and then wouldn't help me out. I went up to Lincoln to stand my trial on the warrant that was out for me, but the territory took a change of venue to Dona Ana, and I knew that I had no show, so I skinned out. When I went up to White Oaks the last time I went there to consult with a lawyer, who had sent for me to come up. But I knew I couldn't stay there, either."

On the morning of the 27th, Garrett, Stewart, and Barney Mason went over to the jail to pick up the prisoners and take them to the train. Garrett had convinced mail contractor Mike Cosgrove, who knew Santa Fe well, to accompany the party. The jailer turned over the Kid and Wilson. When Garrett demanded he bring out Dave Rudabaugh, the jailer refused, saying Rudabaugh had killed a man in Las Vegas and escaped from jail, and they wanted to deal with him themselves. Garrett forcefully pointed out that he had federal charges against Rudabaugh that preempted the territorial ones; with ill grace the prisoner was brought out. Garrett hustled the party over to the train depot.

While they were waiting to leave, a crowd began to gather, many of them armed Hispanics.[13] Garrett and Stewart realized that there was going to be an attempt to take Rudabaugh out and lynch him. He asked Frank Stewart whether he thought they ought to make a fight of it.

"Of course," said Stewart.

"Let's make a good one," Garrett replied.

Like the rest of Garrett's posse, Jim East and Cal Polk had been told their services were no longer required, and had idled over to a saloon.[14]

While we was in there a Mexacan come in drunk and said in spanish to the bartender the Mexacans is agoin to kill them prisners up at the train. I told Jim what he said and we finished up and started to worge the depot and when we got in sight of it I saw there was about 300 Mexacans will all kinds of old rusty goons. . . .

We went to the hotel and got our guns and when we got to the crowd we held our guns drawn by our legs and worked our way thrue the crowd as if we was passengers and when we jumped up on the steps we then turned and threw down on the Mexacans. I lookd and saw Pat Garrett standing in the car door with a 45 in his hand. He said come inside boys and get at a winder. We went in, just at that time Frank Stuart who was at the other door cried out, gentlemen they is agoin to be a fite here and all that wont take a hand in it had better get out. Of corse the drummers and others got their grips and never taken time to tell us goodbye. But they was 2 old long hungry looking men from up about Denver said they had not killed a Mexacan for 2 weeks and was blood thirsty and would go in the fight for pass time. They went down under they seats and draught out some old long buffalo guns and got at a winder. The mob who wanted to linch Billys crowd was increasing all the time and was led by the [deputy] sheriff [Desiderio Romero] who was a Mexacan. Pat Garrett says Boys dont burn powder for nothing. When the first shot is fired, all of you kill a man every shot and we will unchain the prisners and arm them.

We was all at the winders on our kneese with our guns stuck out at it while Pat was at the door and Frank Stuart at the other. I had a bead drawn on a big fat Greezer. They helt us ther in this shape for one our. And all at once a deputy United States Marshal [J. F. Morley] jumped up on the ingin with his 45 in his right hand and he run and grabed the leaver with his left hand and pulled it wide open. The engine spun on track for about 5 minutes and then it run out from among the greezers. So me and Jim went to Santefee with the boys. We got there and landed them in jale and started back the next morning.

When the train reached Santa Fe, Garrett turned his prisoners over to Deputy U.S. Marshal Charles Conklin, who had done some Las Vegas lawing of his own and knew Rudabaugh well. At about 7:30 p.m., the trio were put into a cell already occupied by Edward M. "Choctaw" Kelly, who was awaiting trial for the murder of John Reardon at Carbonateville on October 13.[15] The Kid wasted no time in making plans to get out. On New Year's Day, 1881, he asked for pen and paper and scribbled a note to Governor Wallace, asking to see him "if You can Spare time."[16] As it happened, the governor was on leave in Washington, D.C., so no reply was forthcoming.

On January 3, Rudabaugh went to trial on charges of robbing the U.S. mail and was sentenced to ninety-nine years in jail. This sentence, however, was stayed so that Rudabaugh could be sent to Las Vegas to be tried for the murder of jailer Valdez. Rather than face the music, Rudabaugh decided to see if he couldn't once again dig his way out of trouble, and persuaded the Kid and his fellow prisoners to help. Sheriff Romulo Martinez had paid one of the other inmates to keep an eye on the quartet, however, and on February 28, Martinez and Deputy U.S. Marshal Tony Neis went to the cell, and found an escape tunnel. The prisoners were separated; Billy the Kid was slapped in solitary, shackled to the floor in a cell "where even the light of day is denied admittance and only when some of the jailors or officers enter can he be seen at all."[17]

Shortly after this episode, the Kid sent another note to Wallace.

Dear Sir:
    I wish you would come down to the jail and see me. it will be much to your interest to come and see me. I have some letters which date back two years and there are Parties who are very anxious to get them but I will not dispose of them until I see you. that is if you will come imediatly.
                                                        Yours respect
                                                        Wm. H. Bonney.[18]

He must have felt sure this threat, whatever it was, would bring results; but it did not. Two whole anxious days of waiting later, he tried yet again.

                                                        SANTA FE
                                                        IN JAIL
                                                        March 4, 1881.

Gov Lew Wallace
Dear Sir
    I wrote You a little note the day before yesterday but have received no answer. I Expect you have forgotten what you promised me, this Month two Years ago, but I have not, and I think You had ought to have come and seen me as I requested you to. I have done everything that I promised you I would, and You have done nothing that You promised me.
    I think when You think The matter over, You will come down and See me, and I can then Explain Everything to You.
    Judge Leonard, Passed through here on his way East, in January, and promised to come and See me on his way back, but he did not fulfill his Promise. it looks to me like I am getting left in the Cold. I am not treated right by [U.S.Marshal]

Sherman, he lets Every Stranger that comes to See me through Curiosity in to see me, but will not let a Single one of my friends in, not Even an Attorney.

I guess they mean to Send me up without giving me any Show but they will have a nice time doing it. I am not intirely without friends

I shall Expect to See you Some time today.

Patiently Waiting

I am Very truly Yours, Respt.

Wm. H. Bonney.[19]

The attorney the Kid was talking about was a young fellow named Edgar Caypless, who practiced in Las Vegas and who briefly took an interest in the Kid's plight.[20] He got the Kid to sign over to him the bay mare he had given Frank Stewart, who had in turn given it to the wife of A. Scott Moore, proprietor of the Hot Springs Hotel at Las Vegas. The idea was that Caypless would sue for repossession, and the Kid could pay the attorney out of the proceeds of the sale of the horse. Unfortunately for the Kid, Mrs. Moore expressed her intention of warmly contesting the suit, and Caypless either lost interest or, more likely, could not devote valuable time to it while conducting the defenses of both Dave Rudabaugh and Edward Kelly.

The pages fell off the calendar, and the Kid was told that on March 28 he and Wilson would be taken to La Mesilla for trial at the April term of court. Anger—or fear?—prompted one last attempt to enlist Wallace's help.

SANTA FE NEW MEXICO
March 27, '81.

Gov Lew Wallace
Dear Sir

for the *last time* I ask. Will you keep Your promise. I start below tomorrow. Send Answer by bearer.

Yours respt.
W. Bonney.[21]

There was no answer. While the Kid was writing his desperate notes to Lew Wallace, that worthy was canvassing influential friends, Carl Schurz among them, to lobby the new president, James Garfield, on his behalf as a prospective ambassador. On March 17, Garfield accepted Wallace's resignation as governor, and appointed in his stead his friend and fellow Ohioan, Lionel A. Sheldon. Wallace continued as acting governor while awaiting the appointment he had so long coveted. When the Senate approved him as minister to Turkey, Wallace accepted the post with alacrity, leaving for Crawfordsville on May 30. Before he left New Mexico forever, he did one last thing for Billy the Kid: he signed the warrant authorizing Pat Garrett to hang him.

THE KID'S APOTHEOSIS

IN the year and a half that the Kid had been on the dodge, the world around him had changed. The railroad that now reached all the way down the Rio Grande valley had rendered obsolete a great many things other than the Santa Fe Trail. There was a new feeling in the New Mexico air. The frontier had moved on, to the wild reaches of Arizona's Dragoon Mountains, and boom towns like Tombstone and Globe. The Apaches were tamed. This was a fine, new, growing country: thieves, rustlers, gunfighters, and badmen must no longer be permitted to stand in the way of Progress.

Even the sleepy little hamlet of La Mesilla had grown into a sizable town of two thousand souls, five hundred more than neighboring Las Cruces. On Monday, March 28, the Kid and Billy Wilson were brought across by wagon from the Las Cruces railroad depot and lodged in the La Mesilla jail. It was at the eastern end of the block at whose other end stood the schoolhouse, opposite La Posta and facing the plaza. This simple one-story building on the south side of the square also served as the courthouse of the Third Judicial District. It was

> a room about fourteen feet wide and twice as long, with whitewashed walls and a wooden floor. At the back end of the room is a small platform on which are a table and chair for the judge. On either side of the platform is a small table with two chairs. In one corner of the back wall is a large bookcase with the glass missing from one door. At the other corner is a stove in front of the fireplace. There is no other furniture in the room except sixteen or eighteen wooden benches without backs.[1]

Judge Bristol wasted no time. Case no. 411, *The United States of America vs. Charles Bowdry, Dock Scurlock, Hendry Brown, Henry Antrim alias Kid, John Middleton, Stephen Stevens, John Scroggins, George Coe, and Frederick Wait*, indicted for the murder of A. L. Roberts, was called for Wednesday, March 30.[2] Prosecuting counsel was U.S. District Attorney Sidney M. Barnes; appearing for the defendant, Billy the Kid, was Ira E. Leonard who, in the period since their last meeting, had become a "born again" Christian.

The case was argued over the whole of the following week. On April 5, Leonard withdrew the Kid's plea of not guilty and in its place entered the contention that the United States had no jurisdiction because the killing of Roberts had taken place at Blazer's Mill and not, as alleged, on the Mescalero reservation. It was a technicality, but an effective one. On April 6, Bristol sustained the plea and quashed the case.[3]

Two days later the Kid was back in court, this time to answer for the murder, almost exactly three years earlier, of Sheriff Brady and Deputy George Hindman in cases 531 and 532, *Territory of New Mexico vs. John Middleton, Hendry Brown, and William Bonney, alias Kid, alias William Antrim*. In this, the most emotive of all the charges on which he had been arraigned, the Kid found himself utterly friendless. Ira Leonard, for reasons unknown, did not continue as his counsel, and the court appointed local attorneys Albert Fountain and John Bail, neither of whom had any special understanding of, or sympathy for, the young man they had been assigned to defend.

The jury was composed entirely of Hispanics, their unfamiliar names a confirmation of disinterest, indicating that they had never even indirectly participated in the war and knew nothing about it or the Kid other than what they might have read in a newspaper. Prosecuting the case was Simon B. Newcomb, successor to and close personal friend of the former district attorney of the Third Judicial District, William Rynerson. Appearing against the Kid—as eyewitnesses to the murder of Brady—were Isaac Ellis, Billy Mathews, and Bonnie Baca. No help there: Mathews, Dolan's partner and associate, had been with the sheriff's party that day, and had his own scores to settle with the Kid. Bonnie Baca was another Dolan partisan; Lawrence Murphy had paid his way through college.

The trial took only two days to run its course. On Wednesday, April 13, the jury retired to consider its verdict and in mid-afternoon returned to declare the defendant guilty of murder in the first degree. At a quarter after five, the Kid was brought before Judge Bristol and asked whether he had anything to say before sentence was pronounced. Bonney replied that he had nothing to say.

Bristol intoned the sentence: that the defendant be confined in prison in Lincoln County until, on Friday, May 13, 1881, between 9 a.m. and 3 p.m.,

> he, the said William Bonny, alias Kid, alias William Antrim, be taken from such prison to some suitable and convenient place of execution within said county of Lincoln, by the Sheriff of such county and that then and there, on that day and between the aforesaid hours thereof, by the sheriff of said county of Lincoln, he, the said William Bonney, alias Kid, alias William Antrim, be hanged by the neck until his body be dead.[4]

In the eyes of the law, the Kid had come to the end of the road. There might have been some who thought he ought to have been given more time to prepare a defense, or to summon witnesses who might have helped his attorneys. Some might have argued there was no proof at all that he had been directly responsible for the death of Brady. But there could never really have been any question that he was other than a willing participant in the ambush, and therefore guilty whether he personally fired the fatal shot or not.

It is quite clear just the same that the Kid did not consider the fight over. Two days after he was sentenced to death, he wrote to lawyer Caypless in Santa Fe. "I would have written before this," he apologized, "but could get no paper."

> My United States case was thrown out of court and I was rushed to trial on my Territorial charge. Was convicted of murder in the first degree and am to be hanged on the 13th day of May. Mr. A. J. Fountain was appointed to defend me and has done the best he could for me. He is willing to carry the case further if I can raise the money to bear his expense. The mare is about all I can depend on at present so hope you will settle the case right away and give him the money you get for her. If you do not settle the matter with Scott Moore and have to go to court about it,

either give him [Fountain] the mare or sell her at auction and give him the money. Please do as he wishes in the matter. I know you will do the best you can for me in this. I shall be taken to Lincoln tomorrow. Please write and direct care of Garrett, sheriff. Excuse bad writing. I have my handcuffs on. I remain as ever.

Yours respectfully,
W. H. Bonney[5]

If Caypless ever replied, no record of his reply exists. On the following Saturday night, at about ten o'clock, a heavily armed posse assembled to take the Kid to Lincoln. Deputy Sheriff Dave Woods, who had once arrested Jessie Evans, accompanied by Deputy U.S. Marshal Bob Olinger (fig. 76), had selected five men to accompany the Dougherty wagon: Billy Mathews, John Kinney, D. M. Reade, Tom Williams, and W. A. Lockhart. All were armed to the teeth. No chances were being taken of either an escape or a rescue attempt. If there was any trouble, Bonney would be the first one to be shot.

The Kid was handcuffed and shackled, and chained to the back seat of the ambulance. After a brief stop at the office of the new newspaper *Semi-Weekly* (whose editor reported that the Kid looked quite cheerful), the party set off, with Woods, Reade, Lockhart, and Williams riding guard. Inside the wagon, Kinney sat beside the Kid, Olinger and Mathews opposite. He was truly among friends: if only one of them had made a transcript of their conversation on the 150-mile journey to Lincoln!

And so, on April 21, 1881, they brought the Kid back to Lincoln. Because there was no adequate jail there, they incarcerated him instead in an upstairs room in the old Murphy-Dolan store, recently bought by the county for use as a courthouse.

It was still laid out pretty much as it had been in the days when the House dominated the little world of Lincoln County.[6] A staircase led up to a hallway that ran north-south across the middle of the building. Ahead and to the right was a large storeroom. Ahead and to the left was the room now being used as the sheriff's office. Beyond it, and capable of entry only through the sheriff's office, was a room that had at one time been the private bedroom of Lawrence G. Murphy. It was in this room that the Kid was installed, an irony both might have appreciated.

Across the hall from the sheriff's office and alongside the staircase was the former bedroom of Murphy's housekeeper, Mrs. Lloyd, the one who could outcuss a muleskinner. It was now used as a jail for ordinary prisoners and presently housed some miscreants arrested as a result of a recurrence of the Tularosa Ditch War a little while earlier. As in the Kid's room, there were no bars on the windows or doors. On the other side of the stairs was the big bedroom once shared by Jimmy Dolan and John Riley, now serving as an armory.

Garrett was taking no chances on the Kid. He had special leg shackles made, and the prisoner was kept chained to the hardwood floor at all times. In addition, Bell and Olinger, the deputy U.S. marshals guarding him, had no reason to trust the Kid an inch: Bell had been with the posse at the Greathouse ranch when Jim Carlyle was killed, and Olinger had been around throughout the Lincoln troubles. The deputies drew a chalk line across the center of the room which the Kid was forbidden to cross on pain of death. The two men took turns in maintaining the round-the-clock watch on Billy that Garrett insisted upon. Tradition has it that Bell treated the Kid decently, but that Olinger constantly taunted him about his

FIG. 76. Deputy U.S. marshals Tony Neis (left) and Robert Olinger, March 1, 1881. Photographer Bennett & Brown, Santa Fe. The *New Mexican* remarked Olinger was so big he "had to sit down to keep his head in range of the camera." Note the knife and gunbelt on the floor. Eight weeks after this picture was taken, Olinger was killed by Billy the Kid.

approaching death, and invited him on numerous occasions to make a run for it so that he could have the pleasure of blasting him apart with his favorite Whitneyville shotgun.

On Wednesday, April 27, Garrett left Lincoln on a tax-collecting mission (or, as some others say, to buy lumber for the gallows on which the Kid would be hanged), leaving Olinger and Bell in charge of the prisoners. At noon the following day, Olinger took the prisoners from Mrs. Lloyd's room across to the Wortley Hotel for their midday meal. There exists only one sequential account of what happened, made nearly a decade after the event by Gottfried Gauss, who was the caretaker of the building. "I was crossing the yard behind the courthouse," he said,

> when I heard a shot fired, then a tussle upstairs in the courthouse, somebody hurrying downstairs, and deputy sheriff Bell emerging from the door running toward me. He ran right into my arms, expired the same moment, and I laid him down, dead. That I was in a hurry to secure assistance, or perhaps to save myself, everybody will believe.
>
> When I arrived at the garden gate leading to the street, in front of the courthouse, I saw the other deputy sheriff, Olinger, coming out of the hotel opposite, with the four or five other county prisoners, where they had taken their dinner. I called to him to come quick. He did so, leaving his prisoners in front of the hotel. When he had come close up to me, and while standing not more than a yard apart, I told him that I was just after laying Bell dead on the ground in the yard behind. Before he could reply, he was struck by a well-directed shot fired from a window above us, and fell dead at my feet. I ran for my life to reach my room and safety, when Billy the Kid called to me: "Don't run, I wouldn't hurt you—I am alone, and master not only of the courthouse, but also of the town, for I will allow nobody to come near us." "You go," he said,"and saddle one of Judge [Ira] Leonard's horses, and I will clear out as soon as I can have the shackles loosened from my legs." With a little prospecting pick I had thrown to him through the window he was working for at least an hour, and could not accomplish more than to free one leg. He came to the conclusion to await a better chance, tie one shackle to his waistbelt, and start out. Meanwhile I had saddled a small skittish pony belonging to Billy Burt [the County Clerk], as there was no other horse available, and had also, by Billy's command, tied a pair of red blankets behind the saddle. . . .
>
> When Billy went down stairs at last, on passing the body of Bell he said, "I'm sorry I had to kill him but couldn't help it." On passing the body of Olinger he gave him a tip with his boot, saying "You are not going to round me up again." . . . And so Billy the Kid started out that evening, after he had shaken hands with everybody around and after having had a little difficulty in mounting on account of the shackle on his leg, he went on his way rejoicing.[7]

Gauss's account seems disinterested enough, but it is not at all outside the bounds of possibility that he was aware that someone had furnished the Kid with the gun that Billy used to kill Bell. After all, Gauss had worked for Tunstall; so had the Kid. They had shared the same table, slept on the same floor; the old man had every reason to be sympathetic towards the Kid. His reminiscent account is at best patchy; nor should it be forgotten that his eyesight was at best imperfect. He makes no reference to how Bell was killed, and omits to mention that the Kid used Olinger's own shotgun to kill the deputy, or that Billy Burt's little pony bucked Billy off the first time he tried to mount, ran off, and had to be brought back. The fact that it is midday one moment, evening next, may be explained by the fact that *evening* was a contemporary southwesternism that meant afternoon. By all accounts, the Kid rode out of Lincoln at about 3 p.m.

There have been many, many attempts to reconstruct the events of that April day. Security seems to have been lax; visitors were allowed to come and go freely to see the Kid; Gauss and Sam Corbet were frequent visitors. It was thus, the story goes, that the escape was engineered.[8] Corbet brought the Kid a note telling him there would be a pistol planted in the outhouse in back of the old store; it was put there by Jose Aguayo just before noon on the day of the escape. Whether this story is true or not—and if apocryphal, one would like to have a story half as convincing to replace it—all that is known for sure is that somehow the Kid got a gun and fired twice at the deputy on the staircase. The first shot missed; the second caromed off the right-hand wall and hit Bell beneath the right arm, tearing through his body and emerging beneath the left arm.[9] Gauss rushed out to meet Olinger coming across the street.

"The Kid has killed Bell!" he said.

At the same moment, the Kid who had picked up Olinger's shotgun appeared at the window of the room that had been his prison cell.[10]

"Hello, Bob," he said. "Look up, and see what you get."

"Yes," Olinger said, as he saw him. "And he has killed me, too."

The Kid let him have both barrels. Garrett said Olinger was "hit in the right shoulder, breast and side. He was literally riddled by thirty-six buckshot." Each "buck" pellet weighed about four grams—about a quarter of a pound of lead in all.

Legend has it that the Kid then came out onto the second-story porch of the courthouse, smashed Olinger's gun across the rail and flung the pieces down on the bleeding body, shouting, "And take that to Hell with you!" In fact the spot where Olinger fell is not visible from the porch, a good sixty feet away. Olinger's shotgun is still intact, though it has a repaired stock; it was left in the armory once its purpose had been fulfilled. The Kid armed himself with two pistols and a Winchester, then returned to the porch, where he made his announcement about holding the town and everyone in it.

Although considerably short of definitive, Gottfried Gauss's "eyewitness" account seems to be the only one that exists. Alexander Nunnelly, one of the Tularosa prisoners, added a few descriptive details to fill out the picture; he claimed it was he, not Gauss, who was outside the building when Olinger ran up, and he who recorded the deputy's final, doomed remark; since he was probably on the other side of the street, this seems highly unlikely.[11]

Nunnelly also told how he complained when the Kid took his Winchester. The Kid put it back and selected another; one of the other prisoners objected that the gun was his. Showing what seems in the circumstances to have been almost saintly restraint, the Kid put it back and took a third weapon.

When Gauss saddled Billy Burt's horse, Nunnelly said, the Kid made him help the old man. Since he was a "trusty," Nunnelly objected yet again.

"Don't you think that will have something to do with my trial next month?" he said. "I am up for murder."

"Well," the Kid replied, "you can tell them that I made you do it."

The astonishing fact of the matter is that although apparently everyone in Lincoln saw what happened, not one soul lifted a finger to stop the Kid. Sam Wortley, who was sharing Gauss's room in one of the courthouse outbuildings, actually went in and helped the Kid with his shackles. "It was more than an hour after he killed Olinger and Bell before he left," a bystander testified, continuing

he had at his command eight revolvers and six guns. He stood on the upper porch in front of the building and talked with the people who were in Wortley's, but he would not let anyone come towards him. He told the people that he did not want to kill Bell but, as he ran, he had to. He said he grabbed Bell's revolver and told him to hold up his hands and surrender; that Bell decided to run and he had to kill him. He declared he was "standing pat" against the world; and while he did not wish to kill anybody, if anybody interfered with his attempt to escape, he would kill him.[12]

Garrett concluded that

the inhabitants of the whole town of Lincoln appeared to be terror-stricken. The Kid, it is my firm belief, could have ridden up and down the plaza until dark without a shot having been fired at him, nor an attempt made to arrest him. A little sympathy might have actuated some of them, but most of the people were, doubtless, paralyzed with fear when it was whispered that the dreaded desperado, the Kid, was at liberty and had slain his guards.[13]

Pointing Billy Burt's pony west, Billy the Kid rode out of town. And into legend.

CHAPTER 36

THE MIDNIGHT MAN

BILLY the Kid's escape from Lincoln elevated him almost to legendary status overnight; even the ranks of Tuscany could scarce forbear to cheer, as shown by this item from the *New Mexican*, never a newspaper to praise any supporter of Tunstall and McSween when it could blackguard them.

> The above [account of the escape] is the record of as bold a deed as those versed in the annals of crime can recall. It surpasses anything of which the Kid had been guilty, so far that his past offenses lose much of their heinousness in comparison with it, and it effectually settles the question of whether the Kid is a cowardly cutthroat or a thoroughly reckless and fearless man. Never before has he faced death boldly or run any great risk in the perpetration of his bloody deeds. Bob Olinger used to say that he was a cur, and that every man he had killed had been murdered in cold blood and without the slightest chance of defending himself. The Kid displayed no disposition to correct this until this last act of his when he taught Olinger by bitter experience that his theory was anything but correct.[1]

So the Kid rode out of Lincoln on Billy Burt's pony, stopping at Yginio Salazar's house west of town, where his young friend helped him get the shackles off his feet and rustle up—the exact verb—a good horse. Yginio brought him a prize bay named Don that belonged to Andy Richardson, and the Kid mounted up and moved out.[2]

Displaying the same odd refusal to accept that his luck was running out that he had in Arizona four years earlier, Billy the Kid did not point his pony south to safety. Instead, he returned to his old hangouts around Fort Sumner. Perhaps he wanted to see his *querida*; perhaps it was bravado of the "I'll die before I'll run" variety; probably a little of both of these mixed with more mundane reasons. When J. P. Meadows advised him to hit out for Old Mexico, the Kid replied

> I haven't any money, what would I do in Mexico with no money? I'll have to go back and get a little before I go. Sure as you do, [Meadows] said, Garrett will get you. He said, I have got too many friends up there and I don't believe he will get me, and I can stay there a while and get money enough and then go to Mexico. I said, You'd better go while the going is good, you go back up there and you will get killed or Garrett. He went back to Sumner.[3]

It was a fatal error. Pat Garrett had as good spies there as the Kid had friends to hide and feed him; the long-legged sheriff was perfectly willing to bide his time until he ascertained the Kid's exact whereabouts (fig. 77). To this task he put a number of people, among them Emanuel Brazil and Barney Mason, who was

Garrett's brother-in-law. There were probably others, not the least likely of whom might have been Sabal Gutierrez, who was married to the Kid's *querida*, Celsa.

At this point the accounts diverge. On the one hand there is Garrett's, sparing with detail and careful not to divulge the name of his informants. On another there is that of a newcomer to Lincoln County, John W. Poe, a thirty-year-old Kentuckian who had served as a deputy U.S. marshal and deputy sheriff in the Texas Panhandle; he had replaced Frank Stewart as the New Mexican representative of the same Canadian River cattlemen's association that had sent the posse after the Kid the preceding December (fig. 78).

Poe was living at White Oaks.[4] There he was approached by a man he had known in Texas who told him he had been sleeping in a room at the Dedrick & West livery stable, and had overheard a conversation between the two men which convinced him that the Kid was still in the Fort Sumner area and had actually visited White Oaks twice in the past couple of weeks. Poe rode across to Lincoln to inform Garrett, whom he found "much more skeptical of the truth of the story than I was."

FIG. 77. Patrick Floyd Jarvis Garrett, aged thirty-one. Taken in 1881, about the time he killed the Kid. Photo by Furlong, Las Vegas, N.M.

One good authority suggests that Poe's White Oaks informant was invented to cover up the fact that Peter Maxwell, vastly perturbed at the attention Billy was paying to his teenaged daughter Paulita, sent one of his *vaqueros* down to the Oaks to tell Poe the Kid was in Fort Sumner. Even so, Garrett thought the whole thing hard to believe (he knew as well as, if not better than, anybody that the Kid's sweetheart was a married woman, Celsa Gutierrez), but at Poe's insistence he agreed to check it out.[5]

Poe first wrote his account of events in 1919, and while it does not entirely tally with Garrett's more immediate recollections, both agree on the salient points: that they went down to Roswell to pick up Garrett's deputy, Thomas C. "Kip" McKinney, and set off for Sumner.[6] Garrett's book gives the date of their departure as July 10; his report to the governor, written on July 15, gives it as July 11.[7] He had written to his spy, Emanuel Brazil, asking him to meet them in Arroyo Taiban on the night of the 13th, and gives that as the date of their arrival there. Poe says the following evening; old folks forget, sometimes on purpose.[8]

"It was agreed that as I was not known in Fort Sumner, while the other two were, Garrett having a year or two previously resided there, I should ride into the

FIG. 78. John William Poe. Taken in 1881, at the same time as the Garrett picture. He was thirty-one at this time. Photo by Furlong, Las Vegas, N.M.

place with the object of reconnoitering the ground and gathering such information as was possible," Poe recalled. Garrett and McKinney would remain in Arroyo Taiban, a few miles from town; they would all rendezvous at a preselected spot that night.

Poe rode into town at about ten o'clock, and noticed right away that the atmosphere was very tense. He managed to convince the locals that his cover story was genuine, had a couple of drinks, ate a meal, and loitered around for about three hours in the hope of hearing something about the Kid's whereabouts. When it became apparent nobody was going to tell him anything, he followed Garrett's suggestion and rode over to Milnor Rudolph's ranch at Sunnyside, seven miles north of the fort. Poe did his best to pump Rudolph, but it was apparent that Garrett's friend was too frightened of reprisals from the Kid to say anything about his whereabouts. Accordingly Poe hit out for Punta de la Glorieta for the rendezvous with Garrett. "Garrett seemed to have but little confidence in our being able to accomplish the object of our trip," said Poe, "but said he knew the location of a certain house occupied by a woman in Fort Sumner which the Kid had formerly frequented, and that if he was in or about Fort Sumner, he would most likely be found entering or leaving this house some time during the night."[9]

Garrett differs.[10] "I concluded to go and have a talk with Peter Maxwell, Esq., in whom I felt sure I could rely," he avers. He led the way into town; on the way, they came upon the camp of a man named Jacobs whom Poe knew slightly. Oddly, Poe's account makes no mention of meeting the Texan. They unsaddled their horses, accepted Jacobs's offer of coffee, and then covered the rest of the way into town on foot, concealing themselves at about nine o'clock in the peach orchard on the south side of town. The discrepancy in the two accounts requires particular attention. According to Poe they hid in the shadowy orchard because the moon was shining very brightly.[11] "We kept a fruitless watch here until some time after eleven o'clock, when Garrett stated that he believed we were on a cold trail; that he had very little faith in our being able to accomplish anything when we started on the trip. He proposed that we leave the town without letting anyone know that we had been there in search for the Kid."

Here we have at best a faint-hearted Garrett, possibly even a frightened one. Yet in his own account, he has them cautiously approaching the row of adobes, formerly the quartermaster's storerooms but now mainly occupied by Hispanic families, and skirting around a group of men, one of whom got up and went indoors. This, he learned later, was the Kid, who "went into the house of a Mexican friend, pulled off his hat and boots, threw himself on a bed, and commenced reading a newspaper."

Many accounts have it that the "friend" was Celsa Gutierrez, formerly Martinez, sister of Garrett's first wife. But Celsa was a married woman; she and her husband lived in two rooms in the old quartermaster store. Even if, as tradition has it, he turned a blind eye to his wife's infidelity, it is difficult to believe that Sabal Gutierrez would have permitted her lover to share his home. A more believable scenario would be that the Kid was hiding outside of town with some of Peter Maxwell's sheepherders.[12] He had been on the dodge now for seventy-eight days; hearing that there was to be a *baile* at the Garcia house that Thursday night, he rode in for some fun. During the evening, he took his *querida* out into the cool moonlight and they made love in the peach orchard; theirs were the voices Garrett and his men heard, the Kid the figure they saw rise from the ground, vault the fence, and disappear. Celsa returned home alone; the Kid went to the house of a friend, possibly Bob Campbell.

Meanwhile, Garrett was getting ready to give up and ride out. Poe proposed that before they left, it might be worth going to see Maxwell. The Maxwells lived in the former officers' quarters, a very long two-story, twelve-unit adobe standing end to and flush with the street, having a porch on the south side looking out over the flower garden that stood between the house and the old dance hall (fig. 79). At its southeastern corner was Pete Maxwell's bedroom, one door and window facing south, another east looking out over the old parade ground, with a fireplace on the west wall. The house was encircled by a paling or picket fence, one side of which ran parallel to the street up to and across the porch to the corner of the building. Maxwell's room was simply furnished—a bed, a chest of drawers, a night table—and the door wide open to let in any breath of coolness the night might bring.

"This is Maxwell's room in this corner," Garrett said to Poe and McKinney. "You fellows wait here while I go in and talk to him."

Across the corner of the parade ground, the Kid decided he was hungry, got a butcher knife from the Gutierrez home, and set out to get a steak from Maxwell's meat house, making no attempt to conceal himself. Up to this moment, neither Poe nor McKinney had ever laid eyes on either Pete Maxwell or Billy the Kid, so when Poe saw the Kid approaching in his stocking feet, bareheaded and apparently fastening up his pants, he assumed

> the man approaching was either Maxwell or some guest of his who might have been staying there. He came on until he was almost within arm's length of where I sat, before he saw me, as I was partially concealed from his view by the post of the gate.
>
> Upon his seeing me, he covered me with his six-shooter as quick as lightning, sprang onto the porch, calling out in Spanish, 'Quien es?' (Who is it?)—at the same time backing away from me toward the door through which Garrett only a few seconds before had passed, repeating his query, 'Who is it?' in Spanish several times.[13]

What happened next happened very fast; Poe estimated it at no more than thirty seconds.[14] He stood up and went toward the man, telling him not to be

FIG. 79. Pedro Maxwell's home at Fort Sumner, ca. 1882. Photographer unknown. Billy the Kid was killed in the room on the left-hand front corner. The house was bought by a group of Colorado businessmen in 1884; the drought and depression of 1894 caused the failure of their venture, and they abandoned it, razing the house for lumber.

alarmed, that he would not be hurt, still without the slightest idea who he was talking to. The Kid backed into the doorway, using the thick adobe wall to shield his body, repeating his question for the fourth or fifth time, then called out to Maxwell, "¿Pedro, quien sonos estos hombres afuera?"

"That's him!" Maxwell whispered urgently to Garrett as the Kid came over to the bed. In the darkness, the Kid could see someone sitting beside Maxwell.

"Who is it, Pete?" The Kid stood framed against the moonlit door. "Who's there?"

Garrett drew his gun and fired, throwing himself to the floor as he loosed off his second shot.[15] The first was fatal; the second caromed off the adobe wall and hit a wooden bedstead with a crack loud enough to make Poe, outside, think at first that Garrett had fired three times. He heard "a groan and one or two gasps," then Garrett slid out of the room, placing his back to the wall beside the door. Right behind him, bedclothes clinging to him, came the terrified Pete Maxwell. Poe was so jittery he very nearly shot him, but Garrett knocked his gun down.

"That was the Kid that came in there onto me, and I think I have got him," he said.

"Pat, the Kid would not come to this place; you have shot the wrong man," Poe told him, fueling Garrett's own doubts.

"I'm sure it was him," Garrett insisted, "for I know his voice too well to be mistaken."

Nobody spoke the question they all wanted answered: Was the Kid really dead, or was he lying doggo in there, waiting for someone to poke his head in so he could shoot it off?

A crowd had gathered, and it was less than friendly. Pete Maxwell fetched a tallow candle from his mother's room at the far end of the building and put it on the window sill of his bedroom. The Kid was lying on his back in the middle of the room; Garrett's shot had struck him just above the heart and killed him almost instantaneously. He never even knew who killed him.

So the story ended, and so the legend began.

There have been countless versions of these events since that warm summer night in Fort Sumner. The most endearing of them has it that Garrett found the Kid in bed with Paulita Maxwell and shot him *in flagrante delictu;* the authorized version given above was then cooked up to protect the girl's reputation. Whether the Kid actually departed this vale of tears in such enviable circumstances or not, he achieved in dying a distinction shared by no other western outlaw. On August 18, 1881, this obituary appeared in the London *Times.*[16] Owing nothing to hindsight or recollection, it is unquestionably the first, most immediate, and most convincing account of the Kid's death.

AN AMERICAN DESPERADO

"H.C." writes:—"as many of your readers might like to know the end of one of the principal of those desperadoes mentioned in your Correspondent's letter from the United States, I send you the enclosed. You will see his career has been but a short one."

Extract from the Santa Fe *New Mexican:*—

"William Bonny, *alias* 'the Kid,' is dead. No report could have caused a more general feeling of gratification than this, and when it was further announced that the faithful and brave Pat Garrett, he who has been the mainstay of law and order in Lincoln county, the chief reliance of the people in the dark days, when danger lurked on every hand, has accomplished the crowning feat of his life by bringing down the fierce and implacable foe single-handed, the sense of satisfaction was heightened to one of delight. The following is Sheriff Garrett's official report to the chief executive of the territory. It is concise and simple, in keeping with the character of the writer, and will be found of interest, from the fact that it is the account which is absolutely correct, and because of the characteristics it betrays.

It is as follows:—'Fort Sumner, N.M., July 15.—To his Excellency the Governor of New Mexico.—I have the honour to inform your Excellency that I had received several communications from persons in and about Fort Sumner that William Bonny, *alias* "the Kid," had been there, or in that vicinity for some time. In view of these reports I deemed it my duty to go there and ascertain if there was any truth in them or not, all the time doubting their accuracy; but on Monday, July 11, I left home, taking with me John W. Poe and T. L. McKinney, men in whose courage and sagacity I relied implicitly, and arrived just below Fort Sumner on Wednesday, the 13th. I remained concealed near the houses until night, and then entered the fort about midnight, and went to Mr. P. Maxwell's room. I found him in bed and had just commenced to talk to him about the object of my visit at such an unusual hour, when a man entered the room in stockinged feet, with a pistol in one hand and a knife in the other. He came and placed his hand on the bed just beside me, and in a low whisper, "Who is it?" (and repeated the question) he asked of Mr. Maxwell. I at once recognized the man, and knew he was "the Kid," and reached behind me for my pistol, feeling almost certain of receiving a ball from his at the moment of doing so, as I felt sure he had now recognized me, but fortunately he drew back from the bed at noticing my movement, and although he had his pistol pointed at my breast, he delayed to fire, and asked in Spanish, "Quien es? Quien es?" This gave me time to bring mine to bear on him, and the moment I did so I pulled the trigger and he received his death wound, for the ball struck him in the left breast and pierced his heart. He never spoke, but died in a minute. It was my desire to have been able to take him alive, but his coming upon me so suddenly and unexpectedly leads me to believe that he had seen me enter the room, or had been informed by someone of the fact, and that he came there armed with pistol and knife expressly to kill me if he could. Under that impression I had no alternative but to kill him or to suffer death at his hands. I herewith annex a copy of the verdict rendered by the jury called in by the justice of the peace (*ex officio* coroner), the original of which is in the hands of the prosecuting attorney of the first judicial district.'

The verdict is given in Spanish in Garrett's report, and upon being translated is as follows:—'We, the jury, unanimously say that William Bonny came to his death from a wound in the breast, in the region of the heart, fired from a pistol in the hand of Pat A. Garrett [*sic*]; and our decision is that the action of the said Garrett was justifiable homicide, and we are united in opinion that the gratitude of all the community is due to said Garrett for his action, and that he deserves to be compensated.
—M. Rudolph, foreman, Antonio Saavedra, Pedro Antonio Lucero, Jose Silva, Sabal Gutierrez, Lorenzo Jaramillo.'

All possible honours are being paid to Sheriff Garrett, his slayer, for his brave pursuit of the outlaw. How rightly the people place their trust is shown by the foregoing accounts. Garrett has never ceased to dog the footsteps of the 'Kid.' He said soon after the escape of the criminal that he would 'follow him to the end,' and he has done so with persistency, determination, and bravery through long and anxious months, finally to meet with a success which entitles him to the gratitude and respect of the people of the territory. When trying to surprise his prey he was himself surprised by him. Confronted in a small room by a thoroughly desperate man, with a knife in one hand, while another held a revolver to his breast, Garrett never lost his presence of mind or coolness, but seized the first opportunity offering itself to make use of his skill with his pistol. A second later would have been too late, and a second sooner to attack would have been too soon. He bided his time, and accomplished his end, and he deserves to be richly rewarded. 'Billy the Kid's' funeral took place at Fort Sumner the day after the shooting, and not one of those who were present but rejoiced at his death."

De mortuis nil nisi malum.

CHAPTER 37

FINALE

WITH the death of Billy the Kid it was as if every one of the men who had participated in the years of bloodshed took a vow of silence. Thus, nowhere in the literature of the Lincoln troubles is there any article, any memoir, any reminiscence of the times written between 1882 and the middle 1920s by someone who was actually there. Death, of course, silenced some of them: Chisum, Patrón, Rynerson, and Axtell were gone by the turn of the century. Others—and they included articulate and educated men like Doc Scurlock, who could have enlightened us on much that remains a mystery—categorically refused to discuss the subject. Neither John H. Riley nor Jimmy Dolan left so much as a scrap of paper setting out what they undoubtedly knew. Even George Peppin insisted on letting sleeping dogs lie.

It was not until the arrival of Walter Noble Burns on the scene, like some latter-day Doctor Frankenstein, that the story had life breathed back into it. By that time, nearly every one of those who had supported the House was dead, and Susan McSween was able at last to fit her husband into the martyr's pantheon she had always intended for him.

Jimmy Dolan, whose arrogant pride and combative nature did so much to ignite the conflagration, was ruined by the war, and the rest of his life was speckled with misfortune. In 1882, his first child, named Emil, died at the age of two.[1] Four years later, a few days after giving birth to a daughter, Bessie, Caroline Fritz Dolan died at the age of twenty-five. On February 20, 1888, Dolan married Eva Maria Whitlock, thirty, who had been the children's nurse. It was to prove an unhappy match; a letter from Susan Barber to Fulton of May 27, 1927, indicates it was generally known he mistreated his wife. His tribulations were still not over; a year after Dolan's marriage, his daughter Louise, not yet six, passed away.

Dolan had better luck as a businessman and was well liked. He appropriated Tunstall's land on the Feliz and built a sturdy house not far from the Englishman's original *choza*; it is still there. He also became the owner of the Tunstall store, and re-established himself in the mercantile business there before selling out to Rosenthal & Co. In 1882, he joined William Rynerson in a cattle-raising operation on the Feliz range that later became the Feliz Land & Cattle Company, forerunner of today's Flying H ranch. He served as county treasurer for two terms, 1884 and 1886, and was a member of the territorial senate in 1888. The following year he was appointed receiver of the Land Office. Bad luck still dogged him as he signed the bond of his friend Frank Lesnett, his successor as receiver and later a member of the Roswell board of trustees. In February 1893 Lesnett disappeared,

FIG. 80. James J. Dolan and his wife, Maria Whitlock Dolan. Taken in 1897, a year before his death, at which time he was nearly fifty. Photo by Swartz, Fort Worth, Tex.

leaving his accounts ten thousand dollars short; Dolan had to make good the deficit. In the end, to quote Lily Klasner's hating epitaph, "Dolan drank himself to death."[2] The family persuaded saloonkeepers not to serve him, but he managed to get liquor off others (fig. 80). On February 26, 1898, he collapsed and died at the ranch on the Feliz; there was not even time to call a priest. The cause of death entered in the family bible was "hemorage of stomach." Frank Coe's diagnosis was more brutal—delirium tremens.

Frank Coe himself went on to live a long, rich, and full life, as did his cousin George; both became substantial citizens. Billy Mathews put the past behind him and went on to become a highly respected stockman. John Copeland lived to see the new century, and so did George Peppin, Saturnino Baca, John Kinney, John Riley, Nathan Dudley, Daniel Appel, Taylor Ealy, and Tom Catron. Mathews and Peppin both died in 1904.

Martin Chaves lived until 1931. Yginio Salazar lasted until 1936; George Coe till 1941. Another man who might have told us much but never did, Francisco Gomez, lived until 1946.

Because their part in and contribution to events was so influential, two survivors, Robert Widenmann and Susan McSween, deserve special notice. Robert Widenmann spent the rest of his life haunted by his experiences. The nature and degree of his participation in the shooting war remains obscure. What exactly was his relationship with Tunstall? Was he one of those who killed Brady? Did he try to have Kinney killed? Why did he never go back to New Mexico? We shall never know the answers: if he ever wrote down the truth about his actions, it was destroyed along with all his other papers at the time of his death.

After he said goodbye to her at Las Vegas on October 9, 1878, Robert Widenmann headed east. He may have briefly visited his home at Whitmore Lake; perhaps he went, as he said he would, to see Schurz in Washington. By an extraordinary coincidence, on the very day Widenmann left Las Vegas, J. P. Tunstall had commenced proceedings through the Foreign Office (Britain's equivalent to the State Department) with a view to obtaining an indemnity from the U.S. government.[3] He supported his case with a portfolio of documentation that included excerpts from territorial newspapers and the letters of McSween, Widenmann, Corbet, Gauss, and Susan McSween. These were transmitted to the British ambassador in Washington, Sir Edward Thornton, who in turn placed them before U.S. Attorney General Charles Devens.

On January 10, 1879, J. P. Tunstall indicated to the Marquis of Salisbury in London that Robert Widenmann had arrived from the United States, and offered his personal testimony if it would assist the Foreign Office in pursuing the claim. The records indicate that Widenmann was never called upon.

The story of the Tunstall family's long, sad, and ultimately fruitless attempt to obtain redress from the U.S. government has been told elsewhere; but Widenmann's relationship with them has never been fully explored.[4] As a result, the misconception that he outstayed his welcome in London and was eventually kicked out by the Tunstalls has become accepted as fact. Not so: it is clear from subsequent correspondence between him and the Tunstall family that Widenmann's stay in London was congenial. During his six-month visit, it appears that he made a considerable effort to ingratiate himself with the Tunstalls, perhaps believing in some strange manner that he could take "Dear Harry's" place in the family.

He assisted Mr. Tunstall's understanding of the personalities who had been involved in his son's murder, and explained the nuances in the massive amount of evidence adduced by Frank Angel. He wrote to Probate Judge Florencio Gonzales providing details of debts outstanding against the estate in Lincoln.[5] He drafted a final balance of the Tunstall-McSween account which showed conclusively that McSween's widow had no valid claim against it (although for some strange reason he never presented it to the probate court). He no doubt also assisted the Tunstalls' friend George Parker, who drafted all the letters to the Foreign Office. "Mr. Tunstall lost all hope of compensation through the U.S. Government," Parker recalled in 1925. "He told Wiederman that he could have all he recovered (if anything was left . . . of the property left by John when he was killed) . . . Personally I did not have much confidence in Wiederman exerting himself to recover anything for Mr. Tunstall, but I felt sure he would get some substantial benefit for himself."[6]

From this broad hint and from much other evidence it seems safe to conclude that Widenmann labored under a familiar delusion: that unless he actually strikes you in the face, a man does not actively dislike you.

Such correspondence as has survived indicates that Widenmann left London fired with the determination to go back to Lincoln County; he announced his intention of conferring with Frank Angel as soon as he got to New York. He arrived there from London on Saturday, June 28, and two days later wrote to J. P. Tunstall from the Gilsey House, at Broadway and Twenty-ninth Street, announcing that he was "off to see Mr. Angel in a few minutes and cannot decide on my future movements until I have had a good long talk with him . . . As soon as I have seen Angel and come to some definite conclusion I will write to you again."[7] They did not hear from him for over six months.

The diligent research of his grandson indicates that his discussions with Angel were not encouraging, and he abandoned any plans he might have had to go to New Mexico.[8] The *Michigan Argus* of August 15 noted that he and his sister Pauline were in Ann Arbor, visiting their parents. A little before Christmas, the Tunstalls wrote in puzzled vein to Widenmann's father asking where "Rob" had disappeared to, and enclosing some photographs taken in London.[9]

Widenmann's guilty reply, dated January 13, 1880, once more illustrates his crass exploitation of the relationship. "Dear Mama and Papa," he began,

> Now just you give it to me hot and heavy. I'll take it all, bear it and grin, for I know I deserve it . . . Goodness knows downheartedness has had much to do with my silence, for one never likes to say that so far one has not been successful. But such is the case. . . .
>
> As I wrote you in my last letter, so long, long ago (shame) I saw Mr. Angel and, after a long conference with him, went to Washington and tried to get at those papers. But you catch a yankee giving himself away! Angel also tried his best to aid me but could not do anything, he informed me that the government felt certain England would make a claim on it and wished to keep all the papers in its own hands as far as possible . . . so that was a wild goose chase. I then returned to New York and tried my best to get some capital to go out west again with but was neither then nor since successful . . . I then came home and have been helping father since. . . .
>
> I am hale and hearty as ever though not quite as stout as when I left merry old England. But who could help getting fat and sassy, as they say here, when one is taken as good care of as I was while with you and, what is more, as kindly and lovingly treated as I was. In fact I felt and was as much at home with you as I am in my own home; you can see this from the way in which I have headed my letter. You won't be angry with me, dear Ma and Pa, will you! I can't thank you enough for your kindness and love and only pray the latter may always be retained for me.[10]

With this letter was another to Lillian and Mabel, addressed "My dear, dear little Pets" (using their brother's favorite nickname for them), whose saccharine content surpasses even the one just quoted. "I do wonder how my little wife [Mabel] and my old fatty [Lillian] are getting along without me," he wrote. "Do you still have your romps and blindmans buff with dear old Pa and does Fräulein [the nurse] still scream so? You must write and tell me all you are doing."[11]

J. P. Tunstall wrote to Widenmann on July 19 at Whitmore Lake, sending the news from Lincoln. He had sent Sam Corbet as a gift the deed for the old Mathews-Freeman ranch, but

> Matthews . . . has jumped the Ranch on the Rio Penasco which Corbett had taken up for John, and he is afraid Matthews will cheat him out of it, as he has possession of it—he first entered it under the Home Stead Act and before proving upon it, sold and Quit Claimed Deeded it to McSween or John, he does not remember which and the Quit Claim Deed has been lost, and now Matthews goes to the Land Office and swears it is not Desert Land, from the fact it was farmed before Corbett filed upon it, so Corbett does not know how it will come out.[12]

There had been several letters from Jack Middleton, he went on, "all on the begging strain." Jack had married a fifteen-year-old girl; he had sent them twenty-five dollars as a wedding present. "They say Dolan has come out clear of the murder, it being taken to a court afar off, and they also say he is now very rich, having shares in some very prosperous Mines, and that he is going to marry one of the girls belonging to the Fritz Estate."

It was some time before Widenmann received this letter. Driven by the impulsive restlessness that seems to have plagued him throughout his life, he had left Ann Arbor again. By August, he was back in New York; he wrote to the Tunstalls from Room 8, 132 Front Street. "Many a change has taken place in my life," he wrote.

> I could not get the capital necessary to go West again and at last decided to come here and accept the offer of going into the Coffee and Sugar brokerage business with [he neglected to add the name of the firm]. So here I am tugging away but I can assure you ones path is not exactly strewn with roses. . . .
>
> From New Mexico I have but few news, but they are such that they make every drop of blood in my veins boil every time I think of them. Dolan and his band have taken possession of the Felice and all the other ranches, have now everything in their hands. Oh! for just enough money to get out there and wipe them out! I could do it in three months as clean as a whistle. Now I haven't the necessary cash but I may be able to get it, and then![13]

J. P. Tunstall refrained from either replying or taking the proffered bait; he knew Widenmann would have received the letter sent to Ann Arbor a few days after writing his own. So it was not until December 15 that he reported that although the family had heard nothing yet from the American government about the indemnification claim, they did not "despair of a satisfactory result."[14]

Widenmann replied on February 15, 1881. He was now working for a firm called the Barren Island Manufacturing Company at 36 Broadway, New York; a little while earlier he had met an old friend, "a schoolmate, a young lady whom I have known ever so long, she was once my little lady love years ago, and to be short about it, that settled the matter. In other words, I am engaged to be married (married) just as soon as possible."[15]

There had been a crash in the coffee business; he now had a position with a "manufacturing and exporting establishment," and was "straining every nerve" to get together enough money to buy his father's old business in Ann Arbor. His father, of course, had no business for him to buy; this was his first, but not last, unsubtle proposal that Papa Tunstall finance his endeavors. As for New Mexico,

> not going back there was a great mistake. Large and valuable silver mines have been discovered near Lincoln, business there is excellent and property has increased in value enormously. The ranch alone would have covered all former losses. I am informed that Mrs. McSween now Mrs. Barber, is gradually converting the whole estate to her own private property, and all the others will loose every cent. Those in Lincoln, whom she must fear most, she is buying off and pockets a large balance. From the papers I send you you will have seen that Bonnie has taken a bad end and I should not be surprised that a rope has put on the finishing touch. Dolan is said to be wealthy; he has a half interest in one of the newly discovered mines and has it is said been offered $200,000 for it. The knaves always have the best luck.

In this letter Widenmann referred to the indemnity claim the Tunstalls were pursuing as "our matter." Although they had told him that he could keep whatever he could salvage from the estate, there had never been any suggestion that

Widenmann was to be offered a share of any settlement the family might receive. Whether it was this that cooled the family on "Rob" is not possible to confirm, but the correspondence from their end seems to have ceased from this point.

On November 15, 1881, still at the same address, Widenmann wrote to tell the Tunstalls he was getting married.[16] His prospects had improved, he said, and the date was set: Wednesday, November 23. Elephantinely hinting that he would like them to buy a piano as a wedding present, he said he was puzzled not to have heard from them, but hoped he had their best wishes. No copy of a reply exists. It is possible that J. P. Tunstall's health had by this time failed; with his death seven months later, all correspondence between the family and John Tunstall's former friends and associates ceased.

On November 23, Widenmann married Albertine "Tini" Seiler-Lemke, and they set up house in Brooklyn.[17] August Robert, their first child, was born on January 5, 1883, but lived only one day. The second child, Albertine, was born October 9, 1884, just a few months after the lingering death of Widenmann's father. Concerned about his daughter's health, Widenmann moved his family to a rented house at Nanuet, a village about fifteen miles west of Nyack, N.Y.; sadly, the child died anyway on September 10, 1885.

There were to be two more children born at Nanuet: Elsie, on November 20, 1885, and Adolph Robert on April 18, 1890. There is no precise information on what Widenmann was doing for a living during these years, but since in April 1884 he turns up at a business meeting in Louisville, Ky., representing the New York import-export firm Wm. Foerster & Co., it seems likely he had been with them for some time. Soon after this he became a salesman with a New York piano manufacturer, Alfred Dolge & Son, where he was known as "Bronco Bob" Widenmann.

Widenmann now turned to politics. On January 25, 1892, he was elected chairman of a convention held in New City to choose town officers. He was apparently already widely known for his opposition to the Tammany "machine" run by party bosses Hill, Sheehan, and Murphy. The following month, he published—were memories of former crusades haunting him?—an open letter challenging the "ring" that sought to dominate local politics. He proceeded then to do likewise in person.

In September 1893 he was chosen as one of three delegates to represent Rockland County at the forthcoming state Democratic convention (fig. 81). At that Saratoga convention, on October 6, Judge Isaac Maynard was nominated to continue as judge of the court of appeals. Hardly had the nomination been seconded when Widenmann strode to the platform and launched into a tirade accusing Maynard and Governor Hill of corruption.

Widenmann became something of a hero, and when lawyers of the New York Bar Association met at the end of the month to form a committee (which included Carl Schurz) to bring about the defeat of Maynard in the election, Widenmann was chosen to preside as chairman. His small political star rose over the ensuing years, and in 1895 he was nominated as representative to Congress.

His campaign was a disaster. Adding three years to his age in order to claim service in the Civil War, he decorated himself with the phony title of major and made appearances with a sword strapped to his waist. Out of the 7,611 votes cast in Rockland County, Widenmann polled 165. The party dropped him like a stone; his political career was over before it had properly begun.

At the same time his personal fortunes began to wane. After his wife's death in 1905, he worked only sporadically, if at all, having decided the time had come for his children to support him. A story that he worked for the U.S. Bureau of Fisheries has been discredited, although he may have been employed briefly by the Haverstraw Light & Fuel Gas Co. In 1920, at the age of sixty-eight, he threw himself into yet another of his quixotic crusades, this time an attempt to have the recently proclaimed Eighteenth Amendment repealed. His arguments were dismissed by Chief Justice Smyth. Widenmann appealed, first in the District of Columbia and again (twice) in the Supreme Court. Each time his case was thrown out.

FIG. 81. Robert A. Widenmann, aged forty-one, New York, May 4, 1893. Photographer unknown.

The cost of tilting at these unyielding windmills rendered the family's financial situation critical. Widenmann's response to this was to send his daughter to work and turn the management of the Nanuet farm over to his son. Widenmann and his daughter moved to a wooden bungalow on Willow Road in Haverstraw, now part of Stony Point, N.Y. Elsie stayed with her father and supported him for the rest of his life.

His children remembered him as an ogre and a tyrant. Punishment was administered with a heavy leather belt; the back of a knife blade assured correct table manners. He insisted on German being spoken at home, so Robert and Elsie had to learn English from their playmates and neighbors. To teach his son to swim, Widenmann threw him fully clothed from a bridge into a creek. He taught both children the "quick draw," using a Colt .45 and the silhouette of a man as a target. At Nanuet he kept the window shades drawn at all times, and always carried a gun: no one ever knew why.

Having alienated his son, Widenmann ruined his daughter's life, dominating her so completely that she never married and spent over fifty years after his death living alone. She despised him to her dying day. Immature, impulsive, a bully and a liar to the end, Robert Widenmann died at Haverstraw on April 13, 1930, unloved, unsung, and unremembered.

Unlike Widenmann, Susan McSween stayed put. In the end, she outmaneuvered, outlasted, or outlived all her enemies and fought her way to the position in life she had always wanted. She was brave and she was proud, and right to the very end she never once by so much as the flicker of an eyelid admitted to any of the many accusations leveled against her during her lifetime. Useless to regret that she was never asked the right questions: she probably wouldn't have answered them, anyway.

Whatever doubts there may be about her honesty or her virtue, no one could ever say Susan McSween lacked the courage to speak her mind. The extent of her contribution to the events of the Lincoln County War has never been properly assessed; there is no doubt whatsoever that it was considerably greater than any book yet written has shown. She was the driving force behind McSween, her aspirations firing his ambition first in Kansas and later in Lincoln. She wanted wealth, position, fine clothes, a grand house, and she was not too fussy how she got them. Behind that spirited, defiant, vain, ambitious front she put up it is still possible to discern the headstrong teenage Susanna Hummer, who ran away from home—to what, to where?—and who had never had anything till "Mac" came along.

In typical fashion, Susan McSween concerned herself not at all with the welfare of her one-time protectors after the fighting was over. She had never had much time for the likes of Billy the Kid or those other "foolhardy boys" who had gotten her husband killed. When her ill-advised feud with Dudley ended with his acquittal and departure, she devoted herself instead, with the far from disinterested assistance of Ira Leonard, to the profitable settlement of the estates of Dick Brewer, John Tunstall, and, of course, Alexander McSween.

Her handling of the three estates seems to have met with the approval of the courts, but, as Gottfried Gauss feelingly remarked in a November 22, 1879, letter to J. P. Tunstall, "If it is true what everybody says, the administratrix Mrs. McSween is not going to pay any creditor except herself."[18]

He was not alone in feeling as he did. Both Isaac Ellis and Juan Patrón advised the Tunstall family that Susan was mishandling their son's estate. More interestingly, they later withdrew these allegations completely, lending force to Widenmann's statement that those whom the widow could not get along with, she bought off. Whatever the truth may have been, she ended up with enough money to set herself up as a rancher with a new life partner. His name was George B. Barber, and on the face of it, their marriage was as curious a mismatch as could be imagined.[19]

George Barber had arrived in Lincoln only a few days before the murder of John Tunstall, and in fact sat on the coroner's jury at the Englishman's inquest. He was then thirty-six years of age, with blue eyes and black hair. At 150 lbs. and only 5 ft. 5 in. tall, he must have looked almost diminutive alongside the rangy Susan McSween. More surprising, however, is the fact that he was a chronic invalid (fig. 82).

Born in Milwaukee on May 28, 1846, George Barber was still a schoolboy, albeit having 'sailed before the mast one season on the lakes' when, at age eighteen, he joined the U.S. Navy as a seaman. He saw service on four ships during the Civil War: the gunboats *Clara Dolson* and *Fairy*, the monitor *Oneota*, and the hospital ship *Red Rover*. After the war, he lived for five years at his parents' home in Eagle, Wis., then at Sioux Falls, Dakota Territory, for four more. In 1877, he moved to New Mexico, settling briefly in Colfax County before coming to Lincoln. Along the way he qualified as a surveyor; later, he "read" law under the tutelage of Ira Leonard in Lincoln.

During his war service, Barber contracted chronic hemorrhoids, which resulted in a prolapsed rectum. The pain caused by this (inoperable) condition was so severe as to incapacitate him completely four to eight times a year. During these attacks he had to take to his bed for up to a fortnight, unable to get up or even turn over without assistance. As if all this were not enough, Barber also complained of impaired sight, an enlarged prostate, severe bladder trouble, and chronic tuberculosis. He coughed constantly and spat blood when he had a cold.

Yet in spite of all this, he won the hand of the widow McSween, and they were married on June 20, 1880. It would appear to have been a quiet affair. No mention of it seems to have appeared in the territorial papers, although the *New Mexican* noted that the streets of Lincoln were as dangerous as they had ever been.[20] Over the July 4 holiday, three men, one of them a deputy sheriff, were lynched in Lincoln during an outbreak of mob violence; no further details seem to have reached the newspaper.

FIG. 82. George B. Barber, aged thirty-six, ca. 1882. Photo by Journeay.

The blushing bride (who had reduced her age to thirty-two in the census taken just before the wedding) seems to have wasted no time on honeymooning, devoting herself principally to the affairs of the estates of which she was administratrix. In the case of Dick Brewer she very simply presented to Brewer's aged parents the note against his farm financed by Tunstall and asked them to pay it, or alternately, deed the place to her. The Brewers took the latter course.

Debts to the Tunstall estate from local farmers were by and large worthless, but she made an attempt to collect them. As for the cattle, by the time she disposed of them, they had cost more to collect and herd than they fetched at sale. The store, which she handled on the false premise that it was half owned by McSween, was rented for forty dollars a month; income just about balanced payments for repairs.

Her final report showed assets of $8,386.39 and credits against them totaling $8,888.85.[21] She had sold Tunstall's goods and chattels, valued at $534.00, for $182.00. The cattle, valued (by her, not the appraiser) at $1,200.00, she sold for $976.50. She paid Ira Leonard $600.00 for legal services. There was a loss of over $5,000 on the book accounts, and a further loss of $1,300.00 on the realty. Billy Mathews had reoccupied his place on the Peñasco and defied Corbet to get him off it. George Van Sickle denied he had ever sold his place to Tunstall and challenged Mrs. Barber to prove he had. She could not do so. Gottfried Gauss got $29.90 against his claim for several hundred dollars. Neither Martin Martz nor Ash Upson nor any of Tunstall's Kansas City suppliers got a cent. Administratrix Barber's report was approved by Probate Clerk Sam Corbet on what would have been John Tunstall's thirtieth birthday, March 6, 1883.

On the same day, Susan also presented to the probate court her final settlement of the estate of her former husband.[22] In the matter of the 1878 charge of embezzlement leveled against McSween, Susan counterclaimed through attorney Leonard that Charles Fritz and Emilie Scholand in fact owed his estate ten thousand dollars for "work, labor and services" and eventually ended up making a series of tradeoffs with them and the numerous claimants against McSween's estate.

The attorney had deeded half of his house and the land it stood on to Elizabeth Shield. She disposed of her interest in it to Ira Leonard, who in turn later sold it to Jimmy Dolan. The other part of the land formerly owned by McSween in Lincoln was acquired by Charles Fritz; in 1886, he deeded it to Dolan, who went into business in Tunstall's old store.

All the other lawsuits outstanding against McSween were dropped, for there was nothing in his estate to pay damages, even if won. His notes and accounts, valued at $10,794.97, were worthless. Ira Leonard's fees were $1,200.00. McSween's chattels were valued at $1,853.50: they were sold for $1,200. These included the complete contents of McSween's law office—including that wonderful law library. The purchaser was none other than George B. Barber. It was said he paid $250 for the whole collection.

In 1883, the Barbers bought a ranch at Three Rivers, neighboring and to the north of the old Pat Coghlan ranch east of Tularosa. While her husband offered his services as a surveyor and self-taught lawyer at Lincoln and White Oaks, Susan concentrated on becoming a *ranchera*. A gift of cattle from John Chisum as, one supposes, settlement for services rendered, started her on the road to becoming a highly successful stock raiser, and eventually to fame of a sort as "the Cattle Queen of New Mexico."

Thus Susan McSween Barber at last attained the trappings of means, position, and respect to which she had so long aspired. If the fact that of all his children her father excluded only her from his will bothered her, she put on a bold front; on visits there, she deigned to be fêted and admired by the newspapers of her native state. She is said to have become friendly with the Elkins family, and to have danced with Ambassador Lew Wallace at Elkins's West Virginia home. Her nephew recalled how she loved clothes and jewelry, and "carried a box filled with diamonds, pearls and other gems."[23] She also had a solid gold chain she wore as a necklace.

Her personal life remained unsuccessful. She divorced George Barber on October 16, 1891 on the grounds that he had abandoned her "and failed to contribute to her support for more than one year last past."[24] There may have been other reasons as well. Less than a year later Barber was married by Probate Judge Mickey Cronin to Eugenia Roberts, twenty-two, daughter of Daniel W. and Lou Roberts; the bride's father was sheriff of Lincoln County. That Barber's life with Susan was stormy may be gauged from a notation he made on his pension application in 1915.[25] In reply to the question, "Are you now living with your wife?" Barber replied, "Yes, and happy also." He died of nephritis at Carrizozo on October 24, 1928.

By that time, much had changed. Age was beginning to catch up with Susan McSween Barber (although she gamely understated it in every census that came along, and went to the beauty parlor to have her graying hair dyed). "For goodness sakes, don't think I'm trying to fool anyone," she lied to her relatives (fig. 83).

FIG. 83. Susan McSween Barber, aged seventy-four, Baltimore, Md., 1917. Photographer, her nephew by marriage James Kirkness, Baltimore Photo Co., Lexington St., Baltimore.

"I just hate gray hair." In 1902, no longer able to manage the place alone, she sold Tres Rios to rancher Monroe Harper for $32,000.[26] She may have retained some other lands, because Albert B. Fall gave her two notes of $3,250.00 each, payable June 1, 1918 and 1919, "in part payment for property at Three Rivers."

Mrs. Barber (she never reverted to her former name) bought a house at White Oaks, which had become a ghost of its former self after the gold and silver lodes petered out. Still bad luck pursued her. In the summer of 1923, when she was seventy-eight, her home caught fire, and she jumped fourteen feet from an upstairs window to save her life. She moved to a poky little shack on White Oaks's Lincoln Avenue, and there the writers came, one after another, to ask their questions. And to one after another she told her story, setting the record (as she saw it) straight, and so influencing it way past the grave.

She had already assisted Emerson Hough to write what was to be the first of many, many accounts of the Lincoln County War. After Hough came Maurice Garland Fulton, J. Evetts Haley, and Walter Noble Burns, whose inaccuracies so angered her that she could hardly finish his book. Paradoxically, it was Burns's book that brought her immortality, and elevated Billy the Kid to a pantheon she was unable to understand.

In the summer of 1929, a bad fall incapacitated her; "am still helpless," she wrote Maurice Fulton on February 26, 1930, "am very discouraged."[27] Nonetheless, she was still feisty enough to get angry when she learned that in the Johnny Mack

Brown movie, *Billy the Kid*, she was shown playing "The Star Spangled Banner" on the piano in her burning home, a legend she had always denied. "I think I would have cause for complain whe[n] pure detrimental lies are produced and if our good lord will let me live I shall fight every lie," she promised Fulton.

The good Lord did not let her live to fight every lie. In the winter of 1930, the old lady fell ill with influenza that would not respond to treatment, and sank rapidly. Right up to the end she was still objecting "to being made out a middle-aged woman, when she was much younger," in the movie.[28] At about 7:45 in the evening of Saturday, January 3, 1931, Susanna Hummer McSween Barber breathed her last in the sparsely furnished bedroom of her little house at White Oaks.[29] She died "under almost pioneer conditions; it would have been a false note if there had been electric lights. We had the old kerosene things that resembled those she had in Lincoln," wrote Maurice Fulton, who was there. The following Wednesday, she was buried in the cemetery at White Oaks in a $150 coffin from T. E. Kelleys's Hardware and Sports Shop at Carrizozo.[30]

No other single person knew more of the secret lives of the participants of the Lincoln County War than Susan McSween Barber. Yet never once in all the years she lived did she come even close to admitting that in propagating what became the legend of the Lincoln County War she might have lied. Stubborn, proud, and unrepentant to the end, Susan McSween took her secrets to the grave. And there, she lies.

CHAPTER 38

VALEDICTUM

FUELED by greed, propelled by religious and racial prejudice, by liquor, by firearms, and by some powerful American misbeliefs, the Lincoln County War was based on a whole catalog of self-deceptions. Each side believed it was "us" against "them," Protestants against "dirty Irish cutthroats"; Anglos against Hispanic "greasers"; decent, upright pioneer businessmen challenging and confronting the illegal machinations and extortions of rapacious rivals who would stop at nothing to achieve their ends. Every one of the leading personalities was conditioned by his birth and upbringing to react badly to those opposing him. The result was a physical and chemical reaction that never could have happened had any two of those personalities been removed from the equation.

The Lincoln County War was a false premise pursued to an illogical conclusion. The game, as Tunstall had once put it, was not worth the candle. Nobody ever could have won, and even if anyone had done so it would not have made any difference. The men who had advised John Tunstall that New Mexico was the coming place were right; but that he would have made the fortune he foresaw in the cattle and mercantile trade is extremely unlikely. Certainly the men who took over his range and ran cattle on it did not. Apart from a brief boom in 1885—at which time, following through his plan, Tunstall might have sold out and gone back to England—nobody really made money out of cattle, and after that brief flash of glamor, the industry slid downhill until the Big Die finished it in the winter of 1886–87.

More than thirty years ago, serious treatments of the causes of the Lincoln County War and the motives of its participants were very few. Having no precedent, I had no choice but to set one, and thus in an earlier work viewed the conflict through the refracting lens of John Tunstall's perceptions, lending a bias to my findings which at the time seemed entirely justifiable. After many more years of reflection, of further careful research, it is difficult to maintain that stance.

Perhaps the time has come now to render sterner judgment on Tunstall and especially on Alexander McSween. Although the House was punitively oppressive in a way it is almost impossible to imagine either of them becoming, it is quite obvious that Tunstall and McSween were intent upon a domination of Lincoln County as complete as that of Murphy and Dolan. Perhaps, of the two, they might have been more benevolent. McSween's larger plans did include some— for schools, for churches, for honest politics—which were for the benefit of his fellow man as well as for himself, but that is about all. Always behind the posturing of McSween we descry the shadowy figure of his wife, pushing, needling, cajoling, intent on getting rich.

Fortune-hunting Tunstall, who was a lot more pliable than his jaunty letters to his parents suggest, must have seemed to the McSweens like a God-given opportunity do just that, and they unhesitatingly enlisted him in their own campaign to bring down Murphy and Dolan. Their miscalculation—both of Jimmy Dolan's response, and the reaction to that response of the entire community—was, quite literally, fatal, for if there was a difference between the two factions, it was in the willingness of the House to precipitate violence. Murphy and Dolan used greed, spite, jealousy, racial hatred, and murder without compunction to further their ends. Tunstall's challenge and what Murphy and Dolan saw as McSween's treachery made what ensued, given the time and place, inevitable.

McSween's letters give the strong impression that his most immediate reaction to the murder of his partner was one of dismay. Without Tunstall's money, and no fall-back position, he had only one way to fight the enemy. He knew all the twists and turns of the law; he used that knowledge with as little scruple as he had shown in his other legal maneuverings. Once McSween the lawyer manipulated the law to give the Regulators legal license to kill, he forfeited all credibility, his own pious handwringing notwithstanding. By effectively putting to his followers the question, "If you let these men kill me, who will take my place?" he precipitated murder just as surely as Dolan did by suggesting to the likes of Tom Hill that Tunstall was a menace he would be glad to see removed.

To state the case against the money-hungry McSweens, however, is not in any way to attempt to justify or condone the autocratic arrogance of Murphy or the murderous deviousness of his chief adjutant. If both sides were wrong in what they did and wrong in how they did it, there is no doubt that the actions of the House and its supporters bear even less examination than those of their adversaries. They stand proven embezzlers of government funds, procurers and condoners of violence and murder, extortion and wholesale rustling—men without scruples of any kind.

It is those very facts that make what Tunstall and McSween set out to do all the more reckless. McSween was a highly intelligent man, and he can have been under no misapprehension about the character of the men he was antagonizing. Yet he embarked upon a personal crusade to ruin them. He persuaded Tunstall to set up business in Lincoln and encouraged him in the belief that, within the law, he could continue to attack Jimmy Dolan with impunity. Tunstall made the mistake of believing him and paid for it with his life. Next McSween convinced decent, brave Dick Brewer that he had legal and moral immunity and could exact summary vengeance upon Tunstall's killers. Brewer, who felt guilty because he had abandoned the Englishman, accepted McSween's illegal commission and died trying to effect it. Directly or indirectly, McSween by his intransigence brought about the murder of Sheriff Brady and, by inference, all the others.

Once the killing started, there was no way anyone could stop it, certainly not a man like Dolan, bent on vengeance even at the cost of his own ruin, and most certainly not McSween, who on his dying day was still clinging to the vain hope that justice—that is to say, his personal variety of justice—would triumph, and who probably died unable to comprehend why it would not. As if that were not enough, his wife took up the cudgels after he was killed, prolonging the violence for more than another year. How many men finally died because of the ambitions and machinations of these two as impossible to quantify as it is to define what they died for.

The Lincoln County War established nothing and proved nothing. It did not end so much as sputter out in a gradual, almost reluctant disengagement. Nobody won, everybody lost: Tunstall and McSween their lives and property, Murphy and Dolan their business, half a hundred others their livelihood. In dying, the Lincoln County War effected one other death—that of Lincoln itself. The brief and gaudy years of the little village in the Bonito valley parallel those of its original settler, Avery M. Clenny, who came there in 1855 and who died in 1898. By the time that brave, tough old pioneer had passed on, Lincoln was in a decline from which it never really recovered. Today it lives for only one reason: because it is Billy the Kid's town.

The history ends where the legend began.

The legend never ends.

BIOGRAPHIES

FOUR main biographical strands are woven into the narrative of this book: the lives of John Tunstall, Alexander McSween, Lawrence Murphy, and Billy the Kid. Those of a number of others also emerge with the story: James Dolan, Susan McSween, Robert Widenmann among them. The selection of biographical sketches that follows attempts to document, often for the first time, the lives of some of the lesser known participants in the saga. Please note that the sources listed are not intended to be a comprehensive catalogue of available source material.

ANGEL, FRANK WARNER

Frank Warner Angel, the son of William H. and Harriet (Warner) Angel, was born in Watertown, N.Y., on May 28, 1845. He was thirty-three years old when he arrived in Lincoln County, at which time he was living at 30 Fourth St., Brooklyn, N.Y. An 1868 graduate of the Free Academy (now City College) of New York, he studied law with the New York firm of Barney, Humphrey & Butler, was admitted to the bar in 1869, and later had law offices at 61 Wall St. (fig. 59). On March 18, 1875, he married Sadie Wilcox; they had one child, a daughter. His appointment as special investigator for the Department of Justice commenced April 15 and ended October 5, 1878. That same month, Angel was appointed assistant district attorney for the Eastern District of New York; while in that office, on November 27, 1878, he submitted his report to the attorney general on the murder of Tunstall. He resigned as assistant to U.S. Attorney A. W. Tenney in February 1886. He served as fire commissioner of Jersey City, N.J., 1902–4 and, following an attack of paralysis in 1904, died at his home, 320 Whiting St., Jersey City, on March 15, 1906.

Sources:

Records of Dept. of Justice, NARA; research by Nora Henn, Lincoln, N.M.

ANTRIM, WILLIAM HENRY HARRISON

William Henry Harrison Antrim, fifth of the eight children of Levi and Ida (Lawson) Antrim, both from Ohio, was born at Huntsville, near Anderson, Ind., on December 1, 1842. His father owned a number of hotels in the Anderson area. The other children were Orleana Jane, Thomas, Albert Wood, Levi C., Mary Lawson, Francis Marion, and James Madison. Francis died by drowning at the age of eleven. At the age of twenty-one, while working as a teamster in Philadelphia, William Antrim filed suit against the government for wrongful drafting and took his case successfully to the Supreme Court. By the time its verdict was handed down, Antrim had moved to Indianapolis, where in June 1863 he enlisted as a ninety-day volunteer in Company I, Fifty-fourth Regiment, Indiana Volunteers; he was honorably discharged in September. He lived at Indianapolis until 1869; when his family moved to Kansas in 1870, he settled near what was to become Wichita. He died at Adelaida, Calif., December 10, 1922; the death certificate gives his age as eighty years ten months, suggesting either an 1841 birth or an error by the clerk.

Sources:

Rasch, "Antrim"; Cline, *Antrim and Billy.*

AXTELL, SAMUEL BEACH

Samuel Beach Axtell was born in Franklin County, Ohio, on October 14, 1819. Graduating from Oberlin College, he was admitted to the Ohio bar; in 1851 he went to California and upon the organization of the state into counties was elected district attorney of Amador County. He served two terms in congress as a Democrat, then switched parties; in 1874 he was appointed governor of Utah by President Grant (fig. 51). He became embroiled in a bitter fight between the leaders of the Mormon and anti-Mormon factions in the Republican party there; the death of New Mexico's governor Marsh Giddings providentially offered a means by which Axtell could be extricated from it.

Almost immediately on his assumption of office in New Mexico, a smear campaign was launched by his political opponents, alleging that he was secretly a Mormon bishop charged with converting the people of New Mexico to that faith. For as long as he remained in the Territory, the hapless Axtell was known by the nickname "El Obispo," the Bishop.

Axtell was removed from office subsequent to the Angel investigation. When his long-time friend Gen. James Garfield became president of the United States, he secured for Axtell—in spite of considerable local opposition—the position of chief justice of the Territory of New Mexico, a post Axtell held from 1882 to 1885. He remained in Santa Fe after leaving the bench and died while visiting friends in Morristown, N.J., on August 6, 1891.

Sources:

Twitchell, *Leading Facts*; Keleher, *Violence*; Coe, *Frontier Fighter.*

BACA, SATURNINO

Born in Valencia County, N.M., in 1830, Saturnino Baca served as a U.S. surveyor before the Civil War, and as a first lieutenant in Company E, First New Mexico Cavalry. He saw action at Valverde and served at forts Wingate, Bascom, Defiance, and Stanton. He was a Socorro County member of the territorial legislature when the bill to create Lincoln County was introduced. He married Juana Maria Chaves; there were nine children of the union. Baca played a not-unimportant part in the Lincoln County War and later became a sheep rancher. In 1889 he lost an arm in a shooting incident. Lyon Phillipowski, Sam Corbet, James Brent, Frank Salazar, and Jack Thornton were among his sons-in-law. He died at Lincoln in 1925 (fig. 62).

Lost Treasure

Baca's son Bonifacio "Bonnie" Baca kept a "diary" of the Lincoln County War. Emerson Hough tried to trace it: a letter dated April 30, 1904, from a lawyer named Dabney A. Scales of Memphis, Tenn., confesses Scales's inability to find "the journal" that Baca had loaned him. Hough does not seem to have pursued the matter, and no one seems to know what happened to it. Baca's granddaughter, Rafaelita Pryor, who still lives in Lincoln, says it may have been lost in a fire that destroyed the Baca home. Or is it still somewhere in Tennessee?

Sources:

Emerson Hough Collection, Iowa State University; Traylor, "Facts Regarding the Escape of Billy the Kid."

BAKER, FRANK

Lily Klasner said Frank Baker was the son of a good family of Syracuse, N.Y. He addressed a last letter enclosing his watch and plaited bridle to a Miss Lizzie Lester of that place, "a sweet, fine, educated girl" according to Sallie Chisum, who described both William Morton and Baker as "nice looking chaps with unmistakable marks of culture." Baker may have come to New Mexico from Texas with the Horrells: certainly he was with them when they were under siege from Ham Mills's posse on December 5, 1873. Hough complicates things by saying Baker was part Cherokee, "a well spoken and pleasant man." This is all vastly at odds with Ash Upson's description. "This fellow Baker," he said,

> has shot innocent men when they were on their knees pleading for life. With brutal laugh he has held a pistol to their heads, and after blowing their brains out, kicking the inanimate body and face to a jelly. His countenance was the strongest argument that could be produced for the Darwinian theory. Brutish in expression and feature, he looked a veritable gorilla. He boasts that his father killed 18 men before he was hung in Texas, and that his three brothers had killed a deputy-sheriff in Texas. That he was 22 years of age, the last of the family and had killed 13 men and wanted twenty before he was 25 years old.
>
> I have often heard of the family. Their names are Hart, not Baker. They had no friends and no companions, even among the vilest outlaws, except companions compelled by fear. They were a fearful curse to whatever section they went.

It has not been possible to establish whether the Edward "Little" Hart who participated in the murder of deputy sheriff Joseph Haskins during the Horrell War of 1873, or the Charles Hart involved in the events of July 1878, could have been related to Frank Baker.

There is yet another possibility: William H. Baker, born in 1857, was a friend of rancher Lucien B. "Lute" Jackson, who sold horses to Chisum and Tunstall. Baker and his wife Anne (Brown) claimed to have lived in New Mexico from 1877 to 1879 and later to have moved to Pauls Valley, I.T., where they knew Fred Waite well. The Bakers had several children, one of whom was named Franklin.

Sources:

Klasner, *Girlhood*, 175; Coe, *Frontier Fighter*, 132; Hough, *Outlaw*, 278; research by Donald Lavash; Rasch, "They Fought," 38; Fulton, "Roswell."

BATES, SEBRIAN

Sebrian Bates, who dug Tunstall's grave, worked for the McSweens as a servant. Born in 1842, he grew up in Kentucky, enlisting in the Fifth Kentucky Colored Cavalry as a bugler in 1864; transferred to the Ninth Cavalry in 1866, he re-enlisted in 1872 and saw service as a member of the regimental band at Fort Clark, Tex., and Fort Union and was discharged—dishonorably, according to Dudley—at Fort Stanton in January 1877. He could have been one of a group of musicians, under the command of Lieutenant Taylor of Fort Stanton, who played a Sunday evening concert for Murphy, Baca, and Patrón at Lincoln on March 26, 1876. Then again, perhaps not: At the Dudley Court of Inquiry (DCOI), Chief Musician Charles Spiegel said that Bates had given him troubles "so numerous it is not worth while to give them, caused on account of his habitual drunkenness." Bates "was considered one of the most worthless members of the band. I am speaking morally not profanely. Nobody thought anything of him, he could not be relied on. . . . I would not believe him under oath under any circumstances."

After the troubles, Bates worked for Mrs. McSween for a while, and later as a hired hand on the Coe ranch at Glencoe. He died there in 1910.

Sources:

Dudley to AAAG DNM December 9, 1879, Adjutant General's Office, Cons. File 1405 AGO 1878; *Mesilla Valley Independent,* April 4, 1876; Theisen, "Fight in Lincoln," 183; Judge Advocate General's Office, Records of DCOI, Testimony of Charles Spiegel.

BECKWITH, HENRY M. "HUGH"

Henry M. "Hugh" Beckwith is said to have been born in Alabama, possibly Ashland, since he so named one of his residences. He was forty-four in 1860, which would place his birth in the year 1816. As Jose Enrique (i.e., Joseph Henry) Beckwith, he was married at Santa Fe on December 22, 1849, to Refugia Rascon y Pino, a niece of Nicolas Pino of Galisteo, the "sheep king" of New Mexico. After farming in the Rio Grande valley for some years, in 1855 Beckwith was running a ranch and store near Fort Conrad. By the end of 1859, however, he was reported to be selling liquor to the Indians on the borders of the Mescalero Apache reservation, and at the time the Civil War began, he was running a saloon near Fort Stanton. He was one of the few local men who swore allegiance to the South, and when the Confederates were driven out of the Territory, Beckwith left for El Paso with them. Gen. J. H. Carleton issued urgent orders for his capture; he was taken into custody by a detachment led by Capt. John C. Cremony on September 1, 1862.

Beckwith escaped custody and, although indicted for treason in 1864, managed to evade trial. After the war he settled on the Rio Hondo but relocated in the Seven Rivers area around 1870, at which time there were seven children: Robert (fig. 67), John (fig. 73), Camelia, Josefina, Helen (or Ellen), Elizabeth, and Nicolas. The family prospered, to the extent that it was later remarked they had arrived with one milch cow borrowed from John Chisum and four years later had sixteen hundred head of cattle.

On August 17, 1878, Beckwith shot and killed his son-in-law William H. Johnson at Seven Rivers and was himself severely wounded by Wallace Olinger. He was brought to Lincoln for trial but with the civil authorities there unable to function and the military unwilling to take responsibility for his imprisonment, Beckwith was released. Two years later his wife divorced him and he moved to Texas, where he is said to have been killed during a robbery of his store at Presidio, Tex., in 1892.

Sources:

Wilson, *Merchants*; Rasch and Myers, "Tragedy"; Walker, "California Column."

BERNSTEIN, MORRIS J.

Morris J. Bernstein—whose name is sometimes given as Morris Joseph Bernstein—is said to have been born in London; however, I have personally checked the birth records of England and Wales from 1842 to 1862 without locating anyone of that name. The only candidate is Morice Bernstein, born at 23 Jewry Street, Crutched Friars, London, on February 11, 1856, the son of fancy goods importer Julius and Fanny (Nathan) Bernstein.

Perhaps, then, it was Morice Julius Bernstein who arrived in Santa Fe in the spring of 1873 and went to work as a bookkeeper for Spiegelberg Bros. He was described as a "lively, pleasant, businesslike little gentleman." Some time in 1876, Bernstein moved to the Mescalero Agency as Fred Godfroy's clerk; he also did some bookkeeping for J. J. Dolan & Co. Although traditionally he was seen as a Murphy-Dolan supporter, the few letters he wrote, under the pseudonym "Soapweed," contradict that impression. He seems to have been a feisty young fellow. In his spare time, like another Lincoln County worthy, Doc Scurlock, Bernstein wrote poetry. He was killed on August 5, 1878.

Sources:

Santa Fe New Mexican, April 29, 1873.

BLAIR, THOMAS

Thomas Blair was born Thomas Blair Nichols in Scotland about 1838. He dropped the surname on emigrating to the United States in 1861, enlisted in the army in 1865, and won a commission in 1867. His efforts to relieve the beleaguered Texans during the San Elizario troubles were by all accounts somewhat less than distinguished. In March 1879 he was dismissed from the army for bigamy: he had a wife and child in Scotland. Hence his change of name. After he was released from army custody, he is said to have fled to Maine to escape the wrath of the wealthy Granger family, whose daughter he had married, and seems to have drifted west to California and then back again to Arizona. In September 1879 he applied for the job of post trader's clerk at Camp Thomas, Arizona Territory, was recognized by Captain Stracey, commanding, and was unceremoniously kicked out. He is last heard of at Tombstone, and after that he seems to have disappeared.

Sources:

Rasch, "Fort Stanton," 2; *Santa Fe New Mexican,* September 20, 1879.

BLAZER, JOSEPH HOY

Joseph Hoy Blazer was born in Washington County, Pa., on August 20, 1829. He went to live in Illinois and later in Iowa, where he qualified as a dentist and set up a practice at Mount Pleasant. Blazer served in the Union Army and was invalided out after a horse fell on him. Fearing tuberculosis, he came to San Antonio, Tex., and worked as a teamster. He bought a mule train and freighted to Fort Davis and later El Paso. In 1866 he located on the Tularosa River at a settlement then called Big Fork and bought in with George Nesmith, a former soldier in the California Column turned local farmer, trading his freight team for a share in Nesmith's ranch and sawmill. He was foreman of the Mesilla grand jury in October 1874. In October 1876 he tried to sell the mill and surrounding land to the government as a new Indian reservation for around twenty thousand dollars; agent Fred Godfroy recommended against it. Blazer died October 29, 1898.

Sources:

Research by Melba M. McCaskill, Midland, Tex.; Haley, "Interview with Emma Blazer Thompson."

BOWDRE, CHARLES

Charles Bowdre (the name seems to have been pronounced both Bow-[as in bowel]-dree and bow-[as in bowl]-der) was born in Mississippi around 1848. He is said to have been a cheese maker in Arizona with Doc Scurlock before their arrival in Lincoln in 1875; at that time, according to Jimmy Dolan, they were both flat broke. Although neither of them was an ideal citizen, the House, with startling generosity, sold them a ranch on the Ruidoso River for fifteen hundred dollars, gave them three years to pay, and allowed them some three thousand dollars' worth of credit. Tradition has it that they married sisters, Bowdre taking as his wife Manuela Herrera; this is contradicted by George Coe, who speaks of Bowdre, Scurlock, and Brewer being bachelors in the fall of 1876.

Another theory advanced is that the woman in the photo with Bowdre (fig. 49) is not his wife but a lady named Nellie Pickett, born in Lafayette County, Mo., and raised in Texas, who died at Fort Sumner in August 1882. This charming little nonsense is exploded by the 1880 census records, which show Charlie and Manuela living at Fort Sumner, not to mention the testimony of the posse men who brought in his body.

Poor Charlie Bowdre—one minute "in" with Jessie Evans and the Boys, the next supporting McSween's cause; now Billy the Kid's horse-thieving sidekick, again trying to negotiate a separate peace via J. C. Lea—seems to have suffered from what finally turned out to be a fatal case of indecision. He was killed by Pat Garrett's posse at Stinking Spring

December 21, 1881, and buried alongside Tom O'Folliard at Fort Sumner; later the Kid joined them. The legend on the tombstone says *Pals*, an irony not everyone appreciates.

Sources:

Stanley, *Ike Stockton*; Rasch, "Regulators; *Santa Fe New Mexican*, May 25, 1878; *Albuquerque Review*, August 16, 1882.

BOYLE, ANDREW

Andrew Boyle was born near Brith, in the parish of Dalry, Ayrshire, Scotland, on November 22, 1838. A servant by trade, he was still under legal age when he became Private 1312 in the Seventy-second Highland Regiment of the British Army at Glasgow on January 28, 1856. Although he was awarded two good conduct badges during his service, he was clearly a rowdy: during his ten-year stint he was twice advanced to sergeant and twice court-martialed and reduced to the ranks for drunkenness and riotous conduct. In April 1865 he transferred to the Forty-fifth Regiment of Foot (Infantry) and remained in that regiment until his discharge on grounds of ill health "aggravated by intemperance" at Poona, India, on July 24, 1866. He had served a few days under ten years, most of it in India, which doubtless accounts for McSween's dubbing him "Pasha" Boyle. His discharge papers show he was 5 feet 7½ inches tall, with a fresh complexion, light brown hair, and black eyes.

He and three older brothers, John, Joseph, and James Boyle, emigrated to America in 1867. After some time in Missouri, three of the brothers headed west to Fort Worth, Tex., and later moved to Fort Griffin, where they were joined in 1873 by their widowed mother and sister Elizabeth.

After Elizabeth married Hank C. Smith in May 1874, Andrew drifted farther west and, with John Jones, rented Ham Mills's ranch on the Ruidoso River. When Mills came back to Lincoln in the fall of 1876, Boyle relocated in the Loving's Bend area of the Pecos River. At some point his brother Joe (Elizabeth claimed he was a graduate of Edinburgh University, but no Boyle graduated from there between 1859 and 1888) joined him there. Boyle was a Doña Ana County deputy sheriff at the time of the events under discussion. He died on May 14, either 1882 or 1887—the date on the tombstone is illegible—and is buried at Seven Rivers.

Sources:

British Army, Records, WO97/1528; Curry, *Sun Rising*, 246–59; Rasch, "They Fought," 39–40.

BRADY, WILLIAM

William Brady (fig. 52), eldest son of John and Catherine (Darby) Brady, was born August 16, 1829, in Cavan, County Cavan, Ireland. He was the firstborn of eight children and left Ireland for America early in 1851. On July 11, 1851, he joined the U.S. Army for a five-year hitch, serving in Texas; discharged as a sergeant at the end of his first tour of duty—obviously another tough character who knew how to bounce his knuckles off the skulls of his knotheaded fellow soldiers—Brady re-enlisted in the First Regiment of Mounted Rifles for another five years. Discharged in March 1861 at Fort Craig, he joined the Second New Mexico Volunteer Infantry as first lieutenant and adjutant to its commanding officer, Col. Miguel Pino. On November 16, 1862, he married a widow, Maria Bonifacio Chaves Montoya. He is the subject of a contentious biography (Lavash, *Brady*).

BREWER, RICHARD M.

Richard M. Brewer was born in St. Albans, Vt., on February 19, 1850. His parents were Ransselaer and Phebe (Honsinger) Brewer. Ranse, as he was known, was born in 1820;

his wife, in 1823. They were married by Rev. Charles H. Leonard at Swanton, Vt., on September 1, 1845. They had both grown up in that area: Emanuel Honsinger, Phebe's brother, testified that Ranse "was a neighbor from a lad, & grew to manhood in the neighborhood where I was born." Ranse and Phebe had two children who died in infancy—Samantha, born November 23, 1846, died April 19, 1848, and Josephine, born February 14, died March 4, 1849.

In 1860 the family—by this time there was also a daughter, Lillie, born January 19, 1852—settled in Marshall Township, near Boaz, Richland County, Wis. On September 23, 1861, Ranse Brewer enlisted in Capt. Van S. Bennett's Company I, Twelfth Regiment, Wisconsin Volunteer Infantry. According to the *Richland County Republican*, "[T]here hadn't been time to clear the land when Ranse enlisted in the Union Army. . . . There wasn't an able-bodied man left in the town of Dayton during the war years, and the women and children had to do all the work." So while Ranse served as a nurse in Geneva Hospital, Lawrence, Kans., at Vicksburg, Miss., and at Marietta, Ga., eleven-year-old Dick became the man of the house.

Ranse Brewer was mustered out at Chattanooga, Tenn., October 28, 1864. A second son, Michael, was born March 24, 1866. Soon afterwards the family moved to another farm on Mill Creek, Dayton Township. On April 14, 1870, his daughter Lillie, now a schoolteacher, was married to Benjamin Baxter. Dick Brewer was not at the wedding; by the time it took place, he had left Richland County forever. The family tradition is that he was in love with a girl named Matilda Jane Davis, but they had a quarrel, and he left for the West. In a diary she kept, Matilda Jane, who married Dick's cousin Henry, recorded on February 28, 1874, "It was just five years ago tonight I last saw Dick" i.e., February 28, 1869. The only known photograph of him is said to have been taken at Carthage, Mo., soon afterwards (fig. 24).

What decided him on Lincoln County is not known. It would appear he arrived there sometime in 1870, since the "In Memoriam" notice published after his death notes that some citizens had known him for over eight years. He worked—perhaps as long as four years—for L. G. Murphy & Co. before buying his own place on the Ruidoso River. A blond-haired, blue-eyed, gentle giant with "great arms and huge, strong hands," once known as "the most powerful man in Dayton Township," Brewer won a reputation for himself as a decent, honest, hardworking man. In 1875 his parents traveled out to New Mexico to visit with the son they had not seen for five years. On May 3, 1877, the *Richland County Observer* noted their return "after eighteen months sojourn in New Mexico."

Rensselaer Brewer died of paralysis on Tuesday, November 16, 1897. His wife, Phebe, died April 30, 1914. Lillie Brewer died in 1931. They are buried in Basswood Cemetery, Richland County, Wis. All Dick Brewer's letters home were burned after a family squabble in 1951. The great-grandson of the girl Dick Brewer loved lives today at Richland Center; the Richland County History Room is in the Brewer Public Library.

Sources:

Research by Lewis Ketring, Jr., Los Angeles; Twylah Kepler, Richland Center, Wis.; "Notes on Dick Brewer," Mullin, HHC, courtesy Melba McCaskill.

BRISTOL, WARREN HENRY

Born at Stafford, New York, on March 19, 1823, Warren Henry Bristol (fig. 39) was the son of Dr. Burrage and Sarah (Benham) Bristol, both of Cheshire, Conn. Dr. Bristol served in the War of 1812 as a captain of cavalry before settling in western New York as a farmer. His son Warren was educated at Yates Academy, Lima Seminary, Wilson Collegiate Institute, and finally at Fowler's Law School. He read law in the office of Edward Chase, a brother of Chief Justice Chase, before being admitted to the bar in

Lockport, N.Y. His original intention was to settle in Quincy, Ill.; late in the fall of 1850, en route there, he decided instead to try Minnesota. He worked as a mail carrier between St. Paul and St. Croix before hanging out his shingle in Hennepin County, in the area that would later become Minneapolis. He moved to Redwing and entered a partnership with J. N. Murdock, returning east in the spring of 1854 to be married at Lockport, N.Y., on April 20 to Louisa C. Armstrong of that town. He was elected district attorney of Goodhue County, Minn., and later probate judge. Soon after he served in the state legislature, once in the lower house and twice in the senate. In 1864 he was a member of the Republican convention that renominated Abraham Lincoln at Baltimore. In 1872, President Grant appointed him associate justice of the supreme court of New Mexico; he held this office until 1885, resigning on the election of the Democrat Cleveland. He died at Deming, N.M., on January 12, 1890.

Sources:

Twitchell, *Leading Facts,* 420.

BROWN, HENRY NEWTON

Often referred to inaccurately as "Hendry," Henry Newton Brown was born in the fall of 1857 at Cold Spring Township, near Rolla, Mo. After the death of their parents, he and his sister Ellen, four years his senior, were reared on the farm of an uncle, Andrew Richardson. When Henry was about eighteen, he left Missouri, and worked as a cowboy and buffalo hunter in Texas, where he is said to have killed a man. He drifted into New Mexico in 1876, picking up a job with L. G. Murphy & Co., for whom he worked about eighteen months. When he quit, the company in typical fashion shortchanged him on his wages. Brown is said to have taken himself and his grudge to Chisum, who gave him a job. It would appear that this consisted of some kind of "detached service" as a bodyguard to either Tunstall or McSween, for he became a full-time member of the Regulators. Robert Mullin said that Brown was "a queer character. He neither drank, smoked, nor gambled, which was unusual in that time and place. . . . He was certainly a hired man of Chisum's during most of the Lincoln County War."

After the war, Henry drifted down into Texas and found work on the LIT ranch. He later left Littlefield and worked for Campbell & Ledger trailing horse thieves before becoming a deputy sheriff of Oldham County, Tex., then later again, deputy constable of Tascosa. On July 4, 1882, having been fired from the trail herd that he rode with to Kansas because "he was always on the warpath," Brown was appointed assistant city marshal of Caldwell, Kans. John Ryland, an oldtimer who had known him there, sent me this hitherto unpublished sketch of Brown:

> He was a very quiet man about 5'6" tall, had a very light brown [hair] a blond mustache, wore a sort of business suit, colored shirt, not loud, tie and kerchief around his neck cowboy-style and most of the time, which was a little unusual, he wore shoes but when he wore boots the pants legs were on the outside of the boots. . . . I never liked Brown very well as he was very quiet and to me sort of surly. . . . I dont think he ever was a buffalo hunter nor was he foreman in John S. Chisum outfit like you mentioned.

By December 1882, Brown was marshal of Caldwell, and he served in that capacity until the end of January 1883, when he quit to visit his family in Missouri. The grateful citizens of Caldwell presented him with a gold-mounted Winchester rifle as a going-away present. In March, Brown resumed his duties; over the next year he killed at least two men. On March 26, 1884, he married a local girl, Alice Levagood. Barely a month later, on April 30, 1884, Brown and his deputy, Ben Wheeler, together with William Smith and John Wesley, tried to rob the bank at Medicine Lodge, Kans. In the process Brown killed bank president E. W. Payne, and Wheeler shot down cashier George Geppert. They fled empty-handed and were soon captured by a posse, which took them back to town. At about nine o'clock that night a lynch mob stormed the jail. The prisoners made a run for it; Brown was shot dead. The badly wounded Wheeler and the other two were hanged without ceremony.

A Final Note

Lucius Dills claimed that the Caldwell Henry Brown was not the same man who rode with the Kid but "a counterfeit." The real Henry, he said, was a deputy sheriff in Roswell in 1907–8. Available records do not support the proposition.

Sources:

John Ryland, letter to Nolan, 1955; O'Neal, *Henry Brown*; Rasch, "A Note"; Rickards, "Better for the World" and "More"; Haley, "Interview with Lucius Dills"; research by Elvis Fleming, Roswell, N.M.

BUSHNELL, SAMUEL B. AND CHARLES

Samuel B. Bushnell was born in 1819, and was a resident of Monticello, White County, Ind., when on February 24, 1873, he was appointed Mescalero Apache agent. Doctor Bushnell arrived in Santa Fe March 21, accompanied by his grown son Charles, and reported to Superintendent L. Edwin Dudley before continuing on to Fort Stanton, where he and his son arrived April 2, 1873, to find that Bushnell's predecessor, Andrew J. Curtis, had already left. In July, Charles Bushnell was appointed postmaster at Fort Stanton, ousting L. G. Murphy from that position. On Friday, October 17, 1873, the *Santa Fe New Mexican* reported the death of young Bushnell at Fort Stanton the preceding Monday; he was apparently found dead in his bed. An overdose of laudanum was diagnosed; no further obituary seems to have appeared.

Sources:

Mehren, "Mescalero Apache Reservation"; research by Nora Henn.

CARROLL, HENRY

Henry Carroll (fig. 61), who played a not insignificant role in Lincoln County events, was born in New York City on May 20, 1838. He joined the army as a private and was wounded during the siege of Morris Island, S.C., in July 1863. Commissioned a second lieutenant, Third Cavalry, in 1864, Carroll transferred to the Ninth Cavalry in 1867 and served on the Indian frontier in Texas. Rasch credits him with an 1869 engagement on the Salt Fork of the Brazos River, but no mention of it appears in standard sources. Carroll's company did have a fight with Indians in the Florida Mountains of New Mexico, killing one Indian and capturing eleven head of stock, on September 15, 1876. He was stationed at Fort Union when the Lincoln troubles began, arriving at Fort Stanton only on June 1. He died of blood poisoning in 1908.

Sources:

Record of Engagements, 61; Rasch, "Fort Stanton," 2–3.

CATRON, THOMAS BENTON

Thomas Benton Catron's ancestors immigrated to Virginia from Germany in 1765. He was born on October 6, 1840, the son of John and Mary (Fletcher) Catron of Lafayette County, Mo. After graduating from the University of Missouri in 1860, he almost immediately enlisted in the Confederate Army. He had a dangerous war, participating in the battles of Carthage, Wilson Creek, Dry Fork, Lexington, Pea Ridge, Vicksburg, Corinth, Farmington, Lookout Mountain, Missionary Ridge, and Mobile Bay. At the time of the surrender he was serving with the Third Missouri Battery under the command of Lt. Gen. Richard Taylor.

After the war, Catron (fig. 53) returned to Missouri to study law, but finding that his service in the Confederate Army debarred him, he moved to New Mexico, arriving in Santa Fe July 27, 1866. In somewhat unorthodox sequence, he was appointed district attorney for the Third Judicial District at La Mesilla and admitted to the bar the following year: his friendship with Stephen Elkins proved no handicap at this time. He was thirty-seven when he married Julia A. Walz, twenty-two, on April 28, 1877. Born in Springfield, Ohio, she came from Mankato, Minn. Of the six children born of the marriage, four survived. In order of birth they were: John, born 1878; Charles, born 1879; Thom (who changed his name to Thomas Benton Catron II in 1922), born 1888; and Fletcher, born 1890.

He was a member of the legislative council from Santa Fe County in four legislative assemblies between 1869 and 1872 and was also mayor of Santa Fe. He and his law partner Elkins gained a controlling interest in the First National Bank owned by Lucien B. Maxwell and made a fortune in the land-grant business. After serving as attorney general of New Mexico, Catron was appointed U.S. attorney in 1872. Later he served as U.S. senator. He died on May 21, 1921.

Sources:

Keleher, *Fabulous Frontier*; Westphall, *Catron*. Neither devotes much attention to Elkins and Catron's founding, fostering, and leadership of the Santa Fe Ring; someone should.

CHAPMAN, HUSTON INGRAHAM

The fifth son and seventh child of William Williams and Margaret Fee (Ingraham) Chapman, Huston Ingraham Chapman was born April 28, 1847, in Burlington, Iowa, then a part of Michigan. When he was only seven days old his family—including Sarah Eveline, born 1834; Thomas, born 1836; Arthur, born 1838; James Grimes, born 1840; William Warner, born 1842; and Mary Catherine, born 1844—joined a party of about a hundred emigrants and crossed the plains to Oregon Territory in two ox-drawn wagons, arriving at Marysville (Corwallis) on November 13.

Col. W. W. Chapman was a man of considerable enterprise: Born in Clarksburg, W.Va., in 1808 of Pennsylvania Dutch Quaker stock (which might indicate a reason for his son's affinity with Susan McSween), a schoolmate of Stonewall Jackson, a self-educated lawyer admitted to the bar at age twenty-three, he had already served as prosecuting attorney for Michigan Territory, as the first U.S. attorney for the Territory of Wisconsin, and as congressman for the new state of Iowa when he decided to seek fresh fields. Chapman had married Margaret Fee Ingraham, eighth child and fourth daughter of Col. Arthur Ingraham, a well-known Virginia legislator, in the spring of 1832.

Locating in Salem, Chapman joined a party going to the California goldfields and mined successfully there for a year before returning to Portland, where he purchased a one-third interest in the new town and built a house where the present-day courthouse now stands. He was unquestionably one of the leading founding fathers of the city, as town proprietor, as attorney, as surveyor-general, as commander of the Southern Battalion in the Rogue River Indian War, as a member of the legislature; the list of his many achievements includes the establishment of Portland as a seaport, founding the newspaper *The Oregonian* (which he named), and perhaps his crowning glory, the securing of Portland's eastern railroad connections.

On May 19, 1860, shortly after his thirteenth birthday, Huston (the spelling used by his father) Chapman accidentally shot himself with a shotgun, one barrel loaded with buckshot and the other with birdshot. As a result his left arm was amputated two inches below the shoulder. In a letter written after his son's death, his father said he "spurned the idea that he could not accomplish with one hand anything others could do with two," and that "his energy and enterprise knew no bounds." He was reared in the noisy, crowded family home at 14th and Jefferson (his sister, Sarah, died in 1859 leaving two small children; her mother traveled to St Louis and brought them back to Portland, where she reared them as her own). Huston probably (like his younger brothers Winfield Scott, born July 3, 1850, and Harra Davis, born March 17, 1853) graduated from the Portland Academy and qualified as both a lawyer and engineer. In 1874, Winfield, then chief city surveyor of Portland, surveyed at his own expense part of the railroad line from Salt Lake City to that place; the same year, Harra was in California as assistant engineer on the Southern Pacific, whose last fifty miles of right-of-way into Fort Yuma he constructed.

For many years a resident of Steilacoom, Puget Sound, where he practiced law, Huston Chapman went east in 1877 and joined the AT&SF Railroad, working first on the spur line building to Arkansas City via Winfield, Kans., at which place he probably also practiced law. He remained an employee of the railroad as bridge engineer until the tracks reached Trinidad, Colo., in September 1878, when he quit the company's service. From there he went to Las Vegas, N.M., where he entered a law partnership under the style of Chapman & Quinton; Mrs. McSween seems to have been among his first clients.

W. W. Chapman died October 18, 1892, his wife having predeceased him. "No man, probably," said an obituarist, "ever was so inherently opposed to trickery, machinations, and frauds in politics as he." It remains a mystery why a man so well connected should have done so little to secure an investigation of the death of his son, following Huston Chapman's murder at Lincoln on February 18, 1879.

Sources:

Las Vegas Gazette, March 1, 1879; *The Portland Oregonian,* March 13, 1879, and October 20, 1892; *Salem, Oregon, Statesman,* May 29, 1860; research by Kenneth Lomax, Oregon Historical Society, Portland.

CHAVES Y CHAVES, JOSE

Jose Chaves y Chaves is said to have been born in 1851, which would have made him ~~thirty~~-seven [TWENTY] at the time of the Lincoln County War. A laborer by trade, and something of a hard case by profession, he escaped from the McSween house with the Kid, and later served in the Lincoln County Mounted Riflemen. He is said to have murdered a prisoner in the Lincoln jail in cold blood (perhaps during the mysterious lynchings of July 1881); certainly soon after this he left the area and turned up in Las Vegas, N.M. He is reputed in 1885 to have bested Bob Ford, the man who killed Jesse James, in a shooting match there, and then challenged him to a duel, humiliating Ford to such an extent that he had to quit town.

On October 22, 1892, he was one of a trio of policemen—the other two being Julian Trujillo and Eugenio Alarid—using the badge as cover for membership in a gang known as the Society of Bandits, which lynched a man named Patricio Maes and, four months later, were party to the murder of his brother-in-law Gabriel Sandoval by the head of their gang, saloonkeeper Vicente Silva. In mid-April Silva killed his own wife; suspecting they might be next, his confederates shot him and buried him in the grave they had dug for his wife. A year later, Alarid and Trujillo were arrested and imprisoned for life. Chaves y Chaves skinned out; he was found two months later by either Socorro County sheriff Holm O. Bursum or his special deputy Joe Wiggins (sources differ), herding sheep in Socorro, using the name Joe Gonzales. Tried in June 1895 at Las Vegas and sentenced to death, he was remanded for a new trial by the territorial supreme court. Once again he was sentenced to execution, but this time Governor Miguel Otero, in the face of bitter opposition from the citizens of Las Vegas, commuted his sentence to life imprisonment.

Chaves y Chaves was paroled from the New Mexico penitentiary in 1909 as a reward for assisting prison guards in a riot; he lived for many years in Las Vegas, where he amazed youngsters with his shooting skill and his tall tales, one of which was that it was he, and not Billy the Kid, who shot Sheriff Brady and George Hindman. He is said to have died in Milagro, N.M., on July 17, 1923.

Sources:

Bryan, *Wildest,* 243–44; Rasch, "Regulators," 56–57.

CHISUM, JOHN SIMPSON

There has as yet been no fully documented biography of John Simpson Chisum, who was born on August 15, 1824, at Hardeman, Madison County, Tenn. When Chisum, one of three brothers, was thirteen, the family moved west to Paris, Tex. At the age of thirty, Chisum launched into his career as a cattleman; by 1873 he was occupying a vast stretch of land centered on Bosque Grande on the Pecos River (fig. 6). Presciently anticipating the demise of the cattle industry, he sold out to Hunter & Evans in 1875; much of his later life was plagued by lawsuits brought against him by his rivals. He died at Eureka Springs, Ark., on December 22, 1884.

Sources:

A sketch of Chisum's life and some revealing documents appear in Klasner, *Girlhood,* 309–30. A more fully documented study may be found in Hinton, "Chisum."

COE, BENJAMIN FRANKLIN

Youngest of the four sons of Benjamin and Annie (Kerr [pronounced Kar]) Coe, Benjamin Franklin Coe was born in Moundsville, W. Va., on October 1, 1851. The other three brothers were Louis, Albert, and Jasper. The family settled near Queen City, Mo., and in 1859, Lou joined a wagon train to New Mexico and farmed for a while in the Raton area and in Lincoln County with a friend, Joe Storms. When Lou returned home to marry his childhood sweetheart, his brothers, especially Benjamin Franklin, always known as Frank, were excited by his tales of the West and left home to become buffalo hunters and teamsters.

In 1871, Lou came west again, bringing with him his family and cousin George Washington Coe, and they settled in the Raton area. Jasper "Jap" Newton Coe and his wife Ada (Saunders) Coe also settled nearby, and their first four children, Edward, Ross, Sadie, and Lillie, were born there. The four Coe brothers, Lou, Al, Jap, and Frank, together with cousin George and Ada Saunders's brother, James Albert, known as "Ab," decided it might be profitable for some of them to return to farming in Lincoln County. Accordingly, Frank, Al, Cousin George, and Ab Saunders headed south. Frank, George, and Ab returned to the farm at La Junta on the Rio Hondo, while Al Coe settled on the upper Rio Peñasco at what is now Mayhill.

In October 1876, Frank Coe and Ab Saunders ambushed and nearly killed Juan Gonzales, a local badman who had at one time tried to murder John Riley. Coe is said also to have been one of the group that pursued horse thieves to Puerto de Luna in the summer of 1876 and certainly was one of the men who took Jésus Largo out of the custody of Sheriff Saturnino Baca and lynched him.

After the Lincoln troubles, the Coes went back north to Lou's ranch in San Juan valley near Farmington, where they were joined by Al, now married to Molly Mahill, of the family for whom Mayhill is named. Jap, Frank, and George rented a place on the Animas River about where Aztec, N.M., is now located. Frank was arrested at Santa Fe in May 1879 and charged with murdering "Buckshot" Roberts in the Blazer's Mill fight; he was able to convince the court that although he had been present, it had been in a strictly noncombatant capacity. It transpired he had been mistaken for his cousin George.

Soon thereafter the cousins became embroiled in yet more factional difficulties. They were there or thereabouts when O. H. Hansen and Frank Meyers were liberated from the Farmington jail, and also were instrumental in driving justice of the peace H. H. Halford out of the county. Frank is alleged to have been involved in another lynching in February 1880 and was one of the vigilantes who shot it out the following January with Port Stockton, brother of former Lincoln saloonkeeper Ike, in what became known as the Coe-Stockton feud.

Frank returned to Lincoln County after these troubles were over and met his wife-to-be, Canada-born Helena Anne Tully, who had come via Chicago to live there with her family. They were married February 7, 1881 (fig. 55). Lou Coe stayed in Farmington, bringing his parents out from Missouri to live with him; George Coe also remained in the area.

The Jap Coe family moved to Lompoc, where his wife Ada's family had moved earlier. Their sixth child, Charles, was born there. Al Coe came back to Peñasco, and invited Frank and Helena to join him there. Helena had been ill since the birth of her first child, Sydney (who married Bert Bonnell, whose ranch is the old Jap Coe place), and had to be brought down in a padded wagon. In 1882 Frank and Aunt Ella, as she was known, paid four hundred dollars for the old Dick Brewer place (the actual cycle of ownership was Gylam-Horrell-Brewer-Miller; as a matter of interest, it was sold recently for two and a half million). Frank also built a house on the site of what is now the Ruidoso racetrack.

In 1884, Frank contacted George in Colorado and Jap in California and invited them to join him. Frank and Ella Coe's other children were Wilbur, Annie, and Edith (born October 31, 1896). On the night of October 4, 1898, their daughter Sydney tried to elope with Irvin Lesnett: Frank killed the young man with a shotgun after Irvin fired at him with a Winchester. He was tried and acquitted at Roswell on March 22, 1900. Benjamin Franklin Coe died of pneumonia on September 16, 1931.

Sources:

Research by Cara Mae Coe Smith, El Paso, Tex.; Coe, *Frontier Fighter*; Smith, *The Coe's Go West*; Rasch, "Regulators," 60.

COE, GEORGE WASHINGTON

George Washington Coe, Frank Coe's cousin, was the son of Thomas Coe, who came from Moundsville, W.Va., and settled at Brighton, Washington County, Iowa. George was born there on December 13, 1856, the first of four children left motherless four years later. "Two sisters found pleasant homes," said George, "but my younger sister and I drifted from pillar to post." Their father remarried and the family was reunited in Missouri in 1861. That marriage ended with the death of the wife; while Thomas Coe was serving in the Civil War, George lived with his cousins at Queen City, his sister with an aunt. After the war, Thomas Coe took a third wife, who also died; the fourth was an intolerable stepmother, and when Lou Coe returned to New Mexico, George accompanied him. By 1874 the whole family was relocated in Colfax County.

George Coe was just twenty when he arrived in Lincoln County. He farmed with his cousin Frank for a while, then moved to his own place on the Ruidoso River, with a brother, Jap Coe, farming nearby. He and Doc Scurlock were arrested by Sheriff Brady on suspicion of harboring Frank Freeman (Freeman and Coe were friends, and there is no doubt that Coe helped Freeman after the killing of the soldier in Lincoln); the treatment he received at Brady's hands put him firmly in the McSween camp. George was as active as his cousin Frank in the Farmington troubles; not so involved as to preclude other interests, however, for at the height of the troubles, on November 16, 1879, he married Nebraska-born Phoebe Brown (fig. 56).

They returned to Lincoln County in November 1884, and thereafter George led a peaceful life and lived to see his eight children grow to maturity. Although it must be read with great caution, his autobiography, "as told to Nan Harrison," is a lively and interesting account of his life and times. He died at Roswell on November 14, 1941.

Sources:

Coe, *Frontier Fighter*; Smith, *The Coe's Go West*; Rasch, "Regulators," 57–59, and "Feuding at Farmington."

CORBET, SAMUEL R.

Samuel R. Corbet was born in North Carolina ca. 1850. He became Tunstall's clerk in the summer of 1877 and remained one of his staunchest supporters, particularly in the matter of Dudley's actions during and after the "Big Killing." After the Lincoln troubles, he worked for Isaac Ellis as a clerk. He was a witness at the Dudley Court of Inquiry, and from 1879 to 1880 he was Lincoln postmaster and, in the latter year, deputy probate clerk. In the census that year he gave his occupation as "miner." In 1883 he was probate clerk, and in 1890 county clerk and county superintendent of schools (fig. 68). Shortly after the end of the fighting, Corbet married Teresa Phillipowski, née Padilla, widow of Lyon Phillipowski, who was killed October 21, 1874. Teresa died in the summer of 1882; he then married Josefa Baca. Sometime in the latter part of 1887 he left Lincoln County for Coahuila, Mexico, because of financial difficulties (alleged to have occurred while he had charge of the post office) and marital problems. Of all people, it was to Jimmy Dolan that Corbet turned for help in his time of trouble; it appears Dolan sent him money and did what he could to help, and Corbet later returned to New Mexico. Corbet moved to Texas and married Ola Waddle around 1900. He died in Miller Grove, Texas, in 1923.

Sources:

Research by Lewis Ketring, Jr.; Mullin, "Notes on Sam Corbet," Mullin, HHC, courtesy Melba McCaskill; Fulton-Nolan Correspondence.

DAWSON, BYRON

Byron Dawson was born in Johnson County, Ind., on August 29, 1838. He enrolled as a first sergeant in the Third Cavalry, Forty-fifth Regiment of Indiana Volunteers, in 1862 and was promoted to second lieutenant September 1, 1864. Mustered out as a captain, he accepted a regular army commission as second lieutenant, Ninth Cavalry, in 1866. He was brevetted captain for gallantry in action against Kiowas and Comanches in 1869. Most of his time at Fort Stanton appears to have been spent chasing Apaches; he later served under Gen. George Crook with whom he is seen in a photograph taken at Fort Duchesne, Utah, in 1887. In the same picture, by remarkable coincidence, is Colonel James F. Randlett.

Sources:

Schmitt, *Crook, His Autobiography*, facing p. 236; Rasch, "Fort Stanton," 3–4.

DOLAN, JAMES JOSEPH

There is some slight confusion over the origins of James Joseph Dolan. The register of baptisms for the parish of Loughrea, diocese of Clonfort, County Galway, Ireland, shows that a James Dolan, the son of Patrick and Biddy (Cory) Dolan, was born April 22, 1848, and baptized three days later. This information is confirmed by the entry in the Dolan family bible, although the date May 2, 1848, inscribed on Dolan's tombstone at the Fritz ranch, had been previously accepted by many writers, myself among them. The bible also gives Dolan's age at his death on February 26, 1898, as forty-nine years, nine months, and twenty-nine days, which supports the May birthdate.

In 1824 a John Dolan, tallow chandler, had a business on Main Street, Loughrea; it was no longer there in 1856, lending some support to the family tradition of emigration. Confirmation that the James Dolan discharged at Fort Stanton on April 3, 1869, is the Lincoln County Dolan is still awaited: Dolan told Frank Angel in 1878 that he had lived four years in Lincoln and seven in Fort Stanton. Dolan (figs. 8, 64, 81) became a U.S. citizen April 13, 1874, his sponsors Lyon Phillipowski and John Bolton. He died at his ranch on the Feliz on February 26, 1898. A sketch of his later life forms part of the final chapter of this book.

Sources:

Mullin, "Notes on J. J. Dolan," Mullin, HHC, courtesy Melba McCaskill; research by J. B. Donohoe, Loughrea, 1986; U.S. Dept. of Justice, Angel Report, Deposition of J. J. Dolan.

DOWLIN, PAUL AND WILL

Paul and Will Dowlin were both from Pennsylvania. The third child of Josiah and Elizabeth Dowlin, Paul was born in Greene County, Pa., on December 20, 1828. The other children were Rea, born 1821; Ann, born 1824; John, born 1832; William, born September 2, 1836; and Amos, born 1848. Paul Dowlin first appears in the historical record on November 13, 1861, when he enlisted as a private in Capt. Alonzo C. Adams's C Company, Fourth Regiment of New Mexico Volunteers, at Fort Union, New Mexico. Aged thirty-two, a saddler by occupation, he stood five foot eight, and had gray eyes, light hair, and a florid complexion.

He was a good soldier and rose rapidly through the ranks; by March 1862 he was first sergeant of Company K, First New Mexico Mounted Volunteers; in June 1863 he made second lieutenant, and in November he was appointed acting assistant quartermaster to the Navajo Expedition about to take the field. On March 20, 1864, he became first lieutenant and regimental commander; in October of that year he was assigned to command a detachment escorting a government supply train from Fort Wingate to Fort Whipple, Arizona Territory.

Upon his return to Fort Wingate in March 1865, Dowlin—who had fractured his leg—was assigned to Fort Sumner where, until October of that year, he was in charge of the post commissary. On October 18 he was promoted to captain, Company D; he remained on detached service and, after spending the first three months of 1865 on sick report, requested honorable discharge as he was "unable to perform many of the duties incident to my position." His resignation was accepted, and he was mustered out September 30, 1866.

Exactly when he established the mill at Ruidoso is unclear: the best-informed guesses put it ca. 1868. He was one of the first to file on land there, and his business interests expanded with the influx of new settlers. The following year his brother Will, aged thirty-four, and Will's wife, Clara, joined him; Will became a partner in the firm of Paul Dowlin & Co. In September 1873, when Murphy & Co. were ousted from Fort Stanton, Paul bought the mercantile business and obtained a post trader's license effective December of that year; he took over management of the mercantile business while Will operated the mills on the Ruidoso River. So successful were the brothers that in July 1876 the business was redesignated Paul Dowlin & Brother; at this time Will became a half-owner of the stock and business at the fort, the mill, and all his brother's real and personal property.

That same month Paul Dowlin, who probably already had separated from his common-law wife Placida Valenzuela, entered into an agreement with Indian Agent Williamson D. Crothers to raise and educate his three daughters Francesca, Luisa, and Rufina. He paid Crothers two thousand dollars to take the girls back with him to San Antonio, Tex., reserving the right to have them back should he remarry and wish to bring his children home.

After Paul's murder on April 28, 1877, Will Dowlin was made administrator of his estate and guardian of his children. Later in 1877 he sold the mills to Frank Lesnett and concentrated his energies on the store at Fort Stanton. About 1878 he formed a partnership with John C. DeLany, and on January 5, 1879, they purchased the old Murphy store from Catron, operating it as a mercantile establishment until December 1880, when they went bankrupt.

Clara and Will Dowlin and their three children, Milton, Edwin, and Charles, moved to Las Cruces and were divorced soon afterwards (ca. 1882). Will died in an insane asylum in Pueblo, Colo., in 1884; it was said that he became so despondent over his losses that he never recovered his health.

Sources:

Research by Alice C. Blakestad, Hondo, N.M.; *Santa Fe New Mexican,* August 15, 1876; Las Cruces, *Rio Grande Republican,* December 20, 1884.

DUDLEY, NATHAN AUGUSTUS MONROE

Nathan Augustus Monroe Dudley was born at Lexington, Mass., on August 20, 1825. Appointed first lieutenant in the newly raised Tenth Infantry on March 3, 1855, he saw service in the 1855 campaign against the Sioux in Minnesota, at Fort Kearny, Neb., and—like Lawrence Murphy—in the 1857 "Mormon War" under Gen. Albert Sidney Johnston. On May 7, 1861, he made captain; shortly thereafter, while serving with the Tenth Infantry in Kansas, he became involved in the first of what would be many clashes with his superiors and was court-martialed for "conduct unbecoming." During the Civil War he was stationed in the Gulf states and was brevetted major for gallantry and meritorious service at the battle of Baton Rouge in August 1862, and lieutenant colonel following the battle of Port Hudson in June 1863. He was promoted to the rank of major, Fifteenth Infantry, on September 13, 1864, and later served in Texas. It was there, in 1869, that Dudley first ran afoul of Edward Hatch (fig. 72).

A military court had been convened to try some thirty citizens of Jefferson on charges of opposing the U.S. government by force and lynching three men. During the trial Hatch, like Dudley a member of the court, accepted the hospitality of the father of one of the prisoners, for which action Dudley took him publicly and severely to task. The animosity thus aroused lasted a very long time.

In spite of it, at the beginning of 1865, Dudley was brevetted brigadier general of U.S. Volunteers for gallant and meritorious service during the war. In September 1866 he transferred to the Twenty-fourth Infantry; on December 15, 1870, assigned to the Third Cavalry, he was posted to Camp MacDowell in Arizona Territory. Six months after his arrival, Dudley got into such a blazing row with Capt. Anson Mills, Eighteenth Infantry, that he filed nine charges and twelve specifications against the captain. Not to be outdone, Mills preferred charges against Dudley, claiming that on three occasions he had been too drunk to perform his duties. The ensuing court-martial in October found Dudley guilty of some of the charges leveled against him; he was suspended from rank for sixty days and reprimanded in general orders. In later years, without naming names, Mills described Dudley as a man of overbearing tyrannical disposition, much addicted to drink.

In the winter of 1876, Dudley was given command of Fort Union and, on July 1, was promoted to lieutenant colonel, Ninth Cavalry. Fort Union, however, was under the jurisdiction of his old enemy Hatch, now a colonel. It did not take long for the sparks to fly. By the fall of the following year, Hatch requested permission to relieve Dudley of his command; the request was denied because General Pope, commanding, believed that

Dudley would be just as much of a nuisance wherever he was posted. So on November 26, Hatch threw the book at his contentious junior, leveling five charges and fourteen specifications against him. These included disobedience, disrespect, malicious defamation, false accusation of theft, attempting to coerce a man into marriage, and drunkenness on duty. When he was put under arrest, Dudley shook his finger under Hatch's nose and told him, "I will make your Depot stink, and will make it red hot for some officers at this post before you get through with me."

At the ensuing court-martial, Dudley's defense was skillfully handled by Catron and his then partner, William T. Thornton. Although Dudley was found guilty and suspended from rank and command for three months, forfeiting half his pay, it has to be said he got off very lightly indeed. So lightly that it is easy to believe, as he often boasted, that he had friends in high places. Hatch was bitterly disappointed by the verdict, the more so when the president of the United States, acting on the recommendation of Gen. W. T. Sherman and Brig. Gen. W. McK. Dunn, judge advocate general, remitted the unexecuted portion of the sentence.

Restored to duty, Dudley (fig. 66) assumed command of Fort Stanton on April 5, 1878. More trials still awaited him. He became a full colonel of the First Cavalry in June 1885 and retired from the army on August 20, 1889. Dudley died, bearing the rank of brigadier general, at Roxbury, Mass., on April 29, 1910.

Sources:

Rasch, "A Note," "Trials," and "Fort Stanton."

EALY, TAYLOR FILMORE

Taylor Filmore Ealy, the son of physician John C. Ealy and his wife Anna (Clark), was born September 12, 1848, in Schellsburg, Pa., about 75 miles southeast of Pittsburgh. There were in all seven children: Taylor had two brothers, John and Albert, and four sisters, Mary, Cornelia, Ida, and Anna. A graduate of Washington and Jefferson College, he studied at the Western Theological Seminary in Allegheny, Pa., until 1872, then enrolled in the medical department of the University of Pennsylvania at Philadelphia, graduating in 1874 as a doctor of medicine. On October 1, 1874, he married Mary E. Ramsey at the bride's East Waterford, Pa., home, and immediately thereafter took up an appointment as a teacher in a government school for black children at Fort Arbuckle, I.T., and remained there until late 1876, when responsibility for such schools was allocated to the Baptist Church. Ealy, his wife, and their daughter Anna, born in 1875, returned to Pennsylvania where a second daughter, Ruth, was born in October 1877. The following month, Ealy was offered the opportunity of establishing a new mission and school in Lincoln, N.M.. He accepted and on January 28, 1878, set out for the West with his family and Susan Gates, a young Schellsburg lady recruited as an assistant. After his sojourn in Lincoln, he spent some years as a missionary in Zuni, N.M. He died in his home town of Schellsburg on February 19, 1915.

Sources:

Ealy, *Water*; Bender, *Missionaries*; Ealy, "Medical Missionary."

ELKINS, STEPHEN BENTON

Lawyer, financier, member of Congress, and secretary of war in the Harrison cabinet, Stephen Benton Elkins was born in Perry County, Ohio, on September 26, 1841, the son of a farmer. Soon after his birth the family moved to Missouri, and Elkins was educated in the university of that state, graduating in 1860 in the same class as Thomas Benton Catron. In 1863 he was admitted to the bar and is said to have served in the Union Army, but by 1864 he had located in La Mesilla, N.M., and served in the territorial legislature that year and the next. In 1866 he married Sallie Davis, a Missouri woman; there were two daughters of that marriage.

In 1868 Elkins became first district attorney and then territorial attorney general, in 1869 president of the First National Bank of Santa Fe, U.S. district attorney in 1870 and 1872, and New Mexico's delegate to Congress from 1873 to 1877. During this time, Elkins became a specialist in land grants and made a great deal of money in acquiring and disposing of them. By 1877 he was a very wealthy man; in that year, Elkins moved to West Virginia. His first wife having died, he married Hallie Davis, daughter of the U.S. senator from that State, Henry Gassaway Davis. He managed the presidential campaign of Benjamin Harrison (it is said he was seriously considered as a candidate instead of Harrison but refused to be nominated) and served as secretary of war from 1891 to 1893. He served as senator from West Virginia from 1895 to his death.

It is said that throughout his later life, Elkins's children had no knowledge of their father's earlier life in Missouri and New Mexico and did not learn until after his death that he had been married and had children there. His second wife is said to have sued to prevent Elkins's daughters from coming into any inheritance, and it is also alleged that her father had West Virginia law rewritten to ensure the success of her suit. The most fascinating story I have heard about this family is that Hallie Davis Elkins became very friendly with Susan McSween Barber and that, in the summer of 1892, in the ballroom of the Elkins summer home in Deer Park, Md., Susan danced with another close friend of the family—Lew Wallace. A warts-and-all biography of this remarkable man, who died January 4, 1911, is decades overdue; perhaps one day his family will permit someone to write it.

Sources:

Twitchell, *Leading Facts*, pp.401-02; Matthew Richardson, personal communication, 1986.

EVANS, JESSIE J.

Jessie J. Evans (fig. 33) has been the subject of two biographies, both some way short of definitive. By his own account, Jessie was born in Missouri in 1853; Frank Coe intimates that he was half-Cherokee. Another writer suggests he was a graduate of Washington and Lee College, Va. The *Topeka Daily Commonwealth* of June 26, 1871, reported that a John J. Allen and the Evans family (consisting of father, mother, and son Jesse) were arrested with others for passing counterfeit notes at Elk City, Kans. Jesse, age eighteen, was fined five hundred dollars at the U.S. District Court in Topeka. There is no confirmation that this is the New Mexico Jessie Evans, who appears to have come to Lincoln County from Williamson County, Tex. Lily Klasner has him and Jim McDaniels working for the Jinglebob in the summer of 1873; Evans later testified Chisum employed him to steal horses from the Mescaleros.

Subsequent to the Lincoln troubles, Evans decamped for Arizona; he and Billy Campbell were reported to be at John Slaughter's cattle camp on the Pecos River in May 1879 and, a month later, at La Cienega, near Tucson. On May 19, 1880, he was a member of a gang that robbed a store at Fort Davis; the Texas Rangers were sent for, and on July 3, in a running fight in which George Davis and Ranger George Bingham were killed, Evans was captured. Indicted in October, Evans entered Huntsville Penitentiary December 1, 1880. In May 1882, while on a work detail, Evans escaped from custody and vanished. His first biographer avers that when Evans entered the Huntsville prison in 1880 as prisoner 9078, he volunteered the information that he was born in Missouri in 1853, that he was 5 feet 7 3/4 inches tall, with a fair complexion, gray eyes, and light hair. He had two large scars on his left thigh and a bullet scar above and below his left elbow. In view of the fact that the Lincoln County Jessie Evans is supposed to have had a wrist so badly shattered that he lost the use of it, this seems if anything to cast doubt on the assertion that the Huntsville Evans was the same man, but the rest of the evidence putting him there seems reliable enough.

Many theories about his later life have been advanced, but none substantiated. Emerson Hough's is particularly attractive. In 1959 I asked William V. Morrison, coauthor of *Alias Billy the Kid* (the story of Brushy Bill Roberts, not to be confused with the Cline biography), what documentation he had for the details of Jessie Evans's life after his imprisonment contained in that book. Morrison replied that he "received the Jesse Evans information from his nephew and do[es] not have permission to release it at this time." To my knowledge he never did.

It is said that George Davis, alias Tom Jones, was actually named Dolly Graham and was either Jessie's cousin or brother. In view of Jessie's early association with Pony Diehl, or Deal, who later joined up with Curly Bill Brocius in Tombstone, Ariz., it is tempting to hypothesize a family connection between Jessie, Dolly Graham, and Brocius, whose real name was William Graham and who is said to have been born in Missouri. Pony Diehl, whose real name was Charles Ray, was killed in a gunfight at Clifton, Ariz., in 1882.

Sources:

Bartholomew, *Jesse Evans*; a later biography, McCright and Powell, *Jessie Evans*, adds little to the story. See also Haley, "Interview with Frank Coe," March 20, 1927; Coolidge, *Fighting Men*, 40; Hough, *Outlaw*, 276–77; Klasner, *Girlhood*, 155–57; Mullin, *Chronology*; Rasch, "George Davis"; Rasch, "Jessie J. Evans"; Rasch, "They Fought," 41–44. The death of Pony Deal is in Lake, *Wyatt Earp*, 358.

FOUNTAIN, ALBERT JENNINGS

Albert Jennings Fountain (fig. 34), who was of French Huguenot descent, was (or was he?) born on Staten Island, N.Y., on October 23, 1838. Wherever he was born, he was, in the truest sense of the word, an adventurer; his exploits in Canton and Calcutta, the Nile and Nicaragua, are worthy of, and have been given, a book of their own. Shortly after being admitted to the bar in San Francisco, he was commissioned a lieutenant in the First California Volunteer Infantry. En route to New Mexico with Carleton's Column, he and his command, 110 strong, ran head-on into Cochise and about 1,200 Chiricahuas at Apache Pass, defeating them in a two-day battle. Mustered out in 1864, Fountain was commissioned a captain of volunteer cavalry; later he was appointed custom-house officer at El Paso. He served as a colonel in Benito Juarez's army in Mexico but after the taking of Chihuahua returned to Texas, where in 1868 he was elected to the state senate, eventually becoming its president.

In 1875 he returned to New Mexico and served for a while as district attorney of the Third Judicial District. In 1877 he became copublisher (with John S. Crouch and Thomas Casad) and editor of the *Mesilla Valley Independent*. He was married on October 27, 1862, to Mariana Perez de Ovante, daughter of a prominent Mexican family. They had twelve children. Colonel Fountain quit the editorship of the *Independent* shortly before its demise in the summer of 1879 and went on to figure largely in the history of the Mesilla Valley area. He and his youngest son, Henry, disappeared somewhere between Tularosa and Las Cruces on April 1, 1896. The circumstances of their deaths remain a mystery still, nearly a century later.

Sources:

Smith, "Death in Doña Ana County," parts I and II; Gibson, *Fountain*.

FRANCIS, ALLEN

Allen Francis and his Scottish-born wife had been in Victoria, B.C., Canada, since 1862; he was the town's first American consul. A former newspaperman, Francis hailed from Springfield, Ill. It was at the home of his father, Simeon Francis, that Abraham Lincoln renewed with Mary Todd the friendship that was to lead to their marriage. After Lincoln's assassination, Francis was removed as consul and became a trader in Alaska.

When Tunstall went to live at the Francis home, which was on Pandora Ave., just east of the Metropolitan United Church of today, Allen Francis was still "up North" as a trader. The Francises had six children. In 1876, Allen Bunn Francis, the eldest son, engaged in the fur trade on an island in the Bering Sea; he died in 1886 aged thirty-nine. Another son, Edwin, became deputy collector for the port of Sitka. There were four daughters: one referred to only as Mrs. Hofencamp; Hulda, who had married Byron Z. Holmes of Portland, Ore., in 1871 and gone to live there; and Eliza, the youngest girl, who married William Thomas Gillihan of Portland on November 10 of the same year, and also went to live in that city. She had a daughter, Alice, known to the family as "Allie." In 1878 Francis wrote the Tunstall family that Eliza had tuberculosis and was not expected to live. Allen Francis was killed in a street accident in St. Thomas, Ont., Canada, in 1887; his wife, who had remained in Victoria, died there in 1894 (fig. 5).

Source:

Victoria Daily Colonist, July 23, 1950. Courtesy Provincial Archives, Victoria, B.C., Canada.

FRENCH, JIM

Jim French, not to be confused with Lieutenant James Hansell French who also figured in some of these events, is something of a mystery man: even that redoubtable researcher Philip Rasch was unable to come up with any leads on French's origins; Frank Coe claimed he was half-Cherokee. Variously referred to as "Big Jim" and "Frenchy," he has been labeled by Lincoln tradition as one of Mrs. McSween's lovers; on the available evidence, it seems unlikely. A report filed by Col. G. A. Purington on June 21, 1879, stated that French had been killed in a quarrel over stolen cattle. Since French wrote to Sam Corbet giving his address as Keota, I.T., late in 1878, this would appear to be unlikely. A Jim French was killed during the robbery of a store in Catoosa, Okla., in 1895; although the town is (relatively) near Keota, no connection between this man and the Lincoln County Jim French has yet been made. In 1927, Frank Coe said he had been shot "about three years ago in Oklahoma." Yet another source suggests French went to South America.

Sources:

Haley, "Interview with Frank Coe," March 20, 1927; Utley, *High Noon*, 166; Rasch, "Gunfire", 6; Rasch, "Regulators," 60–61.

FRENCH, JAMES HANSELL

James Hansell French was born in Philadelphia on March 14, 1851, and graduated from West Point in June 1874. He served with the Ninth Cavalry in Texas and Colorado until August 31, 1876, when he resigned because of ill health. Reappointed two years later, he was assigned to Fort Union. He was transferred to Fort Stanton in November 1878. French was killed on January 17, 1880, while serving with a force commanded by Maj. Albert P. Morrow, Ninth Cavalry, in pursuit of the Apache leader Victorio in the San Mateo Mountains.

Sources:

Rasch, "Fort Stanton," 4; *Record of Engagements*, 93.

FRITZ, EMIL CHRISTIAN ADOLF

The second son of Philipp Jakob Friedrich and Caroline (Bofinger) Fritz, Emil Christian Adolf Fritz was born at Eglosheim, near Stuttgart, Germany, on March 3, 1832. Philipp Fritz and Caroline Bofinger were married at Reutlingen, January 25, 1830; at the time of his son's birth Fritz was the steward of a large estate called Monrepos. The first child was Carl Philipp Friedrich, born January 19, 1831, followed by Emil; Christine Mathilde, born July 7, 1833; Marie Luise Amalie, born November 25, 1834; Heinrich Wilhelm Friedrich, born March 19, 1836; Gustav Adolf, born August 23, 1837; Paul Wilhelm Dagobert, born January 23, 1840. After the death of baby Gustav in 1840, Fritz left Monrepos and took over the Lauterbacher Hof at Oedheim, near Heilbron. Three more children were born there: Sophie Caroline Auguste, born April 4, 1841; Ida Johana Elisabeth, born May 8, 1842; and Luise Marie Emilie, born February 20, 1847. Fritz's wife Caroline died October 24, 1854, and he married a thirty-four-year-old widow, Johana Friederike Lechler, née Spittler, on May 8, 1856. There were no children of this marriage.

Emil Fritz (fig. 7) was the first of three Fritz children who immigrated to the United States, probably in the California Gold Rush. He enlisted in the U.S. First Dragoons in 1851 and saw service in the West. He was discharged with the rank of sergeant at Ft. Tejon, Calif., on January 1, 1861. After a spell working in the mines, Fritz was commissioned as captain, Company B, First California Cavalry at Camp Merchant, Calif., on August 16, 1861, and came to New Mexico with Carleton's Column. It was he who led the first Union troops into Tucson on May 20, 1862, seven days after its evacuation by Confederate forces. When his company's term of service expired on August 1, 1864, it was reorganized at Fort Sumner, N.M., where Fritz re-enlisted. He served both there and at Fort Stanton as commanding officer, and was brevetted lieutenant colonel June 7, 1865. It is said he refused a commission in the regular army to go into business with Murphy who, like Fritz, remained a lifelong bachelor. Fritz was staying at his father's home at Jägerstrasse 12, Stuttgart, when his final illness—a combination of heart and kidney disease— overtook him. He died in the Stuttgart Hospital-Church at two o'clock in the afternoon of June 26, 1874, aged forty-two years, three months, and twenty three days, and was buried at five o'clock on June 28. The elder Fritz died soon after his son, April 10, 1876.

FRITZ, CARL PHILLIP FRIEDRICH

Carl Phillip Friedrich "Charlie" Fritz, the oldest son, married Catherine Knebling (b. 1831 in Hamburg, Germany) on May 5, 1856, at Montrose, Pa. Their children were Louise Sophie, born July 28, 1857; Emil Wilhelm, born April 30, 1859; Caroline Franzis, born February 22, 1861; Clara Anna, born January 19, 1863; Henri Frederick, born May 4, 1865; Charles Philip, born June 2, 1867; Willi, born November 3, 1871; and Matilde Louise, born September 22, 1872. With two nubile daughters, Fritz (fig. 27), who came to New Mexico in 1872 at his brother's behest, found his home a favored rendezvous for the blades of Lincoln County. In October 1874, Lt. John W. Wilkinson was married to Fritz's eldest daughter, Louise. Charlie Fritz died at Lincoln on December 2, 1885; some of his grandchildren still live in the area.

FRITZ, LUISE MARIE EMILIE

The youngest sister, Luise Marie Emilie Fritz was married in New York on December 30, 1871, to William Scholand. Since she was scarcely fifteen and it would appear that she was already pregnant, this would doubtless account for her brother's hostility toward her husband after their arrival in Lincoln County in 1872. The couple divorced on April 18, 1876, and Emilie (fig. 26) was awarded custody of the two children, Emilie, age four, and Anna, age two and a half. In 1880 she married a man twenty-five years her senior, David Abraham of Clifton, Ariz.; they moved to Silver City, N.M., in 1883, where they bought and operated the Southern Hotel. In 1885 the household consisted of David Abraham, sixty-two, landlord; Amelia [sic], thirty-seven; Mamie, twelve; and seven boarders. Abraham died in 1894; ten years later Emilie married for the third time. Her husband was a mining man named William McAllister, but he died two years later. Emilie then went to live with her "niece," Mrs. Emil Fritz, of Roswell; between 1915 and 1920 the family moved to Glendale, Calif., where Emilie Fritz Scholand Abraham McAllister died on Sunday, September 7, 1930. Her body was shipped to Silver City for burial in the Masonic Cemetery there alongside the grave of her [step?]daughter Mamie.

Sources:

Genealogical research (USA) Nora Henn, Lincoln, N.M., and Lewis A. Ketring, Los Angeles; (Germany) Friedrich Rupp, Stuttgart. See also Rasch, "Murphy," 64.

GAUSS, GOTTFRIED GEORG

Murphy, McSween, and Godfroy were not alone in having opted out of ecclesiastical life: Gottfried G. Gauss, too, was a failed clergyman (fig. 29). Born in Baden, Württemberg, in 1823 or 1825, he emigrated to America and joined the U.S. Army at Pittsburgh on February 3, 1851. When assigned to Colonel Chandler's Company I, Third Regiment, U.S. Infantry, he was described as being five feet six inches tall, with ruddy complexion, blue eyes, and sandy hair. Army life obviously did not suit him: he deserted on August 22 but was apprehended twelve days later. He served out his five years and was discharged with the rank of private at Fort Craig, N.M. Gauss re-enlisted for thirty dollars' bounty at Albuquerque on March 1, 1856, and did another five years in Maj. O. L. Shepherd's Company B, Third Infantry. Appointed hospital steward March 26, 1857, he was discharged March 1, 1861, at Fort Defiance.

"Persuaded by Colonel [E. S.] Canby to help to subdue the rebellion" (his own words) Gauss enlisted for three years or the duration in the Third Regular New Mexico Mounted Infantry. He served as a hospital steward at Fort Craig until the cessation of hostilities in 1862 and was discharged at Albuquerque with eyesight so poor he "could not recognize an acquaintance ten yards distant," which would seem to dilute somewhat the strength of his later "eyewitness" account of the Kid's escape.

He lived for some years at La Junta in San Miguel County, then came to Lincoln County, where he worked for L. G. Murphy & Co. for about eighteen months. "They cheated me out of what was justly due me; but as I could not help myself I had to take what they gave me," he said. Later he added that he had rented Murphy's brewery and commenced brewing; after two months, when he had four hundred gallons of beer ready, Dolan and Mathews strong-armed him into selling them the beer at 40¢ a gallon, then cut the $160 they owed him to "about $28." This may have been as early as 1869: Kautz writes of a fellow immigrant from Baden who brewed beer locally.

Gauss, who never married, found odd jobs around Lincoln and White Oaks and remained in New Mexico into the mid-1890s, a minor celebrity because of his association with Billy the Kid. He drifted back east and died about March 1902, possibly in Kansas.

Sources:

Deposition of G. Gauss, Angel Report; Military and pension records, NARA; Wallace, "Military Memoir," 243; Fulton-Nolan Correspondence.

GODFROY, FREDERICK CHARLES

Born on the family farm on the north side of the Raisin River on May 15, 1827, Frederick Charles Godfroy was the third of eleven children born to James Jacques "Jock" and Victoria (Navarre) Godfroy of Monroe, Mich., a town later best known for its favorite son, George Armstrong Custer. "Jock" Godfroy, born in Detroit in 1802 of French parents, studied law as a young man but abandoned the profession because of ill health.

Fluent in French, English, and the Indian languages, he formed a partnership with his brother Peter under the style of P & J. J. Godfroy; as well as trading with the Indians, they had a retail establishment on Front and Macomb Streets. When the Indians were removed west of the Mississippi, Godfroy was employed by the government to supervise the operation. A strong advocate of temperance, J. J. Godfroy married Victoria, daughter of Col. Francis and Mary (Suzor) Navarre on September 30, 1823. The Navarres and Godfroys were among the earliest settlers of Frenchtown Township, which later became Monroe. In order of birth their children were John Louis, known as "Columbus", born 1824; Celestine Ann, born 1826; Frederick Charles; Theodore S., born 1829; Alexandrine, born 1830; Hilary, born 1831; Philip Washington, born 1832; Gustave Fernandez, born 1836; Stanislas, born 1838; Victoria Regina, born 1839; and Empress Mary Teresa, born 1841.

Frederick Godfroy (fig. 47), who was intended by his father for the Catholic priesthood, attended parochial school in Monroe and partially completed a course of studies at the University of Michigan at Ann Arbor. The death of his father on May 20, 1847, enabled him to avoid going into the church; preferring business, he instead worked for many years as a clerk in the dry goods store of Charles G. Johnson and also in the Wing & Johnson banking office in Monroe; later he worked at Hillsdale in the Mitchell & Waldron bank. He was married to the daughter of Richard Phillips, of Brest.

It is said that all the "best" people of Monroe were Presbyterians; it might be inferred from McSween's later reference to Godfroy as a "Presbyterian fraud" that it was through connections in his home town that Godfroy obtained his appointment as Mescalero Indian agent, which was announced in the *Santa Fe New Mexican* on April 4, 1876. Opinion seems sharply divided concerning his loyalties during the troubles that followed.

It would appear Godfroy returned east at the time of his mother's death in September 1879. He died of heart disease at the home of his daughter and son-in-law, Kate and Daniel Appel, in Plattsburgh Barracks, N.Y. (almost directly across Lake Champlain from St. Albans, Vt.) on May 15, 1885. His obituary unaccountably gives his name as Fred C. C. Godfroy; the body was taken to Buffalo, N.Y., for interment. His life and career would appear to be a suitable case for much more careful examination.

Sources:

Research by Christine Lynn Kull, archivist, Monroe County Historical Commission, Monroe, Mich.; Richard W. Ward, Plattsburgh, N.Y.

GOODWIN, MILLARD FILLMORE

Millard Fillmore Goodwin was born in New York state on May 25, 1852. He graduated from West Point June 14, 1872, and had seen extensive service in Texas before being posted to Fort Stanton. He played a very active role in Lincoln County events and made no attempt to conceal his antipathy for the McSween faction. Writing much later to Governor Wallace, Billy the Kid advised the governor to "tell the Commanding Officer to Watch Let. Goodwind he would not hesitate to do anything." Later in his career Goodwin served at Fort Bayard and took part in expeditions against the Apaches (fig. 46). He contracted tuberculosis and went on sick leave in August 1882. He died in Yonkers, N.Y., exactly ten years from the day he had served as Dudley's adjutant during the climax of the troubles in Lincoln: July 19, 1888.

Source:

Rasch, "Fort Stanton," 4.

GREATHOUSE, JAMES

Sometimes called "Whiskey Jim," but also known as "Arkansas Jack," which at least indicates where he came from, James Greathouse was part of the cattle-fencing ring that bought from the likes of the Boys, the Rustlers, and later Bonney, and which numbered John Kinney at Las Cruces and Pat Coghlan at Tularosa among its members. He is described as "a large man with a heartless, staring countenance." He was killed by a Socorro badman named Harry A. (Joel) Fowler in 1881.

Sources:

Mullin and Hutchison, *Whiskey Jim*; Cline, "A Cold Night For Angels."

GRZELACHOWSKI, ALEXANDER

Polish-born Alexander Grzelachowski, "Padre Polaco" to the New Mexico Volunteers of the Civil War, was yet another former clergyman; he came to the United States around 1849. Born at Gracina, Poland, in 1824, at the age of twenty-six he was the first resident pastor at French Creek, Avon County, near Cleveland, Ohio. He came to New Mexico at the invitation of Archbishop Lamy. Grzelachowski began his commercial enterprises in Las Vegas and moved to Puerto de Luna in 1874. His lawsuits against John Chisum were among the principal reasons for that worthy's enmity towards and comments about the Pole. Business troubles and poor health hastened Grzelachowski's death on May 24, 1896. The ruins of the store where Billy the Kid ate his last Christmas dinner can still be seen at Puerto de Luna.

Sources:

Klasner, *Girlhood*, 279–80; Hinton, "Chisum"; Kajencki, "Grzelachowski."

HAYS, JOHN COFFEE

Tunstall had first met John Coffee Hays (fig. 19) in 1872, on his arrival at San Francisco en route to Victoria. Hays was born January 28, 1817, at Cedar Lick, Wilson County, Tenn., the same county that Andrew Jackson and Sam Houston came from; there is a family tradition that his grandfather sold Houston the latter's Hermitage estate. The son of Harmon and Elizabeth (Cage) Hays, "Jack," as he was universally known, commenced surveying as a career when he was fifteen, went to Texas during the revolution against Mexico, and, after San Jacinto, served four years on the frontier under Henry W. Karnes and Erastus "Deef" Smith. The enlargement of the Texas Rangers in 1840 led to his appointment at the age of twenty-three as captain of rangers, commanding the San Antonio station, in which role he is credited as having introduced the hostile Comanches along the Pedernales River to the products of Samuel Colt.

In 1847, Hays married Susan Calvert of Alabama; they had six children, of whom only two lived to maturity. Hays served as a colonel of Texas Volunteer Cavalry during the Mexican War and subsequently led an expedition to discover a trade route from San Antonio to Chihuahua. Joining the overland rush to California in 1849, he was elected sheriff of San Francisco the following year, serving in that office until 1853, when he was appointed surveyor general of California. On the expiration of his appointment he retired from public life, devoting himself to private business interests. He died at his home, Fernwood, Piedmont, Alameda County, Calif., on April 23, 1883.

Source:

Greer, *Hays*, is the definitive biography.

HINDMAN, GEORGE

George Hindman (the name may have originally been Heinemann) came from Texas in 1875 with a herd owned by a man named Jordan bound for Arizona. He decided to quit and go to work for Robert Casey on the Feliz, which angered the co-owner of the herd, Bill Humphreys, so much that a gunfight ensued, in which Humphreys got a scalp wound and Hindman's pistol was shot to pieces, some of the bits embedding themselves in his hand. He later worked a farm rented from Casey with Sam Bass. There, according to Lily Klasner, Hindman, "a good, quiet, and inoffensive person," was attacked by a grizzly bear that tore off half his face and crippled his hand and arm. Frank Coe confirms that "Hindman was a crippled man, as a bear up in the mountains had chawed him up, tearing his hands and legs." He also hinted there was a grudge between Hindman and Frank MacNab that harked back to Texas, perhaps the trouble cited above, and that it was MacNab who killed the deputy on the street—not on the steps of San Juan Church, which had not yet been built—on All Fool's Day, 1878.

Sources:

Klasner, *Girlhood*, 153–54, 176–77; Haley, "Interview with Frank Coe," March 20 and August 14, 1927.

HOLLISTER, WILLIAM WELLS

Eighth-generation American William Wells Hollister was born in Licking County, Ohio, on January 12, 1818, the second son and fifth child of John and Philena (Hubbard) Hollister. He attended Kenyon College until an affliction of the eyes forced him to abandon his studies and turn to managing his recently deceased father's thousand-acre farm. In 1852 he crossed the plains to California driving two hundred head of cattle. Together with his brother Joseph Hubbard Hollister, he organized a much larger expedition, consisting of fifty men, nine thousand sheep, two hundred cattle, and some horses. They set out on May 1, 1853, and arrived in California fifteen months later.

In 1861, in conjunction with Joseph Wright Cooper, Thomas Bloodgood, and Albert Dibblee, Hollister bought the great Lompoc and Viaja de Puissance ranchos for sixty thousand dollars. These they later subdivided into farms. Later Hollister joined forces with Flint and Bixby to buy land in Monterey County, the San Justo ranch, where he raised sheep until 1869. On selling out his interests in that year, Hollister moved south to Santa Barbara County, where he and his brother, together with Thomas and Albert Dibblee, bought the Estrada and San Julian rancho from Gasper Orrna. This they later divided, the Dibblees keeping the historic San Julian rancho that had belonged to Jose de la Guerra, one-time comandante of the presidio of Santa Barbara. Hollister retained the Estrada and later added to it the historic Ortega rancho near Garrota: at one time he had an aggregate of some one hundred fifty thousand acres and was the largest wool grower in California.

Hollister (fig. 21) played a very prominent part in the development of Santa Barbara County. It was estimated that he expended nearly half a million dollars in and around the city. In partnership with Thomas Bloodgood Dibblee he owned the hundred-thousand-acre San Julian rancho, which encompassed the former San Julian, Salsipuedes, Espada, Santa Anita, Gaviota, and Las Cruces ranchos; the Gaviota wharf was part of the property, and much of the produce of the Santa Ynez valley was shipped from this point.

Hollister's home, the 2,750-acre Glen Annie ranch, twelve miles west of Santa Barbara, was named for his wife, the former Annie James, daughter of Samuel and Jane James of San Francisco, whom he had married on June 18, 1862. There were six children. Hollister died on August 8, 1886.

Sources:

Hunt, *California and Californians*; Guinn, *History*; research by W. Edwin Gledhill, Santa Barbara Historical Society, and Allan R. Otley, California Section Librarian, California State Library, Sacramento, 1959.

HORRELL, SAMUEL M., JAMES MARTIN, THOMAS L., BENJAMIN F., AND MERRITT

These brothers, the sons of Samuel and Elizabeth (Wells) Horrell, were born in Arkansas. There were eight children in all: William C., born ca. 1839; John W., 1841; Samuel L., 1843; James Martin, three years later; Thomas L., 1850; Benjamin F[ranklin?], 1851; Merritt, 1854; and Sarah Ann, 1857. Old Sam Horrell, born in Kentucky, was the son of Benedict Horrell, a native of Virginia who had settled at Fenton, Hot Springs County. He married sixteen-year-old Arkansas-born Elizabeth Wells around 1837; their sons William, John, Sam, and perhaps James (always known as Mart) were born at Fenton. By 1850, the clan had moved to Caddo Township, Montgomery County, where Tom, Ben, Merritt, and Sarah were born.

Around 1857, the Horrells again moved west and settled on a farm purchased from Mose Jackson about ten miles northeast of Lampasas, Tex. Benedict Horrell, close to seventy at the time of the Civil War, lived adjacent to old Sam with Sam's brother John and sisters Mary, Nancy, and Louisa. Sam's oldest son, William, is thought to have died in the war. He and the next two oldest boys, John and Sam, Jr., served in the Texas State Guards.

In 1868, perhaps following the death of Benedict Horrell, the family sold up its holdings, and driving a herd of about a thousand head, set off for California. They got as far as Las Cruces, N.M., where they sold the herd, and where John Horrell was killed by a man named Early Hubbard in a quarrel over wages. Soon after this, in mid-January 1869, old Sam was killed by Apaches in the San Agustin pass.

The family returned to Texas in the spring of 1869 and settled in the Little Lucies Creek area northeast of Lampasas. By the following year, all but one of the boys—Merritt, who lived with his brother Mart—were family men; even seventeen-year-old Ben had a wife and a baby son. The wives of John, Mart, and Ben Horrell were sisters named, respectively, Sarah, Artemisa, and Martha Grizzell. Of the brothers, only Tom—whose wife Mattie Ann Ausment was an orphan girl the family brought back to Texas from New Mexico—was childless.

In 1873 Merritt Horrell and some others of the clan became embroiled in a fracas with the Texas state police, in which Capt. Tom Williams and four officers were killed; Mart was jailed, along with Allen Whitecraft, James Grizzell, and Jerry Scott. A gang led by Bill Bowen broke open the jail and released them, whereupon they "took to the breaks" for some months before gathering up their stock and a group of relatives and friends with whom they headed for New Mexico in September 1873.

On their return to Texas early in 1874, the Horrells again collided with the law. After several running fights, they settled their difficulties and returned to stock raising. By the beginning of 1877, accusations of rustling were being leveled at them by another local rancher, John Calhoun Pinckney "Pink" Higgins. These came to a head when Merritt Horrell was killed by Higgins in January 1877; the famous Horrell-Higgins feud ensued. It was quelled temporarily by the Texas Rangers in March, blazed up again in June, and ended by "treaty" in July. Accused of the murder of storekeeper J. T. Vaughan, Mart and Tom Horrell were jailed in Meridian, Tex., in September 1878. While still awaiting trial, they were shot to death by a lynch mob on December 15, 1878.

Sam Horrell, the only one of the brothers who had managed to stay out of the troubles, left Texas and lived a long and productive life. He had six children, William, Elmira, Sarah Ann, John Samuel, Merritt, and Benjamin. He died August 8, 1936, and is buried in Eureka, Calif.

All the Horrell widows remarried. In the 1880 Lampasas census, Elizabeth Horrell, sixty-five, appears as the head of a household that included one daughter-in-law, Martha, four grandchildren, and two nephews.

Sources:

Sonnichsen, *I'll Die*; Rasch, "Horrell War"; Haley, "Interview with John Nichols"; U.S. Census, Lampasas County, 1870, 1880; research by James D. Lyman, Dallas; Jeffrey Jackson, Lampasas; Jerry Weddle, Catalina, Ariz.; and Nora Henn, Lincoln, N.M.

HURLEY, JOHN

John Hurley, a New Yorker, was twenty-three at the time of the Lincoln County events. Emerson Hough said he was as brave as a lion and "a very pleasant fellow." At the Dudley Court of Inquiry, he stated that he was a laborer living in Lincoln. He married Ham Mills's daughter Juanita after the death of her first husband, operated a saloon near Fort Stanton and was later manager of DeLany's billiard hall there (fig. 57). Occasionally he served as a deputy sheriff; while serving under Sheriff John Poe in January 1886, he was shot and killed at Chaperito by an escaped rustler named Nicolas Aragon.

Sources:

Hough, *Outlaw*, 279; Rasch, "They Fought," 45–46.

JOHNSON, WILLIAM HARRISON

William Harrison Johnson (or Johnston) claimed to be from Virginia, the son of Dr. William Johnson, graduate of one of the finest medical schools in America. Dr. Johnson moved to Marion, Ohio. His son, William Harrison, enlisted there in the U.S. Army and eventually was discharged in East Texas, where he worked as a cowboy and nursed his friend Wallace Olinger through smallpox. Driving a herd up to New Mexico, Johnson was wounded by Comanches and brought to the Beckwith home. In spite of Hugh Beckwith's opposition, Johnson and Camelia Beckwith were married by the Rev. George G. Smith at Santa Fe's First Presbyterian Church on Christmas Day, 1875. On April 25, 1877, their son William Edward was born. How much of Johnson's account of his life may have been true it is impossible to say. Susan McSween told Fulton that the family later learned Johnson was an outlaw with a wife and several children in Oklahoma or Texas.

Sources:

Barber-Fulton Letters, March 10, 1928; Ball, *Ma'am Jones*; Rasch and Myers, "Tragedy."

JOSEPH, ANTONIO

Twitchell offers a biographical portrait of Antonio Joseph considerably at odds with Tunstall's. He gives Joseph's birthplace as Taos, N.M., on August 25, 1846, and says he was educated at private schools in Taos and Santa Fe, and later at Webster College, St. Louis. He married Elizabeth M. Foree of Clark County, Mo., on March 11, 1881. Joseph held several county offices, was a member of the territorial assembly, and served five times as delegate to the U.S. Congress. He died at his home, Ojo Caliente, on April 18, 1910.

Source:

Twitchell, *Leading Facts*.

KIMBERLY, MARTIN MORSE

Tunstall said Martin Morse Kimberly was born in New England; but he spent his boyhood on Long Island, New York. He came to California in 1851, suffering from a pulmonary complaint. He took up land on Santa Cruz Island in 1854 and after three years regained his health by means of self-administered treatment that included daily sun baths and salt rubs with a gunny sack. He began to farm hogs on the island but was ousted by the Barron and Forbes syndicate on what may have been fraudulent grounds. Kimberly moved to nearby San Nicolas Island, recently abandoned as a penal colony by the Mexican government, filed on 160 acres, and began the sheep venture so admired by Tunstall. He raised some fifteen thousand head of sheep, which provided him with a yearly income of ten thousand dollars, commuting between the island and the mainland on his schooner.

In January 1860 he met Jane Amelia Merritt in San Francisco, shortly after her arrival from the East. Born in New York City on February 13, 1839, Jane was the daughter of Phinias G. Merritt, editor and publisher of the first Republican newspaper in California, *The Republican.*

She and Martin Kimberly were married on Christmas Eve, 1865, and settled in Santa Barbara in a small house on State St. He lost heavily in the drought of 1867, and his sheep venture was wiped out by drought in 1869–70. So desperate did the animals become that before Kimberly abandoned his project, they had turned the island into a desert devoid of vegetation. Only about four thousand sheep remained when Kimberly sold his holdings to a San Francisco banker named Hamilton. With the proceeds of his sale, he purchased a store; later still he purchased a schooner and turned to otter and seal hunting in the northern Pacific for a livelihood. He was reputed to be the best shot in California.

Kimberly (fig. 17) died in 1878 when his ship was lost with all hands in a typhoon off the shores of Japan. His widow and four children—Martin, Morse, Guilford, and Jane, known as Jenny, the last-named born in 1874—remained in Santa Barbara for many years.

Source:

Yule, "Pioneer Mother and Daughter"; research by Allan R. Otley, California State Library, Sacramento, 1959.

KIMBRELL, GEORGE

George Kimbrell—he often signed himself Kimball, but his family said this was the correct spelling—was born in Huntsville, Ark., on March 31, 1842. At age nineteen he came west in the Pike's Peak gold rush of 1859. He got sick while working in Colorado and came to New Mexico the following year. After a short stay at Las Vegas he moved south to Lincoln County in 1863, working there awhile as a government scout. The following year he squatted on Chaves Flats, about twelve miles east of Lincoln. That same year he married Paulita Romero, whose family had come to the area from Manzano. There were four children, a daughter and three sons: John, Boney, and William. As an Anglo married to a Hispanic, Kimbrell was the natural prey of the Horrells, but for some reason they spared his life in 1874 while killing the five Hispanics Kimbrell was traveling with. After a year as sheriff of Lincoln County, Kimbrell was defeated in the next election by Pat Garrett. He served as justice of the peace in his precinct for many years and died at his home in Picacho on March 24, 1925, six days short of his eighty-second birthday.

Sources:

Klasner, *Girlhood; Carrizozo News,* March 28, 1925; Crawford, "Interview with William E. Kimbrell."

KINNEY, JOHN

John Kinney is said to have been born in Hampshire, Mass., in 1847 or 1848; the family migrated west, perhaps to Iowa. He enlisted in the U.S. Cavalry in Chicago on April 13, 1867, giving his occupation as "laborer," and served in Company E, Third Cavalry. He was described as 5 feet 5½ inches tall, with hazel eyes, brown hair, and a ruddy complexion. By his own unreliable account, he was mustered out on April 13, 1873, with the rank of sergeant, at Fort McPherson, Neb. Shortly thereafter he set up in business as a cattleman near Las Cruces; within a few years he was the undisputed kingpin of a substantial rustling operation. After his involvement in the San Elizario troubles, Kinney briefly ran the Exchange Saloon in El Paso, but when the pickings in Lincoln County looked choicer, he quit Texas. After the Lincoln troubles were over, Kinney returned to Las Cruces and the lucrative rustling business. So successful were his activities that they prompted yet another "war," this time pitting Kinney against militia led by Albert Fountain. Kinney was arrested and brought to trial; on April 21, 1883, he was sentenced to five years in Leavenworth, but he served less than three. After a short spell in Texas, Kinney moved to Arizona (fig. 38). On August 25, 1919, he died at Prescott. His obituaries are pure fiction.

Sources:

Rasch, "Kinney"; Mullin, "Here Lies"; *Prescott Journal-Miner*, August 26, 1919; *Prescott Courier*, August 30, 1919.

LEA, JOSEPH C.

Although Joseph C. Lea figured importantly in ridding southeastern New Mexico of the lawless ones, he is largely ignored in books about the Lincoln County troubles; if nothing more, a biographical sketch is overdue. Lea was born in Cleveland, Tenn., on November 8, 1841. He rose to the rank of colonel in the Confederate Army but was known throughout his life as "Captain." After the war he worked his way slowly west, through Georgia, Louisiana, and Mississippi, where on February 3, 1875, he married Sally Wildy at Satartia, Yazoo County. The young couple moved west to Colfax County, N.M., in 1876. Shortly after their first son, Harry, was born there in April 1877, the Leas moved to Roswell. Captain Lea bought out the store/post office and hotel owned by Omaha gambler Van C. Smith and his partner Aaron Wilburn, which were located about a block west of the present-day courthouse. In 1878, Major Wildy, Sally Lea's father, bought from Marion Turner the homestead he had filed on under Van Smith's nose and deeded it to his daughter. These two purchases became the nucleus of what eventually would become vast land holdings in the Roswell area.

Captain Lea, the "Father of Roswell," arranged for his brother Alfred, a surveyor, to come down from Denver and plat the town in November 1885. In 1891 he was responsible for the establishment of what is now the New Mexico Military Institute at Roswell, which had become a county seat when Chaves County was formed from part of Lincoln County in 1889. Also in 1889 the widowed Lea was remarried, to Mabel Day of Coleman, Tex. He was elected the first mayor of Roswell in 1903 and died suddenly, from pneumonia, on February 4, 1904.

Sources:

Fleming and Huffman, eds., *Roundup*.

LEONARD, IRA E.

Ira E. Leonard was born in Connecticut in 1832 but grew up in Batavia, N.Y. He became a lawyer and joined a partnership in Watertown, Wis., in 1860 and ten years later headed west for Jefferson City, Mo., where he became a judge. In 1874 he relocated in Boulder, Colo., and in 1878 moved to Las Vegas, N.M. Like McSween he had come to New Mexico because he was asthmatic. Perhaps this had something to do with Mrs. McSween's selecting him as her attorney: she seems to have been attracted to lawyers with infirmities, and he to ladies with tarnished reputations. Lew Wallace liked Leonard enormously and appointed him his special assistant when he came to Lincoln in March. "You have no idea how pleasant it is to have one hearty assistant and sympathizer in my work," he wrote

Leonard. "To work hard trying to do a little good, but with all the world against you, requires the will of a martyr."

It was Leonard's ambition to become a judge in New Mexico, and specifically to replace the much-criticized Warren Bristol. In this campaign Wallace aided and abetted him, but Leonard was unsuccessful. In 1881, practicing in Lincoln, he excited some scandal in respect of a lady client, Ella Murphy, which led to a shotgun confrontation with Ike Ellis's son Ben. Leonard moved to Socorro and practiced law there for a while, but ill health necessitated his moving to California. While there he sought Wallace's assistance in obtaining an appointment to the New Mexico bench but was again unsuccessful. He was appointed postmaster at Socorro, where he died on July 6, 1889.

Sources:

Rasch, "Leonard"; Wilson, *Merchants.*

LEVERSON, MONTAGUE RICHARD

Montague Richard Leverson was born in London on March 2, 1830, the son of Montague and Elizabeth Levyson. He was obviously a firebrand in his younger days: he claimed acquaintance with Victor Hugo, the French author-agitator Louis Blanc, and others of similar radical fervor. His home was a headquarters for such revolutionaries as Giuseppe Mazzini (1805–72), Felice Orsini (1819–58), and Giuseppe Garibaldi (1807–82); Leverson claimed to have helped organize the latter's 1860 expedition to Sicily, although his name does not appear in any of the standard biographies.

A graduate of the University of London, he appears in London directories for the year 1852 as a patent agent in St. Helen's Gate, Bishopsgate, London. He remained there until 1859, when he entered a partnership under the style Montague Leverson & Hawley, Patent Agents, at the same address. The partnership appears to have been successful. In 1854, Leverson's first published work, *Copyrights and Patents, or property in thought,* was published in London. It appears to have been a proposal to secure copyright in ideas, and is said to have secured the approval of John Stuart Mill. In 1859, Luigi Pianciani fulsomely dedicated his three-volume work, *La Rome des papes,* to Leverson.

He is said to have arrived in the United States in 1865; it may have been earlier, if his boasts of Charles Francis Adams's praise for his (unspecified) "services to the Union" are valid. Against this may be set the fact that in 1866 his monograph, "The Reformers Reform Bill, being a proposed new and comprehensive code of electoral law for the United Kingdom," was published in London. He was certainly in the United States by 1869; on August 29 of that year, his letter advocating effective registration of voters appeared in the *New York Times.* He returned to Europe to obtain degrees at the University of Göttingen in 1872; the following year he was in business as a rancher at Larkspur, Douglas County, near Denver, Colo., and as a lawyer and lecturer in political economy at Golden. Throughout 1874 and 1875 his letters on election laws, public schools, and other topics appeared in the Denver *Rocky Mountain News*; he even found time to draft a new state constitution.

Although he says that he was invited to Lincoln by Juan Patrón, there is evidence that Leverson and John Chisum were business associates, for Leverson unsuccessfully attempted to put up bond for Chisum in January 1878, following Chisum's arrest in Las Vegas, N.M. In 1879 he moved to California, where he practiced law, served in the legislature in 1882, and became an advocate of the doctrines of economist Henry George. He returned east; in 1893 he graduated from the Baltimore Medical College, and in the same year his book, *Thoughts on Institutions of the Higher Education, with a chapter on classical studies,* was published in New York. Now resident in that city, Leverson became deeply interested in the medical research of Pierre Béchamp, and the work of the Anti-Vaccination League.

On May 25, 1911, under the auspices of the British Union for the Abolition of

Vivisection, he delivered a lecture entitled "Pasteur the Plagiarist: The Debt of Science to Béchamp" at Claridge's Hotel in London; the following year his translation of Béchamp's *The Blood and Its Third Anatomical Element* was published in that city. Although New York directories for 1912 show him living at 927 Grant Ave., it would seem likelier that he was in England, preparing a paper setting out the evidence of Pasteur's debt to Béchamp. It appears that he died before it was finished; it was completed by Ethel D. Hume, and published in London in 1923 as *Béchamp or Pasteur*, "founded on a manuscript by Montague R. Leverson and others."

It has not been possible to establish the date and place of Montague Leverson's death; no obituary of him appeared in the *London Times*, nor can any notice of his death be found in British records. As a footnote to his life, his nephew Edwin Leverson married Ada Beddington; as Ada Leverson she became famous as a novelist and as Oscar Wilde's adored "Sphinx."

Sources:

Klasner, *Girlhood*; Nolan, *John Henry Tunstall*; *Who Was Who in America*, vol. 4, 1961–68; Rasch, "Leverson."

LLOYD, STEPHEN W.

Maryland-born Stephen W. Lloyd, known as "Will," was "an elderly sergeant" who had served in Texas, and was honorably discharged at Fort Stanton. Lloyd and his Irish wife Eliza, who had worked as a maid for the officers on the army posts where her husband was stationed, settled on the Pecos River at a place that became known as Lloyd's Crossing. They sold out to Texas cattlemen Tom Toland and W. C. Franks in 1872 and moved up the Rio Hondo to a farm near Casey's Mill.

Mrs. Lloyd had a son Dick from an earlier marriage; he was known both as Dick Kelly and Dick Lloyd. Dick's favorite sport was to get tanked up and "hooraw" the town of Lincoln. He tried the same trick on March 8, 1881, in Maxey, near Camp Thomas, Ariz., where after wounding saloonkeeper Ed Mann, Dick mounted up—the horse was not his own—and rode into O'Neil & Franklin's saloon. A bunch of the local men—among whom were John Ringo and Curly Bill Brocius—were playing serious poker and resented the interruption. About a dozen of them are said to have shot Lloyd, who was killed instantly; O'Neil took the blame, pleaded self-defense, and was acquitted.

Will Lloyd also got mean when he drank: on February 18, 1876, the day John Tunstall left Victoria for the States, he collided with Steve Stanley, reportedly over the property rights to his ranch. The *Las Cruces Eco Del Rio Grande* noted that "pistols were used, and both parties agreed to fire at the word "three" but that Stanley fired before the word was given, wounding Lloyd fatally." Stanley then retreated to his house and refused to surrender to Sheriff Baca. Baca enlisted the aid of Tom Cochrane, George Clark, and John Williams and succeeded in arresting Stanley, who made an appearance before Justice of the Peace Wilson, pleaded self-defense, and was acquitted. Lloyd's wound was not fatal; he was taken to Fort Stanton, yet another gunshot case saved from an early grave by the skills of Post Surgeon Carlos Carvallo.

Sources:

Klasner, *Girlhood*; *Mesilla Valley Independent*, March 7, 1876; *Tombstone Epitaph*, March 10, 1881; research by Chuck Parsons.

LONG, JACK

Jack Long, also known as Barney Longmont, John Mont, John Longmont, Frank Ridden, and Frank Rivers, is another Lincoln County mystery man. He is said to have come to Lincoln County around 1876 and gone to work for Chisum, stealing horses alongside

Jessie Evans and Jim McDaniels; he was at least a part-time member of the Boys. Dudley characterized Long as "one of the most earnest and brave men that I know"; yet the same Long told Dr. Ealy that he would as soon see a whore come to Lincoln as Ealy and "that he had helped hang one preacher in Arizona but he would not help hang me." Lincoln tradition credits Long with being one of the men who killed Alexander McSween. Charles Ballard, placing him in Fort Sumner "shortly after the McSween house-burning," named Long as "the man who murdered Virgil Hervey in Fort Griffin [although] Mont claimed to have killed Hervey accidentally." Garrett (or Upson), characterizing him as "a six-footer, a splendid shot [who] coveted the reputation of a 'bad man' [and] was a boisterous bully," has him backing down in a fracas with the Kid at Fort Sumner around September or October of 1878. He also says Long was killed shortly afterwards at a ranch on the plains by a Mexican named Trujillo, which is certainly thought-provoking but apparently incorrect. Long was back in Lincoln by November, when he was one of those who executed affidavits concerning Susan McSween's character. He appeared at the Dudley Court of Inquiry, where he gave his occupation as laborer. On July 13 he was best man at Jimmy Dolan's wedding. He left Lincoln County for Arizona soon afterwards and disappeared from historical ken.

Sources:

Dudley to AAAG DNM July 20, 1878, File 1405 AGO 1878; Ball, "Charles Ballard"; Bender, *Missionaries*; Garrett, *Authentic Life*, 78–80.

MCDANIELS, JAMES

A more dangerous badman than many better remembered than he, James McDaniels is yet another of whose early life nothing is known. He was a foreman on Chisum's Home Creek ranch in Texas in 1871 and came to New Mexico the following year. He is said to have rescued a bunch of Chisum riders who had been jailed at Las Vegas for killing some of Pedro Maxwell's men; later he is said to have killed a black man, but details are skimpy. During 1874 he, Jessie Evans, Marion Turner, and other Chisum hands were hugely successful in stealing horses from the Mescalero Apaches. He was involved in the deaths of the Mes brothers at Shedd's ranch.

In June 1877, McDaniels and a man named Ben Reinhardt got into a fracas in the Jicarilla mining area and carved each other up with Bowie knives; the "severely stabbed" men were taken to Dow's ranch, where it was believed both would die. Reinhardt was patched up; recovering even faster, McDaniels left with Reinhardt's horse and pistol. On February 23, 1878, in La Mesilla, McDaniels shot and wounded a man named Martin. He turned up at the head of an armed band in Lincoln in April, probably as a Kinney adherent. After the troubles he teamed up with Sam Perry stealing horses or "recovering" them. The *Mesilla Valley Independent* reported on January 4, 1879, that McDaniels had been imprisoned in Chihuahua, but he turned up on February 15 to state that reports of his incarceration had been greatly exaggerated. He was arrested January 7, 1880, on charges that he and Perry had stolen two horses from William Jerroll. On May 6 he was again arrested on larceny charges, this time along with Chris Moessner and James Whittacker. The manner and time of his death are uncertain. One version has it that he died at Las Cruces March 2, 1881; another, that he was killed by police officers near San Geronimo, Tex., in July 1885.

Sources:

Rasch, "They Fought"; *Mesilla Valley Independent,* January 4 and February 15, 1879.

MACNAB, FRANCIS

Other than that he was of Scottish origin and that he worked for Hunter & Evans, little is known about Francis MacNab (this spelling, the one he used himself, would appear to be correct). He enters historical ken on May 6, 1877, when the *Dodge City Times* published a report that a Mr. H. Harrison of Fort Elliott was in the city "hunting for Tipton, alias Frank Hall, Frank McNab, and George Black, who are charged with the murder of the Casner brothers, in the Pan Handle, while herding cattle for Hunter & Evans. The murder was committed for $5,500 in gold twenties which the murderers took from their victims."

This report conflicts directly with another in the same issue, in which one Goodfellow, suspected and accused of complicity in the murder of the Casner brothers, killed a man named Bottom near Fort Elliott and was arrested by the military. On May 19 the *Dodge City Times* printed two further letters, one from a Patrick H. Montage, the other from Harrison, giving completely different versions of the story. The following week, May 26, a further letter revealed that while en route to Sweetwater, Tex., in the custody of the sheriff of that town, Goodfellow had been taken from the sheriff by a band of armed men and hanged forthwith. On June 16, Harrison wrote a sharp rebuttal of the accusations contained in the letter written by Montage, which further muddied the water. MacNab categorically denied the allegations in a June 16 letter from Syracuse, Kans., published in the July 7 issue of the *Dodge City Times*.

He seems eventually to have satisfied the Casners that he was not involved in the murders, which was his good fortune; this bloody little vendetta resulted in the deaths of at least nine men. Later that year, MacNab and Tipton, searching for Hunter & Evans cattle lost on a drive, encountered some Mexicans with a few animals. They killed the Mexicans and drove the cattle to Colorado, where they sold them. Of MacNab, Colonel Dudley later said, "[H]is reputation was as bad as it could be; he was looked upon as an outlaw and a murderer." He was killed at the Fritz ranch below Lincoln, April 29, 1878.

Sources:

Rasch, "Regulators"; Rasch, "Casner Brothers"; Dudley in Judge Advocate General's Office, Records of DCOI. Articles from *Dodge City Times* located by Betty Braddock, Director, Kansas Heritage Center, Dodge City, Kans.

MATHEWS, JACOB BASIL "BILLY"

Jacob Basil "Billy" Mathews was born in Woodbury, Cannon County, Tenn., on May 5, 1847, the son of farmer Walter Mathews and his wife Anna (Ashford). Mathews was one of the few proponents of the troubles who had fought on the Confederate side during the Civil War: he enlisted at McMinnville, Tenn., in Company M, Fifth Tennessee Cavalry, and was discharged at Pulaski, Tenn., in August 1865. In 1867 he located in Gilpin County, Colo., as a miner, and later that year he moved south to Elizabethtown, N.M., where he ran a mining claim for an English syndicate.

About 1874 he located on a tract of land three miles northeast of Roswell, and he farmed there for two years before "squatting" with Frank Freeman on the Peñasco River about seventy-five miles west of Roswell. He sold this ranch to Tunstall although he was not its sole owner, and turned over the job of forage agent to W. W. Paul, about September 1877. Using Tunstall's money, he bought into the Dolan business, partnering Dolan for some years after the war before relocating on the Peñasco River on the range he had once sold to Tunstall, claiming—within legality if not honesty—that Tunstall had never held title to it.

In 1883 he married Dora Bates (fig. 42); there were three children, Ernest, Houston, and Cora. Mathews managed the Peñasco Cattle Co. from 1885 to 1892, in which year both he and Dolan were elected directors of the Peñasco Reservoir & Irrigation Co. As bondsman, Mathews was bankrupted when Frank Lesnett disappeared in February 1893, leaving his accounts ten thousand dollars short; he moved to Roswell and became manager of the Pecos Irrigation & Improvement Co. After further business vicissitudes, he became postmaster at Roswell, and he was serving in that capacity when he died of pneumonia, June 3, 1904.

Sources:

Illustrated History; Rasch, "They Fought"; *Santa Fe New Mexican*, October 2, 1877.

MIDDLETON, JOHN

John Middleton was born in Tennessee; his parents were from Mississippi. He was twenty-six in 1880, which would make his year of birth 1864 or 1865. He said on his deathbed that he fled from his home in Texas after killing a black man and then came to New Mexico; further details were not forthcoming. The fact that the name is not uncommon makes his background difficult to pin down— for example, a John Middleton, former arsonist and proficient horse thief, became the lover of Belle Starr, who deserted her husband to be with him. Whether he or the Lincoln County character was the John Middleton, Jr., who was indicted for horse theft and cattle rustling in Hood County, Tex., in 1874 is not known. (The description is about right, but in both cases the age, thirty-five, is not.) In November 1884 the "Belle Starr" Middleton killed Sheriff J. H. Black of Lamar County, Tex., and fled with an eight-hundred-dollar reward on his head. He drowned while swimming the Poteau River, I.T., in May 1885.

The accepted version of the Lincoln County John Middleton's career is that he came there in 1872 from Kansas, where he had been working for Hunter & Evans, and soon became recognized for marksmanship with both pistol and rifle. It is possible he first worked for the House: Morton and Baker claimed he was a friend. By his own statement, he signed on with Tunstall on October 20, 1877. Middleton left Lincoln County at the end of 1878 and with three hundred dollars borrowed from his employers, Hunter & Evans, started a grocery store at Sun City, Kans. The venture was unsuccessful, and he went back to working cattle, during which time he wrote a number of letters to Tunstall's father from addresses in Kansas asking for recompense for his support of Tunstall: the inference is that McSween had never paid him.

Before Middleton's marriage on December 18, 1879, the elder Tunstall sent him twenty-five dollars as a wedding gift. Middleton's bride was fifteen-year-old Maria H. "Birdie" Colcord, Kentucky-born daughter of cattle herder William Colcord. The Colcords were a wealthy family; they opposed the marriage, which did not last. Middleton died of smallpox in San Lorenzo, N.M., on November 19, 1882; before he died he confessed he had fled Bastrop County, Tex., after a reward of twelve hundred dollars was posted for his arrest on charges of murdering a man at Jim Weaver's ranch at the head of the Nueces River. He suggested someone take his body back to Texas and claim the reward. No one availed themselves of the offer.

Sources:

Rasch, "Regulators"; Mullin, "Noteson John Middleton"; Muskogee, I.T., *The Indian Journal*, May 28, 1885; Middleton to J. P. Tunstall, 1879–81; Silver City *Enterprise*, December 7, 1882.

MILLS, ALEXANDER HAMILTON "HAM"

Alexander Hamilton "Ham" Mills was from Arkansas and was born about 1837. He came to New Mexico around 1868 and about two years later married Maria Hammonds. After the death of Jacob L. Gylam on December 1, 1873, Murphy appointed him sheriff of Lincoln County; no election was held. After first farming on land at "Ashland," Hugh Beckwith's place near Casey's Mill, Mills moved to a small ranch near the confluence of Eagle Creek and the Ruidoso River; because he was contributing half of his crop to the House, it is safe to adduce Murphy financed the move. A lumbering hulk of a man, he was considered—when sober—to be one of the best shots in the county. He deserted his wife and baby daughter and went first to Texas and later to Arizona, possibly settling in Tombstone. He was killed by Mexicans near Georgetown, N.M., at the end of October 1882.

Sources:

Rasch, "Ham Mills"; *Arizona Weekly Star,* April 10, 1879; *New Southwest & Grant County Herald,* November 4, 1882.

MORRIS, HARVEY

Harvey Morris came from a prominent family whose history stretched back to the beginnings of colonial settlement. Of this family was Robert Morris, one of the ablest financiers of the young republic and a signer of the Declaration of Independence. The son of William Archibald and Elizabeth (Quay) Morris, Harvey Morris was born in Friendship, Allegany County, N.Y., in 1848, the sixth of ten children. His father and four of his brothers fought in the Union Army during the Civil War. In November 1865, Charles A. Morris, Harvey's brother, relocated in Fort Scott, Kans., where he was joined the following year by another brother, James William Morris, and in 1868 by his parents. Another brother, John, settled in Kansas City.

At Fort Scott Charles became county treasurer and later, adjutant-general of the state of Kansas. Both he and his brother James commanded troops during the 1874 Indian troubles. That same year he accepted the position of registrar of the U.S. Land Office at Larned, Kans., and moved to that town; his parents and brother James joined him shortly thereafter.

Since Harvey Morris appears in neither the 1870 census for Fort Scott nor the 1875 census for Larned, we must assume he came west some time after 1875 and, perhaps through the acquaintance of his lawyer brother Charles with D. P. Shield, whose practice in Osceola often took him to Fort Scott (equidistant from Osceola and Eureka), received an invitation to come to Lincoln both for his health—Morris was tubercular—and to "read" law in the McSween & Shield practice. No reference to the death of this local man appeared in any of the Larned newspapers of the time, although oddly enough, they noticed the death of Morris Bernstein, who had no local connections.

In 1880, John Middleton wrote to J. P. Tunstall that he "was up to Larned & Saw [Harvey's] Bro C. A. Morris who is U.S. Land Agent. He is trying to work up all the evidence he can get against Col Dudley. I gave him all the information I could & I also gave him your adress." If Morris ever took any action against Dudley, no record of it appears to have survived.

Sources:

United States Biographical Dictionary (Kansas Edition); U.S. Department of the Interior, Pension Applications of William, Charles, and James Morris; newspaper and genealogical research by Betsy Crawford, Fort Larned Historical Society; Mrs. Marcella Speier, Larned; Katy Matthews, Topeka; Betty Braddock, director, Kansas Heritage Trust, Dodge City; and Mary Lou Standish Burt, Angelica, N.Y. John Middleton to J. P. Tunstall, January 19, 1880.

MORTON, WILLIAM SCOTT "BUCK"

William Scott "Buck" Morton was born in Charlotte County, near Richmond, Va., about September 1856. His father was a tobacco planter who fought for the Confederacy and lost everything in the war. There are conflicting family traditions about his youth; Morton's sister said in 1928 that after the death of their mother in 1870, their father moved to New Orleans and Buck was adopted by an uncle in Washington, D.C., Judge

Thomas Tyler Bouldin. "Well educated for his age at leaving school," Morton, oldest of eight children, sold his horse, gun, and watch, and at the age of twenty headed west, first for Denver, where he clerked in a hotel, and then to New Mexico. He was a "very handsome boy, brave and fearless."

In 1962 a daughter of the Quin Morton mentioned in Buck's last letter home stated that Buck was the eldest son of David Holmes and Joanna Tyler Cabell Morton; orphaned after the war, he went west in order to earn money to support his five brothers and sisters.

A James Miller, living at Roswell when Morton was killed, said Buck had lived in Springfield, Mo., before coming to New Mexico; Robert Widenmann claimed Morton had been in Arizona, where he had killed his partner in the mines, one man on the Pecos River, and two others in Lincoln County. Morton had worked as a sixty-dollar-a-month foreman at Dolan's Pecos cow camp from March 1877. Lily Klasner suggested bitter animosity between Morton and the Kid, born when Morton contemptuously kicked the Kid out of the Dolan cow camp on Black River and heightened when the Kid broke up Morton's romance with "the belle of the Pecos valley [Sallie Chisum?]."

There is a tragic footnote to Morton's story: according to family tradition, his eighteen-year-old brother John determined to go to New Mexico, to "learn something and see justice for his dead brother." He kept his family informed about his "futile search" for about a year; then he disappeared without trace and "every effort to find him failed."

Sources:

Barber-Fulton Letters, March 10, 1928; Rasch, "They Fought"; Rasch, File 29; Mullin, "Notes on Buck Morton"; *Cimarron News & Press,* April 11, 1878; Klasner, "The Kid."

OLINGER, JOHN WALLACE

John Wallace Olinger was born in Delphi, Ind., on May 3, 1849. Little is known of his life before his appearance in Lincoln County, although there is testimony to the effect that his mother, Mrs. Stafford, was half-Indian and came from Oklahoma [Indian Territory]. He is said to have been a buffalo hunter at the time William H. Johnson nursed him through smallpox. In later years he married Johnson's widow, Camelia. They apparently separated after thirty years together, and Olinger drifted out to California, where he worked as a gardener in Santa Monica. He died at Valley View Sanatorium, Van Nuys, Calif., on February 25, 1940.

OLINGER, ROBERT

His brother Robert Olinger is likewise a mystery. He is said to have been born in Delphi, Indiana, in 1850. His name is given variously as Robert Charles, Robert M., and Robert Ameridth. Unusual though it is, the last of these seems likeliest, since it was given by Lily Klasner (could she have meant Meredith?), who was engaged to Olinger at the time of his death. According to her the family settled for a while in the Indian Territory. Later, in 1876, Bob joined his brother at Seven Rivers, bringing along their mother, Mrs. Stafford; no Olingers are listed in the voting registrations for that year or for 1877. The 1878 tax assessments show Olinger, also known as "Pecos Bob" and "Big Indian," in partnership with his brother and Charles Kruling. Neither Olinger ever paid real estate taxes in Lincoln County.

Bob Olinger (figs. 63, 76) is described as having been six feet tall, weighing around 240 pounds, having a red complexion and dark eyes, with his hair worn long. He is said to have killed several men, among them Frank Hill, but details are sketchy. His death at the hands of Billy the Kid at Lincoln on April 28, 1881, has ensured Olinger a place in western myth.

Sources:

Klasner, *Girlhood; Cimarron News & Press,* March 11, 1880; Rasch, "They Fought"; Haley, "Interview with Robert A. Casey"; Cline, "Olinger."

PAGUE, SAMUEL SPEECE

Samuel Speece Pague was born in Ohio on April 14, 1855, and had come to Fort Stanton directly after graduating from West Point in 1876. In later years he became an alcoholic and was dismissed from the service; his wife divorced him soon thereafter. He committed suicide in a Chicago flophouse on July 8, 1899.

Sources:

Research by Nora Henn; *Santa Fe Weekly New Mexican,* March 13, 1877; Rasch, "Fort Stanton."

PALMER, FRANCES "FANNY"

The youngest daughter of Mr. and Mrs. Digby Palmer, Frances Palmer, called "Fanny," was eighteen years old in 1862, when the family arrived in Victoria, B.C., Canada, where they ran a dancing school and taught music. Fanny's older sisters, Alice and Lucy, were both married and lived in San Francisco. Although she does not appear in existing biographical sketches of the family, another daughter—referred to by Tunstall as "Mrs. Helen"—seems to have made an extended visit home during the year. All the sisters were accomplished singers, and the Palmer home on Fort St. was the scene of many musical evenings. Fanny Palmer died in the wreck of the steamer *Pacific* in November 1875.

Sources:

Research by Willard Ireland, Provincial Archivist, Victoria, B.C., Canada, 1959; Nolan, *John Henry Tunstall,* 101–2.

PATRON, JUAN BATISTA

Juan Batista Patrón was born in 1850, the son of Isidro and Felipa Patrón. The family came to Placitas around 1870. Surprisingly little is known of his origins; in spite of his comparative youth, he seems to have been looked upon as one of the leading members of the Hispanic New Mexican community (fig. 16). He has been incorrectly credited with attendance at Notre Dame University, Ind.; in this he may have been confused with Bonifacio Baca. Patrón married Beatriz, the sister of Indian agent Lorenzo Labadie. Schoolteacher to the town's children soon after his arrival in Lincoln, he was county clerk at the time of the Horrell War, and in 1876 he served as probate judge. In 1877 he was elected to the territorial legislature and was speaker of the house during the twenty-third assembly convened in January 1878. He left Lincoln at the time of the Big Killing and settled in Puerto de Luna, where he opened a hotel. Reputed to have been quarrelsome and dangerous when drinking, he was killed by a man named Mike Maney in Moore's saloon at Puerto de Luna, April 9, 1884.

Sources:

Las Vegas Daily Optic, April 12 and 15, 1884; Fulton, *Lincoln County War,* 405–9.

PEPPIN, GEORGE WARDEN

George Warden Peppin is said to have been born in Mountville [Montvale?], Vt., in October 1841, but no record of his birth can be found there; in the 1870 census for Lincoln County he gave his birthplace as Ohio and his age as thirty-seven. There is some basis for believing his parents were of French origin, in which case the name might originally have been Pépin, pronounced *pay-pan.* By the time he was twenty, Peppin was in Alleghany, Calif., where he enlisted in Company A, Fifth Regiment California Infantry, and came to New Mexico with Carleton's Column. Mustered out at La Mesilla November 30, 1864, Peppin (fig. 30) drifted up to Lincoln County, where he pursued the trade of mason and builder. He was employed at Fort Stanton during the extensive rebuilding there in 1868–69, and later he built houses at Roswell and Lincoln, including the McSween residence and the new jail. He ran unsuccessfully for the office of sheriff in the first elections held at Rio Bonito precinct in March 1869. Following the death of Hiraldo Jaramillo, Peppin, whose first wife had died, married Jaramillo's young widow. He was an important witness at the Dudley Court of Inquiry in 1879; after a stint as a butcher at Fort Stanton in 1881, he resumed the trade of mason, aided by his son Juan. In 1885 he was elected director of the school board in District No. 1; in 1893 he was jailer in Lincoln and also served as Sheriff George Curry's deputy. Peppin would never speak of the Lincoln troubles after they were over, saying it was his wish to "let sleeping dogs lie." Nevertheless, the old boy was feisty to the end. On May 8, 1901, he was charged with "assault with a deadly weapon," but no true bill was found, so the details of the affray are not known. George Peppin died of "bowel trouble" at his home in Lincoln on September 18, 1904.

Sources:

Research by Nora Henn; Rasch, "They Fought," 54–55.

PERRY, SAMUEL R.

Samuel R. Perry was from Mississippi, where he was born July 31, 1844, the son of Nathanael and A. S. Perry of Hancock County. He was another of the many men around Lincoln crippled by an old (war?) wound, in this instance in the right hip. In 1879, while squatting on a claim a few miles east of Tularosa, he killed an employee, Frank Wheeler; it was claimed that Wheeler had sold some of Perry's cattle and then refused to pay up. There were other versions. He married a young girl named Eolin Bates (a sister of Billy Mathews's wife) when he was fifty-six, an old man by frontier standards. Sam's mother came out from Mississippi and moved in with the couple: the marriage foundered. Perry was killed on November 7, 1901, when he fell off a wagon near his homestead in Perry Canyon.

Sources:

Rasch, "They Fought," 55–56.

PIERCE, MILO LUCIUS

Milo Lucius Pierce was born at Lincoln, Logan County, Ill., on August 13, 1839. He was reared on the family farm and was still living at home at the beginning of the Civil War, at which time he enlisted in Company B, Second Illinois Cavalry. After four years' service he was mustered out at Springfield, Ill., in October 1865. Two years later he moved west to Bates County, Mo., where he worked as an engineer. In January 1872 he again headed west, this time to Waco, Tex. In the fall of that year he moved to New Mexico and went into partnership with Lewis Paxton on a ranch on the Pecos River about forty miles south of Seven Rivers. The following year he became one of the earliest settlers in the Roswell area. He remained in partnership with Paxton until 1881. On April 20 of the following year he was married to the widowed Ella Lea Calfee, a daughter of Joseph C. Lea of Roswell; a son, Milo L., was born on August 6, 1891.

About the time of his marriage, Pierce quit the cattle business and formed Pierce, Lea & Co., sheep breeders and raisers. In 1892 he sold his 480-acre holding to the Pecos Irrigation & Improvement Co., and concentrated on buying and selling real estate; he also owned the largest meat market and butcher shop in the region. He died at Roswell on October 20, 1919.

Sources:

Illustrated History, 624–25; Rasch, "They Fought," 56.

POWELL, THOMAS BENTON "BUCK"

Thomas Benton "Buck" Powell (at the Dudley Court of Inquiry he gave his name as William B. Powell, living at Pope's Crossing) was born in Mississippi on July 24, 1845, but was raised in Texas. A scout for General William R. Shafter against the Comanches in 1869, he came to New Mexico in the 1870s and settled in the Seven Rivers area. He married Eliza Jane Lester (fig. 25), and they reared five sons and three daughters. In 1881 he killed a man at Marfa, Tex., and decamped, forfeiting his bail. He partnered Billy Mathews in a scheme to establish a ranch at Duncan, Ariz., in 1898; it foundered when their foreman absconded with the money. Powell died on his ranch on the Peñasco River, August 31, 1906.

Sources:

Judge Advocate General's Office, Records of DCOI, Deposition of Powell; Rasch, "They Fought," 57.

PURINGTON, GEORGE AUGUSTUS

George Augustus Purington was born in Ohio on July 21, 1837. Although one military historian refers to him as a "plodding mediocrity," he must have been a good soldier: enlisting in the Nineteenth Ohio Volunteer Infantry on April 22, 1861, he came out of the war a colonel of the Second Ohio Volunteer Cavalry, brevetted major for gallant and meritorious service in the Wilderness campaign, lieutenant colonel in the Battle of Winchester, and colonel for yet further gallantry at Cedar Creek (fig. 50). He served later with the Third Cavalry, retired from the army in 1895, and died at Metropolis, Ill., on May 31, 1896.

Sources:

Rasch, "Fort Stanton," 5–6; Utley, *High Noon*, 67.

RANDLETT, JAMES FRANKLIN

James Franklin Randlett, second of the five children of Charles P. and Mary (Hilton) Randlett, was born at Newmarket, Rockingham County, N.H., on December 8, 1832. The others were Charles, born ca. 1829; Martha, born ca. 1835; Ann Mary, born 1841; and Joseph, born 1844. Charles Randlett owned and operated a hotel in Newmarket; apparently the family name was originally Runlett. It appears in the annals of New Hampshire as early as 1652.

James Randlett was educated at the Atkinson Academy in New Hampshire; on August 31, 1856, he and Hannah Hodgdon were married at Barnstead, N.H., by the Rev. Enos George. The groom was working as a machinist at Nashua when he enlisted as a private in Company F of the Third New Hampshire Volunteers on August 15, 1861. He was appointed captain a month later. On April 6, 1864, he was promoted to major; the following May 13 he was wounded in the thigh at Drury's (or Drewry's) Bluff, Va. This did not prevent him from being further promoted to lieutenant colonel on October 15, 1864. He served with Sherman at Charleston, S.C., and following the occupation of Wilmington was made provost marshal of that city. He was mustered out at Nashua, N.H., on July 20, 1865 and was still living there at the end of the year.

He obviously found civilian life unattractive, for he was appointed captain in the regular army on June 6, 1867. He served first with the Thirty-ninth Infantry, was unassigned April 10, 1869, and was assigned to the Eighth Cavalry on December 15, 1870. He was promoted to major, Ninth Cavalry, July 5, 1886, and finally was appointed colonel of the Ninth Cavalry October 14, 1896, retiring on December 8 of that year. He moved to San Diego, Calif., in the fall of 1897. The 1903 directory of the Department of the Interior lists him as agent to the Kiowa from May 13, 1889, to February 2, 1901. The Indian Office Report of 1894, however, lists him as acting agent of the Uintah and Ouray Agency in Utah that year. Another record states he was agent there 1891–93. While at the Kiowa Agency he was asked by the government to select a site for a new town to serve as the county seat of Caddo County, Okla. He chose one between the agency on the north and mission land on the south, in what was then a cornfield. This town was called Anadarko.

It is said that the Indians were so fond of him that upon his retirement a delegation of them went to Washington and threatened to make war unless he was continued in charge of the reservation. He was described at this time as being "an oldtime military man, perhaps a little more on edge than the average run of western military officers."

Randlett (fig. 12) was advanced to colonel on the retired list April 23, 1904. A few miles south of Fort Duchesne, which Randlett commanded when it was a military post, was a village known as Leland; in 1905 it was renamed Randlett in his honor. He died December 12, 1915, at La Mesa, near San Diego, Calif., and was survived by two children, his wife having died in 1911.

Sources:

U.S. Department of the Interior, Pension Application of James Randlett; research by Mrs. Phyllis Longver, Boscawen N.H.; *Army & Navy Journal*, December 25, 1915, courtesy John J. Slonaker, U.S. Army Military History Institute.

REESE, JAMES B.

James B. Reese was a cattleman; he said he had been in New Mexico off and on since 1866, which might indicate he came up from Texas with, or at the same time as, Chisum. Although Joseph Smith's letter to Howard Capper hints that Reese's sympathies lay with the Regulators, he was a paid-up member of the Peppin posse before and during the final fight in Lincoln, and Juan Patrón was convinced on one occasion when Reese marched uninvited into his home that had not Major Mickey Cronin been present, Reese would have killed him. On August 2, 1878, Reese rode into Tularosa from Lincoln, got into a quarrel with the Sanches brothers, Antonio and Juliangero, who were said to be Pat Coghlan's "hit men." The brothers claimed he was riding one of their horses; he was shot in the back of the head by one of them. He was characterized as "a quiet, brave man when sober, but quarrelsome if drunk." They were words that could have served as an epitaph for any of a dozen men in Lincoln County.

Sources:

Mesilla News, August 10, 1878; Rasch, "They Fought," 57–58.

RILEY, JOHN HENRY

As with his partner Jimmy Dolan, there is conflicting evidence concerning the origins of John Henry Riley. The most convincing documentation indicates that he was the son of Patrick J. and Anna (Gogier) Riley, born May 12, 1850, on Valentia Island, County Kerry, Ireland. The family immigrated to America and settled in Baltimore ca. 1862.

Riley's obituary stated he moved to Colorado in 1865, at which time, if the date given on his death certificate is valid, he was only fifteen. He worked for railroad contractor Jim Carlyle—it is not known if this is the same man killed by Billy the Kid—during the building of the Colorado Central Railroad. He first appears in New Mexico as a clerk for Rockwell Blake, a beef contractor who lived near the Mescalero Reservation. He operated a ranch adjacent to John Copeland's place a few miles below Fort Stanton. He became a partner in L. G. Murphy & Co in November 1876 but seems to have carefully avoided direct involvement in the shooting war. Frank Coe characterized him as Murphy and Dolan's "confidence man," a smooth talker who "could make you believe anything, worked in Santa Fe, Albuquerque, and Las Cruces and sent in men to help them. [He] was a damned coward but gave us more dirt than any of them."

He later moved to Las Cruces, where on November 9, 1882, he married Annie Cuniffe, born February 22, 1857; Father Lassaigne officiated, and "almost the entire population of Las Cruces" attended. There were three children: John Dolan, born September 26, 1885; Patrick J., and Genevieve. The family moved to Colorado in 1885, returning to New Mexico in 1889, when Riley was elected assessor of Doña Ana County (fig. 15). Riley's last twelve years were spent at Fowler, Colo., where he had one of the finest hog ranches in the state. He died at Colorado Springs on February 10, 1916.

Sources:

Research by Lewis A. Ketring, Jr.; Rasch, File 29; *Santa Fe New Mexican*, November 21, 1876; Haley, "Interview with Frank Coe," February 20, 1928; *Las Cruces Rio Grande Republican*, November 11, 1898; *Colorado Springs Gazette*, February 11, 1916.

RUDABAUGH, DAVID

David Rudabaugh—correctly Rodenbaugh, but even the name Rudabaugh was often misspelled—is said to have been born July 14, 1854, in Fulton County, Ill. The family must have moved to Ohio soon afterwards, his younger brother and sisters all having been born there. His father, James, was killed in the Civil War; his mother, Susanna Rodenbaugh, never remarried.

In 1870 the widow and her children moved to Kansas and squatted on land at Spring Creek Township, near Eureka. Cemetery records at Eureka indicate that "Sussanna Rodenbaugh," aged eighty-six, died in 1904. The death notice reads "Mrs Susan Rodebaugh [sic], a pioneer resident of Greenwood County, died at her home in North Eureka yesterday at the age of 86 years, 8 months, and 22 days. She was born in Ohio, March 24, 1828."

Exactly when Rudabaugh started his life of crime is uncertain. He is said to have been in Dodge City during the summer of '77; Wyatt Earp claimed to have gone down to Fort Griffin, Doan's Crossing, and the Brazos hunting him, only to find Dave had doubled back and evaded him. On January 27, 1878, Rudabaugh was one of a gang in an unsuccessful train holdup at Kinsley, Kans. He was captured a few days later by a posse led by Bat Masterson. In June 1878 (the newspaper report is dated June 22), when his case was brought to trial, Rudabaugh turned state's evidence and was released. "Rudabaugh . . . was promised entire immunity if he would 'squeal', therefore he squole," said the *Kinsley Graphic*. His partners, Ed West, Tom Gott, and J. D. Green, each got five years in Leavenworth. Rudabaugh was taken with them on the train as far as Newton and there released.

In March 1879, Rudabaugh showed up in Dodge City claiming he was looking for honest work. He may have been present as a Masterson deputy in the Royal Gorge right-of-way fight between the Santa Fe and the Denver & Rio Grande railroads. Here he forged a friendship with John Joshua Webb, who had been party to his original arrest.

By late 1879, Rudabaugh and Webb were both policemen in Las Vegas, N.M.; they used their position as cover for the fact that they were part of the "Dodge City gang," robbing trains and stagecoaches. On November 4 the *Las Vegas Gazette* reported that David Radabaugh [sic] and Joseph Martin, "accused of stage robbing some weeks [ago] were brought in and arraigned. Plead not guilty and in the absence of any prosecution were discharged. The case seems to be involved in mystery. The prosecution failed to appear, and the evidence was of such doubtful character that it was uncertain whether a case could have been made against them or not."

On March 2, 1880, John Webb killed cattleman Michael Kelliher in the Goodlet & Robinson saloon at Las Vegas. He was immediately arrested and charged with complicity in robbery and murder, tried, convicted, and sentenced to hang. On April 30, Rudabaugh tried to break Webb out of jail, killing the jailer, Deputy Sheriff Lino Valdez, in the process. Webb, however, refused to make good his escape. His hanging stayed as a result, Webb engineered another breakout, killing three men in the process. Garrett captured him at Roswell in November 1880 and put him in jail in Las Vegas.

Meanwhile, Rudabaugh (possibly through acquaintance with Charlie Bowdre) joined the Kid's gang. Perhaps "joined forces" would be a better way of putting it: it is said that Rudabaugh was the only man the Kid was afraid of. Almost immediately he was involved with the killing of Jim Carlyle.

On September 19, 1881, while awaiting execution in the San Miguel County jail at Las Vegas, Rudabaugh and fellow prisoners John Webb, Thomas Duffy, and H. S. Wilson somehow obtained a pistol and tried to shoot their way out of the jail. In the ensuing melee, assistant jailer Herculano Chavez killed Duffy. Undaunted by this setback, Rudabaugh, Webb, and five others tunneled out of the jail and escaped on December 3, 1881.

John J. Webb "disappeared." He is said to have resumed an earlier alias of "Samuel King" and died in Arkansas of smallpox in 1882. As for Rudabaugh, he may have gone south to Mexico. On February 18, 1886, in a fracas in a Parral cantina, a man said to have been Rudabaugh killed two men and wounded another, before himself being decapitated by an angry mob. His severed head was then paraded around the plaza on a pole.

A less exciting but possibly more authentic version proposes that, after breaking jail in Las Vegas, Rudabaugh hid out at the home of a friend who helped him reach Mexico. After lying low there for a year or so he joined a trail herd heading into the Niobrara River country and from there moved on to Montana. After working as a top hand there for some years, he acquired his own ranch and married a woman who was one-quarter Indian and who gave him three daughters. When his wife died, Dave started drinking heavily, lost the ranch, went downhill. Later, penniless, he went to live with a daughter in Oregon, where he died in 1928.

Sources:

Research by Helen Bradford, Eureka, Kans.; Lake, *Wyatt Earp*, 191–92; De Arment, *Bat Masterson*, 82–96; Miller and Snell, *Great Gunfighters*, 220–22; Stone, "Notes and Documents," 146–51.

RYNERSON, WILLIAM LOGAN

The giant William Logan Rynerson—he was almost seven feet tall— was a prominent participant in the legal ramifications of the Lincoln County War. He was born February 22, 1828, in Mercer County, Ky. After briefly studying at Franklin College, Ind., he joined the rush to California in 1852. At the outbreak of war he enlisted in the First California Infantry and came to New Mexico with Carleton's California Column. Mustered out at La Mesilla in November 1866, Rynerson took up residence in Las Cruces. On December 15, 1867, he shot and killed John P. Slough, chief justice of New Mexico (and formerly, as a Union colonel of Colorado volunteers, Lawrence Murphy's commanding officer) in the lobby of the Exchange Hotel in Santa Fe. He was tried the following March and acquitted on grounds of self-defense; his attorney was Stephen B. Elkins.

In January 1876, Governor Samuel B. Axtell appointed Rynerson (fig. 43) district attorney for the Third Judicial District, encompassing Doña Ana, Grant, and Lincoln counties; he was reappointed in 1878. After the Lincoln County troubles ended, Rynerson, partnering Dolan, Numa Raymond, and John Lemon, established a ranch, the Feliz Land & Cattle Co., on what would have been Tunstall's range. He died September 26, 1893.

Source:

Miller, "Rynerson."

SAUNDERS, JAMES ALBERT

James Albert Saunders, oldest of the four sons of James W. and Catherine (Wolgamott) Saunders, was born October 14, 1851, in Mount Pleasant, Iowa. "He was an educated man," Frank Coe said, who "lacked but a little of graduating from high school." The other brothers were Robert W., born 1853; Marion B., born 1858; and William C., born 1860. The family had come west to Missouri by way of Ohio—James W. was born at Millersburg, April 7, 1823—and Iowa. A daughter, Ada, married Jasper "Jap" Coe and in 1871 was part of a general exodus of Coes to New Mexico. Ada's brother James Albert, called "Ab," accompanied them, and they settled on land near Raton.

In 1876—possibly attracted by W. W. Broughton's Temperance Colony—the rest of the Saunders family moved out to Lompoc, Calif., where after renting a stock farm for a while, James W. purchased the "Last Chance" ranch in Miguelito Canyon. By this time, "Ab" Saunders (fig. 58) and the Coes had moved down to Lincoln County; Frank Coe dates their arrival May 7, 1875.

After being seriously wounded at the Fritz ranch, Saunders remained in the hospital at Fort Stanton until May 12 and later convalesced at the Ellis hotel. When he was fit enough to travel, Uncle Ike took him down to El Paso, where he caught a stagecoach to his parents' home in California. He died in San Francisco during an operation on his wounded hip, February 5, 1883.

Sources:

Haley, "Interview with Frank Coe," August 14, 1927; research by Lewis A Ketring, Jr.; Smith, *Coes.*

SCURLOCK, JOSIAH GORDON "DOC"

Josiah Gordon "Doc" Scurlock was born at Talapoosa, Ala., on January 11, 1849. His nickname was come by honestly: he is believed to have studied medicine in New Orleans. He was a most unusual gunfighter: a doctor, farmer, poet, teacher, later a linguist and reader of the classics. At the age of twenty (fig. 48) he went to Mexico; fearing tuberculosis, he returned to the States in 1871 and worked for John Chisum in Texas. By May 1875 he was working for Chisum in New Mexico. When his line-riding partner, Newt Huggins, was scalped by Indians "in September 1875," Scurlock rode sixty miles to South Spring and told Chisum he wanted to quit; Chisum refused to let him go or pay him off, whereupon Scurlock stole some of Chisum's horses, two saddles, and a gun and decamped to Arizona. Chisum sent a couple of fighting men after him; when they caught him Scurlock told them why he'd taken the animals, and they told him "he had done the right thing."

He was described as being "five feet eight or ten inches tall, light hair, light complexion, front teeth out, quick spoken." The missing teeth were the result of a shootout over a card game: the bullet took out Doc's teeth and came out the back of his neck without serious damage. The man who fired the shot was not so lucky.

Scurlock family tradition has it that he and Charles Bowdre operated a cheese factory on the Gila River, and that one of their employees was Henry "Kid" Antrim. With financial assistance from L. G. Murphy & Co., Bowdre and Scurlock went into partnership on a Ruidoso ranch, and on October 19, 1876, just a few weeks after accidentally killing his good friend Mike Harkins, Scurlock was married to sixteen-year-old Antonia Miguela Herrera. Altogether they had ten children. Scurlock was active in posses pursuing—and in some cases lynching—the horse thieves infesting the Lincoln area in 1875–76.

After the Lincoln troubles he left New Mexico for Texas, lived awhile in the LX ranch headquarters in Potter County, drifted on to teach school in Vernon, moved on again to Cleburne, near Fort Worth, then Granbury, then Mabank, near Dallas. Throughout the rest of his life Scurlock adamantly dissociated himself from his past; his reluctance to discuss his early life suggests he might have had something to hide. In 1919 the Scurlocks moved to Eastland, Tex., where he died July 25, 1929.

Sources:

Haley, "Interview with Frank Coe," March 20, 1927; *Santa Fe New Mexican*, May 15, 1875; Haley, "Horse Thieves"; Rasch, Buckbee, and Klein, "Many Parts."

SELMAN, JOHN

John Selman was born in Madison County, Ark., on November 16, 1839, the son of an English schoolteacher/farmer. The family—there were five children of whom John was the eldest—moved to Texas in 1858, and after his father's death, Selman became the family provider. He is said to have joined the Confederate Army, served in a noncombatant role in Oklahoma, and deserted in 1863. He and his family moved to a location near Albany, Tex., and in 1864, Selman became a lieutenant in the state militia.

In August 1865, Selman married Edna de Graffenried, and four years later both families relocated in Colfax County, N.M. After a year they returned to Texas and settled in the Fort Griffin area. Selman became a saloonkeeper, and with his partner in crime, Sheriff John Larn, did a little creative rustling on the side. When Larn was lynched early in 1878, Selman fled to New Mexico, leaving his wife to die carrying their fifth child. Remembered chiefly as the brave fellow who shot John Wesley Hardin in the back at El Paso in 1895, he was killed in that same town by George Scarborough on April 5, 1896.

Sources:

Metz, *Selman.*

SHAW, JAMES BARRON

James Barron Shaw was born in London, England, on November 4, 1813. He studied medicine in Inverness for three years before entering University College, London, and spent four years studying there, followed by another at Glasgow University. In August 1836 he became a member of the Royal College of Surgeons. His original choice of career had been the navy; he determined now to take a voyage around the world. On a second voyage, while at Calcutta, he applied for a post as assistant surgeon in an Indian regiment preparing to leave for China, with which country Britain was then at war. After the Treaty of Nankin was signed in 1843, he returned to India and then to England. In 1844 he went to Hong Kong, and he was there when the news of the discovery of gold in California decided him to go there.

He arrived in San Francisco on a Swedish ship in July 1849 and tried his hand as a miner in the Mokelumne River region; shortly thereafter he set up practice in a log cabin at Dry Creek, Tuolumne County. In the winter of 1849–50 he went for the first time to Santa Barbara, and there he practiced until May 1852, when he decided to satisfy his desire to visit Mexico. It was during this visit that he became acquainted with Barron, Forbes & Co., bankers and merchants of New Almaden.

In May 1858 he took charge of the Barron, Forbes interests on Santa Cruz Island— from which that syndicate had just ejected Captain Martin Kimberly—and conducted them successfully for the next sixteen years. The concern was then sold to the Pacific Woollen Mills Co., owned by French and German interests, at which time Shaw turned to ranching on twenty-two thousand acres he had bought at La Laguna de San Francisco y Los Alamos, seventy-two miles from Santa Barbara and alongside the holdings of his friend John S. Bell. After three years, as a result of depredations of bears, pumas, and coyotes, Shaw had fewer sheep than he had started with; he sold off his herds and put the proceeds into shorthorn and Durham cattle. At the same time he disposed of about fifteen thousand acres of his land.

Shaw (fig. 20) married Helen A. Green, a Londoner like himself, in 1861; they had four sons, only one of whom lived to adulthood.

Sources:

W. Edwin Gledhill, Santa Barbara Historical Society, pers. comm., 1959; Guinn, *Historical and Biographical Record.*

SHERMAN, JOHN E., JR.

U.S. Marshal John E. Sherman, Jr., was the son of Judge C. T. Sherman, a respected Cleveland lawyer, the nephew of that renowned soldier, General William Tecumseh Sherman, and brother-in-law of another, General Nelson A. Miles. Through the influence of yet another uncle and namesake, Senator (and later Secretary of the Treasury) John Sherman, in March 1876 he received the appointment to succeed John Pratt as U.S. Marshal for the Territory of New Mexico. He arrived in Santa Fe on May 24. Metz refers to him as an alcoholic. He remained in office until his resignation on March 2, 1882.

Sources:

Ball, *United States Marshals*; Metz, *Garrett*, 83.

SHIELD, DAVID PUGH

David Pugh Shield, one of the six children of Robert Shield, a Columbus, Ohio, lawyer and native of Scotland, was born at Reynoldsburg, Ohio, on December 5, 1835. He was married to Elizabeth Hummer—by the same cleric who had united her parents in matrimony—on November 11, 1869 (figs. 35, 36). Their first child, George, was born in Ohio in 1861; late the following year or early in 1863 they moved to Stockton, and later again to Osceola, Mo. On July 1, 1863, Shield enlisted in the Missouri Militia, served as a sergeant in Company M, Provisional Regiment, later joined Company E, Sixtieth Regiment, and was discharged July 12, 1865.

He was admitted to practice in the St. Clair County Court, Mo., on April 12, 1866, and hung out his shingle with his brother George Whitelaw Shield in offices over the Osceola courtroom. In 1870 he became county attorney; his brother was probate judge. The census for that year lists Shield, thirty-six; his wife, Elizabeth, thirty; son George H., nine; son David C[urtis], six; daughter Mary M., two. Another son, Birdie, was born July 4, 1870, but died at the age of two.

The Shield family arrived in Lincoln in July 1877; Elizabeth Shield may have been suffering from a pulmonary complaint. Shield was admitted to practice law in New Mexico in October 1877; his teenage sons worked for several months in the Tunstall store.

Shield was in Santa Fe when McSween was killed in July 1878 and never returned to Lincoln. He settled in Las Vegas, where he had a brief partnership with lawyer Sidney Wilson; later he set up his own practice at 433½ Grand Ave. and was also a director and secretary of the San Miguel Title & Abstract Co. Shield fell ill in the winter of 1887–88 and died March 6, 1888, of chronic meningitis.

Sources:

Research by Donald Lavash, Santa Fe, N.M.; John Mills, Osceola, Mo.; and Douglas Croy, Las Vegas, N.M.

SIRINGO, CHARLES ANGELO

Charles Angelo Siringo (his father was Italian) was born in Matagorda County, Tex., on February 7, 1855, and died in Hollywood, California, October 19, 1928. His life spans the whole era in which the real-life cowboy was transmuted into the cowboy of Hollywood myth, and he, as much as any man, was responsible for its beginnings. At the age of thirty, considering himself nothing more than an "old, stove-up cowboy," Siringo sat down to write the story of his life. What emerged was *A Texas Cowboy, or, Fifteen Years on the Hurricane Deck of a Spanish Pony*, which came out in 1885 under the imprint of a Chicago publisher with the unlikely name of Umbdenstock. He followed this "cowboy's Bible" with five more books, all drawn from the same well: *A Cowboy Detective* (1912); *Two Evil Isms: Pinkertonism and Anarchism* (1915); *A Lone Star Cowboy* (1919); *Billy the Kid* (1920); and *Riata and Spurs* (1927). Siringo's account of the pursuit of the Kid in *A Texas Cowboy* captures perfectly the improvident, haphazard nature of the part the Texas boys played in the expedition.

Source:

Dobie, "Charles Siringo."

SMITH, VAN C.

Although Lily Klasner, who said he was born in Omaha, described Van C. Smith as "a wealthy gambler and sporting man," John Chisum made no bones about it and called him a pimp, and went on to brand his brother George a thief who had bought himself a sixty-dollar saddle with the proceeds of the stamps sold at the post office and had then decamped for Santa Fe. In 1870, however, Smith himself claimed to have been born in Texas, giving his occupation as salesman and his age as thirty, which would make his birthdate 1839 or 1840. It would appear that all are incorrect.

Born Van Ness Cumming Smith in Ludlow, Windsor County, Vermont, on July 12, 1837, he reached Arizona via California in 1863, where he ranched and later provided the land on which Prescott was built. On May 26, 1864, he was appointed the first sheriff of Yavapai County, serving two months. He is said to have been a friend of Thomas B. Catron, on whose recommendation he settled in what was then called Rio Hondo. Klasner says Smith's father, "Old Man Smith," lived in a *choza* about two miles north of the present town of Roswell at the head of North Spring River on what the local people called El Loma del Viejo, Old Man's Hill. Then Van C. Smith came down from Santa Fe and with his partner Aaron O. Wilburn put up two buildings, one a general store, the other a sort of hotel (another euphemism?). State records show this to have been in December 1871.

The following year, Smith named the settlement Roswell after his father and got the government to establish a post office there. His younger brother George came down to run the store; A.B. Franks and his wife ran the hotel. Smith's "gambler's paradise" failed to materialize and he gave up on the place, leaving Wilburn in charge; Wilburn and Franks had a falling out that ended in Wilburn being badly wounded. Franks drifted on; Van Smith then installed Follett G. Christie as storekeeper.

After his run-in with the Horrell gang in 1874, Smith did not feel life was safe in Roswell and left the area, first for Las Vegas, and then Santa Fe. There he ran a saloon in partnership with Joseph Schwartz; in April 1876 they were also bidders for the contracts to supply beef to forts Wingate, Union, and Stanton, probably in conjunction with John Riley. Nevertheless, it would appear from what Tunstall says that Smith may still have been steering customers towards his "hotel."

He was in Tombstone shortly after the camp was established in 1879, and acted as a deputy to Sheriff John Behan. In 1882, he served as chief of scouts at Fort Cummings,

N.M. Later he prospected and ranched in Mexico. He never married, and died at Prescott, Ariz., on August 29, 1914.

Sources:

Klasner, *Girlhood*; Fleming and Huffman, eds., *Roundup*; Thrapp, *Encyclopedia*. For a character reference on Smith's partner, Schwarz, see Nolan, *John Henry Tunstall*, 164–65.

STONEROAD, GEORGE W.

In *The Life and Death of John Henry Tunstall* (p. 183), I offered a biography of Napoleon Bonaparte Stoneroad that, although at variance with Tunstall's description, seemed to describe the right man but in fact did not. Although obituaries credited him with being the first man to drive sheep successfully from California to New Mexico, it would appear that in fact the drive was made by Napoleon's brother, George W. Stoneroad.

In 1876 the Stoneroad brothers, Napoleon, George W., and Thomas, together with William Dickenson of San Francisco (a brother-in-law) formed a partnership and started east with ten thousand sheep. At the Colorado River, N. B. Stoneroad returned to California, leaving George to take them the rest of the way to New Mexico.

After their arrival in New Mexico, Stoneroad Bros. & Dickenson bought 120,000 acres of grant land and commenced raising sheep. They later turned to raising cattle on a large scale at the Cabra Springs range of 318,000 acres, having abandoned sheep as less profitable.

STONEROAD, NAPOLEON B.

Napoleon B. Stoneroad was born February 11, 1830, in Lawrence County, Ala. He moved his family to New Mexico in 1881 and appears in the Las Vegas City Directory for the year 1882–83 as a sheep dealer, residing at 313 Inter-Ocean West; his brother George is listed as a co-director, with David P. Shield, of the San Miguel County Title & Abstract Co., with offices in the Optic Block on Grand Ave. Napoleon B. Stoneroad died at Las Vegas in February 1900.

Sources:

Research by Richard Terry, supervising librarian, California Section, California State Library, Sacramento; Douglas Croy, Las Vegas, N.M.; Bancroft, *History of Arizona and New Mexico*.

TURNER, JOHN HERBERT

John Herbert Turner was born at Claydon, near Ipswich, Suffolk, England, on May 7, 1834, the son of John and Martha Turner. He received his mercantile education at Whitstable in Kent and emigrated first to Halifax and then to Charlottetown, Prince Edward Island, Canada, in 1856, remaining there until 1860. He returned to England in 1860 to be married to Elizabeth Eilbeck of Whitehaven; his new wife accompanied him to Prince Edward Island. After two more years they came west, and for a time Turner sought his fortune in the Cariboo gold fields. Shortly thereafter, he took up residence in Victoria, B.C., Canada, and in 1863 he entered into a partnership with J. H. Todd at the Victoria Produce Market (fig. 4).

A three-year partnership with J. P. Tunstall and H. C. Beeton was consummated in 1868, and in 1872, when the partnership was renewed, the firm of Turner, Beeton & Tunstall resulted. Always active in civic affairs, Turner served the city of Victoria as alderman (1876–79) and mayor (1879–81). When J. P. Tunstall withdrew in 1882, the business in Victoria became Turner, Beeton & Co., and in London, H. C. Beeton & Co. In 1886, Turner successfully ran for the legislature, and the following year he was appointed finance minister, an office he held three times. In 1895 he became the eleventh premier of British Columbia, serving until 1898, when a change of government placed him in the position of leader of the opposition. He served another year as finance minister in 1900 before returning to London as agent-general until 1915, when he was removed from office. He was reinstated in 1917, but the death of his wife and advancing years brought his political career to an end. He died in London at the age of ninety, in 1923.

Sources:

Imperial Review, November 16, 1908; *Victoria Daily Colonist,* December 11, 1923, and February 27, 1949. Courtesy Provincial Archives, B.C.

TURNER, MARION

Marion Turner is said to have come to Lincoln County in 1872 and homesteaded on land near Roswell. On April 15, 1875, he killed Juan Montoya at Blazer's Mill. Both Billy the Kid and McSween (as "Lincoln") confirmed that Turner had killed the man "to see," as McSween put it, "how a damned Greaser would kick." Turner was another of those employed by John Chisum to steal horses for him; they remained friendly into 1878, when Chisum encouraged Turner to file a Desert Land Act claim on land nominally owned by Van C. Smith and mortgaged for two thousand dollars to Murphy & Co. Shortly thereafter the two men had a falling out, and Turner became one of Chisum's bitterest enemies. Turner sold his Roswell land to the daughter of J. C. Lea on August 1, 1878, making the Lea family owners of the entire townsite. He then shared a place at Seven Rivers with John Jones. In September 1879 he married Fred Godfroy's sixteen-year-old niece Hattie Philips, a union of which the family violently disapproved. They kidnaped her and sent her to a seminary in Godfroy's home town, Monroe, Mich.; a divorce was later arranged. Marion Turner remained in New Mexico into the middle 1880s; what became of him thereafter is not known.

Sources:

Rasch, "They Fought," 61–62; Klasner, *Girlhood,* 284–85.

UPSON, MARSHALL ASHMUN "ASH"

Marshall Ashmun "Ash" Upson is another member of this cast of characters whose life deserves a book-length study. Said to have been a reporter on the *New York Tribune* (although it was to the *Sun* that he was always sending news items), Upson came to the Hondo valley in 1872 via Las Vegas, and before that Santa Fe. He was born in Wolcott, Conn. (or was it South Carolina?), on November 23, 1828, a birthday he would later donate to Billy the Kid. Upson was truly, as he often signed himself, "A Rolling Stone," and this outline of his life is presented somewhat apologetically, for the evidence is mightily garbled.

He worked for a while on James Gordon Bennett's *New York Herald* and perhaps also the *Sun,* made a name for himself on the *Cincinnati Enquirer,* set up the *Leavenworth Herald,* and during the next seven years may or may not (his unsupported testimony is always less than reliable) have wandered around Colorado, Utah, New Mexico, and the Indian Territory, served as an assistant quartermaster in the army, sojourned in Mexico, joined the Arkells in establishing the *Rocky Mountain News,* and also worked for A. W. Simpson on the *Kansas City Commercial Advertiser.*

Small, frail, a heavy drinker, his face badly pitted by smallpox, his nose broken and flat, he worked a small mining claim at Tuerto, N.M., that went bust, filled in as a reporter on the *Elizabethtown Argus,* then at the suggestion of Calvin Simpson, a Las Vegas drummer, came to Lincoln intending to start up a store or a newspaper, or both, in partnership with Alec Duval. The plan did not mature, and he wound up teaching school at the Casey ranch. In 1874 he once more tried mining, this time in the Silver City area. No luck again: the following year Ash was working for the *Mesilla News*. In 1876 he moved to Roswell, got friendly with Van Smith—of whom he spoke highly— and became storekeeper, postmaster, stagecoach agent, notary public, justice of the peace, hog raiser, and farmer. He became a lifelong friend and supporter of Pat Garrett, and died at Uvalde, Tex., October 6, 1894.

Sources:

Keleher, *Violence*, 73–75; Klasner, *Girlhood*, 116–23; Shinkle, *Robert Casey*, 83–88; *Roswell Daily Record*, October 7, 1937; Kelly, "Upson," Mullin, HHC, courtesy Melba McCaskill.

WAITE, FREDERICK TECUMSEH

Frederick Tecumseh Waite, who was part Chickasaw Indian, was the son of Thomas and Catherine (McClure) Waite. He was born September 23, 1853, at Fort Arbuckle, I.T., and educated at Illinois Industrial University in Champaign, and at Bentonville, Ark., before graduating in the spring of 1874 from Mound City Commercial College, St. Louis. He worked for two years in his father's business at Rush Creek, I.T., before going to Colorado and from there came to Lincoln County; he first appears as an employee on the Tunstall ranch in 1877.

After the Lincoln troubles he returned to the Indian Territory, moving in 1886 to the Choctaw Nation. Waite (fig. 41) became a model citizen—an obituary refers to him as a distinguished gentleman, a good speaker, and an excellent writer—and in 1888 was appointed a delegate to the international convention at Fort Gibson. In 1889 he was elected representative of Pickens County, and became speaker of the house; he also became a member of the Indian police force and was a candidate for the senate in 1890. During that year he was elected attorney general of the Chickasaw legislature and later he served as national secretary, which office he was holding at the time of his death, one day after his forty-second birthday, September 24, 1895. He was buried in the family plot at Pauls Valley, about fifty miles south of Oklahoma City.

Source:

Research by Jean LaReau Miller, Oklahoma Historical Society, Oklahoma City; Rasch, "Regulators," 67.

WALLACE, LEWIS

Lewis Wallace (fig. 70) was born at Brockville, Ind., on April 10, 1827. The son of David Wallace, a former governor of the state, he grew up in Brockville and Indianapolis. He had some formal schooling but was largely self-taught. After a brief spell at Wabash College, Wallace worked as a reporter and studied law before raising a volunteer company—at age nineteen—for the Mexican War, serving with it as a second lieutenant in the First Indiana Infantry. After the war he returned to law and in 1849 was admitted to the bar. He practiced law at Covington and later Crawfordsville, Ind., and was elected to the state senate in 1856. In April 1861 he was appointed state adjutant-general and then colonel of the Eleventh Indiana Infantry. Promoted to brigadier general of volunteers in September, he commanded a division under Grant at Fort Donelson and, in March, was promoted to major general of volunteers. He helped relieve Grant at Shiloh (although he was criticized for tardiness in doing so) and took part in the advance on Corinth. He saw further action at Cincinnati, in Kentucky, at Baltimore and the Monocacy River. In May and June 1865 he was a member of the military court that tried the conspirators in the assassination of Abraham Lincoln and was president of the commission that investigated the conduct of Henry Wirz, commandant of Andersonville. After a brief period of service in Mexico, he returned to Indiana to practice law. In 1873 he published his first novel, *The Fair God,* lectured until he tired of it (as he later tired of the law), and unsuccessfully sought an ambassadorship or other political appointment in the Hayes administration.

Appointed governor of New Mexico September 30, 1878, at an annual salary of twenty-four hundred dollars—a post he accepted expecting that President Hayes would promote him to something "more important" within months—Wallace resigned March 17, 1881, and was succeeded by Lionel A. Sheldon, a fellow Ohioan. On May 21, President Garfield sent Wallace's name to the Senate for confirmation as minister to Turkey, a post he held until 1885. He wrote two more books, *The Prince of India* (1893) and his autobiography, which was published posthumously in 1906:

Wallace died at Crawfordsville, Ind., February 15, 1905.

Sources:

Wallace, *Autobiography*; Jones, "Lew Wallace."

WIDENMANN, ROBERT ADOLPH

Robert Adolph Widenmann (fig. 81) has always been one of the more shadowy figures of the Lincoln County War. Thanks to diligent research by his grandson, Robert J. Widenmann, it is now possible to draw a fuller picture than has ever been previously published of this elusive character.

The family has been traced back to Hanss Widenmann, of Blaubeuren, a tiny village in the Swabian Alps about eight miles west of Ulm in what was then the kingdom of Württemberg. Hanss, who died ca. 1635, was the first in a long line of innkeeper-cum-postmasters; Robert Widenmann's grandfather was also a keeper of postal inns and a brewer. He had twelve children; his third child, Karl August, Robert's father, emigrated to America in early 1848, possibly to avoid compulsory military service.

Karl August Widenmann's first three years in America were spent at Germantown, Pa., where he met Pauline Gärttner, also from Württemberg; they were married at Philadelphia on April 8, 1851. Shortly thereafter they moved to Ann Arbor, Mich., where August, as he was known, opened a hardware business in 1852 at the corner of Main and Washington streets. Around 1850 his brother Johann Karl joined him, and in due course the business became known as A. Widenmann & Bro. The arrangement lasted for some years before Karl, who had now anglicized his name to Charles, departed for Vallejo, Calif., where he became a brewer.

August then took another partner; in 1867 the business was known as "August Widenmann & Jacob Schuh." By 1872, Widenmann was operating a "Banking, Passage & Foreign Exchange Office," negotiating bills of exchange and foreign currency, and selling tickets for several passenger lines.

August Widenmann lobbied for more than eight years to obtain the position of Württemberger consul at Ann Arbor; on March 11, 1864, King Wilhelm II made the appointment official. By this time the family had moved from their modest apartment above a store on N. Main St. to a spacious house at the corner of S. Fourth Ave. and Packard. The Widenmanns were pillars of the local community; in the census of 1870 they valued their total assets at about $68,500.

Their first child, born January 24, 1852, was Robert Adolph Widenmann, called "Rob." Five more children followed: Marie, born August 19, 1853; Victor Emanuel, born August 28, 1859; Pauline Caroline, born December 20, 1860; Karl August, born June 22, 1862; and William Adolph, born March 27, 1866. Family tradition has it that while the mother was a strict and God-fearing woman, who believed children should be brought up with a sense of duty and responsibility, the father was a violent, aggressive, bad-tempered petty tyrant who drank heavily and womanized often.

Robert Widenmann was sent first to the German parochial school associated with the Bethlehem Methodist Church; when he expressed a desire to study in Germany, he was installed in the home of his uncle, Dr. Adolph Widenmann, who owned a pharmacy in the little town of Biberach. From there Robert went to live in Stuttgart, probably at the home of another uncle, Karl Heinrich Widenmann, a successful businessman who owned a wholesale drug company, Schmidt & Dihlmann.

It was not long before his behavior and lack of manners alienated his straitlaced relatives; worse, he fell in with two young Americans named Spiers and Leslie, and they became known as "the wild Americans." On one of their sprees, they literally painted a Stuttgart monument red. Needless to say, this did nothing to endear Widenmann to his family or their friends.

By June 1870 he was back in Ann Arbor, probably working for his father—whence the claims Tunstall voices in his behalf—and must have run the business while his father was in Berlin in the spring of 1871. Disaster was in the offing: a year or so later, August fathered an illegitimate child; the parents of the young girl involved demanded an indemnity of ten thousand dollars, threatening prosecution if August refused. Business was already bad, for he had alienated most of his fellow Germans in the local community by this time, and his funds were depleted by his lavish way of life. He mortgaged his share of the business and the building, which he owned. When the panic of 1873 further exacerbated his business losses, August defaulted; his creditor, a man named Fritz Rettich, foreclosed, selling August's business to Jacob Schuh, his former partner.

In a desperate attempt to stave off disaster, Mrs. Widenmann opened their sumptuous house to boarders and established a meat market on the corner of Fourth and Huron streets. The boarders provided only a meager income, and the local Germans boycotted the meat stall; the venture failed within the year. The Widenmanns were now forced to sell their lovely home and rent a house on W. Huron St. Finally, they borrowed some money from brother Charles in Vallejo and purchased an old house with a barn and two acres of land on the east bank of Whitmore Lake, twelve miles north of Ann Arbor. August did some farming for a while; his wife turned their new home into a resort, "Widenmann's Grove."

This scandal to some extent explains Robert Widenmann's reticence and untruths about his background: he was as anxious to keep the scandal quiet as his parents were. A less attractive aspect of his personality is illustrated by the probability that he simply walked away from his father's troubles and left his parents to manage any way they could.

It appears he quit Ann Arbor in 1874 and headed south to Atlanta, Ga. He told Tunstall he was born there; in later years he modified the claim to merely having resided in the city. In August 1875 his sister sent a letter to him at an address in Canton, Miss. From there he may have gone to Colorado. By the time Tunstall met him, he was clearly down and out: indeed, the *Santa Fe New Mexican* later said flatly he had "bummed his way to Colorado." His later life was a series of blunders, misjudgments, and injudicious disasters: it is examined fully in the final chapter of this book. He died at Haverstraw, N.Y., paranoid and forgotten, April 15, 1930.

Source:

Widenmann, "Enigma."

WILSON, JOHN B.

A John B. Wilson was "commissioned a Justice of the Peace in Hamilton County, Illinois, in 1826, 1829, and 1831. He was commissioned quartermaster of the 13th Odd Battalion on 2 January, 1847, but this unit apparently saw no action in the Mexican War," says Rasch. "There is some indication that this man was the Justice Wilson of Lincoln County." However, Wilson himself testified at the Dudley Court of Inquiry that his first name was

Green Wilson, "but my baptismal name is John B. Wilson" and that he had taken the new name at Albuquerque on January 20, 1859. Wilson was later a saloonkeeper in Lincoln, where he is said to have died around the turn of the century.

Sources:

Judge Advocate General's Office, Records of DCOI, Deposition of J. B. Wilson; Rasch, "War in Lincoln County," 11.

CHRONOLOGY

1816	——	Henry M. "Hugh" Beckwith b. Ashland, Ala.
1819	Oct. 14	Samuel Beach Axtell b. nr. Columbus, Ohio.
	——	Samuel Bushnell b.
1821	——	John Bautista (Green) Wilson b. Tennessee.
1822	Mar. 14	Patrick Coghlan b. Clonakilty, Ireland.
1823	Mar. 19	Warren Henry Bristol b. Genessee Co., N.Y.
	——	Alexander Grzelachowski b. Gracina, Poland.
1824	Aug. 15	John Simpson Chisum b. Madison Co., Tenn.
	——	Avery M. Clenny, b. Ohio.
1825	Aug. 20	Nathan Augustus Monroe Dudley b. Lexington, Mass.
	——	Gottfried G. (Godfrey) Gauss b. Württemberg, Germany.
1827	Apr. 10	Lewis Wallace b. Crawfordsville, Ind.
	May 15	Frederick Charles Godfroy b. Monroe, Mich.
1828	Feb. 22	William Logan Rynerson b. Mercer Co., Ky.
	——	Robert Casey b. Ireland.
	——	Stephen Stanley b. Arkansas.
	Nov. 23	Marshall Ashmun "Ash" Upson b. Wolcott, Conn.
	Dec. 20	Paul Dowlin b. Greene Co., Pa.
1829	Aug. 16	William Brady b. Cavan, Ireland.
	Aug. 20	Joseph Hoy Blazer b. Washington Co., Pa.
1830	Mar. 2	Montague Richard Leverson b. London, England.
	——	Isaac Ellis b. Missouri.
	——	Felix McKittrick b. Kentucky.
1831	Jan. 19	Carl Philipp Friedrich (Charles) Fritz b. Eglosheim, Germany.
	Mar. 25	Rolando Guy McLellan b. Prince Edward Island, Canada.
	——	John Newcomb b. Missouri.
	——	George van Sickle b. New Jersey.
1832	Mar. 3	Emil Christian Adolf Fritz b. Eglosheim, Germany.
	——	Ira E. Leonard b. Connecticut.
	——	Samuel Wortley b. Mich.
	Dec. 8	James Franklin Randlett b. Newmarket, N.H.
	Dec. 23	Edward Hatch b. Bangor, Me.
	——	Joseph Storm[s] b. Ohio.
	——	John DeLany b. Ohio.
1833	——	Andrew L. "Buckshot" Roberts, alias Bill Williams, b. Texas(?).
	——	Florencio Gonzales b. New Mexico.
1834	May 13	John Herbert Turner b. Claydon, England.
	——	(also given as 1831) Lawrence Gustave Murphy b. Wexford, Ireland.

1835	Dec. 5	David Pugh Shield b. Reynoldsburg, Ohio.
	———	Daniel Dow b. Iowa.
1836	Sep. 2	William Dowlin b. Greene Co., Pa.
	———	Lyon Phillipowski b. Poland.
1837	Mar. 11	George Washington Smith b. Virginia.
	Jul. 21	George Augustus Purington b. Ohio.
	———	José Montaño b. New Mexico.
	———	Alexander Hamilton Mills b. Arkansas(?).
	———	Jacob L. Gylam b. Ohio.
1838	May 20	Henry Carroll b. New York, N.Y.
	Aug. 13	Milo Lucius Pierce b. Lincoln, Ill.
	Aug. 29	Byron Dawson b. Johnson Co., Ind.
	Oct. 23	Albert Jennings Fountain b. Staten Island, N.Y.
	Nov. 22	Andrew Boyle b. Dalry, Co. Ayr, Scotland.
	———	Thomas Blair (Nichols) b. Scotland(?).
	———	Harvey H. Whitehill b. Ohio.
1839	Nov. 16	John Henry Selman b. Madison Co., Ark.
	———	David C. Warner b. New York.
	———	William Gill b. Pennsylvania.
1840	Oct. 6	Thomas Benton Catron b. Lexington, Mo.
	———	Van C. Smith b. Ludlow, Vt.
1841	Oct. —	George Warden Peppin b. Montvale, Vt. (Ohio?).
	Nov. 8	Joseph Charles Lea b. Cleveland, Tenn.
	———	George Washington b. Texas (?).
	———	John N. Copeland b. Kentucky.
	———	Stephen Benton Elkins b. Ohio.
	———	Joseph LaRue b. New Jersey.
1842	Mar. 31	George Kimbrell b. Huntsville, Ark.
	Dec. 1	William Henry Harrison Antrim b. Huntsville, Ind.
	———	Sebrian Bates b. Kentucky.
1843	———	John H. Farmer b. Missouri.
	———	Joseph R. Haskins b. Michigan.
1844	Jul. 31	Samuel R. Perry b. Hancock Co., Miss.
1845	Jun. 30	Frank Warner Angel b. New York.
	Jul. 24	Thomas Benton "Buck" Powell b. Mississippi.
	Dec. 30	Susanna Ellen Hummer b. Adams Co., Pa.
	———	John Hurley b. New York(?).
	———	Samuel M. Horrell b. Arkansas.
1846	May 28	George B. Barber b. Milwaukee, Wis.
	———	James Martin Horrell b. Arkansas.
1847	Feb. 20	Luise Marie Emilie Fritz b. Oedheim, Germany.
	Apr. 28	Huston Ingraham Chapman b. Burlington, Mich. (Iowa).
	May 5	Jacob Basil "Billy" Mathews b. Cannon Co., Tenn.
	———	William W. Paul b. Illinois.
1848	May 2	(may have been April 22) James Joseph Dolan b. Loughrea, Ireland.
	Sep. 12	Taylor Fillmore Ealy b. Schellsburg, Pa.
	———	Charles Bowdre b. Mississippi
	———	John Kinney b. Hampshire, Mass.
	———	Harvey Morris b. Friendship, Allegany Co., N.Y.
	———	Daniel Dedrick (Dietrich) b. Indiana.
	———	Ed[ward?] Moulton b. Illinois.

1849 Jan. 11   Josiah Gordon "Doc" Scurlock b. Talapoosa, Ala.

     May 3   John Wallace Olinger b. Delphi, Ind.

1850 Feb. 19   Richard M. Brewer b. St Albans, Vt.

     Apr. 9   Emily Francis "Minnie" Tunstall b. London.

     May 12   John Henry Riley b. Valentia Island, Ireland.

     Jun. 5   Patrick Floyd Garrett b. Chambers Co., Ala.

     Oct. 10   Robert W. Beckwith b.

     ———   Robert Ameridth Olinger b. Delphi, Indiana.

     ———   Juan Batista Patrón b. New Mexico.

1851 Mar. 14   James Hansell French b. Philadelphia.

     Jul. 26   L. G. Murphy enlists in U.S. Army at Buffalo, N.Y.

     Oct. 1   Benjamin Franklin Coe b. Moundsville, W.Va.

     Oct. 14   James Abner Saunders b. Mt. Pleasant, Iowa.

     ———   Jose Chaves y Chaves b. New Mexico(?).

     ———   Charles Crawford b. Iowa(?).

     ———   Thomas L. Horrell b. Arkansas.

     ———   William Hudgens b. Pennsylvania.

     ———   Samuel R. Corbet b. Tennessee.

1852 Jan. 16   Robert Adolph Widenmann b. Ann Arbor, Mich.

     May 25   Millard Fillmore Goodwin b. New York.

     ———   Isaac "Ike" Stockton b. Cleburne, Tex.

     ———   Samuel Dedrick (Dietrich) b. Indiana.

     ———   Torreón built at Las Placitas by Enricos Trujillo from Socorro Co.

1853 Mar. 6   John Henry Tunstall b. London, England.

     Sep. 23   Frederick Tecumseh Waite b. Ft. Arbuckle, I.T.

     ———   Jessie J. Evans b. Texas (Missouri?).

     ———   Benjamin F. Horrell b. Arkansas.

1854 Apr. 23   Augustine Montaigue "Gus" Gildea b. DeWitt Co., Tex.

     Jul. 14   David Rudabaugh (Rodenbaugh) b. Fulton Co., Ill.

     Oct. 28   Daniel Mitchell Appel b. Pennsylvania.

     ———   Merritt Horrell b. Arkansas.

     ———   John Middleton b. Tennessee.

     ———   Lucio Montoya b. Manzano, N.M.

1855 Jan. 26   John A. Jones b. Pennsylvania(?).

     Feb. 7   Charles Angelo Siringo b. Matagorda Co., Tex.

     Apr. 14   Samuel Speece Pague b. Ohio.

     ———   John M. Beckwith b.(?)

     ———   Martin Chaves b. Manzano, N.M.(?)

     ———   Joe (Josiah?) Nash b. Alabama.

     ———   Benjamin Ellis b. Iowa.

     May 4   Establishment of Ft. Stanton.

     ———   Avery M. Clenny and David Garland settle near Ft. Stanton.

1856 Jan. 26   John Yeoman Thornton b. Danville, Pa.

     Feb. 11   Morice (Julius?) Bernstein b. London, England.

     Mar. 19   Thomas C. "Kip" McKinney b. Birdville, Tex.

     May 21   L. G. Murphy discharged U.S. Army, Ft. McIntosh.

     May 26   Murphy re-enlists U.S. Army, Ft. McIntosh.

     Jul. 13   George Washington Coe b. Brighton, Iowa.

     Sep.—   William Scott "Buck" Morton b. Richmond, Va.

     Oct. 16   James Perry Jones b. Braxton Co.(?), W.Va.

     ———   Pantaleon Gallegos b. New Mexico.

     ———   Michael J. Harkins b.

1857 May —   David Garland appointed postmaster, Ft. Stanton.

     Fall   Henry Newton Brown b. Rolla, Mo. (also given as 1859).

1858	———	Tom O'Folliard b. Uvalde, Tex.(?).
	———	Lucas Gallegos b. New Mexico.
	Sep. 20	Pablo Alderete appointed alcalde, Placitas.
1859	Jan. 20	Green Wilson baptized Juan Batista Wilson at Albuquerque.
	Nov. 20	Henry McCarty b. New York City(?).
	———	Pvt. Joseph Cummings "accidentally" kills son-in-law of Pablo Alderete at Placitas.
	Dec. 3	Alderete and others kill Private Cummings.
	———	Moses Dedrick (Dietrich) b. Kansas.
1861	Apr. 26	L. G. Murphy discharged U.S. Army, Ft. Fauntleroy.
	Jul. 25	Baylor's Texas Confederates occupy La Mesilla.
	Jul. 27	Murphy enlists in First N.M. Volunteers, Santa Fe.
	Aug. 2	Union forces abandon Ft. Stanton.
	Aug. 13	Confederate troops pillage Placitas.
	Sep. 9	Confederates abandon Ft. Stanton. Placitas is abandoned shortly thereafter.
1862	Jun. —	Settlers move in at Tularosa.
	Jul. —	California Column arrives at La Mesilla.
	Oct. 16	Carson and N.M. Volunteers reoccupy Ft. Stanton.
	Oct. 31	Establishment of Ft. Sumner.
1863	Feb. 14	Yginio Salazar b. Valencia.
1865	Summer	Missouri Plaza (San Jose Valle de Missouri) established 18 mi. upriver from confluence of Hondo and Pecos.
1866	Fall	Lawrence G. Murphy and Emil Fritz mustered out of army at Ft. Stanton. Store and brewery established.
		Joseph H. Blazer buys a share of Nesmith's sawmill at Big Fork, later to be known as Blazer's Mill.
	Oct. 8	William Brady mustered out of army at Ft. Sumner.
	Oct. 11	Charles L. Ballard b. Hays Co., Tex.
		Thomas B. Catron arrives in New Mexico.
1867	———	John Chisum and brother Pitzer settle in New Mexico, establish ranch at Bosque Grande.
	———	Robert Casey takes up land along Feliz River.
	Dec. 17	W. L. Rynerson kills Chief Justice Slough.
1868	———	Work begun on rebuilding Ft. Stanton.
	———	Horrell family set out for California from Texas; reaching Las Cruces, they sell their herd there.
	(Fall?)	John Horrell killed by Early Hubbard in an argument over wages.
1869	Jan. 16	Establishment of Lincoln County, with Placitas (Lincoln) as county seat.
		Jan. (mid) Sam Horrell, Sr., killed by Apaches in San Agustin Pass.
	Mar. 1	First (special) election in Lincoln Co.: Richard Ewan, probate judge, Jesus Sandoval y Serna, sheriff, defeating George W. Peppin.
	Mar. 29	Horrell family at South Spring River en route back to Texas.
	Apr. 3	J. J. Dolan mustered out of army at Ft. Stanton.
	May 12	On resignation of Ewan and Sandoval, L. G. Murphy commissioned probate judge, Mauricio Sanchez as sheriff.
	Jun. 30	Rebuilding work at Ft. Stanton suspended: only the guardhouse completed.
	———	Will Dowlin arrives in Lincoln County.
	Sep. 6	First full election: William Brady elected sheriff, Lincoln Co.

	Oct. 16	Lt. Col. August V. Kautz becomes commanding officer at Ft. Stanton.
	Nov. 14	Mescalero Apaches run off 115 head of cattle belonging to Robert Casey.
	Nov. 18	Lts. Cushing and Yeaton from Ft. Stanton and 32 cavalrymen hit Indian rancheria in Guadalupe Mts., killing "a few" Indians and recovering most of Casey's stock.
	Nov. 23	Expedition returns to Ft. Stanton.
	Dec. 19	Cushing leaves Ft. Stanton with another expedition against Apaches. Yeaton second-in-command, 35 men of Co. F., and 28 civilians.
	Dec. 25	At 4 p.m., Lt. Col. Kautz, commanding, all officers and wives, Charles Fritz, and Paul Dowlin are guests of Murphy and Fritz for Christmas dinner at Ft. Stanton.
	Dec. 26	Cushing attacks Apache village in Guadalupe Mts. Yeaton wounded in chest and wrist.
	Dec. 28	Second attack on Apaches.
1870	Jan. 1	Fritz and Murphy hold a dance at Ft. Stanton.
	Jan. 6	Cushing expedition returns.
	Spring	Dick Brewer arrives in Lincoln Co.
	May 30	Indians, thought to be Navajos, kill two or three Hispanics near Ft. Stanton, stampeding sheep herds, killing cattle, stealing horses.
	Sep. 3	Two soldiers killed at wood camp 5 mi. from Ft. Stanton by Indians.
1871	Jun. 26	John J. Allen and Evans family (consisting of father, mother and son, Jessie, arrested along with others for passing counterfeit money. Jessie (18!) said to have been fined $500 at U.S. District Court Topeka.
	Jul. 12	Emil Fritz insures his life for $10,000 with Merchants Life Insurance Co., of New York.
	Sep.—	William Brady elected to serve in territorial house of representatives; Murphy (unopposed), probate judge. Jacob L. "Jack" Gylam elected sheriff.
	Fall	Alex A. McSween at Washington University Law School, St. Louis.
1872	Apr. 8	Saturnino Baca elected probate judge, defeating William Brady.
	Apr. —	William and Emilie Fritz Scholand arrive at Ft. Stanton. Lt. Col. Kautz replaced as post commander at Ft. Stanton by Capt. Chambers McKibbin. Store, hotel, and gambling parlor established at Rio Hondo on the Pecos by Van C. Smith.
	———	Avery M. Clenny beaten up by Calvin Dotson and George Van Sickle, after which saloonkeeper Pete Bishop kills Dodson.
	May 25(?)	Post office established at Rio Hondo. Name changed to Roswell.
	Aug. 18	John H. Tunstall leaves England for Canada.
	Sep. 25	Tunstall arrives at Victoria, B.C.
	Oct. 25	L. G. Murphy purchases $8,647.50 worth of cattle from John H. Riley to stock his Fairview ranch.
	Fall	Alex A. McSween teaching school at Eureka, Kans.
1873	Feb. 3	Two Hispanics killed by John Copeland and John H. Riley, one at Copeland's ranch, the other near Tularosa.
	Mar. 1	Catherine McCarty marries William H. Antrim at Santa Fe.

Apr. 2	Chisum moves cattle from Black River to new ranch 18 mi. south of Ft. Sumner.
	Samuel B. Bushnell takes over as Indian agent at Ft. Stanton, replacing Andrew J. Curtis.
Apr. 3	Alex A. McSween opens law office, Eureka, Kans.
Apr. 13	Sue E. Homer registers First Presbyterian Church, Atchison, Kans.
Apr. 23	Emil Fritz becomes U.S. citizen.
———	Emilie Scholand abandoned by her husband.
May 18	James J. Dolan tries to kill Capt. James F. Randlett at Ft. Stanton.
May 24	Fight over water rights on Tularosa Creek.
May 29	Military called out to put down trouble. One Hispanic killed.
Jun. 10	Emil Fritz leaves for Germany. Murphy accompanies him to Santa Fe.
Jun. 13	At Santa Fe, Fritz and Murphy sell their Ft. Stanton store to L. Edwin Dudley, superintendent of Indian affairs, for $8,000.
Jul. 15	James Dolan insures his life for $10,000 with Missouri Valley Life Insurance Co., beneficiary Emil Fritz.
Aug. —	In spite of spirited resistance, Indians run off 125 Chisum horses at Bosque Grande.
Aug. 23	Alexander McSween marries Sue E. Homer at Atchison, Kans.; they go to live in Eureka.
Sep. 19	John Bolton appointed first postmaster of Lincoln. Operates from building next door to Patrón store, salary $5 a yr.
Sep. 30	Murphy & Co. evicted from Ft. Stanton.
	Work commenced on "the House."
———	Jacinto Sanchez elected probate judge, defeating William Brady; Juan Patrón elected probate court clerk; Alexander H. "Ham" Mills, sheriff; Manuel Gutierrez, justice of peace; and Juan Martín, constable.
———	Horrells settle on Ruidoso River.
Oct. 23	Paul Dowlin nominated post trader (effective December).
Dec. 1	Ben Horrell, Dave Warner, Jack Gylam, and Juan Martín killed in fight at Lincoln.
Dec. 2	Martin and Thomas Horrell come to Lincoln seeking redress; they are told their brother was killed "while resisting arrest."
Dec. 4	Seferino Trujillo and "another prominent local man" found dead in the pasture of the Horrell ranch.
Dec. 5	Ham Mills and posse go to Horrell ranch: shots fired, but fight abandoned without casualties.
Dec. 20	Horrells shoot up *baile* at Lincoln, killing Isidro Patrón, Isidro Padilla, Mario Balazan, and José Candelaria, also wounding another man and two women, Apolonia Garcia and Pilar Candelaria.
Dec. 21	Juan Patrón leaves for Santa Fe to seek assistance from Gov. Marsh Giddings.
Dec. 24	Capt. E. G. Fechet ordered to take "all available men" and bivouac half a mile from Placita to prevent riot between Americans and Hispanics.
1874 Jan. 4	Some sort of "skirmish" between Americans and Hispanics at San Patricio.
Jan. 7	Gov. Giddings offers reward of $100 each for Crumpton, Scott, and "three other persons, brothers, by the name of Harrold."

Jan. 13	Mass meeting of citizens of Lincoln presided over by L. G. Murphy, with Dolan as secretary. Murphy, William Brady, and José Montaño delegated to form vigilance committee. Vigilance committee formed. Murphy tells Horrells that if they will face trial before a commission consisting of himself, Brady, and José Montaño, he will guarantee their acquittal. Offer is declined.
Jan. 19	Horrells sell their cattle, oxen, and horses to Charles Miller for $9,802.50.
Jan. 20	Sheriff Ham Mills and a posse of about 60 Hispanics surround the Horrell ranch and shoot or drive off all their horses. During the night the Horrells decamp downriver from the Casey ranch.
Jan. 21	Ben Turner killed from ambush. (or 22) Will Casey, Heiskell Jones, Frank McCullum, and Jerry Hocradle go to Horrell ranch to bring over their stock, household goods, and food; returning to Casey's, they are stopped by Hispanics who steal everything.
Jan. 23	Ham Mills and posse return, report to Post Commander John Mason. Mills then returns to Lincoln, where a further posse, led by Jimmy Dolan, is assembling.
Jan. 25	Dolan "posse" goes to Ruidoso, burns down the Horrell ranch, and hauls back all crops and corn to Lincoln. In an ensuing "shooting spree," Steve Stephen is slightly wounded.
Jan. 26	Steve Stanley shoots and wounds (Billy?) Gill for refusing to ride in the Mills posse. The same night, a mob beats and tries to hang a man named (William) Little, but he escapes to Casey's ranch.
Jan. 28	Mills and Juan Patrón leave for Santa Fe to seek assistance again from Gov. Giddings.
Jan. 30	Horrells set off upriver to attack Lincoln, naming as their targets Murphy, Mills, Patrón, Juan Gonzales, Dolan, Stanley, Haskins, William Warnick, and José Montaño. "Little" Hart, C. W. King, and Tom Keenan kill Joe Haskins at Picacho. The projected attack on the town fizzles; the Horrells decide to leave for Texas. En route, they kill 5 Hispanic teamsters hauling corn to Chisum's; relieve Robert Beckwith of his horse, saddle, and pistol; steal 6 head of horses and mules from Van C. Smith's at Roswell.
Feb. 2	Ham Mills and Juan Patrón meet with Gov. Giddings and Col. Gregg, commanding District of New Mexico, in Santa Fe.
Feb. 18(?)	Aaron Wilburn, brother Frank, and party kill Zack Crumpton and 3(?) others at Hueco Tanks, recovering stock stolen from Roswell and Beckwith ranch.
Feb. 20	Wilburn posse returns to Seven Rivers.
Feb. 21	Col. Mickey Cronin appointed post trader, Ft. Stanton.
Mar. 5	On their return to Lampasas, the Horrell clan run into a gunfight in which Jerry Scott and Mart Horrell are wounded.
Mar. end	Grand jury hands down indictments against Edward Hart, C. W. King, James F Randlett, John Walker, one Woods, Edward Keenan, J. D. Scott, Frank Regan, James Wilson, Sam Horrell, Merritt Horrell, James McLaine, Charles Powell, Thomas Bowen, William Applegate, Zachariah Compton, Robert Honeycutt, and Robert Casey.

Apr. 1	J. J. Dolan becomes a partner in L. G. Murphy & Co.
	Williamson D. Crothers replaces Bushnell as Indian agent.
Apr. 4	George Kitt, mining at Silver City, strikes vein assayed at $100 a ton.
Jun. 3	L. G. Murphy & Co. opens for business in Lincoln.
Jun. 26	Emil Fritz dies in Stuttgart, Germany.
Aug. 4	John Tunstall quits Turner home; moves in with Mrs. Allen Francis Aug. 10.
Sep. 16	Catherine Antrim dies at Silver City.
Sep. end	McSweens leave Eureka, Kans.
Oct. 10	James Randlett takes change of venue and is tried as accessory to murder at Socorro district court and acquitted; Robert Casey, indicted on similar charges, is not prosecuted.
Oct. 21	Lyon Phillipowski killed by William Burns, clerk in Murphy store at Lincoln.
Nov. —	José Domingo Valencia kills Daniel Fisher in the dining room of the Worley Hotel.
Dec. 28	*Santa Fe New Mexican* announces that henceforth, L. G. Murphy & Co. will consist of L. G. Murphy and J. J. Dolan.
1875 Mar. 3	Susan and Alexander McSween reach Lincoln. (also given as Mar. 14)
———	Ham Mills kills a black prisoner and flees Lincoln county, renting his farm to Andrew Boyle.
Apr. —	McSween wins his first case in Lincoln Co., defending rancher W. W. Paul on larceny (i.e., rustling) charges.
Apr. 15	Marion Turner kills Juan Montoya at Blazer's Mill "to see how a greaser kicks."
Apr. 21	McSween represents Chisum in tax case brought by acting district attorney Albert J. Fountain.
	Probate judge Murphy appoints William Brady administrator of estate of Emil Fritz.
———	Chisum relocates at South Spring, near Roswell.
Jun. —	Joe Howard fined $20 in district court, La Mesilla, for stealing U.S. property. Cases of Elisha M. Dow and John Bolton, retail liquor dealers, continued.
Jul. 30	Samuel B. Axtell sworn in as governor.
Aug. 1	Robert Casey ambushed and mortally wounded by William Wilson; dies next day.
Aug. 8	At 11 p.m., horse thieves Jesus Mes, Pas Mes, Tomas Madril, and Jermin Aguirre killed by party of masked men at Shedd's ranch.
Aug. 17	J. J. Dolan, in Santa Fe, quoted in *Santa Fe New Mexican* to the effect that "crops in the southeastern part of the Territory promise well."
	Ellen Eveline Casey appointed administratrix of her husband's estate.
Aug. 18	"A Lincoln County Democrat" (J. B. Mathews?) writes to the *Mesilla News* accusing Juan B. Patrón of stealing county taxes.
Aug. 31	Ft. Stanton contracts awarded to José Montaño (100 tons grama hay at $23.35 a ton, and 50 tons bottom hay at $20.90); Luciano Baca (700 cords piñon wood at $3.22); Geo. W. Nesmith (1,300 bushels charcoal at 23¢).
Sep. —	J. G. "Doc" Scurlock alleged to have stolen 3 horses, 2 saddles, and gun from John Chisum and decamped for Arizona.

Sep. 6	Election Day: Stephen B. Elkins, who is in Amsterdam, is re-elected to Congress in absentia, leading to the jibe, "I am ster dam dest candidate vot never vas."
	In local elections, Florencio Gonzales elected probate judge, Saturnino Baca sheriff of Lincoln Co.
Sep. 7	Maj. Williamson D. Crothers reports to *New Mexican* that the "Apaches are quiet on the reservation and more of them are coming in."
Sep. 11	Wm. L. Rynerson reports floods in Las Cruces following heavy rains. "Forty or fifty houses destroyed or washed away. . . . [D]amage estimated at $30,000." No loss of life.
Sep. 15	(also given as September 11 and 20) Juan Patrón shot by John Riley.
Sep. 23	Henry Antrim (McCarty) arrested for theft, Silver City.
Sep. 25	Antrim escapes from jail.
Oct. 10	Ham Mills kills Gregorio Balanzuela in Lincoln.
Oct. 18	William Wilson sentenced to death by hanging.
Oct. —	(between 18 and 23) Wilson tries to escape from Ft. Stanton jail and is "dangerously wounded" by his guard.
Oct. 26	In letter to *New Mexican* agent Crothers seeks relatives of 12-yr.-old girl named Tuaciana recovered from Apaches.
Nov. 2	Mescaleros to be moved to "Brown's ranche on the Tularosa about half a mile above Dr. Blazer's mills," reports *New Mexican*.
Nov. 9	John Chisum receives "eight carloads of blooded bulls and calves (two of the former and six of the latter) which were carefully selected in Kentucky," says *New Mexican*.
Nov. —	John Chisum transfers majority of his stock holdings to Hunter & Evans for a figure variously stated to have been between $219,000 and $312,940.
Dec. 18	Wilson hanged (twice) at Lincoln.
Dec. 19	Tomas Archuleta, McSween servant, stabbed to death by two men from Doña Ana Co.
Dec. 25	William H. Johnson and Camelia Beckwith married at the First Presbyterian Church, Santa Fe.
1876 Jan. 1	Jessie Evans, John Kinney, and others kill 2 soldiers and 1 civilian in a Las Cruces saloon.
Jan. 11	A bill to change the county seat from Lincoln to Dowlin's Mill introduced (unsuccessfully) into the legislature.
Jan. 12	Chisum and attorney Thomas Conway robbed on stagecoach at Cook's Canyon, between Silver City and Mesilla.
Jan. 19	Jessie Evans involved in death of Quirino Fletcher in Las Cruces.
———	William L. Rynerson appointed district attorney, Third Judicial District, La Mesilla.
Feb. 12	"Two American families" settle at Roswell.
Feb. 15	Thieves make an unsuccessful attempt to run off the horses from the Mescalero Apache reservation at Blazer's Mill.
	McSween and Brady travel to Santa Fe for territorial and U.S. district courts.
Feb. 18.	Tunstall leaves Victoria, B.C.
	Stephen Stanley fights duel with S. W. Lloyd; latter seriously wounded. Stanley acquitted by Green Wilson.
———	At special election, new offices of county commissioners filled by Paul Dowlin, Florencio Gonzales, and Dr. J. H. Blazer.

——	Jessie Evans, Frank Freeman, and others kill Pancho Cruz, Roman Mes, and Tomas Cuerele near Shedd's ranch at San Agustin.
Mar. —	(or mid-July) John F. Sherman, Jr., appointed U.S. marshal for Territory of New Mexico.
Mar. 21	J. J. Dolan returns to Lincoln from trip to Texas. John Bolton appointed postmaster ($9 a yr.) and John B. Wilson alcalde ($5 a yr.)
Mar. 26	Lt. Taylor and musicians from Ft. Stanton "serenade" Maj. Murphy, Capt. Baca, and J. B. Patrón in Lincoln.
Apr. 4	Announcement of appointment of Frederick C. Godfroy as new Mescalero agent.
Apr. 16	Emilie Fritz Scholand divorced.
Apr. 21	Gov. Axtell visits Lincoln and Mescalero Agency; addresses citizens evening of April 22. Stays at L. G. Murphy store; during his stay John H. Riley arranges a loan of $1,800 for him.
May 13	Rev. David F. McFarland (who married William Antrim and Catherine McCarty) dies in Lapwai, Idaho Territory.
Jun. 8	Andrew Boyle reports John Jones out with a party hunting horse thieves (Jesús Largo and others).
Jun. 26	Van C. Smith and Joseph Stinson fight duel in plaza at Santa Fe.
Jul. 1	Frederick C. Godfroy takes up appointment as Indian agent, Ft. Stanton. Paul and Will Dowlin announce dissolution "by mutual consent" of firm of Paul Dowlin & Co., which henceforth is to be called "Paul Dowlin & Bro."
Jul. 2	Brady tenders his resignation as administrator of the Fritz estate, to take effect from August.
——	Group of 8 Americans and 75 Hispanics organizes vigilance committee at Lincoln "to combat stock thieves."
Jul. 13	Paul Dowlin pays W. D. Crothers $2,000 to raise and educate his daughters Francesca, Luisa, and Rufina in Valparaiso, Ind.
Jul. 18	(also said to have occurred August) Jesus Largo, horse thief, taken from custody of Sheriff Saturnino Baca and hanged near Lincoln by Frank and George Coe, Doc Scurlock, Charlie Bowdre, and Ab Saunders. A few days later Saunders and Frank Coe kill Nicas Meras in Meras (Baca) Canyon.
Aug. —	McSween ceases to act as attorney for L. G. Murphy & Co.
Aug. 6	Morris J. Bernstein and party of Indians return to Mescalero Agency with 8 horses recovered from thieves in Puerto de Luna and Ft. Sumner.
Aug. 8	At Republican convention in Lincoln organized by Maj. Mickey Cronin, president (José Montaño, vice president, A. A. McSween, secretary), Juan Patrón nominated to represent the county.
Aug. 9	At Lincoln Democratic "convention" (attendance, 8) Murphy and Brady nominated to represent county at territorial Democratic convention in Santa Fe.
Aug. 21	Jerry Dillon appointed constable, Precinct 3 (Dowlin's Mill/Ruidoso).
Sep. 2	Mike G. Harkins (Haskins?) accidentally killed in Murphy carpenter shop by J. G. Scurlock.
Sep. 9	L. G. Murphy and Juan Patrón in Santa Fe to attend conventions.

Sep. 11	Democratic convention held in Santa Fe.
Sep. 14	Republican convention held, Santa Fe.
Sep. 19	Emilie Scholand (sister) and Charles Fritz (brother) named to succeed William Brady as administrator of Emil Fritz estate. McSween continued as counsel.
	Stephen B. Elkins returns to New Mexico after a year's absence.
Sep. 20	Case of *Territory v. Van C. Smith and Joseph Stinson* "for fighting a duel" dismissed for insufficient evidence in Rio Arriba Co.
———	Juan Gonzales and one Kelley try to waylay John H. Riley en route from Santa Fe to Ft. Stanton.
Oct. —	John Chisum goes to Arizona to locate a large herd of cattle on new ranch at Sulphur Springs.
Oct. 19	J. G. Scurlock marries Antonia Miguela Herrera at Lincoln.
Oct. 22	Frank Springer marries Josie Bishop, Las Vegas.
Oct. —	Saturnino Baca, Juan Patrón, and A. A. McSween arrive in Santa Fe.
Oct. 29	Tunstall meets McSween, en route to St. Louis and New York, in Santa Fe.
Oct. —	John Slaughter kills Barney "Buckshot" Gallagher.
Nov. 6	John Tunstall reaches Lincoln for first time.
Nov. 7	*New Mexican* notes Baca, Patrón "late county clerk, and Mr A. A. McSween, a prominent lawyer of Lincoln are sojourners in the city." "Capt. Paul Dowlin, post trader at Fort Stanton is at the Exchange."
	Will Dowlin, Juan Patrón, and Francisco Romero y Lueras elected county commissioners; James H. Farmer, justice of peace; and William Brady, sheriff, Lincoln Co.
Nov. 18	Juan Gonzales shot and killed by sheriff's posse at Bernalillo.
———	Buck Powell kills one Yopp at Wiley's cattle camp on Pecos.
Nov. 21	John H. Riley purchases a junior partnership in L. G. Murphy & Co. Also around this time breaks into McSween's office, smashes furniture, "grossly insults" Mrs. McSween, and vows to run McSween out of country.
Dec. 6	Tunstall back in Lincoln after stay at Jicarilla Station.
	W.W. Campbell kills Thomas King at a Lincoln *baile*, claiming self-defense. I. S. Tesson named as accessory. Campbell acquitted on grounds of self-defense.
Dec. 12	(and 14) McSween, back from New York, writes to Charles Fritz about insurance policy.
Dec. 14	Lincoln Co. Farmers Club formed: L. G. Murphy, president; Wm. Brady and Joe Storms, vice presidents; Morris J. Bernstein, secretary; Charles Fritz, treasurer. Committee: S. W. Lloyd, Saturnino Baca, Francisco Romero y Luceras. Motions entertained from John Newcomb and R. M. Brewer.
Dec. 18	U.S. mail agent Charles Adams reaches Santa Fe with 2 men, Sam Bass and Billy Campbell, wanted for robbing Las Vegas stage in November. Both captured near Ft. Stanton.
Dec. —	(late in month) Frank Freeman shoots and cripples a black soldier at Wortley Hotel and escapes despite pursuit by Sheriff Baca.
Dec. 31	Jesse Wayne Brazel b. near Eureka, Kans.
1877 Jan. 4	Stagecoach robber Bass (Sam Bass?) escapes from Santa Fe jail.

Jan. 7	Chisum pursuing rustlers in El Paso area.
Jan. 10	Brewer sick with smallpox.
Jan. 20	Two Casner brothers robbed and killed at Palo Duro, Tex. Reward of $300 offered for Frank MacNab and Frank Tipton alias Hall.
Jan. 23	J. B. Patrón, Will Dowlin, and Francisco Romero y Lueras named Lincoln Co. commissioners; Ignacio Gavarro, Martin Sanchez, and John Copeland as school commissioners.
Jan. 23(?)	Lucas Gallegos kills a "boy" (Sostero García) at San Patricio.
Jan. 26	John H. Riley at Ft. Bayard.
Jan. 28	John S. Chisum in camp near Goat Mountain, en route from Arizona to El Paso in pursuit of cattle thieves.
Jan. 30	Tunstall and McSween leave Lincoln on circuit of McSween's clients and other legal business.
Feb. 4	Tunstall and McSween at Mesilla.
Feb. 5	John H. Riley at Santa Fe.
Feb. 8	Tunstall makes provisional filing on Feliz land at Las Cruces (2,400 acres[?]).
Feb. 9	McSween acquires 6 acres of land in Lincoln from Murphy "for $1 and other good and sufficient considerations."
Feb. 13	John H. Riley, Capt. Chambers McKibbin, and Wm. Rosenthal leave Santa Fe for Ft. Stanton. They expect to complete the trip in 36 hours.
Feb. 27	Tunstall and McSween in Albuquerque.
Mar. 1	Col. John M. Isaacs badly burned at Ft. Stanton.
Mar. 11	Tunstall and McSween leave Belen.
Mar. 13	J. C. Ramsdell and family leave Silver City for Dowlin's Mill, where they intend to run a hotel.
	Col. Isaacs dies of injuries at Ft. Stanton.
Mar. 14	L. G. Murphy withdraws from business, now run by Dolan and Riley as J. J. Dolan & Co.
Mar.(mid)	Jacob and George Harris, Ezra Lee, and other Mormons settle on land near Bottomless Lakes.
Mar. 21	Tunstall and McSween back at Lincoln.
	Widenmann has arrived from Santa Fe.
Mar. 28	Jim Highsaw kills Richard Smith at Loving's Bend on the Pecos.
Apr. 3	J. J. Dolan reports virulent smallpox among Mescalero Apaches: chiefs Roman, Pinole, and Greeley have died.
Apr. 10	Jimmy Dolan and party of Lincoln men "ambushed" by Chisum men in bloodless clash.
Apr. 19	Tunstall receives first money draft from father.
Apr. 20	Chisum, Wiley, and 30 "warriors" lay siege to the Beckwith ranch at Seven Rivers. After 3 inconclusive days, they pull out.
Apr. 24	Tunstall's "ranch" (probably a *choza*) established on Feliz, "a few miles from Turkey Springs," and manned by new employees, Godfrey Gauss and Frederick T. Waite.
	Contracts to supply fresh beef and beef cattle to forts Bayard, Craig, and Stanton awarded to John H. Riley.
	Formal notice of L. G. Murphy's withdrawal from the firm published in *New Mexican*.
	J. J. Dolan becomes Lincoln postmaster, with post office at the House.
Apr. 28	Paul Dowlin killed by Jerry Dillon.
May 2	One H. Harrison of Ft. Elliott at Dodge City hunting for Frank

MacNab, Tipton, alias Frank Hall, and George Black, charged with murder of Casner brothers in Texas.

May 3   Jimmy Dolan kills Hiraldo Jaramillo at Lincoln.

May 7   Tunstall buys 209 head of Casey cattle at sheriff's auction and drives them to Brewer's ranch.

Thomas B. Catron returns to Santa Fe from Minnesota with his bride, the former Miss Julia Walz.

May 7   Andrew Boyle and Buck Powell try to arrest Chisum; he is too ill with smallpox to be moved.

May 8   L. G. Murphy petitions probate court to ascertain indebtedness of Fritz estate to L. G. Murphy and/or vice versa.

May 10   Andrew Boyle and posse of 14 men serve warrants on Chisum, Wylie, and others for replevin, larceny, and rioting.

May 11   Murphy makes his will bequeathing everything to James J. Dolan.

May 28   Tunstall drives cattle to Feliz (Peñasco?) range (arrives May 30).

Jun. 2   Construction of Tunstall store begun.

Jun. 5   Murphy, Dolan, and Stephen Stanley in Santa Fe.

Jun. 8   Will Dowlin becomes postmaster at Ft. Stanton.

Jun.—   Knife fight at Jicarilla mines between James McDaniels and Mesilla saloonkeeper Ben Rinehart [Reinhardt].

Jun. 16   Francis MacNab, at Syracuse, Kans., denies involvement in the murder of the Casner brothers on the Palo Duro in Texas.

Jun. 23   Tunstall back in Lincoln after trip to Mesilla and Las Cruces.

Jessie Evans acquitted of murder of Quirino Fletcher at La Mesilla.

Jun. —   Grasshopper plague wipes out crops in Rio Arriba area; crops "in flourishing condition" on the Pecos.

Shield to become McSween's partner, firm to be known as McSween & Shield, offices in Tunstall store.

Jul. 1   Widenmann sick with smallpox.

Jul. 7   Tunstall leaves on buying trip to St. Louis.

Jul. —   *Las Cruces Eco del Rio Grande* reports "smallpox raging from Dowlin's Mill to the Pecos."

John Chisum starts for Arizona with 2,500 head of cattle.

David P. Shield, his wife, and 5 children arrive in Lincoln.

Jul. 18   D. P. Shield appointed notary public.

Jul. 19   Donnell, Lawson of New York advises McSween of settlement of Fritz insurance claim.

Capt. G. A. Purington recommends abolition of Mescalero Apache Reservation to accommodate claims of gold, silver, and copper miners who wish to file on land.

Jul. 20   Jessie Evans gang steals horses from Mescalero reservation.

Jul. 24   Tunstall in Kansas City.

Jul. 30   Tunstall's sister Minnie marries L.W.F. Behrens.

J. J. Dolan, in Santa Fe, bids for forage contracts at Ft. Stanton against Pat Coghlan and Willi Spiegelberg.

Summer   Wyatt Earp says Charlie Bowdre, Doc Scurlock, Pat Garrett, Billy Wilson, and Jimmy Carlyle at Dodge City.

———   McSween house and Tunstall store completed.

Isaac Ellis and family arrive from Colfax Co.

Aug. 1   McSween receives Donnell, Lawson letter about settlement of Fritz insurance.

Aug. 5	Frank Freeman and Charlie Bowdre shoot up Lincoln, wounding a soldier. Arrested by Brady, Freeman escapes en route to Ft. Stanton. Bowdre posts $500 bail.
Aug. 11	Jessie Evans gang again raids Mescalero reservation for horses.
Aug 12(?)	One Armstrong killed by posse in Lincoln.
Aug. 14	Formation of Grand Masonic Lodge at Santa Fe. W. L. Rynerson deputy grand master; T. B. Catron grand lecturer; S. B. Newcomb, senior grand warden.
Aug. 15(?)	Frank Freeman killed by posse and soldiers at Bowdre ranch.
Aug. 17	Frank P. Cahill killed at Camp Grant, Ariz., by "Henry Antrim, alias Kid."
Aug. 20	Inception of Tunstall and McSween's private mail service via postmaster Ash Upson at Roswell.
Aug. 23	Ramón García, alias Capitan, kills J. M. Franklin, one of Chisum's men, at Dowlin's Mill.
	García "disappears" en route to Ft. Stanton guardhouse.
Aug. 22	Apache Indian scare at Las Cruces.
Aug. 29	J. J. Dolan & Co. borrows $1,000 from McSween acting for Tunstall.
———	Jessie Evans, Frank Baker, George Davis, and Tom Hill steal mules from Mescalero reservation.
Sep. 3	Tunstall at El Moro.
Sep. 9	Frank Baker and Ponciano kill Benito Cruz during attempted robbery.
Sep. 15	Tunstall ill with smallpox at Las Vegas on return journey from St. Louis.
Sep. 17	Ash Upson appointed notary public.
Sep. 18	Horses belonging to Tunstall and Brewer stolen by Jessie Evans gang.
Sep. 21	Brewer, Scurlock, and Bowdre pursue Evans gang to Shedd ranch at San Agustin pass but are unable to recover horses. Return to Lincoln, meeting Widenmann en route in Las Cruces.
Sep. 22	Widenmann in Las Cruces trying to recover horses.
Sep. end	W. W. Paul appointed forage agent at Rio Peñasco, replacing J. B. Mathews, "who has left that place."
Oct. 8	District court held at San Patricio. In *Territory v. Lucas Gallegos and Catarino Romero* for first-degree murder, McSween & Shield unable to defend accused due to illness in Shield family. Case continued. Court adjourned Oct. 9.
Oct. 9	Tunstall, using as nominees McSween, Brewer, Corbet, Clenny, Gonzales, and Dr. Gurney, files on 3,840 acres of desert land in Feliz valley.
Oct. 12	Brewer raises posse including Sheriff Brady to pursue Evans gang to Seven Rivers.
Oct. 14	Tunstall reaches Lincoln from Las Vegas.
Oct. 17	Evans, Davis, Hill, and Baker arrested at Beckwith ranch.
Oct. 18	Tunstall leaves Lincoln en route to Chisum's ranch.
Oct. 19	On the road, Tunstall encounters Brady posse with Evans and other prisoners, also Dick Brewer.
Oct. 20	The Boys jailed at Lincoln about 2 p.m.
Oct. 27	Brewer leads posse in pursuit of Caseys who have run off Tunstall's cattle and headed for Texas.
	Evans and companions lodged in jail in Lincoln.
	John Middleton begins working for Tunstall.

	Oct. —	Tunstall store opens for business: Samuel Corbet, manager and clerk.
	Nov. 1	John Kinney shoots and wounds Ysabel Barela at Mesilla. Subsequently Leandro Urieta mortally wounded by Sheriff Mariano Barela.
	Nov. 10	*Mesilla News* gives votes for Doña Ana Co. representative to legislature: J. B. Patrón, 275; Florencio Gonzales, 41; Daniel Frietze, 17.
	Nov. 16	The Boys (and Lucas Gallegos) escape from Lincoln jail (late at night or early next day).
	Nov. 27	Court-martial of Lt. Col. N.A.M. Dudley convened at Ft. Union. Counsel for court: T. B. Catron.
	Nov. —	"Kid" Antrim employed by Tunstall.
	Dec. 4	McSween deeds east wing of his house to Elizabeth Shield.
	Dec. 18	McSween and his wife leave Lincoln for Anton Chico, where they are to meet Chisum and travel together to St. Louis.
	Dec. 21	Prompted by J. J. Dolan, Emilie Scholand swears out warrant against McSween for embezzlement.
	Dec. 24	McSween and Chisum "detained" at Las Vegas pending arrival of warrant. Mrs. McSween continues on to St. Louis.
	Dec. 25	Contracts for fresh meat supplies for forts Bayard and Stanton awarded to John H Riley.
1878	Jan. 1	Edgar Walz, Catron's brother-in-law, arrives in Santa Fe from Minnesota.
	Jan. 4	Ordered to La Mesilla for arraignment, McSween leaves Las Vegas in custody of deputy sheriffs Adolph P. Barrier and Antonio Campos.
	Jan. 7	Twenty-third legislative assembly of New Mexico convenes: council representative for Doña Ana, Grant, and Lincoln counties, John H. Crouch; house representatives, Juan B. Patrón and John K. Houston.
	Jan. 9	McSween arrives Lincoln. Word received that Judge Bristol is seriously ill. McSween remains under house arrest.
	Jan. 10	L. G. Murphy claim for $76,000 against Fritz estate dismissed by probate court.
	Jan. 12	Dolan and Riley mortgage everything—the store, the land it stands on, merchandise and accounts, grain, hay, cattle, and horses—to Thomas B. Catron.
	Jan. 17	Tunstall writes to *Mesilla Valley Independent* accusing Brady of misappropriating $1,545.13 tax money paid by McSween.
	Jan. 19	Judge Warren Bristol reported seriously sick at La Mesilla. Series of advertisements in *New Mexican* offering services of blooded livestock owned by Montague R. Leverson. These run until late summer.
	Jan. 21	Party consisting of McSween, Barrier, Tunstall, D. P. Shield, and J. B. Wilson sets out for La Mesilla. St. Louis
	Jan. 26	Party arrives La Mesilla.
	———	Confrontation in La Mesilla between Dolan and Tunstall.
	Feb. 2	Hearing held at home of Judge Warren Bristol in La Mesilla.
	Feb. 4	Hearing concluded (Sunday having intervened). MsSween bound over to April term of court; bail set at $8,000. District Attorney W. L. Rynerson refuses to accept McSween's bondsmen: Barrier instructed to deliver McSween to Sheriff Brady.

Feb. 5   McSween party leaves for Lincoln, reaching Shedd's ranch that night.

Feb. 6   At about 8.30 a.m., Dolan again tries to provoke gunfight with Tunstall in Shedd's corral.

Feb. 7   Writ of attachment on McSween's property issued by Bristol on affidavits of Charles Fritz and Emilie Scholand. Dolan, Evans, Baker, and Hill rush it to Lincoln, passing McSween party.

Feb. 9   Sheriff Brady attaches Tunstall store. Widenmann, protesting, is arrested.

Feb. 10   (morning) Brady attaches property at McSween house.
          (evening) McSween party arrives Lincoln.

Feb. 11   Tunstall sends Gauss to Feliz ranch with mules and horses exempted from Brady's attachment.
          (later in day) Middleton, William McCloskey, Widenmann, Bonney, and Waite also go to the ranch.
          McSween writes to Interior Sec. Carl Schurz accusing Dolan & Co. of fraud at Mescalero Agency.

Feb. 12   Posse led by Jacob B. "Billy" Mathews goes to Feliz. Brewer refuses to turn over stock.
          Widenmann as deputy U.S. marshal threatens to arrest Evans, Baker, and Hill. Stand-off ensues.

Feb. 13   (morning) Posse returns to Lincoln for further instructions. Widenmann, Bonney, and Waite also return to plaza.

Feb. 14   James H. Farmer resigns and John B. Wilson becomes justice of the peace at Lincoln.
          W. L. Rynerson writes to "Friends Riley & Dolan."

Feb. 15   Bonney and Waite prevent Sam Wortley from delivering food to guards at Tunstall store. Bonney challenges one of them, James Longwell, to fight.
          Longwell demurs.
          Eastern Doña Ana Co. annexed to Lincoln Co.
          Tunstall employs "Dutch" Martin Martz.

Feb. 16   L. G. Murphy, "desiring to leave Lincoln Co.," offers his Carrisosa ranch for sale.
          Dolan and Mathews leave town to join party gathering at Paul's ranch under Morton.
          Widenmann, Bonney, and Waite return to Feliz.
          Tunstall rides to Chisum ranch to seek help.

Feb. 17   Unable to get help (Chisum still in jail) Tunstall rides to Feliz. Arrives at about 10 P.M.

Feb. 18   Tunstall, Brewer, Middleton, Bonney, and Widenmann leave for Lincoln with exempted horses.
          Tunstall killed at about 5.30 P.M.
          Mass meeting at McSween house around midnight.

Feb. 19   Taylor F. Ealy, wife, children, and schoolteacher Susan Gates arrive in Lincoln about 11 A.M.
          Brewer and Bonney swear affidavits before J. P. Wilson naming Dolan, Evans, 16 others.
          John Newcomb, Florencio Gonzales, and party recover Tunstall's body. Arrive Lincoln late afternoon.
          Coroner's inquest held at McSween house.
          Warrants issued and handed to Constable Atanacio Martinez.

Feb. 20	Asst. surgeon Lt. Daniel M. Appel conducts post-mortem and embalms body of Tunstall.
	Martinez, with deputized Bonney and Waite, goes to Dolan store to make arrests. Trio arrested by Brady.
	Martinez freed same evening, Waite and Bonney kept in jail.
	Brady tells McSween his new bonds unacceptable.
Feb. 21	McSween has Brady arrested for unlawful appropriation of feed from Tunstall store. Bound over to April term of court.
Feb. 22	Tunstall funeral at 3 p.m. Service conducted by Rev. Dr. Ealy, translated by John B. Wilson.
	Mass meeting follows. Committee interviews Brady but gets short shrift.
	Dolan leaves for La Mesilla.
Feb. 23	Widenmann and detachment of soldiers search Dolan store looking for Evans, Baker, and others, then repossess Tunstall's store. Longwell and 4 other guards jailed overnight.
	McSween and Widenmann write Tunstall family advising of murder.
	Jim McDaniels kills H. Martin (cattle thief) at La Mesilla.
Feb. 24	Rev. Ealy conducts first "Sabbath School" in McSween parlor. Another mass meeting follows: McSween advised to leave town for safety.
Feb. 25	McSween writes to Sir Edward Thornton, British ambassador in Washington; to John Lowrie, Presbyterian Missionary Board, New York; and also makes his will.
	Isaac Ellis appointed administrator of Tunstall's estate.
	Widenmann "poisoned"(?).
Feb. 26	(also given as Feb. 27) Widenmann writes to British ambassador, R. Guy McLellan, and Henry C. Beeton about Tunstall murder.
	McSween leaves town.
Feb. 28	Ealy family move into McSween house.
Mar. 1	Brewer appointed special constable by J. B. Wilson, with Bonney as deputy. Brewer forms posse of about 15 men, called Regulators.
	Widenmann and 15 others who participated in "search" of Dolan store arrested by Brady for "rioting." Bound over to April term of court.
	Construction of 12-ft.-high adobe wall around McSween house begun.
Mar. 2	Regulators leave Lincoln for Pecos.
Mar. 4	Will Dowlin and Asst. Surgeon Appel visit the Ealys.
	Brady writes to Rynerson justifying actions.
Mar. 6	Regulators capture Morton and Baker.
Mar. 8	Regulators at Chisum ranch with prisoners.
Mar. 9	Gov. Axtell visits Lincoln: issues proclamation canceling appointment of J. B. Wilson.
	Jessie Evans wounded, Tom Hill killed during attempted robbery near Tularosa. Evans surrenders to military at Ft. Stanton.
	Morton and Baker killed at Agua Negra. William McCloskey also killed.
	McSween returns to Lincoln about 2 p.m.
Mar. 10	Dolan breaks leg jumping off horse "to shoot an unarmed man."
Mar. 11	McSween with Dep. Barrier, George Washington, and George

Robinson quits Lincoln for Pecos to avoid danger.

Widenmann leaves for Ft. Stanton.

Mar. 12 Jack Long, drunk, threatens Dr. Ealy.

Mar. 21 Widenmann returns to Lincoln.

Mar. 24 John H. Riley, Morris J. Bernstein, and Christian Moesner arrive in Santa Fe with pair of 5 ft. elk antlers(!) and other trophies.

Mar. 28 Kid tries to kill Mathews.

Brady and soldiers at Chisum ranch seeking jurors.

Mar. 29 Widenmann writes to Carl Schurz accusing Dolan & Co. of theft of goods from Indian agency brought in by Steve Stanley.

Capt. Smith agrees McSweens can travel to fort with military detachment. Brady not to serve "alias" warrant.

Mar. 30 *New Mexican* publishes attack on Widenmann.

Mar. 31 McSweens, Chisum, and Leverson leave Chisum ranch.

Heavy rains enforce overnight stay at San Patricio.

Brady and cavalry continue to Lincoln.

Apr. 1 Brady killed with Hindman about 10 A.M.

Unidentified man dies at Murphy-Dolan store when "an old wound bursts" on hearing of assassination.

McSween and party arrive about noon.

McSween arrested by Peppin on alias warrant.

A soldier killed accidentally while trying to pass a sentry at the Murphy-Dolan store.

Apr. 3 McSween taken to Ft. Stanton. Susan McSween accompanies him, returning to Lincoln alone.

Apr. 4 Dick Brewer killed at Blazer's Mill. Andrew L. "Buckshot" Roberts mortally wounded. Middleton and George Coe also wounded and taken to Ft. Stanton by Regulators.

MacNab now takes over as leader.

Apr. 5 Roberts dies around dawn. Buried beside Brewer that afternoon.

(noon) Lt. Col. N.A.M. Dudley assumes command of Ft. Stanton. His first act is to send Lt. Goodwin with escort to protect Bristol and Rynerson en route to Lincoln from Las Cruces.

Apr. 6 McSween applies for protection at Ft. Stanton.

Apr. 8 John Copeland appointed sheriff.

Widenmann, Shield, Washington, and Robinson arrested for murder of Brady and taken to Ft. Stanton. Released from custody, Widenmann and Shield remain at fort.

Warrant for embezzlement served on McSween.

Apr. 10 Copeland sworn in; Scurlock appointed deputy sheriff.

Apr. 13 Grand jury empaneled. Judge Bristol commutes daily from Ft. Stanton.

Grand jury indicts Evans, Hill, and companions for murder of Tunstall.

Apr. 17 McSween writes to Ezra A. Hayt, commissioner for Indian affairs concerning Mescalero Agency; same day, offers J. P. Tunstall's $5,000 reward for arrest and conviction of Tunstall's murderers.

Apr. 18 Grand jury indicts Bonney, Middleton, and Brown for murder of Brady.

Apr. 22 Grand jury indicts Bowdre for murder of Roberts.

Dolan, Evans, and others indicted for cattle theft.

McSween exonerated of embezzlement.

L. G. Murphy seeks protection at Ft. Stanton.

Apr. 23 J. J. Dolan & Co. "temporarily" suspends business.

Apr. 24 End of term of district court. Mass meeting of citizens immediately thereafter passes resolution "requesting" members of "the Irish firm" to leave Lincoln.

Apr. 29 Frank MacNab killed, James "Ab" Saunders wounded, Frank Coe captured near Fritz ranch by Seven Rivers "warriors" en route to "assist" Sheriff Copeland. Saunders taken to fort.
Scurlock becomes Regulators' leader.

Apr. 30 Seven Rivers posse rides into Lincoln, half at Dolan store, others in brush 250 yd. below Ellis's, and surround Ellis place. First shots fired around 9 A.M. (says R. A. Widenmann). Fighting continues all day. George Coe shoots "Dutch Charlie" Kruling in ankle. Claimed 4 Seven Rivers men killed, 2 wounded.
Cavalry arrive at about 5 p.m., arrest Longwell and "30 or 40" others on Copeland's orders, taking them to fort.

May 1 Dolan and Riley announce formal dissolution of J. J. Dolan & Co.
Edgar Walz, Catron's brother-in-law, takes over Dolan interests in Lincoln.
Frank MacNab buried beside Tunstall.

May 2 McSween, Widenmann, Ellis, and others arrested for assault and battery with intent to kill (Widenmann says).
Taken to Ft. Stanton "and closely confined."

May 3 Justice J. G. Trujillo issues warrant at San Patricio for arrest of Beckwith and 20 others accused in murder of MacNab.

May 6 Widenmann becomes administrator of Tunstall estate.

May 8 McSween again writes to Hayt, commissioner for Indian affairs, this time enclosing report of criticisms of Mescalero Agency by grand jury.

May 10 L. G. Murphy, accompanied by Dolan and Longwell, leaves Lincoln Co. for last time.

May 18 *Mesilla Valley Independent* asserts that Murphy, Dolan, and Riley were "kicked off the post" by Dudley.

May 19 Group of 18 Regulators, including Scurlock, Bowdre, Brown, Coe, and Scroggins, raids Dolan-Riley cow camp at Seven Rivers, steals 27 horses, and kills Manuel Segovia, alias "The Indian," a Tunstall posseman.

May 20 Widenmann returns to Lincoln with Brewer cattle.

May 24(?) Frank Warner Angel arrives at Ft. Stanton.

May 28 Axtell dismisses Copeland.

May 30 George Peppin appointed sheriff.

Jun. 13 Widenmann leaves Lincoln for Mesilla with military escort. Party includes Washington, Copeland, Martinez, Robinson, and Gauss.

Jun. 15 Evans taken to Mesilla under escort for trial.

Jun. 17 Wilson tries to sell his house and 8 acres in Lincoln to Ealy for $2,000.

Jun. 18 Act of Congress (Posse Comitatus Act) passed, forbidding military intervention in civil disturbances.
McSween, Patrón, and adherents quit Lincoln, head for San Patricio area.
Peppin reaches Lincoln with military detachment; swears in Long, Powell, Turner, and Chaves y Baca as deputies.

Jun. 22	Kinney gang reaches Lincoln from Mesilla.
Jun. 23	Mathews, Turner, and other Dolan men attend Ealy's Sabbath School in McSween house.
	At La Mesilla, Jessie Evans cleared of stealing government mules.
Jun. 24	(or 25) McSween leaves Lincoln.
Jun. 27	Skirmish at San Patricio between 2 parties. Long posse, supported by Capt. Carroll and 25 men, pursues McSween force into mountains before Dudley recalls Carroll.
	U.S. Marshal John Sherman and Dep. Rosecrans leave Las Cruces to take Nicholas Provencio and Serafin Aragon to Jefferson City, Mo. Provencio to serve 5 yr. in the penitentiary.
Jun. 29	Warrants issued by Wilson for McSween concerning San Patricio fight.
	Juan Patrón, saved by Col. Cronin from being killed by Peppin posse, seeks sanctuary at fort.
Jul. 1	Copeland arrested at his ranch.
Jul. 2	Copeland brought to Lincoln, appeals to Dudley for protection.
	Widenmann testifies at Jessie Evans hearing. Given what he calls "a cathauling" by Judge Bristol.
	Evans released on $5,000 bond, case continued to next term of court.
	Mrs. McSween goes to home of Saturnino Baca and threatens to have him killed if he has sent men after her husband.
Jul. 3	Long posse sacks San Patricio looking for Regulators and McSween.
Jul. 4	Long posse (including Turner, Powell, Beckwith) besieges Chisum ranch where McSween party is hiding.
Jul. 5	Regulators leave Chisum ranch. Very dangerous, Ealy says. "One party in town, another out."
Jul. 8	John Selman gang raids Coe and Saunders ranches.
Jul. 10	Indian scout mounted at Ft. Stanton commanded by Capt. H. Carr.
Jul. 14	McSween and "about forty" men reach Lincoln.
Jul. 15	Dolan party arrives from west. "Yelling and shooting," says Ealy. "About 100 shots fired."
	(evening) Daniel Huff dies of poisoning.
Jul. 16	Intermittent firing all day. Two windows of McSween house shot to pieces.
	Peppin asks Dudley for loan of a howitzer.
	Pvt. Berry Robinson fired on in plaza as he brings Dudley's reply.
	Crawford fatally wounded by Herrera.
	Ben Ellis wounded.
Jul. 18	Thomas Cullins killed(?).
	George Bowers seriously wounded.
Jul. 19	(around noon) Dudley arrives at Lincoln.
	(3–4 p.m.) McSween house fired.
	(around 9 p.m.) "The Big Killing": McSween, Morris, Romero, Zamora, and Beckwith killed. Bowers dies in burning house(?).
	Gonzales and Salazar badly wounded.
Jul. 20	Coroner's inquest on McSween; he is then buried.
	Ealy and Shield families taken to Ft. Stanton when Dudley and troops leave: about 4 p.m. Tunstall store looted.
	Tunstall store looted again.

Jul. 21	Sam Bass killed at Round Rock, Tex.
Jul. 23	Crawford dies at post hospital.
Jul. 29	Capt. Carr's detachment attacks Apaches at Alamosa Canyon.
	Ealy family leaves Ft. Stanton.
	Eclipse of the sun.
———	Frank Wheeler, John Chambers, and another man steal Indian horses near the Nogal. Apaches pursue and recover horses.
	Wheeler and Chambers then steal 50 head of cattle at Tularosa.
Aug. 2	Jim Reese killed at Tularosa by Sanchez brothers.
Aug. 3.	Ealys, Shields, and Mrs. McSween reach Las Vegas.
	Captain John (Navajo scout) kills Apache at Canyon de la Luz.
Aug. 5	Morris J. Bernstein killed at Mescalero Agency.
Aug. 6	Capt. Carroll attacks Apache rancheria at Dog Canyon.
Aug. 7	Axtell telegraphs Carl Schurz news of attack on Mescalero Agency and murder of Bernstein by "McSween band of outlaws."
Aug. 17	Hugh Beckwith kills his son-in-law, William H. Johnson, and is himself wounded by Wallace Olinger.
	Mormon settlers reported leaving the country.
	Frank Warner Angel summoned to Washington by Pres. Hayes. Coes quit Lincoln Co.
	A. J. Fountain relinquishes editorship of *Mesilla Valley Independent* as result of continued ill health.
Aug. 18	Tunstall cattle stolen by Dolan "posse." Bowdre, Middleton, Waite Brown, Scurlock, and Kid at Fort Sumner.
Aug. 19	Warren Bristol takes his wife east for medical treatment.
Aug. 20	Six wagon loads of settlers (Mormons) fleeing from North and South Spring pass through Las Vegas.
Sep. 1	Bowdre and Scurlock move their families from Lincoln to Ft. Sumner.
Sep. 4	Axtell suspended.
Sep. 2	D. P. Shield ordained in Presbyterian service at Anton Chico(?).
Sep. 6	Bowers, O'Folliard, Kid, and Sam Smith run off Charles Fritz's horses.
	John Selman "Scouts" or "Rustlers" rob a man of $40 and kill him (or is this a misplaced version of the death J. H. Tunstall reported in 1876?).
Sep. 14	Abneth McCabe appointed deputy sheriff to arrest Beckwith for murder of Johnson.
Sep. 17	Mrs. McSween flees Lincoln for Las Vegas.
Sep. 23	Judge Bristol announces in *Mesilla Valley Independent* there will be no October term of district court in Lincoln.
Sep. 25	Regulators at Red River Springs according to Sallie Chisum.
Sep. 26	The Rustlers burn Coe ranch, wreck Hudgens saloon near Stanton, and seriously injure one Sheppard (a shepherd?).
Sep. 28	The Rustlers murder Chaves y Sanchez brothers and Lorenzo Lucero; at Martin Sanches farm they kill his son Gregorio.
Sep. 29	Lew Wallace arrives in Santa Fe.
	Dolan leaves Ft. Stanton for Santa Fe.
Sep. 30	The Rustlers rape 2 girls at Bartlett's mill.
	Wallace sworn in as governor.
Sep. end	Widenmann flees La Mesilla, goes to Las Vegas, then Ann Arbor before leaving to visit Tunstall family in London.
Oct. 5	Citizens' posse formed to hunt the Rustlers.

Oct. 7	Hayes issues proclamation.
Oct. 8	Sec. of War McCrary issues general order to military to disperse by force all unlawful assemblages in Territory.
	Probate judge Florencio Gonzales and citizens of Lincoln petition Wallace for protection.
Oct. 10	Dudley writes Wallace "ten murders reported in last fifteen days." Party led by Juan Patrón kills 2 men and hangs 1 said to be Rustlers near Ft. Sumner.
Oct. 12	At Ft. Stanton, 65 horses stolen.
	Group of 7 Americans steals 5,000 sheep near Capitan.
Oct. (mid)	John, Jim, and Will Jones, Marion Turner, George Davis, and others kill 3 (some sources say 9) Hispanics named Feliz south of Black River.
————	(between Oct. 9 and 18) Susan McSween hires Huston I. Chapman in Las Vegas.
Oct. 19	Twenty horses stolen from Mescalero Agency and taken to San Nicolas canyon; 13 head recovered by patrol led by Lt. Smith.
Oct. 20	L. G. Murphy dies at Santa Fe; buried in Masonic and Odd Fellows cemetery.
	Post offices at Roswell, Lloyd's Crossing, and Seven Rivers abandoned.
Oct. 24	Billy the Kid sells Brady's horse to Dr. Henry Hoyt at Tascosa.
Oct. —	(between Oct. 9 and 18) Catron allowed to resign (but continues in office until Jan. when replacement Sidney M. Barnes arrives).
Nov. 3	Attorney Sidney Wilson, former partner of David Shield, sets up for business in Lincoln.
	Sheriff Peppin requests military assistance to arrest "Bowdry, Scurlock, et al."
Nov. 6	(also Nov. 7 and 9) Dudley secures affidavits from Long, Baca, Peppin, Priest, Gomez, and Lts. Smith and Pague attacking Mrs. McSween's character.
Nov. 13	Wallace issues proclamation of amnesty.
Nov. —	Widenmann's bond declared forfeit for nonappearance by Bristol in La Mesilla.
Nov. 21	Dudley's "Open Letter" published.
Nov. 23	Chapman and Mrs. McSween return to Lincoln.
Nov. 30	John Kinney arrested and jailed on charge of murder; principal prosecution witnesses decamp; Kinney takes a change of venue to Grant Co.
Dec. 1	Chapman posts call for public meeting in Lincoln.
Dec. 7	Wallace asks Hatch to remove Dudley.
	"John N. Copeland & Co." open a hotel and saloon at Lincoln.
Dec. 11	Jack Irvin and Charlie Moore, 2 of the Rustlers, found robbed and shot dead at White Sands.
Dec. 13	Sheriff Peppin requests military protection during court session in Lincoln. Lt. French assigned to duty.
	(evening) Lt. French, drunk, tries to assault Huston Chapman. John Copeland shoots 19-yr.-old Juan Mes (Johnny Mace) at Lincoln. Acquitted the following day.
Dec. 14	Board of officers convened at Ft. Stanton to investigate conduct of Lt. French.
Dec. 16	Will Hudgens reports that "a mob" plans to kill Juan Mes and

John Hurley. Both given protection at Ft. Stanton.

Charles Fritz requests military protection from cattle thieves.

Dec. 21 Kinney found not guilty in Grant Co. of murder of Ysabel Barela. Board of officers at Ft. Stanton recommends "no further action" in the case of Lt. French.

Dec. 22 Bonney surrenders to arrest under amnesty; loses nerve and escapes.

Dec. 25 Col. Dudley prohibits civilians from entering Ft. Stanton without a military escort.

Dec. 27 Dolan, Mathews, and Long request protection at Ft. Stanton.

Dec. (end) Widenmann reaches London.

G. W. Peppin resigns as sheriff, declining to serve out term.

1879 Jan. 1 George Kimbrell appointed sheriff.

Jan. 4 New Mescalero agent S. A. Russell appointed.

John Kinney says he plans to move to Silver City.

Frederick C. Godfroy and Ira M. Bond, editor of the *Mesilla News*, accused of smuggling blankets.

Jan. 11 J. B. Wilson informs *Mesilla Valley Independent* that conditions in Lincoln Co. are peaceful.

Jan. 13 Susan McSween appointed administratrix of Brewer, Tunstall, and McSween estates.

Jan. 18 *Mesilla News* reports striking of "peace treaty" between Mrs. McSween and J. J. Dolan.

Feb. 1 Capt. Thomas Blair arrested, charged with bigamy.

Feb. 4 Kate Godfroy married to Dr. D. M. Appel by Rev. Thomas Harwood of La Junta [Hondo], superintendent of the Methodist Episcopalian Mission in New Mexico.

Dr. Blazer reports that the "war element" in Lincoln Co. is "fading."

S. W. Lloyd reports "war" between Hispanics and Apaches.

Feb. 7 John Sherman rescinds Peppin's appointment as deputy U.S. marshal.

Feb. 11 Susan McSween requests military assistance in retrieving Tunstall cattle held at Seven Rivers by Bob Speakes, one of the Rustlers. Request, which Dudley terms "farcical," denied.

Feb. 18 Kimbrell asks military for help in arresting Bonney and Salazar. Lt. Byron Dawson detailed to assist him.

(about 9:15 p.m.) Chapman killed in Lincoln.

Feb. 19 Lt. M. F. Goodwin and 12 men sent to keep order in Lincoln.

Feb. 20 Chapman buried.

J. B. Wilson dismisses lawsuits against Dudley.

Dudley visits Lincoln at request of citizens.

Kimbrell again requests military assistance to arrest Kid and Salazar.

Feb. 23 Posse of 6 soldiers sent to San Patricio by Lt. Goodwin is unsuccessful.

Feb. 25 Posse of soldiers sent to Seven Rivers by Lt. Carroll returns to Roswell with 275 head of Hunter & Evans and Tunstall cattle.

Feb. 27 Wallace again requests imposition of martial law in Lincoln Co.; request denied.

Mar. 1 Wallace and Hatch leave Santa Fe for Lincoln. Hatch orders Dudley to place his command under Wallace.

Mar. 6	Wallace and Hatch arrive Lincoln. Dolan, Evans, Bonney, Campbell, and Mathews arrested and taken to Fort Stanton.
Mar. 7	Wallace again asks Hatch to suspend Dudley.
	Dudley suspended. Capt. Henry Carroll takes command pending return of Purington.
Mar. 13	Wallace forms Lincoln County Riflemen.
Mar. 17	Wallace and Kid meet in Lincoln.
Mar. 18	Evans and Campbell escape from Ft. Stanton. Gov. Wallace offers $1,000 reward. Lincoln County Riflemen (Capt. J. B. Patrón, 1st Lt. B. H. Ellis, 2nd Lt. Martin Sanches) pursue them (unsuccessfully).
Mar. 21	Kid and Scurlock surrender to Kimbrell.
Mar. 22	*Mesilla Valley Independent* reports Joseph C. Lea made postmaster at Roswell.
	J. H. Blazer and Will Dowlin bid for timber contract to build a new military fort at El Paso on the site of Hart's mill (Ft. Bliss).
	John Kinney opens butcher shop in La Mesilla.
Apr. 12	*Mesilla Valley Independent* reports "Texas Jack," soldier who helped Evans and Campbell to escape, captured by military patrol.
	Lincoln Co. deputy sheriff R. M. Gilbert reports 16 in confinement at Ft. Stanton.
Apr. 14	District court convenes in Lincoln.
	Kid testifies about Chapman murder before grand jury.
Apr. 16	Dudley Court of Inquiry (DCOI) convenes at Ft. Stanton.
Apr. 18	Wallace leaves Ft. Stanton for Santa Fe.
Apr. 25	Attempted assassination of Ira E. Leonard.
Apr. 28	Ham Mills passes through Mesilla en route for Arizona from west Texas, plans to settle (in Tombstone?).
Apr. 30	Grand jury adjourns. In all more than 200 indictments found. Lincoln Co. has fewer than 200 voters. Among sentences handed down: Lucas Gallegos, 4th degree murder, 1 yr. in jail; Dan Dedrick, accessory to murder, acquitted. Eli Gray, member of Lincoln Co. militia, accidentally shoots self and dies.
May 6	George A. Rose, alias "Roxy," wounds a soldier in shooting incident at Franklin (El Paso), Tex.
May 8	Agent S. A. Russell arrives at South Fork Agency.
May 10	Presentation commences at DCOI.
	Sebrian Bates in fight at post trader's store with Allen Ballard, whom he hits over the head with an ax handle, leaving Ballard in "a dangerous condition."
May 12	John Kinney decamps for Arizona on hearing of impending arrest.
May 17	*Mesilla Valley Independent* reports gold discovered at Dr. Spencer H. Gurney's "Isabella" mining camp, 8 mi. NE of Lincoln.
	Mickey Cronin, Saturnino Baca also made strikes.
May 24	Evans and Campbell reported to be at John Slaughter's cattle camp on the Pecos.
May 28	Kid testifies at DCOI.
Jun. 4	Evans and Campbell reported at La Cienega, near Tucson.
Jun. 14	Dep. U.S. marshal Charles Conklin brings Frank Coe to La Mesilla in irons for trial for murder of Roberts.
	Coe is exonerated by the court.
	U.S. Marshal Sherman, by failing to bring Scurlock and the

Kid to La Mesilla, makes it impossible for them to be tried during this term of court.

Three counts of resisting arrest against R. A. Widenmann dismissed; he has left the country.

George Washington, attempting to shoot a dog, kills his wife and child with same shot.

Jun. 17	Kid "escapes from custody" in Lincoln.
Jun. 21	"Big Jim" French killed in quarrel over division of spoils near Lincoln (claimed, but unlikely).
Jun. 27	Bristol allows Dolan $3,000 bail at La Mesilla in death of Chapman.
Jul. 5	DCOI ends. Dudley exonerated.
Jul. 13	J. J. Dolan married to Caroline (Lina) Fritz by Rev. J. S. Tafoya (assisted by Mickey Cronin) at A. J. Ballard house, Hondo. The newlyweds leave on a 2 mo. honeymoon.
Jul. 16	Sam Perry kills Frank Wheeler near Hillsboro.
Jul. 22	Dudley transferred to Ft. Union.
Aug. 10	Kid appears in San Miguel Co. district court charged with keeping a gaming table.
Aug. —	Discovery of gold at White Oaks starts "gold rush" and boom town springs up.
Aug. 26	John Jones kills John Beckwith at Nash's *choza* in Pierce Canyon, Seven Rivers.
Aug. 29	Bob Olinger kills John Jones, also accidentally cripples Milo Pierce.
Aug. 30	Stagecoach robbery near Las Vegas attributed to Dave Rudabaugh and John J. Webb.
Sep. 4	Victorio leads Apaches off Mescalero reservation: tells Dr. Blazer "from now on it will be war to the death." Apaches attack troops near Ojo Caliente, killing 8 men and stealing 46 horses.
Sep. 17	Fight between Apaches and civilians near Hillsboro; 10 citizens killed.
Sep. 18	Lt. Byron Dawson ambushed by Apaches. Troops withdraw after being relieved by Capt. C. D. Beyer; 8 killed, 1 wounded.
Sep. 26	Maj. A. P. Morrow attacks Apaches near Ojo Caliente.
Oct. 27	Morrow attacks Apaches again near Corralitos River, Mexico.
Nov. 10	Dudley appears at La Mesilla to stand trial on charges of arson and libel brought by Mrs. McSween; she does not appear. Bench warrant issued for her arrest.
Nov. 17	Susan McSween arrives at La Mesilla.
	Trial of Dudley on charges of arson results in his being acquitted. Further case of libel is dropped.
	Rudabaugh robs train near Las Vegas.
Nov. 23	Dick Hardman shot by unknown parties while in custody at Lincoln.
Dec. 6	Allen J. Ballard shot in back (by mistake?) by unnamed assailant between Lincoln and Hondo.
1880 Jan. 10	Billy the Kid kills Joe Grant at Fort Sumner.
Jan. 12	Morrow attacks Apaches at Puerco River.
Jan. 14	Pat Garrett marries Apolonaria Gutierrez at Ft. Sumner.
Jan. 17	Morrow attacks Apaches in San Mateo Mts. Lt. James Hansell French killed during engagement.
Feb. 3	Morrow again attacks Apaches near Aleman Wells.

Feb. 5	Detachment of troops commanded by Capt. L. H. Rucker routed by Apaches in San Andres Mts.
Mar. 2	John J. Webb kills Michael Kelliher at Las Vegas.
Mar. —	Bob Olinger kills Frank Hill.
	Juanito Mes (Johnny Mace) killed by posse while trying to rob Will Hudgens store.
	Paz Chaves lynched by unknown parties.
Apr. 5	Detachment commanded by Capt. Henry Carroll poisoned by gypsum water at Malpais Spring.
Apr. 6	Carroll's detachment runs into Apaches at Hembrillo Canyon. Two men killed; Carroll wounded.
Apr. 7	Apaches flee in face of reinforcements led by Col. Hatch.
Apr. 9	John J. Webb sentenced to death for murder of Kelliher.
Apr. 12	J. P. Tunstall formally requests $150,000 compensation from U.S. government for death of his son.
Apr. 16	Maj. Morrow attacks Apaches at Dog Canyon.
Apr. 30	Grand jury indicts John Jones and Marion Turner for murder of McSween.
	Dave Rudabaugh tries unsuccessfully to rescue J. J. Webb from Las Vegas jail, killing jailer Lino Valdez in the process.
May 18	(19?) Jessie Evans and others rob Sender & Siebenborn store at Ft. Davis, Tex.
———	Price Stone killed at Lincoln by "One Armed Joe" Murphy; Murphy assassinated while in jail (by Jose Chaves y Chaves?).
Jun. 5	Morrow fights Apaches at Cook's Canyon.
Jun. 20	Susan McSween marries George B. Barber.
Jul. 3	Jessie Evans captured by Texas Rangers in running fight. George Davis and Ranger George Bingham killed.
	New Mexican reports 3 men killed by "mob of reckless men" in Lincoln on consecutive days: victims are a man named Harriman, a deputy sheriff, and a prisoner in the jail.
Aug. 28	Bureau of Indian Affairs bans encroachment of miners and settlers on Mescalero reservation.
Oct. 14	Mexican troops under Gen. Terrazas surround Apaches at Tres Castillos; 78 warriors killed, including Victorio.
Nov. 2	Pat Garrett elected sheriff, Lincoln Co., by 141 majority over George Kimbrell.
Nov. 12	Lew Wallace's novel, *Ben-Hur: A Tale of the Christ*, is published in New York.
Nov. 27	James Carlyle killed at Greathouse & Kuch ranch.
Dec. 1	Jessie Evans enters Huntsville penitentiary.
Dec. 10	Garrett-Stewart posse sets out from Las Vegas to search for the Kid.
Dec. 12	Kid writes letter protesting innocence to Gov. Wallace.
Dec. 15	Wallace offers $500 reward for the Kid.
	Bowdre writes to Capt. Lea asking for help.
	Catron sells the Murphy-Dolan store building to the Lincoln Co. commissioners for use as a jail.
Dec. 18	Some 150 Lincoln Co. residents—among them John Bolton, Dan Dedrick, R. M. Gilbert, James Tomlinson, and George W. Scurlock—petition the president to abolish the Mescalero Apache Reservation and turn the land over to mining use.
Dec. 19	Tom O'Folliard killed at Ft. Sumner.

Dec. 23	Charlie Bowdre killed at Stinking Springs. Kid, Rudabaugh, and Wilson captured by Garrett posse.
Dec. 25	Garrett, Kid, Rudabaugh, and Wilson eat Christmas dinner at Grzelachowski roadhouse in Puerto de Luna.
Dec. 26	Garrett delivers prisoners to Las Vegas jail. Wallace leaves Santa Fe for trip to East.
Dec. 27	Prisoners transferred to Santa Fe by train. Kid, Rudabaugh, and Wilson put in cell with Edward M. "Choctaw" Kelly, accused of murder.
Dec. 28	Rudabaugh pleads guilty to robbing U.S. mail.
1881 Jan. 1	Kid writes to Wallace from jail.
Jan. 3	Rudabaugh tried for robbery and sentenced to life imprisonment. Sentence stayed pending trial for murder.
Jan. 21	Wilson arraigned before Bristol; bond fixed at $5,000. Unable to raise it, he is returned to jail.
Feb. 10	Wallace returns to Santa Fe, leaves immediately for Silver City.
Feb. 28	Attempt by Kid, Rudabaugh, Wilson, and Kelly to dig their way out of jail detected.
Mar. 2	Jim McDaniels dies at Las Cruces.
	Kid writes again to Wallace.
Mar. 4	Kid writes third letter to Wallace from jail.
Mar. 7	Rudabaugh and Kelly taken to Las Vegas for trial.
Mar. 9	Wallace offers his resignation to Pres. Garfield.
	Rudabaugh arraigned at Las Vegas for murder of Valdez. Change of venue granted to Santa Fe.
Mar. 15	Kid indicted for cattle theft by grand jury in San Miguel Co.
Mar. 17	Garfield accepts Wallace's resignation, appoints Lionel A. Sheldon, of Ohio, governor of New Mexico.
Mar. 21	Jim Greathouse arrested at Anton Chico as accessory to Carlyle murder; released on $3,000 bond.
Mar. 27	Kid writes "for the last time I ask" letter to Wallace.
Mar. 30	Wilson tried at La Mesilla. Case continued.
	Kid's first trial commences.
Apr. 6	Ira E. Leonard has Kid's indictment for murder of "Buckshot" Roberts quashed at La Mesilla.
Apr. 8	Kid's second trial commences.
Apr. 9	Kid found guilty of murder of Brady.
Apr. 13	Kid sentenced to be hanged at Lincoln on May 13.
Apr. 15	Kid writes to Edgar Caypless concerning sale of his mare.
	(10 p.m.) Kid, guarded by 7 men, including Mathews, Kinney, and Olinger, taken from La Mesilla to Lincoln.
Apr. 21	Kid jailed in courthouse, former Dolan store.
Apr. 28	Kid escapes, killing Olinger and Bell.
Apr. 29	Coroner's jury headed by Jesus Lueras, justice of the peace, finds that Bell and Olinger were killed by "William Bonney alias Kid."
Apr. 30	Wallace posts a $500 reward for the capture of the Kid. Earlier in the day he had signed his death warrant.
May 8	Thomas C. "Kip" McKinney kills Bob Edwards at Rattlesnake Springs.
May 30	Lew Wallace, appointed minister to Turkey, leaves New Mexico for Crawfordsville.
Jul. 14	Garrett kills the Kid at Ft. Sumner.

J. H. TUNSTALL'S ACCOUNT BOOK

Dr.
Alexʳ A. McSween   in a/c with J. H. Tunstall   Cr.

Mar. 24			*Mar. 20th*		
To amt. Per. Setᵗ		29.50	By Matthews Rent		70.00
" Gold Draft		2425.00	" Brookmire & Ranken		1365.00
" Premᵐ on same		127.63	" Cost of Draft		6.87
" Gold Draft		4812.00	" Safe in Transitu		35.75
" Premium		330.82	" Cost of Draft		.25
" Chq on M.N.B.		174.93	" R. A. Widenmann		220.00
" " " Soule T & W		156.55	" W. R. Arms Co.		455.00
" " " M. N. B.		2000.00	" Cost of Draft		2.27
" " " M. N. B. Draft		1000.00	" Collecting Draft		24.25
" Cash fr. Store Sales		282.90	" Cheque #11		65.00
" Chisum & Hʳ Draft		1000.00	" Otero Sellar & Co.		500.00
" Cash fr. P. Coghlan		47.31	" 610 lbs corn		15.25
" Copeland Note		65.00	" Stove & Pistol		42.50
" W. Dowlin Cash		886.10	" Cost of Draft		.25
" Profit in corn deal		35.83	" Fght on store staty		10.00
		———	" 209 head of cattle		987.40
		13373.57	" [unclear entry]		79.75
					———

Alexʳ A. McSween   In a/c   With J. H. Tunstall

To amt. Bt. Forᵈ		13373.57	*May 18th*		
			By Amt. Bt. Forward		3879.54
To Kennard & Sons		59.40	" G. D. Bowman		25.00
" Jewellry		4.00	" J. H. Farmer Loan		123.47
" Bl. Vinegar		15.55	" Brewer Orders		735.00
" 2 Suits Uclothes		5.25	" S. Wortley		21.75
" Napkins		3.25	" Xpress Ft Stanton		10.70
" Damask		4.25	" " Lincoln		1.00
" Dz L. Hose		3.25	" A. H. Mills		55.00
" 2 Suits for Boys		15.75	June 2 Store Building		166.50
" 1 Suit for Self		14.06	" Chk. F. N. B. Santa Fe		30.00
" Hardware		1.50	" McKitterick		100.00
" 1 LampShade & Br.		2.65	" Watching Horses		.66
15/12/77 Book a/c to date		490.33	9." Store Building		191.25
Shield		90.00	16." " "		83.00
Under Clothing		10.00	23." " "		110.50
			" Bolander		43.42
		———	" Widenmann		25.00
		14093.77			———
					5601.79

Alex. A. McSween   In a/c   With J. H. Tunstall

To Amt Bt Ford.	14093.77		By Amt Bt Ford	5601.79
			" Casey Corn	9.00
			" Freight on safe	39.00
			" Soule T & W	159.40
		June 30	" Store Building	32.37
			" Cheque #246	20.00
			" U.S. Revenue Sep	4.86
			" Terr. License	28.16
		July 7	" Store Building	133.14
			" Cheque Bolander	82.60
			" " Gerdes	24.20
		14	" Store Building	35.63
		21	" " "	25.95
			" Ledger	164.83
			" G. D. Bowman	15.00
			" Skelley Draft	126.63
			" Frght on sacks	163.60
				6666.16

Alex^r A. McSween   In a/c   With J. H. Tunstall

To Amt. Bt. Ford.	14093.77	By Amt. Bt. For^d	6666.16
		" Freight on stove	12.50
		" Matthews Ranch	530.00
		" Widenmann	20.00
		" R. D. Hunter	218.80
		" Freight on Doors&c	72.00
		" Brewer Ranch	170.00
		Matthews Ranch	170.00
		" 3 Feliz Filings	510.00
		" Xpress with Papers	30.00
		" Widenmann	52.40
		" Brewers Ex^n to	65.00
		Las Cruces	
		" Cheque canceller	6.00
		" Note Book	8.50
		" Receipt Book	.75
		" R. D. Hunter Taxes	3059.75
		" License W. Dowlin	389.42
			11981.28

Alex^r A. McSween   In a/c   With J. H. Tunstall

To Amt. B^t For^d.	14093.77	By Amt. B^t For^d	11981.28
		" Taxes Copeland	51.11
		" Cheque JS Chisum	30.00
		" " "	20.00
		" " "	21.95
		" " "	30.00
		" " "	6.00
		" " "	240.00
		" " "	45.00
		" " "	3.00
		" " Hospital	50.00

"	" "	100.00
"	" "	316.00
"	" "	200.00
"	Chisum & Hunter	150.00
"	Taxes J. Newcomb	24.87
"	Romero y Trujillo	2.00
		13271.71

Alex A. McSween   In a/c   With J. H. Tunstall

To Amt B^t For^d	14093.77		By Amt. B^t For^d	13271.71
			Taxes McK^k & Chisum	2.00
			" Brewer & Corbett	4.00
			" Freight on Bk Furniture	11.40
			" Taxes J. H. Blazer	121.05
		[Aug. 29]	J. J. Dolan & Co.	1000.00
			" A. M. Clenny	200.00
			Xpenses	6.00
			Padre for Wool	88.20
			J. B. Wilson	75.00
			" Amt Per Cash Bk. ^97.07- ^32.27	64.80
			" " " " " Page 2	48.90
			" " " " " " 3	1.00
			" ;" " " " 4	8.50
			" " " " " 5	50.48
			Fght on Pistols	.90
			Cash Book 6	76.40
				15034.34

Alex A. McSween   In a/c   With J. H. Tunstall

To Amt Bt. For^d	14093.77	By Amt. Bt. For^d	15034.34
		" Amt Per Cash Book 7	292.15
		" " " " " 8	167.24
		" " " " " 9	67.00
		" Work on Store	18.25
		" " " "	13.50
		" " H Folsom & Co	419.50
		" Otero Sellar & Co.	1176.98
		" 240lbs Soap	26.40
		" 120″ Candles	26.20
		" 130″ Nails	32.50
		" J. H. Farmer	37.90
		" A. M. Clenny	81.00
		" J. B. Patron Brewer	36.20
		" Widenmann at Ellis	4.75
		" Tools for Huff	29.10
		" Paints Brushes &^c	42.90
			17501.91

Alex^r A. McSween   In a/c   With J. H. Tunstall

To Amt. Bt. Ford.	14093.77	By Amt B^t For^d	17501.91
		" Freight on Tools &c	22.00
		" Juan B Patron	112.60
		" " " " Cash	50.00
		" D Huff	83.00
		" Plasterer	5.00
		" C Bowder	36.30
		" E. E. Casey	99.00
		" W. L. Rynerson	75.00
		" Co. Scrip 150	75.00
		" " " 52	26.00
		" Ter^l" 48	36.00
		" " "	75.00
		" West & Blazer	555.35
		" J. B. Wilson	124.39
		" J. B. Wilson Cheque	75.00
		" Lloyd	80.00
			19031.55

Alex^r A. McSween   In a/c   With J. H. Tunstall

To Amt Bt. Ford.	14093.77	By Amt Bt. For^d	19031.55
		" Widenmann	40.00
		" "	50.00
		" Brewer & Paul	10.00
		" McIntosh Brewer	10.00
		Scurlock Chisum	46.00
		" J. H. Blazer	560.40
		" Van Sickles	100.00
		" Harris	149.50
		" Chisum Cheque	68.00
		" Fght South	14.00
		" Chisum Cheque	8.00
		Newcomb "	50.00
		" Corbett	16.75
		Taxes Gonzales	56.00
		Brewer Ellis	11.10
		" D. Dowe	16.00
			20226.30

Alex^r A. McSween   In a/c   With J. H. Tunstall

To Amt Bt. For^d	14093.77	By Amt Bt. For^d	20226.30
		" Blacksmith	8.75
		" W. Dowlin	1258.44
		" "	28.00
		" "	175.00
		" "	70.00
		" Brewer a/c	632.32
		" W Dowlin Dft	300.00
		" Miranda Haul^9	25.00
		" Dodd Brown & Co	25.00
		" 20 Cows @ 14.^00	280.00
		" 20 Calves @ 4^00	80.00

"	9 Yearlings @ 8^{00}	72.00
"	2 2 year olds @ 8^{00}	16.00
"	Van Sickle Wagon	55.00
"	a/c	67.00
"	Mrs Casey (Cattle)	152.00
		23470.81

Alex A McSween	In a/c	With J. H. Tunstall			
To Amt Bt. Ford.	14073.77		By Amt. B^t For^d	23470.81
" W Dowlin	500.00		" Cheque McK^k	6.00
" Brewer Cheque	35.00			
" Chisum & H^r Credit	2250.00			
Balance	6598.04			
	23476.81			23476.81

It was on the basis of this notebook that McSween (and later, his widow) claimed Tunstall owed him money, which he in turn requested that Tunstall's father send to him. However, Robert Widenmann produced a final balancing of the two men's financial affairs that showed a somewhat different picture.

Mrs. A. A. McSween in a/c		with the estate of J. H. Tunstall	
Dr.			**Cr.**
To Store a/c	$789.87		
" ½ of lumber bill	275.67		
" " " " "	120.00		
" Brewer note	2000.00		
" Interest on same 2ys	500.00		
" " " Dolan note	300.00		
" freight of $72-	36.00		
" ½ tools for Huff $29.10	14.55		
" ½ Brushes paints $42.90	21.45		
" ½ freight, tools $22.90	11.45		
" ½ D Huff a/c $83.00	41.50		
" ½ Plasterer $5	2.50		
" ½ Dr Blazer's bill $560.40	280.20		
" ½ freight $14	7.00		
" ½ of store building costs for which he charges himself $1009.99 but which cost over $6000	2000.00		
carried over	6162.19		

Dr. Brought over	6162.19	Brought over	$——
To Cash remittance	484.00	By claim according to book	6598.04
		Balance	48.15
	6646.19		6646.19

To Balance $ 48.15

This would appear to be fairly convincing proof that McSween was trying to appropriate Tunstall's funds and that his wife continued the tradition.

NOTES

CHAPTER ONE

1. Garrett, *Authentic Life,* 7. For the purpose of these notes, I have used the more widely available University of Oklahoma Press edition, first published in 1954. Upson, as noted elsewhere, was born November 23, 1828.

2. U.S. Dept. of the Interior, Bureau of Pensions, pension application of William H. Antrim, dated April 2, 1915, at El Paso, Texas.

3. Rasch and Mullin, "Dim Trails."

4. de Mattos, "Search." The baptismal record originally was located by William J. Carson and first appeared in Mullin, *Boyhood,* 7. In a footnote on p. 24, Mullin gives the date as November 18, not 17.

5. Cline, *Alias,* 11.

6. McCabe, *Lights and Shadows,* 420.

7. Cline, *Alias,* 11.

8. Mullin, *Boyhood,* 11; Cline, *Alias,* 38–45.

9. U.S. Bureau of the Census, 1880 census, Fort Sumner, San Miguel County.

10. Mullin, *Boyhood,* 8–9; Antrim, pension application; Antrim, deposition March 25, 1871, in Deed Book A, Sedgwick County, Kans.; Donald Cline, personal communications, 1986–87. One other theory advanced is that there were two Catherine McCartys and that the one who went to New Orleans was not the Kid's mother but his grandmother, Catherine McCarty's mother-in-law.

11. The Antrim-McCarty wedding is recorded in Book of Marriages A, Santa Fe County, N.M., 35–36; for those who cherish historical coincidences, it is preceded by the January 1, 1873, marriage of Miss Sophie Wollenweber and Paul F. Herlow, who ran the hotel in Santa Fe where Tunstall stayed in 1876. Immediately following is a record of the marriage of Lucien B. Maxwell's physician, Dr. J. H. Shout of Las Vegas, who treated Tunstall in 1877.

12. Cline, "Mystery," 17–19.

13. *Silver City Independent,* March 22, 1932.

14. Mullin, *Boyhood,* 12.

15. Ibid.

16. Ibid.

17. Coe, *Frontier Fighter,* 56. For the purpose of these notes, I have used the Lakeside Press edition, published 1984.

18. Cline, "Mystery," 31.

19. Mullin, *Boyhood,* 12.

CHAPTER TWO

1. For trenchant essays on early-day Eureka, Kans., I am indebted to Helen Bradford, of the Greenwood County Historical Society. It was also she who plodded laboriously through the relevant issues of the *Eureka Herald* for the pieces reproduced in the text.

2. A. A. McSween to J. P. Tunstall, April 17, 1878.

3. Haley, "Interview with Susan E. Barber," August 26, 1927. Hereafter cited as Haley, "Barber interview." I am indebted for this and much other meticulous research at the Haley History Center, Midland, Tex., to Melba M. McCaskill.

4. Canada, Bureau of the Census, Census of 1861, Charlottetown, Prince Edward Island. Research by Mrs. Beryl Barrett, Charlottetown, P.E.I.

5. Scotland, General Register Office, Census of 1851, Edinburgh. One possible candidate was the youngest of five children born to Neil McSween, fifty-five, a crofter, and Marion Ferguson, forty-three, a weaver. The other was the second of four children of Duncan McSween, fifty-five, and his wife Anne, forty. Unfortunately it proved impossible to cross-reference these details with the parish registers of Duirnish, so no further information, such as middle or maiden names, is available. Research by Patricia Phoenix, Edinburgh.

6. Haley, "Barber interview."

7. Ibid.; Nolan, "Search," 288–90.

8. Details of McSween's law school attendance and appearances in city directories were provided by Elizabeth Moss, archives assistant, University Libraries, Washington University, St. Louis. Nolan, "Search," 291.

9. Ida Rodebaugh's family—the correct form is *Rodenbaugh*—were squatters near Spring Creek Township, where McSween originally had taught school. The 1875 census gives the following information:

A. Rodenbaugh 46 F W b Ohio from Iowa
D. Rodenbaugh 21 M W Ill.   Iowa
Z. Rodenbaugh 19 F W Ohio   Iowa
I. Rodenbaugh 15 F W Ohio   Iowa
J. Rodenbaugh 14 M W Ohio   Iowa

Although she was known as Anna, her gravestone (she died in 1904) has the mother's name as Sussanna. Born March 24, 1828, she brought her family to Kansas in 1870. The other son was Joseph, born March 1853. Yet another coincidence: on Verdigris Creek, about ten miles north of Eureka, lived the Brazel family, who had come out from Wisconsin in the spring of 1859. In 1876, Jesse Madison Brazel married a fifteen-year-old girl named Olive Rhodes (there is some doubt about the surname). Their first child was Jesse Wayne Brazel, born on the last day of 1876, later to play a notable role in New Mexico history. Research by Helen Bradford. Nolan, "Dirty Dave," 7–13.

10. There is no record of McSween's naturalization in Baltimore, Md.; Pekin, Ill.; Eureka, Kans.; or Lincoln, N.M. Perhaps it will be found in St. Louis or elsewhere in Missouri, or in Ohio; investigations continue. Research by J. C. Maguire, Jr., Baltimore; V. Tunie Brannan, Carrollton, Ill.; Eleanor Jacoby, Eureka, Kans.; Nora Henn, Lincoln, N.M. Nolan, "Search," 295–96.

11. This item was located by Betty Braddock, director, Kansas Heritage Center, Dodge City.

12. Susan McSween's original marriage certificate was burned with all her possessions in the Lincoln house on July 19, 1878. Copy furnished by Judy Kidwell, records clerk, District Court, Atchison, Kans.; the Sue E. Homer entry in Registration Book, First Presbyterian Church, Atchison, by Carol A. Wagner, church secretary. Nolan, "Search," 297.

13. Neither the 1870 census for Atchison County nor town directories for 1865 and 1870–73 yield mention of any Sue E. Homer/Hummer or Alex A. McSween. There are several Homers in the deed books and census records but nothing at all to link them to Sue E. Homer. Nolan, "Search," 297.

14. Haley, "Barber interview."

15. Research on the McSweens in Pekin and Whitehall, Ill., by Loree Bergerhouse, Tazewell County Genealogical Society, Pekin, Ill., and Helen Widdows Richardson, Greene County Historical and Genealogical Society, Carrollton, Ill. Nolan, "Search," 295–96.

16. Haley, "Barber interview."

17. Because Peter Hummer and his first wife, Elizabeth, were strict Dunkards, we may fairly assume their children were brought up in that faith (although, to confuse matters further, Peter and Elizabeth Hummer were buried in a Friends' graveyard). Susanna Hummer would have needed to convert from Baptism via Catholicism to Presbyterianism between 1870 and 1873; while not impossible, it does tax credulity. Research on the Hummer family by Elizabeth Tangen, Adams County Historical Society, Gettysburg, Pa.

18. A précis of a letter (undated) from Mrs. Quincy W. Hershey, York Springs, Pa., to W. A. Keleher in Mullin, "Notes on Susan E. McSween," states she left home to visit a married sister in Ohio. Research by Melba M. McCaskill.

19. Quincy W. Hershey, interview, *The York Springs Sunday News*, June 3, 1951.

20. Spangler, *The Spangler Annals*, 78.

21. Research by Donald Lavash, Santa Fe, N.M., and John Mills, Osceola, Mo. Nolan, "Search," 294.

22. On the off chance that McSween might have lived or paid taxes in Terre Haute, city directories (for the years 1858, 1863–64, 1868, and 1871–73), census records for 1860 and 1870, various Vigo County histories, and such records as were available for the 1858 Vigo County Landowners Atlas were checked—all without success. Research by Nancy Sherill, Vigo County Public Library, Terre Haute, Ind.

23. Webster was probably the son of William Webster, a farmer of Irish birth, a Wesleyan Methodist by religion; Samuel, nineteen at the time of the 1861 census, was not present when the 1871 census was conducted, although all his brothers and sisters were. In the same 1861 census was a John McSween, aged forty, born in Scotland, and married with two daughters. There, however, the clues peter out; whether Webster might have known McSween before Eureka can probably never be confirmed. Research by Jill and Richard Bickford, visiting Lindsay, Ont.

24. Lincoln County, N.M., records of the Estate of A. A. McSween (hereafter McSween Estate). To give McSween the benefit of any possible doubt, it should also be recorded that

an unattributed note in the Mullin Collection makes the claim that "[McSween] had to borrow some money from a friend in Kansas to make the journey to Lincoln. *He never managed to pay it back*" (Mullin's italics). Although it is extremely unlikely, Webster's funds might—just—have been that loan. Research by Nora Henn and Melba M. McCaskill.

25. These details come, as do all the others about Eureka, from Helen Bradford.

26. Henry, *Conquering Our Great American Plains.*

27. Haley, "Barber interview." Susan McSween's memory again seems to have been faulty (the railroad had not built beyond Granada in the fall of 1874, and remained end-of-track until June 1875). What is harder to establish is whether her unreliability was accidental, or whether she was, to use a recently coined phrase, "economical with the truth."

CHAPTER THREE

1. Nolan, *John Henry Tunstall.*

2. John Partridge Tunstall and his brother-in-law and partner, Henry Coppinger Beeton, originally worked for the London firm of Copestake, Crampton & Co., Ltd., which had offices on Cheapside at the corner of Bow Churchyard (bombed in 1941, the street no longer exists). Tunstall was a traveling salesman, his territory that part of England known as East Anglia. The partnership with John Herbert Turner was begun in 1863 but not formalized until 1868, when Turner came to London. In 1870, Tunstall left the employ of Copestake, Crampton to establish, J. P. Tunstall & Co., Shippers, at 8 Bow Churchyard, London; the family tradition is that his investment was £16,000, then $80,000, a sizable sum. The following year he again visited Victoria. By 1872 the company was listed in London directories as

JOHN P. TUNSTALL & CO.

MERCHANTS AND COMMISSION AGENTS

8 BOW CHURCHYARD, E.C., AND AT

VICTORIA B.C.,

UNDER THE STYLE OF TURNER, BEETON &

TUNSTALL

Nolan, *John Henry Tunstall,* 9–13.

3. Ibid., 17–19. From tenuous internal evidence it would appear that Tunstall's partial blindness was the result of a riding accident. "You know I have very little sight in my right eye," he wrote. "[I]f I lost the other, it would not quite amount to total blindness, though very nearly so. This does not matter atall, for it is a much nicer colour than the other & does not shew any defect & between the two I can see

better than anyone I know." J. H. Tunstall (JHT) to J.P. Tunstall, January 24, 1874. Tunstall's letters and diaries are in the safekeeping of the Tunstall family and have not been made available for general research, although copies of them all are in the author's collection; for this reason I have not felt it necessary to indicate their source.

4. JHT to Major New (a family friend), October 1, 1872.

5. JHT to J. P. Tunstall, January 19, 1873.

6. JHT to J. P. Tunstall, January 2, 1873.

7. JHT to Emily Tunstall (sister), January 12, 1873. The giving of "Mizpah" rings was fashionable for many years. Tunstall's reading of the word misses its import, which was, "God protect and keep you safe for me while we are apart one from another." It may have been this ring that Alexander McSween referred to in 1878 as having been stolen after Tunstall was killed. Tunstall's use of the word *engagement* in relationship to his sister may be seen in one light as his confirmation of their childhood promise to always be true to each other, or in a different light as his unhealthily close attachment to Minnie, which he chose to treat as an "engagement" making him unavailable to any other girl.

8. JHT to J. P. Tunstall, April 3, 1873.

9. Sketches of the lives of Tunstall's friends and acquaintants would seem to be an overload on this narrative, and therefore only the most important of them are included in the biographies. It is evident, however, that Tunstall made a point of cultivating the "right" people. The Finlaysons, Heywoods, Wilsons, Rhodeses, Langleys, and Francises were Victoria's "top drawer" families.

10. JHT, Diary, September 12, 1873, 273.

11. Ibid., September 21, 1873, 276–77.

12. Ibid., November 10, 1873, 297.

13. Ibid., November 12, 1873, 301.

14. Ibid., February 14, 1874, 330.

15. JHT to his family, March 10, 1874.

16. JHT to Emily Tunstall (sister), May 10, 1874.

17. JHT to J. P. Tunstall, June 15, 1874.

18. JHT, Diary, June 17, 1874, 371.

19. Ibid., July 4, 1874, 378.

20. Ibid., August 10, 1874, 385.

21. JHT to Emily Tunstall (sister), August 30, 1874.

22. JHT, Diary, September 1, 1874, 394.

23. Ibid., October 2, 1874, 458. His account of the trip covers pages 392–459, sixty-eight close-written foolscap sheets.

24. Ibid., October 5, 1874, 459.

25. JHT to Emily Tunstall (sister), December 11, 1874.

CHAPTER FOUR

1. Klasner, *Girlhood*, 94.

2. Burns, *Saga*, 21.

3. Rasch, "Murphy," 57.

4. *Santa Fe Weekly New Mexican,* October 26, 1878.

5. On enrollment in Buffalo, N.Y., on July 26, 1851, Murphy said he was twenty-one. His Civil War army records suggest he may have lied about his age. On the muster-in roll at Los Pinos, N.M., dated July 6, 1863, his age is given as twenty-eight; at Fort Canby, N.M., on March 19, 1864, it is thirty. This would place the date of his birth nearer 1834 than the accepted 1830. L. G. Murphy, Military Service Records (MSR), NARA.

6. The activities of the Fifth Infantry at the appropriate times are from Ganoe. The balance of Murphy's service has been reconstructed from his military records. The latter contain numerous examples of Murphy's bold, clear handwriting: it is most certainly not that of a common laborer. Murphy, MSR; Ganoe, *History of the U.S. Army,* 233.

7. Kit Carson to Gen. James H. Carleton, September 23, 1862; Murphy, MSR.

8. Keleher *Turmoil,* 286–90.

9. Murphy, MSR.

10. Keleher, *Turmoil,* 295.

11. Ibid., 304.

12. Ibid., 315.

13. Rasch, "Murphy," 59.

14. Ibid.

15. Keleher, *Turmoil,* 323.

16. Asst. Surgeon J. R. Gibson, quoted in Gorney, *Roots in Lincoln,* 20–21.

17. The exact date of the firm's founding has always been vague; this assertion is based on Murphy's own statement in May 1874: "since we commenced business there nearly eight years ago." L. G. Murphy to Adjutant General, May 25, 1874, Adjutant General's Office, Letters Received, 1871–80, Consolidated File 3211 AGO 1873 (hereafter File 3211 AGO 1873).

18. Church, "Notes." Amelia was the daughter of Irish-born John R. Bolton, a former quartermaster's clerk at Fort Sumner and Fort Stanton who had come west with the army after the Civil War. He settled in Lincoln in 1869 and avoided involvement in the later troubles.

19. J. J. Dolan, MSR.

20. Maryland-born Argalus Garey Hennisee reached the rank of captain in the First Eastern Shore Maryland Infantry during the Civil War. He was appointed second lieutenant of the Nineteenth Infantry on January 22, 1867, and first lieutenant in May the following year. An excess officer after the reorganization of March 1869, he succeeded Lorenzo Labadie as agent to the Mescaleros on July 23, 1869. Assigned to the Eighth Cavalry December 31, 1870, he was still serving at Fort Stanton during the Horrell War. He was later regimental adjutant, Eighth Cavalry, from October 22, 1878, to March 16, 1881. After long and honorable military service in the Second and Ninth Cavalry, he retired with the rank of colonel, Fifth Cavalry, on January 16, 1903.

21. A. G. Hennisee, Report, August 31, 1870, *Report of the Commissioner of Indian Affairs, 1870* (RCIA).

22. Ibid. It should be noted that for all his colorful reports, Hennissee left Fort Stanton without ever having laid eyes on a hostile Mescalero Apache. By all accounts, life on the post was pleasant enough. Col. August V. Kautz, commanding, recalled that on Christmas Eve, 1869, he had champagne, and next day for lunch, Murphy and Fritz served oysters "brought out from the States in cans." At four p.m., all the officers of the post, their hosts, Fritz's brother Charles, and Paul Dowlin had a turkey dinner. On New Year's Day, "Fritz and Murphy had made arrangements for a dance and collected a few of the best women in the country. There were three poor fiddlers, still they made quite a noise and the dance passed off pleasantly and merrily. I left about three in the morning. . . . The supper transpired about midnight and was a very excellent one. Wines and liquors were abundant and freely used but no one was at all troublesome." Wallace "Military Memoir," 246.

23. A. J. Curtis to Nathaniel Pope, September 18, 1871 (RCIA, 1871).

24. The dates of appointment of Indian traders are in William Belknap to Commanding Officer, Fort Stanton, August 20, 1873; Murphy's petition to Belknap, supported by testimonials from Lt. Col. August V. Kautz and seven officers, is dated December 19, 1870 (both in File 3211 AGO 1873). In attempting to untangle the complexities of L. G. Murphy & Co.'s dealings with the army, the Department of the Interior, the Board of Indian Commissioners, and others, I found the following publications helpful: Samek, "No 'Bed of Roses' "; Sonnichsen, *Mescalero Apaches;* Mehren, "Mescalero Apache Reservation"; and *Record of Engagements.*

25. Samuel Bushnell to L. E. Dudley, March 20, 1873, in Mehren, "Mescalero Apache Reservation," 50–51.

26. Ibid.

27. L. E. Dudley to E. P. Smith, April 10, 1873 (RCIA, 1873, 263).

28. J. F. Randlett to Adjutant General, July

22, 1873; Chambers McKibbin to Adjutant General, October 2, 1873 (both in File 3211 AGO 1873).

29. Guardhouse roster, included with McKibbin to Adjutant General, October 2, 1873 (File 3211 AGO 1873).

30. Post Adjutant to L. G. Murphy, May 19, 1873 (File 3211 AGO 1873).

31. J. F. Randlett to Adjutant General, July 18, 1873 (File 3211 AGO 1873).

32. J. F. Randlett to Adjutant General, July 22, 1873 (File 3211 AGO 1873). Parts of Randlett's letter are in Rasch, "Murphy," 67, and Nolan, *John Henry Tunstall*, 186.

33. One or two writers have flirted with the subject of Murphy's possible homosexuality without coming to any conclusion. Frank Coe stated flatly that "Murphy was never married, but he always kept a Mexican woman that came from the high class. He could drink and walk under more whiskey than any man I ever saw." In the absence of real evidence, it might be as well to keep in mind the dictum that an Irish homosexual is a man who prefers women to drink. Haley, "Interview with Frank Coe," March 20, 1927.

34. E. D. Townsend to C. McKibbin, September 30, 1873 (File 3211 AGO 1873). To set the record quite straight, it was not Randlett's letter alone that resulted in the removal from the post of L. G. Murphy & Co., which was mainly the result of Agent Samuel Bushnell's campaign to get rid of the firm. There is no doubt, however, that Randlett's letter was a major factor, also bringing about the dismissal of Capt. Chambers McKibbin as commanding officer.

35. L. E. Dudley to E. P. Smith, April 10, 1873 (RCIA, 1873, 264).

36. L. G. Murphy & Co. accounts, 1873–74, in U.S. Dept. of Justice, Frank W. Angel, "In the Matter of the Cause and Circumstances of the Death of J. H. Tunstall, A British Subject," (hereafter Angel Report).

37. Rasch, "Horrell War."

38. Haley, "Interview with John Nichols."

39. Ibid.

40. Ibid.

41. Haley, "Interview with Bill Jones."

42. *Santa Fe New Mexican*, February 9, 1873.

43. Fulton, *Lincoln County War*, 31. An indictment citing Gallegos for "drawing deadly weapons" was handed down by Judge Bristol at La Mesilla on July 21, 1873; Sheriff Jack Gylam seems to have made no attempt to serve it. Lincoln County Papers, Weisner Collection, New Mexico State University.

44. Fulton, *Lincoln County War*, 31, places

the shooting of Patrón in February 1875, citing the *Mesilla News* of September 18 and the *Grant County Herald* of eight days later. In fact, the story in the *News* dates the affray the preceding Wednesday, September 15. The *New Mexican* reported the Patrón shooting Tuesday, September 21, 1875, concurring with the *News* that it happened the preceding Wednesday. Further confirmation is provided by Tunstall's letter of November 16, 1876, to his family. The killing of the two Hispanics took place in 1873, not 1875; it was the opening scene in the racial disharmony of that year.

45. Rasch, "Tularosa Ditch War," 230. I prefer the alternative spelling of the place name, which originated with the rose-tinted reeds bordering the river there (*tule rosa*), but to conform with present-day usage, I have kept the form *Tularosa* throughout.

46. Haley, "Interview with Robert A. Casey."

47. Ibid.

48. Jacinto Gonzales and Manuel Gutierrez to Marsh Giddings, December 26, 1873 (Dept. of the Interior, Letters Received 1849–1907).

49. Church, "Early Days in Roswell."

50. Haley, "Interview with Robert Casey."

51. Haley, "Interview with Frank Coe," March 20, 1927.

52. Ibid.

53. Maj. John Mason, commanding Fort Stanton, reported that "the Texans were murdered in cold blood, one at least [Ben Horrell, just twenty years old] while on his knees—badly wounded, had surrendered and begged for mercy was inhumanly murdered by having been pierced by nine balls—his body then taken and thrown across the creek near the town." During the night someone cut off Horrell's finger to steal his ring. Juan Martín's body lay in the street until next morning, when it was discovered that someone had carved a cross on his forehead. Mason to Adjutant General, December 25, 1873 (Letters Received, District of New Mexico [DNM] HQ, 1865–90, M1088 Roll 20); Burns, *Saga*, 35; Hough, *Outlaw*, 201; Rasch, "Horrell War,"; Fulton, "Harrell War of 1873"; Haley, "Interview with Bill Jones"; Fulton-Nolan correspondence, 1953–55.

54. Mason to Gutierrez, December 2, 1873 (Dept. of Interior, Letters Received 1849–1907).

55. Gonzales and Gutierrez to Giddings, December 26 (Dept. of Interior, Letters Received 1849–1907).

56. Mason to Adjutant General, December 25.

57. The indictments date these events vari-

ously December 10, which was a Wednesday; December 15, a Monday; and December 20, a Saturday. Juan Patrón, an eyewitness, confirms the last date as correct. Arrest Warrant Nos. 22, 28, 46, 64, 67, 68, 78, and 81; copies in Weisner Collection. *New Mexican*, January 9, 1874.

58. Haley, "Interview with Bill Jones"; "Interview with Frank Coe," March 20, 1927.

59. Haley, "Interview with Frank Coe."

60. Keleher, *Violence*, 13; *New Mexican*, January 9, 1874.

61. Klasner, *Girlhood*, 106. Mason's wording, however, suggests that the killer was not himself Hispanic. Mason to Adjutant General, December 25. The Horrells left Turner where he fell; Robert Casey buried him later at Picacho. George Kimbrell, who was also married to a Hispanic woman, is said to have been with the five Hispanics killed by the Horrells; he "somehow managed to come out of the affair with his life." Klasner, *Girlhood*, 106–7.

62. Maj. Wm. Redwood Price to (John Loud) Assistant Adjutant General, District of New Mexico (hereafter AAG DNM), January 28, 1874; quoted in Wilson, *Merchants*, 45–46.

63. The sequence of events set forth is distilled from a number of accounts, the most precise of which are Mason to Adjutant General, December 25, 1873, and Maj. Wm. R. Price to AAG DNM, February 5, 1874. Haley, "Interview with William Casey" and "Interview with Frank Coe," March 20, 1927, and Klasner, *Girlhood*, 105–7, are vague about dates and the sequence of events but add valuable detail that the spare military reports omit. The indictments date the Haskins murder February 8 and state that Haskins was shot in the head, body, and back. Incidentally, Sheriff Ham Mills claimed to have ridden nearly 2,400 miles trying unsuccessfully to serve the warrants. Arrest Warrant Nos. 3, 12, 67, 68, 76, 78, and 81; copies in Weisner Collection. Zack Crumpton, Bill Applegate, Little Hart, J. D. Scott, and John Walker of the Horrell crowd elected to steal two horses and four mules belonging to either Aaron Wilburn or Van Smith; Wilburn got up a party, pursued them, sneaked up on their camp at Hueco Tanks while they were still asleep, and killed Crumpton and Stills (Klasner says all of them). Klasner, *Girlhood*, 106–7; Fulton, "Harrell War of 1873"; *New Mexican*, March 13, 1874.

64. *New Mexican*, January 27, 1874.

65. W. D. Crothers to L. E. Dudley, April 6, 1874, in Mehren, "Mescalero Apache Reservation," 86–87.

66. Randlett was charged with having "feloniously, unlawfully, and from a premeditated design" incited, aided, counseled, procured, and advised Zachariah Compton, John Walker (a soldier in the U.S. Army), and J. D. Scott "to make an assault then and there"—December 15—on the four men killed at the *baile*. Witnesses against Randlett listed in Indictment 22 of the April grand jury included Charles Miller, Eugene Dow, Ham Mills, L. B. Anderson, J. R. Bolton, and a soldier named Whiting of D Troop, Eighth Cavalry. At the October term, Randlett—Paul Dowlin is unaccountably listed as a codefendant—secured a change of venue to Socorro County. Weisner Collection.

67. Following Randlett's complaints, rancher James Trainor of Pecos, Tex., alleged that Apaches from the Mescalero reservation had killed a herder and stolen mules and horses. At the end of August, Maj. William R. Price and five troops of Eighth Cavalry were dispatched to Fort Stanton to investigate. Price's arrival stiffened Bushnell's backbone sufficient to bring about the ejection of L. G. Murphy & Co. It was in response to all this—Randlett's accusations, their banishment, and Price's report to the adjutant general—that Murphy presented his case. James Trainor to Lt. Gen. P. H. Sheridan, July 30, 1873, in Mehren, "Mescalero Apache Reservation," 70–71; Price to AAAG DNM, November 25, 1873, cited in Wilson, *Merchants*; L. G. Murphy to William Belknap (File 3211 AGO 1873).

68. An undated newspaper clipping, apparently from the *New Mexican*, states that the case was tried October 10, 1874: "Several witnesses were examined on the part of the Territory, and we learn that the evidence was of such a character that the jury returned their verdict without leaving their seats. Robert Casey, well-known resident of Lincoln county, was also indicted at the same time in four cases of the same nature. . . . [T]he presenters after examining the evidence did not risk a trial but entered a nol pros in all the cases against Mr Casey."

69. Mehren, "Mescalero Apache Reservation," 83–88.

70. U.S. Dept. of Interior, Bureau of Indian Affairs, Selected Documents Relating to Mescalero Apache Indian Agency (hereafter MAIA).

CHAPTER FIVE

1. Garrett, *Authentic Life*, 11.

2. Fulton, "Apocrypha of Billy the Kid." At the time, Fulton was still interested in researching the Kid's background. He had already persuaded Susan McSween Barber to write a bundle of notes correcting Burns's *Saga*, a waste of resources comparable to having Pat Garrett comment on the movie "Young Guns." None of

this material appeared in the version of Garrett's *Authentic Life* that Fulton edited; he later became impatient with those who continued to follow the Kid's faint historical trail and devoted himself to documented research. The fruits of his years of concentration on the Kid are to be found in Hunt, *Tragic Days.*

3. Cline, *Alias,* 31.

4. *Grant County Herald,* September 18, 1875.

5. *Grant County Herald,* September 26, 1875.

6. Cline, *Alias,* 34–35; Mullin, *Boyhood.*

7. *The Mustang,* April 14, 1950; quoted in Rasch and Mullin, "New Light," 4.

8. For the "New York theory," see Cline, *Alias,* 36–43.

9. This outline of the Kid's activities is based upon the meticulous research into his "missing" years conducted by Jerry Weddle of Catalina, Ariz.; it places the Kid squarely where logic has always insisted he must have been. Weddle, "Apprenticeship."

10. Mullin, *Boyhood,,* 15.

11. Denton, "Billy the Kid's Friend."

12. Miles L. Wood, "Reminiscences," n.d. [1920], courtesy Jerry Weddle; Weddle, "Apprenticeship."

13. Deposition of Louis C. Hartman, February 16, 1877, courtesy Jerry Weddle; Weddle, "Apprenticeship."

14. Wood, "Reminiscences"; Weddle, "Apprenticeship."

CHAPTER SIX

1. Deposition of A. A. McSween, ca. June 1, 1878, Angel Report. The statement that the McSweens were penniless when they arrived was made in a letter dated April 18, 1878, purportedly written by Marion Turner (but probably the work of Ash Upson, who more than once used the semiliterate Turner's name to conceal his own partisanship). *Las Vegas Gazette,* May 14, 1878.

2. Church, "Notes."

3. Barber-Fulton Letters, June 27, 1926.

4. Ibid.

5. That the citizens of Lincoln were aware their taxes were being misappropriated is not in doubt; who was responsible is another matter. "A Lincoln County Democrat" pointed the finger.

Mister Editer: When the *Borderer* newspaper come in this week I look in it and find the name of Juan B Patron of Lincoln county the Democratic candidate for representative to the legislater. Now I reckon this is the same Juan B Patron what used to be the probate clerk of the county and the same feller what got kicked out of being Assessor of the county because he got cotched in swindlin the people, and the same man who was twice indicted by the Grand Jury at the last Court on account of his robbin the county and the same Patron who was been doin the dirty work of the swindlin ring that have been rulin Lincoln county and a disgustin of every honest man and democrat in the county.

Now Mr Editer I dont hold to be much of a writer or a politicion, I always pays my debts and my taxes here in Lincoln county and the corrupt ring that rules this county has never paid a cent of these taxes that I work hard for, but has put the money in their pockets and the county and the Territory has got no benefits of it and that's what's the matter with Hanner and thats the reason a Grand Jury of good Democrats put inditements against Juan B Patron for swindlin the county.

Mr Editer I fought the war on the wrong side but I done my duty like a man because I thort I was in the rite and I goin to do it now. I never had much show at schoolin by my old man, he says to me when I left home in old Tennessee, says he, my boy you always play your hand fair, and when you cotch cheatin round the bord you just go for the feller whats doin it . . . we got a mean thievin ring in this county what steals all the taxes, and the honest men here are tryin to brake it up and we dont want no Juan B Patron because he's in with that ring and so far as his politics hes nothin but a Maverick anyhow. Patron would be a radical in a minit if he think Juan B Patron would make anythin out of it.

We did want old man Chisum rite bad to be our candidate, hes a square man and a good man and a good democrat, but if we cant get him, dont take Patron, take somebody else, take a bull calf that cant do us no harm if he dont do any good, give us some man that the King of Lincoln dont own, somebody that dont belong to no thievin ring and put this in your paper if you can read it and if you wont put it in for the sake of honesty, let me know and I pay you if I have to sell a cow. (*Mesilla News,* August 18, 1875)

6. The Mesilla grand jury, foreman Dr. Joseph Blazer, had inquired into allegations of fraud and irregularities at the Mescalero Apache Indian Reservation during the preceding October term of district court but handed down no indictments. The following spring, Michael

Clark, a former employee of Paul Dowlin, alleged that Crothers sold 105 pounds of agency coffee and 125 pounds of sugar to Rushwood Black of Blazer's Mills, whose wife was Dr. Blazer's housekeeper. Crothers's son Oren, employed at the agency as issuing clerk, testified it was a loan. A procession of bit players—John Bolton, John Copeland, Dr. Blazer, William H. McCloskey, the Dowlin brothers, Charlie Scase, Michael Harkins, and Sam Smith—gave affidavits; McNulta probably couldn't draw any more of a conclusion from them than we can today. U.S. Dept. of the Interior, Bureau of Indian Affairs, MAIA.

7. Fulton, *Lincoln County War*, 50. Maj. Williamson Crothers, who came from Valparaiso, Ind., had taken office at the agency in April 1874; he lasted less than a year. It might be said that he won the battle but lost the war. Citing poor health and sickness in the family, he resigned February 9, 1876; when he left for San Antonio and later returned east. Paul Dowlin paid him two thousand dollars to take his daughters Francesca, Luisa, and Rufina with him to educate them and bring them up as ladies. Research by Alice Blakestad, Hondo, N.M.

8. *Pueblo Colorado Chieftain*, December 3, 1875; *Las Vegas Gazette*, November 15, 1875; JHT to J. P. Tunstall, June 24, 1875. To muddy the water still further, the *Mesilla News* put the price at $312,940. Clarke, *Chisum*, 33.

9. Klasner, *Girlhood*, 142.

10. Ibid. Abneth [or Abner] W. McCabe, "Uncle Mac" to the Casey children, came from Virginia and had arrived in New Mexico by way of Lampasas, Tex. He worked as a storekeeper and accountant for Casey and, about August 1875, went to work for Chisum at the Bosque Grande ranch. His last appearance in the annals of Lincoln County was when he was appointed deputy sheriff on September 14, 1878, to arrest Hugh Beckwith for the murder of William Johnson. Lily Klasner said he relocated at Lampasas; he is thereafter lost to history. Ibid., 137, 146.

11. Klasner, *Girlhood*, 4.; Shinkle, *Robert Casey*, 15–32. The latter work is weakened by contradictory statements and the lack of an index but is a valuable antidote to the Klasner book. Susan McSween made some strong accusations against the Caseys: "And they tell you the Caseys had lots of friends then why was it in the mouths of everybody that Casey & wife had been tried for murdering a brother in law for his money in Texas. . . . Their son Add killed 'Buck Guyse' some years after that over some land matter & it was said that Lillie the sister held him. The sister Mrs Clasner was tried for theft and sentenced to the Penitentiary for two years.

That is the kind of good family they were." Mrs. McSween's allegations are well founded; on April 24, 1896, in a dispute over water rights, Robert "Add" Casey, Lily, and her husband Joe Klasner got into a violent argument with William H. "Buck" Guyse (or Guise) in which Guyse was shot dead in circumstances less than straightforward. The records of the trial are missing from the Lincoln County files and the state records. For sparing details, see Shinkle, *Robert Casey*, 170–71; Barber-Fulton Letters, October 3, 1930.

12. Klasner, *Girlhood*, 118.

13. Ibid.

14. Deposition of Juan B. Patrón, June 6, 1878, Angel Report.

15. Barber-Fulton Letters, March 10, 1928.

16. *Weekly New Mexican*, September 7, 1875.

17. Shinkle, *Robert Casey*, 140.

18. Ibid., 127.

19. *New Mexican*, September 21, 1875.

20. In the matter of killing Balansuela [the correct spelling appears to have been Valenzuela], Mills was indicted for manslaughter; he was also under indictment for embezzling three thousand dollars of county tax funds. At which session of district court these cases were heard—if at all—is not clear. On June 8, 1876, Andrew Boyle wrote his sister he was in New Mexico and told her he had "started farming at last" at Ham Mills's ranch on the Ruidoso, which he was renting. Of Mills he had this to say: "He killed a Mexican last March and shot at J. B. Wilson, Justice of the Peace, and skinned out for Texas. I do not think he will come back [although] he is under $1000 bond for his appearance at the next district court." Either this letter was written a year earlier than the date given, or Boyle was unaware that Mills had killed Balansuela and thought he had skinned out because of the earlier killing. Mills worked for the House as a teamster. Boyle's letter goes on to say Mills owed the House ten thousand dollars, which might have been an equally persuasive reason for taking a Texas rest cure. Lincoln County, District Court Records, Cases 151 and 163; Curry, *Sun Rising*, 247–48.

21. *Weekly New Mexican*, October 26, 1875. The newspaper's informant was John H. Riley.

22. Klasner, *Girlhood*, 134.

23. Ibid.

24. *New Mexican*, December 21, 1875. Also in Keleher, *Violence*, 18.

CHAPTER SEVEN

1. JHT to J. P. Tunstall, September 15, 1875.

2. Tunstall's thoughts and letters on the subject of sheep farming are set out in full in Nolan, *John Henry Tunstall*, 73–96.

3. JHT to J. P. Tunstall, January 3, 1876.
4. JHT to J. P. Tunstall, February 3, 1876.
5. JHT, Diary, February 23, 1876, 465.
6. Ibid., 466.
7. Ibid., 467.
8. Ibid., 468.
9. Ibid., 470.
10. Ibid., 471.
11. Ibid., 472–73.
12. Ibid., March 10, 1875, 484.
13. Ibid., 484–45.
14. Ibid., March 11, 1876, 487.
15. Ibid., March 27, 1876, 505.
16. JHT to J. P. Tunstall, May 2, 1876.
17. JHT to J. P. Tunstall, May 11, 1876.
18. JHT to J. P. Tunstall, June 17, 1876.
19. Ibid.
20. JHT to J. P. Tunstall, June 20, 1876.
21. Ibid.
22. JHT to J. P. Tunstall, June 24, 1876.
23. JHT to J. P. Tunstall, July 15, 1876.
24. Ibid.
25. JHT to J. P. Tunstall, August 4, 1876. Tunstall carried on his diary until his return to San Francisco; the last entry is dated July 29. It ends, without comment, at p. 518.
26. Ibid.
27. JHT to J. P. Tunstall, August 15, 1876.
28. JHT to his family, July 10, 1876.

CHAPTER EIGHT

1. JHT to J. P. Tunstall, August 15, 1876.
2. An aside: On October 5, 1876, Laura, daughter of Bradley Barlow, co-owner of Barlow & Sanderson's Southern Overland Stage Company, was married to Frederick A. Metcalf of New York. The ceremony took place at St. Albans, Vt. I have often wondered if there was any connection between the Barlow and Brewer families, and if it was thus that Vermonter Dick Brewer first came, via Missouri, to New Mexico. *Las Vegas Gazette*, October 21, 1876.
3. JHT to J. P. Tunstall, August 15, 1876.
4. *Santa Fe New Mexican*, August 15, 1876.
5. Fulton attributes the theft of horses that brought about Bernstein's expedition to the Mes brothers, who had shifted their headquarters from La Boquilla on the Rio Hondo to the Fort Sumner area. This cannot be correct, but what is certain is that horses were stolen from the reservation, and when the newly appointed agent, Frederick Godfroy, could get no help from the military to pursue the thieves, he sent Bernstein and a party of Indians after them, with

eminently satisfactory results. An attempt to sort out the different gangs of horse thieves and their proclivities is made in chapter 11. Fulton, *Lincoln County War*, 66; Haley, "Horse Thieves."

6. JHT to J. P. Tunstall, August 15, 1876.
7. JHT to Emily Tunstall (mother), August 25, 1876.
8. JHT to Emily Tunstall (sister), August 17, 1876.
9. JHT to J. P. Tunstall, September 5, 1876.
10. JHT to J. P. Tunstall, August 24, 1876.
11. JHT to J. P. Tunstall, September 1, 1876.
12. JHT to J. P. Tunstall, September 5, 1876.
13. JHT to J. P. Tunstall, September 11, 1876.
14. JHT to J. P. Tunstall, September 21, 1876.
15. Ibid.
16. JHT to J. P. Tunstall, September 22, 1876. Plaza del Alcalde, to give it its correct name, had been the county seat of Rio Arriba County since 1860. On April 15, 1876, storekeeper and hotelier Louis Clark, a leading citizen, was assassinated there. The *New Mexican's* report:

> As far as we can learn [he] had taken some gentlemen to their bedrooms in a house about a hundred yards north of his own and on his return he was shot; the bullet passed through the upper part of the right lung, leaving a large track, and it is presumed from the nature of the wound that the ball was an explosive one; Clark was discovered by his clerk running towards his store crying out that he was murdered and upon reaching his own portal fell down; he was carried into the house where anything possible was done to alleviate his pains, but he suffered great agony until death relieved him. . . . The presumption in Plaza Alcalde as to the party who committed the deed is against a person named [Diego?] Archuleta; he had been refused credit at Clark's store, was drunk and violent during the day, was seen on the spot where Clark was murdered but a short time before its committal, did not sleep at his own house that night, and has not been seen since. (*New Mexican*, April 18, 1876)

17. An account of the comedy appears in the *New Mexican* of June 27, 1876. Subsequent to their brawl, Stinson and Smith expressed regret for their actions, and professed great friendship for each other.

18. JHT to J. P. Tunstall, September 24, 1876.

19. JHT to J. P. Tunstall, October 7, 1876.

20. JHT to Emily Tunstall (sister), October 18, 1876.

21. JHT to J. P. Tunstall, October 7, 1876.

22. JHT to J. P. Tunstall, October 9, 1876.

23. JHT to J. P. Tunstall, October 22, 1876. The Argyle Rooms Tunstall refers to were a London public dance hall. Harry Mottley had opened his "Centennial Hall and Terpsichorean Academy" on July 4, 1876. It stood at the corner of Centennial Ave. and the Levee. Mottley raised bail and was set free.

24. JHT to J. P. Tunstall, October 28, 1876.

25. Ibid.

CHAPTER NINE

1. Wallace, "Military Memoir," 247.

2. JHT to his family, November 16, 1876.

3. Ibid.

4. Ibid. A vignette of how the natives saw Tunstall also exists. "The first time I saw him," George Coe recalled, "he was dressed in knee pants and had stockings up to his knees." Haley, "Interview with George Coe," March 20, 1927.

5. See chapter 6, note 20; Mullin, "Notes on A. H. 'Ham' Mills."

6. JHT to his family, November 16, 1876.

7. Coe, *Frontier Fighter*, 66–67. Another version of this story, which Coe, chronologically inaccurate as always, dates October 1877, bears only passing resemblance to the one in the book. In this one, Coe states that King goosed the girl at the dance, simultaneously squawling like a cat. "There was an American there, courting her. The two nearly ran together but they stopped them. But this fellow took it to heart and was not satisfied." The next day Campbell turned up at the Coe place. "I heard him say with an oath that he wanted Tom to squawl like a cat or he would blow his brains out. Tom would not squawl so he pulled his six-shooter and shot him through five times. This fellow was farming the Gonzales place. Murphy & Dolan told him to get out of the country and they took his crops" (Haley, "Interview with George Coe," March 20, 1927).

8. *Weekly New Mexican*, December 19, 1876.

9. JHT to his family, November 16, 1876.

10. JHT to his family, December 6, 1876.

11. Ibid. Although there does not seem to be any further record of the activities of the Lincoln County Farmers' Club, many of its officers were to play prominent roles in coming events. Joe Storms, "ragged, half starved and lousy," as Abneth McCabe described him, had come to Lincoln County with Jap Coe in 1866 and now farmed adjacent to Avery M. Clenny at La Junta, or Hondo; he is said to have later bought the Lou Coe place, on which he went broke and later committed suicide. Clenny, by trade a monte dealer, had come in with the California Column and ran a saloon and gambling house. Will Lloyd we encountered in chapter 6; John Newcomb, "a gambler and whiskey drinker" from Fort Wayne, Ind., had a small farm on the Ruidoso River. Within two years he would become one of Tunstall's pallbearers. Klasner, *Girlhood*, 171; Haley, "Interview with Frank Coe," August 17, 1927.

12. *Weekly New Mexican*, February 13, 1877. In another version, the fight began when Powell came out of a *choza* and startled some cattle Yopp was trying to pen. Yopp "abused [Powell] dreadfully for . . . making a lot of extra trouble for him," and drew his gun, whereupon Powell shot him. Klasner, *Girlhood*, 209.

13. Emily Tunstall (mother) to JHT, February 27, 1877.

14. *New Mexican*, January 9, 1877.

15. JHT to Lillian Tunstall, January 14, 1877. Tunstall's long account of his first visit to Lincoln and his later experiences with Dick Brewer have never been found; my remarks are based on the reactions to what he wrote expressed by his mother and sister Emily (Minnie) in their [unpublished] letters to him.

16. *Weekly New Mexican*, January 30, 1877. Gallegos was indicted for murder, and his attorney, Alexander McSween, won a continuance to the October term of court. Gallegos meanwhile languished in jail; he was still there when the Boys were broken out the following November. It was not until the April 1879 term of court at Lincoln that he was found guilty of fourth-degree murder and sentenced to a year in jail. *Mesilla News*, May [date illegible], 1879.

17. Alexander McSween to Charles Fritz, December 12, 1876. R. G. McCubbin Collection.

18. Alexander McSween to Charles Fritz, December 14, 1876, in records of the Estate of Emil Fritz, Lincoln County (hereafter cited as Fritz Estate). Lt. John F. Wilkinson married Louise Sophie Fritz on October 15, 1874. Louise's sister Caroline was sixteen going on seventeen; Jimmy Dolan, although twelve years her senior, was already calling upon her. Research by Nora Henn.

19. Deposition of A. A. McSween, Angel Report.

20. Barber-Fulton Letters, March 11 and May 30, 1928.

21. For the full provisions of the Desert Land

Act, enacted March 31, see *New Mexican*, April 24, 1877.

22. John H. Riley, down at Fort Bayard setting up his bids for 1877–78 beef contracts, sent a note to the *New Mexican* dated January 26, 1877, recounting that "Lieut. [H. H.] Wright [Ninth Cavalry] who left this post on a scout a few days since met a party of Indians who had stolen and killed some cattle on the Mimbres, and had an engagement, killing six Indians and capturing some horses and arms." The official report of this engagement, which took place on January 24, put the number killed at five, with several wounded. In another engagement near Bosque Grande, Lt. Charles D. Beyer, Ninth Cavalry, and a detachment of ten men pursued twenty-five hostile Indians to their encampment, which was destroyed, a number of horses being captured. *New Mexican*, April 24, 1877.

23. JHT to J. P. Tunstall, March 9, 1877.

24. Emily Tunstall (mother) to JHT, February 27, 1877. Tunstall's eagerness to buy cattle may have encouraged him to believe that anything Murphy and Dolan could do, he could do, too. Andrew Boyle later testified to Inspector E. C. Watkins that Dick Brewer, acting as agent for McSween and Tunstall, had traveled throughout the county offering to buy cattle and horses without close examination of their origins, providing only that they were not from Chisum's herds. It would appear that the offer of "half the animal's resale value" met with some success. Watkins, "Examination of Charges Against F. C. Godfroy, Indian Agent, Mescalero, N.M., 1878," in U.S. Dept. of the Interior, Bureau of Indian Affairs (hereafter cited as Watkins Report).

25. JHT to J. P. Tunstall, March 9, 1877.

26. JHT to J. P. Tunstall, March 12, 1877.

27. Ibid.

28. JHT to J. P. Tunstall, March 23, 1877.

29. A long, but circumspect account of Isaacs's death, datelined Jicarilla Mines, N.M., March 27, 1877, and written by Tunstall's friend L. G. Taylor, district recorder, appeared in the *New Mexican* of April 3. The presence at Fort Stanton of U.S. postal inspector Charles Adams, sometimes referred to as General Adams, cannot be confirmed; he had been at Stanton immediately before Christmas to take Sam Bass and Billy Campbell to Santa Fe.

30. JHT to J. P. Tunstall, March 23, 1877.

31. Ibid.

32. Book B, Contracts, Agreements and Leases, and Deed Book B, Lincoln County, N.M.

33. The *New Mexican* noted the changed ownership on April 24, 1877:

By referring to an advertisement elsewhere in today's paper it will be seen that Col. L. G. Murphy, the popular and well-known head of the extensive mercantile firm of L. G. Murphy & Co. at Lincoln, N.M., has withdrawn his name from the partnership. The business will be continued by the two remaining members of the old firm, Mr Jas. J. Dolan and our enterprising young friend John H. Riley (the latter of whom is now in this city) under the name Jas. J. Dolan & Co.

Details of the awards for supplying fresh beef were published in the same edition. The price Tunstall paid Mathews is from his account book (see appendix 3); Susan Barber documents his purchase of the ambulance and mules, and Mathews's apprehension, in Barber-Fulton Letters, March 10, 1928.

34. JHT to J. P. Tunstall, March 23, 1877.

35. The actual promissory note, signed by Brewer, is in McSween Estate. Robert Mullin believed that after delivering to the House his wheat and everything else he grew for two seasons, Brewer was given notice to quit or pay his debts in full; unable to do the latter and unwilling to do the former, Brewer agreed to sign the note. Reference to Tunstall's account book and Widenmann's final balancing of the two accounts proves incontrovertibly that when the widow McSween had Brewer's parents sign the properties over to her, claiming their son owed McSween the money, she was lying.

Dolan's side of the story appeared more than a year later.

R. M. Brewer I always considered an honest man and treated him as such until he became contaminated with Mr. McSween, his "legal advisor." It didn't take Mr McSween long to initiate him into the way he should go, as it was only a short time after they became acquainted that Mr Brewer came to me and offered to sell me about twenty head of beef steers, he knowing them to be the property of Mr Chisum, and that they were taken out of a herd of Mr Chisum's which passed his ranch on the Ruidoso a few days before. I was much surprised at Brewer, as I always thought him honest. I told him I would not buy or have anything to do with the cattle, and advised him to turn them over to the owner.

He (Brewer) next tried to defraud us, on advice received from Mr McSween, out of two of our ranches situated on the Ruidoso, which we had rented to him on leaving our employ, by entering them under the Desert Land Act, but failed to prove up on his right. The circumstances are well known to Mr [George D.] Bowman of the Land Office and another gentleman living in the Mesilla valley and Lincoln County. Mr Brewer is owing our firm over two thousand dollars. (*New Mexican*, May 16, 1878)

36. JHT to J. P. Tunstall, March 23, 1877.

37. JHT to J. P. Tunstall, March 30, 1877. That the smallpox plague was anything but abated is confirmed in a letter Dolan wrote to Riley at Santa Fe, published in the *New Mexican* of April 3.

SMALL POX:—A letter to Mr J. H. Riley in this city . . . announces that the small pox has broken out with great virulence among the Indians of the Mescalero Apache reservation, creating great consternation among them. Three chiefs, Roman, headchief, and Pinole and Greeley have died.

The accuracy of this report is questionable; Roman, at least, appears to have been alive and active long after this time. Sonnichsen, *Mescalero Apaches*, 199.

38. Ibid. The seven-page letter, taken in conjunction with the expenditures dated March 20 in Tunstall's account book ($1,365 with Brookmire & Ranken, merchants of St. Louis, and a further $500 with Otero Sellar & Co.), would seem to indicate that Tunstall started storekeeping long before work was even begun on the store building. His interest in the hay contracts is easy to understand: the amounts of money involved were substantial. Bids to supply forage for Fort Stanton were invited in July; Willi Spiegelberg, Pat Coghlan, and Jimmy Dolan competed as follows:

Spiegelberg: All the grama hay wanted at $31.00 [a ton]; bottom hay at $19.00.
Coghlan, 100 tons of bottom hay at $18.00.
Dolan, Grama hay, $33.70; 50 tons bottom hay $19.00.

George Coe claimed he and his clan brought the first mowing machine to Lincoln County from Colfax County in March 1876. If so, it would appear this was the one to which Tunstall referred. Coe, *Frontier Fighter*, 65.

39. JHT to J. P. Tunstall, March 31, 1877.

CHAPTER TEN

1. Barber-Fulton Letters, March 10, 1928.

2. Ibid.

3. Hinton, "Chisum," 196. This and Rasch, "Pecos War," remain the most reliable versions of these events.

4. Boyle's report, which is quoted throughout this passage, appeared in the *Mesilla Valley Independent*, June 23, 1877.

5. *Grant County Herald*, August 24, 1878.

6. JHT to J. P. Tunstall, April 17, 1877.

7. JHT, unaddressed note endorsed "Rec'd 8 May 77" by J. P. Tunstall. J. P. Tunstall had suggested that if he had the deeds to the land, he could raise extra capital. This is part of Tunstall's explanation of why there were none.

8. JHT to J. P. Tunstall, April 20, 1877.

9. JHT to J. P. Tunstall, April 21, 1877.

10. The careful research of his grandson makes it possible to glean the grains of truth from the chaff of Widenmann's bluster. "His parents are German" was true; that they lived in Georgia was not. The travels around Germany and Switzerland were probably fact; on the basis of such French as Tunstall uses in his correspondence, Widenmann's fluency would not have had to be great. The "banking" experience—in his deposition to Angel, Widenmann referred to himself as a "merchant and banker"—and the Bremen Steamship Co. job could be extrapolated from the Ann Arbor business, and the chemical factory from the family firm in Stuttgart. Whether Widenmann ever truly ran a ranch in Colorado has never been established. Widenmann, "Enigma."

11. A. A. McSween to J. P. Tunstall April 17, 1878.

12. JHT to J. P. Tunstall, April 22, 1877.

13. JHT to J. P. Tunstall, April 24, 1877. Tunstall's account book shows he ordered the harness he was so eager to have from Bolanders, the saddlers in Santa Fe, at a cost of $126.02: obviously, only the best was good enough.

14. Ibid. Tunstall's account book was a record of his contra account with McSween; the lawyer kept a matching one that is notable for the fact that it frequently fails to match. Tunstall shows one payment of $510.00 for "3 Feliz filings" and two other payments totaling $40.00 to Land Office clerk George Bowman (probably registration fees). McSween's entry states simply "By U.S. lands $850." At twenty-five cents an acre, this would indicate a filing of either 2,040 acres (Tunstall) or 3,040 acres (McSween). It seems clear that there were later filings: Sam Corbet's listing of Tunstall's proxies shows himself, McSween, Brewer, Florencio Gonzales, Avery Clenny, and Dr. Spencer Gurney. If each filed on 640 acres, the figure would have been 3,840 acres; McSween's April 17 letter to J. P. Tunstall [q.v.] confirms this as the correct figure. Later, Huston Chapman, as lawyer to the estate, defined the holding only as "over 2500 acres." It was clearly much larger. In 1879, Ellen Casey inquired at the Land Office in La Mesilla about the land on which the spring at the head of the Rio Feliz was located. She was informed that it

had been filed upon under the Desert Land Act on October 9, 1877, by Trinidad Delgado. Delgado was one of the many local farmers who pledged their crops to Tunstall that summer and may therefore have been yet another of his proxies. McSween's account book, Angel Report; H. I. Chapman to J. P. Tunstall, February 10, 1879; Mullin, "Notes on Sam Corbet"; Shinkle, *Robert Casey*, 96.

15. Haley, Barber interview.

16. JHT to J. P. Tunstall, April 24, 1877.

17. J. P. Tunstall to JHT, March 24, 1877.

18. Capt. Paul Dowlin—the family insists this is correct, although the firm's letterheads give the name as Dowling—was another member of the military coterie that ran things in Lincoln County; a one-time (albeit briefly) commanding officer of Fort Stanton, he had settled on the Ruidoso and built the mill and a lodging house alongside it run by J. C. Ramsdell, who had brought his family there from Silver City in March 1877. Frank Coe said Dillon

> was fired by Paul because of his jealousy concerning Jerry's relations with his wife. Jerry claimed he was innocent of any indiscretion and went back to Dowling's Mill. . . . Paul jerked his gun but it caught and Jerry shot first with a Carbine, missed, then took his six-shooter and shot him just above the eye. He came down to my place and told me what he had done. He laid out at a spring up in the canons. He was not going to leave until he had seen Bill Dowling and had made some settlement over the killing. I took Bill up there, kept them from getting into a shooting, and mediated between them.

That there may have been more to the story than this may be inferred from the fact that a William Green was also indicted for the murder. *New Mexican*, May 8, 1877; Haley, "Interview with Frank Coe," August 17, 1927.

19. JHT to J. P. Tunstall, May 7, 1877.

20. Barber-Fulton Letters, March 10, 1928. The court records list the complainants as James L. Johnson et al., of Santa Fe. Civil cases 747 and 748, First Judicial District Court Records, Santa Fe County. The amount involved was $154.61. *New Mexican*, March 6, 1877.

21. JHT to J. P. Tunstall, May 20, 1877.

22. Barber-Fulton letters, March 10, 1928..

23. JHT to J. P. Tunstall, May 17, 1877.

24. JHT to J. P. Tunstall, May 20, 1877.

25. JHT to J. P. Tunstall, May 22, 1877.

26. JHT to J. P. Tunstall, May 27, 1877.

27. Robert A. Widenmann to J. P. Tunstall, April 28, 1878.

28. JHT to J. P. Tunstall, May 27, 1877.

29. Ibid. The "deed" Tunstall executed was little more than a power of attorney. It was dated at Brewer's Ranch May 23, 1877, and was witnessed by Gauss and Samuel R. Corbet. This document, which Widenmann insisted upon calling a will, is reproduced in full in Nolan, *John Henry Tunstall*, 240.

CHAPTER ELEVEN

1. Tunstall wrote Otero, Sellar on May 1, 1877, enclosing a deposit check of three hundred dollars. He requested them to make arrangements to freight to Lincoln the wool he had bought in April, and he ordered a variety of goods that included three Colt .45 six-shooters, five hundred rounds of ammunition, three hundred pounds of plug and two hundred of smoking tobacco, tools, padlocks, and ladders, and also a suit, probably for himself, "dark grey color, heavy tweed." He specified a sack coat with hip pockets and outside and inside breast pockets, with vest to match, chest thirty-eight inches, arm twenty-seven, waist thirty-three, leg inseam thirty-five. JHT to J. P. Tunstall, April 22, 1877; JHT to Otero, Sellar & Co., May 1, 1877. Gross, Kelly & Co. Collection, University of New Mexico. Courtesy Jerry Weddle.

2. Barber-Fulton Letters, n.d. The wording of the note is sufficiently ambiguous to make it equally likely that Mrs. Barber was referring to L. G. Murphy & Co. In the absence of any hard facts, the matter of which building became what is based mostly on guesswork. Maurice G. Fulton wrote that the former Murphy branch store became the McSween home in 1876; it was enlarged into the "new" house in the summer of 1877. On the other hand, Robert N. Mullin, a tireless researcher into the topography of early Lincoln, told me he never was able to find any evidence that Tunstall had conducted business out of any building other than his big store: the discovery of Tunstall's notebook might be classed as that evidence. The "old man"—it would appear anyone aged fifty or over was called an old man—"they" (later) poisoned was Daniel Huff. Fulton-Nolan correspondence 1953–55; Mullin-Nolan correspondence, 1952–72.

3. Fergusson, *Rio Grande*.

4. The descriptions of the law office, Tunstall's rooms, and the McSween house are reconstructions based on the inventory taken by Sheriff Brady at the time he attached McSween's property. McSween Estate.

5. JHT to his family, June 4, 1877.

6. In chilling detail, Frank Coe dates these events subsequent to "one day in August," when they first heard Largo had been captured. He

was "a large man, over six feet tall," Coe said, a "gross featured black Mexican [whose] nose had been broken and was mashed flat."

Captain Baca was sheriff and there were several Mexicans with him helping guard the prisoner who they had in a buggy. George Coe, a big husky boy, stepped out from behind the willows and threw his Winchester down on Baca and it scared those Mexicans to death. He told Baca to come up to him and then told him what to do. He was given very definite instructions to ride back, also that he was not to know anything of the party, and that he was to say nothing. He promised gladly. We took Largo up a canon about 600 yards to the south of the Bonito. We made him walk in front of us. After we had come about this distance Bowdre said: "This is all right, and if they want him let them come up and carry him out." I got off my horse and Largo looked at the horse and at the pinon by which we had stopped and knew what was up. Doc Scurlock had punched cattle with Largo [for Chisum] and Largo tried to impress him, crying "Doc! Doc!" but Scurlock brushed him aside saying he did not know him. We had Largo climb on the horse and he did. We tried to get him to tell who his men were but he would not. He took his medicine pretty good. . . . We did not shoot him after hanging him as we did not have the ammunition to waste (Haley, "Interview with Frank Coe," August 17, 1927).

7. *New Mexican*, November 18, 1876. The "good looking" Gonzales, "a Spaniard, and light complexioned," a former Santa Fe Trail freighter who lived on the north side of the Lincoln street, a little east of the courthouse, was also renowned for having brought an American whore out with him from Leavenworth; she died at Lincoln in the black smallpox epidemic the following spring. Haley, "Interview with Frank Coe," August 17, 1927.

8. Reference has already been made to the horse thieves of Lincoln County. This is merely an attempt to put the various confused tales into correct historical sequence, although whether or not that will ever be possible is another matter: for instance, how many horse thieves named Mes were there all together? As for the Meras, Gonzales, and Largo gang, they must have been operating in 1876 because Saturnino Baca ceased to be sheriff at the end of that year.

9. The appearance here of Sam Bass presents a fascinating little conundrum hitherto unexamined in books about his brief career. According to Lily Klasner, Bass had a place on the Feliz in

partnership with George Hindman. She misremembered Bass as "a refugee in New Mexico. I believe the robbery of the U.P. train was his first exploit as a bandit, and it was shortly after this that he came into New Mexico. The usual statement is that he hid out in the Panhandle, but as a matter of fact he was up on our Feliz place." Lily was confusing what she knew then with what she learned later: the Bass gang did not hold up the U.P. train at Big Spring, Neb., until September 18, 1877. Adding that he also had a wife living with him, Klasner goes on to say that Sam got into a shooting scrape up at the Mathews-Freeman place on the Peñasco. As with everything she says, it is difficult to be precise about the timing, but it was "after father's death," that is to say, after August 1875. Ellen Casey swore out a complaint against Bass, and a warrant was issued, but Sam had skipped. "The next grand jury [October 1876?] brought in an indictment, but Bass was never found and brought back to Lincoln county."

There is no mention of any of this in Wayne Garde's definitive biography of Bass. Ramon Adams, usually reliable, dismisses Klasner's account out of hand: "The Texas Sam Bass was never in New Mexico, nor was he married, and the Union Pacific robbery was not his first exploit as a bandit," he snaps. It is always dangerous to be so dogmatic: for in the *New Mexican* of December 12, 1876, is the following item:

Special Mail Agent Adams arrived yesterday from Fort Stanton bringing with him the two men captured in that vicinity suspected of being of the party that robbed the stage near Las Vegas last month. The prisoners are heavily ironed and are confined in the county jail; their names are Bliss [sic] and Campbell.

Two related stories appeared in the *Weekly New Mexican* of January 9, 1877. The first noted that [o]ne of the men confined in the county jail charged with robbing the stage near Las Vegas last November made his escape early Thursday evening while the guard was closing up for the night. In some way he had managed to unlock his irons and while the guard's back was turned, he jumped down the stairs and ran up the street where he was soon lost sight of in the crowd. Until we have a more secure jail building than the present one, these frequent escapes may be expected.

This story had originally appeared on Saturday, January 6. Coincidentally,

U.S. Mail Agent Adams came in on Saturday evening's coach. With him came a sheriff from Nebraska with a requisition for the man Bass whom Gen. Adams captured down in Lincoln county, and had been here in jail on suspicion of being one of the stage robbers. Bass is wanted on a charge of murder committed in Nebraska over a year ago and the officers were rather disgusted when they heard of his escape.

A later story adds that the guard, a former southern mail driver named S. B. Applegate, was arrested and jailed on a charge of "having assisted the escape of Bass, the mail robber and murderer from Nebraska," and that he "allowed him to escape for a consideration." Was this man Lily Klasner's misremembered Sam Bass, on his way to brief fame and early death? It's a tantalizing proposition. Klasner, *Girlhood*, 154, 157–58; Adams, *More Burs Under the Saddle*, 87; Gard, *Sam Bass; New Mexican*, January 16, 1877.

10. Dated June 2 in JHT to his family, June 4, 1877.

11. Dated June 3, ibid.

12. Ibid.

13. JHT to J. P. Tunstall, n.d. [end May 1877].

14. JHT to J. P. Tunstall, June 8, 1877.

15. JHT to J. P. Tunstall, June 23, 1877.

16. JHT to J. P. Tunstall, July 1, 1877.

17. *New Mexican*, June 28, 1877.

18. JHT to J. P. Tunstall, July 1, 1877.

19. Lincoln County, tax assessment records, 1877. Courtesy Donald Cline.

20. Copies of the Tunstall check for two thousand dollars and the tax check paid to Brady were included as exhibits with the Angel Report. The Tunstall-McSween bank accounts are in Special Collections, Zimmerman Library, University of New Mexico. Courtesy Jan Barnhart.

21. Lavash, *Brady*, 63–67. The author's interpretation of the Tunstall-McSween financial transactions is unaccountably hostile.

22. JHT to J. P. Tunstall, July 1, 1877.

CHAPTER TWELVE

1. *New Mexican*, July 3, 1877.

2. The *New Mexican* of Saturday, 20 January, 1877, published news of Chisum's activities, datelined January 7, "in camp in full sight of Goat Mountain."

John S. Chisum [is] making a hasty trip to El Paso on the track of some cattle thieves. . . . He was going on horseback with a pack mule and came from Arizona where he had been since last October locating a large herd of cattle on a new ranche. . . . [H]is herd numbers some 40,000 head, with headquarters on the Pecos river in Lincoln county, but . . . it is increasing to such an

extent that he is compelled to hunt up new ranges in isolated regions further west. At his ranche on the Pecos and with his hands elsewhere he employs ninety herders whom he furnishes with horses, wagons, camp equipage and provisions; . . . within the past two years he has purchased $25,000 worth of improved stock from Kentucky. He gave us a graphic description of his encounter (with your Mr Conway) with road agents in Cook's Cañon [on January 12 the preceding year] when he lost a fine gold watch and about $200 in money; he has heard of his watch in Chihuahua, Mexico, and intends to try and purchase it back.

3. *New Mexican*, July 17, 1877.

4. *Mesilla Valley Independent*, July 28, 1877.

5. *New Mexican*, July 30, 1877.

6. The most damning affidavits were those made by Francisco Gómez, George Peppin, Saturnino Baca, and John Long; the first three, and one by John Priest, were made November 6, 1878; those of Lts. S. S. Pague and G. W. Smith, November 7. Long's affidavit, dated November 9, is of value for reasons other than this.

Susan McSween never forgot—or forgave—those who had circulated this scurrilous gossip. In her defense it must be said that the accusations made against her were designed to discredit her in her quest to bring Dudley to book for his actions—or rather, lack of them—in connection with the death of her husband. However, the evidence of Francisco Gomez seems quite conclusive; there are hints and gossip aplenty to suggest later liaisons. While readers will go wherever their sympathies or judgment lead, it is my opinion that, on balance, while she was no better than she had to be, Susan McSween was not a trollop. Judge Advocate General's Office, "Records Relating to the Dudley Court of Inquiry" (hereafter DCOI).

7. Florencio Gonzales and Charles Fritz to Donnell, Lawson & Co., August 1, 1877. Fritz Estate, courtesy Nora Henn; quoted in Keleher, *Violence*, 34.

8. Donnell, Lawson & Co. to A. A. McSween, Esq., July 19, 1877. Exhibit 7 with deposition of McSween, Angel Report.

9. Petition of A. A. McSween, August 1, 1877. Fritz Estate.

10. As in the matter of his wife, so with McSween's maneuverings in the probate court: readers must follow their own judgment. Some see McSween's actions as clever manipulation of the law enabling him to keep, and later embezzle, the Fritz insurance money; others, the determined efforts of an honest man to ensure that the money was not paid over until proper settlement

was assured. It is said (but not, as far as I know, documented) that in later years Susan McSween admitted that the Fritz insurance money had been used to build the house and store; it would seem far likelier that it was eaten up financing McSween's war on Dolan.

11. *Arizona Weekly Star*, August 23, 1877. Gus Gildea, who claimed to have witnessed the killing, stated categorically that Cahill was a blacksmith and that he was known as "Windy" because he was a blowhard. "He would throw Billy to the floor, ruffle his hair, slap his face and humiliate him before the men in the saloon." Denton, "Billy the Kid's Friend"; the *Weekly Star* account of the killing first appeared in Mazzanovich, "Tony Tells About the Kid."

12. Mullin, *Boyhood*, 17. This would appear to be a misplacing by Mullin of the events related earlier.

13. Miles Leslie Wood, "Biographical Sketch," Office of Arizona Historian, Phoenix, June 30, 1911. Courtesy Jerry Weddle.

14. *Arizona Citizen*, August 25, 1877. In this account, the Kid was referred to as "Austin Antrim."

15. Cline, *Alias*, 53.

16. Ibid., 51. Gildea's account supports the proposition that the Kid skinned out. After killing Cahill, he "squirmed free and ran to the door, vaulted into the saddle on John Murphey's racing pony and left Fort Grant." Denton, "Billy the Kid's Friend."

17. *Mesilla Valley Independent*, July 21, 1877.

18. Ibid., July 13, 1878.

19. *Mesilla News*, January 11, 1876.

20. *Weekly New Mexican*, January 22, 1876.

21. Doña Ana County, District Court Records, case 322; *New Mexican*, February 8, 1876. On receiving the news of his son's death, Frank Fletcher, who had a place a few miles from town, said philosophically, "Well, he has killed two men but will kill no more."

22. *Grant County Herald*, July 14, 1877.

23. *Mesilla Valley Independent*, July 21, 1877.

24. *Grant County Herald*, July 21, 1877.

25. In a precis of an unsigned letter to M. G. Fulton, a Shield descendant (probably Minnie Shield Zimmerman) says that "Shield and wife . . . moved to Missouri and at this time Mrs. Shield had some sort of disease, which her sister, the newly [married?] Mrs. McSween wrote to her and said could be cured in the dry climate of New Mexico" (Mullin, "Notes on David P. Shield").

26. *Mesilla Valley Independent*, September 8, 1877.

27. Ibid.

28. Coe, *Frontier Fighter*, 72.

29. *Mesilla Valley Independent*, September 8, 1877.

30. Fulton, *Lincoln County War*, 81.

31. *Mesilla Valley Independent*, September 8, 1877.

32. Rasch, "Pecos War," 108. Another version of the Franklin killing has it that he got drunk and started abusing the cook, Miguel Tayas. Tayas shot Franklin, and the cowboys were going to hang him on the spot. "Chisum interfered and said to take him to Fort Stanton, thirty miles away. He gave his boys the wink, meaning to let him make a break and then get him before he got away. . . . Near the mouth of Gavilan Canon . . . he commenced to run and they all began shooting and he ran through the bullets, got into heavy timber, and got away" (Haley, "Interview with Frank Coe," August 14, 1927).

33. The scope of Tunstall's shopping spree— the range of goods he bought must really have had eyes popping when they arrived in Lincoln—may be gauged from the invoices and the like from which this information is extracted. Lincoln County, Records of the Estate of J. H. Tunstall (hereafter Tunstall Estate). Courtesy Nora Henn.

34. JHT to J. P. Tunstall, August 1, 1877.

35. JHT to J. P. Tunstall, August 19, 1877.

36. No doubt the arrangements pleased McSween, too; at their business meeting, the attorney required Dolan and Riley to sell to him, for $250, the remainder of the forty-acre tract of land on which his house and Tunstall's store stood. McSween now owned all the land on the north side of the street from his house to a point near the jail. Lincoln County, Contracts, Agreement & Leases, Book B, 79–80; Deed Book B, 19–21. Courtesy Nora Henn.

CHAPTER THIRTEEN

1. *Mesilla Valley Independent*, September 29, 1877.

2. JHT to J. P. and Mrs. Tunstall, November 29, 1877. Warren Shedd was from St. Louis. He purchased the ranch, with its natural spring, from merchant Thomas Bull of La Mesilla and set up business as an innkeeper and merchant; later he built a large stagecoach station and hotel on the site, followed by a dance hall and gambling parlor. Liquor, gambling, and girls made it an attractive watering hole for the likes of Jessie Evans and the Boys.

3. The Barelas were prominent in Las Cruces affairs; the family owned stores and a hotel. Frank Angel was not impressed by Sheriff Barela: "not reliable," he sniffed, "a Ring tool." Mariano

Barela's brother and one-time deputy, Manuel, was lynched in Las Vegas in June 1879 after committing a particularly gratuitous murder. Theisen, "Angel's Notes"; *Mesilla News*, June 14; *Mesilla Valley Independent*, June 15, 1879.

4. Barber-Fulton Letters, March 10, 1928.

5. Klasner, "The Kid."

6. *Mesilla Valley Independent*, October 13, 1877. John Swisshelm, to give him his correct name, was a silver miner who in 1879 had a claim at Whitewater Basin in the Chiricahua Mountains.

7. Klasner, "The Kid."

8. One of the most convincing versions of the Kid's movements at this time was given by Robert Casey, confirming in many ways his sister Lily's unpublished version. It is cited in Shinkle, *Robert Casey*, 103–5. For the others, see Coe, *Frontier Fighter*, 49–50; Ball, *Ma'am Jones*, 118–23; Lavash, *Brady*, 66–67. The claims of all these parties are reminiscent of Thomas Heywood's seven cities, which "warred for Homer being dead / Who living had no roof to shroud his head."

9. Klasner, "The Kid."

10. Ibid.

11. On May 7, Tunstall noted that the staff on his Feliz "ranch" consisted of himself, Brewer, Widenmann, a cook [Gauss], and "a boy." Of the later employees, Fred Waite was twenty-four, and John Middleton a year younger; unless he was one of the Shield teenagers, the identity of the "boy" remains a mystery. JHT to J. P. Tunstall, May 7, 1877.

12. JHT to Emily Tunstall (sister), September 6, 1877. Emily Frances Tunstall and Louis Wilhelm Frederick Behrens, a partner in the firm of Behrens & Landsberg, 12 Little Tower St., London, were married by the Reverend Malden at St. Lawrence Parish Church; the bride wore a dark green traveling dress with a matching green felt hat; the groom wore a dark blue sailor suit. The best man was Behrens's friend Willy Habel, whom Minnie described as "tall, dark, clever and quiet, very kind looking." Emily Tunstall to JHT, August 6, 1877.

13. JHT to J. P. and Mrs. Tunstall, September 17, 1877.

14. JHT to J. P. and Mrs. Tunstall, November 29, 1877. Tunstall's comments on the death rate contradict local reports to the effect that "the small pox is on the decline. This week the number of deaths have been much less than for weeks previous. People do not need to stay away from town for fear of contracting the disease as there is but slight danger of catching it in the business portion of town" (*Las Vegas Gazette*, October 13, 1877).

15. An unsigned letter datelined San Patricio, October 8, outlined the proceedings of court there, and noted that the cases of Lucas Gallegos and Catarino Romero were continued to the next term of court because McSween could not defend them due to sickness in the Shield family. *New Mexican*, October 23, 1877.

The tradition that one of the Shield children died in Lincoln is difficult to document. The Osceola, Mo., census of 1870 showed the Shields with only three children. Certainly there were five when the family arrived in Lincoln in the summer of 1877. Most accounts of the family's escape from the McSween house in July 1878 give the number of children present then as five (although one or two say four). As far as is known, no Shield children were born in Lincoln. The 1880 Las Vegas census shows five children, the youngest, Edgar, having been born there in 1878. If this is so, and there were five children when the family arrived in the summer of 1877, it would seem probable that one child did indeed succumb to smallpox in October 1877.

16. The Ellises were originally from Missouri and had settled in Kansas; they fell in with the Coes heading west on the Santa Fe Trail in 1873 and were their neighbors for a while in Colfax County. "Mr Ellis and family, consisting of two grown sons [Ben and Will] and one of five or six summers, are here from Colfax county about three months since," said the same anonymous correspondent. "He bought the property belonging to Daniel Dow in this county. Mr Ellis appears to be doing a thriving business. He is just the [sort of] man we want in our county, and I hope many more like him will come in." *New Mexican*, October 23, 1877.

17. JHT to J. P. and Mrs. Tunstall, October 16, 1877.

18. JHT to J. P. and Mrs. Tunstall, November 29, 1877.

19. Ibid. The dialogue is taken directly from the letter.

20. Ibid.

21. *Independent*, October 27, 1877.

22. The succeeding narrative is extracted from JHT to J. P. and Mrs. Tunstall, November 29, 1877.

CHAPTER FOURTEEN

1. JHT to J. P. and Mrs. Tunstall, November 29, 1877.

2. Klasner, *Girlhood*, 148. Another version of the Casey story is in Shinkle, *Robert Casey*, 151–53. Tunstall, who might have been expected to do so, does not mention Brewer's "ar-

rest" of Will and Ad Casey; if it happened, no record seems to have survived.

3. JHT to J. P. and Mrs. Tunstall, November 29, 1877. In January 1932, Riley Lake of Lake City, Kans., told M. G. Fulton that Middleton was "dark complected; a full face; black eyes; height about 5'10"; weight about 180; heavy black moustache; the earmarks of a general westerner. Very quiet and feared nothing or nobody." Mullin, "Notes on John Middleton."

4. JHT to J. P. and Mrs. Tunstall, November 29, 1877.

5. The Las Vegas Gazette of August 4, 1877, noted the completion of the McSween house.

A. A. McSween Esq. has built a new dwelling house in Lincoln, also a building for business purposes in which he will have one of the nicest and best furnished offices in the Territory—also a bank, the Lincoln County Bank, and a store. The proprietors of the Bank are J. S. Chisum, Esq., Roswell, A. A. McSween, Esq., Lincoln, and Col. R. D. Hunter of St. Louis. The safes and necessary paraphernalia are en route.

The inclusion of the name of R. D. Hunter as a proprietor (and the absence of Tunstall's) may safely be taken as an error on the part of Editor Koogler, who probably got his information at second, third, or even fourth hand.

6. Klasner refers to Avery Clenny as "Old Man Clene," contemporary usage indicating the advanced age of fifty or more, and relates how subsequent to Clenny being badly beaten up by Cal Dotson and "S. W. VanSickle" in 1872, saloonkeeper Pete Bishop killed Dotson and wounded Van Sickle, whose ranch Tunstall bought. The ranch was located on the Peñasco. James Farmer had a place seven miles from Fort Stanton "right down the creek just this side of Lincoln," and John Copeland and his wife, Sarah, shared a ranch located eight miles southwest of Fort Stanton with Copeland's brother and his wife. Klasner, Girlhood, 209–10; DCOI.

7. There had been considerable local controversy over the building of the new jail; Peppin submitted a bill to the county for three thousand dollars which, even though it was reduced to seventeen hundred, had to be paid by borrowing from the school fund.

8. JHT to J. P. and Mrs. Tunstall, November 29, 1877.

9. Deposition of A. A. McSween, Angel Report.

10. JHT to J. P. and Mrs. Tunstall, November 29, 1877.

11. Deposition of A. A. McSween, Angel Report.

12. Ibid.

13. JHT to J. P. and Mrs. Tunstall, November ber 29, 1877. Tunstall's observation that it was impossible to get within a mile of the Brewer place without being seen vividly emphasizes the radical changes that have taken place in the topography of the Ruidoso valley. Today, after more than a century of tree planting and farming, the one-time Brewer farm lies in a tree-shaded, fertile declivity below and to the left of U.S. 70. It is almost invisible from a few hundred yards away.

14. Independent, December 15, 1877. McSween's reference to "Pasha" Boyle is a sneer at that worthy's British Army service in India.

15. Klasner, Girlhood, 174.

16. JHT to J. P. and Mrs. Tunstall, December 6, 1877.

17. The story of the San Elizario "Salt Wars" is told in some detail in Sonnichsen, Ten Texas Feuds. A long report describing the sequence of events, copied from the Las Cruces Eco del Rio Grande, appeared in the New Mexican, January 1, 1878. Kinney's involvement is covered in Rasch, "Kinney," 11.

18. JHT to J. P. and Mrs. Tunstall, November ber 29, 1877.

19. Mesilla Valley Independent, November 3, 1877; Rasch, "Kinney." John Kinney gave his own version of events a week later. It merits reproduction if only to preserve the magnificent hyperbole of the dialogue that ensued when he and Barela confronted each other.

I went to the house of Urieta . . . and asked him if he had anything against me; he said "No!" I shook hands with him and left with —— and very near Ramon Gonzales's old house, where Mr —— and I were talking of a horse of mine which was shot, he (Barela) came out and began to speak to me, and the conversation was this: He said he was a man and liked bad men. I said, "You can't like me, I am a good man." He said that he was a man and I said that I was not a woman. He said, "I am a man, I will show you." He said, "look! look!! look!!!" and put his hand on his Winchester rifle as if to pull [it] from the scabbard, when I pulled my pistol and shot. He was under the influence of whiskey while I was just as sober as a man could be. The man who says that I put my pistol in Charlie Bull's face is telling what is not so. The man who informed me that Barela had no rifle has told you a falsehood, for he had a new one and I can prove it. You will oblige me very much if you would correct this statement in your last paper. Your old friend till death, John Kenney [sic]. (Mesilla Valley Independent, November 10, 1877)

An item in the Mesilla News of August 8, 1878,

suggests Widenmann's adventures were somewhat less glorious than he painted them. He "was going to do a lot of killing over here once before," said the *News*, "but he only got a couple of men killed. Some were scared into behaving themselves, at least for a time, while he sneaked off for his field of operations in Lincoln county under McSween."

So the jury remains out; but if he *was* involved, this would certainly account for Kinney's animosity toward the Tunstall-McSween interests in general and Widenmann in particular, and would lend considerable weight to the latter's claims that during the summer of 1878, when he was virtually a prisoner in Mesilla, his life was in constant danger.

20. JHT to J. P. and Mrs. Tunstall, November 29, 1877.

21. Widenmann to J. P. and Mrs. Tunstall, December 7, 1877. Tunstall's letters give no indication of where he went on the December trip. Lavash claims that Tunstall and Chisum "made frequent trips to the Oklahoma Territory where Tunstall eventually purchased horses. The animals were to be placed on the Chisum South Spring Ranch near Roswell until Tunstall could locate them on permanent pasture land in Lincoln County." Authority for this statement is an undated bill of sale from one Lute Jackson of Marietta, I.T., to John Chisum, with Tunstall shown as witness. There is no mention of Jackson, or any reference to trips into Indian Territory, with or without Chisum, in any of Tunstall's papers. In this particular instance, however, the trip was certainly not made with Chisum, who was still in jail in Las Vegas. Lavash, *Brady*, 59.

CHAPTER FIFTEEN

1. Lincoln County, Deed Book B. Courtesy Nora Henn.

2. Civil case 140, Lincoln County District Court Records.

3. Deposition of J. J. Dolan, Angel Report.

4. *New Mexican*, May 18, 1878.

5. The documents relating to the Fritz-Scholand writ of attachment can be found in civil case 141, Lincoln County District Court Records.

6. Chisum's narrative is in Klasner, *Girlhood*, 261–82. McSween's corrective version is in Deposition of A. A. McSween, Angel Report.

7. JHT to J. P. and Mrs. Tunstall, November 29, 1877.

8. Mrs. Allen Francis to J. P. and Mrs. Tunstall, April 26, 1878.

9. Dated January 6, 1878, in JHT to J. P. and Mrs. Tunstall, November 29, 1877.

10. Bristol's illness was reported in the *New Mexican*, January 19, 1878.

11. Lincoln County, Probate Court Journal, 1876–81, 58–59.

12. *Las Cruces Eco*, January 10, 1878.

13. Ibid. Quoted in Fulton, *Lincoln County War*, 99.

14. Lincoln County, Contracts, Agreements and Leases, Book B.

15. Deposition of A. A. McSween, Angel Report.

16. *Mesilla Valley Independent*, January 26, 1878.

17. According to Widenmann, Dolan confronted Tunstall in La Mesilla and demanded satisfaction. Deposition of R. A. Widenmann, Angel Report.

18. JHT to J. P. Tunstall, January 22, 1878.

19. *New Mexican*, February 10, 1878. The same issue carried an announcement of the birth of a twelve-pound boy, born on the morning of February 4, later christened John Catron.

20. JHT to J. P. Tunstall, January 30, 1878.

21. *Mesilla Valley Independent*, April 27, 1878.

22. Depositions of James Longwell, Adolph P. Barrier, and David P. Shield, Angel Report.

23. Deposition of A. P. Barrier, Angel Report.

24. The account of events at Shedd's ranch and after is compiled from the depositions of McSween, Widenmann, Barrier, and J. J. Dolan, Angel Report.

25. Doña Ana County, District Court Records, Civil Case 141.

26. Deposition of Widenmann, Angel Report.

27. Deposition of McSween, Angel Report.

28. R. A. Widenmann to J. P. Tunstall, February 9, 1878.

29. *New Mexican*, May 4, 1878. The Tunstall-Chisum letter was quoted in an editorial; the newspaper does not seem to have been called on to explain how it became privy to the contents of a private letter that, it is quite certain, Chisum would never have shown its editors. There is no correspondence of any kind between Chisum and Tunstall in the papers preserved by the Tunstall family.

CHAPTER SIXTEEN

1. Deposition of James Longwell, Angel Report. Follett G. Christie, a former California miner who had probably come to New Mexico with Carleton, was a clerk at the Dolan store, and had previously worked for Van Smith and been deputy postmaster at Roswell. James Longwell (the name sometimes incorrectly rendered

Longwill) may have been from the Santa Fe area; it was to there he retreated after the murder of Brady, playing no further part in Lincoln County affairs. Robert Mullin, who knew him at El Paso in later years, could never persuade Longwell to talk about his part in the events of 1878. Mullin-Nolan Correspondence; Mullin, "Notes on Ash Upson."

2. Deposition of R. A. Widenmann, Angel Report.

3. McSween to Carl Schurz, February 11, 1878. U.S. Dept. of the Interior, Bureau of Indian Affairs, Letters Received, 1878. A corrective note: the statement made over the years by earlier writers to the effect that Widenmann had some "pull" with the secretary of the interior because his father had emigrated to America on the same boat as Schurz would seem to require revision. Karl August Widenmann emigrated to the United States in 1848; Schurz in 1852. They were not even from the same town in Württemberg. Widenmann, "Enigma."

4. Deposition of A. A. McSween, Angel Report.

5. Deposition of Widenmann, Angel Report.

6. Deposition of Godfrey Gauss, Angel Report.

7. Deposition of Widenmann, Angel Report.

8. Deposition of J. B. Mathews, Angel Report.

9. Deposition of Widenmann, Angel Report.

10. Deposition of McSween, Angel Report. The matter of how the Rynerson letter to "Friends Dolan & Riley" was made public is examined in a later chapter. A minor point that has bothered some writers is Rynerson's remark about there being no Hell. At the end of 1877 the renowned preacher and lecturer Henry Ward Beecher had given a speech in which he discounted the doctrine of Hell, which had excited great controversy. It is to this that Rynerson was referring. *Weekly New Mexican*, January 1, 1878.

11. Fulton, "Calendar of Tunstall's Last Three Months."

12. Deposition of McSween, Angel Report.

13. Fritz Estate.

14. Deposition of Widenmann, Angel Report.

15. Deposition of Gauss, Angel Report.

16. Deposition of Widenmann, Angel Report.

17. Deposition of Mathews, Angel Report.

18. Ibid.

19. Deposition of Gauss, Angel Report.

20. Deposition of Mathews, Angel Report.

21. Ibid. Mathews lied under oath: not only were Evans, Baker, and Hill in the posse, but also Andrew Roberts, Ham Mills, Tom Moore, Juan Silva, Felipe Mes, E. H. Wakefield, Sam Perry, Pablo Pino, Charlie Woltz, Tom Green, Charles Marshall, a man called Ponciacho, and perhaps others.

22. Deposition of Samuel R. Perry, Angel Report.

23. Deposition of Widenmann, Angel Report. Widenmann's statement that Tunstall had no gun meant no rifle or carbine. According to McSween, Tunstall was carrying two pistols. One of these was the 7½-inch-barreled Colt .45 Frontier Model Serial No. 28190, probably bought by Tunstall from Folsoms in Kansas City in 1877, now in the possession of the Tunstall family. The second pistol, if there was one, would have been Tunstall's "British Bulldog," as he called it. A solid-frame, double-action "Bulldog" revolver was manufactured by Webley & Scott, Birmingham, England, in various calibers. A handgun called the "British Bulldog" was made by Forehand and Wadsworth of Worcester, Mass., in three models: a .32 caliber seven-shot; a .38 six-shot; and a .44 five-shot. Whichever model Tunstall may have had, there is no clue as to what became of it.

24. Deposition of John Middleton, Angel Report.

CHAPTER SEVENTEEN

1. Deposition of John Patton, Angel Report.

2. Deposition of Albert Howe, Angel Report.

3. Before he left the United States for England in the fall of 1878, Robert Widenmann wrote a short essay entitled "Border Troubles in Lincoln Co., N.M.," leaving it with his family in Ann Arbor. Mich. It runs to about fifteen hundred words and is essentially an indictment of the activities of Murphy, Dolan, Riley, and Axtell. In closing, Widenmann had this to say:

Governor Axtell pretends that there is no such combination in existence as the N. Mexican Ring. A pocket book that J. H. Riley has lost some time ago contains among other interesting notices the following cypher names of the N.M. Ring:

T. B. Catron (U.S. Attorney)	Grapes
L. G. Murphy	Box
Maj. Godfroy (Ind. Agent)	Hampton
Indians	Trees
W. L. Rynerson (Dist. Attorney)	Oyster
1st Nat. Bank, Santa Fe	Terror
2nd Nat. Bank, Santa Fe	Fearful

This is only a part of the Ring which operates in Southern New Mexico. In the northern part of the Territory there are probably things kept in the same shape.

Some other code names: Morris Bernstein was "Soapweed," Spiegelberg was "Sugar," and Staab was "Earth." Most evocative of all, the code name the House gave Alexander McSween was "Diablo." Dolan and Riley claimed Widenmann stole papers containing this information when he searched the Murphy store. Widenmann, "Border Troubles"; Mullin-Nolan Correspondence.

4. Details of how Tunstall's body was located and brought down from the canyon were given to Maurice G. Fulton by Ramón Baragón. Fulton to Col. T. T. Behrens (Minnie Tunstall Behrens's son), July 1, 1927.

5. Deposition of Florencio Gonzales, Angel Report.

6. Deposition of J. B. Wilson, Angel Report; Nolan, *John Henry Tunstall*, 285.

7. Bender, *Missionaries*, 18.

8. Deposition of D. M. Appel, Angel Report. Quoted in Nolan, *John Henry Tunstall*, 286–87. On June 1, 1878, Appel submitted his account, for "professional services to J. H. Tunstall, and for making a post-mortem examination of, and embalming his body, $100.00," to the executors of Tunstall's estate. He obviously got short shrift there, for on October 8 he wrote directly to J. P. Tunstall in London asking for settlement. Another letter headed Fort Supply, Indian Territory, and dated September 20, 1880, repeated the request. On November 19, J. P. Tunstall referred him to Susan McSween, administratrix of Tunstall's estate. At this juncture, Appel obviously gave up: there is no indication in the records of the estate that he was ever paid. Tunstall Estate.

9. The threats made against Martínez are documented in the deposition of Lieutenant Goodwin, Angel Report.

10. Ealy, "Medical Missionary."

11. G. A. Purington to AAAG, Santa Fe, February 21, 1878. District of New Mexico, Letters Received by Headquarters. AGO, Letters Received, Consolidated File 1405 AGO 1878 (hereafter File 1405 AGO 1878).

12. The exact location of McSween's "private cemetery" is uncertain: it was somewhere beyond the east wall of the corral behind the Tunstall store. That wall no longer exists but stood approximately on the line dividing what is now the Penfield property and the store. There is a Lincoln tradition to the effect that all the bodies were later taken up and reburied at the rear of the Penfield property. As nearly as can be guessed, Tunstall's grave is somewhere between the privy and the patch of weeds in back of the Penfield house. In 1927, Col. T. T. Behrens, an army engineer, hired about thirty laborers and dug over a considerable patch of ground in that area: they found the skeleton of a child and the well-preserved body of a man with a long red flowing beard. Behrens always believed

this to have been the body of Alexander McSween. Mary S. Behrens, widow of Colonel Behrens, told this story to the author in 1957.

13. Deposition of A. A. McSween, Angel Report.

14. A. A. McSween to J. P. Tunstall, February 23, 1878. The appointment of Isaac Ellis was handled throughout by McSween: all the relevant documents are in his handwriting. Ellis entered bond of ten thousand dollars, and letters of administration were issued by Probate Judge Florencio Gonzales on 25 February. Oddly enough, on the initial petition, where Tunstall's age was to be entered, McSween wrote "not known." Tunstall Estate.

15. R. A. Widenmann to J. P. Tunstall, February 23, 1878. Widenmann is in error saying Tunstall's body reached Lincoln on Wednesday. Appel conducted his postmortem that day. The body was brought in the preceding evening.

CHAPTER EIGHTEEN

1. As well as Bonney and Waite, Middleton, Scurlock, the two Coes, MacNab, Corbet, Washington, Robinson, and four or five Hispanics went along as backup. Lincoln County, District Court Journal, 1875–79, 264–91. Deposition of G. A. Purington, Angel Report.

2. There is much family testimony to Widenmann's mean streak. Widenmann, "Enigma."

3. Deposition of M. F. Goodwin, Angel Report.

4. Deposition of G. W. Peppin, civil case 141, Lincoln County, District Court.

5. A. A. McSween to J. P. Tunstall, February 24, 1878. A reward offer, as discussed in a subsequent chapter, appeared in the *Mesilla Valley Independent* on May 11 and 18. Ironically it appeared directly adjacent to Dolan's "Card to the Public" announcing the cessation of trading due to conditions in Lincoln County.

6. Taylor F. Ealy to John C. Ealy (father), February 25, 1878; Bender, *Missionaries*, 21.

7. Lincoln County, Probate Court Journal, 1876–81, 100–102; A. A. McSween to Sir Edward Thornton, February 24, 1878, in British Foreign Office, File F05-1965; Angel Report.

8. A. A. McSween to John C. Lowrie, February 25, 1878, in U.S. Dept. of the Interior, Bureau of Indian Affairs, Letters Received, 1878.

9. R. A. Widenmann to Mrs. Emily Tunstall, February 26, 1878.

10. R. A. Widenmann to J. P. Tunstall, February 28, 1878.

11. Bender, *Missionaries*, 22.

CHAPTER NINETEEN

1. Keegan, *Face of Battle*, 114–16.

2. Exactly how and where did the Regulators capture Morton and Baker? Taking their cue from Upson, most writers say something like "at the lower crossing of the Penasco" which is a little inexact. "Pecos" (a *nom de plume* employed by John Chisum), informed the *Las Vegas Gazette* on March 9 that they were taken "after a chase of more than six miles, in the bottom of the banks of the Pecos." Frank Coe said they were caught in a dugout at Seven Rivers. "Uncle Jim" Miller's brother, who talked to Morton at South Spring, told him they holed up in a patch of tule reeds and the Regulators burned them out. Morton said that "he never felt the cold sweat run down his legs before as it did when he stepped out of the burning tule with his hands up," which has a certain ring to it. Rasch is the only writer who is specific: he avers that Morton and Baker were captured, after a six-mile chase, at the Seven Rivers ranch of "Cap" Amazon Howell. Tom Cochrane, who had also been a member of the Tunstall posse, was with them; he escaped capture by hiding in a corn crib. Keleher, *Violence*, 97–98; Haley, "Interview with Frank Coe," August 14, 1927; Mullin, "Notes on J. M. Miller"; Fulton, *Lincoln County War*, 138; Burns, *Saga*, 86; Garrett, *Authentic Life*, 53; Rasch, "War in Lincoln County," 3. Lloyd's involvement is mentioned in Klasner, *Girlhood*, 60.

3. R. A. Widenmann to J. P. Tunstall, March 6, 1878.

4. Bender, *Missionaries*, 24.

5. William H. McCloskey had been around Lincoln County for some years; in 1875, he was working as a teamster and Spanish interpreter for Indian Agent Williamson Crothers at Fort Stanton.

6. W. S. Morton to H. H. Marshall, March 8, 1878; *Mesilla Valley Independent*, April 14, 1878.

7. *Mesilla Valley Independent*, March 16, 1878.

8. A. A. McSween to J. P. Tunstall, April 4, 1878.

9. R. A. Widenmann to *Cimarron News and Press*, March 30, 1878. *Cimarron News and Press*, April 11, 1878.

10. A letter from "XYZ" to the *Albuquerque Review* of March 30, 1878, claims, on what authority it is not known, that McCloskey objected to the Regulators killing Morton and Baker with their hands tied (which would seem to be a very fine point of etiquette indeed), whereupon "Young Kid Antrim shot him." Baker had five

bullets in him, and Morton was shot ten times, nine in the body and one in the head. Rasch says both men were shot eleven times; Utley agrees. Although Upson claimed to have seen the bodies when they were brought to Roswell, I have based my version on correspondence with Fulton, who got his information from Francisco Gutierrez, the sheepherder who buried them. Rasch, "War in Lincoln County," 4; Utley, *High Noon*, 58; Fulton-Nolan Correspondence, September 5, 1954. Upson's letter (unsigned) appeared in the *Mesilla Valley Independent*, March 16, 1878.

11. R. A. Widenmann to *Cimarron News and Press*, March 30, 1878; *Cimarron News and Press*, April 11, 1878.

12. *New Mexican*, March 16, 1878.

13. *Weekly New Mexican*, March 23, 1878.

14. *Weekly New Mexican*, April 6, 1878.

15. A hitherto unpublished account fixes the date of Hill's demise as March 14. It appeared in the *Cimarron News and Press* on March 28, 1878, excerpted from the *Mesilla Valley Independent*.

OUR PET BANDITTI
—
How They Amuse Themselves
—

Hon H. J. Cuniffe our Probate Judge has received the following letter from Tulerosa. The men spoken of are some of our pet banditti who are now taking a little relaxation *after their arduous labors as a sheriff's posse in Lincoln county:*

Tulerosa, March 14 1878.

Mr Cuniffe:

Albino Carrio begs me to inform you that a band of men tried to drive him from his ranche and are taking away his water where he is irrigating his land, and have shot at him. Yesterday they stole a horse from me, broken open my trunks taking out all clothing and throwing it around, built a fire under my wagon, shot my driver in the leg, and took several articles from the wagon with them. [The next sentence is illegible].

John Wagner.
Julian Guerra,
Justice of Peace.
Jose Ma. Carillo.

LATER: It is reported that Wagner has been killed and that there has been a desperate fight between the citizens and outlaws, but we can trace the report to no reliable source. The same report says that JESSIE EVANS has been killed by the citizens, but we don't believe it because it is too good to be true.

MORE KILLING

—

The Banditti at Work Again!!

—

As we go to press the report comes to us that Mr
Warner (Wagner) and party driving 4,000 head
of sheep from California to [Concho], Texas,
were attacked by our pet banditti near Tulerosa
day before yesterday (the 14th inst.) The Justice
of the Peace has sent in for assistance and from
the meagre report sent by him to the Probate
Judge we gather the following account of the
affair. Mr Warner and two others of his party
were watering the sheep when they were attacked by the bandits in force; a desperate fight
ensued in which Warner was killed; of the banditti Tom Hill is said to have been killed. We
give the report as we received it, not vouching
for its correctness.

A descriptive vignette by Frank Coe adds a
little detail. Hill and Evans were "down untying
the horses from the picket pins and he turned
loose on them. He shot Hill as he was stooping
over. The bullet hit him from the back in the
hip and came out at his throat." Evans nearly
bled to death on his way down to Tulerosa; he
was brought up to Stanton in an ambulance.
Haley, "Interview with Frank Coe," August 14,
1927.

16. J. H. Turner to H. C. Beeton, March 19,
1878.

17. H. C. Beeton to Robert Widenmann,
March 19, 1878.

18. Florence Beeton to J. P. Tunstall, March
22, 1878.

19. H. C. Beeton to William Brooke Herford, March 22, 1878.

20. H. C. Beeton to J. P. Tunstall, March
23, 1878.

21. R. A. Widenmann to H. C. Beeton,
March 30, 1878.

22. R. A. Widenmann, "Border Troubles in
Lincoln County," undated ms. (March 30,
1878) on Lincoln County Bank letterhead.

CHAPTER TWENTY

1. His biographer states that "countless" bullets riddled Brady's body; other writers put the
number between eight and sixteen, the figure
given by his family. The Lincoln tradition is that
Frank MacNab killed George Hindman; both
were from Texas, "and there seemed to be a
grudge between them." The Kid later told Mrs.
McSween he was shooting at Mathews. Chavez
y Chavez's claims are in Bryan, Wildest, 244.
Lavash, Brady, 106; Cline, Alias, 66–67; Rasch,
"War in Lincoln County," 5; Haley, "Interview
with Frank Coe," March 20, 1927.

2. Juan Peppin, who was ten or twelve in
1878, later became his father's associate in adobe
and stone work. M. G. Fulton, "Interview with
Juan Peppin, Artesia, N.M. [ca. 1930]"; research by Melba McCaskill.

3. Bender, Missionaries, 28. Ealy's bigotry is
revealed in a letter dated March 19, 1878, to
Sheldon Jackson, editor of The Rocky Mountain
Presbyterian in Denver.

They are persecuting [McSween] partly because he is a Presbyterian. He has been
arrested and has offered bail; but they refuse
it. Just because they want to get him out of
Lincoln. He refuses to go to Jail, because
they have threatened his life. He is now a
refugee. I can see no dishonor in it. They
are a dirty set of Irish cut throats and you
know what their religion is. They drink
whiskey, gamble and nothing is too bad for
them. (Jackson Correspondence, vol. 7,
Presbyterian Historical Society, Philadelphia, courtesy Mary Plummer)

4. Mesilla Valley Independent, March 30,
1878.

5. File 1405 AGO 1878; Lavash, Brady, 98.

6. File 1405 AGO 1878.

7. Deposition of S. B. Axtell, Angel Report.

8. Taylor Ealy noted on March 3 that "one
of the worst men in the County broke his leg
while trying to shoot an unarmed man in the
streets of Lincoln. Jumped from his horse before
stopping him. I am careful to keep in at night
and am out very little in daylight." Unfortunately for all of us, Ealy did not see fit to mention
the object of Dolan's homicidal attentions. Nor
did he say Dolan was drunk. However, shortly
after M. G. Fulton made contact with Ealy's wife
Mary, Robert Mullin sent him a note to ask if
he knew how Dolan came to fall off his horse.
On it in Fulton's crabbed handwriting is the tart
comment, "He fell off the water wagon first."
Ealy, "Medical Missionary."

9. Montague R. Leverson to His Excellency
Sir Edward Thornton, March 16, 1878. British
Foreign Office (BFO) File F05-1965. Leverson's
letters are quoted, for the most part in full, in
Nolan, John Henry Tunstall, 292–314.

10. M. R. Leverson to President R. B. Hayes,
March 16, 1878. Ibid.

11. M. R. Leverson to John Sherman, Jr.,
March 20, 1878, Ritch Collection.

12. M. R. Leverson to Sen. H. B. Anthony,
March 20, 1878, in BFO File F05-1965. Leverson's note to Butler has not survived; the one
he wrote to Senator Anthony has. His rhetoric
appears to have signally failed to excite that
worthy, who merely forwarded the letter to Carl
Schurz, noting that it "contains all the knowl-

13. M. R. Leverson to Sir Edward Thornton, March 21, 1878. Ibid.

14. M. R. Leverson to Carl Schurz, March 25, 1878. Ibid.

15. Bender, *Missionaries*, 29. Almost coincident with this, Colonel Purington was writing, "I apprehend no further troubles in civil matters. The court is expected to meet next Monday." G. A. Purington to AAAG, DNM, March 29, 1878, in File 1405 AGO 1878.

16. *Cimarron News & Press*, April 4 and 11, 1878. The first editorial took issue with a *New Mexican* story of March 30, headlined

DISGRACEFUL EXHIBITION
A DEPUTY U.S. MARSHAL SEEKS
BRITISH PROTECTION
AN OFFICER OF THE COURT
SLANDERS
THEM TO A FOREIGN
GOVERNMENT

The letter from Widenmann to McLellan published in our last issue deserves further notice from the fact that U.S. Marshal Sherman has reappointed him and thus endorsed his ignorant and slanderous utterances.

If naught else, the *New Mexican* piece at least dates Widenmann's reinstatement as a deputy U.S. marshal; the rest was inflated rhetoric the *News and Press* was happy to puncture.

In frothy rage the *New Mexican* observes that Widenmann, a U.S. officer and so forth, etc., goes to the British Minister "with his complaint that a murder has been committed." Truly, he must be an overparticular sort of an official if he complains of so trivial an occurrence. . . .

"What has Attorney General Devens done that he should be ignored?" it cries. We are sure we don't know, but we expect he is getting used to it, as the *New Mexican* took especial pleasure in announcing that he had been snubbed by [territorial] Attorney General Breeden.

A week later, the *News & Press* again came to Widenmann's defense when the Santa Fe paper claimed that by his failure to arrest the Boys, Widenmann was responsible for the death of Tunstall.

Now taking into consideration that . . . Sheriff Brady found it necessary to write his special deputy special instructions not to employ notorious outlaws in his posse, and that he, Sheriff Brady, was often in their company, indeed had one in his company at the time of his death; and taking also into consideration that the Governor, when it became necessary, called in the military to protect these men, is it to be wondered that Mr Widenmann found their arrest a difficult matter to accomplish?

Language is strained by the *New Mexican* to find epithets bad enough to fling at Widenmann because he could not arrest somebody for stealing U.S property, but we have failed to find in its columns any denunciation for the officials who employed bandits and escaped jail birds in their service, or for those who planned and executed the assassination of J. H. Tunstall. That paper, which so long denied the existence of outlaws and bandits in that region, may dodge the real issue, but the people will not forget it.

17. H. C. Beeton to Robert Widenmann, March 21, 1878.

18. R. A. Widenmann to H. C. Beeton, March 31, 1878.

19. M. R. Leverson to President R. B. Hayes, April 2, 1878, in BFO File F05-1965. He also claimed he had been assured on good authority that even though Brady had warned Hispanic New Mexicans who refused to accompany him that they would be fined fifty dollars for so refusing, the sheriff was still unable to enlist possemen. "When we get the $50.00 [to pay the fine] we will pay it," the citizens said. "But if you call on us to go in pursuit of the murderers of Mr Tunstall we will go at once." Nolan, *John Henry Tunstall*, 309.

20. On his return to Las Vegas, Barrier, a paperhanger by trade, was promptly arrested for contempt of court (in not handing McSween over to Brady) on his return to Lincoln. He gave bonds for his appearance at court in the Third Judicial District the following October and was discharged. *Las Vegas Gazette*, May 4, 1878.

21. Edith Crawford, "Interview with Francisco Trujillo."

22. *Weekly New Mexican*, June 15, 1878.

23. M. R. Leverson to President R. B. Hayes, April 2, 1878, in BFO File F05-1965.

24. Barber-Fulton Letters, October 12, 1927, and March 21, 1928.

25. Lavash, *Brady*, 105.

26. Cline, *Alias*, 66. Cline also argues that Brady and his deputies were on horseback at the time of the shooting, but the case for this is less convincing.

27. Lavash, *Brady*, 105. In a footnote (p. 108) the author categorically states that Brady and Hindman were shot in the back but neglects to add how he knows. A more enduring story, that Hindman called for water and was being helped

toward Ike Stockton's saloon when a second shot felled him, is accepted by Fulton and supported by Doctor Ealy's testimony. Frank Coe says Hindman "ran forty yards before he was shot through." Lavash says merely that Hindman died "within minutes" (p.106), while Cline claims eyewitnesses (unnamed) testified that Hindman "never moved or spoke save for a slight twitch of the hand" after he was shot. Fulton, *Lincoln County War*, 159; Bender, *Missionaries*, 30; Haley, "Interview with Frank Coe," March 20, 1927; Cline, *Alias*, 66.

28. Some accounts also have Washington and Robinson in the corral, unarmed. Whether Widenmann participated in the ambush cannot be established; many were convinced he did. A letter signed "Citizen" dated Las Cruces, August 2, asked:

Did not Widenmann almost run over one or two influential citizens as he jumped over the adobe wall of the corral and ran with a gun and two pistols? After he had fired his gun did he not quickly change for another gun that had not been fired, and when he arrived in the presence of certain persons did he not ask them to look that the gun was not fired off?

Good questions; but Widenmann never answered them. When asked to explain why he needed a rifle and two pistols to feed a dog, he replied that the dog was vicious and he was afraid it might bite him. This was the reason the *New Mexican* and the *News* referred to him so contemptuously as "the dog feeder." Fulton, *Lincoln County War*, 162; *Mesilla News*, August 8, 1878; Rasch, "War in Lincoln County," 11.

29. There has been some difference of opinion as to the identities of the wounded men. Mary Ealy was quite specific: she said that French was "pretty badly wounded and the Dr dressed his wounds." Added to the statement of Frank Coe that both were hit by the same bullet, this would seem to dispose of the argument; and since French, like the Kid, was back in action just a couple of days later at Blazer's Mill, it is safe to assume neither wound was really serious. Mary Ealy to M. G. Fulton, January 18, 1928. L. O. Ealy Collection, University of Arizona, Tucson; Haley, "Interview with Frank Coe," March 20, 1927.

30. Ealy, "The Lincoln County War as I Saw It," unpublished ms. in L. O. Ealy Collection; Fulton, *Lincoln County War*, 159.

CHAPTER TWENTY-ONE

1. Bender, *Missionaries*, 30.
2. Lavash, *Brady*, 109.

3. M. R. Leverson to President R. B. Hayes, April 1, 1878, BFO F05-1965.
4. Ibid.
5. Ibid.
6. Leverson's note to Carl Schurz:

Lincoln, N.M. 1 April 1878.
Hon Carl Schurz
Dear Sir
Since I wrote my letter to the president this forenoon, some of the deputies of the late Sheriff *aided by the Commander of the Post* and a company of Cavalry have dared to search the houses of citizens here without warrant or authority of any kind and have arrested just whom they pleased being persons who had as much to do with the killing of the sheriff as you had—among them the deputy of the U.S. Marshall of New Mex.

Once again, a footnote in a different hand pointed out that "Wiederman, Dep. U.S. Marshall, was in the corral with the party who shot Brady and Hindman."
7. The dialogue is in Leverson's April 1 letter to Hayes; see note 3 above.
8. *Cimarron News & Press*, April 11, 1878. M. R. Leverson to President R. B. Hayes, April 2, 1878, BFO F05-1965.
9. Carl Schurz to Charles Devens, April 1, 1878, BFO F05-1965; H. C. Beeton to Secretary of State, Canada, April 2, 1878; William Brooke Herford to P. H. Sheridan, April 4, and Sheridan to W. T. Sherman, April 5, 1878, File 1405 AGO 1878; Taylor Ealy to Congressman Rush Clark, April 5, 1878, File 1405 AGO 1878.
10. H. C. Beeton to J. P. Tunstall, April 7, 1878.
11. Ibid.; Frank Springer to Rush Clark, April 9, 1878, File 1405 AGO 1878.
12. Dudley to AAAG DNM, April 5, 1878, DCOI.
13. Coe, *Frontier Fighter*, 90; Burns, *Saga*, 95; Haley, "Interview with Frank Coe," March 20, 1927; *Independent*, June 14, 1879.
14. M. G. Fulton to W. A. Carrell, April 19, 1930.
15. My reconstruction of the fight at Blazer's Mill draws on information from Coe, *Frontier Fighter*, 93–101; Burns, *Saga*, 92–100; testimony of David Easton, DCOI; Rickards, *Gunfight at Blazer's Mill*; Blazer, "Fight at Blazer's Mill"; *Independent*, April 13, 1878. Who exactly was Buckshot Roberts? Burns said he was a Texan, a former army sergeant and Texas Ranger. He killed a man and, when the Rangers came to arrest him, was riddled with bullets in the fight that ensued. Frank Coe confirmed that Roberts came from Texas, had been a soldier at Fort Stanton, and was a deserter and a horse thief. It

will be recalled that under his "other" name, Bill Williams, he was involved in the Horrell War, which offers the possibility that he came up from Texas with them. McSween, on the other hand, labeled him a member of the Jessie Evans gang. Burns, *Saga*, 92–93; Haley, "Interview with Frank Coe," March 20, 1927; *Cimarron News & Press*, April 18, 1878.

16. Blazer, "Fight at Blazer's Mill," 208.

17. Ibid., 209. The house in which Roberts made his stand burned down in 1886.

CHAPTER TWENTY-TWO

1. A. A. McSween to J. P. Tunstall, April 4, 1878.

2. *Cimarron News & Press*, April 18, 1878. A garbled account of Dick Brewer's life appeared in the *Richland Observer*, Richland Center, Wis., June 21, 1963; author Harry Johnson avers that Brewer's parents received news of his death by telegraph from Susan McSween.

Some hundred and fifty citizens of Lincoln appended their names to an "In Memoriam" eulogy to Brewer written by McSween; it did not list all the signatories, but those named included John Chisum, I. Ellis & Sons, Merchants, G. B. Barber, Juan Patrón, Jose Montaño, McSween, Shield, John Copeland, John Newcomb, Taylor F. Ealy, the Dow brothers, R. M. Gilbert, A. Wilson, and W. Fields. *Cimarron News & Press*, May 2, 1878.

3. A. A. McSween to Col. N.A.M. Dudley, April 6, 1878, DCOI.

4. A. A. McSween to J. P. Tunstall, April 6, 1878.

5. L. G. Murphy to Col. N.A.M. Dudley, April 6, 1878, DCOI.

6. R. A. Widenmann to J. P. Tunstall, April 12, 1878.

7. *Independent*, April 27, 1878. Quoted in Fulton, *Lincoln County War*, 196–99.

8. R. A. Widenmann to J. P. Tunstall, April 16, 1878.

9. That the mystery man was considered to be one of the posse which killed Tunstall is borne out by McSween's April 17 letter to Minnie Tunstall Behrens saying that "seven of his murderers" were now dead: Morton, Baker, Hill, Brady, Hindman, Roberts, and ——? Widenmann is emphatic that this was one of the February 18 possemen. Yet later, when he testified to Angel concerning the disposition of those who had been in the posse, he did not mention this man's death at all.

10. A. A. McSween to J. P. Tunstall, April 17, 1878.

11. A. A. McSween to Emily Tunstall Behrens, April 17, 1878.

12. R. A. Widenmann to Emily Tunstall Behrens, April 17, 1878. Widenmann's peculiar phraseology—and this is but one of numerous examples—"the dreadful news only reached you after you had been prepared to receive them," is due to the fact that in German the word *nachrichten*, meaning news or tidings, is plural. He implies that by the time his and McSween's letters reached London the Tunstalls were already aware of John's death. The family tradition is that the news came by telegraph; it would seem probable that John H. Turner, having cabled the news to Henry Beeton in Milwaukee on March 19, also sent word to London in the same manner.

13. A. A. McSween to J. P. Tunstall, April 17, 1878.

14. Ibid. Most of the 3,840 acres Tunstall filed on seem to have been in the Feliz and Peñasco valleys; by filing along both sides of the upper reaches of both rivers, he would have controlled most of the range between the Pecos and the Mescalero reservation. In addition he had an interest in a number of other ranches, Brewer's and George van Sickle's among them. Corbet filed on the Mathews-Freeman place; the deed locates the ranch on the SW¼ of the SE¼ and the W½ of the SW¼ and the SE¼ of the SW¼ of section 3 & the SE¼ of Section 4 & the NE¼ of Section 10 & the S½ of the NW¼ & N½ of the SW¼ of Section 11, in Township 16, South of Range 16 East. The filings were made at La Mesilla on October 9, 1877. On the same day, Trinidad Delgado filed on land surrounding the headspring of the Rio Feliz.

Robert Mullin said Tunstall's

> headquarters consisted of a small stone cottage and a horse corral, located in Township 15 South, Range 17 East, at the south end of Lincoln canyon at a small spring which fed into the Rio Felix, just west of [what became] the Dolan ranch. . . . When I searched out the spot many years ago, the property on which this stood was owned by the Gorman family; I was shown a building made of stone and was told that the stone had come from the Tunstall house or the stone wall of the corral, I forget now which. (Mullin-Nolan correspondence, September 28, 1959)

15. *Independent*, April 27, 1878. The Dolan crowd circulated allegations that the grand jury had brought in verdicts favorable to the McSween party because they were terrified. In a long editorial overview of Lincoln County events commencing with the arguments over the Fritz Estate, the *New Mexican* said:

> But it is not generally known that the men who killed Roberts had gone to the agency

to look for the court that was expected from Mesilla, as it is believed upon good evidence, for the purpose of killing the judge and district attorney. They had made their threats that no court should be held in Lincoln county, and when it was held, it was held with a guard of soldiers to protect the court.

We are also informed that the grand jury was terrorized and frightened into doing just as these outlaws dictated—that they were told that a hundred men were in arms in the mountains and would deal out vengeance on those who did not obey their dictates. In this way the court was practically a farce.

If any of this bothered U.S. Marshal John Sherman, Jr., he gave no sign of it: he had applied for a month's leave on April 16 and, when this was turned down, accepted a shorter furlough. The same issue of the *New Mexican* reported he had left for Cleveland to attend the wedding of his cousin, the daughter of Secretary of the Treasury John Sherman, to Sen. Don Cameron of Pennsylvania. *New Mexican*, May 4, 1878.

16. *Independent*, May 5, 1878.

17. Ibid.

18. *New Mexican*, April 17, 1878.

19. *New Mexican*, February 23, 1878; ibid., January 19–April 4, 1878.

20. *New Mexican*, April 20, 1878.

21. Ibid. McSween secured a reply to Riley and "Cow Boy" in the *New Mexican* the following week. After demolishing Riley's protestations, he turned to "Cow Boy's" allegations and did the same with them. His letter is quoted in its entirety in Fulton, *Lincoln County War*, 189–92. In addition, under the pen name "Stanton," he furnished the *Cimarron News & Press* with a further installment of his version of events. Isaac Ellis used McSween's letter as the basis for one of his own to the *Trinidad Enterprise and Chronicle*. As Fulton remarks, these charges and countercharges changed very few opinions. Strangely, while denying every other charge made by "Cow Boy," McSween neglected to correct the statement that Shield had fled Missouri to escape his creditors; perhaps it touched a raw nerve.

22. *New Mexican*, April 27, 1878.

23. Exhibit 77-12, DCOI.

24. DCOI, vol. 2; *Independent*, May 4, 1878.

25. A copy of the resolution is in File 1405 AGO 1878.

CHAPTER TWENTY-THREE

1. R. A. Widenmann to J. P. Tunstall, April 25, 1878.

2. R. A. Widenmann to J. P. Tunstall, April 28, 1878.

3. Widenmann did not get around to making a balance sheet of the Tunstall estate until he got to London at the beginning of 1879. It is included with Tunstall's account book in appendix 3. Taken in conjunction with McSween's pleas for reimbursement, based on the account books, and his widow's later claims against the estate, it is a damning document. The notebooks show an outstanding amount in McSween's favor of $6,598.04. Widenmann's final rendering shows a balance of $48.15, and effectively destroys McSween's claim that Tunstall owed him money. Further, in dealing with the Tunstalls, McSween never mentioned interest on the loan to Dolan or the fact that it was Tunstall, and not he, who had advanced the money with which Dick Brewer paid off the note on his ranch.

4. A. A. McSween to J. P. Tunstall, April 28, 1878.

5. *New Mexican*, May 11, 1878; *Independent*, May 18, 1878.

6. It would be interesting to know the identity of "S" of Silver City; I am tempted to think it was Stanley because his last recorded public act in Lincoln County was on May 28, 1878, when he provided Inspector E. C. Watkins, investigating the running of the Mescalero Agency, with a telling affidavit about the inner workings of L. G. Murphy & Co. Immediately thereafter, Stanley, along with brother-in-law Ham Mills, quit Lincoln County for good. *Grant County Herald*, June 8, 1878.

7. Coe, *Frontier Fighter*, 117.

8. Widenmann to J. P. Tunstall, April 28, 1878.

9. A. A. McSween to J. P. Tunstall, May 9, 1878. R. A. Widenmann to J. P. Tunstall, May 11, 1878.

10. G. W. Smith to Post Adjutant, May 1, 1878, File 1405 AGO 1878.

11. Coe, *Frontier Fighter*, 122. His chronology is very unreliable. Ab Saunders was out of hospital by mid-May, when he was moved to the Ellis house to recuperate. Isaac Ellis to Commanding Officer, Fort Stanton, May 12, 1878, File 1405 AGO 1878.

12. Fulton, *Lincoln County War*, 216–17. Because his name was found in Riley's notebook, and because he was later killed by the gang that had once called itself the Regulators, many writers have assumed Bernstein, who worked for the House, was one of its adherents and supporters. There is no doubt he was on very friendly terms with Jimmy Dolan, but for all that, he managed to remain on good terms with those hostile to the Dolan cause as well.

13. W. L. Rynerson to A. A. McSween, May 2, 1878, quoted in Fulton, *Lincoln County War*, 221–22.

14. *Weekly New Mexican*, May 11, 1878.

15. Petition to Col. N.A.M. Dudley, signed by twenty-four Seven Rivers ranchers, and also Dolan, Walz, and "L. G. Murphy for himself and others," May 1, 1878, File 1405 AGO 1878.

A report filed by Corporal Thomas Dale, Company H, Ninth Cavalry, detailed by Dudley on April 23 to assist Copeland, was bitingly critical of Copeland's conduct. "I were [sic] called upon to visit the House of Mr Murphy by John Copeland the Renegade or the Sheriff, so I went with him but let me state that the Renegade was drunk," said Dale. "I have noticed the Sheriff being too intoxicated to lead a body of soldiers," he went on. Copeland "stayed at McSween's all the time, he kept his horse at McSween's and he boarded there. he kept his arms there and was there on the 30th when the riot commenced." Report of Corp. Thos. Dale to Col. N.A.M. Dudley, May 1, 1878, File 1405 AGO 1878.

16. *New Mexican*, May 11, 1878.

17. J. Copeland to Col. N.A.M. Dudley, May 1; D. M. Easton to Dudley, May 1; M. F. Goodwin to Post Adjutant, May 6, File 1405 AGO 1878.

18. M. F. Goodwin to Post Adjutant, May 6, 1878, File 1405 AGO 1878. Goodwin sent Scurlock ("a very bad man, the worst in the bunch"), Widenmann, Scroggins, Washington, Gonzales, Isaac and Ben Ellis, and Stanley to the fort on May 2 (Corbet was ill and had been left in Lincoln) under escort by one L. Sneley, deputy sheriff of Lincoln County. Whence he came and whither he went, history does not record. This appears to have been the only duty in that role he ever undertook. L. Sneley to Col. N.A.M. Dudley, May 2, 1878, File 1405 AGO 1878.

19. J. Copeland to Col. N.A.M. Dudley, May 4; Copeland to Dudley, May 7; Dudley to AAAG DNM, May 11 and 18, 1878, File 1405 AGO 1878.

20. R. A. Widenmann to J. P. Tunstall, May 11, 1878.

21. BFO F05-1965.

22. Charles Devens to John S. Sherman, in Instruction Book B; Devens's follow-up letter of May 4 concerning Buisson in Letter Book M; Angel's expense account statements in Contingent & Miscellaneous Accounts #6; all in U.S. Department of Justice, NARA.

23. C. Devens to F. W. Angel, May 4, 1878, Letter Book M, U.S. Department of Justice, NARA. Pierre Buisson (or Boisson), a Frenchman, and a woman named Tomasa Gallegos were shotgunned to death at Las Vegas on December 15, 1877, by an Italian named Giovanni Dugl. In June 1879, still awaiting disposition of his case, Dugl was taken from his cell in Las Vegas jail and lynched, along with Manuel Barela, who was the immediate object of the mob's attention. *Independent*, June 14, 1879.

24. Confusion concerning fighting that took place away from—sometimes well over a hundred miles away from—Lincoln itself was common and, in the circumstances, understandable. It would appear that while Scurlock's posse was raiding Dolan's cow camp, Captain Johnson and the Seven Rivers men, only a mile or so away, avoided the larger force. It could well be that a few days later this band, en route to Lincoln, skirmished with Widenmann, Smith, and Newcomb on the Peñasco or the Feliz.

Billy Weir, or Wier, appears briefly in Ball, *Ma'am Jones*, 127–29. The *Independent's* report that he had been killed in the Regulator raid was in error; he was interviewed at length in 1937 by J. Evetts Haley, at which time, on the subject of the war, he made the memorable observation, "That insurance business was what started it all, and then they all wanted to kill somebody. Every sonofabitch over there wanted to kill somebody." Haley, "Interview with William Weir"; *Independent*, May 25, 1878.

25. *New Mexican*, June 1, 1878. When word of the Regulator raid on the Dolan camp reached him on May 30, Tom Catron wrote to Axtell. Those were *his* cattle down there, not Dolan or Riley's. He demanded that

some steps be taken to disarm all parties there carrying arms, and that the military may be instructed to see that they keep the peace.

I am informed that the sheriff keeps with his deputies large armed posses, who are of one faction only and who take occasion at all times to kill persons and take property of the other faction whenever they get an opportunity.

There is no power, from what I can learn, that can keep the peace in the county except the military, of whom both parties have a healthy dread.

Axtell snapped to attention and requested General Hatch to send troops to the Pecos to protect Catron's property; Hatch complied forthwith. On June 7 a detachment of troops led by Captain Purington started down to Roswell, drawing sarcastic comments about the military being used as "Catron's cowboys." T. B. Catron to S. B.

Axtell; Axtell to General Hatch, May 30; Hatch to Commanding Officer, Fort Stanton, June 1; subsequent correspondence, including instructions from Pope countermanding Hatch's authorization: File 1405 AGO 1878.

26. R. A. Widenmann to J. P. Tunstall, May 14, 1878.

27. Fulton, *Lincoln County War*, 236–37.

28. Ealy, "Medical Missionary."

29. Fulton, *Lincoln County War*, 231.

30. Specimen of Proclamation in DCOI; also File 1405 AGO 1878.

CHAPTER TWENTY-FOUR

1. *Weekly New Mexican*, May 10, 1878.

2. When he wasn't running to the fort scared out of his wits, Copeland seems to have spent most of his time drunk. As noted earlier (chapter 23, note 15), Cpl. Thomas Dale bore witness to Copeland's partisanship. On the day of the collision between Johnson's posse and the Regulators, he said, "Today there is great excitement in the town and the Sheriff cannot be found the house of McSween's is in a perfect fog from the smoke of powder. oh where is the Sheriff? don't know if I am not mistaken the Sheriff was in McSween's house when the shooting commenced." Report of Cpl. Thomas Dale to Commanding Officer, May 1, 1878, File 1405 AGO 1878.

3. If "El Gato" seriously believed McSween had paid Copeland three thousand dollars to be sheriff, the merest glance at the attorney's finances, as indicated by his bank statements and his constant pleas to the Tunstall family for financial assistance, would have disabused him of the notion immediately. McSween simply did not have that kind of money. There is further support for this conclusion in Widenmann's letter of June 3 to J. P. Tunstall: the fact that Isaac Ellis was billing the Tunstall estate for feeding and boarding the Regulators indicates they were being paid in kind rather than cash.

4. *Weekly New Mexican*, May 18 and May 25, 1878.

5. Bender, *Missionaries*, 46. Postmaster Dolan's cavalier attitude to the sanctity of the mails has already been remarked on; it may be safely assumed his men respected it even less. Tunstall and McSween made a private arrangement with Ash Upson in August 1877 to have their mail separated out and sent up to Lincoln in a special sealed sack from Roswell so that it would not pass through Dolan's hands. After McSween's death, Taylor Ealy noted, "It was said there was half a bushel of his mail found. It had been buried in an arroya [sic] and this high wind uncovered it. As it was all found in one place it could not have leaked out of his mail sack." Bender, *Missionaries*, 46.

6. R. A. Widenmann to J. P. Tunstall, May 27, 1878.

7. In *John Henry Tunstall*, 332, I remarked, "If there is any other record of McLellan's participation in Lincoln County affairs, the writer has seen no reference to it. . . . Governor Axtell's reply to McLellan would be an interesting document."

It transpires that McLellan continued to correspond with J. P. Tunstall for some time, and that Axtell's reply to him, dated April 13, survived:

Affairs in Lincoln Co are in a very sad condition. Since Tunstall was killed, Sheriff Brady and at least four of the posse have been shot and killed and two of the Tunstall party if not more.

I will send you such printed accounts as may come into my hands.

Attorney General [of the United States at Washington] Devens has requested the United States Attorney here, T. B. Catron, to furnish him statements of the affair. His attention was called to it by Sir Edward Thornton.

Widerman is under arrest as an accomplice in murdering Sheriff Brady.

Very truly yours,

S. B. Axtell,
Gov. N.M.

Enclosing Axtell's letter with his own, written on April 24, McLellan confessed his helplessness to J. P. Tunstall:

I have just read an extract from a New Mexico paper giving an account of the shooting of Sheriff Brady and four of his posse, and that McSween had to leave the country and that Widerman was in prison. Now I fully realize how these events may endanger the property of your late son and how by some act of omission by the officials of the Territory, or of those to whom you gave the Power of Attorney, all or most may be lost, and I hardly know how to advise you, as I do not know either the reliability or the capacity of those intrusted by you in these matters. . . .

If the *authorities* or anyone acting under authority of the government of the Territory, or of the Republic, murdered or participated in, or conspired in the murder of your son, or destroy his property, it is a fit case for demand on the United States Government for damages— decidedly so.

J. P. Tunstall traced an emphatic ring around this last paragraph: he had probably not realized that he might have a case for indemnification until McLellan wrote. The correspondence petered out inconclusively in June, and McLellan seems to have had nothing more to do with Lincoln County matters. R. G. McLellan to J. P. Tunstall, April 24, 1878.

8. R. A. Widenmann to J. P. Tunstall, May 27, 1878.

9. Theisen, "Angel's Notes," 368.

10. R. A. Widenmann to J. P. Tunstall, June 3, 1878.

11. Only a few days earlier, on May 24, Huff, who lived in a small house next to the *torreón*, had found an unidentified dead man buried in his yard. Rasch, "War in Lincoln County," 8.

12. A. A. McSween to J. P. Tunstall, June 5, 1878.

13. Axtell apparently appointed George Peppin sheriff on the recommendation of William Rynerson; why Rynerson thought Peppin especially qualified for the task is not known.

14. R. A. Widenmann to J. P. Tunstall, June 11, 1878.

15. *Mesilla News,* August 10, 1878.

16. Watkins's report contains testimony from thirty-five witnesses, many of whom also supplied affidavits to Angel and appeared at the Dudley Court of Inquiry. Watkins Report.

17. Ibid.

18. Ibid.

19. Ibid.

20. Angel recommended Godfroy's suspension effective August; he was to be replaced by James A. Broadhead, who was appointed September 10. When Broadhead got to Lincoln County at the end of October and saw what conditions were like, he beat a hasty retreat back whence he had come because, as the *Rocky Mountain Sentinel* of November 1 put it, "he had also taken up the foolish idea that unless he as agent should allow contractors for supplies at the agency to cheat and steal from the Indians, they would either kill him or trump up some charges against him and have him removed." The *Independent* of January 4, 1879, noted the appointment of a new Indian agent, S. A. Russell, who arrived May 9.

21. R. A. Widenmann to J. P. Tunstall, June 11, 1878.

22. In line with their new legal standing, Peppin's possemen began calling themselves the "law and order" party; the discredited Regulators, according to Gus Gildea, were now dubbed "Modocs," presumably on the old basis that the only good one was a dead one. Rasch, "Gildea," 4.

23. G. Peppin to Col. N.A.M. Dudley, June 18, 1878, presenting his credentials, together with U.S. Marshal Sherman's warrants for Bowdre, Scurlock, the Kid, et al. Dudley placed lieutenants Goodwin and Pague with twenty-seven enlisted men at his disposal. File 1405 AGO 1878.

24. Dudley later praised Goodwin for "very judiciously" refusing to enter Lincoln in such company. Kinney and his band took one direction, the soldiers and Peppin another. When they reached town the soldiers set up a cordon and Peppin searched for the wanted men without success. Col. N.A.M. Dudley to AAAG DNM, June 22, 1878, File 1405 AGO 1878.

25. Wilson's revised offer is documented in a letter Ealy wrote, on the letterhead of John H. Tunstall, to Sheldon Jackson.

Our work here is encourageing. We greatly need a house to hold our services in. There is a property [the courthouse, which stood on Wilson's land] here in the centre of town—containing a room large enough to hold three hundred people. I tried to buy it & was asked $2,000 for it—now I am offered the same for $700 & a span of mules. The property contains about five acres of *fenced land.* I will give $50 of my salary towards purchasing it for the Ch. I can have all the papers drawn up ect by a lawyer who will give his services. I will agree to raise something in addition to what I offer of my salary—from the people, but how much cannot say. I find Pres[byterians] scattered up and down this canon & we in a private house & they will not come to a parlor as they would to a Ch. I have a small school of 20 scholars, half Americans, half Mexicans. They do not pay me any money but give a little of such as they have. Let me hear from you at once on the subject of purchasing the property. Court is held in the house & they pay $5 per day rent. I want to keep the school & that is the best place in town for it, we can get it for $700 cash I know. (Taylor F. Ealy to Sheldon Jackson, June 15, 1878, Sheldon Jackson Correspondence, vol. 8, Presbyterian Historical Society, Philadelphia. Courtesy Mary Plummer.)

26. A note from someone who signed himself "Scrope" (Dolan?), datelined Fort Stanton, June 18, indicated the whereabouts of the McSween party. Near Dowlin's Mill, it said, Dolan's Mexican driver and an employee of Doctor Blazer's met Copeland who called him in Mexican a d-d s- of a b-, said he was a d-d spy and ought to be shot. He also told Blazer's man that a party was at the Mills waiting for Peppin but that he did not want to be con-

sidered one of them. . . .I suppose Widenmann or someone at Cruces or Mesilla notified the "Regulators" that Peppin was coming and as I was along it may be ticklish for me to go to the Plaza but I will go. (*Mesilla News*, June 29, 1878)

27. *Independent*, June 22, 1878; also *Mesilla News*, 29 June. The existence or otherwise of Susan McSween's piano is one that inexplicably has occupied the attention of a number of writers ever since Walter Noble Burns pictured her playing "The Star Spangled Banner" as her house burned down over her head. The evidence pro and con, including the mortgage to Isaac Ellis, is examined in Henn, "Was A Piano in the McSween House?"

28. The letter he wrote that day is datelined Lincoln; of course, it may well have been written elsewhere.

29. A. A. McSween to J. P. Tunstall, June 24, 1878. No monument was ever erected over Tunstall's unmarked grave, a subject examined earlier. A "death card" issued shortly after the news of Tunstall's murder was received in London indicates the epitaph it might have borne:

In Remembrance of
John Henry Tunstall
The Only Beloved Son Of
John Partridge and Emily Tunstall
Who Died February 18th, 1878,
In Lincoln County, New Mexico,
Aged 24 Years.

"Weep ye not for the dead, neither bemoan him: but weep sore for him that goeth away: for he shall return no more, nor see his native country."
JER.22 ch. 10 v.

J. P. Tunstall did write to Robert Eagle, who, by the time the letters arrived, had resigned from his post with the Merchants National Bank. In letters dated September 19 and October 3, 1878, Eagle offered to be of any assistance he could. It would appear the Tunstalls abandoned the idea.

30. For a description of the San Juan fiesta, see Church, "Notes."

31. Bender, *Missionaries*, 48.

32. *Weekly New Mexican*, July 6, 1878.

33. Affidavit, June 27, 1878, File 1405 AGO 1878.

34. In spite of these attempts to make it appear he did, it is almost impossible to believe McSween ever really used a gun. It was, very simply, against his religion. A letter from someone called "Julius" (Bernstein?) claimed he was "clean shaven and wearing a very large hat." Sun-swarthy, thinned down, moustache shaved off, and wearing a big sombrero: even if he wasn't a fighting man, McSween probably looked like one. *Mesilla News*, July 6, 1878.

35. J. Isaacs and J. N. Coe to Rutherford B. Hayes, June 22, 1878; Montague R. Leverson to Carl Schurz, June 28, 1878. U.S. Department of Justice, 44-4-8, RG 60, NARA.

CHAPTER TWENTY-FIVE

1. On May 25, Dudley had encountered Widenmann and young Ben Ellis swaggering around Fort Stanton bandoliered and armed to the teeth, "both walking Gatlin guns or equivalent to a well-armed detachment," he snorted, and ordered them off the post. Col. N.A.M. Dudley to AAAG DNM, May 25, 1878, File 1405 AGO 1878.

2. The requests for protection, affidavits, and details of the escort are in DCOI.

3. John Sherman to Col. N.A.M. Dudley, June 12, 1878, File 1405 AGO 1878. *New Mexican*, June 8 and 15, 1878. The *Independent*, June 22, 1878, carried a vignette of Jessie Evans enjoying his "vacation" in Room 2 of the Barela Hotel.

4. R. A. Widenmann to J. P. Tunstall, July 26, 1878.

5. *Mesilla News*, July 6, 1878.

6. Ibid.

7. *Weekly New Mexican*, July 27, 1878.

8. There is one other possibility: they were pressed men. That this may have been so is hinted at in an affidavit made by Yginio Salazar, who testified "Mr. McSween come to me at the Berando and told me if I did not go with him he would fine me fifty dollars that he knew I had a good gun and wanted me to go with him." Affidavit of Hinio (sic) Salazar, July 20, 1878, File 1405 AGO 1878.

9. G. W. Peppin affidavit, June 24, 1878, File 1405 AGO 1878.

10. Col. N.A.M. Dudley to AAAG DNM, June 29, 1878, File 1405 AGO 1878.

11. Ibid.; Col. N.A.M. Dudley to G. W. Peppin, July 3, 1878, File 1405 AGO 1878. He also declined a request from Postmaster Dolan, who asked for troops to protect the mails. Lieutenant Carroll, who had tracked the McSween party over the mountains south of the Ruidoso, then back north to Hondo, where they had stopped for food at Coe's ranch, and from there north by northwest to the Blue Water road, was not sorry to abandon the pursuit. It was a "toilsome and disagreeable march," he said, and such work was "the most disagreeable duty that can be assigned either officer or soldier." Henry Carroll to Post Adjutant, July 1, 1878, File 1405 AGO 1878.

12. "Lincoln," who claimed that the Regulators now numbered two hundred, went on to say

that L. G. Murphy had written to Florencio Gonzales demanding he deny signing a petition sent to the governor asking for the removal of Peppin; and that anyway, Axtell could not remove Peppin even if he wanted to. "No doubt," he commented tartly, "he knows whereof he writes." *Cimarron News & Press*, July 25, 1878. Quoted in Fulton, *Lincoln County War*, 243–46.

13. Affidavit of R. B. Copeland, July 13; handwritten petition from San Patricio families, July 11, 1878. File 1405 AGO 1878. Copeland was the brother of the former sheriff; they worked an Eagle Creek ranch on shares. Copeland himself was hiding out at the fort, as was Juan Patrón. Among familiar names on the petition were those of Trujillo, Chavez, Garcia, Gutierrez, Jaramillo, Lucero, Sanchez, Sedillo, and Miranda.

14. Barber, "Notes of Correction."

15. Testimony of Saturnino Baca, DCOI.

16. Hinton, "Chisum," 324. George Coe said that on the morning of the Fourth, he and the Kid, Henry Brown, and some others went over to Ash Upson's post-office-cum-store. While they were there they saw a "big outfit" coming, and fogged it for Chisum's. "There was about twenty five of them and only four or five of us," Coe recalled. "They never got close enough to hit us. . . . They thought they would take the ranch, and we fought around there most of the day. They stayed off on the prairie too far for our bullets to reach them. We stayed up all night, but they never charged us." Haley, "Interview with George Coe," March 20, 1927.

17. *Las Vegas Gazette*, July 20, 1878; quoted in Keleher, *Violence*, 139.

18. Rasch and Myers, "Tragedy," 3–4.

19. "Regulator" to E. Walz, July 13, with T. Blair to Post Adjutant, July 23, 1878, File 1405 AGO 1878; quoted in Fulton, *Lincoln County War*, 246–47. Bowdre's handwriting was identified by the recipient, Walz.

20. Isaac Ellis, affidavit, July 12, 1878, in DCOI, also File 1405 AGO 1878.

21. Col. N.A.M. Dudley to AAAG DNM, July 13, 1878, File 1405 AGO 1878. On July 15, Scurlock swore an affidavit before Juan Patrón. "I have been accused of attempting to kill Mrs. Brady and also with threatening the life of General Dudley. Most positively deny both accusations as there is no real foundation for either." File 1405 AGO 1878.

22. In his report of July 15, Daniel Appel testified he met the Kinney/Powell reinforcements on their way into Lincoln; the wind was blowing strongly, whirling dust high in the air and making visibility patchy. Appel warned the

possemen that McSween had invested the town and there was no way they could get in there. They "rushed on at ful galop and I heard shooting as soon as they reached Wortley's hotel. I heard about twenty shots fired but as it was growing dusk I left for the post." D. Appel to Post Adjutant, July 15, 1878, File 1405 AGO 1878.

23. A. A. McSween to S. Baca and Baca to Col. N.A.M. Dudley, July 15, 1878, DCOI.

24. D. Appel to Post Adjutant, July 15, 1878, File 1405 AGO 1878. Also in DCOI.

25. Bender, *Missionaries*, 50–51.

26. Ibid.

27. G. W. Peppin to Col. N.A.M. Dudley, July 16, 1878, File 1405 AGO 1878; also in DCOI. I first encountered Peppin's request for the loan of a howitzer in a western by Nelson C. Nye, *Pistols for Hire*, and for years believed it to have been invented by the novelist. It is still hard to believe, and harder still to believe that Dudley and his officers gave the request serious consideration, but the documents are there to prove they did.

28. Col. N.A.M. Dudley to AAAG DNM, July 16, 1878, File 1405 AGO 1878.

29. Testimony of Pvt. Berry Robinson, in "Proceedings of a Board of Officers," July 17, 1878, File 1405 AGO 1878. Also in DCOI.

30. The other man Saturnino Baca saw running down the hill after Crawford was shot was Lucio Montoya, George Peppin's nephew. Testimony of Saturnino Baca, DCOI.

31. Burns, *Saga*, 120–21.

32. Testimony of G. A. Purington, DCOI.

33. Ibid.

34. Bender, *Missionaries*, 51–52.

35. Testimony of Andrew Keefe, DCOI.

36. Bender, *Missionaries*, 52.

37. Joseph Smith to Howard Capper, July 19, 1878. Rasch, "Five Days," 303.

38. Testimony of J. J. Dolan, S. G. Beard, and J. A. Tomlinson in DCOI.

39. Testimony of J. Patrón, ibid.

40. Col. N.A.M. Dudley to AAAG DNM, July 20, 1878, File 1405 AGO 1878; also in DCOI.

41. Testimony of Alex Rudder, DCOI.

42. Testimony of J. B. Wilson, ibid.

CHAPTER TWENTY-SIX

1. Unless otherwise noted, all the documentary evidence cited in this chapter is from DCOI.

2. Bender, *Missionaries*, 55.

3. A. A. McSween to Ash Upson, July 19, 1878, McSween Estate.

4. DCOI.

5. Testimony of D. Appel, DCOI. Other tes-

timony indicates that the camp stretched east from a point opposite Montaño's store to one opposite Patrón's.

6. D. G. McSwain, JAG, to AAG DMO, September 23, 1879. Findings on DCOI, ibid., and File 1405 AGO 1878.

7. Testimony of Sue E. McSween, DCOI.

8. Testimony of G. A. Purington, D. Appel, M. F. Goodwin, G. W. Peppin, G. Washington, Teresa Phillipowski, Josefita Montaño, Martin Chaves, et al., DCOI.

9. Testimony of D. Appel, Isaac Ellis, Andrew Keefe, et al., DCOI.

10. Testimony of Sue E. McSween, DCOI.

11. Col. N.A.M. Dudley to AAAG DNM, July 20, 1878, File 1405 AGO 1878. Also in DCOI.

12. Ibid.

13. Ibid.; testimony of G. W. Peppin, Isaac Ellis, John Long, James Bush, and Houston Lusk, DCOI.

14. Testimony of Col. N.A.M. Dudley, Wilson, and many others, DCOI. The witnesses testifying to whether or not Dudley threatened to put Wilson in irons were about evenly divided; the threat is certainly typical, a perfect example of Dudley's notoriously short fuse.

15. Testimony of Sue E. McSween, DCOI.

16. Testimony of Sue E. McSween and G. W. Peppin, DCOI.

17. Testimony of Sue E. McSween, Col. N.A.M. Dudley, G. A. Purington, M. F. Goodwin, A. Keefe, T. Baker, et al., DCOI. The witnesses were not in main at odds about the burden of the conversation, only its tone: Mrs. McSween and her supporters claiming Dudley was angry, rude, and unsympathetic, the military witnesses claiming he was courteous and kind despite great provocation to be otherwise.

18. Testimony of G. W. Peppin, G. Washington, M. Chaves, G. A. Purington, S. R. Corbet, A. Keefe, H. Lusk, et al., DCOI. Keefe denied the Gatling gun had been aimed as stated, but he was alone in this claim. It was probably the hail of bullets directed at them by Peppin's men which drove off the Regulators, not the gun: Martin Chaves stated he did not even see it.

19. Testimony of M. Turner, A. Boyle, Bob Olinger, Joseph Nash, M. Pierce, and G. W. Peppin, et al., DCOI.

20. Barber-Fulton Letters, June 13, 1926.

21. My authority for stating that Elizabeth Shield was pregnant comes from the fact that her son, Edgar Shield, gave his date of birth as 1878 and the place as Las Vegas. Mrs. Shield went to Las Vegas immediately after the death of McSween. Set against this evidence is Dudley's statement that Mrs. Shield had five children with her when she sheltered at the fort. Col. N.A.M. Dudley to AAAG NMD, July 27, 1878, File 1405 AGO 1878.

22. Testimony of J. Long, A. Boyle, and Buck Powell, DCOI.

23. "All day, when we had nothing better to do," Coe recalled, "we made that [outhouse] our target and shot it full of holes. The result was that [Long] was forced to crawl down into the pit rather than meet certain death. He afterwards remarked that it was the most gruesome experience of his life but beat dying all hollow at that." Coe, *Frontier Fighter*, 169.

24. Barber, "Notes of Correction."

25. Ibid.

26. Haley, "Interview with Susan E. Barber."

27. Mrs. Ealy to D. Appel, n.d., File 1405 AGO 1878. Also in DCOI. Taylor Ealy wrote a number of versions of the events of the Five Days, most of them many years later. His most immediate account, addressed to Sheldon Jackson, was written August 5 at Las Vegas; a slightly longer one on August 21 from Anton Chico, where Ealy was staying on his way back to Las Vegas after having taken Susan Gates to her new teaching post at Agua Negra, near Cimarron.

I was in Lincoln when McSween was killed. Saw more than I ever thought could be tolerated in the U.S. or Territories. That poor man was assinated most barberously. Perhaps you will be very anxious to know what I saw. I will briefly state them to you.

July 14th, Mr. McSween and about 40 men came in to the town of Lincoln. There was not a shot fired. I nor my family did not know that they had entered. It was just as the moon rose after dark. Part of the Sherriff's posse were out of town. They were sent for next day, and reached town about sun-set. Came in riding at full speed and hollowing and before getting off their horses began firing at McSween's house. About 100 shots fired. And for five days firing was kept up in the near center of town. All McSweens side withdrew except himself and ten men who remained with him in his own house. About two hours after the troops came in, Mrs. Shields house, which adjoined McSweens was fired, while she (Mrs. S.) and family were removing property—her little girl stepping in the oil which was poured on the floor. About the same time, or shortly after, McSween house was fired by means of coal oil. The Sheriffs posse were stationed around the house and kept firing all the time. Any attempt to escape would have been death. The eleven men inside were almost burnt alive when about dark they attempted to escape from the east room yet remaining unconsumed by the flames— were shot! Not all. Some I believe got off— but the Noble McSween was killed. Our house was between the firing and we were not offered protection until about dusk. Miss Gates went at the risk of her life and asked an escort of soldiers. The Col. immediately sent an escort. (Sheldon Jackson Letters, vol. 8, Presbyterian Historical Society. Courtesy Mary Plummer.)

Ealy also sent Jackson a piece for publication in the *Rocky Mountain Presbyterian,* but Jackson decided against publishing it. Bender, *Missionaries,* 62.

28. Mrs. Ealy to Col. N.A.M. Dudley, July 19, 1878, File 1405 AGO 1878. Testimony of T. Ealy, D. Appel, Blair, George Murison, and Frederick Berghold, DCOI.

29. Testimony of G. A. Purington and D. Appel, DCOI.

30. Testimony of D. Appel, DCOI.

31. Testimony of W. Bonney, DCOI.

32. Testimony of A. Boyle, DCOI. Another account of the Big Killing, claimed to be that of an eyewitness, signed "A Looker On" and dated Lincoln, July 30, appeared in the *Independent.* It adds little to what is already known, except to say that after pitching camp, Dudley sent "three soldiers to the house of McSween who remained near the house until the sheriff's posse had time to set the house on fire, after which the soldiers withdrew."

"Looker On" went on to offer the dubious observation that of the eleven men in the house besides McSween, several were "quiet, inoffensive Mexican citizens." *Independent,* August 10, 1878.

33. Susan McSween to J. P. Tunstall, August 28, 1878.

34. DCOI. Exactly who killed whom will probably never be known. McSween's body had five bullets in it; Morris, one; Romero, three in body and legs; Zamora, eight shots in the body; and Robert Beckwith, two shots, in the head and wrist. There is at least partial ground for believing that Beckwith was shot accidentally by either his own brother or, more probably, John Jones, a mistake that may have had considerable bearing on later events. Report of Coroner's Jury, July 20, 1878, File 1405 AGO 1878, quoted in Fulton, *Lincoln County War,* 274; Hall, "Recollections"; Fulton, *Lincoln County War,* 272.

35. Coe, *Frontier Fighter,* 182.

36. Ibid. Burns, *Saga,* 142, repeats the story.

Neither Bates nor Washington referred to this when testifying to the Dudley Court of Inquiry.

37. Yginio Salazar (I have preferred to spell his name as it appears on his tombstone) was born February 14, 1863, and was therefore just a few months past his *fifteenth* birthday at the time of these events. He told his story many, many times. Most often it was Boyle who kicked him; sometimes, Kinney. Three years before his death on January 7, 1936, he told the version reproduced in Pryor, "Siege of the McSween House." The Kinney version is in Haley, "Interview with Yginio Salazar." See also, among other sources, Coe, *Frontier Fighter,* 182–83, and Burns, *Saga,* 142–48.

CHAPTER TWENTY-SEVEN

1. The events of July 20 and the days immediately following have been in main reconstructed from the testimonies of Col. N.A.M. Dudley, G. W. Peppin, D. Easton, D. Appel, et al., DCOI, and Doctor Ealy in Bender, *Missionaries,* 55–63.

2. Proceedings of Coroner's Jury, July 20, 1878, File 1405 AGO 1878. Quoted in Fulton, *Lincoln County War,* 274.

3. Col. N.A.M. Dudley to AAAG DNM July 23, 1878, File 1405 AGO 1878. Testimony of G. W. Peppin, D. Easton, and D. Appel, DCOI.

4. S. R. C.[orbet] to R. A. Widenmann, July 20, 1878.

5. Bender, *Missionaries,* 54–55.

6. Col. N.A.M. Dudley to AAAG DNM, July 23, File 1405 AGO 1878.

7. Testimony of D. M. Appel, DCOI.

8. Col. N.A.M. Dudley to AAAG DNM, July 20, 1878, File 1405 AGO 1878; testimony in DCOI.

9. Col. N.A.M. Dudley to AAAG DNM, July 20, 1878, File 1405 AGO 1878.

10. Col. N.A.M. Dudley to AAAG DNM, July 23, 1878, File 1405 AGO 1878.

11. Testimony of D. Easton, DCOI.

12. Col. N.A.M. Dudley to AAAG DNM, July 27, 1878, File 1405 AGO 1878; Bender, *Misionaries,* 56.

13. Ealy, *Water,* 73–74.

14. Dol. N.A.M. Dudley to T. Ealy, July 23, 1878. DCOI; quoted in Bender, *Missionaries,* 57–58.

15. On July 10, Dudley sent out an Indian scout of seventy men under the command of Capt. Henry Carroll, supported by lieutenants G. W. Smith and Harry Wright, the latter in charge of the Navajo scouts. While Taylor Ealy was whining about not being given permission

to preach to the soldiers, Dudley was awaiting word from the scout he had authorized. He was not kept waiting long.

On July 27, the patrol struck Indian sign, and two days later came upon an encampment of Mescaleros in Alamosa canyon up in the Sacramentos. A short, sharp engagement ensued in which three Indians were killed, one wounded, and another taken prisoner. The soldiers captured twelve horses, a mule, and much camp equipment.

On August 3 Captain John, a Navajo scout, killed another Apache in Canyon de La Luz; three days later, guided by John Copeland (not the sheriff), Henry Carroll, sixteen enlisted men and five Navajo scouts stumbled upon a large rancheria in Dog Canyon, a well-watered spot on the main highway used by Apaches going to or coming from the mountains. An inconclusive running fight ensued in which some horses were killed. The Indians scattered in parties of two and three and made their escape. Carroll and Smith brought their detachments in just in time to become embroiled in the killing of Bernstein at the agency. There are hints in later testimony that there was some connection between the killing of the Apaches by the Navajo scouts, and the ensuing death of Bernstein. *Independent*, August 17, 1878.

16. Fulton, *Lincoln County War*, 281–82.

17. Susan McSween to J. P. Tunstall, July 25, 1878.

18. Mullin, "Notes on Jim French." Dudley clearly thought otherwise. Just a few weeks later, he noted that French was in Lincoln, "almost every night, leaving early in the morning. He generally stops at the house where Mrs. McSween lives." And again, "French makes his headquarters with Mrs. McSween." Dudley to AAAG DNM, August 24 and September 7, 1878, File 1405 AGO 1878.

19. M. R. Leverson to Hon. Carl Schurz, July 30, 1878, BFO F05-1965.

20. M. R. Leverson to President R. B. Hayes, July 30, 1878, BFO F05-1965.

21. The item appeared in the *Denver News* on or about July 31. It was reprinted in the *Las Animas Leader*, August 9, 1878.

22. M. R. Leverson to Hon. Carl Schurz, July 31, 1878. U.S. Department of Justice, 44-4-8-3, RG 60, NARA. Leverson was not, of course, invited to become governor of New Mexico. He lost interest in Lincoln County matters as enthusiastically as he had taken them up, and involved himself in other and to him more profitable pursuits. On January 19, 1879, at which time Leverson was using the columns of the *Denver Tribune* to propose himself for the task of revising the code of the Colorado legislature, the *New Mexican* could not resist taking one last swipe at him, labeling him a "dead beat and tramp . . . notorious throughout this section for his ignorant and presumptuous interference in our local affairs." This was his last appearance in the annals of New Mexico.

23. Col. N.A.M. Dudley to AAAG DNM, July 27, 1878, File 1405 AGO 1878.

24. Haley, "Interview with Frank Coe," August 14, 1927. There may be a grain of truth in the Wheeler story; at around this time Wheeler, John Chambers, and another man stole Indian horses near the Nogal. When the Indians pursued them and recovered the horses, Wheeler and Chambers moved on to Tularosa, where they stole fifty head of cattle. *Independent*, August 17, 1878.

25. Thomas Blair to Post Adjutant, August 9, 1878, File 1405 AGO 1878. Interpreter Jose Carrillo, who spoke Spanish and Apache, was forty-one years of age at this time; he had been employed at the agency "from about the time the Indians killed the other interpreter in November, 1872." He was paid $125 a quarter plus rations for himself and his wife and five children.

26. Testimony of F. C. Godfroy, File 1405 AGO 1878.

27. Col. N.A.M. Dudley to AAAG DNM, August 10, 1878, File 1405 AGO 1878. Goodwin followed a "party sixteen in number" to Scurlock's ranch, where he abandoned the chase and turned back. M. F. Goodwin to Col. N.A.M. Dudley, August 7, 1878, ibid.

28. Enclosed with Dudley's weekly report. Col. N.A.M. Dudley to AAAG DNM, August 8, 1878, ibid.

29. Thomas Blair to Post Adjutant, August 9, 1878, ibid.

30. Ibid.

31. *Las Vegas Gazette*, September 14, 1878. John O'Brien, an employee at the agency, provided a further confused account of the day's events.

About 40 men came to the issue house on Monday at 3 o'clock P.M. I was down at Dr. Blazer's house at the time and did not see the party myself. I heard heavy firing up about the issue room and soon Mr. Godfroy sent word down that Bernstine was killed. Godfroy came down soon and said they had fired six shots at him. He escaped, I was in Blazer's house while shooting was going on. Bernstine was at the issue room when about 40 men came down the road on the Ruidoso side from the north. Mr. Bernstine went out to see who they were when he was shot and killed. Godfroy came down soon after and sent me off with despatches. I don't know who the attacking party were: they were all Americans. Don't know their object. They took some horses belonging to Godfroy, the agent, and Carrillo, the interpreter. They were leaving when I left, but still fighting, I could hear the firing. They were fighting the Indians. Lt. Smith with 3 or 4 men was at the mill, and started upon down quick, but I left before I learned the result, I met 6 men at the cañon coming into Tulerosa; they ordered me back but I refused to go. They chased me 5 miles. I left Tulerosa about 9 o'clock that night, my horse gave out, and I walked about 35 miles that night. Six men got after me at White Sands and I ran into the mountains. I overtook a train 15 miles from Shedd's; my tongue had swollen out of my mouth, and I gave the owner of the train 35 cts. for a drink of water. I got a horse from Mr. Shedd and came on in.

O'Brien's account exaggerates the size of the party and confuses the sequence of events (Lieutenant Smith said Bernstein was killed at two, not three) but it is a valuable reminder of the dangers inherent in riding alone in those lonely mountains, where a wagon boss would demand thirty-five cents for water from a man dying of thirst, and around the next bend in the trail you might encounter a party of armed men ready to kill you for your money, your weapons, your horse, or simply for the hell of it. *Independent*, August 10, 1878.

32. Thomas B. Baker to Post Adjutant, September 5, 1878, File 1405 AGO 1878.

33. "In my judgment," Dudley provocatively commented later, "the whole trouble at the Agency on the 5th inst. was brought about by the continual personal misunderstandings between Dr. Blazer, Bernstein and Godfray [*sic*]." Col. N.A.M. Dudley to AAAG DNM, August 27, 1878, ibid.

CHAPTER TWENTY-EIGHT

1. S. R. Corbet to J. P. Tunstall, August 13, 1878. No letter from Dudley to the Tunstall family has ever come to light, neither in the records of the U.S. Army nor in the papers so carefully preserved by the elder Tunstall, who surely would have capitalized upon such a missive in his later campaign for indemnification against the U.S. government. There is no doubt that it was written, since on June 30 Isaac Ellis asked J. P. Tunstall to send him a copy (which was probably the one Corbet read). From what Corbet says, it was sent in April shortly after the

murder of Brady. It is hard to imagine Dudley sticking his neck out so far as to accuse McSween and Widenmann of murdering Tunstall. What seems likelier is that he claimed that by their actions (or lack of them) Widenmann and McSween had brought about Tunstall's death. This was a twist on the old *New Mexican* ploy, implying that if Widenmann had arrested the Boys when he was supposed to, they never could have killed Tunstall.

2. Barber-Fulton Letters, March 10, 1928. Other sources suggest that the quarrel was precipitated when Johnson learned Beckwith had registered ownership of the ranch in his name alone; Mrs. McSween's suggestion seems more likely.

3. Fort Stanton, Letters Received, 1879. On September 14, Abneth McCabe was appointed deputy sheriff; he arrested Beckwith for murder and took him before Justice Wilson in Lincoln, who committed him to the keeping of the sheriff or his deputies. McCabe applied to have Beckwith placed in the guardhouse, but Dudley declined.

"There being no jail, no funds, no jailer in the County, this villionous murderer was allowed to go free," said Dudley. "He was seen some sixty miles south of here en route to the region of his former home on the 18th inst. McCabe told me he would be killed there on sight, but the greater fear is that he may kill one or more of his family first."

In point of fact, after he left Fort Stanton, Hugh Beckwith went to Texas and came back only occasionally to New Mexico; an unconfirmed story has it that he was beaten to death during a robbery at his store in Presidio, Tex., in 1892. Dudley to AAAG DNM, September 21, 1878, File 1405 AGO 1878; Rasch and Myers, "Tragedy," 5.

4. The *Independent* marked Frank Angel's departure from the Territory on August 31 by noting

> That Angel has gone home to heaven at 63 Liberty Street [New York]. Selah!
>> I wish I was an angel
>> And with the angels stand
>> With Governor Axtell on my head
>> And a New Mexican in my hand.

This was fairly broad humor: it was already widely known that Axtell was finished. He was suspended on September 4, and there were "plenty of rumors" that Catron would be next. *Independent*, September 7, 1878.

5. G. Gauss to J. P. Tunstall, August 22, 1878. On the same day, Sam Corbet wrote to Lee Kayser to say Gauss had returned the preceding night, but brought no cattle with him.

"These nine men that was here went out there [to the Tunstall ranch] and taken everything, even old Gauss's clothes," he reported. "They taken old Martin Martz wagon and team so that brakes any sale of them." S. R. Corbet to Lee Kayser, August 22, 1878, File 1405 AGO 1878.

When J. P. Tunstall received Gauss's plaintive letter, he wrote Isaac Ellis for information. Ellis replied, "As regards this business of Mr. G Gauss I know that the Estate is indebted to him also to one Mr. Martin Martz in a much larger sum. Messrs Martz and Gauss having had charge of the cattle for a considerable length of time. Not having seen Mr. Gauss for some time cannot say just how much the Estate owes him. Will attend to this matter in the course of two or three weeks." He went on to say that the store was still standing but in a very bad condition: rain coming in through the unfinished roof was making large holes in the walls. The barn had also been washed away. A letter from David Shield advised him that Widenmann had left Las Vegas for the East, "without giving anyone charge of anything." Never a man to miss a chance to turn a dime into a dollar, Ellis offered to pay $250 of indebtedness if J. P. Tunstall would send him the "undivided ½ interest of said building as it was owned in that shape by Mesrs Tunstall & McSween." Isaac Ellis to J. P. Tunstall, October 15, 1878.

Two weeks later he advised that Gauss's claim against the estate was for $175 and Martin Martz's for $300. Both, he said, were

poor men but honest industrious and upright, have lived on Felix Ranch when it would have been impossible to have procured the services of any one else. Mr. Martz was taken prisoner . . . when they the "Rustlers" took the cattle. Mr. Martz was taken to Black River and mad[e] to cook and drive his own team and wagon under peril of his life. Mr. Martz was alowed to return with nothing save his Team and wagon. These men have lived on the ranch owned by your son for six months and in this whole time their lives have been in danger. I know their claims to be true and if anyone by right should be paid they should. I will send Mr. Angel's report &c as soon as posible we have not been able to get hold of it yet. (Isaac Ellis to J. P. Tunstall, October 31, 1878)

6. *Independent,* August 24, 1878.

7. John Middleton to R. A. Widenmann, August 30, 1878. Middleton's reference to George Washington harks back to when that worthy was arrested at San Patricio; in his anxiety to save his own skin, Washington said just

about anything his captors wanted to hear, including the "fact" that Widenmann had been one of those who killed Sheriff Brady.

"There is thirty armed men between old Fort Sumner and Roswell," Dudley reported. "Scurlock and Middleton is reported to be with the party. Kinney and his party I am unable to locate just now positively. Another party of some fifteen men are in the mountains near Tularosa. the two Coe brothers are in this band." Dudley to AAAG DNM, September 7, 1878, File 1405 AGO 1878.

8. In an "extra" to his report of that day, Dudley sent word to Santa Fe that Bowers and Smith had run off the Fritz horses at gunpoint. Dudley to AAAG DNM, September 7, 1878, File 1405 AGO 1878.

9. R. A. Widenmann to J. P. Tunstall, September 2, 1878. A postscript to this letter somewhat diminished Mrs. McSween's cries of destitution: McSween, he said, had insured his life for ten thousand dollars, "so Mrs. McS will not at least be in want." Generous-hearted old John Partridge Tunstall sent her five hundred dollars anyway.

A minor mystery: where—and more specifically upon what—did Widenmann live during his long stay in La Mesilla? He had no money worth mentioning, and no means of obtaining any. There is no record of Tunstall's father sending him money, and he seems to have avoided finding work. Did he run up bills and then, as he had done at Santa Fe, "skip" without paying? Did he invent a "robbery" of Tunstall's valuables so he could sell them?

His statement that he might bring his brother out to collect Tunstall's outstanding accounts is a typical piece of bombast: his oldest brother Victor was not yet nineteen; Karl August was sixteen; and William, twelve. Widenmann, *Genealogy.*

10. Samuel R. Corbet to J. P. Tunstall, September 23, 1878. Corbet's letter got some of it wrong: neither Judge Bristol nor Marshal Sherman was removed from office.

11. The best source of information on the depredations of the Rustlers is Dudley's weekly reports. Dudley to AAAG DNM, September 28 and 29, October 3, 5, 10, and 19, 1878, File 1405 AGO 1878.

12. Astonishing as it may seem, while half a dozen gangs of cutthroats plundered and killed as they pleased in Lincoln County, a pleasant little party of four ladies and four gentlemen left La Mesilla on a camping and hunting excursion. The party left La Mesilla on September 11, driving a coach and four mules, and stayed overnight at Coghlan's in Tularosa, where they were enter-

tained by that "genial" old thief and his lady; next day they called at Blazer's Mill, then camped at Dowlin's. On the third day "we wended our way up the Rui Doso some six miles . . . where we pitched our tents and all prepared for a few days of good jolly camp life." After a stay of three days, they made their way to Fort Stanton.

It is impossible to go into details or state even a small part of the kindnesses received at the hands of the ladies at the post without filling all your columns. Suffice it to say that to Mrs. and Miss Godfroy, Miss Lulu Philips, Mrs. Lt. Goodwin, Mrs. Lt. Smith, General Dudley, Capt. Carr, Drs. Lyon and Appel, and Lts. Smith, Pague, and Harry Wright, with his guitar we owe two of the most pleasant days of our lives.

On their way home, the eightsome camped a few days more on Eagle Creek, where they were joined for a while by Captain Carroll, Doctor Lyon, and Lee Kayser, Dowlin's clerk. They headed back via Tularosa, where they met Lieutenant Goodwin, stationed there until October 1, then continued blithely on down to La Mesilla. "The general impression seems to be," wrote "Matt," "that the outlaws and bandits have all left that part of the country as none of them have been seen of late, and law-abiding citizens feel more secure than they have felt for months past." Comment would appear unnecessary. *Independent*, September 23, 1878.

13. S. R. Corbet to J. P. Tunstall, October 1, 1878.

14. Keleher, *Violence*, 167–68.

15. W. Bristol to J. Sherman, October 4, 1878, Wallace Collection.

16. Lew Wallace telegram to Carl Schurz, October 5, 1878, Wallace Collection.

17. Printed copies of the proclamation are in File 1405 AGO 1878 and Wallace Collection.

18. Dudley to AAAG DNM, October 19, 1878, File 1405 AGO 1878. One of the best sources for information on the Rustlers was the Kid, who was down in the Panhandle while the gang was scourging Lincoln. In March 1879 he told Lew Wallace that

before they organized as "Rustlers" they had been Peppin's posse. They came from Texas. Jake Owens was conspicuous amongst them. They were organized before the burning of McSween's house, and after that they went on their first trips down country as far as Coe's ranch and thence to the Feliz, where they took Tunstall's cattle. Martin [Martz] (known to Sam Corbett) was in charge of the Tunstall cattle and was taken prisoner and saw them kill one of

their own party. On the same trip they burned Lola Wise's house, and took her horses. Coe at the time was ranching at the house. On this trip they moved behind a body of soldiers, one company, and a company of Navaho scouts. They moved in sight of the soldiers, taking horses, insulting women. . . . They stopped on the Pecos at Seven Rivers. Collins [Caleb Hall], now at Silver City, was one of the outfit—nicknamed the Prowler by the cowboys. ("Statement by Kid, made Sunday night, March 29, 1879," Wallace Collection)

19. Murphy died in a charity ward; St. Vincent's Hospital was also an asylum. Only the *New Mexican* and the *Independent* printed obituaries, and neither tells us anything new about the man. The *Independent* was almost perfunctory:

Lawrence G. Murphy died in Santa Fe on the 20th ult. at 7 o'clock A.M. He was buried by the Masonic and Odd Fellows fraternities of Santa Fe in the Masonic and Odd Fellows cemetery in the presence of a large concourse of citizens. Major Lawrence Gustave Murphy was an Irishman by birth and a graduate of Maynooth College, Ireland. He came to the United States at an early age and shortly after joined the U.S. army. He served as a Quartermaster Sergeant during his enlistment and on leaving the Army became a citizen of New Mexico.

Upon the breaking out of the War, Major Murphy was among the first to volunteer and was appointed Regimental Quartermaster of the first New Mexico Volunteers commanded by Col. St. Vrain. He afterwards became Regimental Adjutant in the regiment commanded by Col. Kit Carson and in 1863 was promoted to the rank of Captain. In 1865 his regiment was disbanded and he was honorably mustered out of the service. Since then he had resided in Lincoln where he was engaged in the mercantile business. He was for a time Probate Judge of Lincoln County and held other positions of honor and trust. (*Independent*, November 2, 1878)

There were a few lines more about his membership in the Masonic and Odd Fellows organizations, and the formal resolutions passed by those fraternities expressing regret at his passing, but nothing further. Others were less forgiving. "The Sisters of Charity would not let him have whiskey," said Frank Coe, "and that cut his living off. He died in a short time and everybody rejoiced over it." Haley, "Interview with Frank Coe," March 20, 1927.

CHAPTER TWENTY-NINE

1. Rasch, Buckbee, and Klein, "Many Parts," 12.

2. Coe, *Frontier Fighter,* 200.

3. Rasch, Buckbee, and Klein, "Many Parts"; Rickards, "Better For the World," 4.

4. Hoyt, *Frontier Doctor,* 154–56.

5. Lew Wallace to Carl Schurz, October 22, 1878, Wallace Collection.

6. Sue E. McSween to J. P. Tunstall, August 28, completed at Las Vegas, October 7, 1878. In spite of Susan McSween's expectations, the nearest General Sherman came to Lincoln County was a quick trip down the Rio Grande valley and across Arizona on his way to San Francisco.

7. Sue E. McSween to Mrs. Emily Tunstall, October 8, 1878.

8. Ibid. The McSween cemetery was on open ground to the east of and behind the corral in back of the Tunstall store. Susan McSween gives the number "burried" there as seven. The "four who fell in the cause" would be Tunstall, Frank MacNab, Harvey Morris, and McSween. The "friends" would seem to have been Daniel Huff, one or more of the Shield children, and a baby daughter of Ike Stockton who died in the small-pox epidemic of 1877. Huston Chapman was also buried there later. No tombstones were ever erected, nor, as far as can be ascertained, was the ground ever consecrated. Fulton said that when he visited the site with her in the late 1920s, Mrs. Barber was unable to tell him the location of her husband's grave. Fulton-Nolan Correspondence.

9. Sue E. McSween to J. P. Tunstall, October 18, 1878.

10. H. I. Chapman to Governor Wallace, October 24, 1878, Exhibit #4, DCOI.

11. Lew Wallace to Edward Hatch, October 28, 1878, Exhibit 10, DCOI.

12. Exhibit 8, DCOI.

13. Ibid.

14. Ibid.

15. Ibid.

16. Ibid.

17. Ibid.

18. Lew Wallace to Carl Schurz, November 8, 1878, Wallace Collection.

19. *Independent,* November 23, 1878. Also published (in English and Spanish) in the *New Mexican* and the *Mesilla News.*

20. *Weekly New Mexican,* December 14; *Mesilla News,* December 21, 1878.

21. H. I. Chapman to Governor Wallace, November 25, 1878, Exhibit #23, DCOI.

22. H. I. Chapman to Governor Wallace, November 29, 1878, Exhibit #24, DCOI.

23. Isaac Ellis to J. P. Tunstall, November 29, 1878.

24. H. I. Chapman to Governor Wallace, November 29, 1878, Exhibit #24, DCOI.

25. Sue E. McSween to J. P. Tunstall, November 30, 1878. She got the store anyway: at the December 13 sitting of the probate court, despite opposition from Isaac Ellis, she was appointed administratrix of both Tunstall's and Brewer's estates. She moved into what had been her husband's law office while she pursued her feud with Dudley and took care of business. Neither Tunstall's nor Brewer's family received one red cent; indeed, she persuaded Ranse Brewer to deed her his son's ranch to pay off the "debt" to her husband's estate.

26. Col. N.A.M. Dudley to AAAG DNM December 9, 1878, enclosing a specimen of the hand-lettered notice, File 1405 AGO 1878.

CHAPTER THIRTY

1. The account of events in Lincoln and all documents quoted are from the depositions and/or reports of Dudley, French, Chapman, Keton, Horton, Washington, Sidney Wilson, and others, DCOI. Mrs. McSween does not appear to have been asked to testify.

2. Special Orders No. 156, December 13; deposition of George W. Peppin, December 15, 1878. Proceedings of a Board of Officers, Exhibit #28, DCOI.

3. Deposition of Maximiano de Guevara, DCOI.

4. Deposition of James H. French, DCOI.

5. Deposition of H. I. Chapman, DCOI.

6. Depositions of Pvts. Louis Horton, Shannon Keton, and trumpeter George Washington (not to be confused with the Lincoln man of the same name), DCOI.

7. Mes, or Maes, was (and still is) a common name in New Mexico; indeed, there is a Maes family in Lincoln today. Garrett notes a December 1880 encounter with "Juanito Maes, a noted desperado, thief and murderer" at Puerto de Luna, for years a favorite hideout of Lincoln's Hispanic rustling gangs. The connection is tenuous; the *New Mexican* later reported the name of this man as Juan Silva, although it may have been an alias. The Juan Mes/ Johnny Mace of this fracas was killed by a posse led by Deputy Sheriff Longworth in March 1880 while—showing a distinct lack of gratitude—trying to rob Hudgens's store. Garrett, *Authentic Life,* 107–8; *Cimarron News and Press,* March 11, 1880.

8. Lt. J. H. French to Recorder, Board of Officers, Supplemental Report, December 19, 1878, DCOI. Col. N.A.M. Dudley to AAAG DNM, December 15, 1878, DCOI.

9. Deposition of Sidney Wilson, DCOI. Sidney Wilson was a Colorado lawyer recently arrived in Lincoln, a former partner of General Danforth in a Las Vegas law firm. He remained long enough to handle a batch of habeas corpus writs at the spring 1879 term of court, and then dropped out of sight; George Coe hints that he absconded.

10. Deposition of H. I. Chapman, DCOI.

11. Deposition of G. W. Peppin, DCOI.

12. Special Orders No. 157, December 14, 1878, DCOI.

13. Col. N.A.M. Dudley to AAAG DNM, December 15, 1878, DCOI.

14. Special Orders No. 158, December 16, 1878, DCOI.

15. Col. N.A.M. Dudley to AAAG DNM, December 17, 1878, DCOI.

16. Ibid.

17. General Orders No. 62, December 20, 1878, DCOI.

18. Special Orders No. 167, December 27, 1878, DCOI.

19. J. J. Dolan to Governor Wallace, December 31, 1878, Wallace Collection. Copy in Mullin, "Notes on J. J. Dolan." Courtesy Melba McCaskill.

CHAPTER THIRTY-ONE

1. Peppin's resignation is cited in Fulton, *Lincoln County War*, 318; but did he tender it? Dudley reported the sheriff's dissatisfaction (in very similar terms) as early as the first week of December. At the end of January, however, Dudley said Kimbrell had "not yet received his papers and has not assumed the functions of his office. Sheriff Peppin is making no arrests." John Sherman did not rescind Peppin's commission as deputy U.S. marshal until February 17, 1879. Col. N.A.M. Dudley to AAAG DNM, 7 December, 1878, and January 26, 1879; J. Sherman to G. W. Peppin, February 17, 1879. File 1405 AGO 1878.

2. *Independent*, November 30, 1878; *Grant County Herald*, December 17, 1878. On March 22, 1879, the *Independent* reported that Kinney had opened a butcher shop in the Rafael Bernindas building "at the corner of Church and 3rd Streets near the old stand of Seraño Lopez." On May 17 came the news that Kinney had left "abruptly" for Arizona shortly before further warrants could be served on him. He was not gone long; he still had some significant appearances to

make in the annals of New Mexico. *Independent*, May 17, 1879; Rasch, "Kinney," 11–12.

3. Tunstall Estate. The list of Tunstall's uncollectible notes—virtually all of them for goods advanced against future harvests—is a veritable roll call of those who had either fled the county or been rendered unable to meet their obligations by events: Thomas Cochrane, Richard Ewan, J. B. Mathews, John Hurley, Godfrey Gauss, Jake Harris, Sam Wortley, S. W. Lloyd, and A. H. Mills among the Anglos; and an even longer list of Hispanics that included Atanacio Martínez, Jose Miguel Sedillo, Trinidad Delgado, Jose Miranda, Maximiano de Guevara, Bernabel Mes, and the Baragon brothers.

4. McSween Estate.

5. *Independent*, January 25, 1879.

6. That Wilson was acting as Wallace's informant, not to say spy, is evident from their correspondence. On February 6, Wallace wrote

Your favors are both to hand and place me under renewed obligation. I have seen Marshal Sherman as you requested, and, he replied that he would not now appoint a deputy in Lincoln County. As the matter is his exclusively, we will have to wait his pleasure.

I suppose you saw the Mesilla Independent, containing your letters in full: also the Sentinel, (Santa Fe) with the extracts from your favor to me. The comments in both papers were in the right direction, and particularly gratifying.

By the way, be good enough to send me certified copies of the affidavits lodged in your office against Col. Dudley and Lt. French, with the warrants issued upon them. Also furnish me with a certified statement of the proceedings to date against those officers. The use I have for them I will explain when I see you.

Very respectfully,

Your friend, Lew Wallace (Lew Wallace to J. B. Wilson, February 6, 1879, DCOI)

It should perhaps be explained that in using the word *favors* Wallace was referring to Wilson's letters and not to favors done or received.

7. *Independent*, February 8, 1879. Frederick Godfroy, meanwhile, was in some sort of trouble at the border, where he and Ira M. Bond, editor of the *Mesilla News*, had tried unsuccessfully to smuggle fifteen bales of Mexican blankets into the States without paying the duty, giving the editor of the *Independent* a stick with which he continued to beat Bond for months. In May, the new Indian agent, S. A. Russell, arrived at the agency, and Godfroy moved in with his daughter and son-in-law at Fort Stanton. He seems to

have lived with them for the rest of his life. *Independent*, January 4, May 8, and May 31, 1879.

8. Col. N.A.M. Dudley to AAAG DNM, February 8, 1879, DCOI.

9. H. I. Chapman to J. P. Tunstall, February 10, 1878. Quoted in Fulton, *Lincoln County War*, 320–21; and in Nolan, *John Henry Tunstall*, 396–98.

10. Lew Wallace to D. Shield, February 11; D. Shield to Colonel Hatch, February 12, 1879; endorsement by secretary of war, February 25, 1879. All in File 1405 AGO 1878.

11. *Las Vegas Gazette*, March 1, 1879.

12. Sue E. McSween to Col. N.A.M. Dudley, February 11, 1879, DCOI; also in File 1405 AGO 1878.

13. Col. N.A.M. Dudley to AAAG, February 15; Dudley to Sue E. McSween, February 13, 1878. File 1405 AGO 1878. Capt. Henry Carroll had been ordered to take station at Roswell for the protection of citizens there on November 4. His instructions were to divide his command, part of it patrolling the road between Roswell and Fort Sumner, the balance the road between Roswell and Seven Rivers. On February 1, 1879, one Emil Powers, newly appointed constable for Precinct No. 5, requested military assistance from Carroll "to search for and recover certain stolen stock, on the Pecos river, or elsewhere in the Territory."

Carroll furnished him with men, and the party set off for the south, with the results stated in his February 25 report. The Las Cruces newspaper, *Thirty Four*, March 19, 1879, averred that 138 head of Tunstall cattle were turned over to Mrs. McSween. This makes the situation appear simpler than it actually was. When the cattle arrived at Lincoln, Mrs. McSween sent Sam Smith to identify them and bring them back; Carroll's orders, however, were to hand all recovered stock over to the sheriff. Later they were taken to Brewer's ranch and then on to the Copeland place, where Sam Smith guarded them until they were sold to Lee Kayser for a thousand dollars, only a few dollars more than it had cost to find and recover them. E. Powers to H. Carroll, February 1; Col. N.A.M. Dudley to H. Carroll, February 4; Carroll to Post Adjutant, February 25, 1879. All in DCOI.

A long article complaining about his "mistreatment" by Carroll and Deputy Gilbert, signed by Marion Turner but probably written by Ash Upson, appeared in the *Mesilla News*, August 16, 1881.

14. H. Carroll to Post Adjutant, February 25, 1879, DCOI. Dudley vented his spleen in his weekly report. There were not ten head of beef cattle in the whole herd, he frothed. The whole thing was a fraud, the more painful because "I have on two or more occasions . . . saved the life of this young lad, Walz, for I believe he is not of age yet"—a claim Walz later refuted. Col. N.A.M. Dudley to AAAG DNM, February 18; E. Walz to Col. Hatch, June 5, 1879. File 1405 AGO 1878.

15. The Kid's state of mind before the Chapman killing is confirmed in a letter from Sam Corbet to John Middleton, February 3, 1880.

16. The Kid's note to Evans obviously was shown around; Dudley saw it on the morning of February 18. The version of events that follows is taken from the testimony of witnesses in military reports and newspaper accounts. G. Kimbrell to Col. N.A.M. Dudley, February 18 and 19; B. Dawson to Post Adjutant, February 19; Col. N.A.M. Dudley to AAAG DNM, February 19, 1879. All in File 1405 AGO 1878. *Independent*, July 5, 1879.

17. *Roswell Daily Record*, December 26, 1955. This was an article written by Charles L. Ballard, son of A. J. Ballard, a former buffalo hunter who came to Lincoln County from Fort Griffin in November 1878 and established a store nine miles below Lincoln. Ballard was an eyewitness to the events of February 18, 1879. In the same article, his son also claimed that when "they did finally make friends . . . my father invited all to have supper at our house which they did."

18. Col. N.A.M. Dudley to AAAG DNM, February 21, 1879, DCOI; also in File 1405 AGO 1878.

19. G. Kimbrell to Col. N.A.M. Dudley, February 18, 1879, File 1405 AGO 1878. The Kid told Kimbrell flatly that he would not be taken alive if the warrants Kimbrell held were for murder. This doubtless compounded Kimbrell's difficulties in finding deputies. Col. N.A.M. Dudley to AAAG DNM, February 19, File 1405 AGO 1878.

20. The conversations are principally from the report in the *Independent*, July 5, 1879, and an account signed "Max" in the *Las Cruces Thirty Four*, March 5, 1879. I have put it into what seems to be logical sequence.

21. B. Dawson to Post Adjutant, February 19, 1879, File 1405 AGO 1878.

22. G. Kimbrell to Col. N.A.M. Dudley, February 19; Lieutenant Goodwin to Dudley, February 20, 1879. DCOI; also in File 1405 AGO 1878. The petition indicates which of Lincoln's citizens were still around: J. B. Wilson, Benjamin Ellis, Jose Montaño, Doctor Gurney, Juan Patrón, Susan McSween, Sam Corbet, Sidney Wilson, J. A. Tomlinson, A. J. Ballard, Saturnino and Bonifacio Baca, George Kim-

brell, Lee Kayser, Esteban Chávez, David Easton, John Copeland, Santiago Mes y Trujillo, Anton Jose García, W. H. Wilson, Edgar Walz, G. S. Redman, and Francisco Romero y Valencia.

CHAPTER THIRTY-TWO

1. L. Wallace to E. Hatch, February 27, 1879, File 1405 AGO 1878. L. Wallace to C. Schurz, February 27, 1879, Wallace Collection.

2. J. B. Wilson to Col. N.A.M. Dudley, n.d. (ca. February 20, 1879), Letters Received, Fort Stanton, RG 98 NARA, in Rasch, File 12; Col. N.A.M. Dudley to AAAG DNM, March 1, 1879, File 1405 AGO 1878.

3. L. Wallace to C. Schurz, March 21, 1879, Wallace Collection. Dolan had gone to some lengths to ingratiate himself with Wallace. Soon after the governor promulgated his amnesty, Dolan called on him in Santa Fe to offer his support. Hard upon the governor's arrival, there was an attempt to hold up Wallace's ambulance between Fort Stanton and Lincoln. Dolan supposedly was under "house arrest" at Fort Stanton but had been leaving at will. This had led to a report that he had been one of the holdup men. The accusation, Dolan said, was "basely false, and I feel confident that it is a ruse resorted to by my treacherous enemies with a view to prejudicing you against me." In spite of this, he hoped he could still look to Wallace as a friend. J. J. Dolan to L. Wallace, March 14, 1879, Wallace Collection.

Fifteen days later, on March 29, Dolan was again expressing concern at being accused of threatening Wallace's life. From the wording of his letter a cynical reader might be tempted to conclude he was doing just that.

Attorney [Sidney] Wilson told me yesterday that your life was threatened, and told it in such a manner that I was compelled to believe that you considered me the author, and that in case it should happen, my life would be taken in one hour after &c. Governor, I can't believe for a moment that you would do me such an injustice as to think that I was connected in any way with said threat, and won't until I see or hear from you. Still, this move, with my present condition [on Wallace's orders, he was now in close confinement] and the many rumors about the underhand work which is going on against me, makes me feel anything but happy.

I don't doubt in the least but what there are bad men running over the country that

would kill any man, friend or enemy, should either be in their way; therefore you can't be too careful.

I have good reason for believing that there are now men in the Plaza who would kill you in a moment, providing they were certain they could get away with it, and that I would suffer thereby. I wish that I could believe [illegible] when those making the threat intended to carry it out. I would try to convince you that such was not my nature. I sincerely hope that the report will prove without foundation. I don't write this to you as Governor of New Mexico, or with the expectation of influencing your official actions toward me in any manner whatsoever. It is simply because you have commanded my respect from the first time we met that I look upon you as a friend, and it grieves me to think you give such reports credence.

I learned yesterday that my pony has been stolen from the corral [at the] Carisosa Ranch by the two men who escaped from here [Campbell and Evans]. The pony is known all through southern New Mexico as being mine, and when seen with those men, another report will be circulated that I am aiding them. (J. J. Dolan to L. Wallace, March 29, 1879, Wallace Collection)

Dolan was also busily writing to the newspapers asking them to publish "cards" inviting his friends to ignore the accusations being leveled at him. It is hard to avoid the feeling that, like Shakespeare's lady, the gentleman protested far too much. Perhaps Governor Wallace thought so, too. Mesilla News, 22 March, 1879; J. J. Dolan to L. Wallace, March 14 and 29, 1879, Wallace Collection (typescript copies in Mullin, HHC).

4. L. Wallace to E. Hatch, and Special Orders No. 34, March 6, 1879, DCOI.

5. L. Wallace to C. Schurz, March 21, 1879, Wallace Collection; L. Wallace to E. Hatch, March 7, 1879, File 1405 AGO 1878. Wallace's accusations against Dudley are (and were) impossible to substantiate. He picked up a story about Dudley having "loaned" money to Campbell—with whom he was on friendlier terms than might have been expected—when the latter returned to Fort Stanton after the killing of Chapman; this seemed to indicate Dudley's involvement. Equally damning was Campbell's boast that he had promised Dudley he would kill the attorney and Charlie Scase, yet even this does not really hang together. While Dudley might have had a motive for wanting to get rid

of Chapman, no case can be made for his wanting to kill Scase, an employee at the Mescalero reservation.

The facts would appear to be that Scase (acting for Mrs. McSween) and Campbell (acting for Catron) had locked horns down on Seven Rivers, and when Campbell learned Scase was in Lincoln, went hunting for him. Testimony adduced at the Dudley Court of Inquiry indicated that Scase sought protection at the fort, which Dudley agreed to give him; when it transpired that he was going to be quartered with the black troopers, the offended Scase declined the offer and departed for parts unknown.

The real question is: Who was W. W. "Billy" Campbell?

Burns claimed his real name was Ed Richardson; this was the name of a well-known gold camp desperado of the 1850s. It was later stated that Campbell had killed "three men in the buffalo country in cold blood" (presumably before arriving in Lincoln County). But where he came from remains unknown.

Ira Leonard's partner George Taylor made the assertion— which Lew Wallace believed to his dying day—that Campbell was really Jesse James. A Lincoln tradition has it that Campbell's real name was Hines and he was a former member of the James gang. A man named John (Jack) Hines of Jackson County, suspected of involvement in a bank robbery attributed to the James boys at Richmond, Mo., on May 22, 1867, fled thereafter; nothing else is known about him.

The probability is that Campbell was a stagecoach robber from the Las Vegas area, possibly one of the Hoodoo Brown bunch; he killed Thomas King in cold blood in Lincoln around November (December 6?), 1876, and was acquitted by bumbling J. B. Wilson on a plea of self-defense; was arrested at or near Fort Stanton with Sam (Frank?) Bass (Bliss?) by special mail agent and post office investigator Charles Adams. Both men were taken to Santa Fe to await transportation December 11, 1876, suspected of "being of the party that robbed the stage near Las Vegas last month."

Early Thursday evening, January 4, 1877, Bass "the mail robber and murderer from Nebraska," escaped; there is no mention of what happened to Campbell. He was away from the scene for about two years, reappearing at Seven Rivers in 1879 as one of those who drove the Catron cattle up to Lincoln. It is possible he was in jail, although there is no record of any prisoner by that name in the penitentiaries at Jefferson City and Leavenworth on the relevant dates.

Arrested by the military on Wallace's orders on March 6, 1879, and confined in the Fort Stanton jail, Campbell and Jessie Evans escaped March 19 with the aid of a soldier known as "Texas Jack"; on May 24 they were reported to be at John Slaughter's cattle camp on the Pecos at Seven Rivers; on June 4 at La Cienega, near Tucson, Ariz.

In December 1881 Campbell and a partner, one Joe Waters, attempted to assassinate William Blanchard, owner of a trading post at Sunset Crossing, eight miles east of Winslow, Ariz. In the shootout that followed, Blanchard and a customer named Joe Barrett were killed and Waters slightly wounded. Blanchard's partner Joseph H. Breed formed a posse and brought in Campbell and his partner, returning them to the county jail at St. Johns, from which place they were shortly thereafter taken and lynched.

T. Smith to L. Wallace, March 13, 1879, Wallace Collection; G. Taylor to R. B. Hayes, April 4, 1879, in Rasch, File 2; *New Mexican*, December 10, 1876; Burns, *Saga*, 163; Triplett, *Jesse James*, 34; Thrapp, *Encyclopedia*, 218.

6. Col. N.A.M. Dudley to Adjutant General, March 13; Col. N.A.M. Dudley to J. Sherman, March 18; Ira E. Leonard to Secretary of War G. W. McCrary, March 4, 1879. All in File 1405 AGO 1878.

7. Endorsement of Secretary of War G. W. McCrary, March 18, 1879; John Pope to War Department, March 28, 1879. Both in File 1405 AGO 1878.

8. L. Wallace to C. Schurz, March 21, 1879, Wallace Collection. Wallace apparently was unaware that the half-naked bodies of Jim (or Jack) Irvin[g], "aged about 30," shot in the side of the neck, and Thomas (or Charley) Moore, "aged about 20, sometimes called Windy" (a member of the Tunstall posse), shot in the left eye and the back of the head (after which both had been again shot in the chest), had been found near the White Sands the preceding December, or that Roscoe Bryant had been killed by his fellow Rustlers somewhere between the Feliz and Seven Rivers. *Independent* and *Mesilla News*, December 14, 1878.

9. File 1405 AGO 1878. The Hispanics who feature in Carroll's macabre story were killed in October 1878. For what it is worth, which may not be much, Susan Barber told Fulton that a man named Hart (Jones?) was "found in the river with his head cut off. Then there was a dreadful howl made and was put upon the few mexicans who were living there. The Mexicans were leaving in their wagons then some parties

followed them killed every one of them and brought all their holdings wagon horses clothing &c with them and kept them."

The facts seem to be that a party of eight or nine men and women started off from Black River to sell farm produce in Texas. They were overtaken by John, Jim, and William Jones, George Davis, Turner, Hall, Johnson, and others. Accusing the Hispanics of having murdered Hart Jones, they arrested four of them. These were taken down the road a short distance and shot (other sources say that all nine were killed).

To further add to the confusion, Burns offers a story about a man named Hart not unlike Susan McSween's, while Leon Metz says John Selman killed Ed Hart in September 1878. Rasch, File 29; Barber-Fulton Letters, March 21, 1928; Burns, *Saga*, 44; Metz, *Selman*, 101. For the Jones family's version, Ball, *Ma'am Jones*, 125–29.

10. The Kid's letters, *seriatim*, and the governor's replies, are from the Wallace Collection, with the exception of the first, which was owned by his grandson and is now on display at the Lincoln County Heritage Trust.

11. *Indianapolis World*, June 8, 1902.

12. *Independent*, March 29, 1879.

13. The fifty-strong Lincoln County Rifles unit was disbanded in July 1879; its campaign records are in the Territorial Archives of New Mexico, NMSRCA. For a roster, see Fulton, *Lincoln County War*, 340.

14. J. B. Wilson to L. Wallace, May 18, 1879, Wallace Collection.

15. *Independent*, April 12, 1879.

16. L. Wallace to C. Schurz, March 31, 1879, Wallace Collection.

17. "Statement by Kid," March 29, 1879, Wallace Collection. For a sketch of Gildea's life, see Rasch, "Gildea."

18. L. Wallace to R. B. Hayes, via C. Schurz, and Wallace to C. Schurz, March 31 and April 4, 1879, Wallace Collection.

19. Ira E. Leonard to L. Wallace, April 12, 1879, Wallace Collection. Leonard may have been blackening Dr. Spencer Gurney's name needlessly: the good doctor really was doing some serious prospecting (although whether as a cover while he ran supplies to Evans and Campbell is another matter) because gold had been discovered at Gurney's mining camp eight miles northeast of Lincoln. George Barber was named recorder of the mining district; Cronin, Baca, and Gurney all had made good finds, and Gurney planned to call his strike the Isabella. This would appear to have been the precursor of the big White Oaks boom. *Independent*, May 17, 1879.

20. A full account of the court proceedings at Lincoln appeared in both the *Independent* and the *Grant County Herald* of May 10.

21. Ira E. Leonard to L. Wallace, April 20, 1879, Wallace Collection. Leonard's friend George Taylor, a cousin of President Hayes, passed along a story that Leonard hadn't bothered to tell Wallace:

I thought I would give you a little sketch of matters here as some things that have happened after you left [on the 18th] may be interesting to you.

Last night two of those outlawed scoundrels who are so numerous around here made a dash through the town on horseback and fired into our building.

Judge Leonard had changed the place of his bed and they seemed to be aware of the fact for the bullets were directed where he lay, fortunately the side of the house was struck and no damage done, but had they not been going to rapidly when they fired they may have accomplished their purpose which was evidently to kill or injure the Judge so he cannot prosecute them.

Col. Rynerson, the prosecuting attorney for the territory is either afraid of or anxious to screen these villains you have arrested; he is entering into his work with no spirit and leaves all the work for the Judge, only interfering to raise obstacles in the way of bringing the rascals to justice. I have no confidence in him, he has been engaged in numerous scrapes himself, and can't help but have a fellow feeling for men who are in the same trouble he has been in himself.

[Sidney] Wilson (lawyer living at Lincoln) is in great trouble, the men who employed him are now to get back their horses and arms from him; he is denouncing them as a set of —— cutthroats and murderers and swearing he will never defend another one of them. He told me he had heard them make desperate threats against parties who had been prominent in arresting them, and particularly against Judge Leonard, against whom they were very hostile. Singularly they have no feeling against Rynerson but all their animosity is directed against the Judge. (G. Taylor to L. Wallace, April 25, 1879, Wallace Collection)

22. All the details pertaining to the Dudley Court of Inquiry are from the official record, DCOI.

23. Ira E. Leonard to L. Wallace, May 19, 1879, Wallace Collection.

24. Ira E. Leonard to L. Wallace, June 6, 1879, Wallace Collection.

25. Wallace was not the only one to disagree violently with the verdict of the court of inquiry, which he dubbed "one of the most extraordinary tribunals ever assembled." D. G. Swaine of the judge advocate general's department in Washington, reviewing the evidence, stated that he had little doubt of Dudley's partiality on July 19—his handling of the burials of McSween and Beckwith were quoted as one example—nor did he doubt that soldiers had fired on the burning house. No attempt had been made to accept McSween's surrender, nor to prevent Peppin's men mingling with the soldiers as they passed through town. Adding to all these Dudley's treatment of Wilson, and his personally handing the warrant for McSween's arrest to the sheriff, his presence during the looting of the store, and much else, "the conclusion is irresistible that Dudley both actively and passively aided and abetted the Sheriff's party in its doings."

That, unquestionably, would be the verdict of any impartial witness. But the judge advocate general's final recommendation to the secretary of war was that "it would not be in the best interests of the public or military service to attempt to bring Colonel Dudley to trial by court martial." L. Wallace to C. Schurz, July 30, 1879, Wallace Collection; D. G. Swaine, JAG, Washington, to AAG Dept. of Missouri, September 29, and JAG to Secretary of War G. W. McCrary, October 22, 1879, File 1405 AGO 1878.

CHAPTER THIRTY-THREE

1. L. Wallace to C. Schurz, June 11, 1879, File 1405 AGO 1878. Quoted in Keleher, *Violence*, 240–42; Fulton, *Lincoln County War*, 368–69.

2. *Las Cruces Thirty Four*, July 9, 1879.

3. *Independent*, July 5, 1879.

4. There seems to be no question about it: Dolan was a brazen liar. As noted previously, he had sent a "card" to the newspapers referring to the "very serious charges . . . preferred against me" and asking his "friends and the public to refrain from judging me until such time as the charges are properly and thoroughly investigated before the courts." Rather than print this homily, the *Thirty Four* commented that the denial was a weak one, and asked why he had not tried to prevent the crime. Writing from Fort Stanton on March 24 he replied:

My first knowledge [that Chapman was in Lincoln] was when I met him on the evening of the occurrence after dark on his arrival entering the house of Mrs McSween, where a party of citizens were assembled, Mrs McSween giving a Musical entertainment. Salutations passed between us, he expressing himself as being pleased with the proceedings of the afternoon. I [replied] in like manner, after which we parted, he retiring to his room. This was the last time I saw Mr Chapman. (*Mesilla News*, 5 April, 1879)

5. *Weekly New Mexican*, July 26, 1879. It would appear Allen Ballard had a penchant for trouble. During the Dudley Court of Inquiry he was in a fight with Sebrian Bates at the post trader's; Bates bent an ax handle over his head, leaving Ballard in what was considered "a dangerous condition." Early in December, he was shot and seriously wounded "on the road between Lincoln and his place. He was travelling with another man and on the way the latter fell behind Ballard and shot him in the back and then made his escape." No amplification appeared, so the motive and outcome are unknown. Ballard died soon after of complications ensuing from the wounding. *Mesilla News*, (?) May, 1879 (Vol. 6, No. 27); *New Mexican*, December 13, 1879.

6. Dolan's trials are recorded in Socorro County District Court Book A, 6th day, October 1879 term, as Criminal Cases 92 and 98, November 1; Peppin's trial, Criminal Case 102, was heard four days later.

7. Details of the Apache breakout assembled from Sonnichsen, *Mescalero Apaches*, and *Record of Engagements*. See also Terrell, *Apache Chronicle*; Thrapp, *Conquest of Apacheria*. During the fight following the ambush of Dawson's detachment, 2nd Lt. Matthias Day won the unique distinction of being the first soldier to be threatened with a court-martial and awarded the Medal of Honor for the same action: the gallant rescue of a wounded enlisted man. Thrapp, *Conquest of Apacheria*, 184.

8. Lew Wallace's novel, *Ben-Hur, A Tale of the Christ*, was completed in the early spring of 1880 and published on November 13 of that year by Harper & Bros. It was an immediate success; the first printing sold out immediately, and the book went on to become one of the most successful ever published. It was filmed several times; the best-known versions are the 1925 silent movie starring Francis X. Bushman and Ramon Novarro, and the spectacular 1959 version featuring Charlton Heston.

9. *Weekly New Mexican,* September 20, 1879.

10. Ibid. Susan McSween told Fulton that Pierce's wound resulted in an amputation, and that for the rest of his life the old warrior wore a wooden leg. Other sources state that after his recovery, Pierce attended a celebration dance. He bent down to pick up a dropped handkerchief and was unable to straighten up again, and thereafter had to use a cane. Either way, Pierce was whole enough to marry his partner Capt. J. C. Lea's widowed sister, Ella Calfee, in 1883. Barber-Fulton Letters, March 10, 1928; Rasch, File 29; Rasch, "They Fought"; Poe, *Buckboard Days,* 183–88.

11. L. Wallace to C. Schurz, September 15, 1879, Wallace Collection.

One other succinct version of the fight, admittedly hearsay, does exist; it is that of Ash Upson, who told Ad Casey:

John Jones killed John Beckwith at Paxton's cow camp 40 miles below Seven Rivers. Jones charged Beckwith with stealing his cattle. A few days afterwards, John Jones rode into Paxton's camp alone. Paxton, Pierce, Bob Olinger, Buck Powell, [Jim] Ramer and Billy Smith was there. John was shot twice in the back and twice in the back of the head. All four of the balls went through, killing him instantly. Pierce was badly shot above the hip, and was taken to Fort Stockton. I was down at Seven Rivers since the family, especially Mrs Jones, feel very bad. (M. A. Upson to Ad Casey, September 9, 1879)

12. *Trinidad News,* August 5, 1879.

13. *Weekly New Mexican,* November 15, 1879.

14. Col. N.A.M. Dudley to Charles Devens, attorney general, September 16, 1879; Col. N.A.M. Dudley to AAAG Dept. of Missouri, December 12, 1879. Both in File 1405 AGO 1878.

15. Haley, Barber interview.

16. Dudley's attorney was jubilant. "General Dudley triumphantly acquitted yesterday after long fierce trial," he telegraphed Washington. "Jury out but a moment great applause by people. It is time prosecutions against him had ceased. Inform Adjutant General."

17. *Weekly New Mexican,* December 6, 1879. Barnes to Charles Devens, November 30, 1879, File 1405 AGO 1878.

18. As is evident from the fact that he had brought his wife down, Dudley was convinced he would be returned to command at Fort Stanton. In fact he was given command of Fort Union and, following extended and meritorious

service against the Apaches (he, too, had his brush with Victorio in 1880), he was promoted colonel and transferred to Fort Custer, Mont. After more Indian fighting he was retired from the service in 1889 and died in 1910. Some lines from Edward Hatch to Lew Wallace, written shortly before the court of inquiry, might stand as his epitaph: "If Dudley had not been so constantly under the influence of alcohol while at Stanton, he might have managed matters very well. I attach most of his troubles to drink." E. Hatch to L. Wallace, April 9, 1879, Wallace Collection.

19. It is difficult to separate fact from folklore in the matter of Billy the Kid's life at this time, especially insofar as it refers to his sweethearts, mistresses, live-in partners, or whatever you want to call them. The names of Nasaria Yerby, Celsa Gutierrez, and Paulita Maxwell occur most frequently, but there are many other claimants. In 1971, when I first met her, Eve Ball told me that the Kid's son, who had lived "not far away" from her home in Ruidoso, had died "a few years" earlier. She would not reveal his name. Robert Mullin also spent years tracking down such tales: for some, but by no means all of them, see Metz, *Garrett,* 49, and Cline, *Alias,* 87–88.

20. The world owes the Dedrick brothers (the name comes in a variety of spellings; originally it was Dietrich) a special debt: it was they who preserved the only extant tintype of Billy the Kid (see figure 74 in chapter 34). In 1949, Frank L. Upham, Dan Dedrick's nephew, gave the tintype to his daughter-in-law. In 1986 it was donated to the Lincoln County Heritage Trust, where it may be seen along with Upham's authentication.

21. Hertzog, *Little Known Facts,* 8.

22. Garrett, *Authentic Life,* 86.

23. The Garrett-Upson version of Scurlock's departure, albeit written tongue in cheek, is worth noting. Ibid.; Rasch, Buckbee, and Klein, "Many Parts."

24. *Las Vegas Daily Optic,* n.d., in Hertzog, *Little Known Facts,* 10. Frank Lloyd, a former cowboy, said that

the Kid killed a fellow in Sumner called Texas Red. He came up to kill the Kid from down in Texas. . . . We were out shooting at a mark. . . . All of us were as drunk as four hundred dollars. . . . We went into the store to get a drink after shooting and Texas Red who had been with us made a remark as he put his hand on his gun and stepped off to face the bunch. "Billy, I'll draw first blood for the drinks." Billy said: "I'll go you," and broke his neck, while Texas Red never got his six-shooter out of the scabbard." (Haley, "Interview with Frank Lloyd")

25. Garrett, *Authentic Life,* 90–91.

26. Patrick Floyd Jarvis Garrett was born in Chambers County, Ala., on June 5, 1850. It seems pointless to repeat yet again the familiar details of his early life; instead, the reader is referred to Leon Metz's fine biography. Metz, *Garrett,* 3–41.

27. Ibid., 55–56.

28. Ibid., 58. Although his name appeared in Garrett's *Authentic Life,* 98–100, nobody thought to check up on the Lincoln County activities of Azariah F. Wild until the 1970s, when Leon Metz unearthed his "perceptive, but often inaccurate" reports. Wild submitted daily accounts of his activities in New Mexico from September 1880 until he returned to his New Orleans base in January 1881. They are in U.S. Treasury Department, Secret Service Division, "Records of U.S. Secret Service Agents, 1875–1936."

29. Metz, *Garrett,* 59.

30. Ibid.

31. *Lincoln County Leader,* December 7, 1889. Very little is known about the dead man. A James Carlyle figured in the Adobe Walls fight in July 1874, Wyatt Earp mentioned that there was a James Carlysle at Dodge City in the summer of 1877; whether these are the same person as the man killed at the Greathouse ranch cannot be established. Burns suggested that the Kid threatened to kill Carlyle when he realized that Carlyle had his gloves; he then relented. The Kid himself hinted at other reasons. He told Frank Coe, "There is more to that killing than I care to go into or to have people know, but if I were to tell the story in full, public opinion would justify me. . . . The trouble started in Silver City but I have never told it and now I want the cause of it all to be buried with him."

As to who actually killed Carlyle, Deputy U.S. Marshal James W. Bell, a member of the posse who would later be the Kid's guard at Lincoln, told a reporter about seeing Billy Wilson at the Las Vegas depot when the mob came after Dave Rudabaugh. Wilson asked Bell for help.

Bell replied: "That is a hard thing to ask of me after you killed Carlyle in cold blood, as you did." Wilson hung his head and replied: "I didn't shoot at him and tried to keep the others from doing so."

Rudabaugh overhearing this last remark of Wilson's, put in with, "You are a damned liar. We all three shot at him. You and I fired one shot apiece and the Kid twice."

Miller and Snell, *Great Gunfighters,* 196;

Lake, *Wyatt Earp,* 168; Burns, *Saga;* Otero, *The Real Billy the Kid,* 145–50; *Las Vegas Daily Optic,* January 21, 1881, 202.

32. On all the available evidence, it would appear that in his long editorial, J. W. Koogler, a close friend of Huston Chapman and Ira Leonard, was the first person ever to refer to Bonney in print as "Billy the Kid." *Las Vegas Gazette,* December 3, 1880.

33. W. H. Bonney to Governor Wallace, December 12, 1880, Wallace Collection.

34. Territorial Archives of New Mexico, Executive Record Book No. 2, 1867–82, 473. Reproduced in Poe, *Death of Billy the Kid,* xxii.

CHAPTER THIRTY-FOUR

1. Whether it is genuine is another matter. None of the other possemen who wrote about these events mentioned Polk's presence; it does seem unlikely, although not impossible, that Garrett would have taken an unblooded teenager along. However, Polk claims to have begun his account in 1896, at which time only Garrett and Siringo had written about the pursuit. It is possible, perhaps probable, that Polk assimilated much of his information from others who were there. Either way, his idiosyncratic style beautifully portrays the undisciplined, hell-raising way Siringo's cowboys acted. Polk (Siringo refers to him as Cal Pope) was born near Paris in Caldwell County, Tex., on January 8, 1863. He died in 1904 after accidentally shooting himself with his own gun. Polk, "Life of C. W. Polk." His account is reproduced here by courtesy of his granddaughter, Mrs. Jessie Polk McVicker. A complete transcript appears in Earle, *Capture of Billy the Kid.*

2. Garrett, *Authentic Life,* 101; Metz, *Garrett,* 62. The George Davis captured by Garrett at Bosque Grande was not the one who had been a member of the Jessie Evans gang. That worthy went to Texas, where he was indicted in December 1879 for the murder of one C. C. Eden. He then linked up with Jessie Evans and what was left of the old gang. They moved down to the Fort Davis–Fort Stockton area in Texas and took up their old profession of rustling. John Selman, one-time leader of the Rustlers, had taken the rank of captain and the name of John Tyson and set up a butcher shop at Fort Davis; this provided Jessie and the Boys with a safe outlet for stolen beef. It was just like the good old days in the Mesilla valley, but the Boys were greedy.

At around 5 p.m. on May 19, 1880, Jessie Evans, Bud Graham (alias Ace Carr), and Bud's brother Charlie robbed the Sender & Siebenborn store in Fort Davis of some two hundred dollars' worth of firearms and another eight hundred or so in cash. The indignant citizens petitioned the governor for help from the Texas Rangers and posted a reward of eleven hundred dollars. A detachment of nine, led by Sergeant Ed Sieker, forced-marched to Fort Stockton, which they reached on June 6; a further unit, led by Sergeant L. B. Caruthers, headed for Fort Davis, arriving the same day.

On July 3, while scouting near Cibola Creek, eighteen miles north of Presidio, a Ranger detail ran down the gang, and in a running fight that lasted about an hour, killed George Davis (alias Dolly Graham, alias Tom Jones, among others), and captured Evans, Selman, and Bud Graham. One Ranger, George Bingham, was killed. The prisoners were thrown into the Fort Davis slammer to await trial. It was a vile place known as the Bat Cave, located in a cellar beneath the sheriff's office and cut from solid rock. Exit and entry were through a trapdoor in the floor; there was no light. Lt. Charles L. Nevill arrived on August 6 to take command, and two days later Sieker left for Austin taking John Selman along to be handed over to the sheriff of Comanche County. On August 26, after returning from a scout against Victorio's Apaches, Nevill reported that the prisoners were "getting very restless."

I have a letter they wrote to a friend of Evans in New Mexico calling himself Billy Antrum to cause their rescue, and to use his words he was "in a damned tight place only 14 Rangers here any time, ten on a scout and only four in camp right now," and that Antrum and a few men could take them out very easy and if he could not do it now meet him on the road to Huntsville as he was certain to go. I understand this man Antrum is a fugitive from some where and a noted desperado. If he comes down and I expect he will, I will enlist him and put him in the same mess with Evans & Co. (Rasch, "Davis")

Since Nevill had intercepted their letter, it is difficult to imagine how the Kid could have known that Jessie and his partners were in jail, and even more difficult to believe he would have made any effort to deliver him. As he said himself, the Kid was "all for Billy."

After an abortive attempt to dig themselves out, the outlaws went to trial. The Davis family managed to keep their boys out of jail. The disposition of Gunter's case is unknown; he seems to have been sent to the penitentiary. The jury in Evans's trial for the murder of Ranger Bingham decided he was "guilty of murder in the second degree & ses his punishment to con-

finement in the State penitentiary for ten years." He escaped in 1882 and was never seen again. Some people believe that Brushy Bill Roberts was actually Jessie come back. I am not one of them. Bartholomew, *Jesse Evans*; Metz, *Selman*; Rasch, "Davis."

3. Garrett, *Authentic Life*, 105–6.

4. C. Bowdre to Captain Lea, December 15, 1880, in Hertzog, *Little Known Facts*, 14. Bowdre also wrote to the acting governor, W. G. Ritch, proposing to surrender if the indictments against him were dropped; the *New Mexican* unsympathetically observed that the authorities would probably have turned him down. Not that it mattered: "Charlie is now where no indictments will reach him." *New Mexican*, December 29, 1880.

5. Polk, "Life of C. W. Polk."

6. Garrett, *Authentic Life*, 110–11.

7. Polk, "Life of C. W. Polk."

8. Metz, *Garrett*, 76.

9. Polk, "Life of C. W. Polk." Garrett makes no mention of Bowdre's firing his pistols at the posse; from his account it is clear he wishes the reader to know that he took the first shot at Bowdre. "I gave the signal by bringing my gun up to my shoulder, my men raised, and seven bullets sped on their errand of death." Bousman says, "We all took a shot at him"; Jim East said only Garrett and Lee Hall fired. Garrett's account says he "laid [Bowdre] gently on my blankets, and he died almost immediately." Polk's matter-of-fact version suggests Charlie received no such comfort. Earle, *Capture of Billy the Kid*, 53, 84; Garrett, *Authentic Life*, 125.

10. Garrett, *Authentic Life*, 127.

11. Kajencki, "Grzelachowski," 254.

12. All quotations from Morrison, *Billy the Kid: Las Vegas Newspaper Accounts*.

13. Garrett, *Authentic Life*, 129–30. Garrett's version of events tends always to play down the number of men supporting him and play up the number opposing. This is true of events at the Las Vegas depot.

14. Polk, "Life of C. W. Polk." In fact, Morley did not drive the train, and the mob was nearer thirty than three hundred—but Cal Polk captures the tension of the scene perfectly. In a postscript to his service as a posseman, Polk added,

in a few days we saw in paper that Stuart and Garrett had got $1800 reward for ketching the Kids band. So when Frank Stuart come down to the White Oaks and we wanted our part of the reward. He denied getting it for a while. But when we put a rope round his neck and led him out to a big pine tree and threw the rope over a big limb and told him to say his prairs as this was the last chance to say them, he looked up at the limb and said Boys I did get that monnie and I will whack it up with you all rather than to die. And this he did and left the out fit.

15. Rasch, "Curious Case."

16. W. H. Bonney to Gov. Lew Wallace, January 1, 1881, Wallace Collection.

17. The Sheriff found "the bed ticking was filled with stones and earth, and, removing the mattress, they found a deep hole. . . . [B]y concealing the loose earth in the bed and covering the hole with it [the prisoners] had almost reached the street without awakening the suspicions of the guard." *New Mexican*, March 1, 1881; Rasch, "Curious Case."

18. W. H. Bonney to Gov. Lew Wallace, March 2, 1881, Wallace Collection.

19. W. H. Bonney to Gov. Lew Wallace, March 4, 1881, Wallace Collection.

20. Rudabaugh's Las Vegas trial took place on or about March 9; the court appointed W. H. Whiteman and Edgar Caypless as defense attorneys. They filed a motion for change of venue, which was granted by Judge Bradford Lebaron Prince, acting this time in his territorial office. Rudabaugh was then tried for murder in Santa Fe, and sentenced to death. An appeal to the Supreme Court was unsuccessful. In Kelly's case, Caypless went to extraordinary lengths to get his client off, even resorting to a subterfuge. It made no difference: Kelly was sentenced to death. Undeterred, Caypless fought on, and managed to get Kelly's death sentence commuted to life imprisonment. Rasch, "Curious Case."

21. W. H. Bonney to Gov. Lew Wallace, March 27, 1881, Wallace Collection.

CHAPTER THIRTY-FIVE

1. Mullin, *Item from Old Mesilla.*

2. Doña Ana County, District Court Records, Criminal Case Files.

3. Keleher, *Violence*, 315. Keleher provides by far the fullest and most detailed account of the Kid's trials, 312–18.

4. Doña Ana County, District Court Records, Criminal Case Files.

5. Keleher, *Violence*, 320–21. The author credits original publication of the letter to *History of the Mesilla Valley* by George Griggs, who established the Billy the Kid Museum in La Mesilla. As noted earlier, Caypless was an unusually persistent attorney. He pursued the case of the Kid's horse and won a judgment of fifty dollars in San Miguel County court late in July 1881;

by this time the Kid had no need of money. Cline, "Battle."

6. J. C. DeLany and Will Dowlin, post traders, had bought the old Murphy building with a view to going into business in Lincoln. They defaulted on their mortgage and the property reverted to Thomas B. Catron. In January 1881 he struck a deal with the county commissioners, who intended to convert the building into a new courthouse. It was the only building in town considered secure enough to house the Kid.

7. *Lincoln County Leader*, January 15, 1890.

8. The "onlie true begetter" of this story seems to have been Francisco "Frank" Salazar who, like Corbet, was Saturnino Baca's son-in-law. Salazar told it to Fulton, who told it to Robert Mullin, who told the world. The alternative versions are variations on the theme of the Kid's slipping his irons, which were double the usual weight, over his small wrists and hands. He hit Bell over the head—the deputy's scalp was cut—then grabbed his gun. Cline asserts (without substantiating documentation) that the Kid was not allowed visitors, and that he did not know of and never found the pistol in the outhouse, which Garrett located shortly after the escape. Cline, *Alias*, 106.

9. There are numerous theories about the killing of Bell: that he was coming up the stairs, that he was running down them, that he was already at the bottom and heading for the doorway when the Kid shot him, and so on. Garrett's testimony is the most solid: he says Bell was hit under the right arm, the bullet passing through his body and coming out under the left arm. "The ball had hit the wall on Bell's right," he says, "caromed [i.e., glanced off at an angle], passed through his body, and buried itself in an adobe [wall] on his left. There was no other proof besides the marks on the walls."

How many times did the Kid fire? According to Maurice G. Fulton, when he first saw the building in the 1920s there were "any number of bullet holes"; he had a photograph "taken in the 1930s prior to the restoration which shows *three.*" He went on to say that J. Smith Lea, who arrived in Lincoln to be Garrett's deputy and jailer a few days after the escape, assured him that Garrett made a careful investigation, and reached the conclusions which are embodied in his book. Fulton's conclusion: Bell was coming up the stairs. Garrett, *Authentic Life*, 138–39; Fulton, *Lincoln County War*, 393–95; Fulton-Nolan Correspondence, December 31, 1953.

10. *Lincoln County Leader*, January 15, 1890; Meadows with Fulton, "Billy the Kid as I Knew Him."

11. *Alamogordo News*, June 25, 1936.

12. Anonymous, April 29, 1881, in *Grant County Herald*, May 14, 1881.

13. Garrett, *Authentic Life*, 139.

CHAPTER THIRTY-SIX

1. *New Mexican*, May 4, 1881.

2. Hunt, *Tragic Days*, 296.

3. Meadows, "Reminiscences," February 26, 1931. Quoted in Hunt, *Tragic Days*, 301.

4. Poe, *Death of Billy the Kid*, 12–15.

5. Metz, *Garrett*, 98.

6. Brininstool, "Billy the Kid."

7. Garrett, *Authentic Life*, 143.

8. Poe, *Death of Billy the Kid*, 16.

9. Ibid., 27–28.

10. Garrett, *Authentic Life*, 144.

11. Poe, *Death of Billy the Kid*, 28–29.

12. Metz, *Garrett*, 99–100.

13. Poe, *Death of Billy the Kid*, 31–34.

14. Ibid., 42.

15. Garrett, *Authentic Life*, 147.

16. *The Times*, London, August 13, 1881.

CHAPTER THIRTY-SEVEN

1. A family bible lists the family as follows:
Emil, born at Spring Ranch, May 2nd, 1880.
Caroline F " " " " February 19th, 1882.
Louise " " Lincoln, Nov'r 30th, 1883.
Bessie" " " Sept. 20th, 1886.
James Joseph Dolan, Born in Loughrea, County Galway, Ireland, May 2nd, 1848.
Maria Eva Whitlock, Born in Floyd County, Indiana, December 20th, A.D. 1858.
Dolan and Eva Whitlock were married in a civil ceremony at Lincoln by Chief Justice Elisha V. Long. As to her comments anent the unhappiness of the match, it might be as well to bear in mind that Susan Barber had no cause to love Dolan and plenty to slander him. Research by Lewis A. Ketring, Jr.

2. Klasner, *Girlhood*; Haley, "Interview with Frank Coe," March 20, 1927.

3. BFO File F05-1965.

4. Nolan, *John Henry Tunstall*, 418–37.

5. Tunstall Estate.

6. George Parker to T. T. Behrens, 19 August, 1925.

7. R. A. Widenmann to J. P. Tunstall, June 30, 1879.

8. Widenmann, "Enigma."

9. J. P. Tunstall to K. A. Widenmann, December 16, 1879.

10. R. A. Widenmann to J. P. and Emily Tunstall, January 13, 1880.

11. R. A. Widenmann to Lilian and Mabel Tunstall, January 13, 1880.

12. J. P. Tunstall to R. A. Widenmann, July 19, 1880.

13. R. A. Widenmann to the Tunstall family, August 7, 1880.

14. J. P. Tunstall to R. A. Widenmann, December 15, 1880.

15. R. A. Widenmann to the Tunstall family, August 15, 1881.

16. R. A. Widenmann to the Tunstall family, November 15, 1881.

17. This and the succeeding biographical material is from Widenmann, "Enigma."

18. G. Gauss to J. P. Tunstall, November 22, 1879.

19. Biographical details from pension application, U.S. Department of the Interior, Bureau of Pensions.

20. *New Mexican*, July 19, 1880. The newspaper called it "another reign of terror," reporting that on three consecutive nights, the 3rd, 4th, and 5th of July, violence again stalked the streets of Lincoln. The first night a man named only as Harriman got drunk and was jailed; during the night "a mob of reckless men" broke into the jail and riddled him with bullets. The following night, the mob surrounded the jail and killed a deputy sheriff, and the next night hanged yet another prisoner.

21. Tunstall Estate.

22. McSween Estate.

23. Quincy W. Hershey, interview.

24. She filed for divorce September 15; the decree was granted on the date stated but not apparently filed until the following year. Mullin, "Notes on Susan E. McSween."

25. Pension application, U.S. Department of the Interior, Bureau of Pensions.

26. Mullin, "Notes on Susan E. McSween."

27. *Lincoln County News*, June 21, 1929.

28. M. G. Fulton to W. A. Carrell, January 25, 1931.

29. Ibid.

30. Lincoln County, Estate of Susan E. Barber.

BIBLIOGRAPHY

PUBLISHED SOURCES

Adams, Ramon L. F. *More Burs Under the Saddle.* Norman: University of Oklahoma Press. 1979.

Andreas, A. T. *History of the State of Kansas.* Chicago: A. T. Andreas, 1883.

Ball, Eve. "Charles Ballard, 'Lawman' of the Pecos." *English Westerners Brand Book* 7(4) (July 1965): 1–6.

———. *Ma'am Jones of the Pecos.* Tucson: University of Arizona Press, 1969.

Ball, Larry D. *The United States Marshals of New Mexico and Arizona Territories, 1846–1912.* Albuquerque: University of New Mexico Press, 1978.

Bancroft, Hubert Howe. *A History of Arizona and New Mexico, 1530–1888.* San Francisco: The History Company, 1889.

Bartholomew, Ed. *Jesse Evans, A Texas Hide-Burner.* Houston: Frontier Press of Texas, 1955.

Beauvais, John Robert, and Thomas William Merlan, eds. *Lincoln, New Mexico: A Plan for Preservation and Growth.* Santa Fe: New Mexico State Planning Office, 1974.

Bender, Norman J. *Missionaries, Outlaws and Indians: Taylor F. Ealy at Lincoln and Zuni, 1878–1881.* Albuquerque: University of New Mexico Press, 1984.

Blazer, Paul A. "The Fight at Blazer's Mill: A Chapter in the Lincoln County War." *Arizona and the West* 6 (Autumn 1964): 203–10.

Brayer, Herbert O. *William Blackmore: A Case Study in the Economic Development of the West.* Denver, 1948.

Brininstool, E. A. "Billy the Kid." *Wide World Magazine* (December 1919).

Bryan, Howard. *Wildest of the Wild West: True Tales of a Frontier Town on the Santa Fe Trail.* Santa Fe: Clear Light Publishers, 1988.

Burns, Walter Noble. *The Saga of Billy the Kid.* Garden City, N.Y.: Doubleday, Page, 1926.

Church, Amelia Bolton. "Early Days in Roswell and Southeast New Mexico." In J. D. Shinkle, *Reminiscences of Roswell Pioneers,* 96–97. Roswell, N.M.: Hall-Poorbaugh Press, 1966.

———. "Notes for [an] Informal Talk on Her Recollections of Life, February 16, 1950." In J. R. Beauvais and T. W. Merlan, eds., *Lincoln, New Mexico: A Plan for Preservation and Growth,* 135–38. Santa Fe: State Planning Office, 1974.

Clarke, Mary Whatley. *John Chisum: Jinglebob King of the Pecos.* Austin, Tex.: Eakins Press, 1984.

Cline, Donald. "A Cold Night for Angels." *Real West* (December 1984): 32–52.

———. "Robert Olinger, Outlaw and Lawman Killer." *NOLA Quarterly* 9(4) (Spring 1985): 11–13.

———. *Alias Billy the Kid: The Man Behind the Legend.* Santa Fe: Sunstone Press, 1986.

———. "Battle over Billy the Kid's Horse." *NOLA Quarterly* 12(3) (Winter 1988): 12.

———. "The Mystery of Billy the Kid's Home." *NOLA Quarterly* 13(2) (Fall 1988): 16–19.

———. *Antrim and Billy.* College Station, Tex.: Creative Publishing, 1990.

Coe, George. *Frontier Fighter*. Ed. Doyce B. Nunis, Jr. Chicago: Lakeside Press, R. R. Donnelley & Sons, 1984.

Commissioner of Indian Affairs. *Report to the Secretary of the Interior for the Year 1870*. Washington, D.C.: Government Printing Office, 1870.

——. *Report to the Secretary of the Interior for the Year 1871*. Washington, D.C.: Government Printing Office, 1871.

——. *Annual Report to the Secretary of the Interior for the Year 1872*. Washington, D.C.: Government Printing Office, 1872.

——. *Annual Report to the Secretary of the Interior for the Year 1873*. Washington, D.C.: Government Printing Office, 1873.

Coolidge, Dane. *Fighting Men of the West*. New York: E.P. Dutton, 1932.

Curry, W. Hubert. *Sun Rising on the West: The Saga of Henry Clay and Elizabeth Smith*. Crosbyton, Tex.: Crosby County Pioneer Memorial, 1979.

De Arment, Robert. *Bat Masterson: The Man and the Legend*. Norman: University of Oklahoma Press, 1979.

de Mattos, Jack. "The Search for Billy the Kid's Roots—Is Over!" *Real West* 23 (January 1980): 20–25.

Denton, J. Fred. "Billy the Kid's Friend Tells for First Time of Thrilling Incidents." *Tucson Daily Citizen*, March 28, 1931.

Dobie, J. Frank. "A Note on Charles Siringo, Writer and Man." In *Charles A. Siringo, A Texas Cowboy*, i–xl. New York: William Sloane Associates, 1950.

Dykes, J. C. *Billy the Kid: The Bibliography of a Legend*. Albuquerque: University of New Mexico Press, 1952.

Ealy, Mary R. "Reminiscences of Old Lincoln." *New Mexico Magazine* 32 (March 1954): 17, 42–43.

Ealy, Ruth R. "A Medical Missionary." *New Mexico Magazine* 32 (March 1954): 16, 38–39.

——. *Water in a Thirsty Land*. N.p., 1955. Privately printed.

Earle, James H., ed. *The Capture of Billy the Kid*. College Station, Tex.: Creative Publishing, 1988.

Ellis, Bruce T., ed. "Lincoln County Postscript: Notes on Robert A. Widenmann by His Daughter, Elsie Widenmann." *New Mexico Historical Review* 50(3) (July 1975): 213–30.

Fergusson, Harvey. *Rio Grande*. New York: Knopf, 1933.

Fleming, Elvis E., and Minor S. Huffman, eds. *Roundup on the Pecos*. Roswell, N.M.: Chaves County Historical Society, 1978.

Fulton, Maurice G. "Apocrypha of Billy the Kid." In *Folk Say: A Regional Miscellany*, ed. B. A. Botkin. Norman: University of Oklahoma Press, 1930.

——. "Roswell in Its Early Years." *Roswell Daily Record*, October 7, 1937.

——. "The Harrell War of 1873." *English Westerners Brand Book* 3(3) (January 1957): 3–6.

——. *History of the Lincoln County War*. Ed. Robert N. Mullin. Tucson: University of Arizona Press, 1975.

Ganoe, William Addleman. *A History of the United States Army*. New York: Appleton-Century, 1942.

Gard, Wayne. *Sam Bass*. Boston: Houghton Mifflin, 1936.

Garrett, Pat F. *The Authentic Life of Billy the Kid, the Noted Desperado of the Southwest*. Ed. and with an introduction by Maurice Garland Fulton. New York: Macmillan, 1927.

——. *The Authentic Life of Billy the Kid, the Noted Desperado of the Southwest*. With introduction by J. C. Dykes. Norman: University of Oklahoma Press, 1954.

Gibson, Arrell M. *The Life and Death of Colonel Albert Jennings Fountain*. Norman: University of Oklahoma Press, 1965.

Gorney, Carole. *Roots in Lincoln: A History of Fort Stanton Hospital*. Santa Fe: New Mexico State Planning Office, 1969.

Greer, James Kimmins. *Colonel Jack Hays: Texas Frontier Leader and California Builder*. New York: Dutton, 1952.

Guinn, James M. *A Historical and Biographical Record of Southern California*. Chicago: Chapman, 1902.

——. *A History of the State of California, Central Coast*. Chicago: Chapman, 1903.

Haley, J. Evetts. "Horse Thieves." *Southwest Review* 15 (Spring 1930): 317–32.

Henn, Nora. "Was a Piano in the McSween House During the Five Day Battle?" *Real West Annual* (Spring 1985): 26–29.

Henry, Stuart. *Conquering Our Great American Plains*. New York: Dutton, 1930.

Hertzog, Peter. *Little Known Facts About Billy the Kid*. Santa Fe, N.M.: The Press of the Territorian, 1964.

Hinton, Harwood P. "John Simpson Chisum, 1877–84." *New Mexico Historical Review* 31(3) (July 1956): 177–205; 31(4) (October 1956): 310–37; 32(1) (January 1957): 53–65.

Horn, Calvin. *New Mexico's Troubled Years*. Albuquerque: Horn & Wallace, 1963.

Hough, Emerson. *The Story of the Outlaw*. New York: A. L. Burt, 1907.

Hoyt, Henry F. *A Frontier Doctor*. Ed. Doyce B. Nunis, Jr. Chicago: Lakeside Press, R. R. Donnelley & Sons, 1979.

Hunt, Frazier. *The Tragic Days of Billy the Kid*. New York: Hastings House, 1956.

Hunt, Rockwell D. *California and Californians*. Vol. 3. San Francisco: Lewis, 1932.

Illustrated History of New Mexico, An. Chicago: Lewis, 1895.

Jones, Oakah L. "Lew Wallace: Hoosier Governor of Territorial New Mexico." *New Mexico Historical Review* 60(2) (April 1985): 129–58.

Kajencki, Francis C. "Alexander Grzelachowski: Pioneer Merchant of Puerto de Luna, New Mexico." *Arizona and the West* 26(3) (Autumn 1984): 243–60.

Keegan, John. *The Face of Battle*. London: Jonathan Cape, 1976.

Keleher, William A. *Turmoil in New Mexico, 1848–68*. Santa Fe, N.M.: Rydal Press, 1952.

———. *Violence in Lincoln County, 1869–1881*. Albuquerque: University of New Mexico Press, 1957.

———. *The Fabulous Frontier: Twelve New Mexico Items*. Albuquerque: University of New Mexico Press, 1962.

Kelly, Charles. *The Outlaw Trail, A History of Butch Cassidy and the Wild Bunch*. New York: Devin-Adair, 1959.

Klasner, Lily Casey. *My Girlhood Among Outlaws*. Ed. Eve Ball. Tucson: University of Arizona Press, 1972.

Lake, Stuart N. *Wyatt Earp. Frontier Marshal*. Boston: Houghton Mifflin, 1931.

Lamar, Howard. *The Far Southwest, 1846–1912: A Territorial History*. New Haven, Conn.: Yale University Press, 1966.

Lavash, Donald. *William Brady: Tragic Hero of the Lincoln County War*. Santa Fe, N.M.: Sunstone Press, 1986.

Mazzanovich, Anton. "Tony Tells About the Kid." *Tombstone Epitaph*, March 9, 1933.

McCabe, James D. *Lights and Shadows of New York Life, or, Sights and Sensations of the Great City*. Philadelphia: National Publishing, 1872.

McCright, Grady C., and James H. Powell. *Jessie Evans: Lincoln County Badman*. College Station, Tex.: Creative Publishing, 1983.

Metz, Leon C. *John Selman: Texas Gunfighter*. New York: Hastings House, 1966.

———. *Pat Garrett: The Story of a Western Lawman*. Norman: University of Oklahoma Press, 1974.

Miller, Darlis A. "William Logan Rynerson in New Mexico, 1862–93." *New Mexico Historical Review* 48(2) (April 1973): 101–32.

Miller, Nyle H., and Joseph W. Snell. *Great Gunfighters of the Kansas Cowtowns*. Lincoln: University of Nebraska Press, 1967.

Morrison, John W. *The Life of Billy the Kid, A Juvenile Outlaw*. New York: John W. Morrison, n.d. [1881].

Morrison, William V. *Billy the Kid: Las Vegas Newspaper Accounts of His Career*. Waco, Tex., 1958.

Mullin, Robert N. *A Chronology of the Lincoln County War*. Santa Fe, N.M.:Press of the Territorian, 1966.

———. *The Boyhood of Billy the Kid*. Monograph 17, Southwestern Studies 5(1). El Paso: Texas Western Press, University of Texas at El Paso, 1967.

———. "Here Lies John Kinney." *The Journal of Arizona History* 14 (Autumn 1973): 223–42.

———. *An Item from Old Mesilla*. N.p., n.d. Privately printed.

Mullin, Robert N., and W. H. Hutchinson. *Whiskey Jim and a Kid Named Billie*. Clarendon, Tex.: Clarendon Press, 1967.

Nolan, Frederick W. "A Sidelight on the Tunstall Murder." *New Mexico Historical Review* 31(3) (July 1956): 206–22.

———. "John H. Tunstall, Merchant." *The English Westerners Brand Book* 4(5) (March 1958): 2–10.

——. *The Life and Death of John Henry Tunstall.* Albuquerque: University of New Mexico Press, 1965.

——. "The Search for Alexander McSween." *New Mexico Historical Review* 62(2) (July 1987): 287–301.

——. " 'Dirty Dave' Rudabaugh, The Kid's Worst Friend." *The Kid* (3) (December 1989): 7–13.

Nordhoff, Charles. *California for Health, Pleasure, and Residence.* London: Sampson Low Marston Low & Searle, 1873.

Nye, Nelson C. *Pistols for Hire: A Tale of the Lincoln County War and the West's Most Desperate Outlaw William (Billy the Kid) Bonney.* New York: Macmillan, 1941.

O'Neal, Bill. *Henry Brown, The Outlaw Marshal.* College Station, Tex.: Creative Publishing, 1980.

Otero, Miguel A. *The Real Billy the Kid: With New Light on the Lincoln County War.* New York: Rufus Rockwell Wilson, 1936.

Pearson, Jim Berry. *The Maxwell Land Grant.* Norman: University of Oklahoma Press, 1961.

Poe, John W. *The Death of Billy the Kid.* Introduction by Maurice Garland Fulton. Boston: Houghton Mifflin, 1933.

Poe, Sophie A. *Buckboard Days.* Ed. Eugene Cunningham. Caldwell, Idaho: Caxton Printers, 1936.

Pryor, Rafaelita. "Siege of the McSween House." *Frontier Times* (May 1969): 24–25, 54–56.

Rasch, Philip J. "A Note on N.A.M. Dudley." *Westerners Brand Book (Los Angeles)* 3 (1949): 207–14.

——. "Henry Newton Brown." *Westerners Brand Book (Los Angeles)* 5 (1953): 58–67.

——. "The Twenty One Men He Put Bullets Through." *New Mexico Folklore Record* 9 (1954–55): 8–14.

——. "Five Days of Battle." *Westerners Brand Book (Denver)* 11 (1955): 295–323.

——. "The Horrell War." *New Mexico Historical Review* 31(3) (July 1956): 223–31.

——. "A Man Called Antrim." *Westerners Brand Book (Los Angeles)* 6 (1956): 48–54.

——. "The Pecos War." *Panhandle-Plains Historical Review* 29 (1956): 101–11.

——. "The Rise of the House of Murphy." *Westerners Brand Book (Denver)* 12 (1956): 53–84.

——. "Prelude to War: The Murder of John Henry Tunstall." *Westerners Brand Book (Los Angeles)* 7 (1957): 78–96.

——. "More on the McCartys." *English Westerners Brand Book* 3(6) (April 1957): 3–9.

——. "Exit Axtell: Enter Wallace." *New Mexico Historical Review* 32(3) (July 1957): 231–45.

——. "The Murder of Huston I. Chapman." *Westerners Brand Book (Los Angeles)* 8 (1959): 69–82.

——. "The Story of Jessie J. Evans." *Panhandle-Plains Historical Review* 33 (1960): 108–21.

——. "The Men at Fort Stanton." *English Westerners Brand Book* 3(3) (April 1961): 2–7.

——. "The Short Life of Tom O'Folliard." *Potomac Westerners Corral Dust* 6 (May 1961): 9–11, 14.

——. "John Kinney—King of the Rustlers." *English Westerners Brand Book* 4(1) (October 1961): 10–12.

——. "George Washington of Lincoln County." *Washington D.C. Westerners Corral Dust* 6 (December 1961): 45–46.

——. "A. Ham Mills—Sheriff of Lincoln County." *English Westerners Brand Book* 5(3) (April 1962): 11–12.

——. "The Mystery of George Davis." *English Westerners Brand Book* 4(4) (July 1962): 2–5.

——. "War in Lincoln County." *English Westerners Brand Book* 6(4) (July 1964): 2–11.

——. "The Would-Be Judge: Ira E. Leonard." *Denver Westerners Roundup* 20 (July 1964): 13–17.

——. "The Loquacious Mr. Leverson." *Westerners Brand Book, New York* 11(4) (1964): 92–93.

——. "He Rode with the Kid: The Life of Tom Pickett." *English Westerners Tenth Anniversary Publication* (1964): 11–15.

——. "The Trials of Lieutenant-Colonel Dudley." *English Westerners Brand Book* 7(2) (January 1965): 1–7.

——. "Feuding at Farmington." *New Mexico Historical Review* 40(3) (July 1965): 214–32.

——. "The Governor Meets the Kid." *English Westerners Brand Book* 8(3) (April 1966): 5–12.

——. "The Murder of the Casner Brothers." *Los Angeles Westerners Branding Iron* 83 (March 1967): 9–12.

——. "Gunfire in Lincoln County." *English Westerners Brand Book* 9(3) (April 1967): 6–11.

——. "The Tularosa Ditch War." *New Mexico Historical Review* 43(3) (July 1968): 229–35.

——. "They Fought for the House." In *Portraits in Gunsmoke*, ed. Jeff Burton, 34–64. London: English Westerners Society, 1971.

——. "These Were the Regulators." In *Ho! For the Great West*, ed. Barry C. Johnson, 50–69. London: English Westerners Society, 1980.

——. "Gus Gildea—An Arizone [*sic*] Pioneer." *English Westerners Brand Book* 23(2) (Summer 1985): 1–7.

——. "The Curious Case of Edward M. Kelly." *NOLA Quarterly* 22(2) (Fall 1987): 8, 16–17.

Rasch, Philip J., Joseph E. Buckbee, and Karl K. Klein. "Man of Many Parts." *English Westerners Brand Book* 5(2) (January 1963): 9–12.

Rasch, Philip J., and Robert N. Mullin. "New Light on the Legend of Billy the Kid." *New Mexico Folklore Record* 7 (1952–53): 1–5.

——. "Dim Trails: The Pursuit of the McCarty Family." *New Mexico Folkore Record* 8 (1953–54): 6–11.

Rasch, Philip J., and Lee Myers. "The Tragedy of the Beckwiths." *English Westerners Brand Book* 5(4) (July 1963): 1–6.

Record of Engagements with Hostile Indians Within the Military Division of the Missouri from 1868–1882. Washington, D.C.: Government Printing Office, 1882.

Rickards, Colin W. "Better for the World That He Is Gone." *English Westerners Brand Book* 2(3) (April 1960): 2–8.

——. "More on Henry Newton Brown." *English Westerners Brand Book* 3(1) (October 1960): 8–10.

——. *The Gunfight at Blazer's Mill.* Southwestern Studies, Monograph 40. El Paso: University of Texas at El Paso, 1974.

Samek, Hana. "No 'Bed of Roses': The Career of Four Mescalero Indian Agents, 1871–1878." *New Mexico Historical Review* 57(2) (April 1982): 136–57.

Sands, Frank. *A Pastoral Prince: The History and Reminiscences of J. W. Cooper.* Santa Barbara, Calif., 1893.

Schmitt, Martin F., ed. *General George Crook, His Autobiography.* Norman: University of Oklahoma Press, 1960.

Shinkle, James D. *Reminiscences of Roswell Pioneers.* Roswell, N.M.: Hall-Poorbaugh Press, 1966.

——. *Robert Casey and the Ranch on the Rio Hondo.* Roswell, N.M.: Hall-Poorbaugh Press, 1970.

Smith, Cara Mae Coe Marable. *The Coe's Go West.* El Paso, Tex., 1988.

Smith, William R. "Death in Doña Ana County, Part I." *English Westerners Brand Book* 9(2) (January 1967): 1–12.

——. "Death in Doña Ana County, Part II." *English Westerners Brand Book* 9(3) (April 1967): 1–5.

Sonnichsen, C. L. *Ten Texas Feuds.* Albuquerque: University of New Mexico Press, 1957.

——. *The Mescalero Apaches.* Norman: University of Oklahoma Press, 1958.

——. *I'll Die Before I'll Run: The Story of the Great Feuds of Texas.* New York: Devin-Adair, 1962.

Sonnichsen, C. L., and William V. Morrison. *Alias Billy the Kid.* Albuquerque: University of New Mexico Press, 1955.

Spangler, Edward W. *The Spangler Annals.* York, Pa., 1896.

Stanley, F. [pseudonym of Fr. Stanley Crocchiola.] *The Private War of Ike Stockton.* Denver: World Press, 1959.

Stone, Stephen A. "Notes and Documents [Dave Rudabaugh]." *New Mexico Historical Review* 23(2) (April 1948): 146–54.

Terrell, John Upton. *Apache Chronicle.* New York: World, 1972.

Theisen, Lee Scott. "The Fight in Lincoln, N.M., 1878: The Testimony of Two Negro Participants." *Arizona and the West* 12 (Summer 1970): 173–98.

——. "Frank Warner Angel's Notes on New Mexico Territory, 1878." *Arizona and the West* 18(4) (Winter 1976): 333–70.

Thrapp, Dan L. *The Conquest of Apacheria.* Norman: University of Oklahoma Press, 1967.

——. *Encyclopedia of Frontier Biography.* 3 vols. Rev. ed. Spokane: Arthur H. Clarke Co., 1990.

Traylor, Leslie. "Facts Regarding the Escape of Billy the Kid." *Frontier Times* 13 (July 1936): 506–13.

Triplett, Frank. *The Life, Times and Treacherous Death of Jesse James.* Ed. Joseph Snell. Chicago: Swallow Press, 1970.

Twitchell, Ralph Emerson. *The Leading Facts of New Mexican History.* 5 vols. Cedar Rapids, Iowa: Torch Press, 1912.

United States Biographical Dictionary (Kansas Edition). N.p., 1879.

Utley, Robert M. *Four Fighters of Lincoln County.* Albuquerque: University of New Mexico Press, 1986.

———. *High Noon in Lincoln, Violence on the Western Frontier.* Albuquerque: University of New Mexico Press, 1987.

———. *Billy the Kid: A Short and Violent Life.* Lincoln: University of Nebraska Press, 1989.

Walker, Henry P. "Soldier in the California Column: The Diary of John W. Teal." *Arizona and the West* 13 (Spring 1971): 33–82.

Wallace, Andrew. "Duty in the District of New Mexico: A Military Memoir." *New Mexico Historical Review* 50(3) (July 1975): 231–62.

Wallace, Lew. *An Autobiography.* 2 vols. New York: Harper & Bros., 1906.

Walz, Edgar. *Retrospection.* Santa Fe, N.M., 1931.

Weddle, Jerry. "Apprenticeship of an Outlaw: Billy the Kid in Arizona." *Journal of Arizona History* (Autumn 1990): 233–52.

Westphall, Victor. *Thomas Benton Catron and His Era.* Tucson: University of Arizona Press, 1973.

Who Was Who in America. Vol. 4, 1961–68. Chicago: Marquis Who's Who, n.d. (1969?).

Widenmann, Robert J., trans. *A Genealogy of the Widenmann Family.* Brønshøj, Denmark, 1978.

Wilson, John P. *Merchants, Guns, and Money: The Story of Lincoln County and Its Wars.* Santa Fe: Museum of New Mexico Press, 1987.

Wing, Talcott E., ed. *History of Monroe County, Michigan.* New York: Munsell & Co., 1890.

Yule, Dorothy A. "The Kimberlys: Santa Barbara's Pioneer Mother and Daughter." *The Grizzly Bear Magazine (Los Angeles)* 57(342): 2–3.

UNPUBLISHED SOURCES

Barber, Susan E. Notes of Correction on *The Saga of Billy the Kid.* [1926].

———. Letters to Maurice G. Fulton. Special Collections, University of Arizona, Tucson. Cited as Barber-Fulton Letters.

Beeton, Florence. Letter to J. P. Tunstall, March 22, 1878.

Beeton, Henry C.
    Letters to Robert Widenmann, 1878.
    Letters to J. P. Tunstall, 1878.
    Letters to William Brooke Herford, 1878.
    Copies of letters to Sir Edward Thornton and Secretary of State, Canada, 1878.

    Originals in collection of Hilary Tunstall-Behrens, London; copies in author's collection.

Bonney, W.H. "Statement by the Kid, Made Sunday Night March 29, 1879." Wallace Collection.

Bradford, Helen. "The First Twenty Years of the M. E. Church [of Eureka, Kansas]." Greenwood County Historical Society, Eureka, Kans.

Chapman, Huston I. Letter to J. P. Tunstall, 1879. Original in collection of Hilary Tunstall-Behrens; copy in author's collection.

Corbet, Samuel R.
    Letters to J.P. Tunstall, 1878.
    Letters to John Middleton, 1878.
    Letter to R. A. Widenmann, July 20, 1878.

    Originals in collection of Hilary Tunstall-Behrens, London; copies in author's collection.

Letter to John Middleton February 3, 1880. Fulton Papers, Box 11, Folder 8, Special Collections, University of Arizona, Tucson.

Crawford, Edith.
    Interview with Francisco Trujillo, May 10, 1937.
    Interview with William E. Kimbrell, August 9, 1938.

    WPA Files, New Mexico State Record Center and Archive (NMSRCA).

Dobler, Grace. "History of Eureka." Greenwood County Historical Society, Eureka, Kans.

Ealy, Lawrence O. Collection of correspondence, diaries and memoirs of Taylor F. and Mary Ealy. Special Collections, University of Arizona, Tucson.

Ellis, Ben H. Letters to J. P. Tunstall, 1879. Originals in collection of Hilary Tunstall-Behrens; copies in author's collection.

Ellis, Isaac, Letters to J. P Tunstall, 1878. Originals in collection of Hilary Tunstall-Behrens; copies in author's collection.

Francis, Mrs. Allen. Letter to J. P. Tunstall, n.d. Original in collection of Hilary Tunstall-Behrens; copy in author's collection.

Fulton, Maurice G., Interview with Juan Peppin, Artesia, N.M. [1930]. Robert N. Mullin Collection, Haley History Center, Midland, Tex. Cited as Mullin, HHC.

————. Correspondence with W. A. Carrell, 1929–31. Carrell Collection, Lincoln County Heritage Trust, Lincoln, N.M.

————. Correspondence with Col. T. T. Behrens and other members of the Tunstall family, 1927–54. Author's collection.

————. Correspondence with Frederick Nolan, 1953–55. Author's collection.

————. "Calendar of Tunstall's Last Three Months." Undated ms. [ca. 1954]. Author's collection.

Gauss, Gottfried G. Letters to J. P. Tunstall, 1878–79. Originals in collection of Hilary Tunstall-Behrens; copies in author's collection.

Haley, J. Evetts.
    Interview with Susan E. Barber, August 26, 1927.
    Interview with Robert A. Casey, June 25, 1937.
    Interview with Frank Coe, March 20, 1927.
    Interview with Frank Coe, August 14 and 17, 1927.
    Interview with Frank Coe, February 20, 1928.
    Interview with George Coe, March 20, 1927.
    Interview with George Coe, August 12 and 18, 1927.
    Interview with George Coe, June 12, 1939.
    Interview with Lucius Dills, August 5, 1937.
    Interview with Bill Jones, January 13, 1927.
    Interview with Frank Lloyd, August 18, 1927.
    Interview with John Nicholls, May 15, 1927.
    Interview with Yginio Salazar, August 17, 1927.
    Interview with Emma Blazer Thompson, October 14, 1927.

    All in Haley History Center, Midland, Tex.

————. Interview with William Wier, June 22, 1937. Vandale Collection, Barker History Center, University of Texas, Austin.

Hall, Mrs. Caleb. "Recollections of My Grandmother, Mrs Caleb Hall." Unsigned ms., n.d. Mullin, HHC.

Hough, Emerson. Correspondence. Hough Collection, Iowa State University, Iowa City.

Jackson, Sheldon. Correspondence. Presbyterian Historical Society, Philadelphia.

Kelly, Thomas Fulton. "The Life of M. A. Upson (from Original Letters)." Mullin, HHC.

Klasner, Lily Casey, "The Kid." Unsigned ms., n.d. Lillian Klasner Collection, Harold B. Lee Library, Brigham Young University, Provo, Utah.

Leverson, M. R. Letter to John Sherman, Jr., March 20, 1878. Ritch Collection, Henry E. Huntington Library, San Marino, Calif.

McLellan, R. G. Letters to J. P. Tunstall. Originals in collection of Hilary Tunstall-Behrens; copies in author's collection.

McSween, Alexander A. Letters to J. P. Tunstall, 1878. Originals in collection of Hilary Tunstall-Behrens; copies in author's collection.

————. Letter to Charles Fritz, December 12, 1876. R. G. McCubbin Collection, El Paso, Tex.

————. Letter to Emily Tunstall Behrens, April 17, 1878. Original in collection of Hilary Tunstall-Behrens; copy in author's collection.

McSween, Sue E. Letters to J. P. and Mrs. Emily Tunstall, 1878. Originals in collection of Hilary Tunstall-Behrens; copies in author's collection.

Meadows, J. P., in collaboration with Maurice G. Fulton. "Billy the Kid as I Knew Him." N. d. Philip J. Rasch files, Lincoln County Heritage Trust, Lincoln, N.M.

Mehren, Lawrence L. "A History of the Mescalero Apache Reservation, 1869–1881." M.A. thesis, University of Arizona, [1968].

Middleton, John. Letters to J. P. Tunstall, 1879–81.
  Letter to R. A. Widenmann, August 30, 1878.
  Originals in collection of Hilary Tunstall-Behrens; copies in author's collection.

Morton, W. S. Letter to H. H. Marshall, March 8, 1878. R. G. McCubbin Collection, El Paso, Tex.

Mullin, Robert N. Correspondence with Frederick Nolan, 1952–72. Author's collection.
————. Notes on Dick Brewer.
  Notes on Sam Corbet.
  Notes on J. J. Dolan.
  Notes on Jim French.
  Notes on A. A. McSween.
  Notes on Susan E. McSween.
  Notes on John Middleton.
  Notes on J. M. Miller.
  Notes on A. H. "Ham" Mills.
  Notes on Buck Morton.
  Notes on David P. Shield.
  Notes on Ash Upson.

  All in Mullin, HHC.

Murphy, Lawrence G. Records of Service in Regular Army (Veterans' Records); Records of Service in Civil War (Compiled Service Records of Volunteer Union Soldiers, New Mexico; microfilm M427 roll 15). National Archives and Records Administration (NARA). Cited as MSR, NARA.

Parker, George. Letter to T. T. Behrens, August 19, 1925. Original in collection of Hilary Tunstall-Behrens; copy in author's collection.

Polk, Cal. "Life of C. W. Polk, Commenced January 25, 1896." Jessie Polk McVicker, Burneyville, Okla.

Rasch, Philip J. Correspondence with Frederick Nolan, 1954–88. Author's collection.
————. Research File 12: The Murder of Huston Chapman.
  Research File 28: The Horrell War.
  Research File 29: They Fought for the House, vol. 1.

  All in Lincoln County Heritage Trust, Lincoln, N.M.

Ryland, John. Correspondence with Frederick Nolan, 1954–55. Author's collection.

Tunstall, John H. Account Book [with A. A. McSween].
  Diary, August 18, 1872–July 29, 1876.
  Letters written from Victoria, B.C., September 1872–December 1875.
  Letters written from California, March 6–August 4, 1876.
  Letters written from Santa Fe, N.M., August 15–October 28, 1876.
  Letters written from Lincoln County, N.M., December 6, 1876–January 30, 1878.

  Originals in collection of Hilary Tunstall-Behrens; microfilm and copies in author's collection.

Tunstall, John Partridge, Mrs. Emily, and Emily ("Minnie").
  Letters to J. H. Tunstall, August 1872–February 1878.

  Originals in collection of Hilary Tunstall-Behrens; microfilm and copies in author's collection.

Tunstall, John Partridge. Letters to:
  Dr. Appel, 1880.
  Samuel Corbet, 1879.
  Robert Eagle, 1880.
  Ben H. Ellis, 1880.
  Isaac Ellis, 1879.

Godfrey Gauss, 1879.

John Middleton, 1879–80.

R. Guy McLellan, 1879.

Juan Patrón, 1881.

Karl August Widenmann, 1879.

Robert Widenmann, 1880.

Originals in collection of Hilary Tunstall-Behrens, London; microfilm in author's collection.

Turner, J. H. Telegram to H. C. Beeton, March 19, 1878. Original in collection of Hilary Tunstall-Behrens, London; microfilm in author's collection.

Upson, M. A. Letter to Adam Casey, September 9, 1879. Lillian Casey Klasner Collection, Harold B. Lee Library, Brigham Young University, Provo, Utah.

Widenmann, Robert A. Letters to J. P. and Mrs. Emily Tunstall, and Mrs. Emily Behrens, December 1877–November 1881.

Letters to H. C. Beeton, 1878.

Letter to *Cimarron News & Press*, March 30, 1878 [copy].

Originals in collection of Hilary Tunstall-Behrens, London; microfilm in author's collection.

———. "Border Troubles in New Mexico." Undated ms. on Lincoln County Bank letterhead.[March 30, 1878].

Original in collection of Hilary Tunstall-Behrens, London; microfilm in author's collection.

Widenmann, Robert J. "Lincoln County Enigma: Robert A. Widenmann." Unpublished ms., n.d. (1985?) Copy in author's collection.

———. Correspondence with Frederick Nolan, 1984–88. Author's collection.

Wood, Miles L. "Reminiscences," n.d. [1920]. University of Arizona Library, Tucson.

———. Biographical sketch, June 30, 1911. Office of Arizona Historian, Phoenix.

DOCUMENTARY RECORDS

Adjutant General's Office (AGO). Letters received, 1871–80.

Consolidated File 3211 AGO 1873. Microfilm M666 roll120. NARA.

Consolidated File 554 AGO 1874. Microfilm M666 roll 142. NARA.

Consolidated File 1405 AGO 1878. Microfilm M666 rolls 397–98. NARA.

British Army. Records of the service of Andrew Boyle: WO97/1528. Public Records Office, Kew, England.

British Foreign Office (BFO). "Correspondence Respecting the Murder of Mr J H Tunstall on the 18th February, 1878, in Lincoln County, New Mexico, United States, 1878–86." File FO5-1965, Public Records Office, Kew, England.

Canada, Bureau of the Census.

Census of 1861, Charlottetown, Prince Edward Island.

Census of 1861, Lindsay, Ontario.

Census of 1871, Lindsay, Ontario.

District of New Mexico.

Letters received by headquarters, 9th Military District, 1865–90. Microfilm M1088 rolls 20 (1873) and 36(January–March 1879). NARA.

Letters sent by headquarters, 9th Military District, 1878–81. Microfilm M1072 roll 6. NARA.

Doña Ana County, N.M.

District Court Records, Cases 141, 322.

Criminal Case Files 531-32.

NMSRCA.

First National Bank of Santa Fe, N.M. Accounts of John H. Tunstall and Alexander McSween. Special Collections, Zimmerman Library, University of New Mexico, Albuquerque.

First Presbyterian Church, Atchison, Kans. Registration Book.

Gross, Kelly & Co. Collection. Special Collections, Zimmerman Library, University of New Mexico, Albuquerque.

Judge Advocate General's Office. Records Relating to the Dudley Court of Inquiry (DCOI). RG 153, CQ 1284, NARA.

Lincoln County, N.M.
    Contracts, Agreements and Leases, Book B.
    Deed Book B.
    Estate of Susan E. Barber.
    Estate of Emil Fritz.
    Estate of A. A. McSween.
    Estate of John H. Tunstall.
    Probate Court Journal, December 1876–May 1881.

    All in Lincoln County Courthouse, Carrizozo, N.M.

    District Court Records, Lincoln County, Civil Cases 140, 141, 151, 163. District Court Journal, 1875–79, Lincoln County.
    Tax Assessment Records, Lincoln County.
    Voting Lists, Lincoln County.
    Poll and Tally Books, Lincoln County.

    All in NMSRCA.

Loughrea, diocese of Clonfort, Galway, Ireland. Parish records.

Santa Fe County, N.M.
    Book of Marriages A.
    First Judicial District Court, Cases 747-48, NMSRCA.

Sedgwick County, Kans. Deed Book A.

Scotland, General Register Office. Census of 1851.

Socorro County, N.M. District Court Book A, October 1879 term. NMSRCA.

Territorial Archives of New Mexico. Executive Record Book 2, 1867–82. NMSRCA.

U.S. Army Continental Commands, Fort Stanton, N. M. Entry 8: Letters received, 1873; 1878; January 1, 1879–May 1879. RG 393. NARA.

U.S. Bureau of the Census.
    Census of 1850, Adams County, Pa.
    Census of 1850, Franklin County, Ark.
    Census of 1860, Adams County, Pa.
    Census of 1860, Vigo County, Ind.
    Census of 1860, Richland County, Wis.
    Census of 1870, Atchison and Atchison County, Kans.
    Census of 1870, Fort Scott, Kans.
    Census of 1870, Greenwood County, Kans.
    Census of 1870, Lampasas County, Tex.
    Census of 1870, Larned, Kans.
    Census of 1870, Lincoln County, N.M.
    Census of 1870, New York (Manhattan).
    Census of 1870, Osceola, Mo.
    Census of 1870, Vigo County, Ind.
    Census of 1875, Greenwood County, Kans.
    Census of 1880, Lampasas County, Tex.
    Census of 1880, Lincoln County, N.M.
    Census of 1880, San Miguel County, N.M.

U.S. Department of the Interior, Bureau of Indian Affairs. Selected Documents Relating to Mescalero Apache Indian Agency (MAIA). University of New Mexico Library, Albuquerque Microfilm E99 M45 U55x.

Letters Received, Ind. Div. 1849–1907 RG 48 NARA.

Letters Received, 1878. RG 75 NARA.

Letters Received, Office of Indian Affairs, 1855–1881. M234-563 RG 75 NARA.

U.S. Department of the Interior, Bureau of Pensions.
  Pension applications of:
      William H. H. Antrim
      George B. Barber
      Ransselaer Brewer
      Charles A. Morris
      James W. Morris
      William Morris
      Gottfried Gauss
      William A. Morris
      James F. Randlett
  All in NARA.
U.S. Department of Justice.
  Instruction Book B.
  Letter Book M.
  Contingent & Miscellaneous Accounts #6.
  Angel, Frank W. "In the Matter of the Cause and Circumstances of the Death of J. H. Tunstall, a British Subject" (cited as Angel Report). 44-4-8-3, RG 60, NARA.
  Angel, Frank W. Examination of Charges Against F. C. Godfroy, Indian Agent, Mescalero, N.M., October 2, 1878. (Report 1981, Inspector E. C. Watkins; cited as Watkins Report). M319-20 and L147, 44-4-8, RG 75, NARA.
U.S. Treasury Department, Secret Service Division.
  Records of U.S. Secret Service Agents, 1875–1936.
  Reports of Special Operative Azariah F. Wild.
  Microfilm T915 roll 308. RG 87, NARA.
Wallace (Lew) Collection, William Henry Smith Memorial Library, Indiana Historical Society, Indianapolis. Wallace Papers.
Weisner Collection, New Mexico State University, Las Cruces. Lincoln County Papers.

NEWSPAPERS AND PERIODICALS

Alamogordo [N.M.] News.
Albuquerque [N.M.] Review.
Army & Navy Journal, The.
Carrizozo [N.M.] News.
Cimarron [N.M.] News & Press.
Colorado Springs [Colo.] Gazette.
[Denver] Rocky Mountain Presbyterian.
[Denver] Rocky Mountain Sentinel.
Denver Tribune.
Dodge City [Kans.] Times.
Eureka [Kans.] Herald.
Imperial Review, The.
Indianapolis World.
Kinsley [Kans.] Graphic.
Larned [Kans.] Press, The.
[Larned, Kans.] Pawnee Herald.
Las Animas [Colo.] Leader.
Las Cruces [N.M.] Eco del Rio Grande.

Las Cruces, [N.M.] Rio Grande Republican.
Las Cruces [N.M.] Thirty Four.
Las Vegas [N.M.] Daily Optic.
Las Vegas [N.M.] Gazette.
Lincoln County [N.M.] Leader.
London [England] Times, The.
Mesilla [N.M.] News.
Mesilla [N.M.] Valley Independent.
Monroe [Mich.] Democrat.
[Muskogee, I.T.] The Indian Journal.
New York Sun.
New York Times.
[Oklahoma City] Chickasaw Nation.
Omaha [Neb.] Republican.
Plattsburgh [N.Y.] Sentinel.
Portland [Ore.] Oregonian, The.
Prescott [Ariz.] Courier.
Prescott [Ariz.] Journal-Miner.
Pueblo [Colo.] Colorado Chieftain.
Richland County [Wis.] Republican.
Richland [Wis.] Observer.
Roswell [N.M.] Daily Record.
[Salem, Ore.] The Statesman.
San Francisco Call.
Santa Fe New Mexican.
[Santa Fe] Weekly New Mexican.
[Silver City, N.M.] Enterprise.
[Silver City, N.M.] Grant County Herald.
Silver City [N.M.] Independent.
Silver City [N.M.] Mining Life.
[Silver City, N.M.] Newman's Semi-Weekly.
[Silver City, N.M.] New Southwest & Grant County Herald.
Tombstone [Ariz.] Epitaph.
Topeka [Kans.] Commonwealth.
Trinidad [Colo.] News.
[Tucson] Arizona Citizen [became the Daily Citizen].
[Tucson] Arizona Weekly Star.
Victoria [B.C.] Daily Colonist.
Victoria [B.C.] Times.
[White Oaks, N.M.] Lincoln County Leader.
Wichita [Kans.] Eagle.
York Springs [Pa.] Sunday News, The.

INDEX

Because of the frequency with which they occur, the names of Lincoln and Lincoln County have been omitted from the index; because of the multiplicity of place-names generated by the biographical sketches and chronology, only the most significant city, town, and county names have been included.